A Dictionary of American Idioms

Third Edition

Adam Makkai
M. T. Boatner
J. E. Gates

Revised and thoroughly updated by
Adam Makkai
Professor of Linguistics
University of Illinois at Chicago

BARRON'S

REF
423.1
mak
1·01

International Standard Book Number 0-8120-1248-8

Library of Congress Catalog Card Number 94-79207

PRINTED IN THE UNITED STATES OF AMERICA
19 18 17 16 15 14 13 12 11

Contents

Acknowledgments

This dictionary is the result of the work of many hands. It was first published in 1966 in West Hartford, Connecticut, and later republished in 1969, copyrighted by the American School of the Deaf under the title *A Dictionary of Idioms for the Deaf,* edited by Maxine Tull Boatner, project director, aided by chief linguistic advisor, J. Edward Gates. The consulting committee consisted of Dr. Edmund E. Boatner, Dr. William J. McClure, Dr. Clarence D. O'Connor, Dr. George T. Pratt, Jack Brady, M.A., Richard K. Lane, and Professor H. A. Gleason, Jr., of the Hartford Seminary Foundation. Special editors for various subcategories, such as usage, sport terms, etc., were Elizabeth Meltzer, and E. Ward Gilman; Loy E. Golladay helped as language consultant with reviewing and editing. Definers were Edmund Casetti, Philip H. Cummings, Anne M. Driscoll, Harold J. Flavin, Dr. Frank Fletcher, E. Ward Gilman; Loy E. Golladay, Dr. Philip H. Goepp, Dr. Beatrice Hart, Dr. Benjamin Keen, Kendall Litchfield, Harold E. Niergarth, Ruth Gill Price, Thomas H. B. Robertson, Jess Smith, Rhea Talley Stewart, Harriet Smith, Elizabeth D. Spellman, John F. Spellman, and George M. Swanson, Barbara Ann Kipfer, and Justyn Moulds. The following have cooperated as simplifiers: Linda Braun, Dr. G. C. Farquhar, Carey S. Lane, Wesley Lauritsen, Nellie MacDonald, Ruth S. McQueen, and Donald Moores. In 1975 an edition was prepared for Barron's Educational Series, by the well-known expert on idioms Professor Adam Makkai of the University of Illinois at Chicago Circle.

For the second edition, Professor Makkai deleted obsolete material, updated old entries, and added hundreds of modern idiomatic phrases to the collection. Many of these new entries were of the slang character, originating within recent cultural movements; others reflect the popular usage of specialized areas of endeavor, including computer technology. Professor Robert A. Hall, Jr. of Cornell reviewed the manuscript of the revision and made invaluable suggestions.

In this new, thoroughly revised and updated third edition, Professor Makkai added *more than 2,000* new entries, making it the largest dictionary of American idioms available on the market today.

The ever-increasing international demand for more and better dictionaries of American idioms necessitated the inclusion of eight foreign language prefaces explaining what idioms are and how this book works. We wish to acknowledge the help of the following individuals in preparing these foreign language prefaces:

Arabic: Muhammad Q. Muhammad, M.A. (UIC), Embassy of the Republic of Qatar.
Chinese: Professor Guo Yianzhong, University of Hangzhou, P.R.C.
French: Professor Jean-Luc Garneau, Lake Forest College.
German: Doris Jutta Glatzl, M.A. (UIC), Department of German.
Italian: Professor Marcel Danesi, University of Toronto.
Japanese: Richard Goris, Shubun International, Tokyo.
Russian: Maya Aleksandrovna Glinberg, M.A., University of Moscow.
Spanish: Verónica Cortés, M.A. (UIC), Department of Linguistics.

We also acknowledge with thanks the numerous inquiries and letters from readers of this dictionary. Their questions and suggestions have been a most welcome source of inspiration for further research. Once again we encourage all interested users of this book to jot down any queries, suggestions, and questions that occur. Please send all such correspondence to the Editor, c/o Barron's Educational Series, 250 Wireless Blvd., Hauppauge, NY 11788, USA.

The Most Useful Dictionary of American Idioms

As you compare this *Dictionary of American Idioms* with similar works, please be aware that you are holding the most comprehensive dictionary of its kind on the market:

- More than 8,000 entries taken from real life and based on actual observations of how Americans use them.
- A dictionary with an international scope that aims at anybody whose native language was not American English. Prefaces written in nine languages help explain what an idiom is, what kinds there are, and how they work.
- A totally revised and updated edition that capitalizes on its astounding past success and brings brand-new idioms from all areas of human endeavor.
- Logical ordering of information that includes the parts of the sentence, clear explanations, enlightening examples, and cross-references in alphabetical order on every pertinent page.

Introduction

WHAT IS AN IDIOM?

If you understand every word in a text and still fail to grasp what the text is all about, chances are you are having trouble with the idioms. For example, suppose you read (or hear) the following:

Sam is a real cool cat. He never blows his stack and hardly ever flies off the handle. What's more, he knows how to get away with things . . . Well, of course, he is getting on, too. His hair is pepper and salt, but he knows how to make up for lost time by taking it easy. He gets up early, works out, and turns in early. He takes care of the hot dog stand like a breeze until he gets time off. Sam's got it made; this is it for him.

Needless to say, this is not great literary style, but most Americans, especially when they converse among themselves, will use expressions of this sort. Now if you are a foreigner in this country and have learned the words *cool* 'not very warm,' *cat* 'the familiar domestic animal,' *blow* 'exhale air with force,' *stack* 'a pile of something, or material heaped up,' *fly* 'propel oneself in the air by means of wings,' *handle* 'the part of an object designed to hold by hand'—and so forth you will still not understand the above sample of conversational American English, because this basic dictionary information alone will not give you the meaning of the forms involved. An idiom—as it follows from these observations—is the assigning of a new meaning to a group of words which already have their own meaning. Below you will find a 'translation' of this highly idiomatic, colloquial American English text, into a more formal, and relatively idiom free variety of English:

Sam is really a calm person. He never loses control of himself and hardly ever becomes too angry. Furthermore, he knows how to manage his business financially by using a few

tricks . . . Needless to say, he, too, is getting older. His hair is beginning to turn gray, but he knows how to compensate for wasted time by relaxing. He rises early, exercises, and goes to bed early. He manages his frankfurter stand without visible effort, until it is someone else's turn to work there. Sam is successful; he has reached his life's goal.

Now if you were to explain how the units are organized in this text, you would have to make a little idiom dictionary. It would look like this:

to be a (real) cool cat	to be a really calm person
to blow one's stack	to lose control over oneself, to become mad
to fly off the handle	to become excessively angry
what's more	furthermore, besides, additionally
to get away with something	to perpetrate an illegitimate or tricky act without repercussion or harm
of course	naturally
to be getting on	to age, to get older
pepper and salt	black or dark hair mixed with streaks of gray
to make up for something	to compensate for something
lost time	time wasted, time spent at fruitless labor
to take it easy	to relax, to rest, not to worry
to get up	to rise from bed in the morning or at other times
to work out	to exercise, to do gymnastics
to turn in	to go to bed at night
like a breeze	without effort, elegantly, easily

time off	period in one's job or place of employment during which one is not performing one's services
to have got it made	to be successful, to have arrived
this is it	to be in a position or in a place, or to have possession of an object, beyond which more of the same is unnecessary

Many of the idioms in this little sample list can be found in this dictionary itself. The interesting fact about most of these idioms is that they can easily be identified with the familiar parts of speech. Thus some idioms are clearly verbal in nature, such as *get away with, get up, work out,* and *turn in.* An equally large number are nominal in nature. Thus *hot dog* and *cool cat* are nouns. Many are adjectives, as in our example *pepper and salt* meaning *'black hair mixed with gray.'* Many are adverbial, as the examples *like the breeze* 'easily, without effort,' *hammer and tongs* 'violently' (as in *she ran after him hammer and tongs),* and so forth. These idioms which correlate with the familiar parts of speech can be called *lexemic idioms.*

The other most important group of idioms are of larger size. Often they are an entire clause in length, as our examples to *fly off the handle,* 'lose control over oneself,' and to *blow one's stack,* 'to become very angry.' There are a great many of these in American English. Some of the most famous ones are: to *kick the bucket* 'die,' *to be up the creek* 'to be in a predicament or a dangerous position,' to *be caught between the devil and deep blue sea* 'to have to choose between two equally unpleasant alternatives,' to *seize the bull by the horns* 'to face a problem and deal with it squarely,' and so on. Idioms of this sort have been called *tournures* (from the French), meaning 'turns of phrase,' or simply *phraseological idioms.* What they have in common is that they do not readily correlate with a given grammatical part of speech and require a paraphrase longer than a word.

Their form is set and only a limited number of them can be said or written in any other way without destroying the meaning of the idiom. Many of them are completely rigid and cannot show up in any other form whatever. Consider the idiom *kick the bucket,* for example. In the passive voice, you get an unacceptable form such as *the bucket has been kicked by the cowboy,* which no longer means that the 'cowboy died.' Rather it means that he struck a pail with his foot. Idioms of this type are regarded as *completely frozen forms.* Notice, however, that even this idiom can be inflected for tense, e.g., it is all right to say *the cowboy kicked the bucket, the cowboy will kick the bucket, he has kicked the bucket,* etc. Speakers disagree as much as do grammarians whether or not, for example, it is all right to use this idiom in the gerund form (a gerund being a noun derived from a verb by adding *-ing* to it, e.g., *singing* from *sing, eating* from *eat,* etc.) in *His kicking the bucket surprised us all.* It is best to avoid this form.

The next largest class of idioms is that of well established sayings and proverbs. These include the famous types of *don't count your chickens before they're hatched* (meaning 'do not celebrate the outcome of an undertaking prematurely because it is possible that you will fail in which case you will look ridiculous'); *don't wash your dirty linen in public* (meaning 'do not complain of your domestic affairs before strangers as it is none of their business'), and so forth. Many of these originate from some well known literary source or come to us from the earliest English speakers of the North American Continent.

Lack of predictability of meaning (or precise meaning) is not the only criterion of idiomaticity. Set phrases or phraseological units are also idiomatic, even though their meanings may be transparent. What is idiomatic (unpredictable) about them is their construction. Examples include *How about a drink? What do you say, Joe?* (as a greeting); *as a matter of fact, just in case; just to be on the safe side,* and many more.

Another important case of idiomaticity is the one-word idiom that occurs when a word is used in a surprisingly different meaning from the original one. Examples include *lemon,* said of bad watches, cars, or machines in general; and *dog,* said of a bad date or a bad exam. (*My car is a lemon, my math exam was a dog.*)

Why is English, and especially American English, so heavily idiomatic? The most probable reason is that as we develop new concepts, we need new expressions for them, but instead of creating a brand new word from the sounds of the language, we use some already existent words and put them together in a new sense. This, however, appears to be true of all known languages. There are, in fact, no known languages that do not have some idioms. Consider the Chinese expression for 'quickly,' for example. It is *mǎ shāng,* and translated literally it means 'horseback.' Why should the concept of 'quick' be associated with the back of a horse? The answer reveals itself upon a moment's speculation. In the old days, before the train, the automobile, and the airplane, the fastest way of getting from one place to the other was by riding a horse, i.e., on horseback. Thus Chinese *mǎ shāng* is as if we said in English *hurry up! We must go 'on horseback,'* i.e., 'Hurry up! We must go quickly.' Such a form would not be unintelligible in English at all, though the speaker would have to realize that it is an idiom, and the foreigner would have to learn it. However, in learning idioms a person may make an incorrect guess. Consider the English idiom *Oh well, the die is cast!* What would you guess this means—in case you don't know it? Perhaps you may guess that the speaker you heard is acquiescing in something because of the *Oh well* part. The expression means 'I made an irreversible decision and must live with it.' You can now try to reconstruct how this idiom came into being: The image of the die that was cast in gambling cannot be thrown again; that would be illegal; whether you have a one, a three, or a six, you must face the consequences of your throw, that is, win or lose, as the case may be. (Some people may know that the phrase was used by Caesar when he crossed the Rubicon, an event that led to war.)

How, then, having just learned it, will you use this idiom correctly? First of all, wait until you hear it from a native speaker in a natural context; do not experiment yourself with using an idiom until you have mastered the basics of English grammar. Once you have heard the idiom being used more than once, and fully understand its meaning, you can try using it yourself. Imagine that you have two job offers, one sure, but lower paying, and one that pays more, but is only tentative. Because of nervousness and fear of having no job at all, you accept the lower paying job, at which moment the better offer comes through and naturally you feel frustrated. You can then say *Oh well, the die is cast . . .* If you try this on a native speaker and he looks at you with sympathy and does not ask 'what do you mean?'—you have achieved your first successful placement of a newly learned idiom in an appropriate context. This can be a rewarding experience. Americans usually react to foreigners more politely than do people of other nations, but they can definitely tell how fluent you are. If a person always uses a bookish, stilted expression and never uses an idiom in the right place, he might develop the reputation of being a dry, unimaginative speaker, or one who is trying to be too serious and too official. *The use of idioms is, therefore, extremely important. It can strike a chord of solidarity with the listener.* The more idioms you use in the right context, the more at ease Americans will feel with you and the more they will think to themselves 'this is a nice and friendly person—look at how well he expresses himself!'

We will now take a look at some practical considerations regarding the use of *A Dictionary of American Idioms.*

HOW TO USE THIS DICTIONARY

This dictionary can be used successfully by nonnative speakers of English, students, workers, immigrants—in short, anybody who wants to make his English more fluent, more idiomatic. It contains phrases of the types mentioned above, lexemic idioms, phrase idioms, and proverbial idioms, that have a special meaning. When a phrase has a special meaning that you cannot decode properly by looking up and understanding the individual words of which it is composed, then you know you are dealing with an idiom. You may already know some of these idioms or may be able to imagine what they mean. Look in the book for any of the following idioms that you may already know well, this will help you to understand how you should use this book: *boyfriend, girl friend, outer space, piggy bank, get even, give up, going to, keep on, keep your mouth shut, lead somebody by the nose, look after, show off, throw away, all over, in love, mixed-up, out of this world, throw away, I'll say, both X and Y.*

A dictionary is like any other tool: You must familiarize yourself with it and learn how to use it before it begins to work well for you. Study the directions carefully several times, and practice looking up idioms. That way, searching for an idiom and finding it will become second nature to you. If you hear an idiomatic expression that is not in this book, after using it for a while, you will develop the ability to track down its meaning and write it down for yourself. Keep your own idiom list at home, right beside your regular dictionary. If you read a technical text, or a novel or a newspaper article and do not understand an expression, look it up in your regular school dictionary first; if you do not find it, try this one.

How do you find out if this dictionary can help you understand a hard sentence? Sometimes you can easily see what the phrase is, as with *puppy love, fun house, dog-eat-dog, mixed-up.* If not, pick out an important word from the most difficult part and look for that. If it is the first word in the idiom, you will find the whole phrase, followed by an explanation. Thus the expression *bats in the belfry* is listed in this dictionary under *b,* the word *bats.* If the word you picked is not the first word, you will find a list of idioms that contain that word. For example the word *toe* will be found in entries such as *curl one's hair OR curl one's toes, on one's toes, step on the toes (of somebody).* You may, of course, find that the reason why you do not understand a particular sentence is not because of any idioms in it, in that case your regular dictionary will be of help to you. Also, there are more idioms than listed in this book; only the most frequently occurring in *American English* are included. British English, for example, or the English spoken in Australia, certainly has many idiomatic expressions that are not a part of American English.

TYPES OF ENTRY

This dictionary contains four kinds of entry: *main entries, run-on entries, cross reference entries,* and *index entries.* A main entry includes a full explanation of the idiom. A run-on entry is a phrase which is derived from another idiom but would be separated from it if it entered at its own alphabetical place. These derived idioms have been run on at the end of the main entry (e.g., *fence-sitter* at *sit on the fence)* with an illustration and a paraphrase; an extra explanation has been added when understanding the derivative from the main explanation seemed difficult. When an idiom has come to be used as more than one part of speech, a separate entry has been made for each usage.

A cross-reference entry guides you to a definition in another place. Suppose you want to look up *cast in one's lot with.* You can look under *cast,* and under *lot;* but the cross-reference entry will send you to *throw* in the phrase *throw in one's lot with.* The reason for this is that *cast* is a much rarer word nowadays and so the usual, more frequent form of this idiom starts with the verb *throw.*

An index entry directs you to all other entries containing the index word. Thus the word *chin* is followed by the phrases of which it is a part, e.g., *keep one's chin up, stick one's chin (or neck) out, take it on the chin, up to the chin in.*

PARTS OF SPEECH LABELS

Those idioms that correlate with a well-defined grammatical form class carry a part of speech label. Sometimes, as with many prepositional phrases, a double label had to be assigned because the given phrase has two grammatical uses, e.g., *in commission* can be either adverbial or adjectival. Many prepositional phrases are adverbial in their literal sense, but adjectival in their nonpredictable, idiomatic sense. *v.* stands for verb; it was assigned to phrases containing a verb and an adverb; verb and preposition; or verb, preposition, and adverb. *v. phr.* stands for 'verbal phrase'; these include verbs with an object, verbs with subject complement, and verbs with prepositional phrase.

RESTRICTIVE USAGE LABELS

You must pay particular attention to whether it is appropriate for you to use a certain idiom in a certain setting. The label *slang* shows that the idiom is used only among very close friends who are quite familiar with one another. *Informal* indicates that the form is used in conversation but should be avoided in formal composition. *Formal* indicates the opposite, this is a form that people usually do not say, but they will write it in an essay or will state it in a speech or a university lecture. *Literary* alerts you to the fact that people are usually aware that the form is a quotation; it would be inappropriate for you to use these too often. *Vulgar* indicates that you should altogether avoid the form; recognizing it may, of course, be important to you as you can judge a person by the language he uses. *Substandard* labels a form as chiefly used by less educated people; *nonstandard* means that a phrase is felt to be awkward. *Archaic* (rarely used in this book) means that the form is heavily restricted to Biblical or Shakespearean English. *Dialect* means that the form is restricted to its geographical source; e.g., *chiefly British* means that Americans seldom use it, *Southern* means that the form is of much higher currency in the South of the United States than in the North.

Adam Makkai, Ph.D.
Professor of Linguistics
University of Illinois at Chicago
Executive Director and Director of
Publications, Linguistic Association of
Canada and the United States (LACUS), Inc.

مقدمه

ماهو مصطلح؟

اذا كنت تعرف معنى كل كلمة في نص من النصوص وما زلت لاتفهم النص فلربما كنت تستصعب فهم المصطلحات . دعني اضرب لك مثلا فيما اعني. افرض انك تقرا (او تسمع) مايلى .

Sam is a real cool cat. He never blows his stack and hardly ever flies off the handle . what's more, he knows how to get away with things....well,of course, he is getting on, too. His hair is pepper and salt, but he knows how to make up for lost time by taking it easy. He gets up early, works out, and turns it early. He takes care of the hot dog stand like a breeze until he gets time off. Sam's got it made; this is it for him.

لا داعي في ان اقول ان هذا الاسلوب ليس ادبيا رفيعا ، بل ان معظم الامريكين ، وعلى الاخص عندما يتحدثون فيما بينهم، يستعملون مصطلحات من هذا النوع . فاذا كنت اجنبيا في هذه البلاد وتعلمت ان الكلمة cool بمعنى"بارد" و cat بمعنى "قط" وblow بمعنى "ينفخ" و stack بمعنى "كومة" وfly بمعنى "يطير" و handle بمعنى "مقبض" وهكذا فسوف لا تستطيع مع ذلك فهم الانموذج المذكور اعلاه من لغة المحادثة الانكليزية ـ الامريكية لان هذه المعلومات المعجمية الاساسية وحدها لا تعطيك معاني الكلمة في تركيباتها المختلفة . مصطلح ـ كما يتضح مما سبق ـ هو اعطاء معان جديدة لعدد من الكلمات التي تحوي بنفسها معان مستقلة .

فيما يلي نورد لك ترجمة عربية خالية نوعامان المصطلحات (واضحة) لهذا النص الذي يحتوي على عدد كبير من المصطلحات العامية الامريكية .

سام شخص هادئ حقا. لا يفقد ضبط نفسه وقلما يغضب . وبالاضافة الى هذا فانه يعرف كيف يدير اموره المالية باستعمال حيلة ، فهو حقا قد تقدم في السن وبدأ الشيب يخط شعره ولكنه يعرف كيف يعوض عن الوقت الضائع بتلقي الامور

بسهولة . فانه يستيقظ مبكرا ، يتريض وينام مبكرا . ويدير امور دكانه الصغير١ الذي يبيع فيه المآنق بسهولة حتى ينتهي وقت عمله . سام شخص ناجح قد حصل على ما اراد .

فاذا اردنا شرح الوحدات التي تؤلف هذا النص فسوف نضع معجما اصطلاحيا صغيرا وسيكون كما يلي .

to be a (real) cool cat .... كـان٢ هادئا (حـقا)
to blow one's stack ...... فقد التسلط على نفسه
to fly off the handle ..... غضب غضبا شديدا
what's more .. بالاضافة الى هذا . علاوة على ذلك
to get away with some thing ... تملص من المأزق
of course .... طبعــا
to be getting on .... تقدم في السن
pepper and salt شعر وخطه الشيب . شعر اسود ابيض
to make up for something .. عوض عن شيء ..
lost time .... وقت ضـائع
to take it easy................... تلقى الامور بسهولة
to get up .... استيـقـظ
to work out .... عمل تمارين رياضيــة
to turn in .... نام . عاد الى فراشه ليلا
to take care of .... ادار . اهتم بـ
like a breeze .... بسهولة . بدون صعوبة
time off .... الوقت الذي لا يشتغل فيه الانسان
to have got it made .... حـقق . حـصل على
this is it.. كون الانسان في موقف حصل فيه على كل مايريد ..

كثير من المصطلحات المذكورة في هذه القائمة الانموذجية الصغيرة تستطيع ان تجدها في هذا المعجم نفسه. والحقيقة التي يجدر ذكرها هنا هي ان معظم هذه المصطلحات تتفق مع قواعد النحو المعروفة في اللغة الانكليزية حيث نلاحظ بوضوح ان بعض هذه المصطلحات فعلية بطبيعتها مثل get up, get away with, turn in, work out الخ. وبعضها الاخر اسمية بطبيعتها مثل White House, hot dog كما نرى البعض كصفات في مبناها كما هو الحال في pepper and salt والبعض الاخر احوال مثل like the breeze بسهولة hammer an

و نهايتها تشير الى ان ليس هنالك اجماع في ان هذه الصيغة منفق عليها ام لا . واننا لنقترح عدم استعمالها .

و القسم الكبير الاخر من المصطلحات هو الاقوال والامثال التي رسخت في الكلام . و هذه تضم الامثال المعروفة مثل don't count your chickens before they're hatched (اي "لاتحسين نتائج العمل قبل الاوان لانك قد تفشل فيه فتكون في موقف سخري ") ، don't wash your dirty linen in public (اي لاتشكي امورك الحاليه امام الغرباء لان ذلك لا يعنيهم ") و هكذا . وكثير من هذه المصطلحات جاءت عن مصادر ادبية معروفة او جاءت عن المتحدثين الاقدمين بالانكليزية في القارة الامريكية الشمالية التي كانت المصطلحات قسما من ثقافتهم الكلامية .

قد تعجب لماذا كانت اللغة الانكليزية ، و على الاخص الامريكية ، مليئة بالمصطلح و المصطلح ؟ ان احسن التعليلات الممكنة هو انه عندما تنضج فكرة ما فاننا نحتاج الى طريقة جديدة للتعبير عنها فعوضا عن ايجاد كلمة جديدة في اللغة فاننا نستعمل بعض ما هو جاهز من الكلمات بوضعها مع بعضها في معنى جديد . و هذا ، على كل حال ، يبدو صحيحا في جميع اللغات المعروفة ، اذ لا توجد في الحقيقة لغة معروفة بدون بعض المصطلحات على الاقل . لناخذ مثلا التعبير الصيني للكلمة "بسرعة " وهو ما شائك وترجمة الحرفية " ظهر حصان . " قد يسأل سائل ما هي العلاقة بين فكرة السرعة و ظهر الحصان ؟ و الجواب يظهر لنا في لحظة من التأمل . فان في الزمن القديم قبل اختراع القطار والسيارة والطائرة فان اسرع الطرق للوصول من مكان الى اخر هو عن طريق ركوب الخيل ــ اي على ظهر حصان . فان التعبير ماشائك باللغة الصينية هو كأننا نقول "هيا بنا لنذهب على ظهور الخير" او" هيا بنا لنذهب سريعا" . صيغة كهذه لا يستعصي فهمها بالانكليزية على الاطلاق ولكن على المتحدث ان يقدر ان ذلك مصطلح وعلى الاجنبي ان يتعلمه .

عندما اقول "لايستعصي فهمها" اعني بذلك ان التعبيرين "ظهر الحصان" و "بسرعة" ليسا بعيدين الواحد عن الاخر في المعنى حتى ولو كان الشخص لم يسمع ان ما شائك تعني بسرعة فانه قد يقدر المعنى . ومع ذلك فان الشخص قد يقدر تقديرا مغلوطا . فلو اخذنا في نظر الاعتبار المصطلح الانكليزي oh well, the die is cast ٤ فماذا تقدر معنى ذلك ــ ان كنت لاتعرفه ؛ ربما بسبب القسم الاول من الجملة oh well

بشده ، بعنف . كما هو في المثل الاتي she ran after him hammer and tongs و هكذا .

هذه المصطلحات التي تلائم القواعد النحوية المعروفة يمكن ان ندعوها lexemic idioms مصطلحات معجمية.

اما القسم المهم الاخر من المصطلحات فانه يهوي كمية اكبر من المصطلحات و هي تتالف على الاغلب من جمل مثل to fly off the handle,to blow one's stack فان اللغة الانكليزية الامريكية تحوي على عدد كبير من هذا الصنف . و فيما يلي نورد بعض المصطلحات المشهورة من هذا النوع . "to kick the bucket" "مـــات" "to be up the creek" "وقع في موقف حرج او خطر" "to be caught between the devil and deep blue sea" اضطر الاختيار بين موقفين ليسا مرغوبين". "to seize the bull by the horns" واجه مشكلة و تلقاها بصورة مباشرة" و هكذا . مصطلحات من هذا النوع تدعى tournures (عن الفرنسية) بمعنى جملة مغيرة ٢ او مصطلحات بصورة جمل . والمشترك في هذه المصطلحات انها لا تخضع الى الصيغ النحوية المعروفة و تتطلب شرحا اطول من كلمة .

ولقد وضعت صيغ هذه المصطلحات بحث ان القليل منها يمكن ان يقال او يكتب بصورة اخرى بدون تغير معنى المصطلح و كثير منها جامدة لايمكن ان تظهر في اي صيغة اخرى . فلو اخذنا المصطلح kick the bucket في نظر الاعتبار مثلا و غير ناه الى صيغة المبني للمجهول فاننا سنحصل على صيغة غير مقبولة مثل the bucket has been kicked by the cowboy الذي لا يعني ان راعي البقر قد مات ولكنه يعني ان راعي البقر قد ضرب الدلو برجله . مصطلحات كهذه تعتبر صيغا جامده على الاطلاق . ومن الجدير بالملاحظة هنا ان هذا المصطلح مع كونه جامدا يمكن استعماله في الازمنة المختلفة اذ يمكن ان تقول the cowboy kicked the bucket او cowboy the cowboy has او will kick the bucket او kicked the bucket الخ . و يختلف المتحدثون كما يختلف النحويون في استعمال الصيغة التي ندعوها بالانكليزية the gerund form (و هو اشتقاق الاسم من الفعل باضافة ing مثل singing من sing و eating من eat الخ) كما هو الحال في His kicking the bucket surprised us all? فان علامة الاستفهام في بداية الجملة ؟

تستطيع ان تقدران المتحددث يوافق في شيء ما . ولكن التعبير يعني " لقد قررت قرارا غير قابل للتغيير وعلي ان اتقبله " . حاول الان ان تحقق كيف نشأ هذا المصطلح . ان الزهر الذي رمي في المقامرة لايمكن رميه ثانية لان ذلك يعتبر غير قانوني . فان كان عدد النقاط على الزهر واحدة او ثلاثة او ستة عليك ان تتحمل نتائج ما رميت ، اي انك ستربح او تخسر كما يقتضيه الموقف (قد يعرف البعض بان يوليوس قيصر قد استعمل هذه الجملة عندما عبر نهر روبيكان مما ادى الى حرب).

فكيف اذاً تستعمل هذا المصطلع بصورة صحيحة بمجرد العلم به ؟ عليك اولا ان تنتظر حتى تسمعه من مواطن امريكي يستعمله في الموضع الطبيعي . لاتحاول بنفسك استعماله حتى تتقن اسس قواعد اللغة الانكليزية . وعندما تلاحظ استعماله اكثر من مرة و تفهم تماما معناه تستطيع حينئذ استعماله بنفسك . تصور انه قد عرضت عليك وظيفتان ، واحدة مضمونة ولكنها بمرتب بسيط والثاني تجريبية ولكنها بمرتب اعلى ، فتوخيا لتوتر الاعصاب والخوف من عدم الحصول على عمل فانك ستختار الوظيفة ذات المرتب البسيط . وعندما يتضح لك انك قد نلت العرض الافضل و تشعر بالطبع بالخيبة يمكنك ان تقول حينذاك oh well, the die is cast. فاذا استعملت هذا المصطلح مع مواطن امريكي و نظر اليك مشاركا لك في شعورك دون ان يسالك " ماذا تعني ؟ " فانك قد استعملت المصطلح الجديد في المناسبة الملائمة . وتكون قد نلت بهذه التجربة ما اردت . فان المواطنين الامريكين يعاملون الاجانب بصورة عامة بادب اكثر مما يفعله شعب اخر ولكنهم يستطيعون ان يدركوا تماما ان كنت تحسن الكلام ام لا . فاذا كان الانسان يستعمل دائما تعبيرات ادبية من الكتب ولا يستعمل المصطلحات في المواضع المناسبة على الاطلاق فلربما يعرف بين الناس كمتحدث غير مرن وليس ذا خيال او كانسان جدي او رسمي . ان استعمال المصطلحات اذاً حيوي جدا قد يضرب على وتر مشترك من قلب المستمع . وكلما اكثرت في استعمال المصطلحات في المواضع المناسبة فانك ترى ان المواطنين الامريكين يشعرون بالتقارب اليك ويكون ظنهم فيك " انه شخص لطيف المعشر ـ انظر كيف يعبر عن نفسه جيداً .

و الان سننظر الى بعض الامثلة العملية التي وردت في هذا المعجم الذي دعوناه معجم المصطلحات الامريكية .

كيفية استعمال هذا المعجم

ان هذا المعجم قد وضع لغير المواطنين الامريكين كالتلاميذ والعمال والمهاجرين ـ باختصار لكل شخص يريد ان تكون انكليزيته طلقة تتخللها المصطلحات اذ انه يحوي على جمل من النوع المذكور اعلاه ، مصطلحات معجمية ، مصطلحات جملية و مصطلحات مثلية ، تحمل معان خاصة . عندما يكون للجملة معنى خاص يصعب تفسيره عن طريق فهم معاني الكلمات المؤلفة منها فان هذه الجملة مصطلح . ربما تكون قد تعرفت على بعض هذه المصطلحات او قد تستطيع تقدير معناها . فتش في هذا الكتاب عن المصطلحات التالية التي يجوز انك تعرفها جيدا فهذا مما يساعدك على فهم طريقة استعمال هذا الكتاب : give up, going to, keep on, keep your mouth shut, boyfriend, girlfriend, show off, throw away, all over, in love, outer space, piggy bank, get even, throw away, out of this world, mixed up, lead somebody by the nose, look after, show off, I'll say, both x and y.

ان المعجم كأي آلة اخرى يجب ان تتعرف على طريقة استعماله جيدا قبل استخدامه في عملك . اقرا التعليمات بعناية مرات عديدة وتمرن على تفتيش المصطلحات فيه . و هكذا فانك سترى ان تفتيش المصطلحات وايجادها سيصبح امرا طبيعيا لديك . واذا سمعت تعبيرا اصطلاحيا لا تجده في هذا الكتاب فانك بعد استعماله قليلا ستجد في نفسك القابلية في تتبع معناه فسجله لنفسك . احتفظ بقائمة مصطلحاتك في البيت الى جانب معجمك المعتاد . وابعث لنا بملاحظاتك . واذا قرأت مقالا علميا او رواية او مقال صحفيا واستصعبت فهم مصطلح ما ، فتش عنه في المعجم المدرسي العادي اولا وان لم تجده حاول ان تجده في هذا المعجم .

كيف تعلم ان هذا المعجم سيساعدك على فهم جملة صعبة؟ فانك احيانا تستطيع بسهولة معرفة التعبير كما هو الحـــال mixed-up, dog-eat-dog, fun house, puppy love وان لم تكن لك معرفة به فاختر احدى الكلمات المهمة من القسم الصعب في الجملة و حاول ان تجده في هذا المعجم . فان كانت الكلمة هي الاولى في المصطلح فانك ستجد التعبير كله متبوعا بالشرح . وهكذا فانك ستجد التعبير bats in the belfry في المعجم تحت كلمة bats واذا كانت

الكلمة التي اخترتها ليست بالكلمة الاولى فانك ستجد مجموعة من المصطلحات التي تتضمنها الكلمة . وعلى سبيل المثل فان الكلمة toe ستقع في مواضع مثل : "curl one's hair" او OR "curl one's toes," "step on the toes (of somebody)," "on one's toes" . وقد تجد و لا شك ان السبب في عدم فهم جملة ما ليس بسبب مصطلح و في هذه الحالة فانك ستجد العون في معجم عادي . و هنالك بالطبع مصطلحات لا يتضمنها هذا المعجم حيث اننا نقدم هنا المصطلحات الانكليزيةالامريكية الاكثر استعمالا فقط . اما اللغةالانكليزية البريطانية واللغة الانكليزية الاسترالية فهن يحوين مصطلحات وتعبيرات لاتجدها في اللغة الانكليزية الامريكية . ان المعجم الذي سيضم كل مصطلحات اللغة الانكليزية المستعملة في كل مكان سيكون المعجم العالمي للمصطلحات الانكليزية فانه لا يوجد مثل هذا المعجم حاليا و يجدر الاهتمام بتاليفه .

انواع المداخل (المواضع)

يتضمن هذا المعجم اربعة انواع من المداخله : المدخل الرئيسي ، المدخل المستمر ، المدخل المرجعي و المدخل الفهرسي . فالمدخل الرئيسي يضم شرحا كاملا للمصطلح والمدخل المستمر هو تعبير مشتق من مصطلح اخر ولكنه يكون مستقلا عنه اذا دخل في موضعه حسب الاحرف الهجائية . هذه المصطلحات المشتقة تكُون استمرارا للمداخل الرئيسية فان fence-sitter كمدخل مستمر يكون كمدخل رئيسي في (sit on the fence) مع شرح وايضاح . ويضاف الى ذلك شرح اضافي عندما يبدو ان فهم المشتق من الشرح الرئيسي صعب . و عندما يكون المصطلح مستعملا في اكثر من موضوع واحد من مواضيع النحو و في نفس الصورة فقد وضعنا له مدخلا في كل موضوع .

اما المدخل المرجعي فانه كمرجع يشير الى تعريف في موضع اخر . فالنفرض انك تريد ان تفتش عن cast in one's lot with فانك تستطيع ان نفتش ذلك في cast و lot ولكن المدخل المرجعي سيرجع بك الى throw. لأن الكلمة cast نادرة اليوم . الصورة الاكثر استعمالا في هذا المصطلح تبدا بالفعل throw .

اما المدخل الفهرسي فهو يشير الى جميع المداخل الاجرى التي تحتوي الكلمة المفهرسة و هكذا فان الكلمة take مثلا يتبعها التعبيرات التي تتضمنها مثل it on the chin

chin, stick one's chin (or neck) out, keep one's chin up, up to the chin.

العلامات النحوية

المصطلحات المعجمية (كما شرحناها سابقا) لها تسمية نحوية كما هو الحال في كثير من اشباه الجمل التي تحوي حرفا من احرف الجر فقد وضعناها في موضعين لان لها استعمالين نحويين فان شبه الجملة in commission يمكن ان تكون في الانكليزية حال و صفة فكثير من اشباه الجمل هذه تكون احوالا حسب المعنى الحرفي ولكنها صفات حسب المعنى الاصطلاحي غير المتوقع .

v علامة للفعل verb و قد وضعت للتعبيرات التي تحوي فعلا وحالا او فعلا او حرف جر او فعلا وحرف جر مع حال .

v.phr. علامة الجملة الفعلية 'verbal phrase' و هذه تتضمن فعلا ومفعولا به او فعلا و فاعلا او فعلا وشبه جملة من الجار والمجرور .

علامات لا ستعمالات محدودة

عليك ، كمتكلم غير مواطن ، ان توجه اهتمامك فيما اذا كان من اللائق بك استعمال مصطلح ما في تركيب معين . فالعلامة slang تشير الى ان المصطلح يستعمل فقط بين اصدقاء مقربين يعرف بعضهم البعض معرفة تامة . والعلامة Informal تشير الى ان المصطلح يستعمل في الحديث ولكن من المستحسن تجنب استعماله في كتابة رسمية . والعلامة Formal تشير العكس اي ان هذه الصيغة لاتستعمل في الحديث بل في كتابة المقالات او خلال محاضرة جامعية . والعلامة Literary تنبهك الى ان الناس عادة على علم بان هذه الصيغة مقتبسة معروفة ويكون من الغريب استعمالها كثيرا . والعلامة Vulgar تشير الى وجوب عدم استعمال هذه الصيغة ولكن معرفتها مهمة جدا اذ يحكم الناس على الشخص بلغته . والعلامة Substandard تدل على ان هذه الصيغة تستعمل على الاخص بين الناس الذين يتميزون بثقافة واطئة . والعلامة nonstandard تعني ان الجملة نفسها تعتبر ثقيلة على السمع . اما العلامة Archaic (التي قل استعمالها في هذا المعجم)[فانها تعني بان هذه الصيغة غير مستعملة في الانكليزية العصرية] والعلامة Regional تشير بان استعمال الصيغة تتحدد في مقاطعات خاصة مثلا chiefly British تعني ان الصيغة يندر استعمالها بين الامريكين .

الولايات المتحدة اكثر من شمالها .

امـا الصـيـغ التي ظهرت مـؤخـرا - في سـت او سـبع السنوات الاخيرة فقد جمعناها في ملحق لهذا المعجم .

ملاحظات .

١- في الاصل الانكليزي استعملت الكلمة stand وهى تعني دكانا صغيرا مصنوعا من الخشب او الصفيح . و هو ما يدعونه في بعض البلدان العربية بالعامية سقفية اوكشك .

الدكتور آدم ماكاي
استاذ اللغات في جامعة الينوي في شيكاغو .

٢- استعملنا الفعل الماضي في الترجمة وليس المصدر كمـا هو في الاصل الانكليزي لان المتبع في المعاجم العربية هو استعمال الفعل الماضي .

٣- جملة تغير معنى كلماتها الى معنى اخر .

٤- الترجمة الحرفية للمصطلح هي "طيب ، الزهر قدرمي" (الزهر هنا هو زهر الطاولة) .

٥- ترجمنا الكلمة entry بالكلمة مدخل التي تدل على الموضع الذي تدخل الكلمة فيه .

序　言

一、什麼是成語

在閱讀英語時，如果你明白句子中每一個詞的意義，却不懂整個句子的意思，那很可能是遇到了成語問題。例如，你若讀到或聽到下面這段話，就會遇到這個問題。

Sam is a real cool cat. He never blows his stack and hardly ever flies off the handle. What's more, he knows how to get away with things . . . Well, of course, he is getting on, too. His hair is pepper and salt, but he knows how to make up for lost time by taking it easy. He gets up early, works out, and turns in early. He takes care of the hot dog stand like a breeze until he gets time off. Sam's got it made; this is it for him.

毋庸違言，這段話不太文雅，但大都數美國人，尤其是他們自己互相交談時，往往都會這麼說的。如果你是美國的外國人，當你聽到這段話時，儘管懂得那些單詞的意義，例如，*cool* 意思是 "凉的"，*cat* 意思是 "貓" *blow* 意思是 "吹"，*stack* 意思是 "一堆東西"，*fly* 意思是 "飛" *handle* 意界是 "把手"，等等，可是，你仍不明白這段口語體的美國英語到底說的是什麼意思，因為，詞典上所給予的這些單詞的基本含義不能提供上述表達方式的意義。從以上例子的分析，我們就可以知道，所謂成語，是指賦予了新的意義的一個詞組，儘管該詞組中的每個單詞各具其本身獨立的意義。現在，我們把這一段充滿成語而又非常通俗的美國英語 "譯" 為成語相對較少而又較正式的文體；

Sam is a really calm person. He never loses control of himself and hardly ever becomes too angry. Furthermore, he knows how to manage his business financially by using a few tricks . . . Needless to say, he, too, is getting older. His hair is beginning to turn grey, but he knows how to compensate for wasted time by relaxing. He rises early, exercises, and goes to bed early. He man-ages his frankfurter dispensary without visible effort until it is someone else's turn to work there. Sam is successful, he has reached his life's goal.

薩姆是個頭腦冷靜的人。他從不失去自控，也很少不發雷霆。而且，他也懂得怎樣玩弄一些小詭計賺錢。……當然，他人也漸漸老了，黑髮中出現了白髮。但他懂得如何把日子過得悠閑些，以贖回虛度的光陰。他早上起得很早，然後鍛煉身體，晚上也很早上床睡覺。他管理自己的那個熱狗攤，顯得輕鬆自如，直到別人接他的班。薩姆很成功。他已經達到了他人生的目標。

如果你想了解這些詞組是怎樣組成的，就得編一個小小的成語詞典。該詞典的樣子大致如下：

to be a (real) cool cat	頭腦冷靜的人
to blow one's stack	失去自制
to fly off the handle	大發雷霆
what's more	而且
to get away with something	做成（某壞事或錯事而未被發覺或受處分）
of course	當然
to be getting on	變老
pepper and salt	（頭髮）黑白參雜的
to make up for something	補償，瀰補
lost time	浪費的時間
to take it easy	休息，不憂慮
to get up	起床
to work out	鍛煉身體
to turn in	上床睡覺
to take care of sg.	照管
like a breeze	毫不費力地
time off	下班時間
to have got it made	成功，達到
this is it	達到了目標

上面列出的這些成語都能在本詞典中查到，有趣的是，大多數成語都能與我們所熟悉的語法中詞類相對應。有些成語很

明顯相當於動詞，如 *get away with, work out, turn in* 等。不少成語具有名詞性質，如 *hot dog* （熱狗，麵包夾香腸）和 *White House* "白宮，美國總統官邸"。還有很多成語相當於形容詞，如 *pepper and salt* "黑白參雜的（頭髮）"；另一些成語又具有副詞性質，如 *like a breeze* "輕鬆自如地"，*hammer and tongs* "拼命地，竭盡全力地"，(*She ran after him hammer and tongs* "她拼命追求他。"）如此等等，不一而足。這些與語法中的詞類相關的成語，稱之為詞彙成語，即這類成語以詞彙為單位。

另一類重要的成語組成的單位較大，有時往往有一個子句那麼長。例如 *to blow one's stack* "失去自制"和 *to fly off the handle* "大發雷霆"就屬此類。在美國英語中，這類成語很多。下面幾個就是大家都熟悉的成語：

to kick the bucket	死
to be up the creek	遭到困難
to be caught between the devil and deep blue sea	處於困境 進退兩難
to seize the bull by the horns	不畏艱險

這類成語曾經被稱之為 *tournures* 該詞源自法語），意即具有短語的特色，可簡單地稱作"短語成語"。這類成語的共同特點是，它們並不與語法裡的某一詞類相關聯，並且需用不至一個詞才能把意思解釋清楚。

這類成語的形式是固定的，只有少數成語在使用時可以有變化而仍不損其原意。許多成語是完全固定不變的，無論如何不能以別的形式出現。試以成語 *kick the bucket* 為例。如果把這一成語用在被動語態中，*The bucket has been kicked by the cowboy*，這種用法就不對了。因為句子的意思不再是"那牛仔死了"，而是說"那牛仔用脚踢了那只桶"。這類成語可謂是"全凍式"，即其形式是完全固定不變的。然而，值得注意的是，即使是這類成語，也可以用在不同的時態中。例如，我們可以說：

The cowboy kicked the bucket.
The cowboy will kick the bucket.
He has kicked the bucket. 等等。

但這類成語是否可以以動名詞形式出現，語法家和普通大衆都莫衷一是，意見不一。我們的建議是最好盡量避免使用動名詞形式。所謂動名詞，就是在動詞後加上 *-ing* 變成名詞。例如，我們應避免使用下面的形式：

His kicking the bucket surprised us call.

另一大類成語是人們常用的諺語。例如，大家熟悉的有： *Don't count your chickens before they're hatched.*

別在蛋未孵化之前先數小鷄。

這句話的意思是"事情未成功以前，別先慶祝，因為可能會失敗；如果失敗，那就被人笑話了。"意即"別指望得太早"。

Don't wash your dirty linen in public.

別在大庭廣衆面前洗自己的髒被單。

這句話的意思是"不要在陌生人面前談家醜，因為跟他們無關"，意即"家醜不可外揚。"

許多這類成語出自文學名著或早期北美演說家的演講詞。

為什麼英語，尤其是美國英語，成語這麼豐富呢？最可能的原因是，當新概念形成時，我們需要有新的表達方式。有時，我們不想創造新詞，而是用原有的詞，組成新的意義。這種用已有的詞，組成新的表達方式，在世界各國語言中都是存在的。事實上，就我們所知，沒有一種語言是沒有成語的。例如，在漢語中，表示"快"的意思用"馬上"這一表達方式。如果其譯成英語，意即" *horse back* "（在）馬背（上）。那麼，"快"的意思又怎麼會跟"馬背"聯系在一起呢？原來，在古代，在火車、汽車和飛機出現之前，從一個地方到另一個地方最快的方法就是騎馬，也就是"在馬背上"，意思是"趕快！我們得快走。"這種表達方式在英語裡也不是不可理解的，只是說話的人必須知道，這是成語，外國人得學習方能懂得。但在學習成語時，我們往往會猜錯意思。試以英語成語 *Oh well, the die is cast!* 為例，如果你不知道這一成語，你猜會是什麼意思呢？也許，因為這句中有 *Oh well* 這兩個詞，你會以為說話者是在默然同意某件事情。其實，這句話的意思是："我已作了不可挽回的決定，後果如何我也只

能忍受了。"意即"木已成舟"（事已定局，無法挽回了。）現在，再試想一下這個成語是如何來的。想像一下，在賭博時，骰子一擲出就不能再擲了，想拿回來再投就算犯規。不管你投出幾點，是三是六，是輸是贏，你都得接受。可能有人知道，公元前四十九年凱撒越過魯比孔河與羅馬執政龐培決戰時曾用過此語。

那麼，學了這個成語後，怎樣才能正確使用呢？首先，你得聽到以英語為母語的人在自然的場合下使用這個成語。在自己沒有掌握成語的基本含義之前，千萬別急於使用。在你多次聽到別人使用這一成語並徹底了解了成語的意義之後，才可以自己試着使用。譬如，你找到兩個工作。一個肯定能得到，但薪水低；另一個薪水高，但沒把握得到。由於憂慮和担心什麼工作都找不到，你接受了那份低薪的工作。就在那個時候，那份高薪工作也通過了。你自然感到失望，這時，你就可以說："*Oh well, the die is cast . . .*"如果這句語你是對以英語為母語的人說的，他聽了之後用同情的眼光注視着你，也沒有問你"你是什麼意思？"那就表明，你第一次在適當的場合正確地使用了這一成語。這於你可算是一次有益的經驗。美國人對外國人要比其他國家的人對外國人有禮貌，但他們完全知道你的英語是否熟練。如果一個人老是用文縐縐的、誇張不自然的詞句，而從不使用成語，那別人就會認為他是一個死板的人，一個乏味的人，要不就認為他是太嚴肅了，太官氣十足了。所以，使用成語是十分重要的。使用成語能使聽話人起共鳴。在適當的場合，你成語使用越多，美國人跟你談話就會越感到自在；他們在心里越是會這麼想："這個人多好，多友善——看看他自己的思想表達得多好啊！"

下面我們談談這本《美國成語詞典》的使用方法。

二、如何使用這本詞典

這本詞典是為非英語民族的學生、工人和移民編寫的。總之，任何人若想學會說流利而地道的英語，都可使用本詞典。詞典中包括前面所談到的三類成語，即詞彙成語、短語成語和諺語成語。這些成語都有其特定的意義。當一個短語具有特定的意義，光從短語中的單詞的意義你無法解釋整個短語的意思，那你就可能遇到了成語。你也許已經知道了一些成語，也能猜出這些成語的意義。現在，請你在本詞典中查閱一下下列成語的意義，這會幫助你了解怎樣使用這本詞典，儘管其中的有些成語你已知道，但也務必查一下。這些成語是：

boy friend, girl friend, outer space, piggy bank, get even, give up, going to keep on, keep your mouth shut, lead somebody by the nose, look after, show off, throw away, all over, in love, mixed-up, out of this world, I'll say, both X and Y.

詞典像其他工具一樣，你必須熟悉它，並學會如何使用，才能更好地為你服務。應該反復仔細地研讀使用說明，並練習查成語。只有這樣，你才能得心應手地查出成語，並了解成語的意義。以後，你如果聽到一個習慣的表達方式，但在本詞典中又查不到，在你使用本詞典相當一段時間之後，你就會自己找出那個習慣用語的意義，並自己把它記下來。把自己記下來的這些成語放在家中自己常用的詞典旁邊。在你閱讀科技文章、小說或新聞時，若碰到你不懂的表達方式，先查一下你常用的詞典；若查不到，則可試試查這本詞典。

如何知道這本詞典可以幫助你了解難句呢？有時，你一眼就可以知道一些短語的意思，例如 *puppy love, fun house, dog-eat-dog, mixed up* 等。如果不懂，就找出難住你的那個短語中最重要的詞查一下。如果這個詞是短語中的第一個詞，你就會發現整個短語，短語後面就是解釋。例如，短語 *bats in the belfry*，在本詞典中就列在字母 *b* 下面的 *bats* 這一詞下。如果你查閱的詞不是短語中的第一個詞，你就會發現包含這個詞的好幾個成語。例如，在 *toe* 這一詞條下，列出了下列成語：*curl one's hair OR curl one's toes, on one's toes, step on the toes (of somebody)*

當然，有時候你不懂整個句子的意思並不是因為其中包含的成語的關係，那你就可以查一下普通詞典。當然，也有許多成語沒有列入本詞典，這裡，我們只收入了最常用的美國成語。例如，英國英語或澳大利亞英語中，也有許多習慣表達方式，但那些不屬於美國英語，當然就不包括在本詞典之內了。

三、詞條類型

本詞典的詞條包括四種類型，即主詞條，內詞條，參照詞條和索引詞條。主詞條包括對成語完整的釋義。內詞條是指從另一個成語派生出來的短語，若以短語本身的字母排列，就會與這個成語分開，所以把派生的成語附在主詞條之後。例如，*fence-sitter* 附在 *sit on the fence* 之後，並加以解釋；如果光看主詞條的解釋對理解派生的成語有困難，則另加說明如果一個成語可以作不同的詞類使用，也以不同的詞類分別列入詞條。

參照詞條使你能在另一個地方找到釋義。假如，你要查成語 *cast in one's lot with*，你查 *lot* 或 *throw* 詞條，你得到的是 *throw in one's lot with* 這一短語。其原因是，*cast* 一詞現在已很少用了，在這一成語中，現在更常用的是 *throw* 一詞。

索引詞條可使你找到包含該索引詞的其他所有的條目。例如，在 *chin* 一詞後，列出了包含這一詞的所有的短語：*keep one's chin up, stick one's chin (or neck) out, take it on the chin, up to the chin.*

四、詞類標記

每條成語凡是與語法中的詞類相關聯的，均標上詞類標記。有的成語有兩種詞類標記，如介詞短語，因為這類成語能有兩種語法作用。例如，*in commission*

這一短語，既可用作形容詞，也可用作副詞。許多介詞短語其詞面意義往往作副詞用，其不可預測的習慣意義，往往又用作形容詞。V 表示動詞，這類短語包含一個動詞和一個副詞，或一個動詞和一個介詞，或一個動詞，一個介詞和一個副詞。*V. phr.* 表示動詞短語。這類短語包括動詞及其賓語，動詞及其主語補語，以及動詞及其詞短語。

五、慣用法標記

使用成語，需特別注意場合是否合適。現把成語的習慣用法的標記分別說明如下：

Slang: 俚語，只用於十分熟悉的好朋友之間。

Informal: 非正式用語，用於日常談話中，但應避免使用在書面語中。

Formal: 正式用語，與上述非正式用語相反，一般不用於日常談話中，而用於文章中，正式演說中，或大學講課中。

Literary: 文學用語，一般都用在引語中，應避免經常使用這類成語。

Vulgar: 粗俗語，應完全避免使用這類成語。當然，很重要的一點是，你經常可以從使用的語言判斷一個人。

Substandard: 不規范用語，主要用於教育水平不太高的人們之間。

Nonstandard: 非標准用語，這類成語使人聽了感到別扭。

Archaic: 古體詞，現已不通用。

Chiefly British: 主要用於英國英語中，美國人很少用。

Southern: 南方英語，指在美國南方用得多，北方很少用。

原序作者：馬亞當教授，
美國芝加哥伊利諾大學語言系
原序翻譯：郭建中教授，
中國杭州大學外語學院

Préface

QU'EST-CE QUE C'EST QU'UNE EXPRESSION IDIOMATIQUE?

Lorsqu'on comprend chaque mot d'un texte et qu'on n'en arrive tout de même pas à le déchiffrer, dans bien de cas c'est dû à une mauvaise compréhension des expressions idiomatiques. Le texte qui suit illustre ce que je veux dire. Disons que vous lisez (ou entendez) ce qui va suivre :

Sam is a real cool cat. He never blows his stack and hardly ever flies off the handle. What's more, he knows how to get away with things . . . Well, of course, he is getting on, too. His hair is pepper and salt, but he knows how to make up for lost time by taking it easy. He gets up early, works out, and turns in early. He takes care of the hot dog stand like a breeze until he gets time off. Sam's got it made: this is it for him.

Il va sans dire que ce texte n'est pas du meilleur style littéraire, mais la plupart des Américains, quand ils bavardent, emploient des expressions de ce genre. Or, si l'on est un étranger dans ce pays, et si l'on a appris les mots *cool* « pas très chaud », *cat* « l'animal domestique familier », *blow* « expulser de l'air avec force », *stack* « un tas de quelque chose » ou « matériel empilé », *fly* « se déplacer dans l'air au moyen d'ailes », *handle* « la partie d'un objet par laquelle on le tient dans la main », ... et ainsi de suite, l'on ne pourra quand même pas comprendre l'échantillon donné ci-dessus, d'anglais américain employé dans la conversation, car ces seuls renseignements de base que fournit le dictionnaire ne vous révéleront pas la signification des formes employées dans le texte idiomatique. Un idiotisme, — comme nous l'indiquent ces observations — consiste à attacher une nouvelle signification à un groupe de mots qui ont déjà leur propre signification. Vous trouverez ci-dessous une « traduction » de ce texte écrit en

anglais américain très idiomatique et familier, en une variété d'anglais plus conventionnel et d'où, dans la mesure du possible, les expressions idiomatiques sont absentes.

Sam is really a calm person. He never loses control of himself and hardly ever becomes too angry. Furthermore, he knows how to manage his business financially by using a few tricks . . . Needless to say, he, too, is getting older. His hair is beginning to turn gray, but he knows how to compensate for wasted time by relaxing. He rises early, exercises, and goes to bed early. He manages his frankfurter dispensary without visible effort, until it is someone else's turn to work there. Sam is successful, he has reached his life's goal.

Si l'on voulait expliquer comment les unités sont disposées dans ce texte, il en sortirait un petit dictionnaire d'expressions idiomatiques à l'aspect suivant :

to be a (real) cool cat	être une personne très calme
to blow one's stack	perdre son sang froid, se fâcher
to fly off the handle	se mettre très en colère
what's more	depuis, d'ailleurs, en outre
to get away with something	perpétrer un acte illégitime ou rusé, sans répercussion ni mal
of course	naturellement
to be getting on	vieillir
pepper and salt	cheveux noirs ou foncés bariolés de gris
to make up for something	compenser pour quelque chose
lost time	temps perdu, temps passé à un travail infructueux
to take it easy	se détendre, ne pas s'inquiéter

to get up	se lever le matin ou à tout autre moment
to work out	faire de l'exercice, de la gymnastique
to turn in	aller se coucher le soir
to take care of something	s'occuper de quelque chose, en prendre soin
like a breeze	sans effort, élégamment, facilement
time off	période de temps où l'on ne travaille pas
to have got it made	avoir du succès, avoir réussi
this is it	être dans une situation où un endroit, ou posséder un objet à un tel degré qu'en avoir davantage n'est pas nécessaire

Un grand nombre d'idiotismes contenus dans cette courte liste d'exemples-ci paraissent aussi dans le dictionnaire.

Il est intéressant de remarquer que la plupart de ces idiotismes se laissent facilement classifier sous les rubriques grammaticales bien connues des (parties du discours). Ainsi, certains idiotismes appartiennent clairement à la classe du verbe, tels que *get away with, get up, work out, turn in*, etc. D'autres, tout aussi nombreux, appartiennent à la classe du substantif. Par exemple, *hot dog* « saucisse entre deux morceaux de pain », *White House* « résidence officielle du président des Etats-Unis », sont des noms. Plusieurs sont des adjectifs comme dans notre exemple *pepper and salt*, qui veut dire « cheveux noirs bariolés de gris ». Plusieurs sont des adverbes comme dans les exemples *like the breeze* « facilement, sans effort », *hammer and tongs* « viollement » (comme dans l'expression *she ran after him hammer and tongs,*) et ainsi de suite.

Les idiotismes qui appartiennent à une classe grammaticale bien définie peuvent être appelés *idiotismes lexémiques*.

Les idiotismes faisant partie de l'autre groupe le plus important forment des expressions plus longues. Ils sont souvent de la longueur d'une locution entière, par exemple, *to fly off the handle,* « perdre son sang froid » et *to blow one's stack* « se mettre en colère ». Il y en a plusieurs de cette catégorie en anglais américain. Parmi les plus célèbres nous trouvons : *to kick the bucket* « mourir », *to be up the creek* « être dans une situation dangereuse », *to be caught between the devil and the deep blue sea* « devoir choisir entre deux situations également peu plaisantes », *to seize the bull by the horn*s « faire face à un problème et le résoudre honnêtement », etc. Ces idiotismes portent le nom de tournures (d'après le français) qui veut dire (tours de phrases), ou simplement idiotismes phraséologiques. Ce qu'ils ont tous en commun, c'est qu'il serait difficile de les ranger sous une classe grammaticale donnée (partie du discours) et qu'une paraphrase d'un seul mot ne suffirait pas à les expliquer.

Leur forme est figée et seulement un nombre limité de ces idiotismes phraséologiques peuvent se dire ou s'écrire d'une façon différente sans détruire la signification de l'idiotisme. Il en est beaucoup qui sont complètement figés et qui ne peuvent apparaître sous aucune autre forme que ce soit. Prenons comme exemple l'idiotisme *kick the bucket*. Si l'on met cette expression au passif, le résultat est inacceptable (*the bucket has been kicked by the cowboy)* ce qui ne veut plus dire que « le cowboy est mort » mais qu'il a frappé du pied une chaudière. Les expressions idiomatiques de ce genre sont considérées comme des formes complètement figées. Il est à remarquer cependant, que ces idiotismes portent la marque des inflexions temporelles, e.g., l'on peut dire *the cowboy kicked the bucket, the cowboy will kick the bucket, he has kicked the bucket,* etc. Les sujets parlant tout comme les grammairiens ne s'entendent pas touchant l'emploi de ces idiotismes au gérondif (un gérondif étant un nom dérivé d'un verbe auquel on ajoute la forme *-ing*, e.g., *singing*, de *sing*, *eating*, de *eat*, etc.) Comme dans ?*His kicking the bucket surprised us all?* (Les points d'interrogation placés au début et à la fin de l'expression indiquent qu'il n'existe pas de commun accord sur la grammaticalité ou la non-grammaticalité de cette expression; nous vous conseillons de l'éviter).

La catégorie d'expressions idiomatiques qui se révèle ensuite la plus grande c'est celle bien connue des dictons et des proverbes. Parmi ces idiotismes apparaissent les types célèbres du *don't count your chickens before they're hatched* (ce qui veut dire « ne vous réjouissez pas trop tôt des résultats d'une entreprise, car il est possible que vous échouiez et que vous ayez l'air ridicule ») *don't wash your dirty linen in public* (voulant dire « ne vous plaignez point de vos problèmes de famille devant des étrangers car ça ne les regarde pas »), ainsi de suite. De ces expressions idiomatiques un grand nombre ont vu le jour dans quelque oeuvre littéraire bien connue ou nous viennent des premiers habitants du Continent Nord Américain à parler anglais. Cette littérature avait influencé leur culture linguistique à eux aussi.

Pourquoi l'anglais, et surtout l'anglais américain, sont-ils aussi peuplés d'idiotismes? C'est là un fait intrigant. La raison la plus plausible, c'est que, développant de nouveaux concepts, nous avons besoin de nouvelles expressions pour les exprimer, mais au lieu de créer un mot de toute pièce à partir des sons de la langue, nous employons plutôt des mots déjà en existence et nous les mettons ensemble en leur donnant une nouvelle signification. Il semble que cela serait vrai de toutes les langues connues. Il n'existe, en effet, aucune langue connue qui n'ait au moins quelques idiotismes. Citons l'expression chinoise pour « vite » par exemple. C'est *mǎ shāng,* et traduite littéralement cette expression veut dire « à dos de cheval ». Pourquoi—peut-on se demander—l'idée de « vitesse » devrait-elle être associée au dos d'un cheval? Quelques moments de réflexion ont vite fait de nous révéler la réponse. Dans le bon vieux temps avant l'avènement du train, de l'automobile et de l'avion, c'était le cheval qui fournissait le moyen le plus rapide de se rendre d'un endroit à un autre. L'expression chinoise *mǎ shāng* est donc comparable à ce qu'on pourrait dire en anglais *hurry up! "We must go on horse back"* i.e., « Dépêche-toi! Nous devons aller vite ». Une telle forme serait tout à fait compréhensible en anglais, bien que le sujet parlant dût se rendre compte que c'est un idiotisme, et que l'étranger dût faire l'effort pour l'apprendre. En disant que ces expressions ne sont pas inintelligibles, je veux dire que « à dos de cheval » et « vite » ne sont pas tellement éloignés l'un de l'autre quant à leur signification : même si l'on n'avait jamais entendu dire que *mǎ shāng* veut dire « vite » il est fort possible qu'on puisse en deviner la signification. Mais il se peut aussi que l'on ne devine pas juste. Prenons l'idiotisme anglais *Oh well, the die is cast!* Quelle en serait la signification selon vous—au cas où vous ne connaissiez pas cette expression? A cause du *Oh well,* il se peut que vous pensiez que le sujet parlant donne son consentement à quelque proposition. L'expression veut dire « J'ai pris une décision sur laquelle je ne peux pas revenir et je dois l'accepter ». L'on peut maintenant essayer de reconstruire l'apparition de cet idiotisme : ce qui apparaît sur les dés jetés au jeu ne peut pas être changé ; ce serait illégal ; que vous obteniez un un, un trois ou un six, il vous faut accepter les conséquences de votre jeu, c'est-à-dire, gagner ou perdre, selon le cas. (Il y a des gens qui savent peut-être que cette expression a été employée par César au moment où il traversait le Rubicon et que cette action causa la guerre).

Après avoir appris cet idiotisme, comment l'exploierez-vous correctement? Tout d'abord, attendez de l'entendre de la bouche de celui dont l'anglais est la langue maternelle et utilisé dans un contexte naturel; n'essayez pas d'employer un idiotisme avant d'avoir fait l'apprentissage des règles fondamentales de grammaire anglaise. Après avoir entendu l'expression idiomatique plus d'une fois et en ayant compris toute la signification, c'est le moment de l'employer vous-mêmes. Imaginez qu'on vous fait deux offres d'emploi, l'un certain, mais à un salaire moindre et l'autre à un meilleur salaire, mais qui n'est que provisoire. Parce que vous êtes nerveux et que vous avez peur de n'avoir aucun emploi, vous acceptez l'emploi au salaire plus bas. A ce moment la meilleure offre se réalise et vous vous sentez naturellement contrarié. Vous pouvez alors dire *Oh well, the die is cast...* Si vous faites cet essai avec quelqu'un dont l'anglais est la langue maternelle et s'il vous regarde tendrement sans vous demander *"What do you mean?"* «Que voulez-vous dire?»—vous avez réussi à employer votre premier idiotisme avec succès dans un contexte approprié. C'est là une agréable expérience. Les Américains indigènes acceptent les étrangers plus poliment d'ordinaire que les autres nations, mais ils peuvent sans contredit, porter un jugement sur votre connaissance de la langue. Si l'on emploie toujours une expression livresque et recherchée, ne pouvant jamais utiliser un idiotisme en temps et lieu, l'on s'attirera sans doute la réputation d'être un locuteur plat et sans imagination, ou de quelqu'un qui essaie d'être trop sérieux ou trop officiel. *L'emploi d'idiotismes est par conséquent d'une importance extrême. Il peut faire naître de la sympathie chez celui qui vous écoute.* Plus vous utilisez d'idiotismes dans le bon contexte et plus les Américains se sentiront à l'aise avec vous et plus ils se diront « voilà un chic type—regarde comme il s'exprime bien! »

Arrêtons-nous maintenant à quelques considérations pratiques sur notre *Dictionary of American Idioms*.

COMMENT UTILISER LE DICTIONNAIRE

Ce dictionnaire a été compilé pour les gens dont l'anglais n'est pas la langue maternelle, qu'ils soient étudiants, ouvriers, immigrants, bref pour tous ceux qui veulent améliorer leur anglais et le rendre plus idiomatique. Il contient des expressions appartenant aux catégories dont on a fait mention plus haut, idiotismes léxémiques, idiotismes phraséologiques, et idiotismes proverbiaux, qui ont une signification particulière. Quand une expression a une signification particulière qu'on ne peut pas déchiffrer adéquatement en cherchant dans le dictionnaire et en comprenant chaque mot dont elle est formée, l'on a alors affaire à un idiotisme. Il est possible que vous connaissiez déjà quelques-unes de ces expressions idioma-

tiques et que vous puissiez en imaginer la signification. Cherchez dans le dictionnaire l'un ou l'autre des idiotismes suivants que vous connaissez peut-être déjà bien : ceci vous aidera à comprendre comment utiliser ce livre : *boyfriend* «ami», *girl friend* «amie», *outer space* «l'espace», *piggy bank* «tire-lire», *get even* «se venger», *going to* «aller», *keep on* «continuer à», *keep your mouth shut* «taisez-vous», *lead somebody by the nose* «mener par le bout du nez», *look after* «s'occuper de», *show off,* «faire parade de», *throw away* «gaspiller», *all over* «partout», *in love* «amoreux», *mixed-up* «troublé», *out of this world* «fantastique», *I'll say* «dites donc», *both x and y* «à la fois x et y».

Il en est d'un dictionnaire comme de tout autre outil : il faut apprendre à le connaître et à s'en servir avant qu'en retour cet outil nous rende service. Etudiez les modes d'emploi avec soin plusieurs fois, et cherchez des idiotismes dans le dictionnaire à plusieurs reprises. De cette manière chercher un idiotisme et le trouver deviendront pour vous seconde nature. Si vous entendez une expression idiomatique qui n'est pas dans ce livre, après l'avoir employée un certain temps, vous pourrez en identifier la signification et l'ajouter vous-même à la liste. Dressez votre propre liste d'idiotismes chez vous, juste à côté de votre dictionnaire usuel. Faites-nous parvenir vos observations et vos remarques. Si vous faites la lecture d'un texte de prose technique, ou d'un roman ou d'un article de journal et que vous ne comprenez pas une expression, cherchez-la dans votre dictionnaire habituel d'abord; si vous ne la trouvez pas, essayez ensuite le dictionnaire que voici.

Comment vérifier que ce dictionnaire peut vous aider à comprendre une phrase difficile? Parfois la locution saute aux yeux, comme dans le cas de *puppy love, fun house, dog-eat-dog, mixed-up.* Si ce n'est pas aussi évident, choisissez un mot important tiré de la partie la plus difficile de l'expression et cherchez-le dans le dictionnaire. Si c'est là le premier mot de l'idiotisme, vous allez trouver la locution entière suivie d'une explication. Ainsi l'expression *bats in the belfry* «araignée au plafond», apparaît dans le dictionnaire sous la lettre *b,* le mot *bats.* Si le mot choisi n'est pas le premier mot, vous trouverez une liste d'idiotismes qui renferment ce mot. Par exemple, le mot *toe* se trouvera sous les entrés *curl one's hair* OU *curl one's toes,* OU *one's toes, step on the toes (of somebody)*. Il se peut, naturellement, que vous découvriez que ce n'est pas à cause de la présence d'un idiotisme dans une phrase que vous ne la comprenez pas; dans ce cas, votre dictionnaire de tous les jours vous viendra en aide. Il y a aussi, il va sans dire, plus d'idiotisme que ce dictionnaire n'en contient: nous ne donnons ici que les idiotismes les plus fréquemment employés en *anglais américain.* L'anglais d'Angleterre, par exemple, ou l'anglais parlé en Australie, renferme, bien sûr, plusieurs idiotismes qui n'existent pas en anglais américain. Un dictionnaire qui contiendrait tous les idiotismes de la langue anglaise où qu'elle se parle, serait un dictionnaire *interdialectal des idiotismes anglais.* Ce livre n'existe pas présentement, mais devrait éventuellement être compilé.

GENRES D'ENTRÉE

Ce dictionnaire renferme quatre sortes d'entrée : *entrées principales, entrées dérivées, entrées de références* et *entrées d'index.* Une entrée principale contient une explication complète de l'idiotisme. Une entrée dérivée est une locution qui est dérivée d'un autre idiotisme mais qui en serait séparée si elle apparaissait dans l'ordre alphabétique qui lui est assigné. Les idiotismes dérivés ont été placés à la fin de l'entrée principale (e.g., *fence-sitter* à *sit on the fence)* suivis d'une illustration et d'une paraphrase; on a ajouté une explication supplémentaire quand il nous a semblé qu'il serait difficile de comprendre l'explication de la locution dérivée à partir de l'explication de la locution de base. Quand un idiotisme en est venu à être employé sous plus d'une des parties du discours sans changer de forme, on a créé une entré séparée pour chacun.

Une entrée de référence vous guide vers une définition donnée à un autre endroit. Disons que vous voulez chercher *cast in one's lot with.* Vous pouvez chercher sous *cast* et sous *lot*: mais l'entrée de référen-ce vous référera à *throw* dans la locution *throw in one's lot with.* C'est que *cast* est un mot beaucoup plus rare aujourd'hui et ainsi, la forme habituelle et plus fréquente de cet idiotisme commence par le verbe *throw.*

Une entrée d'index vous renverra à toutes les autres entrés contenant le mot de l'index. Par exemple, le mot *chin* est suivi des locutions dont il fait partie, e.g., *keep one's chin up, stick one's chin (or neck) out, take it on the chin, up to the chin.*

ETIQUETTES INDIQUANT LA PARTIE DU DISCOURS

Les idiotismes lexémiques (tels que présentés plus haut) sont porteurs d'une étiquette de partie du discours. Parfois, comme dans le cas de plusieurs locutions adverbiales, une double étiquette doit leur être attachée, parce que la locution en question a deux emplois grammaticaux, e.g., *in commission* peut être soit adverbe soit adjectif. Plusieurs locutions prépositionnelles sont des adverbes dans leur sens littéral, mais sont des adjectifs dans leur sens idiomatique.

V. veut dire verbe: il a été attaché aux locutions contenant un verbe et un adverbe: un verbe et une préposition: ou un verbe, une préposition et un adverbe. *V. Phr.* veut dire "verbal phrase" (prédicat): sont inclus sous cette étiquette les verbes qui ont un objet, les verbes qui ont un sujet et les verbes attachés à une locution prépositionelle.

ETIQUETTES DÉCRIVANT L'USAGE DES IDIOTISMES

Il est important pour vous, dont l'anglais n'est pas la langue maternelle de réfléchir à l'emploi que vous faites d'un certain idiotisme dans un certain contexte. L'étiquette *informal* «langue familière» indique que la forme s'emploie en conversation mais devrait être évitée en composition. *Formal* «langue recherchée» indique le contraire: c'est une forme que les gens n'emploient pas d'habitude en conversation mais qu'ils écriront volontiers dans une dissertation et dont ils se serviront lorsqu'ils donnent une conférence à l'université. *Literary* «langue littéraire» vous éveille au fait que les gens savent en général que la forme est une citation; vous auriez l'air bizarre si vous employiez ces expressions trop souvent. *Vulgar* «vulgaire» indique que vous devriez éviter cette forme complètement. *Substandard* «inférieure au niveau moyen» veut dire qu'une forme n'est employée que par ceux qui sont moins instruits; *nonstandard* «qui n'est pas standard» signifie qu'une locution semble être une gaucherie d'expression. *Regional labels* «régionalisme» sont ce qui nous révèlent l'origine géographique d'une forme et l'emploie qu'on en fait dans ce milieu, e.g., *chiefly British* «strictement anglais d'Angleterre» veut dire que les Américains n'emploient cette expression que rarement, *Southern* «du sud» signifie qu'une forme est beaucoup plus fréquente au sud qu'au nord des Etats-Unis.

Les formes qui sont récentes, ayant fait leur entrée dans la langue pendant ces six ou sept dernières années, apparaissent dans un appendice faisant suite au texte principal du dictionnaire.

Adam Makkai/Jean-Luc Garneau

Vorwort

WAS IST EIN IDIOM?

Wenn wir jedes Wort in einem Text verstehen, und den Sinn des Ganzen doch nicht begreifen, dann müssen wir davon ausgehen, daß uns die Idiomatismen verwirren. Nehmen wir zum Beispiel an, daß jemand das Folgende liest, oder hört:

Sam is a real cool cat. He never blows his stack and hardly ever flies off the handle. What's more, he knows how to get away with things . . . Well, of course, he is getting on, too. His hair is pepper and salt, but he knows how to make up for lost time by taking it easy. He gets up early, works out, and turns in early. He takes care of the hot dog stand like a breeze until he gets time off. Sam's got it made; this is it for him.

Die Bemerkung, daß wir es hier nicht mit einem gehobenen literarischen Stil zu tun haben, erübrigt sich; die meisten Amerikaner werden jedoch die in der vorliegenden Textpassage vorkommenden Ausdrücke oft gebrauchen, besonders wenn sie im vertrauten Kreis miteinander reden. Ein Fremder oder ein erst kürzlich in dieses Land Eingewanderter wird zwar schon früher gelernt haben, daß *cool* 'kühl', *cat* 'Katze', *blow* 'blasen, wehen', *stack* 'Haufen, Stapel', *fly* 'fliegen', *handle* 'Griff, Stiel, Öhr', etc. bedeuten, es folgt daraus aber bei weitem nicht, daß die obige amerikanisch-englische Gabrauchssprache auch verstanden wird, da eine leicht zu handhabenbe Wörterbuchinformation allein nicht genügen kann, den Sinn der vorliegenden Formen zu enthüllen. Wie aus diesen Beobachtungen hervorgeht, ist ein Idiom nichts anderes, als eine Gruppe von Wörtern, die einzeln und ursprünglich eine andere Bedeutung haben, einen neuen Sinn zu verleihen. Die 'Übersetzung' dieses vertraulich-slangartigen Textes in eine troken-formalere und verhältnismäßig idiomentfrei englische Fassung könne so lauten:

Sam is really a calm person. He never loses control of himself and hardly ever becomes too angry. Furthermore, he knows how to manage his business financially by using a few tricks . . . Needless to say, he, too, is getting older. His hair is beginning to turn gray, but he knows how to compensate for wasted time by relaxing. He rises early, exercises, and goes to bed early. He manages his frankfurter stand without visible effort, until it is someone else's turn to work there. Sam is successful; he has reached his life's goal.

Sam ist wirklich ein ruhiger Mensch Er verliert niemals die Beherrschung, und wird fast nie allzu ärgerlich. Außerdem weiß er darüber Bescheid, wie er seine finanziellen Geschäfte mittels einiger Kniffe zu führen hat... Selbstverständlich ist auch er nicht mehr der Jüngste. Seine Haare werden langsam grau, aber er weiß, daß man die verlorengegangene Zeit durch Gemütsruhe ersetzen kann. Er steht früh auf, turnt, und geht früh zu Bett. Er versieht die Arbeit in seinem Heißwurst-Verkaufsstand ohne sichtliche Anstrengung, bis ihn dort jemand ablöst. Sam ist erfolgreich, er hat sein Lebensziel erreicht.

Wenn wir nun die Struktur der phraseologischen Einheiten des Slangtextes zu erklären versuchten, so wäre das Ergebnis unserer Arbeit ein kleines idiomatisches Wörterbuch, das wie folgt aussehen würde:

to be a (real) cool cat	'eine wirkliche ruhiger Mensch sein'
to blow one's stack	'die Beherrschung verlieren, plötzlich in Wut geraten'
to fly off the handle	'sich erzürnen, ärgerlich werden'
what's more	'außerdem, darüberhinaus'

to get away with something	'eine gesetzwirdrige oder knifflige Handlung vornehmen und mit heiler Haut davonkommen'
of course	'selbstverständlich, natürlich'
to be getting on	'älter werden', 'altern'
pepper and salt	'mit grauen Strähnen vermischte dunkle Haarfarbe'
to make up for something	'gutmachen, kompensieren'
lost time	'durch sinnlose Betätigung verschwendete Zeit'
to take it easy	'sich keine Sorgen machen', 'sich nicht aus der Ruehe bringen lassen'
to get up	'aufstehen'
to work out	'turnen'
to turn in	'abends zu Bett gehen'
to take care of something	'sich für etwas Sorge tragen', 'sich um etwas kümmern'
like a breeze	'ohne Anstrengung, leicht'
time off	'Freizeit'
to have got it made	'erfolgreich sein, es geschafft haben'
this is it	'das ist es, in einer Lage sein, in der man sein Zeit erreicht hat'

Viele Idiome der vorliegenden kleinen Wortauslese sind in diesem Wörterbuch zu finden. Bemerkenswert ist gerade jener Umstand, daß die meinsten dieser Idiome leicht mit den herkömmlichen, allgemein üblichen Satzteilen zu identifizieren sind. Manche sind offensichtlich verbaler Natur, z.B. *get away with, get up, work out, turn in*, usw. Ebenso häufig sind die Idiome von substantivischem Charakter, beispielsweise *hot dog* (nicht 'heisser Hund', sondern 'heißes Würstchen mit Senf und/oder anderen Beilagen zwischen zwei länglichen Brötchen'), *White House* 'das Weiße Haus, Residenz des Präsidenten der Vereinigten Staaten', usw. Viele haben eine prädikative Funktion, wie *pepper and salt* 'ergrauende, dunkle Haare', andere wiederum sind adverbialer Natur, wie in unserem Beispiel: *like a breeze* ('ohne Anstrengung, leicht'/oder wie in der Redewendung *hammer and tongs* (nicht 'hammer und Kneifzange' sondern 'heftig, gewaltsam').

Die Idiome, die in einem bestimmten Zusammenhang mit den bekannten Bestandteilen eines Satzes stehen, werden LEXEMISCHE IDIOME 'lexemic idioms' genannt.

Die andere, sehr wichtige Gruppe von Idiomen besteht aus längeren formelhaften Redewendungen. Oft machen solche Idiome einen ganzen kleinen Satz aus, wie unsere Beispiele *to fly off the handle* 'sich erzürnen, ärgerlich werden' und *to blow one's stack* 'die Beherrschung verlieren'. Davon gibt es im Amerikanischen Englisch eine große Anzahl. Hier sind einige der bekanntesten: *to kick the bucket* 'sterben', *to be up the creek* 'in der Klemme sitzen', usw. Diese Idiome heißen 'tournures', auf gut Deutsch Redewendungen, laut linguistischer Definition, phraseologische Einheiten.

Ihre Form ist festgeleft, und lediglich eine geringe Anzahl solcher Idiome kann umgewandelt oder anders gesagt werden, ohne ihren ursprünglichen Sinn zu verlieren. Manche von ihnen sind völlig unveränderbare Redewendungen.

Die nächste wichtige Klasse von Idiomen bilden die bekannten Sprüche und Sprichwörter.

Warum ist die englische Sprache und besonders ihre amerikanische Variante dermaßen reich an Idiomen? Höchst wahrscheinlich liegt es daran, daß in einer schnell sich entwickelnden großindustriellen Gesellschaft Tag für Tag neue Begriffe und sprachliche Konzepte entstehen und immer mehr neue Benennungen und Ausdrücke zur Kommunikation benötigt werden. Die menschliche Natur mit unserer angeborenen Bequemlichkeit ist aber so beschaffen, daß wir anstatt aus dem phonetischen Bestand der Sprache brandneue Wörter zu schöpfen, lieber die schon vorhandenen Wörter gebrauchen, indem wir sie in einer neuen sinntragenden Form zusammenstellen. Dies scheint jedoch auf alle Sprachen zuzutreffen.

TIPS FÜR DEN GEBRAUCH DIESES WÖRTERBUCHS

Dieses Wörterbuch der Idiome wurde für jene Studenten, Berufstätige und Einwanderer zusammengestellt, die Englisch schon gelernt haben, aber die Sprache fließender und natürlicher sprechen wollen. Es enthält die oben angeführten Arten von Redewendungen: Lexemische, phraseologische, und spruchartige Idiome, deren spezifischer Sinn nicht mit der Einzelbedeutung der darin vorkommenden Wörter identifiziert werden kann. Der Leser wird die Bedeutung mancher Idiome von vorherein kennen, die meisten aber werden für ihn wahrscheinlich neu sein. Der Gebrauch diese Nachschlagewerkes wird beträchtlich erleichtert, wenn wir nach allgemein verbreiteten Ausdrücken suchen, wie z.B. *boyfriend, girl friend, outer space, piggy bank, get even, give up, going to, keep on, keep your mouth shut.*

Ein Wörterbuch ist, wie jedes andere Werkzeug: Man muß sich damit vertraut machen, bevor es einem nützen kann. Es ist also ratsam, die folgende Anleitung aufmerksam durchzulesen und zu üben, wie und wo man die gesuchten Idiome im Buch findet. Bald wird es mit automatischer Leichtigkeit gehen. Sollten wir einen idiomatischen Ausdruck hören, der in diesem Wörterbuch nicht enthalten ist, dann wird die Übung zur Fähigkeit beitragen, den Sinn eines Idioms selbst zu entschlüsseln. Es ist empfehelenswert ein kleines Wörterbuch der Idiome für den Eigengebrauch anzulegen. Der Verleger zeigt sich dankbar für alle Bemerkungen und Vorschläge der Leser.

Wenn irgendetwas in einem Fachtext, Roman oder Zeitungsartikel unverständlich ist, kann man vorerst im allgemeinen Schul- oder im erläuternden Wörterbuch nachschlagen; fehlt dort das Gesuchte, dann verspricht dieses Wörterbuch mehr Erfolg.

Wie findet man heraus, ob dieses Werk beim Verstehen eines schwierigen englischen Satzes Hilfestellung leistet? Manchmal sind auch unbekannte Ausdrücke mittels der Struktur der Wortzusammensetzungen einfach zu lösen, wie *puppy love, fun house, dog-eat-dog, mixed-up.* Ist der Ausdruck aber doch nicht zu enträt- seln, so ist es am besten, ein wichtiges Wort des schwierigsten Teiles nachzuschlagen. Steht das gesuchte Wort am Anfang des Idioms, so wird der ganze Satz(teil) samt Erklärung bei diesem Wort zu finden sein. Der Ausdruck *bats in the belfry* (nicht 'Fledermäuse im Kirchturm' sondern 'er ist nicht richtig im Oberstübchen', 'er ist meschugge', 'übergeschnappt') steht unter dem Buchstaben 'B' beim Wort *bats.* Ist das gewählte Wort nicht das erste im Satz, dann finden wir eine ganze Liste von Idiomen, die dieses Wort enthalten. Zum Beispiel das Wort *toe* 'Zehe' ist in den folgenden Ausdrücken zu finden: *Curl one's hair or curl one's toes, on one's toes, step on the toes (of somebody).* Es kann natürlich vorkommen, daß man einen Satz nicht deshalb mißversteht (oder gar nicht versteht), weil Idiome darin vorkommen, sondern nur deswegen, weil uns auch die Ursprüngliche Bedeutung der Wörter unbekannt ist. Es versteht sich von selbst, daß in diesem Fall ein allgemeines Wörterbuch benützt werden soll. Natürlich gibt es mehr Idiome als in diesem Band erhalten sind; dieses Buch enthält nur die meistgebrauchten Idiome des Amerikanischen English. Das Britische Englisch und das in Australien gesprochene Englisch weisen sicherlich manche idiomatische Wendungen auf, die nicht zum Bestandteil der nordamerikanischen Sprache geworden sind. Ein Wörterbuch, das alle Idiome der englischen Sprache enthielte, wäre ein unterdialektisches Wörterbuch der englischen Idiome. Ein solches Buch gibt es vorläufig nicht, wir wollen aber hoffen, daß die Zusammenstellung dieses erwünschten Werkes lediglich eine Zeitfrage ist.

ARTEN VON EINTRAGUNGEN

In diesem Wörterbuch finden wir vier Arten von Eintragungen: Haupteintragungen, Ableitungseintragungen, Referenzeintragungen und Index-Eintragungen. Eine Haupteintragung enthält die volle Erklärung des Idioms. Eine Ableitungseintragung ist ein Ausdruck, der von einem anderen Idiom herrührt, der aber von seinem Ursprung getrennt wäre, wenn er seine einreihung laut Alphabet erhielte.

Diese abgeleiteten Idiome finden sich im vorliegenden Wörterbuch im Anschluß an die Haupteintragung, so wie der Ausdruck *fence sitter* unter der Haupteintragung *sit on the fence*, also bei 'S' und nicht by 'F' vorkommt. Die Erläuterung, wie dieser Ausdruck zu gebrauchen ist, wird auch in der Haupteintragung gegeben, aber es wurden überall dort Sondererklärungen beigefügt, wo das Verstehen des abgeleiteten Idioms aufgrund der ursprünglichen Redewendung schwierig gewesen wäre. Wenn ein gegebenes Idiom als unterschiedlicher Satzteil gebraucht wird, erscheint jeder Satzteil in diesem Band als Sondereintragung. Eine anderswo hinweisende Eintragung dient dazu, eine Erklärung zu finden, die an einer anderen Stelle im Wörterbuch enthalten ist. Die Index-Eintragung führt zu allen Ausdrücken, die das gesuchte Stichwort enthalten.

SATZTEILBEZEICHNUNGEN

Da (wie schon erörtert worden ist) die lexemischen Idiome mit Satzteilen identifizierbar sind, wurden sie mit Satzteilbezeichnungen versehen. Es kommt oft vor, daß ein englisches Idiom eine syntaktische Doppelrolle innehat. Das ist eine bekannte Schwierigkeit dieser Sprache. Im Falle eines einfachen Wortes sieht das so aus: *man* kann ein Hauptwort sein, wie in diesem Satz: *he is a good man* 'er ist ein guter Mensch', es kann aber ebenso als Zeitwort dienen: *John will man the post tonight* 'heute nacht wird John den Posten besetzen/übernehmen'. Diese syntaktische Pluralität besteht auch bei mehrteiligen Idiomen. Der Ausdruck *in commission* 'in Betrieb sein' kann sowohl prädikativ als auch adverbial sein. Viele präpositionalen Wortgruppen sind adverbialer Art in ihrem engsten Sinn, aber adjektivisch in ihrer unvorhersehbaren idiomatischen Bedeutung.

Das Zeichen *v* steht für 'verb' d.h. 'Zeitwort', und wurde solchen Wortgruppen zugeteilt, die ein Zeitwort und ein Bestimmungswort, oder ein Zeitwort und ein Verhältniswort, oder alle drei enthalten.

Die Abkürzung *v. phr.* steht für *verbal phrase*, d.h. für solche längeren Ausdrücke, die verbalen Charakter im Satz haben; diese beinhalten Zeitwörter mit einem Objekt, Zeitwörter mit erweitertem Subjekt und Zeitwörter mit präpositionalen Wortverbindungen.

GEBRAUCHSHINWEISE

Derjenige, der Englisch nicht als seine Muttersprache spricht, muß besonders darauf achten, ob der Gebrauch gewisser Idiome in einer Bestimmten Umgebung passend ist oder nicht. Die Bezeichnung *slang* weist darauf hin, daß das Idiom nur im engen Freundeskreis angewandt werden soll. *Informal* 'ungebunden' macht darauf aufmerksam, daß diese Form im Gespräch volkommen einwandfrei, aber in schriftlicher Fassung zu vermeiden ist. *Formal* bezeichnet das Gegenteil; solche Ausdrücke hören wir im gesprochenen Englisch selten, wärend sie ziemlich häufig in der Schriftsprache und in Vorlesungen vorkommen. *Literary* ist ein Hinweis darauf, daß wir mit einem literarischen Zitat zu tun haben, und diejenigen, die das gebrauchen, wissen zumeist Bescheid (obwohl nicht ausnahmslos), aber ein Ausländer soll mit Zitaten vorsichtig umgehen. *Vulgar* bezeichnet, daß der Ausdruck zu vermeiden ist. Natürlich kann es nicht schaden, wenn mach auch diese Art von Idiomen kennt und versteht, da der von einem Menschen gern gebrauchte Wortschatz nicht wenig zu seiner Beurteilung beiträgt. Regionale Bezeichnungen sind einschränkender Natur, und geben die geographische Herkunft und Verbreitung einer Ausdrucksform an. *Chiefly British* bedeutet 'in England üblich', aber in Nordamerika selten zu hören. *Southern* bedeutet daß das Idiom in den Südstaaten viel beliebter ist, als im nördlichen Teil der USA.

Adam Makkai/Doris Jutta Glatzl

Premessa

CHE COS'E' UN'ESPRESSIONE IDIOMATICA?

Se non si capisce ciascuna parola in un certo testo e non si riesce ad interpretare tale testo, il motivo sicuro per questo è la presenza nel testo di espressioni idiomatiche sconosciute. Per esempio, supponiamo che si è presentati con il seguente testo:

Sam is a real cool cat. He never blows his stack and hardly ever flies off the handle. What's more, he knows how to get away with things . . .Well, of course, he is getting on, too. His hair is pepper and salt, but he knows how to make up for lost time by taking it easy. He gets up early, works out, and turns in early. He takes care of the hot dog stand like a breeze until he gets time off. Sam's got it made; this is it for him.

Va senza dire che non si tratta di un testo di grande qualità letteraria, ma la maggior parte degli americani, specialmente quando conversano tra di loro, utilizzano espressioni proprio come quelle contenute in questo testo. Se non si conosce la cultura americana, pur conoscendo vocaboli come *cool* "fresco," *cat* "gatto," *blow* "soffiare," *stack* "mucchio," *fly* "volare," *handle* "maniglia, manico," e così via, non si sarà in grado di capire il testo riportato sopra, per il motivo che le definizioni di un vocabolario regolare non forniranno i significati idiomatici delle parole. Ma sono proprio questi significati che si dorvano conoscere per interpretare il testo nella sua globalità. L'uso idiomatico di una parola sta, ovviamente, nell'assegnare un nuovo significato alla stessa parola. Ecco, perciò, una "traduzione" letterale del testo idiomatico riportato sopra. Questa riflette uno stile più formale e privo relativamente di idiomaticità:

Sam is really a calm person. He never loses control of himself and hardly ever becomes too angry. Further-more, he knows how to manage his business financially by using a few tricks . . . Needless to say, he, too, is getting older. His hair is beginning to turn gray, but he knows how to compensate for wasted time by relaxing. He rises early, exercises, and goes to bed early. He manages his frankfurter stand without visible effort, until it is someone else's turn to work there. Sam is successful; he has reached his life's goal.

Ora, se si dovesse spiegare come sono organizzate le unità in questo testo, si avrebbe bisogno di un dizionarietto di espressioni idiomatiche che avrebbe la seguente forma:

to be a (real) cool cat	essere una persona molto calma
to blow one's stack	perdere l'auto-controllo, arrabbiarsi
to fly off the handle	arrabbiarsi fortemente
what's more	per di più
to get away with something	cavarsela
of course	certo, naturalmente
to be getting on	invecchiarsi
pepper and salt	capelli che stanno diventando grigi
to make up for something	riprendere, riacquistare, rifare
lost time	tempo perduto
to take it easy	stare calmo, non preoccuparsi
to get up	alzarsi dal letto
to work out	fare esercizio, fare ginnastica
to turn in	andare a dormire la sera
to take care of something	pensarci
like a breeze	con facilità, facilmente, senza alcuno sforzo
time off	tempo libero
to have got it made	essere arrivato, avere successo
this is it	avercela fatta

Gran parte delle espressioni in questo elenco sono ritrovabili nel presente dizionario. E' interessante notare che esse sono classificabili secondo le cosiddette "parti del discorso": e cioè, dal punto di vista grammaticale alcune fungono da verbi (*get away with, get up, work out, turn in*, ecc.), alcune da nomi (*hot dog, White House* "Casa Bianca,") altre da aggettivi (*pepper and salt*), altre ancora da avverbi (*like the breeze, hammer and tongs* "in modo violento,") e così via. Le espressioni che si possono correlare alle parti del discorso sono *lessemi idiomatici*.

L' altro tipo di espressione idiomatica di una certa frequenza nel discorso comune è costituito da frasi intere come *to fly off the handle* "perdere l'auto-controllo" e *to blow one's stack* "arrabbiarsi fortemente." Ce ne sono veramente tante in inglese di frasi di questo tipo, alcune delle quali sono assai famose: *to kick the bucket* "morire," *to be up the creek* "essere in pericolo," *to be caught between the devil and the deep blue sea* "essere tra l'incudine ed il martello," *to seize the bull by the horns* "risolvere un problema concretamente," e così via. In francese, espressioni di questo tipo si chiamano *tournures*, e cioè, "giri di parole," ma si possono anche denominare semplicemente delle *frasi idiomatiche*. La loro caratteristica saliente è il fatto che non sono assegnabili facilmente ad una parte del discorso, e, per di più, che sono esplicabili nei termini di una parafrasi.

La loro forma è fissa e non può essere alterata senza modificare il significato. Sono delle "formule rigide" che non si possono parafrasare, né facilmente spiegare. L'espressione *to kick the bucket*, per esempio, non può essere modificata in nessuna maniera: la forma passiva *the bucket has been kicked by the cowboy* non significa più che "il cowboy è morto," ma invece che "il cowboy ha dato un calcio al secchio." Espressioni di questo tipo sono *forme completamente fisse*, anche se possono essere modificate in quanto al loro tempo verbale: *the cowboy kicked the bucket, the cowboy will kick the bucket, he has kicked the bucket*, ecc. le quali significano irspettivamente che il cowboy "morì," "morirà," e "è morto." Solo il caso del gerundio (forma verbale terminante in *-ing*) presenta un'ambiguità interpretativa, per cui è meglio evitare frasi tipo *His kicking the bucket surprised us all.*

Un altro tipo assai consistente di espressioni idiomatiche è costituito dai detti e dai proverbi, e cioè, da espressioni come *don't count your chickens before they're hatched* ("una rondine non fa primavera,") *don't wash your dirty linen in public* ("non far conoscere agli altri i propri problemi domestici,") ecc. Molte di queste espressioni hanno una lunga ed illustre tradizione letteraria, essendo state tramandate al continente americano dai primi parlanti d'inglese.

Perché è così "idiomatico" l'inglese, specialmente nella sua versione americana? La risposta più probabile a questo quesito è il bisogno di creare nuovi significati semplicemente ricombinando le parole già esistenti nella lingua, ed evitando perciò d'inventare nuove parole in base alle risorse fonetiche della lingua. Questa forma di creatività si manifesta in tutte le lingue del mondo. Non esiste una lingua che non abbia espressioni idiomatiche. In cinese, per esempio, l'espressione *mǎ shāng* "velocemente," significa letteralmente "groppa di cavallo." In che modo è associabile il concetto di "velocemente" con una "groppa di cavallo?" La risposta risulta ovvia se si considera che prima dell'avvento del treno, dell'automobile, e dell'aeroplano, il modo più veloce per giungere a destino era a cavallo. Quindi, l'espressione cinese *mǎ shāng* corrisponde all'inglese *hurry up! We must go on horse back* ("Andiamo velocemente"). Tali forme, quindi, non sono affatto incomprensibili, ma uno studente straniero della lingua le dovrà imparare correttamente, altrimenti rischia di essere incompreso. Si consideri, per esempio, l'espressione *Oh well, the die is cast!* Cosa significa? Ovviamente, contiene un elemento di sorpresa, visto la presenza dell'interiezione *Oh well*. Essa significa: "Ho sbagliato, e dovrò accettarne le conseguenze!" Da un punto di vista etimologico tale espressione deriva probabilmente dal fatto che nei giochi d'azzardo una volta che è stato buttato giù un dado sul tavolo, non importerà se dimostra il numero uno, tre, o sei; il fatto sta che bisognerà accettarne le conseguenze, per cui si potrà vincere o perdere. Alcuni pensano, invece, che tale frase fu usata da Cesare quando attraversò il Rubicone, azione dalla quale conseguì una guerra.

Come sarà possibile usare un'espressione come questa, appena determinato il suo significato? Anzitutto, sarà necessario ascoltare come viene usata nei suoi contesti naturali da parlanti nativi; non è consigliabile usarla senza conoscere prima la grammatica dell'inglese. In seguito a diverse osservazioni circa il suo uso coretto, si sarà più in grado di usarla per conto proprio. Ecco uno scenario plausibile in proposito: Poniamo che un individuo riceva due offerte di impiego, uno delle quali ha prospettive di stipendio più alto; e poniamo l'individuo accetti quella meno lucrosa per qualche motivo; allora l'espressione *Oh well, the die is cast*, è del tutto applicabile alla situazione in questione. Un parlante nativo che sentirà tale espressione in riferimento a questo scenario la capirà perfettamente, e la troverà del tutto adatta. Anche se gli americani tendono ad essere assai tolleranti rispetto agli stranieri, sanno giudicare correttamente il livello di competenza linguistica raggiunto da un qualsiasi straniero. Chi usa uno stile troppo formale e letterale è spesso giudicato come troppo serio e uggioso. *Perciò, l'abilità di padroneggiare le espressioni idiomatiche è importantissima, poiché consente di avvicinarsi all'interlocutore.* Più espressioni idiomatiche si conoscono, più probabile è un tale avvicinamento.

COME USARE QUESTO DIZIONARIO

Chi non consoce la lingua inglese come un nativo, non importa a quale ambito sociale appartenga, può facilmente usare questo dizionario allo scopo di rendere la propria conoscenza della lingua più idiomatica. Esso contiene i tipi d'espressione menzionati sopra: *frasi idiomatiche, forme fisse,* ecc. Le espressioni idiomatiche si riconoscono subito quando il significato non è determinaibile in base al significato delle singole parole che le compongono. Alcune di queste saranno già familiari al lettore, il quale potrà ricercarle facilmente nel presente libro: *boyfriend, girl friend, outer space, piggy bank, get even, give up, going to, keep on, keep your mouth shut,* *lead someone by the nose, look after, show off, throw away, all over, in love, mixed-up, out of this world, throw away, I'll say, both X and Y.*

Questo dizionario è uno strumento che si deve conoscere prima di usare. Quindi, sarà necessario leggere le sue didascalie con attenzione e fare qualche "prova iniziale," ricercando in esso diverse espressioni idiomatiche. In tal modo sarà molto più facile familiarizzarsi con questo strumento, utilizzandolo assieme ad un vocabolario normale quando si leggono testi tecnici, romanzi, o anche articoli di giornale. Chi desidera veramente imparare a parlare idiomaticamente dovrà notare per iscritto qualsiasi espressioni che vuole veramente imparare, appena l'avrà ritrovata nel dizionario.

Questo dizionario sarà anche utile per l'interpretazione di intere frasi. Se la frase contiene un'espressione come *puppy love, fun house, dog-eat-dog, mixed-up*, si potrà semplicemente ricercarla in modo alfabetico; diversamente, sarà necessario determinare qual è parola chiave in una data espressione e poi ricercarla in modo alfabetico. Se è la prima parola dell'espressione, allora è proprio questa che si dovrà ricercare alfabeticamente: per esempio, l'espressione *bats in the belfry* appare alfabeticamente in rapporto alla parola *bats*. Se invece non è la prima parola, bisognerà seguire un'altra modalità di ricerca: per esempio, la parola *toe* in una data espressione sarà ritrovata come una voce in *curl one's hair, curl one's toes, on one's toes, step on the toes (of somebody)*. Ovviamente, nel caso di espressioni non-idiomatiche, si dovrà consultare un vocabolario regolare. E' da notare che non è stato possibile includere in questo dizionario tutte le espressioni idiomatiche dell'inglese parlato in America. Inoltre, nell'inglese parlato in Gran Bretagna in Australia esistono frasi idiomatiche che non fanno parte del repertorio espressivo dell'inglese parlato sul continente nordamericano.

TIPO DI VOCI RACCOLTE IN QUESTO DIZIONARIO

Ci sono quattro tipi di voce raccolti in questo dizionario: *voci principali, voci continuate o unite, voci di richiamo,* e *voci indice.* Nel caso di *voci principali* si tratta di un'espressione spiegata nella sua totalità. Nel caso di una *voce continuata* si tratta di un'espressione derivata da un'altra che altrimenti sarebbe separata da essa se fosse messa in ordine alfabetico (per es., *fence-sitter* viene collocata dopo *sit on the fence* e poi illustrata o spiegata secondo la necessità); un'espressione che appartiene a più di una parte del discorso viene spiegata separatamente. Le voci di richiamo permettono di ricercare frasi come *cast in one's lot with* sia in base a *cast* che a *lot.* In questo caso il lettore troverà la voce nel contesto di *throw in one's lot with* per il motivo che *cast* è una parola di scarsa frequenza, mentre *throw* è di frequenza elevata. Infine, la voce indice permette di ritrovare tutte le altre voci che la contengono: per es., la parola *chin* è seguita dalle espressioni di cui è una componente, e cioè, *keep one's chin up, stick one's chin (or neck) out, take it on the chin, up to the chin.*

VOCI CLASSIFICATE SECONDO LE PARTI DEL DISCORSO

Le espressioni che corrispondono a specifiche parti del discorso saranno classificate in modo correlativo. Per esempio, le espressioni preposizionali sono assegnate a due categorie grammaticali: e.g., *in com-mission* può essere usata sia come frase aggettivale che come avverbiale. E' da notare che molte di queste espressioni sono avverbiali quando vengono usate con un significato letterale, ma aggettivali quando sono usate in modo idiomatico. La sigla *v.* rappresenta un verbo; e cioè essa indica le espressioni contenenti un verbo e un avverbio, un verbo e una preposizione, oppure un verbo, una preposizione e un avverbio. La sigla *v. phr.* indica qualsiasi frase verbale (verbo più complemento, verbo più frase preposizionale, ecc.).

VOCI CON USI RESTRITTIVI

E' ovviamente importante saper usare una qualsiasi espressione in modo appropriato; perciò l'etichetta *slang* indica che è da usare solo con amici che si conoscono intimamente; *uso informale* indica che è da usare sollo nelle conversazioni informali, e *uso formale* nei testi, orali o scritti, che esigono un livcllo più formale di discorso; *uso letterario* indica che si tratta di una citazione, e che, quindi, è da usare di rado; *volgare* indica che è da evitare, anche se viene usata da qualche nativo; *substandard* indica un uso incolto, e *nonstandard* un uso grossalano; *arcaico* indica un uso ormai sorpassato; *regionale* indica un uso ristretto ad un'area geografica (*generalmente britannico* indica uno scarso uso in America, e *meridionale* un uso particolarmente caratteristico nel sud degli Stati Uniti).

Adam Makkai/Marcel Danesi

序文

イディオムとは何か

あるテキストに分からない単語は一つもないのに、全体で一体どういう意味なのか理解できないとしたら、その原因は恐らくイディオムにあるだろう。たとえば次の文章を読んだ(または聞いた)としよう。

Sam is a real cool cat. He never blows his stack and hardly ever flies off the handle. What's more, he knows how to get away with things...Well, of course, he is getting on, too. His hair is pepper and salt, but he knows how to make up for lost time by taking it easy. He gets up early, works out, and turns in early. He takes care of the hot dog stand like a breeze until he gets time off. Sam's got it made; this is it for him.

言うまでもなく、これはすぐれた文学的文体ではないが、大概のアメリカ人は、特に彼ら同士で話す時には、この種の表現を使うだろう。さて、もしあなたがアメリカにいる外国人で、cool「涼しい、冷静な」、cat「ねこ」、blow「吹く」、stack「堆積」、fly「飛ぶ」、handle「取手」等々の単語を学んでいたとしても、上に挙げた会話体のアメリカ英語は分からないだろう。辞書の与えるこういった基礎的な知識だけではここで使われたいろいろな形の意味は与えられないからである。イディオムとは—今言ったことから分かるように—すでにそれぞれ自身の意味を持っている一群の語に新しい意味を付与することである。下に示すのは、この高度にイディオマティックな口語アメリカ英語のテキストを、もっと形式張っていて、比較的イディオムを用いない英語に翻訳したものである。

Sam is really a calm person. He never loses control of himself and hardly ever becomes too angry. Furthermore, he knows how to manage his business financially by using a few tricks... Needless to say, he, too, is getting older. His hair is beginning to turn grey, but he knows how to compensate for wasted time by relaxing. He rises early, exercises, and goes to bed early. He manages his frankfurter dispensary without visible effort, until it is someone else's turn to work there. Sam is successful, he has reached his life's goal.

さて、もしこのテキストで意味の単位が如何に構成されているかを説明するとしたら、イディオム小辞典を作らねばならないだろう。それは次のようになるだろう。

to be a (real) cool cat	本当に落ち着いた人だ
to blow one's stack	自制を失う、かっとなる
to fly off the handle	激怒する
what's more	さらに、その上
to get away with something	(罰せられたりせずに)ある事をうまくやり遂げる
of course	もちろん
to be getting on	年をとる
pepper and salt	(頭髪が)ごま塩
to make up for something	ある事の埋め合わせをする
lost time	むだにした時間
to take it easy	気楽にやる、のんきにやる
to get up	起床する
to work out	体操をする
to turn in	就寝する
to take care of something	ある事の面倒を見る
like a breeze	たやすく
time off	休み時間
to have got it made	成功する
this is it	これで終わりだ

この小さな見本のリストに挙げたイディオムの多くはこの辞書に見出される。興味深いことに、これらのイディオムの大多数は我々が親しんでいるいずれかの品詞に容易に当てはめることができる。たとえば get away with, get out, turn in のようなイディオムは明らかに動詞的である。同様に多数のイディオムは名詞的である。たとえば hot dog「ホット・ドッグ」や White House「ホワイト・ハウス」は名詞である。上の文にある「ごま塩」の意味の pepper and salt のような形容詞的なものも多い。like the breeze「たやすく」、hammer and tongs「激しく」(たとえば She ran after him hammer and tongs.「彼女は猛烈に彼の後を追った」)など多くは副詞的である。このように我々が親しんでいる品詞と関連しているイディオムを「語彙

的イディオム」(lexemic idiom)と呼ぶことができる。

　もう一つの大変重要なイディオムのグループはもっと形が大きい。上例の to fly off the handle「自制を失う」や to blow one's stack「激怒する」のように、しばしば一つの節(clause)全体の長さに近い。このようなイディオムはアメリカ英語には非常に多い。最も有名なものを幾つか挙げれば、to kick the bucket「死ぬ」、to be up the creek「苦境にある」、to be caught between the devil and deep blue sea「二つのいやなことのどちらかを選ばねばならない、進退きわまる」、to seize the bull by the horns「敢然と難局に当たる」などである。この種のイディオムは「言い回し」(フランス語から来たtournure)または「句イディオム」(phraseological idiom)と呼ばれている。それらに共通しているのは、それらがある文法的品詞とすぐには関連せずに、2語以上のパラフレーズを必要とすることである。

　これらのイディオムの形は固定していて、ごく少数のものを除けば、別の言い方や書き方をすると、イディオムの意味が破壊されてしまう。多くのものは完全に固定していて、それ以外の形で現われることはあり得ない。たとえば kick the bucket というイディオムを考えて頂きたい。これを受動態にすれば、たとえば The bucket has been kicked by the cowboy のようになるが、これはイディオムとしては受け入れられず、もはや「カウボーイは死んだ」ではなく、「カウボーイが足でバケツをけった」という意味になる。しかしながら、注意して頂きたいが、このイディオムでも時制によって変化させることはできるのである。たとえば The cowboy kicked the bucket, The cowboy will kick the bucket, He has kicked the bucket、などと言ってもよい。たとえば、His kicking the bucket surprised us all.のようにこのイディオムを動名詞(sing から singing, eat からeating のように動詞に -ingをつけて派生した名詞を動名詞と言う)の形で使ってよいかどうかについては、文法家も一般の話し手も意見が一致しない。この形は避けるのが一番よい。

　次に大きなイディオムのクラスは十分確立した言い習わしや諺である。これには Don't count your chickens before they're hatched.「失敗してみっともないことになりかねないから仕事の結果も分からないうちから祝ったりするな、捕らぬたぬきの皮算用」とかDon't wash your dirty linen in public.「家庭の問題について関係ない他人にぐちをこぼすな、内輪の恥をさらけ出すな」といった有名なタイプが含まれる。これらの多くはよく知られた文学的な出所から出ていたり、北米大陸で最も早く英語を話した人々から我々に伝えられたものである。

　なぜ英語、それも特にアメリカ英語にはこんなにイディオムが多いのだろうか。我々が新しい概念を発達させるにつれてそのために新しい表現を必要とするが、我々の言語の音から全く新しい語を造り出す代わりに、我々はすでに存在する二つ以上の語を使って、それらを合わせて新しい意味を持たせる、というのが一番有力な理由であろう。しかし、これはこれまでに知られているすべての言語について言えることである。事実、イディオムを持たない言語はない。たとえば「速く」という意味の中国語の表現を考えてみよう。それは mǎ shāng（馬上）で、文字通りに訳せば 'horse back' という意味である。どうして「速い」という概念が馬の背と結び付けられるのだろうか。一寸考えれば答えは明らかになる。昔、まだ汽車も自動車もない頃、ある場所から他の場所へ行く一番速い方法は馬に、つまり馬の背に乗ることだった。そこで中国語の mǎ shāng は英語ならば Hurry up! We must go 'on horse back'. つまり Hurry up! We must go quickly. と言うようなものである。このような形は英語でも決して理解できないことはないだろうが、話し手はそれがイディオムだと悟らねばならないだろうし、外国人はそれを学ばねばならないだろう。しかしながら、イディオムを学ぶ時に、人は不正確な推測をすることがある。英語のイディオム Oh well, the die is cast! を考えて頂きたい。あなたはこれがどんな意味だと思うだろうか—あなたがそれを知らなかったとして。Oh well という部分があるので、恐らくこの話し手は何かに仕方なく従っているのだとあなたは推測するだろう。この表現の意味は「取り返しのつかない決定をしてしまってそれに従わねばならない」ということである。今このイディオムの生成過程を再建してみることができる。賭博で投げられたさいは2度投げることはできない。それは規則違反である。1が出ようと、3が出ようと、6が出ようと、投げた結果に甘んじなければならない、つまり、場合に応じて勝つか負けるかしなければならない。(この句はシーザーがルビコン川を渡った時に使って、その結果戦争になったということを知っている人もいるだろう。)

それでは、たった今このイディオムを覚えて、あなたはそれを正確に使えるだろうか。まず第一に、英語を母国語とする人が自然な文脈の中で使うのを聞くまで待たなければならない。英文法の基礎をマスターするまでは、自分でイディオムを使う実験をしてはならない。そのイディオムが使われるのを２回以上聞いてその意味が十分に分かったら、自分で使ってみてもよい。一方は確実だが給料は低く、他方は給料は多いが仮りである二つの仕事の話があったと想像してみるとよい。臆病と完全な失職の恐れのために低い給料の仕事を承諾した丁度その時に、もっとよい話が舞い込んで、あなたは当然気をくじかれる。その時、Oh well, the die is cast...と言えるのである。これを英語を母国語とする人に使ってみて、相手が同情の色を見せ、そして What do you mean? と言わなければ、あなたは覚えたてのイディオムを適切な文脈に使うことに初めて成功したわけである。これは貴重な体験になる。生粋のアメリカ人はふつう他の国の人々よりも外国人に対して丁寧な反応を示すが、彼らはあなたがどの位流暢に話すかはっきり言うことができる。もしいつも堅苦しく大げさな表現を使って、適切な場所にイディオムを使わなければ、その人は無味乾燥で想像力のない話し手か、あまりにまじめで形式張ろうとしている話し手だという評判を得るかもしれない。<u>したがって、イディオムの使用は極めて大切である。それは聞き手との連帯感を呼び起こすことができるのである。</u>あなたが正しい文脈でイディオムをたくさん使えば使うほど、生粋のアメリカ人はあなたに対してくつろいだ気持になり、それだけ一層「これはよい親しみのある人だ―実にうまく自分の考えを話すことができる」と心の中で思うだろう。

　次に『現代熟語辞典』の使い方に関する幾つかの実際的な問題を見ることにしよう。

本辞典の使い方

　この辞典は英語を母国語としない人、学生、労働者、移住者―要するに英語をもっと流暢にもっとイディオマティックに使いたいと思っている人が使うと効果があるだろう。本辞典には上に挙げた型の句、すなわち特別の意味を持った語彙的イディオム (lexemic idiom)、句イディオム (phrase idiom)、諺的イディオム (proverbial idiom) が載せてある。あなたがある句を構成している個々の語を辞書で

調べて分かっても、その句が持つ特別な意味を正しく理解できない時に、その句はイディオムである。イディオムの幾つかをあなたはすでに知っているかもしれないし、あるいはその意味を想像できるかもしれない。すでによく知っているかもしれないが、次のイディオムのどれでも本辞典で引いてみると、この辞典の使い方を理解するのに役立つだろう。: boy friend, girl friend, outer space, piggy bank, get even, give up, going to, keep on, keep your mouth shut, lead somebody by the nose, look after, show off, throw away, all over, in love, mixed-up, out of this world, I'll say, both X and Y.

　辞書も他の道具と同じである。それがあなたのためによく働いてくれるためには、あなたがそれに慣れ親しんで、使い方を学ばねばならない。使用法指示を何度も注意深く読んで、イディオムを調べる練習をしなさい。そのように、イディオムを捜して見つければ、それはあなたの第二の天性になるだろう。本辞典をしばらく使った後で、ここに載っていないイディオマティックな表現を耳にしたら、その意味を突き止めてそれを自分で書き留める力がついているだろう。あなた自身のイディオムのリストを家のふつうの辞書のすぐそばに置きなさい。専門書や小説や新聞記事を読んで分からない表現があったら、まずふつうの学校用辞書を調べて、そこに見つからなかったら、この辞典を使いなさい。

　この辞典が難文の理解を助けるかどうか、どうしたら分かるだろうか。puppy love, fun house, dog-eat-dog, mixed-up などのように句がどれだかすぐに分かることもあるだろう。もし分からなければ、一番難しい部分から重要な１語を取り出して、それを捜しなさい。もしそれがイディオムの最初の語ならば、句全体が見つかり、その後に説明がある。たとえば bats in the belfry という表現は本辞典はbのbatsの所に挙げてある。取り出した語がイディオムの最初の語でない場合は、その語を含むリストを見い出すだろう。たとえば、toe という語は curl one's hair / curl one's toe, on one's toe, step on the toes (of somebody) の項に見い出される。もちろん、ある文が分からない理由がイディオムのためでないこともあるだろうが、その場合には、ふつうの辞書が役に立つだろう。また、イディオムの数は本辞典に載っているよりも多い。ここに載せたのはアメリカ英語で最もよく使われるものだけである。たとえばイギリス英語や

オーストラリアで話される英語には確かにアメリカ英語にはないイディオマティックな表現が沢山ある。

項目の型

　本辞典には4種類の項目がある。独立項目、追い込み項目、相互参照項目、索引項目である。独立項目はイディオムの完全な説明を含んでいる。追い込み項目は他のイディオムから派生しているがそのアルファベットの位置に置かれると基本的なイディオムから離れてしまう句である。これらの派生イディオムは独立項目の終わりに追い込んで(たとえば fence-sitter は sit on the fence の項にある) 説明とパラフレーズをつけた。主要項目の説明から派生項目を理解することが難しいと思われる場合にはさらに説明をつけた。イディオムが二つ以上の品詞に用いられる場合は、それぞれの用法を別見出しにした。

　相互参照項目はその定義が別の場所にあることを示す。たとえば cast in one's lot with を調べたいと思ったとしよう。あなたは cast と lot の項を見ることができるが、相互参照項目によって throw in one's lot with という句を参照するように指示される。これは cast が今日ではずっとまれな語なので、このイディオムのふつうの、もっと頻度の高い形は throw という動詞で始まるからである。

　索引項目は索引語を含む他のすべての項目を指示する。たとえば chin という語の後に、keep one's chin up, stick one's chin (or neck) out, take it on the chin, up to the chin など chin を含む句が挙げてある。

品詞表示

　はっきりした文法形式類と関連するイディオムには品詞表示がつけられている。たとえば、〔動〕は、「動詞」及び「動詞句」を表し、「動詞＋副詞」、「動詞＋前置詞」、「動詞＋前置詞＋副詞」(以上、原著ではv.と表示)、「動詞＋目的語」、「動詞＋主格補語」、「動詞＋前置詞句」(以上、原著ではv. phr. と表示)を含む。品詞表示にはその他、〔名〕〔代〕〔形〕〔副〕〔前〕〔接〕〔感〕がある。また、多くの前置詞句の場合のように、ある句が二つの文法的用法を持っているために、二つの表示をつけなければならないこともあった。たとえば in commission は副詞的か形容詞的かである。そのような時は〔副、形〕と表示した。前置詞句の多くは文字通りの意味では副詞的であるが、予言できないイディオマティックな意味では形容詞的である。

用法指示

　あるイディオムをある環境で使うことが適切かどうかに特に注意を払わねばならない。sl. (slang 「俗語」) はあるイディオムがお互いにごく親しい友人の間でだけ使われていることを示す。inf. (informal 「口語的」) はある形が会話では用いられるが、改まった作文では避けるべきことを示す。form. (formal 「形式張った」) はその反対で、通常話す時には使わず、エッセイで書いたり、講演や大学の講義で用いる形である。lit. (literary 「文学的」) は、人々がその形が引用であることを知っているということに注意を喚起するのであって、こういう形をあまり使うのは不適当である。(卑語) (vulgar 「卑俗な」) はその形を全く避けるべきことを示す。使用する言葉によって人を判断することができるのだから、その形を卑俗だと分かることはもちろん重要である。(非標準語) は、substandard 「標準語以下の」—主に教育の低い人々が使う形を示す—及び nonstandard 「非標準語の」—ある句がぎこちないと感じられるという意味である—を示す。(古風) (archaic 「古風な」、本書ではまれにしか用いていない) はある形が現代英語ではもはや用いられないことを意味する。regional labels 「地域表示」はある形の地理的起源と使用を示す。たとえば (英国語法) (Chiefly British 「主に英国」) はアメリカ人はめったに使わないという意味であり、(南部方言) (Southern 「南部」) はある形が米国北部よりも南部でずっとよく行われていることを意味する。

Adam Makkai/Guo Yianzhong

Предисловие

ЧТО ТАКОЕ ИДИОМА?

Если в незнакомом тексте Вы понимаете каждое слово, но не можете понять смысла, Ваши затруднения, вероятно, вызваны идиоматическими выражениями. Предположим, Вы прочитали или услышали следующий текст:

Sam is a real cool cat. He never blows his stack and hardly ever flies off the handle. What's more, he knows how to get away with things . . . Well, of course, he is getting on, too. His hair is pepper and salt, but he knows how to make up for lost time by taking it easy. He gets up early, works out, and turns in early. He takes care of the hot dog stand like a breeze until he gets time off. Sam's got it made; this is it for him.

Очевидно, что этот стиль нельзя назвать строго литературным, но, тем не менее, американцы в разговоре друг с другом часто употребляют такие выражения. Если Вы иностранец и знаете слова *cool* (прохладно), *cat* (кошка), *blow* (дуть), *stack* (куча), *fly* (лететь), *handle* (ручка) и т.д., Вы не поймете данный образец разговорного американского английского языка, потому что те переводы слов, которые находятся в обычных английских словарях, не дадут Вам точного значения приведенных выше выражений. Из этого следует, что идиома — это новое, неожиданное значение группы слов, каждое из которых обладает своим собственным значением. Ниже Вы найдете перевод этого разговорного и нелитературного текста на более формальный вариант американского диалекта:

Sam is really a calm person. He never loses control of himself and hardly ever becomes too angry. Furthermore, he knows how to manage his business financially by using a few tricks . . . Needless to say, he, too, is getting older. His hair is beginning to turn gray, but he knows how to compensate for wasted time by relaxing. He rises early, exercises, and goes to bed early. He manages his frankfurter stand without visible effort, until it is someone else's turn to work there. Sam is successful; he has reached his life's goal.

Сэм очень тихий человек. Он никогда не теряет контроль над собой и редко сердится. Кроме того, он знает, как вести свое дело с финансовой точки зрения, употребляя некоторые хитрости . . . Безусловно, он тоже стареет. Его волосы седеют, но он умеет восстанавливать потраченные силы отдыхом. Он рано встает, делает гимнастику и рано ложится. Со своей работой в колбасном магазине он справляется без особого труда, успевая все сделать до того, как его сменят. Сэм вполне счастлив, — он достиг цели своей жизни.

Идиоматические выражения, употребленные в этом тексте, можно организовать в следующий небольшой словарь:

to be a (real) cool cat	«быть очень спокойным человеком»
to blow one's stack	«потерять контроль над собой, рассердиться»
to fly off the handle	«прийти в ярость»
what's more	«помимо этого, кроме того»
to get away with something	«смошенничать, оставшись безнаказанным»
of course	«конечно»
to be getting on	«постареть»
pepper and salt	«седеющие черные или темные волосы»

to make up for something lost time	«восполнить что-то» «потерянное время»
to take it easy	«не обращать внимания»
to get up	«встать утром»
to work out	«делать гимнастику»
to turn in	«лечь спать»
to take care of something	«отвечать за что-то»
like a breeze	«легко, элегантно, без усилий»
time off	«время отдыха»
to have got it made	«быть счастливым, довольным, удачливым»
this is it	«вот и все, что нужно»

Некоторые идиомы из этого небольшого списка можно найти в нашем словаре. Большая часть идиом принадлежит обыкновенным грамматическим классам или частям речи. Так, например, некоторые идиомы по своей природе—типичные глаголы: *get away with, get up, work out, turn in* и т.д. Не меньшее число идиоматических выражений—имена. Так, *hot dog* (сосиска в хлебе), *The White House* (Белый Дом—официальная резиденция американского президента)—имена существительные. Некоторые из идиом—имена прилагательные; так, в нашем примере *pepper and salt* (седеющие черные или темные волосы) обозначает цвет волос. Многие из этих выражений, как, например, *like a breeze* (легко), *hammer and tongs* (*violently*, насильственно)—наречия. Идиоматические выражения, относящиеся к одному из обыкновенных грамматических классов, называются *лексемными идиомами* (*lexemic idioms*).

Вторая основная группа идиом состоит из фраз, таких как наши примеры *to fly off the handle* (потерять контроль над собой) и *to blow one's stack* (прийти в ярость). В американском варианте английского языка подобные выражения встречаются очень часто. Некоторые из наиболее известных следующие: *to kick the bucket* (*die*, умереть, сыграть в ящик, отбросить копыта), *to be up the creek* (*in danger*, быть в опасности), *to seize the bull by the horns* (*face a problem squarely*, разрешать проблему или задачу, стоящую перед нами, взять быка за рога) и т.д. Идиомы этой группы называются *оборотами* речи, по-английски *tournures* (из французского языка). Они не принадлежат одному какому-либо грамматическому классу (*части речи*), и переводить их нужно не словом, а группой слов.

Форма подобных идиоматических выражений устоялась; многие из них совсем «застыли» и не могут функционировать в другой форме. Рассмотрим, например, идиому *to kick the bucket* (*die*, умереть). Употребив эту форму в пассивном залоге, мы отказываемся от идиоматического смысла, получив выражение *the bucket has been kicked by the cowboy* (ковбой ударил ведро ногой). Впрочем, даже это выражение может изменяться по времени, так как мы можем сказать *the cowboy kicked the bucket, the cowboy will kick the bucket, the cowboy has kicked the bucket* и т.д. Проблема, можно ли употреблять это идиоматическое выражение в герундивной форме (*герундив*, gerundive—слово, производное от глагола с помощью суффикса *-ing*, например, *singing* от *sing, eating* от *eat* и т.д.), не решена окончательно учеными-лингвистами и носителями языка. Правильная эта форма или нет, мы не рекомендуем употреблять выражения типа *his kicking the bucket surprised us all.*

Следующий большой класс идиом состоит из поговорок, таких как *don't count your chickens before they're hatched* (*do not celebrate the outcome of an undertaking prematurely—you may fail and will look ridiculous);* буквально: «не считайте кур, пока они не вылупились из яиц»; русский вариант поговорки звучит: «цыплят по осени считают». Большое число поговорок пришло в американский вариант английского языка из литературных источников или же от первых английских иммигрантов в Америку.

Своим рождением идиомы обязаны тому, что мы чаще используем уже существующие слова для выражения новых идей, чем создаем новые слова с помощью фонем языка. Фактически нет языков, в которых не было бы идиом. Возьмем, например, слова *ма шанг*, китайское выражение, которое значит «быстро». Переведенное дословно, оно означает «лошадиная спина». Связь понятий *лошадиной спины* и *быстроты* очевидна: раньше, до появления поезда, автомобиля и самолета, быстрее всего было путешествовать верхом на лошади. Китайское выражение *ма шанг* было бы аналогом русской фразы: «Торопитесь, нам надо ехать *на лошадиной спине*!» Такая форма была бы вполне понятной носителю русского языка, но иностранец должен был бы понять, что это идиома. Даже если иностранец никогда не слышал выражения *ма шанг* (лошадиная спина), он может догадаться, что это значит; однако, во многих случаях подобные догадки ошибочны.

Например, возьмем английскую идиому *the die is cast* (жребий брошен). Вряд ли, не зная ее точного выражения, Вы догадаетесь, что это выражение значит: «Я решил, и больше не могу изменить свое решение». Зная точное значение, Вы можете догадаться, как возникло это идиоматическое выражение: кость, брошенная во время игры в кости, по правилам может быть брошена только один раз, независимо от результата. Многие знают, что эту фразу произнес Юлий Цезарь, когда перешел Рубикон, что явилось началом войны.

Как научиться употреблять идиоматическое выражение правильно? Прежде всего, подождите, пока Вы не услышите идиому от человека, для которого американский английский—родной язык. Если Вы неоднократно слышали идиому и вполне поняли ее значение, Вы сами можете начать употреблять это выражение. Предположим, молодая девушка очень хочет выйти замуж. Она может выбирать между двумя возможными женихами, назовем их Павел и Николай. Павел немолод, некрасив и небогат, но он уже сделал предложение и готов жениться хоть завтра. Николай красив и богат, но он пока не собирается жениться и неизвестно, женится ли когда-нибудь. После некоторого раз-

мышления девушка решает принять предложение Павла, боясь остаться старой девой. Если вскоре после свадьбы Николай признается ей, что мечтает быть ее мужем, нашей героине останется только сказать *"Oh, well, the die is cast..."* («Что делать, жребий брошен»). Если, оказавшись в подобной ситуации, Вы произносите эту фразу, беседуя с американцем, и он смотрит на Вас с сочувствием и не переспрашивает: «Что Вы имеете в виду?»—считайте, что Вы достигли первого успеха, употребив новую идиому в правильном контексте. Американцы относятся к иностранцам более лояльно, чем другие нации, но они, конечно, оценят, сколь бегло Вы говорите по-английски. Использование идиом поможет Вам установить контакт со слушателем и избежать репутации «слишком серьезного» человека. Чем больше идиом Вы употребляете в правильном контексте, тем лучше о Вас будут думать Ваши собеседники.

КАК ПОЛЬЗОВАТЬСЯ ЭТИМ СЛОВАРЕМ?

Словарь был составлен для людей, говорящих по-английски, но не родившихся в Америке. Словарь содержит *лексемные идиомы, фразеологические единицы* и *поговорки*, имеющие особенное значение. Возможно, некоторые из идиоматических выражений Вам уже знакомы, и Вы понимаете, что они означают. Найдите в словаре перевод одной из следующих идиом, значение которой Вы уже знаете,—это поможет Вам понять, как пользоваться этой книгой: *boyfriend, girl friend, piggy bank, get even, give up, going to, keep on, keep your mouth shut, lead somebody by the nose, look after, show off, throw away, all over, in love, mixed-up, out of this world, I'll say.*

Чтобы научиться пользоваться словарем, несколько раз внимательно изучите предписания и попрактикуйтесь в нахождении значения идиоматических выражений. Если Вы услышите идиому, которой нет в книге, то, имея некоторый опыт работы с нашим словарем, Вы сможете найти ее значение и выписать его для себя. Заведите Ваш собственный список идиом и храните его вместе с Вашим обычным словарем. Пошлите нам Ваши наблюдения и замечания.

Как узнать, поможет ли Вам «Словарь идиом» понять трудную фразу? Иногда догадаться, о чем идет речь, не сложно, как в выражениях *puppy love, fun house, dog-eat-dog, mixed-up*. Если же Вы не можете перевести выражение, выберите основное слово из самой трудной части и найдите его в словаре. Если это первое слово идиомы, Вы найдете всю фразу и перевод к ней. Таким образом, выражение *bats in the belfry* напечатано в этом словаре под буквой *b*, слово *bats*. Если слово, которое Вы выбрали, не первое слово идиомы, Вы найдете список идиом, которые содержат это слово. Например, слово *toe* (палец ноги) Вы найдете в статьях *curl one's hair or curl one's toes, on one's toes, step on the toes (of somebody)*. Конечно, Вы можете столкнуться с тем, что не понимаете некоторые фразы, потому что Вам незнакомы обыкновенные слова, а не из-за обилия идиоматических выражений. В этом случае Вам поможет обычный словарь. Обратите внимание, что в этом словаре приведены наиболее употребительные выражения только американского английского языка, без учета идиоматики, например, британского или австралийского диалектов. Словарь, содержащий идиомы всех диалектов английского языка, был бы *международным словарем английских идиоматических выражений*. В настоящее время такой книги нет, но надеемся, что в будущем она будет написана.

ТИПЫ СЛОВАРНЫХ СТАТЕЙ

Этот словарь содержит четыре типа статей: *Главные статьи, продолжающиеся статьи, статьи-ссылки и указательные статьи. Главная статья* включает полное объяснение идиомы. *Продолжающаяся статья* — фраза, происходящая от другой идиомы, но которая была бы самостоятельной единицей, если бы она была напечатана в своем собственном алфавитном месте. Эти производные идиомы приводятся в конце главной статьи, например, *fence sitter* «человек, сидящий на заборе» в конце статьи *sit on the fence* «сидеть на заборе». В тех случаях, когда понять производную форму, опираясь на основное объяснение, затруднительно, приводятся дополнительные объяснения. Если идиома может употребляться в форме различных частей речи, приводится отдельная статья на каждый случай.

Ссылки показывают, что объяснение можно найти в другом месте. Предположим, Вы хотите посмотреть выражение *cast in one's lot with* (решить стать соучастниками или партнерами). Вы можете посмотреть на слово *cast* (бросать) или на слово *lot* (судьба); ссылка направит Вас к слову *throw* в фразе *throw in one's lot with*. Причиной этого является тот факт, что слово *cast* (бросать)—употребляется в сегодняшнем английском языке гораздо режеъ чем слово *throw*. Следовательно, более распространенная форма этой идиомы начинается глаголом *throw*.

Указательная статья ведет нас ко всем другим статьям, содержащим искомое слово. Таким образом, слово *chin* (подбородок) сопровождается фразами, в которых Вы найдете слово *chin*, таких как *keep one's chin up, stick one's chin (OR neck) out, take out, take it on the chin, up to the chin*.

УКАЗАТЕЛИ ЧАСТЕЙ РЕЧИ

Лексемные идиомы, которые мы обсуждали раньше, сопровождены указателем части речи. В некоторых случаях, таких, как, скажем, в случае предложных фраз, употреблен двойной указатель, потому что данная фраза имеет два грамматических употребления. Буква *v* значит *verb* (глагол); она напечатана в фразах, содержащих глагол и наречие, или глагол и предлог, или все три, то есть глагол, предлог и наречие. Сокращение *v. phr.* означает *"verbal phrase"* как, например, *look up, look in* и т.д., то есть сочетание глагола с существительным: глагол с дополнением, глагол с подлежащим и глагол с предложной фразой.

ОГРАНИЧИТЕЛЬНЫЕ УКАЗАТЕЛИ

Иностранцу, для которого американский английский—неродной язык, следует обратить особое внимание на то, в какой ситуации какую идиому можно употреблять. В этом читателю словаря помогут ограничительные указатели. Так, указатель *slang* (слэнг) показывает, что идиома употребляется только в фамильярном разговоре очень близкими друзьями. Указатель *informal* (неформальный) показывает, что выражение может употребляться в разговоре, но не должно встречаться в формальных сочинениях. Указатель *formal* (формальный) имеет противоположное значение; он указывает, что форма употребляется только в научных работах или при чтении лекции в университете. Указатель *literary* (литературный) напоминает, что интересующая Вас идиома—широко известная цитата; ее не стоит употреблять слишком часто. Указатель *vulgar* (вульгарный, грубый) показывает, что Вам не следует употреблять эту форму. Однако, иметь представление о подобных формах необходимо, чтобы иметь возможность судить о людях по языку, который они употребляют. Указатель *substandard* (не соответствующий языковой норме) показывает, что форма употребляется малообразованными людьми; *nonstandard* (нестандартный) значит, что фраза неуклюжая. Указатель *archaic* (архаический) редко употребляется в этой книге; он означает, что форма очень редка в современном английском языке. Географические указатели показывают, где идиома образовалась и где употребляется. *Chiefly British* (главным образом британское) значит, что американцы редко употребляют эту форму; *southern* (южный) значит, что идиома употребляется чаще на юге США, чем на севере. Молодые формы, которые образовались не более шести или семи лет назад, находятся в приложении к главному словарю.

Adam Makkai/Maya Aleksandrovna Glinberg

Prefacio

¿QUÉ ES UN MODISMO?

Si usted entiende todas las palabras de un texto y aún no comprende su significado, es posible que tenga dificultad con los modismos. Por ejemplo, suponga que usted lee (u oye) lo siguiente:

Sam is a real cool cat. He never blows his stack and hardly ever flies off the handle. What's more, he knows how to get away with things . . . Well, of course, he is getting on, too. His hair is pepper and salt, but he knows how to make up for lost time by taking it easy. He gets up early, works out, and turns in early. He takes care of the hot dog stand like a breeze until he gets time off. Sam's got it made; this is it for him.

No es necesario mencionar que tal párrafo carece de estilo literario, pero la mayoría de los estadounidenses, especialmente en conversación, usan expresiones de este tipo. Si usted es un extranjero en E.U.A. y ha aprendido las palabras *cool* (frío a tibio), *cat* (gato, animal común doméstico), *blow* (expirar aire con fuerza), *stack* (pila de cosas u objetos amontonados), *fly* (impulsarse por el aire), *handle* (parte de un objeto designada a tomarse con la mano), todavía no comprenderá el párrafo recién visto porque esta información básica de diccionario no es suficiente para darle el significado a la combinación de palabras usadas. Un modismo—como puede verse—es la asignación de un nuevo significado a un grupo de palabras que ya tienen su propio significado. Observe en el siguiente párrafo cómo ese texto lleno de modismos típicos del inglés estadounidense común se traduce a una versión más formal y relativamente exenta de modismos:

Sam is really a calm person. He never loses control of himself and hardly ever becomes too angry. Furthermore, he knows how to manage his business financially by using a few tricks . . . Needless to say, he, too, is getting older. His hair is beginning to turn gray, but he knows how to compensate for wasted time by relaxing. He rises early, exercises, and goes to bed early. He manages his frankfurter stand without visible effort, until it is someone else's turn to work there. Sam is successful; he has reached his life's goal.

Si uno fuera a explicar cómo están organizadas las palabras en este texto, crearía un pequeño diccionario de modismos que tendría la siguiente forma:

to be a (real) cool cat	ser realmente calmo, ser sumamente tranquilo
to blow one's stack	perder el control, enojarse
to fly off the handle	enfurecerse
what's more	además, de paso, adicionalmente
to get away with something	cometer un acto ilegítimo o tramposo sin repercusiones o daño
of course	naturalmente
to be getting on	envejecer
pepper and salt	cabello negro u oscuro, tornándose canoso
to make up for something	recuperar algo
lost time	tiempo perdido, tiempo desperdiciado
to take it easy	descansar, despreocuparse
to get up	levantarse
to work out	hacer ejercicio, hacer gimnasia
to turn in	acostarse
to take care of something	ocuparse de algo, encargarse de algo, cuidar algo
like a breeze	sin esfuerzo, elegantemente, fácilmente
time off	período de inactividad en el empleo o en el sitio de empleo

to have got it made	tener buen éxito, haber cumplido
this is it	estar en una posición o en un sitio, o tener posesión de un objeto, tras lo cual más no es necesario

Muchos de los modismos en esta pequeña lista de ejemplos pueden ser hallados en este mismo diccionario. Lo interesante de la mayoría de estos modismos es que pueden ser identificados fácilmente con las partes de la oración. De esta manera algunos modismos son claramente de naturaleza verbal, tales como *get away with, get up, work out, turn in*, etc. Una gran cantidad son de naturaleza nominal, como *hot dog* y *cool cat*, es decir, son sustantivos. Muchos son adjetivos, como en el ejemplo *pepper and salt* (cabello tornándose canoso), indicativo del color del cabello. Otros son adverbiales, como los ejemplos *like the breeze* (fácilmente, sin esfuerzo) y *hammer and tongs* (violentamente).

Estos modismos que correlacionan con las familiares partes de la oración se pueden llamar modismos lexémicos.

El otro grupo importante de modismos es más grande. Frecuentemente son del tamaño de una oración completa, como son nuestros ejemplos *to fly off the handle* (enfurecerse) y *to blow one's stack* (perder el control). El inglés norteamericano se caracteriza por tener muchos de este grupo. Algunos de los más famosos son *to kick the bucket* (morirse), *to be up the creek* (estar en un aprieto o en una situación peligrosa), *to be caught between the devil and the deep blue sea* (tener que optar entre dos alternativas igualmente desagradables), *to seize the bull by the horns* ("tomar el toro por los astas", es decir, enfrentarse con un problema y tratarlo con equidad), y otros. Los modismos de este tipo se llaman *tournures* (del francés), "giros de frase", o simplemente modismos *fraseológicos*. Lo que tienen en común es que no se correlacionan fácilmente con una parte de la oración determinada y requieren una paráfrasis mayor que una mera palabra.

Su forma es fija y solamente un número limitado de estos modismos puede ser dicho o escrito de cualquier otra forma sin destruir su significado. Muchos de ellos son completamente rígidos y no pueden tener ninguna otra forma. Considere el modismo *kick the bucket,* por ejemplo. Si se pone en voz pasiva, se obtiene una forma tan inaceptable como *the bucket has been kicked by the cowboy,* la cual ya no indica que murió el vaquero, sino que éste pateó el balde. Modismos de este tipo son considerados *formas completamente congeladas*. Fíjese, sin embargo, que hasta este modismo puede ser conjugado: por ejemplo, es correcto decir *the cowboy kicked the bucket* o *the cowboy will kick the bucket.*

El próximo grupo de modismos importante es el de los refranes y proverbios. Estos incluyen ejemplos tan conocidos como *don't count your chickens before they're hatched* (no celebre el resultado de una empresa prematura pues, de fracasar ésta, sufrirá el ridículo): *don't wash your dirty linen in public* ("la ropa sucia se lava en casa") y otros. Muchos de éstos tuvieron origen en fuentes literarias muy conocidas o vienen a nosotros de los primitivos colonos norteamericanos, para quienes dichos, refranes y proverbios eran parte de su cultura oral.

¿Por qué es el inglés, y especialmente el inglés estadounidense, tan sobrecargado de modismos? Mientras desarrollamos nuevos conceptos, necesitamos nuevas expresiones para ellos, pero en vez de crear una nueva palabra de los sonidos de la lengua, preferimos usar palabras existentes y las combinamos para obtener un nuevo sentido. Esto, sin embargo, parece ocurrir en todas las lenguas. Considere la expresión china *mă shāng* para "rápidamente". Traducida al pie de la letra, *mă shāng* significa "lomo de caballo" y uno se pregunta por qué el concepto de "rapidez" está asociado con el lomo del caballo. Reflexionemos un momento. En tiempos pasados, antes de que se inventaran el tren, el automóvil y en avión, la manera más rápida de llegar de un lugar a otro era montado a caballo, es decir, a lomo de caballo. Por esto, *mă shāng* equivale a "¡vamos a galopar!" y, por extensión, "¡apurémonos!" En español, "vamos a galopar" sería fácilmente comprendido por todos y todos sabrían que se trata de un modismo, mientras que el extranjero tendría que aprenderlo como tal.

No obstante, hay ocasiones en que la persona puede adivinar incorrectamente. Considere el modismo inglés *Oh well, the die is cast!* Si desconoce su significado, ¿qué le sugiere esta frase? Tal vez por la expresión *Oh well* puede suponer que el que lo dijo está consintiendo a algo. Sin embargo, este modismo significa "Tomé una decisión y ahora tengo que vivir con ella". Al tratar de reconstruir este modismo aparece la imagen del dado tirado. Recordamos, entonces que, según las reglas del juego de dados, la tirada puede ser una sola sean cuales sean las consecuencias. La frase fue usada por César cuando cruzó el Rubicón, un evento, que desencadenó la guerra.

¿Cómo, entonces, acabando de aprenderlo, va usted a usar este modismo correctamente? Antes que nada, asegúrese de conocer los rudimentos básicos de la gramática inglesa. Luego, escuche como lo emplea la persona cuyo idioma materno es el inglés. Después de haber escuchado más de una vez el uso del modismo y comprender completamente su significado, podrá usarlo usted mismo. Imagínese tener dos ofertas de trabajo, una segura, pero de menos salario, y otra que pague más, pero sólo tentativa. Nervioso y atemorizado de terminar sin empleo alguno, acepta la de menor sueldo, pocas horas antes de recibir una oferta definitiva por el trabajo mejor pagado. La frustración lo lleva entonces a exclamar, *Oh well, the die is cast . . .* Y si un norteamericano lo oye, asiente con comprensión y no le pregunta—¿qué dijo?—ha logrado usted su primer éxito en el uso correcto de un modismo recientemente aprendido. Los estadounidenses suelen tratar a los extranjeros con más cortesía que los de otras naciones, pero prefieren a los que se les asemejan. Si una persona siempre usa expresiones versadas y afectadas y jamás usa un modismo en el momento apropiado, puede obtener la reputación de ser un orador pedante y sin imaginación, o uno demasiado serio y formal. El uso de modismos es, por consiguiente, de suma importancia pues puede establecer lazos de solidaridad con el oyente. Mientras más modismos use dentro del contexto apropiado, más cómodos se sentirán los estadounidenses con usted y más se dirán "¡qué simpática y amable es esta persona y qué bien se expresa!"

Veremos ahora algunas consideraciones prácticas con relación al presente libro.

COMO USAR ESTE DICCIONARIO

Recapitulemos. Cuando una frase tiene un significado especial que nadie puede descifrar correctamente aun cuando las palabras individuales que la componen son comprendidas fácilmente, se trata de un modismo. Este diccionario se destina a personas de habla no inglesa...estudiantes, obreros, profesionales, todos los que deseen perfeccionar su inglés y mejorar su posición social. Contiene frases con significado especial de los tipos anteriormente mencionados, es decir, modismos lexémicos, modismos fraseológicos y proverbios. Sugerimos buscar en el libro algunos modismos que Ud. indudablemente ya conoce como práctica para el uso adecuado de este libro: *boyfriend, girl friend, outer space, piggy bank, get even, give up, going to, keep on, keep your mouth shut, lead somebody by the nose, look after, show off, throw away, all over, in love, mixed-up, out of this world, throw away, I'll say.*

Un diccionario es como cualquier otra herramienta: Debe familiarizarse con él y aprender a usarlo antes de obtener buenos resultados. Repase las instrucciones y practique buscando modismos determinados. Semejante práctica le familiarizará hasta tal punto con los modismos que le permitirá deducir el significado de muchos modismos desconocidos que escucha por primera vez. Mantenga su propia lista de modismos en casa, al lado de su diccionario corriente. Al leer un texto técnico, o una novela o un artículo de periódico y no comprender una expresión, búsquela primero en su diccionario corriente y, si no lo encuentra, recurra al volumen que ahora lee.

¿Cómo puede saber usted si este diccionario puede ayudarle a entender una oración difícil? Algunas veces el modismo es de fácil interpretación, como en el caso de *puppy love, fun house, dog-eat-dog, mixed-up.* En los demás casos, seleccione una palabra clave de la parte más difícil de la oración y búsquela. Si es la primera palabra del modismo, encontrará la frase completa, seguida por una explicación. Así, la expresión *bats in the belfry* se encuentra en este diccionario bajo la *b,* en la palabra *bats.* Si la palabra que usted escogió no es la primera, encontrará una lista de modismos que contienen esa palabra. Por ejemplo, la palabra *toe* se encontrará bajo expresiones como *curl one's hair* o *curl one's toes, on one's toes, step on the toes (of somebody)*. Podría ocurrir, por supuesto, que la razón de no comprender una oración sea ajena a todo modismo: en ese caso, recurra a su diccionario corriente. También, por supuesto, hay muchos más modismos de los que se encuentran en este libro: le damos aquí los más frecuentemente usados en los Estados Unidos. El inglés británico, por ejemplo, o el inglés hablado en Australia posee muchos modismos que no forman parte del inglés estadounidense. Un diccionario que contenga todos los modismos de la lengua inglesa mundial no existe en el presente, aunque tarde o temprano saldrá a luz.

TIPOS DE ARTICULOS

Este diccionario contiene cuatro clases de artículos: artículos principales, artículos continuados, artículos de referencias cruzadas, y artículos alfabéticos. Un artículo principal incluye una explicación completa del modismo. Un artículo continuado es una frase derivada de otro modismo pero que estaría separada de éste si hubiese sido anotada en orden alfabético. Estos modismos derivados han sido añadidos al final del artículo principal (por ejemplo, *fencesitter* en *on the fence*) y van acompañados de una segunda explicación cuando el derivado de la explicación principal es difícil de comprender.

Un artículo de referencia cruzada le guía a una definición en otro sitio. Suponga que desea encontrar *cast in one's lot with.* Puede buscar bajo *cast* y bajo *lot,* pero el artículo de referencia cruzada lo encauzará al término *throw* en la frase *throw in one's lot with.* La razón para esto es que *cast* es una palabra mucho menos usada en la actualidad, siendo *throw* la versión más corriente y frecuente de este modismo.

Un artículo alfabético lo dirige a todos los otros artículos que contienen la palabra en orden alfabético. Así, la palabra *chin* es seguida por las frases donde se encuentra, por ejemplo, *keep one's chin up, stick one's chin out, take it on the chin, up to the chin.*

CLASIFICACIONES SEGUN LAS PARTES DE LA ORACION

Los modismos lexémicos antes vistos van acompañados por indicadores de la parte de la oración a la cual están vinculados. Algunas veces, como con muchas frases preposicionales, una segunda clasificación ha sido necesaria porque la frase obtenida tiene dos usos gramaticales: por ejemplo, *in commission* puede ser adverbial o adjetival.

v indica verbo y fue designada a frases que contienen un verbo y un adverbio, verbo y preposición o verbo, preposición y adverbio.

v. phr. indica "frase verbal" e incluye a verbos con un objeto, verbos con un complemento de sujeto y verbos con frases preposicionales.

CLASIFICACIONES RESTRICTIVAS

Le aconsejamos determinar en cada ocasión si es apropiado o no usar determinado modismo. La clasificación *slang* indica que el modismo es usado solamente entre íntimos amigos. *Informal* señala que la expresión es usada en conversación, pero que debiera evitarse en una composición formal. *Formal* indica lo contrario: ésta es una forma que la gente generalmente no emplea al hablar, sino que utiliza por escrito en un ensayo o durante un discurso universitario. *Literary* le advierte que el modismo es una cita conocida y que sería poco apropiado usarla muy seguido. *Vulgar* es señal de evitar este modismo por completo, aunque reconociendo que su conocimiento puede serle importante para juzgar al usuario. *Substandard* indica que el modismo es empleado principalmente por gente poco educada. *Nonstandard* significa que la frase resultante de este modismo es torpe y debiera evitarse. *Archaic* (raramente usada en este libro) significa que el modismo pertenece al inglés bíblico o antiguo. Algunos modismos se identifican según su origen geográfico; por ejemplo, *chiefly British* significa que los estadounidenses raramente lo usan; *Southern* significa que el modismo es mucho más corriente en el sur de los Estados Unidos que en el norte.

Adam Makkai/Verónica Cortés

A Dictionary of American Idioms

abide by *v.* To accept and obey; be willing to follow. ♦*A basketball player may know he did not foul, but he must abide by the referee's decision.* ♦*The members agree to abide by the rules of the club.*

a bit *n., informal* A small amount; some. ♦*There's no sugar in the sugar bowl, but you may find a bit in the bag.* ♦*If the ball had hit the window a bit harder, it would have broken it.*—Often used like an adverb. ♦*This sweater scratches a bit.*—Also used like an adjective before *less, more.* ♦*Janet thought she could lose weight by eating a bit less.* ♦*"Have some more cake?" "Thanks. A bit more won't hurt me."*—Often used adverbially after verbs in negative, interrogative, and conditional sentences, sometimes in the form *one bit.* ♦*"Won't your father be angry?" "No, he won't care a bit."* ♦*Helen feels like crying, but I'll be surprised if she shows it one bit.*—Sometimes used with *little* for emphasis, also in the emphatic form *the least bit.* ♦*"Wasn't Bob even a little bit sorry he forgot his date?" "No, Bob wasn't the least bit sorry."* Syn. A LITTLE. Compare A FEW. Contrast A LOT.

about face *n.* A sudden change of course or a decision opposite to what was decided earlier. ♦*Her decision to become an actress instead of a dentist was an about face from her original plans.*

about one's ears *or* **around one's ears** *adv. phr.* To or into complete collapse, defeat, or ruin; to the destruction of a person's plans, hopes, or happiness.— ♦*They planned to have factories all over the world but the war brought their plans down about their ears.* ♦*John hoped to go to college and become a great scientist some day, but when his father died he had to get a job, and John's dreams came crashing around his ears.* Compare ON ONE'S HEAD.

about time *n. phr.* Finally, but later than it should have been; at last. ♦*Mother said, "It's about time you got up, Mary."* ♦*The basketball team won last night. About time.*

about to **1.** Close to; ready to.—Used with an infinitive. ♦*We were about to leave when the snow began.* ♦*I haven't gone yet, but I'm about to.* Compare GOING TO, ON THE POINT OF. **2.** *informal* Having a wish or plan to.—Used with an infinitive in negative sentences. ♦*Freddy wasn't about to give me any of his ice-cream cone.* ♦*"Will she come with us?" asked Bill. "She's not about to," answered Mary.*

above all *adv. phr.* Of first or highest importance; most especially. ♦*Children need many things, but above all they need love.* Syn. FIRST AND LAST.

above suspicion *adj. phr.* Too good to be suspected; not likely to do wrong. ♦*The umpire in the game must be above suspicion of supporting one side over the other.*

absent without leave (AWOL) *adj.* Absent without permission; used mostly in the military. ♦*Jack left Fort Sheridan without asking his commanding officer, and was punished for going AWOL.*

absentia See IN ABSENTIA.

Acapulco gold *n., slang* Marijuana of an exceptionally high quality. ♦*Jack doesn't just smoke pot, he smokes Acapulco gold.*

accord See OF ONE'S OWN ACCORD *or* OF ONE'S OWN FREE WILL.

according as *conj.* **1.** Depending on which; whichever. ♦*You may take an oral or written exam according as you prefer.* **2.** Depending on whether; if. ♦*We will play golf or stay home according as the weather is good or bad.*

according to *prep.* **1.** So as to match or agree with; so as to be alike in. ♦*Many words are pronounced according to the spelling but some are not.* ♦*The boys were placed in three groups according to height.* **2.** On the word or authority of. ♦*According to the Bible, Adam was the first man.*

according to one's own lights *adv. phr.* In accordance with one's conscience or inclinations. ♦*Citizens should vote according to their own lights.*

account See CALL TO ACCOUNT, CHARGE

ACCOUNT, LEAVE OUT OF ACCOUNT, ON ACCOUNT, ON ACCOUNT OF, ON ONE'S ACCOUNT, ON ONE'S OWN ACCOUNT, SAVINGS ACCOUNT, TAKE INTO ACCOUNT.

ace See WITHIN AN ACE OF.

ace in the hole *n. phr.* **1.** An ace given to a player face down so that other players in a card game cannot see it. ♦ *When the cowboy bet all his money in the poker game he did not know that the gambler had an ace in the hole and would win it from him.* **2.** *informal* Someone or something important that is kept as a surprise until the right time so as to bring victory or success. ♦ *The football team has a new play that they are keeping as an ace in the hole for the big game.* ♦ *The lawyer's ace in the hole was a secret witness who saw the accident.* Compare CARD UP ONE'S SLEEVE.

Achilles' heel *n. phr., literary* A physical or psychological weakness named after the Greek hero Achilles who was invulnerable except for a spot on his heel. ♦ *John's Achilles' heel is his lack of talent with numbers and math.*

acid head *n., slang* A regular user of LSD on whom the hallucinogenic drug has left a visible effect. ♦ *The reason John acts so funny is that he is a regular acid head.*

acid rock *n., slang* A characteristic kind of rock in which loudness and beat predominate over melody; especially such music as influenced by drug experiences. ♦ *John is a regular acid rock freak.*

acorn See GREAT OAKS FROM LITTLE ACORNS GROW.

acoustic perfume *n., slang* Sound for covering up unwanted noise, such as music over loudspeakers in a noisy construction area. ♦ *Let's get out of here—this acoustic perfume is too much for my ears.*

acquire a taste for *v. phr.* To become fond of something; get to like something. ♦ *Jack acquired a taste for ripe cheeses when he went to France.*

across the board *adv. phr.* **1.** So that equal amounts of money are bet on the same horse to win a race, to place second, or third. ♦ *I bet $6 on the white horse across the board.*—Often used with hyphens as an adjective. ♦ *I made*

an across-the-board bet on the white horse. **2.** *informal* Including everyone or all, so that all are included. ♦ *The President wanted taxes lowered across the board.*—Often used with hyphens as an adjective. ♦ *The workers at the store got an across-the-board pay raise.*

across the tracks See THE TRACKS.

act See READ THE RIOT ACT.

act high and mighty *v. phr.* To wield power; act overbearingly; order others around; look down on others. ♦ *Paul is an inexperienced teacher and he acts high and mighty with his students.*

actions speak louder than words What you do shows your character better and is more important than what you say.—A proverb. ♦ *John promised to help me, but he didn't. Actions speak louder than words.* ♦ *Joe is very quiet, but actions speak louder than words. He is the best player on the team.*

act of faith *n. phr.* An act or a deed that shows unquestioning belief in someone or something. ♦ *It was a real act of faith on Mary's part to entrust her jewelry to her younger sister's care.*

act of God *n.* An occurrence (usually some sort of catastrophe) for which the people affected are not responsible; said of earthquakes, floods, etc. ♦ *Hurricane Andrew destroyed many houses in Florida, but some types of insurance did not compensate the victims, claiming that the hurricane was an act of God.* See: FICKLE FINGER OF FATE.

act one's age *or* **be one's age** *v. phr.* To do the things that people expect someone of your age to do, not act as if you were much younger than you are. ♦ *Mr. O'Brien was playing tag with the children at the party. Then Mrs. O'Brien said, "Henry! Act your age!" and he stopped.*

actor See BAD ACTOR.

act out *v.* **1.** To show an idea, story, or happening by your looks, talk, and movements. ♦ *He tried to act out a story that he had read.* **2.** To put into action. ♦ *All his life he tried to act out his beliefs.*

act up *v., informal* **1.** To behave badly; act rudely or impolitely. ♦ *The dog acted up as the postman came to the door.* **2.** To work or run poorly (as a machine); skip; miss. ♦ *The car acted up because the spark plugs were dirty.*

add fuel to the flame *v. phr.* To make a bad matter worse by adding to its cause; spread trouble, increase anger or other strong feelings by talk or action. ♦ *By criticizing his son's girl, the father added fuel to the flame of his son's love.* ♦ *Bob was angry with Ted and Ted added fuel to the flame by laughing at him.*

add insult to injury *v. phr.* **1.** To hurt someone's feelings after doing him harm. ♦ *He added insult to injury when he called the man a rat after he had already beaten him up.* **2.** To make bad trouble worse. ♦ *We started on a picnic, and first it rained, then to add insult to injury, the car broke down.*

addition See IN ADDITION.

address See PUBLIC-ADDRESS SYSTEM.

add the finishing touches *v. phr.* To complete; finish. ♦ *Mary's first novel promised to be excellent; however, her editor suggested that she should add some finishing touches before accepting it.*

add up *v.* **1.** To come to the correct amount. ♦ *The numbers wouldn't add up.* **2.** *informal* To make sense; be understandable. ♦ *His story didn't add up.*

add up to *v.* **1.** To make a total of; amount to. ♦ *The bill added up to $12.95.* **2.** *informal* To mean; result in. ♦ *The rain, the mosquitoes, and the heat added up to a spoiled vacation.*

ad lib *v. phr.* To improvise; interpolate during speech. ♦ *When the actress forgot her lines during the second act, she had to ad lib in order to keep the show going.*

advance See IN ADVANCE *or* IN ADVANCE OF.

advantage See TAKE ADVANTAGE OF, TO ADVANTAGE.

a few *n. or adj.* A small number (of people or things); some. ♦ *The dry weather killed most of Mother's flowers, but a few are left.* ♦ *In the store, Mary saw many pretty rings and bracelets, and she wanted to buy a few of them.* ♦ *After the party, we thought that no one would help clean up, but a few couples did.* ♦ *Alice wanted to read a few pages more before she stopped.*—Usually *a few* is different in meaning from *few*, which emphasizes the negative; *a few* means 'some,' but *few* means 'not many.' ♦ *We thought no one would come to lunch, but a few came.* ♦ *We thought many people would come to lunch, but few came.* But sometimes *a few* is used with only, and then it is negative. ♦ *We thought many people would come to lunch, but only a few came.*—Sometimes used like an adverb. ♦ *Three students have no seats; we need a few more chairs.* ♦ *If we can set up chairs faster than people come and sit in them, we will soon be a few ahead.*—Sometimes used with *very* for emphasis. ♦ *Uncle Ralph gave away almost all of his sea shells, but he still had a very few left.* Compare A LITTLE. Contrast A LOT, QUITE A FEW.

affair See LOVE AFFAIR.

afoul of *prep.* **1.** In collision with. ♦ *The boat ran afoul of a buoy.* **2.** In or into trouble with. ♦ *The thief ran afoul of the night watchman.* ♦ *Speeders can expect to fall afoul of the law sometimes.*

afraid of one's shadow *adj. phr., informal* Scared of small or imaginary things; very easily frightened; jumpy; nervous. ♦ *Mrs. Smith won't stay alone in her house at night; she is afraid of her own shadow.* ♦ *Johnny cries whenever he must say hello to an adult; he is afraid of his own shadow.*

a friend in need is a friend indeed A genuine friend on whom one can always depend.—A proverb; often shortened to "a friend in need..." ♦ *When John's house burned down, his neighbor Jim helped him and his family with shelter, food and clothing. John said, "Jim, a friend in need is a friend indeed—this describes you."*

after a fashion *adv. phr.* Not very well or properly; poorly. ♦ *He played tennis after a fashion.* ♦ *The roof kept the rain out after a fashion.* Compare IN A WAY.

after all *adv. phr.* **1.** As a change in plans; anyway.—Used with emphasis on *after.* ♦ *Bob thought he couldn't go to the party because he had too much homework, but he went after all.* **2.** For a good reason that you should remember.—Used with emphasis on *all.* ♦ *Why shouldn't Betsy eat the cake? After all, she baked it.*

after a while *informal or* **in a while** *adv. phr.* Later, at some time in the future; after a time that is not short and not long. ♦ *"Dad, will you help me make this model plane?" "After a while, Jimmy, when I finish reading the newspaper."* ♦ *The boys gathered some wood, and in a while, a hot fire was burning.* Syn. BY AND BY. Contrast RIGHT AWAY.

after hours *adv. or adj. phr.* Not during the regular, correct, or usual time; going on or open after the usual hours. ♦ *The store was cleaned and swept out after hours.* ♦ *The children had a secret after hours party when they were supposed to be in bed.*

after one's own heart *adj. phr., informal* Well liked because of agreeing with your own feelings, interests, and ideas; to your liking—agreeable. Used after *man* or some similar word. ♦ *He likes baseball and good food; he is a man after my own heart.* ♦ *Thanks for agreeing with me about the class party; you're a girl after my own heart.* Compare SEE EYE TO EYE.

after the dust clears/when the dust settles *adv. phr.* When a troubling, confusing, or disastrous event is finally over. ♦ *John invited Tim for dinner, but since Tim's father had just died, he replied, "Thanks. I'd like to come after the dust settles."*

again See COME AGAIN, EVERY NOW AND THEN *or* EVERY NOW AND AGAIN, NOW AND THEN *or* NOW AND AGAIN, OFF AGAIN, ON AGAIN *or* ON AGAIN, OFF AGAIN, SOMETHING ELSE AGAIN, THEN AGAIN, TIME AND AGAIN, YOU SAID IT *or* YOU CAN SAY THAT AGAIN.

against it See UP AGAINST IT.

against the clock See AGAINST TIME.

against the current *or* **against the stream** See SWIM AGAINST THE CURRENT.

against the grain *adv. phr.* **1.** Across rather than with the direction of the fibers (as of wood or meat). ♦ *He sandpapered the wood against the grain.* **2.** So as to annoy or trouble, or to cause anger or dislike.—Usually follows *go.* ♦ *His coarse and rude ways went against the grain with me.* ♦ *It went against the grain with him to have to listen to her gossip.* Compare RUB THE WRONG WAY.

against time *or* **against the clock** *adv. phr.* **1.** As a test of speed or time; in order to beat a speed record or time limit. ♦ *John ran around the track against time, because there was no one else to race against.* **2.** As fast as possible; so as to do or finish something before a certain time. ♦ *It was a race against the clock whether the doctor would get to the accident soon enough to save the injured man.* **3.** So as to cause delay by using up time. ♦ *The outlaw talked against time with the sheriff, hoping that his gang would come and rescue him.*

age See ACT ONE'S AGE *or* BE ONE'S AGE, DOG'S AGE *or* COON'S AGE, LEGAL AGE *or* LAWFUL AGE, OF AGE, OVER AGE, UNDER AGE.

agent See FREE AGENT.

Agent Orange *n.* A herbicide used as a defoliant during the Vietnam War, considered by some to cause birth defects and cancer, hence, by extension, an instance of 'technological progress pollution.' ♦ *If things continue as they have, we'll all be eating some Agent Orange with our meals.*

ago See WHILE AGO.

agree with *v.* To have a good effect on, suit. ♦ *The meat loaf did not agree with him.* ♦ *The warm, sunny climate agreed with him, and he soon grew strong and healthy.*

ahead See DEAD AHEAD, GET AHEAD.

ahead of *prep.* **1.** In a position of advantage or power over. ♦ *He studies all the time, because he wants to stay ahead of his classmates.* **2.** In front of; before. ♦ *The troop leader walked a few feet ahead of the boys.* **3.** Earlier than; previous to, before. ♦ *Betty finished her test ahead of the others.*

ahead of the game *adv. or adj. phr., informal* **1.** In a position of advantage; winning (as in a game or contest); ahead (as by making money or profit); making it easier to win or succeed. ♦ *The time you spend studying when you are in school will put you ahead of the game in college.* ♦ *After Tom sold his papers, he was $5 ahead of the game.* **2.** Early; too soon; beforehand. ♦ *When Ralph came to school an hour early, the janitor said, "You're ahead of the game."* ♦ *John studies his lessons* *only one day early; if he gets too far ahead of the game, he forgets what he read.*

ahead of time *adv. phr.* Before the expected time; early. ♦ *The bus came ahead of time, and Mary was not ready.* ♦ *The new building was finished ahead of time.* Contrast BEHIND TIME.

a hell of a *or* **one hell of a** *adj., or adv. phr. informal* Extraordinary; very. ♦ *He made a hell of a shot during the basketball game.* ♦ *Max said seven months was a hell of a time to have to wait for a simple visa.* ♦ *The fall Max took left one hell of a bruise on his knee.*

aim See TAKE AIM.

air See BUILD CASTLES IN THE AIR, CLEAR THE AIR, GIVE ONESELF AIRS, GET THE AIR at GET THE BOUNCE 1., GIVE THE AIR at GIVE THE BOUNCE 1., IN THE AIR, INTO THIN AIR, LEAVE HANGING *or* LEAVE HANGING IN THE AIR, ON THE AIR, OUT OF THIN AIR, UP IN THE AIR, WALK ON AIR.

airbus *n.* A trade name, also used informally for a wide-bodied airplane used chiefly as a domestic passenger carrier. ♦ *Airbuses don't fly overseas, but mainly from coast to coast.*

air one's dirty linen in public *or* **wash one's dirty linen in public** *v. phr.* To talk about your private quarrels or disgraces where others can hear; make public something embarrassing that should be kept secret. ♦ *Everyone in the school knew that the superintendent and the principal were angry with each other because they aired their dirty linen in public.* ♦ *No one knew that the boys' mother was a drug addict, because the family did not wash its dirty linen in public.*

airquake *n.* An explosive noise of undetermined origin usually heard in coastal communities and appearing to come from some higher point in elevation. ♦ *What was that awful noise just now?—I guess it must have been an airquake.*

air shuttle *n., informal* Air service for regular commuters operating between major cities at not too far a distance, e.g., between Boston and New York City; such flights operate without reservation on a frequent schedule.

♦ *My dad takes the air shuttle from Boston to New York once a week.*

a la *prep.* In the same way as; like. ♦ *Billy played ball like a champion today, a la the professional ball players.* ♦ *Joe wanted to shoot an apple off my head a la William Tell.* [From French *à la,* in the manner of.]

albatross around one's neck *n. phr., literary* Guilt, the haunting past, an unforgettable problem. ♦ *Even though it was an accident, John's father's death has been an albatross around John's neck.* Compare MONKEY ON ONE'S BACK.

alert See ON THE ALERT.

a little *n. or adj.* A small amount (of); some.—Usually *a little* is different in meaning from *little,* which emphasizes the negative; *a little* means 'some'; but *little* means 'not much.' We say ♦ *"We thought that the paper was all gone, but a little was left."* But we say, ♦ *"We thought we still had a bag of flour, but little was left."* Also, we say, ♦ *"Bob was sick yesterday, but he is a little better today."* But we say, ♦ *"Bob was sick yesterday, and he is little better today."* Sometimes *a little* is used with *only,* and then it is negative. ♦ *We thought we had a whole bag of flour, but only a little was left.* ♦ *We have used most of the sugar; but a little is left.* ♦ *We did not eat all the cake; we saved a little of it for you.* ♦ *I'm tired; I need a little time to rest.* ♦ *Where is the paper? I need a little more.*—Often used like an adverb. ♦ *Usually the teacher just watched the dancing class, but sometimes she danced a little to show them how.* ♦ *The children wanted to play a little longer.*—Sometimes used with *very* for emphasis. ♦ *The sick girl could not eat anything, but she could drink a very little tea.* Syn. A BIT. Compare A FEW. Contrast A LOT, QUITE A LITTLE.

a little bird told me To have learned something from a mysterious, unknown, or secret source. ♦ *"Who told you that Dean Smith was resigning?" Peter asked. "A little bird told me," Jim answered.*

a little knowledge is a dangerous thing *literary* A person who knows a little about something may think he knows it all and make bad mistakes.—A proverb. ◆*John has read a book on driving a car and now he thinks he can drive. A little knowledge is a dangerous thing.*

alive See COME ALIVE, KNOW ——— IS ALIVE, LOOK ALIVE, SKIN ALIVE.

alive and kicking *adj. phr.* Very active; vigorous; full of energy. ◆*Grandpa was taken to the hospital with pneumonia, but he was discharged yesterday and is alive and kicking.*

alive with *prep., informal* Crowded with; filled with. ◆*The lake was alive with fish.* ◆*The stores were alive with people the Saturday before Christmas.*

all See AFTER ALL, AND ALL, AT ALL, BEAT ALL *or* BEAT THE DUTCH, FOR ALL, FOR ALL ONE IS WORTH, FOR ALL ONE KNOWS, FOR ALL THE WORLD, FOR GOOD *also* FOR GOOD AND ALL, FROM THE BOTTOM OF ONE'S HEART *or* WITH ALL ONE'S HEART, HAVE ALL ONE'S BUTTONS *or* HAVE ALL ONE'S MARBLES, IN ALL, JUMP ON *or* JUMP ALL OVER *or* LAND ALL OVER, KNOW-IT-ALL, ON ALL FOURS, ONCE AND FOR ALL, PUT ALL ONE'S EGGS IN ONE BASKET, STRIKE ALL OF A HEAP, WALK OVER *or* WALK ALL OVER *or* STEP ALL OVER.

all along *or* (*informal*) **right along** *adv. phr.* All the time; during the whole time. ◆*I knew all along that we would win.* ◆*I knew right along that Jane would come.*

all at once *adv. phr.* **1.** At the same time; together. ◆*The teacher told the children to talk one at a time; if they all talked at one time, she could not understand them.* ◆*Bill can play the piano, sing, and lead his orchestra all at once.* **2.** *or* **all of a sudden** Without warning; abruptly; suddenly; unexpectedly. ◆*All at once we heard a shot and the soldier fell to the ground.* ◆*All of a sudden the ship struck a rock.* Compare AT ONCE.

all better *adj. phr.* Fully recovered; all well again; no longer painful.— Usually used to or by children. ◆*"All better now," he kept repeating to the little girl.*

all but *adv. phr.* Very nearly; almost. ◆*Crows all but destroyed a farmer's field of corn.* ◆*The hikers were exhausted and all but frozen when they were found.*

all ears *adj. phr., informal* Very eager to hear; very attentive.—Used in the predicate. ◆*Go ahead with your story; we are all ears.* ◆*When John told about the circus, the boys were all ears.*

alley See BLIND ALLEY, DOWN ONE'S ALLEY *or* UP ONE'S ALLEY.

alley cat *n., slang* **1.** A stray cat. **2.** A person (usually a female) of rather easy-going, or actually loose sexual morals; a promiscuous person. ◆*You'll have no problem dating her; she's a regular alley cat.*

all eyes *adj. phr., informal* Wide-eyed with surprise or curiosity; watching very closely.—Used in the predicate. ◆*At the circus the children were all eyes.*

all gone *adj. phr.* Used up; exhausted (said of supplies); done with; over with. ◆*We used to travel a lot, but, alas, those days are all gone.*

all here See ALL THERE.

all hours *n. phr., informal* Late or irregular times. ◆*The boy's mother said he must stop coming home for meals at all hours.* ◆*He stayed up till all hours of the night to finish his school work.*

all in *adj. phr., informal* Very tired; exhausted. ◆*The players were all in after their first afternoon of practice.* Syn. PLAYED OUT, WORN OUT.

all in a day's work *or* **all in the day's work** *adj. phr., informal* Unpleasant or bad but to be expected; not harder than usual; not unusual. ◆*Keeping ants away from a picnic lunch is all in the day's work.* ◆*When the car had a flat tire, Father said that it was all in a day's work.* Compare PAR FOR THE COURSE, PUT UP WITH.

all in all¹ *n. phr., literary* The person or thing that you love most. ◆*She was all in all to him.* ◆*Music was his all in all.*

all in all² *or* **in all** *adv. phr.* When everything is thought about; in summary; altogether. ◆*All in all, it was a pleasant day's cruise.* ◆*All in all, the pilot of an airplane must have many abilities and years of experience before he can be appointed.* Compare ON THE WHOLE 1. ◆*Counting the balls on the green, we have six golf balls in all.*

all in good time *adv. phr.* Some time soon, when the time is ripe for an event to take place. ◆*"I want to get married, Dad," Mike said. "All in good time, Son," answered his father.*

all in one piece *adv. phr.* Safely; without damage or harm. ♦*John's father was terribly concerned when his son was sent to war as a pilot, but he came home all in one piece.*

all kinds of *adj. phr., informal* Plenty of. ♦*People say that Mr. Fox has all kinds of money.* ♦*When Kathy was sick, she had all kinds of company.* Compare GREAT DEAL.

all manner of *adj. phr., formal* Many different kinds of; all sorts of. ♦*In a five-and-ten-cent store you can buy all manner of things.*

all of *adj. phr., informal* **1.** At least the amount or number of; fully; no less than. ♦*It was all of ten o'clock before they finally started.* ♦*She must have paid all of $50 for that hat.* **2.** Showing all the signs of; completely in.—Used with *a.* ♦*The girls were all of a twitter before the dance.* ♦*Mother is all of a flutter because of the thunder and lightning.* ♦*The dog was all of a tremble with cold.*

all of a sudden See ALL AT ONCE 2.

all out *adv. phr., informal* With all your strength, power, or determination; to the best of your ability; without holding back.—Usually used in the phrase *go all out.* ♦*We went all out to win the game.* ♦*John went all out to finish the job and was very tired afterwards.* Compare ALL THE WAY 2, FULL TILT, GO THE WHOLE HOG, GO TO ANY LENGTH, LEAVE A STONE UNTURNED, WITH MIGHT AND MAIN.

all-out effort *n.* A great and thorough effort at solving a given problem. ♦*The President is making an all-out effort to convince Congress to pass the pending bill on health care.*

all-out war *n.* Total war including civilian casualties as opposed to a war that is limited only to armies. ♦*Hitler was waging an all-out war when he invaded Poland.*

all over *adv. phr.* **1.** In every part; everywhere. ♦*He has a fever and aches all over.* ♦*I have looked all over for my glasses.* Compare FAR AND WIDE. **2.** *informal* In every way; completely. ♦*She is her mother all over.* **3.** *informal* Coming into very close physical contact, as during a violent fight; wrestling. ♦*Before I noticed what happened, he was all over me.*

all over but the shouting *adv. phr., informal* Finally decided or won; brought to an end; not able to be changed. ♦*After Bill's touchdown, the game was all over but the shouting.* ♦*John and Tom both tried to win Jane, but after John's promotion it was all over but the shouting.*

all over someone See FALL ALL OVER SOMEONE.

allowance See MAKE ALLOWANCE.

allow for *v.* To provide for; leave room for; give a chance to; permit. ♦*She cut the skirt four inches longer to allow for a wide hem.* ♦*Democracy allows for many differences of opinion.*

all right¹ *adv. phr.* **1.** Well enough. *The new machine is running all right.* **2.** *informal* I am willing; yes. ♦*"Shall we watch television?" "All right."* Compare VERY WELL. **3.** *informal* Beyond question, certainly.—Used for emphasis and placed after the word it modifies. ♦*It's time to leave, all right, but the bus hasn't come.*

all right² *adj. phr.* **1.** Good enough; correct; suitable. ♦*His work is always all right.* **2.** In good health or spirits; well. ♦*"How are you?" "I'm all right."* **3.** *slang* Good. ♦*He's an all right guy.*

all right for you *interj.* I'm finished with you! That ends it between you and me!—Used by children. ♦*All right for you! I'm not playing with you any more!*

all roads lead to Rome *literary* The same end or goal may be reached by many different ways.—A proverb. ♦*"I don't care how you get the answer," said the teacher, "All roads lead to Rome."*

all set *adj. phr.* Ready to start. ♦*"Is the plane ready for take-off?" the bank president asked. "Yes, Sir," the pilot answered. "We're all set."*

all shook up *also* **shook up** *adj., slang* In a state of great emotional upheaval; disturbed; agitated. ♦*What are you so shook up about?*

all systems go *Originally from space English, now general colloquial usage.* Everything is complete and ready for action; it is now all right to proceed. ♦*After they wrote out the invitations, it was all systems go for the wedding.*

all the¹ *adj. phr., dial.* The only. ♦*A hut was all the home he ever had.*

all the² *adv. phr.* Than otherwise; even.—Used to emphasize comparative adjectives, adverbs, and nouns. ♦ *Opening the windows made it all the hotter.* ♦ *Take a bus instead of walking and get home all the sooner.* ♦ *If you don't eat your dessert, all the more for us.*

all the better See ALL THE 2.

all the ——er *substandard* The —— est; as ... as.—Used with a comparative adjective or adverb and subordinate clause in place of a superlative adjective or adverb. ♦ *That was all the bigger he grew.* ♦ *Is that all the faster you can go?*

all there *or* **all here** *adj. phr., informal* Understanding well; thinking clearly; not crazy.—Usually used in negative sentences. ♦ *Joe acted queerly and talked wildly, so we thought he was not all there.*

all the same¹ *or* **all one** *n. phr.* Something that makes no difference; a choice that you don't care about. ♦ *If it's all the same to you, I would like to be waited on first.* ♦ *You can get there by car or by bus—it's all one.*

all the same² *or* **just the same** *adv. phr., informal* As if the opposite were so; nevertheless; anyway; anyhow; still. ♦ *Everyone opposed it, but Sally and Bob got married all the same.* ♦ *Mary is deaf, but she takes tap dancing lessons just the same.* Compare AT THAT 3, IN SPITE OF.

all the thing *or* **all the rage, the in thing** *n. phr.* The fashionable or popular thing to do, the fashionable or most popular artist or form of art at a given time. ♦ *After "The Graduate" Dustin Hoffman was all the rage in the movies.* ♦ *It was all the thing in the late sixties to smoke pot and demonstrate against the war in Vietnam.*

all the time *adv. phr.* **1.** *or* **all the while** During the whole period; through the whole time. ♦ *Mary went to college in her home town and lived at home all the while.* ♦ *Most of us were surprised to hear that Mary and Tom had been engaged all year, but Sue said she knew it all the time.* **2.** Without stopping; continuously ♦ *Most traffic lights work all the time.* **3.** Very often; many times. ♦ *Ruth talks about her trip to Europe*

all the time, and her friends are tired of it.

all the way *or* **the whole way** *adv. phr.* **1.** From start to finish during the whole distance or time. ♦ *Jack climbed all the way to the top of the tree.* ♦ *Joe has played the whole way in the football game and it's almost over.* **2.** In complete agreement; with complete willingness to satisfy.—Often used in the phrase *go all the way with.* ♦ *I go all the way with what George says about Bill.* ♦ *Mary said she was willing to kiss Bill, but that did not mean she was willing to go all the way with him.* ♦ *The bank was willing to lend Mr. Jones money to enlarge his factory but it wasn't willing to go all the way with his plans to build another in the next town.* Compare ALL OUT, GO THE WHOLE HOG.

all the worse See ALL THE 2.

all thumbs *adj., informal* Awkward, especially with your hands; clumsy. ♦ *Harry tried to fix the chair but he was all thumbs.*

all told *adv. phr., informal* Counting or including everything. ♦ *Including candy sale profits we have collected $300 all told.*

all to the good See TO THE GOOD.

all up *adj. phr., informal* Near to certain death or defeat without any more chance or hope. ♦ *With their ammunition gone the patrol knew that it was all up with them.*

all very well *adj.* All right; very good and correct; very true.—Usually followed by a *but* clause. ♦ *It's all very well for you to complain but can you do any better?* ♦ *It's all very well if Jane comes with us, but how will she get back home?* Compare WELL AND GOOD.

all walks of life *n. phr.* All socioeconomic groups; all professions and lines of work. ♦ *A good teacher has to be able to communicate with students from all walks of life.* ♦ *A clever politician doesn't alienate people from any walk of life.*

all wet *adj., slang* Entirely confused or wrong; mistaken. ♦ *When the Wright brothers said they could build a flying machine, people thought they were all wet.* ♦ *If you think I like baseball, you're all wet.* Compare OFF ONE'S ROCKER.

all wool and a yard wide *adj. phr.* Of fine character; especially, very generous and kind-hearted. ◆ *He's a wonderful brother—all wool and a yard wide.*

all work and no play makes Jack a dull boy Too much hard work without time out for play or enjoyment is not good for anyone.—A proverb. ◆ *Bill's mother told him to stop studying and to go out and play, because all work and no play makes Jack a dull boy.*

all year round *adv. phr.* Always; all the time; throughout all seasons of the year. ◆ *In California the sun shines all year round.*

alone See LET ALONE *or* LEAVE ALONE, LET WELL ENOUGH ALONE *or* LEAVE WELL ENOUGH ALONE.

along See ALL ALONG *or* RIGHT ALONG, COME ALONG, GET ALONG, GO ALONG, RUN ALONG, STRING ALONG.

along for the ride *adv. phr., informal* Being in a group for the fun or the credit without doing any of the work. ◆ *He wants no members in his political party who are just along for the ride.*

along in years *or* **on in years** *adj. phr.* Elderly; growing old. ◆ *As Grandfather got on in years, he became quiet and thoughtful.* ◆ *Our dog isn't very playful because it is getting on in years.*

alongside of *prep.* **1.** At or along the side of. ◆ *We walked alongside of the river.* **2.** Together with. ◆ *I played alongside of Tom on the same team.* Compare SHOULDER TO SHOULDER, SIDE BY SIDE. **3.** *informal* Compared with or to; measured next to. ◆ *His money doesn't look like much alongside of a millionaire's.*

a lot *n., informal* A large number or amount; very many or very much; lots. ◆ *I learned a lot in Mr. Smith's class.* ◆ *A lot of our friends are going to the beach this summer.*—Often used like an adverb. ◆ *Ella is a jolly girl; she laughs a lot.* ◆ *Grandfather was very sick last week, but he's a lot better now.* ◆ *You'll have to study a lot harder if you want to pass.*—Also used as an adjective with *more, less,* and *fewer.* ◆ *There was a good crowd at the game today, but a lot more will come next week.*—Often used with *whole* for emphasis. ◆ *John has a whole lot of marbles.* ◆ *Jerry is a whole lot taller than he was*

a year ago. Compare GOOD DEAL, GOOD MANY, A NUMBER. Contrast A FEW, A LITTLE.

aloud See THINK ALOUD *or* THINK OUT LOUD.

alpha wave *n.* A brain wave, 8–12 cycles per second, associated with a state of relaxation and meditation and, hence, free of anxieties. ◆ *Try to produce some alpha waves; you will instantly feel a lot better.*

alter See CIRCUMSTANCES ALTER CASES.

always See GRASS IS ALWAYS GREENER ON THE OTHER SIDE OF THE FENCE.

ambulance chaser *n.* An attorney who specializes in representing victims of traffic accidents. By extension, a lawyer of inferior rank or talent. ◆ *Don't hire Cohen; he's just another ambulance chaser.*

American plan *n.* A system of hotel management in which meals are included with the room, as opposed to the European plan that does not include meals. ◆ *American tourists in Europe sometimes expect that their meals will be included, because they are used to the American plan.*

amount to *v.* Signify; add up to. ◆ *John's total income didn't amount to more than a few hundred dollars.*

a must *n.* **1.** An inevitability; a necessity. *Visas in many foreign countries are a must.* **2.** An extremely interesting or memorable event, such as a free concert given by an international celebrity. ◆ *Alfred Brendel's Beethoven master classes are open to the public and are not to be missed; they're a must.*

anchor See AT ANCHOR.

—— **and** —— **1.** *—And* is used between repeated words to show continuation or emphasis. ◆ *When the children saw the beautiful Christmas tree they looked and looked.* ◆ *Old Mr. Bryan has known Grandfather for years and years, since they were boys.* ◆ *Billy dived to the bottom of the lake again and again, looking for the lost watch.* ◆ *Everyone wished the speaker would stop, but he talked on and on.* Compare THROUGH AND THROUGH. **2.** *—When and* is used between words with opposite meaning, it often emphasizes how much you mean. ◆ *Mr. Jones worked early and late to earn enough to live.*

♦ *The parents hunted high and low for the lost child.* Compare DAY AND NIGHT, FROM ———— TO, INSIDE AND OUT.

and all *informal* And whatever goes with it; and all that means. ♦ *We don't go out much nowadays, with the new baby and all.* ♦ *Jack's employer provided the tools and all.*

and how! *interj. informal* Yes, that is certainly right!—Used for emphatic agreement. ♦ *"Did you see the game?" "And how!"* ♦ *"Isn't Mary pretty?" "And how she is!"* Syn. YOU BET, YOU SAID IT. Compare BUT GOOD.

and so forth *or* **and so on** And more of the same kind; and further amounts or things like the ones already mentioned. ♦ *The costumes were red, pink, blue, purple, yellow, and so forth.* Compare WHAT HAVE YOU.

and the like *n. phr.* Things of a similar nature. ♦ *I like McDonald's, Wendy's, Kentucky Fried Chicken, and the like.* ♦ *When I go out to the beach I take towels, a mat, suntan lotion, and the like.*

and then some And a lot more; and more too. ♦ *It would cost all the money he had and then some.* ♦ *Talking his way out of this trouble was going to take all his wits and then some.*

and what not See WHAT NOT.

angel dust *n., slang* Phencyclidine, an addictive hallucinatory narcotic drug extremely dangerous to the users' health, also called PCP. ♦ *Mike has gone from grass to angel dust; he will end up in the morgue.*

another See DANCE TO ANOTHER TUNE.

answer back See TALK BACK.

answer for *v.* **1.** To take responsibility for; assume charge or supervision of. ♦ *The secret service has to answer for the safety of the President and his family.* **2.** To say you are sure that (someone) has good character or ability; guarantee: sponsor. ♦ *When people thought Ray had stolen the money, the principal said, "Ray is no thief. I'll answer for him."* **3.** Take the blame or punishment for. ♦ *When Mother found out who ate the cake, Tom had to answer for his mischief.*

answer one's calling *v. phr.* To fulfill one's destiny in terms of work or profession by doing what one has a talent for. ♦ *Don answered his calling when*

he became a chiropractor. Susy answered her calling when she became a violinist.

answer the call of nature *or* **obey the call of nature** *v. phr., slang* To go to the bathroom to relieve oneself by urinating or defecating. ♦ *Ted was hiking in the mountains when suddenly he had to answer the call of nature but since there was no bathroom in the woods, he excused himself and disappeared behind the bushes.*

answer to *v.* To be named; go by a certain name or designation; be accountable. ♦ *When you walk my dog, please remember that he answers to the name "Caesar."* ♦ *As head of the company she does not have to answer to anyone.*

ante up *v., informal* To produce the required amount of money in order to close a transaction; to pay what one owes. ♦ *"I guess I'd better ante up if I want to stay an active member of the Association," Max said.*

ants in one's pants *n. phr., slang* Nervous over-activity; restlessness. ♦ *Jane can not sit still; she has ants in her pants.* ♦ *You have ants in your pants today. Is something wrong?*

a number *n.* A rather large number; numbers.—Used when there are more than several and fewer than many. ♦ *The parents were invited to see the program, and a number came.* ♦ *We knew the Smiths rather well; we had visited them a number of times.*—Used like an adjective before *less, more.* ♦ *We have not set up enough folding chairs; we need a number more.* Compare QUITE A FEW.

any See HARDLY ANY *or* SCARCELY ANY.

any number *n., informal* A large number; many. ♦ *There are any number of reasons for eating good food.* ♦ *Don't ask George what his excuse is. He can invent any number.* Compare A LOT, A NUMBER, GOOD MANY.

any old how / any old way *adv. phr., informal* Doing something in a casual, haphazard, or careless way. ♦ *"John," the teacher said, "you can't just do your homework any old way; you must pay attention to my instructions!"*

any port in a storm Any help is welcome in an emergency.—A proverb. ♦ *The motel we stopped in was nothing* *to brag about, but we were so exhausted that it was a clear case of any port in a storm.*

anything See HAVE NOTHING ON *or* NOT HAVE ANYTHING ON, IF ANYTHING.

anything but *adv. phr.* Quite the opposite of; far from being. ♦ *I don't mean he's lazy—anything but!* ♦ *The boys knew they had broken the rules, and they were anything but happy when they were called to the office.*

anything like *or* **anywhere near** *adv.* Nearly.—Used in negative, interrogative, and conditional sentences, often in the negative forms *nothing like* or *nowhere near.* ♦ *It's not anything like as hot today as it was yesterday.* ♦ *Do you think that gold ring is worth anywhere near a hundred dollars?* ♦ *Today's game was nowhere near as exciting as yesterday's game.* ♦ *Studying that lesson should take nothing like two hours.*

anywhere near See ANYTHING LIKE *or* ANYWHERE NEAR.

any which way See EVERY WHICH WAY.

apart See JOKING ASIDE *or* JOKING APART, POLES APART, TELL APART.

apart from *or* **aside from** *prep. phr.* Beside or besides; in addition to. ♦ *The children hardly see anyone, apart from their parents.* ♦ *Aside from being fun and good exercise, swimming is a very useful skill.* Syn. EXCEPT FOR, OUTSIDE OF.

ape See GO APE.

appear See SPEAK OF THE DEVIL AND HE APPEARS.

appearance See PUT IN AN APPEARANCE *also* MAKE AN APPEARANCE.

apple See POLISH THE APPLE.

applecart See UPSET THE APPLECART *or* UPSET ONE'S APPLECART.

apple of one's eye *n. phr.* Something or someone that is adored; a cherished person or object. ♦ *Charles is the apple of his mother's eye.* ♦ *John's first car was the apple of his eye. He was always polishing it.*

apple-pie order *n. phr., informal* Exact orderly arrangement, neatness; tidy arrangement. ♦ *The house was in apple-pie order.* ♦ *Like a good secretary, she kept the boss's desk in apple-pie order.*

apple polisher; apple polishing See POLISH THE APPLE.

approval See ON APPROVAL.

a pretty pass *n. phr.* An unfortunate condition; a critical state. ♦ *While the boss was away, things at the company had come to a pretty pass.*

apron See TIED TO ONE'S MOTHER'S APRON STRINGS.

apropos of *prep., formal* In connection with; on the subject of, about; concerning. ♦ *Apropos of higher tuition, Mr. Black told the boy about the educational loans that banks are offering.* ♦ *Mr. White went to see Mr. Richards apropos of buying a car.*

arm See GIVE ONE'S RIGHT ARM, KEEP AT A DISTANCE *or* KEEP AT ARM'S LENGTH, SHOT IN THE ARM, TAKE UP ARMS, TWIST ONE'S ARM, UP IN ARMS, WITH OPEN ARMS, COST AN ARM AND A LEG.

arm and a leg *n., slang* An exorbitantly high price that must be paid for something that isn't really worth it. ♦ *It's true that to get a decent apartment these days in New York you have to pay an arm and a leg.*

armed to the teeth *adj. phr.* Having all needed weapons; fully armed. ♦ *The paratroopers were armed to the teeth.*

arm in arm *adv. phr.* With your arm under or around another person's arm, especially in close comradeship or friendship. ♦ *Sally and Joan were laughing and joking together as they walked arm in arm down the street.* ♦ *When they arrived at the party, the partners walked arm in arm to meet the hosts.* Compare HAND IN HAND.

around one's ears See ABOUT ONE'S EARS.

around the clock *also* **the clock around** *adv. phr.* For 24 hours a day continuously all day and all night. ♦ *The factory operated around the clock until the order was filled.* ♦ *He studied around the clock for his history exam.*—**round-the-clock** *adj.* ♦ *That filling station has round-the-clock service.*

around the corner *adv. phr.* Soon to come or happen; close by; near at hand. ♦ *The fortune teller told Jane that there was an adventure for her just around the corner.*

arrest See UNDER ARREST.

as See FOR AS MUCH AS, INASMUCH AS.

as a last resort *adv. phr* In lieu of better things; lacking better solutions. ♦ *"We'll sleep in our sleeping bags as a* *last resort," John said, "since all the motels are full."*

as a matter of fact *adv. phr.* Actually; really; in addition to what has been said; in reference to what was said.— Often used as an interjection. ♦ *It's not true that I cannot swim; as a matter of fact, I used to work as a lifeguard in Hawaii.* ♦ *Do you think this costs too much? As a matter of fact, I think it is rather cheap.*

as an aside *adv. phr.* Said as a remark in a low tone of voice; used in theaters where the actor turns toward the audience as if to 'think out loud.' ♦ *During the concert Tim said to his wife as an aside, "The conductor has no idea how to conduct Beethoven."*

as a rule *adv. phr.* Generally; customarily. ♦ *As a rule, the boss arrives at the office about 10 A.M.*

as an old shoe See COMFORTABLE AS AN OLD SHOE, COMMON AS AN OLD SHOE.

as ——— as——— —Used with an adjective or adverb in a comparison or with the effect of a superlative. ♦ *John is as tall as his father now.* ♦ *I didn't do as badly today as I did yesterday.* ♦ *John's father gave him a hard job and told him to do as well as possible.* ♦ *The sick girl was not hungry, but her mother told her to eat as much as she could.*—Also used in the form *so ——— as* in some sentences, especially negative sentences. ♦ *This hill isn't nearly so high as the last one we climbed.*—Often used in similes (comparisons that are figures of speech). ♦ *The baby mouse looked as big as a minute.* ♦ *Jim's face was red as a beet after he made the foolish mistake.*— Most similes in conventional use are clichés, avoided by careful speakers and writers.

as best one can *adv. phr.* As well as you can; by whatever means are available; in the best way you can. ♦ *The car broke down in the middle of the night, and he had to get home as best he could.* ♦ *George's foot hurt, but he played the game as best he could.* ♦ *The girl's mother was sick, so the girl got dinner as best she could.*

as catch can See CATCH AS CATCH CAN.

as far as *or* **so far as** *adv. phr.* **1.** To the degree or amount that; according to what, how much, or how far. ♦ *John*

did a good job as far as he went, but he did not finish it. ♦ *So far as the weather is concerned, I do not think it matters.* ♦ *As far as he was concerned, things were going well.* **2.** To the extent that; within the limit that. ♦ *He has no brothers so far as I know.* Compare FOR ALL 2.

as far as that goes *or* **as far as that is concerned** *or* **so far as that is concerned** *also* **so far as that goes** *adv. phr.* While we are talking about it; also; actually. ♦ *You don't have to worry about the girls. Mary can take care of herself, and as far as that goes, Susan is pretty independent, too.* ♦ *I didn't enjoy the movie, and so far as that is concerned, I never like horror movies.* Syn. FOR THAT MATTER, IN FACT. Compare COME TO THINK OF IT.

as follows A list of things that come next; what is listed next.—Followed by a colon. ♦ *My grocery list is as follows: bread, butter meat, eggs, sugar.* ♦ *The names of the members are as follows: John Smith, Mary Webb, Linda Long, Ralph Harper.* ♦ *The route is as follows: From City Hall go south on Main Street to Elm Street, east on Elm to 5th Street, and south on 5th two blocks to the school.*

as for *prep.* **1.** In regard to; speaking of; concerning. ♦ *We have plenty of bread, and as for butter, we have more than enough.* **2.** Speaking for. ♦ *Most people like the summer but as for me, I like winter much better.* Compare FOR ONE'S PART.

as good as *adv. phr.* Nearly the same as; almost. ♦ *She claimed that he as good as promised to marry her.* ♦ *He as good as called me a liar.* ♦ *We'll get to school on time, we're as good as there now.* ♦ *The man who had been shot was as good as dead.*—Often used without the first *as* before adjectives. ♦ *When the car was repaired, it looked good as new.*

as good as a mile See MISS IS AS GOOD AS A MILE.

as good as one gets See GIVE AS GOOD AS ONE GETS.

as good as one's promise See AS GOOD AS ONE'S WORD.

as good as one's word *or* **good as one's word** *adj. phr.* Trustworthy; sure to keep your promise. ♦ *The coach said* he would give the players a day off if they won, and he was as good as his word. ♦ *We knew she was always good as her word, so we trusted her.*

as hard as nails *adj. phr.* Very unfeeling; cruel, and unsympathetic. ♦ *Uncle Joe is as hard as nails; although he is a millionaire, he doesn't help his less fortunate relatives.*

aside See JOKING ASIDE, SET ASIDE.

aside from See APART FROM.

aside of *prep., dialect* Beside; by the side of. ♦ *Mary sits aside of her sister on the bus.*

as if *or* **as though** *conj.* **1.** As (he, she, it) would if; in the same way one would if seeing to show. ♦ *The baby laughed as if he understood what Mother said.* ♦ *The book looked as though it had been out in the rain.* ♦ *The waves dashed on the rocks as if in anger.* **2.** That. ♦ *It seems as if you are the first one here.*

as if one has come out of a bandbox See LOOK AS IF ONE HAS COME OUT OF A BANDBOX.

as is *adv.* Without changes or improvements; with no guarantee or promise of good condition.—Used after the word it modifies. ♦ *They agree to buy the house as is.* ♦ *He bought an old car as is.* Compare AT THAT 1.

as it were *adv. phr.* As it might be said to be; as if it really were; seemingly.— Used with a statement that might seem silly or unreasonable, to show that it is just a way of saying it. ♦ *In many ways children live, as it were, in a different world from adults.* ♦ *The sunlight on the icy branches made, as it were, delicate lacy cobwebs from tree to tree.* Compare SO TO SPEAK.

ask See FOR THE ASKING.

ask for *v., informal* To make (something bad) likely to happen to you; bring (something bad) upon yourself. ♦ *Charles drives fast on worn-out tires; he is asking for trouble.* ♦ *The workman lost his job, but he asked for it by coming to work drunk several times.* Compare HAVE IT COMING, SERVE RIGHT, SIGN ONE'S OWN DEATH WARRANT.

ask for one's hand *v. phr.* To ask permission to marry someone. ♦ *"Sir,"* John said timidly to Mary's father, *"I*

came to ask for your daughter's hand."

ask for the moon *or* **cry for the moon** *v. phr.* To want something that you cannot reach or have; try for the impossible. ♦ *John asked his mother for a hundred dollars today. He's always asking for the moon.* Compare PROMISE THE MOON.

asleep at the switch *adj. phr.* **1.** Asleep when it is one's duty to move a railroad switch for cars to go on the right track. ♦ *The new man was asleep at the switch and the two trains crashed.* **2.** *informal* Failing to act promptly as expected; not alert to an opportunity. ♦ *When the ducks flew over, the boy was asleep at the switch and missed his shot.*

as likely as not *adv. phr.* Probably. ♦ *As likely as not, he will disappear forever.*

as long as *or* **so long as** *conj.* **1.** Since; because; considering that. ♦ *As long as you are going to town anyway, you can do something for me.* **2.** Provided that; if. ♦ *You may use the room as you like, so long as you clean it up afterward.*

as luck would have it *adv. clause* As it happened; by chance; luckily or unluckily. ♦ *As luck would have it, no one was in the building when the explosion occurred.* ♦ *As luck would have it, there was rain on the day of the picnic.*

as much *n.* The same; exactly that. ♦ *Don't thank me, I would do as much for anyone.* ♦ *Did you lose your way? I thought as much when you were late in coming.*

as much as *adv. phr.* **1.** *or* **much as** Even though; although. ♦ *As much as I hate to do it, I must stay home and study tonight.* **2.** *or* **so much as** Just the same as; almost; practically; really. ♦ *By running away he as much as admitted that he had taken the money.* ♦ *You as much as promised you would help us.* ♦ *The clerk as much as told me that I was a fool.* Compare AS GOOD AS. **3.** See FOR AS MUCH AS.

as of *prep.* At or until (a certain time). ♦ *I know that as of last week he was still unmarried.* ♦ *As of now we don't know much about Mars.*

as one goes See PAY AS ONE GOES.

as one man *adv. phr.* Unanimously; together; involving all. ♦ *The audience arose as one man to applaud the great pianist.*

as regards *prep.* Regarding; concerning;

about. ♦ *You needn't worry as regards the cost of the operation.* ♦ *He was always secretive as regards his family.*

as soon as *conj.* Just after; when; immediately after. ♦ *As soon as the temperature falls to 70, the furnace is turned on.* ♦ *As soon as you finish your job let me know.* ♦ *He will see you as soon as he can.*

as the crow flies *adv. clause* By the most direct way; along a straight line between two places. ♦ *It is seven miles to the next town as the crow flies, but it is ten miles by the road, which goes around the mountain.*

as the story goes *adv. phr.* As the story is told; as one has heard through rumor. ♦ *As the story goes, Jonathan disappeared when he heard the police were after him.*

as though See AS IF.

as to *prep.* **1.** In connection with; about; regarding. ♦ *There is no doubt as to his honesty.* ♦ *As to your final grade, that depends on your final examination.* Syn. WITH RESPECT TO. **2.** According to; following; going by. ♦ *They sorted the eggs as to size and color.*

as usual *adv. phr.* In the usual way; as you usually do or as it usually does. ♦ *As usual, Tommy forgot to make his bed before he went out to play.* ♦ *Only a week after the fire in the store, it was doing business as usual.*

as well *adv. phr.* **1.** In addition; also, too; besides. ♦ *The book tells about Mark Twain's writings and about his life as well.* ♦ *Tom is captain of the football team and is on the baseball team as well.* **2.** Without loss and possibly with gain. ♦ *After the dog ran away, Father thought he might as well sell the dog house.* ♦ *Since he can't win the race, he may as well quit.* ♦ *It's just as well you didn't come yesterday, because we were away.*

as well as *conj.* In addition to; and also; besides. ♦ *Hiking is good exercise as well as fun.* ♦ *He was my friend as well as my doctor.* ♦ *The book tells about the author's life as well as about his writings.*

as yet *adv. phr.* Up to the present time; so far; yet. ♦ *We know little as yet about the moon's surface.* ♦ *She has not come as yet.*

as you please **1.** As you like, whatever

you like or prefer; as you choose. ♦ *You may do as you please.* **2.** *informal* Very.—Used after an adjective or adverb often preceded by *as.* ♦ *There was Tinker, sitting there, cheerful as you please.* ♦ *She was dressed for the dance and she looked as pretty as you please.*

at a blow *or* **at a stroke** *or* **at one stroke** *adv. phr.* Immediately; suddenly; with one quick or forceful action. ♦ *The pirates captured the ship and captured a ton of gold at a blow.* ♦ *A thousand men lost their jobs at a stroke when the factory closed.* ♦ *All the prisoners escaped at one stroke.* Compare AT ONCE, AT ONE TIME.

at all *adv. phr.* At any time or place, for any reason, or in any degree or manner.—Used for emphasis with certain kinds of words or sentences. **1.** Negative ♦ *It's not at all likely he will come.* **2.** Limited ♦ *I can hardly hear you at all.* **3.** Interrogative ♦ *Can it be done at all?* **4.** Conditional ♦ *She will walk with a limp, if she walks at all.* Syn. IN THE LEAST.

at all costs *adv. phr.* At any expense of time, effort, or money. Regardless of the results. ♦ *Mr. Jackson intended to save his son's eyesight at all costs.* ♦ *Carl is determined to succeed in his new job at all costs.*

at all events See IN ANY CASE.

at all hazards *adv. phr.* With no regard for danger; at any risk; regardless of the chances you must take. ♦ *The racer meant to win the 500-mile race at all hazards.*

at all hours *adv. phr.* Any time; all the time; at almost any time. ♦ *The baby cried so much that we were up at all hours trying to calm her down.*

at a loss *adj. phr.* In a state of uncertainty; without any idea; puzzled. ♦ *A good salesman is never at a loss for words.* ♦ *When Don missed the last bus, he was at a loss to know what to do.*

at anchor *adj. phr.* Held by an anchor from floating away; anchored. ♦ *The ship rode at anchor in the harbor.*

at any rate *adv. phr.* In any case; anyhow. ♦ *It isn't much of a car, but at any rate it was not expensive.* Compare AT LEAST 2, IN ANY CASE.

at a premium *adv. phr.* At a high price due to special circumstances. ♦*When his father died, Fred flew to Europe at a premium because he had no chance to buy a less expensive ticket.*

at arm's length See KEEP AT A DISTANCE *or* KEEP AT ARM'S LENGTH.

at a set time *prep. phr.* At a particular, pre-specified time. ♦*Do we have to eat in this hotel at a set time, or may we come down whenever we want?*

at a snail's pace See SNAIL'S PACE.

at a straw See GRASP AT STRAWS.

at a stroke See AT A BLOW *or* AT A STROKE.

at a time *adv. phr.* At once; at one time; in one group or unit; together. ♦*He checked them off one at a time as they came in.* ♦*He ran up the steps two at a time.* See EVERY OTHER. ♦*They showed up for class three and four at a time.*

at bay *adv. or adj. phr.* In a place where you can no longer run away; unable to go back farther; forced to stand and fight, or face an enemy; cornered. ♦*The dog ran the rat into a corner, and there the rat turned at bay.* ♦*The police chased the thief to a roof, where they held him at bay until more policemen came to help.* Compare BRING TO BAY.

at best *or* **at the best** *adv. phr.* **1.** Under the best conditions; as the best possibility. ♦*A coal miner's job is dirty and dangerous at best.* ♦*We can't get to New York before ten o'clock at best.* Compare AT MOST. Contrast AT WORST. **2.** In the most favorable way of looking at something; even saying the best about the thing. ♦*The treasurer had at best been careless with the club's money, but most people thought he had been dishonest.*

at both ends See BURN THE CANDLE AT BOTH ENDS.

at call *adj. or adv. phr.* **1.** Ready or nearby for use, help, or service; on request. ♦*Thousands of auto insurance agents all over the country are at the insured person's call, wherever he may travel.* **2.** At the word of command; at an order or signal. ♦*The dog was trained to come at call.*

at close range *adv. phr.* Close by; in proximity. ♦*The police officer fired at the fleeing murder suspect at close range.*

at cross purposes *adv. phr.* With opposing meanings or aims; with opposing effect or result; with aims which hinder or get in each other's way. ♦*Tom's parents acted at cross purposes in advising him; his father wanted him to become a doctor; but his mother wanted him to become a minister.*

at death's door *adj. or adv. phr.* Very near death; dying. ♦*He seemed to be at death's door from his illness.*

at each other's throats *prep. phr.* Always arguing and quarreling. ♦*Joan and Harry have been at each other's throats so long that they have forgotten how much they used to love one another.*

at ease *or* **at one's ease** *adj. or adv. phr.* **1.** In comfort; without pain or bother. ♦*You can't feel at ease with a toothache.* **2.** *or* **at one's ease** Comfortable in one's mind; relaxed, not troubled.—Often used in the phrase *put at ease* or *put at one's ease.* ♦*We put Mary at her ease during the thunderstorm by reading her stories.* Compare AT HOME 2. Contrast ILL AT EASE, ON EDGE. **3.** Standing with your right foot in place and without talking in military ranks. ♦*The sergeant gave his men the command "At ease!"* Compare PARADE REST.

at every turn *adv. phr.* Every time; all the time; continually without exception. ♦*Because of his drinking, the man was refused a job at every turn.*

at face value *prep. phr.* What one can actually hear, read, or see; literally. ♦*John is so honest that you can take his words at face value.* ♦*This store's advertisements are honest; take them at face value.*

at fault *adj. phr.* Responsible for an error or failure; to blame. ♦*The driver who didn't stop at the red light was at fault in the accident.* ♦*When the engine would not start, the mechanic looked at all the parts to find what was at fault.* Syn. IN THE WRONG.

at first *adv. phr.* In the beginning; at the start. ♦*The driver didn't see the danger a first.* ♦*At first the job looked good to Bob, but later it became tiresome.* ♦*There was a little trouble at first, but things soon were quiet.*

at first blush *adv. phr.* When first seen; without careful study. ♦*At first blush* *the offer looked good, but when we studied it, we found things we could not accept.*

at first glance *or* **at first sight** *adv. or adj. phr.* After a first quick look. ♦*At first sight, his guess was that the whole trouble between the two men resulted from personalities that did not agree.* ♦*Tom met Mary at a party, and it was love at first sight.*

at great length *prep. phr.* **1.** In great detail. ♦*Jim told us the story of his life at great length.* **2.** For a long time. ♦*The boring speaker rambled on at great length.*

at half mast *prep. phr.* Halfway up or down; referring primarily to flagposts, but may be used jokingly. ♦*When a president of the United States dies, all flags are flown at half mast.*

at hand *also* **at close hand** *or* **near at hand** *adv. phr.* **1.** Easy to reach; nearby. ♦*When he writes, he always keeps a dictionary at hand.* **2.** *formal* Coming soon; almost here. ♦*Examinations are past and Commencement Day is at hand.*

at heart *adv. phr.* **1.** In spite of appearances; at bottom; in reality. ♦*His manners are rough but he is a kind man at heart.* **2.** As a serious interest or concern; as an important aim or goal. ♦*He has the welfare of the poor at heart.*

at home *adv. or adj. phr.* **1.** In the place where you live or come from. ♦*I went to his house, but he was not at home.* ♦*Americans abroad are protected by the government like Americans at home.* **2.** Knowing what to do or say; familiar; comfortable. ♦*Charles and John enjoy working together because they feel at home with each other.* ♦*The politician was at home among poor farmers and among rich factory owners.* ♦*Make the new student feel at home in your school.* ♦*Would you be at home driving a truck?* ♦*Jim always lived by a lake, and he is at home in the water.* ♦*Tom has read many books about missiles and is at home in that subject.* Syn. AT EASE 2. Compare IN ONE'S ELEMENT, MAKE ONESELF AT HOME. Contrast AT A LOSS.

at issue *adj. phr.* **1.** In dispute; to be settled by debate, by vote, by battle, or by some other contest. ♦*His good name was at issue in the trial.* ♦*The independence of the United States from England was at issue in the Revolutionary War.* Compare IN QUESTION. **2.** Not in agreement; in conflict; opposing. ♦*His work as a doctor was at issue with other doctors' practice.* Syn. AT ODDS.

at it *adj. phr.* Busily doing something; active. ♦*His rule for success was to keep always at it.* ♦*The couple who owned the little cleaning shop were at it early and late.* ♦*Mr. Curtis heard a loud crash in the next apartment—the neighbors were at it again.*

at large *adv. or adj. phr.* **1.** Not kept within walls, fences, or boundaries; free. ♦*The killer remained at large for weeks.* Compare AT LIBERTY. ♦*Cattle and sheep roamed at large on the big ranch.* **2.** In a broad, general way; at length; fully. ♦*The superintendent talked at large for an hour about his hopes for a new school building.* **3.** As a group rather than as individuals; as a whole; taken together. ♦*The junior class at large was not interested in a senior yearbook.* **4.** As a representative of a whole political unit or area rather than one of its parts; from a city rather than one of its wards, or a state rather than one of its districts. ♦*He was elected congressman at large.* ♦*Aldermen are voted for at large.*

at last *also* **at long last** *adv. phr.* After a long time; finally. ♦*The war had been long and hard, but now there was peace at last.* ♦*The boy saved his money until at last he had enough for a bicycle.*

at least *adv. phr.* **1.** *or* **at the least** At the smallest guess; no fewer than; no less than. ♦*You should brush your teeth at least twice a day.* ♦*At least three students are failing in mathematics.* ♦*Mr. Johnson must weigh 200 pounds at least.* Compare ALL OF. **2.** Whatever else you may say; anyhow; anyway. ♦*It was a clumsy move, but at least it saved her from getting hit.* ♦*She broke her arm, but at least it wasn't the arm she writes with.* ♦*The Mortons had fun at their picnic yesterday—at least the children did—they played while their parents cooked the food.* ♦*He's not coming—at least that's what he said.* Compare AT ANY RATE.

at leisure *adj. or adv. phr.* **1.** Not at work; not busy; with free time; at rest. ♦ *Come and visit us some evening when you're at leisure.* **2.** *or* **at one's leisure** When and how you wish at your convenience; without hurry. ♦ *John made the model plane at his leisure.* ♦ *You may read the book at your leisure.*

at length *adv. phr.* **1.** In detail; fully. ♦ *You must study the subject at length to understand it.* ♦ *The teacher explained the new lesson at length to the students.* **2.** In the end; at last; finally. ♦ *The movie became more and more exciting, until at length people were sitting on the edge of their chairs.*

at liberty *adv. or adj. phr.* Free to go somewhere or do something; not shut in or stopped. ♦ *The police promised to set the man at liberty if he told the names of the other robbers.* ♦ *I am sorry, but I am not at liberty to come to your party.* Compare AT LARGE 1.

at loggerheads *adj. or adv. phr.* In a quarrel; in a fight; opposing each other. ♦ *The two senators had long been at loggerheads on foreign aid.* ♦ *Because of their barking dog, the Morrises lived at loggerheads with their neighbors.* Compare AT ODDS.

at long last See AT LAST.

at loose ends *adj. phr.* Without a regular job or settled habits; uncertain what to do next; having nothing to do for a while; undecided; unsettled; restless. ♦ *Feeling at loose ends, I went for a long walk.* ♦ *He had finished college but hadn't found a job yet, so he was at loose ends.*

at most *or* **at the most** *adv. phr.* By the largest or most generous guess; at the upper limit; by the maximum account; not more than; at best; at worst. ♦ *It was a minor offense at most.* ♦ *He had been gone 15 minutes at the most.* ♦ *Their new house lot is a quarter acre at most.*

at odds *adj. phr.* In conflict or disagreement; opposed. ♦ *The boy and girl were married a week after they met and soon found themselves at odds about religion.* Compare AT LOGGERHEADS.

at once *adv. phr.* **1.** Without delay; right now or right then; immediately. ♦ *Put a burning match next to a piece of paper and it will begin burning at once.*

♦ *Mother called the children to lunch, and Paul came at once, but Brenda stayed in the sand pile a little longer.* Syn. RIGHT AWAY *or* RIGHT OFF. Compare ALL AT ONCE 2.

at one *adj. phr.* **1.** In union or harmony; in agreement or sympathy. Not usually used informally. ♦ *He felt at one with all the poets who have sung of love.* **2.** Of the same opinion, in agreement. ♦ *Husband and wife were at one on everything but money.* Contrast AT ODDS.

at one fell swoop See IN ONE FELL SWOOP.

at one's beck and call *or* **at the beck and call of** *adj. phr.* Ready and willing to do whatever someone asks; ready to serve at a moment's notice. ♦ *A good parent isn't necessarily always at the child's beck and call.*

at one's best *prep. phr.* In best form; displaying one's best qualities. ♦ *Tim is at his best when he has had a long swim before a ballgame.* ♦ *Jane rested before the important meeting because she wanted to be at her best.*

at one's door *or* **at one's doorstep** *adv. phr.* **1.** Very close; very near where you live or work. ♦ *Johnny is very lucky because there's a swimming pool right at his doorstep.* ♦ *Mr. Green can get to work in only a few minutes because the subway is at his door.* **2.** See LAY AT ONE'S DOOR.

at one's ease See AT EASE 2.

at one's elbow *adv. phr.* Close beside you; nearby. ♦ *The President rode in an open car with his wife at his elbow.* ♦ *Mary practiced for several years to become a champion swimmer and her mother was always at her elbow to help her.* Contrast BREATHE DOWN ONE'S NECK.

at one's feet *adv. phr.* Under your influence or power. ♦ *She had a dozen men at her feet.* ♦ *Her voice kept audiences at her feet for years.* Compare THROW ONESELF AT SOMEONE'S FEET.

at one's fingertips *adv. phr.* **1.** Within easy reach; quickly touched; nearby. ♦ *Seated in the cockpit, the pilot of a plane has many controls at his fingertips.* **2.** Readily usable as knowledge or skill; familiar. ♦ *He had several languages at his fingertips.* ♦ *He had the* *whole design of the machine at his fingertips.*

at one's heels *adv. phr.* Close behind; as a constant follower or companion. ♦ *The boy got tired of having his little brother at his heels all day.* ♦ *John ran by the finish line with Ned at his heels.* ♦ *Bad luck followed at his heels all his life.*

at one's leisure See AT LEISURE 2.

at one's service *adv. phr.* **1.** Ready to serve or help you; prepared to obey your wish or command; subject to your orders. ♦ *He placed himself completely at the President's service.* ♦ *"Now I am at your service," the dentist told the next patient.* **2.** Available for your use; at your disposal. ♦ *He put a car and chauffeur at the visitor's service.*

at one stroke See AT A BLOW *or* AT ONE STROKE.

at one's wit's end *or* **at wits end** *adj. phr.* Having no ideas as to how to meet a difficulty or solve a problem; feeling puzzled after having used up all of your ideas or resources; not knowing what to do; puzzled. ♦ *He had approached every friend and acquaintance for help in vain, and now he was at his wit's end.* ♦ *The designer was at his wit's end: he had tried out wings of many different kinds but none would fly.* Compare AT A LOSS, END OF ONE'S ROPE.

at one's word See TAKE AT ONE'S WORD.

at one time *adv. phr.* **1.** In the same moment; together. ♦ *Let's start the dance again all at one time.* ♦ *Mr. Reed's bills came all at one time and he could not pay them.* Syn. AT THE SAME TIME 1. **2.** At a certain time in the past; years ago. ♦ *At one time people thought that Minnesota was not a good place to live.* ♦ *At one time most school teachers were men, but today there are more women than men.*

at pains *adj. phr.* Making a special effort. ♦ *At pains to make a good impression, she was prompt for her appointment.*

at present *adv. phr.* At this time; now. ♦ *It took a long time to get started, but at present the road is half finished.* ♦ *At present the house is empty, but next week a family will move in.*

at random *adv. phr.* With no order, plan, or purpose; in a mixed-up, or thoughtless way. ♦ *He opened the letters at random.* ♦ *His clothes were scattered about the room at random.*

at sea¹ *adv. or adj. phr.* **1.** On an ocean voyage; on a journey by ship. ♦ *They had first met at sea.* **2.** Out on the ocean; away from land. ♦ *By the second day the ship was well out at sea.* ♦ *Charles had visited a ship in dock, but he had never been on a ship at sea.*

at sea² *adj. phr.* Not knowing what to do; bewildered; confused; lost. ♦ *The job was new to him, and for a few days he was at sea.* ♦ *When his friends talked about chemistry, Don was at sea, because he did not study chemistry.* Compare AT A LOSS.

at sight *or* **on sight** *adv. phr.* **1.** The first time the person or thing is seen; as soon as the person or thing is seen. ♦ *First graders learn to read many words on sight.* ♦ *Mary had seen many pictures of Grandfather, so she knew him on sight.* Compare AT ONCE 1. **2.** On demand, on asking the first time. ♦ *The money order was payable at sight.*

at sixes and sevens *adj. phr.* Not in order; in confusion; in a mess. ♦ *He apologized because his wife was away and the house was at sixes and sevens.* ♦ *Our teacher had just moved to a new classroom, and she was still at sixes and sevens.* ♦ *After the captain of the team broke his leg, the other players were at sixes and sevens.*

at ——— stage of the game *adv. phr.* At (some) time during an activity; at (some) point. ♦ *At that stage of the game, our team was doing so poorly that we were ready to give up.* ♦ *It's hard to know what will happen at this stage of the game.* ♦ *At what stage of the game did the man leave?*

at stake *adj. phr.* Depending, like a bet, on the outcome of something uncertain; in a position to be lost or gained. ♦ *The team played hard because the championship of the state was at stake.* ♦ *The farmers were more anxious for rain than the people in the city because they had more at stake.* Compare HANG IN THE BALANCE.

at straws See GRASP AT STRAWS.

at swords' points *adj. phr.* Ready to start fighting; very much opposed to each; other hostile; quarreling. ♦ *The dog's barking kept the Browns at swords' points with their neighbors for months.* ♦ *The mayor and the reporter were always at swords' points.*

at table See AT THE TABLE; WAIT AT TABLE.

at that *adv. phr., informal* **1.** As it is; at that point; without more talk or waiting. ♦ *Ted was not quite satisfied with his haircut but let it go at that.* **2.** In addition; also. ♦ *Bill's seat mate on the plane was a girl and a pretty one at that.* **3.** After all; in spite of all; anyway. ♦ *The book was hard to understand, but at that Jack enjoyed it.* Syn. ALL THE SAME.

at the best See AT BEST.

at the bit See CHAMP AT THE BIT.

at the drop of a hat *adv. phr., informal* **1.** Without waiting; immediately; promptly. ♦ *If you need a babysitter quickly, call Mary, because she can come at the drop of a hat.* Compare ON THE SPUR OF THE MOMENT. **2.** Whenever you have a chance; with very little cause or urging. ♦ *At the drop of a hat, he would tell the story of the canal he wanted to build.* ♦ *He was quarrelsome and ready to fight at the drop of a hat.*

at the eleventh hour *prep. phr.* At the last possible time. ♦ *Aunt Mathilda got married at the eleventh hour; after all, she was already 49 years old.*

at the end of one's rope See END OF ONE'S ROPE.

at the kill See IN AT THE KILL.

at the least See AT LEAST.

at the mercy of *or* **at one's mercy** *adj. phr.* In the power of; subject to the will and wishes of; without defense against. ♦ *The champion had the other boxer at his mercy.* ♦ *The picnic was at the mercy of the weather.* ♦ *The small grocer was at the mercy of people he owed money to.*

at the most See AT MOST.

at the outset *adv. phr.* At the start; at the beginning. ♦ *"You'll live in the cheaper barracks at the outset; later you can move into the better cabins," the camp director said to the new boys.*

at the outside *adv. phr.* Maximally; at the utmost. ♦ *This old house can cost no more than $40,000 at the outside.*

at the point of *prep.* Very near to; almost at or in. ♦ *When Mary broke her favorite bracelet, she was at the point of tears.* ♦ *The boy hurt in the accident lay at the point of death for a week, then he got well.* Compare ABOUT TO 1, ON THE POINT OF.

at the ready *adj. phr.* Ready for use. ♦ *The sailor stood at the bow, harpoon at the ready, as the boat neared the whale.*

at the same time *adv. phr.* **1.** In the same moment; together. ♦ *The two runners reached the finish line at the same time.* Syn. AT ONCE, AT ONE TIME. **2.** In spite of that fact; even though; however; but; nevertheless. ♦ *John did pass the test; at the same time, he didn't know the subject very well.*

at the seams See BURST AT THE SEAMS.

at the table *or* **at table** *adv. phr.* At a meal; at the dinner table. ♦ *The telephone call came while they were all at table.*

at the tip of one's tongue *or* **on the tip of one's tongue** *adv. phr. informal* **1.** Almost spoken; at the point of being said. ♦ *It was at the tip of my tongue to tell him, when the phone rang.* ♦ *John had a rude answer on the tip of his tongue, but he remembered his manners just in time.* **2.** Almost remembered; at the point where one can almost say it but cannot because it is forgotten. ♦ *I have his name on the tip of my tongue.*

at the top of one's voice *or* **at the top of one's lungs** *adv. phr.* As loud as you can; with the greatest possible sound; very loudly. ♦ *He was singing at the top of his voice.* ♦ *He shouted at the top of his lungs.*

at this rate *or* **at that rate** *adv. phr.* At a speed like this or that; with progress like this or that. ♦ *John's father said that if John kept going at that rate he would never finish cutting the grass.* ♦ *So Johnny has a whole dollar! At this rate he'll be a millionaire.* ♦ *"Three 100's in the last four tests! At this rate you'll soon be teaching the subject," Tom said to Mary.*

at times *adv. phr.* Not often; not regularly; not every day; not every week; occasionally; sometimes. ♦ *At times Tom's mother lets him hold the baby.*

♦ *You can certainly be exasperating, at times!* ♦ *We have pie for dinner at times.* Syn. FROM TIME TO TIME, NOW AND THEN, ONCE IN A WHILE.

at will *adv. phr.* As you like; as you please or choose freely. ♦ *Little Bobby is allowed to wander at will in the neighborhood.* ♦ *With an air conditioner you can enjoy comfortable temperatures at will.*

at wits end See AT ONE'S WIT'S END.

at work *adj. phr.* Busy at a job; doing work. ♦ *The teacher was soon hard at work correcting that day's test.* ♦ *Jim is at work on his car.*

at worst *or* **at the worst** *adv. phr.* **1.** Under the worst conditions; as the worst possibility. ♦ *When Don was caught cheating in the examination he thought that at worst he would get a scolding. Compare* AT MOST. Contrast AT BEST. **2.** In the least favorable view, to say the worst about a thing. ♦ *The treasurer had certainly not stolen any of the club's money; at worst, he had forgotten to write down some of the things he had spent money for.*

aught See FOR AUGHT at FOR ALL 2, FOR ALL ONE KNOWS.

Aunt Tom *n., slang, originally from Black English* A successful professional or business woman who, due to her success in a masculine profession, doesn't care about the women's liberation movement or the passing of the Equal Rights Amendment to the U.S. Constitution. ♦ *Hermione is a regular Aunt Tom, she'll never vote for the ERA.*

avail See TO NO AVAIL *or* OF NO AVAIL.

average See ON AN AVERAGE *or* ON THE AVERAGE, LAW OF AVERAGES.

awe See STAND IN AWE OF.

awkward age *n.* Adolescence; awkwardness during adolescence. ♦ *Sue used to be an "ugly duckling" when she was at the awkward age, but today she is a glamorous fashion model.*

AWOL See ABSENT WITHOUT LEAVE.

ax to grind *n. phr. informal* Something to gain for yourself: a selfish reason. ♦ *In praising movies for classroom use he has an ax to grind; he sells motion picture equipment.* ♦ *When Charles told the teacher he saw Arthur copying his homework from Jim, he had an ax to grind; Arthur would not let Charles copy from him.*

babe in the woods n. phr. A person who is inexperienced or innocent in certain things. ◆ *He is a good driver, but as a mechanic he is just a babe in the woods.* Compare OVER ONE'S HEAD, BEYOND ONE'S DEPTH.

baby See WAR BABY.

baby boom n. A sudden increase in the birth rate. ◆ *The universities were filled to capacity due to the baby boom that followed World War II.*

baby grand n. A small grand piano no longer than three feet, maximally four feet. ◆ *This apartment can't take a regular grand piano, so we'll have to buy a baby grand.*

baby kisser n., slang A person campaigning for votes in his quest for elected political office; such persons often kiss little children in public. ◆ *Nixon was a baby kisser when he ran for Vice President with Eisenhower.*

back See BACK OF or IN BACK OF, BEHIND ONE'S BACK, BRUSH BACK, COME BACK, CUT BACK, DOUBLE BACK, DRAW BACK, DROP BACK, EYES IN THE BACK OF ONE'S HEAD, FADE BACK, FALL BACK, FALL BACK ON, FLANKER BACK, FROM WAY BACK, GET BACK AT, GET ONE'S BACK UP, GIVE THE SHIRT OFF ONE'S BACK, GO BACK ON, HANG BACK, HARK BACK, HOLD BACK, LIKE WATER OFF A DUCK'S BACK, LOOK BACK, OFF ONE'S BACK, ON ONE'S BACK, PAT ON THE BACK, PIGGY-BACK, PIN ONE'S EARS BACK, PUT BACK THE CLOCK or TURN BACK THE CLOCK, PUT ONE'S BACK TO IT, SCRATCH ONE'S BACK, SET BACK, SET BACK ON ONE'S HEELS, SIT BACK, STAB IN THE BACK, TAKE A BACK SEAT, TAKE BACK, TALK BACK also ANSWER BACK, TURN ONE'S BACK ON, WEIGHT OF THE WORLD ON ONE'S SHOULDERS or WORLD ON ONE'S BACK, WHILE BACK.

back and forth adv. Backwards and forwards. ◆ *The chair is rocking back and forth.* ◆ *The tiger is pacing back and forth in his cage.* Compare TO AND FRO.

back away v. To act to avoid or lessen one's involvement in something; draw or turn back; retreat. ◆ *The townspeople backed away from the building plan when they found out how much it would cost.*

back door n., slang, citizen's band radio jargon Rear of vehicle. ◆ *I am watching your back door.*

back down or **back off** v., informal To give up a claim; not follow up a threat. ◆ *Bill said he could beat Ted, but when Ted put up his fists Bill backed down.* ◆ *Harry claimed Joe had taken his book, but backed down when the teacher talked with him.* Syn. BEAT A RETREAT. Compare BACK OUT, GIVE IN, GO BACK ON 1.

back in circulation adv. phr. **1.** Socially active once again (said about people); back on the dating circuit after a divorce or a romantic breakup. ◆ *Now that Sally is divorced from Jim she is back in circulation.* **2.** Once again available to the public (said about types of paper money, rare coins, or other commercially available goods). ◆ *In the USA the two-dollar bill was back in circulation for a short time only in the 1950s and 1960s.*

back number n. Something out of fashion, or out of date. ◆ *Among today's young people a waltz like "The Blue Danube" is a back number.*

backfire v. To misfire; to have a reverse effect from what was intended. ◆ *Mimi's gossip about the Head of the Department backfired when people began to mistrust her.*

backhanded compliment n. phr. A remark that sounds like a compliment but is said sarcastically. ◆ *"Not bad for a girl" the coach said, offering a backhanded compliment.*

back of or **in back of** prep. **1.** In or at the rear of; to the back of; behind. ◆ *The garage is back of the house.* ◆ *Our car was in back of theirs at the traffic light.* **2.** informal Being a cause or reason for; causing. ◆ *Hard work was back of his success.* ◆ *The principal tried to find out what was back of the trouble on the bus.* **3.** informal In support or encouragement of; helping. ◆ *Jones will be elected because many powerful men are back of him.* ◆ *Get in back of your team by cheering them at the game.*

back out *v. phr.* **1.** To move backwards out of a place or enclosure. ♦*Bob slowly backed his car out of the garage.* **2.** To withdraw from an activity one has promised to carry out. ♦*Jim tried to back out of the engagement with Jane, but she insisted that they get married.* Compare BEG OFF, GO BACK ON.

back seat See TAKE A BACK SEAT.

backseat driver *n., informal* A bossy person in a car who always tells the driver what to do. ♦*The man who drove the car became angry with the back seat driver.*

back street *n.* A street not near the main streets or from which it is hard to get to a main street. ♦*We got lost in the back streets going through the city and it took us a half hour to find our way again.* Compare SIDE STREET.

back talk *n.* A sassy, impudent reply. ♦*Such back talk will get you nowhere, young man!* See TALK BACK.

back the wrong horse *v. phr.* To support a loser. ♦*In voting for George Bush, voters in 1992 were backing the wrong horse.*

back-to-back *adv.* **1.** Immediately following. ♦*The health clinic had back-to-back appointments for the new students during the first week of school.* **2.** Very close to, as if touching. ♦*Sardines are always packed in the can back-to-back. The bus was so full that people had to stand back-to-back.*

back to the salt mines *informal* Back to the job; back to work; back to work that is as hard or as unpleasant as working in a salt mine would be.—An overworked phrase, used humorously. ♦*The lunch hour is over, boys. Back to the salt mines!* ♦*"Vacation is over," said Billy. "Back to the salt mines."*

back to the wall *or* **back against the wall** *adv. phr.* In a trap, with no way to escape; in bad trouble. ♦*The soldiers had their backs to the wall.* ♦*He was in debt and could not get any help; his back was against the wall.* ♦*The team had their backs to the wall in the second half.* Compare BETWEEN THE DEVIL AND THE DEEP BLUE SEA, LAST DITCH, ON THE SPOT, UP AGAINST IT.

back up *v.* **1.** To move backwards. ♦*The train was backing up.* **2.** To help or be ready to help; stay behind to help; agree with and speak in support of. ♦*Jim has joined the Boy Scouts and his father is backing him up.* ♦*The principal backs up the faculty.* ♦*Jim told us what had happened and Bob backed him up.* Compare BACK OF 3, STAND BY 4. **3.** To move behind (another fielder) in order to catch the ball if he misses it. ♦*The shortstop backed up the second baseman on the throw.*

backward See BEND OVER BACKWARD *or* LEAN OVER BACKWARD; FALL OVER BACKWARDS *or* FALL OVER ONESELF.

backward and forward *or* **backwards and forwards** *adv. phr.* To the full extent; in all details; thoroughly; completely. ♦*He understood automobile engines backwards and forwards.* ♦*He knew basketball rules backwards and forwards.* ♦*I explained matters to him so that he understood backwards and forwards how it was.*

bacon See BRING HOME THE BACON.

bad See GO FROM BAD TO WORSE, IN A BAD WAY, IN BAD, IN ONE'S BAD GRACES, LEAVE A BAD TASTE IN ONE'S MOUTH, NOT BAD *or* NOT SO BAD *or* NOT HALF BAD, ON ONE'S BAD SIDE, TOO BAD, WITH BAD GRACE.

bad actor *n., informal* A person or animal that is always fighting, quarreling, or doing bad things. ♦*The boy was a bad actor and nobody liked him.*

bad blood *n., informal* Anger or misgivings due to bad relations in the past between individuals or groups. ♦*There's a lot of bad blood between Max and Jack; I bet they'll never talk to each other again.* Compare BAD SHIT.

bad egg *n., slang* A ne'er-do-well; good-for nothing; a habitual offender. ♦*The judge sent the bad egg to prison at last.* Contrast GOOD EGG.

bad mouth (someone) *v., slang* To say uncomplimentary or libelous things about someone; deliberately to damage another's reputation. ♦*It's not nice to bad mouth people.*

bad news *n., slang* An event, thing, or person which is disagreeable or an unpleasant surprise. ♦*What's the new professor like?—He's all bad news to me.*

bad paper *n., slang* **1.** A check for which there are no funds in the bank. **2.** Counterfeit paper money. ♦*Why are* *you so mad?—I was paid with some bad paper.*

bad shit *n., vulgar, avoidable* An unpleasant event or situation, such as a long lasting and unsettled quarrel or recurring acts of vengeance preventing two people or two groups from reaching any kind of reconciliation. ♦ *There is so much bad shit between the two gangs that I bet there will be more killings this year.* Compare BAD BLOOD.

bad trip *n., slang, also used colloquially* A disturbing or frightening experience, such as terrifying hallucinations, while under the influence of drugs; hence, by colloquial extension any bad experience in general. ♦ *Why's John's face so distorted?—He had a bad trip.* ♦ *How was your math exam?—Don't mention it; it was a bad trip.*

bag See GRAB BAG, IN THE BAG, LEAVE HOLDING THE BAG, LET THE CAT OUT OF THE BAG.

bag and baggage *adv., informal* With all your clothes and other personal belongings, especially movable possessions; completely. ♦ *If they don't pay their hotel bill they will be put out bag and baggage.*

baggage See BAG AND BAGGAGE.

bail See JUMP BAIL or SKIP BAIL.

bail out¹ *v.* **1.** To secure release from prison until trial by leaving or promising money or property for a while. ♦ *When college students got into trouble with the police, the college president would always bail them out.* **2.** *informal* To free from trouble by giving or lending money. ♦ *He started a small business, which prospered after his father had to bail him out a couple of times.*

bail out² *v.* To jump from an airplane and drop with a parachute. ♦ *When the second engine failed, the pilot told everyone to bail out.*

bail out³ *v.* To dip water from a filling or leaking boat; throw water out of a boat to prevent its sinking. ♦ *Both men were kept busy bailing out the rowboat after it began to leak.*

bait See FISH OR CUT BAIT.

bake See HALF-BAKED.

baker's dozen *n., informal* Thirteen. ♦ *"How many of the jelly doughnuts,*

Sir?" the salesclerk asked. "Oh, make it a baker's dozen."

balance See HANG IN THE BALANCE, OFF BALANCE.

ball See BASE ON BALLS, CARRY THE BALL, FLY BALL, FOUL BALL, GET THE BALL ROLLING, SET THE BALL ROLLING, START THE BALL ROLLING, GOPHER BALL, GROUND BALL, HAVE A BALL, HAVE SOMETHING ON THE BALL, JUMP BALL, KEEP THE BALL ROLLING, LONG BALL, ON THE BALL, PASSED BALL, PLAY BALL.

ball game *n., slang, also informal* The entire matter at hand; the whole situation; the entire contest. ♦ *You said we can get a second mortgage for the house?! Wow! That's a whole new ball game.*

ball of fire *n., informal* A person with great energy and ability; a person who can do something very well. ♦ *He did poorly in school but as a salesman he is a ball of fire.* ♦ *The new shortstop is a good fielder but certainly no ball of fire in batting.* Compare HOT NUMBER, HOT ONE.

balloon See TRIAL BALLOON, LEAD BALLOON.

ballot stuffing See STUFF THE BALLOT BOX.

ball up *v., slang* To make a mess of; confuse. ♦ *Don't ball me up.* ♦ *Hal balled up the business with his errors.*—Often used in the passive. ♦ *He was so balled up that he did not know if he was coming or going.* Compare MIXED UP.

baloney *n., informal* Nonsense, unbelievable, trite, or trivial. ♦ *John brags that he's won the $10 million lottery, and I think it's just a lot of baloney.* ♦ *"Will you marry Joe?" mother asked. "Baloney," Susie answered with a disgusted look.* ♦ *Do you still believe all that baloney about socialism excluding free enterprise? Look at China and Hungary.*

banana oil *n., slang* Flattery that is an obvious exaggeration; statements that are obviously made with an ulterior motive. ♦ *Cut out the banana oil; flattery will get you nowhere!*

band See BEAT THE BAND.

bandbox See LOOK AS IF ONE HAS COME OUT OF A BANDBOX.

band together *v. phr.* To join a group to exert united force. ♦ *The inhabitants of* *the ecologically threatened area banded together to stop the company from building new smokestacks.*

bandwagon See JUMP ON THE BANDWAGON.

bandy about *v. phr.* To spread rumors or whisper secrets. ♦ *The news of Jim and Mary's divorce was bandied about until everyone at the office had heard it.*

bang up *adj., informal* Very successful; very good; splendid; excellent. ♦ *The football coach has done a bang-up job this season.* ♦ *John did a bang-up job painting the house.* Syn. FIRST-CLASS.

bank See PIGGY BANK.

bank on *v., informal* To depend on; put one's trust in; rely on. ♦ *He knew he could bank on public indignation to change things, if he could once prove the dirty work.* ♦ *The students were banking on the team to do its best in the championship game.* Syn. COUNT ON.

bar See BEHIND BARS, PARALLEL BARS.

bargain See DRIVE A BARGAIN, IN THE BARGAIN *or* INTO THE BARGAIN.

bargain for *or* **bargain on** *v.* To be ready for; expect. ♦ *When John started a fight with the smaller boy he got more than he bargained for.* ♦ *The final cost of building the house was much more than they had bargained on.* Compare COUNT ON.

barge in *v. phr., informal* To appear uninvited at someone's house or apartment, or to interrupt a conversation. ♦ *I'm sorry for barging in like that, Sir, but my car died on me and there is no pay phone anywhere.* ♦ *I'm sorry for barging in while you two are having a discussion, but could you please tell me where the nearest exit is?*

bark up the wrong tree *v. phr., informal* To choose the wrong person to deal with or the wrong course of action; mistake an aim. ♦ *If he thinks he can fool me, he is barking up the wrong tree.* ♦ *He is barking up the wrong tree when he blames his troubles on bad luck.* ♦ *The police were looking for a tall thin man, but were barking up the wrong tree; the thief was short and fat.*

bark worse than one's bite *informal* Sound or speech more frightening or worse than your actions. ♦ *The small dog barks savagely, but his bark is worse than his bite.* ♦ *The boss sometimes talks roughly to the men, but they*

know that his bark is worse than his bite. ♦ *She was always scolding her children, but they knew her bark was worse than her bite.*

barn See LOCK THE BARN DOOR AFTER THE HORSE IS STOLEN.

barrel See OVER A BARREL *also* OVER THE BARREL, SCRAPE THE BOTTOM OF THE BARREL.

barrelhead See CASH ON THE BARRELHEAD.

bar the door See CLOSE THE DOOR.

base See FIRST BASE, GET TO FIRST BASE *or* REACH FIRST BASE, LOAD THE BASES *or* FILL THE BASES, OFF BASE, SECOND BASE, STOLEN BASE, THIRD BASE.

base on balls *n.* First base given to a baseball batter who is pitched four balls outside of the strike zone. ♦ *He was a good judge of pitchers and often received bases on balls.*

basket See PUT ALL ONE'S EGGS IN ONE BASKET.

basket case *n., slang, also informal* **1.** A person who has had both arms and both legs cut off as a result of war or other misfortune. **2.** A helpless person who is unable to take care of himself, as if carted around in a basket by others. ♦ *Stop drinking, or else you'll wind up a basket case!*

bat See AT BAT, GO TO BAT FOR, RIGHT AWAY *or* RIGHT OFF *also* RIGHT OFF THE BAT.

bat an eye *or* **bat an eyelash** *v. phr., informal* To show surprise, fear, or interest; show your feelings.—Used in negative sentences. ♦ *When I told him the price of the car he never batted an eye.* ♦ *Bill told his story without batting an eyelash, although not a word of it was true.* Compare STRAIGHT FACE.

bath See SPONGE BATH, THROW THE BABY OUT WITH THE BATH.

bats in one's belfry *or* **bats in the belfry** *n. phr., slang* Wild ideas in his mind; disordered senses; great mental confusion. ♦ *When he talked about going to the moon he was thought to have bats in his belfry.*

bat the breeze See SHOOT THE BREEZE.

batting average *n. phr.* Degree of accomplishment (originally used as a baseball term). ♦ *Dr. Grace has a great batting average with her heart transplant operations.*

battle See HALF THE BATTLE.

battle of nerves *n. phr.* A contest of wills during which the parties do not fight physically but try to wear each other out. ♦ *It has been a regular battle of nerves to get the new program accepted at the local state university.* See WAR OF NERVES.

bawl out *v., informal* To reprove in a loud or rough voice; rebuke sharply; scold. ♦ *The teacher bawled us out for not handing in our homework.* Compare HAUL OVER THE COALS, LIGHT INTO, TELL A THING OR TWO.

bay See AT BAY, BRING TO BAY.

be See LET BE, TO-BE.

beach See NOT THE ONLY PEBBLE ON THE BEACH.

beach bunny *n., slang* An attractive girl seen on beaches—mostly to show off her figure; one who doesn't get into the water and swim. ♦ *What kind of a girl is Susie?—She's a beach bunny; she always comes to the Queen's Surf on Waikiki but I've never seen her swim.*

bead See DRAW A BEAD ON.

be a fly on the wall *v. phr.* To eavesdrop on a secret conversation. ♦ *How I wish I could be a fly on the wall to hear what my fiance's parents are saying about me!*

be a good hand at *v. phr.* To be talented, gifted, or skilled in some activity. ♦ *Florian is a good hand at both gardening and building.*

beam See OFF THE BEAM, ON THE BEAM.

bean See FULL OF BEANS, SPILL THE BEANS, USE ONE'S HEAD *or* USE ONE'S BEAN.

be an item *v. phr.* To be a couple; belong to one another. ♦ *No one is surprised to see them together anymore; it is generally recognized that they are an item.*

be a poor hand at *v. phr.* To be inept, untalented, or clumsy in some activity. ♦ *Archibald is a poor hand at tennis so no one wants to play with him.* Contrast BE A GOOD HAND AT.

be at pains *v. phr.* To be extremely desirous to do something; to take the trouble to do something. ♦ *The captain was at pains to see that everybody got safely into the lifeboats.*

bear See GRIN AND BEAR IT, LOADED FOR BEAR.

bear a grudge *v. phr.* To persist in bearing ill feeling toward someone after a quarrel or period of hostility. ♦ *Come on, John, be a good sport and don't bear a grudge because I beat you at golf.* Contrast BURY THE HATCHET.

bear a hand See LEND A HAND.

beard See LAUNCH UP ONE'S SLEEVE *or* LAUGH IN ONE'S SLEEVE *or* LAUGH IN ONE'S BEARD.

bear down *v.* **1.** To press or push harder; work hard at; give full strength and attention. ♦ *She is bearing down in her studies to win a scholarship.* ♦ *The baseball pitcher is bearing down.* ♦ *The pitcher bore down on the star batter.* ♦ *Teachers of the deaf bear down on English.* ♦ *The sergeant bears down on lazy soldiers.* Contrast LET UP 2b. **2.** To move toward in an impressive or threatening way.—Often used with *on.* ♦ *While he was crossing the street a big truck bore down on him.* ♦ *The little ship tried to escape when the big pirate ship bore down.* ♦ *After the boys threw the snowballs they saw a large lady bearing down upon them from across the street.*

bear down on *or* **upon** *v. phr.* To draw constantly nearer with great speed and force. ♦ *The police cars were bearing down on the bank robbers' get-away car.*

bear fruit *v. phr.* To yield results. ♦ *We hope that the company's new investment policy will bear fruit.*

bear in mind See IN MIND.

bear in the air *or* **bear in the sky** *n. phr., slang, citizen's band jargon* A police helicopter flying overhead watching for speeders. ♦ *Slow down, good buddy, there's a bear in the air.*

bear off the palm See CARRY OFF THE PALM.

bear one's cross See CARRY ONE'S CROSS.

bear out *v.* To show to be right; prove; support. ♦ *Modern findings do not bear out the old belief that the earth is flat.* ♦ *Seward's faith in his purchase of Alaska was borne out, even though it was once called "Seward's Folly."*

bear trap *n., slang, citizen's band radio jargon* A police radar unit designed to catch speeders. ♦ *Watch the bear trap at exit 101.*

bear up *v.* **1.** To hold up; carry; support; encourage. ♦ *The old bridge can hardly bear up its own weight any more.* ♦ *He was borne up by love of country.* **2.** To keep up one's courage or strength; last.—Often used with *under.* ♦ *This boat will bear up under hurricane winds.* ♦ *She bore up well at the funeral.* Syn. STAND UP. Compare CARRY ON.

bear watching *v. phr.* **1.** To be worth watching or paying attention to; have a promising future. ♦ *That young ball player will bear watching.* **2.** To be dangerous or untrustworthy. ♦ *Those tires look badly worn; they will bear watching.* Compare KEEP AN EYE ON.

bear with *v., formal* To have patience with; not get angry with. ♦ *Your little sister is sick. Try to bear with her when she cries.* ♦ *It is hard to bear with criticism.* Syn. PUT UP WITH. Compare CARRY ONE'S CROSS.

beat See HEART SKIP A BEAT, OFF THE BEATEN TRACK.

beat about the bush *or* **beat around the bush** *v. phr., slang* To talk about things without giving a clear answer; avoid the question or the point. ♦ *He would not answer yes or no, but beat about the bush.* ♦ *He beat about the bush for a half hour without coming to the point.* Compare BESIDE THE POINT. Contrast COME TO THE POINT.

beat all *or* **beat the Dutch** *v. phr., informal* To be strange or surprising. ♦ *John found a box full of money buried in his garage. Doesn't that beat all!* ♦ *It beats the Dutch how Tom always makes a basket.*

beat all hollow *also* **beat hollow** *v. phr., slang* To do much better than; to beat very badly. ♦ *We beat their team all hollow.* ♦ *As a speaker, he beats us all hollow.*

beat a retreat *v. phr.* **1.** To give a signal, esp. by beating a drum, to go back. ♦ *The Redcoats' drums were beating a retreat.* **2.** To run away. ♦ *They beat a retreat when they saw that they were too few.* ♦ *The cat beat a hasty retreat when he saw the dog coming.* Compare BACK DOWN, FALL BACK.

beat around the bush See BEAT ABOUT THE BUSH.

beat down *v.* **1.** To crush or break the spirit of; win over; conquer. ♦ *All their*

defenses were beaten down by the tanks. **2.** *informal* **a.** To try to get reduced; force down by discussing. ♦ *Can we beat down the price?* **b.** To persuade or force (someone) to accept a lower price or easier payments. ♦ *He tried to beat us down, so we did not sell the house.* **3.** To shine brightly or hotly. ♦ *At noon the sun beat down on our heads as we walked home.*

beaten path *n. phr.* The usual route or way of operating that has been conventionally established. ♦ *If we always follow the beaten path, we'll never have the courage to try something new.*

beaten track *n.* See BEATEN PATH.

beat hollow See BEAT ALL HOLLOW.

beat into one's head *v. phr., informal* To teach by telling again and again; repeat often; drill, also, to be cross and punish often. ♦ *Tom is lazy and stubborn and his lessons have to be beaten into his head.* ♦ *I cannot beat it into his head that he should take off his hat in the house.*

beat it *v., slang* To go away in a hurry; get out quickly. ♦ *When he heard the crash he beat it as fast as he could.*—Often used as a command. ♦ *The big boy said, "Beat it, kid. We don't want you with us."* Compare CLEAR OUT 2, LIGHT OUT, HEAD FOR THE HILLS.

beat one to it *v. phr.* To arrive or get ahead of another person. ♦ *I was about to call you, John, but you have beat me to it! Thanks for calling me.*

beat one's brains out *or* **beat one's brains** *v. phr., slang* To try very hard to understand or think out something difficult; tire yourself out by thinking. ♦ *It was too hard for him and he beat his brains out trying to get the answer.* ♦ *Some students are lazy, but others beat their brains and succeed.*

beat one's gums *v. phr., slang* To engage in idle talk, or meaningless chatter; generally to talk too much. ♦ *"Stop beating your gums, Jack," Joe cried. "I am falling asleep."* Compare CHEW THE FAT *or* CHEW THE RAG, SHOOT THE BREEZE *or* BAT THE BREEZE *or* FAN THE BREEZE *or* SHOOT THE BULL.

beat one's head against a wall *v. phr.* To struggle uselessly against something that can't be beaten or helped; not succeed after trying very hard. ♦ *Trying to* *make him change his mind is just beating your head against a wall.*

beat the band *adv. phr., informal* At great speed; with much noise or commotion.—Used after *to.* ♦ *The fire engines were going down the road to beat the band.* ♦ *The audience cheered and stamped and clapped to beat the band.*

beat the bushes *also* **beat the brush** *v. phr., informal* To try very hard to find or get something. ♦ *The mayor was beating the bushes for funds to build the playground.* Contrast BEAT ABOUT THE BUSH *or* BEAT AROUND THE BUSH .

beat the drum *v. phr.* To attract attention in order to advertise something or to promote someone, such as a political candidate. ♦ *Mrs. Smith has been beating the drum in her town in order to get her husband elected mayor.*

beat the gun See JUMP THE GUN.

beat the —— out of *or* **lick the —— out of** *or* **whale the —— out of** *v. phr., informal* To beat hard; give a bad beating to.—Used with several words after *the,* as *daylights, living daylights, tar.* ♦ *The big kid told Charlie that he would beat the daylights out of him if Charlie came in his yard again.*

beat the meat *v. phr., vulgar, avoidable* To masturbate (said primarily of men). ♦ *"So what did you do for sex in prison for seven years?" Joe asked. "Well, unless you want to become gay, you can beat the meat and that's about it," Max answered.*

beat the pants off *v. phr.* **1.** To prevail over someone in a race or competition. ♦ *Jim beat the pants off George in the swimming race.* **2.** To give someone a severe physical beating. ♦ *Jack beat the pants off the two young men who were trying to hold him up in Central Park.*

beat the rap *v. phr.* To escape the legal penalty one ought to receive. ♦ *In spite of the strong evidence against him, the prisoner beat the rap and went free.*

beat the shit out of *v. phr., vulgar, avoidable* See KNOCK THE LIVING DAYLIGHTS OUT OF.

beat time *v. phr.* To follow the rhythm of a piece of music by moving one's fingers or feet. ♦ *Jack was beating time with his foot during the concert, which annoyed his neighbor.*

beat to *v., informal* To do something before someone else does it. ♦ *I was waiting to buy a ticket but only one ticket was left, and another man beat me to it.* ♦ *We were planning to send a rocket into space but the Russians beat us to it.* Compare GET THE JUMP ON.

beat to the punch *or* **beat to the draw** *v. phr., slang* To do something before another person has a chance to do it. ♦ *John was going to apply for the job, but Ted beat him to the draw.* ♦ *Lois bought the dress before Mary could beat her to the punch.*

beat up *v., informal* To give a hard beating to; hit hard and much; thrash; whip. ♦ *When the new boy first came, he had to beat up several neighborhood bullies before they would leave him alone.—*Used with *on* in substandard speech. ♦ *The tough boy said to Bill, "If you come around here again, I'll beat up on you."*

beauty sleep *n.* A nap or rest taken to improve the appearance. ♦ *She took her beauty sleep before the party.* ♦ *Many famous beauties take a beauty sleep every day.*

beaver *n., slang, vulgar, avoidable, citizen's band radio jargon* A female, especially one driving along the highway and operating a CB radio. ♦ *I didn't know there was a beaver aboard that eighteen wheeler.*

because of *prep.* On account of; by reason of; as a result of. ♦ *The train arrived late because of the snowstorm.*

beck See AT ONE'S BECK AND CALL.

become of *v. phr.* To happen to; befall. ♦ *What will become of the children, now that both parents are in jail?*

bed See GET UP ON THE WRONG SIDE OF THE BED, GO TO BED WITH THE CHICKENS, MAKE ONE'S BED AND LIE IN IT, PUT TO BED.

bed of nails *n. phr.* A difficult or unhappy situation or set of circumstances. ♦ *"There are days when my job is a regular bed of nails," Jim groaned.* Contrast BED OF ROSES.

bed of roses *or* **bowl of cherries** *n. phr.* A pleasant easy place, job, or position; an easy life. ♦ *A coal miner's job is not a bed of roses.* ♦ *After nine months of school, summer camp seemed a bowl of cherries.* Compare IN CLOVER, LIFE OF RILEY.

bed of thorns *n. phr.* A thoroughly unhappy time or difficult situation. ♦ *I'm sorry I changed jobs; my new one turned out to be a bed of thorns.* See BED OF NAILS.

bee See BIRDS AND THE BEES.

beef about *v. phr.* To complain about something. ♦ *Stop beefing about your job, Jack. You could have done a lot worse!*

beef up *v., informal* To make stronger by adding men or equipment; make more powerful; reinforce. ♦ *The general beefed up his army with more big guns and tanks.* ♦ *The university beefed up the football coaching staff by adding several good men.*

bee in one's bonnet *n. phr., informal* A fixed idea that seems fanciful, odd, or crazy. ♦ *Robert Fulton had a bee in his bonnet about a steamboat.* ♦ *Grandmother has some bee in her bonnet about going to the dance.*

beeline See MAKE A BEELINE FOR.

be even-Steven *v. phr.* To be in a position of owing no favors or debt to someone. ♦ *Yesterday you paid for my lunch, so today I paid for yours; now we're even-Steven.*

before long *adv. phr.* In a short time; without much delay; in a little while, soon. ♦ *Class will be over before long.* ♦ *We were tired of waiting and hoped the bus would come before long.*

before one can say Jack Robinson *adv. cl., informal* Very quickly; suddenly.— An overused phrase. ♦ *Before I could say Jack Robinson, the boy was gone.* Compare IN A FLASH, RIGHT AWAY.

before swine See CAST PEARLS BEFORE SWINE *or* CAST ONE'S PEARLS BEFORE SWINE.

before you know it *adv. phr.* Sooner than one would expect. ♦ *Don't despair; we'll be finished with this work before you know it!*

beg See BEGGING.

be game *v. phr.* To be cooperative, willing, sporting. ♦ *When I asked Charlie to climb Mount McKinley with us, he said he was game if we were.*

beggars can't be choosers People who can not choose what they will have, must accept what they get; if you are not in control, you must take what you can get. ♦ *We wanted to leave on the train in the morning but it doesn't go until afternoon, so we must go then. Beggars can't be choosers.* ♦ *Mary got a red dress from her sister, although she didn't like red. She kept it because she said beggars should not be choosers.* Compare LOOK A GIFT HORSE IN THE MOUTH.

begin with *adv. phr.* As a preliminary statement; in the first place. ♦ *To begin with, you are far too young to get married.*

beg off *v.* To ask to be excused. ♦ *Father told Tom to rake the yard, but Tom tried to beg off.* ♦ *Mrs. Crane accepted an invitation to a luncheon, but a headache made her beg off.* Compare BACK OUT.

beg the question *v. phr., literary* To accept as true something that is still being argued about, before it is proved true; avoid or not answer a question or problem. ♦ *The girls asked Miss Smith if they should wear formal dresses to the party; Miss Smith said they were begging the question because they didn't know yet if they could get permission for a party.* ♦ *Laura told Tom that he must believe her argument because she was right. Father laughed and told Laura she was begging the question.* Compare TAKE FOR GRANTED.

behalf See IN BEHALF OF *or* ON BEHALF OF, IN ONE'S BEHALF *or* ON ONE'S BEHALF.

behavior See ON ONE'S GOOD BEHAVIOR.

be hard on *v. phr.* To be strict or critical with another; be severe. ♦ *"Don't be so hard on Jimmy," Tom said. "He is bound to rebel as he gets older."*

behind See DRY BEHIND THE EARS, FALL BEHIND, GET BEHIND, HANG BACK *or* HANG BEHIND.

behind bars *adv. phr.* In jail; in prison. ♦ *He was a pickpocket and had spent many years behind bars.* ♦ *That boy is always in trouble and will end up behind bars.*

behind one's back *adv. phr.* When one is absent; without one's knowledge or consent; in a dishonest way; secretly; sneakily. ♦ *Say it to his face, not behind his back.* ♦ *It is not right to criticize a person behind his back.* Contrast TO ONE'S FACE.

behind the eight-ball *adj. phr., slang* In a difficult position; in trouble. ♦ *Mr.*

Thompson is an older man, and when he lost his job, he found he was behind the eight-ball. ♦ *Bill can't dance and has no car, so he is behind the eight-ball with the girls.* Compare HAVE TWO STRIKES AGAINST ONE 2, IN A HOLE.

behind the scenes *adv. phr.* Out of sight; unknown to most people; privately. ♦ *Much of the banquet committee's work was done behind the scenes.* ♦ *John was president of the club, but behind the scenes Lee told him what to do.*

behind the times *adj. phr.* Using things not in style; still following old ways; old-fashioned. ♦ *Johnson's store is behind the times.* ♦ *The science books of 30 years ago are behind the times now.* ♦ *Mary thinks her parents are behind the times because they still do the foxtrot and don't know any new dances.*

behind time *adv. or adj. phr.* **1a.** Behind the correct time; slow. ♦ *That clock is behind time.* **1b.** Behind schedule; late. ♦ *The train is running behind time today.* **2.** Not keeping up; not at the proper time; overdue. ♦ *Your lessons are good, but why are you behind time?* ♦ *We are behind time in paying the rent.* Contrast AHEAD OF TIME, IN TIME, ON TIME.

be-in *n., slang, hippie culture* A gathering or social occasion with or without a discernible purpose, often held in a public place like a park or under a large circus tent. ♦ *The youngsters really enjoyed the great springtime jazz be-in at the park.*

be in a stew *v. phr.* To be worried, harassed, upset. ♦ *Al has been in a stew ever since he got word that his sister was going to marry his worst enemy.*

being See FOR THE TIME BEING.

be in labor *v. phr.* To be in parturition; experience the contractions of childbirth. ♦ *Jane had been in labor for eight hours before her twin daughters were finally born.*

be in someone else's shoes *v. phr.* To be in someone else's situation. ♦ *Fred has had so much trouble recently that we ought to be grateful we're not in his shoes.*

be into something *v. phr., informal* To have taken something up partly as a hobby, partly as a serious interest of sorts (basically resulting from the new consciousness and self-realization movement that originated in the late Sixties). ♦ *Roger's wife is into women's liberation and women's consciousness.* ♦ *Did you know that Syd is seriously into transcendental meditation?* ♦ *Jack found out that his teenage son is into pot smoking and gave him a serious scolding.*

be itching to *v. phr.* To have a very strong desire to do something. ♦ *Jack is itching to travel abroad.*

be it so See SO BE IT.

belabor the point *v. phr.* To overexplain something to the point of obviousness, resulting in ridicule. ♦ *"Lest I belabor the point," the teacher said, "I must repeat the importance of teaching good grammar in class."*

belfry See BATS IN ONE'S BELFRY *or* BATS IN THE BELFRY.

believe See MAKE BELIEVE, SEEING IS BELIEVING.

believe one's ears *v. phr.* **1.** To believe what one hears; trust one's hearing.— Used with a negative or limiter, or in an interrogative or conditional sentence. ♦ *He thought he heard a horn blowing in the distance, but he could not believe his ears.* **2.** To be made sure of (something). ♦ *Is he really coming? I can hardly believe my ears.*

believe one's eyes *v. phr.* **1.** To believe what one sees; trust one's eyesight.— Used with a negative or limiter or in an interrogative or conditional sentence. ♦ *Is that a plane? Can I believe my eyes?* **2.** To be made sure of seeing something. ♦ *She saw him there but she could hardly believe her eyes.*

bell See RING A BELL, WITH BELLS ON.

bellyache *v.* To constantly complain. ♦ *Jim is always bellyaching about the amount of work he is required to do.*

belly up *adj., informal* Dead, bankrupt, or financially ruined. ♦ *Tom and Dick struggled on for months with their tiny computer shop, but last year they went belly up.*

belly up *v., informal* To go bankrupt, become afunctional; to die. ♦ *Uncompetitive small businesses must eventually all belly up.*

below par *adj. or adv.* Below standard. ♦ *Bob was fired because his work has* *been below par for several months now.* Contrast UP TO PAR *or* UP TO SNUFF.

below the belt *adv. phr.* **1.** In the stomach; lower than is legal in boxing. ♦ *He struck the other boy below the belt.* **2.** *informal* In an unfair or cowardly way; against the rules of sportsmanship or justice; unsportingly; wrongly. ♦ *It was hitting below the belt for Mr. Jones's rival to tell people about a crime that Mr. Jones committed when he was a young boy.* ♦ *Pete told the students to vote against Harry because Harry was in a wheelchair and couldn't be a good class president, but the students thought Pete was hitting below the belt.*

belt See BELOW THE BELT, SEAT BELT, TIGHTEN ONE'S BELT, UNDER ONE'S BELT.

belt out *v., slang* To sing with rough rhythm and strength; shout out. ♦ *She belted out ballads and hillbilly songs one after another all evening.* ♦ *Young people enjoy belting out songs.*

be my guest *v. phr.* Feel free to use what I have; help yourself. ♦ *When Suzie asked if she could borrow John's bicycle, John said, "Be my guest."*

beneath one *adj. phr.* Below one's ideals or dignity. ♦ *Bob felt it would have been beneath him to work for such low wages.*

bench See ON THE BENCH, WARM THE BENCH.

bench warmer See WARM THE BENCH.

bend over backward *or* **lean over backward** *v. phr., informal* To try so hard to avoid a mistake that you make the opposite mistake instead; do the opposite of something that you know you should not do; do too much to avoid doing the wrong thing; also, make a great effort; try very hard. ♦ *Instead of punishing the boys for breaking a new rule, the principal bent over backward to explain why the rule was important.* ♦ *Mary was afraid the girls at her new school would be stuck up, but they leaned over backward to make her feel at home.* Compare GO OUT OF ONE'S WAY.

benefit See GIVE THE BENEFIT OF THE DOUBT.

bent on *or* **bent upon** Very decided, determined, or set. ♦ *The sailors were bent on having a good time.* ♦ *The policeman saw some boys near the*

school after dark and thought they were bent on mischief. ♦ *The bus was late, and the driver was bent upon reaching the school on time.*

be nuts about *v. phr.* To be enthusiastic or very keen about someone or something; be greatly infatuated with someone. ♦ *Hermione is nuts about modern music.* ♦ *"I am nuts about you, Helen," Jim said. "Please let's get married!"*

be off *v. phr.* **1.** *v.* To be in error; miscalculate. ♦ *The estimator was off by at least 35% on the value of the house.* **2.** *v.* To leave. ♦ *Jack ate his supper in a hurry and was off without saying goodbye.* **3.** *adj.* Cancelled; terminated. ♦ *The weather was so bad that we were told that the trip was off.* **4.** *adj.* Crazy. ♦ *I'm sure Aunt Mathilda is a bit off; no one in her right mind would say such things.* **5.** *adj.* Free from work; having vacation time. ♦ *Although we were off for the rest of the day, we couldn't go to the beach because it started to rain.*

be on *v. phr.* **1.** To be in operation; be in the process of being presented. ♦ *The news is on now on Channel 2; it will be off in five minutes.* **2.** To be in the process of happening; to take place. ♦ *We cannot travel now to certain parts of Africa, as there is a civil war on there right now.*

be one's age See ACT ONE'S AGE.

be oneself *v.* To act naturally; act normally without trying unduly to impress others. ♦ *Just try being yourself; I promise people will like you more.*

be on the outs with *v. phr.* To not be on speaking terms with someone; be in disagreement with someone. ♦ *Jane and Tom have been on the outs with one another since Tom started to date another woman.*

be on the rocks See ON THE ROCKS, GO ON THE ROCKS.

be on the verge of *v. phr.* To be about to do something; be very close to. ♦ *We were on the verge of going bankrupt when, unexpectedly, my wife won the lottery and our business was saved.*

be on the wagon See ON THE WAGON, FALL OFF THE WAGON.

be on to *v. phr.* To understand the motives of someone; not be deceived. ♦ *Jack keeps telling us how wealthy his family is, but we are on to him.*

be over v. phr. To be ended; be finished. ♦ *The show was over by 11 P.M.* ♦ *The war will soon be over.*

be out v. phr. **1.** To not be at home or at one's place of work. ♦ *I tried to call but they told me that Al was out.* **2.** To be unacceptable; not be considered; impossible. ♦ *I suggested that we hire more salespeople but the boss replied that such a move was positively out.* **3.** To be poorer by; suffer a loss of. ♦ *Unless more people came to the church picnic, we realized we would be out $500. at least.* **4.** To be in circulation, in print, published. ♦ *Jane said that her new novel won't be out for at least another month.* **5.** A baseball term indicating that a player has been declared either unfit to continue or punished by withdrawing him. ♦ *The spectators thought that John was safe at third base, but the umpire said he was out.*

be out to v. phr. To intend to do; to plan to commit. ♦ *The police felt that the gang may be out to rob another store.*

berth See GIVE A WIDE BERTH.

be set on or **upon** v. phr. To be determined about something. ♦ *Tom is set upon leaving his Chicago job for Tokyo, Japan, although he speaks only English.*

beside oneself adj. phr. Very much excited; somewhat crazy. ♦ *She was beside herself with fear.* ♦ *He was beside himself, he was so angry.* ♦ *When his wife heard of his death, she was beside herself.*

beside the point or **beside the question** adj. or adv. phr. Off the subject; about something different. ♦ *What you meant to do is beside the point; the fact is you didn't do it.* ♦ *The judge told the witness that his remarks were beside the point.* Compare BEAT AROUND THE BUSH, NEITHER HERE NOR THERE.

best See AS BEST ONE CAN, AT BEST, FOR THE BEST, GET THE BETTER OF or GET THE BEST OF, HAD BETTER or HAD BEST, HE LAUGHS BEST WHO LAUGHS LAST, MAKE THE BEST OF, PUT ONE'S BEST FOOT FORWARD, SECOND BEST, TO THE BEST OF ONE'S KNOWLEDGE, WITH THE BEST or WITH THE BEST OF THEM.

best bib and tucker or **Sunday best** or **Sunday go-to-meeting clothes** n. phr., informal Best clothes or outfit of clothing. ♦ *The cowboy got all dressed up in his best bib and tucker to go to the dance.* ♦ *Mary went to the party in her Sunday best and made a hit with the boys.* Compare GLAD RAGS.

best man n. The groom's aid (usually his best friend or a relative) at a wedding. ♦ *When Agnes and I got married, my brother Gordon was my best man.*

best seller n. An item (primarily said of books) that outsells other items of a similar sort. ♦ *Catherine Neville's novel The Eight has been a national best seller for months.* ♦ *Among imported European cars, the Volkswagen is a best seller.*

bet See YOU BET or YOU BET YOUR BOOTS or YOU BET YOUR LIFE.

be the making of v. phr. To account for the success of someone or something. ♦ *The strict discipline that we had to undergo in graduate school was the making of many a successful professor.* ♦ *The relatively low cost and high gas mileage are the making of Chevrolet's Geo Metro cars.*

bet one's boots or **bet one's bottom dollar** or **bet one's shirt** v. phr., informal **1.** To bet all you have. ♦ *This horse will win. I would bet my bottom dollar on it.* ♦ *Jim said he would bet his boots that he would pass the examination.* **2.** or **bet one's life.** To feel very sure; have no doubt. ♦ *Was I scared when I saw the bull running at me? You bet your life I was!*

bet on the wrong horse v. phr., informal To base your plans on a wrong guess about the result of something; misread the future; misjudge a coming event. ♦ *To count on the small family farm as an important thing in the American future now looks like betting on the wrong horse.* ♦ *He expected Bush to be elected President in 1992 but as it happened, he bet on the wrong horse.*

better See ALL BETTER, DISCRETION IS THE BETTER PART OF VALOR, FOR BETTER OR WORSE, FOR THE BETTER, GET THE BETTER OF, GO ———ONE BETTER, HAD BETTER, HALF A LOAF IS BETTER THAN NONE or HALF A LOAF IS BETTER THAN NO BREAD, SEE BETTER DAYS, THINK BETTER OF.

better half n., informal One's marriage partner (mostly said by men about their wives.) ♦ *"This is my better half, Mary," said Joe.*

better late than never It is better to come or do something late than never. ♦ *The firemen didn't arrive at the house until it was half burned, but it was better late than never.* ♦ *Grandfather is learning to drive a car. "Better late than never," he says.* Compare HALF A LOAF IS BETTER THAN NONE.

better than *prep. phr.* More than; greater than; at a greater rate than. ♦ *The car was doing better than eighty miles an hour.* ♦ *It is better than three miles to the station.*

between See BETWIXT AND BETWEEN, COME BETWEEN, FEW AND FAR BETWEEN.

between a rock and a hard place See BETWEEN THE DEVIL AND THE DEEP BLUE SEA.

between life and death *adv. phr.* In danger of dying or being killed; with life or death possible. ♦ *He held on to the mountainside between life and death while his friends went to get help.* ♦ *The little sick girl lay all night between life and death until her fever was gone.*

between the devil and the deep blue sea *or literary* **between two fires** *or* **between a rock and a hard place** *adv. phr.* Between two dangers or difficulties, not knowing what to do. ♦ *The pirates had to fight and be killed or give up and be hanged; they were between the devil and the deep blue sea.* ♦ *The boy was between a rock and a hard place; he had to go home and be whipped or stay in town all night and be picked up by the police.* ♦ *When the man's wife and her mother got together, he was between two fires.* Compare COMING AND GOING 2, IN A BIND.

between the eyes See HIT BETWEEN THE EYES.

between the lines See READ BETWEEN THE LINES.

between two fires See BETWEEN THE DEVIL AND THE DEEP BLUE SEA.

between two shakes of a lamb's tail See BEFORE ONE CAN SAY JACK ROBINSON.

be up to no good *v. phr., informal* To be plotting and conniving to commit some illegal act or crime. ♦ *"Let's hurry!" Susan said to her husband. "It's dark here and those hoodlums obviously are up to no good."*

be up to something *v. phr., informal* **1.** To feel strong enough or knowledgeable enough to accomplish a certain task. ♦ *Are you up to climbing all the way to the 37th floor?* ♦ *Are we up to meeting the delegation from Moscow and speaking Russian to them?* **2.** Tendency to do something mischievous. ♦ *I'm afraid Jack is up to one of his old tricks again.*

beyond measure *adj. or adv. phr., formal* So much that it can not be measured or figured without any limits. ♦ *With her parents reunited and present at her graduation, she had happiness beyond measure.* ♦ *No one envied him for he was popular beyond measure.*

beyond one's depth *adj. or adv. phr.* **1.** Over your head in water; in water too deep to touch bottom. ♦ *Jack wasn't a good swimmer and nearly drowned when he drifted out beyond his depth.* **2.** In or into something too difficult for you; beyond your understanding or ability. ♦ *Bill decided that his big brother's geometry book was beyond his depth.* ♦ *Sam's father started to explain the atom bomb to Sam but he soon got beyond his depth.* ♦ *When Bill played checkers against the city champion, Bill was beyond his depth.* Compare OVER ONE'S HEAD 1.

beyond one's means *adj. phr.* Too expensive, not affordable. ♦ *Unfortunately, a new Mercedes Benz is beyond my means right now.*

beyond one's nose See SEE BEYOND ONE'S NOSE.

beyond question[1] *adj. phr.* Not in doubt certain; sure.—Used in the predicate. ♦ *People always believe anything that Mark says; his honesty is beyond question.* Contrast IN QUESTION.

beyond question[2] *or* **without question** *adv. phr.* Without doubt or argument; surely; unquestionably. ♦ *Beyond question, it was the coldest day of the winter.* ♦ *John's drawing is without question the best in the class.*

beyond reasonable doubt *adv. phr. formal and legal* Virtually certain; essentially convincing. ♦ *The judge instructed the jurors to come up with a verdict of guilty only if they were convinced* *beyond a reasonable doubt that Algernon was the perpetrator.*

beyond the pale *adv. or adj. phr.* In disgrace; with no chance of being accepted or respected by others; not approved by the members of a group. ♦ *After the outlaw killed a man he was beyond the pale and not even his old friends would talk to him.* ♦ *Tom's swearing is beyond the pale; no one invites him to dinner any more.*

beyond the shadow of a doubt *adv. phr., formal and legal* Absolutely certain, totally convincing. ♦ *Fred burglarized Mrs. Brown's apartment, beyond the shadow of a doubt.*

bib See BEST BIB AND TUCKER.

bide one's time *v. phr.* To await an opportunity; wait patiently until your chance comes. ♦ *Refused work as an actor, Tom turned to other work and bided his time.* ♦ *Jack was hurt deeply, and he bided his time for revenge.*

bid fair *v., literary* To seem likely; promise. ♦ *He bids fair to be a popular author.* ♦ *The day bids fair to be warm.*

big See IN A BIG WAY, LITTLE FROG IN A BIG POND, LITTLE PITCHERS HAVE BIG EARS, TALK BIG, TOO BIG FOR ONE'S BREECHES, WHAT'S THE BIG IDEA.

big as life *or* **large as life** *adj. phr.* **1.** or **life-size** The same size as the living person or thing. ♦ *The statue of Jefferson was big as life.* ♦ *The characters on the screen were life-size.* **2.** or **big as life and twice as natural** *informal* In person; real and living. ♦ *I had not seen him for years, but there he was, big as life and twice as natural.*

big cheese *or* **big gun** *or* **big shot** *or* **big wheel** *or* **big wig** *n., slang* An important person; a leader; a high official; a person of high rank. ♦ *Bill had been a big shot in high school.* ♦ *John wanted to be the big cheese in his club.* Compare WHOLE CHEESE.

big daddy *n., slang, informal* The most important, largest thing, person or animal in a congregation of similar persons, animals, or objects. ♦ *The whale is the big daddy of everything that swims in the ocean.* ♦ *The H-bomb is the big daddy of all modern weapons.* ♦ *Al Capone was the big daddy of organized crime in Chicago during Prohibition.*

big deal *interj., slang, informal* (loud stress on the word *deal*) Trifles; an unimportant, unimpressive thing or matter. ♦ *So you became college president—big deal!*

big frog in a small pond *n. phr., informal* An important person in a small place or position; someone who is respected and honored in a small company, school, or city; a leader in a small group. ♦ *As company president, he had been a big frog in a small pond, but he was not so important as a new congressman in Washington.* Contrast LITTLE FROG IN A BIG POND.

bigger than one's stomach See EYES BIGGER THAN ONE'S STOMACH.

big hand *n.* Loud and enthusiastic applause. ♦ *When Pavarotti finished singing the aria from Rigoletto, he got a very big hand.*

big head *n., informal* Too high an opinion of your own ability or importance; conceit. ♦ *When Jack was elected captain of the team, it gave him a big head.* Compare SWELLED HEAD.

big house *n.* A large jail or prison. ♦ *The rapist will spend many years in the big house.*

big lie, the *n., informal* A major, deliberate misrepresentation of some important issue made on the assumption that a bold, gross lie is psychologically more believable than a timid, minor one. ♦ *We all heard the big lie during the Watergate months.* ♦ *The pretense of democracy by a totalitarian regime is part of the big lie about its government.*

big mouth *or* **big-mouthed** See LOUD MOUTH, LOUD-MOUTHED.

big shot *or* **big wig** *n.* An important or influential person. ♦ *Elmer is a big shot in the State Assembly.*

big stink *n., slang* A major scandal; a big upheaval. ♦ *I'll raise a big stink if they fire me.*

big time *n., informal* **1.** A very enjoyable time at a party or other pleasurable gathering. ♦ *I certainly had a big time at the club last night.* **2.** The top group; the leading class; the best or most important company. ♦ *After his graduation from college, he soon made the big time in baseball.* ♦ *Many young actors go to Hollywood, but few of them reach the big time.*

big-time *adj.* Belonging to the top group; of the leading class; important. ♦*Jean won a talent contest in her home town, and only a year later she began dancing on big-time television.* ♦*Bob practices boxing in the gym every day; he wants to become a big time boxer.*— Often used in the phrase *big-time* operator. ♦*Just because Bill has a new football uniform he thinks he is a big-time operator.* Compare SHOW OFF. Contrast SMALL-TIME.

big top *n.* The main tent under which a circus gives its show; the circus and circus life. ♦*Lillian Leitzel was one of the great stars of the big top.* ♦*The book tells of life under the big top.*

big wheel *n., informal* An influential or important person who has the power to do things and has connections in high places. ♦*Uncle Ferdinand is a big wheel in Washington; maybe he can help you with your problem.*

big yawn *n.* A very boring person, story or event. ♦*I love my grandma very much, but the stories she tells sure are a yawn.*

bill See CLEAN BILL OF HEALTH, FILL THE BILL.

bind See DUTY BOUND, IN A BIND, MUSCLE BOUND, ROOT-BOUND.

bingo card *n., slang* A response card, bound into a periodical, containing numbers keyed to editorial or advertising matter, giving the reader the opportunity to send for further information by marking the numbers of the items he is interested in; such a card can be mailed free of charge. ♦*Jack thinks he is saving time by filling out bingo cards instead of writing a letter.*

bird See EARLY BIRD CATCHES THE WORM *or* EARLY BIRD GETS THE WORM, EAT LIKE A BIRD, FINE FEATHERS DO NOT MAKE FINE BIRDS, FOR THE BIRDS, KILL TWO BIRDS WITH ONE STONE.

bird has flown *slang* The prisoner has escaped; the captive has got away. ♦*When the sheriff returned to the jail, he discovered that the bird had flown.*

bird in the hand is worth two in the bush (a) Something we have, or can easily get, is more valuable than something we want that we may not be able to get; we shouldn't risk losing something sure by trying to get something that is not sure.—A proverb. ♦*Johnny has a job as a paperboy, but he wants a job in a gas station. His father says that a bird in the hand is worth two in the bush.*

bird of a different feather *n. phr.* A person who is free thinking and independent. ♦*Syd won't go along with recent trends in grammar; he created his own. He is a bird of a different feather.*

birds of a feather flock together People who are alike often become friends or are together; if you are often with certain people, you may be their friends or like them.—A proverb. ♦*Don't be friends with bad boys. People think that birds of a feather flock together.*

birds and the bees (the) *n. phr., informal* The facts we should know about our birth. ♦*At various ages, in response to questions, a child can be told about the birds and the bees.*

bird watcher *n.* A person whose hobby is to study birds close-up in their outdoor home. ♦*A bird watcher looks for the first robin to appear in the spring.*

birthday suit *n.* The skin with no clothes on; complete nakedness. ♦*The little boys were swimming in their birthday suits.*

bit See A BIT, CHAMP AT THE BIT, FOUR BITS, QUITE A LITTLE *or* QUITE A BIT, SIX BITS, TAKE THE BIT IN ONE'S MOUTH, TWO BITS.

bitch See SON OF A BITCH.

bite See BARK WORSE THAN ONE'S BITE, PUT THE BITE ON, ONCE BITTEN, TWICE SHY *at* BURNT CHILD DREADS THE FIRE.

bite off more than one can chew *v. phr., informal* To try to do more than you can; be too confident of your ability. ♦*He bit off more than he could chew when he agreed to edit the paper alone.* ♦*He started to repair his car himself, but realized that he had bitten off more than he could chew.*

bite one's head off *v. phr.* To answer someone in great anger; answer furiously. ♦*I'm sorry to tell you that I lost my job, but that's no reason to bite my head off!*

bite one's lips *v. phr.* To force oneself to remain silent and not to reveal one's feelings. ♦*I had to bite my lips when I heard my boss give the wrong orders.*

bite the dust *v. phr., informal* **1.** To be killed in battle. ♦*Captain Jones dis-*

charged his gun and another guerrilla bit the dust. **2.** To fall in defeat; go down before enemies; be overthrown; lose. ♦ *Our team bit the dust today.*

bite the hand that feeds one *v. phr.* To turn against or hurt a helper or supporter; repay kindness with wrong. ♦ *He bit the hand that fed him when he complained against his employer.*

bitter See TO THE BITTER END.

bitter pill *n.* Something hard to accept; disappointment. ♦ *Jack was not invited to the party and it was a bitter pill for him.*

black See BLACK AND WHITE, IN THE BLACK, LOOK BLACK, POT CALLS THE KETTLE BLACK.

black and blue *adj.* Badly bruised. ♦ *Poor Jim was black and blue after he fell off the apple tree.*

black and white *n. phr.* **1.** Print or writing; words on paper, not spoken; exact written or printed form. ♦ *He insisted on having the agreement down in black and white.* ♦ *Mrs. Jones would not believe the news, so Mr. Jones showed her the article in the newspaper and said, "There it is in black and white."* **2.** The different shades of black and white of a simple picture, rather than other colors. ♦ *He showed us snapshots in black and white.*

black-and-white *adj.* Divided into only two sides that are either right or wrong or good or bad, with nothing in between; thinking or judging everything as either good or bad. ♦ *Everything is black-and-white to Bill; if you're not his friend, you are his enemy.* ♦ *The old man's religion shows his black-and-white thinking; everything is either completely good or completely bad.*

black day *n.* A day of great unhappiness; a disaster. ♦ *It was a black day when our business venture collapsed.*

black eye *n.* **1.** A dark area around one's eye due to a hard blow during a fight, such as boxing. ♦ *Mike Tyson sported a black eye after the big fight.* **2.** Discredit. ♦ *Bob's illegal actions will give a black eye to the popular movement he started.*

blackout *n.* **1.** The darkening of a city during an air raid by pulling down all curtains and putting out all street lights. ♦ *The city of London went through numerous blackouts during World War II.* **2.** A cessation of news by the mass media. ♦ *There was a total news blackout about the kidnapping of the prime minister.*

black out *v.* **1.** To darken by putting out or dimming lights. ♦ *In some plays the stage is blacked out for a short time and the actors speak in darkness.* ♦ *In wartime, cities are blacked out to protect against bombing from planes.* **2.** To prevent or silence information or communication; refuse to give out truthful news. ♦ *In wartime, governments often black out all news or give out false news.* ♦ *Dictators usually black out all criticism of the government.* ♦ *Some big games are blacked out on television to people who live nearby.* **3.** *informal* To lose consciousness; faint. ♦ *It had been a hard and tiring day, and she suddenly blacked out.*

black sheep *n.* A person in a family or a community considered unsatisfactory or disgraceful. ♦ *My brother Ted is a high school dropout who joined a circus; he is the black sheep in our family.*

blame See TO BLAME.

blank check *n.* **1.** A bank check written to a person who can then write in how much money he wants. ♦ *John's father sent him a blank check to pay his school bills.* **2.** *informal* Permission to another person to do anything he decides to do. ♦ *The teacher gave the pupils a blank check to plan the picnic.*

blanket See WET BLANKET.

blast off *v.* **1.** To begin a rocket flight. ♦ *The astronaut will blast off into orbit at six o'clock.* **2.** *Also* **blast away** *informal* To scold or protest violently. ♦ *The coach blasted off at the team for poor playing.*

blaze a trail *v. phr.* **1.** To cut marks in trees in order to guide other people along a path or trail, especially through a wilderness. ♦ *Daniel Boone blazed a trail for other hunters to follow in Kentucky.* **2.** To lead the way; make a discovery; start something new. ♦ *Henry Ford blazed a trail in manufacturing automobiles.* ♦ *The building of rockets blazed a trail to outer space.* See TRAILBLAZER.

bleep out See BLIP OUT.
bless one's heart *v. phr.* To thank someone; consider one the cause of something good that has happened. ♦ *Aunt Jane, bless her heart, left me half a million dollars!*
blessing See MIXED BLESSING.
blind See FLY BLIND.
blind alley *n.* **1.** A narrow street that has only one entrance and no exit. ♦ *The blind alley ended in a brick wall.* **2.** A way of acting that leads to no good results. ♦ *John did not take the job because it was a blind alley.* ♦ *Tom thought of a way to do the algebra problem, but he found it was a blind alley.*
blind as a bat/beetle/mole/owl *adj. phr.* Anyone who is blind or has difficulty in seeing; a person with very thick glasses. ♦ *Without my glasses I am blind as a bat.*
blind date *n.* An engagement or date arranged by friends for people who have not previously known one another. ♦ *A blind date can be a huge success, or a big disappointment.*
blind leading the blind One or more people who do not know or understand something trying to explain it to others who do not know or understand. ♦ *Jimmy is trying to show Bill how to skate. The blind are leading the blind.*
blind spot *n.* **1.** A place on the road that a driver cannot see in the rearview mirror. ♦ *I couldn't see that truck behind me, Officer, because it was in my blind spot.* **2.** A matter or topic a person refuses to discuss or accept. ♦ *My uncle Ted has a real blind spot about religion.*
blink See ON THE BLINK.
blip out *or* **bleep out** *v. phr., informal* To delete electronically a word on television or on radio either because it mentions the name of an established firm in a commercial or because it is a censored word not allowed for television audiences, resulting in a sound resembling the word "bleep." ♦ *What was the old product they compared Spic-n-Span to?—I don't know; they've bleeped it out.*
blitz See SAFETY BLITZ.
block See CHIP OFF THE OLD BLOCK, KNOCK ONE'S BLOCK OFF, ON THE BLOCK.

blockhead *n., informal* An unusually dense, or stupid person whose head is therefore exaggeratedly compared to a solid block of wood. ♦ *Joe is such a blockhead that he flunked every course as a freshman.*
blood See DRAW BLOOD, FLESH AND BLOOD, IN COLD BLOOD, IN ONE'S BLOOD *or* INTO ONE'S BLOOD, MAKE ONE'S BLOOD BOIL *or* MAKE THE BLOOD BOIL, NEW BLOOD, OUT OF ONE'S BLOOD, RUN IN THE BLOOD *or* RUN IN THE FAMILY, SPORTING BLOOD, SWEAT BLOOD, WARM ONE'S BLOOD.
blood and thunder *n. phr.* The violence and bloodshed of stories that present fast action rather than understanding of character. ♦ *Crime movies and westerns usually have lots of blood and thunder.*—Often used like an adjective. ♦ *John likes to watch blood-and-thunder stories on television.*
blood freezes See BLOOD RUNS COLD.
blood is thicker than water Persons of the same family are closer to one another than to others; relatives are favored or chosen over outsiders. ♦ *Mr. Jones hires his relatives to work in his store. Blood is thicker than water.*
blood runs cold *also* **blood freezes** *or* **blood turns to ice** You are chilled or shivering from great fright or horror; you are terrified or horrified.—Usually used with a possessive. ♦ *The horror movie made the children's blood run cold.* ♦ *Mary's blood froze when she had to walk through the cemetery at night.* ♦ *Oscar's blood turned to ice when he saw the shadow pass by outside the window.* Compare HAIR STAND ON END, THE CREEPS.
blood turns to ice See BLOOD RUNS COLD.
bloody See SCREAM BLOODY MURDER.
blot out *v. phr.* **1.** To obstruct; cover; obscure. ♦ *The high-rise building in front of our apartment house blots out the view of the ocean.* **2.** To wipe out of one's memory. ♦ *Jane can't remember the details when she was attacked in the streets; she blotted it out of her memory.*
blow See AT A BLOW, BODY BLOW, COME TO BLOWS, IT'S AN ILL WIND THAT BLOWS NOBODY GOOD, WAY THE WIND BLOWS *or* HOW THE WIND BLOWS.

blow a fuse or **blow a gasket** or **blow one's top** or **blow one's stack** v. phr., slang   To become extremely angry; express rage in hot words. ♦ When Mr. McCarthy's son got married against his wishes, he blew a fuse. ♦ When the umpire called Joe out at first, Joe blew his top and was sent to the showers. Syn. BLOW UP 1b, FLIP ONE'S LID, LOSE ONE'S TEMPER. Compare BLOW OFF STEAM 2.

blow great guns   See GREAT GUNS.

blow hot and cold   v. phr.   To change your ways or likes often; be fickle or changeable. ♦ Tom blows hot and cold about coming out for the baseball team; he cannot decide. ♦ Mary blew hot and cold about going to college; every day she changed her mind. ♦ The boys will get tired of Ann's blowing hot and cold.

blow in   v., slang   To arrive unexpectedly or in a carefree way. ♦ The house was already full of guests when Bill blew in. Compare SHOW UP 3.

blow into   v., slang   To arrive at (a place) unexpectedly or in a carefree way. ♦ Bill blows into college at the last minute after every vacation. ♦ Why Tom, when did you blow into town?

blow off steam   See LET OFF STEAM.

blow one's brains out   v. phr.   **1.** To shoot yourself in the head. ♦ Mr. Jones lost all his wealth, so he blew his brains out. **2.** slang   To work very hard; overwork yourself. ♦ The boys blew their brains out to get the stage ready for the play. ♦ Mary is not one to blow her brains out. Compare BREAK ONE'S NECK.

blow one's cool   v. phr., slang, informal   To lose your composure or self-control. ♦ Whatever you say to the judge in court, make sure that you don't blow your cool.

blow one's lines or **fluff one's lines**   v. phr., informal   To forget the words you are supposed to speak while acting in a play. ♦ The noise backstage scared Mary and she blew her lines.

blow one's mind   v. phr., slang, informal; originally from the drug culture   **1.** To become wildly enthusiastic over something as if understanding it for the first time in an entirely new light. ♦ Read Lyall Watson's book Supernature, it will simply blow your mind! **2.** To lose one's ability to function, as if due to an overdose of drugs. ♦ Joe is entirely

incoherent—he seems to have blown his mind. Contrast BLOW ONE'S COOL.

blow one's own horn or **toot one's own horn**   v. phr., slang   To praise yourself; call attention to your own skill, intelligence, or successes; boast. ♦ People get tired of a man who is always blowing his own horn. ♦ A person who does things well does not have to toot his own horn; his abilities will be noticed by others.

blow one's top   v. phr.   To become very excited, angry, hysterical, or furious. ♦ "No need to blow your top, Al," his wife said, "just because you lost a few dollars."

blow out   v. phr.   **1.** To cease to function; fail; explode (said of tires and fuses). ♦ The accident occurred when Jim's tire blew out on the highway. ♦ The new dishwasher blew out the fuses in the whole house. **2.** To extinguish. ♦ Jane blew out her birthday cake candles before offering pieces to the guests.

blowout   n.   **1.** An explosion of a tire or a fuse. ♦ Jim's van veered sharply to the right after his car had a blowout. **2.** A big party. ♦ After graduation from college, my son and his friends staged a huge blowout.

blow over   v.   To come to an end; pass away with little or no bad effects. ♦ The sky was black, as if a bad storm were coming, but it blew over and the sun came out. ♦ They were bitter enemies for a while, but the quarrel blew over. ♦ He was much criticized for the divorce, but it all blew over after a few years.

blow taps   v. phr.   To sound the final bugle call of the evening in a camp or military base. ♦ After taps is blown the boy scouts go to their bunks to sleep.

blow the gaff   v. phr.   To open one's mouth to reveal a secret. ♦ When Al cheated on his wife, his younger brother blew the gaff on him.

blow the lid off   v. phr., informal   Suddenly to reveal the truth about a matter that has been kept as a secret either by private persons or by some governmental agency. ♦ The clever journalists blew the lid off the Watergate cover-up.

blow the whistle on   v. phr., slang   **1.** To inform against; betray. ♦ The police caught one of the bank robbers, and he *blew the whistle on two more.* **2.** To act against, stop, or tell people the secrets of (crime or lawlessness). ♦ *The mayor blew the whistle on gambling.* ♦ *The police blew the whistle on hot rodding.*

blow up *v.* **1a.** To break or destroy or to be destroyed by explosion. ♦ *He blew up the plane by means of a concealed bomb.* ♦ *The fireworks factory blew up when something went wrong in an electric switch.* **1b.** *informal* To explode with anger or strong feeling; lose control of yourself. ♦ *When Father bent the nail for the third time, he blew up.* Compare BLOW A FUSE. **1c.** To stop playing well in a game or contest, usually because you are in danger of losing or are tired; *especially*: To lose skill or control in pitching baseball. ♦ *The champion blew up and lost the tennis match.* ♦ *Our team was behind but the pitcher on the other team blew up and we got the winning runs.* **2.** *informal* To be ruined as if by explosion; be ended suddenly. ♦ *The whole scheme for a big party suddenly blew up.* **3a.** To pump full of air; inflate. ♦ *He blew his tires up at a filling station.* **3b.** To make (something) seem bigger or important. ♦ *It was a small thing to happen but the newspapers had blown it up until it seemed important.* **4.** To bring on bad weather; also, to come on as bad weather. ♦ *The wind had blown up a storm.* ♦ *A storm had blown up.* **5.** To copy in bigger form; enlarge. ♦ *He blew up the snapshot to a larger size.*

blow up in one's face *v. phr., informal* To fail completely and with unexpected force. ♦ *The thief's plan to rob the bank blew up in his face when a policeman stopped him.*

blue See BETWEEN THE DEVIL AND THE DEEP BLUE SEA, BOLT FROM THE BLUE, ONCE IN A BLUE MOON, OUT OF THE BLUE *or* OUT OF A CLEAR BLUE SKY.

blue around the gills See GREEN AROUND THE GILLS.

blue collar worker *n. phr.* A manual laborer who is probably a labor union member. ♦ *Because Jack's father is a blue collar worker, Jack was so anxious to become an intellectual.* Contrast WHITE COLLAR WORKER.

blue in the face *adj. phr., informal* Very angry or upset; excited and very emo-

tional. ♦ *Tom argued with Bill until he was blue in the face.* ♦ *Mary scolded Jane until she was blue in the face, but Jane kept on using Mary's paints.*

blue Monday *n.* A Monday when you have to work after a happy weekend. ♦ *It was blue Monday and John nodded sleepily over his books.* ♦ *Housewives sometimes wish they could sleep through blue Monday.*

blue-pencil *v.* To edit. ♦ *The editor blue-penciled John's manuscript.*

bluff See CALL ONE'S BLUFF.

blurt out *v. phr.* To suddenly say something even if one was not planning to do so, or if it was not expected of them. ♦ *"My brother Bob is in jail," Tony blurted out, before anybody could stop him.*

blush See AT FIRST BLUSH.

board See ACROSS THE BOARD, COLLEGE BOARDS, GO BY THE BOARD *or* PASS BY THE BOARD, ON BOARD, SANDWICH BOARD.

boat See BURN ONE'S BRIDGES *also* BURN ONE'S BOATS, IN THE SAME BOAT, MISS THE BOAT, ROCK THE BOAT.

bobby-soxer *n.* A teen-aged girl. (1940s idiom) ♦ *My two daughters, age 13 and 14, are typical bobby-soxers.*

bob up See POP UP 1.

body See KEEP BODY AND SOUL TOGETHER.

body blow *n., informal* A great disappointment; a bitter failure. ♦ *When he failed to get on the team it came as a body blow to him.*

body English *n., informal* The wishful attempt to make a ball move in the right direction after it has been hit or let go, by twisting the body in the desired direction. ♦ *He tried to help the putt fall by using body English.*

bog down *v. phr.* To be immobilized in mud, snow, etc.; slow down. ♦ *Our research got bogged down for a lack of appropriate funding.* ♦ *Don't get bogged down in too much detail when you write an action story.*

bog down, to get bogged down *v. phr., mostly intransitive or passive* **1.** To stop progressing; to slow to a halt. ♦ *Work on the new building bogged down, because the contractor didn't deliver the needed concrete blocks.* **2.** To become entangled with a variety of obstacles making your efforts unproductive or unsatisfying. ♦ *The novelist wrote little last summer because she got bogged down in housework.*

boggle the mind *v. phr., informal* To stop the rational thinking process by virtue of being too fantastic or incredible. ♦ *It boggles the mind that John should have been inside a flying saucer!*

boil See MAKE ONE'S BLOOD BOIL *or* MAKE THE BLOOD BOIL.

boil down *v.* **1.** To boil away some of the water from; make less by boiling. ♦ *She boiled down the maple sap to a thick syrup.* ♦ *The fruit juice boiled down until it was almost not good for jelly.* **2.** To reduce the length of; cut down; shorten. ♦ *The reporter boiled the story down to half the original length.* **3.** To reduce itself to; come down to; be briefly or basically. ♦ *The whole discussion boils down to the question of whether the government should fix prices.*

boil over *v. phr.* **1.** To rise due to boiling and overflow down the sides of a pan or a pot. ♦ *"Watch out!" Jane cried. "The milk is boiling over on the stove!"* **2.** To become enraged to the point of being unable to contain oneself. ♦ *John took a lot of abuse from his boss, but after 25 minutes he suddenly boiled over and told him what he thought of him.*

boiling point *n.* **1.** The temperature at which a liquid boils. ♦ *The boiling point of water is 212° Fahrenheit.* **2.** The time when you become very angry. ♦ *He has a low boiling point.* ♦ *After being teased for a long time, John reached the boiling point.* ♦ *When John made the same mistake for the fourth time, his teacher reached the boiling point.* Compare BLOW UP. 1b, MAKE ONE'S BLOOD BOIL.

bolt from the blue *n. phr.* Something sudden and unexpected; an event that you did not see coming; a great and usually unpleasant surprise; shock. ♦ *We had been sure she was in Chicago, so her sudden appearance was a bolt from the blue.* ♦ *His decision to resign was a bolt from the blue.* Compare OUT OF THE BLUE.

bombshell See EXPLODE A BOMBSHELL.

bond See SAVINGS BOND.

bone See BRED IN THE BONE, FEEL IN ONE'S BONES *or* KNOW IN ONE'S BONES, FUNNY BONE, MAKE NO BONES, SKIN AND BONES, T-BONE STEAK, WORK ONE'S FINGERS TO THE BONE.

bonehead *n., slang* An unusually dense or stupid person. ♦ *John is such a bonehead—small wonder he flunks all of his courses.*

bone of contention *n. phr.* Something to fight over; a reason for quarrels; the subject of a fight. ♦ *The boundary line between the farms was a bone of contention between the two farmers.* ♦ *The use of the car was a bone of contention between Joe and his wife.*

bone to pick *or* **crow to pick** *n. phr., informal* A reason for dispute; something to complain of or argue about.— Often used jokingly. ♦ *"I have a bone to pick with you," he said.* ♦ *There was always a crow to pick about which one would shave first in the morning.* Compare BONE OF CONTENTION.

bone up *v., informal* To fill with information; try to learn a lot about something in a short time; study quickly. ♦ *Carl was boning up for an examination.* ♦ *Jim had to make a class report the next day on juvenile delinquency, and he was in the library boning up on how the courts handle it.*

bonnet See BEE IN ONE'S BONNET.

book See CLOSED BOOK, CLOSE THE BOOKS, HIT THE BOOKS, KEEP BOOKS, NOSE IN A BOOK, ONE FOR THE BOOKS, READ ONE LIKE A BOOK, TALKING BOOK, THROW THE BOOK AT.

boom See LOWER THE BOOM.

boot See DIE IN ONE'S BOOTS, IN ONE'S SHOES *also* IN ONE'S BOOTS, LICK ONE'S BOOTS, SHAKE IN ONE'S SHOES *or* SHAKE IN ONE'S BOOTS, TO BOOT, TOO BIG FOR ONE'S BREECHES *or* TOO BIG FOR ONE'S BOOTS, YOU BET *or* YOU BET YOUR BOOTS.

boot hill *n.* A cemetery in the old Wild West where cowboys and cops and robbers used to be buried with their boots on. Hence, jokingly, any cemetery. ♦ *Good old Joe, the cowboy, is resting comfortably in the nearby boot hill.*

boot out See KICK OUT.

boot strap See PULL ONESELF UP BY THE BOOTSTRAPS.

border on *v. phr.* To be adjacent to; come close to; adjoin. ♦ *Our village borders on the Mississippi River.* ♦ *John's actions border on irresponsibility.*

bore to death See TO DEATH.

bore to tears *v. phr.* To fill with tired dislike; tire by dullness or the same old thing bore. ♦ *The party was dull and Roger showed plainly that he was bored to tears.* ♦ *Mary loved cooking, but sewing bores her to tears.*

born See NATURAL-BORN, TO THE MANNER BORN.

born out of wedlock *adj. phr.* Born to parents who are not married to each other; without legal parents. ♦ *Sometimes when a married couple can't have children, they adopt a child who was born out of wedlock.* ♦ *Today we no longer make fun of children born out of wedlock.*

born with a silver spoon in one's mouth *adj. phr.* Born to wealth and comfort; provided from birth with everything wanted; born rich. ♦ *The stranger's conduct was that of a man who had been born with a silver spoon in his mouth.* Compare WELL-HEELED.

born yesterday *adj. phr.* Inexperienced and easily fooled; not alert to trickery; easily deceived or cheated.—Usually used in negative sentences. ♦ *When Bill started the new job, the other workers teased him a little, but he soon proved to everyone that he wasn't born yesterday.* ♦ *I won't give you the money till I see the bicycle you want to sell me. Do you think I was born yesterday?* Compare NOBODY'S FOOL.

borrow See LIVE ON BORROWED TIME.

borrow trouble *v. phr.* To worry for nothing about trouble that may not come; make trouble for yourself needlessly. ♦ *Don't borrow trouble by worrying about next year. It's too far away.* ♦ *You are borrowing trouble if you try to tell John what to do.* Compare ASK FOR, CROSS ONE'S BRIDGES BEFORE ONE COMES TO THEM, CRY BEFORE ONE IS HURT.

bosom friend *n. phr.* A very close friend; an old buddy with whom one has a confidential relationship. ♦ *Sue and Jane have been bosom friends since their college days.*

boss See STRAW BOSS.

boss one around *v. phr.* To keep giving someone orders; to act overbearingly toward someone. ♦ *"If you keep bossing me around, darling," Tom said to Jane, "the days of our relationship are surely numbered."*

botch up *v. phr.* To ruin, spoil, or mess something up. ♦ *"I botched up my chemistry exam," Tim said, with a resigned sigh.*

both See CUT BOTH WAYS, PLAGUE ON BOTH YOUR HOUSES.

both —— and *coord. conj.* Used to emphasize that two or more things are talked about. ♦ *Both Frank and Mary were at the party.* ♦ *Millie is both a good swimmer and a good cook.* ♦ *In the program tonight Mary will both sing and dance.* ♦ *The frog can move quickly both on land and in the water.* Compare AS WELL AS. Contrast EITHER OR.

bothered See HOT AND BOTHERED.

bottle blond *n., slang* A person who is obviously not a natural blond but whose hair is artificially colored. ♦ *I doubt that Leonora's hair color is natural; she strikes me as a bottle blond.*

bottleneck *n.* A heavy traffic congestion. ♦ *In Chicago the worst bottleneck is found where the Kennedy and the Eden's expressways separate on the way to the airport.*

bottle up *v.* **1.** To hide or hold back; control. ♦ *There was no understanding person to talk to, so Fred bottled up his unhappy feeling.* **2.** To hold in a place from which there is no escape; trap. ♦ *Our warships bottled up the enemy fleet in the harbor.*

bottom See BET ONE'S BOOTS *or* BET ONE'S BOTTOM DOLLAR, FROM THE BOTTOM OF ONE'S HEART, FROM —— TO ——, GET TO THE BOTTOM OF, HIT BOTTOM *or* TOUCH BOTTOM, ROCK BOTTOM, SCRAPE THE BOTTOM OF THE BARREL.

bottom dollar *n., v. phr., informal* One's last penny, one's last dollar. ♦ *He was down to his bottom dollar when he suddenly got the job offer.*

bottom drop out *or* **bottom fall out** *v. phr. informal* **1.** To fall below an earlier lowest price. ♦ *The bottom dropped out of the price of peaches.* **2.** To lose all cheerful qualities; become very unhappy, cheerless, or unpleasant. ♦ *The bottom dropped out of the day for John when he saw his report card.* ♦ *The bottom fell out for us when the game ended with our team on the two-yard line and six points behind.*

bottom line *n., informal* (stress on *line*) **1.** The last word on a controversial issue; a final decision. ♦ *"Give me the bottom line on the proposed merger,"* said John. **2.** The naked truth without embellishments. ♦ *Look, the bottom line is that poor Max is an alcoholic.* **3.** The final dollar amount; for example, the lowest price two parties reach in bargaining about a sale. ♦ *"Five-hundred,"* said the used car dealer, *"is the bottom line. Take it or leave it."*

bottom line *v., informal* (stress on *bottom*) To finish; to bring to a conclusion. ♦ *Okay, you guys, let's bottom line this project and break for coffee.*

bottom out *v. phr.* To reach the lowest point (said chiefly of economic cycles). ♦ *According to the leading economic indicators the recession will bottom out within the next two months.*

bounce See GET THE BOUNCE, GIVE THE BOUNCE.

bound See BIND, BY LEAPS AND BOUNDS, OUT OF BOUNDS, WITHIN BOUNDS.

bound for *adj. phr.* On the way to; going to. ♦ *I am bound for the country club.* ♦ *The ship is bound for Liverpool.*

bound up with *v. phr.* To be connected; be involved with. ♦ *Tuition at our university is bound up with the state budget.*

bow See TAKE A BOW.

bow and scrape *v.* To be too polite or obedient from fear or hope of gain; act like a slave. ♦ *The old servant bowed and scraped before them, too obedient and eager to please.*

bowl of cherries See BED OF ROSES.

bowl over *v., informal* **1.** To knock down as if with a bowled ball. ♦ *The taxi hit him a glancing blow and bowled him over.* **2.** To astonish with success or shock with misfortune; upset; stun. ♦ *He was bowled over by his wife's sudden death.* ♦ *The young actress bowled over everybody in her first movie.*

bow out *v., informal* To give up taking part; excuse yourself from doing any more; quit. ♦ *Mr. Black often quarreled with his partners, so finally he bowed out of the company.* ♦ *While the movie was being filmed, the star got sick and had to bow out.* **2.** To stop working after a long service; retire. ♦ *He bowed out as train engineer after forty years of railroading.*

box See IN A BIND *or* IN A BOX, PENALTY BOX, PRESS BOX, STUFF THE BALLOT BOX, VOICE BOX.

box office *n., informal* **1.** The place at movies and theaters where tickets may be purchased just before the performance instead of having ordered them through the telephone or having bought them at a ticket agency. ♦ *No need to reserve the seats; we can pick them up at the box office.* **2.** A best selling movie, musical, or drama (where the tickets are all always sold out and people line up in front of the box office). ♦ *John Wayne's last movie was a regular box office.* **3.** Anything successful or well liked. ♦ *Betsie is no longer box office with me.*

boy See ALL WORK AND NO PLAY MAKES JACK A DULL BOY, FAIR-HAIRED BOY, MAMA'S BOY, OLD BOY, SEPARATE THE MEN FROM THE BOYS.

boyfriend *n., informal* **1.** A male friend or companion. ♦ *"John and his boyfriends have gone to the ball game,"* said his mother. **2.** A girl's steady date, a woman's favorite man friend; a male lover or sweetheart. ♦ *Jane's new boyfriend is a senior in high school.* Contrast GIRL FRIEND.

boys will be boys Boys are only children and must sometimes get into mischief or trouble or behave too roughly. ♦ *Boys will be boys and make a lot of noise, so John's mother told him and his friends to play in the park instead of the back yard.*

brain See BEAT ONE'S BRAINS OUT, BLOW ONE'S BRAINS OUT, ON THE BRAIN, RACK ONE'S BRAIN, GET ONE'S BRAINS FRIED.

brain bucket *n., slang* A motorcycle helmet. ♦ *If you want to share a ride with me, you've got to wear a brain bucket.*

brain drain *n., informal* **1.** The loss of the leading intellectuals and researchers of a country due to excessive emigration to other countries where conditions are better. ♦ *Britain suffered a considerable brain drain to the United States after World War II.* **2.** An activity requiring great mental concentration resulting in fatigue and exhaustion ♦ *That math exam I took was a regular brain drain.*

brain-storm *v.* To have a discussion among fellow researchers or co-workers on a project in order to find the best solution to a given problem. ♦ *Dr. Watson and his research assistants are brain-storming in the conference room.*

brainstorm *n.* A sudden insight; a stroke of comprehension. ♦ *Listen to me, I've just had a major brainstorm, and I think I found the solution to our problem.*

brain trust *n.* A group of specially trained, highly intelligent experts in a given field. ♦ *Albert Einstein gathered a brain trust around himself at the Princeton Institute of Advanced Studies.*

brake See RIDE THE BRAKE.

branch off *v.* To go from something big or important to something smaller or less important; turn aside. ♦ *At the bridge a little road branches off from the highway and follows the river.* ♦ *Martin was trying to study his lesson, but his mind kept branching off onto what girl he should ask to go with him to the dance.*

branch out *v.* To add new interests or activities; begin doing other things also. ♦ *First Jane collected stamps; then she branched out and collected coins, too.* ♦ *John started a television repair shop; when he did well, he branched out and began selling television sets too.*

brand-new *also* **bran-new** *adj.* As new or fresh as when just made and sold by the manufacturer; showing no use or wear. ♦ *He had taken a brand-new car from the dealer's floor and wrecked it.* ♦ *In Uncle Tom's trunk, we found a wedding ring, still in its little satin-lined box, still brand-new.*

brass See DOUBLE IN BRASS, GET DOWN TO BRASS TACKS.

brass hat *n., slang* **1.** A high officer in the army, navy, or air force. ♦ *The brass hats in Washington often discuss important secrets.* **2.** Any person who has a high position in business, politics,

or other work. ♦ *Mr. Woods, the rich oil man, is a political brass hat.*

brass tacks See GET DOWN TO BRASS TACKS.

brave it out *v. phr.* To endure something difficult or dangerous through to the end; keep on through trouble or danger. ♦ *It was a dangerous ocean crossing in wartime, but captain and crew braved it out.*

brazen it out *v. phr.* To pretend you did nothing wrong; be suspected, accused, or scolded without admitting you did wrong; act as if not guilty. ♦ *The teacher found a stolen pen that the girl had in her desk, but the girl brazened it out; she said someone else must have put it there.*

bread See HALF A LOAF IS BETTER THAN NONE, KNOW WHICH SIDE ONE'S BREAD IS BUTTERED ON, TAKE THE BREAD OUT OF ONE'S MOUTH.

bread and butter[1] *n. phr.* The usual needs of life; food, shelter, and clothing. ♦ *Ed earned his bread and butter as a bookkeeper, but added a little jam by working with a dance band on weekends.*

bread and butter[2] *adj.* Thanking someone for entertainment or a nice visit; thank-you. ♦ *After spending the weekend as a guest in the Jones' home, Alice wrote the Joneses the usual bread-and-butter letter.* SEE BREAD AND BUTTER LETTER.

bread and butter[3] *interj., informal* Spoken to prevent bad luck that you think might result from some action. ♦ *We'd say "Bread and butter!" when we had passed on opposite sides of a tree.*

bread-and-butter letter *n.* A written acknowledgment of hospitality received. ♦ *Jane wrote the Browns a bread-and-butter letter when she returned home from her visit to them.*

breadbasket *n., slang* The stomach. ♦ *John is stuffing his breadbasket again.*

break See COFFEE BREAK.

break away *or* **break loose** *v. phr.* To liberate oneself from someone or something. ♦ *Jane tried to break loose from her attacker, but he was too strong.*

break camp *v. phr.* To take down and pack tents and camping things; take your things from a camping place. ♦ *The scouts broke camp at dawn.*

break down *v.* (stress on *down*) **1.** To smash or hit (something) so that it falls; cause to fall by force. ♦ *The firemen broke down the door.* **2.** To reduce or destroy the strength or effect of; weaken; win over. ♦ *By helpful kindness the teacher broke down the new boy's shyness.* ♦ *Advertising breaks down a lot of stubbornness against change.* **3.** To separate into elements or parts; decay. ♦ *Water is readily broken down into hydrogen and oxygen.* ♦ *After many years, rocks break down into dirt.* **4.** To become unusable because of breakage or other failure; lose power to work or go. ♦ *The car broke down after half an hour's driving.* ♦ *His health broke down.* ♦ *When the coach was sick in bed, the training rules of the team broke down.* Compare GO BACK ON 2.

breakdown See NERVOUS BREAKDOWN.

breaker See JAW-BREAKER.

break even *v. phr., informal* (stress on *even*) To end a series of gains and losses having the same amount you started with; have expenses equal to profits; have equal gain and loss. ♦ *The storekeeper made many sales, but his expenses were so high that he just broke even.* ♦ *If you gamble you are lucky when you break even.*

break-even *n.* The point of equilibrium in a business venture when one has made as much money as one had invested, but not more—that would be "profit." ♦ *"We've reached the break-even point at long last!"—Max exclaimed with joy.*

break ground *v. phr.* To begin a construction project by digging for the foundation; especially, to turn the formal first spadeful of dirt. ♦ *City officials and industrial leaders were there as the company broke ground for its new building.* See BREAK NEW GROUND.

break in *v.* (stress on *in*) **1a.** To break from outside. ♦ *The firemen broke in the door of the burning house.* **1b.** To enter by force or unlawfully. ♦ *Thieves broke in while the family was away.* **2.** To enter suddenly or interrupt. ♦ *A stranger broke in on the meeting without knocking.* ♦ *The secretary broke in to say that a telegram had arrived.*

Compare CUT IN 2. **3.** To make a start in a line of work or with a company or association; begin a new job. ♦ *He broke in as a baseball player with a minor league.* **4.** To teach the skills of a new job or activity to. ♦ *An assistant foreman broke in the new man as a machine operator.* **5.** To lessen the stiffness or newness of by use. ♦ *He broke in a new pair of shoes.* ♦ *Breaking in a new car requires careful driving at moderate speeds.*

break-in *n.* (stress on *break*) A robbery; a burglary. ♦ *We lost our jewelry during a break-in.*

break into *v.* **1.** To force an entrance into; make a rough or unlawful entrance into. ♦ *Thieves broke into the store at night.* **2.** *informal* To succeed in beginning (a career, business, or a social life) ♦ *He broke into television as an actor.* **3.** To interrupt. ♦ *He broke into the discussion with a shout of warning.* **4.** To begin suddenly. ♦ *He broke into a sweat.* ♦ *She broke into tears.* ♦ *The dog heard his master's whistle and broke into a run.*

break new ground *v. phr.* **1.** To start a new activity previously neglected by others; do pioneering work. ♦ *Albert Einstein broke new ground with his theory of relativity.* **2.** To begin something never done before. ♦ *The school broke new ground with reading lessons that taught students to guess the meaning of new words.*

break off *v.* **1.** To stop suddenly. ♦ *The speaker was interrupted so often that he broke off and sat down.* ♦ *When Bob came in, Jean broke off her talk with Linda and talked to Bob.* **2.** *informal* To end a friendship or love. ♦ *I hear that Tom and Alice have broken off.* ♦ *She broke off with her best friend.*

break one's balls *v. phr., slang, vulgar, avoidable* To do something with maximum effort; to do something very difficult or taxing ♦ *I've been breaking my balls to buy you this new color TV set and you aren't the least bit appreciative!* Compare BREAK ONE'S NECK.

break one's heart *v. phr.* To discourage greatly; make very sad or hopeless. ♦ *His son's disgrace broke his heart.* ♦ *When Mr. White lost everything he* *had worked so hard for, it broke his heart.*

break one's neck *v. phr., slang* To do all you possibly can; try your hardest.—Usually used with a limiting adverb or negative. ◆*John nearly broke his neck trying not to be late to school.* ◆*Mother asked Mary to go to the store when she was free, but not to break her neck over it.*

break one's word *v. phr.* To renege on a promise. ◆*When Jake broke his word that he would marry Sarah, she became very depressed.*

break out *v.* **1.** To begin showing a rash or other skin disorder.—Often used with *with.* ◆*He broke out with scarlet fever.* **2.** To speak or act suddenly and violently. ◆*He broke out laughing.* ◆*She broke out, "That is not so!"* **3.** To begin and become noticeable. ◆*Fire broke out after the earthquake.* ◆*War broke out in 1812.* Compare FLARE UP. **4.** *informal* To bring out; open and show. ◆*When word of the victory came, people began breaking out their flags.* ◆*When Mr. Carson's first son was born, he broke out the cigars he had been saving.*

break the ice *v. phr., informal* **1.** To conquer the first difficulties in starting a conversation, getting a party going, or making an acquaintance. ◆*To break the ice Ted spoke of his interest in mountain climbing, and they soon had a conversation going.* ◆*Some people use an unusual thing, such as an unusual piece of jewelry, to break the ice.* **2.** To be the first person or team to score in a game. ◆*The Wolves broke the ice with a touchdown.*

break the record *v. phr.* To set or to establish a new mark or record. ◆*Algernon broke the record in both the pentathlon and the decathlon and took home two gold medals from the Olympics.*

break through *v.* To be successful after overcoming a difficulty or bar to success. ◆*Dr. Salk failed many times but he finally broke through to find a successful polio vaccine.* ◆*Jim studied very hard this semester in college, and he finally broke through onto the Dean's List for the first time.*

breakthrough *n.* A point of sudden success after a long process of experimentation, trial and error. ◆*The U.S. Space Program experienced a major breakthrough when Armstrong and Aldrin landed on the moon in June of 1969.*

break up *v. phr.* To end a romantic relationship, a marriage, or a business partnership. ◆*Tom and Jane broke up because Tom played so much golf that he had no time for her.*

break up *v.* **1.** To break into pieces. ◆*The workmen broke up the pavement to dig up the pipes under it.* ◆*River ice breaks up in the spring.* **2.** *informal* To lose or destroy spirit or self-control.—Usually used in the passive. ◆*Mrs. Lawrence was all broken up after her daughter's death, and did not go out of the house for two months.* Compare CRACK UP, GO TO PIECES. **3.** To come or to put to an end, especially by separation; separate. ◆*Some men kept interrupting the speakers, and finally broke up the meeting.* ◆*The party broke up at midnight.*—Often used in the informal phrase *break it up.* ◆*The boys were fighting, and a passing policeman ordered them to break it up.* Compare CUT OUT 1. **4.** *informal* To stop being friends. ◆*Mary and June were good friends and did everything together, but then they had a quarrel and broke up.* Compare BREAK OFF.

break-up *n.* The end of a relationship, personal or commercial. ◆*The break-up finally occurred when Smith and Brown decided to sue each other for embezzlement.*

break with *v.* To separate yourself from; end membership in; stop friendly association with ◆*He broke with the Democratic party on the question of civil rights.* ◆*He had broken with some friends who had changed in their ideas.*

breast See MAKE A CLEAN BREAST OF.

breath See CATCH ONE'S BREATH, DRAW A LONG BREATH *or* TAKE A LONG BREATH, HOLD ONE'S BREATH, IN THE SAME BREATH, OUT OF BREATH, SAVE ONE'S BREATH, SECOND WIND *also* SECOND BREATH, TAKE ONE'S BREATH AWAY, UNDER ONE'S BREATH, WASTE ONE'S BREATH.

breathe down one's neck *v. phr., informal* To follow closely; threaten from behind; watch every action. ♦ *Too many creditors were breathing down his neck.* ♦ *The carpenter didn't like to work for Mr. Jones, who was always breathing down his neck.*

breathe easily *or* **breathe freely** *v.* To have relief from difficulty or worry; relax; feel that trouble is gone; stop worrying. ♦ *Now that the big bills were paid, he breathed more easily.* ♦ *His mother didn't breathe easily until she got home that night.*

breathe one's last *v. phr.* To die. ♦ *The wounded soldier fell back on the ground and breathed his last.*

bred in the bone *adj. phr.* Belonging to your nature or character, especially from early teaching or long habit; natural from belief or habit; believing deeply. ♦ *The Willett children's cleanness is bred in the bone.* Often used, with hyphens before the noun. ♦ *Joe is a bred-in-the-bone horseman; he has been riding since he was six.* Contrast SKIN-DEEP.

breeches See TOO BIG FOR ONE'S BREECHES.

breeze SEE SHOOT THE BREEZE *or* BAT THE BREEZE *or* FAN THE BREEZE, WIN IN A WALK *or* WIN IN A BREEZE.

breeze in *v. phr., slang, informal* To walk into a place casually (like a soft blowing wind). ♦ *Betsie breezed in and sat down at the bar.*

brew See HOME BREW.

brick See MAKE BRICKS WITHOUT STRAW.

brick wall See STONE WALL.

bridge See BURN ONE'S BRIDGES, CROSS A BRIDGE BEFORE ONE COMES TO IT, WATER OVER THE DAM *or* WATER UNDER THE BRIDGE.

brief See HOLD A BRIEF FOR, IN BRIEF *or* IN SHORT *or* IN A WORD.

bright and early *adj. phr.* Prompt and alert; on time and ready; cheerful and on time or before time. ♦ *He came down bright and early to breakfast.* ♦ *She arrived bright and early for the appointment.*

bring about *v.* To cause; produce; lead to. ♦ *The war had brought about great changes in living.* ♦ *Drink brought about his downfall.*

bring around *or* **bring round** *v.* **1.** *informal* To restore to health or consciousness cure. ♦ *He was quite ill, but good nursing brought him around.* Compare

BRING TO 1. **2.** To cause a change in thinking; persuade; convince; make willing. ♦ *After a good deal of discussion he brought her round to his way of thinking.*

bringdown *n., slang, informal* **1.** (from *bring down,* past *brought down*). A critical or cutting remark said sarcastically in order to deflate a braggard's ego. ♦ *John always utters the right bringdown when he encounters a braggard.* **2.** A person who depresses and saddens others by being a chronic complainer. ♦ *John is a regular bringdown.*

bring down *v. phr., slang, informal* **1.** To deflate (someone's ego). ♦ *John brought Ted down very cleverly with his remarks.* **2.** To depress (someone). ♦ *The funeral brought me down completely.*

bring down about one's ears *or* **bring down around one's ears** See ABOUT ONE'S EARS.

bring down the house *v. phr., informal* To start an audience laughing or clapping enthusiastically. ♦ *The principal's story was funny in itself and also touched their loyalties, so it brought down the house.* ♦ *The President made a fine speech which brought down the house.*

bring home *v.* To show clearly; emphasize; make (someone) realize; demonstrate. ♦ *The accident caused a death in his family, and it brought home to him the evil of drinking while driving.* ♦ *A parent or teacher should bring home to children the value and pleasure of reading.*

bring home the bacon *v. phr., informal* **1.** To support your family; earn the family living. ♦ *He was a steady fellow, who always brought home the bacon.* **2.** To win a game or prize. ♦ *The football team brought home the bacon.*

bring in *v.* In baseball: To enable men on base to score, score. ♦ *Dick's hit brought in both base runners.* ♦ *A walk and a triple brought in a run in the third inning.*

bring into line *v. phr.* To make someone conform to the accepted standard. ♦ *Sam had to be brought into line when he refused to take his muddy shoes off the cocktail table.*

bring off v. To do (something difficult); perform successfully (an act of skill); accomplish (something requiring unusual ability). ◆ *By skillful discussion, Mr. White had brought off an agreement that had seemed impossible to get.* ◆ *He tried several times to break the high jump record, and finally he brought it off.* Compare PUT OVER 2.

bring on v. To result in; cause; produce. ◆ *The murder of Archduke Franz Ferdinand in the summer of 1914 brought on the First World War.* ◆ *Spinal meningitis brought on John's deafness when he was six years old.* ◆ *Reading in a poor light may bring on a headache.*

bring out v. **1.** To cause to appear; make clear. ◆ *His report brought out the foolishness of the plan.* ◆ *Brushing will bring out the beauty of your hair.* **2.** To help (an ability or skill) grow or develop. ◆ *The teacher's coaching brought out a wonderful singing voice of great power and warmth.* **3.** To offer to the public by producing, publishing, or selling. ◆ *He brought out a new play.* ◆ *The company brought out a line of light personal airplanes.*

bring round See BRING AROUND.

bring suit against v. phr. To sue someone in a court of law. ◆ *Fred brought suit against Tom for fraud and embezzlement.*

bring to v. (stress on *to*) **1.** To restore to consciousness; wake from sleep, anesthesia, hypnosis, or fainting. ◆ *Smelling salts will often bring a fainting person to.* Compare BRING AROUND 1. **2.** To bring a ship or boat to a stop. ◆ *Reaching the pier, he brought the boat smartly to.*

bring to a close v. phr. To terminate; cause to end. ◆ *The meeting was brought to an abrupt close when the speaker collapsed with a heart attack.*

bring to a head v. phr. To cause some activity to reach the point of culmination. ◆ *Time is running out, gentlemen, so let us bring this discussion to a head.*

bring to bay v. phr. To chase or force into a place where escape is impossible without a fight; trap; corner. ◆ *The police brought the robber to bay on the roof and he gave up.* ◆ *The fox was brought to bay in a hollow tree and the dogs stood around it barking.* Compare AT BAY.

bring to heel See TO HEEL.

bring to light v. phr. To discover (something hidden); find out about; expose. ◆ *Many things left by the ancient Egyptians in tombs have been brought to light by scientists and explorers.* ◆ *His enemies brought to light some foolish things he had done while young, but he was elected anyway because people trusted him.* Compare COME TO LIGHT.

bring to one's knees v. phr. To seriously weaken the power or impair the function of. ◆ *The fuel shortage brought the automobile industry to its knees.*

bring to pass v. phr., informal To make (something) happen; succeed in causing. ◆ *By much planning, the mother brought the marriage to pass.* ◆ *The change in the law was slow in coming, and it took a disaster to bring it to pass.* Compare BRING ABOUT, COME TO PASS.

bring to terms v. phr. To make (someone) agree or do; make surrender. ◆ *The two brothers were brought to terms by their father for riding the bicycle.* ◆ *The war won't end until we bring the enemy to terms.* Contrast COME TO TERMS.

bring up v. **1.** To take care of (a child); raise, train, educate. ◆ *He gave much attention and thought to bringing up his children.* ◆ *Joe was born in Texas but brought up in Oklahoma.* **2.** informal To stop; halt.—Usually used with short. ◆ *He brought the car up short when the light changed to red.* ◆ *Bill started to complain, I brought him up short.* **3.** To begin a discussion of; speak of; mention. ◆ *At the class meeting Bob brought up the idea of a picnic.*

bring up the rear v. phr. **1.** To come last in a march, parade, or procession; end a line. ◆ *The fire truck with Santa on it brought up the rear of the Christmas parade.* ◆ *The governor and his staff brought up the rear of the parade.* **2.** informal To do least well; do the most poorly of a group; be last. ◆ *In the race, John brought up the rear.* ◆ *In the bas-*

ketball tournament, our team brought up the rear.

bring *or* **wheel in** *or* **out** *or* **up the big guns** *v. phr.* To make use of a concealed plan in order to defeat an opponent in an argument or in a game, debate, or competition. ◆ *The new computer software company decided to bring out the big guns to get ahead of the competition.*

broke See GO BROKE, GO FOR BROKE, STONE-BROKE *or* DEAD BROKE *or* FLAT BROKE, STRAW THAT BROKE THE CAMEL'S BACK.

Bronx cheer *n. phr., slang* A loud sound made with tongue and lips to show opposition or scorn. ◆ *When he began to show anti-union feelings, he was greeted with Bronx cheers all around.*

broom See NEW BROOM SWEEPS CLEAN.

broth See SCOTCH BROTH.

brow See BY THE SWEAT OF ONE'S BROW.

brown See DO UP BROWN.

brown-bagger *n., slang, informal* A person who does not go to the cafeteria or to a restaurant for lunch at work, but who brings his homemade lunch to work in order to save money. ◆ *John became a brown-bagger not because he can't afford the restaurant, but because he is too busy to go there.*

brown-nose *v., slang, avoidable, though gaining in acceptance* To curry favor in a subservient way, as by obviously exaggerated flattery. ◆ *Max brown-noses his teachers, that's why he gets all A's in his courses.* Compare POLISH THE APPLE.

brown paper bag *n., slang, citizen's band radio jargon* An unmarked police car. ◆ *The beaver got a Christmas card because she didn't notice the brown paper bag at her back door.* See PLAIN WHITE WRAPPER.

brown study *n. phr.* A time of deep thought about something; a deep thoughtful mood. ◆ *When his wife found him, he had pushed away his books and was in a brown study.*

brush See BEAT THE BUSHES *or* BEAT THE BRUSH.

brush aside *v. phr.* To ignore; give no reply. ◆ *Brushing aside the editor's comments, the young novelist proceeded with his story, which was subsequently rejected by the publisher.*

brush back *v.* To throw a baseball pitch close to. ◆ *The pitcher threw a high inside pitch to brush the batter back.* Syn. DUST OFF.

brushoff See GET THE BRUSHOFF, BRUSH OFF *or* GIVE THE BRUSHOFF.

brush off *or* **give the brush off** *v. phr.* **1.** To refuse to hear or believe; quickly and impatiently; not take seriously or think important. ◆ *John brushed off Bill's warning that he might fall from the tree.* ◆ *I said that it might rain and to take the bus, but Joe gave my idea the brushoff.* ◆ *Father cut his finger but he brushed it off as not important and kept working.* **2.** *informal* To be unfriendly to; not talk or pay attention to (someone); get rid of. ◆ *Mary brushed off Bill at the dance.* ◆ *I said hello to Mr. Smith, but he gave me the brushoff.* Compare COLD SHOULDER, HIGH-HAT. Contrast GET THE BRUSH OFF.

brush up *or* **brush up on** *v.* To refresh one's memory of or skill at by practice or review; improve; make perfect. ◆ *She spent the summer brushing up on her American History as she was to teach that in the fall.* ◆ *He brushed up his target shooting.*

bubble gum music *n., slang* The kind of rock'n'roll that appeals to young teenagers. ◆ *When will you learn to appreciate Mozart instead of that bubble gum music?*

bubble trouble *n., slang, citizen's band radio jargon* Tire trouble, flat tire. ◆ *The eighteen wheeler ahead of me seems to have bubble trouble.*

buck See FAST BUCK *or* QUICK BUCK, PASS THE BUCK.

bucket See KICK THE BUCKET, RAIN CATS AND DOGS *or* RAIN BUCKETS.

bucket of bolts *n., slang* A very old and shaky car that barely goes. ◆ *When are you going to get rid of that old bucket of bolts?*

buckle See BUCKLE DOWN *or* KNUCKLE DOWN.

buckle down *or* **knuckle down** *v.* To give complete attention (to an effort or job); attend. ◆ *They chatted idly for a few moments then each buckled down to work.* ◆ *Jim was fooling instead of studying; so his father told him to buckle down.*

buck passer, buck-passing See PASS THE BUCK.

buck up *v. phr., informal* To make or become more cheerful; make or become free from discouragement; become more hopeful. ♦*After the heavy rain, the scoutmaster bucked up the boys by leading them in a song.* ♦*Tom was disappointed that he didn't make the team; but he soon bucked up.*

bud See NIP IN THE BUD.

bug-eyed *adj., slang* Wide-eyed with surprise. ♦*He stood there bug-eyed when told that he had won the award.*

buggy-whip *n., slang* An unusually long, thin radio antenna on a car that bends back like a whip when the car moves fast. ♦*He's very impressed with himself ever since he got a buggy whip.*

bughouse¹ *n., slang* An insane asylum. ♦*They took Joe to the bughouse.*

bughouse² *adj., slang* Crazy, insane. ♦*Joe's gone bughouse.*

bug in one's ear *n. phr., informal* A hint; secret information given to someone to make him act; idea. ♦*I saw Mary at the jeweler's admiring the diamond pin; I'll put a bug in Henry's ear.*

build See JERRY-BUILT.

build a fire under *v. phr.* To urge or force (a slow or unwilling person) to action; get (someone) moving; arouse. ♦*The health department built a fire under the restaurant owner and got him to clean the place up by threatening to cancel his license.*

build castles in the air *or* **build castles in Spain** *v. phr.* To make impossible or imaginary plans, dream about future successes that are unlikely. ♦*He liked to build castles in the air, but never succeeded in anything.* ♦*To build castles in Spain is natural for young people and they may work hard enough to get part of their wishes.*

build on sand *v. phr.* To lay a weak or insufficient foundation for a building, a business, or a relationship. ♦*"I don't want to build my business on sand,"* John said, *"so please, Dad, give me that loan I requested."*

build up *v.* **1.** To make out of separate pieces or layers; construct from parts. ♦*Johnny built up a fort out of large balls of snow.* ♦*Lois built up a cake of three layers.* **2.** To cover over or fill up with buildings. ♦*The fields where Tom's father played as a boy are all built up now.* ♦*A driver should slow down when he comes to an area that is built up.* **3a.** To increase slowly or by small amounts; grow. ♦*John built up a bank account by saving regularly.* ♦*The noise built up until Mary couldn't stand it any longer.* **3b.** To make stronger or better or more effective. ♦*Fred exercised to build up his muscles.* ♦*Joanne was studying to build up her algebra.* **3c.** *informal* To advertise quickly and publicize so as to make famous. ♦*The press agent built up the young actress.* ♦*The movie company spent much money building up its new picture.*

build up to *v. phr.* To be in the process of reaching a culmination point. ♦*The clouds were building up to a violent storm.* ♦*Their heated words were building up to a premature divorce.*

bull See HIT THE BULLS-EYE, SHOOT THE BREEZE *or* SHOOT THE BULL, TAKE THE BULL BY THE HORNS.

bullet lane *n., slang, citizen's band radio jargon* The passing lane. ♦*Move over into the bullet lane, this eighteen wheeler is moving too slow.*

bull in a china shop *n. phr.* A rough or clumsy person who says or does something to anger others or upset plans; a tactless person. ♦*We were talking politely and carefully with the teacher about a class party, but John came in like a bull in a china shop and his rough talk made the teacher say no.*

bull session *n., slang* A long informal talk about something by a group of persons. ♦*After the game the boys in the dormitory had a bull session until the lights went out.*

bullshit *n., vulgar, but gaining in acceptance by some* Exaggerated or insincere talk meant to impress others. ♦*"Joe, this is a lot of bullshit!"*

bullshit *v., vulgar to informal, gaining in social acceptance by some* To exaggerate or talk insincerely in an effort to make yourself seem impressive. ♦*"Stop bullshitting me, Joe, I can't believe a word of what you're saying."*

bullshit artist *n., slang, vulgar, but gaining in social acceptance* A person who habitually makes exaggerated or insincerely flattering speeches designed to impress others. ♦ *Joe is a regular bull-shit artist, small wonder he keeps getting promoted ahead of everyone else.*

bum around *v. phr., slang* To aimlessly wander in no definite direction, like a vagabond. ♦ *Jim had been bumming around in the desert for three days and nights before he was able to remember how he got there in the first place.*

bump See GOOSE BUMPS.

bump into *v., informal* To meet without expecting to; happen to meet; come upon by accident. ♦ *Mary was walking down the street, when she suddenly bumped into Joan.* ♦ *Ed was surprised to bump into John at the football game.* Syn. RUN INTO.

bump off *v., slang* To kill in a violent way; murder in gangster fashion. ♦ *Hoodlums in a speeding car bumped him off with Tommy guns.*

bum's rush *n. phr., slang* Throwing or pushing someone out from where he is not wanted. ♦ *When John tried to go to the party where he was not invited, Bill and Fred gave him the bum's rush.* ♦ *Tom became too noisy, and he got the bum's rush.* **2.** To hurry or rush (someone). ♦ *The salesman tried to give me the bum's rush.*

bum steer *n.* Wrong or misleading directions given naively or on purpose. ♦ *Man, you sure gave me a bum steer when you told me to go north on the highway; you should have sent me south!*

bundle of laughs *n. phr.* A very amusing person, thing, or event. ♦ *Uncle Lester tells so many jokes that he is a bundle of laughs.*

bundle up See WRAP UP 1.

burn See EARS BURN, KEEP THE HOME FIRES BURNING, MONEY TO BURN.

burn a hole in one's pocket *v. phr.* To make you want to buy something; be likely to be quickly spent. ♦ *Money burns a hole in Linda's pocket.* ♦ *The silver dollar that Don got for his birthday was burning a hole in his pocket, and Don hurried to a dime store.*

burn down *v. phr.* To burn to the ground; be totally gutted by fire. ♦ *The old frame house burned down before the firefighters could get to it.*

burn in effigy See HANG IN EFFIGY.

burn one's bridges *also* **burn one's boats** *v. phr.* To make a decision that you cannot change; remove or destroy all the ways you can get back out of a place you have got into on purpose; leave yourself no way to escape a position. ♦ *Bob was a good wrestler but a poor boxer. He burned his boats by letting Mickey choose how they would fight.* ♦ *When Dorothy became a nun, she burned her bridges behind her.*

burn one's fingers *v. phr., informal* To get in trouble doing something and fear to do it again; learn caution through an unpleasant experience. ♦ *He had burned his fingers in the stock market once, and didn't want to try again.* ♦ *Some people can't be told; they have to burn their fingers to learn.*

burn out *v. phr.* **1.** To destroy by fire or by overheating. ♦ *Mr. Jones burned out the clutch on his car.* **2.** To destroy someone's house or business by fire so that they have to move out. ♦ *Three racists burned out the Black family's home.* **3a.** To go out of order; cease to function because of long use or overheating. ♦ *The light bulb in the bathroom burned out, and Father put in a new one.* ♦ *The electric motor was too powerful, and it burned out a fuse.* **3b.** To break, tire, or wear out by using up all the power, energy, or strength of. ♦ *Bill burned himself out in the first part of the race and could not finish.* ♦ *The farmer burned out his field by planting the same crop every year for many years.*

burn-out *n.* A point of physical or emotional exhaustion. ♦ *There are so many refugees all over the world that charitable organizations as well as individuals are suffering from donor burn-out.*

burn rubber *v. phr., slang* **1.** To start up a car or a motorcycle from dead stop so fast that the tires leave a mark on the road. ♦ *The neighborhood drag racers burned a lot of rubber—look at the marks on the road!* **2.** To leave in a hurry. ♦ *I guess I am going to have to burn rubber.*

burnt child dreads the fire *or* **once bitten, twice shy** A person who has suffered from doing something has learned to avoid doing it again.—A proverb. ♦ *Once Mary had got lost when her mother took her downtown. But a burnt child dreads the fire, so* *now Mary stays close to her mother when they are downtown.*

burn the candle at both ends *v. phr.* To work or play too hard without enough rest; get too tired. ♦ *He worked hard every day as a lawyer and went to parties and dances every night; he was burning the candle at both ends.*

burn the midnight oil *v. phr.* To study late at night. ♦ *Exam time was near, and more and more pupils were burning the midnight oil.*

burn to a crisp *v. phr.* To burn black; burn past saving or using especially as food. ♦ *While getting breakfast, Mother was called to the telephone, and when she got back, the bacon had been burned to a crisp.*

burn up *v.* **1.** To burn completely; destroy or be destroyed by fire. ♦ *Mr. Scott was burning up old letters.* ♦ *The house burned up before the firemen got there.* **2.** *informal* To irritate, anger, annoy. ♦ *The boy's laziness and rudeness burned up his teacher.* ♦ *The breakdown of his new car burned Mr. Jones up.*

burn up the road *v. phr., informal* To drive a car very fast. ♦ *In his eagerness to see his girl again, he burned up the road on his way to see her.* ♦ *Speed demons burning up the road often cause accidents.*

burst at the seams *v. phr., informal* To be too full or too crowded. ♦ *John ate so much he was bursting at the seams.* ♦ *Mary's album was so full of pictures it was bursting at the seams.*

burst into *v. phr.* **1.** To enter suddenly. ♦ *Stuart burst into the room, screaming angrily.* **2.** To break out. ♦ *The crowd burst out cheering when the astronauts paraded along Fifth Avenue.*

burst into flames *v. phr.* To begin to burn suddenly. ♦ *The children threw away some burning matches and the barn burst into flames.*

burst into tears *v. phr.* To suddenly start crying. ♦ *Mary burst into tears when she heard that her brother was killed in a car accident.*

burst with joy or pride *v. phr.* To be so full of the feeling of joy or pride that one cannot refrain from showing one's exuberant feelings. ♦ *Armstrong and Aldrin burst with pride when they*

stepped out on the moon in July, 1969.

bury one's head in the sand   See HIDE ONE'S HEAD IN THE SAND.

bury the hatchet *v. phr., informal* To settle a quarrel or end a war; make peace. ♦ *The two men had been enemies a long time, but after the flood they buried the hatchet.* Compare MAKE UP 5.

bus   See MISS THE BOAT *or* MISS THE BUS.

bush   See BEAT ABOUT THE BUSH, BIRD IN THE HAND IS WORTH TWO IN THE BUSH.

bushel   See HIDE ONE'S LIGHT UNDER A BUSHEL.

bushes   See BEAT THE BUSHES.

business   See DO THE BUSINESS, HAVE NO BUSINESS, LAND-OFFICE BUSINESS, MEAN BUSINESS, MONKEY BUSINESS, THE BUSINESS.

bust up *v. phr., slang* To terminate a partnership, a relationship, a friendship, or a marriage. ♦ *If Jack keeps drinking the way he does, it will bust up his marriage to Sue.*

busy work *n.* Work that is done not to do or finish anything important, but just to keep busy. ♦ *When the teacher finished all she had to say it was still a half hour before school was over. So she gave the class a test for busy work.*

but for   See EXCEPT FOR.

but good *adv. phr., informal* Very much so; thoroughly; completely; forcefully.—Used for emphasis. ♦ *Jack called Charles a bad name, and Charles hit him, but good.* ♦ *Tom fell and broke his leg. That taught him but good not to fool around in high trees.* Compare AND HOW.

but not least   See LAST BUT NOT LEAST.

butter   See BREAD AND BUTTER.

butterflies in one's stomach *n. phr.* A queer feeling in the stomach caused by nervous fear or uncertainty; a feeling of fear or anxiety in the stomach. ♦ *When Bob walked into the factory office to ask for a job, he had butterflies in his stomach.*

butter up *v., informal* To try to get the favor or friendship of (a person) by flattery or pleasantness. ♦ *He began to butter up the boss in hope of being given a better job.* Compare POLISH THE APPLE.

butter wouldn't melt in one's mouth *informal* You act very polite and friendly but do not really care, you are very nice to people but are not sincere. ♦ *The new secretary was rude to the other workers, but when she talked to the boss, butter wouldn't melt in her mouth.*

butt in *v., slang* To join in with what other people are doing without asking or being asked; interfere in other people's business; meddle. ♦ *Mary was explaining to Jane how to knit a sweater when Barbara butted in.* Often used with *on.* ♦ *John butted in on Bill and Tom's fight, and got hurt.* Compare HORN IN.

button See HAVE ALL ONE'S BUTTONS, ON THE BUTTON, PUSH THE PANIC BUTTON.

button down *v., slang* (stress on *down*) To state precisely, to ascertain, to pin down, to peg down. ♦ *First let's get the facts buttoned down, then we can plan ahead.*

button-down *attrib. adj., slang* (stress on *button*) Well-groomed, conservatively dressed. ♦ *Joe is a regular button-down type.*

buttonhole *v.* To approach a person in order to speak with him or her in private. ♦ *After waiting for several hours, Sam managed to buttonhole his boss just as she was about to leave the building.*

button one's lip *also* **zip one's lip** *v. phr., slang* To stop talking; keep a secret; shut your mouth; be quiet. ♦ *The man was getting loud and insulting and the cop told him to button his lip.* ♦ *John wanted to talk, but Dan told him to keep his lip buttoned.* Syn. KEEP ONE'S MOUTH SHUT, SHUT UP.

buy for a song *v. phr.* To buy something very cheaply. ♦ *Since the building on the corner was old and neglected, I was able to buy it for a song.*

buy off *v.* To turn from duty or purpose by a gift. ♦ *When the police threatened to stop the gambling business, the owner bought them off.* ♦ *The Indians were going to burn the cabins, but the men bought them off with gifts.* Compare PAY OFF.

buy out *v.* **1.** To buy the ownership or a share of; purchase the stock of. ♦ *He bought out several small stockholders.* **2.** To buy all the goods of; purchase the merchandise of. ♦ *Mr. Harper bought*

out a nearby hardware store. Contrast SELL OUT.

buy up *v. phr.* To purchase the entire stock of something. ♦ *The company is trying to buy up all the available shares.*

buzz See GIVE A RING *also* GIVE A BUZZ.

buzz word *n.* A word that sounds big and important in a sentence but, on closer inspection, means little except the speaker's indication to belong to a certain group. ♦ *The politician's speech was nothing but a lot of misleading statements and phony promises hidden in a bunch of buzz words.*

by See TOO ———BY HALF.

by a hair See HANG BY A THREAD *or* HANG BY A HAIR

by *or* **in my book** *adv. phr.* In my opinion; as far as I am concerned; in my judgment. ♦ *By my book, Mr. Murgatroyd is not a very good department head.*

by all means *also* **by all manner of means** *adv. phr.* Certainly, without fail. ♦ *He felt that he should by all means warn Jones.* Contrast BY NO MEANS.

by all odds *adv. phr.* Without question; certainly. ♦ *He was by all odds the strongest candidate.* ♦ *By all odds we should win the game, because the other team is so weak.* Compare FAR AND AWAY.

by a long shot *adv. phr., informal* By a big difference; by far.—Used to add emphasis. ♦ *Bert was the best swimmer in the race, by a long shot.* Often used with a negative. ♦ *Tom isn't the kind who would be fresh to a teacher, by a long shot.* ♦ *Our team didn't win—not by a long shot.* Compare MISS BY A MILE.

by a mile See MISS BY A MILE.

by and by *adv.* After a while; at some time in the future; later. ♦ *Roger said he would do his homework by and by.* ♦ *The mother knew her baby would be a man by and by and do a man's work.* Syn. AFTER A WHILE.

by and large *adv. phr.* As it most often happens; more often than not; usually; mostly. ♦ *There were bad days, but it was a pleasant summer, by and large.* ♦ *By and large, women can bear pain better than men.* Syn. FOR THE MOST PART, ON THE WHOLE 2.

by any means See BY NO MEANS.

by a thread See HANG BY A THREAD.

by chance *adv. phr.* Without any cause or reason; by accident; accidentally. ♦ *Tom met Bill by chance.* ♦ *The apple fell by chance on Bobby's head.*

by choice *adv. phr.* As a result of choosing because of wanting to; freely. ♦ *John helped his father by choice.* ♦ *Mary ate a plum, but not by choice. Her mother told her she must eat it.*

by dint of *prep.* By the exertion of; by the use of; through. ♦ *By dint of sheer toughness and real courage, he lived through the jungle difficulties and dangers.* ♦ *His success in college was largely by dint of hard study.*

bye See BY THE WAY *also* BY THE BYE.

by ear *adv. phr.* **1.** By sound, without ever reading the printed music of the piece being played. ♦ *The church choir sang the hymns by ear.* **2.** Waiting to see what will happen. ♦ *I don't want to plan now; let's just play it by ear.*

by far *adv. phr.* By a large difference; much. ♦ *His work was better by far than that of any other printer in the city.* ♦ *The old road is prettier, but it is by far the longer way.* Compare FAR AND AWAY.

by fits and starts *or* **jerks** *adv. phr.* With many stops and starts, a little now and a little more later; not all the time; irregularly. ♦ *He had worked on the invention by fits and starts for several years.* ♦ *You will never get anywhere if you study just by fits and starts.* Compare FROM TIME TO TIME, OFF AND ON.

bygone See LET BYGONES BE BYGONES.

by heart *adv. phr.* By exact memorizing; so well that you remember it; by memory. ♦ *The pupils learned many poems by heart.* ♦ *He knew the records of the major league teams by heart.*

by hook or by crook *adv. phr.* By honest ways or dishonest in any way necessary. ♦ *The wolf tried to get the little pigs by hook or by crook.* ♦ *The team was determined to win that last game by hook or by crook, and three players were put out of the game for fouling.*

by inches *adv. phr.* By small or slow degrees; little by little; gradually. ♦ *The river was rising by inches.* ♦ *They got a heavy wooden beam under the barn for a lever, and managed to move it by inches.* ♦ *He was dying by inches.*

by leaps and bounds *adv. phr.* With long steps; very rapidly. ♦ *Production in the factory was increasing by leaps and bounds.* ♦ *The school enrollment was going up by leaps and bounds.*

by means of *prep.* By the use of; with the help of. ♦ *The fisherman saved himself by means of a floating log.* ♦ *By means of monthly payments, people can buy more than in the past.*

by mistake *adv. phr.* As the result of a mistake; through error. ♦ *He picked up the wrong hat by mistake.*

by no means *or* **not by any means** *also* **by no manner of means** *or* **not by any manner of means** *adv. phr.* Not even a little; certainly not. ♦ *He is by no means bright.* ♦ *"May I stay home from school?" "By no means."* ♦ *Dick worked on his project Saturday, but he is not finished yet, by any means.* Contrast BY ALL MEANS.

B.Y.O. *(Abbreviation) informal* Bring Your Own. Said of a kind of party where the host or hostess does not provide the drinks or food but people bring their own.

B.Y.O.B. *(Abbreviation) informal* Bring Your Own Bottle. Frequently written on invitations for the kind of party where people bring their own liquor.

by oneself *adv. phr.* **1.** Without any others around; separate from others; alone. ♦ *The house stood by itself on a hill.* ♦ *Tom liked to go walking by himself.* ♦ *Betty felt very sad and lonely by herself.* **2.** Without the help of anyone else; by your own work only. ♦ *John built a flying model airplane by himself.* ♦ *Lois cleaned the house all by herself.*

by one's own bootstraps See PULL ONESELF UP BY THE BOOTSTRAPS.

by storm See TAKE BY STORM.

by surprise See TAKE BY SURPRISE.

by the board See GO BY THE BOARD *also* PASS BY THE BOARD.

by the bootstraps See PULL ONESELF UP BY THE BOOTSTRAPS.

by the bye See BY THE WAY.

by the dozen *or* **by the hundred** *or* **by the thousand** *adv. phr.* Very many at one time; in great numbers. ♦ *Tommy ate cookies by the dozen.* Often used in the plural, meaning even larger numbers. ♦ *The ants arrived at the picnic by the* *hundreds.* ♦ *The enemy attacked the fort by the thousands.*

by the horns See TAKE THE BULL BY THE HORNS.

by the hundred See BY THE DOZEN.

by the nose See LEAD BY THE NOSE.

by the piece *adv. phr.* Counted one piece at a time, separately for each single piece. ♦ *John bought boxes full of bags of potato chips and sold them by the piece.* ♦ *Mary made potholders and got paid by the piece.*

by the seat of one's pants See FLY BY THE SEAT OF ONE'S PANTS.

by the skin of one's teeth *adv. phr.* By a narrow margin; with no room to spare; barely. ♦ *The drowning man struggled, and I got him to land by the skin of my teeth.* ♦ *She passed English by the skin of her teeth.* Compare SQUEAK THROUGH, WITHIN AN ACE OF *or* WITHIN AN INCH OF.

by the sweat of one's brow *adv. phr.* By hard work; by tiring effort; laboriously. ♦ *Even with modern labor-saving machinery, the farmer makes his living by the sweat of his brow.*

by the thousand See BY THE DOZEN.

by the way *also* **by the bye** *adv. phr.* Just as some added fact or news; as something else that I think of.—Used to introduce something related to the general subject, or brought to mind by it. ♦ *We shall expect you; by the way,* *dinner will be at eight.* ♦ *I was reading when the earthquake occurred, and, by the way, it was* The Last Days of Pompeii *that I was reading.*

by the wayside See FALL BY THE WAYSIDE.

by turns *adv. phr.* First one and then another in a regular way; one substituting for or following another according to a repeated plan. ♦ *On the drive to Chicago, the three men took the wheel by turns.* ♦ *The teachers were on duty by turns.* ♦ *When John had a fever, he felt cold and hot by turns.* Syn. IN TURN. Compare TAKE TURNS.

by virtue of *also* **in virtue of** *prep.* On the strength of; because of; by reason of. ♦ *By virtue of his high rank and position, the President takes social leadership over almost everyone else.* ♦ *Plastic bags are useful for holding many kinds of food, by virtue of their clearness, toughness, and low cost.* Compare BY DINT OF.

by way of *prep.* **1.** For the sake or purpose of; as. ♦ *By way of example, he described his own experience.* **2.** Through; by a route including; via. ♦ *He went from New York to San Francisco by way of Chicago.*

by word of mouth *adv. phr.* From person to person by the spoken word; orally. ♦ *The news got around by word of mouth.* ♦ *The message reached him quietly by word of mouth.*

cahoots See IN LEAGUE WITH *or* IN CAHOOTS WITH.

Cain See RAISE CAIN.

cake See EAT-ONE'S CAKE AND HAVE IT TOO, PAT-A-CAKE, TAKE THE CAKE.

calculated risk *n.* An action that may fail but is judged more likely to succeed. ♦ *The sending of troops to the rebellious island was a calculated risk.*

calf love See PUPPY LOVE.

call See AT CALL, AT ONE'S BECK AND CALL, CLOSE CALL, ON CALL, PORT OF CALL, POT CALLS THE KETTLE BLACK, WITHIN CALL.

call a halt *v. phr.* To give a command to stop. ♦ *The scouts were tired during the hike, and the scoutmaster called a halt.* ♦ *When the children's play, got too noisy, their mother called a halt.*

call a spade a spade *v. phr.* To call a person or thing a name that is true but not polite; speak bluntly; use the plainest language. ♦ *A boy took some money from Dick's desk and said he borrowed it, but I told him he stole it; I believe in calling a spade a spade.*

call down *also* **dress down** *v., informal* To scold. ♦ *Jim was called down by his teacher for being late to class.* ♦ *Mother called Bob down for walking into the kitchen with muddy boots.* Compare CALL ON THE CARPET, CHEW OUT, BAWL OUT, READ THE RIOT ACT.

call for *v.* **1.** To come or go to get (someone or something). ♦ *John called for Mary to take her to the dance.* Syn. PICK UP. **2.** To need; require. ♦ *The cake recipe calls for two cups of flour.* ♦ *Success in school calls for much hard study.*

call girl *n., slang* A prostitute catering to wealthy clientele, especially one who is contacted by telephone for an appointment. ♦ *Rush Street is full of call girls.*

calling down *also* **dressing down** *n. phr., informal* A scolding; reprimand. ♦ *The judge gave the boy a calling down for speeding.*

call in question *or* **call into question** *or* **call in doubt** *v. phr.* To say (something) may be a mistake; express doubt about; question. ♦ *Bill called in ques-tion Ed's remark that basketball is safer than football.*

call it a day *v. phr.* To declare that a given day's work has been accomplished and go home; to quit for the day. ♦ *"Let's call it a day," the boss said, "and go out for a drink."* ♦ *It was nearly midnight, so Mrs. Byron decided to call it a day, and left the party, and went home.* ♦ *The four golfers played nine holes and then called it a day.* Compare CLOSE UP SHOP.

call it a night *v. phr.* To declare that an evening party or other activity conducted late in the day is finished. ♦ *I am so tired that I am going to call it a night and go to bed.*

call it quits *v. phr., informal* **1.** To decide to stop what you are doing; quit. ♦ *When Tom had painted half the garage, he called it quits.* **2.** To agree that each side in a fight is satisfied; stop fighting because a wrong has been paid back; say things are even. ♦ *Pete called Tom a bad name, and they fought till Tom gave Pete a bloody nose; then they called it quits.* **3.** To cultivate a habit no longer. ♦ *"Yes, I called it quits with cigarettes three years ago."*

call names *v. phr.* To use ugly or unkind words when speaking to someone or when talking about someone.—Usually used by or to children. ♦ *Bill got so mad he started calling Frank names.*

call off *v.* To stop (something planned); quit; cancel. ♦ *When the ice became soft and sloppy, we had to call off the ice-skating party.* ♦ *The baseball game was called off because of rain.*

call on *or* **call upon** *v.* **1.** To make a call upon; visit. ♦ *Mr. Brown called on an old friend while he was in the city.* **2.** To ask for help. ♦ *He called on a friend to give him money for the busfare to his home.*

call one's bluff *v. phr., informal* To ask someone to prove what he says he can or will do. (Originally from the card game of poker.) ♦ *Tom said he could jump twenty feet and so Dick called his bluff and said "Let's see you do it!"*

call one's shot *v. phr.* **1.** To tell before firing where a bullet will hit. ♦ *An* *expert rifleman can call his shot regularly.* ♦ *The wind was strong and John couldn't call his shots.* **2.** *or* **call the turn** To tell in advance the result of something before you do it. ♦ *Mary won three games in a row, just as she said she would. She called her turns well.* ♦ *Nothing ever happens as Tom says it will. He is very poor at calling his turns.*

call on the carpet *v. phr., informal* To call (a person) before an authority (as a boss or teacher) for a scolding or reprimand. ♦ *The worker was called on the carpet by the boss for sleeping on the job.* ♦ *The principal called Tom on the carpet and warned him to stop coming to school late.*

call the roll *v. phr.* To read out the names on a certain list, usually in alphabetical order. ♦ *The sergeant called the roll of the newly enlisted volunteers in the army.*

call the shots *v. phr., informal* To give orders; be in charge; direct; control. ♦ *Bob is a first-rate leader who knows how to call the shots.* ♦ *The quarterback called the shots well, and the team gained twenty yards in five plays.* Syn. CALL THE TUNE.

call the tune *v. phr., informal* To be in control; give orders or directions; command. ♦ *Bill was president of the club but Jim was secretary and called the tune.* ♦ *The people supported the mayor, so he could call the tune in city matters.* Syn. CALL THE SHOTS.

call the turn See CALL ONE'S SHOT 2.

call to account *v. phr.* **1.** To ask (someone) to explain why he did something wrong (as breaking a rule). ♦ *The principal called Jim to account after Jim left school early without permission.* **2.** To scold (as for wrong conduct); reprimand. ♦ *The father called his son to account for disobeying him.*

call to arms *v. phr.* To summon into the army. ♦ *During World War II millions of Americans were called to arms to fight for their country.*

call to mind *v. phr.* To remember; cause to remember. ♦ *Your story calls to mind a similar event that happened to us a few years back.*

call to order *v. phr.* **1.** To open (a meeting) formally. ♦ *The chairman* called the committee to order. ♦ *The president pounded with his gavel to call the convention to order.* **2.** To warn not to break the rules of a meeting. ♦ *The judge called the people in the court room to order when they talked too loud.*

call out *v. phr.* **1.** To shout; speak loudly. ♦ *My name was called out several times, but I was unable to hear it.* **2.** To summon someone. ♦ *If the rioting continues, the governor will have to call out the National Guard.*

call up *v.* **1.** To make someone think of; bring to mind; remind. ♦ *The picture of the Capitol called up memories of our class trip.* **2.** To tell to come (as before a court). ♦ *The district attorney called up three witnesses.* **3.** To bring together for a purpose; bring into action. ♦ *Jim called up all his strength, pushed past the players blocking him, and ran for a touchdown.* ♦ *The army called up its reserves when war seemed near.* **4.** To call on the telephone. ♦ *She called up a friend just for a chat.*

call upon See CALL ON.

calm down *v. phr.* To become quiet; relax. ♦ *"Calm down, Mr. Smith," the doctor said with a reassuring smile. "You are going to live a long time."*

camel See STRAW THAT BROKE THE CAMEL'S BACK *at* LAST STRAW.

camp See BREAK CAMP.

campaign See WHISPERING CAMPAIGN.

camp follower *n.* **1.** A man or woman who goes with an army, not to fight but to sell something. ♦ *Nowadays camp followers are not allowed as they were long ago.* **2.** A person who goes with a famous or powerful person or group in hope of profit. ♦ *A man who runs for president has many camp followers.*

camp out *v.* To live, cook, and sleep out of doors (as in a tent). ♦ *We camped out near the river for a week.*

can See AS BEST ONE CAN, CATCH AS CATCH CAN.

canary See LOOK LIKE THE CAT THAT ATE THE CANARY *or* LOOK LIKE THE CAT THAT SWALLOWED THE CANARY.

cancel out *v.* To destroy the effect of; balance or make useless. ♦ *The boy got an "A" in history to cancel out the "C" he got in arithmetic.* ♦ *Our track team won the mile relay to cancel out the* *other team's advantage in winning the half-mile relay.* ♦ *Tom's hot temper cancels out his skill as a player.*

cancer stick *n., slang* A cigarette. ♦ *Throw away that cancer stick! Smoking is bad for you!*

candle BURN THE CANDLE AT BOTH ENDS, GAME IS NOT WORTH THE CANDLE, HOLD A CANDLE.

canned heat *n.* Chemicals in a can which burn with a hot, smokeless flame. ♦ *Some people use canned heat to keep food warm.* ♦ *The mountain climbers used canned heat for cooking.*

canned laughter *n., informal* The sounds of laughter heard on certain television programs that were obviously not recorded in front of a live audience and are played for the benefit of the audience from a stereo track to underscore the funny points. ♦ *"How can there be an audience in this show when it is taking place in the jungle?—Why, it's canned laughter you're hearing."*

canned music *n.* Recorded music, as opposed to music played live. ♦ *"Let us go to a real concert, honey," Mike said. "I am tired of all this canned music we've been listening to."*

canoe See PADDLE ONE'S OWN CANOE.

can of worms *n., slang, informal* **1.** A complex problem, or complicated situation. ♦ *Let's not get into big city politics—that's a different can of worms.* **2.** A very restless, jittery person. ♦ *Joe can't sit still for a minute—he is a can of worms.*

can't help but *(informal)* ALSO *(formal)* **cannot but** *v. phr.* To be forced to; can only; must. ♦ *When the streets are full of melting snow, you can't help but get your shoes wet.* ♦ *When a friend gave Jim a ticket to the game, he couldn't help but go.* ♦ *When a close friend dies, you cannot but feel sad.* Compare CAN HELP, HAVE TO.

can't make an omelette without breaking (some) eggs To achieve a certain goal one must sometimes incur damage, experience difficulties, or make sacrifices.—A proverb. ♦ *When we drove across the country, we put a lot of mileage on our car and had a flat tire, but it was a pleasant trip. "Well, you can't make an omelette without breaking some eggs," my wife said with a smile.*

can't see the wood for the trees *or* **can't see the woods for the trees** *or* **can't see the forest for the trees** *v. phr.* To be unable to judge or understand the whole because of attention to the parts; criticize small things and not see the value or the aim of the future achievement. ♦ *Teachers sometimes notice language errors and do not see the good ideas in a composition; they cannot see the woods for the trees.* ♦ *The voters defeated a bond issue for the new school because they couldn't see the forest for the trees; they thought of their taxes rather than of their children's education.* ♦ *We should think of children's growth in character and understanding more than of their little faults and misdeeds; some of us can't see the wood for the trees.*

cap See FEATHER IN ONE'S CAP, SET ONE'S CAP FOR, PUT ON ONE'S THINKING CAP.

cap the climax *v. phr.* To exceed what is already a high point of achievement. ♦ *Sam's piano recital was great, but Bill's performance capped the climax.*

card See CREDIT CARD, FLASH CARD, HOUSE OF CARDS, IN THE CARDS *or* ON THE CARDS, LAY ONE'S CARDS ON THE TABLE, PLAY ONE'S CARDS RIGHT, PUT ONE'S CARDS ON THE TABLE, STACK THE CARDS, TRUMP CARD.

cards stacked against one See STACK THE CARDS.

card up one's sleeve *n. phr., informal* Another help, plan, or argument kept back and produced if needed; another way to do something. ♦ *John knew his mother would lend him money if necessary, but he kept that card up his sleeve.* ♦ *Bill always has a card up his sleeve, so when his first plan failed he tried another.* Compare ACE IN THE HOLE 2.

care See COULDN'T CARE LESS, HAVE A CARE, GIVE A HANG *or* CARE A HANG, TAKE CARE.

carpet See CALL ON THE CARPET, MAGIC CARPET, ROLL OUT THE RED CARPET.

car pool *n.* A group of people who own cars and take turns driving each other to work or on some other regular trip. ♦ *It was John's father's week to drive his own car in the car pool.*

carriage trade *n., literary* Rich or upper class people. ♦ *The hotel is so expensive that only the carriage trade stays there.*

♦ *The carriage trade buys its clothes at the best stores.*

carrot and stick *n. phr.* The promise of reward and threat of punishment, both at the same time. ♦ *John's father used the carrot and stick when he talked about his low grades.*

carry See CASH-AND-CARRY.

carry a torch *or* **carry the torch** *v. phr.* **1.** To show great and unchanging loyalty to a cause or a person. ♦ *Although the others gave up fighting for their rights, John continued to carry the torch.* **2.** *informal* To be in love, usually without success or return. ♦ *He is carrying a torch for Anna, even though she is in love with someone else.*

carry a tune *v. phr.* To sing the right notes without catching any false ones. ♦ *Al is a wonderful fellow, but he sure can't carry a tune and his singing is a pain to listen to.*

carry away *v.* To cause very strong feeling; excite or delight to the loss of cool judgment. ♦ *The music carried her away.* ♦ *He let his anger carry him away.*—Often used in the passive. ♦ *She was carried away by the man's charm.* ♦ *He was carried away by the sight of the flag.*

carry coals to Newcastle *v. phr.* To do something unnecessary; bring or furnish something of which there is plenty. ♦ *The man who waters his grass after a good rain is carrying coals to Newcastle.* ♦ *Joe was carrying coals to Newcastle when he told the doctor how to cure a cold.* [Newcastle is an English city near many coal mines, and coal is sent out from there to other places.]

carrying charge *n.* An extra cost added to the price of something bought on weekly or monthly payments. ♦ *The price of the bicycle was $50. Jim bought it for $5.00 a month for ten months plus a carrying charge of $1 a month.*

carry off *v.* **1.** To cause death of; kill. ♦ *Years ago smallpox carried off hundreds of Indians of the Sioux tribe.* Compare WIPE OUT. **2.** To succeed in winning. ♦ *Bob carried off honors in science.* ♦ *Jim carried off two gold medals in the track meet.* **3.** To succeed somewhat unexpectedly in. ♦ *The spy planned to deceive the enemy soldiers and carried it off very well.* ♦ *In the class play, Lloyd carried off his part surprisingly well.*

carry ———— off one's feet See KNOCK OFF ONE'S FEET, SWEEP OFF ONE'S FEET.

carry off the palm *or* **bear off the palm** *v. phr., literary* To gain the victory; win. ♦ *John carried off the palm in the tennis championship match.* ♦ *Our army bore off the palm in the battle.* [From the fact that long ago a palm leaf was given to the winner in a game as a sign of victory.]

carry on *v.* **1.** To work at; be busy with; manage. ♦ *Bill and his father carried on a hardware business.* ♦ *Mr. Jones and Mr. Smith carried on a long correspondence with each other.* **2.** To keep doing as before; continue. ♦ *After his father died, Bill carried on with the business.* ♦ *The colonel told the soldiers to carry on while he was gone.* ♦ *Though tired and hungry, the Scouts carried on until they reached camp.* Compare BEAR UP 2, GO ON **3a.** *informal* To behave in a noisy, foolish, and troublesome manner. ♦ *The boys carried on in the swimming pool until the lifeguard ordered them out.* **3b.** *informal* To make too great a show of feeling, such as anger, grief, and pain. ♦ *John carried on for ten minutes after he hit his thumb with the hammer.* Compare TAKE ON 4. **4.** *informal* To act in an immoral or scandalous way; act disgracefully. ♦ *The townspeople said that he was carrying on with a neighbor girl.*

carry one's cross *or* (*literary*) **bear one's cross** *v. phr.* To live with pain or trouble; keep on even though you suffer or have trouble. ♦ *Weak ankles are a cross Joe carries while the other boys play basketball.* ♦ *We didn't know the cheerful woman was bearing her cross, a son in prison.*

carry out *v.* To put into action; follow; execute. ♦ *The generals were determined to carry out their plans to defeat the enemy.* ♦ *John listened carefully and carried out the teacher's instructions.*

carry over *v.* **1.** To save for another time. ♦ *The store had some bathing suits it had carried over from last year.* ♦ *What you learn in school should carry over into adult life.* **2.** To transfer (as a figure) from one column, page, or book to another. ♦ *When he added up the figures, he carried over the total into the next year's account book.* **3.** To continue in another place. ♦ *The story was carried over to the next page.*

carry the ball *v. phr., informal* To take the most important or difficult part in an action or business. ♦ *None of the other boys would tell the principal about their breaking the window, and John had to carry the ball.* ♦ *When the going is rough, Fred can always be depended on to carry the ball.*

carry the banner *v. phr.* To support a cause or an ideal with obvious advocacy. ♦ *Our college is carrying the banner for saving the humpback whale, which is on the list of endangered species.*

carry the day *v. phr., informal* To win completely; to succeed in getting one's aim accomplished. ♦ *The defense attorney's summary before the jury helped him carry the day.*

carry the torch See CARRY A TORCH.

carry the weight of the world on one's shoulders See WEIGHT OF THE WORLD ON ONE'S SHOULDERS.

carry through *v.* **1a.** To put into action. ♦ *Mr. Green was not able to carry through his plans for a hike because he broke his leg.* **1b.** To do something you have planned; put a plan into action. ♦ *Jean makes good plans but she cannot carry through with any of them.* Compare GO THROUGH WITH, CARRY OUT. **2.** To keep (someone) from failing or stopping; bring through; help. ♦ *When the tire blew out, the rules Jim had learned in driving class carried him through safely.*

carry weight *n.* To be influential; have significance and/or clout; impress. ♦ *A letter of recommendation from a full professor carries more weight than a letter from an assistant professor.*

cart before the horse (to put) *n. phr., informal* Things in wrong order; something backwards or mixed up.—An overused expression. Usually used with *put* but sometimes with *get* or *have.* ♦ *When the salesman wanted money for goods he hadn't delivered, I told him he was putting the cart before the horse.* ♦ *To get married first and then get a job is getting the cart before the horse.*

cart off *or* **cart away** *v., informal* To take away, often with force or with rough handling or behavior. ♦ *The police carted the rioters off to jail.* ♦ *When Bobby wouldn't eat his supper, his mother carted him away to bed.*

carved *or* **chiseled** *or* **inscribed in granite / written in stone** *adj. phr.* Holy; unchangeable; noble and of ancient origin. ♦ *You should wear shoes when you come to class, although this is not carved in granite.* ♦ *The Constitution of the United States is so hard to change that one thinks of it as written in stone.*

case See BASKET CASE, CIRCUMSTANCES ALTER CASES, COUCH CASE, GET DOWN TO BRASS TACKS *also* GET DOWN TO CASES, IN ANY CASE, IN CASE *or* IN THE EVENT, IN CASE OF *also* IN THE EVENT OF, VANITY CASE.

case in point *n. phr.* An example that proves something or helps to make something clearer. ♦ *An American can rise from the humblest beginnings to become President. Abraham Lincoln is a case in point.*

case the joint *v. phr., slang* **1.** To study the layout of a place one wishes to burglarize. ♦ *The hooded criminals carefully cased the joint before robbing the neighborhood bank.* **2.** To familiarize oneself with a potential workplace or vacation spot as a matter of preliminary planning. ♦ *"Hello Fred," he said. "Are you working here now?" "No, not yet," Fred answered. "I am merely casing the joint."*

cash See COLD CASH.

cash-and-carry[1] *adj.* Selling things for cash money only and letting the customer carry them home, not having the store deliver them; *also* sold in this way. ♦ *This is a cash-and-carry store only.* ♦ *You can save money at a cash-and-carry sale.*

cash-and-carry[2] *adv.* With no credit, no time payments, and no deliveries. ♦ *Some stores sell cash-and-carry only.* ♦ *It is cheaper to buy cash-and-carry.*

cash crop *n.* A crop grown to be sold. ♦ *Cotton is a cash crop in the South.* ♦ *They raise potatoes to eat, but tobacco is their cash crop.*

cash in *v.* **1.** To exchange (as poker chips or bonds) for the value in money.

♦ *He paid the bill by cashing in some bonds.* ♦ *When the card game ended, the players cashed in their chips and went home.* **2.** *or* **cash in one's chips** *slang* To die. ♦ *When the outlaw cashed in his chips, he was buried with his boots on.* ♦ *He was shot through the body and knew he was going to cash in.*

cash in on *v., informal* To see (a chance) and profit by it; take advantage of (an opportunity or happening). ♦ *Mr. Brown cashed in on people's great interest in camping and sold three hundred tents.*

cash on the barrelhead *n. phr., informal* Money paid at once; money paid when something is bought. ♦ *Father paid cash on the barrelhead for a new car.* ♦ *Some lawyers want cash on the barrelhead.* Compare COLD CASH.

cast *or* **shed** *or* **throw light upon** *v. phr.* To explain; illuminate; clarify. ♦ *The letters that were found suddenly cast a new light on the circumstances of Tom's disappearance.* ♦ *Einstein's General Theory of Relativity threw light upon the enigma of our universe.*

cast about *also* **cast around** *v., literary* **1.** To look everywhere; search. ♦ *The committee was casting about for an experienced teacher to take the retiring principal's place.* **2.** To search your mind; try to remember something; try to think of something. ♦ *The teacher cast about for an easy way to explain the lesson.* ♦ *Jane cast around for a good subject for her report.*

cast down *adj.* Discouraged; sad; unhappy.—Used less often than the reverse form, *downcast.* ♦ *Mary was cast down at the news of her uncle's death.* ♦ *Charles felt cast down when he lost the race.*

cast in one's lot with *formal* See THROW IN ONE'S LOT WITH.

castle in the air See BUILD CASTLES IN THE AIR.

castles in Spain See CASTLES IN THE AIR.

cast off *v.* **1a.** *or* **cast loose** To unfasten; untie; let loose (as a rope holding a boat). ♦ *The captain of the boat cast off the line and we were soon out in open water.* **1b.** To untie a rope holding a boat or something suggesting a boat. ♦ *We cast off and set sail at 6 A.M.* **2.** To knit the last row of stitches. ♦ *When*

she had knitted the twentieth row of stitches she cast off. **3.** To say that you do not know (someone) any more; not accept as a relative or friend. ♦ *Mr. Jones cast off his daughter when she married against his wishes.*

cast one's lot with See THROW IN ONE'S LOT WITH.

cast out *v., formal* To force (someone) to go out or away; banish; expel. ♦ *After the scandal, he was cast out of the best society.* Compare CAST OFF 3.

cast pearls before swine *or* **cast one's pearls before swine** *n. phr., literary* To waste good acts or valuable things on someone who won't understand or be thankful for them, just as pigs won't appreciate pearls.—Often used in negative sentences. ♦ *I won't waste good advice on John any more because he never listens to it. I won't cast pearls before swine.*

cast the first stone *v. phr., literary* To be the first to blame someone, lead accusers against a wrongdoer. ♦ *Jesus said that a person who was without sin could cast the first stone.* ♦ *Although Ben saw the girl cheating, he did not want to cast the first stone.*

cast up *v. literary* **1.** To turn or direct upward; raise. ♦ *The dying missionary cast up his eyes to heaven and prayed.* **2.** *archaic* To do sums; do a problem in addition; add. ♦ *Cast up 15, 43, 27, and 18.* ♦ *When John had all the figures, he cast them up.*

cat See COPY CAT, CURIOSITY KILLED THE CAT, FRAIDY-CAT *or* FRAID-CAT *or* SCAREDY CAT *or* SCARED-CAT, HOLY CATS, LET THE CAT OUT OF THE BAG, LOOK LIKE THE CAT THAT ATE THE CANARY, PLAY CAT AND MOUSE WITH, RAIN CATS AND DOGS.

catch SEE EARLY BIRD CATCHES THE WORM, FAIR CATCH, SHOESTRING CATCH.

catch-as-catch-can¹ *adv. phr.* In a free manner; in any way possible; in the best way you can. ♦ *On moving day everything is packed and we eat meals catch-as-catch-can.*

catch-as-catch-can² *adj. phr.* Using any means or method; unplanned; free. ♦ *Rip van Winkle seems to have led a catch-as-catch-can life.* ♦ *Politics is rather a catch-as-catch-can business.* Compare HIT-OR-MISS.

catch at *v.* **1.** To try to catch suddenly; grab for. ♦ *The boy on the merry-go-round caught at the brass ring, but did not get it.* **2.** To seize quickly; accept mentally or physically. ♦ *The hungry man caught at the sandwich and began to eat.* ♦ *Joe caught at Bill's offer to help.*

catch at a straw See GRASP AT STRAWS.

catch cold *v. phr.* **1.** *or* **take cold** To get a common cold-weather sickness that causes a running nose, sneezing, and sometimes sore throat and fever or other symptoms. ♦ *Don't get your feet wet or you'll catch cold.* **2.** *informal* To catch unprepared or not ready for a question or unexpected happening. ♦ *I had not studied my lesson carefully, and the teacher's question caught me cold.* ♦ *The opposing team was big and sure of winning, and they were caught cold by the fast, hard playing of our smaller players.*

catch (someone) dead *v. phr., informal* To see or hear (someone) in an embarrassing act or place at any time. Used in the negative usually in the passive. ♦ *You won't catch Bill dead taking his sister to the movies.* ♦ *John wouldn't be caught dead in the necktie he got for Christmas.*

catch fire *v. phr.* **1.** To begin to burn. ♦ *When he dropped a match in the leaves, they caught fire.* **2.** To become excited. ♦ *The audience caught fire at the speaker's words and began to cheer.* ♦ *His imagination caught fire as he read.*

catch flat-footed See FLAT-FOOTED 2.

catch forty winks See FORTY WINKS.

catch hold of *v. phr.* To grasp a person or a thing. ♦ *"I've been trying to catch hold of you all week," John said, "but you were out of town."* ♦ *The mountain climber successfully caught hold of his friend's hand and thereby saved his life.*

catch it *or* **get it** *v. phr., informal* To be scolded or punished.—Usually used of children. ♦ *John knew he would catch it when he came home late for supper.* ♦ *Wow, Johnny! When your mother sees those torn pants, you're going to get it.* Compare GET WHAT'S COMING TO ONE. Contrast GIVE IT TO 2.

catch it in the neck *or* **get it in the neck** *v. phr., slang* To be blamed or punished. ♦ *Tom got it in the neck because he forgot to close the windows when it rained.* ♦ *Students get it in the neck when they lose library books.* Compare CATCH IT, GET WHAT'S COMING TO ONE.

catch off balance *v. phr.* To confront someone with physical force or with a statement or question he or she is not prepared to answer or deal with; to exploit the disadvantage of another. ♦ *The smaller wrestler caught his opponent off balance and managed to throw him on the floor in spite of his greater weight and strength.* ♦ *Your question has caught me off balance; please give me some time to think about your problem.*

catch off guard *v. phr.* To challenge or confront a person at a time of lack of preparedness or sufficient care. ♦ *The suspect was caught off guard by the detective and confessed where he had hidden the stolen car.*

catch on *v., informal* **1.** To understand; learn about.—Often used with *to.* ♦ *You'll catch on to the job after you've been here awhile.* ♦ *Don't play any tricks on Joe. When he catches on, he will beat you.* **2.** To become popular; be done or used by many people. ♦ *The song caught on and was sung and played everywhere.* **3.** To be hired; get a job. ♦ *The ball player caught on with a big league team last year.*

catch one's breath *v. phr.* **1.** To breathe in suddenly with fear or surprise. ♦ *The beauty of the scene made him catch his breath.* Compare TAKE ONE'S BREATH AWAY. **2a.** To rest and get back your normal breathing, as after running. ♦ *After running to the bus stop, we sat down to catch our breath.* **2b.** To relax for a moment after any work. ♦ *After the day's work we sat down over coffee to catch our breath.*

catch one's death of *or* **take one's death of** *v. phr., informal* To become very ill with (a cold, pneumonia, flu). ♦ *Johnny fell in the icy water and almost took his death of cold.* Sometimes used in the short form *"catch your death."* ♦ *"Johnny! Come right in here and put your coat and hat on. You'll catch your death!"*

catch one's eye *v. phr.* To attract your attention. ♦ *I caught his eye as he* *moved through the crowd, and waved at him to come over.* ♦ *The dress in the window caught her eye when she passed the store.*

catch red-handed *v. phr.* To apprehend a person during the act of committing an illicit or criminal act. ♦ *Al was caught red-handed at the local store when he was trying to walk out with a new camera he had not paid for.*

catch sight of *v. phr.* To see suddenly or unexpectedly. ♦ *Allan caught sight of a kingbird in a maple tree.* Contrast LOSE SIGHT OF.

catch some rays *v. phr., slang, informal* To get tanned while sunbathing. ♦ *Tomorrow I'll go to the beach and try to catch some rays.*

catch some Z's *v. phr., slang, informal* To take a nap, to go to sleep. (Because of the *z* sound resembling snoring.) ♦ *I want to hit the sack and catch some Z's.*

catch-22 *n., informal* From Joseph Heller's novel *Catch-22*, set in World War II. A regulation or situation that is self-contradictory or that conflicts with another regulation. In Heller's book it referred to the regulation that flight crews must report for duty unless excused for reasons of insanity, but that any one claiming such an excuse must, by definition, be sane. ♦ *Government rules require workers to expose any wrongdoing in their office, but the Catch-22 prevents them from their doing so, because they are not allowed to disclose any information about their work.* **2.** A paradoxical situation. ♦ *The Catch-22 of job-hunting was that the factory wanted to hire only workers who had experience making computers but the only way to get the experience was by working at the computer factory.*

catch up *v.* **1.** To take or pick up suddenly; grab (something). ♦ *She caught up the book from the table and ran out of the room.* **2.** To capture or trap (someone) in a situation; concern or interest very much.—Usually used in the passive with *in.* ♦ *The Smith family was caught up in the war in Europe and we did not see them again till it was over.* ♦ *We were so caught up in the movie we forgot what time it was.* Compare MIX UP. **3.** To go fast enough

or do enough so as not to be behind; overtake; come even.—Often used with *to* or *with.* ♦ *Johnny ran hard and tried to catch up to his friends.* ♦ *Mary missed two weeks of school; she must work hard to catch up with her class.* Compare UP TO. **4.** To find out about or get proof to punish or arrest.— Usually used with *with.* ♦ *A man told the police where the robbers were hiding, so the police finally caught up with them.* **5.** To result in something bad; bring punishment.—Usually used with *with.* ♦ *The boy's fighting caught up with him and he was expelled from school.* ♦ *Smoking will catch up with you.* Compare CHICKENS COME HOME TO ROOST. **6.** To finish; not lose or be behind.—Used with *on* and often in the phrase *get caught up on.* ♦ *Frank stayed up late to get caught up on his homework.* ♦ *I have to catch up on my sleep.* ♦ *We caught up on all the latest news when we got back to school and saw our friends again.* Syn. KEEP UP.

catch with one's pants down *v. phr., slang* To surprise someone in an embarrassing position or guilty act. ♦ *They thought they could succeed in the robbery, but they got caught with their pants down.* ♦ *When the weather turned hot in May, the drive-in restaurant was caught with its pants down, and ran out of ice cream before noon.*

cat got one's tongue You are not able or willing to talk because of shyness. Usually used about children or as a question to children. ♦ *Tommy's father asked Tommy if the cat had got his tongue.* ♦ *The little girl had a poem to recite, but the cat got her tongue.* Compare LOSE ONE'S TONGUE.

cat has nine lives A cat can move so fast and jump so well that he seems to escape being killed many times. ♦ *We thought our cat would be killed when he fell from the roof of the house. He was not, but he used up one of his nine lives.*

cathouse *n., slang* A house of ill repute, a house of prostitution. ♦ *Massage parlors are frequently cathouses in disguise.*

cat's meow *or* **cat's pajamas** *n. slang* Something very wonderful, special, or good. ♦ *John's new bike is really the cat's meow.* ♦ *Mary's party is going to* *be the cat's pajamas.*

caught short *adj. phr., informal* Not having enough of something when you need it. ♦ *Mrs. Ford was caught short when the newspaper boy came for his money a day early.* ♦ *The man was caught short of clothes when he had to go on a trip.*

cause eyebrows to raise *v. phr.* To do something that causes consternation; to shock others. ♦ *When Algernon entered Orchestra Hall barefoot and wearing a woman's wig, he caused eyebrows to raise.*

cause tongues to wag See TONGUES TO WAG.

caution See THROW CAUTION TO THE WINDS.

cave in *v.* **1.** To fall or collapse inward. ♦ *The mine caved in and crushed three miners.* ♦ *Don't climb on that old roof. It might cave in.* **2.** *informal* To weaken and be forced to give up. ♦ *The children begged their father to take them to the circus until he caved in.* ♦ *After the atomic bomb, Japan caved in and the war ceased.*

cease fire *v.* To give a military command ordering soldiers to stop shooting. ♦ *"Cease fire!" the captain cried, and the shooting stopped.*

cease-fire *n.* A period of negotiated nonaggression, when the warring parties involved promise not to attack. ♦ *Unfortunately, the cease-fire in Bosnia was broken many times by all parties concerned.*

ceiling See HIT THE CEILING *or* HIT THE ROOF.

cent See TWO CENTS, WORTH A CENT.

center See FRONT AND CENTER, OFF-CENTER, SHOPPING CENTER.

century See TURN OF THE CENTURY.

C.E.O. *n.* Abbreviation of "Chief Executive Officer." The head of a company, factory, firm, etc. ♦ *We are very proud of the fact that our C.E.O. is a young woman.*

ceremony See STAND ON CEREMONY.

certain See FOR SURE *or* FOR CERTAIN.

chain gang *n.* A group of convicts or slaves in the old South who were chained together. ♦ *Chain gangs are no longer an acceptable way of punishment, according to modern criminologists.*

chain letter *n.* A letter which each person receiving it is asked to copy and send to several others. ♦ *Most chain letters die out quickly.*

chain-smoke *v.* To smoke cigarettes or cigars one after another without stopping. ♦ *Mr. Jones is very nervous. He chain-smokes cigars.* **chain smoker** *n.* ♦ *Mr. Jones is a chain smoker.* **chain-smoking** *adj. or n.* ♦ *Chain smoking is very dangerous to health.*

chain stores *n.* A series of stores in different locations, joined together under one ownership and general management. ♦ *The goods in chain stores tend to be more uniform than in independent ones.*

chained to the oars *adj. phr.* The condition of being forced to do strenuous and unwelcome labor against one's wishes for an extended period of time. ♦ *Teachers in large public schools frequently complain that they feel as if they had been chained to the oars.*

chair See MUSICAL CHAIRS.

chalk See WALK THE CHALK.

chalk up *v., informal* **1.** To write down as part of a score; record. ♦ *The scorekeeper chalked up one more point for the home team.* **2.** To make (a score or part of a score); score. ♦ *The team chalked up another victory.* ♦ *Bob chalked up a home run and two base hits in the game.* ♦ *Mary chalked up good grades this term.*

champ at the bit *v. phr.* To be eager to begin; be tired of being held back; want to start. ♦ *The horses were champing at the bit, anxious to start racing.* ♦ *As punishment John was kept after school for two hours. He was champing at the bit to go out.*

chance See BY CHANCE, FAT CHANCE, STAND A CHANCE, TAKE A CHANCE.

chance it *v. phr.* To be willing to risk an action whose outcome is uncertain. ♦ *"Should we take the boat out in such stormy weather?" Jim asked. "We can chance it," Tony replied. "We have enough experience."*

chance on *also* **chance upon** *v.* To happen to find or meet; find or meet by accident. ♦ *On our vacation we chanced upon an interesting antique store.* ♦ *Mary dropped her ring in the yard, and Mother chanced on it as she was raking.* Syn. HAPPEN ON. Compare

RUN INTO.

change See RING THE CHANGES.

change color *v. phr.* **1.** To become pale. ♦ *The sight was so horrible that Mary changed color from fear.* ♦ *Bill lost so much blood from the cut that he changed color.* **2.** To become pink or red in the face; become flushed; blush. ♦ *Mary changed color when the teacher praised her drawing.* ♦ *Tom got angry at the remark and changed color.*

change hands *v. phr.* To change or transfer ownership. ♦ *Ever since our apartment building changed hands, things are working a lot better.*

change horses in the middle of a stream or **change horses in midstream** *v. phr.* To make new plans or choose a new leader in the middle of an important activity. ♦ *When a new President is to be elected during a war, the people may decide not to change horses in the middle of a stream.*

change off *v., informal* To take turns doing something; alternate. ♦ *John and Bill changed off at riding the bicycle.* ♦ *Bob painted one patch of wall and then he changed off with Tom.*

change of heart *n. phr.* A change in the way one feels or thinks about a given task, idea or problem to be solved. ♦ *Joan had a change of heart and suddenly broke off her engagement to Tim.* ♦ *Fred got admitted to medical school, but he had a change of heart and decided to go into the Foreign Service instead.*

change of life *n. phr.* The menopause (primarily in women). ♦ *Women usually undergo a change of life in their forties or fifties.*

change of pace *n. phr.* **1.** A quick change in what you are doing. ♦ *John studied for three hours and then read a comic book for a change of pace.* ♦ *The doctor told the man he needed a change of pace.*

change one's mind *v. phr.* To alter one's opinion or judgment on a given issue. ♦ *I used to hate Chicago, but as the years passed I gradually changed my mind and now I actually love living here.*

change one's tune *v. phr., informal* To make a change in your story, statement, or claim; change your way of acting. ♦ *The man said he was innocent, but when they found the stolen money in his pocket he changed his tune.* ♦ *Bob was rude to his teacher, but she threatened to tell the principal and he changed his tune.* Syn. SING A DIFFERENT TUNE.

change up See LET UP 4.

character See IN CHARACTER.

charge See CARRYING CHARGE, CHARGE OFF 2, IN CHARGE, IN CHARGE OF, TAKE CHARGE.

charge account *n.* An agreement with a store through which you can buy things and pay for them later. ♦ *Mother bought a new dress on her charge account.* ♦ *Mr. Jones has a charge account at the garage on the corner.*

charge off *v.* **1.** To consider or record as a loss, especially in an account book. ♦ *The store owner charged off all of the last season's stock of suits.* Syn. WRITE OFF 1. **2.** or **charge up** *informal* To accept or remember (something) as a mistake and not worry about it any more.—Often used with *to experience.* ♦ *He charged off his mistakes to experience.* Syn. CHALK UP. Compare CHARGE TO.

charge something to something *v.* **1.** To place the blame on; make responsible for. ♦ *John failed to win a prize, but he charged it to his lack of experience.* ♦ *The coach charged the loss of the game to the team's disobeying his orders.* **2.** To buy something on the credit of. ♦ *Mrs. Smith bought a new pocketbook and charged it to her husband.* ♦ *Mr. White ordered a box of cigars and had it charged to his account.*

charge up *v. phr.* **1.** To submit to a flow of electricity in order to make functional. ♦ *I mustn't forget to charge up my razor before we go on our trip.* **2.** To use up all the available credit one has on one's credit card(s). ♦ *"Let's charge dinner on the Master Card,"* *Jane said. "Unfortunately I can't," Jim replied. "All of my credit cards are completely charged up."*

charge with *v. phr.* To accuse someone in a court of law. ♦ *The criminal was charged with aggravated kidnapping across a state line.*

charmed life *n.* A life often saved from

danger; a life full of lucky escapes. ♦ *He was in two airplane accidents, but he had a charmed life.* ♦ *During the war a bullet knocked the gun out of his hand, but he had a charmed life.*

chase See GIVE CHASE, GO CHASE ONE-SELF, LEAD A MERRY CHASE.

chase after See RUN AFTER.

chase around See RUN AROUND.

cheapskate *n., informal* A selfish or stingy person; a person who will not spend much.—An insulting term. ♦ *None of the girls like to go out on a date with him because he is a cheap-skate.*

cheat on someone *v. phr., informal* To be unfaithful (to one's wife or husband, or to one's sweetheart or fiancee). ♦ *It is rumored that Joe cheats on his wife.*

check See BLANK CHECK, CLAIM CHECK, DOUBLE CHECK, IN CHECK, RAIN CHECK, RUBBER CHECK, SALES CHECK.

check in *v.* **1a.** To sign your name (as at a hotel or convention). ♦ *The last guests to reach the hotel checked in at 12 o'clock.* Contrast CHECK OUT. **1b.** *informal* To arrive. ♦ *The friends we had invited did not check in until Saturday.* **2.** To receive (something) back and make a record of it. ♦ *The coach checked in the football uniforms at the end of the school year.* ♦ *The students put their books on the library desk, and the librarian checked them in.*

check off *v.* To put a mark beside (the name of a person or thing on a list) to show that it has been counted. ♦ *The teacher checked off each pupil as he got on the bus.* ♦ *Bill wrote down the names of all the states he could remember, and then he checked them off against the list in his book.* Compare TICK OFF.

check on someone/thing *or* **check up on someone/thing** *v.* To try to find out the truth or rightness of; make sure of; examine; inspect; investigate. ♦ *We checked on Dan's age by getting his birth record.* ♦ *Mrs. Brown said she heard someone downstairs and Mr. Brown went down to check up on it.* ♦ *You can check on your answers at the back of the book.* ♦ *The police are checking up on the man to see if he has a police record.* ♦ *Grandfather went to have the doctor check on his health.* Compare LOOK INTO, LOOK OVER.

check out *v.* **1a.** To pay your hotel bill and leave. ♦ *The last guests checked out of their rooms in the morning.* Contrast CHECK IN. **1b.** *informal* To go away; leave. ♦ *I hoped our guest would stay but he had to check out before Monday.* Compare CHECK IN. **2a.** To make a list or record of. ♦ *They checked out all the goods in the store.* **2b.** To give or lend (something) and make a record of it. ♦ *The boss checked out the tools to the workmen as they came to work.* **2c.** To get (something) after a record has been made of it. ♦ *I checked out a book from the library.* **3.** *informal* To test (something, like a part of a motor). ♦ *The mechanic checked out the car battery.* ♦ *"He checked out from the motel at nine," said the detective, "then he checked out the air in the car tires and his list of local clients."* **4.** *slang* To die. ♦ *He seemed too young to check out.*

check up *v.* To find out or try to find out the truth or correctness of something; make sure of something; investigate. ♦ *Mrs. Brown thought she had heard a burglar in the house, so Mr. Brown checked up, but found nobody.* ♦ *Bill thought he had a date with Janie, but phoned her to check up.*

check-up *n.* A periodic examination by a physician or of some equipment by a mechanic. ♦ *I am overdue for my annual physical check-up.* ♦ *I need to take my car in for a check-up.*

check with *v. phr.* **1.** To consult. ♦ *I want to check with my lawyer before I sign the papers.* **2.** To agree with. ♦ *Does my reconciliation of our account check with the bank statement?*

cheek See TURN THE OTHER CHEEK.

cheer See BRONX CHEER.

cheer on *v. phr.* To vociferously encourage a person or a team during a sports event. ♦ *The spectators at the stadium cheered on their home team.*

cheer up *v.* **1.** To feel happy; stop being sad or discouraged; become hopeful, joyous, or glad. ♦ *Jones was sad at losing the business, but he cheered up at the sight of his daughter.* ♦ *Cheer up! The worst is over.* **2.** To make cheerful or happy. ♦ *The support of the students cheered up the losing team and they played harder and won.* ♦ *We went to* *the hospital to cheer up a sick friend.* ♦ *Flowers cheer up a room.*

cheese See BIG CHEESE, WHOLE CHEESE.

cheesebox *n., slang* A small, suburban house built by a land developer available at low cost and resembling the other houses around it. ♦ *They moved to a suburb, but their house is just a cheesebox.*

cheesecake *n., slang, informal* A showing of the legs of an attractive woman or a display of her breasts as in certain magazines known as cheesecake magazines. ♦ *Photographer to model: "Give us some cheesecake in that pose!"*

cherry farm *n., slang* A correctional institution of minimal security where the inmates, mostly first offenders, work as farmhands. ♦ *Joe got a light sentence and was sent to a cherry farm for six months.*

chest See OFF ONE'S CHEST, ON ONE'S CHEST.

chew See BITE OFF MORE THAN ONE CAN CHEW.

chew out *v., slang* To scold roughly. ♦ *The boy's father chewed him out for staying up late.* ♦ *The coach chews out lazy players.* Syn. BAWL OUT, CALL ON THE CARPET, HAUL OVER THE COALS.

chew the fat *or* **chew the rag** *v. phr., slang* To talk together in an idle, friendly fashion; chat. ♦ *We used to meet after work, and chew the fat over coffee and doughnuts.* ♦ *The old man would chew the rag for hours with anyone who would join him.*

chew the scenery *v. phr., slang* To act overemotionally in a situation where it is inappropriate; to engage in histrionics. ♦ *I don't know if Joe was sincere about our house, but he sure chewed up the scenery!*

chicken See COUNT ONE'S CHICKENS BEFORE THEY ARE HATCHED, GO TO BED WITH THE CHICKENS, SPRING CHICKEN.

chicken-brained *adj.* Stupid; narrow-minded; unimaginative. ♦ *I can't understand how a bright woman like Helen can date such a chicken-brained guy as Oliver.*

chicken feed *n., slang* A very small sum of money. ♦ *John and Bill worked very hard, but they were only paid chicken*

feed. ♦ *Mr. Jones is so rich he thinks a thousand dollars is chicken feed.*

chicken-hearted *adj.* Cowardly; excessively timid. ♦ *"Come on, let's get on that roller coaster," she cried. "Don't be so chicken-hearted."* See CHICKEN-LIVERED.

chicken-livered *adj., slang, colloquial* Easily scared; cowardly. ♦ *Joe sure is a chicken-livered guy.* See CHICKEN-HEARTED.

chicken out *v. phr., informal* To stop doing something because of fear; to decide not to do something after all even though previously having decided to try it. ♦ *I used to ride a motorcycle on the highway, but I've chickened out.* ♦ *I decided to take flying lessons but just before they started I chickened out.*

chickens come home to roost *informal* Words or acts come back to cause trouble for a person; something bad you said or did receives punishment; you get the punishment that you deserve. ♦ *Fred's chickens finally came home to roost today. He was late so often that the teacher made him go to the principal.*—Often used in a short form. ♦ *Mary's selfishness will come home to roost some day.*

chicken switch *n., slang, Space English* **1.** The emergency eject button used by test pilots in fast and high flying aircraft by means of which they can parachute to safety if the engine fails; later adopted by astronauts in space capsules. ♦ *Don't pull the chicken switch, unless absolutely necessary.* **2.** The panic button; a panicky reaction to an unforeseen situation, such as unreasonable or hysterical telephone calls to friends for help. ♦ *Joe pulled the chicken switch on his neighbor when the grease started burning in the kitchen.*

child See BURNT CHILD DREADS THE FIRE, WITH CHILD.

children and fools speak the truth Children and fools say things without thinking; they say what they think or know when grown-ups might not think it was polite or wise to do so.—A proverb. ♦ *"Uncle Willie is too fat," said little Agnes. "Children and fools speak the truth," said her father.*

children should be seen and not heard

A command issued by adults to children ordering them to be quiet and not to interrupt.—A proverb. ♦ *Your children should not argue so loudly. Haven't you taught them that children should be seen and not heard?*

child's play *adj.* Easy; requiring no effort. ♦ *Mary's work as a volunteer social worker is so agreeable to her that she thinks of it as child's play.*

chill See SPINE-CHILLING.

chime in *v.* **1.** *informal* To join in. ♦ *The whole group chimed in on the chorus.* ♦ *When the argument got hot, John chimed in.* **2.** To agree; go well together.—Usually used with *with.* ♦ *Dick was happy, and the holiday music chimed in with his feelings.* ♦ *When Father suggested going to the shore for the vacation, the whole family chimed in with the plan.*

chin See KEEP ONE'S CHIN UP, STICK ONE'S NECK OUT *or* STICK ONE'S CHIN OUT, TAKE IT ON THE CHIN, UP TO THE CHIN IN.

china shop See BULL IN A CHINA SHOP.

China syndrome *n., informal* From the title of the movie with Jane Fonda and Jack Lemmon. The possibility that an industrial nuclear reactor might explode, literally affecting the other side of the planet (as if by eating a hole through the earth all the way to China.) ♦ *Antinuclear demonstrators are greatly worried about the China syndrome.*

chip See CASH IN ONE'S CHIPS *at* CASH-IN, IN THE CHIPS. LET THE CHIPS FALL WHERE THEY MAY, FISH-AND-CHIPS, WHEN THE CHIPS ARE DOWN.

chip in *or* **kick in** *v., informal* To give together with others, contribute. ♦ *The pupils chipped in a dime apiece for the teacher's Christmas present.* ♦ *All the neighbors kicked in to help after the fire.* ♦ *Lee chipped in ten points in the basketball game.* ♦ *Joe didn't say much but chipped in a few words.*

chip off the old block *n. phr.* A person whose character traits closely resemble those of his parents. ♦ *I hear that Tom plays the violin in the orchestra his father conducts; he sure is a chip off the old block.*

chip on one's shoulder *n. phr., informal* A quarrelsome nature; readiness to be angered. ♦ *He went through life with a chip on his shoulder.* ♦ *Jim often gets into fights because he goes around with a chip on his shoulder.*

chips See WHEN THE CHIPS ARE DOWN.

chisel *or* **muscle in on** *v. phr.* To illegitimately and forcefully intrude into someone's traditional sales or professional arena of operation. ♦ *Tim has a good sales territory, but he is always afraid that someone might chisel in on it.* ♦ *Las Vegas casino owners are concerned that the Mafia might muscle in on their territory.*

choice See BY CHOICE, FIELDER'S CHOICE.

choke off *v.* To put a sudden end to; stop abruptly or forcefully. ♦ *It was almost time for the meeting to end, and the presiding officer had to move to choke off debate.* ♦ *The war choked off diamond shipments from overseas.*

choke up *v.* **1a.** To come near losing calmness or self-control from strong feeling; be upset by your feelings. ♦ *When one speaker after another praised John, he choked up and couldn't thank them.* ♦ *When Father tried to tell me how glad he was to see me safe after the accident, he choked up and was unable to speak.* **1b.** *informal* To be unable to do well because of excitement or nervousness. ♦ *Bill was a good batter, but in the championship game he choked up and did poorly.* **2.** To fill up; become clogged or blocked; become hard to pass through. ♦ *The channel had choked up with sand so that boats couldn't use it.*

choose See PICK AND CHOOSE.

chooser See BEGGARS CAN'T BE CHOOSERS.

choose up sides *v. phr.* To form two teams with two captains taking turns choosing players. ♦ *The boys chose up sides for a game of softball.* ♦ *Tom and Joe were the captains. They chose up sides.*

chop See LICK ONE'S CHOPS.

chow line *n., slang* A line of people waiting for food. ♦ *The chow line was already long when John got to the dining hall.* ♦ *The soldiers picked up trays and got into the chow line.*

Christmas See FATHER CHRISTMAS.

Christmas card *n., slang, citizen's band radio jargon* A speeding ticket. ♦ *Smokey just gave a Christmas card to* *the eighteen wheeler we passed.*

Christmas club *n.* A plan for putting money in the bank to be saved for Christmas shopping. ♦*John deposits $10 each week in the Christmas club.* ♦*The woman will get her Christmas club money on December 10.*

chum around with *v. phr.* **1.** To be close friends with someone. ♦*They have been chumming around with one another for quite some time.* **2.** To travel around with someone. ♦*Jack is planning to chum around with Tim in Europe this summer.*

cigar-store Indian *n. phr.* A wooden statue of an Indian which in the past was placed in front of a cigar store. ♦*A cigar store Indian used to mean a cigar store in the same way a barber pole still means a barber shop.*

circle See COME FULL CIRCLE, IN A CIRCLE *or* IN CIRCLES, RUN CIRCLES AROUND *also* RUN RINGS AROUND.

circulation See IN CIRCULATION, OUT OF CIRCULATION.

circumstance See UNDER THE CIRCUMSTANCES *also* IN THE CIRCUMSTANCES.

circumstances alter cases *formal* The way things are, or happen, may change the way you are expected to act. ♦*John's father told him never to touch his gun, but one day when Father was away, John used it to shoot a poisonous snake that came into the yard. Circumstances alter cases.*

circus See THREE-RING CIRCUS.

citizen See SENIOR CITIZEN.

civil See KEEP A CIVIL TONGUE IN ONE'S HEAD.

claim See STAKE A CLAIM.

claim check *n.* A ticket needed to get back something. ♦*The man at the parking lot gave Mrs. Collins a claim check.* ♦*The boy put the dry cleaning claim check in his billfold.* ♦*The man told Mary the pictures would be ready Friday and gave her a claim check.*

clamp down *v., informal* To put on strict controls; enforce rules or laws. ♦*After the explosion, police clamped down and let no more visitors inside the monument.* ♦*The school clamped down on smoking.* ♦*When the crowds became bigger and wilder, the police clamped down on them and made everyone go home.*

clam up *v., slang* To refuse to say any-thing more; stop talking. ♦*The suspect clammed up, and the police could get no more information out of him.*

class See HIGH-CLASS, SECOND CLASS.

clay See FEET OF CLAY.

clay pigeon *n., slang, informal* **1.** A popular target at practice shooting made of clay and roughly resembling a pigeon; an easy target that doesn't move. ♦*All he can shoot is a clay pigeon.* **2.** A person who, like a clay pigeon in target practice, is immobilized or is in a sensitive position and is therefore easily criticized or otherwise victimized. ♦*Poor Joe is a clay pigeon.* **3.** A task easily accomplished like shooting an immobile clay pigeon. ♦*The math exam was a clay pigeon.*

clean See COME CLEAN, KEEP ONE'S NOSE CLEAN, MAKE A CLEAN BREAST OF, NEW BROOM SWEEPS CLEAN, TAKE TO ONE'S HEELS, *also* SHOW A CLEAN PAIR OF HEELS.

clean bill of health *n. phr.* **1.** A certificate that a person or animal has no infectious disease. ♦*The government doctor gave Jones a clean bill of health when he entered the country.* **2.** *informal* A report that a person is free of guilt or fault. ♦*The stranger was suspected in the bank robbery, but the police gave him a clean bill of health.*

clean break *n. phr.* A complete separation. ♦*Tom made a clean break with his former girlfriends before marrying Pamela.*

cleaners See TO TAKE TO THE CLEANERS.

clean hands *n. phr., slang* Freedom from guilt or dishonesty; innocence. ♦*John grew up in a bad neighborhood, but he grew up with clean hands.* ♦*There was much proof against Bill, but he swore he had clean hands.*

clean out *v.* **1.** *slang* To take everything from; empty; strip. ♦*George's friends cleaned him out when they were playing cards last night.* ♦*The sudden demand for paper plates soon cleaned out the stores.* **2.** *informal* To get rid of; remove; dismiss. ♦*The new mayor promised to clean the crooks out of the city government.*

clean slate *n. phr.* A record of nothing but good conduct, without any errors or bad deeds; past acts that are all good without any bad ones. ♦*Johnny was sent to the principal for whispering.*

He had a clean slate so the principal did not punish him. ♦ *Mary stayed after school for a week, and after that the teacher let her off with a clean slate.* Compare TURN OVER A NEW LEAF.

clean sweep *n. phr.* A complete victory. ♦ *Our candidate for the United States Senate made a clean sweep over his opponent.*

clean up *v. phr.* **1.** To wash and make oneself presentable. ♦ *After quitting for the day in the garage, Tim decided to clean up and put on a clean shirt.* **2.** To finish; terminate. ♦ *The secretary promised her boss to clean up all the unfinished work before leaving on her Florida vacation.* **3.** *informal* To make a large profit. ♦ *The clever investors cleaned up on the stock market last week.*

clean-up *n.* **1.** An act of removing all the dirt from a given set of objects. ♦ *What this filthy room needs is an honest clean-up.* **2.** The elimination of pockets of resistance during warfare or a police raid. ♦ *The FBI conducted a clean-up against the drug pushers in our district.*

clear See COAST IS CLEAR, IN THE CLEAR, OUT OF THE BLUE *or* OUT OF A CLEAR SKY *or* OUT OF A CLEAR BLUE SKY, SEE ONE'S WAY CLEAR, STEER CLEAR OF.

clear-cut *adj.* Definite; well defined. ♦ *The president's new policy of aggressive action is a clear-cut departure from his old methods of unilateral appeasement.*

clear-eyed *adj.* Understanding problems or events clearly; being able to tell very well the results of a way of acting. ♦ *Tom is very clear-eyed. He knows he doesn't have much chance of winning the race, but he will try his best.* ♦ *He is a clear-eyed and independent commentator on the news.*

clear one's name *v. phr.* To prove someone is innocent of a crime or misdeed of which he has been accused. ♦ *The falsely accused rapist has been trying in vain to clear his name.*

clear out *v.* **1.** To take everything out of; empty. ♦ *When Bill was moved to another class he cleared out his desk.* **2.** *informal* To leave suddenly; go away; depart. ♦ *The cop told the boys to clear out.* ♦ *Bob cleared out without paying his room rent.* ♦ *Clear out of here! You're bothering me.* Compare BEAT IT.

clear the air *v. phr.* To remove angry feelings, misunderstanding, or confusion. ♦ *The President's statement that he would run for office again cleared the air of rumors and guessing.* ♦ *When Bill was angry at Bob, Bob made a joke, and it cleared the air between them.*

clear the decks *v. phr.* To put everything in readiness for a major activity; to eliminate unessentials. ♦ *The governor urged the State Assembly to clear the decks of all but the most pressing issues to vote on.*

clear up *v.* **1.** To make plain or clear; explain; solve. ♦ *The teacher cleared up the harder parts of the story.* ♦ *Maybe we can clear up your problem.* **2.** To become clear. ♦ *The weather cleared up after the storm.* **3.** To cure. ♦ *The pills cleared up his stomach trouble.* **4.** To put back into a normal, proper, or healthy state. ♦ *The doctor can give you something to clear up your skin.* ♦ *Susan cleared up the room.* **5.** To become cured. ♦ *This skin trouble will clear up in a day or two.*

clerk See ROOM CLERK *or* DESK CLERK.

cliffdweller *n., slang, informal* A city person who lives on a very high floor in an apartment building. ♦ *Joe and Nancy have become cliffdwellers—they moved up to the 30th floor.*

cliffhanger *n., informal* A sports event or a movie in which the outcome is uncertain to the very end keeping the spectators in great suspense and excitement. ♦ *Did you see* The Fugitive? *It's a regular cliffhanger.*

climb See SOCIAL CLIMBER.

climb on the bandwagon See ON THE BANDWAGON.

climb the wall *v. phr., slang. informal* **1.** To react to a challenging situation with too great an emotional response, frustration, tension, and anxiety. ♦ *By the time I got the letter that I was hired, I was ready to climb the wall.* **2.** To be so disinterested or bored as to be most anxious to get away at any cost. ♦ *If the chairman doesn't stop talking, I'll climb the wall.*

clinging vine *n.* A very dependent woman; a woman who needs much love and encouragement from a man.

♦ *Mary is a clinging vine; she cannot do anything without her husband.*

cling to one's mother's apron strings See TIED TO ONE'S MOTHER'S APRON STRINGS.

clip joint *n. slang* A low-class night club or other business where people are cheated. ♦ *The man got drunk and lost all his money in a clip joint.* ♦ *The angry woman said the store was a clip joint.*

clip one's wings *v. phr.* To limit or hold you back, bring you under control; prevent your success. ♦ *When the new president tried to become dictator, the generals soon clipped his wings.* ♦ *Jim was spending too much time on dates when he needed to study so his father stopped his allowance; that clipped his wings.*

cloak-and-dagger *adj.* Of or about spies and secret agents. ♦ *It was a cloak-and-dagger story about some spies who tried to steal atomic secrets.* ♦ *The book was written by a retired colonel who used to take part in cloak-and-dagger plots.* [From the wearing of cloaks and daggers by people in old adventure stories.] Compare BLOOD AND THUNDER.

clock See AGAINST TIME *or* AGAINST THE CLOCK, AROUND THE CLOCK *or* THE CLOCK AROUND, PUT BACK THE CLOCK *or* TURN BACK THE CLOCK, GO LIKE CLOCKWORK *or* GO OFF LIKE CLOCKWORK, TURN THE CLOCK BACK.

clock watcher *n. phr., informal* A worker who always quits at once when it is time; a man who is in a hurry to leave his job. ♦ *When Ted got his first job, his father told him to work hard and not be a clock watcher.*

close at hand *adj. phr.* Handy; close by; within one's range. ♦ *My calendar isn't close at hand, so I can't tell you whether we can come next week or not.* ♦ *I always keep my pencils and erasers close at hand when I work on a draft proposal.*

close call *or* **shave** *n. phr.* A narrow escape. ♦ *That sure was a close call when that truck came near us from the right!* ♦ *When Tim fell off his bicycle in front of a bus, it was a very close shave.*

closed book *n.* A secret; something not known or understood. ♦ *The man's early life is a closed book.* ♦ *For Mary,*

science is a closed book. ♦ *The history of the town is a closed book.*

closed-door *adj.* Away from the public; in private or in secret; limited to a few. ♦ *The officers of the club held a closed-door meeting.* ♦ *The committee decided on a closed-door rule for the investigation.* Compare IN PRIVATE.

close down *or* **shut down** *v.* To stop all working, as in a factory; stop work entirely; *also:* to stop operations in. ♦ *The factory closed down for Christmas.* ♦ *The company shut down the condom plant for Easter.*

closed shop *n. phr.* **1.** A plant or factory that employs only union workers. ♦ *Our firm has been fighting the closed shop policy for many years now.* **2.** A profession or line of work dominated by followers of a certain mode of thinking and behaving that does not tolerate differing views or ideas. ♦ *Certain groups of psychologists, historians, and linguists often behave with a closed-shop mentality.* Contrast OPEN SHOP.

close in *v.* To come in nearer from all sides. ♦ *We wanted the boat to reach shore before the fog closed in.*—Often used with *on.* ♦ *The troops were closing in on the enemy.*

close its doors *v. phr.* **1.** To keep someone or something from entering or joining; become closed. ♦ *The club has closed its doors to new members.* **2.** To fail as a business; go bankrupt. ♦ *The fire was so damaging that the store had to close its doors.* ♦ *Business was so poor that we had to close our doors after six months.* Compare CLOSE THE DOOR. Contrast OPEN ITS DOORS.

close-knit *adj.* Closely joined together by ties of love, friendship, or common interest; close. ♦ *The Joneses are a close-knit family.* ♦ *The three boys are always together. They form a very close-knit group.*

close one's eyes *or* **shut one's eyes** *v. phr.* To refuse to see or think about. ♦ *The park is beautiful if you shut your eyes to the litter.* ♦ *The ice was very thin, but the boys shut their eyes to the danger and went skating.* Compare OPEN ONE'S EYES.

close out *v.* To sell the whole of; end (a business or a business operation) by selling all the goods; *also,* to sell your stock and stop doing business. ♦ *The store closed out its stock of garden supplies.* ♦ *Mr. Jones closed out his grocery.* ♦ *Mr. Randall was losing money in his shoe store, so he decided to close out.*

close quarters *n. phr.* Limited, cramped space. ♦ *With seven boy scouts in a tent, they were living in very close quarters.*

close ranks *v. phr.* **1.** To come close together in a line especially for fighting. ♦ *The soldiers closed ranks and kept the enemy away from the bridge.* **2.** To stop quarreling and work together; unite and fight together. ♦ *The Democrats and Republicans closed ranks to win the war.* ♦ *The leader asked the people to close ranks and plan a new school.*

close shave See CLOSE CALL.

closet See SKELETON IN THE CLOSET.

close the books *v. phr.* To stop taking orders; end a bookkeeping period. ♦ *The tickets were all sold, so the manager said to close the books.* ♦ *The department store closes its books on the 25th of each month.*

close the door *or* **bar the door** *or* **shut the door** *v. phr.* To prevent any more action or talk about a subject. ♦ *The President's veto closed the door to any new attempt to pass the bill.* ♦ *Joan was much hurt by what Mary said, and she closed the door on Mary's attempt to apologize.* ♦ *After John makes up his mind, he closes the door to any more arguments.* Contrast OPEN THE DOOR.

close to home *adv. phr.* Too near to someone's personal feelings, wishes, or interests. ♦ *When John made fun of Bob's way of walking, he struck close to home.* ♦ *When the preacher spoke about prejudice, some people felt he had come too close to home.*

close-up *n.* A photograph, motion picture, or video camera shot taken at very close range. ♦ *Directors of movies frequently show close-ups of the main characters.*

close up shop *v. phr.* **1.** To shut a store at the end of a day's business, *also,* to end a business. ♦ *The grocer closes up shop at 5 o'clock.* ♦ *After 15 years in business at the same spot, the garage closed up shop.* **2.** *informal* To stop some activity; finish what you are

doing. ♦ *After camping out for two weeks, the scouts took down their tents and closed up shop.* ♦ *The committee finished its business and closed up shop.* Compare CALL IT A DAY.

clothes See BEST BIB AND TUCKER *or* SUNDAY-GO-TO-MEETING CLOTHES.

clothing See WOLF IN SHEEP'S CLOTHING.

cloud See EVERY CLOUD HAS A SILVER LINING, IN THE CLOUDS, ON CLOUD NINE, UNDER A CLOUD.

clover See FOUR-LEAF CLOVER, IN CLOVER *or* IN THE CLOVER.

club See CHRISTMAS CLUB.

cluck and grunt *n., slang, avoid it in restaurants* The familiar restaurant dish of ham and eggs; since ham is made of pork (and pigs grunt) and eggs come from hens (which cluck.) ♦ *"I am sorry I can't fix you an elaborate meal, but I can give you a quick cluck and grunt."*

clutch See RIDE THE BRAKE.

coal See CARRY COALS TO NEWCASTLE, HAUL OVER THE COALS *or* RAKE OVER THE COALS, HEAP COALS OF FIRE ON ONE'S HEAD.

coast is clear No enemy or danger is in sight; there is no one to see you. ♦ *When the teacher had disappeared around the corner, John said, "Come on, the coast is clear."* ♦ *The men knew when the night watchman would pass. When he had gone, and the coast was clear, they robbed the safe.* ♦ *When Father stopped the car at the stop sign, Mother said, "The coast is clear on this side."*

coat tail See ON ONE'S COAT TAILS.

cock See GO OFF HALF-COCKED *also* GO OFF AT HALF COCK.

cock-and-bull story *n. phr.* An exaggerated or unbelievable story. ♦ *"Stop feeding me such cock-and-bull stories,"* the detective said to the suspect.

cockeyed *adj.* Drunk; intoxicated. ♦ *Frank has been drinking all day and, when we met, he was so cockeyed he forgot his own address.*

cocksure *adj.* Overconfident; very sure. ♦ *Paul was cocksure that it wasn't going to snow, but it snowed so much that we had to dig our way out of the house.*

C.O.D. *n. phr.* Abbreviation of "cash on delivery." ♦ *If you want to receive a piece of merchandise by mail and pay* *when you receive it, you place a C.O.D. order.*

coffee break *n.* A short recess or time out from work in which to rest and drink coffee. ◆ *The girls in the office take a coffee break in the middle of the morning and the afternoon.*

coffee hour *n.* A time for coffee or other refreshments after a meeting; a time to meet people and have refreshments. ◆ *After the business meeting we had a coffee hour.* ◆ *The Joneses had a coffee hour so their visitor could meet their neighbors.*

coffee table *n.* A low table used in a living room. ◆ *There were several magazines on the coffee table.*

coffin nail *n., slang* A cigarette. ◆ *"I stopped smoking," Algernon said. "In fact, I haven't had a coffin nail in well over a year."*

cog See SLIP A COG *or* SLIP A GEAR.

coin money *or* **mint money** *v. phr., informal* To make a lot of money quickly; profit heavily; gain big profit. ◆ *Fred coined money with many cigarette vending machines and juke boxes.*

cold See BLOOD RUNS COLD, BLOW HOT AND COLD, CATCH COLD *or* TAKE COLD, IN COLD BLOOD, OUT COLD, OUT IN THE COLD, PASS OUT 2, STONE-COLD, STOP COLD, THROW COLD WATER ON.

cold cash *or* **hard cash** *n.* Money that is paid at the time of purchase; real money; silver and bills. ◆ *Mr. Jones bought a new car and paid cold cash for it.* ◆ *Some stores sell things only for cold cash.* Compare CASH ON THE BARRELHEAD.

cold comfort *n.* Something that makes a person in trouble feel very little better or even worse. ◆ *When Tim lost the race, it was cold comfort to him to hear that he could try again in two weeks.* ◆ *Mary spent her vacation sick in bed and Jane's letter about her trip was cold comfort.*

cold feet *n. phr., informal* A loss of courage or nerve; a failure or loss of confidence in yourself. ◆ *Ralph was going to ask Mary to dance with him but he got cold feet and didn't.*

cold fish *n., informal* A queer person; a person who is unfriendly or does not mix with others. ◆ *No one knows the new doctor, he is a cold fish.* ◆ *Nobody*

invites Eric to parties because he is a cold fish.

cold-shoulder *v., informal* To act towards a person; with dislike or scorn; be unfriendly to. ◆ *Fred cold-shouldered his old friend when they passed on the street.* ◆ *It is impolite and unkind to cold-shoulder people.* Compare BRUSH OFF 2, HIGH-HAT, LOOK DOWN ONE'S NOSE AT.

cold shoulder *n., informal* Unfriendly treatment of a person, a showing of dislike for a person or of looking down on a person.—Used in the clichés *give the cold shoulder* or *turn a cold shoulder to* or *get the cold shoulder.* ◆ *When Bob asked Mary for a date she gave him the cold shoulder.* ◆ *The membership committee turned a cold shoulder to Jim's request to join the club.*

cold snap *n.* A short time of quick change from warm weather to cold. ◆ *The cold snap killed everything in the garden.*

cold turkey *adv., slang, informal* **1.** Abruptly and without medical aid to withdraw from the use of an addictive drug or from a serious drinking problem. ◆ *Joe is a very brave guy; he kicked the habit cold turkey.* **2.** *n.* An instance of withdrawal from drugs, alcohol, or cigarette smoking. ◆ *Joe did a cold turkey.*

cold war *n.* A struggle that is carried on by other means and not by actual fighting; a war without shooting or bombing. ◆ *After World War II, a cold war began between Russia and the United States.*

collar See HOT UNDER THE COLLAR, ROMAN COLLAR, SAILOR COLLAR.

collective farm *n.* A large government-run farm made by combining many small farms. ◆ *The Russian farmers used to live on collective farms.*

collector's item *n.* Something rare or valuable enough to collect or save. ◆ *Jimmy's mother found an old wooden doll in the attic that turned out to be a collector's item.*

College Boards *n.* A set of examinations given to test a student's readiness and ability for college. ◆ *John got a high score on his College Boards.* ◆ *College Boards test both what a student has learned and his ability to learn.*

color See CHANGE COLOR, GIVE COLOR TO or LEND COLOR TO, HAUL DOWN ONE'S COLORS, HORSE OF A DIFFERENT COLOR, NAIL ONE'S COLORS TO THE MAST, OFF-COLOR or OFF-COLORED, SAIL UNDER FALSE COLORS, SEE THE COLOR OF ONE'S MONEY, SHOW ONE'S COLORS, WITH FLYING COLORS.

color guard n. A military guard of honor for the flag of a country; also: a guard of honor to carry and protect a flag or banner (as of a club). ♦ *There were four Marines in the color guard in the parade.* ♦ *Bob was picked to be a color guard and to carry the banner of the drum corps at the football game.*

color scheme n. A plan for colors used together as decoration. ♦ *The color scheme for the dance was blue and silver.* ♦ *Mary decided on a pink and white color scheme for her room.*

comb See FINE-TOOTH COMB.

come See CHICKENS COME HOME TO ROOST, CROSS A BRIDGE BEFORE ONE COMES TO IT, EASY COME–EASY GO, FIRST COME–FIRST SERVED, GET WHAT'S COMING TO ONE, HAVE IT COMING, HOW COME also HOW'S COME, IF WORST COMES TO WORST, JOHNNY-COME-LATELY, KNOW ENOUGH TO COME IN OUT OF THE RAIN, KNOW IF ONE IS COMING OR GOING, LOOK AS IF ONE HAS COME OUT OF A BANDBOX, SHIP COME IN.

come about v. To take place; happen; occur. ♦ *Sometimes it is hard to tell how a quarrel comes about.* ♦ *When John woke up he was in the hospital, but he didn't know how that had come about.*

come a cropper 1. To fall off your horse. ♦ *John's horse stumbled, and John came a cropper.* 2. To fail. ♦ *Mr. Brown did not have enough money to put into his business and it soon came a cropper.* Compare RIDING FOR A FALL.

come across v. 1. or **run across** To find or meet by chance. ♦ *He came across a dollar bill in the suit he was sending to the cleaner.* ♦ *The other day I ran across a book that you might like.* ♦ *I came across George at a party last week; it was the first time I had seen him in months.* Compare COME ON 3, RUN INTO 3b. 2. To give or do what is asked. ♦ *The robber told the woman to come across with her purse.* ♦ *For hours the police questioned the man suspected of* kidnapping the child, and finally he came across with the story.

come again v., informal Please repeat; please say that again.—Usually used as a command. ♦ *"Harry has just come into a fortune," my wife said. "Come again?" I asked her, not believing it.* ♦ *"Come again," said the hard-of-hearing man.*

come alive or **come to life** v. 1. informal To become alert or attentive; wake up and look alive; become active. ♦ *When Mr. Simmons mentioned money, the boys came alive.* ♦ *Bob pushed the starter button, and the engine came alive with a roar.* 2. To look real; take on a bright, natural look. ♦ *Under skillful lighting, the scene came alive.* ♦ *The President came alive in the picture as the artist worked.*

come along v. To make progress; improve; succeed. ♦ *He was coming along well after the operation.* ♦ *Rose is coming right along on the piano.*

come a long way v. phr. To show much improvement; make great progress. ♦ *The school has come a long way since its beginnings.* ♦ *Little Jane has come a long way since she broke her leg.*

come apart at the seams v. phr., slang, informal To become upset to the point where one loses self-control and composure as if having suffered a sudden nervous breakdown. ♦ *After his divorce Joe seemed to be coming apart at the seams.*

come around See COME ROUND.

come at v. 1. To approach; come to or against; advance toward. ♦ *The young boxer came at the champion cautiously.* 2. To understand (a word or idea) or master (a skill); succeed with. ♦ *The sense of an unfamiliar word is hard to come at.*

come back v., informal 1. To reply; answer. ♦ *The lawyer came back sharply in defense of his client.* ♦ *No matter how the audience heckled him, the comedian always had an answer to come back with.* 2. To get a former place or position back, reach again a place which you have lost. ♦ *After a year off to have her baby, the singer came back to even greater fame.* ♦ *It is hard for a retired prize fighter to come back and beat a younger man.*

comeback n., v. phr., slang, citizen's band

radio jargon A return call. ◆ *Thanks for your comeback.*

come back to earth *or* **come down to earth** *v. phr.* To return to the real world; stop imagining or dreaming; think and behave as usual. ◆ *After Jane met the movie star it was hard for her to come back to earth.* ◆ *Bill was sitting and daydreaming so his mother told him to come down to earth and to do his homework.* Compare COME TO ONE'S SENSES, DOWN-TO-EARTH. Contrast IN THE CLOUDS.

come between *v.* To part; divide; separate. ◆ *John's mother-in-law came to live in his home, and as time passed she came between him and his wife.* ◆ *Bill's hot rod came between him and his studies, and his grades went down.*

come by *v.* To get; obtain; acquire. ◆ *A good job like that is hard to come by.* ◆ *Money easily come by is often easily spent.* ◆ *How did she come by that money?*

come by honestly *v. phr., informal* To inherit (a characteristic) from your parents. ◆ *Joe comes by his hot temper honestly; his father is the same way.*

come clean *v. phr., slang* To tell all; tell the whole story; confess. ◆ *The boy suspected of stealing the watch came clean after long questioning.*

comedown *n.* Disappointment; embarrassment; failure. ◆ *It was quite a comedown for Al when the girl he took for granted refused his marriage proposal.*

come down *v.* **1.** To reduce itself; amount to no more than.—Followed by *to.* ◆ *The quarrel finally came down to a question of which boy would do the dishes.* Syn. BOIL DOWN 3. **2.** To be handed down or passed along, descend from parent to child; pass from older generation to younger ones. ◆ *Mary's necklace had come down to her from her grandmother.*

come down hard on *v., informal* **1.** To scold or punish strongly. ◆ *The principal came down hard on the boys for breaking the window.* **2.** To oppose strongly. ◆ *The minister in his sermon came down hard on drinking.*

come down in the world *v. phr.* To lose a place of respect or honor, become lower (as in rank or fortune). ◆ *The stranger plainly had come down a long*

way in the world. Compare DOWN ON ONE'S LUCK.

come down off one's high horse *v. phr.* To become less arrogant; to assume a more modest disposition. ◆ *The boastful candidate for Congress quickly came down off his high horse when he was soundly beaten by his opponent.*

come down on like a ton of bricks *v. phr., slang* To direct one's full anger at somebody. ◆ *When the janitor was late for work, the manager came down on him like a ton of bricks.*

come down to earth See COME BACK TO EARTH.

come down with *v., informal* To become sick with; catch. ◆ *We all came down with the mumps.* ◆ *After being out in the rain, George came down with a cold.*

come from far and wide *v. phr.* To originate or hail from many different places. ◆ *The students at this university come from far and wide and speak many languages.*

come full circle *v. phr., informal* **1.** To become totally opposed to one's own earlier conviction on a given subject. ◆ *Today's conservative businessperson has come full circle from former radical student days.* **2.** To change and develop, only to end up where one started. ◆ *From modern permissiveness, ideas about child raising have come full circle to the views of our grandparents.*

come hell or high water *adv. phr., informal* No matter what happens; whatever may come. ◆ *Grandfather said he would go to the fair, come hell or high water.* Compare COME WHAT MAY, THROUGH THE MILL.

come home to roost See CHICKENS COME HOME TO ROOST.

come in *v.* **1.** To finish in a sports contest or other competition. ◆ *He came in second in the hundred-yard dash.* **2.** To become the fashion; begin to be used. ◆ *Swimming trunks for men came in after World War I; before that men used full swim suits.*

come in for *v.* To receive. ◆ *He came in for a small fortune when his uncle died.* ◆ *His conduct came in for much criticism.*

come in handy *v. phr., informal* To prove useful. ♦ *Robinson Crusoe found tools in the ship which came in handy when he built a house.* ♦ *The French he learned in high school came in handy when he was in the army in France.*

come into *v.* To receive, especially after another's death; get possession of. ♦ *He came into a lot of money when his father died.* ♦ *He came into possession of the farm after his uncle died.*

come into one's own *v. phr.* To receive the wealth or respect that you should have. ♦ *John's grandfather died and left him a million dollars; when John is 21, he will come into his own.* ♦ *With the success of the Model T Ford, the automobile industry came into its own.*

come natural See COME EASY.

come of *v.* **1.** To result from. ♦ *After all the energy we spent on that advertising campaign, absolutely nothing came of it.* **2.** To become of; happen to. ♦ *"Whatever became of your son, Peter?"*

come of age See OF AGE.

come off *v.* **1.** To take place; happen. ♦ *The picnic came off at last, after being twice postponed.* **2.** *informal* To do well; succeed. ♦ *The attempt to bring the quarreling couple together again came off, to people's astonishment.*

come off it *also* **get off it** *v. phr., slang* Stop pretending; bragging; or kidding; stop being silly.—Used as a command. ♦ *"So I said to the duchess…" Jimmy began. "Oh, come off it," the other boys sneered.* ♦ *Fritz said he had a car of his own. "Oh, come off it," said John. "You can't even drive."*

come off *or* **through with flying colors** *v. phr.* To succeed; triumph. ♦ *John came off with flying colors in his final exams at college.*

come off second best *v. phr.* To not win first but only second, third, etc. place. ♦ *Our home team came off second best against the visitors.* ♦ *Sue complains that she always comes off second best when she has a disagreement with her husband.*

come on *v.* **1.** To begin; appear. ♦ *Rain came on toward morning.* ♦ *He felt a cold coming on.* **2.** To grow or do well; thrive. ♦ *The wheat was coming on.* ♦ *His business came on splendidly.* **3.**

or **come upon.** To meet accidentally; encounter; find. ♦ *He came on an old friend that day when he visited his club.* ♦ *He came upon an interesting idea in reading about the French Revolution.* Syn. COME ACROSS, HAPPEN ON. **4.** *informal* Let's get started; let's get going; don't delay; don't wait.—Used as a command. ♦ *"Come on, or we'll be late," said Joe, but Lou still waited.* **5.** *informal* Please do it!—Used in begging someone to do something. ♦ *Sing us just one song, Jane, come on!* ♦ *Come on, Laura, you can tell me. I won't tell anybody.*

come-on *n., slang* An attractive offer made to a naive person under false pretenses in order to gain monetary or other advantage. ♦ *Joe uses a highly successful come-on when he sells vacant lots on Grand Bahama Island.*

come one's way *v. phr.* To be experienced by someone; happen to you. ♦ *Tom said that if the chance to become a sailor ever came his way, he would take it.* ♦ *I hope bad luck isn't coming our way.* ♦ *Luck came Bill's way today and he hit a home run.* Compare GO ONE'S WAY, IN ONE'S FAVOR.

come on strong *v. phr., slang* To overwhelm a weaker person with excessively strong language, personality, or mannerisms; to insist extremely strongly and claim something with unusual vigor. ♦ *Joe came on very strong last night about the War in Indochina; most of us felt embarrassed.*

come out *v.* **1.** *Of a girl:* To be formally introduced to polite society at about age eighteen, usually at a party; begin to go to big parties. ♦ *In society, girls come out when they reach the age of about eighteen, and usually it is at a big party in their honor; after that they are looked on as adults.* **2.** To be published. *The book came out two weeks ago.* **3.** To become publicly known. ♦ *The truth finally came out at his trial.* **4.** To end; result; finish. ♦ *How did the story come out?* ♦ *The game came out as we had hoped.* ♦ *The snapshots came out well.* **5.** To announce support or opposition; declare yourself (for or against a person or thing). ♦ *The party leaders came out for an acceptable candidate.* ♦ *Many Congressmen came out*

against the bill. **6.** See GO OUT FOR.—
coming-out *adj.* Introducing a girl to polite society. ♦ *Mary's parents gave her a coming-out party when she was 17.*

come out for *v. phr.* To support; declare oneself in favor of another, especially during a political election. ♦ *Candidates for the presidency of the United States are anxious for the major newspapers to come out for them.*

come out in the open *v. phr.* **1.** To reveal one's true identity or intentions. ♦ *Fred finally came out in the open and admitted that he was gay.* **2.** To declare one's position openly. ♦ *The conservative Democratic candidate came out in the open and declared that he would join the Republican party.*

come out with *v. phr.* **1.** To make a public announcement of; make known. ♦ *He came out with a clear declaration of his principles.* **2.** To say. ♦ *He comes out with the funniest remarks you can imagine.*

come over *v.* To take control of; cause sudden strong feeling in; happen to. ♦ *A sudden fit of anger came over him.* ♦ *A great tenderness came over her.* ♦ *What has come over him?*

come round *or* **come around** *v.* **1.** To happen or appear again and again in regular order. ♦ *And so Saturday night came around again.* ♦ *I will tell him when he comes round again.* **2.** *informal* To get back health or knowledge of things; get well from sickness or a faint. ♦ *Someone brought out smelling salts and Mary soon came round.* ♦ *Jim has come around after having had stomach ulcers.* **3.** To change direction. ♦ *The wind has come round to the south.* **4.** *informal* To change your opinion or purpose to agree with another's. ♦ *Tom came round when Dick told him the whole story.*

come through *v., informal* To be equal to a demand; meet trouble or a sudden need with success; satisfy a need. ♦ *When the baseball team needed a hit, Willie came through with a double.* ♦ *John needed money for college and his father came through.*

come to *v.* (stress on *to*) **1.** To wake up after losing consciousness; get the use

of your senses back again after fainting or being knocked out. ♦ *She fainted in the store and found herself in the first aid room when she came to.* ♦ *The boxer who was knocked out did not come to for five minutes.* ♦ *The doctor gave her a pill and after she took it she didn't come to for two days.* Compare BRING TO. **2.** (stress on *come*) To get enough familiarity or understanding to; learn to; grow to.—Used with an infinitive. ♦ *John was selfish at first, but he came to realize that other people counted, too.* ♦ *During her years at the school, Mary came to know that road well.* **3.** To result in or change to; reach the point of; arrive at. ♦ *Mr. Smith lived to see his invention come to success.* ♦ *Grandfather doesn't like the way young people act today; he says, "I don't know what the world is coming to."* **4.** To have something to do with; be in the field of; be about.—Usually used in the phrase *when it comes to.* ♦ *Joe is not good in sports, but when it comes to arithmetic he's the best in the class.* ♦ *The school has very good teachers, but when it comes to buildings, the school is poor.*

come to a dead end *v. phr.* To reach a point from which one cannot proceed further, either because of a physical obstacle or because of some forbidding circumstance. ♦ *Our car came to a dead end; the only way to get out was to drive back in reverse.* ♦ *The factory expansion project came to a dead end because of a lack of funds.*

come to blows *v. phr.* To begin to fight. ♦ *The two quarreling boys came to blows after school.* ♦ *The two countries came to blows because one wanted to be independent from the other.*

come to grief *v. phr.* To have a bad accident or disappointment; meet trouble or ruin; end badly; wreck; fail. ♦ *Bill came to grief learning to drive a car.* ♦ *Nick's hopes for a new house came to grief when the house he was building burned down.* ♦ *The fishing boat came to grief off Cape Cod.*

come to grips with *v. phr.* **1.** To get hold of (another wrestler) in close fighting. ♦ *After circling around for a minute, the two wrestlers came to grips with each other.* **2.** To struggle seriously with (an idea or problem). ◆ *Mr. Blake's teaching helps students come to grips with the important ideas in the history lesson.* ◆ *Harry cannot be a leader, because he never quite comes to grips with a problem.* Compare COME TO TERMS 2.

come to hand *v. phr.* To be received or obtained. ◆ *Father's letter was mailed from Florida last week and came to hand today.* ◆ *The new books came to hand today.* ◆ *New information about the boy's disappearance came to hand yesterday.*

come to heel See TO HEEL.

come to life See COME ALIVE.

come to light *v. phr.* To be discovered; become known; appear. ◆ *John's thefts from the bank where he worked came to light when the bank examiners made an inspection.* ◆ *When the old woman died it came to light that she was actually rich.* ◆ *New facts about ancient Egypt have recently come to light.* Compare BRING TO LIGHT.

come to mind *v. phr.* To occur to someone. ◆ *A new idea for the advertising campaign came to mind as I was reading your book.*

come to nothing *also formal* **come to naught** *v. phr.* To end in failure; fail; be in vain. ◆ *The dog's attempts to climb the tree after the cat came to nothing.*

come to one's senses *v. phr.* **1.** Become conscious again; wake up. ◆ *The boxer was knocked out and did not come to his senses for several minutes.* ◆ *The doctors gave Tom an anesthetic before his operation; then the doctor took out Tom's appendix before he came to his senses.* Compare COME TO 1. **2.** To think clearly; behave as usual or as you should; act sensibly. ◆ *A boy threw a snowball at me and before I could come to my senses he ran away.* ◆ *Don't act so foolishly. Come to your senses!* Contrast OUT OF ONE'S HEAD.

come to pass *v. phr., literary* To happen; occur. ◆ *Strange things come to pass in troubled times.* ◆ *It came to pass that the jailer visited him by night.* ◆ *His hopes of success did not come to pass.* Compare BRING TO PASS, COME ABOUT.

come to terms *v. phr.* To reach an agreement. ◆ *Management and the labor union came to terms about a new*

arrangement and a strike was prevented.

come to the point *or* **get to the point** *v. phr.* To talk about the important thing; reach the important facts of the matter; reach the central question or fact. ◆ *Henry was giving a lot of history and explanation, but his father asked him to come to the point.* ◆ *A good newspaper story must come right to the point and save the details for later.* Contrast BEAT ABOUT THE BUSH.

come to think of it *v. phr., informal* As I think again; indeed; really. ◆ *Come to think of it, he has already been given what he needs.* ◆ *Come to think of it, I should write my daughter today.*

come true *v.* To really happen; change from a dream or a plan into a fact. ◆ *It took years of planning and saving, but their seagoing vacation came true at last.* ◆ *It was a dream come true when he met the President.* ◆ *His hope of living to 100 did not come true.*

come up *v.* **1.** To become a subject for discussion or decision to talk about or decide about. ◆ *"He was a good salesman, and price never came up until the very last," Mary said.* ◆ *The question of wage increases came up at the board meeting.* ◆ *Mayor Jones comes up for reelection this fall.* **2.** To be equal; match in value.—Used with *to.* ◆ *The new model car comes up to last year's.* **3.** To approach; come close. ◆ *We saw a big black bear coming up on us from the woods.* ◆ *Christmas is coming up soon.* ◆ *The team was out practicing for the big game coming up.* **4.** To provide; supply; furnish.—Used with *with.* ◆ *For years Jones kept coming up with new and good ideas.* ◆ *The teacher asked a difficult question, but finally Ted came up with a good answer.*

come up in the world *or* **rise in the world** *v. phr.* To gain success, wealth, or importance in life; rise to a position of greater wealth or importance. ◆ *He had come up in the world since he peddled his wife's baked goods from a pushcart.* Compare GET AHEAD. Contrast COME DOWN IN THE WORLD.

come up smelling like a rose *v. phr.* To escape from a difficult situation or misdeed unscathed or without punishment.

♦*It is predicted that Congressman Brown, in spite of the current investigation into his financial affairs, will come up smelling like a rose at the end.*

come up to *v. phr.* To equal. ♦ *The meals cooked in most restaurants do not come up to those prepared at home.*

come up with *v. phr.* **1.** To offer. ♦ *We can always depend on John Smith to come up with a good solution for any problem we might have.* **2.** To produce on demand. ♦ *I won't be able to buy this car, because I cannot come up with the down payment you require.* **3.** To find. ♦ *How on earth did you come up with such a brilliant idea?*

come upon See COME ON 3.

come what may *adv. phr.* Even if troubles come; no matter what happens; in spite of opposition or mischance. ♦ *Charles has decided to get a college education, come what may.* ♦ *The editor says we will publish the school paper this week, come what may.*

comfort See COLD COMFORT.

comfortable as an old shoe *adj. phr., informal* Pleasant and relaxed; not stiff, strict or too polite; easy to talk and work with. ♦ *The stranger was as comfortable as an old shoe, and we soon were talking like old friends.*

coming and going *or* **going and coming** *adv. phr.* **1.** Both ways; in both directions. ♦ *The truck driver stops at the same cafe coming and going.* ♦ *John was late. He got punished both going and coming; his teacher punished him and his parents punished him.* **2.** Caught or helpless; in your power; left with no way out of a difficulty.—Used after *have.* ♦ *If Beth stayed in the house, Mother would make her help with the cleaning; if she went outside, Father would make her help wash the car—they had her coming and going.* ♦ *Uncle Mike is a good checker player, and he soon had me beat coming and going.* Compare BETWEEN THE DEVIL AND THE DEEP BLUE SEA.

coming out See COME OUT 1.

coming out party *n. phr.* A debutante party in which a young girl is formally introduced to society. ♦ *Coming out parties used to be more popular in the early twentieth century than nowadays, primarily because they cost a lot of money.*

comings and goings *n. pl., informal* **1.** Times of arriving and going away; movements. ♦ *I can't keep up with the children's comings and goings.* **2.** Activities; doings; business. ♦ *Mary knows all the comings and goings in the neighborhood.*

command module *n., Space English* **1.** One of the three main sections of the basic Apollo spacecraft. It weighs six tons and is cone shaped. It contains crew compartments and from it the astronauts can operate the lunar module (LM), the docking systems, etc. **2.** *Informal transferred sense.* The cockpit, the chief place where a person does his most important work. ♦ *My desk is my command module.*

commission See IN COMMISSION *or* INTO COMMISSION, OUT OF COMMISSION.

common See IN COMMON.

common as an old shoe *adj. phr., informal* Not showing off; not vain; modest; friendly to all. ♦ *Although Mr. Jones ran a large business, he was common as an old shoe.* ♦ *The most famous people are sometimes as common as an old shoe.*

common ground *n.* Shared beliefs, interests, or ways of understanding; ways in which people are alike. ♦ *Bob and Frank don't like each other because they have no common ground.* ♦ *The only common ground between us is that we went to the same school.* Compare IN COMMON.

common touch *n.* The ability to be a friend of the people; friendly manner with everyone. ♦ *Voters like a candidate who has the common touch.*

company See KEEP COMPANY, PART COMPANY.

company man *n., informal* A worker who always agrees with management rather than labor.—Usually used to express dislike or disapproval. ♦ *Joe was a company man and refused to take a part in the strike.* Compare YESMAN.

compare notes *v. phr., informal* To exchange thoughts or ideas about something; discuss together. ♦ *Mother and Mrs. Barker like to compare notes about cooking.*

compliment See RETURN THE COMPLIMENT.

conclusion See JUMP TO A CONCLUSION.

condition See IN SHAPE *or* IN CONDITION, IN THE PINK *or* IN THE PINK OF CONDITION, ON CONDITION THAT, OUT OF SHAPE *or* OUT OF CONDITION.

conference See PRESS CONFERENCE.

congregate housing *n., informal* A form of housing for elderly persons in which dining facilities and services are shared in multiple dwelling units. ♦*Jerry put Grandma in a place where they have congregate housing.*

conk out *v. phr., slang, informal* To fall asleep suddenly with great fatigue or after having drunk too much. ♦*We conked out right after the guests had left.*

consent See SILENCE GIVES CONSENT.

consequence See IN CONSEQUENCE, IN CONSEQUENCE OF.

consideration See IN CONSIDERATION OF.

consumer goods *or* **consumer items** *n.* Food and manufactured things that people buy for their own use. ♦*In time of war, the supply of consumer goods is greatly reduced.*

content See TO ONE'S HEART'S CONTENT.

contention See BONE OF CONTENTION.

contrary See ON THE CONTRARY, TO THE CONTRARY.

control room *n.* A room containing the panels and switches used to control something (like a TV broadcast). ♦*While a television program is on the air, engineers are at their places in the control room.*

control tower *n.* A tower with large windows and a good view of an airport so that the traffic of airplanes can be seen and controlled, usually by radio. ♦*We could see the lights at the control tower as our plane landed during the night.*

conversation See MAKE CONVERSATION.

conversation piece *n.* Something that interests people and makes them talk about it; something that looks unusual, comical, or strange. ♦*Uncle Fred has a glass monkey on top of his piano that he keeps for a conversation piece.*

conviction See HAVE THE COURAGE OF ONE'S CONVICTIONS.

cook See SHORT-ORDER COOK, WHAT'S UP *or* WHAT'S COOKING.

cook one's goose *v. phr., slang* To ruin someone hopelessly; destroy one's future expectations or good name. ♦*The bank treasurer cooked his own goose when he stole the bank's funds.* ♦*She cooked John's goose by reporting what she knew to the police.* ♦*The dishonest official knew his goose was cooked when the newspapers printed the story about him.*

cook up *v., informal* To plan and put together; make up; invent. ♦*The boys cooked up an excuse to explain their absence from school.*

cool See PLOW ONE'S COOL.

cool as a cucumber *adj. phr., informal* Very calm and brave; not nervous, worried, or anxious; not excited; composed. ♦*Bill is a good football quarterback, always cool as a cucumber.*

cool customer *n.* Someone who is calm and in total control of himself; someone showing little emotion. ♦*Jim never gets too excited about anything; he is a cool customer.*

cool down *or* **cool off** *v.* **1.** To lose or cause to lose the heat of any deep feeling (as love, enthusiasm, or anger); make or become calm, cooled or indifferent; lose interest. ♦*A heated argument can be settled better if both sides cool down first.* ♦*John was deeply in love with Sally before he left for college, but he cooled off before he got back.* ♦*Their friendship cooled off when Jack gave up football.* ♦*The neighbor's complaint about the noise cooled the argument down.*

cool one's heels *v. phr., slang* To be kept waiting by another's pride or rudeness; be forced to wait by someone in power or authority; wait. ♦*He cooled his heels for an hour in another room before the great man would see him.* ♦*I was left to cool my heels outside while the others went into the office.*

coon's age See DOG'S AGE.

coop See FLY THE COOP.

coop up *v. phr.* To hedge in; confine; enclose in a small place. ♦*How can poor Jane work in that small office, cooped up all day long?*

cop a feel *v. phr., vulgar, avoidable* To attempt to arouse sexually by manual contact, usually by surprise. ♦*John talks big for a 16 year old, but all he's ever done is cop a feel in a dark movie* *theater.* Compare FEEL UP. Contrast COP A PLEA.

cop a plea *v. phr., slang, colloquial* To plead guilty during a trial in the hope of getting a lighter sentence as a result. ◆ *The murderer of Dr. Martin Luther King, Jr., copped a plea of guilty, and got away with a life sentence instead of the death penalty.*

cop out *v. phr., slang, informal* To avoid committing oneself in a situation where doing so would result in difficulties. ◆ *Nixon copped out on the American people with Watergate.*

cop-out *n. phr., slang, informal* An irresponsible excuse made to avoid something one has to do, a flimsy pretext. ◆ *Come on, Jim, that's a cheap cop-out, and I don't believe a word of it!*

copy cat *n.* Someone who copies another person's work or manner.— Usually used by children or when speaking to children. ◆ *He called me a copy cat just because my new shoes look like his.*

corn ball *n., slang, informal* **1.** A superficially sentimental movie or musical in which the word *love is* mentioned too often; a theatrical performance that is trivially sentimental. ◆ *That movie last night was a corn ball.* **2.** A person who behaves in a superficially sentimental manner or likes performances portraying such behavior. ◆ *Suzie can't stand Joe; she thinks he's a corn ball.*

corn belt *n.* **1.** The Midwest; the agricultural section of the United States where much corn is grown. ◆ *Kansas is one of the states that lies within the corn belt.*

corner See AROUND THE CORNER, CUT CORNERS, FOUR CORNERS, OUT OF THE CORNER OF ONE'S EYE.

cost a bomb *or* **an arm and a leg** *v. phr.* To be extremely expensive. ◆ *My new house has cost us an arm and a leg and we're almost broke.*

cotton See ON TOP OF THE WORLD *also* SITTING ON HIGH COTTON.

cotton picking, cotton-pickin' *adj., slang, colloquial* Worthless, crude, common, messy. ◆ *Keep your cotton picking hands off my flowers!* ◆ *You've got to clean up your room, son, this is a cotton-pickin' mess!*

couch case *n., slang, informal* A person judged emotionally so disturbed that

people think he ought to see a psychiatrist (who, habitually, make their patients lie down on a couch). ◆ *Joe's divorce messed him up so badly that he became a couch case.*

couch doctor *n., slang, colloquial* A psychoanalyst who puts his patients on a couch following the practice established by Sigmund Freud. ◆ *I didn't know your husband was a couch doctor, I thought he was a gynecologist!*

couch potato *n.* A person who is addicted to watching television all day. ◆ *Poor Ted has become such a couch potato that we can't persuade him to do anything.*

cough up *v., slang* **1.** To give (money) unwillingly; pay with an effort. ◆ *Her husband coughed up the money for the party with a good deal of grumbling.* **2.** To tell what was secret; make known. ◆ *He coughed up the whole story for the police.*

couldn't care less *v. phr., informal* To be indifferent; not care at all. ◆ *The students couldn't care less about the band; they talk all through the concert.* Also heard increasingly as *could care less* (nonstandard in this form.)

counsel See KEEP ONE'S OWN COUNSEL.

count See STAND UP AND BE COUNTED.

countdown *n., Space English, informal* **1.** A step by-step process which leads to the launching of a rocket. ◆ *Countdown starts at 23:00 hours tomorrow night and continues for 24 hours.* **2.** Process of counting inversely during the acts leading to a launch; liftoff occurs at zero. **3.** The time immediately preceding an important undertaking, borrowed from Space English. ◆ *We're leaving for Hawaii tomorrow afternoon; this is countdown time for us.*

counter See UNDER THE COUNTER.

count heads *or* **count noses** *v. phr., informal* To count the number of people in a group. ◆ *On the class picnic, we counted heads before we left and when we arrived to be sure that no one got lost.* ◆ *The usher was told to look out into the audience and count noses.*

count off *v.* **1.** To count aloud from one end of a line of men to the other, each man counting in turn. ◆ *The soldiers* counted off from right to left. **2.** To place into a separate group or groups by counting. ♦ *The coach counted off three boys to carry in the equipment.* ♦ *Tom counted off enough newspapers for his route.*

count on *v.* **1.** To depend on; rely on; trust. ♦ *The team was counting on Joe to win the race.* ♦ *I'll do it; you know you can count on me.* ♦ *The company was counting on Brown's making the right decision.* Syn. BANK ON. **2.** See FIGURE ON 2.

count one's chickens before they're hatched *v. phr., informal* To depend on getting a profit or gain before you have it; make plans that suppose something will happen; be too sure that something will happen. Usually used in negative sentences. ♦ *When Jim said that he would be made captain of the team, John told him not to count his chickens before they were hatched.* ♦ *Maybe some of your customers won't pay, and then where will you be? Don't count your chickens before they're hatched.*

count out *v.* **1.** To leave (someone) out of a plan; not expect (someone) to share in an activity; exclude. ♦ *"Will this party cost anything? If it does, count me out, because I'm broke."* ♦ *When the coach was planning who would play in the big game he counted Paul out, because Paul had a hurt leg.* **2.** To count out loud to ten to show that (a boxer who has been knocked down in a fight) is beaten or knocked out if he does not get up before ten is counted. ♦ *The champion was counted out in the third round.* **3a.** To add up; count again to be sure of the amount. ♦ *Mary counted out the number of pennies she had.* **3b.** To count out loud, (especially the beats in a measure of music). ♦ *The music teacher counted out the beats "one-two-three-four," so the class would sing in time.*

count to ten *v. phr., informal* To count from one to ten so you will have time to calm down or get control of yourself; put off action when angry or excited so as not to do anything wrong. ♦ *Father always told us to count to ten before doing anything when we got angry.* Compare KEEP ONE'S HEAD.

Contrast BLOW A FUSE, FLY OFF THE HANDLE.

county mounty *n., slang, citizen's band radio jargon* Sheriff's deputy. ♦ *The county mounties are parked under the bridge.*

courage See HAVE THE COURAGE OF ONE'S CONVICTIONS, SCREW UP ONE'S COURAGE.

course See IN DUE COURSE, MATTER OF COURSE, OF COURSE, PAR FOR THE COURSE.

court See DAY IN COURT, FRONT COURT, HOLD COURT, KANGAROO COURT.

cousin See FIRST COUSIN, SECOND COUSIN.

cover See FROM COVER TO COVER *at* FROM ———TO 3, UNDER COVER.

cover a lot of ground *v. phr.* To process a great deal of information and various facts. ♦ *Professor Brown's thorough lecture on asteroids covered a lot of ground today.*

covered-dish supper *or* **potluck supper** A meal to which each guest brings a share of the food. ♦ *Dolly made a chicken casserole for the covered-dish supper.*

cover girl *n.* A pretty girl or woman whose picture is put on the cover of a magazine. ♦ *Ann is not a cover girl, but she is pretty enough to be.*

cover ground *or* **cover the ground** *v. phr.* **1.** To go a distance; travel. ♦ *Mr. Rogers likes to travel in planes, because they cover ground so quickly.* **2.** *informal* To move over an area at a speed that is pleasing; move quickly over a lot of ground. ♦ *The new infielder really covers the ground at second base.* ♦ *Herby's new car really covers ground!* **3.** To give or receive the important facts and details about a subject. ♦ *If you're thinking about a trip to Europe, the airline has a booklet that covers the ground pretty well.* ♦ *The class spent two days studying the Revolutionary War, because they couldn't cover that much ground in one day.*

cover one's tracks *or* **cover up one's tracks** *v. phr.* **1.** To hide and not leave anything, especially foot marks, to show where you have been, so that no one can follow you. ♦ *The deer covered his tracks by running in a stream.* **2.** *informal* To hide or not say where you have been or what you have done; not tell why you do something or what you plan to do. ♦ *The boys covered their tracks when they went swimming by saying that they were going for a walk.* Compare COVER UP 1.

cover the waterfront *v. phr.* To talk or write all about something; talk about something all possible ways. ♦ *The principal pretty well covered the waterfront on student behavior.*

cover up *v., informal* **1.** To hide something wrong or bad from attention. ♦ *The spy covered up his picture-taking by pretending to be just a tourist.* ♦ *A crooked banker tried to cover up his stealing some of the bank's money by starting a fire to destroy the records.* Compare COVER ONE'S TRACKS 2. **2.** *In boxing:* To guard your head and body with your gloves, arms, and shoulders. ♦ *Jimmy's father told him to cover up and protect his chin when he boxed.* **3.** To protect someone else from blame or punishment; protect someone with a lie or alibi.—Often used with *for.* ♦ *The teacher wanted to know who broke the window and told the boys not to try to cover up for anyone.* ♦ *The burglar's friend covered up for him by saying that he was at his home when the robbery occurred.*

cover-up *n., slang* A plan or excuse to escape blame or punishment; lie, alibi. ♦ *When the men robbed the bank, their cover-up was to dress like policemen.* ♦ *Joe's cover-up to his mother after he had been fighting was that he fell down.*

cow See HOLY CATS *or* HOLY COW, SACRED COW.

cowboy *n., slang, informal* A person who drives his car carelessly and at too great a speed in order to show off his courage. ♦ *Joe's going to be arrested some day—he is a cowboy on the highway.*

cow college *n., slang* **1.** An agricultural college; a school where farming is studied. ♦ *A new, bigger kind of apple is being grown at the cow college.* **2.** A new or rural college not thought to be as good as older or city colleges. ♦ *John wanted to go to a big college in New York City, not to a cow college.*

cow's tail *n., dialect* A person who is behind others. ♦ *John was the cow's tail at the exam.* ♦ *Fred was always the old cow's tail for football practice.*

cozy up *v., slang* To try to be close or friendly; try to be liked.—Usually used with *to.* ♦ *John is cozying up to Henry so he can join the club.*

crack See HARD NUT TO CRACK *or* TOUGH NUT TO CRACK.

crack a book *v. phr., slang* To open a book in order to study.—Usually used with a negative. ♦ *John did not crack a book until the night before the exam.* ♦ *Many students think they can pass without cracking a book.*

crack a bottle *v. phr.* To open a new bottle of alcoholic beverage. ♦ *On birthdays it is customary to crack a bottle and offer one's best wishes.*

crack a joke *v. phr., informal* To make a joke; tell a joke. ♦ *The men sat around the stove, smoking and cracking jokes.*

crack a smile *v. phr., informal* To let a smile show on one's face; permit a smile to appear. ♦ *Bob told the whole silly story without even cracking a smile.* ♦ *Scrooge was a gloomy man, who never cracked a smile.* ♦ *When we gave the shy little boy an ice cream cone, he finally cracked a smile.*

crack down *v. phr., informal* To enforce laws or rules strictly; require full obedience to a rule. ♦ *After a speeding driver hit a child, the police cracked down.*—Often used with *on.* ♦ *Police suddenly cracked down on the selling of liquors to minors.* ♦ *The coach cracked down on the players when he found they had not been obeying the training rules.*

crack of dawn *n. phr.* The time in the morning when the sun's rays first appear. ♦ *The rooster crows at the crack of dawn and wakes up everybody on the farm.*

cracked up *adj. phr., informal* Favorably described or presented; praised.—Usually used in the expression *not what it's cracked up to be.* ♦ *The independent writer's life isn't always everything it's cracked up to be.* ♦ *In bad weather, a sailing cruise isn't what it's cracked up to be.*

cracking See GET CRACKING—*at* GET GOING 2.

crackpot *n., attrib. adj., informal* **1.** *n.* An eccentric person with ideas that don't make sense to most other people. ♦ *Don't believe what Uncle Noam tells you—he is a crackpot.* **2.** *attrib. adj.* ♦ *That's a crackpot idea.*

crack the whip *v. phr., informal* To get obedience or cooperation by threats of punishment. ♦ *If the children won't behave when I reason with them, I have to crack the whip.*

crack up *v.* **1.** To wreck or be wrecked; smash up. ♦ *The airplane cracked up in landing.* ♦ *He cracked up his car.* **2.** *informal* To become mentally ill under physical or mental overwork or worry. ♦ *He had kept too busy for years, and when failures came, he cracked up.* ♦ *It seemed to be family problems that made him crack up.* **3.** burst into laughter *or* cause to burst into laughter. ♦ *That comedian cracks me up.*

cradle See ROB THE CRADLE.

cradle robber, cradle robbing See ROB THE CRADLE.

cramp See WRITER'S CRAMP.

cramp one's style *v. phr., informal* To limit your natural freedom; prevent your usual behavior; limit your actions or talk. ♦ *It cramped his style a good deal when he lost his money.* ♦ *Army rules cramped George's style.*

crash dive *n.* A sudden dive made by a submarine to escape an enemy; a dive made to get deep under water as quickly as possible. ♦ *The captain of the submarine told his crew to prepare for a crash dive when he saw the enemy battleship approaching.*

crash-dive *v.* **1.** To dive deep underwater in a submarine as quickly as possible. ♦ *We shall crash-dive if we see enemy planes coming.* **2.** To dive into (something) in an airplane. ♦ *When the plane's motor was hit by the guns of the enemy battleship, the pilot aimed the plane at the ship and crash-dived into it.*

crash the gate *v. phr., slang* To enter without a ticket or without paying; attend without an invitation or permission. ♦ *Bob got into the circus without paying. He crashed the gate.* ♦ *Three boys tried to crash the gate at our party but we didn't let them in.*

craw See STICK IN ONE'S CRAW.

crawl up See RIDE UP.

crazy *or* **mad** *or* **nuts about** *adj. phr., informal* Excessively fond of; infatu-

ated with. ♦ *Jack is totally nuts about Liz, but she is not too crazy about him.*

cream See VANISHING CREAM.

cream of the crop *n. phr.* The best of a group; the top choice. ♦ *May Queen candidates were lovely, but Betsy and Nancy were the cream of the crop.* ♦ *The students had drawn many good pictures and the teacher chose the cream of the crop to hang up when the parents came to visit.*

creature of habit *n. phr.* A person who does things out of habit rather than by thought. ♦ *Our boss is a creature of habit, so let us not confuse him with too many new ideas.*

credibility gap *n., hackneyed phrase, politics* An apparent discrepancy between what the government says and what one can observe for oneself. ♦ *There was a tremendous credibility gap in the USA during the Watergate years.*

credit See DO CREDIT.

creek See UP THE CREEK *or* UP THE CREEK WITHOUT A PADDLE.

creep See THE CREEPS.

creep up on *v.* **1.** To crawl towards; move along near the ground; steal cautiously towards so as not to be seen or noticed. ♦ *The mouse did not see the snake creeping up on it over the rocks.* ♦ *Indians were creeping up on the house through the bushes.* **2.** *or* **sneak up on** To come little by little; arrive slowly and unnoticed. ♦ *The woman's hair was turning gray as age crept up on her.* ♦ *Winter is creeping up on us little by little.* ♦ *The boys didn't notice the darkness creeping up on them while they were playing.* Compare COME OVER.

crew See SECTION GANG *or* SECTION CREW.

crew cut *or* **crew haircut** *n.* A boy's or man's hair style, cut so that the hair stands up in short, stiff bristle. ♦ *Many boys like to get crew cuts during the summer to keep cooler.*

crisp See BURN TO A CRISP.

crocodile tears *n.* Pretended grief; a show of sorrow that is not really felt. ♦ *When his rich uncle died, leaving him his money, John shed crocodile tears.* [From the old legend that crocodiles make weeping sounds to attract victims and then shed tears while eating them.]

crook See BY HOOK OR BY CROOK.

crop See CASH CROP, CREAM OF THE CROP, STICK IN ONE'S CRAW *or* STICK IN ONE'S CROP.

crop out *v.* To appear at the surface; come through or show through from hiding or concealment. ♦ *Rocks often crop out in New England pasture land.* ♦ *A hidden hate cropped out in his words.*

cropper See COME A CROPPER.

crop up *v.* To come without warning; appear or happen unexpectedly. ♦ *Problems cropped up almost every day when Mr. Reed was building his TV station.* ♦ *Serious trouble cropped up just when Martin thought the problem of his college education was solved.* Compare TURN UP.

cross See AT CROSS PURPOSES, CARRY ONE'S CROSS, DOUBLE CROSS, KEEP ONE'S FINGERS CROSSED *at* CROSS ONE'S FINGERS 1b.

cross a bridge before one comes to it *v. phr.* To worry about future events or trouble before they happen—Usually used in negative sentences, often as a proverb. ♦ *"Can I be a soldier when I grow up, Mother?" asked Johnny. "Don't cross that bridge until you come to it," said his mother.* Compare BORROW TROUBLE.

cross-check¹ *v.* To test the truth of by examining in different ways or by seeing different reports about. ♦ *If you see something in a book that may not be true, be sure to crosscheck it in other books.*

cross-check² *n.* The testing of the truth of by checking one report against another or others. ♦ *A cross-check with other books will show us if this story is true.*

cross fire *n.* **1.** Firing in a fight or battle from two or more places at once so that the lines of fire cross. ♦ *The soldiers on the bridge were caught in the cross fire coming from both sides of the bridge.* **2.** Fast or angry talking back and forth between two or more people; *also,* a dispute; a quarrel. ♦ *There was a cross fire of excited questions and answers between the parents and the children who had been lost in the woods.* ♦ *The principal and the graduates quarreled about the football*

team, and the coach was caught in the cross fire and lost his job.

cross one's fingers *v. phr.* **1a.** To cross two fingers of one hand for good luck. ♦ *Mary crossed her fingers during the race so that Tom would win.* **1b.** *or* **keep one's fingers crossed** *informal* To wish for good luck. ♦ *Keep your fingers crossed while I take the test.* **2.** To cross two fingers of one hand to excuse an untruth that you are telling. ♦ *Johnny crossed his fingers when he told his mother the lie.*

cross one's heart *or* **cross one's heart and hope to die** *v. phr., informal* To say that what you have said is surely true; promise seriously that it is true.— Often used by children in the longer form. Children often make a sign of a cross over the heart as they say it, for emphasis. ♦ *"Cross my heart, I didn't hide your bicycle," Harry told Tom.* ♦ *"I didn't tell the teacher what you said. Cross my heart and hope to die," Mary said to Lucy.*

cross one's mind *or* **pass through one's mind** *v. phr.* To be a sudden or passing thought; be thought of by someone; come to your mind; occur to you. ♦ *At first Bob was puzzled by Virginia's waving, but then it crossed his mind that she was trying to tell him something.* ♦ *When Jane did not come home by midnight, many terrible fears passed through Mother's mind.*

cross one's path *v. phr.* To meet or encounter someone; to come upon someone more by accident than by plan. ♦ *Surprisingly, I crossed John's path in Central Park one afternoon.*

cross street *n.* A street that crosses a main street and runs on both sides of it. ♦ *Elm Street is a cross street on Main Street and there is a traffic light there.* Compare THROUGH STREET.

cross swords *v. phr., literary* To have an argument with; fight.—Often used with *with.* ♦ *Don't argue with the teacher; you're not old enough to cross swords with her.*

cross the wire *v. phr.* To finish a race. ♦ *The Russian crossed the wire just behind the American.*

cross up *v., informal* **1.** To block or upset; throw into confusion or disorder. ♦ *We were going to catch him at* the gate, but he crossed us up by going in the back way. ♦ Father crossed up the surprise party we had planned for him by not getting back in time. **2.** To deceive or be false to. ♦ George crossed up his partner by selling a lot of things secretly.

crow See EAT CROW.

crow before one is out of the woods v. phr. To be glad or brag before you are safe from danger or trouble.—Usually used in negative sentences, often as a proverb, "Don't crow before you are out of the woods." ♦ John thought his team would win because the game was almost over, but he didn't want to crow before they were out of the woods. Often used in a short form, out of the woods. ♦ Mary nearly died during the operation, and she is not out of the woods yet.

crown jewels n. pl. The crown, staff, and jewels used for the crowning of a king or queen; the crown and jewels representing royal power and authority. ♦ The crown jewels are handed down from one king to the next when the new king is crowned.

crow to pick See BONE TO PICK or CROW TO PICK.

crust See UPPER CRUST.

crux of the matter n. phr. The basic issue at hand; the core essence that one must face. ♦ The crux of the matter is that he is incompetent and we will have to fire him.

cry See FAR CRY, FOR CRYING OUT LOUD, HUE AND CRY.

cry or **scream bloody murder** v. phr. To bitterly and loudly complain against an indignity. ♦ Pete cried bloody murder when he found out that he didn't get the promotion he was hoping for.

cry before one is hurt or **holler before one is hurt** v. phr., informal To complain when there is no reason for it; become upset because you are worried or afraid—Used in negative sentences. ♦ When Billy went to the barber, he began to cry before the barber cut his hair and his father told him not to cry before he was hurt.—Often used as a proverb. ♦ John was worried because he would soon have a new boss. His mother said, "Don't cry before you're hurt!" Syn. BORROW TROUBLE.

cry buckets v. phr. To shed an excessive amount of tears. ♦ Grandma is crying buckets over the loss of our cat .

cry for or **cry out for** v., informal To need badly; be lacking in. ♦ It has not rained for two weeks and the garden is crying for it. ♦ The school is crying out for good teachers.

cry out v. **1.** To call out loudly; shout; scream. ♦ The woman in the water cried out "Help!" **2.** To complain loudly; protest strongly.—Used with against. ♦ Many people are crying out against the new rule.

cry out for See CRY FOR.

cry over spilled milk or **cry over spilt milk** v. phr., informal To cry or complain about something that has already happened; be unhappy about something that cannot be helped. ♦ After the baby tore up Sue's picture book, Sue's mother told her there was no use crying over spilled milk. ♦ You have lost the game but don't cry over spilt milk. Compare MAKE ONE'S BED AND LIE IN IT, WATER OVER THE DAM or WATER UNDER THE BRIDGE.

crystal ball n. A ball, usually made of quartz crystal (glass) that is used by fortune-tellers. ♦ The fortune-teller at the fair looked into her crystal ball and told me that I would take a long trip next year. **2.** Any means of predicting the future. ♦ My crystal ball tells me you'll be making the honor roll.

crystal gazing n. The attempt to predict future events. ♦ The magician's specialty was crystal gazing.

cry uncle See SAY UNCLE.

cry wolf v. phr. To give a false alarm; warn of a danger that you know is not there. ♦ The general said that the candidate was just crying wolf when he said that the army was too weak to fight for the country. [From an old story about a shepherd boy who falsely claimed a wolf was killing his sheep, just to start some excitement.]

cub scout n. A member of the Cub Scouts, the junior branch of the Boy Scouts for boys 8–10 years of age. ♦ Jimmie is only seven, too young to be a Cub Scout.

cucumber See COOL AS A CUCUMBER.

cudgel See TAKE UP THE CUDGELS FOR.

cudgel one's brains See BEAT ONE'S BRAINS OUT.

cue in *v. phr., informal* To add new information to that which is already known. ♦ *Let's not forget to cue in Joe on what has been happening.*

cuff See OFF-THE-CUFF, ON THE CUFF.

culture vulture *n., slang, informal* A person who is an avid cultural sightseer, one who seeks out cultural opportunities ostentatiously, such as going to the opera or seeing every museum in a town visited, and brags about it. ♦ *My Aunt Mathilda is a regular culture vulture; she spends every summer in a different European capital going to museums and operas.*

cup See IN ONE'S CUPS.

cup of tea *also* **dish of tea** *n. phr., informal* **1.** Something you enjoy or do well at; a special interest, or favorite occupation. Used with a possessive. ♦ *You could always get him to go for a walk: hiking was just his cup of tea.* Compare DOWN ONE'S ALLEY. **2.** Something to think about; thing; matter. ♦ *That's another cup of tea.* Compare KETTLE OF FISH.

curb service *n.* Waiting on customers while they sit in their cars. ♦ *Families with small children often look for hamburger stands that offer curb service.*

curiosity killed the cat *informal* Getting too nosy may lead a person into trouble.—A proverb. ♦ *"Curiosity killed the cat," Fred's father said, when he found Fred hunting around in closets just before Christmas.*

curl See PIN CURL.

curl one's hair *v. phr., slang* To shock; frighten; horrify; amaze. ♦ *Wait till you read what it says about you—this'll curl your hair.* ♦ *The movie about monsters from another planet curled his hair.*

curl up *v.* **1a.** To become curly or wavy. ♦ *Bacon curls up when it is cooked.* **1b.** To roll oneself into a ball. ♦ *Tim curled up in bed and was asleep in five minutes.* **2.** See FOLD UP.

current See SWIM AGAINST THE CURRENT.

curry favor *v.* To flatter or serve someone to get his help or friendship. ♦ *Joe tried to curry favor with the new teacher by doing little services that she didn't really want.* ♦ *Jim tried to curry favor with the new girl by telling her she was the prettiest girl in the class.* Compare POLISH THE APPLE.

curve See THROW A CURVE.

cut See FISH OR CUT BAIT.

cut a class *v. phr.* To be truant; to deliberately miss a class and do something else instead. ♦ *"If you keep cutting classes the way you do, you will almost surely flunk this course," John's professor said to him.*

cut a figure *v. phr.* To make a favorable impression; carry off an activity with dignity and grace. ♦ *With his handsome face and sporty figure, Harry cuts quite a figure with all the ladies.*

cut across *v.* **1.** To cross or go through instead of going around; go a short way. ♦ *John didn't want to walk to the corner and turn, so he cut across the yard to the next street.* **2.** To go beyond to include; stretch over to act on; affect. ♦ *The love for reading cuts across all classes of people, rich and poor.*

cut-and-dried *adj. phr.* Decided or expected beforehand; following the same old line; doing the usual thing. ♦ *The decision of the judge was cut-and-dried.* ♦ *The ways of the king's court were cut-and-dried.* ♦ *People at the convention heard many cut-and-dried speeches.*

cut and run *v., informal* To abandon an unfavorable situation. ♦ *When the price of coffee dropped sharply many investors wanted to cut and run.*

cut a swathe *v. phr.* **1a.** To mow a path through a field. ♦ *The farmer cut a swathe through the high grass with his scythe.* **1b.** To cut down as if by mowing. ♦ *The machine gun cut a swathe in the lines of enemy soldiers.* **2.** *informal* To attract notice; make an impression; seem important. ♦ *The movie star cut a wide swathe when he walked down the street.* ♦ *John tries to show off and cut a big swathe with the girls.* Compare GO OVER 6, MAKE A HIT.

cut back *v.* **1.** To change direction suddenly while going at full speed. ♦ *The halfback started to his left, cut back to his right, and ran for a touchdown.* **2.** To use fewer or use less. ♦ *After the big job was finished, the builder cut back the number of men working for him.* ♦ *The school employed forty teachers until a lower budget forced it to cut back.*

cut back *v. phr.* To diminish; lessen; decrease (said of budgets). ♦ *The state had to cut back on the university budget.*

cutback *n.* An act of decreasing monetary sources. ♦ *The cutback in military spending has caused many bases to be closed.*

cut both ways *or* **cut two ways** *v. phr.* To have two effects; cause injury to both sides. ♦ *People who gossip find it cuts both ways.*

cut corners *v. phr.* **1.** To take a short way; not go to each corner. ♦ *He cut corners going home in a hurry.* **2.** To save cost or effort; manage in a thrifty way; be saving. ♦ *John's father asked him to cut corners all he could in college.* **3.** To do less than a very good job; do only what you must do on a job. ♦ *He had cut corners in building his house, and it didn't stand up well.*

cut down *v.* To lessen; reduce; limit. ♦ *Tom had to cut down expenses.* ♦ *The doctor told Mr. Jones to cut down on smoking.*

cut down to size *v. phr., informal* To prove that someone is not as good as he thinks. ♦ *The big boy told John he could beat him, but John was a good boxer and soon cut him down to size.* Syn. PUT IN ONE'S PLACE.

cut ice *v. phr., informal* To make a difference; make an impression; be accepted as important.—Usually used in negative, interrogative, or conditional sentences. ♦ *When Frank had found a movie he liked, what others said cut no ice with him.* ♦ *Jones is democratic; a man's money or importance never cuts any ice with him.* ♦ *Does comfort cut any ice with you?* ♦ *I don't know if beauty in a woman cuts any ice with him.*

cut in *v.* **1.** To force your way into a place between others in a line of cars, people, etc.; push in. ♦ *After passing several cars, Fred cut in too soon and nearly caused an accident.*—Often used with *on.* ♦ *A car passed Jean and cut in on her too close; she had to brake quickly or she would have hit it.* ♦ *The teacher beside the lunch line saw Pete cut in, and she sent him back to wait his turn.* **2.** To stop a talk or program for a time; interrupt. ♦ *While Mary and Jim were talking on the porch, Mary's little brother cut in on them and began to tell about his fishing trip.* ♦ *While we were watching the late show, an announcer cut in to tell who won the election.* Syn. BREAK IN 2. **3.** *informal* To tap a dancer on the shoulder and claim the partner. ♦ *Mary was a good dancer and a boy could seldom finish a dance with her; someone always cut in.*—Often used with *on.* ♦ *At the leap year dance, Jane cut in on Sally because she wanted to dance with Sally's handsome date.* **4.** To connect to an electrical circuit or to a machine. ♦ *Harry threw the switch and cut in the motor.* ♦ *The airplane pilot cut in a spare gas tank.* **5.** *informal* To take in; include. ♦ *When John's friends got a big contract, they cut John in.*

cut into *v.* **1.** To make less; reduce. ♦ *The union made the company pay higher wages, which cut into the profits.* ♦ *The other houses got old and shabby, and that cut into the value of his house.* ♦ *At first Smith led in votes, but more votes came in and cut into his lead.* **2.** To get into by cutting in. ♦ *She heard the other women gossiping and cut into the talk.* ♦ *While Bill was passing another car, a truck came around a curve heading for him, and Bill cut back into line quickly.*

cut loose *v.* **1.** To free from ties or connections, cut the fastenings of. ♦ *The thief hastily cut the boat loose from its anchor.* Compare LET LOOSE 1a. **2.** *informal* To break away from control; get away and be free. ♦ *The boy left home and cut loose from his parents' control.* **3.** *informal* To behave freely or wildly. ♦ *The men had come to the convention to have a good time, and they really cut loose.* ♦ *When he got the news of his job promotion, Jack cut loose with a loud "Yippee!"* Compare LET GO 6.

cut no ice *v. phr.* To have no effect; achieve no result; be insignificant. ♦ *The fact that the accused is a millionaire will cut no ice with this particular judge.*

cut off *v.* **1.** To separate or block. ♦ *The flood cut the townspeople off from the rest of the world.* ♦ *The woods cut off the view.* ♦ *His rudeness cuts him off from friends he might have.* **2.** To interrupt or stop. ♦ *The television show was cut off by a special news report.* ♦ *We were told to pay the bill or the water would be cut off.* **3.** To end the life of; cause the death of. ♦ *Disease cut Smith off in the best part of life.* **4.** To give nothing to at death; leave out of a will. ♦ *Jane married a man her father hated, and her father cut her off.* ♦ *Frank's uncle cut him off without a penny.* **5.** To stop from operating; turn a switch to stop. ♦ *The ship cut off its engines as it neared the dock.* Syn. SHUT OFF, TURN OFF.

cut off one's nose to spite one's face *v. phr.* To suffer from an action intended originally to harm another person. ♦ *In walking out and leaving his employer in the lurch, John really cut off his nose to spite his face, since no business wanted to hire him afterwards.*

cut offs *n., colloquial* Pants cut to the length of shorts and usually left unhemmed so as to look old and worn, e.g., considered cool and elegant. ♦ *Jack always wears cut-offs during the summer.*

cut one's eyeteeth on See CUT TEETH 2.

cut one's losses *v. phr.* To stop spending time, money, or energy on unprofitable projects and concentrate on what goes well. ♦ *"Just cut your losses, Jim," his father suggested, "and get on with the rest of your life."*

cut one's teeth on See CUT TEETH 2.

cut one's throat *v. phr., informal* To spoil one's chances; ruin a person. ♦ *He cut his own throat by his carelessness.* ♦ *The younger men in the company were cutting each other's throats in their eagerness to win success.* ♦ *John cut Freddie's throat with Mary by telling her lies.*

cut out¹ *v., slang* **1.** To stop; quit. ♦ *All right, now—let's cut out the talking.* ♦ *He was teasing the dog and Joe told him to cut it out.* Compare BREAK UP 3. **2.** To displace in favor. ♦ *Tony cut Ed out with Mary.* ♦ *John cut out two or three other men in trying for a better job.*

cut out² *adj.* **1.** Made ready; given for action; facing. ♦ *Mary agreed to stay with her teacher's children all day; she did not know what was cut out for her.*—Often used in the phrase *have one's work cut out for one.* ♦ *If Mr.*

Perkins wants to become a senator, he has his work cut out for him. **2.** Suited to; fitted for. ♦ *Warren seemed to be cut out for the law.* ♦ *It was clear very early that Fred was cut out to be a doctor.*

cut rate¹ *n.* A lower price; a price less than usual. ♦ *Toys are on sale at the store for cut rates.*

cut-rate² *adj.* Sold for a price lower than usual; selling cheap things. ♦ *If you buy cut-rate things, be sure they are good quality first.* ♦ *John's brother bought a cut-rate bicycle at the second-hand store.* ♦ *There is a cut-rate drug-store on the corner.*

cut short *v.* To stop or interrupt suddenly; end suddenly or too soon. ♦ *Rain cut short the ball game.* ♦ *An auto accident cut short the man's life.* ♦ *When Dick began to tell about his summer vacation the teacher cut him short, saying "Tell us about that another time."*

cut teeth *v. phr.* **1.** To have teeth grow out through the gums. ♦ *The baby was cross because he was cutting teeth.* **2.** *or* **cut eye teeth** *informal* To learn something very early in life; gain experience; start by learning or doing.— Used with a possessive, usually used with *on.* ♦ *The professional ball player cut his teeth on a baseball bat in the sandlots.* ♦ *Mr. Jones's company is building the new Post Office in town but Mr. Jones cut his eye teeth as a carpenter.*

cut the ground from under *v. phr. informal* To make (someone) fail; upset the plans of; spoil the argument for (a person) in advance. ♦ *Paul wanted to be captain but we cut the ground from under him by saying that Henry was the best player on the team.* ♦ *Several workers applied for the retiring foreman's job, but the owner cut the ground from under them by hiring a foreman from another company.*

cut the mustard *v. phr., slang* To do well enough in what needs to be done; to succeed. ♦ *His older brothers and sisters helped Max through high school, but he couldn't cut the mustard in college.*

cut-throat *adj.* Severe; intense; unrelenting. ♦ *There is cut-throat competi-*

tion among the various software companies today.

cut to pieces *v. phr.* **1.** To divide into small parts with something sharp; cut badly or completely. ◆ *Baby has cut the newspaper to pieces with scissors.* **2.** To destroy or defeat completely. ◆ *The soldiers were cut to pieces by the Indians.* ◆ *When Dick showed his book report to his big sister for correction, she cut it to pieces.*

cut to the bone *v. phr.* To make (something) the least or smallest possible amount; reduce severely; leave out everything extra or unnecessary from. ◆ *Father cut Jane's allowance to the bone for disobeying him.* ◆ *When father lost his job, our living expenses had to be cut to the bone.*

cut to the quick *v. phr.* To hurt someone's feelings deeply. ◆ *The children's teasing cut Mary to the quick.*

cut two ways See CUT BOTH WAYS.

cut up *v.* **1.** *informal* To hurt the feelings of; wound.—Usually used in the passive. ◆ *John was badly cut up when Susie gave him back his ring.* **2.** *slang* To act funny or rough; clown. ◆ *Joe would always cut up if there were any girls watching.* ◆ *At the party Jim and Ron were cutting up and broke a chair.* Compare FOOL AROUND.

dab See SMACK-DAB *or* SMACK-TO DAB.

dagger See CLOAK-AND-DAGGER, LOOK DAGGERS.

daily dozen *n., informal* Gymnastic exercises; *especially,* several different exercises done daily. ♦ *The boys did their daily dozen early each morning.*

daisy See PUSH UP DAISIES.

dam See WATER OVER THE DAM.

damn See GIVE A HANG, NOT WORTH A TINKER'S DAMN.

damned if one does, damned if one doesn't *adj. phr.* No matter what one does, someone is likely to criticize one. ♦ *No matter what decisions I make, there are always some people who will approve them and those who won't. It is a classical case of "damned if I do, damned if I don't."*

dance See SONG AND DANCE.

dance to another tune *v. phr.* To talk or act differently, usually better because things have changed; be more polite or obedient because you are forced to do it. ♦ *Johnny refused to do his homework but punishment made him dance to another tune.* Compare CHANGE ONE'S TUNE, SING A DIFFERENT TUNE.

dander See GET ONE'S BACK UP, GET ONE'S DANDER UP *or* GET ONE'S IRISH UP.

dandy See JIM-DANDY.

dangerous See A LITTLE KNOWLEDGE IS A DANGEROUS THING.

dare say *v. phr.* To think probable; suppose; believe.—Used in first person. ♦ *Mary is unhappy now but I dare say she will be laughing about this tomorrow.* ♦ *There is no more ice cream on the table, but I dare say we can find some in the kitchen.*

dare one to do something *v. phr.* To challenge someone to do something. ♦ *"I dare you to jump off that rock into the sea," Fred said to Jack.*

dark See IN THE DARK, SHOT IN THE DARK, WHISTLE IN THE DARK.

darken one's door *or* **darken the door** To appear, as in a doorway; enter someone's home or establishment.—Used in negative imperative sentences especially with *never* and *again.* ♦ *If you leave this house now, never darken my door again.* ♦ *After a son shamed his father by having to go to prison, the father told him never to darken his door again.*

dark horse *n., informal* A political candidate little known to the general voting public; a candidate who was not expected to run. ♦ *Every once in a while a dark horse candidate gets elected President.*

dark of the moon *n. phr., literary* A time when the moon is not shining or cannot be seen. ♦ *It was the dark of the moon when the scouts reached camp and they had to use flashlights to find their tents.* Contrast FULL OF THE MOON.

dash cold water on See THROW COLD WATER ON.

dash light *n.* A light on the front inside of a car or vehicle. ♦ *Henry stopped the car and turned on the dash lights to read the road map.*

dash off *v.* To make, do, or finish quickly; especially, to draw, paint, or write hurriedly. ♦ *Ann took out her drawing pad and pencil and dashed off a sketch of the Indians.* ♦ *John can dash off several letters while Mary writes only one.* ♦ *Charles had forgotten to write his English report and dashed it off just before class.*

date See DOUBLE-DATE, TO DATE.

date back *v. phr.* To go back to a given period in the past. ♦ *My ancestors date back to the sixteenth century.*

dawn on *v.* To become clear to. ♦ *It dawned on Fred that he would fail the course if he did not study harder.*

day See ALL IN A DAY'S WORK, CALL IT A DAY, CARRY THE DAY, EVERY DOG HAS HIS DAY, FATHER'S DAY, FOREVER AND A DAY, GOOD DAY, MAKE A DAY OF IT, NAME DAY, NIGHT AND DAY, ONE OF THESE DAYS, *or* SOME OF THESE DAYS, PASS THE TIME OF DAY, RAINY DAY, SAVE THE DAY, SEE BETTER DAYS, THAT'LL BE THE DAY.

day and night *or* **night and day** *adv.* **1.** For days without stopping; continually. Syn. AROUND THE CLOCK. ♦ *Some filling stations on great highways are open day and night 365 days a year.*

♦ *The three men took turns driving the truck, and they drove night and day for three days.* **2.** Every day and every evening. ♦ *The girl knitted day and night to finish the sweater before her mother's birthday.*

day by day *adv.* Gradually. ♦ *The patient got better day by day.*

day in and day out *or* **day in, day out** *adv. phr.* Regularly; consistently; all the time; always. ♦ *He plays good tennis day in and day out.*—Also used with several other time words in place of *day: week, month, year.* ♦ *Every summer, year in, year out, the ice cream man comes back to the park.*

day in court *n. phr.* A chance to be heard; an impartial hearing; a chance to explain what one has done. ♦ *The letters from the faculty members to the dean gave Professor Smith his day in court.*

daylight See SCARE OUT OF ONE'S WITS *or* SCARE THE DAYLIGHTS OUT OF, SEE DAYLIGHT.

daylight saving time *also* **daylight saving** *or* **daylight time** *or* **fast time** *n.* A way of keeping time in summer that is one or two hours ahead of standard time.—Abbreviation DST. ♦ *Many places in the United States keep their clocks on daylight saving time in the summer; in this way people get up earlier and have more free time in the afternoon and evening while it is still daylight.* ♦ *Father said that next week it will get dark later because we will change to daylight saving time.* ♦ *We go off daylight saving in the fall.* Compare CENTRAL TIME. Contrast STANDARD TIME.

daylight robbery See HIGHWAY ROBBERY.

daydream *v.* To spend time in reverie; be absentminded during the day. ♦ *John spends so much time daydreaming that he never gets anything done.*

day of grace *n. phr.* An extension period after the due date of some contract or bond. ♦ *The premium is due on the first of each month, but they allow ten days of grace.*

day of reckoning *n. phr.* **1.** A time when one will be made to account for misdeeds. ♦ *When the criminal was caught and brought to trial his victims said, "finally, the day of reckoning has come."* **2.** A time when one's will and

judgment are severely tested. ♦ *"You always wanted to run the department," the dean said to Professor Smith. "Now here is your chance; this is your day of reckoning."*

day off *n.* A day on which one doesn't have to work, not necessarily the weekend. ♦ *Monday is his day off in the restaurant, because he prefers to work on Saturdays and Sundays.*

day-to-day *adj.* Daily; common; everyday. ♦ *For best results, students' homework should be checked on a day-to-day basis.*

days are numbered (Someone or something) does not have long to live or stay. ♦ *The days of the old school building are numbered.* ♦ *When a man becomes ninety years old, his days are numbered.*

dazzle See RAZZLE-DAZZLE.

dead See CATCH DEAD, DROP DEAD, STONEDEAD.

dead ahead *adv., informal* Exactly in front; before. ♦ *The school is dead ahead about two miles from here.* ♦ *Father was driving in a fog, and suddenly he saw another car dead ahead of him.*

deadbeat *n., slang* A person who never pays his debts and who has a way of getting things free that others have to pay for. ♦ *You'll never collect from Joe—he's a deadbeat.*

dead and buried *adj. phr.* Gone forever. ♦ *Slavery is dead and buried in twentieth-century America.*

dead as a doornail *adj. phr.* Completely dead without the slightest hope of resuscitation. ♦ *This battery is dead as a doornail; no wonder your car won't start.*

dead broke See STONE-BROKE.

dead center *n.* The exact middle. ♦ *The treasure was buried in the dead center of the island.* Often used like an adverb. ♦ *The arrow hit the circle dead center.*

dead duck *n., slang* A person or thing in a hopeless situation or condition; one to whom something bad is sure to happen. ♦ *When the pianist broke her arm, she was a dead duck.*

deadhead *n., slang* An excessively dull or boring person. ♦ *You'll never get John to tell a joke—he's a deadhead.*

dead letter *n. phr.* An undeliverable letter that ends up in a special office holding such letters. ♦ *There is a dead letter office in most major cities.*

deadline *n.* A final date by which a project, such as a term paper, is due. ♦ *The deadline for the papers on Shakespeare is November 10.*

dead loss *n. phr.* A total waste; a complete loss. ♦ *Our investment in Jack's company turned out to be a dead loss.*

dead on one's feet *adv. phr., informal* Very tired but still standing or walking; too tired to do more; exhausted. ♦ *Jimmy never leaves a job unfinished. He continues to work even when he's dead on his feet.* ♦ *After the soldiers march all night, they are dead on their feet.* Compare DEAD TIRED, WEAR OUT 2.

deadpan *adj., adv., slang* With an expressionless or emotionless face; without betraying any hint of emotion. ♦ *She received the news of her husband's death deadpan.*

dead pedal *n., slang, citizen's band radio jargon* A slow moving vehicle. ♦ *Better pass that eighteen wheeler, Jack; it's a dead pedal.*

dead ringer *n. phr.* A person who strongly resembles someone else. ♦ *Charlie is a dead ringer for his uncle.*

dead set against *adj. phr.* Totally opposed to someone or something. ♦ *Jack is dead set against the idea of marriage, which upsets Mary.*

dead tired *adj. phr., informal* Very tired; exhausted; worn out. ♦ *She was dead tired at the end of the day's work.* Compare DEAD ON ONE'S FEET.

dead to rights *adv. phr., informal* Without a chance of escaping blame; proven wrong. ♦ *Mother had Bob dead to rights, because she caught him with his hand in the cookie jar.* ♦ *The police caught the man dead to rights.*

dead to the world *adj. phr., informal* 1. Fast asleep. ♦ *Tim went to bed very late and was still dead to the world at 10 o'clock this morning.* 2. As if dead; unconscious. ♦ *Tom was hit on the head by a baseball and was dead to the world for two hours.*

dead-end *n.* A street closed at one end; a situation that leads nowhere. ♦ *Jim drove into a dead-end street and had to back out.* ♦ *Mary was in a dead-end job.*

dead-end *v.* To not continue normally but end in a closure (said of streets). ♦ *Our street dead-ends on the lake.*

deaf See TURN A DEAF EAR TO.

deal See GOOD DEAL *or* GREAT DEAL, NEW DEAL, NO DEAL, THINK A GREAT DEAL OF, WHEEL AND DEAL.

deal in *v. phr.* To sell; do business in a certain commodity. ♦ *Herb's firm deals in sporting goods.*

deal with *v. phr.* 1. To conduct negotiations or business dealings with. ♦ *John refuses to deal with the firm of Brown and Miller.* 2. To handle a problem. ♦ *Ted is a very strong person and dealt with the fact that his wife had left him much better than anyone else I know.*

dealer See WHEELER-DEALER *at* WHEEL AND DEAL.

dear See FOR DEAR LIFE.

Dear John letter *n. phr.*—A note or a letter informing one that a romantic relationship or a marriage is over. ♦ *Jane left a "Dear John letter" on the table and went home to live with her parents.*

dear me *interj.* Used to show surprise, fear, or some other strong feeling. ♦ *Dear me! My purse is lost, what shall I do now?*

death See AT DEATH'S DOOR, BETWEEN LIFE AND DEATH, CATCH ONE'S DEATH OF *or* TAKE ONE'S DEATH OF, SIGN ONE'S OWN DEATH WARRANT, TO DEATH.

death knell *n. formal* 1. The ringing of a bell at a death or funeral. ♦ *The people mourned at the death knell of their friend.* 2. *literary* Something which shows a future failure. ♦ *Bill's poor grade on his final examination sounded the death knell of his hope to be a doctor.* ♦ *His sudden deafness was the death knell of his hope to become President.*

death on *adj. phr., informal* 1. Very successful in meeting or dealing with. ♦ *Joe is death on fast balls. He usually knocks them out of the park.* 2. Disliking or strongly against; very strict about. ♦ *The new teacher is death on students who come late to class.* ♦ *The twins' grandmother is death on smoking.*

deck See HIT THE DECK, ON DECK.

decked out *adj. phr., informal* Dressed in fancy clothes; specially decorated for some festive occasion. ♦ *The school band was decked out in bright red uniforms with brass buttons.* ♦ *Main Street was decked with flags for the Fourth of July.*

declare See I DECLARE.

deep See BETWEEN THE DEVIL AND THE DEEP BLUE SEA, GO OFF THE DEEP END, IN DEEP, KNEE-DEEP.

deep-six *v., slang* To throw away; dispose of. ♦ *As the police boat came near, the drug smugglers deep-sixed their cargo.* (An expression originally used by sailors, suggesting throwing something into water six fathoms deep.)

deep water *n.* Serious trouble or difficulty. ♦ *When Dad tried to take Mom's place for a day, he found himself in deep water.*

defense See ZONE DEFENSE.

defiance See IN DEFIANCE OF.

degree See TO A DEGREE, TO THE NTH DEGREE.

deliver the goods *v. phr.* **1.** To carry things and give them to the person who wants them. ♦ *Lee delivered the goods to the right house.* **2.** *slang* To succeed in doing well what is expected. ♦ *The new pitcher delivered the goods by striking out 20 men in his first game.* ♦ *This personal computer surely delivers the goods.* Compare BRING HOME THE BACON.

delta wave *n., informal, semi-technical* A brain wave 1-3 cycles per second, associated with very deep sleep. ♦ *Good night, honey, I'm off to produce some delta waves.* Compare CATCH SOME Z'S, HIT THE HAY *or* HIT THE SACK.

demand See IN DEMAND.

Dennis the Menace *n. phr.* After the notorious television character played by a young boy who always creates trouble for the grownups. Any hyperactive little boy who needs calming down. ♦ *"Your son, Joey, is becoming a regular 'Dennis the Menace',"* Jane said to Elvira.

dent See MAKE A DENT IN.

deposit See ON DEPOSIT.

depth See BEYOND ONE'S DEPTH.

desk clerk See ROOM CLERK.

detective See HOUSE DETECTIVE.

devil See BETWEEN THE DEVIL AND THE DEEP BLUE SEA, FULL OF THE OLD NICK *or* FULL OF THE DEVIL, GIVE THE DEVIL HIS DUE, GO TO THE DEVIL, PLAY THE DEVIL WITH, RAISE THE DEVIL, SPEAK OF THE DEVIL AND HE APPEARS.

devil-may-care *adj.* Not caring what happens; unworried. ♦ *Johnny has a devil-may-care feeling about his school work.* ♦ *Alfred was a devil-may-care youth but became more serious as he grew older.*

devil-may-care attitude *n. phr.* An attitude of no concern for financial or other loss. ♦ *"Easy come, easy go," John said in a devil-may-care attitude when he lost all of his money during a poker game.*

devil of it *or* **heck of it** *n. phr.* **1.** The worst or most unlucky thing about a trouble or accident; the part that is most regrettable. ♦ *Andy lost his notebook, and the devil of it was that the notebook contained all his homework for the coming week.* ♦ *When I had a flat tire, the devil of it was that my spare tire was flat too.* **2.** Fun from doing mischief.—Used after *for.* ♦ *The boys carried away Miss White's front gate just for the devil of it.*

devil to pay *n. phr.* Great trouble.—Used after *the.* ♦ *There'll be the devil to pay when the teacher finds out who broke the window.* ♦ *When Jim wrecked his father's car, there was the devil to pay.*

dewey-eyed See MISTY-EYED.

diamond in the rough *n. phr.* A very smart person without a formal education who may have untutored manners. ♦ *Jack never went to school but he is extremely talented; he is a veritable diamond in the rough.*

dibs See TO HAVE DIBS ON *or* TO PUT DIBS ON.

dice See NO DEAL *or* NO DICE.

Dick See TOM, DICK AND HARRY.

die See CROSS ONE'S HEART *or* CROSS ONE'S HEART AND HOPE TO DIE, DO-OR-DIE, NEVER SAY DIE.

die away *or* **die down** *v.* To come slowly to an end; grow slowly less or weaker. ♦ *The wind died down.* ♦ *The music died away.* ♦ *He waited until the excitement had died down.* ♦ *His mother's anger died away.*

die in one's boots *or* **die with one's boots on** *v. phr., informal* To be killed or hanged rather than die in bed. ♦ *The badmen of the Old West usually died in their boots.* ♦ *The robber said he wanted to die with his boots on.*

die is cast *v. phr., literary* To make an irrevocable decision. (From Julius Caesar's famous words in Latin, *alea iacta est,* when he crossed the river Rubicon, which meant war.) ♦ *Everything was ready for the invasion of Europe, the die had been cast, and there was no turning back now.*

die off *v.* To die one at a time. ♦ *The flowers are dying off because there has been no rain.*

die on the vine *or* **wither on the vine** *v. phr.* To fail or collapse in the planning stages. ♦ *The program for rebuilding the city died on the vine.*

die out *v.* To die or disappear slowly until all gone. ♦ *This kind of bird is dying out.* ♦ *If you pour salt water on grass, it dies out.* ♦ *The American colonists started colleges so that learning would not die out.*

difference See MAKE A DIFFERENCE, SPLIT THE DIFFERENCE.

different See SING A DIFFERENT TUNE *or* WHISTLE A DIFFERENT TUNE.

dig down *v., slang* To spend your own money. ♦ *The school let the club use the bus and driver free for their trip, but they had to dig down to pay for gas and meals.* ♦ *"So you broke Mrs. Brown's window?" Tom's father said, "You'll have to dig down and pay for it."*

dig in *v., informal* **1.** To dig ditches for protection against an enemy attack. ♦ *The soldiers dug in and waited for the enemy to come.* **2a.** To go seriously to work; work hard. ♦ *John dug in and finished his homework very quickly.* **2b.** To begin eating. ♦ *Mother set the food on the table and told the children to dig in.*

dig out *v.* **1.** To find by searching; bring out (something) that was put away. ♦ *Jack dug his sled out of the cellar.* ♦ *The newspaper printed an old story dug out of their records.* Compare DIG UP. **2.** *informal* To escape.—Usually used with *of.* Often used in the phrase *dig oneself out of a hole.* ♦ *The pitcher dug himself out of a hole by striking the batter out.*

dig up *v., informal* To find or get (something) with some effort. ♦ *Sue dug up*

some useful material for her English composition. ♦ *Jim asked each boy to dig up twenty-five cents to pay for the hot dogs and soda.* Compare DIG OUT.

dilemma See HORNS OF A DILEMMA.

dim See TAKE A DIM VIEW OF.

dime a dozen *adj. phr., informal* Easy to get and so of little value; being an everyday thing because there are many of them; common. ♦ *Mr. Jones gives A's to only one or two students, but in Mr. Smith's class, A's are a dime a dozen.*

dime store *or* **five-and-dime** *or* **five-and-ten** *n. phr.* A store that sells things that cost little. ♦ *Charles bought a pencil at the five-and-dime.*

dine out *v. phr.* To not eat at home but to go to a restaurant. ♦ *"Let's dine out tonight, honey," she said to her husband. "I am tired of cooking dinner every night."* See EAT OUT.

dint See BY DINT OF.

dip into *v. phr.* **1.** To scan or sample lightly and briefly (said of printed materials). ♦ *I didn't get a chance to read all of* War and Peace, *but I dipped into it here and there.* **2.** To take money out of a savings account or a piggy bank. ♦ *I am sorry to have to say that I had to dip into the piggy bank; I took out $6.75.*

dirt See EAT DIRT, HIT THE DIRT, PAY DIRT.

dirt cheap *adj.* Extremely inexpensive. ♦ *The apartment we are renting is dirt cheap compared to other apartments of similar size in this neighborhood.*

dirty See AIR ONE'S DIRTY LINEN IN PUBLIC *or* WASH ONE'S DIRTY LINEN IN PUBLIC.

dirty look *n., informal* A look that shows dislike. ♦ *Miss Parker sent Joe to the principal's office for giving her a dirty look.*

dirty old man *n. phr.* An older man who shows an unhealthy interest in young girls. ♦ *"Stay away from Uncle Algernon, Sally," her mother warned. "He is a dirty old man."*

dirty one's hands *or* **soil one's hands** *v. phr.* To lower or hurt one's character or good name; do a bad or shameful thing. ♦ *The teacher warned the children not to dirty their hands by cheating in the examination.* ♦ *I would not soil my hands by going with bad people and doing bad things.*

dirty story *n. phr.* An improper or obscene story. ♦ *Uncle Bill is much too fond of telling dirty stories in order to embarrass his friends.*

dirty trick *n. phr.* A treacherous action; an unfair act. ♦ *That was a dirty trick John played on Mary when he ran away with her younger sister.*

disappear *or* **evaporate** *or* **vanish into thin air** *v. phr.* To disappear quickly, without leaving a trace. ♦ *Money seems to disappear into thin air these days.* ♦ *Jack just vanished into thin air before the meeting had started.*

discretion See THROW CAUTION TO THE WINDS *also* THROW DISCRETION TO THE WINDS.

discretion is the better part of valor *literary* When you are in danger or trouble, good sense helps more than foolish risks; it is better to be careful than to be foolishly brave.—A proverb. ♦ *When you are facing a man with a knife, discretion is the better part of valor.*

dish See COVERED-DISH SUPPER.

dish of tea See CUP OF TEA.

dish out *v.* **1.** To serve (food) from a large bowl or plate. ♦ *Ann's mother asked her to dish out the beans.* **2.** *informal* To give in large quantities. ♦ *That teacher dished out so much homework that her pupils complained to their parents.* **3.** *slang* To scold; treat or criticize roughly. ♦ *Jim likes to dish it out, but he hates to take it.* Compare HAND OUT.

dish the dirt *v. phr., slang* To gossip, to spread rumors about others. ♦ *Stop dishing the dirt, Sally, it's really quite unbecoming!*

disk jockey *n.* An employee at a radio station or in a dance club who puts on the records that will be broadcast. ♦ *Jack is working as a disk jockey at the local FM station.*

dispose of *v.* **1.** To throw away; give away, or sell; get rid of. ♦ *John's father wants to dispose of their old house and buy a new one.* ♦ *The burglars had difficulty in disposing of the stolen jewelry.* **2.** To finish with; settle; complete. ♦ *The boys were hungry, and quickly disposed of their dinner.* ♦ *The committee soon disposed of all its business.* **3.** To destroy or defeat. ♦ *The champion disposed of the other fighter by knocking him out in the second round.* ♦ *Our planes disposed of two enemy planes.*

dispute See IN DISPUTE.

distance See KEEP AT A DISTANCE, KEEP ONE'S DISTANCE.

ditch See LAST DITCH.

dive See GO INTO A TAIL SPIN *or* GO INTO A NOSE DIVE.

do See HAVE DONE, HAVE DONE WITH, HAVE TO DO WITH, LET GEORGE DO IT, LET ONE'S RIGHT HAND KNOW WHAT ONE'S LEFT HAND IS DOING, LET'S DON'T, MAKE DO, WELL-TO-DO, WHAT'S UP *or* WHAT'S DOING.

do a double take *v. phr., informal* To look again in surprise; suddenly understand what is seen or said. ♦ *John did a double take when he saw Bill in girls' clothes.* ♦ *When Evvie said she was quitting school, I did a double take.*

do a job on *v. phr., slang* To damage badly; do harm to; make ugly or useless. ♦ *The baby did a job on Mary's book.* ♦ *Jane cut her hair and really did a job on herself.*

Doakes See JOE DOAKES.

do a stretch *v. phr.* To spend time in jail serving one's sentence. ♦ *Jake has disappeared from view for a while; he is doing a stretch for dope smuggling.*

do away with *v.* **1.** To put an end to; stop. ♦ *The teachers want to do away with cheating in their school.* ♦ *The city has decided to do away with overhead wires.* Compare RID OF. **2.** To kill; murder. ♦ *The robbers did away with their victims.*

do by someone *or* **something** *v.* To deal with; treat.—Used with a qualifying adverb between *do* and *by.* ♦ *Andy's employer always does very well by him.*

do credit *or* **do credit to** *also (informal)* **do proud** To add to or improve the reputation, good name, honor, or esteem of; show (you) deserve praise. ♦ *Your neat appearance does you credit.* ♦ *Mary's painting would do credit to a real artist.*

doctor See JUST WHAT THE DOCTOR ORDERED.

doctor up *v. phr.* To meddle with; adulterate. ♦ *You don't have to doctor up this basic salad with a lot of extras as I am trying to lose weight.*

do duty for *v. phr.* To substitute for; act in place of. ♦ *The bench often does duty for a table.*

Doe See JOHN DOE.

doesn't add up to a can of beans *v. phr.* To be of little or no value. (Said of plans, ideas, etc.) ♦ *"That's a fairly interesting concept you got there, Mike, but the competition is bound to say that it doesn't add up to a can of beans."*

do for *v., informal* To cause the death or ruin of; cause to fail.—Used usually in the passive form *done for.* ♦ *The poor fellow is done for and will die before morning.* ♦ *Andy's employer always does very well by him.* ♦ *If Jim fails that test, he is done for.*

dog See EVERY DOG HAS HIS DAY, GO TO THE DOGS, HOT DOG, LEAD A DOG'S LIFE, LET SLEEPING DOGS LIE, RAIN CATS AND DOGS.

dog days *n. phr.* The hottest days of the year in the Northern Hemisphere (July and August). (The ancient Romans associated this time with the "Dog Star"—Sirius—which becomes visible in the heavens at this time of year.) ♦ *"The dog days are upon us," John said. "It's time to go swimming in the lake."*

dog-eat-dog[1] *n.* A way of living in which every person tries to get what he wants for himself no matter how badly or cruelly he must treat others to get it; readiness to do anything to get what you want. ♦ *In some early frontier towns it was dog-eat-dog.*

dog-eat-dog[2] *adj.* Ready or willing to fight and hurt others to get what you want. ♦ *During the California gold rush, men had a dog-eat-dog life.*

doghouse See IN THE DOGHOUSE.

dog in the manger *n. phr.* A person who is unwilling to let another use what he himself has no use for. ♦ *Although Valerie lives alone in that big house, she is like a dog in the manger when it comes to letting someone sharing it with her.*

dog one's steps *v. phr.* To follow someone closely. ♦ *All the time he was in Havana, Castro's police were dogging his steps.*

dog's age *or* **coon's age** *n., informal* A very long time. Usually used after *for* or *in* with a negative. ♦ *Charlie Brown!*

I haven't seen you for a coon's age. ♦ *Father hasn't had a night out with the boys in a dog's age.* ♦ *I waited for him for a dog's age, but he didn't come.* Syn. MONTH OF SUNDAYS.

dog's life *n. phr.* A life of misery, poverty, and unhappiness. ♦ *Diogenes, the Greek philosopher, lived a dog's life inside an empty barrel.*

do in *v., slang* **1.** To ruin; destroy. ♦ *Mr. Smith's business was done in by a fire that burned down his store.* **2a.** To kill; murder. ♦ *The poor man was done in by two gangsters who ran away after the crime.* **2b.** To make tired; exhaust. ♦ *The boys were done in after their long hike.* Syn. WEAR OUT 2. **3.** To cheat; swindle. ♦ *Mr. Jones was done in by two men who claimed to be collecting money for orphans and widows.*

doing See NOTHING DOING.

do justice to *v. phr.* **1.** To do (something) as well as you should; do properly. ♦ *Barbara had so many things to do that she could not do justice to her lessons.* ♦ *The newspaper man did not do justice to the story.* **2.** To eat or drink with enthusiasm or enjoyment. ♦ *The boy did justice to the meal.*

dole out *v. phr.* To measure out sparingly. ♦ *Since the water ration was running low in the desert, the camp commandant doled out small cups of water to each soldier.*

dollar See BET ONE'S BOTTOM DOLLAR *at* BET ONE'S BOOTS, FEEL LIKE A MILLION *or* FEEL LIKE A MILLION DOLLARS, LOOK LIKE A MILLION DOLLARS.

doll up *v., slang* **1.** To dress in fine or fancy clothes. ♦ *The girls dolled up for the big school dance of the year.* ♦ *The girls were all dolled up for the Christmas party.* **2.** To make more pretty or attractive. ♦ *The classrooms were all dolled up with Christmas decorations.* Compare DECKED OUT.

done for *adj. phr.* Finished; dead. ♦ *When the police burst in on the crooks, they knew they were done for.*

done to a turn See TO A T *or* TO A TURN.

done with *adj. phr.* Finished; completed. ♦ *As soon as you're done with your work, give us a call.*

don't cross your bridges until you come to them See CROSS A BRIDGE BEFORE ONE COMES TO IT.

don't cry before you're hurt See CRY BEFORE ONE IS HURT.

don't let's See LET'S DON'T.

don't look a gift horse in the mouth See LOOK A GIFT HORSE IN THE MOUTH.

do one a good turn *v. phr.* To perform an act of kindness, friendship, or help to another person, unselfishly, without expectation of reward. ♦ *"I'll be happy to help you any time you need it," John said. "After all you have done me so many good turns."*

do one good *v. phr.* To benefit. ♦ *The fresh air will do you good after having been inside the house all day.*

do one good *or* **do one's heart good** *v. phr.* To give satisfaction; please; gratify. ♦ *It does my heart good to see those children play.*

do one's best *v. phr.* To perform at one's optimum capacity; spare no effort in fulfilling one's duties. ♦ *"I've really done my best teaching you people," the tired professor said on the last day of classes. "I hope you got something out of this course."*

do one's bit *or* **part** *v. phr.* To shoulder one's share of responsibility in a communal undertaking; shirk one's obligation. ♦ *"Let me go home and rest, fellows," John said. "I think I've done my bit for this project."*

do one's thing *or* **do one's own thing** *v. phr., informal* **1.** To do what one does well and actually enjoys doing. ♦ *Two thousand fans paid $15 each to hear the rock group do their thing.* **2.** To follow one's bent; for example, to be engaged in left-wing politics, some sort of meditation, or use of drugs (particularly in the sixties). ♦ *The hippies were doing their own thing when the cops came and busted them.* **3.** To be engaged in an unusual activity that strikes others as odd. ♦ *Leave Jim alone, he's just doing his own thing when he's standing on his head.*

do one's worst *v. phr.* To do one's utmost by resorting to every foul means possible. ♦ *Hitler did his worst to drive out the Allied invasion from Europe, but he failed.*

door See AT DEATH'S DOOR, AT ONE'S DOOR, CLOSED-DOOR, CLOSE ITS DOORS, CLOSE THE DOOR *or* BAR THE DOOR *or* SHUT THE DOOR, DARKEN ONE'S DOOR, *or* DARKEN THE DOOR, FOOT IN THE DOOR, KEEP THE WOLF FROM THE DOOR, LAY AT ONE'S DOOR, LOCK THE BARN DOOR AFTER THE HORSE IS STOLEN, NEXT DOOR, OPEN ITS DOORS, OPEN THE DOOR, SHOW THE DOOR, SLAM THE DOOR IN ONE'S FACE *at* IN ONE'S FACE.

do-or-die *adj.* Strongly decided, very eager and determined. ♦ *With a real do-or-die spirit the team scored two touchdowns in the last five minutes of the game.* ♦ *The other army was larger but our men showed a do-or-die determination and won the battle.*

doorstep See AT ONE'S DOOR *or* AT ONE'S DOOR-STEP.

do over *v. phr.* **1.** To renovate; redecorate. ♦ *The new owners are going to do over the entire building in the fall.* **2.** To repeat. ♦ *Please do that math problem over until you get it right.*

dope out *v., slang* To think of something that explains. ♦ *The detectives tried to dope out why the man was murdered.* Syn. FIGURE OUT.

do proud See DO CREDIT.

do someone out of something *v., informal* To cause to lose by trickery or cheating. ♦ *The clerk in the store did me out of $2.00 by overcharging me.*

dose of one's own medicine *or* **taste of one's own medicine** *n. phr.* Being treated in the same way you treat others; something bad done to you as you have done bad to other people. ♦ *Jim was always playing tricks on other boys. Finally they decided to give him a dose of his own medicine.*

dot See ON THE DOT *also* ON THE BUTTON.

do tell *interj., informal* An inelegant expression used to show that you are a little surprised by what you hear. ♦ *"You say George is going to get married after all these years? Do tell!" said Mrs. Green.* Syn. YOU DON'T SAY.

do the business *v. phr., informal* To do what is needed or wanted; get the job done; take proper action. ♦ *The boys had trouble in rolling the stone, but four of them did the business.* ♦ *When the little boy cut his finger a bandage did the business.*

do the honors *v. phr.* To act as host or hostess (as in introducing guests, carving, or paying other attentions to guests.) ♦ *The president of the club will do the honors at the banquet.*

do the trick *v. phr., informal* To bring success in doing something; have a desired result. ♦ *Jim was not passing in English, but he studied harder and that did the trick.* ♦ *The car wheels slipped on the ice, so Tom put sand under them, which did the trick.* Compare TURN THE TRICK.

do things by halves *v. phr.* To do things in a careless and incomplete way. ♦ *When he reads a book he always does it by halves; he seldom finishes it.*

do time *or* **doing time** See DO A STRETCH.

do to death *v. phr.* To overdo; do something so often that it becomes extremely boring or tiresome. ♦ *The typical car chase scene in motion pictures has been done to death.*

dot the i's and cross the t's *v. phr.* To be careful, thorough, and pay close attention to detail. ♦ *"The best way to get an A on the final exam," the teacher said, "is for every one to dot the i's and cross the t's."* Compare MIND ONE'S P'S AND Q'S.

double back *v.* **1.** To turn back on one's way or course. ♦ *The escaped prisoner doubled back on his tracks.* **2.** To fold over; usually in the middle. ♦ *The teacher told Johnny to double back the sheet of paper and tear it in half.*

double check *n.* A careful second check to be sure that something is right; a careful look for errors. ♦ *The policeman made a double check on the doors in the shopping area.*

double-check *v.* **1.** To do a double check on; look at again very carefully. ♦ *When the last typing of his book was finished, the author double-checked it.* **2.** To make a double check; look carefully at something. ♦ *The proofreader double-checks against errors.*

double-cross *v.* To promise one thing and deliver another; to deceive. ♦ *The lawyer double-crossed the inventor by manufacturing the gadget instead of fulfilling his promise to arrange a patent for his client.* Compare SELL DOWN THE RIVER, TWO-TIME.

double date *n., informal* A date on which two couples go together. ♦ *John and Nancy went with Mary and Bill on a double date.*

double-date *v., informal* To go on a double date; date with another couple. ♦ *John and Nancy and Mary and Bill double-date.*

double duty *n.* Two uses or jobs; two purposes or duties. ♦ *Matthew does double duty. He's the janitor in the morning and gardener in the afternoon.* ♦ *Our new washer does double duty; it washes the clothes and also dries them.*

double-header *n.* Two games or contests played one right after the other, between the same two teams or two different pairs of teams. ♦ *The Yankees and the Dodgers played a double-header Sunday afternoon.* ♦ *We went to a basketball double-header at Madison Square Garden and saw Seton Hall play St. John's and N.Y.U. play Notre Dame.*

double nickel *adv., slang, citizen's band radio jargon* The nationally enforced speed limit on some highways—55 MPH. ♦ *We'd better go double nickel on this stretch, partner; there's a bear in the air.*

double-park *v.* To park a car beside another car which is at the curb. ♦ *Jimmy's father double-parked his car and the police gave him a ticket.* ♦ *If you double-park, you block other cars from passing.*

double-talk *n.* **1.** Something said that is worded, either on purpose or by accident, so that it may be understood in two or more different ways. ♦ *The politician avoided the question with double-talk.* **2.** Something said that does not make sense; mixed up talk or writing; nonsense. ♦ *The man's explanation of the new tax bill was just a lot of double-talk.*

double up *v.* **1.** To bend far over forward. ♦ *Jim was hit by the baseball and doubled up with pain.* **2.** To share a room, bed, or home with another. ♦ *When relatives came for a visit, Ann had to double up with her sister.*

doubt See GIVE THE BENEFIT OF THE DOUBT, NO DOUBT.

do up *v.* **1a.** To clean and prepare for use or wear; launder. ♦ *Ann asked her mother to do up her dress.* **1b.** To put in order; straighten up; clean. ♦ *At camp* the girls have to do up their own cabins. **2.** To tie up or wrap. ♦ *Joan asked the clerk to do up her purchases.* **3a.** To set and fasten (hair) in place. ♦ *Grace helped her sister to do up her hair.* Compare PUT UP. **3b.** *informal* To dress or clothe. ♦ *Suzie was done up in her fine new skirt and blouse.*

do up brown *v. phr., slang* To do in a thorough or complete way. ♦ *When Jim does a job, he does it up brown.*

do well by *v. phr.* To benefit; help; treat exceptionally well. ♦ *In his will Grandpa did well by all of his grandchildren and left each of them one million dollars.*

do with *v.* **1.** To find enough for one's needs; manage.—Usually follows *can.* ♦ *Some children can do with very little spending money.* Compare GET ALONG, MAKE DO. **2.** To make use of; find useful or helpful.—Follows *can* or *could.* ♦ *After a hard day's work, a man can do with a good, hot meal.* ♦ *After cleaning out the basement, the boy could do with a bath.*

do without *or* **go without** *v.* **1.** To live or work without (something you want); manage without. ♦ *Ann said that she likes candy, but can do without it.* ♦ *We had to go without hot food because the stove was broken.* **2.** To live or work without something you want; manage. ♦ *If George cannot earn money for a bicycle, he will have to do without.* Compare GET ALONG, GET BY.

down and out *adj. phr.* Without money; without a job or home; broke. ♦ *Poor Sam lost his job after his wife had left him; he is really down and out.*

down-and-outer *n. phr.* A person who has lost everything and is penniless. ♦ *Joe goes from shelter to shelter asking for food and a place to sleep; he's become a regular down-and-outer.*

down-at-heel *or* **down-at-the-heel** *or* **down-at-the-heels** *adj.* Poorly kept up or dressed shabby; not neat; sloppy. ♦ *John is always down-at-the-heels, but his sister is always very neat.* ♦ *Old houses sometimes look down-at-the-heel.*

down east *or* **Down East** *n.* The northeast coastal part of the United States and part of Canada; *especially:* the coastal parts of Maine. ♦ *Many people in Boston like to go down east for their summer vacation.* Compare I WOULDN'T DO IT FOR A FARM DOWN EAST.

down in the dumps *or* **down in the mouth** *adj. phr., informal* Sad or discouraged; gloomy; dejected. ♦ *The boys were certainly down in the dumps when they heard that their team had lost.*

down on *adj. phr., informal* Having a grudge against; angry at. ♦ *John is down on his teacher because she gave him a low grade.*

down one's alley *or* **up one's alley** *adj. phr., slang* Suited to your tastes and abilities; what you like or like to do. ♦ *Baseball is right down Jim's alley.* Compare CUP OF TEA.

down one's neck See BREATHE DOWN ONE'S NECK.

down one's nose See LOOK DOWN ONE'S NOSE.

down one's throat See JUMP DOWN ONE'S THROAT, SHOVE DOWN ONE'S THROAT *or* RAM DOWN ONE'S THROAT.

down on one's luck *adj., informal* Having bad luck; having much trouble; not successful in life. ♦ *Harry asked me to lend him ten dollars, because he was down on his luck.* ♦ *The teacher is easy on Jane because Jane has been down on her luck lately.* Compare HARD ROW TO HOE, HARD SLEDDING, ON ONE'S UPPERS.

down payment *n.* A retainer paid to a prospective seller. ♦ *How much of a down payment do you require for this new car?*

down the drain *adj. or adv. phr., informal* Wasted; lost. ♦ *It is money down the drain if you spend it all on candy.* ♦ *Our plans to go swimming went down the drain when it rained.* Compare GO BY THE BOARD.

down the hatch! *v. phr., informal* Let us drink! ♦ *When we celebrated Mom's birthday, we all raised our glasses and cried in unison, "Down the hatch!"*

down the line *adv. phr., informal* **1.** Down the road or street; straight ahead. ♦ *The church is down the line a few blocks.* **2.** All the way; completely; thoroughly. ♦ *Bob always follows the teacher's directions right down the line.*

down-to-earth *adj.* Showing good sense; practical. ♦ *The committee's first plan* *for the party was too fancy, but the second was more down-to-earth.* ♦ *Mr. Jenkins never seems to know what is happening around him, but his wife is friendly and down-to-earth.* Compare COME BACK TO EARTH.

down to the wire *adj., slang* **1.** Running out of time, nearing a deadline. ♦ *Bob is down to the wire on his project* **2.** Being financially almost broke, being very low on cash or other funds. ♦ *We can't afford going to a restaurant tonight—we're really down to the wire!*

down with a disease *adj. phr.* Ill or sick. ♦ *Aunt Liz is down with the flu this week; she has to stay in bed.*

dozen See BY THE DOZEN, DAILY DOZEN, DIME A DOZEN, SIX OF ONE AND HALF-A-DOZEN OF THE OTHER.

drag in *v.* To insist on bringing (another subject) into a discussion; begin talking about (something different.) ♦ *No matter what we talk about, Jim drags in politics.* ♦ *Whenever anyone mentions travel, Grace has to drag in the trip to Mexico she took ten years ago.*

drag on *or* **drag out** *v.* **1.** To pass very slowly. ♦ *The cold winter months dragged on until we thought spring would never come.* **2.** To prolong; make longer. ♦ *The meeting would have been over quickly if the members had not dragged out the argument about dues.*

drag on the market *n. phr.* An article for which the demand has fallen off thus causing an oversupply. ♦ *Your type of word processor went out of style and is now a drag on the market.*

drag oneself up by one's boot straps See PULL ONESELF UP BY THE BOOT STRAPS.

drag one's feet *or* **drag one's heels** *v. phr.* To act slowly or reluctantly. ♦ *The children wanted to watch television, and dragged their feet when their mother told them to go to bed.* ♦ *The city employees said the mayor had promised to raise their pay, but was now dragging his feet.*

drag out See DRAG ON.

drag race *n., slang* An automobile race in which the drivers try to cover a certain distance (usually one quarter mile) in the shortest possible time. ♦ *Drag races are often held on airport*

landing strips. ♦ *Holding drag races is a good way to stop teenage hot rod racing on public highways.* Compare DRAG STRIP.

drag strip *n., slang* A place where drag races are held. ♦ *Before the race Paul loaded his racer onto the trailer to take it out of town to the drag strip for the race.* Compare DRAG RACE.

drain See DOWN THE DRAIN.

draw See BEAT TO THE PUNCH *or* BEAT TO THE DRAW.

draw a bead on *v. phr. informal* **1.** To aim at; sight (with a gun). ♦ *The deer bounded into the forest before the hunters could draw a bead on them.* ♦ *John drew a bead on the elk, but didn't have the heart to pull the trigger.* **2.** To take (something) as an aim or goal. ♦ *"I'm drawing a bead on the Literary Society president's office,"* said Tom. **3.** To use as a target of attack; criticize. ♦ *Whenever a politician makes a mistake, his opponents are ready to draw a bead on him.*

draw a blank *v. phr., informal* **1.** To obtain nothing in return for an effort made or to get a negative result. ♦ *I looked up all the Joneses in the telephone book but I drew a blank every time I asked for Archibald Jones.* **2.** To fail to remember something. ♦ *I am trying to think of the name but I keep drawing a blank.* **3.** To be consistently unsuccessful at doing something. ♦ *I keep trying to pass that math exam but each time I try it I draw a blank.*

draw a conclusion *v. phr.* To make an inference. ♦ *After he failed to keep an appointment with me for the third time, I drew the conclusion that he was an unreliable person.*

draw a line *or* **draw the line** *v. phr.* **1.** To think of as different. ♦ *The law in this country draws a line between murder and manslaughter.* ♦ *Can you draw the line between a lie and a fib?* **2.** To set a limit to what will be done; say something cannot be done. ♦ *We would like to invite everybody to our party, but we have to draw a line somewhere.*—Often used with *at.* ♦ *Mrs. Jones draws the line at permitting the children to play in their father's den.* ♦ *People fighting for their freedom often do not draw the line at murder.*

draw a long breath *or* **take a long breath**
v. phr. To breathe deeply when getting ready to speak or act. ♦ *Father asked who broke the window. Jim drew a long breath and admitted that he had done it.* ♦ *The salesman took a long breath and started his talk.*

draw a parallel *v. phr.* To make a comparison. ♦ *It is easy to draw a parallel between the characters of Saint Francis of Assisi and Great Saint Theresa of Aquila, but this doesn't mean that all saints are alike.*

draw and quarter *v. phr. literary* **1.** To execute someone in the barbaric medieval fashion of having him torn into four pieces by four horses tearing his body in four different directions. ♦ *The captured foreign marauders were drawn and quartered by the angry citizens of ancient Frankfurt.* **2.** To punish someone very severely. ♦ *"If you miss another homework assignment, John," the teacher said, "I'll have you drawn and quartered."*

draw aside *v. phr.* To separate; take to one side. ♦ *He drew her aside and whispered into her ear, "Johanna, please marry me!"*

draw back *v.* To move back; back away; step backward; withdraw; move away from. ♦ *When the man spotted the rattlesnake, he drew back and aimed his shotgun.* ♦ *The children drew back from the dog when it barked at them.* ♦ *When the pitcher drew back his arm to pitch the ball, Tom ran as fast as he could to steal second base.* ♦ *Some juice from the grapefruit that Father was eating squirted in his eye and he drew back in surprise.* Compare DROP BACK.

drawback *n.* Disadvantage; obstacle; hindrance. ♦ *The biggest drawback of Bill's plan is the cost involved.*

draw blood *v. phr., informal* To make someone feel hurt or angry. ♦ *If you want to draw blood, ask Jim about his last money-making scheme.* ♦ *Her sarcastic comments drew blood.*

drawer See TOP-DRAWER.

draw fire *v. phr.* **1.** To attract or provoke shooting; be a target. ♦ *The general's white horse drew the enemy's fire.* **2.** To bring criticism or argument; make people say bad things about you. ♦ *Having the newest car in your group is sure to draw fire.*

drawing card *n.* The most important figure in a multi-person event; the top entertainer during a show; the best professor or researcher at a university, etc. ♦ *During the concert series Barbra Streisand was the biggest drawing card.* ♦ *The biggest drawing card at many a university is the resident Nobel Laureate.*

draw in one's horns See PULL IN ONE'S HORNS.

draw interest *v. phr.* To earn interest on invested capital. ♦ *My savings account draws 4.5% interest.*

draw lots *v. phr.* To select at random from a series in order to determine precedents or apportionment. ♦ *The refugees to be evacuated drew lots on who would get a place on the first airplane out of the besieged city.*

draw near *v. phr.* To approach; come near. ♦ *The time is drawing near when this century will end and the next will begin.*

draw off *v. phr.* To drain away; deflect. ♦ *A light flanking attack was made in order to draw off the enemy's fire.*

draw on *v. phr.* **1.** To arrive; approach. ♦ *As midnight drew on, the New Year's Eve party grew louder and louder.* **2.** To secure funds from a bank or person. ♦ *Jack kept drawing on his bank account so much that several of his checks bounced.*

draw out *v. phr.* **1.** To take out; remove. ♦ *Johnny drew a dollar out of the bank to buy his mother a present.* ♦ *The hunter drew out his gun and shot the snake.* **2.** To make (a person) talk or tell something. ♦ *Jimmy was bashful but Mrs. Wilson drew him out by asking him about baseball.* **3.** To make come out; bring out. ♦ *The bell of the ice-cream truck drew the children out of the houses.* ♦ *Mary was drawn out of her silence by Billy's jokes.* **4.** To make longer or too long; stretch. ♦ *The Smiths drew out their vacation at the beach an extra week.* ♦ *It was a long drawn out meeting because everybody tried to talk at once.* ♦ *Mary and her mother drew out their goodbyes so long at the bus station that Mary almost missed the bus.*

draw the fire of See DRAW OFF.

draw the line See DRAW A LINE.

draw to a close *v. phr.* To finish; terminate; come to an end. ♦ *The meeting drew to a close around midnight.*

draw up *v.* **1.** To write (something) in its correct form; put in writing. ♦ *The rich man had his lawyers draw up his will so that each of his children would receive part of his money when he died.* **2.** To plan or prepare; begin to write out. ♦ *The two countries drew up a peace treaty after the war ended.* ♦ *Plans are being drawn up for a new school next year.* Compare WRITE UP. **3.** To hold yourself straight or stiffly, especially because you are proud or angry. ♦ *When we said that Mary was getting fat, she drew herself up angrily and walked out of the room.* **4.** To stop or come to a stop. ♦ *The cowboy drew up his horse at the top of the hill.* ♦ *A big black car drew up in front of the house.* Syn. PULL UP.

dread See BURNT CHILD DREADS THE FIRE.

dream of *v.* To think about seriously; think about with the idea of really doing; consider seriously.—Usually used with a negative. ♦ *I wouldn't dream of wearing shorts to church.*

dressing down *n., informal* A scolding. ♦ *The sergeant gave the soldier a good dressing down because his shoes were not shined.*

dress a window See WINDOW DRESSING.

dress like a million dollars See BEST BIB AND TUCKER.

dress up *v.* **1a.** To put on best or special clothes. ♦ *Billy hated being dressed up and took off his best suit as soon as he got home from church.* **1b.** To put on a costume for fun or clothes for a part in a play. ♦ *Mary was dressed up to play Cinderella in her school play.* **2.** To make (something) look different; make (something) seem better or more important. ♦ *A fresh coat of paint will dress up the old bicycle very much.* ♦ *Tommy dressed up the story of what he did on vacation and made it seem twice as interesting as it was.*

dressed fit to kill See BEST BIB AND TUCKER.

dressed like a peacock See BEST BIB AND TUCKER.

dribs and drabs *n. phr.* Portions; small bits. ♦ *John paid Oliver back what he owed him in dribs and drabs.*

drift off *v. phr.* **1.** To fall asleep. ♦ *He kept nodding and drifting off to sleep while the lecturer was speaking.* **2.** To depart; leave gradually. ♦ *One by one, the sailboats drifted off over the horizon.*

drink down *v. phr.* To drink in one gulp; swallow entirely. ♦ *Steve was so thirsty that he drank down six glasses of orange juice in rapid succession.*

drink in *v. phr.* To absorb with great interest. ♦ *The tourists stood on the beach drinking in the wonderful Hawaiian sunset.*

drink like a fish *v. phr.* To drink (alcoholic beverages) in great quantities; to be addicted to alcohol. ♦ *John is a nice guy but, unfortunately, he drinks like a fish.*

drink up *v. phr.* To finish drinking; empty one's glass. ♦ *"Drink up that cough syrup," the nurse said, "and never mind the taste."*

drive See LINE DRIVE.

drive a bargain *v. phr.* **1.** To buy or sell at a good price; succeed in a trade or deal. ♦ *Tom's collie is a champion; it should be easy for Tom to drive a bargain when he sells her puppies.* ♦ *Father drove a hard bargain with the real estate agent when we bought our new house.* **2.** To make an agreement that is better for you than for the other person; make an agreement to your advantage. ♦ *The French drove a hard bargain in demanding that Germany pay fully for World War I damages.*

drive a hard bargain See DRIVE A BARGAIN.

drive at *v.* To try or want to say; mean.—Used in the present participle. ♦ *John did not understand what the coach was driving at.* ♦ *He had been talking for half an hour before anyone realized what he was driving at.*

drive home *v. phr.* To argue convincingly; make a strong point. ♦ *The doctor's convincing arguments and explanation of his X-ray pictures drove home the point to Max that he needed surgery.*

drive-in *adj./n.* A kind of movie theater, fast food restaurant, or church, where the customers, spectators, or worshippers do not leave their automobiles but are served the food inside their cars, can watch a motion picture from inside their cars, or can participate in a religious service in their cars. ♦ *Let's not waste time on the road; let's just eat at the next drive-in restaurant.* ♦ *There is a drive-in theater not far from where we live.* ♦ *Max and Hilde go to a drive-in church every Sunday.*

drive like Jehu *v. phr., informal* To drive very fast, carelessly or recklessly. ♦ *When Joe is late for work, he drives like Jehu.*

drive one ape, bananas, crazy, mad *or* **nuts** *v. phr., informal* To irritate, frustrate, or tickle someone's fancy so badly that they think they are going insane. ♦ *"Stop teasing me, Mary,"* John said. *"You are driving me nuts."* ♦ *"You are driving me bananas with all your crazy riddles,"* Steve said.

drive one round the bend *v. phr., informal* To upset someone so much that they think they are going crazy. ♦ *"Slow down, please,"* Miss Jones cried. *"You are driving me around the bend!"* Contrast DRIVE ONE APE, BANANAS, ETC.

driver See BACKSEAT DRIVER.

drive to the wall *v. phr.* To defeat someone completely; to ruin someone. ♦ *Poor Uncle Jack was driven to the wall by his angry creditors when his business failed.* Compare GO TO THE WALL.

drive someone bananas *or* **drive someone nuts** *or* **drive someone ape** *v. phr., slang informal* To excite someone to the point that he or she goes out of his or her mind; to drive someone crazy. ♦ *You're driving me bananas/nuts with that kind of talk!*

drop See AT THE DROP OF A HAT, BOTTOM DROP OUT, JAW DROP *or* JAW DROP A MILE.

drop a line *v. phr.* To write someone a short letter or note. ♦ *Please drop me a line when you get to Paris; I'd like to know that you've arrived safely.*

drop back *v.* To move or step backwards; retreat. ♦ *The soldiers dropped back before the enemy's attack.* ♦ *The quarterback dropped back to pass the football.* Compare DRAW BACK, FADE BACK, FALL BACK.

drop by *or* **stop by** *v.* **1.** or **drop around** To make a short or unplanned visit; go

on a call or errand; stop at someone's home. ♦ *Drop by any time you're in town.* ♦ *My sister dropped around last night.* ♦ *Don't forget to stop by at the gas station.* Syn. DROP IN. **2.** or **drop into** To stop (somewhere) for a short visit or a short time. ♦ *We dropped by the club to see if Bill was there, but he wasn't.* ♦ *I dropped into the drugstore for some toothpaste and a magazine.*

drop by the wayside See FALL BY THE WAYSIDE.

drop dead *v., slang* To go away or be quiet; stop bothering someone.— Usually used as a command. ♦ *"Drop dead!"* Bill told his little sister when she kept begging to help him build his model airplane. ♦ *When Sally bumped into Kate's desk and spilled ink for the fifth time, Kate told her to drop dead.* Compare BEAT IT, GET LOST.

drop in *v.* To make a short or unplanned visit; pay a call.—Often used with *on.* ♦ *We were just sitting down to dinner when Uncle Willie dropped in.* ♦ *The Smiths dropped in on some old friends on their vacation trip to New York.* Syn. DROP BY, RUN IN 2.

drop in the bucket *n. phr.* A relatively small amount; a small part of the whole. ♦ *Our university needs several million dollars for its building renovation project; $50,000 is a mere drop in the bucket.*

drop name *v. phr.* To impress people by mentioning famous names. ♦ *He likes to pretend he's important by dropping a lot of names.*

drop off *v.* **1.** To take (someone or something) part of the way you are going. ♦ *Joe asked Mrs. Jones to drop him off at the library on her way downtown.* **2.** To go to sleep. ♦ *Jimmy was thinking of his birthday party as he dropped off to sleep.* **3.** To die. ♦ *The patient dropped off in his sleep.* **4.** or **fall off** To become less. ♦ *Business picked up in the stores during December, but dropped off again after Christmas.* Contrast PICK UP 14.

dropout *n.* Someone who did not finish school, high school and college primarily. ♦ *Tim is having a hard time getting a better job as he was a high-school dropout.* ♦ *Jack never got his B.A. as he became a college dropout.*

drop out v. To stop attending; quit; stop; leave. ♦ *In the middle of the race, Joe got a blister on his foot and had to drop out.* ♦ *Teenagers who drop out of high school have trouble finding jobs.*

drown one's sorrows or **drown one's troubles** v. phr., informal To drink liquor to try to forget something unhappy. ♦ *When his wife was killed in an auto accident, Mr. Green tried to drown his sorrows in whiskey.* ♦ *When Fred lost his job and had to give up his new car, he tried to drown his troubles at the nearest tavern.*

drown one's troubles See DROWN ONE'S SORROWS.

drown out v. To make so much noise that it is impossible to hear (some other sound). ♦ *The children's shouts drowned out the music.* ♦ *The actor's words were drowned out by applause.*

drum up v. **1.** To get by trying or asking again and again; attract or encourage by continued effort. ♦ *The car dealer tried to drum up business by advertising low prices.* **2.** To invent. ♦ *I will drum up an excuse for coming to see you next week.* Syn. MAKE UP 2, THINK UP.

dry See CUT AND DRIED, HIGH AND DRY.

dry behind the ears adj. phr., informal Experienced; knowing how to do something. Usually used in the negative. ♦ *John had just started working for the company, and was not dry behind the ears yet.* Compare KNOW ONE'S WAY AROUND. Contrast WET BEHIND THE EARS.

dry out v. phr. To cure an alcoholic. ♦ *A longtime alcoholic, Uncle Steve is now in the hospital getting dried out.*

dry up v. **1.** To become dry. ♦ *The reservoir dried up during the four-month drought.* **2.** To disappear or vanish as if by evaporating. ♦ *The Senator's influence dried up when he was voted out of office.* **3.** slang To stop talking.—Often used as a command. ♦ *"Dry up!" Tony said angrily when his friend told him for the third time that he had made a mistake in his theme.* Syn. SHUT UP 1.

dual highway See DIVIDED HIGHWAY.

duck See DEAD DUCK, KNEE HIGH TO A GRASSHOPPER or KNEE HIGH TO A DUCK, LAME DUCK, LIKE WATER OFF A DUCK'S BACK.

duckling See UGLY DUCKLING.

duck out v. phr. To avoid; escape from something by skillful maneuvering. ♦ *Somehow or other Jack always manages to duck out of any hard work.*

duck soup n., slang **1.** A task easily accomplished or one that does not require much effort. ♦ *That history test was duck soup.* **2.** A person who offers no resistance; a pushover. ♦ *How's the new history teacher?—He's duck soup.*

duddy See FUDDY-DUDDY.

due See GIVE ONE'S DUE, GIVE THE DEVIL HIS DUE, IN DUE COURSE at IN GOOD TIME.

due to prep. Because of; owing to; by reason of. ♦ *His injury was due to his careless use of the shotgun.* ♦ *Joe's application to the University was not accepted due to his failing English.*

dull See ALL WORK AND NO PLAY MAKES JACK A DULL BOY.

dumb bunny n., slang, informal Any person who is gullible and stupid. ♦ *Jack is a regular dumb bunny.*

dumbwaiter n. A small elevator for carrying food, dishes, etc., from one floor to another in hotels, restaurants, or large homes. ♦ *The banquet was delayed because the dumbwaiter broke down and the food had to be carried upstairs by hand.*

dumps See DOWN IN THE DUMPS or DOWN IN THE MOUTH.

dust See BITE THE DUST, KICK UP A FUSS or KICK UP A DUST, WATCH ONE'S DUST, AFTER THE DUST CLEARS/WHEN THE DUST SETTLES.

dust off v., informal **1.** To get ready to use again. ♦ *Four years after he graduated from school, Tom decided to dust off his algebra book.* **2.** To throw a baseball pitch close to. ♦ *The pitcher dusted off the other team's best hitter.* Syn. BRUSH BACK.

Dutch See BEAT ALL or BEAT THE DUTCH, GO DUTCH, IN DUTCH.

dutch treat n., informal A meal in a restaurant or an outing at the movies, concert, or theater where each party pays his or her own way. ♦ *"I am willing to accept your invitation," Mary said, "but it will have to be Dutch treat."*

duty See DO DUTY FOR, DOUBLE DUTY, HEAVY DUTY, OFF DUTY, ON DUTY.

duty bound adj. phr. Forced to act by what you believe is right. ♦ *Abraham*

Lincoln walked miles once to return a few pennies that he had overcharged a woman because he felt duty bound to do it. ♦*John felt duty bound to report that he had broken the window.*

duty calls *n. phr.* One must attend to one's obligations. ♦*"I'd love to stay and play more poker," Henry said, "but duty calls and I must get back to the office."*

dwell on *or* **dwell upon** *v.* To stay on a subject; not leave something or want to leave; not stop talking or writing about. ♦*Joe dwelt on his mistake long after the test was over.* ♦*Our eyes dwelled on the beautiful sunset.* ♦*The principal dwelled on traffic safety in his talk.* Compare HARP ON. Contrast TOUCH ON.

dyed-in-the-wool *adj. phr. Thoroughly committed; inveterate; unchanging. He is a died-in-the-wool Conservative Republican.*

dying to *adj. phr.* Having a great desire to; being extremely eager to. ♦*Seymour is dying to date Mathilda, but she keeps refusing him.*

each and every *adj. phr.* Every.—Used for emphasis. ◆ *The captain wants each and every man to be here at eight o'clock.* ◆ *The teacher must learn the name of each and every pupil.* Syn. EVERY SINGLE.

each other *or* **one another** *pron.* Each one the other; one the other. ◆ *That man and his wife love each other.* ◆ *Bill and Mary gave one another Christmas presents last year.* ◆ *All the children at the party were looking at one another trying to recognize one another in their masks and costumes.* ◆ *The birds fought each other over the bread.*

eager beaver *n. phr., slang* A person who is always eager to work or do anything extra, perhaps to win the favor of his leader or boss. ◆ *Jack likes his teacher and works hard for her, but his classmates call him an eager beaver.* ◆ *The man who was promoted to be manager was an eager beaver who got to work early and left late and was always offering to do extra work.*

eagle eye *n.* Sharp vision like that of an eagle; the ability to notice even the tiniest details. ◆ *The new boss keeps an eagle eye on all aspects of our operation.*

ear See ABOUT ONE'S EARS *or* AROUND ONE'S EARS, BELIEVE ONE'S EARS, DRY BEHIND THE EARS, FLEA IN ONE'S EAR, GIVE AN EAR TO *or* LEND AN EAR TO, GO IN ONE EAR AND OUT THE OTHER, JUG-EARED, LITTLE PITCHERS HAVE BIG EARS, MUSIC TO ONE'S EARS, PIN ONE'S EARS BACK, PLAY BY EAR, PRICK UP ONE'S EARS, ROASTING EAR, TURN A DEAF EAR, UP TO THE CHIN IN *or* UP TO THE EARS IN, WET BEHIND THE EARS.

early See BRIGHT AND EARLY.

early bird *n* An early riser from bed. ◆ *Jane and Tom are real early birds; they get up at 6 A.M. every morning.*

early bird catches the worm *or* **early bird gets the worm** A person who gets up early in the morning has the best chance of succeeding; if you arrive early or are quicker, you get ahead of others.—A proverb. ◆ *When Billy's father woke him up for school he said, "The early bird catches the worm."* ◆ *Charles began looking for a summer job in January; he knows that the early bird gets the worm.* Compare FIRST COME, FIRST SERVED.

earn one's keep *v. phr.* To merit one's salary or keep by performing the labor or chores that are expected of one. ◆ *John earned his keep at the music conservatory by dusting off all the musical instruments every day.*

earnest See IN EARNEST.

ears burn *informal* To feel embarrassment or shame at hearing others talk about you. ◆ *Joan overheard the girls criticizing her and it made her ears burn.* ◆ *Joe's ears burned when he heard his classmates praising him to each other.*

earth See COME BACK TO EARTH *or* COME DOWN TO EARTH, DOWN-TO-EARTH, IN THE WORLD *or* ON EARTH, MOVE HEAVEN AND EARTH.

ear to the ground *n. phr., informal* Attention directed to the way things are going, or seem likely to go, or to the way people feel and think. ◆ *The city manager kept an ear to the ground for a while before deciding to raise the city employees' pay.* ◆ *Reporters keep an ear to the ground so as to know as soon as possible what will happen.*

ease See AT EASE *or* AT ONE'S EASE, ILL AT EASE.

ease off *or* **ease up** *v.* To make or become less nervous; relax; work easier. ◆ *When the boss realized that John had been overworking, he eased off his load.* ◆ *With success and prosperity, Mr. Smith was able to ease off.* Compare LET UP 3.

easily See BREATHE EASILY *or* BREATHE FREELY.

east See DOWN EAST.

easy See FREE AND EASY, GET OFF EASY, ON EASY STREET, TAKE IT EASY *or* GO EASY *or* TAKE THINGS EASY.

easygoing *adj.* Amiable in manner; relaxed; not excited. ◆ *Because Al has an easygoing personality, everybody loves him.*

easy as pie See PIECE OF CAKE.

easy come, easy go *truncated sent. informal* Something you get quickly and easily may be lost or spent just as easily. ♦ *Grandfather thought Billy should have to work for the money Father gave him, saying "Easy come, easy go."*

easy does it *informal* Let's do it carefully, without sudden movements and without forcing too hard or too fast; let's try to just hard enough but not too hard. ♦ *"Easy does it," said the boss as they moved the piano through the narrow doorway.* Compare TAKE IT EASY.

easy mark *n.* A foolishly generous person; one from whom it is easy to get money. ♦ *Bill is known to all the neighborhood beggars as an easy mark.* See SOFT TOUCH.

easy money *n. informal* Money gained without hard work; money that requires little or no effort. ♦ *The movie rights to a successful play mean easy money to the writer of the play.* ♦ *Young people who look for easy money are usually disappointed.*

eat See DOG-EAT-DOG, LIVE HIGH OFF THE HOG *or* EAT HIGH ON THE HOG, LOOK LIKE THE CAT THAT ATE THE CANARY.

eat away *v.* **1.** To rot, rust, or destroy. ♦ *Rust was eating away the pipe.* ♦ *Cancer ate away the healthy flesh.* See EAT OUT 2. **2.** To gradually consume. ♦ *The ocean waves were gradually eating the volcanic rocks until they turned into black sand.*

eat away at *v. phr.* To psychologically gnaw at; to worry someone. ♦ *Fear of the comprehensive examination was eating away at Sam.*

eat crow *v. phr.* To admit you are mistaken or defeated; take back a mistaken statement. ♦ *John had boasted that he would play on the first team; but when the coach did not choose him, he had to eat crow.* ♦ *Fred said he could beat the new man in boxing, but he lost and had to eat crow.* Compare BACK DOWN, EAT HUMBLE PIE, EAT ONE'S WORDS.

eat dirt *v. phr., informal* To act humble; accept another's insult or bad treatment. ♦ *Mr. Johnson was so much afraid of losing his job that he would eat dirt whenever the boss got mean.*

eat (live) high on the hog *or* **eat (live) high off the hog** *v. phr.* To eat or live well or elegantly. ♦ *For the first few*

days after the check arrived, they ate high on the hog. Compare IN CLOVER *or* IN THE CLOVER, ON EASY STREET.

eat humble pie *v. phr.* To be humbled; to accept insult or shame; admit your error and apologize. ♦ *Tom told a lie about George, and when he was found out, he had to eat humble pie.* ♦ *In some old stories a boy with a stepfather has to eat humble pie.*

eating one *v. phr.* To cause someone to be angry or ill-humored. ♦ *We can't figure out what's eating Burt, but he hasn't spoken one pleasant word all day.*

eat like a bird *v. phr.* To eat very little; have little appetite. ♦ *Mrs. Benson is on a diet and she eats like a bird.* ♦ *Alice's mother is worried about her; she eats like a bird and is very thin.* Contrast EAT LIKE A HORSE.

eat like a horse *v. phr.* To eat a lot; eat hungrily. ♦ *The harvesters worked into the evening, and then came in and ate like horses.* Contrast EAT LIKE A BIRD.

eat one out of house and home *v. phr.* **1.** To eat so much as to cause economic hardship. ♦ *Our teenaged sons are so hungry all the time that they may soon eat us out of house and home.* **2.** To overstay one's welcome. ♦ *We love Bob and Jane very much, but after two weeks we started to feel that they were eating us out of house and home.*

eat one's cake and have it too *v. phr.* To use or spend something and still keep it; have both when you must choose one of two things. Often used in negative sentences. ♦ *Roger can't make up his mind whether to go to college or get a job. You can't eat your cake and have it too.* ♦ *Mary wants to buy a beautiful dress she saw at the store, but she also wants to save her birthday money for camp. She wants to eat her cake and have it too.*

eat one's heart out *v. phr.* To grieve long and hopelessly; to become thin and weak from sorrow. ♦ *For months after her husband's death, Joanne simply ate her heart out.* ♦ *We sometimes hear of a dog eating its heart out for a dead owner.*

eat one's words *also* **swallow one's words** *v. phr.* To take back something you have said; admit something is not true. ♦ *John had called Harry a* *coward, but the boys made him eat his words after Harry bravely fought a big bully.* Compare EAT CROW.

eat out *v.* **1.** To eat in a restaurant; eat away from home. ♦ *Fred ate out often even when he wasn't out of town.* **2.** To rust, rot, or be destroyed in time. ♦ *Rust had eaten out the gun barrel.* See EAT AWAY.

eat out of one's hand *v. phr., informal* To trust someone fully; believe or obey someone without question. ♦ *The governor has the reporters eating out of his hand.* ♦ *Helen is so pretty and popular that all the boys eat out of her hand.*

eat up *v.* **1.** To eat all of. ♦ *After hiking all afternoon, they quickly ate up all of the dinner.* **2.** To use all of. ♦ *Idle talk had eaten up the hour before they knew it.* **3.** *slang* To accept eagerly; welcome. ♦ *The girls told John he was a hero because he made the winning touchdown, and he ate up their praise.* ♦ *Jim told Martha that she was as smart as she was beautiful and Martha ate it up.*

edge See HAVE AN EDGE ON, ON EDGE, SET ONE'S TEETH ON EDGE, TAKE THE EDGE OFF, THE EDGE.

edge away *v. phr.* To withdraw or retreat gradually. ♦ *Frightened by the growling tiger guarding its catch, the hunter carefully edged away.*

edge in *v.* To move slowly; get in quietly, especially with some difficulty, by force or without a big enough opening. ♦ *People had crowded around the senator, but Don succeeded in edging in.* ♦ *Harry edged the book in on the shelf.*

edge in (on) *v. phr.* **1.** To gradually approach an individual or a group with the intent of taking over or wielding power. ♦ *Jack was edging in on the firm of Smith and Brown and after half a year actually became its vice president.* **2.** To approach for capture (said of a group). ♦ *The hunters were edging in on the wounded leopard.*

edge on *adv. phr.* Edgewise; with the narrow side forward. ♦ *The board struck him edge on.*

edge out *v.* To defeat in competition or rivalry; take the place of; force out. ♦ *Harry edged out Tom for a place in Mary's affections.* ♦ *Signal lights on cars have gradually edged out hand signals.*

edgeways See GET A WORD IN *or* GET A WORD IN EDGEWISE, *also* GET A WORD IN EDGEWAYS.

edgewise See GET A WORD IN *or* GET A WORD IN EDGEWAYS.

education See HIGHER EDUCATION.

effect See IN EFFECT, INTO EFFECT, SOUND EFFECTS, TAKE EFFECT, TO THAT EFFECT, TO THE EFFECT THAT.

effigy See HANG IN EFFIGY *or* BURN IN EFFIGY.

egg See BAD EGG, GOOD EGG, KILL THE GOOSE THAT LAID THE GOLDEN EGG, LAY AN EGG, PUT ALL ONE'S EGGS IN ONE BASKET, ROTTEN EGG.

egg on *v.* To urge on; excite; lead to action. ♦ *Joe's wife egged him on to spend money to show off.* ♦ *The big boys egged on the two little boys to fight.* Compare PUT UP 6.

either a feast or a famine See FEAST OR A FAMINE.

either hide or hair See HIDE OR HAIR.

eke out *v.* **1.** To fill out or add a little to; increase a little. ♦ *Mr. Jones eked out a country teacher's small salary by hunting and trapping in the winter.* ♦ *The modest meal was eked out with bread and milk.* **2.** To get (little) by hard work; to earn with difficulty. ♦ *Fred eked out a bare living by farming on a rocky hillside.*

elbow See AT ONE'S ELBOW, ELBOW ROOM, RUB ELBOWS, UP TO THE CHIN IN *or* UP TO THE ELBOWS IN.

elbow grease *n.* Exertion; effort; energy. ♦ *"You'll have to use a little more elbow grease to get these windows clean,"* Mother said to Ed.

elbow one's way into *or* **out of** *v. phr.* To force entry into a place by using one's elbows. ♦ *The bus was so crowded that, in order to get off in time, we had to elbow our way to the exit door.*

elbow room *n.* Adequate space to move around or to work in. ♦ *He doesn't require a huge office, but we must at least give him elbow room.*

element See IN ONE'S ELEMENT, OUT OF ONE'S ELEMENT.

eleventh hour *adj. phr.* Pertaining to the last minutes; the last opportunity to accomplish a task. ♦ *The editors made several eleventh hour changes in the headlines of the morning paper.*

else See SOMETHING ELSE AGAIN.

emcee See MASTER OF CEREMONIES.

end See AT LOOSE ENDS, AT ONE'S WITS' END, BURN THE CANDLE AT BOTH ENDS, GO OFF THE DEEP END, HAIR STAND ON END, HOLD ONE'S END UP *or* HOLD UP ONE'S END *or* KEEP ONE'S END UP *or* KEEP UP ONE'S END, LIVING END, LOOSE ENDS, MAKE AN END OF, MAKE ENDS MEET, NO END, NO END TO *or* NO END OF, ON END, PUT AN END TO, REAR END, SHORT END, SPLIT END, TAG END *or* TAIL END, TIGHT END, TO THE BITTER END, WORLD WITHOUT END.

end for end *adv. phr.* In a reversed or opposite position (as upside down or backwards); the other way around; over. ◆ *The box turned end for end as it fell, and everything spilled out.* ◆ *The wind caught the canoe and turned it end for end.*

end in itself *n. phr.* Something wanted for its own sake; a purpose, aim, or goal we want for itself alone and not as a way to something else. ◆ *The miser never spent his gold because for him it was an end in itself.*

end of one's rope *or* **end of one's tether** *n. phr., informal* The end of your trying or imagining; the last of your ability, or ideas of how to do more. ◆ *Frank was out of work and broke, and he was at the end of his rope.* ◆ *The doctor saw that Mother had reached the end of her tether, and told us to send her away for a holiday.* Compare AT ONE'S WIT'S END, FED UP, UP AGAINST IT, UP A TREE.

end of the road *or* **end of the line** *n. phr.* The final result or end (as of a way of action or behavior); the condition that comes when you can do no more. ◆ *He had left a trail of forgery and dishonesty across seven states; he had got out of each trouble with a new trick. Now the police had caught up with him, and it was the end of the road.* ◆ *"When I get to the end of the line," Jones thought, "I'd like my children to like and respect me still."*

end run *n.* A football play in which a back tries to run around one end of the opponent's line. ◆ *Smith's end run scored the winning touchdown.*

end up *v.* **1.** To come to an end; be ended or finished; stop. ◆ *How does the story end up?* **2.** To finally reach or arrive; land. ◆ *I hope you don't end up in jail.* **3.** *informal* To die, be killed. ◆ *The gangster ended up in the electric chair.* **4.** *or* **finish up.** To put an end to; finish; stop. ◆ *The politician finally ended up his speech.* Syn. WIND UP.

end zone *n.* Either of the marked areas behind the goal line. ◆ *He caught a pass in the end zone for a touchdown.*

engage in small talk *v. phr.* To converse with a stranger or casual acquaintance about matters of no great importance in order to make the time go faster. ◆ *The patients in the doctor's waiting room engaged in small talk complaining about the hot weather.*

English See BODY ENGLISH.

enjoy oneself *v. phr.* To have a good time; be happy; feel pleasure. ◆ *Mary enjoyed herself at the party.* ◆ *"Enjoy yourselves, children," Mother urged the guests at our party.*

enlarge on *or* **enlarge upon** *or* **expand on** *or* **expand upon** *v.* To talk or write more about; say or explain more completely or at greater length. ◆ *The teacher enlarged on the uses of atomic power.*

en masse *adv. phr.* As a group; in one big mass or group.—Used after the word it modifies. ◆ *The school turned out en masse to cheer the returning astronaut.*

enough See GIVE ONE ENOUGH ROPE, AND HE WILL HANG HIMSELF, KNOW ENOUGH TO COME IN OUT OF THE RAIN, LET WELL ENOUGH ALONE, SURE-ENOUGH.

enough is enough That's enough, let's not have any more; that will do, let's cut it short; that's the limit, let's stop there. ◆ *"I don't mind good clean fun, but enough is enough," the principal said.*

enterprise See FREE ENTERPRISE.

entry See PORT OF ENTRY.

envy See GREEN WITH ENVY.

equal to *adj. phr.* Able to meet, do, or control; able to do something about. ◆ *The situation took quick thinking, but John was equal to it.* ◆ *When a guest upset the coffee pot, Mrs. Smith's tact and quickness of mind were equal to the occasion.*

equal to the occasion *adj. phr.* Capable of handling the situation. ◆ *Although* *he had never before assisted in child-birth, the taxi driver proved equal to the occasion and helped deliver the baby in his cab.*

error See TRIAL AND ERROR.

evaporate into thin air See DISAPPEAR INTO THIN AIR.

eve See ON THE EVE OF.

even See BREAK EVEN, GET EVEN, ON AN EVEN KEEL.

evening See GOOD EVENING.

even so *adv.* Although that is true; nevertheless; still. ◆ *The fire was out, but even so, the smell of smoke was strong.*

event See IN ANY CASE *or* AT ALL EVENTS, IN ANY CASE *also* IN ANY EVENT *or* AT ALL EVENTS, IN CASE *or* IN THE EVENT, IN CASE OF *also* IN THE EVENT OF.

ever See FOREVER AND EVER, HARDLY EVER *or* SCARCELY EVER.

ever so much *adv.* Very much; truly. ◆ *I am ever so much in your debt for your kind assistance when I needed it most.*

every See AT EVERY TURN, EACH AND EVERY.

every cloud has a silver lining Every trouble has something hopeful that you can see in it, like the bright edge around a dark cloud.—A proverb. ◆ *The doctor told Tommy to cheer up when he had measles. "Every cloud has a silver lining," he said.* Compare IT'S AN ILL WIND THAT BLOWS NOBODY GOOD.

every dog has his day Everyone will have his chance or turn; everyone is lucky or popular at some time.—A proverb. ◆ *Mary will be able to go to dances like her sister when she grows up. Every dog has his day.*

every inch *adv. phr.* To the last part, in every way; completely. ◆ *He was every inch a man.* ◆ *Henry looked every inch a soldier.*

every last See EVERY SINGLE.

every last man *also* **every man jack** *n. phr.* Every single man; each man without exception. ◆ *I want every last man to be here on time tomorrow morning.* ◆ *Every man jack of you must do his duty.*

every man jack See EVERY LAST MAN.

every now and then *or* **every now and again** *or* **every so often** *or* **every once in a while** *adv. phr.* At fairly regular intervals; fairly often; repeatedly.

◆ *John comes to visit me every now and then.* ◆ *It was hot work, but every so often Susan would bring us something cold to drink.* Compare NOW AND THEN.

every other *adj. phr.* Every second; every alternate. ◆ *The milkman comes every other day.* ◆ *On St. Patrick's Day, it seems as if every other man you meet is wearing a shamrock.*

every single *or* **every last** *adj. phr.* Every.—Used for emphasis. ◆ *She dropped the box, and when she opened it, every single glass was broken.* ◆ *When she got home she found every last tomato in the box was rotten.* Syn. EACH AND EVERY.

every so often See EVERY NOW AND THEN.

everything See HOLD IT *or* HOLD EVERYTHING.

every time one turns around *adv. phr.*, *informal* Very often. ◆ *Mr. Winston must be rich. He buys a new suit every time he turns around.* ◆ *No, Charles—I can't drive you to the park every time I turn around.*

every which way *also* **any which way** In all directions. ◆ *Bricks and boards were scattered in confusion on the ground every which way, just as they had fallen after the tornado.* Compare HELTER-SKELTER.

evidence See IN EVIDENCE.

example See FOR EXAMPLE, MAKE AN EXAMPLE OF.

except for *or formal* **but for** *prep.* **1.** With the exception of; if (a certain person or thing) were left out; omitting. ◆ *Except for John, the whole class passed the test.* **2.** Without. ◆ *I'd have been lost but for you.*

exception See TAKE EXCEPTION TO.

exception proves the rule Something unusual that does not follow a rule tests that rule to see if it is true; if there are too many exceptions, the rule is no good.—A proverb. ◆ *Frank is very short but is a good basketball player. He is the exception that proves the rule.*

excuse oneself *v. phr.* **1.** To think of reasons for not being to blame; think yourself not at fault. ◆ *John excused himself for his low grades on the ground that the teacher didn't like him.* **2.** To ask to be excused after doing something impolite. ♦*John excused himself for his tardiness, saying his watch was wrong.* **3.** To ask permission to leave a group or place. ♦*The committee meeting lasted so long that Mr. Wilkins excused himself to keep an appointment.* ♦*John had to go to the dentist's, so he excused himself and left the classroom.*

exert oneself *v. phr.* To make an effort; try hard; work hard. ♦*Susan exerted herself all year to earn good marks.* ♦*Jerry exerted himself to please the new girl.*

expand on *or* **expand upon** See ENLARGE ON *or* ENLARGE UPON.

explain away *v.* To explain (something) so that it does not seem true or important. ♦*John explained away his unfinished homework by showing the teacher his broken arm in a cast.* ♦*It is hard to explain away Abraham Lincoln's dream about being dead, which he had a few days before he was shot.* ♦*The man could not explain away the gun and the marked money from the bank robbery that the police found in his car.*

explain oneself *v. phr.* **1.** To make your meaning plainer; make your first statement clear. ♦*When we didn't understand Fritz, he went on to explain himself.* **2.** To give a good reason for something you did or failed to do which seems wrong. ♦*When Jack brought Mary home at three o'clock in the morning, her father asked him to explain himself.*

explode a bombshell *v. phr., informal* To say something startling; suggest or show something astonishing or shocking. ♦*The police exploded a bombshell when they arrested the kindly old banker for stealing money from the bank.* ♦*The principal exploded a bombshell by cancelling the dance as a penalty.* ♦*Political leaders exploded a bombshell when they picked the young lawyer to run for mayor.*

express oneself *v. phr.* To say what you think or feel; put your thoughts or feelings into words by speaking or writing. ♦*The boy expressed himself well in debate.* ♦*The mayor expressed himself as opposed to any borrowing.*

extend one's sympathy to *v. phr.* To offer one's condolences on the occasion of a death or similarly tragic event. ♦*All of Tom's colleagues extended their sympathy to him when his wife and daughter were killed in a car accident.*

eye See APPLE OF ONE'S EYE, BAT AN EYE *or* BAT AN EYELASH, BELIEVE ONE'S EYES, CATCH ONE'S EYE, CLEAR-EYED, CLOSE ONE'S EYES *or* SHUT ONE'S EYES, EYES OPEN, EYE OUT, EYE TO, FEAST ONE'S EYES ON, FOUR-EYES, GET THE EYE, GIVE THE EYE, GREEN-EYED MONSTER, HALF AN EYE, HAVE AN EYE ON, HAVE EYES ONLY FOR, HIT BETWEEN THE EYES, IN ONE'S MIND'S EYE, IN THE PUBLIC EYE, KEEP AN EYE ON *or* KEEP ONE'S EYE ON, KEEP ONE'S EYES PEELED *or* KEEP ONE'S EYES SKINNED, LAY EYES ON *or* SET EYES ON, LOOK IN THE EYE, MAKE EYES AT, MEET ONE'S EYE, MISTY-EYED *or* DEWEY-EYED, ONE EYE ON, OPEN ONE'S EYES *or* OPEN UP ONE'S EYES, OUT OF THE CORNER OF ONE'S EYE, PULL THE WOOL OVER ONE'S EYES, SEE EYE TO EYE, SHUT-EYE, SIGHT FOR SORE EYES, STARS IN ONE'S EYES, ROUND-EYED *or* WIDE-EYED *also* LARGE-EYED, PRIVATE EYE, TO THE EYE, UP TO THE CHIN IN *or* UP TO THE EYES IN, WEATHER EYE.

eyebrow See RAISE EYEBROWS.

eye-catcher *n.* Something that strongly attracts the eye. See CATCH ONE'S EYE. ♦*That new girl in our class is a real eye-catcher.*

eye-catching See CATCH ONE'S EYE.

eye-filling *adj., literary* Attractive to the eye; beautiful; especially grand; splendid; majestic. ♦*The mountains in the distance were an eye-filling sight.*

eye for an eye and a tooth for a tooth A blow or injury should be given back as hard as each one that is received; every crime or injury should be punished or paid back. ♦*In ancient times if a man's eye was put out by his enemy, he might get revenge by putting his enemy's eye out. This was the rule of "an eye for an eye and a tooth for a tooth."* Sometimes used in a short form. ♦*Churches today teach that we should forgive people who hurt us, not follow the rule of "an eye for an eye."* [From the old command in the Bible meaning when you pay back a person, you should not hurt him more than he hurt you.]

Compare DOG EAT DOG, GIVE AS GOOD AS ONE GETS, TIT FOR TAT.

eye-opener See OPEN ONE'S EYES.

eye out Careful watch or attention; guard.—Used after *keep, have* or *with.* ♦ *Keep an eye out. We're close to Joe's house.* Usually used with *for.* ♦ *Mary has her eye out for bargains.* ♦ *They went through the woods very quietly, with an eye out for Indians.* Compare LOOK OUT 2, ON GUARD, ON THE ALERT, ON THE WATCH.

eyes are bigger than one's stomach *informal* You want more food than you can eat. ♦ *Annie took a second big helping of pudding, but her eyes were bigger than her stomach.* ♦ *"Your eyes are bigger than your stomach," mother told little Tommy when he piled up food on his plate.*

eye shadow *n. phr.* A cream used to darken the eyelids in order to make the eyes more noticeable. ♦ *Jane's mother told her that girls in the ninth grade shouldn't be using eye shadow.*

eyes in the back of one's head *n. phr., informal* Ability to know what happens when your back is turned. ♦ *Mother must have eyes in the back of her head, because she always knows when I do something wrong.*

eyes open 1. Careful watch or attention; readiness to see—Usually used with *for.* ♦ *Keep your eyes open for a boy in a red cap and sweater.* ♦ *The hunter had his eyes open for rabbits.* ♦ *They drove on with their eyes open for a gas station.* Syn. EYE OUT, KEEP ONE'S EYES PEELED. **2.** Full knowledge; especially of consequences; understanding of what will or might result.—Used with *have* or *with.* ♦ *Automobile racing is dangerous. Bob went into it with his eyes open.* ♦ *Betty had her eyes open when she got married.* Contrast CLOSE ONE'S EYES.

eyes pop out *informal* (You) are very much surprised.—Used with a possessive noun or pronoun. ♦ *Mary's eyes popped out when her mother entered her classroom.* ♦ *When Joan found a clock radio under the Christmas tree, her eyes popped out.*

eye teeth See CUT ONE'S EYE TEETH ON *at* CUT TEETH 2.

eye to 1. Attention to.—Usually used with *have* or *with.* ♦ *Have an eye to spelling in these test papers.* **2.** Plan for, purpose of.—Usually used with *have* or *with.* ♦ *Save your money now with an eye to the future.* ♦ *John is going to college with an eye to becoming a lawyer.*

face See BLUE IN THE FACE, CUT OFF ONE'S NOSE TO SPITE ONE'S FACE, FLY IN THE FACE OF, HATCHET FACE, HIDE ONE'S FACE, IN ONE'S FACE, IN THE FACE OF, LONG FACE, LOOK IN THE EYE *or* LOOK IN THE FACE, MAKE A FACE, ON THE FACE OF IT, SAVE FACE, SET ONE'S FACE AGAINST, SHOOT OFF ONE'S MOUTH *or* SHOOT OFF ONE'S FACE, SHOW ONE'S FACE, SLAP IN THE FACE, STARE IN THE FACE, STRAIGHT FACE, THROW IN ONE'S FACE, TO ONE'S FACE.

face down *v. phr.* To get the upper hand over someone by behaving forcefully; disconcert someone by the displaying of great self-assurance. ♦*The night guard faced down the burglar by staring him squarely in the face.* Contrast FACE UP.

face lift *n. phr.* **1.** A surgical procedure designed to make one's face look younger. ♦*Aunt Jane, who is in her seventies, had an expensive face lift and now she looks as if she were 40.* **2.** A renovation, a refurbishing. ♦*Our house needs a major face lift to make it fit in with the rest of the neighborhood.*

face-saver, face-saving See SAVE FACE.

face the music *v. phr., informal* To go through trouble or danger, especially because of something you did; accept your punishment. ♦*The boy was caught cheating in an examination and had to face the music.* ♦*The official who had been taking bribes was exposed by a newspaper, and had to face the music.* ♦*George knew his mother would cry when he told her, but he decided to go home and face the music.* Compare MAKE ONE'S BED AND LIE IN IT, PAY THE PIPER, TAKE ONE'S MEDICINE.

face-to-face *adv. phr.* **1.** With your face looking toward the face of another person; each facing the other. ♦*Turning a corner, he found himself face-to-face with a policeman.* ♦*The two teams for the spelling bee stood face-to-face on opposite sides of the classroom.* ♦*The church and the school stand face-to-face across the street.* **2.** In the presence of another or others. ♦*She was thrilled to meet the President face-to-face.* ♦*I have heard about him, but I never met him face-to-face.* Compare IN PERSON. **3.** To the point where you must do something.—Used with *with.* ♦*The solution of the first problem brought him face-to-face with a second problem.* Compare UP AGAINST.

face-to-face *adj.* Being in the presence of a person; being right with someone. ♦*The British prime minister came to Washington for a face-to-face meeting with the President.*

face up to *v. phr.* **1.** To bravely confront a person or a challenge; admit.. ♦*Jack doesn't want to face up to the fact that Helen doesn't love him anymore.* ♦*Jane cannot face up to her mother-in-law who always wins every argument they have.* **2.** To confess something to someone; confess to having done something. ♦*Jim had to face up to having stolen a sweater from the department store.* Contrast FACE DOWN.

face value *n.* **1.** The worth or price printed on a stamp, bond, note, piece of paper money, etc. ♦*The savings bond had a face value of $25.* **2.** The seeming worth or truth of something. ♦*She took his stories at face value and did not know he was joking.*

faced with *adj. phr.* Confronted with. ♦*We were all faced with the many wars that broke out in the wake of the collapse of communism.*

fact See IN FACT, MATTER-OF-FACT.

facts of life *n. phr.* **1.** The truth which we should know about sex, marriage, and births. ♦*His father told him the facts of life when he was old enough.* **2.** The truths one learns about people and their good and bad habits of life, work or play. ♦*As a cub reporter he would learn the facts of life in the newspaper world.*

fade back *v.* To back away from the line before passing in football. ♦*The quarterback is fading back to pass.* Compare DROP BACK.

fail See WITHOUT FAIL.

fail to do *v. phr.* To neglect to do something that is expected of one. ♦*Tom waited for Jane for nearly an hour, but* *she failed to show up.*

fair See BID FAIR, PLAY FAIR.

fair and square *adv. phr., informal* Without cheating; honestly. ♦ *He won the game fair and square.*

fair catch *n.* A catch of a kicked football by a player after he holds up his hand to show that he will not run with the ball. ♦ *He saw that he would not be able to run with the ball, so he signalled for a fair catch.*

fair-haired boy *n., informal* A person that gets special favors; favorite; pet. ♦ *If he wins the election by a large majority, he will become his party's fair-haired boy.* ♦ *The local boy playing first base could do no wrong; he was the fair-haired boy of the fans.* ♦ *Charles was a good student and behaved very well; he became the teacher's fair-haired boy.*

fair play *n.* Equal and right action (to another person); justice. ♦ *The visiting team did not get fair play in the game.* ♦ *The judges decided against Bob, but he said that he had gotten fair play.* ♦ *Sally's sense of fair play made her a favorite with her classmates.*

fair sex *n., informal* Women in general; the female sex. ♦ *"Better not use four-letter words in front of a member of the fair sex," Joe said.*

fair shake *n., informal* Honest treatment. ♦ *Joe has always given me a fair shake.*

fair-weather friend *n.* A person who is a friend only when you are successful. ♦ *Everyone knows that John's only a fair-weather friend.*

fairy godmother *n.* **1.** A fairy believed to help and take care of a baby as it grows up. **2.** A person who helps and does much for another. ♦ *The rich man played fairy godmother to the boys and had a baseball field made for them.* ♦ *Jane was a fairy godmother to her poorer friends.*

fairy tale *or* **story** *n.* An inaccurate, even false account of something; a result of wishful thinking. ♦ *Jeff said he was going to be promoted soon, but we all suspect that it is only one of his customary fairy tales.*

faith See GOOD FAITH, ON FAITH.

fall See BOTTOM DROP OUT OR BOTTOM FALL OUT, RIDING FOR A FALL.

fall all over *v. phr., informal* To show too much love or thanks toward (someone). ♦ *She must love him. Every time you see them, she's falling all over him.* ♦ *When Bob found the lady's ring and returned it, she fell all over him.*

fall asleep at the switch *v. phr.* To fail to perform an expected task; be remiss in one's duty. ♦ *The two airplanes wouldn't have collided, if the control tower operator hadn't fallen asleep at the switch.* ♦ *The dean promised our department $250,000 but the foundation never sent the money because someone in the dean's office fell asleep at the switch.*

fall away *v. phr.* To decline; diminish. ♦ *I was shocked to see how haggard Alan looked; he seems to be falling away to a shadow.*

fall back *v.* To move back; go back.— Usually used with a group as subject. ♦ *The army fell back before their stubborn enemies.* ♦ *The crowd around the hurt boy fell back when someone shouted "Give him air!"* Compare DROP BACK, GIVE WAY.

fall back on *or* **fall back upon** *v.* **1.** To retreat to. ♦ *The enemy made a strong attack, and the soldiers fell back on the fort.* **2.** To go for help to; turn to in time of need. ♦ *When the big bills for Mother's hospital care came, Joe was glad he had money in the bank to fall back on.* ♦ *If Mr. Jones can't find a job as a teacher, he can fall back on his skill as a printer.*

fall behind *v.* To go slower than others and be far behind them. ♦ *When the campers took a hike in the woods, two boys fell behind and got lost.* ♦ *Frank's lessons were too hard for him, and he soon fell behind the rest of the class.* ♦ *Mary was not promoted because she dreamed too much and fell behind in her lessons.*

fall by the wayside *also* **drop by the wayside** *v. phr.* To give up or fail before the finish. ♦ *The boys tried to make a 50-mile hike, but most of them fell by the wayside.* ♦ *George, Harry, and John entered college to become teachers, but Harry and John fell by the wayside, and only George graduated.*

fall down on the job *v. phr., informal* To fail to work well. ♦ *The boss was disap-*

pointed when his workers fell down on the job.

fall due *or* **come** *or* **become due** *v. phr.* To reach the time when a bill or invoice is to be paid. ♦*Our car payment falls due on the first of every month.*

fall flat *v., informal* To be a failure; fail. ♦*The party fell flat because of the rain.* ♦*His joke fell flat because no one understood it.*

fall for *v., slang* **1.** To begin to like very much. ♦*Dick fell for baseball when he was a little boy.* **2.** To begin to love (a boy or a girl.) ♦*Helen was a very pretty girl and people were not surprised that Bill fell for her.* **3.** To believe (something told to fool you.) ♦*Nell did not fall for Joe's story about being a jet pilot.*

fall from grace *v. phr.* To go back to a bad way of behaving; do something bad again. ♦*The boys behaved well during dinner until they fell from grace by eating their dessert with their fingers instead of their forks.* ♦*The boy fell from grace when he lied.*

fall guy *n. slang* The "patsy" in an illegal transaction; a sucker; a dupe; the person who takes the punishment others deserve. ♦*When the Savings and Loan Bank failed, due to embezzlement, the vice president had to be the fall guy, saving the necks of the owners.*

fall in *v.* **1.** To go and stand properly in a row like soldiers. ♦*The captain told his men to fall in.* Contrast FALL OUT 3. **2.** to collapse. ♦*The explosion caused the walls of the house to fall in.*

fall in for *v.* To receive; get. ♦*The boy fell in for some sympathy when he broke his leg.* ♦*The team manager fell in for most of the blame when his team lost the playoffs.*

falling-out *n.* Argument; disagreement; quarrel. ♦*Mary and Jane had a falling-out about who owned the book.* ♦*The boys had a falling-out when each said that the other had broken the rules.*

fall in line *or* **fall into line** See IN LINE, INTO LINE.

fall in love See IN LOVE.

fall in *or* **into place** *v. phr.* To suddenly make sense; find the natural or proper place for the missing pieces of a puzzle. ♦*When the detectives realized that a* second man was seen at the place of the murder, the pieces of the puzzle began to fall into place.

fall in with *v., informal* **1.** To meet by accident. ♦*Mary fell in with some of her friends downtown.* **2.** To agree to help with; support. ♦*I fell in with Jack's plan to play a trick on his father.* **3.** To become associated with a group detrimental to the newcomer. ♦*John fell in with a wild bunch; small wonder he flunked all of his courses.* Compare PLAY ALONG.

fall into the habit of *v. phr.* To develop the custom of doing something. ♦*Jack has fallen into the bad habit of playing poker for large sums of money every night.*

fall off See DROP OFF 4.

fall off the wagon *v. phr., slang alcoholism and drug culture* To return to the consumption of an addictive, such as alcohol or drugs, after a period of abstinence. ♦*Poor Joe has fallen off the wagon again—he is completely incoherent today.*

fall on *or* **fall upon** *v.* **1.** To go and fight with; attack. ♦*The robbers fell on him from behind trees.* **2.** *formal* To meet (troubles). ♦*The famous poet fell upon unhappy days.*

fallout *n.* **1.** Result of nuclear explosion; harmful radioactive particles. *Some experts consider fallout as dangerous as the bomb itself.* **2.** Undesirable aftereffects in general. ♦*As a fallout of Watergate, many people lost their faith in the government.*

fall out *v.* **1.** To happen. ♦*As it fell out, the Harpers were able to sell their old car.* Compare TURN OUT 6. **2.** To quarrel; fight; fuss; disagree. ♦*The thieves fell out over the division of the loot.* **3.** To leave a military formation. ♦*You men are dismissed. Fall out!* Contrast FALL IN. **4.** To leave a building to go and line up. ♦*The soldiers fell out of the barracks for inspection.*

fall over backwards *or* **fall over oneself** *v. phr.* To do everything you can to please someone; try very hard to satisfy someone. ♦*The hotel manager fell over backwards to give the movie star everything she wanted.* ♦*The boys fell over themselves trying to get the new girl's attention.*

fall over yourself See FALL OVER BACKWARDS.

fall short *v.* To fail to reach (some aim); not succeed. ♦*His jump fell three inches short of the world record.* ♦*The movie fell short of expectations.* Contrast MEASURE UP.

fall through *v., informal* To fail; be ruined; not happen or be done. ♦*Jim's plans to go to college fell through at the last moment.* ♦*Mr. Jones' deal to sell his house fell through.* Contrast COME OFF.

fall to *v.* **1.** To begin to work. ♦*The boys fell to and quickly cut the grass.* Syn. TURN TO **2.** To begin to fight. ♦*They took out their swords and fell to.* **3.** To begin to eat. ♦*The hungry boys fell to before everyone sat down.* **4.** Begin; start. ♦*The old friends met and fell to talking about their school days.*

fall to pieces *v. phr.* To disintegrate; collapse. ♦*After the death of Alexander the Great, his empire started to fall to pieces.*

fall wide of the mark See WIDE OF THE MARK.

false See PLAY ONE FALSE, SAIL UNDER FALSE COLORS.

family See RUN IN THE BLOOD *or* RUN IN THE FAMILY, IN A FAMILY WAY.

family tree *n.* Ancestry. ♦*My family tree can be traced back to the sixteenth century.*

famine See FEAST OR A FAMINE.

fancy doing something—An expression of surprise. ♦*Fancy meeting you here in such an unexpected place!*

fancy pants *n., slang* A man or boy who wears clothes that are too nice or acts like a woman or girl; sissy. ♦*The first time they saw him in his new band uniform, they yelled "Hey, fancy pants, what are you doing in your sister's slacks?"*

fan See HIT THE FAN.

fan out *v. phr.* To spread in several directions. ♦*The main road fans out at the edge of the forest in four different directions.*

fan the breeze *v. phr.* **1.** See SHOOT THE BREEZE. **2.** To swing and miss the ball in baseball. ♦*The batter tried to hit a home run, but he fanned the breeze.*

far See AS FAR AS *or* SO FAR AS, SO FAR *also* THUS FAR, BY FAR, FEW AND FAR BETWEEN, SO FAR, SO GOOD.

far afield *adj. phr.* Remote; far from the original starting point. ♦*When we started to discuss theology, Jack was obviously getting far afield from the subject at hand.*

far and away *adv. phr.* Very much. ♦*The fish was far and away the biggest ever caught on the lake.* Compare BY FAR, HEAD AND SHOULDERS 2.

far and near *n. phr.* Far places and near places; everywhere. ♦*People came from far and near to hear him speak.*

far and wide *adv. phr.* Everywhere, in all directions. ♦*The wind blew the papers far and wide.* ♦*My old school friends are scattered far and wide now.* ♦*The movie company looked far and wide for a boy to act the hero in the new movie.* Compare ALL OVER.

farfetched *adj.* Exaggerated; fantastic. ♦*Sally told us some farfetched story about having been kidnapped by little green men in a flying saucer.*

far cry *n.* Something very different. ♦*His last statement was a far cry from his first story.* ♦*The first automobile could run, but it was a far cry from a modern car.*

far from it *adv. phr.* Not even approximately; not really at all. ♦*"Do you think she spent $100 on that dress?" Jane asked. "Far from it," Sue replied. "It must have cost at least $300."*

far gone *adj. phr.* In a critical or extreme state. ♦*He was so far gone by the time the doctor arrived, that nothing could be done to save his life.*

farm See COLLECTIVE FARM.

farm out *v.* **1.** To have another person do (something) for you; send away to be done. ♦*Our teacher had too many test papers to read, so she farmed out half of them to a friend.* **2.** To send away to be taken care of. ♦*While Mother was sick, the children were farmed out to relatives.* **3.** To send a player to a league where the quality of play is lower. ♦*The player was farmed out to Rochester to gain experience.*

far-out *adj.* **1.** Very far away; distant. ♦*Scientists are planning rocket trips to the moon and far-out planets.* **2.** *informal* Very different from others; queer; odd, unusual. ♦*He enjoyed being with beatniks and other far-out people.* ♦*Susan did not like some of the* *paintings at the art show because they were too far-out for her.*

fashion See AFTER A FASHION, HIGH FASHION *or* HIGH STYLE.

fast See HARD-AND-FAST, PLAY FAST AND LOOSE.

fast and furious *adj. or adv. phr.* Very fast; with much speed and energy. ♦*He was mowing the grass at a fast and furious rate.* ♦*When I last saw her she was driving fast and furious down the street.* Compare GREAT GUNS.

fast buck *or* **quick buck** *slang* Money earned quickly and easily, and sometimes dishonestly. ♦*You can make a fast buck at the golf course by fishing balls out of the water trap.* ♦*He isn't interested in a career; he's just looking for a quick buck.*

fast talker *n., slang, informal* A con artist or a swindler, one who is particularly apt to get away with illegitimate transactions because of the clever way he talks. ♦*I wouldn't trust Uncle Joe if I were you,—he is a fast talker.*

fast time See DAYLIGHT SAVING TIME.

fasten on *v. phr.* To attach; tie something to make it secure. ♦*"Fasten on your life jackets when you get into the life boats," the captain said.*

fat See CHEW THE FAT.

fat chance *n. phr., slang* Little or no possibility; almost no chance. ♦*A high school team would have a fat chance of beating a strong college team.* ♦*Jane is pretty and popular; you will have a fat chance of getting a date with her.* Compare GHOST OF A.

fat city *n., slang* A state of contentment due to wealth and position. ♦*Bully for the Smiths; they have arrived in Fat City.*

fate See TEMPT FATE *or* TEMPT THE FATES.

father See LIKE FATHER, LIKE SON.

Father Christmas *n., British* The joyful spirit of Christmas; Santa Claus. ♦*English children look forward to the visit of Father Christmas.*

Father's Day *n.* The third Sunday in June set aside especially to honor fathers whether living or dead. ♦*The children gave nice presents to their father on Father's Day.*

fat is in the fire Something has happened that will cause trouble or make a bad situation worse. ♦*He found out you took it? Well, the fat's in the fire now.*

fat of the land *n. phr.* The best and richest food, clothes, everything. ♦*When I'm rich I'll retire and live off the fat of the land.*

fault See AT FAULT, FIND FAULT, TO A FAULT.

faultfinding *n.* Recrimination; nagging; criticism. ♦*All of this constant fault-finding will only to lead to trouble between you and your wife.*

favor See CURRY FAVOR, IN FAVOR OF.

favorite son *n.* A man supported by his home state for President. ♦*At a national convention, states often vote for their favorite sons first; then they change and vote for another man.*

fear See FOR FEAR.

fear and trembling *or* **fear and trepidation** *n. phr.* Great fear. ♦*He came in fear and trembling to tell his father he had a bad report card.*

feast one's eyes on *v. phr.* To look at and enjoy very much. ♦*He feasted his eyes on the beautiful painting.*

feast or a famine *n. phr.* Plenty or very little; big success or bad failure. ♦*In this business it's either a feast or a famine.* ♦*He is very careless with his money, it is always a feast or a famine with him.*

feather See BIRDS OF A FEATHER FLOCK TOGETHER, TAR AND FEATHER, FINE FEATHERS DO NOT MAKE FINE BIRDS, FUSS AND FEATHERS, MAKE THE FEATHERS FLY, RUFFLE FEATHERS.

feather in one's cap *n. phr.* Something to be proud of; an honor. ♦*It was a feather in his cap to win first prize.* [From the medieval practice of placing a feather in the helmet of one who won honors in battle.]

feather one's nest *v. phr., informal* **1.** To use for yourself money and power, especially from a public office or job in which you are trusted to help other people. ♦*The rich man told his lawyer to use his money after he died to build a hospital for poor people, but the lawyer feathered his own nest with the money instead.* ♦*The man feathered his nest in politics by getting money from contractors who built roads.* Syn. LINE ONE'S POCKETS. **2.** To make your home pleasant and comfortable; furnish and decorate your house. ♦ *Furniture stores welcome young couples who want to feather their nests.*

fed up *(informal)* ALSO *(slang)* **fed to the gills** *or* **fed to the teeth** *adj. phr.* Having had too much of something; at the end of your patience; disgusted; bored; tired. ♦ *People get fed up with anyone who brags all the time.* ♦ *I've had enough of his complaints. I'm fed up.* ♦ *He was fed to the teeth with television and sold his set to a cousin.* ♦ *John quit football because he was fed to the gills with practice.* Compare SICK AND TIRED.

feed See BITE THE HAND THAT FEEDS ONE, CHICKEN FEED, OFF FEED *or* OFF ONE'S FEED, SPOON FEED.

feel See GET THE FEEL OF *and* HARD FEELING.

feel a draft *v. phr., slang* To have the sensation that one is not welcome in a place; that one has gotten a cold reception. ♦ *Let's go, Suzie, I feel a draft.*

feel for someone *v. phr., informal* To be able to sympathize with someone's problems. ♦ *I can really feel for you, John, for losing your job.*

feel free to do *v. phr.* To take the liberty to engage in an activity. ♦ *Please feel free to take off your jackets; this is an informal party.*

feel in one's bones *or* **know in one's bones** *v. phr.* To have an idea or feeling but not know why. ♦ *I feel in my bones that tomorrow will be a sunny day.* ♦ *I know in my bones that God will protect us.*

feel like *v., informal* To want to do or have. ♦ *I don't feel like running today.* ♦ *I just don't feel like pancakes this morning.*

feel like a million *or* **feel like a million dollars** *v. phr., informal* To be in the best of health and spirits. ♦ *I feel like a million this morning.* ♦ *He had a headache yesterday but feels like a million dollars today.* Compare LOOK LIKE A MILLION.

feel like a new man *v. phr.* To feel healthy, vigorous, and well again after a major physical illness or emotional upheaval. ♦ *Ted felt like a new man after his successful heart bypass operation.*

feel like two cents See TWO CENTS.

feel low *v. phr.* To be depressed; be in low spirits. ♦ *I don't know what's the matter with Mary, but she says she has been feeling very low all afternoon.*

feel no pain *v. phr., slang* To be drunk. ♦ *After a few drinks, the man felt no pain and began to act foolishly.*

feel one's oats *v. phr., slang* **1.** To feel frisky or playful; be eager and excited. ♦ *The horses were feeling their oats.* ♦ *When they first got to camp, the boys were feeling their oats.* **2.** To act in a proud or important way. ♦ *The new gardener was feeling his oats and started to boss the other men.*

feel one's way *v. phr.* To proceed cautiously by trial and error; probe. ♦ *I won't ask her to marry me directly; I will feel my way first.*

feel *or* **look small** *v. phr.* To have the impression that one is insignificant, foolish, or humiliated. ♦ *"I feel small next to Hemingway," the young student of creative writing said.*

feel out *v.* To talk or act carefully with someone and find what he thinks or can do. ♦ *The pupils felt out the principal about a party after the game.* ♦ *John felt out his father about letting him have the car that evening.* ♦ *At first the boxers felt each other out.* Compare SOUND OUT.

feel out of place *v. phr.* To experience the sensation of not belonging in a certain place or company. ♦ *Dave felt out of place among all those chess players as he knows nothing about chess.*

feel the pinch *v. phr.* To be short of money; experience monetary difficulties. ♦ *If we are going to have a recession, everybody will feel the pinch.*

feel up *v. phr., vulgar, avoidable* To arouse sexually by manual contact. ♦ *You mean to tell me that you've been going out for six months and he hasn't ever tried to feel you up?* Contrast COP A FEEL.

feel up to something *v. phr., informal* To feel adequately knowledgeable, strong, or equipped to handle a given task. ♦ *Do you feel up to jogging a mile a day with me?* Contrast BE UP TO SOMETHING.

feet See FOOT.

feet of clay *n. phr.* A hidden fault or weakness in a person which is discovered or shown. ♦ *The famous general* *showed he had feet of clay when he began to drink liquor.* ◆ *The banker seemed to be honest, but he had feet of clay and was arrested for stealing.*

feet on the ground *n. phr.* An understanding of what can be done; sensible ideas. Used with a possessive. ◆ *John has his feet on the ground; he knows he cannot learn everything at once.* ◆ *Ted dreams of sudden riches, but Henry keeps his feet on the ground and expects to work for his money.* ◆ *Mrs. Smith was a dreamer, but her husband was a man with his feet on the ground.* Contrast IN THE CLOUDS.

fell See AT ONE FELL SWOOP.

fellow See HAIL-FELLOW-WELL-MET, REGULAR GUY *or* REGULAR FELLOW.

fellow traveller *n.* A sympathizer with a political movement who does not officially belong to the political party in question. ◆ *Many Germans after World War II were innocently accused of being fellow travellers of Nazism.* ◆ *During the McCarthy era, many Americans were accused of being Communist fellow travellers.*

fence See GRASS IS ALWAYS GREENER ON THE OTHER SIDE OF THE FENCE, MEND ONE'S FENCES, ON THE FENCE.

fence in *or* **hedge in** *or* **hem in** *v.* To keep (someone) from doing what he or she would like to do. Usually used in the passive. ◆ *Mary felt fenced in because her father would not let her drive a car or have dates with boys.* ◆ *John didn't like his job because he had to do the same kind of work all the time. He felt that he was hemmed in.*

fence-sitter *n.* A person unable to pick between two sides; a person who does not want to choose. ◆ *Daddy says he is a fence-sitter because he doesn't know which man he wants for President.*

fence-sitting *n. or adj.* Choosing neither side. ◆ *You have been fence-sitting for too long. It is time you made up your mind.* Contrast MAKE UP ONE'S MIND, TAKE SIDES.

fence with *or* **spar with** *v.* To talk with (someone) as if you were fighting like a swordsman or boxer; to give skillful answers or arguments against (someone). ◆ *The governor was an expert at fencing with reporters at press conferences.*

ferret out *literary or* **smell out** *or* **sniff out** *v.* To hunt or drive from hiding; to bring out into the open; search for and find. ◆ *John ferreted out the answer to the question in the library.* ◆ *Jane smelled out the boys' secret hiding place in the woods.*

few See MAN OF FEW WORDS, NOT A FEW, QUITE A FEW.

few and far between *adj. phr.* Not many; few and scattered; not often met or found; rare.—Used in the predicate. ◆ *People who will work as hard as Thomas A. Edison are few and far between.* ◆ *Places where you can get water are few and far between in the desert.* ◆ *Really exciting games are few and far between.*

fickle finger of fate See ACT OF GOD.

fiddle See PLAY SECOND FIDDLE.

fiddle around See FOOL AROUND 3.

fiddler See PAY THE PIPER *or* PAY THE FIDDLER.

fiddle with *v. phr.* To carelessly play with something. ◆ *If Jimmy continues to fiddle with our computer, he is liable to ruin it.*

field See CENTER FIELD, LEFT FIELD, OUT IN LEFT FIELD, PLAY THE FIELD, RIGHT FIELD.

field goal *n.* **1.** A score in football made by kicking the ball over the bar between the goal posts. ◆ *The Giants were not able to make a touchdown but they kicked two field goals.* Compare EXTRA POINT. **2.** A score in basketball made by a successful shot through the basket not made on a free throw. ◆ *A field goal counts two points.* Compare FOUL SHOT, FREE THROW.

fifth See TAKE THE FIFTH.

fifth column *n. phr.* A group or organization within a country that works to bring about the country's downfall, usually through acts of espionage and sabotage. ◆ *The Communist party in the United States was considered by Senator McCarthy to be the Soviet Union's fifth column.*

fifty-fifty[1] *adv., informal* Equally; evenly. ◆ *The two boys divided the marbles they won fifty-fifty.* ◆ *When Dick and Sam bought an old car, they divided the cost fifty-fifty.*

fifty-fifty[2] *adj., informal* **1.** Divided or shared equally. ◆ *It will be a fifty-fifty* *arrangement; half the money for me and half for you.* **2.** Half for and half against; half good and half bad. ♦ *There is only a fifty-fifty chance that we will win the game.* Compare HALF AND HALF.

fight against time See RACING TO STAND STILL.

fight fire with fire *v. phr. slightly formal, of Biblical origin* To fight back in the same way one was attacked; make a defense similar to the attack. ♦ *The candidate was determined to fight fire with fire in the debate.*

fight it out See SLUG IT OUT.

fighting chance *n. phr.* A chance that necessitates struggle and courage; a slim chance. ♦ *The doctor told the family that Jack had a fighting chance to recover.* ♦ *Our business lost a lot of money, but we have a fighting chance to stage a comeback.*

fight off *v. phr.* **1.** To struggle against someone so as to free oneself; push an attacker back. ♦ *Suzy fought off her two attackers in Central Park with a couple of karate chops.* **2.** To strive to overcome something negative. ♦ *After twelve hours at the computer terminal, Jane had to fight off her overwhelming desire to go to sleep.*

fight shy of *v. phr.* To avoid; escape from. ♦ *Jack always fights shy of anything that even remotely resembles serious work.*

fight tooth and nail See TOOTH AND NAIL.

figure in *v.* **1.** *informal* To add to a total; remember to put down in figures. ♦ *We figured in the travel expenses but forgot the cost of meals.* **2.** To have a part in; be partly responsible for. ♦ *Joe figured in all our touchdowns.* ♦ *Mary's good grades figured in her choice as class president.*

figure on *v.* **1.** To expect and think about while making plans. ♦ *We did not figure on having so many people at the picnic.* ♦ *He figured on going to town the next day.* Syn. PLAN ON. **2.** To depend on; be sure about. ♦ *You can figure on him to be on time.* Syn. COUNT ON.

figure out *v.* **1.** To find an answer by thinking about (some problem or difficulty); solve. ♦ *Tom couldn't figure out the last problem on the arithmetic test.*

♦ *Sam couldn't figure out how to print a program until the teacher showed him how.* ♦ *Mary couldn't figure out why her cake tasted so funny until she found salt mixed in the sugar bag.* Compare FIND OUT 1. **2.** To learn how to explain; understand. ♦ *Laurence is an odd boy; I can't figure him out.* Compare MAKE OUT 2.

figure up *v. phr.* To calculate; add up. ♦ *If you can figure up how many phone calls I've made from your home, I will pay you right away.*

fill in *v.* **1.** To write words needed in blanks; put in; fill. ♦ *You should fill in all the blanks on an application for a job.* **2.** *informal* To tell what you should know. ♦ *The new boy didn't know the rules so Bob filled him in.* ♦ *The teacher filled in Mary about class work done while she was sick.* **3.** To take another's place; substitute. ♦ *The teacher was sick and Miss Jones filled in for her.*

fill (in) the gap *v. phr.* To supply a missing piece of information; provide a clue during the course of solving a mystery. ♦ *Sherlock Holmes said, "These fingerprints are bound to fill the gap in our investigation."*

fill one's shoes *v. phr.* To take the place of another and do as well; to substitute satisfactorily for. ♦ *When Jack got hurt, the coach had nobody to fill his shoes.* ♦ *Joe hopes to fill his father's shoes.* See IN ONE'S SHOES.

fill out *v.* **1.** To put in what is missing; complete; finish; *especially,* to complete (a printed application blank or other form) by writing the missing facts in the blank spaces; to write down facts which are asked for in (a report or application.) ♦ *After Tom passed his driving test he filled out an application for his driver's license.* ♦ *The policeman filled out a report of the accident.* **2.** To become heavier and fatter; gain weight. ♦ *When Bill was nineteen he began to fill out.* ♦ *The girl was pale and thin after her sickness, but in a few months she filled out.*

fill the bases See LOAD THE BASES.

fill the bill *v. phr., informal* To be just what is needed; be good enough for something; be just right. ♦ *The boss was worried about hiring a deaf boy,* *but after he tried Tom out for a few weeks, he said that Tom filled the bill.* ♦ *I thought I would need a special tool, but this wrench fills the bill.*

fill up *or* **fill it up** *or* **fill her up**   *v. phr.* To fill entirely. (Said by the driver of a car to a gas station attendant). ♦ *When the attendant asked Andrew how much gas he wanted in the tank, Andrew replied, "Fill her up."*

filthy lucre   *n.*, *informal* Money, especially when thought of as bad or shameful. ♦ *When the rich gambler tried to make Sarah marry him, she said, "Keep your filthy lucre—I shall marry the man I love."*—Sometimes used in a joking way. ♦ *"Come and let's get rid of some filthy lucre."*

filthy rich   *adj. phr.* Extremely rich but without cultural refinement; nouveau riche. ♦ *"The Murgatroyds are filthy rich,"* Ted complained. *"They are rolling in money but they never learned how to behave properly at a dinner table."*

finders keepers *or* **finders keepers, losers weepers** *informal* Those who find lost things can keep them.—Used usually by children to claim the right to keep something they have found. ♦ *I don't have to give it back; it's finders keepers.* ♦ *Finders keepers, losers weepers! It's my knife now!*

find fault   *v. phr.* To find something wrong; complain; criticize. ♦ *She tries to please him, but he always finds fault.* ♦ *They found fault with every box I made.* Compare JUMP ON, PICK AT 3.

find it in one's heart   *v. phr.* To be able or willing because of your nature. ♦ *He could not find it in his heart to tell her about her mother's death.* ♦ *Can you find it in your heart to forgive me?* ♦ *He could never find it in his heart to be mean to a dog.*

find one's ———   *v. phr.* To become able to use (some power of the body or mind.) ♦ *In the program for the parents, John was nervous and could not speak at first; then he found his tongue.* ♦ *The young bird had just found its wings.* ♦ *The baby was just beginning to find his feet.* ♦ *The question surprised him, and it was a minute before he found his tongue.*

find oneself   *v. phr.* To find out what one is fitted for and succeed in that. ♦ *Mary*

tried several lines of work, but at last found herself as a teacher. ♦ *Sometimes young people move around a long time from job to job before they find themselves.*

find *or* **get one's bearings**   *v. phr.* To know where one is or where one is headed. ♦ *"Without a compass,"* the sergeant warned the enlisted men, *"you will never find your bearings in the desert."*

find out   *v.*   **1.** To learn or discover (something you did not know before.) ♦ *One morning the baby found out for the first time that she could walk.* ♦ *I don't know how this car works, but I'll soon find out.* ♦ *He watched the birds to find out where they go.* ♦ *Mary was angry when Jane found out her secret.* **2.** To get facts; to get facts about. ♦ *He wrote to find out about a job in Alaska.* ♦ *She found out how much the house would cost.* **3.** To discover (someone) doing wrong; catch. ♦ *Some children are bad when no one is watching them, but they are usually found out.* ♦ *The boy knew that if he cheated on the test the teacher would find him out.*

find out the hard way   See HARD WAY.

fine feathers do not make fine birds *literary* A person who wears fine clothes may not be as good as he looks.—A proverb. ♦ *Mary is pretty and she wears pretty clothes, but she is very mean. Fine feathers do not make fine birds.* Compare HANDSOME IS AS HANDSOME DOES.

fine kettle of fish   See KETTLE OF FISH.

fine-tooth comb   *n. phr.* Great care; careful attention so as not to miss anything. ♦ *The police searched the scene of the crime with a fine-tooth comb for clues.* ♦ *My room is so clean you couldn't find dirt if you went over it with a fine-tooth comb.* Compare LEAVE NO STONE UNTURNED.

finger   See BURN ONE'S FINGERS, CROSS ONE'S FINGERS, *or* KEEP ONE'S FINGERS CROSSED, LAY A FINGER ON, LIFT A FINGER, PUT ONE'S FINGER ON *also* LAY ONE'S FINGER ON, SLIP THROUGH ONE'S FINGERS, SNAP ONE'S FINGERS AT, STICKY FINGERS, TWIST AROUND ONE'S LITTLE FINGER, WORK ONE'S FINGERS TO THE BONE.

finger in the pie   *n. phr.*, *informal* Something to do with what happens;

part interest or responsibility. ◆ *When the girls got up a Christmas party, I felt sure Alice had a finger in the pie.* ◆ *The Jones Company was chosen to build the new hospital and we knew Mr. Smith had a finger in the pie.* ◆ *Jack is a boy with a finger in every pie at school, from dramatics to football.* Compare HAVE A HAND IN, TOO MANY IRONS IN THE FIRE.

fingertip See AT ONE'S FINGERTIPS.

finish up See END UP 4.

fire See BALL OF FIRE, BETWEEN THE DEVIL AND THE DEEP BLUE SEA *or* BETWEEN TWO FIRES, BUILD A FIRE UNDER, BURNT CHILD DREADS THE FIRE, CATCH FIRE, DRAW FIRE, FAT'S IN THE FIRE, FIGHT FIRE WITH FIRE, HANG FIRE, HEAP COALS OF FIRE ON ONE'S HEAD, HOLD ONE'S FIRE *or* HOLD FIRE, IRON IN THE FIRE, KEEP THE HOME FIRES BURNING, LINE OF FIRE, ON FIRE, OPEN FIRE, OUT OF THE FRYING PAN INTO THE FIRE, PLAY WITH FIRE, PULL ONE'S CHESTNUTS OUT OF THE FIRE, SET FIRE TO, SET THE WORLD ON FIRE, TILL THE LAST GUN IS FIRED *or* UNTIL THE LAST GUN IS FIRED, UNDER FIRE.

firebug *n.* An arsonist; one who willfully sets fire to property. ◆ *The police caught the firebug just as he was about to set another barn ablaze in the country.*

firing squad *n.* A group of soldiers chosen to shoot a prisoner to death or to fire shots over a grave as a tribute. ◆ *A dictator often sends his enemies before a firing squad.* ◆ *The dead general was honored by a firing squad.*

first See AT FIRST BLUSH, AT FIRST SIGHT, CAST THE FIRST STONE, GET TO FIRST BASE *or* REACH FIRST BASE, IN THE FIRST PLACE, OF THE FIRST WATER .

firsthand *adj.* Fresh; genuine; from the original source. ◆ *John says he got the information firsthand from the president himself.*

first and foremost *adv. phr.* As the most important thing; first. ◆ *First and foremost they needed food.* ◆ *I want you to remember to pay that bill first and foremost.* ◆ *First and foremost, we must keep America free.*

first and last *adv. phr.* Most noticeably; all the time; chiefly. ◆ *He was first and last a school teacher.* ◆ *Steven joined the army because first and last he wanted to help his country.* Syn. ABOVE ALL.

first base *n. phr.* **1.** The base that must be touched first by a baseball player after batting. ◆ *He got to first base on four balls.* **2.** See GET TO FIRST BASE.

first class *n.* **1.** The first rank; the highest class; the best group. ◆ *The pianist was quite good but he was not in the first class.* **2.** The most expensive or comfortable class of travel; the best or one of the best groups in which to travel, especially by ship, train, or airplane. ◆ *Most people can't afford the first class when they take a long journey by ship.* **3.** The way of sending all mail that includes letters and post cards, anything written by hand or typewriter, and anything sealed so that it cannot be inspected, and that is the most expensive class of mail but receives the best treatment. ◆ *The usual way to send a letter is by first class.* Compare SECOND CLASS, THIRD CLASS.

first-class¹ *adj.* **1.** Of the highest class or best kind; excellent; first-rate. ◆ *Jane did a first-class job of repairing the coat.* ◆ *It was a first-class TV program.* Compare TOP-NOTCH. **2.** Of the best or most expensive class of travelling. ◆ *Mr. Jones bought a first-class plane ticket to Chicago.* **3.** Belonging to the class of mail for sending letters, post cards, and handwritten or typewritten mail that is sealed. ◆ *It is expensive to send a heavy letter by first-class mail.*

first-class² *adv.* With the best material; in the best or most expensive way. ◆ *When Mr. Van Smith goes anywhere he always travels first-class.* ◆ *"How did you send the package?" "First-class."*

first come, first served *truncated sent. informal* If you arrive first, you will be served first; people will be waited on in the order they come; the person who comes first will have his turn first. ◆ *Get in line for your ice cream, boys. First come, first served.* ◆ *The rule in the restaurant is first come, first served .* ◆ *The team's owners announced that tickets for the World Series would be sold on a first come, first served basis only.* ◆ *There are only a few seats left so it's first come, first served.* Compare EARLY BIRD CATCHES THE WORM.

first cousin *n.* The child of your aunt or uncle. ◆ *Tom's only first cousin was Ralph, the son of his Uncle John.*

first of all *adv. phr.* Chiefly; primarily; as the first thing. ♦ *After we get to Chicago, we will, first of all, try to find a reliable used car.*

first off *adv. phr., informal* Before anything else; first. ♦ *First off, I want you to mow the lawn.*

first-run *adj. phr.* Shown for the first time; new. ♦ *The local theater showed only first-run movies.*

first stone See CAST THE FIRST STONE.

first string[1] *n., informal* **1.** The best group of players on a team; first team; A team. ♦ *Dick loved basketball and practiced hard until he was put on the first string.* **2.** The best group of workers. ♦ *Tom learned his trade so well that his boss soon called him one of his first string.*

first-string *adj., informal* **1.** On the starting team or A team. ♦ *He was the first-string quarterback.* **2.** Of the best quality; foremost. ♦ *He was the least expensive of the city's first-string lawyers.*

first thing off the bat *adv. phr.* Immediately; at once. ♦ *He called home from Paris first thing off the bat as he stepped off the plane.*

first things first Other things must wait until the most important and necessary things are done. ♦ *Study your lessons before you go out to play. First things first.*

fish See COLD FISH, KETTLE OF FISH, NEITHER FISH NOR FOWL, NOT THE ONLY FISH IN THE SEA, OTHER FISH TO FRY.

fish-and-chips *n. phr.* Fried fish and french fried potatoes. ♦ *The family went to a drive-in restaurant and had fish-and-chips.*

fish for *v., informal* To try to get or to find out (something), by hinting or by a roundabout way to try to lead someone else to give or tell you what you want by hinting. ♦ *Jerry was always fishing for an invitation to Bob's house.* ♦ *Near examination time, some of the students fish for information.*

fish for a compliment *v. phr.* To try to make someone pay a compliment. ♦ *When Jim showed me his new car, I could tell that he was fishing for a compliment.*

fish fry *n.* An outdoor party or picnic at which fish are fried and eaten. ♦ *The*

guests at the fish fry caught and cooked their own fish.

fish in muddy *or* **troubled waters** *v. phr.* To take advantage of a troubled or confusing situation; seek personal advantage. ♦ *With the police disorganized after the collapse of communism in Europe, many criminals started to fish in troubled waters.*

fish or cut bait *v. phr., informal* **1.** Decide what you want to do and stop wasting time; either act now or give someone else a chance or turn. ♦ *Jack couldn't decide whether to go to college or get a job, so his father told him to fish or cut bait.* ♦ *"Buy the kind of ice cream you want or give someone else in line a chance. Fish or cut bait!"* Compare MAKE UP ONE'S MIND. **2.** either try hard and do your best, or quit. ♦ *Frank missed football practice so often that the coach told him to fish or cut bait.*

fish out of water *n. phr.* A person who is out of his proper place in life; someone who does not fit in. ♦ *Because Ed could not swim, he felt like a fish out of water at the beach.* ♦ *She was the only girl at the party not in a formal dress and she felt like a fish out of water.* Compare OUT OF ONE'S ELEMENT, OUT OF PLACE.

fish story *n. phr.* An unlikely or improbable tale. ♦ *Hunters and fishermen often exaggerate their successes by telling fish stories.*

fist See HARD-FISTED.

fit See BY FITS AND STARTS, GIVE FITS, HAVE A FIT *or* HAVE FITS, IF THE SHOE FITS, WEAR IT, SEE FIT *also* THINK FIT, SURVIVAL OF THE FITTEST.

fit as a fiddle *adj. phr.* In very good health. ♦ *The man was almost 90 years old but fit as a fiddle.* ♦ *Mary rested at home for a few weeks after her operation; then she felt fit as a fiddle.*

fit for *v. phr.* To be suited for; be prepared for. ♦ *"What kind of job is Ted fit for?"* the social worker asked.

fit in with *v. phr.* To fall into agreement or accord with. ♦ *His plans to take a vacation in early July fit in perfectly with the university schedule.*

fit like a glove *v. phr.* To fit perfectly. ♦ *Her new dress fits her like a glove.*

fit out *or* **fit up** *v.* To give things needed; furnish. ♦ *The soldiers were fitted out* *with guns and clothing.* ♦ *The government fitted out warships and got sailors for them.* ♦ *The house was fitted out very nicely.* ♦ *He fitted his room up as a photographic laboratory.*

fit the bill See FILL THE BILL.

fit to a T See TO A T.

fit to be tied[1] *adj. phr., informal* Very angry or upset. ♦ *She was fit to be tied when she saw the broken glass.*

fit to be tied[2] *adv. phr., substandard* Very hard.—Used for emphasis. ♦ *Uncle Willie was laughing fit to be tied at the surprised look on Mother's face.*

five o'clock shadow *n. phr.* A very short growth of beard on a man's face who did shave in the morning but whose beard is so strong that it is again visible in the afternoon. ♦ *"You have a five o'clock shadow, honey," Irene said, "and we're going to the opera. Why don't you shave again quickly?"*

fix See GET A FIX *or* GIVE SOMEONE A FIX, GET A FIX ON.

fix someone's wagon *or* **fix someone's little red wagon** *v. phr., informal* **1.** (Said to a child as a threat) to administer a spanking. ♦ *Stop that right away or I'll fix your (little red) wagon!* **2.** (Said of an adult) to thwart or frustrate another, to engineer his failure. ♦ *If he sues me for slander, I will counter-sue him for malicious prosecution. That will fix his wagon!*

fix someone up with *v. phr., informal* To help another get a date with a woman or man by arranging a meeting for the two. ♦ *Say Joe, can you possibly fix me up with someone this weekend? I am so terribly lonesome!*

fix up *v. phr.* **1.** To repair. ♦ *The school is having the old gym fixed up.* **2.** To arrange. ♦ *I think I can fix it up with the company so that John gets the transfer he desires.* **3.** To arrange a date that might lead to a romance or even to marriage. ♦ *Mary is a great matchmaker; she fixed up Ron and Betty at her recent party.*

fizzle out *v., informal* **1.** To stop burning; die out. ♦ *The fuse fizzled out before exploding the firecracker.* **2.** To fail after a good start; end in failure. ♦ *The power mower worked fine for a while but then it fizzled out.* ♦ *The party*

fizzled out when everyone went home early.

flag down *v., informal* To stop by waving a signal flag or as if waving a signal flag. ♦ *The signalman flagged down the freight train.* ♦ *A policeman flagged down the car with his flashlight.*

flakeball *or* **flake** *n., slang, drug culture* A disjointed, or "flaky" person, who is forgetful and incoherent, as if under the influence of narcotics. ♦ *Hermione is a regular flakeball.* Compare SPACED OUT.

flame See ADD FUEL TO THE FLAME, GO UP IN FLAMES.

flanker back *n.* A football back who can play far to the outside of his regular place. ♦ *The coach is still looking for a speedy boy to play flanker back.*

flare up *v.* **1.** To burn brightly for a short time especially after having died down. ♦ *The fire flared up again and then died.* **2.** To become suddenly angry. ♦ *The mayor flared up at the reporter's remark.* ♦ *The mother flared up at her children.* **3.** To begin again suddenly, especially for a short time after a quiet time. ♦ *Mr. Gray's arthritis flared up sometimes.* ♦ *Even after they had conquered the country, revolts sometimes flared up.*

flare-up *n.* The reoccurrence of an infection or an armed conflict. ♦ *He had a flare-up of his arthritis. There was a bad flare-up of hostilities in some countries.*

flash See IN A FLASH.

flash card *n.* A card with numbers or words on it that is used in teaching a class. ♦ *The teacher used flash cards to drill the class in addition.*

flash in the pan *n. phr., slang* A person or thing that starts out well but does not continue. ♦ *The new quarterback was a flash in the pan.* ♦ *Mary got 100 on the first test in arithmetic but it was just a flash in the pan because she failed in arithmetic.*

flat See FALL FLAT, IN NO TIME *or* IN NOTHING FLAT, LEAVE FLAT.

flat as a pancake *adj. phr.* Very level; very flat; having no mountains or hills. ♦ *A great part of the American Midwest is as flat as a pancake.*

flat broke See STONE-BROKE.

flatfoot *n., slang, derogatory* A policeman. ♦ *"What does Joe do for a living?—He's a flatfoot."*

flat-footed *adj., informal* **1.** Straightforward; forthright; direct; outright. ♦ *The governor issued a flat-footed denial of the accusation.* ♦ *He came out flat-footed against the idea.* **2.** Not ready; not prepared;—usually used with *catch.* ♦ *The teacher's question caught Tim flat-footed.* ♦ *Unexpected company at lunch time caught Mrs. Green flat-footed.*

flat-out *adv. phr., informal* **1.** Without hiding anything; plainly; openly. ♦ *The student told his teacher flat-out that he was not listening to her.* **2.** At top speed; as fast as possible. ♦ *He saw two men running flat-out from the wild rhinoceros.*

flatter oneself To be sure of your own talent or skill; highly confident. ♦ *I flatter myself that I am a better swimmer than he is.*

flea in one's ear *n. phr., informal* An idea or answer that is not welcome; an annoying or surprisingly sharp reply or hint. ♦ *I'll put a flea in his ear if he bothers me once more.*

flea market *n. phr.* A place where antiques, second-hand things, and cheap articles are sold, and especially one in the open air. ♦ *The local antique dealers held a flea market and fair on the high-school athletic field.* ♦ *There are many outdoor flea markets in Europe.*

flesh See IN PERSON *also* IN THE FLESH, NEITHER FISH NOR FOWL *also* NEITHER FISH, FLESH, NOR FOWL, PRESS THE FLESH, THORN IN THE FLESH.

flesh and blood *n.* **1.** A close relative (as a father, daughter, brother); close relatives. Used in the phrase *one's own flesh and blood.* ♦ *Such an answer from her—and she's my own flesh and blood, too!* **2.** The appearance of being real or alive. ♦ *The author doesn't give his characters any flesh and blood.* **3.** The human body. ♦ *Before child labor laws, small children often worked 50 or 60 hours a week in factories. It was more than flesh and blood could bear.*

flesh out *v., informal* **1.** To add to; make fuller, bigger, or longer. ♦ *The author fleshed out his story by adding more about his war experiences.* **2.** *also* **flesh up** To become heavier, put on weight, or flesh. ♦ *He lost weight after his ill-*ness *but is beginning to flesh out again.* See FILL OUT.

flesh up See FLESH OUT 2.

fling oneself at See THROW ONESELF AT.

fling oneself at someone's head See THROW ONESELF AT SOMEONE'S HEAD.

flip-flop[1] *v., informal* To alternate the positions of; exchange the places of; switch. ♦ *The football coach had one play in which he flip-flopped his left halfback and fullback.*

flip-flop[2] *n., informal* A complete change; a switch from one thing to an entirely different one. ♦ *John wanted to be a carpenter like his father, but when he saw the print shop he did a flip-flop and now he's learning printing.*

flip-flop[3] *adj. phr., informal* Involving or using a change from one of two places, positions, or alternatives to the other. ♦ *The machine was controlled by a flip-flop switch.* ♦ *The football coach hoped to surprise his opponents by using a flip-flop offense.*

flip one's lid *also* **flip one's wig** *slang* **1.** To lose one's temper. ♦ *When that pushy salesman came back Mom really flipped her lid.* Compare BLOW A FUSE. **2.** To lose your mind; become insane. ♦ *When he offered me three times the pay I was getting, I thought he had flipped his lid.* **3.** To become unreasonably enthusiastic. ♦ *She flipped her lid over a hat she saw in the store window.* ♦ *He's flipped his lid over that new actress.*

flip out *v. phr., slang, informal* To go insane, to go out of one's mind. ♦ *It is impossible to talk to Joe today—he must have flipped out.*

flock See BIRDS OF A FEATHER FLOCK TOGETHER.

floor See GROUND FLOOR, MOP THE FLOOR WITH, WALK THE FLOOR.

floor one *v. phr.* To overwhelm; astound; nonplus. ♦ *John's sudden announcement that he would retire floored all of us in the office.*

floorwalker *n.* A section manager in a department store. ♦ *To exchange this pair of shoes, you must first get the floorwalker's approval.*

flop See FLIP-FLOP.

flower child *n., slang, informal* **1.** A young person who believes in nonviolence and carries flowers around to symbolize his peace-loving nature. ♦ *Flower children are supposed to be nonviolent, but they sure make a lot of noise when they demonstrate!* **2.** Any person who cannot cope with reality. ♦ *"Face facts, Suzie, stop being such a flower child!"*

flower power *n., slang* The supposed power of love and nonviolence as intended to be used by members of the anti-culture to change American society. ♦ *The young people were marching for flower power.*

fluff one's lines See BLOW ONE'S LINES.

fluff stuff *n., slang, citizen's band radio jargon* Snow. ♦ *We can expect some fluff stuff this afternoon.*

flunk out *v. phr.* To have to withdraw from school or college because of too many failing grades. ♦ *Fred flunked out of college during his junior year.*

flush it *v. phr., slang* **1.** To fail (something). ♦ *I really flushed it in my math course.* **2.** *interj., used imperatively* Expression registering refusal to believe something considered stupid or false. ♦ *"You expect me to buy that story? Flush it!"*

fly See BIRD HAS FLOWN, GO FLY A KITE, MAKE THE FEATHERS FLY, MAKE THE FUR FLY, ON THE FLY, POP FLY, SACRIFICE FLY.

fly at one's throat *v. phr.* To attack you suddenly with great anger. ♦ *When Tom called Dick a bad name, Dick flew at his throat.*

fly ball *n.* A baseball hit high into the air. ♦ *He hit an easy fly ball to center field.*

fly blind *v. phr.* **1.** To fly an airplane by instruments alone. ♦ *In the heavy fog he had to fly blind.* **2.** *informal* To do something without understanding what you are doing. ♦ *I'm glad the car runs now; I was flying blind when I fixed it.* ♦ *He's flying blind when he talks about philosophy.*

fly-by-night[1] *adj.* Set up to make a lot of money in a hurry, then disappear so people can't find you to complain about poor work, etc.; not trustworthy; not reliable. ♦ *Mrs. Blank bought her vacuum cleaner from a new company; when she tried to have it fixed, she found it was a fly-by-night business.*

fly-by-night[2] *n., informal* **1.** A company that sells many cheap things for a big profit and then disappears. ♦ *A dependable company honors its guarantees, but a fly-by-night only wants your money.* **2.** A person who does not pay his bills, but sneaks away (as at night.) ♦ *Hotels are bothered by fly-by-nights.*

fly by the seat of one's pants *v. phr., slang* To fly an airplane by feel and instinct rather than with the help of the instruments. ♦ *Many pilots in World War I had to fly by the seat of their pants.*

flying See WITH FLYING COLORS.

flying high *adj., slang* Very happy; joyful. ♦ *Jack was flying high after his team won the game.* Compare IN THE CLOUDS, ON TOP OF THE WORLD.

flying start See GET OFF TO A FLYING START.

flying tackle *n., informal* A tackle made by jumping through the air at the person to be tackled. ♦ *Most football coaches don't want their players to make flying tackles.* ♦ *The policeman stopped the burglar with a flying tackle.*

flying wedge *n., informal* **1.** An offensive formation in football in which players link arms and line up to form a "V" with the ball carrier in the middle. ♦ *The flying wedge was so dangerous and hurt so many players that rules have forbidden it for over 50 years.* **2.** A group (as of guards or policemen) who use a "V" formation to help someone get through a crowd. ♦ *Police had to form a flying wedge to get the movie star through the crowd of autograph hunters.*

fly in the face of *or* **fly in the teeth of** *v. phr.* To ignore; go against; show disrespect or disregard for. ♦ *You can't fly in the face of good business rules and expect to be successful.* ♦ *Floyd's friends tried to help him, but he flew in the teeth of their advice and soon became a drunkard.*

fly in the ointment *n. phr., informal* An unpleasant part of a pleasant thing; something small that spoils your fun. ♦ *We had a lot of fun at the beach; the only fly in the ointment was George's cutting his foot on a piece of glass.* ♦ *Your new job sounds too good to be* *true—interesting work, high pay, short hours. Isn't there any fly in the ointment?*

fly off the handle *v. phr., informal* To become very angry. ♦ *John flew off the handle whenever Mary made a mistake.* ♦ *The children's noise made the man next door fly off the handle.* Syn. LOSE ONE'S TEMPER.

fly the coop *v. phr., slang* To leave suddenly and secretly; run away. ♦ *The robbers flew the coop before the police arrived.* ♦ *His partner flew the coop with all the money.*

flying visit *n. phr.* A visit of very short duration. ♦ *Tom came to New York for only a flying visit.* ♦ *We had hardly eaten lunch when he had to leave.*

flying saucer See U.F.O.

fly into a rage or temper *v. phr.* To become very angry. ♦ *Each time we mention the name of her ex-husband, she flies into a rage.*

foam at the mouth *v. phr., slang* To be very angry, like a mad dog. ♦ *By the time Uncle Henry had the third flat tire he was really foaming at the mouth.*

fob off *v., informal* **1.** To get something false accepted as good or real. ♦ *The peddler fobbed off pieces of glass as diamonds.* Syn. PALM OFF, PASS OFF. **2.** To put aside; not really answer but get rid of. ♦ *Her little brother asked where she was going, but she fobbed him off with an excuse.*

fog See IN A FOG.

foggy bottom *n., slang* An area in downtown Washington, D.C. where many offices of the Department of State are located; hence figuratively, the U.S. Department of State. ♦ *The press secretary gave us a lot of foggy bottom double-talk about the hostage crisis in the Near East.*

fold up *v., informal* To collapse; fail. ♦ *The team folded up in the last part of the season.* ♦ *The new restaurant folded up in less than a year.* Compare FALL APART.

folk See WEE FOLK.

follow See AS FOLLOWS.

follower See CAMP FOLLOWER.

follow in one's footsteps *also* **follow in one's tracks** *v. phr.* To follow someone's example; follow someone exactly. ♦ *He followed in his father's*

footsteps and became a doctor. Compare LIKE FATHER, LIKE SON.

follow one's heart *v. phr.* To do what one wishes to do rather than to follow the voice of reason. ♦ *Instead of accepting a lucrative job in his father's business, Jim followed his heart and became a missionary in the jungle.*

follow one's nose *v. phr., informal* **1.** To go straight ahead; continue in the same direction. ♦ *Just follow your nose and you'll get there.* **2.** To go any way you happen to think of. ♦ *Oh, I don't know just where I want to go. I'll just follow my nose and see what happens.*

follow out *v. phr., informal* **1.** To do fully; finish (what you are told to do.) ♦ *The boy followed out the instructions and made a fine model plane.* Compare FOLLOW THROUGH. **2.** To keep working at (something) until it is finished; give (something) your attention until it comes to an end or conclusion. ♦ *The student followed out all the index references in the encyclopedia until he found what he wanted to know.* Compare FOLLOW UP.

follow suit *v. phr.* **1.** To play a card of the same color and kind that another player has put down. ♦ *When diamonds were led, I had to follow suit.* **2.** To do as someone else has done; follow someone's example. ♦ *When the others went swimming, I followed suit.*

follow through *v. phr.* **1.** To finish a movement that you have started; continue an action to its natural ending. ♦ *A football passer should follow through after he throws the ball.* **2.** To finish an action that you have started. ♦ *Bob drew plans for a table for his mother, but he did not follow through by making it.*

follow up *v. phr., informal* **1.** To chase or follow closely and without giving up. ♦ *The Indians followed up the wounded buffalo until it fell dead.* **2.** Make (one action) more successful by doing something more. ♦ *After Mary sent a letter to apply for a job; she followed it up by going to talk to the personnel manager.* ♦ *The doctor followed up Billy's operation with x-rays and special exercises to make his foot stronger.* Compare FOLLOW OUT, FOLLOW THROUGH 2. **3a.** To hunt for (more news about something that has already been in the newspapers, radio or TV news); find more about. ♦ *The day after news of the fire at Brown's store, the newspaper sent a reporter to follow up Mr. Brown's future plans.* **3b.** To print or broadcast (more news about some happening that has been in the news before). ♦ *The fire story was printed Monday, and Tuesday's paper followed it up by saying that Mr. Brown planned to build a bigger and better store at the same place.*

follow-up *n.* Additional work or research by means of which an earlier undertaking's chances of success are increased. ♦ *I hope you'll be willing to do a bit of follow-up.*

fond of Having a liking for; attracted to by strong liking. ♦ *Alan is fond of candy.* ♦ *Uncle Bill was the children's favorite, and he was fond of them too.*

food for thought *n. phr.* Something to think about or worth thinking about; something that makes you think. ♦ *The teacher told John that she wanted to talk to his father, and that gave John food for thought.* ♦ *There is much food for thought in this book.*

fool See CHILDREN AND FOOLS SPEAK THE TRUTH, MAKE A FOOL OF.

fool and his money are soon parted A foolish person soon wastes his money.—A proverb. ♦ *Jimmy spends all his pennies for candy. A fool and his money are soon parted.*

fool around *or* **mess around** *or* **play around** *or* **monkey around** *v., informal* **1.** To spend time playing, fooling, or joking instead of being serious or working; waste time. ♦ *If you go to college, you must work, not fool around.* ♦ *The boys fooled around all afternoon in the park.* Compare CUT UP 2. To treat or handle carelessly. ♦ *Bob cut himself by fooling around with a sharp knife.* ♦ *Suzie says she wishes John would quit playing around with the girls and get married.* **3.** *or* **fiddle around** To work or do something in an irregular or unplanned way; tinker. ♦ *Jimmy likes to monkey around with automobile engines.* ♦ *Alice is fooling around with the piano in her spare time.* cf. fuck around.

fool around See MESS AROUND.

fool away *or* **fritter away** *v., informal* To waste foolishly. ♦ *Paul failed history because he fooled away his time instead of studying.* ♦ *The man won a lot of money, but he soon frittered it away and was poor again.*

foolish See PENNY WISE AND POUND FOOLISH.

foolproof *adj.* So constructed that not even a fool can spoil it; easy. ♦ *This entrance examination is so easy that it is actually foolproof.*

fool's paradise See LIVE IN A FOOL'S PARADISE.

foot See AT ONE'S FEET, COLD FEET, DEAD ON ONE'S FEET, DRAG ONE'S FEET, FROM HEAD TO FOOT, GET OFF ON THE WRONG FOOT, GET ONE'S FEET WET, HAND AND FOOT, KEEP ONE'S FEET, KNOCK OFF ONE'S FEET, LAND ON ONE'S FEET, LET GRASS GROW UNDER ONE'S FEET, ONE FOOT IN THE GRAVE, ON FOOT, ON ONE'S FEET, PLAY FOOTSIE, PUT ONE'S BEST FOOT FORWARD, PUT ONE'S FOOT DOWN, PUT ONE'S FOOT IN IT, SET FOOT, SHOE ON THE OTHER FOOT, STAND ON ONE'S OWN FEET, SWEEP OFF ONE'S FEET, THINK ON ONE'S FEET, THROW ONESELF AT SOMEONE'S FEET.

footed See FLAT FOOTED.

foot in the door *n. phr., informal* The first step toward getting or doing something; a start toward success; opening. ♦ *Don't let Jane get her foot in the door by joining the club or soon she'll want to be president.*

footstep See FOLLOW IN ONE'S FOOTSTEPS.

foot the bill *v. phr.* To cover the expenses of; pay for something. ♦ *The bride's father footed two-thirds of the bill for his daughter's wedding.* Compare PICK UP THE TAB.

footloose and fancy-free *adj. phr.* Free and free to do what one wants (said of unmarried men). ♦ *Ron is a merry bachelor and seems to enjoy greatly being footloose and fancy-free.*

for a fall See RIDING FOR A FALL.

for all **1.** In spite of; even with, despite.—Used for contrast. ♦ *For all his city ways, he is a country boy at heart.* ♦ *There may be mistakes occasionally,, but for all that, it is the best book on the subject.* ♦ *For all his money, he was very unhappy.* **2.** *also*

for aught To the extent that.—Used like a negative with *care* and *know.* ♦ *For all I care, you can throw it away.* ♦ *For all he knows, we might be in Boston.* Compare AS FAR AS 2, ONCE AND FOR ALL.

for all one cares *adv. phr.* In the opinion of one who is not involved or who does not care what happens. ♦ *For all Jane cares, poor Tom might as well drop dead.*

for all one is worth With all of your strength; as hard as you can. ♦ *Roger ran for all he was worth to catch the bus.*

for all one knows *adv. phr.* According to the information one has; probably. ♦ *For all we know, Ron and Beth might have eloped and been married in a French chateau.*

for all that *adv. phr.* In spite of what has been said, alleged, or rumored. ♦ *Well, for all that, we think that she is still the most deserving candidate for Congress.*

for all the world *adv. phr.* **1.** Under no circumstances. ♦ *Betty said she wouldn't marry Jake for all the world.* **2.** Precisely; exactly. ♦ *It began for all the world like a successful baseball season for the UIC Flames, when suddenly they lost to the Blue Demons.*

for a loop See KNOCK FOR A LOOP *or* THROW FOR A LOOP.

for a loss See THROW FOR A LOSS.

for a ride See TAKE FOR A RIDE.

for as much as *conj., formal* Because; since. ♦ *For as much as the senator is eighty years old, we feel he should not run for reelection.* Syn. INASMUCH AS.

for a song *adv. phr., informal* At a low price; for a bargain price; cheaply. ♦ *He sold the invention for a song and its buyers were the ones who got rich.* ♦ *They bought the house for a song and sold it a few years later at a good profit.*

for aught See FOR ALL 2.

for bear See LOADED FOR BEAR.

for better or worse *or* **for better or for worse** *adv. phr.* **1.** With good or bad effect, depending on how one looks at the matter. ♦ *The historian did justice, for better or worse, to the careers of several famous men.* **2.** Under any eventuality; forever; always. ♦ *Alex and Masha decided to leave Moscow and come to Chicago, for better or for*

worse. **3.** *(Marriage vows)* Forever, for as long as one may live. ♦ *With this ring I thee wed, for richer or poorer, in sickness and in health, for better or worse, til death do us part.*

forbid See GOD FORBID.

for broke See GO FOR BROKE.

force See IN FORCE, JOIN FORCES.

force one's hand *v. phr.* To make you do something or tell what you will do sooner than planned. ♦ *Ben did not want to tell where he was going, but his friend forced his hand.* ♦ *Mr. Smith planned to keep his land until prices went up, but he had so many doctor bills that it forced his hand.*

force play *or* **force-out** *n.* A play in baseball in which a runner is out because he does not run to the next base before the fielder with the ball touches the base. ♦ *Bob was out at second base when Joe hit into a force play.*

for certain See FOR SURE.

for crying out loud *informal* Used as an exclamation to show that you feel surprised or cross. ♦ *For crying out loud, look who's here!* ♦ *For crying out loud! that's the third time you've done it wrong.* Compare FOR ONE'S SAKE.

for days on end *adv. phr.* For a long time; for many days. ♦ *The American tourists tried to get used to Scottish pronunciation for days on end, but still couldn't understand what the Scots were saying.*

for dear life *adv. phr.* As though afraid of losing your life. ♦ *He was running for dear life toward town.* ♦ *When the horse began to run, she held on for dear life.*

fore See TO THE FORE.

foremost See FIRST AND FOREMOST.

forest See CAN'T SEE THE WOOD FOR THE TREES *or* CAN'T SEE THE FOREST FOR THE TREES.

forever and a day *adv. phr., informal* For a seemingly endless time; forever; always. Used for emphasis. ♦ *We waited forever and a day to find out who won the contest.* ♦ *They promised to remain friends forever and a day.*

forever and ever *adv. phr.* Forever; always.—Used for emphasis, usually about spiritual things. ♦ *God will live forever and ever.*

for example *or* **for instance** *adv. phr.* As an example; as proof; to give an example or illustration. ♦ *Not only rich men become President. For example, Lincoln was born poor.* ♦ *There are jobs more dangerous than truck driving; for instance, training lions.* Compare FOR ONE THING.

for fear Because of fear. ♦ *He left an hour early for fear of missing his train.* ♦ *She worried for fear that the child would be hurt.*

for fear of *adv. phr.* Because of being afraid of something; on account of being scared. ♦ *Dave refuses to go to Europe for fear of an airplane crash and for fear of a shipwreck.*

for free *adj. phr. substandard* Without having to pay; free. ♦ *Hey you guys, look at this balloon! They're for free down at the new store.*

for fun *prep. phr.* As amusement, not seriously, as a joke. ♦ *Let's try to play Beethoven's Emperor Concerto together, you on one piano, and I on another one.* Compare IN FUN.

forget See FORGIVE AND FORGET.

forget oneself *v. phr.* To do something one should have remembered not to do; do something below one's usual conduct although one knows better; let one's self-control slip. ♦ *He forgot himself only once at dinner—when he belched.* ♦ *He knew he should hold his temper, but because of the trouble he forgot himself and began to shout.*

forgive and forget *v.* To have no bad feelings about what happened in the past. ♦ *After the argument the boys decided to forgive and forget.* Syn. LET BYGONES BE BYGONES, LIVE AND LET LIVE.

for good *also* **for good and all** Permanently, forever, for always. ♦ *The lost money was gone for good.* ♦ *He hoped that the repairs would stop the leak for good.* ♦ *When John graduated from school, he decided that he was done with study for good and all.* Syn. FOR KEEPS 2.

for good measure *adv. phr.* As something more added to what is expected or needed; as an extra. ♦ *He sold me the car at a cheap price and included the radio for good measure.* ♦ *She puts in the spices the recipe calls for and* then adds an extra pinch for good measure. Compare IN THE BARGAIN, TO BOOT.

for granted See TAKE FOR GRANTED.

for Heaven's sake! *adv. phr.* Please. ♦ *"Help me, for Heaven's sake!" the injured man cried.*

for hours on end *adv. phr.* For many hours; for a very long time. ♦ *We have been trying to get this computer going for hours on end, but we need serious professional help.*

for instance See FOR EXAMPLE.

for it See RUN FOR IT.

for keeps *adv. phr.* **1.** For the winner to keep. ♦ *They played marbles for keeps.* **2.** *informal* For always; forever. ♦ *He left town for keeps.* Syn. FOR GOOD. **3.** Seriously, not just for fun. ♦ *This is not a joke, it's for keeps.*—Often used in the phrase *play for keeps.* ♦ *The policeman knew that the robber was trying to shoot him. He was playing for keeps.*

forked tongue See SPEAK WITH A FORKED TONGUE.

fork over a lot of money *v. phr.* To pay an excessive amount of money often unwillingly. ♦ *"According to my divorce decree," Alan complained, "I have to fork over a lot of money to my ex-wife every month."*

fork over *or* **fork out** *also* **fork up** *v.* To pay; pay out. ♦ *He had to fork over fifty dollars to have the car repaired.* Compare HAND OVER.

for laughs *adv. phr.* For pleasure; for fun; as a joke. ♦ *The college boys climbed up into the girls' dorms and stole some of their dresses just for laughs, but they were punished all the same.*

for love or money *adv. phr.* For anything; for any price. Used in negative sentences. ♦ *I wouldn't give him my dog for love or money.* Compare FOR ALL THE WORLD 1.

form See RAN TRUE TO FORM.

for no man See TIME AND TIDE WAIT FOR NO MAN.

for one As the first of several possible examples; as one example. ♦ *Many people do not like certain foods. I for one do not like cabbage.*—Also used with similar words instead of *one.* ♦ *Several materials can be used to make* *the box: plywood, for one; masonite, for another; sheet metal, for a third.*

for one's money *prep. phr.* Regarding one's endorsement or support; as far as one is concerned. ♦*For my money, the best candidate for Congress is Ms. Smith.*

for one's part *also* **on one's part** *adv. phr.* As far as you are concerned; the way you feel or think. ♦*I don't know about you, but for my part I don't want to go to that place.* Compare AS FOR.

for one thing *adv. phr.* As one thing of several; as one in a list of things. ♦*The teacher said, "You get a low mark, for one thing, because you did not do your homework."* ♦*The house was poorly built; for one thing, the roof leaked.* Compare FOR EXAMPLE, IN THE FIRST PLACE.

for real[1] *adj. phr., informal* Not practice or play; earnest, real, serious. ♦*The war games were over now. This battle was for real.*

for real[2] *adv. phr., substandard* Not for practice; really; seriously. ♦*Let's do our work for real.*

for one's sake *adv. phr., informal* Used with different possessive nouns to show surprise, crossness, or impatience. ♦*For heaven's sake, where did you come from?* ♦*For Pete's sake, look who's here!* ♦*Well, for pity's sake, I wish you'd told me sooner.* ♦*Oh, for gosh sake, let me do it.*

for shame *interj.* Shame on you; you should be ashamed of yourself.—An exclamation no longer in common use, having been largely replaced by *shame on you.* ♦*"For shame, John, taking the toy from your baby brother!"*

for short *adv. phr.* So as to make shorter; as an abbreviation or nickname. ♦*The boy's name was Humperdink, or "Dink" for short.* ♦*The National Broadcasting Company is called NBC for short.*

for sure *or* **for certain** *adv. phr.* **1.** Without doubt; certainly; surely. ♦*He couldn't tell for sure from a distance whether it was George or Tom.* ♦*He didn't know for certain which bus to take.* ♦*I know for certain that he has a car.* **2.** *slang* Certain. ♦*"That car is smashed so badly it's no good any more." "That's for sure!"* Compare SURE THING.

fort See HOLD THE FORT.

forth See AND SO FORTH, BACK AND FORTH, CALL FORTH, HOLD FORTH, SET FORTH.

for that matter *adv. phr.* With regard to that; about that. ♦*I don't know, and for that matter, I don't care.* ♦*Alice didn't come, and for that matter, she didn't even telephone.* Compare MATTER OF FACT.

for the asking *adv. phr.* By asking; by asking for it; on request. ♦*John said I could borrow his bike any time. It was mine for the asking.* ♦*Teacher said her advice was free for the asking.*

for the best *adj. or adv. phr.* good or best; not bad as thought; lucky; well, happily. ♦*Maybe it's for the best that your team lost; now you know how the other boys felt.* ♦*John's parents thought it would be for the best if he stayed out of school for the rest of the year.* Often used in the phrase *turn out for the best.* ♦*You feel unhappy now because you got sick and couldn't go with your friends, but it will all turn out for the best.* Compare TURN OUT 6. Contrast FOR THE WORSE.

for the better *adj. or adv. phr.* With a better result; for something that is better. ♦*The doctor felt that moving Father to a dry climate would be for the better.* ♦*The new large print in the book is a change for the better.* Compare TAKE A TURN. Contrast FOR THE WORSE.

for the birds *adj. phr., slang* Not interesting; dull; silly; foolish; stupid. ♦*I think history is for the birds.* ♦*I saw that movie. It's for the birds.*

for the books See ONE FOR THE BOOKS.

for the devil *or* **heck** *or* **the hell of it** *adv. phr.* For no specific reason; just for sport and fun. ♦*We poured salt into Uncle Tom's coffee, just for the heck of it.* See DEVIL OF IT.

for the hills See HEAD FOR THE HILLS.

for the life of one *adv., informal* No matter how hard you try.—Used for emphasis with negative statements. ♦*I can't for the life of me remember his name.*

for the moon See ASK FOR THE MOON *or* CRY FOR THE MOON.

for the most part *adv. phr.* In general; mostly; most of the time; commonly;

generally. ♦ *European countries are, for the most part, tired of war.* Syn. BY AND LARGE, ON THE WHOLE.

for the nonce See FOR THE TIME BEING.

for the ride See ALONG FOR THE RIDE.

for the sake of, *or* **for one's sake** *adv. phr.* On behalf of; for the benefit of. ♦ *For the sake of truth and freedom, Dr. Sakharov, the Soviet dissident, was willing to be banished from Moscow.* ♦ *"Do it for my sake, please!" Tom begged.*

for the time being *also literary* **for the nonce** *adv. phr.* For now; for a while; temporarily. ♦ *I haven't any note paper, but this envelope will do for the time being.* ♦ *She hasn't found an apartment yet; she's staying with her aunt for the time being.*

for the world See NOT FOR THE WORLD.

for the worse *adj. phr. or adv. phr.* For something that is worse or not as good, with a worse result. ♦ *He bought a new car but it turned out to be for the worse.* ♦ *The sick man's condition changed for the worse.* Compare TAKE A TURN. Contrast FOR THE BETTER.

for to *prep. phr., dialect* So that you can; to. ♦ *Simple Simon went a-fishing for to catch a whale.* Syn. IN ORDER TO.

forty winks *n. phr., informal* A short period of sleep; a nap. ♦ *When the truck driver felt sleepy, he stopped by the side of the road to catch forty winks.* Compare SHUT-EYE.

forward See BACKWARD AND FORWARD, LOOK FORWARD TO, PUT ONE'S BEST FOOT FORWARD.

forward wall *n.* The line of a football team. ♦ *Princeton's line outplayed the Rutgers forward wall.*

for you See THAT'S ———FOR YOU.

foul ball *n.* A batted baseball that lands outside the foul line. ♦ *Mickey hit a long foul ball that landed on the roof.*

foul line *n.* **1.** Either of two lines separating fair from foul ground in baseball. ♦ *Willie hit the ball just inside the foul line for a double.* **2.** A line across the upper end of a bowling alley across which a bowler must not step. ♦ *John bowled a strike but it didn't count because he stepped over the foul line.* **3.** A line on the floor in front of the basket in basketball, from which foul shots are made. ♦ *Tony scored eight points from the foul line.*

foul out *v.* **1.** To make an out in baseball by hitting a foul fly ball that is caught. ♦ *He fouled out to the catcher.* **2.** To be forced to leave a basketball game because of getting more than the limit number of personal fouls. ♦ *A professional basketball player is allowed six personal fouls before fouling out.*

foul play *n.* Treachery; a criminal act (such as murder). ♦ *After they discovered the dead body, the police suspected foul play.* ♦ *"She must have met with foul play," the chief inspector said when they couldn't find the 12-year-old girl who had disappeared.*

foul shot *n.* A free throw given in basketball to a player who has been fouled. ♦ *Tony was given two foul shots when he was fouled while trying to shoot.* Compare FIELD GOAL 2, FREE THROW.

foul up *v., informal* **1.** To make dirty. ♦ *The birds fouled up his newly washed car.* **2.** To tangle up. ♦ *He tried to throw a lasso but he got the rope all fouled up.* **3.** To ruin or spoil by stupid mistakes; botch. ♦ *He fouled the whole play up by forgetting his part.* **4.** To make a mistake; to blunder. ♦ *Blue suit and brown socks! He had fouled up again.* **5.** To go wrong. ♦ *Why do some people foul up and become criminals?*

foul-up *n.* (stress on *foul*) **1.** *informal* A confused situation; confusion; mistake. ♦ *The luncheon was handled with only one or two foul-ups.* **2.** *informal* A breakdown. ♦ *There was a foul-up in his car's steering mechanism.* **3.** *slang* A person who fouls up or mixes things. ♦ *He had gotten a reputation as a foul-up.*

foundation garment *n.* A close-fitting garment designed for women to wear underneath their clothes to make them look slim; a piece of woman's underwear. ♦ *Jane wears a foundation garment under her evening dress.*

four See HIT ON ALL FOUR, ON ALL FOURS.

four bits *n., slang* Fifty cents. ♦ *Tickets to the play are four bits," said Bill.* Compare TWO BITS.

four corners *n.* All parts of a place. ♦ *People came from the four corners of the world to see him.* ♦ *He has been to the four corners of the country.*

Compare ALL OVER.

four-eyes *n., slang* A person who wears glasses.—A rude expression. ♦*Hey, four-eyes, come over here.*

four-leaf clover *n.* A small green plant with four leaves which many people think means good luck because clover plants usually have three leaves. ♦*John has a four-leaf clover in his pocket. He thinks he will have good luck now .*

fourth class *n.* A class of mail that is not sealed and weighs a pound or more, that includes things that are bought and sold and sent in the mail, and printed things that are not second or third class mail. ♦*Bill sent away 98 cereal box tops and a dollar and got back a sheriff's badge and gun in the mail by fourth class.*

fourth-class[1] *adj.* Belonging to the fourth class of mail. ♦*The package weighed a pound and a half, so it had to be sent by fourth-class mail.*

fourth-class[2] *adv.* By fourth-class mail. ♦*How did the company mail the package? Fourth-class.*

fourth world *n., informal* The poor nations of the world, as distinguished from the oil-rich nations of the third world. ♦*Sri Lanka will never join OPEC, since it is a fourth world nation.*

fowl See NEITHER FISH NOR FOWL.

fox and geese *n. phr.* A tag game in which the player representing the fox tries to catch one of the players representing geese as they run around the outside of a circle.

fraidy-cat *or* **fraid-cat** *or* **scaredy-cat** *or* **scared cat** *n., informal* A shy person; someone who is easily frightened.— Usually used by or to children. ♦*Tom was a fraidy-cat and wouldn't go in the water.*

frame of mind *n. phr.* One's mental outlook; the state of one's psychological condition. ♦*There is no use trying to talk to him while he is in such a negative frame of mind.*

freak *n., slang* **1.** A good, or well-liked person, the opposite of a square, someone with long hair and who is likely (or known) to be a marijuana smoker or a drug user. Also said of homosexuals. ♦*Is Joe a square, establishment type?—Oh no, he's a regular*

freak. **2.** ——**freak** An enthusiast, a person who does or cultivates something in excess. ♦*Ellen is a film-freak.*

freak-out[1] *n., slang* An act of losing control; a situation that is bizarre or unusual. ♦*The party last night was a regular freak-out.*

freak out[2] *v. phr., slang* To lose control over one's conscious self due to the influence of hallucinogenic drugs. ♦*Joe freaked out last night.*

free See FOR FREE, MAKE FREE, MAKE FREE WITH, OF ONE'S OWN ACCORD *or* OF ONE'S OWN FREE WILL.

free agent *n.* A professional player who does not have a contract with a team. ♦*The Giants signed two free agents who had been released by the Cardinals.*

free and easy *adj.* Not strict; relaxed or careless. ♦*The teacher was free and easy with his students.* ♦*He had a free and easy way of acting that attracted many friends.* ♦*They were free and easy with their money and it was soon gone.*

free ball *n.* A ball in football that is in play, that is not in the possession of anyone, that is not a legally thrown forward pass, and that belongs to the first team which can grab it. ♦*A Notre Dame player fell on a free ball and recovered it for his team.*

free enterprise *n. phr.* A system in which private business is controlled by as few government rules as possible. ♦*The United States is proud of its free enterprise.*

free hand *n.* Great freedom. ♦*The teacher had a free hand in her classroom.* ♦*Bob put paint on the fence with a free hand.* Compare FREE REIN.

freeload *v.* To have oneself supported in terms of food and housing at someone else's expense. ♦*When are you guys going to stop freeloading and do some work?*

free rein *n.* Freedom to do what you want. ♦*The king had free rein in his country.* ♦*Father is strict with the children, but Mother gives them free rein.* Compare FREE HAND.

free throw *n.* A shot at the basket in basketball without interference from opponents. ♦*Mike scored the winning point on a free throw.* Compare FIELD

GOAL 2, FOUL SHOT.

free-for-all *n.* **1.** Unlimited, free access to something everybody wants. ♦ *The Smith's party was a lavish free-for-all; everybody could eat and drink as much as they wanted.* **2.** A barroom, tavern, or street fight in which everybody participates. ♦ *The celebration after the soccer game victory turned into an uncontrollable free-for-all.*

freeze See BLOOD RUNS COLD *or* BLOOD FREEZES.

freeze one's blood See BLOOD RUNS COLD.

freeze out *v., informal* To force out or keep from a share or part in something by unfriendly or dishonest treatment. ♦ *The other boys froze John out of the club.*

freeze over *v.* To become covered with ice. ♦ *The children wanted the lake to freeze over so they could ice-skate.*

French fried potato *or* **French fry** *n.* A narrow strip of potato fried in deep fat.—Usually used in the plural. ♦ *Sue ordered a hamburger and french fries.*

French leave *n.* The act of slipping away from a place secretly and without saying good-bye to anyone. ♦ *"It's getting late," Rob whispered to Janet. "Let's take French leave and get out of here."*

fresh from *adj.* Recently returned from; experienced in. ♦ *Tom was fresh from two years in Paris and was very condescending in matters pertaining to cuisine and wines.*

friction tape *n.* Black cloth tape with one sticky side used around electric wires. ♦ *The boy fixed his cracked baseball bat with some friction tape.*

Friday See GIRL FRIDAY.

friend See BOY FRIEND, FAIR-WEATHER FRIEND, GIRL FRIEND, LADY FRIEND, MAKE FRIENDS.

friends with Friendly to; a friend of. ♦ *Alice found several girls to be friends with on the first day of school.* ♦ *At first I didn't like John, but now I am friends with him.*

frightened out of one's wits See OUT OF ONE'S WITS.

frightened to death See TO DEATH.

fritter away See FOOL AWAY.

fro See TO AND FRO.

frog See BIG FROG IN A SMALL POND, LITTLE FROG IN A BIG POND.

from bad to worse See GO FROM BAD TO WORSE.

from grace See FALL FROM GRACE.

from hand to hand *adv. phr.* From one person to another and another. ♦ *The box of candy was passed from hand to hand.* ♦ *Jane brought her engagement ring, and it passed from hand to hand until all the girls had admired it.*

from hand to mouth See LIVE FROM HAND TO MOUTH.

from little acorns See GREAT OAKS FROM LITTLE ACORNS GROW.

from Missouri *adj. phr., slang* Doubtful; suspicious. ♦ *Don't try to fool me. I'm from Missouri.*

from mouth to mouth *adv. phr.* See BY WORD OF MOUTH.

from pillar to post *adv. phr.* From one place to another many times. ♦ *Sarah's father changed jobs several times a year, and the family was moved from pillar to post.*

from rags to riches *adv. phr.* Suddenly making a fortune; becoming rich overnight. ♦ *The Smiths went from rags to riches when they unexpectedly won the lottery.*

from scratch *adv. phr., informal* With no help from anything done before; from the beginning; from nothing. ♦ *Dick built a radio from scratch.* ♦ *In sewing class, Mary already knew how to sew a little, but Jane had to start from scratch.* Compare FROM THE GROUND UP.

from the bottom of one's heart *or* **with all one's heart** *adv. phr.* With great feeling; sincerely. ♦ *A mother loves a baby from the bottom of her heart.* ♦ *John thanked his rescuer from the bottom of his heart.* ♦ *The people welcomed the returning soldiers from the bottom of their hearts.*

from the door See KEEP THE WOLF FROM THE DOOR.

from the ground up *adv. phr.* From the beginning; entirely; completely. ♦ *After the fire they had to rebuild their cabin from the ground up.* ♦ *Sam knows about baseball from the ground up.* ♦ *The new cars have been changed from the ground up.*

from the heart *adv.* Sincerely; honestly. ♦ *John always speaks from the heart.*

from the word "go" *adv. phr.* From start to finish; completely. ♦ *He may look French but he is a New Yorker from the word "go."*

from time to time *adv. phr.* Not often; not regularly; sometimes; occasionally; at one time and then again at another time. ♦ *Even though the Smiths have moved, we still see them from time to time.* ♦ *Mother tries new recipes from time to time, but the children never like them.* Syn. NOW AND THEN, AT TIMES, ONCE IN A WHILE. Compare BY FITS AND STARTS, OFF AND ON.

from —— to —— **1.** Used with a repeated word to show that something keeps on. Without ending. ♦ *The world grows wiser from age to age.* ♦ *He goes from day to day without changing his necktie.*—Also used in a short form like an adjective. ♦ *The superintendent spends more time on plans for the future, and the principal handles the day-to-day problems of the school.* **2.** Used with a repeated word to show that something happens again and again. ♦ *She sells face cream from door to door.* ♦ *The artist goes from place to place painting pictures.*—Also used in a short form like an adjective. ♦ *Mr. Roberts began as a door-to-door salesman, and now is president of the company.* **3.** Used with words showing opposite or extreme limits, often to emphasize that something is very large or complete. ♦ *The eagle's wings measured six feet from tip to tip.* ♦ *Sarah read the book from cover to cover.* ♦ *Mrs. Miller's dinner included everything from soup to nuts.* ♦ *That book is a bestseller from Maine to California.* ♦ *The captain looked the boy over from head to foot.* ♦ *The dog sniffed the yard from end to end in search of a bone.* ♦ *This new car has been redesigned from top to bottom.* ♦ *That bookstore has books on everything from archery to zoology.* ♦ *The television show was broadcast from coast to coast.* ♦ *He knows mathematics from A to Z.*—Sometimes used in a short form like an adjective. ♦ *The airplane made a non-stop coast-to-coast flight.*

from under See OUT FROM UNDER, PULL THE RUG OUT FROM UNDER.

from way back *adv. phr.* From a pre-vious time; from a long time ago. ♦ *They have known one another from way back when they went to the same elementary school.*

front See IN FRONT OF.

front and center *adv., slang* Used as a command to a person to go to someone who wants him. ♦ *Front and center, Smith. The boss wants to see you.*

front court *n.* The half of a basketball court that is a basketball team's offensive zone. ♦ *The guard brought the ball up to the front court.*

front office *n., informal* The group of persons who manage a business; the officers. ♦ *The front office decides how much the workers are paid.*

frown upon *v. phr.* To look with disfavor upon somebody or something. ♦ *Everybody in her family frowns upon her attachment to him.*

fruitcake See NUTTY AS A FRUITCAKE.

fry See OTHER FISH TO FRY, OUT OF THE FRYING PAN INTO THE FIRE, SMALL FRY.

fuck around *v. phr., vulgar, avoidable* **1.** To be promiscuous. ♦ *John fucks around with the secretaries.* **2.** To play at something without purpose, to mess around. ♦ *He doesn't accomplish anything, because he fucks around so much.*

fuck off *v. phr., vulgar, avoidable* **1.** Go away! ♦ *Can't you see you're bothering me? Fuck off!* **2.** To be lazy. ♦ *John said "I don't feel like working, so I'll fuck off today."* Compare BEAT IT, GOOF OFF.

fuck up *v. phr., vulgar, avoidable* To make a mess of something or oneself. ♦ *Because he was totally unprepared, he fucked up his exam.* ♦ *He is so fucked up he doesn't know whether he is coming or going.*

fuck-up *n. vulgar, avoidable* A mess; a badly botched situation. ♦ *What a fuck-up the dissolution of the USSR created!*

fuddy-duddy *n.* A person whose ideas and habits are old-fashioned. ♦ *His students think Professor Jones is an old fuddy-duddy.*

fuel See ADD FUEL TO THE FLAME.

full See HAVE ONE'S HANDS FULL, IN FULL SWING, TO THE FULL.

full blast *adv.* At full capacity. ♦ *With all the research money at their disposal,* *the new computer firm was going ahead full blast.*

full-bodied *adj.* Mature; of maximum quality. ♦ *The wines from that region in California have a rich, full-bodied flavor.*

full-fledged *adj.* Having everything that is needed to be something; complete. ♦ *A girl needs three years of training to be a full-fledged nurse.* ♦ *The book was a full-fledged study of American history.*

full of beans *adj. phr., slang* **1.** Full of pep; feeling good; in high spirits. ♦ *The football team was full of beans after winning the tournament.* ♦ *The children were full of beans as they got ready for a picnic.* **2.** *also* **full of prunes.** Being foolish and talking nonsense. ♦ *You are full of prunes; that man's not 120 years old.*

full of it See FULL OF THE OLD NICK.

full of oneself *adj. phr., informal* Interested only in yourself. ♦ *Joe would be a nice boy if he would stop being so full of himself.* Compare BIG HEAD.

full of prunes See FULL OF BEANS 2.

full of the moon *n. phr., literary* The moon when it is seen as a full circle; the time of a full moon. ♦ *The robbers waited for a dark night when the full of the moon was past.* Contrast DARK OF THE MOON.

full of the Old Nick *or* **full of the devil** *or* **full of it** *adj. phr., informal* Always making trouble; naughty; bad. ♦ *That boy is full of the Old Nick.*

full tilt *adv.* At full speed; at high speed. ♦ *He ran full tilt into the door and broke his arm.*

fun See MAKE FUN OF.

fun and games *n., slang, informal* **1.** A party or other entertaining event. **2.** Something trivially easy. **3.** Petting, or sexual intercourse. **4.** (Ironically) An extraordinary difficult task. ♦ *How was your math exam? (With a dismayed expression):—Yeah, it was all fun and games, man.*

fun house *n.* A place where people see many funny things and have tricks played on them to make them laugh or have a good time. ♦ *The boys and girls had a good time looking at themselves in mirrors in the fun house.*

funny bone *n.* **1.** The place at the back of the elbow that hurts like electricity when accidentally hit. ♦ *He hit his funny bone on the arm of the chair.* **2.** *or informal* **crazy bone** Sense of humor; understanding jokes. ♦ *Her way of telling the story tickled his funny bone.*

fur See MAKE THE FUR FLY.

furious See FAST AND FURIOUS.

fuse See BLOW A FUSE.

fuss See KICK UP A FUSS.

fuss and feathers *n., informal* Unnecessary bother and excitement. ♦ *She is full of fuss and feathers this morning.*

gab See GIFT OF GAB *or* GIFT OF THE GAB.

gaff See STAND THE GAFF.

gain ground *v. phr.* **1.** To go forward; move ahead. ◆ *The soldiers fought hard and began to gain ground.* **2.** To become stronger; make progress; improve. ◆ *The sick man gained ground after being near death.* ◆ *Under Lincoln, the Republican Party gained ground.* Contrast LOSE GROUND.

gallery See PLAY TO THE GALLERY.

gallon See TEN-GALLON HAT.

gallows' humor *n. phr.* Bitter joke(s) that make fun of a very serious matter, e.g. death, imprisonment, etc. ◆ *When the criminal was led to the electric chair on Monday morning, he said, "Nice way to start the week, eh?"*

game See AHEAD OF THE GAME, LOVE GAME, NAME OF THE GAME, PLAY THE GAME, AT ——— STAGE OF THE GAME.

game at which two can play *n. phr.* A plan, trick, or way of acting that both sides may use. ◆ *Rough football is a game two can play.* ◆ *Politics is a game at which two can play.*

game is not worth the candle *literary* What is being done is not worth the trouble or cost; the gain is not worth the effort. ◆ *I don't want to walk so far on such a hot day. The game is not worth the candle.*

game is up *or slang* **jig is up** The secret or plan won't work; we are caught or discovered. ◆ *The game is up; the teacher knows who took her keys.* ◆ *The jig's up; the principal knows the boys have been smoking in the basement.* Compare FAT IS IN THE FIRE.

gang See ROAD GANG, SECTION GANG.

gang up on *or* **gang up against** *v. phr., informal* To jointly attack someone, either physically or verbally; take sides in a group against an individual. ◆ *The class bully was stronger than all the other boys, so they had to gang up on him to put him in his place.* Compare LINE UP, 4b.

garbage down *v. phr., slang* To eat eagerly and at great speed without much regard for manners or social convention. ◆ *The children garbaged down their food.*

garden apartment *n.* An apartment with a garden near it. ◆ *The couple live in a garden apartment.*

garment See FOUNDATION GARMENT.

gas See STEP ON IT *or* STEP ON THE GAS.

gasket See BLOW A FUSE *or* BLOW A GASKET.

gas up *v., informal* **1.** To fill the gasoline tank of. ◆ *The mechanics gassed up the planes for their long trip.* **2.** To fill the tank with gasoline. ◆ *The big truck stopped at the filling station and gassed up.*

gate See GET THE BOUNCE *or* GET THE GATE, GIVE THE BOUNCE *or* GIVE THE GATE.

gate crasher See CRASH THE GATE.

gather See ROLLING STONE GATHERS NO MOSS.

gather in *v. informal* To catch. ◆ *The end gathered in the pass and went over for a touchdown.*

gauntlet See RUN THE GAUNTLET, THROW DOWN THE GAUNTLET.

gay nineties *n.* The years between 1890 and 1900; remembered as a happy exciting time. ◆ *Ladies wore large hats in the gay nineties.* ◆ *Picnics were popular in the gay nineties.*

gaze See CRYSTAL GAZING.

gear See HIGH GEAR, SLIP A COG *or* SLIP A GEAR, THROW OUT OF GEAR.

geese See FOX AND GEESE.

gee whiz *interj., informal* Used as an exclamation to show surprise or other strong feeling. Rare in written English. ◆ *Gee whiz! I am late again.*

general See IN GENERAL.

generation gap *n., informal, hackneyed phrase* The difference in social values, philosophies, and manners between children and their parents, teachers and relatives which causes a lack of understanding between them and frequently leads to violent confrontations. ◆ *My daughter is twenty and I am forty, but we have no generation gap in our family.*

generous to a fault *adj. phr.* Excessively generous. ◆ *Generous to a fault, my Aunt Elizabeth gave away all her rare books to her old college.*

George See LET GEORGE DO IT.

get See GIVE AS GOOD AS ONE GETS, EARLY BIRD CATCHES THE WORM *or* EARLY BIRD GETS THE WORM, GO-GETTER, TELL ONE WHERE TO GET OFF.

get about See GET AROUND *at* 1b.

get a black eye *v. phr.* **1.** To receive a dark ring around the eye after being hit by someone's fist or an object. ♦ *In the fistfight Tom got a black eye from Pete.* ♦ *Sue got a black eye when she ran into a tree.* **2.** To have one's character denigrated. ♦ *Our firm received a black eye because of all the consumer complaints that were lodged against our product.*

get a break *v. phr.* To receive a stroke of luck. ♦ *Bill got a break when he won the lottery.*

get across *v.* **1.** To explain clearly, make (something) clear; to make clear the meaning of. ♦ *Mr. Brown is a good coach because he can get across the plays.* Syn. PUT ACROSS. **2.** To become clear. ♦ *The teacher tried to explain the problem, but the explanation did not get across to the class.*

get after *v., informal* **1.** To try or try again to make someone do what he is supposed to do. ♦ *Ann's mother gets after her to hang up her clothes.* **2.** To scold or make an attack on. ♦ *Bob's mother got after him for tracking mud into the house.* ♦ *The police are getting after the crooks in the city.*

get ahead *v.* **1.** *informal* To become successful. ♦ *Mr. Brown was a good lawyer and soon began to get ahead.* ♦ *The person with a good education finds it easier to get ahead.* **2.** To be able to save money; get out of debt. ♦ *In a few more years he will be able to get ahead.* ♦ *After Father pays all the doctor bills, maybe we can get a little money ahead and buy a car.*

get a load of *v. phr., slang* **1.** To take a good look at; see (something unusual or interesting.)—Often used to show surprise or admiration. ♦ *Get a load of that pretty girl!* ♦ *Get a load of Dick's new car!* Compare LOOK OVER. **2.** To listen to carefully or with interest, especially exciting news.—Often used as a command: **1.** *Get a load of this: Alice got married yesterday!*

get along *also* **get on** *v.* **1.** To go or move away; move on. ♦ *The policeman told the boys on the street corner to get along.* **2.** To go forward; make progress; advance. ♦ *John is getting along well in school. He is learning more every day.* Syn. GET AHEAD. **3.** To advance; become old or late. ♦ *It is getting along towards sundown.* ♦ *Grandmother is 68 and getting along.* **4.** To get or make what you need; manage. ♦ *It isn't easy to get along in the jungle.* ♦ *We can get along on $100 a week.* Compare DO WITHOUT 2, GET BY, MAKE DO. **5.** To live or work together in a friendly way; agree, cooperate; not fight or argue. ♦ *We don't get along with the Jones family.* ♦ *Jim and Jane get along fine together.* ♦ *Don't be hard to get along with.*

get a fix *or* **give a fix** *v. phr., slang, drug culture* To provide (someone) with an injection of narcotics. ♦ *The neighborhood pusher gave Joe a fix.* Contrast GET A FIX ON.

get a fix on *v. phr., informal* Receive a reading of a distant object by electronic means, as by radar or sonar. ♦ *Can you get a fix on the submarine?* Contrast GET A FIX.

get a grip on *v. phr.* To take firm control of something. ♦ *If Tim wants to keep his job, he had better get a grip on himself and start working harder.* Contrast LOSE ONE'S GRIP.

get a head start on *v. phr.* To receive preliminary help or instruction in a particular subject so that the recipient is in a favorable position compared to his or her peers. ♦ *At our school, children get a head start on their reading ability thanks to a special program.*

get a kick out of *v. phr.* To be greatly thrilled; derive pleasure from. ♦ *Tom and Marty get a kick out of playing four hands on the piano.*

get a line on *v. phr.* To receive special, sometimes even confidential information about something. ♦ *Before Bill accepted his new position, he got a line on how the business was being run.*

get a move on *informal or slang* **get a wiggle on** *v. phr.* To hurry up; get going.—Often used as a command. ♦ *Get a move on, or you will be late.*

get a raise *v. phr.* To receive an increment in salary. ♦ *Because of his good work, Ted got a raise after May 1.*

get a rise out of *v. phr., slang* **1.** To have some fun with (a person) by making (him) angry; tease. ♦ *The boys get a rise out of Joe by teasing him about his girl friend.* **2.** *vulgar, avoidable* To be sexually aroused (said of males) ♦ *Jim always gets a rise out of watching adult movies.*

get (all) dolled up See DOLL UP.

get along *or* **on in years** *v. phr.* To age; grow old. ♦ *My father is getting along in years; he will be ninety on his next birthday.*

get an earful *v. phr., informal* To hear more (of usually unwelcome news) than one expects or wishes to hear. ♦ *I asked how Tim and his wife were getting along, and I certainly got an earful.* Contrast SAY A MOUTHFUL.

get around *v.* **1a.** To go to different places; move about. ♦ *Mary's father really gets around; Monday he was in Washington; Wednesday he was in Chicago; and today he is in New York.* ♦ *Fred broke his leg, but he is able to get about on crutches.* **1b.** *or* **get about** To become widely known especially by being talked about. ♦ *Bad news gets around quickly.* **2a.** *informal* To get by a trick or flattery what you want from (someone). ♦ *Mary knows how to get around her father.* **2b.** *informal* To find a way of not obeying or doing; escape from. ♦ *Some people try to get around the tax laws.* ♦ *John did not weigh enough to join the Navy, but he got around that; he drank a lot of water before his physical examination.*

get around to *v.* To do (something) after putting it off; find time for. ♦ *Mr. Lee hopes to get around to washing his car next Saturday.*

get at *v.* **1.** To reach an understanding of; find out the meaning. ♦ *This book is very hard to get at.* **2.** To do harm to. ♦ *The cat is on the chair trying to get at the canary.* Compare GET BACK AT. **3.** To have a chance to do; attend to. ♦ *I hope I have time to get at my homework tonight.* Compare GET TO 2. **4.** To mean; aim at; hint at. ♦ *What was Betty getting at when she said she knew our secret?* ♦ *What the teacher was getting at in this lesson was that it is important to speak correctly.* Syn. DRIVE AT. Compare GET ACROSS.

getaway car *n. phr.* A vehicle parked near the scene of a crime in which the criminals escape. ♦ *The police intercepted the getaway car at a major crossroads.*

get away *v.* **1.** To get loose or get free; become free from being held or controlled; succeed in leaving; escape. ♦ *As Jim was trying the bat, it got away from him and hit Tom.* ♦ *Someone left the door open, and the puppy got away.* ♦ *Mary tried to catch a butterfly, but it got away from her.* ♦ *The bank robbers used a stolen car to get away.* ♦ *If Mr. Graham can get away from his store this afternoon, he will take Johnny fishing.* **2.** To begin; start. ♦ *We got away early in the morning on the first day of our vacation.* ♦ *The race got away to a fast start.* Compare GET OFF 3, START IN, START OUT.

get away with *v., informal* To do (something bad or wrong) without being caught or punished. ♦ *Some students get away without doing their homework.* See GET BY 3.

get away with murder *v. phr., informal* To do something very bad without being caught or punished. ♦ *John is scolded if he is late with his homework, but Robert gets away with murder.* ♦ *Mrs. Smith lets her children get away with murder.*

get a wiggle on See GET A MOVE ON.

get a word in *or* **get a word in edgewise** *also* **get a word in edgeways** *v. phr.* To find a chance to say something when others are talking. ♦ *The little boy listened to the older students and finally got in a word.* ♦ *Mary talked so much that Jack couldn't get a word in edgewise.*

get back at *v., informal* To do something bad to (someone who has done something bad to you) hurt in return. ♦ *John played a joke on Henry, and next day Henry got back at him.* ♦ *The elephant waited many years to get back at the man who fed him red pepper.* Syn. PAY BACK, SETTLE A SCORE, TIT FOR TAT. Compare GET AT 2, GET EVEN.

get back on one's feet *v. phr.* To once again become financially solvent; regain one's former status and income, or health. ♦ *Max got back on his feet soon after his open heart surgery. Tom's*

*business was ruined due to the infla-
tion, but he got back on his feet again.*
get behind *v.* **1.** To go too slowly; be
late; do something too slowly. ◆ *The
post office got behind in delivering
Christmas mail.* Syn. FALL BEHIND.
Contrast KEEP UP. **2.** *informal* To support; help. ◆ *A club is much better if
members get behind their leaders.* ◆ *We
got behind Mary to be class president.*
Compare BACK OF 3. **3.** *informal* To
explain; find out the reason for. ◆ *The
police are questioning many people to
try and get behind the bank robbery.*
Syn. GET TO THE BOTTOM OF.
get busy *v. phr.* To accelerate the pace
in one's activities. ◆ *We've got to get
busy if we want to make the deadline.*
get by *v., informal* **1.** To be able to go
past; pass. ◆ *The cars moved to the curb
so that the fire engine could get by.* **2.**
To satisfy the need or demand. ◆ *Mary
can get by with her old coat this winter.*
◆ *The janitor does just enough work to
get by.* Syn. GET ALONG 4. **3.** Not to be
caught and scolded or punished. ◆ *The
soldier thought he could get by with his
dirty rifle.* ◆ *The boy got by without
answering the teacher's question
because a visitor came in.* Compare
GET AWAY WITH.
get carried away with See CARRY AWAY.
get couthed up *v. phr., slang* To get oneself dressed up neatly and look elegant
and presentable. ◆ *What are you getting all couthed up for?* (This derives
from *uncouth* 'outlandish, ill-man-
nered' by leaving off the prefix *un-*.)
get cracking *v. phr., slang, informal* To
hurry up, to start moving fast. (Used
mostly as an imperative). ◆ *Come on,
you guys, let's get cracking!* (Let's
hurry up!) Compare GET GOING 2.
get credit for *v. phr.* To be given points
of merit, recognition, or praise for
labor or intellectual contribution.
◆ *Our firm got a lot of credit for developing parts of the space shuttle.*
Contrast GIVE CREDIT FOR.
get one down *v. phr., informal* **1.** To
make (someone) unhappy; cause low
spirits; cause discouragement. ◆ *Low
grades are getting Helen down.* ◆ *Three
straight losses got the team down.* **2.** To
swallow; digest. ◆ *The medicine was so
bitter I couldn't get it down.* **3.** To

depress a person's spirit. ◆ *Working at
such an awful job got Mike down.*
get down cold *v. phr.* To memorize perfectly. ◆ *Terry got the text of his speech
down cold.*
get down off your high horse See OFF
ONE'S HIGH HORSE.
get down to *v., informal* To get started
on, being on. ◆ *Joe wasted a lot of time
before he got down to work.* ◆ *Let's get
down to work.* Compare GET AT 3, GET
GOING, GET TO.
get down to brass tacks *also* **get down to
cases** *v. phr., informal* To begin the
most important work or business; get
started on the most important things to
talk about or know. ◆ *The men talked
about little things and then got down to
brass tacks.* ◆ *A busy doctor wants his
patients to get down to brass tacks.*
get down to business *or* **work** *v. phr.* To
start being serious; begin to face a
problem to be solved, or a task to be
accomplished. ◆ *Gentlemen, I'm afraid
the party is over and we must get down
to business.*
get down to work See GET DOWN TO
BUSINESS.
get even *v., informal* **1.** To owe nothing.
◆ *Mr. Johnson has a lot of debts, but in
a few years he will get even.* **2.** To do
something bad to pay someone back
for something bad; get revenge; hurt
back. *Jack is waiting to get even with
Bill for tearing up his notebook.* ◆ *Last
April First Mr. Harris got fooled by
Joe, and this year he will get even.*
Compare GET BACK AT.
get going *v., informal* **1.** To excite; stir
up and make angry. ◆ *The boys' teasing
gets John going.* ◆ *Talking about her
freckles gets Mary going.* **2.** *or chiefly
British* **get cracking** To begin to move;
get started. ◆ *The teacher told Walter to
get going on his history lesson.* ◆ *The
foreman told the workmen to get
cracking.* ◆ *Let's get going. It's almost
supper time.* Compare GET DOWN TO,
STEP LIVELY.
get gray hair *or* **get gray** *v. phr., informal*
To become old or gray from worrying;
become very anxious or worried.
Often used with *over.* ◆ *"If John
doesn't join the team, I won't get gray
hair over it," the coach said.* ◆ *Naughty
children are why mothers get gray.*

Compare GIVE GRAY HAIR.

get his *or* **hers** *v. phr.* To receive one's proper reward or punishment. ♦ *Tim will get his when his wife finds out that he's been seeing other women.*

get hitched *v. phr.* To get married. ♦ *After a long period of dating, Fred and Mary finally got hitched.*

get hold of *v.* **1.** To get possession of. ♦ *Little children sometimes get hold of sharp knives and cut themselves.* **2.** To find a person so you can speak with him. ♦ *Mr. Thompson spent several hours trying to get hold of his lawyer.*

get in *v. phr.* **1.** To be admitted. ♦ *Andy wants to go to medical school but his grades aren't good enough for him to get in.* **2.** To arrive. ♦ *What time does the plane from New York get in?* **3.** To enter. ♦ *"Get in the car, and let's go," Tom said in a hurry.* **4.** To put in stock; receive. ♦ *The store just got in a new shipment of shoes from China.*

get in on *v. phr.* To be permitted to participate; become privy to; be included. ♦ *This is your chance to get in on a wonderful deal with the new company if you're willing to make an investment.*

get in on the ground floor *v. phr.* To be one of the first members or employees to participate in the growth of a firm, educational institution, etc. ♦ *Elliott got in on the ground floor and made a fortune at the company.* ♦ *Mr. Smith who joined the new college as an instructor, got in on the ground floor, and wound up as its president after twenty years.*

get in on the *or* **one's act** *v. phr.* To do something because others are engaged in the same act; join others. ♦ *John's business is succeeding so well that both of his brothers want to get in on the act.*

get in one's hair See IN ONE'S HAIR.

get in one's way See IN ONE'S WAY.

get into See BE INTO SOMETHING.

get into line *v. phr.* To cooperate; conform. ♦ *The maverick members of the party were advised to get into line unless they wanted to be expelled.* Contrast OUT OF LINE.

get in touch with See IN TOUCH.

get involved with See BE INVOLVED WITH.

get in with *v. phr.* To join up with; begin to associate with; be accepted by. ♦ *He got in with the wrong gang of boys and wound up in jail.* ♦ *She got in with her father's firm and made a successful career of it.*

get in wrong *v. phr.* To incur the anger or dislike of someone; come into disfavor. ♦ *Although he means well, Fred is always getting in wrong with someone at the office.*

get it *v.* **1.** See CATCH IT. **2.** To understand; comprehend; grasp. ♦ *"I can't get it," John said. "Why do you spend so much on clothes."*

get it all together *v. phr.* **1.** To be in full possession and control of one's mental faculties; have a clear purpose well pursued. ♦ *You've sure got it all together, haven't you?* **2.** Retaining one's self-composure under pressure. ♦ *A few minutes after the burglars left he got it all together and called the police.* **3.** To be well built, stacked (said of girls and women.) ♦ *Sue's sure got it all together, hasn't she?*

get it in the neck See CATCH IT IN THE NECK.

get (it *or* **something) in** *or* **into one's head** *v. phr.* To become possessed of an idea; develop a fixed idea. ♦ *Jack got it into his head to become a marine and nothing we could say would make him change his mind.*

get lost *v. phr., slang* Go away!—Used as a command. ♦ *Get lost! I want to study.* ♦ *John told Bert to get lost.* Compare DROP DEAD.

get mixed up See MIXED UP.

get next to See BE CLOSE TO.

get off *v.* **1.** To come down from or out of. ♦ *The ladder fell, and Tom couldn't get off the roof.* ♦ *The bus stopped, the door opened, and Father got off.* **2.** To take off. ♦ *Joe's mother told him to get his wet clothes off.* **3.** To get away; leave. ♦ *Mr. Johnson goes fishing whenever he can get off from work.* ♦ *William got off early in the morning.* **4.** To go free. ♦ *Mr. Andrews got off with a $5 fine when he was caught passing a stop sign.* **5.** To make (something) go. ♦ *The halfback got off a long pass.* ♦ *John got a letter off to his grandmother.* **6.** To tell. ♦ *The governor got off several jokes at the beginning of his speech.*

get off cheap *v. phr.* **1.** To receive a lesser punishment than one deserves. ♦ *Ted could have been sentenced to fif-*

teen years in prison; he got off cheap by receiving a reduced sentence of five years. **2.** To pay less than the normal price. ♦*If you had your car repaired for only $75, you got off cheap.* Contrast GET AWAY WITH.

get off easy *v. phr., informal* To have only a little trouble; escape something worse. ♦*The children who missed school to go to the fair got off easy.* ♦*John got off easy because it was the first time he had taken his father's car without permission.*

get off it See COME OFF IT.

get off one's back *v. phr., slang, colloquial* To stop criticizing or nagging someone. ♦*"Get off my back! Can't you see how busy I am?"*

get off one's case *or* **back** *or* **tail** *v. phr.* To stop bothering and constantly checking up on someone; quit hounding one. ♦*"Get off my case!" he cried angrily. "You're worse than the cops."* Contrast ON ONE'S CASE.

get off one's chest See OFF ONE'S CHEST.

get off one's tail *v. phr., slang* To get busy, to start working. ♦*OK you guys! Get off your tails and get cracking!*

get off on the wrong foot *v. phr.* To make a bad start; begin with a mistake. ♦*Peggy got off on the wrong foot with her new teacher; she chewed gum in class and the teacher didn't like it.*

get off the ground *v. phr., informal* To make a successful beginning; get a good start; go ahead; make progress. ♦*Our plans for a party didn't get off the ground because no one could come.*

get off the hook See OFF THE HOOK.

get off to a flying *or* **running start** *v. phr.* To have a promising or successful beginning. ♦*Ron got off to a flying start in business school when he got nothing but A's.*

get on *or* **get onto** *v., informal* **1.** To speak to (someone) roughly about something he did wrong; blame; scold. ♦*Mrs. Thompson got on the girls for not keeping their rooms clean.* ♦*The fans got on the new shortstop after he made several errors.* Syn. JUMP ON. **2.** See GET ALONG. **3.** To grow older. ♦*Work seems harder these days; I'm getting on, you know.*

get one's See GET WHAT'S COMING TO ONE.

get one's back up *v. phr., informal* To become or make angry or stubborn. ♦*Fred got his back up when I said he was wrong.* ♦*Our criticisms of his actions just got his back up.*

get one's brains fried *v. phr., slang also used colloquially* **1.** To sit in the sun and sunbathe for an excessive length of time. ♦*Newcomers to Hawaii should be warned not to sit in the sun too long—they'll get their brains fried.* **2.** To get high on drugs. ♦*He can't make a coherent sentence anymore—he's got his brains fried.*

get one's dander up *or* **get one's Irish up** *v. phr.* To become or make angry. ♦*The boy got his dander up because he couldn't go to the store.* ♦*The children get the teacher's dander up when they make a lot of noise.* Compare BLOW A FUSE.

get one's ducks in a row *v. phr., informal* To get everything ready. ♦*The scoutmaster told the boys to get their ducks in a row before they went to camp.* ♦*Mr. Brown got his ducks in a row for his trip.* Compare LINE UP.

get one's feet on the ground See FEET ON THE GROUND.

get one's feet wet *v. phr., informal* To begin; do something for the first time. ♦*The party was at Bill's house and when Ruth and I got there the party had already started. "Jump right in and don't be afraid to get your feet wet," said Bill.* ♦*"It's not hard to dance once you get your feet wet," said the teacher.*

get one's fingers burned See BURN ONE'S FINGERS.

get one's foot in the door See FOOT IN THE DOOR.

get one's goat *v. phr., informal* To make a person disgusted or angry. ♦*The boy's laziness all summer got his father's goat.* ♦*The slow service at the cafe got Mr. Robinson's goat.*

get one's hands on See LAY ONE'S HANDS ON.

get one's number *or* **have one's number** *v. phr., informal* To find out or know what kind of person somebody is. ♦*The boys soon had the new student's number.* ♦*The girls got their new roommate's number the first week of school.*

get one's rear in gear *v. phr., slang* To hurry up, to get going. ♦*I'm gonna have to get my rear in gear.*

get one's second wind See SECOND WIND.

get one's teeth into or **sink one's teeth into** *v. phr., informal* To have something real or solid to think about; go to work on seriously; struggle with. ◆*After dinner, John got his teeth into the algebra lesson.* ◆*Frank chose a subject for his report that he could sink his teeth into.*

get one's tongue See CAT GET ONE'S TONGUE.

get on in years See ALONG IN YEARS.

get on one's good side *v. phr.* To gain the favor of someone; flatter or please another. ◆*A clever lobbyist knows how to get on the good side of both the House of Representatives and the Senate.*

get on one's nerves *v. phr.* To make you nervous. *John's noisy eating habits get on your nerves.* ◆*Children get on their parents' nerves by asking so many questions.*

get on the ball See ON THE BALL.

get on the bandwagon See JUMP ON THE BANDWAGON.

get on the good side of See ON THE GOOD SIDE OF.

get on the stick *v. phr., slang, informal* To get moving; to stop being idle and to start working vigorously. ◆*All right, man, let's get on the stick!* Compare ON THE BALL, GET OFF ONE'S TAIL.

get on to one *v. phr.* To figure someone out; understand what someone else is up to. ◆*The FBI is on to Jim's secret trading with the enemy.*

get one wrong *v. phr.* To misinterpret; misunderstand another. ◆*Don't get me wrong; I didn't mean to criticize you.*

get or **have one's say** See DAY IN COURT.

get out *v. phr.* **1.** leave or depart. ◆*"Get out of here!" the teacher shouted angrily to the misbehaving student.* ◆*"Driver, I want to get out by the opera."* **2.** To publish; produce. ◆*Our press is getting out two new books on ecology.* **3.** To escape; leak out. ◆*We must not let the news about this secret invention get out.*

get out in the open See OUT IN THE OPEN.

get out of *v. phr.* **1.** To be excused from; avoid. ◆*He got out of jury duty because of his illness.* **2.** To gain from; extract from. ◆*Tom complained that he didn't*

get anything out of the course on grammar.

get out of the way See OUT OF THE WAY.

get out of hand See OUT OF HAND, OUT OF CONTROL.

get over *v.* **1.** To finish. ◆*Tom worked fast to get his lesson over.* **2.** To pass over. ◆*It was hard to get over the muddy road.* **3.** To get well from; recover from. ◆*The man returned to work after he got over his illness.* **4.** To accept or forget (a sorrow or surprise.) ◆*It is hard to get over the death of a member of your family.* ◆*We could not get over the speed of Mary's recovery from pneumonia.*

get rattled *v. phr.* To become confused, overexcited, or nervous. ◆*The thief got so rattled when he saw the police following him that he drove his car into a ditch.*

get rid of See RID OF.

get set *v. phr.* To get ready to start. ◆*The runners got set.* ◆*The seniors are getting set for the commencement.*

get short shrift See SHORT SHRIFT.

get something out of one's system *v. phr.* **1.** To eliminate some food item or drug from one's body. ◆*John will feel much better once he gets the addictive sleeping pills out of his system.* **2.** To free oneself of yearning for something in order to liberate oneself from an unwanted preoccupation. ◆*Ted bought a new cabin cruiser that he'd been wanting for a long time, and he says he is glad that he's finally got it out of his system.*

get something over with See OVER WITH 1.

get something straight *v. phr.* To clearly comprehend an issue. ◆*"Let me get this straight," Burt said. "You want $85,000 for this miserable shack?"*

get stoned *v. phr., slang* To become very drunk or high on some drug. ◆*Poor Fred was so stoned that Tom had to carry him up the stairs.* Compare THREE SHEETS TO THE WIND.

get straight See GO STRAIGHT; GO LEGIT.

get stuck *v. phr.* **1.** To be victimized; be cheated. ◆*The Smiths sure got stuck when they bought that secondhand car; it broke down just two days after they got it.* **2.** To become entrapped or embroiled in a physical, emotional, or social obstacle so as to be unable to free oneself. ♦ *Last winter our car got stuck in the snow and we had to walk home.* ♦ *Poor Jeff is stuck in a terrible job.* ♦ *Tom and Jane are stuck in a bad marriage.*

get (all) the breaks *v. phr.* To be fortunate; have luck. ♦ *That fellow gets all the breaks! He's been working here only six months, and he's already been promoted to vice president!*

get the air See GET THE BOUNCE 1.

get the ax *v. phr., slang* **1.** To be fired from a job. ♦ *Poor Joe got the ax at the office yesterday.* **2.** To be dismissed from school for improper conduct, such as cheating. *Joe got caught cheating on his final exam and he got the ax.* **3.** To have a quarrel with one's sweetheart or steady ending in a termination of the relationship. ♦ *Joe got the ax from Betsie—they won't see each other again.*

get the ball rolling *or* **set the ball rolling** *or* **start the ball rolling** *informal* To start an activity or action; make a beginning; begin. ♦ *George started the ball rolling at the party by telling a new joke.* Compare KEEP THE BALL ROLLING.

get the better of *or* **get the best of** *v. phr.* **1.** To win over, beat; defeat. ♦ *Our team got the best of the visitors in the last quarter.* ♦ *George got the better of Robert in a game of checkers.* ♦ *When the opposing player fouled John, John let his anger get the better of his good sense and hit the boy back.* ♦ *Dave wanted to study till midnight, but sleepiness got the best of him.* Compare RUN AWAY WITH 1. **2.** *or* **have the best of** *or* **have the better of** To win or be ahead in (something); gain most from (something.) *Bill traded an old bicycle tire for a horn; he got the best of that deal.* ♦ *Our team had the best of it today, but they may lose the game tomorrow.* ♦ *The champion had all the better of it in the last part of the fight.* Contrast GET THE WORST OF.

get the boot *or* **the gate** *or* **the sack** See GET THE AXE.

get the bounce *or* **get the gate** *v. phr., slang* **1.** *or* **get the air** To lose one's sweetheart; not be kept for a friend or lover. ♦ *Joe is sad because he just got*

the gate from his girl. ♦ *Shirley was afraid she might get the air from her boyfriend if she went out with other boys while he was away.* **2.** *or* **get the sack** *also* **get the hook** To be fired; lose a job. ♦ *Uncle Willie can't keep a job; he got the sack today for sleeping on the job.* ♦ *You're likely to get the bounce if you are absent from work too much.* Contrast GIVE THE BOUNCE.

get the brush-off *v. phr., slang* **1.** To be paid no attention; not be listened to or thought important. ♦ *My idea for a party got the brush-off from the other children.* **2.** To be treated in an unkind or unfriendly way; be ignored. ♦ *Frank and Jane had an argument, so the next time he telephoned her, he got the brush-off.* Compare COLD SHOULDER, HIGH-HAT. Contrast BRUSH OFF.

get the cart before the horse See CART BEFORE THE HORSE.

get the eye *v. phr., informal* **1.** To be looked at, especially with interest and liking. ♦ *The pretty girl got the eye as she walked past the boys on the street corner.* **2.** To be looked at or stared at, especially in a cold, unfriendly way. ♦ *When Mary asked if she could take home the fur coat and pay later, she got the eye from the clerk.* Contrast GIVE THE EYE.

get the feel of *v. phr.* To become used to or learn about, especially by feeling or handling; get used to the experience or feeling of; get skill in. ♦ *John had never driven a big car, and it took a while for him to get the feel of it.* ♦ *You'll get the feel of the job after you've been there a few weeks.*

get the go-ahead *or* **the green light** *v. phr.* To receive the permission or signal to start or to proceed. ♦ *We had to wait until we got the go-ahead on our research project.*

get the goods on *or* **have the goods on** *v. phr. slang* To find out true and, often, bad information about; discover what is wrong with; be able to prove the guilt of. ♦ *Tell the truth, Johnny. We know who your girl is because we've got the goods on you.* ♦ *The police had the goods on the burglar before he came to trial.* Compare HAVE SOMETHING ON.

get the hook See GET THE BOUNCE 2.

get the inside track See INSIDE TRACK.

get the jitters *v. phr.* To become very nervous or excited. ♦*I always get the jitters when I sit in an airplane that's about to take off.*

get the jump on *or* **have the jump on** *v. phr., slang* To get ahead of; start before (others); have an advantage over. ♦*Don't let the other boys get the jump on you at the beginning of the race.* ♦*Our team got the jump on their rivals in the first minutes of play, and held the lead to win.*

get the last laugh See HAVE THE LAST LAUGH.

get the lead out of one's pants *v. phr., slang* To get busy; work faster. ♦*The captain told the sailors to get the lead out of their pants.* ♦*The coach told the players to get the lead out of their pants.*

get the lowdown on *v. phr.* To receive the full inside information on a person or thing. ♦*We need to get the lowdown on Peter before we can decide whether or not to hire him.*

get the message *or* **get the word** *v. phr., slang* To understand clearly what is meant. ♦*The principal talked to the students about being on time, and most of them got the message.* ♦*Mary hinted to her boyfriend that she wanted to break up, but he didn't get the message.* Compare THE PICTURE.

get the picture See THE PICTURE.

get the runaround See RUN AROUND.

get the sack *v. phr., slang* **1.** To be fired or dismissed from work. ♦*John got the sack at the factory last week.* **2.** To be told by one's lover that the relationship is over. ♦*Joanna gave Sam the sack.* See GET THE AX *and* GET THE BOUNCE 2.

get the show on the road *v. phr., informal* To start a program; get work started. ♦*It was several years before the rocket scientists got the show on the road.* Compare GET THE BALL ROLLING.

get the third degree See THIRD DEGREE.

get the upper hand on See UPPER HAND.

get the word See GET THE MESSAGE.

get the works See THE WORKS.

get the worst of *also* **have the worst of** *v. phr.* To lose; be defeated or beaten in; suffer most. ♦*Joe got the worst of the argument with Molly.* Often used in the phrase *the worst of it. If you start a fight with Jim, you may get the worst of it.* ♦*Bill had the worst of it in his race with Al.* ♦*Jack traded his knife for a few marbles; he got the worst of it in that trade.* ♦*The driver of the car got the worst of it in the accident.* Contrast GET THE BETTER OF 2.

get through *v. phr.* **1.** To finish. ♦*Barry got through his homework by late evening.* **2.** To pass a course or an examination. ♦*I got through every one of my courses except mathematics.*

get through one's head *v. phr.* **1.** To understand or believe. ♦*Jack couldn't get it through his head that his father wouldn't let him go to camp if his grades didn't improve.* ♦*At last Mary got it through her head that she had failed to pass the test.* **2.** To make someone understand or believe. ♦*I'll get it through his head if it takes all night.*

get through to *v.* To be understood by; make (someone) understand. ♦*The little boy could not get through to his housemother.* ♦*Deaf people sometimes find it hard to get through to strangers.* ♦*When the rich boy's father lost his money, it took a long time for the idea to get through to him that he'd have to work and support himself.*

get to *v. phr., informal* **1.** To begin by chance; begin to.—Used with a verbal noun or an infinitive. ♦*George meant to save his dollar, but he got to thinking how good an ice cream cone would taste, and he spent it.* ♦*On a rainy day, Sally got to looking around in the attic and found some old pictures of Father.* ♦*I got to know Mary at the party.* ♦*I was just getting to know John when he moved away.* Compare TAKE TO 2. **2.** To have a chance to; be able to. *The Taylors wanted to go to the beach Saturday, but it rained and they didn't get to.* ♦*Did you get to see the king?* Compare GET AT 3. **3.** See HAVE TO.

get to first base *or* **reach first base** *v. phr.* To make a good start; really begin; succeed. ♦*Joe had a long paper to write for history class, but when the teacher asked for it, Joe hadn't got to first base yet.* ♦*Suppose Sam falls in love with Betty. Can he even get to first base with her?* ♦*George wants to go to* *college and become a teacher, but I'll be surprised if he even reaches first base.* ♦ *If you don't dress neatly, you won't get to first base when you look for a job.* Compare FIRST BASE.

get together *v.* To come to an agreement; agree. ♦ *Mother says I should finish my arithmetic lesson, and Father says I should mow the lawn. Why don't you two get together?*

get-together *n.* A party; a gathering. ♦ *I hate to break up this nice get-together but we must leave.* ♦ *We manage to have a get-together with our old friends once or twice a year.*

get to the bottom of *v. phr.* To find out the real cause of. ♦ *The superintendent talked with several students to get to the bottom of the trouble.* ♦ *The doctor made several tests to get to the bottom of the man's headaches.* Compare GET TO THE HEART OF.

get to the heart of *v. phr.* To find the most important facts about or the central meaning of; understand the most important thing about. ♦ *You can often get to the heart of people's unhappiness by letting them talk.* ♦ *"If you can find a topic sentence, often it will help you get to the heart of the paragraph," said the teacher.*

get to the point See COME TO THE POINT.

get two strikes against one See TWO STRIKES AGAINST.

get underway *v. phr.* To set out on a journey; start going. ♦ *We are delighted that our new Ph.D. program finally got underway.*

get under one's skin *v. phr.* To bother; upset. ♦ *The students get under Mary's skin by talking about her freckles.* ♦ *Children who talk too much in class get under the teacher's skin.*

get up *v.* **1.** To get out of bed. ♦ *John's mother told him that it was time to get up.* **2.** To stand up; get to your feet. ♦ *A man should get up when a woman comes into the room.* **3.** To prepare; get ready. ♦ *Mary got up a picnic for her visitor.* ♦ *The students got up a special number of the newspaper to celebrate the school's 50th birthday.* **4.** To dress up. *One of the girls got herself up as a witch for the Halloween party.* **5.** To go ahead. ♦ *The wagon driver shouted, "Get up!" to his horses.*

get up *or* **rise with the chickens** *v. phr.* To rise very early in the morning. ♦ *All the farmers in this village get up with the chickens.* Contrast GO TO BED WITH THE CHICKENS.

get-up *n.* (stress on *get)* Fancy dress or costume. ♦ *Some get-up you're wearing!*

get-up-and-go *also* **get-up-and-get** *n. phr., informal* Energetic enthusiasm; ambitious determination; pep; drive; push. ♦ *Joe has a lot of get-up-and-go and is working his way through school.*

get up on the wrong side of the bed *v. phr., informal* To awake with a bad temper. ♦ *Henry got up on the wrong side of the bed and wouldn't eat breakfast.* ♦ *The man went to bed very late and got up on the wrong side of the bed.*

get up the nerve *v. phr.* To build up your courage until you are brave enough; become brave enough. ♦ *Jack got up the nerve to ask Ruth to dance with him.* ♦ *The hungry little boy got up nerve to ask for another piece of cake.*

get used to See USED TO.

get warmed up See WARM UP.

get what's coming to one *or slang* **get one's** *v. phr.* To receive the good or bad that you deserve; get what is due to you; get your share. ♦ *At the end of the movie the villain got what was coming to him and was put in jail.* ♦ *John didn't think he was getting what was coming to him, so he quit the job.* ♦ *Mother told Mary that she'd get hers if she kept on being naughty.* Compare CATCH IT, HAVE IT COMING, SERVE RIGHT.

get wind of *v. phr.* To get news of; hear rumors about; find out about. ♦ *The police got wind of the plans to rob the bank.* ♦ *The captain didn't want the sailors to get wind of where the ship was going.*

get wise *v. phr., slang* To learn about something kept secret from you; become alert. ♦ *One girl pretended to be sick on gym days when she had athletics, until the teacher got wise and made her go anyway.* ♦ Often used with *to. The boys got wise to Jack's fondness for bubble gum.* ♦ *If you don't get wise to yourself and start studying, you will fail the course.* Compare CATCH ON, SEE THROUGH. Contrast IN THE DARK.

get with it *v. phr., slang* To pay attention; be alive or alert; get busy. The students get with it just before examinations. ♦ *The coach told the team to get with it.* Compare ON THE BALL.

ghost See GIVE UP THE GHOST.

ghost of a Least trace of; slightest resemblance to; smallest bit even of; a very little. Usually used with *chance* or *idea* in negative sentences, or with *smile.* ♦ *There wasn't a ghost of a chance that Jack would win.* ♦ *We didn't have the ghost of an idea where to look for John.* ♦ *The teacher scolded Harold for drawing a funny picture on the chalkboard, but she had a ghost of a smile.* Compare FAT CHANCE.

ghost-writer *n.* A writer whose identity remains a secret and who writes for another who receives all the credit. ♦ *It is rumored that John Smith's best-selling novel was written by a ghost-writer.*

gift of gab *or* **gift of the gab** *n. phr., informal* Skill in talking; ability to make interesting talk that makes people believe you. ♦ *Many men get elected because of their gift of gab.* ♦ *Mr. Taylor's gift of gab helped him get a good job.*

gild the lily *also* **paint the lily** *v. phr.* To add unnecessarily to something already beautiful or good enough. ♦ *To talk about a beautiful sunset is to gild the lily.* ♦ *For the beautiful girl to use makeup would be to gild the lily.* ♦ *Frank's father is a millionaire, but Frank gilds the lily by saying he is a billionaire.*

gill See FED TO THE GILLS *at* FED UP, GREEN AROUND THE GILLS *or* PALE AROUND THE GILLS.

gilt-edged *adj.* Of the highest quality. ♦ *Government saving bonds are considered by many to be a gilt-edged investment.*

gin mill *n., slang* A bar where liquor is sold. ♦ *Rush Street in Chicago is full of gin mills.* Syn. SPEAKEASY.

G.I. or "government issue" *n.* An American soldier. ♦ *After the war many GI's were able to get a free education.*

gird one's loins *v. phr., literary* To prepare for action; get ready for a struggle or hard work. ♦ *David girded up his*

loins and went out to meet the giant Goliath. ♦ *Seniors must gird their loins for the battles of life.*

girl Friday *n.* A very dependable and helpful female office worker; *especially* a secretary. *Miss Johnson is the manager's girl Friday.* ♦ *There was an advertisement in the newspaper for a girl Friday.*

girl friend *n., informal* **1.** A female friend or companion. ♦ *Jane is spending the night at her girl friend's house.* **2.** A boy's steady girl; the girl or woman partner in a love affair; girl; sweetheart. ♦ *John is taking his girl friend to the dance.* Contrast BOYFRIEND.

give See SILENCE GIVES CONSENT.

give a buzz See GIVE A RING.

give a cold shoulder See COLD SHOULDER.

give a hand See LEND A HAND.

give a hang *or* **care a hang** *v. phr., informal* To have any interest or liking; care.—Used also with other words in the place of *hang,* such as *damn, rap, straw;* usually used in the negative. ♦ *You can quit helping me if you want to. I don't give a hang.* ♦ *Some people don't care a rap about sports.* ♦ *Bruce never goes to the dances; he does not care a straw about dancing.*

give a hard time *v. phr., informal* **1.** To give trouble by what you do or say; complain. ♦ *Jane gave her mother a hard time on the bus by fighting with her sister and screaming.* ♦ *Don't give me a hard time, George. I'm doing my best on this job.* Compare GIVE FITS. **2.** To get in the way by teasing or playing; kid. ♦ *Don't give me a hard time, boys. I'm trying to study.* Compare ACT UP, IN ONE'S HAIR.

give-and-take *n. phr.* **1.** A sharing; giving and receiving back and forth between people; a giving up by people on different sides of part of what each one wants so that they can agree. ♦ *Jimmy is too selfish.* ♦ *He has no notion of give-and-take with the other children but wants everything for himself.* ♦ *There has to be give-and-take between two countries before they can be friends.* Compare LIVE AND LET LIVE. **2.** Friendly talking or argument back and forth. Friendly sharing of ideas which may not agree; also: an exchange of teasing remarks. ♦*After the meeting there was a lot of give-and-take about plans for the dance.*

give an ear to *or* **lend an ear to** *v. phr., literary* To listen to. ♦*Children should give an ear to their parents' advice.* ♦*The king lent an ear to the complaints of his people.*

give a pain *v. phr., slang* To make (you) disgusted; annoy. ♦*Ann's laziness gives her mother a pain.* ♦*John's bad manners give his teacher a pain.* Compare PAIN IN THE NECK.

give as good as one gets *v. phr.* To be able to give back blow for blow; defend yourself well in a fight or argument. *The Americans gave as good as they got in the war with the English.* ♦*George gave as good as he got in his fight with the older boy.* Compare EYE FOR AN EYE, GAME AT WHICH TWO CAN PLAY.

give away *v.* **1.** To give as a present. ♦*Mrs. Jones has several kittens to give away.* **2.** To hand over (a bride) to her husband at the wedding. ♦*Mr. Jackson gave away his daughter.* **3.** To let (a secret) become known; tell the secret of. ♦*The little boy gave away his hiding place when he coughed.* ♦*Mary said she didn't care anything about John, but her blushing face gave her away.* Compare SPILL THE BEANS, LET THE CAT OUT OF THE BAG. **4.** See GIVE ONE-SELF AWAY.

giveaway *or* **dead giveaway** *n.* (stress on *give*) **1.** An open secret. ♦*By mid-afternoon, it was a dead giveaway who the new boss would be.* **2.** A forced or sacrifice sale at which items are sold for much less than their market value. ♦*The Simpson's garage sale was actually a big giveaway.* **3.** A gift; something one doesn't have to pay for. ♦*The tickets to the concert were a give-away.*

give a wide berth *v. phr.* To keep away from; keep a safe distance from. ♦*Mary gave the barking dog a wide berth.* ♦*Jack gave a wide berth to the fallen electric wires.* ♦*After Tom got Bob into trouble, Bob gave him a wide berth.*

give birth to *v. phr.* **1.** To bear live offspring. ♦*The mother gave birth to twin baby girls.* **2.** To bring about; create;

occasion. ♦*Beethoven gave birth to a new kind of symphony.*

give chase *v. phr.* To chase or run after someone or something. ♦*The dog saw a rabbit and gave chase.* ♦*The policeman gave chase to the man who robbed the bank.*

give color to *or* **lend color to** *v. phr.* To make (something) seem true or likely. ♦*The boy's torn clothes gave color to his story of a fight.* ♦*The way the man ate lent color to his story of near starvation.*

give credence to *v. phr.* **1.** To be willing to believe that something is true. ♦*Larry gave credence to the rumor that Fred used to be a convict.* ♦*Give no credence to the rumor that our state is bankrupt; nothing could be farther from the truth.*

give fits *v. phr. informal* To upset; bother very much. ♦*Paul's higher grades give John fits.* ♦*The short guard gave his tall opponent fits.* Compare GIVE A HARD TIME.

give forth *v. phr.* To emit; produce. ♦*When the gong was struck it gave forth a rich, resounding sound.*

give free rein to See GIVE REIN TO.

give gray hair *v. phr., informal* To make (someone) anxious, confused, or worried. ♦*The traffic problem is enough to give a policeman gray hairs.* Compare GET GRAY HAIR.

give ground *v. phr.* To go backward under attack; move back; retreat. ♦*After fighting for a while the troops slowly began to give ground.* ♦*Although they were outnumbered by the enemy, the men refused to give ground.* Compare DRAW BACK, DROP BACK, LOSE GROUND. Contrast HOLD ONE'S GROUND, STAND OFF, STAND ONE'S GROUND, STAND PAT, STAVE OFF.

give her the gun See GIVE IT THE GUN.

give in *v.* To stop fighting or arguing and do as the other person wants; give someone his own way; stop opposing someone. ♦*Mother kept inviting Mrs. Smith to stay for lunch, and finally she gave in.* ♦*After Billy proved that he could ride a bicycle safely, his father gave in to him and bought him one.* Compare GIVE UP, SAY UNCLE.

give it some thought *v. phr.* To wait and see; consider something after some time has elapsed. ♦*"Will you buy my car?" Fred asked. "Let me give it some thought," Jim answered.* Contrast SLEEP ON.

give it the gun *or* **give her the gun** *v. phr., slang* To gun or speed up a motor; make a car, airplane, or something driven by a motor go faster. ♦*The race driver gave it the gun.* ♦*The speedboat pilot gave her the gun.* Compare STEP ON IT.

give it to *v. phr., informal* **1.** To give punishment to; beat. ♦*The crowd yelled for the wrestler to give it to his opponent.* Syn. LET HAVE IT. **2.** To scold. ♦*Jerry's mother gave it to him for coming home late.* Compare GIVE A PIECE OF ONE'S MIND, LACE INTO. Contrast CATCH IT.

give it to one straight *v. phr.* To be direct; be frank. ♦*I asked the doctor to give it to me straight how long I have to live.*

give no quarter *v. phr.* To be ruthless and show no mercy. ♦*The enemy soldiers gave no quarter and shot all the prisoners.*

give notice *v. phr.* To inform an employer, an employee, a landlord, or a tenant of the termination of a contractual agreement of service or tenancy. ♦*Max gave notice at the bank where he was working.* ♦*Sally was given notice by her landlord.*

given to *adj. phr.* Having a tendency to; addicted to. ♦*Phil is given to telling fantastic tales about his chateau in France.*

give off *v.* To send out; let out; put forth. ♦*Rotten eggs give off a bad smell.* ♦*Burning leaves give off thick smoke.* Syn. GIVE OUT 2.

give of oneself *v. phr., literary* To give your time and effort to help others. ♦*You should give of yourself sometimes.* ♦*During World War II, Governor Baldwin gave of himself by sweeping the halls of a hospital every afternoon.*

give one a dressing down See DRESSING DOWN.

give one a free hand See FREE HAND.

give one a (good) going-over See GO OVER 1.

give one a lift *v. phr.* **1.** To give someone a ride. ♦*Jack gave me a lift in his new*

car. **2.** To comfort someone. ♦*Talking to my doctor yesterday gave me a lift.*

give one an inch, and he will take a mile If you give some people a little or yield anything, they will want more and more; some people are never satisfied. ♦*I gave Billy a bite of candy and he wanted more and more.* ♦*If you give him an inch, he'll take a mile.* ♦*The counselor said to Jack, "No, I can't let you get a haircut until Saturday. It's against the rules, and if I give an inch, someone will take a mile."*

give one a piece of one's mind *v. phr., informal* To scold angrily; say what you really think to (someone). ♦*Mr. Allen gave the other driver a piece of his mind.* ♦*The sergeant gave the soldier a piece of his mind for not cleaning his boots.* Syn. TELL OFF. Compare BAWL OUT, DRESS DOWN, GIVE IT TO, TONGUE LASHING.

give one a ring *also informal* **give a buzz** To call on the telephone. ♦*Mrs. Jacobs promised to give her husband a ring in the afternoon.* ♦*Alice will give her friend a buzz tonight.*

give one enough rope and he will hang himself *informal* Give a bad person enough time and freedom to do as he pleases, and he may make a bad mistake or get into trouble and be caught.—A proverb. ♦*Johnny is always stealing and hasn't been caught. But give him enough rope and he'll hang himself.* Often used in a short form, *give one enough rope.* ♦*Mother didn't know who robbed the cookie jar, but she thought she could catch him if she gave him enough rope.*

give one pause *v. phr.* To astonish someone; cause one to stop and think. ♦*"Your remark gives me pause," Tom said, when Jane called him an incurable gambler.*

give one short shrift See SHORT SHRIFT.

give oneself airs *v. phr.* To act proud; act vain. ♦*Mary gave herself airs when she wore her new dress.* ♦*John gave himself airs when he won first prize.*

give oneself away *v. phr.* To show guilt; show you have done wrong. ♦*The thief gave himself away by spending so much money.* ♦*Carl played a joke on Bob and gave himself away by laughing.* Compare GIVE AWAY.

give oneself up *v.* To stop hiding or running away; surrender. ♦ *The thief gave himself up to the police.* ♦ *Mr. Thompson hit another car, and his wife told him to give himself up.* Compare TURN IN.

give oneself up to *v. phr.* Not to hold yourself back from; let yourself enjoy. ♦ *Uncle Willie gave himself up to a life of wandering.* ♦ *John came inside from the cold and gave himself up to the pleasure of being in a warm room.* Compare ENJOY ONESELF, LET ONESELF GO.

give one some of his or her own medicine *v. phr.* To treat someone the way he or she treats others (used in the negative). ♦ *The gangster beat up an innocent old man, so when he resisted arrest, a policeman gave him a little of his own medicine.*

give one's due *v. phr.* To be fair to (a person), give credit that (a person) deserves. ♦ *The boxer who lost gave the new champion his due.* ♦ *We should give a good worker his due.* Compare GIVE THE DEVIL HIS DUE.

give one's right arm for *v. phr.* To give something of great value; sacrifice. ♦ *During our long hike in the desert, I would have given my right arm for an ice cold drink.*

give one's word *v. phr.* To seriously promise. ♦ *"You gave me your word you would marry me," Mary bitterly complained, "but you broke your word."*

give one the eye *v. phr., slang* **1.** To look at, especially with interest and liking. ♦ *A pretty girl went by and all the boys gave her the eye.* **2.** To look or stare at, especially in a cold or unfriendly way. ♦ *Mrs. Jones didn't like Mary and didn't speak. She just gave her the eye when they met on the street.*

give one the works See THE WORKS.

give or take *v. phr.* To add or subtract. Used with a round number or date to show how approximate it is. ♦ *The house was built in 1900, give or take five years.*

give out *v.* **1.** To make known; let it be known; publish. ♦ *Mary gave out that she and Bob were going to be married.* **2.** To let escape; give. ♦ *The cowboy gave out a yell.* Syn. GIVE OFF, LET GO.

3. to give to people; distribute. ♦ *The barber gives out free lollipops to all the children.* Compare HAND OUT, PASS OUT. **4.** To fail; collapse. *Tom's legs gave out and he couldn't run any farther.* ♦ *The chair gave out under the fat man.* Compare WEAR OUT. **5.** To be finished or gone. ♦ *When the food at the party gave out, they bought more.* ♦ *The teacher's patience gave out.* Syn. RUN OUT, RUN SHORT. Compare USE UP, WEAR OUT. **6.** *slang* Not to hold back; act freely; let yourself go.—Often used in the imperative. ♦ *You're not working hard, Charley. Give out!* **7.** *informal* To show how you feel. ♦ *When Jane saw the mouse, she gave out with a scream.* ♦ *Give out with a little smile.* Compare LET GO.

give pause *v. phr.* To cause you to stop and think; make you doubt or worry. ♦ *The heavy monthly payments gave Mr. Smith pause in his plans to buy a new car.* ♦ *The bad weather gave Miss Carter pause about driving to New York City.*

give place to See GIVE RISE TO.

give rein to *or* **give free rein to** *v. phr.* To remove all restrictions or limitations from someone or something. ♦ *When she wrote her first mystery novel, the talented novelist gave rein to her imagination.*

give rise to *v. phr.* To be the reason for; cause. A *branch floating in the water gave rise to Columbus' hopes that land was near.* ♦ *John's black eye gave rise to rumors that he had been in a fight.*

give someone his rights *or* **read someone his rights** *v. phr., informal* **1.** The act of advising arrested criminals that they have the right to remain silent and that everything they say can be held against them in a court of law; that they have the right to the presence of an attorney during questioning and that if they can't afford one and request it, an attorney will be appointed for them by the State. ♦ *The cops gave Smith his rights immediately after the arrest.* **2.** To sever a relationship by telling someone that he or she can go and see a divorce lawyer or the like. ♦ *Sue gave Mike his rights before she slammed the door in his face.* Compare READ THE RIOT ACT.

give the air See GIVE THE BOUNCE 1.

give the ax   *v. phr., colloquial*   **1.** Abruptly to finish a relationship. ♦ *She gave me the ax last night.* **2.** To fire an employee in a curt manner. ♦ *His boss gave John the ax last Friday.*

give the benefit of the doubt   *v. phr.* To believe (a person) is innocent rather than guilty when you are not sure. ♦ *The money was stolen and John was the only boy who had known where it was, but the teacher gave him the benefit of the doubt.* ♦ *George's grade was higher than usual and he might have cheated, but his teacher gave him the benefit of the doubt.*

give the bounce *or* **give the gate** *v. phr., slang* **1.** *or* **give the air** To stop being a friend or lover to (a person); separate from. ♦ *Mary gave John the bounce after she saw him dating another girl.* ♦ *Bill and Jane had an argument and Bill is giving her the gate.* **2.** *or* **give the sack** *also* **give the hook** To fire from a job; dismiss. ♦ *The ball team gave Joe the gate because he never came to practice.* Contrast GET THE BOUNCE.

give the creeps See THE CREEPS.

give the devil his due *v. phr.* To be fair, even to someone who is bad; tell the truth about a person even though you don't like him. ♦ *I don't like Mr. Jones, but to give the devil his due, I must admit that he is a good teacher.*

give the gate See GIVE THE BOUNCE.

give the glad eye *v. phr., slang* To give (someone) a welcoming look as if saying "come over here, I want to talk to you." ♦ *I was surprised when Joe gave me the glad eye.*

give the go-by *v. phr.* To pay no attention to a person; avoid. ♦ *John fell in love with Mary, but she gave him the go-by.* ♦ *The boy raised his hand to answer the question, but the teacher gave him the go-by.* Compare THE RUNAROUND.

give the high sign See HIGH SIGN.

give the hook See GIVE THE BOUNCE 2.

give the lie to *v. phr., literary* **1.** To call (someone) a liar. ♦ *The police gave the lie to the man who said that he had been at home during the robbery.* **2.** To show (something) to be false; prove untrue. ♦ *The boy's dirty face gave the lie to his*

answer that he had washed.

give the sack See GIVE THE BOUNCE 2.

give the shirt off one's back *v. phr., informal* To give away something or everything that you own. ♦ *He'd give you the shirt off his back.*

give the show away *v. phr.* To reveal a plan or information that is supposed to be secret. ♦ *You have read further in the book than I have, but please don't tell me where the treasure was buried; otherwise you'd be giving the show away.*

give the slip *v.* To escape from (someone); run away from unexpectedly; sneak away from. ♦ *An Indian was following, but Boone gave him the slip by running down a hill.* ♦ *Some boys were waiting outside the school to beat up Jack, but he gave them the slip.*

give signs of See SHOW SIGN(S) OF; SHOW NO SIGN OF.

give the willies *v. phr.* To cause someone to be uncomfortable, fearful, or nervous. ♦ *Sue hates to camp out in a tent; the buzzing of the mosquitoes gives her the willies.*

give thought to   *v. phr.* To consider; think about. ♦ *Have you given any thought to the question of how to sell Grandpa's old house?* Contrast GIVE IT SOME THOUGHT.

give to understand *v. phr., informal* **1.** To make a person think that something is true but not tell him; suggest; hint. ♦ *Mr. Johnson gave Billy to understand that he would pay him if he helped him clean the yard.* **2.** To make a person understand by telling him very plainly or boldly. ♦ *Frank was given to understand in a short note from the boss that he was fired.*

give up *v.* **1a.** To stop trying to keep; surrender; yield. ♦ *The dog had the ball in his mouth and wouldn't give it up.* ♦ *Jimmy is giving up his job as a newsboy when he goes back to school.* Compare GIVE ONESELF UP, HAND OVER, LET GO 1a. Contrast HOLD ON TO. **1b.** To allow; permit. ♦ *Ford gave up two walks in the first inning.* **2.** To stop doing or having; abandon; quit. ♦ *The doctor told Mr. Harris to give up smoking.* ♦ *Jane hated to give up her friends when she moved away.* Compare LEAVE OFF, PART WITH. **3.** To stop hoping for, waiting for, or trying to do. ♦*Johnny was given up by the doctors after the accident, but he lived just the same.* ♦*When Mary didn't come by nine o'clock, we gave her up.* ♦*I couldn't do the puzzle so I gave it up.* **4.** To stop trying; quit; surrender. ♦*The war will be over when one of the countries gives up.* ♦*The other team gave up after we scored three touchdowns.* Compare GIVE IN 2, RESIGN ONESELF, THROW IN THE SPONGE.

give (one) up for *v. phr.* To abandon hope for someone or something. ♦*After Larry had not returned to base camp for three nights, his fellow mountain climbers gave him up for dead.*

give up the ghost *v. phr.* To die; stop going. ♦*After a long illness, the old woman gave up the ghost.* ♦*The motor turned over a few times and gave up the ghost.*

give up the ship *v. phr.* To stop fighting and surrender; stop trying or hoping to do something. ♦*"Don't give up the ship, John," said his father when John failed a test.*

give voice *v. phr., formal* To tell what you feel or think; especially when you are angry or want to object.—Used with *to.* ♦*The students gave voice to their pleasure over the new building.* ♦*Little Willie gave voice to his pain when the dog bit him by crying loudly.* Compare CRY OUT, SPEAK OUT.

give way *v.* **1.** To go back; retreat. ♦*The enemy army is giving way before the cannon fire.* Compare FALL BACK. **2.** To make room, get out of the way. ♦*The children gave way and let their mother through the door.* Compare MAKE WAY. **3.** To lose control of yourself; lose your courage or hope; yield. ♦*Mrs. Jones didn't give way during the flood, but she was very frightened.* Compare GIVE UP, LOSE ONE'S HEAD. **4.** To collapse; fail. ♦*The river was so high that the dam gave way.* ♦*Mary's legs gave way and she fainted.* Compare GIVE OUT 4, LET GO 1a. **5.** To let yourself be persuaded; give permission. ♦*Billy kept asking his mother if he could go to the movies and she finally gave way.* Compare GIVE IN.

give way to *v. phr.* **1a.** To make room for; allow to go or pass; yield to. ♦*John gave way to the old lady and let her pass.* **1b.** To allow to decide. ♦*Mrs. Rogers gave way to her husband in buying the car.* **1c.** To lose control of (your feelings), not hold back. ♦*Timmy gave way to his feelings when his dog died.* **2.** *or* **give place to.** To be replaced by. ♦*Radio has given way to television in popularity.* ♦*When she saw the clowns, the little girl's tears gave way to laughter.*

glad hand *n., informal* A friendly handshake; a warm greeting. ♦*Father went to the front door to give Uncle Fred the glad hand when he arrived.* ♦*The politician went down the street on election day giving everyone the glad hand.*

glad rags *n., slang* Clothes worn to parties or on special occasions; best clothes. ♦*Mrs. Owens put on her glad rags for the party.* Compare BEST BIB AND TUCKER,

glance See AT FIRST GLANCE *or* AT FIRST SIGHT.

glance off *v. phr.* To ricochet. ♦*The bullet glanced off the wall and wounded an innocent bystander.*

glass See PEOPLE WHO LIVE IN GLASS HOUSES SHOULD NOT THROW STONES, SAFETY GLASS.

glasses See LOOK AT THE WORLD THROUGH ROSE-COLORED GLASSES.

glass jaw *n., slang* The inability of a boxer to get a hard punch on the jaw without being knocked out; a tendency to be knocked out easily. ♦*He would have been champion except for his glass jaw.*

globe-trotter *n.* One who has travelled far and wide. ♦*Tim and Nancy are regular globe-trotters; there are few countries they haven't been to.*

glory See IN ONE'S GLORY.

gloss over *v.* To try to make what is wrong or bad seem right or not important; try to make a thing look easy; pretend about; hide. ♦*Billy broke a window and Mother tried to gloss it over by saying it wouldn't cost much to have it fixed, but Father spanked Billy anyway.* ♦*John glossed over his mistake by saying that everybody did the same thing.*

glove See FIT LIKE A GLOVE, HAND IN GLOVE *or* HAND AND GLOVE, HANDLE WITH GLOVES.

glutton for punishment *n. phr.* A

greedy person; someone who wants too much of something, such as food or drink, which will make him sick. ♦ *Fred eats so much red meat that he is a regular glutton for punishment.*

go See HERE GOES, HERE GOES NOTHING, BEST BIB AND TUCKER *or* SUNDAY-GO-TO-MEETING CLOTHES, COMINGS AND GOINGS, EASY COME EASY GO, GET GOING, GET-UP-AND-GO, HAVE A GO AT, HEART GOES OUT TO, KNOW WHETHER ONE IS COMING OR GOING, LET GO, MAKE A GO OF, NO DEAL *or* NO GO, ON THE GO, PAY AS ONE GOES, TOUCH AND GO.

go about *v.* **1.** To be busy with; keep busy at or working on; start working on; do. ♦ *Bobby is going about his homework very seriously tonight.* ♦ *Just go about your business and don't keep looking out of the window.* ♦ *How will you go about building the bird house?* Syn. GO AT 2. **2a.** To move from one place or person to another. ♦ *Some people go about telling untrue stories.* **2b.** To go together.—Usually used with *with.* ♦ *Mother doesn't want me to go about with Jane and her friends any more.* Syn. GO AROUND 1b.

go about one's business *v. phr.* To mind one's own affairs. ♦ *Fred kept bothering me with his questions all day, so I finally told him to go about his business and leave me alone.*

go after *v.* To try to get. ♦ *"First find out what job you want and then go after it," said Jim's father.*

go against the grain See AGAINST THE GRAIN 2.

go ahead *v.* To begin to do something; not wait. ♦ *The teacher told the students not to write on the paper yet, but John went ahead and wrote his name.* ♦ *"May I ask you a question?" "Go ahead."* Compare GO ON 1.

go astray *v. phr.* To become lost. ♦ *The letter has obviously gone astray; otherwise it would have been delivered a long time ago.*

goal See FIELD GOAL.

goal line *n.* A line that marks the goal in a game (as football.) ♦ *The fullback went over the goal line from five yards out.*

goal line stand *n.* A strong defensive effort right in front of the goal line. ♦ *A*

goal line stand by the home team held the visitors on the two-yard line.

go all the way with See ALL THE WAY.

go along *v.* **1.** To move along; continue. ♦ *Uncle Bill made up the story as he went along.* Compare GO ON 1. **2.** To go together or as company; go for fun.—Often used with *with. Mary went along with us to Jane's house.* ♦ *John just went along for the ride to the ball game. He didn't want to play.* ♦ *When one filling station cuts gasoline prices, the others usually go along.* **3.** To agree; cooperate.—Often used with *with.* ♦ *"Jane is a nice girl." "I'll go along with that," said Bill.* ♦ *Just because the other boys do something bad, you don't have to go along with it.*

go ape *v. phr., slang* To become highly excited or behave in a crazy way. ♦ *Amy went ape over the hotel and beautiful beaches.* ♦ *The electric door opener malfunctioned and caused the garage door to go ape.*

go around *v.* **1a.** To go from one place or person to another. *Mr. Smith is going around looking for work.* ♦ *Don't go around telling lies like that.* ♦ *Chicken pox is going around the neighborhood.* ♦ *A rumor is going around school that we will get the afternoon off.* **1b.** To go together; keep company.—Usually used with *with.* ♦ *Bill goes around with boys older than he is because he is big for his age.* Syn. GO ABOUT 2b. **2.** To be enough to give to everyone; be enough for all. ♦ *There are not enough desks to go around in the classroom.*

go around in circles See IN A CIRCLE.

goat See GET ONE'S GOAT.

goat *v.* **1.** To start to fight with; attack. ♦ *The dog and the cat are going at each other again.* **2.** To make a beginning on; approach; tackle. ♦ *How are you going to go at the job of fixing the roof?* Compare START IN. Syn. GO ABOUT 1.

go at it hammer and tongs *v. phr., informal* **1.** To attack or fight with great strength or energy; have a bad argument. ♦ *Bill slapped George's face and now they're going at it hammer and tongs in back of the house.* ♦ *Helen and Mary have been arguing all day, and now they are going at it hammer and tongs again.* **2.** To start or do something with much strength, energy, or enthusiasm. ♦ *The farmer had to chop down a tree and he went at it hammer and tongs.* ♦ *Charles had a lot of homework to do and he went at it hammer and tongs till bedtime.* Compare IN EARNEST, WITH MIGHT AND MAIN.

go AWOL See ABSENT WITHOUT LEAVE.

go back on *v. phr.* **1.** To turn against; not be faithful or loyal to. ♦ *Many of the man's friends went back on him when he was sent to prison.* ♦ *The boy's father told him not to go back on his promise.* Compare BACK DOWN, TURN ONE'S BACK. **2.** To fail to do necessary work; not work. ♦ *Grandfather's eyes are going back on him.* Compare BREAK DOWN 4, GIVE OUT.

go back on one's word *v. phr.* To renege; break a promise. ♦ *Patrick went back on his word when he refused to marry Karen in spite of his earlier promise.*

go *or* **be on the rocks** See ON THE ROCKS.

go *or* **be on the wagon** See ON THE WAGON. Contrast FALL OFF THE WAGON.

go bail for *v. phr.* To advance the necessary money as security in order to release an accused person until trial. ♦ *The arrested driver had no trouble finding someone to go bail for him.*

go begging *v. phr.* To be not needed or wanted. ♦ *Many old homes in the city go begging.* ♦ *Most of the apples on the market went begging.*

go broke *v. phr., slang* To lose all one's money; especially by taking a chance; owe more than you can pay. ♦ *The inventor went broke because nobody would buy his machine.* ♦ *Dan had a quarter but he went broke matching pennies with Fred.*

go-between *n.* An intermediary. ♦ *They expect Mr. Smith to act as a go-between in the dispute between management and labor.*

go bust *v. phr., slang* To become bankrupt. ♦ *Our company lost a lot of money and went bust.* Compare BELLY UP.

go-by See GIVE THE GO-BY.

go by *v.* **1.** To go or move past; pass. ♦ *Bob had to go by the post office on his way to school, so he mailed the letter.* **2.** To follow; copy; obey. ♦ *Mother goes by a pattern when she* makes a dress. ♦ *You will find Main Street without trouble if you go by Father's directions.* ♦ *If you ride a bicycle, you must go by the rules of the road.* **3.** To be known by; be called. ♦ *Many actors do not go by their real names.* ♦ *Fred goes by the nickname of Chubby.* **4.** To pass; be over; end. ♦ *Time goes by quickly on vacation.* ♦ *The horse and buggy days have gone by.* ♦ *The flowers have all gone by. What will I do for a bouquet?* **5.** To stop for a short visit; go to someone's house for a short while. ♦ *"Have you seen Bill lately?" "Yes, I went by his house last week."* Compare STOP BY.

go by the board *also* **pass by the board** *v. phr.* To go away or disappear forever; be forgotten or not used. ♦ *Tom had several chances to go to college, but he let them go by the board.* ♦ *Grandfather said he was too old to go to the beach.* ♦ *"Those days have passed by the board," he said.* Compare DOWN THE DRAIN.

go by the name of *v. phr.* To be called. ♦ *Adolf Schicklegruber went by the name of Adolf Hitler.*

go chase oneself *v. phr., slang* Go away and stop being a nuisance. ♦ *John's father was busy and told him to go chase himself.* ♦ *The owner of the store told the boys in front to go chase themselves.* Compare BEAT IT, GO JUMP IN THE LAKE.

God See IN THE LAP OF THE GODS *also* ON THE KNEES OF THE GODS, MY GOD *or* MY GOODNESS, WOULD THAT *or* WOULD GOD.

God forbid *interj.* May God prevent (something from happening); I hope that will not happen or is not true. ♦ *Someone told the worried mother that her son might have drowned. She said, "God forbid!"* ♦ *God forbid that the dam break and flood the valley!* Compare PERISH THE THOUGHT.

Godfrey See GREAT GODFREY.

God knows *or* **goodness knows** *or* **heaven knows** *informal* **1.** Maybe God knows but I don't know and no one else knows.—Often used with only. ♦ *Do you know where Susan is? God only knows!* **2.** Surely; certainly. ♦ *Goodness knows, the poor man needs the money.* ♦ *Heaven only knows, I* *have tried hard enough.*

Godmother See FAIRY GODMOTHER.

go down *v. phr.* **1.** To deteriorate in quality. ♦ *This hotel, which used to be one of the best, has gone down during the past few years.* **2.** To become lower in price. ♦ *It is said that the price of milk is expected to go down soon.* **3.** To sink. ♦ *The* Titanic *went down with a lot of people aboard.*

go down in history *or* **go down in the records** *v. phr.* To be remembered or recorded for always. ♦ *The lives of great men go down in history.* ♦ *Babe Ruth went down in history as a home run hitter.* ♦ *The boy's straight A's for four years of college went down in the records.* ♦ *The President said that the day the war ended would go down in history.*

go down the drain *v. phr.* To be lost or wasted forever. ♦ *If he doesn't pass the bar examination tomorrow, his best efforts to become a lawyer will go down the drain.*

God tempers the wind to the shorn lamb *literary* A person who is already helpless will not have more trouble; you will not have more trouble than you can bear. ♦ *After Mr. Smith lost his job, the Smith's house caught fire, but the fire was put out before much harm was done. Mr. Smith said, "God tempers the wind to the shorn lamb."* Contrast IT NEVER RAINS BUT IT POURS.

go Dutch *v. phr., informal* To go out for fun together but have each person pay for himself. ♦ *High school students often go Dutch to basketball games.* ♦ *Sometimes boys and girls go Dutch on dates.* ♦ *The girl knew her boyfriend had little money, so she offered to go Dutch.* Compare DUTCH TREAT.

go easy See TAKE IT EASY 1.

go fly a kite *v. phr., slang* To go away; leave. Usually used as a command, to show that you do not accept someone's ideas. ♦ *Harry was tired of John's advice and told him to go fly a kite.* ♦ *After Mary stood around telling Sue what was wrong with her dress, Sue told her to go fly a kite.* Compare DROP DEAD, GO JUMP IN THE LAKE.

go for *v. phr., informal* **1.** To try to get; aim for; try for. ♦ *Our team is going for the championship in the game tonight.* ♦ *The dog went for Bob's leg.* **2.** To

favor; support; like. *Little Susie really goes for ice cream.* ♦ *Bob goes for Jane in a big way.* **3.** To attack; begin to fight or argue with. ♦ *The Indian jumped out of the bush and went for Daniel. Molly went for James about being late as soon as he got home.*

go for a spin *v. phr.* To go for a ride in a car. ♦ *Billy has invited us to go for a spin in his new car.*

go for broke *v. phr., slang* To risk everything on one big effort; use all your energy and skill; try as hard as possible. ♦ *The racing car driver decided to go for broke in the biggest race of the year.* Compare ALL-OUT.

go for nothing *also formal* **go for naught** *v. phr.* To count for nothing; be useless; be wasted. ♦ *What the teacher said went for nothing because the pupils did not pay attention.* ♦ *I hope that all your good work doesn't go for naught.* Compare IN VAIN.

go from bad to worse *adv. phr.* To change from a bad position or condition to a worse one; become worse. ♦ *Dick's typing went from bad to worse when he was tired.* ♦ *Jack's conduct in school has gone from bad to worse.* Compare OUT OF THE FRYING PAN INTO THE FIRE.

go from strength to strength *v. phr.* To move forward, increasing one's fame, power, or fortune in a series of successful achievements. ♦ *Our basketball team has gone from strength to strength.*

go-getter *n.* A person who works hard to become successful; an active, ambitious person who usually gets what he wants. ♦ *The governor of the state has always been a go-getter.* ♦ *The best salesmen are the go-getters.*

go-go *adj., slang, informal* **1.** vigorous youthful, unusually active. ♦ *Joe is a go-go kind of guy.* **2.** Of a discotheque or the music or dances performed there. **3a.** unrestrained **3b.** very up-to-date, hip. ♦ *Mary wore handsome go-go boots to the discotheque last night.*

go great guns See GREAT GUNS.

go halfway *or* **go halfway to meet one** *or* **meet one halfway** *v. phr.* To give up part of what you want or to do your share in reaching an agreement with someone. ♦ *Our neighbors are willing* *to go halfway to meet us and pay their share for a fence between our houses.* ♦ *Bob wants to make up after your fight and you should meet him halfway.* ♦ *If you're willing to go halfway with us, we'll be friends again.* ♦ *Bill met Mary halfway after their argument.*

go halves *v. phr., informal* To share half or equally become partners. ♦ *The boys went halves in raising pigs.* ♦ *The men are going halves in a new business.* ♦ *The girl bought a box of candy and went halves with her roommate.*

go hang *v. phr., slang* **1.** To stop being of interest or importance; be forgotten.— Usually used with *let*. ♦ *Mr. Johnson let his business go hang after his wife died.* **2.** To leave you alone; not bother. ♦ *When the neighbor told Father how to manage his children, Father told him to go hang.* Compare TELL WHERE TO GET OFF.

go hard with *v. phr.* To be painful, troublesome, or hard for; happen or result badly for.—Used after *it*. ♦ *It will go hard with you if I catch you smoking.*

go haywire *v. phr., informal* Mixed-up, out of order, not in regular working condition. ♦ *My electric typewriter has gone all haywire; I have to call the repair man.*

go hog wild *v. phr., slang* To become extremely agitated and go out of control. ♦ *After the soccer game was won, the fans went hog wild.*

go in a circle *or* **go in circles** See IN A CIRCLE.

go in for *v. phr., informal* To try to do; take part in; take pleasure in. ♦ *Most girls do not go in for rough games.* ♦ *Mrs. Henry goes in for simple meals.* Compare GO INTO 3, TAKE UP 5b.

going and coming See COMING AND GOING.

going for one *adj. phr.* Working to help; in one's favor. ♦ *The young woman surely will get the job; she has everything going for her.*

going on *adv. phr.* Almost; nearly. ♦ *Joe is going on six years old.* ♦ *It is going on six o'clock.*

going through changes *v. phr., slang, informal* To be in trouble, to have difficulties, to be trapped in unfavorable circumstances. ♦ *"What's the matter with Joe?"—"He's going through changes."*

going to Can be expected to; planning to.—Used after *is* (or *was*, etc.), with an infinitive, in the same way *will* is used, to show future. ♦ *Some day that big tree is going to rot and fall.* ♦ *Look at those dark clouds. It's going to rain.* ♦ *The boys are going to practice football this afternoon.* ♦ *For a minute Ben thought the car was going to hit him.* ♦ *I was going to attend the meeting, but after supper I forgot about it.* Sometimes used without the infinitive. ♦ *That worn rope hasn't broken yet, but it's going to.* ♦ *Put some more wood on the fire. "I'm going to."* Compare ABOUT TO 1.

go in one ear and out the other *v. phr., informal* To be not really listened to or understood; be paid no attention. ♦ *The teacher's directions to the boy went in one ear and out the other.* ♦ *Mother scolded Martha, but it went in one ear and out the other.*

go into *v.* **1a.** To go or fit inside of; able to be put in. ♦ *The table is too big to go into the closet.* **1b.** To be able to be divided into; be divisible into. ♦ *Two goes into four two times.* **2.** To enter a state or condition of; pass into. *John went into a fit of temper when he didn't get his own way.* ♦ *The sick man went into a coma.* ♦ *The country went into mourning when the king died.* **3.** To be busy in or take part in; enter as a job or profession. ♦ *The mayor went into politics as a very young man.* ♦ *Mr. Johnson is going into business for himself.* ♦ *Bill wants to go into law when he gets out of school.* Compare GO IN FOR, TAKE UP 5b. **4.** To start to talk about; bring up the subject of; examine. ♦ *We'll talk about the dead mouse after dinner, Billy. Let's not go into it now.* ♦ *The teacher went into the subject of newspapers today.* Compare LOOK INTO.

go into a huddle *v. phr.* **1.** To gather close together as a team in a football game, usually to find out your team's next play. ♦ *The football team which has the ball goes into a huddle before every play to get orders on what play they will use.* **2.** *informal* To talk together privately about something; discuss something where others cannot hear. ♦ *The man went into a huddle* *with his lawyers before answering the question.* ♦ *The doctors went into a huddle and decided to operate.*

go into a nose dive See GO INTO A TAIL SPIN.

go into a tailspin *or* **go into a nose dive** *v. phr., informal* To fall or go down badly; collapse; give up trying. ♦ *The team went into a tailspin after their captain was hurt, and they were badly beaten.* **2.** *informal* To become very anxious, confused, or mentally sick; give up hope. ♦ *The man went into a tailspin after his wife died and he never got over it.*

go into orbit *v. phr., slang* **1.** To become very happy or successful. ♦ *Our team has gone into orbit.* Compare FLY HIGH. **2.** To lose one's temper or control completely; become very angry. ♦ *John was afraid his father would go into orbit when he found out about the car accident.* Compare HIT THE CEILING.

go it *v. phr., informal* **1.** To go fast; run hard; not to spare yourself.—Often used as a command. ♦ *The coach yelled to the runner to go it.* ♦ *At the party the girls cheered for their partners to go it.* ♦ *The boys called, "Go it!" to the dog chasing the cat.* **2.** To live; continue to do or work. ♦ *John wants to leave home and go it alone.* Compare ON ONE'S OWN.

go jump in the lake *v. phr., informal* To go away and quit being a bother. ♦ *George was tired of Tom's advice and told him to go jump in the lake.* Compare GO CHASE YOURSELF, GO FLY A KITE.

gold See HEART OF GOLD.

golden See KILL THE GOOSE THAT LAID THE GOLDEN EGG.

goldfish bowl *n., slang, informal* **1.** A situation in which it is not possible to keep things secret for any length of time. ♦ *Washington Society is a goldfish bowl.* **2.** An apartment or place that provides no privacy for its occupant, e.g., an office that has too many windows. ♦ *Joe's office is a goldfish bowl, that's why I didn't let him kiss me there.*

golf widow *n., informal* A woman whose husband is often away from home playing golf. ♦ *Mrs. Thompson didn't like being a golf widow.*

go legit *v. phr.* To start practicing a legitimate business after having been operating outside of the law. ♦ *"The old days are over," the crime boss said to his friends. "We are going legit as of right now."*

go like clockwork *or* **go off like clockwork** *v. phr., informal* To run smoothly and regularly like the workings of a clock; go smoothly and without difficulty; go on time or as planned. ♦ *The car's motor went like clockwork after Bob fixed it.* ♦ *The birthday party went off like clockwork and everyone had a good time.*

go native *v. phr.* To behave like a native (said of European Americans in tropical countries). ♦ *Mainlanders often go native in Hawaii.*

gone goose *also* **gone gosling** *n., slang* A person for whom there is no hope. ♦ *Herbert's grades have been so low that he is a gone goose for the year.* ♦ *The man was a gone gosling when a policeman caught him breaking the store window.*

gone with the wind *adj. phr.* Gone forever; past; vanished. ♦ *All the Indians who used to live here are gone with the wind.* ♦ *Joe knew that his chance to get an "A" was gone with the wind when he saw how hard the test was.* Compare DOWN THE DRAIN.

good See AS GOOD AS, AS GOOD AS ONE GETS, BUT GOOD, DO ONE GOOD, FOR GOOD, FOR GOOD MEASURE, GET THE GOODS ON, HOLD GOOD, IN GOOD, IN GOOD FAITH, IN GOOD TIME, IN ONE'S GOOD GRACES, IT'S AN ILL WIND THAT BLOWS NOBODY GOOD, MAKE GOOD, MISS IS AS GOOD AS A MILE, NO GOOD, ON ONE'S GOOD BEHAVIOR, ON ONE'S GOOD SIDE, SO FAR, SO GOOD, STAND IN GOOD STEAD, TO THE GOOD, WELL AND GOOD, WITH GOOD GRACE.

good and—— *adv., informal* Very; completely. ♦ *John's father was good and mad when John came home late.* ♦ *Jack knew good and well that Tom had thrown the snowball at him.* ♦ *I pushed Bill good and hard.* ♦ *Susan wouldn't come out till she was good and ready.* ♦ *I beat Joe good and proper in the game of marbles.*

good as See AS GOOD AS.

good as one's promise See AS GOOD AS

ONE'S WORD.

good as one's word   See AS GOOD AS ONE'S WORD.

good buddy   *n., slang, citizen's band radio jargon*   Salutation used by truckers and automobile drivers who have CB radios. ♦*What's the Smokey situation, good buddy?*

good command   See HAVE A GOOD COMMAND OF.

good day   *interj.*   Hello or goodbye.— Used as a formal greeting or salute when you meet or leave someone during the day. ♦*Miss Rogers said, "Good day!" when she met her friend on the street.* ♦*Mr. Lee said "Good day!" and left the office.*

good deal *or* **great deal**   *n., informal*   A large amount; much.—Used with *a*. ♦*Mrs. Walker's long illness cost her a good deal.* ♦*George spends a great deal of his time watching television.*—Often used like an adverb. ♦*Cleaning up after the party took a great deal more work than the girls expected.* ♦*Usually it takes Father half an hour to drive to work, but in bad weather it takes a good deal longer.* ♦*Mother likes the gloves Mary gave her, and she uses them a good deal.* ♦*George is a good deal like his father; they both love to eat.* Syn. A LOT, QUITE A LITTLE. Compare ALL KINDS OF, GOOD MANY. Contrast A LITTLE.

good egg   *slang or informal*   **good scout**   *n. phr.*   A friendly, kind or good-natured person, a nice fellow. ♦*Tommy is such a good egg that everybody wants to be his friend.* Syn. REGULAR GUY. Contrast BAD EGG.

good evening   *interj.*   Hello or goodbye.—Used as a formal greeting or salute when you meet or leave someone in the evening. ♦*When the TV program began, an announcer appeared and said, "Good evening, everyone."* ♦*Finally Aunt May stood up and said, "I will not sell the house. Good evening, Mr. Flynn."*

good faith   *n.*   **1.** Belief in another person's honesty; trust. ♦*Uncle Dick let me have the keys to his candy store to show his good faith.*—Often used in the phrase *in good faith.* ♦*The teacher accepted Bob's excuse for being late in good faith.* **2.** Honesty of purpose; trustworthiness. ♦*John agreed to buy Ted's bicycle for $20, and he paid him $5 right away to show his good faith.*

good for *or* **hurrah for**   *adj. phr.*   Used with a name or pronoun to praise someone. ♦*Good for George! He won the 100-yard dash.* ♦*You got 100 on the test? Hurrah for you.*

good-for-nothing   *adj. phr.*   Worthless. ♦*While Janice works hard each day, her good-for-nothing husband hangs around in the bars.*

good grief!   *interj., informal*   Wow! Indication of surprise, good or bad. ♦*"Good grief," Joe cried out loud. "Is this all you will pay me for my hard work?"* ♦*What a figure Melanie has, good grief! I wonder if she would be willing to go out with me.* Compare GOODNESS GRACIOUS!, HEAVENLY DAYS!, HOLY CATS *or* HOLY COW *or* HOLY MACKEREL *or* HOLY MOSES. See GOODNIGHT 2.

good head on one's shoulders   *n. phr.*   Good sense; good judgment. ♦*Jack has a good head on his shoulders; he never drives too fast.* ♦*Alice is a girl with a good head on her shoulders, she always keeps good company.* ♦*George showed he had a good head on his shoulders by refusing to cheat.*

good many *or* **great many**   *n. or adj.*   A large number (of); very many. Used with *a*. ♦*We found some fall flowers, but the frost had already killed a good many.* ♦*A great many of the houses were knocked down by the earthquake.* ♦*Tom has a good many friends at school.* ♦*Mary has a great many ideas for interesting programs.* Syn. QUITE A FEW. Compare A LOT, ANY NUMBER, GOOD DEAL. Contrast A FEW.

good nature   *n.*   Readiness to please others and to be pleased. Cheerfulness, pleasantness. ♦*Everybody likes Mr. Crowe because of his good nature.* ♦*Miss Reynolds was remembered by her students for her good nature.*

goodness   See HONEST-TO-GOODNESS, MY GOD *or* MY GOODNESS.

goodness gracious   *interj., slightly archaic*   Exclamation of surprise and a certain degree of disapproval. ♦*"Can my boyfriend stay overnight, Dad?" Melanie asked. "Goodness gracious, most certainly not!" her father replied.*

"What would the neighbors think?"

goodness knows See GOD KNOWS.

good night *interj.* **1.** Used as a polite phrase when you leave someone at night. ♦ *"Good night!" said Bob as he left Dick's house after the party. "I'll see you in the morning."* ♦ *Bill said good night to his parents and went upstairs to bed.* **2.** *or* **good grief**—Used to show surprise and often some fear or anger. ♦ *Mr. Johnson's eyes opened wide when he saw the fish his little boy had caught, and said, "Good night!"* ♦ *Mother was angry and said to Mary, "Good grief! Haven't you started the dishes yet?"*

good riddance *n.* A loss that you are glad about. Often used as an exclamation, and in the sentence *good riddance to bad rubbish.* To show that you are glad that something or somebody has been taken or sent away. ♦ *The boys thought it was good riddance when the troublemaker was sent home.* ♦ *When Mr. Roberts' old car was stolen he thought it was good riddance.* ♦ *Betty thought it was good riddance when her little brother broke his toy drum.* ♦ *"I'm going and won't come back," said John. "Good riddance to bad rubbish!" said Mary.*

goods See DELIVER THE GOODS, CONSUMER GOODS .

good show! *adj. phr.* Excellent; terrific; wonderful. ♦ *"Good show, boys!" the coach cried, when our team won the game.*

good scout See GOOD EGG.

go off *v.* **1.** To leave; to depart. ♦ *Helen's mother told her not to go off without telling her.* **2a.** To be fired; explode. ♦ *The firecracker went off and scared Jack's dog.* **2b.** To begin to ring or buzz. ♦ *The alarm clock went off at six o'clock and woke Father.* **3.** To happen. ♦ *The party went off without any trouble.* ♦ *The parade went off without rain.*

go off half-cocked *also* **go off at half cock** *v. phr., informal* To act or speak before getting ready; to do something too soon. ♦ *Bill often goes off half cocked.* ♦ *Mr. Jones was thinking about quitting his job, but his wife told him not to go at half cock.*

go off like clockwork See GO LIKE CLOCKWORK.

go off the deep end *or* **go overboard** *v. phr., informal* To act excitedly and without careful thinking. ♦ *John has gone off the deep end about owning a motorcycle.* ♦ *Mike warned his roommate not to go off the deep end and get married.* ♦ *Some girls go overboard for handsome movie and television actors.*

goof off *v., slang* To loaf or be lazy; not want to work or be serious; fool around. ♦ *Tom didn't get promoted because he goofed off all the time and never did his homework.* ♦ *If you goof off on the job too much, you'll be fired.*

go off in a huff *v. phr.* To depart in anger. ♦ *Marian went off in a huff just because Jeff failed to open the door for her.*

go on *v.* **1a.** To continue; not stop. ♦ *After he was hit by the ball, Billy quit pitching and went home, but the game went on.* ♦ *The TV picture began to jump, and it went on like that until Father turned a knob.* ♦ *I asked Jane a question but she went on reading and didn't answer.* ♦ *Mother told Jim to stop, but he went on hitting Susan.* Syn. KEEP ON. **1b.** To continue after a pause; begin with the next thing. ♦ *"Go on! I'm listening," said Mother.* ♦ *The teacher pointed to the map, and went on, "But the land that Columbus came to was not India."*—Often used before an infinitive. ♦ *Father said Mother had gone to the hospital, and went on to say that Grandmother was coming to take care of us.* **1c.** *Of time:* To pass. ♦ *As time went on, Mary began to wonder if John had forgotten their date.* ♦ *The years went on, and Betty's classmates became gray-haired men and women.* **2.** To happen. ♦ *Mr. Scott heard the noise and went to see what was going on in the hall.* ♦ *The teacher knows what goes on when she leaves the room.* Syn. TAKE PLACE. **3.** To talk for too long, often angrily. ♦ *We thought Jane would never finish going on about the amount of homework she had.* **4.** To fit on; be able to be worn. ♦ *My little brother's coat wouldn't go on me. It was too small.* **5.** Stop trying to fool me; I don't believe you.—Used as a command, sometimes with *with.* ♦ *When Father told Mother she was the prettiest girl in the world, Mother just said, "Oh, go on, Charles."* ♦ *"Aunt*

May, your picture is in the paper." "Go on with you, boy!"

go on record *v. phr.* To make an official statement as opposed to an informal one; say something officially that may be quoted with the person's name added for reference. ♦*I want to go on record that I oppose the merger with the firm of Catwallender and Swartvik.*

go on the rocks See ON THE ROCKS.

go one's way *v. phr.* **1.** To start again or continue to where you are going. ♦*The milkman left the milk and went his way.* ♦*The man stopped and asked me for a match, then went his way.* Compare GO ALONG, GO ON. **2.** To go or act the way you want to or usually do. ♦*Joe just wants to go his way and mind his own business.* ♦*Don't tell me how to do my job. You go your way and I'll go mine.* ♦*George was not a good sport; when the game did not go his way, he became angry and quit.*

goose See COOK ONE'S GOOSE, FOX AND GEESE, KILL THE GOOSE THAT LAID THE GOLDEN EGG, GONE GOOSE.

goose bumps *or* **goose pimples** *n. plural, informal* Small bumps that come on a person's skin when he gets cold or afraid. ♦*Nancy gets goose bumps when she sees a snake.* ♦*Ann, put on your sweater; you're so cold you have goose pimples on your arms.*

go *or* **drive to the wall** See TO THE WALL.

go out *v. phr.* **1.** To pass out of date or style. ♦*Short skirts are gradually going out.* **2.** To stop giving off light or burning. ♦*Put more wood on the fire or it will go out.* **3.** To leave. ♦*When I called Sue, her mother said that she had just gone out.*

go out for *or* **come out for** *v. phr.* To try for a place on (an athletic team.) ♦*Ten boys went out for track that spring.* ♦*The coach asked Tom why he didn't come out for basketball.*

go out of business *v. phr.* To cease functioning as a commercial enterprise. ♦*The windows of the store are all boarded up because they went out of business.*

go out of one's way *v. phr.* To make an extra effort; do more than usual. ♦*Jane went out of her way to be nice to the new girl.* ♦*Don did not like Charles, and he went out of his way to*

say bad things about Charles. Compare BEND OVER BACKWARD, KNOCK ONESELF OUT.

go out the window *v. phr., informal* To go out of effect; be abandoned. ♦*During the war, the school dress code went out the window.*

go over *v.* **1.** To examine; think about or look at carefully. ♦*The teacher went over the list and picked John's name.* ♦*The police went over the gun for fingerprints.* **2.** To repeat; do again. ♦*Don't make me go all over it again.* ♦*We painted the house once, then we went over it again.* ♦ **3.** To read again; study. ♦*After you finish the test, go over it again to look for mistakes.* ♦*They went over their lessons together at night.* **4.** To cross; go to stop or visit; travel. ♦*We went over to the other side of the street.* ♦*I'm going over to Mary's house.* ♦*We went over to the next town to the game.* **5.** To change what you believe. ♦*Father is a Democrat, but he says that he is going over to the Republicans in the next election.* ♦*Many of the natives on the island went over to Christianity after the white men came.* **6.** To be liked; succeed.—Often used in the informal phrase *go over big.* ♦*Bill's joke went over big with the other boys and girls.* ♦*Your idea went over well with the boss.*

go over like a lead balloon *v. phr., informal* To fail to generate a positive response or enthusiasm; to meet with boredom or disapproval. ♦*The president's suggested budget cuts went over like a lead balloon.* ♦*Jack's off-color jokes went over like a lead balloon.*

go over one's head *v. phr.* **1.** To be too difficult to understand. ♦*Penny complains that what her math teacher says simply goes over her head.* **2.** To do something without the permission of one's superior. ♦*Fred went over his boss's head when he signed the contract on his own.*

go over with a fine-tooth comb See FINE-TOOTH COMB.

gopher ball *n., slang* A baseball pitch that is hit for a home run. ♦*The pitcher's only weakness this year is the gopher ball.*

go places See GO TO TOWN 2.

go sit on a tack *v. slang* Shut up and go away; stop bothering.—Usually used as a command and considered rude. ♦ *Henry told Bill to go sit on a tack.* Compare GO JUMP IN THE LAKE.

gosling See GONE GOOSE *also* GONE GOSLING.

go somebody one better *v. phr., informal* To do something better than (someone else); do more or better than; beat. ♦ *Bill's mother gave the boys in Bill's club hot dogs for refreshments, so Tom's mother said that she would go her one better next time by giving them hot dogs and ice cream.* ♦ *John made a good dive into the water, but Bob went him one better by diving in backwards.*

go stag *v. phr.* **1.** To go to a dance or party without a companion of the opposite sex. ♦ *When Sally turned him down, Tom decided to go stag to the college prom.* **2.** To participate in a party for men only. ♦ *Mrs. Smith's husband frequently goes stag, leaving her at home.*

go steady *v. phr.* To go on dates with the same person all the time; date just one person. ♦ *At first Tom and Martha were not serious about each other, but now they are going steady.* ♦ *Jean went steady with Bob for a year; then they had a quarrel and stopped dating each other.* Syn. KEEP COMPANY. Contrast PLAY THE FIELD.

go straight *v. phr., slang* To become an honest person; lead an honest life. ♦ *After the man got out of prison, he went straight.* ♦ *Mr. Wright promised to go straight if the judge would let him go free.*

got a thing going *v. phr., slang, informal* To be engaged in a pleasurable or profitable activity with someone else as a partner either in romance or in mutually profitable business. ♦ *"You two seem to have got a thing going, haven't you?"* ♦ *"You've got a good thing going with your travel bureau, why quit now?"*

go the rounds *v. phr.* To pass or be told from one person to another; spread among many people. ♦ *There is a rumor going the rounds that Mr. Norton will be the new superintendent.* ♦ *The story about Mr. Cox's falling into the lake is making the rounds.* Syn. GO AROUND.

go the whole hog *or* **go whole hog** *v. phr., informal* To do something com-

pletely or thoroughly; to give all your strength or attention to something. ♦ *When Bob became interested in model airplanes, he went the whole hog.* ♦ *The family went whole hog at the fair, and spent a lot of money.* Compare ALL OUT, ALL THE WAY, SHOOT THE WORKS.

go through *v.* **1.** To examine or think about carefully; search. ♦ *I went through the papers looking for Jane's letter.* ♦ *Mother went through the drawer looking for the sweater.* Syn. GO OVER **2.** To experience; suffer; live through. ♦ *Frank went through many dangers during the war.* **3.** To do what you are supposed to do; do what you promised. ♦ *I went through my part of the bargain, but you didn't go through your part.* Syn. CARRY OUT. **4.** To go or continue to the end of; do or use all of. ♦ *Jack went through the magazine quickly.* ♦ *We went through all our money at the circus.* Syn. RUN THROUGH. **5.** To be allowed; pass; be agreed on. ♦ *I hope the new law we want goes through Congress.* ♦ *The sale of the store went through quickly.*

go through hell and high water *v. phr., informal* To go through danger, or trouble. ♦ *John is ready to go through hell and high water to help his chum.* ♦ *The soldiers went through hell and high water to capture the fort.* Compare COME HELL OR HIGH WATER, THROUGH THE MILL.

go through the motions *v. phr.* To pretend to do something by moving or acting as if you were really doing it; do something without really trying hard or caring. ♦ *Jane was angry because she couldn't go out, and when her mother said to dust her room she just went through the motions.* ♦ *The team was so far behind in the game that they just went through the motions of playing at the end.*

go through with *v. phr.* To finish; do as planned or agreed; not stop or fail to do. ♦ *The boys don't think Bob will go through with his plans to spend the summer at a camp.* ♦ *Mr. Trent hopes the city won't go through with its plans to widen the street.* Syn. CARRY OUT. Compare CARRY THROUGH, LIVE UP TO.

go to *v.* To be ready to do; start doing

something. ♦ *When Jack went to write down the telephone number, he had forgotten it.*

go to any length *v. phr.* To do everything you can. ♦ *Bill will go to any length to keep Dick from getting a date with Mary.* Compare ALL-OUT.

go to bat for *v. phr., informal* To help out in trouble or need; give aid to. ♦ *Everybody else thought Billy had broken the window, but Tom went to bat for him.* ♦ *Mary went to bat for the new club program.* ♦ Syn. STAND UP FOR.

go to bed with the chickens *v. phr., informal* To go to bed early at night. ♦ *On the farm John worked hard and went to bed with the chickens.* ♦ *Mr. Barnes goes to bed with the chickens because he has to get up at 5 A.M.*

go together *v.* **1.** To go with the same boy or girl all the time; date just one person. Herbert and Thelma go together. Compare GO STEADY, GO WITH 2, KEEP COMPANY. **2.** To be suitable or agreeable with each other; match. ♦ *Roast turkey and cranberries go together.* ♦ *Ice cream and cake go together.* ♦ *Green and yellow go together.*

go to great lengths See GO TO ANY LENGTH.

go to hell See GO TO THE DEVIL.

go to it! *v. phr.* An expression of encouragement meaning go ahead; proceed. ♦ *"Go to it!" my father cried enthusiastically, when I told him I had decided to become a doctor.*

go to one's head *v. phr.* **1.** To make one dizzy. ♦ *Beer and wine go to a person's head.* ♦ *Looking out the high window went to the woman's head.* **2.** To make someone too proud; make a person think he is too important. ♦ *Being the star player went to John's head.* ♦ *The girl's fame as a movie actress went to her head.*

go to pieces *v. phr.* To become very nervous or sick from nervousness; become wild. ♦ *Mrs. Vance went to pieces when she heard her daughter was in the hospital.* ♦ *The man went to pieces when the judge said he would have to go to prison for life.* ♦ *Mary goes to pieces when she can't have her own way.*

go to pot *v. phr., informal* To be ruined; become bad; be destroyed. ♦ *Mr.*

Jones' health has gone to pot. ♦ *The motel business went to pot when the new highway was built.* Compare GO TO WRACK AND RUIN, GO TO THE DOGS.

go to prove See GO TO SHOW.

go to seed *or* **run to seed** *v. phr.* **1.** To grow seeds. ♦ *Onions go to seed in hot weather.* **2.** To lose skill or strength; stop being good or useful. ♦ *Sometimes a good athlete runs to seed when he gets too old for sports.* ♦ *Mr. Allen was a good carpenter until he became rich and went to seed.*

go to show *or* **go to prove** *v. phr., informal* To seem to prove; act or serve to show (a fact); demonstrate.— Often used after *it.* ♦ *Our team beat a bigger team, and it just goes to show you can win if you play hard enough.* ♦ *The hard winter at Valley Forge goes to show that our soldiers suffered a great deal to win the Revolution.*

go to the chair *v. phr.* To be executed in the electric chair. ♦ *After many stays of execution, the criminal finally had to go to the chair.*

go to the devil *v. phr., informal* **1.** To go away, mind your own business.—Used as a command; considered rude. ♦ *George told Bob to go to the devil.* ♦ *"Go to the devil!" said Jack, when his sister tried to tell him what to do.* **2.** To become bad or ruined; become useless. ♦ *The boy got mixed up with bad company and began to steal and rob his friends. He went to the devil.* ♦ *Mr. Jones went to the devil after he lost his business.*

go to the dogs *v. phr., informal* To go to ruin; to be ruined or destroyed. ♦ *The man went to the dogs after he started drinking.* ♦ *After the death of the owner, the business went to the dogs.* ♦ *The team went to the dogs when its best players got hurt.* Compare GO TO POT.

go to the trouble *or* **take the trouble** *v. phr.* To make trouble or extra work for yourself; bother. ♦ *John told Mr. Brown not to go to the trouble of driving him home.* ♦ *Since your aunt took the trouble to get you a nice birthday present, the least you can do is to thank her.* Compare PUT OUT 5.

go to town *v. phr., slang* **1.** To do something quickly or with great force or energy; work fast or hard. ♦ *The boys went to town on the old garage, and had it torn down before Father came home from work.* ♦ *While Sally was slowly washing the dishes, she remembered she had a date with Pete that evening; then she really went to town.* Compare IN NO TIME, MAKE TIME. Contrast TAKE ONE'S TIME. **2.** *or* **go places.** To do a good job; succeed. ♦ *Our team is going to town this year.* ♦ *We have won all five games that we played.* ♦ *Dan was a good student and a good athlete; we expect him to go places in business.*

go to waste *v. phr.* To be wasted or lost; not used. ♦ *The strawberries went to waste because there was nobody to pick them.* ♦ *Joe's work on the model automobile went to waste when he dropped it.* Compare IN VAIN.

go to wrack and ruin *v. phr.* To fall apart and be ruined; to become useless. ♦ *The barn went to wrack and ruin after the farmer moved.* ♦ *The car will soon go to wrack and ruin standing out in all kinds of weather.*

go under *v.* **1.** To be sunk. ♦ *The ship hit an iceberg and went under.* **2.** To fail; be defeated. ♦ *The filling station went under because there were too many others on the street.*

go under the hammer *v. phr.* To be auctioned off. ♦ *Our old family paintings went under the hammer when my father lost his job.*

go up *v.* **1.** To go or move higher; rise. ♦ *Many people came to watch the weather balloon go up.* ♦ *The path goes up the hill.* **2.** To be able to become heard; become loud or louder. ♦ *A shout went up from the crowd at the game.* **3.** Grow in height while being built; to be built. ♦ *The new church is going up on the corner.* **4.** To increase. ♦ *Prices of fruit and vegetables have gone up.*

go up in smoke *or* **go up in flames** *v. phr.* To burn; be destroyed by fire. **1.** ♦ *The house went up in flames.* ♦ *The barn full of hay went up in smoke.* **2.** Disappear; fail; not come true. ♦ *Jane's hopes of going to college went up in smoke when her father lost his job.* ♦ *The team's chances to win went up in smoke when their captain was hurt.*

go up in the air *v. phr.* To become angry; lose one's temper. ♦ *Herb is so irritable these days that he goes up in the air for no reason at all.*

gourd See SAW WOOD *or* SAW GOURDS.

go with *v.* **1.** To match; to look good with. ♦ *A yellow blouse goes with her blonde hair.* ♦ *The woman bought a purse to go with her new shoes.* **2.** To go out in the company of. *Tom goes with the girl who lives across the street.*

go without See DO WITHOUT.

go without saying *v. phr.* To be too plain to need talking about; not be necessary to say or mention. ♦ *It goes without saying that children should not be given knives to play with.* ♦ *A person with weak eyes should wear glasses. That goes without saying.*

go wrong *v. phr.* **1.** To fail; go out of order. ♦ *Something went wrong with our car and we stalled on the road.* **2.** To sink into an immoral or criminal existence. ♦ *In a large city many young people go wrong every year.*

gown See TOWN AND GOWN.

grab bag *n.* **1.** A bag from which surprise packages are chosen; a bag in which there are many unknown things. ♦ *The woman paid a quarter for a chance at the grab bag.* ♦ *The children brought packages to be sold from the grab bag at the school carnival.* **2.** A group of many different things from which to choose; a variety. ♦ *The TV program was a grab bag for young and old alike.*

grab off *v., informal* To take quickly; take or grab before anybody else can; choose for yourself. ♦ *The people who got to the show first grabbed off the best seats.* ♦ *The women hurried to the store to grab off the things on sale.* ♦ *The prettiest girls at the dance were grabbed off for partners first.* Compare SNAP UP.

grabs See UP FOR GRABS.

grace See FALL FROM GRACE, IN ONE'S BAD GRACES, IN ONE'S GOOD GRACES, WITH BAD GRACE, WITH GOOD GRACE.

grace period *or* **period of grace** *n.* The time or extra time allowed in which to do something. ♦ *Most insurance companies have a grace period of one month for payments.* ♦ *The teacher gave the class a week's period of grace to finish workbooks.*

grade See MAKE THE GRADE.

grain See AGAINST THE GRAIN, TAKE WITH A GRAIN OF SALT.

grand slam *n.* A home run hit when there are three men on the bases. ♦ *Tony's grand slam won the game for the Yankees, 4–0.*

grandstand *v., slang, informal* To show off, to perform histrionics needlessly. ♦ *Stop grandstanding and get down to honest work!*

grandstander *n., slang, informal* A showoff, a person who likes to engage in histrionics. ♦ *Many people think that Evel Knievel is a grandstander.*

granted See TAKE FOR GRANTED.

grasp at straws *or* **clutch at straws** *v. phr.* To depend on something that is useless or unable to help in a time of trouble or danger; try something with little hope of succeeding. ♦ *To depend on your memory without studying for a test is to grasp at straws.* ♦ *The robber clutched at straws to make excuses. He said he wasn't in the country when the robbery happened.*

grass See LET GRASS GROW UNDER ONE'S FEET, SNAKE IN THE GRASS.

grasshopper See KNEE-HIGH TO A GRASSHOPPER

grass is always greener on the other side of the fence *or* **grass is always greener on the other side of the hill** We are often not satisfied and want to be somewhere else; a place that is far away or different seems better than where we are. ♦ *John is always changing his job because the grass always looks greener to him on the other side of the fence.*

grave See ONE FOOT IN THE GRAVE, TURN IN ONE'S GRAVE *or* TURN OVER IN ONE'S GRAVE.

graveyard shift *n. phr.* The work period lasting from sundown to sunup, when one has to work in the dark or by artificial light. ♦ *"Why are you always so sleepy in class?" Professor Brown asked Sam. "Because I have to work the graveyard shift beside going to school," Sam answered.*

gravy See PAN GRAVY.

gravy train *n., slang, informal* The kind of job that brings in a much higher income than the services rendered would warrant. ♦ *Jack's job at the Athletic Club as Social Director is a regular gravy train.*

gray See GET GRAY HAIR *or* GET GRAY, GIVE GRAY HAIR.

grease-ball *n., slang, derogatory* (avoid) An immigrant from a southern country, such as Mexico, Italy, or Spain; a person with oily looking black hair. ♦ *Mr. White is a racist; he calls Mr. Lopez from Tijuana a grease-ball because he has dark hair.*

grease monkey *n., slang* **1.** A person who greases or works on machinery; a mechanic or worker in a garage or gasoline station. ♦ *Hey, grease monkey, fill up my gas tank!* ♦ *The grease monkey was all dirty when he came out from under the car.* **2.** Airplane mechanic. ♦ *Jack was a grease monkey in the Air Force.*

grease one's palm *or* **grease the palm** *slang* **1.** To pay a person for something done or given, especially dishonestly; bribe. ♦ *Some politicians will help you if you grease their palms.* **2.** To give a tip; pay for a special favor or extra help. ♦ *We had to grease the palm of the waiter to get a table in the crowded restaurant.*

grease the wheels *v. phr., informal* To do something or act to make something go smoothly or happen in the way that is wanted. ♦ *Mr. Davis asked a friend to grease the wheels so he could borrow money from the bank.* ♦ *William's father tried to grease the wheels for him to get a new job.*

greasy spoon *n., informal* Any small, inexpensive restaurant patronized by workers or people in a hurry; a place not noted for its excellence of cuisine or its decor. ♦ *I won't have time to eat lunch at the club today; I'll just grab a sandwich at the local greasy spoon.*

great See THINK A GREAT DEAL OF.

great deal See GOOD DEAL.

great Godfrey *or* **great guns** *or* **great Scott** *interj., informal* A saying usually used to show surprise or anger. ♦ *Great Godfrey! Uncle Willie is sitting on top of the flagpole!* ♦ *Great guns! The lion is out of his cage.* ♦ *Great Scott! Who stole my watch?*

great guns *adv. phr., informal* **1.** Very fast or very hard.—Usually used in the phrases *blow great guns, go great guns.* ♦ *The wind was blowing great guns,* and big waves beat the shore. ♦ *The men were going great guns to finish the job.* Compare FAST AND FURIOUS. **2.** Very well; successfully. ♦ *Smith's new store opened last week and it's going great guns.*

great many See GOOD MANY.

great oaks from little acorns grow As great oak trees grow from tiny acorns, so many great people or things grow from a small and unimportant beginning, so be patient.—A proverb. ♦ *Many great men were once poor, unimportant boys. Great oaks from little acorns grow.*

Great Scott See GREAT GODFREY.

green See GRASS IS ALWAYS GREENER ON THE OTHER SIDE OF THE FENCE *or* GRASS IS ALWAYS GREENER ON THE OTHER SIDE OF THE HILL.

green around the gills *or* **pale around the gills** *adj. phr., slang* Pale-faced from fear or sickness; sickly; nauseated. ♦ *Bill's father took him for a ride in his boat while the waves were rough, and when he came back he was green around the gills.* ♦ *The car almost hit Mary crossing the street, and she was pale around the gills because it came so close.*—Also used with other prepositions besides *around*, as *about, at, under,* and with other colors, as *blue, pink, yellow, white.*

green-eyed monster *n. phr.* Jealousy; envy. ♦ *When John's brother got the new bicycle, the green-eyed monster made John fight with him.*

green power *n., slang, informal* The social prestige or power money can buy one. ♦ *In American political elections the candidates that win are usually the ones who have green power backing them.*

green thumb *n., informal* A talent for gardening; ability to make things grow.—Considered trite by many. ♦ *Mr. Wilson's neighbors say his flowers grow because he has a green thumb.*

green with envy *adj. phr.* Very jealous; full of envy. ♦ *Alice's girlfriends were green with envy when they saw her new dress.* ♦ *The other boys were green with envy when Joe bought a second-hand car.* Compare GREEN-EYED MONSTER.

grief See COME TO GRIEF, GOOD GRIEF, GOOD NIGHT 2 *or* GOOD GRIEF.

grin and bear it *v. phr., informal* To be as cheerful as possible in pain or trouble; do something without complaining. ♦ *The doctor told Mrs. Howard that she had to stop eating sweets if she wanted to lose weight, and she tried to grin and bear it.* ♦ *If you must have a tooth drilled, all you can do is grin and bear it.* Compare MAKE THE BEST OF, PUT UP WITH.

grind See AX TO GRIND.

grindstone See KEEP ONE'S NOSE TO THE GRINDSTONE.

grind to a halt *v. phr., informal* To slow down and stop like a machine does when turned off. ♦ *The old car ground to a halt in front of the house.* ♦ *The Cardinals' offense ground to a halt before the stubborn Steeler defense.*

grip See COME TO GRIPS WITH, LOSE ONE'S GRIP.

groove See IN THE GROOVE.

gross out *v., slang* To commit a vulgar act; to repel someone by saying a disgusting or vulgar thing. ♦ *You are going to gross out people if you continue talking like that.*

gross-out session *n., slang, avoidable* A verbal contest between teen-agers in which the object of the game is to see who can be more disgusting or vulgar than anybody else. ♦ *When Jim got home he found his two teen-age sons engaged in a gross-out session; he bawled them out and cut their weekly allowance.*

ground See BREAK GROUND, COMMON GROUND, COVER GROUND *or* COVER THE GROUND, CUT THE GROUND FROM UNDER, EAR TO THE GROUND, FEET ON THE GROUND, GAIN GROUND, GET OFF THE GROUND, GIVE GROUND, HAPPY HUNTING GROUND, HOLD ONE'S GROUND, LOSE GROUND, MIDDLE GROUND, RUN INTO THE GROUND, STAMPING GROUND, STAND ONE'S GROUND, FROM THE GROUND UP.

ground ball *n.* A ball batted onto the ground in baseball; a grounder. ♦ *Taylor hit a ground ball to the short-stop.*

ground floor *n.* **1.** First floor of a house or building. ♦ *Mrs. Turner has an apartment on the ground floor.* **2.** *informal* The first or best chance, especially in a business. ♦ *That man got rich because he got in on the ground floor of the television business.*

ground rule *n.* **1.** A rule in sports that is made especially for the grounds or place where a game is played.—Usually used in the plural. ♦ *There was such a big crowd at the baseball game, that the ground rules of the field were changed in case a ball went into the crowd.* **2.** A rule, usually not written, of what to do or how to act in case certain things happen.—Usually used in the plural. ♦ *When you go to a new school, you don't know the ground rules of how you are supposed to behave.*

grow See GREAT OAKS FROM LITTLE ACORNS GROW, LET GRASS GROW UNDER ONE'S FEET.

growing pains *n.* **1.** Pains in children's legs supposed to be caused by changes in their bodies and feelings as they grow. ♦ *The little girl's legs hurt, and her mother told her she had growing pains.* **2.** *informal* Troubles when something new is beginning or growing. ♦ *The factory has growing pains.*

grow on *or* **grow upon** *v.* **1.** To become stronger in; increase as a habit of. ♦ *The habit of eating before going to bed grew upon John.* **2.** To become more interesting to or liked by. ♦ *The more Jack saw Mary, the more she grew on him.* ♦ *Football grew on Billy as he grew older.*

grow out of *v. phr.* **1.** To outgrow; become too mature for. ♦ *As a child he had a habit of scratching his chin all the time, but he grew out of it.* **2.** To result from; arise. ♦ *Tom's illness grew out of his tendency to overwork and neglect his health.*

grow up *v.* To increase in size or height; become taller or older; reach full height. **1.** ♦ *Johnny is growing up; his shoes are too small for him.* ♦ *I grew up on a farm.* ♦ *The city has grown up since I was young.* **2.** To become adult in mind or judgment; become old enough to think or decide in important

matters. ♦ *Tom wants to be a coach when he grows up.* ♦ *Grow up, you're not a baby any more!*

grudge See NURSE A GRUDGE.

guard See COLOR GUARD, OFF GUARD, ON GUARD.

guest See BE MY GUEST.

gum up *v., slang* To cause not to work or ruin; spoil; make something go wrong.—Often used in the phrase *gum up the works.* ♦ *Jimmy has gummed up the typewriter.* Syn. THROW A MONKEY WRENCH.

gun See BIG CHEESE *or* BIG GUN, GIVE IT THE GUN *or* GIVE HER THE GUN, GREAT GODFREY *or* GREAT GUNS, JUMP THE GUN, SON OF A GUN, STICK TO ONE'S GUNS *or* STAND BY ONE'S GUNS, TILL THE LAST GUN IS FIRED *or* UNTIL THE LAST GUN IS FIRED.

gun for *v., informal* **1.** To hunt for with a gun; look hard for a chance to harm or defeat. ♦ *The cowboy is gunning for the man who stole his horse.* ♦ *Bob is gunning for me because I got a higher mark than he did.* **2.** To try very hard to get. ♦ *The man is gunning for first prize in the golf tournament.*

gung-ho *adj., colloquial* Enthusiastic, full of eagerness in an uncritical or unsophisticated manner. ♦ *Suzie is all gung-ho on equal rights for women, but fails to see the consequences.*

gut feeling *n. phr.* An instinctive reaction. ♦ *I have a gut feeling that they will never get married in spite of all they say.*

gut reaction *n. phr.* A mental or physical response that springs from one's depths. ♦ *My gut reaction was to get out of here as fast as possible.*

gut talk *n. phr.* Sincere, honest talk. ♦ *We admire people who speak gut talk and tell exactly what they think and feel.*

guts See HATE ONE'S GUTS, HAVE THE GUTS TO DO SOMETHING.

guy See REGULAR GUY, WISE GUY.

hackle See RAISE HACKLES *or* RAISE ONE'S HACKLES.

had as soon *or* **had as lief** See AS SOON.

had better *or* **had best** *informal* Should; must. ◆ *I had better leave now, or I'll be late.* ◆ *If you want to stay out of trouble, you had best not make any mistakes.* ◆ *Jim decided he had better do his homework instead of playing ball.*

had rather *or* **had sooner** *v.* To choose to (do one thing instead of another thing); like better to; would prefer to.—Used with an infinitive without *to.* ◆ *My aunt invited me to the movies, but I said I had rather go on a picnic with the girls.* ◆ *I had sooner live in the city than on a farm.*

hail See WITHIN CALL *or* WITHIN HAIL.

hail-fellow-well-met[1] *adj. phr.* Talking easily and in a friendly way to everyone you meet. ◆ *John won the election as class president because he was hail-fellow-well-met.*

hail-fellow-well-met[2] *n. phr.* A good friend and companion; buddy; pal. ◆ *John just moved to town but he and the boys in the neighborhood are already hail-fellows-well-met.*

hail from *v., informal* To have your home in; come from; be from; *especially,* to have been born and raised in. ◆ *Mrs. Gardner hails from Mississippi.* ◆ *Mr. Brown and Mr. White are old friends because they both hail from the same town.*

hair See CURL ONE'S HAIR, GET GRAY HAIR *or* GET GRAY, GIVE GRAY HAIR, HANG BY A THREAD *or* HANG BY A HAIR, HIDE OR HAIR *or* HIDE NOR HAIR, IN ONE'S HAIR, LET ONE'S HAIR DOWN, OUT OF ONE'S HAIR, SPLIT HAIRS, TEAR ONE'S HAIR.

haircut place *n., slang, citizen's band radio jargon* Bridge or overpass with tight clearance. ◆ *Are we going to make it in that haircut place?*

hairdo *n.* Style or manner of arranging, combing, or wearing one's hair. ◆ *"How do you like my new hairdo?" Jane asked, as she left the beauty parlor.*

hair stand on end *informal* The hair of your head rises stiffly upwards as a sign or result of great fright or horror. ◆ *When he heard the strange cry, his hair stood on end.* ◆ *The sight of the dead man made his hair stand on end.* Compare BLOOD RUN COLD, HEART IN ONE'S MOUTH, HEART STAND STILL, JUMP OUT OF ONE'S SKIN, SPINE-CHILLING.

hale and hearty *adj. phr.* In very good health; well and strong. ◆ *Grandfather will be 80 years old tomorrow, but he is hale and hearty.* ◆ *That little boy looks hale and hearty, as if he is never sick.*

half See GO HALVES, GO OFF HALF-COCKED *also* GO OFF AT HALF COCK, IN HALF, SIX OF ONE AND HALF-A-DOZEN OF THE OTHER, TIME AND A HALF, TOO—BY HALF.

half a chance *or* **a half chance** *n.* An opportunity; a reasonable chance. ◆ *Just give yourself half a chance and you will quickly get used to your new job.*

half a loaf is better than none *or* **half a loaf is better than no bread** Part of what we want or need is better than nothing.—A proverb. ◆ *Albert wanted two dollars for shoveling snow from the sidewalk but the lady would only give him a dollar. And he said that half a loaf is better than none.* Compare BETTER LATE THAN NEVER.

half a mind *also* **half a notion** *n. phr., informal* A wish or plan that you have not yet decided to act on; a thought of possibly doing something.—Used after *have* or *with* and before *to* and an infinitive. ◆ *I have half a mind to stop studying and walk over to the brook.* ◆ *Jerry went home with half a mind to telephone Betty.*

half-and-half[1] *adj.* As much one thing as the other. ◆ *We asked the coach if more boys than girls were interested in debating, and he said it was about half-and-half.* ◆ *The show last night was neither very good nor very poor—just half-and-half.* Compare FIFTY-FIFTY.

half-and-half[2] *n.* A mixture of milk and cream in equal parts, used with cereal or coffee. ◆ *John uses half-and-half with his cereal, but his wife, who is dieting, uses milk.*

half an eye *n. phr.* A slight glance; a

quick look. ♦*The substitute teacher could see with half an eye that she was going to have trouble with the class.* ♦*While Mary was cooking she kept half an eye on the baby to see that he didn't get into mischief.*

half bad See NOT BAD.

half-baked *adj., informal* Not thought out or studied thoroughly; not worth considering or accepting. ♦*We wish Tom would not take our time at meetings to offer his half-baked ideas.* ♦*We cannot afford to put the government in the hands of people with half-baked plans.*

half-hearted *adj.* Lacking enthusiasm or interest. ♦*Phil made several half-hearted attempts to learn word processing, but we could see that he didn't really like it.*

half-holiday *n.* A day on which you get out of school or work in the afternoon. ♦*The principal said that Tuesday would be a half-holiday.*

half the battle *n. phr.* A large part of the work. ♦*When you write an essay for class, making the outline is half the battle.* ♦*To see your faults and decide to change is half the battle of self-improvement.*

half-time *n.* A rest period in the middle of certain games. ♦*I saw Henry at the football game and I went over and talked to him at half-time.* ♦*The pep squad put on a drill at half-time when we played basketball with our old rivals.*

halfway See GO HALFWAY *or* MEET ONE HALF-WAY *or* GO HALFWAY TO MEET ONE.

halt See CALL A HALT, GRIND TO A HALT.

ham actor *n. phr., slang* An untalented actor; someone who tries so hard to act that his performance becomes foolishly exaggerated. ♦*Fred is a ham actor who, instead of memorizing his lines, keeps moving around in a ridiculous way.*

ham-handed *adj., slang* **1.** Having very large hands. ♦*Pete is a big, ham-handed man who used to be a football player.* **2.** See HEAVY-HANDED.

ham it up *v. phr., slang* To do more than look natural in acting a part; pretend too much; exaggerate. ♦*When Tom told the teacher he was too sick to do* homework, he really hammed it up. ♦*The old-fashioned movies are funny to us because the players hammed it up.* Compare LAY IT ON.

hammer See GO AT IT HAMMER AND TONGS, UNDER THE HAMMER.

hammer and tongs *adv. phr.* Violently. ♦*Mr. and Mrs. Smith have been at it all day, hammer and tongs.*

hammer at *or* **hammer away at** *v.* **1.** To work steadily at; keep at. ♦*That lesson is not easy, but hammer away at it and you will get it right.* **2.** To talk about again and again; emphasize. ♦*The speaker hammered at his opponent's ideas.*

hammer out *v.* **1.** To write or produce by hard work. ♦*The President sat at his desk till midnight hammering out his speech for the next day.* **2.** To remove, change, or work out by discussion and debate; debate and agree on (something). ♦*Mrs. Brown and Mrs. Green have hammered out their difference of opinion.* ♦*The club members have hammered out an agreement between the two groups.* Compare IRON OUT.

Hancock See JOHN HANCOCK *or* JOHN HENRY.

hand See AT HAND, BIRD IN THE HAND IS WORTH TWO IN THE BUSH, BITE THE HAND THAT FEEDS ONE, CLEAN HANDS, DIRTY ONE'S HANDS, EAT OUT OF ONE'S HAND, FORCE ONE'S HAND, FREE HAND, FROM HAND TO HAND, GLAD HAND, HAM-HANDED, HANG HEAVY *or* HANG HEAVY ON ONE'S HANDS, HAT IN HAND, HAVE A HAND IN, HAVE ONE'S HANDS FULL, HEAVY-HANDED, IN HAND, JOIN FORCES *or* JOIN HANDS, KEEP ONE'S HAND IN, LAY HANDS ON, LAY ONE'S HANDS ON *or* GET ONE'S HAND ON *or* PUT ONE'S HAND ON, LEND A HAND *or* GIVE A HAND *or* BEAR A HAND, LET ONE'S LEFT HAND KNOW WHAT ONE'S RIGHT HAND IS DOING, LIFT A FINGER *or* LIFT A HAND *also* RAISE A HAND, LIVE FROM HAND TO MOUTH, MANY HANDS MAKE LIGHT WORK, OFF ONE'S HANDS, ON HAND, ON ONE'S HANDS, ON THE OTHER HAND, OUT OF HAND, PLAY INTO ONE'S HANDS, PUT ONE'S HAND TO *or* SET ONE'S HAND TO *or* TURN ONE'S HAND TO, PUT ONE'S HAND TO THE PLOW, ROB THE TILL *or* HAVE ONE'S HAND IN THE TILL, SECTION HAND, SIT

ON ONE'S HANDS, TAKE ONE'S LIFE IN ONE'S HANDS, TAKE THE LAW INTO ONE'S OWN HANDS, THROW UP ONE'S HANDS, THROW UP ONE'S HANDS IN HORROR, TIE ONE'S HANDS, TRY ONE'S HAND, UPPER HAND *or* WHIP HAND, WASH ONE'S HANDS OF.

hand and foot *adv. phr.* **1.** So that the hands and feet cannot be used.—Used with *bind* or a synonym. ♦ *The robbers bound him hand and foot and left him on the floor.* **2.** So that no free action is possible.—Used with *bind* or a synonym. ♦ *If Mr. Jones signs that paper, he will be bound hand and foot.* **3.** See WAIT ON HAND AND FOOT.

hand and glove See HAND IN GLOVE.

hand down *v.* To arrange to give or leave after death. ♦ *Joe will have his father's gold watch because it is handed down in the family.* ♦ *In old times, property was usually handed down to the oldest son at his father's death.* Compare PASS ON.

hand in See TURN IN 1.

hand in glove *or* **hand and glove** *adj. or adv. phr.* Very close or friendly; working together; in very close agreement or cooperation, especially for bad purposes. ♦ *The Navy and the Coast Guard work hand and glove, especially in war time.* ♦ *Judges and others in high office sometimes are hand in glove with gangsters to cheat and steal.*

hand in hand *adv. phr.* **1.** Holding hands. ♦ *Bob and Mary walked along hand in hand in the park.* Compare ARM IN ARM. **2.** Accompanying each other; together; closely connected.— Used with *go.* ♦ *Ignorance and poverty often go hand in hand.* ♦ *Selfishness and unhappiness often go hand in hand.*

hand it to *v. phr., informal* To admit the excellence of; give credit or praise to. ♦ *You have to hand it to Jim; he is very careful and hard-working in all he does.* ♦ *The teacher said, "I hand it to Jane for the way she managed the Music Club."* Syn. TAKE OFF ONE'S HAT TO.

handle See FLY OFF THE HANDLE.

handle to one's name *n. phr., slang* A special title used before your name. ♦ *Jim's father has a handle to his name. He is Major Watson.* ♦ *Bob came back*

from the University with a handle to his name and was called Dr. Jones.

handle with gloves *or* **handle with kid gloves** *v. phr., informal* **1.** To treat very gently and carefully. ♦ *An atomic bomb is handled with kid gloves.* **2.** To treat with great tact and diplomacy. ♦ *Aunt Jane is so irritable that we have to treat her with kid gloves.*

hand-me-down *n., informal* Something given away after another person has no more use for it; especially, used clothing. ♦ *Alice had four older sisters, so all her clothes were hand-me-downs.*

hand off *v.* To hand the football to another back. ♦ *The quarterback faked to the fullback and handed off to the halfback.*

hand on *v.* To pass along to the next person who should have it. ♦ *Everyone in class should read this, so when you have finished, please hand it on.* ♦ *In the early days, news was handed on from one person to another.*

handout *n.* **1.** A free gift of food, clothes, etc. ♦ *The homeless people were standing in a long line for various handouts.* **2.** A typed and photocopied sheet or sheets of paper outlining the main points made by a speaker. ♦ *Please look at page three of the handout.*

hand out *v., informal* To give (things of the same kind) to several people. ♦ *The teacher handed out the examination papers.* ♦ *At the Christmas party Santa Claus handed out the presents under the tree.* ♦ *Handing out free advice to all your friends will not make them like you.* Compare GIVE OUT 3.

hand over *v.* To give control or possession of; give (something) to another person. ♦ *When the teacher saw Johnny reading a comic book in study period, she made him hand over the book.* ♦ *When Mr. Jones gets old, he will hand over his business to his son.* Syn. FORK OVER, GIVE UP 1, TURN OVER 3.

hand over fist *adv. phr., informal* Fast and in large amounts. ♦ *Fred may get a pony for Christmas because his father is making money hand over fist.* ♦ *Business is so bad that the store on the corner is losing money hand over fist.*

hand over hand *adv. phr.* By taking hold with one hand over the other alternately. ♦ *The only way to climb a rope is hand over hand.*

hand-pick *v., informal* To choose very carefully. ♦ *This debating team should win because its members are all hand-picked.* ♦ *The political bosses hand-picked a man for mayor who would agree with them.*

hands-down *adj., informal* **1.** Easy. ♦ *The Rangers won a hands-down victory in the tournament.* **2.** Unopposed; first; clear. ♦ *Johnny was the hands-down favorite for president of the class.*

hands down *adv., informal* **1.** Without working hard; easily. ♦ *The Rangers won the game hands down.* **2.** Without question or doubt; without any opposition; plainly. ♦ *Johnny was hands down the best player on the team.*

hands off *informal* Keep your hands off or do not interfere; leave that alone.— Used as a command. ♦ *I was going to touch the machine, but the man cried, "Hands off!" and I let it alone.*

hands-off *adj., informal* Leaving alone, not interfering; inactive. ♦ *The United States told the European governments to follow a hands-off policy toward Latin America.* ♦ *I did not approve of his actions, but I have a hands-off rule in personal matters, so I said nothing.*

handsome is as handsome does *informal* A person must act well and generously so that he will be truly worth respecting.—A proverb. ♦ *Everyone thinks that Bob is a very handsome boy, but he is very mean too. Handsome is as handsome does.* Compare FINE FEATHERS DO NOT MAKE FINE BIRDS.

hands up *informal* Hold up your hands! Put your hands up high and keep them there!— Used as a command. ♦ *The sheriff pointed his gun at the outlaws and called out, "Hands up!"* Syn. REACH FOR THE SKY.

hand something to someone on a silver platter *v. phr.* To give a person a reward that has not been earned. ♦ *The lazy student expected his diploma to be handed to him on a silver platter.*

hand to hand *adv. phr.* Close together, near enough to hit each other. ♦ *The two soldiers fought hand to hand until one fell badly wounded.* ♦ *In modern naval warfare, men seldom fight hand to hand.* Compare FACE TO FACE.

hand-to-hand *adj.* Close to each other; near enough to hit each other. ♦ *The result of the battle was decided in hand-to-hand combat.* ♦ *When the police tried to break up the riot, there was hand-to-hand fighting with fists, stones, and clubs.* Compare FACE-TO-FACE.

hand-to-mouth *adj.* Not providing for the future; living from day to day; not saving for later. ♦ *Many native tribes lead a hand-to-mouth existence, content to have food for one day at a time.* ♦ *John is not a saving boy; he spends his money without thought for the future, and lives a hand-to-mouth life.* See LIVE FROM HAND TO MOUTH.

handwriting on the wall *n. phr.* A sign that something bad will happen. ♦ *When Bill's team lost four games in a row, he saw the handwriting on the wall.* ♦ *John's employer had less and less work for him; John could read the handwriting on the wall and looked for another job.*

hang See GO HANG, GIVE A HANG *or* CARE A HANG, GIVE ONE ENOUGH ROPE, AND HE WILL HANG HIMSELF, LEAVE HANGING *or* LEAVE HANGING IN THE AIR.

hang around *v., informal* **1.** To pass time or stay near without any real purpose or aim; loaf near or in. ♦ *The principal warned the students not to hang around the corner drugstore after school.* Compare HANG OUT 1. **2.** To spend time or associate. ♦ *Jim hangs around with some boys who live in his neighborhood.*

hang back *or* **hang off** *or* **hang behind 1.** To stay some distance behind or away, be unwilling to move forward. ♦ *Mary offered the little girl candy, but she was shy and hung back.* **2.** To hesitate or be unwilling to do something. ♦ *Lou wanted Fred to join the club, but Fred hung off.*

hang behind See HANG BACK 1.

hang by a hair See HANG BY A THREAD.

hang by a thread *or* **hang by a hair** *v. phr.* To depend on a very small thing; be in doubt. ♦ *For three days Tom was so sick that his life hung by a thread.* ♦ *As Joe got ready to kick a field goal, the result of the game hung by a hair.* Compare HANG IN THE BALANCE.

hanger See CREPE HANGER.

hang fire *v. phr.* **1.** To fail or be slow in shooting or firing. ♦ *Smith pulled the trigger, but the gun hung fire and the deer escaped.* **2.** To be slow in beginning; to be delayed; to wait. ♦ *The boys' plans for organizing a scout troop hung fire because they could not find a man to be scoutmaster.*

hang heavy *or* **hang heavy on one's hands** *v. phr.* To pass slowly or uninterestingly; be boring with little to do. ♦ *The vacation time hung heavy on Dick's hands because all his friends were away at camp.* Compare ON ONE'S HANDS.

hang in effigy *or* **burn in effigy** *v. phr.* To hang or burn a figure, usually a stuffed dummy, representing a person who is disliked or scorned. ♦ *When the high school team lost the championship game, the coach was hung in effigy by the townspeople.* ♦ *During World War II, Hitler was sometimes burned in effigy in the United States.*

hang in the balance *v. phr.* To have two equally possible results; to be in doubt; be uncertain. ♦ *Until Jim scored the winning touchdown, the outcome of the game hung in the balance.* ♦ *She was very sick and her life hung in the balance for several days.* Compare HANG BY A THREAD.

hang in (there) *v. phr., slang, informal* To persevere; not to give up; to stick to a project and not lose faith or courage. ♦ *Hang in there old buddy; the worst is yet to come.*

hang it *interj. informal* An exclamation used to express annoyance or disappointment. ♦ *Oh, hang it! I forgot to bring the book I wanted to show you.* ♦ *Hang it all, why don't you watch where you're going?*

hang off See HANG BACK.

hang on *v.* **1.** To hold on to something, usually tightly. ♦ *Jack almost fell off the cliff, but managed to hang on until help came.* Syn. HOLD ON 1. **2a.** To continue doing something; persist. ♦ *The grocer was losing money every day, but he hung on, hoping that business would improve.* Compare HOLD OUT, STICK OUT **2b.** To hold a lead in a race or other contest while one's opponents try to rally. ♦ *The favorite horse opened an early lead and hung on to win as two* other horses almost passed him in the final stretch. ♦ *Bunning, staked to a 6–0 lead in the first inning, hung on to beat the Dodgers 6–4.* **3.** To continue to give trouble or cause suffering. ♦ *Lou's cold hung on from January to April.* **4.** To continue listening on the telephone. ♦ *Jerry, asked John, who had called him on the phone, to hang on while he ran for a pencil and a sheet of paper.* Compare HOLD ON 3.

hang one on *v. phr., slang* **1.** To give a heavy blow to; hit hard. ♦ *The champion hung one on his challenger in the second round and knocked him out of the ring.* **2.** To get very drunk. *After Smith lost his job, he went to a bar and hung one on.*

hang one's head *v. phr.* To bend your head forward in shame. ♦ *Johnny hung his head when the teacher asked him if he broke the window.* Compare HIDE ONE'S HEAD.

hang on the words of *also* **hang on the lips of** *v. phr.* To listen very attentively to. ♦ *Ann hangs on every word of her history teacher and takes very careful notes.* ♦ *As he went on with his speech, his auditors, deeply interested, hung on his lips.*

hang on to *v.* To hold tightly; keep firmly. ♦ *The child hung on to its mother's apron, and would not let go.* ♦ *John did not like his job, but decided to hang on to it until he found a better one.*

hang on to one's mother's apron strings See TIED TO ONE'S MOTHER'S APRON STRINGS.

hang on to your hat *or* **hold on to your hat** *or* **hold your hat** *v. phr., informal* **1.** Watch out; be prepared.—Used as a command, usually to warn of an unexpected action. ♦ *"Hold on to your hat," said Jim as he stepped on the gas and the car shot forward.* **2.** Get ready for a surprise.—Used as a command, usually to warn of unexpected news. ♦ *"Hold on to your hat," said Mary. "Jim asked me to marry him."*

hang out *v.* **1.** *slang* To spend your time idly or lounging about. ♦ *The teacher complained that Joe was hanging out in poolrooms instead of doing his homework.* Compare HANG AROUND 1. **2.** *slang* To live; reside. ♦ *Two policemen* *stopped the stranger and asked him where he hung out.* **3.** To reach out farther than the part below. ◆ *The branches of the trees hung out over the road.* ◆ *The upper floor of that house hangs out above the first.*

hang out one's shingle *v. phr., informal* To give public notice of the opening of an office, especially a doctor's or lawyer's office, by putting up a small signboard. ◆ *The young doctor hung out his shingle and soon had a large practice.*

hangover *n.* A bad feeling of nausea and/or headache the day after one has had too much to drink. ◆ *Boy, did I have a hangover after that party yesterday!*

hang over *v.* **1.** To be going to happen to; threaten. ◆ *Great trouble hangs over the little town because its only factory has closed down.* **2.** To remain to be finished or settled. ◆ *The committee took up the business that hung over from its last meeting.*

hang over one's head *v. phr.* To be a danger or threat to you.—An overused phrase. ◆ *Over Jimmy's head hung the teacher's suspicion that Jimmy had cheated in the final examination.* ◆ *Death hangs over a bullfighter's head every time he performs.*

hang round See HANG AROUND.

hang ten *v., slang* **1.** To be an outstanding performer on a surfboard or on a skateboard (referring to the user's ten toes). ◆ *I bet I am going to be able to hang ten if you let me practice on your skateboard .* **2.** To be a survivor despite great odds. ◆ *Don't worry about Jack, he can hang ten anywhere!*

hang together *v.* **1.** To stay united; help and defend one another. ◆ *The club members always hung together when one of them was in trouble.* Syn. STICK TOGETHER. Compare STAND BY, STAND UP FOR. **2.** *informal* To form a satisfactory whole; fit together. ◆ *Jack's story of why he was absent from school seems to hang together.*

hang up *v.* **1.** To place on a hook, peg, or hanger. ◆ *When the children come to school, they hang up their coats in the cloakroom.* **2a.** To place a telephone receiver back on its hook and break the connection. ◆ *Carol's mother told* her she had talked long enough on the phone and made her hang up. **2b.** To put a phone receiver back on its hook while the other person is still talking.—Used with on. ◆ *I said something that made Joe angry, and he hung up on me.* **3a.** *informal* To cause to be stuck or held so as to be immovable.—Usually used in the passive. ◆ *Ann's car was hung up in a snowdrift and she had to call a garageman to get it out.* **3b.** *informal* To stick or get held so as to be immovable. ◆ *A big passenger ship hung up on a sandbar for several hours.* **4.** *informal* To cause a wait; delay. ◆ *Rehearsals for the school play were hung up by the illness of some of the actors.* **5.** *informal* To set (a record.) ◆ *Bob hung up a school record for long distance swimming.*

hang-up *n., informal* (stress on *hang*) **1.** A delay in some process. ◆ *The mail has been late for several days; there must be some hang-up with the trucks somewhere.* **2.** A neurotic reaction to some life situation probably stemming from a traumatic shock which has gone unconscious. ◆ *Doctor Simpson believes that Suzie's frigidity is due to some hang-up about men.*

happen on *or* **happen upon** *v. literary* To meet or find accidentally or by chance. ◆ *The Girl Scouts happened on a charming little brook not far from the camp.* ◆ *At the convention I happened upon an old friend I had not seen for years.* Syn. CHANCE ON, COME ACROSS 1, 3. Compare HIT ON.

happy See STRIKE A HAPPY MEDIUM, TRIGGER HAPPY *at* QUICK ON THE TRIGGER.

happy as the day is long *adj. phr.* Cheerful and happy. ◆ *Carl is happy as the day is long because school is over for the summer.*

happy-go-lucky See FOOTLOOSE AND FANCY-FREE.

happy hour *n., informal* A time in bars or restaurants when cocktails are served at a reduced rate, usually one hour before they start serving dinner. ◆ *Happy hour is between 6 and 7 P.M. at Celestial Gardens.*

happy hunting ground *n. phr.* **1.** The place where, in American Indian belief, a person goes after death;

heaven. ♦ *The Indians believed that at death they went to the happy hunting ground.* **2.** *informal* A place or area where you can find a rich variety of what you want, and plenty of it. ♦ *The forest is a happy hunting ground for scouts who are interested in plants and flowers.* ♦ *Shell collectors find the ocean beaches happy hunting grounds.*

hard See GIVE A HARD TIME, GO HARD WITH, SCHOOL OF HARD KNOCKS.

hard-and-fast *adj.* Not to be broken or changed; fixed; strict. ♦ *The teacher said that there was a hard-and-fast rule against smoking in the school.*

hard as nails *adj. phr., informal* **1.** Not flabby or soft; physically very fit; tough and strong. ♦ *After a summer of work in the country, Jack was as hard as nails, without a pound of extra weight.* **2.** Not gentle or mild; rough; stern. ♦ *Johnny works for a boss who is as hard as nails and scolds Johnny roughly whenever he does something wrong.*

hard-boiled *adj.* Unrefined; tough; merciless. ♦ *"Because you were two minutes late," my hard-boiled boss cried, "I will deduct fifteen minutes worth from your salary!"*

hard cash See COLD CASH.

hard feeling *n.* Angry or bitter feeling; enmity.—Usually used in the plural. ♦ *Jim asked Andy to shake hands with him, just to show that there were no hard feelings.* ♦ *Bob and George once quarreled over a girl, and there are still hard feelings between them.*

hard-fisted *adj.* **1.** Able to do hard physical labor; strong. ♦ *Jack's uncle was a hard-fisted truck driver with muscles of steel.* **2.** Not gentle or easy-going; tough; stern. ♦ *The new teacher was a hard-fisted woman who would allow no nonsense.* **3.** Stingy or mean; not generous with money. ♦ *The hard-fisted banker refused to lend Mr. Jones more money for his business.*

hard going *adj. phr.* Fraught with difficulty. ♦ *Dave finds his studies of math hard going.*

hardheaded *adj.* Stubborn; shrewd; practical. ♦ *Don is a hardheaded businessman who made lots of money, even during the recession.*

hardhearted *adj.* Unsympathetic; mer-

ciless. ♦ *Jack is so hardhearted that even his own children expect nothing from him.*

hard-hitting *adj.* Working hard to get things done; strong and active; stubbornly eager. ♦ *The boys put on a hard-hitting drive to raise money for uniforms for the football team.* ♦ *He is a hard-hitting and successful football coach.*

hard line *n. phr.* Tough political policy. ♦ *Although modern economists were trying to persuade him to open up to the West, Castro has always taken the hard line approach.*

hard-liner *n.* A politician who takes the hard line. See HARD LINE.

hard luck See TOUGH LUCK.

hardly any *or* **scarcely any** Almost no or almost none; very few. ♦ *Hardly any of the students did well on the test, so the teacher explained the lesson again.* ♦ *Charles and his friends each had three cookies, and when they went out, hardly any cookies were left.*

hardly ever *or* **scarcely ever** *adv. phr.* Very rarely; almost never; seldom. ♦ *It hardly ever snows in Florida.* ♦ *Johnny hardly ever reads a book.*

hard-nosed *adj., slang* Tough or rugged; very strict; not weak or soft; stubborn, especially in a fight or contest. ♦ *Joe's father was a hard-nosed army officer who had seen service in two wars.* ♦ *Pete is a good boy; he plays hard-nosed football.* Compare HARD-BOILED.

hard nut to crack *also* **tough nut to crack** *n. phr., informal* Something difficult to understand or to do. ♦ *Tom's algebra lesson was a hard nut to crack.* ♦ *Mary found knitting a hard nut to crack.* Compare HARD ROW TO HOE.

hard of hearing *adj.* Partially deaf. ♦ *Some people who are hard of hearing wear hearing aids.*

hard-on *n. vulgar, avoidable.* An erection of the male sexual organ.

hard put *or* **hard put to it** *adj.* In a difficult position; faced with difficulty; barely able. ♦ *John was hard put to find a good excuse for his lateness in coming to school.* ♦ *The scouts found themselves hard put to it to find the way home.*

hard row to hoe *or* **tough row to hoe** *n. phr.* A hard life to live; a very hard job to do. ♦ *She has a hard row to hoe with*

six children and her husband dead.
♦ *Young people without enough education will have a tough row to hoe when they have to support themselves.* Syn. HARD SLEDDING. Compare DOWN ON ONE'S LUCK, HARD NUT TO CRACK.

hard sell *n., informal* A kind of salesmanship characterized by great vigor, aggressive persuasion, and great eagerness on the part of the person selling something; opposed to 'soft sell'. ♦ *Your hard sell turns off a lot of people; try the soft sell for a change, won't you?*

hard sledding *or* **rough sledding** *or* **tough sledding** *n., informal* Difficulty in succeeding or making progress. ♦ *Jane had hard sledding in her math course because she was poorly prepared.* ♦ *When Mr. Smith started his new business, he had tough sledding for a while but things got better.*

hard-top *n.* **1.** A car that has a metal roof; a car that is not a convertible. ♦ *Every spring Mr. Jones sells his hard-top and buys a convertible.* **2.** *or* **hardtop convertible** A car with windows that can be completely lowered with no partitions left standing, and with a top that may or may not be lowered. ♦ *Mr. Brown's new car is a hardtop convertible.*

hard up *adj., informal* Without enough money or some other needed thing. ♦ *Dick was hard up and asked Lou to lend him a dollar.* ♦ *The campers were hard up for water because their well had run dry.* Compare UP AGAINST IT.

hard way *n.* The harder or more punishing of two or more ways to solve a problem, do something, or learn something.—Used with *the.* ♦ *The mayor refused the help of the crooks and won the election the hard way by going out to meet the people.* ♦ *The challenger found out the hard way that the champion's left hand had to be avoided.*

hare See MAD AS A HATTER *or* MAD AS A MARCH HARE, RUN WITH THE HARE AND HUNT (RIDE) WITH THE HOUNDS.

harebrained *adj.* Thoughtless; foolish. ♦ *Most of the harebrained things Ed does may be attributable to his youth and lack of experience.*

hark back *v. literary* **1.** To recall or turn back to an earlier time or happening.

♦ *Judy is always harking back to the good times she had at camp.* **2.** To go back to something as a beginning or origin. ♦ *The cars of today hark back to the first automobiles made about 1900.* ♦ *The slit in the back of a man's coat harks back to the days when men rode horseback.*

harp away at *or* **on** *v.* To mention again and again. ♦ *In his campaign speeches, Jones harps on his rival's wealth and powerful friends.*

Harry See TOM, DICK, AND HARRY.

harum-scarum[1] *adv., informal* In a careless, disorderly or reckless way. ♦ *Jim does his homework harum-scarum, and that is why his schoolwork is so poor.*

harum-scarum[2] *adj., informal* Careless, wild, or disorderly in one's acts or performance; reckless. ♦ *Jack is such a harum-scarum boy that you can never depend on him to do anything right.*

hash See SETTLE ONE'S HASH, SLING HASH.

hash house *n., slang* An eating place where cheap meals are served. ♦ *Joe and his friends went to a hash house around the corner after the game.*

hash out *v., informal* To talk all about and try to agree on; discuss thoroughly. ♦ *The teacher asked Susan and Jane to sit down together and hash out their differences.* ♦ *The students hashed out the matter and decided to drop it.*

hash up *v., slang* **1.** To make a mess of; do badly. ♦ *Bob really hashed up that exam and failed the course.* **2.** To bring to life; remember and talk about. ♦ *The teacher advised Sue not to hash up old bitterness against her schoolmates.*

haste See MAKE HASTE.

hat See AT THE DROP OF A HAT, BRASS HAT, HANG ON TO YOUR HAT *or* HOLD ON TO YOUR HAT *or* HOLD YOUR HAT, HIGH-HAT, KEEP UNDER ONE'S HAT, OLD HAT, PULL OUT OF A HAT, TAKE OFF ONE'S HAT TO, TALK THROUGH ONE'S HAT, TEN-GALLON HAT, THROW ONE'S HAT IN THE RING.

hat in hand *adv. phr., informal* In a humble and respectful manner. ♦ *They went hat in hand to the old woman to ask for her secret recipe.*

hatch See COUNT ONE'S CHICKENS BEFORE THEY ARE HATCHED.

hatchet See BURY THE HATCHET.

hatchet face *n.* A long narrow face with sharp parts; also, a person with such a face. ♦*Johnny was sent to the principal's office because he called his teacher old hatchet face.* ♦*He was hatchet-faced and not at all handsome.*

hatchet job *n. phr., slang* **1.** The act of saying or writing terrible things about someone or something, usually on behalf of one's boss or organization. ♦*When Phil makes speeches against the competition exaggerating their weaknesses, he is doing the hatchet job on behalf of our president.* **2.** A ruthless, wholesale job of editing a script whereby entire paragraphs or pages are omitted. ♦*Don, my editor, did a hatchet job on my new novel.*

hatchet man *n., colloquial* **1.** A politician or newspaper columnist whose job is to write and say unfavorable things about the opposition. ♦*Bill Lerner is the hatchet man for the Mayor's Party; he smears all the other candidates regularly.* **2.** An executive officer in a firm whose job it is to fire superfluous personnel, cut back on the budget, etc., in short, to do the necessary but unpleasant things. ♦*The firm hired Cranhart to be hatchet man; his title is that of Executive Vice President.*

hate one's guts *v. phr., slang* To feel a very strong dislike for someone. ♦*Dick said that he hated Fred's guts because Fred had been very mean to him.*

hats off to *or* **one's hat is off to** *truncated phr. informal* Used to recognize and praise a job well-done. ♦*Hats off to anyone who runs the twenty-six mile race.* ♦*My hat is off to the chef who created this delicious meal.* Compare TAKE OFF ONE'S HAT TO.

hatter See MAD AS A HATTER.

haul See LONG HAUL.

haul down *v., informal* **1.** To catch (as a ball) usually after a long run. ♦*Willie hauled down a long fly to center field for the third out.* ♦*The star halfback hauled down the pass for a touchdown.* **2.** To tackle in football. ♦*Ted was hauled down from behind when he tried to run with the ball.*

haul down one's colors *or* **strike one's colors** *v. phr* **1.** To pull down a flag, showing you are beaten and want to stop fighting. ♦*After a long battle, the pirate captain hauled down his colors.* **2.** To admit you are beaten; say you want to quit. ♦*After losing two sets of tennis, Tom hauled down his color.*

haul in *or* **haul up** *or* **pull in** *v. slang* To bring before someone in charge for punishment or questioning; arrest. ♦*John was hauled in to court for speeding.* ♦*The tramp was hauled up for sleeping on the sidewalk.* Compare CALL ON THE CARPET.

haul in one's horns See PULL IN ONE'S HORNS.

haul off *v.* To move suddenly.—Used with *and* usually before a verb like *hit* or *kick.* ♦*Ed hauled off and hit the other boy in the nose.* ♦*Lee hauled off and threw a touchdown pass.*

haul over the coals *or* **rake over the coals** *v. phr.* To criticize sharply; rebuke; scold. ♦*The sergeant raked the soldier over the coals for being late for roll call.* Syn. DRESS DOWN.

have See CAT HAS NINE LIVES, ONE'S CAKE AND HAVE IT TOO, EVERY CLOUD HAS A SILVER LINING, EVERY DOG HAS HIS DAY, HAVE NOTHING ON *or* HAVE ANYTHING ON, LITTLE PITCHERS HAVE BIG EARS, *or an important word after this in the sentence.*

have *or* **get** *or* **develop a crush on** *v. phr.* To be infatuated with someone. ♦*Walter has a terrible crush on his English teacher, but she is a lot older and doesn't take it seriously.*

have a ball *v. phr., slang* Enjoy yourself very much; have a wonderful time. ♦*Johnny had a ball at camp.* ♦*Mary and Tim have a ball exploring the town.* ♦*After their parents left, the children had a ball.* Syn. HAVE A TIME 2.

have a bone to pick See BONE TO PICK.

have a care *v. phr., formal* To be careful what you do. ♦*Jane, have a care what you're doing with that valuable glass.* ♦*The judge told him to have a care what he said in court.*

have a field day *v. phr.* To enjoy great success or unlimited opportunity. ♦*The visiting basketball team was so weak that our school had a field day scoring one point after another.*

have a finger in the pie See FINGER IN THE PIE.

have a fit *or* **have fits** *or* **throw a fit** *v. phr.* **1.** To have a sudden illness with stiffness or jerking of the body. ♦*Our dog had a fit yesterday.* **2.** *informal* To become angry or upset. ♦*Father will throw a fit when he sees the dent in the car.* ♦*Howard will have a fit when he learns that he lost the election.* ♦*When John decided to drop out of college, his parents had fits.*

have a go at *v. phr., informal* To try, especially after others have tried. ♦*Bob asked Dick to let him have a go at shooting at the target with Dick's rifle.* ♦*She had a go at archery, but did not do very well.*

have a good head on one's shoulders *v. phr.* To be smart; intelligent; well educated. ♦*Rob is not the handsomest guy in the world but the girls appreciate him because he has a good head on his shoulders.*

have a (good) head for *v. phr.* To have a special talent in a certain area. ♦*Joan has quite a good head for business administration.*

have a (good) mind to *v. phr.* To consider doing; intend to with a high degree of probability. ♦*I have a good mind to tell my boss that he doesn't know how to run our enterprise.*

have a hand in *v. phr.* To have a part in or influence over; to be partly responsible for. ♦*Sue's schoolmates respect her and she has a hand in every important decision made by the Student Council.* ♦*Ben had a hand in getting ready the Senior play.* Compare FINGER IN THE PIE.

have a heart *v. phr., informal* To stop being mean; be kind, generous, or sympathetic. ♦*Have a heart, Bob, and lend me two dollars.* ♦*Have a heart, Mary, and help me with this lesson.* ♦*He didn't know if the teacher would have a heart and pass him.*

have a heart-to-heart talk *v. phr.* To confide in someone with great intimacy. ♦*Jill and her mother had a heart-to-heart talk before she decided to move in with Andrew.*

have all one's buttons *or* **have all one's marbles** *v. phr., slang* To have all your understanding; be reasonable.—Usually used in the negative or conditionally. ♦*Mike acts sometimes as if he* didn't have all his buttons. ♦*He would not go to town barefooted if he had all his marbles.*

have a mind of one's own *v. phr.* To be independent in one's thinking and judgment. ♦*Tom has always had a mind of his own so there is no use trying to convince him how to vote.*

have an affair with *v. phr.* To have a sexual relationship with someone, either before marriage or outside of one's marriage. ♦*Tom and Jane had a long and complex affair but they never got married.*

have an ear for *v. phr.* To have a keen perception; have a taste or a talent for; be sensitive to something. ♦*I have no ear whatsoever for foreign languages or music.*

have an ear to the ground See EAR TO THE GROUND.

have an edge on *v. phr., informal* **1.** To have an advantage over someone or something else in the course of an evaluative comparison. ♦*I can't beat you at tennis, but I have an edge on you in ping-pong.* **2.** To be mildly intoxicated; to have had a few drinks. ♦*Joe sure had an edge on when I saw him last night.* Compare EDGE ON.

have an eye for *v. phr.* To be able to judge correctly of; have good taste in. ♦*She has an eye for color and style in clothes.* ♦*He has an eye for good English usage.*

have an eye on *or* **have one's eye on** *v. phr., informal* **1.** To look at or think about (something wanted); have a wish for; have as an aim. ♦*I bought ice cream, but Jimmy had his eye on some candy.* ♦*John has his eye on a scholarship so he can go to college.* Compare IN MIND. **2.** See KEEP AN EYE ON 1.

have an eye out See EYE OUT.

have an eye to See EYE TO.

have an itch for *or* **to do** See BE ITCHING TO.

have a nodding acquaintance with See NODDING ACQUAINTANCE.

have a price on one's head See PRICE ON ONE'S HEAD.

have a rough idea about See ROUGH IDEA.

have a say in *or* **a voice in** *v. phr.* To have the right to express one's opinion or cast a vote in a pending matter.

♦ *Our boss is friendly and democratic; he always encourages us to have a say in what we will do next.*

have a screw loose   *v. phr., slang*   To act in a strange way; to be foolish. ♦ *Now I know he has a screw loose—he stole a police car this time.* ♦ *He was a smart man but had a screw loose and people thought him odd.*

have a snowball's chance in hell   *v. phr.* To be condemned to failure; enjoy a zero chance of success. ♦ *Pessimists used to think that we had a snowball's chance in hell to put a man on the moon; yet we did it in July, 1969.*

have a soft spot in one's heart for   *v. phr.* To be sympathetically inclined towards; entertain a predilection for. ♦ *Ron always had a soft spot in his heart for intellectual women wearing miniskirts.*

have a sweet tooth   *v. phr.* To be excessively fond of dessert items, such as ice cream, pies, etc. ♦ *Jill has a sweet tooth; she always orders apple pie after a meal in a restaurant.*

have a time   *v. phr., informal*   **1.** To have trouble; have a hard time. ♦ *Poor Susan had a time trying to get the children to go to bed.* ♦ *John had a time passing his math course.* **2.** To have a good time; to have fun.—Used with a reflexive pronoun. ♦ *Bob had himself a time going to every night club in town.* ♦ *Mary had herself a time dancing at the party.* Syn. HAVE A BALL.

have a way with   *v. phr.* To be able to lead, persuade, or influence. ♦ *Dave has such a way with the campers that they do everything he tells them to do.* ♦ *Ted will be a good veterinarian, because he has a way with animals.*

have a word with   *v. phr.*   **1.** To talk, discuss, or speak briefly with. ♦ *Robert, I need to have a word with you about tomorrow's exam.* **2.** To engage in a sincere discussion with the purpose of persuading the other person or let him or her know of one's dissatisfaction. ♦ *Our boss has been making funny decisions lately; I think we ought to have a word with him.*

have been around   *v. phr., informal* Have been to many places and done many things; know people; have experience and be able to take care of your-self. ♦ *Uncle Willie is an old sailor and has really been around.* ♦ *Betty likes to go out with Jerry, because he has been around.* ♦ *It's not easy to fool him; he's been around.* Compare GET AROUND, KNOW ONE'S WAY AROUND.

have dibs on *or* **put dibs on**   *v. phr., slang* To demand a share of something or to be in line for the use of an object usable by more than one person. ♦ *Don't throw your magazine away! I put (my) dibs on it, remember?*

have done   *v., formal*   To stop; finish. ♦ *When the teacher had done, she asked for questions from the class.* ♦ *If you have done, I will explain the matter.*

have done with   *v.* To stop doing or using something. ♦ *When you have done with that paintbrush, Barbara, I would like to use it.* ♦ *I wish you would have done with your criticisms.*

have eyes only for   *v. phr.* To see or want nothing else but; give all your attention to; be interested only in. ♦ *Of all the horses in the show, John had eyes only for the big white one.* ♦ *All the girls liked Fred, but he had eyes only for Helen.*

have fits   See HAVE A FIT.

have got to   *v. phr.*   Must; be in great need to do something; be obliged to. ♦ *I am sorry but we have got to leave, otherwise, we'll miss the last train.*

have had it   *v. phr., slang* To have experienced or suffered all you can; to have come to the end of your patience or life. ♦ *"I've had it," said Lou, "I'm resigning from the job of chairman right now."* ♦ *When the doctor examined the man who had been shot, he said, "He's had it."*

have hair   *v. phr., slang* To possess courage, fortitude, guts, sex-appeal. ♦ *I like him, he's got a lot of hair.*

have *or* **hold the whip over**   *v. phr.* To control; dominate. ♦ *Eugene has always held the whip over his younger brothers and sisters.*

have in mind   *v. phr.* To plan; intend; select. ♦ *We don't know whom our boss has in mind for the new position.*

have in one's hair   See IN ONE'S HAIR.

have in the palm of one's hand   *v. phr.* To completely control; have a project finished, all wrapped up. ♦ *Our boss felt that if he could calm his critics he* *would soon have the entire factory in the palm of his hand.*

have it *v. phr.* **1.** To hear or get news; understand. ♦*I have it on the best authority that we will be paid for our work next week.* **2.** To do something in a certain way. ♦*Make up your mind, because you can't have it both ways. You must either stay home or come with us.* ♦*Bobby must have it his way and play the game by his rules.* **3.** To claim; say. ♦*Rumor has it that the school burned down.* ♦*Gossip has it that Mary is getting married.* ♦*The man is very smart the way his family has it, but I think he's silly.* **4.** To allow it— Usually used with *will* or *would* in negative sentences. ♦*Mary wanted to give the party at her house, but her mother wouldn't have it.* Syn. HEAR OF, STAND FOR. **5.** To win. ♦*When the senators vote, the ayes will have it.* **6.** To get or find the answer; think of how to do something. ♦*"I have it!" said John to Mary. "We can buy Mother a nice comb for her birthday."* **7.** *informal* To have an (easy, good, rough, soft) time; have (certain kinds of) things happen to you; be treated in a (certain) way by luck or life. ♦*Everyone liked Joe and he had it good until he got sick.* ♦*Mary has it easy; she doesn't have to work.* **8.** See AS LUCK WOULD HAVE IT.

have it all over See HAVE IT OVER.

have it coming *v. phr.* To deserve the good or bad things that happen to you. ♦*I feel sorry about Jack's failing that course, but he had it coming to him.* ♦*Everybody said that Eve had it coming when she won the scholarship.* Compare ASK FOR, GET WHAT'S COMING TO ONE, SERVE RIGHT.

have it in for *v. phr., informal* To wish or mean to harm; have a bitter feeling against. ♦*George has it in for Bob because Bob told the teacher that George cheated in the examination.* ♦*After John beat Ted in a fight, Ted always had it in for John.*

have it made *v. phr., slang* To be sure of success; have everything you need. ♦*With her fine grades Alice has it made and can enter any college in the country.* ♦*The other seniors think Joe has it made because his father owns a big factory.*

have it out *v. phr.* To settle a difference by a free discussion or by a fight. ♦*Joe called Bob a bad name, so they went back of the school and had it out. Joe got a bloody nose and Bob got a black eye.* ♦*The former friends finally decided to have it out in a free argument and they became friends again.*

have it over *or* **have it all over** *v. phr.* To be better than; be superior to. ♦*Anne has it all over Jane in looks and charm.* ♦*A professional golfer usually has it all over an amateur.* ♦*A jeep has it over a regular car on rough mountain trails.* Compare BEAT ALL HOLLOW.

have kittens *v. phr., slang* To become very much worried or upset. ♦*Mrs. Jones was having kittens because it was very late and Susan wasn't home yet.* Compare HAVE A FIT.

have lots (everything) going for one *v. phr.* To have abilities or qualities that help in achieving one's goal; assets working in one's favor. ♦*The young woman will surely get the job; she has everything going for her.*

have money to burn See MONEY TO BURN.

have no business *v. phr.* To have no right or reason. ♦*Jack had no business saying those nasty things about Dick.* ♦*Vern's mother told him he had no business going swimming that day.*

have none of *v. phr.* To refuse to approve or allow. ♦*The teacher said she would have none of Mike's arguing.* ♦*When the fullback refused to obey the captain, the captain said he would have none of that.*

have nothing on *or* **not have anything on** *v. phr.* Not to be any better than; to have no advantage over. ♦*Susan is a wonderful athlete, but when it comes to dancing she has nothing on Mary.* ♦*Even though he is older, John has nothing on Peter in school.* ♦*Although the Smiths have a Rolls Royce, they have nothing on the Jones' who have a Cadillac and a Jaguar.* **2.** To have no information or proof that someone broke the law. ♦*Mr. James was not worried when he was arrested because he was sure they had nothing on him.* ♦*Mr. Brown was an honest politician and they had nothing on him.*

have nothing to do with *v. phr.* To not be involved with; not care about.

♦ *Our firm has nothing to do with oil from the Near East; we are interested in solar energy.*

have no use for See NO USE.

have on *v.* **1.** To be dressed in; wear. ♦ *Mary had on her new dress.* **2.** To have (something) planned; have an appointment; plan to do. ♦ *Harry has a big weekend on.* ♦ *I'm sorry I can't attend your party, but I have a meeting on for that night.* **3.** See HAVE NOTHING ON, HAVE SOMETHING ON.

have one's ass in a sling *v. phr., slang, vulgar, avoidable* To be in an uncomfortable predicament; to be in the doghouse; to be at a disadvantage. ♦ *Al sure had his ass in a sling when the boss found out about his juggling the account.*

have one's cake and eat it too *v. phr.* To enjoy two opposite advantages. ♦ *You can either spend your money going to Europe or save it for a down payment on a house, but you can't do both. That would be having your cake and eating it, too.*

have one's ear *v. phr.* To have access to someone in power; receive audiences rather frequently. ♦ *The national security advisor has the president's ear.*

have one's ears on *v. phr., slang, citizen's band radio jargon* To have one's CB radio in receiving condition. ♦ *Good buddy in the eighteen wheeler southbound, got your ears on?*

have oneself *v. phr., nonstandard* To enjoy—Sometimes used in very informal speech to provide emphasis. ♦ *As soon as their parents left, the boys had themselves some fun.* ♦ *After working hard all day, John had himself a good night's sleep.*

have one's feet planted firmly in the ground See FEET ON THE GROUND.

have one's fill *v. phr.* To be satisfied; be surfeited; be overindulged. ♦ *Howard says he's had his fill of expensive golf tournaments in Europe.*

have one's fling *v. phr.* To have one or more romantic and/or sexual experiences, usually before marriage. ♦ *Jack has had his fling and now seems to be ready to get married and settle down.*

have one's hand in the till See ROB THE TILL.

have one's hands full *v. phr.* To have as much work as you can do; be very

busy. ♦ *The plumber said that he had his hands full and could not take another job for two weeks.* ♦ *With three small children to take care of, Susie's mother has her hands full.*

have one's hands tied See TIED ONE'S HANDS.

have one's head in the sand See HIDE ONE'S HEAD IN THE SAND.

have one's head screwed on backwards *v. phr.* To lack common sense; behave in strange and irrational ways. ♦ *Henry seems to have his head screwed on backwards; he thinks the best time to get a suntan is when it is raining and to sleep with his shoes on.*

have one's heart in the right place See HEART IS IN THE RIGHT PLACE.

have one's hide *v. phr., informal* To punish severely. ♦ *John's mother said she would have his hide if he was late to school again.*

have one's nose to the grindstone See KEEP ONE'S NOSE TO THE GRINDSTONE.

have one's number See GET ONE'S NUMBER.

have one's wings clipped See CLIP ONE'S WING.

have one's wits about one *v. phr.* To be alert; remain calm; not panic. ♦ *Sam was the only one who kept his wits about him when the floodwaters of the Mississippi broke into our yard.*

have one's work cut out See CUT OUT 1.

have on the ball See ON THE BALL.

have qualms about *v. phr.* To feel uneasy about; hesitate about something. ♦ *Mike had no qualms in telling Sue that he was no longer in love with her.*

have rocks in one's head *v. phr., informal* To be stupid; not have good judgment. ♦ *When Mr. James quit his good job with the coal company to begin teaching school, some people thought he had rocks in his head.*

have second thoughts about See SECOND THOUGHT(S).

have seen better days See SEE BETTER DAYS.

have someone by the balls *v. phr., slang, vulgar, avoidable* To have someone at a disadvantage or in one's power. ♦ *The kidnappers had the company by the balls for six long weeks.*

have something going for one *v. phr., slang, informal* To have ability, talent;

good looks, and/or influence in important places helping one to be successful. ♦ *Well now, Pat Jones, that's another story—she's got something going for her.*

have something on *v. phr., informal* To have information or proof that someone did something wrong. ♦ *Mr. Jones didn't want to run for office because he knew the opponents had something on him.* ♦ *Mr. Smith keeps paying blackmail to a man who has something on him.* ♦ *Although Miss Brown is not a good worker, her boss does not fire her because she has something on him.* Compare GET THE GOODS ON. Contrast HAVE NOTHING ON.

have something on the ball *v. phr., slang, colloquial* To be smart, clever; to be skilled and have the necessary know-how. ♦ *You can trust Syd; he's got a lot on the ball* OR *he's got something on the ball.*

have sticky fingers See STICKY FINGERS.

have *or* **take a shot at** See HAVE GO AT.

have the best of *or* **have the better of** See GET THE BETTER OF 2.

have the better of *or* **have the best of** See GET THE BETTER OF.

have the cart before the horse See CART BEFORE THE HORSE.

have the constitution of an ox *v. phr.* To be able to work extremely hard and to have the stamina to overcome misfortune. ♦ *Stan, who has lost both of his parents within one year and is constantly working late, seems to be indestructible, as if he had the constitution of an ox.*

have the courage of one's convictions *v. phr.* To be brave enough to act according to your beliefs. ♦ *Steve showed that he had the courage of his convictions by refusing to help another student cheat in the exam.* ♦ *Owen knew that Pete had started the fight, but he was afraid to say so; he did not have the courage of his convictions.*

have the goods on See GET THE GOODS ON.

have the guts to do something *v. phr., informal* To be brave enough to do something difficult or dangerous. ♦ *Jack wants to marry Jill, but he doesn't have the guts to pop the question.*

have the jump on See GET THE JUMP ON.

have the last laugh *or* **get the last laugh** *v. phr.* To make someone seem foolish for having laughed at you. ♦ *Other schools laughed at us when our little team entered the state championship, but we had the last laugh when we won it.* Compare HE LAUGHS BEST WHO LAUGHS LAST, TURN THE TABLES.

have the laugh on *v. phr.* To emerge as the victor. ♦ *We were trying to fool Paul by setting him up with a blind date who was reportedly unattractive, but he had the laugh on us when this girl turned out to be beautiful.*

have the lead *v. phr.* To occupy the most prominent part in something. ♦ *Maria has the lead in our school play.*

have the makings of *v. phr.* To possess the basic ingredients; have the basic qualities to do something. ♦ *Tom is still young but he seems to have the makings of an excellent pianist.*

have the right-of-way *v. phr.* To have priority in proceeding in traffic on a public highway while other vehicles must yield and wait. ♦ *"Go ahead," he said. "We have the right-of-way at this intersection."*

have the time of one's life See TIME OF ONE'S LIFE.

have the worst of See GET THE WORST OF.

have to *or* **have got to** *v., informal* To be obliged or forced to; need to; must. ♦ *Do you have to go now?* ♦ *He had to come. His parents made him.* ♦ *I have got to go to the doctor.* ♦ *I have to go to Church.*

have to do with *v. phr.* **1.** To be about; be on the subject of or connected with. ♦ *The book has to do with airplanes.* **2.** To know or be a friend of; work or have business with.—Usually used in negative sentence. ♦ *Tom said he didn't want to have anything to do with the new boy.* ♦ *I had nothing to do with the party; I was home that night.*

have too many irons in the fire See TOO MANY IRONS IN THE FIRE.

have two strikes against one *or* **have two strikes on one** *v. phr., informal* To have things working against you; be hindered in several ways; be in a difficult situation; be unlikely to succeed. ♦ *Children from the poorest parts of a city often have two strikes against them* *before they enter school.* ♦ *George has two strikes against him already. Everybody is against what he wants to do.* Compare BEHIND THE EIGHT BALL. [In baseball, three strikes are out. If the umpire calls two strikes against the batter, he has only one strike left and will be out if he gets one more strike.]

haw See HEM AND HAW.

hay See HIT THE HAY.

haystack See NEEDLE IN A HAYSTACK.

haywire See GO HAYWIRE.

hazard See AT ALL HAZARDS.

haze See IN A FOG *or* IN A HAZE.

head See ACID HEAD, BEAT INTO ONE'S HEAD, BEAT ONE'S HEAD AGAINST A WALL, BIG HEAD, COUNT HEADS, EYES IN THE BACK OF ONE'S HEAD, FROM HEAD TO FOOT, GET THROUGH ONE'S HEAD, GOOD HEAD ON ONE'S SHOULDERS, GO TO ONE'S HEAD, HANG ONE'S HEAD, HAVE ONE'S HEAD IN THE SAND, HAVE ROCKS IN ONE'S HEAD, HEAP COALS OF FIRE ON ONE'S HEAD, HIT THE NAIL ON THE HEAD, HANG OVER ONE'S HEAD, HIDE ONE'S FACE OR HIDE ONE'S HEAD, HOLD ONE'S HEAD UP, KEEP A CIVIL TONGUE IN ONE'S HEAD, KEEP ONE'S HEAD, LOSE ONE'S HEAD, MAKE HEAD OR TAIL OF, OFF THE TOP OF ONE'S HEAD, ON ONE'S HEAD, OUT OF ONE'S HEAD, *also* OFF ONE'S HEAD, OVER ONE'S HEAD, PRICE ON ONE'S HEAD, PUT THEIR HEADS TOGETHER *or* LAY THEIR HEADS TOGETHER, SWELLED HEAD, TAKE INTO ONE'S HEAD, TELL —— ——WHERE TO GET OFF *or* TELL —— WHERE TO HEAD IN, THROW ONESELF AT SOMEONE'S HEAD *or* FLING ONESELF AT SOMEONE'S HEAD, TURN ONE'S HEAD, USE ONE'S HEAD.

head above water *n. phr.* out of difficulty; clear of trouble. ♦ *How are your marks at school? Are you keeping your head above water?* ♦ *Business at the store is bad. They can't keep their heads above water.*

head and shoulders *adv. phr.* **1.** By the measure of the head and shoulders. ♦ *The basketball player is head and shoulders taller than the other boys.* **2.** By far; by a great deal; very much. ♦ *She is head and shoulders above the rest of the class in singing.* See FAR AND AWAY.

header See DOUBLE-HEADER.

head for *v. phr.* To go in the direction of. ♦ *We left early in the morning and headed for Niagara Falls.*

head for the hills *v. phr., informal* To get far away in a hurry; run away and hide.—Often used imperatively. ♦ *Head for the hills. The bandits are coming.* ♦ *He saw the crowd chasing him, so he headed for the hills.* ♦ *When they saw the mean boy coming, they all headed for the hills.* Compare BEAT IT, LIGHT OUT, TAKE TO THE WOODS.

head-hunting *n., slang, informal* **1.** The custom of seeking out, decapitating, and preserving the heads of enemies as trophies **2.** A search for qualified individuals to fill certain positions. ♦ *The president sent a committee to the colleges and universities to do some head-hunting; we hope he finds some young talent.* **3.** A systematic destruction of opponents, especially in politics. ♦ *Billings was hired by the party to do some head-hunting among members of the opposition.*

head in the clouds See IN THE CLOUDS.

head in the sand See HIDE ONE'S HEAD IN THE SAND.

head off *v.* **1.** To get in front of and stop, turn back, or turn aside. ♦ *The sheriff said to head the cattle thieves off at the pass.* **2.** To block; stop; prevent. ♦ *He will get into trouble if someone doesn't head him off.*

head-on *adj. or adv. phr.* **1.** With the head or front pointing at; with the front facing; front end to front end. ♦ *Our car skidded into a head-on crash with the truck.* ♦ *In the fog the boat ran head-on into a log.* ♦ *There is a head-on view of the parade from our house.* Compare FACE-TO-FACE. Contrast REAR-END. **2.** In a way that is exactly opposite; against or opposed to in argument. ♦ *If you think a rule should be changed, a head-on attack against it is best.* ♦ *Tom did not want to argue head-on what the teacher said, so he said nothing.*

head out *v.* **1.** To go or point away. ♦ *The ship left port and headed out to sea. The car was parked beside the house. It was headed out towards the street.* **2.** *informal* Leave; start out. ♦ *I have a long way to go before dark. I'm going to head out.*

head over heels *also* **heels over head 1a.** In a somersault;; upside down; head first. ♦ *It was so dark Bob fell head over heels into a big hole in the ground.* Compare UPSIDE DOWN. **1b.** In great confusion or disorder; hastily. ♦ *The children all tried to come in the door at once, head over heels.* Compare TOPSY-TURVY. **2.** *informal* Completely; deeply. ♦ *He was head over heels in debt.* ♦ *She was head over heels in love.*

head shrinker *n., slang, informal* A psychoanalyst, also called a *shrink.* ♦ *Forrester is falling apart; his family physician sent him to a head shrinker (to a shrink).*

head start *n.* **1.** A beginning before someone; lead or advantage at the beginning. ♦ *The other racers knew they couldn't catch Don if he got too big a head start.* ♦ *Joe has a head start. He began to study earlier than we did.* **2.** A good beginning. ♦ *Let's get a head start in painting the house by getting up early.* ♦ *The teacher gave the class a head start on the exercise by telling them the answers to the first two problems.* Compare RUNNING START.

heads or tails *n. phr.* The two sides of a coin, especially when the coin is tossed in the air in order to decide which of two alternatives are to be followed. ♦ *Tom tossed a quarter in the air and said, "Tails, I win; heads you win."*

heads up *interj., informal* Keep your head up and be careful or ready.—Used as a warning to prepare for something or clear the way ♦ *"Heads up!" said the waiter carrying the hot food.* ♦ *Heads up, boys! A train is coming.* ♦ *Heads up, now! You can do better than that.* Syn. LOOK ALIVE, LOOK OUT.

heads-up *adj., informal* Wide-awake; alert; watchful; intelligent. ♦ *You must play hard, heads-up baseball to win this game.* Compare ON ONE'S TOES, ON THE BALL.

head up *v., informal* **1.** To be at the head or front of. ♦ *The elephants headed up the whole parade.* **2.** To be the leader or boss of. ♦ *Mr. Jones will head up the new business.* ♦ *The class planned a candy sale, and they elected Mary to head it up.*

health See CLEAN HILL OF HEALTH.

heap See STRIKE ALL OF A HEAP.

heap coals of fire on one's head *v. phr., literary* To be kind or helpful to someone who has done wrong to you, so that he is ashamed. ♦ *Alice heaped coals of fire on Mary's head by inviting her to a party after Mary had gossiped about her.* ♦ *Jean Valjean stole the Bishop's silver, but the Bishop heaped coals of fire on his head by giving the silver to him.*

hear See WILL NOT HEAR OF.

hear a pin drop *v. phr.* Absolute silence. ♦ *It's so quiet in the room you could hear a pin drop.*

heart See AFTER ONE'S OWN HEART, AT HEART, EAT ONE'S HEART OUT, BREAK ONE'S HEART, BY HEART, CHANGE OF HEART, CROSS ONE'S HEART, DO ONE GOOD *or* DO ONE'S HEART GOOD, FIND IT IN ONE'S HEART, FROM THE BOTTOM OF ONE'S HEART *or* WITH ALL ONE'S HEART, FROM THE HEART, GET TO THE HEART OF, HAVE A HEART, HEAVY HEART, LOSE HEART, LOSE ONE'S HEART, OPEN HEART, OPEN ONE'S HEART, SEARCH ONE'S HEART, SET ONE'S HEART ON, TAKE HEART, TAKE TO HEART, TO ONE'S HEART'S CONTENT, WEAR ONE'S HEART ON ONE'S SLEEVE.

heartbreaker *n.* One with numerous admirers of the opposite sex; one with whom others fall in love readily. ♦ *Tom, who has four girls in love with him at college, has developed the reputation of being a heartbreaker.*

heart and soul[1] *n.* Eager love; strong feeling; great enthusiasm. Often used with a singular verb. ♦ *When Mr. Pitt plays the piano, his heart and soul is in it.* ♦ *John plays tennis badly, but with heart and soul.* ♦ *Mary wanted a puppy with all her heart and soul.*

heart and soul[2] *adv.* Wholly and eagerly; with all one's interest and strength; completely. ♦ *Will you try to make our city a better place? Then we are with you heart and soul.* ♦ *Mike was heart and soul against the new rules.* Compare BODY AND SOUL.

heart goes out to *formal* You feel very sorry for; you feel pity or sympathy for.—Used with a possessive. ♦ *Frank's heart went out to the poor children playing in the slum street.* ♦ *Our hearts went out to the young mother whose child had died.*

hear the beat *or* **see the beat** *v. phr., dialect* To hear of or to see someone or something better or surpassing.— Usually used in negative or interrogative sentences and often followed by *of.* ♦*I never heard the beat! John swam all the way across the river. Did you ever hear the beat of it?* ♦*The juggler spun a table around on the tip of his finger. I never saw the beat of that.*

heart in one's mouth *or* **heart in one's boots** A feeling of great fear or nervousness.—Often considered trite. ♦*Charles got up to make his first speech with his heart in his mouth.* ♦*My heart was in my mouth as I went into the haunted house.* ♦*When the bear came out of the woods towards us, our hearts were in our mouths.* Compare HAIR STAND ON END.

heart is in the right place *or* **have one's heart in the right place.** To be kindhearted, sympathetic or well-meaning; have good intentions. ♦*All the tramps and stray dogs in the neighborhood knew that Mrs. Brown's heart was in the right place.* ♦*Tom looks very rough but his heart is in the right place.*

heart miss a beat See HEART SKIP A BEAT.

heart of gold *n. phr.* A kind, generous, or forgiving nature. ♦*John has a heart of gold. I never saw him angry at anyone.* ♦*Mrs. Brown is a rich woman with a heart of gold.* Compare GOOD AS GOLD, HEART IN THE RIGHT PLACE.

heart of stone *n. phr.* A nature without pity. ♦*Mr. Smith has a heart of stone. He whipped his horse until it fell down.*

heart-searching See SEARCH ONE'S HEART.

heart set See SET ONE'S HEART ON.

heart sink To lose hope, courage, or eagerness; be very disappointed. ♦*The soldiers' hearts sank when they saw that they were surrounded by Indians.* ♦*The children were happy because they were going to the beach to swim, but their hearts sank when it began to rain.*

heart skip a beat *or* **heart miss a beat 1.** The heart leaves out or seems to leave out a beat; the heart beats hard or leaps from excitement or strong feeling.—Often considered trite. ♦*When Paul saw the bear standing in front of him, his heart skipped a beat.*

2. To be startled or excited from surprise, joy, or fright. ♦*When Linda was told that she had won, her heart missed a beat.*

heart stand still *v. phr.* To be very frightened or worried. ♦*Johnny's heart stood still when he saw his dog run into the street in front of a car.* ♦*Everybody's heart stood still when the President announced that war was declared.* Compare HAIR STAND ON END.

heart-to-heart *adj.* Speaking freely and seriously about something private. ♦*The father decided to have a heart-to-heart talk with his son about smoking.* ♦*She waited until they were alone so she could have a heart-to-heart talk with him.* Compare MAN-TO-MAN.

hearty See HALE AND HEARTY.

heat See CANNED HEAT.

heave in sight *v. phr.* To seem to rise above the horizon at sea and come into sight; come into view; become visible.—Usually used of ships. ♦*A ship hove in sight many miles away on the horizon.*

heaven See MOVE HEAVEN AND EARTH, WOULD THAT *or* WOULD HEAVEN.

heaven knows *or* **heaven only knows** See GOD KNOWS.

heavenly days! *interj., informal* Exclamation of amazement and disbelief with negative coloring. ♦*Heavenly days! Look what happened! The dog did it again on the Persian carpet!* Compare GOOD GRIEF!

heave to *v.* To bring a ship to a stop; bring a sailing ship to a standstill by setting the sails in a certain way. ♦*"Heave to!" the captain shouted to his crew.* ♦*We fired a warning shot across the front of the pirate ship to make her heave to.*

heave up See THROW UP.

heavy See HANG HEAVY *or* HANG HEAVY ON ONE'S HANDS, HOT AND HEAVY.

heavy-duty *adj.* Made for long or hard use; very strong. ♦*The lumberman used heavy-duty trucks for hauling logs down the mountains.* ♦*The workers in the steel mill have heavy-duty gloves for handling hot steel.* ♦*Mrs. Carlson bought a heavy-duty cleanser to clean her greasy oven.*

heavy-footed *adj.* **1.** Slow and clumsy in walking or movement; awkward in using your feet. ♦*The fat man tried to* dance, but he was too heavy-footed. ♦ *Martha is not fat, but she is heavy-footed and walks noisily.* **2.** Awkward in choice and order of words; not smooth and graceful; clumsy. ♦ *In Mary's compositions, the words seem to dance, but John's compositions are always heavy-footed.* **3.** *or* **lead-footed** *informal* Likely to drive an automobile fast. ♦ *Jerry is a bad driver because he is too heavy-footed.* Compare STEP ON IT.

heavy-handed *adj.* **1.** Not skillful or graceful; clumsy. ♦ *George is heavy-handed and seldom catches the ball.* ♦ *My sister plays the piano badly; she is too heavy-handed.* ♦ *Tim told a heavy-handed joke about the principal's baldness that embarrassed everyone.* **2.** Likely to hit or punish hard; harsh or cruel in making (someone) obey. ♦ *Years ago many fathers were heavy-handed bosses in their homes.* ♦ *Many American colonists believed that the English tax collectors were too heavy-handed.* ♦ **3.** See HAM-HANDED.

heavy heart *n. phr.* A feeling of being weighed down with sorrow; unhappiness. ♦ *They had very heavy hearts as they went to the funeral.*

heck See RAISE THE DEVIL *or* RAISE HECK *or* RAISE HOB *or* RAISE NED.

heck of it See DEVIL OF IT.

hedge about *or* **hedge in 1.** To surround with a hedge or barrier; protect or separate by closing in. ♦ *The house is hedged about with bushes and trees.* ♦ *The little garden is hedged in to keep the chickens out.* **2.** To keep from getting out or moving freely; keep from acting freely; block in. ♦ *The boys are hedged in today. They can only play in the backyard.* ♦ *The king said he could not make new laws if he was so hedged in by old ones.* Syn. FENCE IN.

hedged in See FENCED IN.

heed See TAKE HEED.

heel See AT ONE'S HEELS, COOL ONE'S HEELS, DOWN AT-THE-HEEL *or* DOWN-AT-HEEL, DRAG ONE'S FEET *or* DRAG ONE'S HEELS, HEAD OVER HEELS, KICK UP ONE'S HEELS, ON ONE'S HEELS *or* ON THE HEELS OF, SET BACK ON ONE'S HEELS *or* KNOCK BACK ON ONE'S HEELS, TAKE TO ONE'S HEELS *also* SHOW A CLEAN PAIR OF HEELS, TO HEEL, TURN ON ONE'S HEEL, WELL-HEELED.

heels over head See HEAD OVER HEELS.

he laughs best who laughs last A person should go ahead with what he is doing and not worry when others laugh at him. When he succeeds he will enjoy laughing at them for being wrong more than they enjoyed laughing at him.—A proverb. ♦ *Everyone laughed at Mary when she was learning to ski. She kept falling down. Now she is the state champion. He laughs best who laughs last.* Compare CHANGE ONE'S TUNE, LAST LAUGH, LAUGH ON THE OTHER SIDE OF ONE'S MOUTH, SHOE ON THE OTHER FOOT.

hell See COME HELL OR HIGH WATER, GO THROUGH HELL AND HIGH WATER, HELL-ON-WHEELS, LIKE HELL, TO HELL WITH, UNTIL HELL FREEZES OVER, WHEN HELL FREEZES OVER.

hell and high water *n. phr.* Troubles or difficulties of any kind. ♦ *After John's father died he went through hell and high water, but he managed to keep the family together.* Compare COME HELL OR HIGH WATER.

hell-on-wheels *n., slang* A short-tempered, nagging, or crabby person especially one who makes another unhappy by constantly criticizing him even when he has done nothing wrong. ♦ *Finnegan complains that his wife is hell on wheels; he is considering getting a divorce.*

help See CAN HELP, CAN'T HELP BUT *or* CANNOT BUT, SO HELP ME.

help oneself *v. phr.* To take what you want; take rather than ask or wait to be given. ♦ *Help yourself to another piece of pie.* ♦ *John helped himself to some candy without asking.*

help out *v.* **1.** To be helpful or useful; help sometimes or somewhat. ♦ *Mr. Smith helps out with the milking on the farm.* ♦ *Tom helps out in the store after school.* **2.** To help (someone) especially in a time of need; aid; assist. ♦ *Jane is helping out Mother by minding the baby.* ♦ *When John couldn't add the numbers, the teacher helped him out.*

helter-skelter *adv.* **1.** At a fast speed, but in confusion. ♦ *The batted ball broke Mr. Jones's window, and the boys ran away helter-skelter.* ♦ *When* the bell rang, the pupils ran helter-skelter out of the door. **2.** In a confusing group; in disorder. ♦ *The movers piled the furniture helter-skelter in the living room of the new house.* ♦ *Mary fell down and her books, papers, and lunch landed helter-skelter over the sidewalk.* Compare EVERY WHICH WAY.

he-man *n., informal* A man who is very strong, brave, and healthy. ♦ *Larry was a real he-man when he returned from service with the Marines.*

hem and haw *v. phr.* **1.** To pause or hesitate while speaking, often with little throat noises. ♦ *The man was a poor lecturer because he hemmed and hawed too much.* **2.** To avoid giving a clear answer; be evasive in speech. ♦ *The principal asked Bob why he was late to school, and Bob only hemmed and hawed.* Compare BEAT AROUND THE BUSH.

hem in *or* **hem around** *or* **hem about** *v.* **1.** To put something around, or to be placed around; surround. ♦ *Mountains hemmed the town in on all sides.* ♦ *As soon as Tom and Bob started to fight, they were hemmed around by other boys.* **2.** See FENCE IN.

hen See MAD AS A HORNET, *or* MAD AS HOPS *or* MAD AS A WET HEN.

hen party *n. phr., informal* A party to which only women or girls are invited. ♦ *The sorority gave a hen party for its members.* Contrast STAG PARTY. See GO STAG.

Henry See JOHN HANCOCK *or* JOHN HENRY.

her See GIVE IT THE GUN *or* GIVE HER THE GUN.

herd See RIDE HERD ON.

here See ALL THERE *or* ALL HERE, NEITHER HERE NOR THERE, SAME HERE.

here and now[1] *adv. phr.* At this very time and place; right now; immediately. ♦ *I want my dime back, and I want it here and now.* Compare THEN AND THERE.

here and now[2] *n.* The present time and place; today. ♦ *He enjoys the pleasures of the here and now and never worries about the future.* ♦ *"I want my steak here and now!"*

here and there *adv. phr.* **1.** In one place and then in another. ♦ *I looked here and there for my pen, but I didn't look* everywhere. ♦ *Here and there in the yard little yellow flowers had sprung up.* **2.** In various directions. ♦ *We went here and there looking for berries.* Compare HITHER AND THITHER.

here goes *interj., informal* I am ready to begin; I am now ready and willing to take the chance; I am hoping for the best.—Said especially before beginning something that takes skill, luck, or courage. ♦ *"Here goes!" said Charley, as he jumped off the high diving board.* ♦ *"Here goes!" said Mary as she started the test.*

here goes nothing *interj., informal* I am ready to begin, but this will be a waste of time; this will not be anything great; this will probably fail.—Used especially before beginning something that takes skill, luck or courage. ♦ *"Here goes nothing," said Bill at the beginning of the race.*

hide See HAVE ONE'S HIDE, TAN ONE'S HIDE.

hide one's face *or* **hide one's head** *v. phr.* **1.** To lower your head or turn your face away because of shame or embarrassment. ♦ *The teacher found out that Tom had cheated, and Tom hid his head.* ♦ *When Bob said how pretty Mary was, she blushed and hid her face.* **2.** To feel embarrassed or ashamed. ♦ *We will beat the other team so badly that they will hide their heads in shame.*

hide one's head in the sand *or* **bury one's head in the sand** *or* **have one's head in the sand** To keep from seeing, knowing, or understanding something dangerous or unpleasant; to refuse to see or face something. ♦ *If there is a war, you cannot just bury your head in the sand.*

hide one's light under a bushel *v. phr.* To be very shy and modest and not show your abilities or talents; be too modest in letting others see what you can do. ♦ *When Joan is with her close friends she has a wonderful sense of humor, but usually she hides her light under a bushel.* ♦ *Mr. Smith is an expert in many fields, but most people think he is not very smart because he hides his light under a bushel.* ♦ *All year long Tommy hid his light under a bushel and the teacher was surprised to see how* *much he knew when she read his exam paper.*

hide or hair *or* **hide nor hair** *n. phr., informal* A sign or trace of someone that is gone or lost; any sign at all of something missing. Usually used in negative or interrogative sentence. ♦*Tommy left the house this morning and I haven't seen hide or hair of him since.* ♦*A button fell off my coat and I could find neither hide nor hair of it.*

hide out *v. phr.* To go into hiding, as in the case of a criminal on the run. ♦*He tried to hide out but the police tracked him down.*

hideout *n.* A place where one hides. ♦*The wanted criminal used several hideouts but he was captured in the end.*

high See COME HELL OR HIGH WATER, FLYING HIGH, GO THROUGH HELL AND HIGH WATER, HELL AND HIGH WATER, HIT THE HIGH SPOTS, LIVE HIGH OFF THE HOG *or* EAT HIGH ON THE HOG, OFF ONE'S HIGH HORSE, ON TOP OF THE WORLD *or* SITTING ON TOP OF THE WORLD *also (Southern)* SITTING ON HIGH COTTON, RIDING HIGH.

high and dry *adv. or adj. phr.* **1.** Up above the water; beyond the reach of splashing or waves. ♦*Mary was afraid she had left her towel where the tide would reach it, but she found it high and dry.* ♦*When the tide went out the boat was high and dry.* **2.** Without anyone to help; alone and with no help. ♦*When the time came to put up the decorations, Mary was left high and dry.* ♦*At first the other boys helped, but when the work got hard, Bob found himself high and dry.* Compare LEAVE IN THE LURCH, OUT IN THE COLD.

high and low *adv.* Everywhere. ♦*The police were searching for the criminal high and low, but they couldn't find him.*

high-and-mighty *adj., informal* Feeling more important or superior to someone else; too proud of yourself. ♦*John wasn't invited to the party, because he acted too high-and-mighty.* ♦*Mary become high-and-mighty when she won the prize, and Joan would not go around with her any more.* Compare STUCK-UP.

high as a kite *adj.* **1.** As excited and happy as one can possibly be. ♦*When Eric won the lottery he was high as a kite.* **2.** Intoxicated or under the influence of some drug. ♦*Jeff has been drinking again and he is high as a kite.* Compare THREE SHEETS IN/TO THE WIND.

highbrow *adj.* Very well educated or even over-educated; belonging to the educated middle class; sophisticated. ♦*Certain novels are not for everyone and are considered as highbrow entertainment.* Contrast LOW BROW.

high camp *n., slang, show business* **1.** Kitsch, or pretentious material in bad taste that is still liked by higher class audiences. ♦*The* Potsdam Quartet *is a play full of high camp.* **2.** An exaggerated movie or theater scene that loses believability. ♦Scarecrow and Mrs. King *and* Sledge Hammer *are so full of high camp that no sensible people watch them anymore.* **middle camp** and **low camp** refer to theatrical kitsch preferred by middle class and low class audiences, respectively.

high-class *adj.* Of the best quality; very good; superior.—Avoided by many careful speakers. ♦*When Mr. Brown got a raise in pay, Mrs. Brown started to look for a high-class apartment.* ♦*Mrs. Smith always gets her clothing at high-class shops.* ♦*Mr. Jones always gets his office workers from Burns Agency because they have high-class help.* Compare FIRST-CLASS.

higher education *n.* Schooling after graduation from high school, especially in a college or university. ♦*Tom plans to get his higher education at the state university.*

higher-up *n., informal* One of the people who has one of the more important positions in an organization; an important official. ♦*The teacher's problem was discussed by the higher-ups.* ♦*The local officers of the scout group approved the plan, but the state higher-ups did not accept it.*

high fashion *or* **high style** *n. phr.* The new style in women's dress set each season by designers in Paris or other fashion centers and accepted by fashionable women. ♦*The high styles designed in Paris are often quickly copied by makers of cheap clothing.*

high gear *n. phr., informal* Top speed; full activity. ♦*Production got into high* *gear after the vacation.* ♦ *An advertising campaign for the new toothpaste promptly moved into high gear.*

high-handed *adj.* Depending on force rather than right; bossy; dictatorial. ♦ *With high-handed daring, John helped himself to the best food on the table.* ♦ *Mr. Smith was a high-handed tyrant in his office.*

high-hat[1] *adj., slang* Treating others as inferior; acting above others. ♦ *It was an expensive place to eat, and the customers were likely to be a little high-hat.* ♦ *Jones acted high-hat toward anyone poorer than he.*

high-hat[2] *v., slang* To treat others as inferior; look down on. ♦ *After she had married a rich man, Mary high-hatted her former friends.* ♦ *"Don't high-hat me," Fred warned, when Harry began to walk away as if he didn't know him.* Compare BRUSH OFF.

high jinks *n. phr., informal* Noisy or rough gaiety; wild play; tricks. ♦ *The sailors were on shore leave, and high jinks were to be expected.* ♦ *The high school seniors engaged in high jinks after commencement.*

high off the hog See LIVE HIGH OFF THE HOG.

high on *adj. phr.* **1.** Intoxicated on some drug or alcoholic drink. ♦ *Rob was severely scolded by the dean for always being high on marijuana.* **2.** Enthusiastic about something. ♦ *Jeff is high on Beethoven and Brahms.*

high place *n. phr.* A position of responsibility, honor, and power. ♦ *Jones had reached a high place in the government at Washington.*

high seas *n. phr.* The open ocean, not the waters near the coast. ♦ *It was a big powerful liner built to sail on the high seas.* ♦ *The ships of every country have the right to sail on the high seas.*

high season *n. phr.* The time of year when the largest number of passengers are travelling; the time when airfare costs more. ♦ *We had to pay $100 more for our tickets because it was the high season.* Contrast LOW SEASON.

high sign *n. phr., informal* A silent signal of recognition, greeting, or warning; an open or secret signal between two persons.—Used with *get* or *give.* ♦ *The Joneses saw us across the*

hotel dining room and gave us the high sign. ♦ *John could see that Grace wanted to tell him something, but he got her attention and frowned. She got the high sign and waited until the teacher had moved on before speaking.*

high-sounding *adj.* Sounding important; said for showing off; too fancy. ♦ *The politician's speech was full of high-sounding words.* ♦ *Mr. Brown filled his son with many high-sounding ideas about life.*

high-strung *adj.* Nervous; sensitive; tense. ♦ *Gary has been rather high-strung lately because of too much work at the office.*

high style See HIGH FASHION.

hightail it *v. phr., slang* To travel fast; move rapidly. ♦ *After school, Frank would hightail it home.* ♦ *The two men who held up the bank hightailed it out of town.*

high time *adj. phr., used predicatively* (stress on *time*) Dire, necessary, and sufficient circumstances prompting action. ♦ *It is high time we sold the old house; it will fall apart within a year.*

highway See DIVIDED HIGHWAY *or* DUAL HIGHWAY.

highway robbery *n. phr.* **1.** A hold-up of or theft from a person committed on an open road or street usually by an armed man. ♦ *Highway robbery was common in England in Shakespeare's day.* **2.** An extremely high price or charge; a profiteer's excessive charge. ♦ *To someone from a small town, the prices of meals and theater tickets in New York often seem to be highway robbery.*

hill See GRASS IS ALWAYS GREENER ON THE OTHER SIDE OF THE FENCE *or* GRASS IS ALWAYS GREENER ON THE OTHER SIDE OF THE HILL, HEAD FOR THE HILLS.

hilt See TO THE HILT *or* UP TO THE HILT.

hinge on *or* **hinge upon** *v.* To depend on as decisive; be decided by. ♦ *In a dictatorship, everything hinges on one man.* ♦ *A tobacco grower's income for the year may hinge on what the weather is like in a few summer weeks.*

hired man *n. phr.* A man employed to do jobs every day about a house or farm. ♦ *The hired man was sick, and a lot of the daily chores were not done.*

hire out *v., informal* **1.** To accept a job; take employment. ♦ *Frank hired out as a saxophonist with a dance band.* **2.** To rent (as owner). ♦ *John used to hire out his tractor sometimes when he didn't need it himself.*

history See GO DOWN IN HISTORY *or* GO DOWN IN THE RECORDS.

hit See HARD-HITTING, MAKE A HIT, SMASH HIT.

hit and miss See HIT OR MISS.

hit-and-run *adj.* **1.** Of or about an accident after which a motorist drives away without giving his name and offering help. ♦ *Judges are stern with hit-and-run drivers.* **2.** Striking suddenly and leaving quickly. ♦ *The bandits often made hit-and-run attacks on wagon trains.*

hit below the belt See BELOW THE BELT.

hit between the eyes *v. phr., informal* To make a strong impression on; surprise greatly. ♦ *Helen hit Joe right between the eyes the moment he saw her.* ♦ *It was a wonderfully lifelike picture, and it hit Sol right between the eyes.* ♦ *To learn that his parents had endured poverty for his sake hit John between the eyes.*

hit bottom *or* **touch bottom** *v. phr., informal* **1.** To be at the very lowest. ♦ *In August there was a big supply of corn and the price hit bottom.* ♦ *When Johnny failed the exam his spirits hit bottom.* **2.** To live through the worst; not to be able to go any lower. ♦ *After all their troubles, they thought they had hit bottom and then something else happened.* ♦ *When they lost all their money they thought they had touched bottom and things would have to get better.*

hitch one's wagon to a star *v. phr.* To aim high; follow a great ambition or purpose. ♦ *In trying to be a famous pianist, Mary had hitched her wagon to a star.* ♦ *John hitched his wagon to a star and decided to try to become President.*

hither and thither *or* **hither and yon** *adv. phr., literary* In one direction and then in another. ♦ *Bob wandered hither and thither looking for a playmate.* Compare HERE AND THERE.

hither and yon See HITHER AND THITHER.

hit home *v. phr.* To go directly to the mark; strike a vulnerable spot. ♦ *His* remark hit home when he referred to those who do not contribute sufficiently to the college fund drive.

hit it off *v. phr., informal* To enjoy one another's company; be happy and comfortable in each other's presence. ♦ *Tom and Fred hit it off well with each other.* ♦ *Mary and Jane hit it off from the first.* Syn. GET ALONG.

hit on *or* **hit upon** *v.* To happen to meet, find, or reach; to choose or think by chance. ♦ *John hit on a business that was just starting to grow rapidly.* ♦ *There seemed to be several explanations of the crime, but the detectives hit on the right one the first time.* Compare HAPPEN ON.

hit on all cylinders *v. phr.* **1.** To run smoothly or at full power without any missing or skipping.—Said of a motor. ♦ *The mechanic tuned the car engine until it was hitting on all cylinders.* **2.** *informal* To think or work well; to use all your ability. ♦ *The football team was hitting on all cylinders and scored a big victory.* ♦ *Bob began to write his examination, and found himself hitting on all cylinders.*

hit one's stride *v. phr.* **1.** To walk or run at your best speed; reach your top speed or game. ♦ *After walking the first mile, Jim was just hitting his stride.* ♦ *The horse began to hit his stride and moved ahead of the other horses in the race.* **2.** To do your best work; do the best job you are able to. ♦ *Mary didn't begin to hit her stride in school until the fifth grade.*

hit-or-miss *also* **hit-and-miss** *adj.* Unplanned; uncontrolled; aimless; careless. ♦ *John did a lot of hit-or-miss reading, some of it about taxes.* ♦ *Mary packed her bag in hurried, hit-or-miss fashion.*

hit or miss *also* **hit and miss** *adv.* In an unplanned or uncontrolled way; aimlessly; carelessly. ♦ *George didn't know which house on the street was Jane's, so he began ringing doorbells hit or miss.*

hit parade *n.* **1.** A list of songs or tunes arranged in order of popularity. ♦ *Tom was overjoyed when his new song was named on the hit parade on the local radio station.* **2.** *slang* A list of favorites in order of popularity. ♦ *Jack is no longer number one on Elsie's hit parade.*

hitter See PINCH HIT, PINCH HITTER, PULL HITTER.

hit the books *v. phr., informal* To study your school assignments, prepare for classes. ◆ *Jack broke away from his friends, saying, "I've got to hit the books."*

hit the bull's-eye *v. phr., informal* To go to the important part of the matter; reach the main question. ◆ *John hit the bull's-eye when he said the big question was one of simple honesty.*

hit the ceiling *or* **hit the roof** *v. phr., slang* To become violently angry; go into a rage. ◆ *When Elaine came home at three in the morning, her father hit the ceiling.* ◆ *Bob hit the roof when Joe teased him.* Syn. BLOW A FUSE.

hit the deck *v. phr.* To get up from bed, to start working. (From sailor's language as in *"All hands on the deck!"*) ◆ *OK boys, it's time to hit the deck!*

hit the dirt *v. phr., slang military* To take cover under gunfire by falling on the ground. ◆ *We hit the dirt the moment we heard the machine gun fire.*

hit the fan *v. phr., informal* To become a big public problem or controversy. ◆ *The whole mess hit the fan when the judge was arrested for drunken driving for the second time.*

hit the hay *or* **hit the sack** *v. phr., slang* To go to bed. ◆ *The men hit the hay early, in order to be out hunting at dawn.* ◆ *Louis was so tired that he hit the sack soon after supper.*

hit the high spots *v. phr.* To consider, mention, or see only the more important parts of something such as a book, war, or school course. ◆ *In his lecture, the speaker hit the high spots of his subject.* ◆ *The first course in general science hits only the high spots of the physical sciences.* ◆ *The Bakers went to the fair for one day, and only hit the high spots.*

hit the jackpot *v. phr., slang* To be very lucky or successful. ◆ *Mr. Brown invented a new gadget which hit the jackpot.* ◆ *Mrs. Smith hit the jackpot when she got Lula for a maid.*

hit the nail on the head *v. phr.* To get something exactly right; speak or act in the most fitting or effective way. ◆ *The mayor's talk on race relations hit the nail on the head.*

hit the road *v. phr., slang* **1.** To become a wanderer; to live an idle life; become a tramp or hobo. ◆ *When Jack's wife left him, he felt a desire to travel, so he hit the road.* **2.** To leave, especially in a car. ◆ *It is getting late, so I guess we will hit the road for home.* ◆ *He packed his car and hit the road for California.*

hit the roof See HIT THE CEILING.

hit the sack See HIT THE HAY.

hit the sauce *v. phr., slang* To drink alcoholic beverages—especially heavily and habitually. ◆ *When Sue left him, Joe began to hit the sauce.*

hit the spot *v. phr., informal* To refresh fully or satisfy you; bring back your spirits or strength—used especially of food or drink. ◆ *A cup of tea always hits the spot when you are tired.* ◆ *Mother's apple pie always hits the spot with the boys.*

hit town *v. phr.* To arrive in town. ◆ *Give me a phone call as soon as you hit town.*

hit upon See HIT ON.

hob See PLAY THE DEVIL WITH *or* PLAY HOB WITH.

hoe See HARD ROW TO HOE *or* TOUGH ROW TO HOE.

hoe one's own row *v. phr.* To make your way in life by your own efforts; get along without help. ◆ *David's father died when he was little, and he has always had to hoe his own row.* Syn. PADDLE ONE'S OWN CANOE, STAND ON ONE'S OWN FEET.

hog See EAT (LIVE) HIGH ON THE HOG *or* EAT (LIVE) HIGH OFF THE HOG, GO THE WHOLE HOG *or* GO WHOLE HOG, ROAD HOG.

hog-tie *v., informal* **1.** To tie (an animal) so it is unable to move or escape. ◆ *The Cowboy caught a calf and hog-tied it.* **2.** To make someone unable to act freely; limit. ◆ *The welfare worker wanted to help at once, but rules and regulations hog-tied her, so she could only report the case.*

hoist with one's own petard *adj. phr.* Caught in your own trap or trick. ◆ *Jack carried office gossip to the boss until he was hoisted by his own petard.* [From Shakespeare; literally, blown up with one's own bomb.]

hold See GET HOLD OF, LAY HOLD OF, LEAVE HOLDING THE BAG *or* LEAVE HOLDING THE SACK.

hold a brief for *v. phr.* To argue in support of; defend.—Usually used with a negative. ♦ *I hold no brief for John, but I do not think he was responsible for the accident.* ♦ *The lawyer said he held no brief for thievery, but he considered the man should be given another chance.*

hold a candle to *also* **hold a stick to** *v. phr.* To be fit to be compared with; be in the same class with.—A trite phrase used in negative, interrogative, and conditional sentences. ♦ *Henry thought that no modern ball club could hold a candle to those of 50 years ago.*

hold all the trumps *v. phr.* To have the best chance of winning; have all the advantages; have full control. ♦ *Most of the team wants John for captain and he is the best player. He will be elected captain because he holds all the trumps.* ♦ *Freddy has a quarter and I have no money, so he holds all the trumps and can buy whatever he wants with it.*

hold back *v.* **1.** To stay back or away; show unwillingness. ♦ *The visitor tried to get the child to come to her, but he held back.* ♦ *John held back from social activity because he felt embarrassed with people.* **2.** To keep someone in place; prevent from acting. ♦ *The police held back the crowd.*

hold court *v. phr.* **1.** To hold a formal meeting of a royal court or a court of law. ♦ *Judge Stephens allowed no foolishness when he held court.* **2.** *informal* To act like a king or queen among subjects. ♦ *Even at sixteen, Judy was holding court for numbers of charmed boys.*

hold down *v.* **1.** To keep in obedience; keep control of; continue authority or rule over. ♦ *Kings used to know very well how to hold down the people.* **2.** *informal* To work satisfactorily at. ♦ *John had held down a tough job for a long time.*

hold everything See HOLD IT.

hold fire See HOLD ONE'S FIRE.

hold forth *v.* **1.** To offer; propose. ♦ *As a candidate, Jones held forth the promise of a bright future.* **2.** To speak in public; preach.—Usually used with little respect. ♦ *Senator Smith was holding forth on free trade.*

hold good *v.* **1.** To continue to be good; last. ♦ *The coupon on the cereal box offered a free toy, but the offer held good only till the end of the year.* ♦ *Attendance at the basketball games held good all winter.* **2.** To continue; endure; last. ♦ *The demand for new houses held good all that year.* ♦ *The agreement between the schools held good for three years.* See HOLD TRUE.

hold it *or* **hold everything** *v. phr., informal* To stop something one is doing or getting ready to do.—Usually used as a command. ♦ *The pilot was starting to take off, when the control tower ordered "Hold it!"*

hold off *v.* **1a.** To refuse to let (someone) become friendly. ♦ *The president's high rank and chilly manner held people off.* Compare KEEP AT A DISTANCE. **1b.** To be rather shy or unfriendly. ♦ *Perkins was a scholarly man who held off from people.* Compare KEEP AT A DISTANCE. **2.** To keep away by fighting; oppose by force. ♦ *The man locked himself in the house and held off the police for an hour.* **3.** To wait before (doing something); postpone; delay. ♦ *Jack held off paying for the television set until the dealer fixed it.* ♦ *Mr. Smith held off from building while interest rates were high.*

hold on *v.* **1.** To keep holding tightly; continue to hold strongly. ♦ *As Ted was pulling on the rope, it began to slip and Earl cried, "Hold on, Ted!"* Syn. HANG ON. **2.** To wait and not hang up a telephone; keep a phone for later use. ♦ *Mr. Jones asked me to hold on while he spoke to his secretary.* **3.** To keep on with a business or job in spite of difficulties. ♦ *It was hard to keep the store going during the depression, but Max held on and at last met with success.* **4.** *informal* To wait a minute; stop.—Usually used as a command. ♦ *"Hold on!" John's father said, "I want the car tonight."*

hold one's breath *v. phr.* **1.** To stop breathing for a moment when you are excited or nervous. ♦ *The race was so close that everyone was holding his breath at the finish.* **2.** To endure great nervousness, anxiety, or excitement. ♦ *John held his breath for days before he got word that the college he chose had accepted him.*

hold one's end up *or* **hold up one's end** *or* **keep one's end up** *or* **keep up one's end** *v. phr., informal* To do your share of work; do your part. ♦ *Mary washed the dishes so fast that Ann, who was drying them, couldn't keep her end up.* ♦ *Susan kept up her end of the conversation, but Bill did not talk very much.* ♦ *Bob said he would lend me his bicycle if I repaired the flat tire, but he didn't keep up his end of the bargain.*

hold one's fire *or* **hold fire** *v. phr.* To keep back arguments or facts; keep from telling something. ♦ *Tom could have hurt Fred by telling what he knew, but he held his fire.* ♦ *Mary held fire until she had enough information to convince the other club members.*

hold one's head up *v. phr.* To show self-respect; not be ashamed; be proud. ♦ *When Mr. Murray had paid off his debts, he felt that he could hold his head up again.*

hold one's horses *v. phr., informal* To stop; wait; be patient.—Usually used as a command. May be considered rude. ♦ *"Hold your horses!" Mr. Jones said to David when David wanted to call the police.*

hold one's nose to the grindstone See KEEP ONE'S NOSE TO THE GRINDSTONE.

hold one's own *v. phr.* To keep your position; avoid losing ground; keep your advantage, wealth, or condition without loss. ♦ *Mr. Smith could not build up his business, but he held his own.* ♦ *The team held its own after the first quarter.* ♦ *Mary had a hard time after the operation, but soon she was holding her own.*

hold one's peace *v. phr., formal* To be silent and not speak against something; be still; keep quiet. ♦ *I did not agree with the teacher, but held my peace as he was rather angry.* Compare HOLD ONE'S TONGUE

hold one's temper *or* **keep one's temper** *v. phr.* To make yourself be quiet and peaceful; not become angry. ♦ *The meeting will go smoothly if the president keeps his temper.* ♦ *Dave can't keep his temper when he drives in heavy traffic.* Contrast LOSE ONE'S TEMPER, BLOWS ONE'S STACK.

hold one's tongue *v. phr.* To be silent; keep still; not talk.—May be consid-

ered rude. ♦ *The teacher told Fred to hold his tongue* ♦ *If people would hold their tongues from unkind speech, fewer people would be hurt*

hold on to *v. phr.* **1a.** *or* **hold to** To continue to hold or keep; hold tightly. ♦ *When Jane played horse with her father, she held on to him tightly.* ♦ *The teacher said that if we believed something was true and good we should hold on to it.* ♦ *The old man held on to his job stubbornly and would not retire.* **1b.** To stay in control of. ♦ *Ann was so frightened that she had to hold on to herself not to scream.* Contrast LET GO. **2.** To continue to sing or sound. ♦ *The singer held on to the last note of the song for a long time.*

hold on to your hat See HANG ON TO YOUR HAT.

holdout *n.* A rebel who refuses to go with the majority. ♦ *Sam was a lone holdout in town; he refused to sell his old lakefront cottage to make place for a skyscraper.*

hold out *v. phr.* **1.** To put forward; reach out; extend; offer. ♦ *Mr. Ryan held out his hand in welcome.* ♦ *The clerk held out a dress for Martha to try on.* ♦ *The Company held out many fine promises to Jack in order to get him to work for them.* **2.** To keep resisting; not yield; refuse to give up. ♦ *The city held out for six months under siege.* Compare HANG ON, HOLD ON. **3.** To refuse to agree or settle until one's wishes have been agreed to. ♦ *The strikers held out for a raise of five cents an hour.* **4.** *slang* To keep something from; refuse information or belongings to which someone has a right. ♦ *Mr. Porter's partner held out on him when the big payment came in.* ♦ *Mother gave Bobby cookies for all the children in the yard, but he held out on them and ate the cookies himself.* ♦ *John knew that the family would go to the beach Saturday, but he held out on his brother.*

hold out an olive branch See BURY THE HATCHET.

holdover *n.* **1.** A successful movie or theater production that plays longer than originally planned. ♦ *Because of its great popularity,* Star Wars *was a holdover in most movie theaters.* **2.** A reservation not used at the time intended, but used later. ♦ *They kept my seat at the opera as a holdover because I am a patron.*

hold over *v.* **1.** To remain or keep in office past the end of the term. ♦ *The city treasurer held over for six months when the new treasurer died suddenly.* ♦ *The new President held the members of the Cabinet over for some time before appointing new members.* **2.** To extend the engagement of; keep longer. ♦ *The theater held over the feature film for another two weeks.* **3.** To delay action on; to postpone; to defer. ♦ *The directors held over their decision until they could get more information.*

hold still *v. phr.* To remain motionless. ♦ *"Hold still," the dentist said. "This won't hurt you at all."*

hold the bag *v. phr.* To be made liable for or victimized. ♦ *We went out to dinner together but when it was time to pay I was left holding the bag.*

hold the fort *v. phr.* **1.** To defend a fort successfully; fight off attackers. ♦ *The little group held the fort for days until help came.* **2.** *informal* To keep a position against opposing forces. ♦ *Friends of civil liberties held the fort during a long debate.* **3.** *informal* **to keep service or operations going** ♦ *It was Christmas Eve, and a few workers held the fort in the office.* ♦ *Mother and Father went out and told the children to hold the fort.*

hold the line *v. phr.* To keep a situation or trouble from getting worse; hold steady; prevent a setback or loss. ♦ *The mayor held the line on taxes.* ♦ *The company held the line on employment.*

hold the stage *v. phr.* **1.** To continue to be produced and to attract audiences. ♦ *"Peter Pan" holds the stage year after year at its annual Christmas showing in London.* **2.** To be active in a group; attract attention. ♦ *We had only an hour to discuss the question and Mr. Jones held the stage for most of it.* ♦ *Jane likes to hold the stage at any party or meeting, so she does and says anything.*

hold to See HOLD ON TO.

hold true *or* **hold good** *v. phr.* To remain true. ♦ *It has always held true that man cannot live without laws.*

♦ *Bob is a good boy and that holds true of Jim.*

holdup *n.* **1.** Robbery. ♦ *John fell victim to a highway holdup.* **2.** A delay, as on a crowded highway. ♦ *Boy we're late! What's causing this holdup?*

hold up *v.* **1.** To raise; lift. ♦ *John held up his hand.* **2.** To support; bear; carry. ♦ *The chair was too weak to hold up Mrs. Smith.* **3.** To show; call attention to; exhibit. ♦ *The teacher held up excellent models of composition for her class to imitate.* **4.** To check; stop; delay. ♦ *The wreck held up traffic on the railroad's main line tracks.* **5.** *informal* To rob at gunpoint. ♦ *Masked men held up the bank.* **6.** To keep one's courage or spirits up; remain calm; keep control of oneself. ♦ *The grieving mother held up for her children's sake.* **7.** To remain good; not get worse. ♦ *Sales held up well.* ♦ *Our team's luck held up and they won the game.* ♦ *The weather held up and the game was played.* **8.** To prove true. ♦ *The police were doubtful at first, but Tony's story held up.* **9.** To delay action; defer; postpone. Often used with *on.* ♦ *The college held up on plans for the building until more money came in.* ♦ *The President held up on the news until he was sure of it.*

hold up one's end See HOLD ONE'S END UP.

hold water *v. phr.* **1.** To keep water without leaking. ♦ *That pail still holds water.* **2.** *informal* To prove true; stand testing; bear examination.—Usually used in negative, interrogative, or conditional sentences. ♦ *Ernest told the police a story that wouldn't hold water.*

hold your hat See HANG ON TO YOUR HAT.

hole See ACE IN THE HOLE, BURN A HOLE IN ONE'S POCKET, IN A HOLE *or* IN A SPOT, IN THE HOLE, OUT OF THE HOLE, SQUARE PEG IN A ROUND HOLE.

hole in See HOLE UP.

hole in one *n. phr.* A shot in golf that is hit from the tee and goes right into the cup. ♦ *Many golfers play for years before they get a hole in one.*

hole-in-the-wall *n. phr.* A small place to live, stay in, or work in; a small, hidden, or inferior place. ♦ *The jewelry store occupied a tiny hole-in-the-wall.* ♦ *When Mr. and Mrs. Green were first* *married, they lived in a little hole-in-the-wall in a cheap apartment building.* **2.** *slang, citizen's band radio jargon.* A tunnel. ♦ *Let's get through this hole in the wall, then we'll change seats.*

hole out *v.* To finish play in golf by hitting the ball into the cup. ♦ *The other players waited for Palmer to hole out before they putted .*

hole up *also* **hole in** *v., slang* To take refuge or shelter; put up; lodge. ♦ *After a day's motoring, Harry found a room for rent and holed up for the night.* ♦ *The thief holed up at an abandoned farm.* ♦ *"Let's hole in," said Father as we came to a motel that looked good.*

holiday See HALF-HOLIDAY.

holier-than-thou *adj.* Acting as if you are better than others in goodness, character, or reverence for God; acting as if morally better than other people. ♦ *Most people find holier-than-thou actions in others hard to accept.* ♦ *After Mr. Howard stopped smoking, he had a holier-than-thou manner toward his friends who still smoked.*

holistic health *n., informal, semi-technical* The maintenance of health and the avoidance of disease through such psychogenic practices and procedures as biofeedback, meditation, alternative methods of childbirth, and avoidance of drugs. ♦ *The Murgatroyds are regular holistic health freaks—why, they won't even take aspirin when they have a headache.*

holler before one is hurt See CRY BEFORE ONE IS HURT.

hollow See BEAT ALL HOLLOW *also* BEAT HOLLOW.

hollow out *v.* To cut or dig out or to cut or dig a hole in; make a cut or cave in; excavate. ♦ *The soldier hollowed out a foxhole in the ground to lie in.* ♦ *The Indians used to hollow out a log to make a canoe.* ♦ *Joe's father hollowed out a pumpkin to make a jack-o'-lantern.*

holy cats *or* **holy cow** *or* **holy mackerel** *or* **holy Moses** *interj., informal*—Used to express strong feeling (as astonishment, pleasure, or anger); used in speech or when writing conversation. ♦ *"Holy cats! That's good pie!" said Dick.* ♦ *"Holy cow! They can't do that!" Mary said when she saw the boys hurting a much smaller boy.*

holy terror *n., informal* A very disobedient or unruly child; brat. ♦ *All the children are afraid of Johnny because he's a holy terror.*

home See AT HOME, BRING HOME, BRING HOME THE BACON, CHICKENS COME HOME TO ROOST, CLOSE TO HOME, CONVALESCENT HOME *or* NURSING HOME *or* REST HOME, KEEP THE HOME FIRES BURNING, MAKE ONESELF AT HOME, NOBODY HOME, WRITE HOME ABOUT.

home brew *n. phr.* A beer or other malt liquor made at home, not in a brewery. ♦ *Home brew reached its greatest popularity in America during national prohibition.*

home on *or* **home in on** *v.* To move toward a certain place by following a signal or marker. ♦ *The airplane homed in on the radio beacon.* ♦ *The ship homed on the lights of New York harbor.*

home plate *n.* The base in baseball where the batter stands and that a runner must touch to score. ♦ *The runner slid across home plate ahead of the tag to score a run.*

home run *n.* A hit in baseball that allows the batter to run around all the bases and score a run. ♦ *Frank hit a home run over the left field wall in the second inning.*

honest broker *n. phr.* A person hired or appointed to act as an agent in a legal, business, or political situation where impartial advice is needed in order to settle a dispute. ♦ *Michael has been asked to act as an honest broker to settle the argument between the employees and the management.*

honestly See COME BY HONESTLY.

honest to goodness *or* **honest to God** *adj. phr., informal* Really; truly; honestly.—Used to emphasize something said. ♦ *When we were in Washington, we saw the President, honest to goodness.* ♦ *"Honest to goodness, Jane, I think you are the messiest girl in the world," said Mother.*

honest-to-goodness *or* **honest-to-God** *adj. phr., informal* Real; genuine.—Used for emphasis. ♦ *She served him honest-to-goodness deep dish apple pie.* ♦ *It was the first honest-to-goodness baseball game he'd seen since going abroad.*

honeymoon is over The first happy period of friendship and cooperation between two persons or groups is over. ♦ *A few months after a new President is elected, the honeymoon is over and Congress and the President begin to criticize each other.* ♦ *The honeymoon was soon over for the new foreman and the men under him.*

honky-tonk *n.* A cheap nightclub or dance hall. ♦ *There were a number of honky-tonks near the army camp.*

honor See DO THE HONORS, IN HONOR OF, ON ONE'S HONOR.

hook See BY HOOK OR BY CROOK, GET THE HOOK *at* GET THE BOUNCE 2, GIVE THE HOOK *at* GIVE THE BOUNCE 2, OFF THE HOOK.

hooked on *adj.* **1.** Addicted to a substance such as cigarettes, coffee, tea, drugs, or alcohol. ♦ *Fred is hooked on grass, but Tim is only hooked on tea.* **2.** Enthusiastic or very supportive of something. ♦ *I am hooked on the local symphony.*

hookey See PLAY HOOKEY.

hook, line and sinker *adv. phr., informal* Without question or doubt; completely. ♦ *Johnny was so easily fooled that he fell for Joe's story, hook, line and sinker.* ♦ *Mary was such a romantic girl that she swallowed the story Alice told her about her date, hook, line and sinker.* ♦ *Bobby trusted Jim so he was taken in by his hard-luck story hook, line and sinker.*

hookup *n.* A connection, electrical or otherwise, between two instruments or two individuals. ♦ *Edwin and Hermione are a perfect couple; they have got the right hookup.*

hook up *v. phr.* To connect or fit together. ♦ *The company sent a man to hook up the telephone.* ♦ *They could not use the gas stove because it had not been hooked up.*

hoop See JUMP THROUGH A HOOP.

hop See MAD AS A HORNET *or* MAD AS HOPS.

hop, skip and a jump See STONE'S THROW.

hope See CROSS ONE'S HEART *or* CROSS ONE'S HEART AND HOPE TO DIE, IN HOPES.

hope against hope *v. phr.* To try to hope when things look black; hold to hope in bad trouble. ♦ *The mother continued to hope against hope although the plane was hours late.* ♦ *Jane hoped against hope that Joe would call her.*

hop to it *v. phr., slang* To get started; start a job; get going. ♦ *"There's a lot to do today, so let's hop to it,"* the boss said.

hopped up *adj., slang* **1.** Doped with a narcotic drug. ♦ *Police found Jones hiding in an opium den, among other men all hopped up with the drug.* **2.** Full of eagerness; excited. ♦ *Fred was all hopped up about going over the ocean.*

horn See BLOW ONE'S OWN HORN *or* TOOT ONE'S OWN HORN, PULL IN ONE'S HORNS *or* DRAW IN ONE'S HORNS, TAKE THE BULL BY THE HORNS.

hornet See MAD AS A HORNET *or* MAD AS HOPS *or* MAD AS A WET HEN, STIR UP A HORNET'S NEST.

horn in *v., slang* To come in without invitation or welcome; interfere. Often used with *on.* ♦ *Jack would often horn in on conversations discussing things he knew nothing about.* ♦ *Lee horned in on Ray and Annie and wanted to dance with Annie.* Compare BUTT IN.

horns of a dilemma *n. phr.* Two choices possible in a situation in which neither is wanted. Usually used after *on.* ♦ *Joe found himself on the horns of a dilemma; if he went to work, he'd miss seeing Mary; if he stayed out, he'd be too broke to take her anywhere.*

horror See THROW UP ONE'S HANDS IN HORROR.

horse See BET ON THE WRONG HORSE, CART BEFORE THE HORSE, CHANGE HORSES IN THE MIDDLE OF THE STREAM *or* CHANGE HORSES IN MIDSTREAM, EAT LIKE A HORSE, HOLD ONE'S HORSES, IRON HORSE, LOCK THE BARN DOOR AFTER THE HORSE IS STOLEN, LOOK A GIFT HORSE IN THE MOUTH, OFF ONE'S HIGH HORSE, ON ONE'S HIGH HORSE, PUT ONE'S MONEY ON A SCRATCHED HORSE, STRAIGHT FROM THE HORSE'S MOUTH.

horsefeathers! *n. phr., slang* **1.** Not true; I don't believe what you're saying. ♦ *"Horsefeathers!" Brad cried. "I can't believe a word of what you said about Jessica."* **2.** Exclamation of disgust. ♦ *"Horsefeathers!" Fred cried.*

"We've just missed the bus." Compare FIDDLESTICKS, BULLSHIT.

horselaugh *n. phr.* A loud, sarcastic, and derisive laugh. ♦ *When the speaker praised politics as one of the oldest and noblest professions, his audience of college students gave him a horselaugh.*

horse around *v., slang* To join in rough teasing; play around. ♦ *They were a bunch of sailors on shore leave, horsing around where there were girls and drinks.* ♦ *John horsed around with the dog for a while when he came in from school.*

horse of a different color *or* **horse of another color** *n. phr., informal* Something altogether separate and different. ♦ *Anyone can be broke, but to steal is a horse of a different color.* ♦ *Do you mean that the boy with that pretty girl is her brother? I thought he was her boyfriend. Well, that's a horse of another color.*

horse opera *n. phr.* A Western movie in which cowboys and horses play a major part. ♦ *John Wayne played in many horse operas.*

horseplay *n.* Rough, practical joking. ♦ *The newlyweds couldn't get a wink of sleep all night because there was a lot of yelling and screaming outside of their window—the usual horseplay.*

horse sense *n., informal* A good understanding about what to do in life; good judgment; wisdom in making decisions. ♦ *Bill had never been to college, but he had plenty of horse sense.* ♦ *Some people are well educated and read many books, but still do not have much horse sense.*

horse trade *n.* **1.** The sale of a horse or the exchange of two horses. ♦ *It was a horse trade in which the owner of the worse animal gave a rifle to make the trade equal.* **2.** *informal* A business agreement or bargain arrived at after hard and skillful discussion. ♦ *Party leaders went around for months making horse trades to get support for their candidate.* ♦ *The horse trade finally called for a new car for the radio station in exchange for several weeks of advertising for the car dealer.*

hot See BLOW HOT AND COLD, MAKE IT HOT.

hot air *n., informal* Nonsense, exaggerated talk, wasted words characterized by emotion rather than intellectual content. ♦ *That was just a lot of hot air what Joe said.*

hot and bothered *adj., informal* Excited and worried, displeased, or puzzled.—A hackneyed phrase. *Fritz got all hot and bothered when he failed in the test.* ♦ *Leona was all hot and bothered when her escort was late in coming for her.* ♦ *Jerry was hot and bothered about his invention when he couldn't get it to work.* ♦ *It is a small matter; don't get so hot and bothered.*

hot and heavy *adv. phr., informal* Strongly; vigorously; emphatically. ♦ *Fred got it hot and heavy when his wife found out how much he had lost at cards.* ♦ *The partners had a hot and heavy argument before deciding to enlarge their store.*

hot dog *n. phr., informal* A frankfurter or wiener in a roll. ♦ *The boys stopped on the way home for hot dogs and coffee.*

hot dog *interj., informal* Hurrah!—A cry used to show pleasure or enthusiasm. ♦ *"Hot dog!" Frank exclaimed when he unwrapped a birthday gift of a small record player.*

hot dog roast See WIENER ROAST.

hot number *n., slang* A person or thing noticed as newer, better, or more popular than others. ♦ *The boys and girls thought that song was a hot number.* ♦ *The new car that Bob is driving is a real hot number.* ♦ *John invented a new can opener that was a hot number in the stores.*

hot off the press *adj. phr.* Just appeared in print. ♦ *This is the latest edition of the* Chicago Tribune; *it's hot off the press.*

hot one *n., slang, informal* ♦ Something out of the ordinary; something exceptional, such as a joke, a person whether in terms of looks or intelligence. ♦ *Joe's joke sure was a hot one.* ♦ *Sue is a hot one, isn't she?*

hot potato *n., informal* A question that causes strong argument and is difficult to settle. ♦ *Many school boards found segregation a hot potato in the 1960s.*

hot rod *n., informal* An older automobile changed so that it can gain speed quickly and go very fast. ♦ *Hot rods are used by young people especially in drag racing.*

hot seat *n., slang* **1.** The electric chair used to cause death by electrocution in legal executions. ◆ *Many a man has controlled a murderous rage when he thought of the hot seat.* **2.** *informal* A position in which you can easily get into trouble. ◆ *A judge in a beauty contest is on the hot seat. If he chooses one girl, the other girls will be angry with him.*

hot stuff *n., slang, citizen's band radio jargon* Coffee. ◆ *Let's stop and get some hot stuff.*

hot under the collar *adj. phr., informal* Angry. ◆ *Mary gets hot under the collar if you joke about women drivers.* ◆ *Tom got hot under the collar when his teacher punished him.*

hot water *n. informal* Trouble.—Used with *in, into, out, of.* ◆ *John's thoughtless remark about religion got John into a lot of hot water.* ◆ *It was the kind of trouble where it takes a friend to get you out of hot water.*

hound See ROCK HOUND, RUN WITH THE HARE AND HUNT (RIDE) WITH THE HOUNDS.

hour See AFTER HOURS, ALL HOURS, COFFEE HOUR, ON THE HOUR, ZERO HOUR.

house See BOARDING HOUSE REACH, BRING DOWN THE HOUSE, FUN HOUSE, HASH HOUSE, KEEP HOUSE, ON THE HOUSE, PARISH HOUSE, PEOPLE WHO LIVE IN GLASS HOUSES SHOULD NOT THROW STONES, PLAGUE ON BOTH YOUR HOUSES *or* PLAGUE O' BOTH YOUR HOUSES, PUT ONE'S HOUSE IN ORDER *or* SET ONE'S HOUSE IN ORDER.

housebroken *adj.* Trained to go outside to relieve themselves (said of domestic pets, primarily dogs). ◆ *All young puppies must eventually be housebroken.*

house detective *n.* A detective employed by a hotel, store, or other business to watch for any trouble. ◆ *The one-armed man sweeping the bank floor was really the house detective.*

house of cards *n. phr.* Something badly put together and easily knocked down; a poorly founded plan, hope, or action. ◆ *John's business fell apart like a house of cards..*

house of ill fame *or* **of ill repute** *n. phr.* A bordello; a brothel. ◆ *At the edge of town there is a house of ill repute run by a Madame who used to be a singer in a bar.*

housetop See SHOUT FROM THE HOUSETOPS *or* SHOUT FROM THE ROOFTOPS.

hover over *v. phr.* **1.** To remain close or above. ◆ *The rescue helicopter was carefully hovering above the stranded rock climbers.* **2.** To watch over; supervise. ◆ *"Mother!" Phillip cried, "if you don't stop hovering over me, I'll go bananas!"*

how See AND HOW!

how about *or* **what about** *interrog.*— Used to ask for a decision, action, opinion, or explanation. **1.** Will you have or agree on? ◆ *How about another piece of pie?* ◆ *What about a game of tennis?* ◆ *How about going to the dance with me Saturday?* **2.** Will you lend or give me? ◆ *How about five dollars until Friday?* ◆ *What about a little help with these dishes?* **3.** What is to be done about? ◆ *What about the windows? Shall we close them before we go?* **4.** How do you feel about? What do you think about? What is to be thought or said? ◆ *What about women in politics?* ◆ *How about this button on the front of the typewriter?*

how about that *or* **what about that** *informal* An expression of surprise, congratulation, or praise. ◆ *When Jack heard of his brother's promotion, he exclaimed, "How about that!"* ◆ *Bill won the scholarship! What about that!*

how come *informal also nonstandard* **how's come** *interrog.* How does it happen that? Why? ◆ *How come you are late?* ◆ *You're wearing your best clothes today. How come?* Compare WHAT FOR.

how do you do *formal* How are you?— Usually as a reply to an introduction; it is in the form of a question but no answer is expected. ◆ *"Mary, I want you to meet my friend Fred. Fred, this is my wife, Mary." "How do you do, Mary?" "How do you do, Fred?"*

how goes it? *v. phr. interrog.* How are you and your affairs in general progressing? ◆ *Jim asked Bill, "how goes it with the new wife and the new apartment?"*

howling success *n., informal* A great success; something that is much praised;

something that causes wide enthusiasm. ♦ *The party was a howling success.* ♦ *The book was a howling success.*

how's come See HOW COME.

how so *interrog.* How is that so? Why is it so? How? Why? ♦ *I said the party was a failure and she asked. "How so?"* ♦ *He said his brother was not a good dancer and I asked him, "How so?"*

how's that *informal* What did you say? Will you please repeat that? ♦ *"I've just been up in a balloon for a day and a half." "How's that?"* ♦ *"The courthouse is on fire." "How's that again?"*

how the land lies See LAY OF THE LAND.

how the wind blows See WAY THE WIND BLOWS.

huddle See GO INTO A HUDDLE.

hue and cry *n.* **1.** An alarm and chase after a supposed wrongdoer; a pursuit usually by shouting men. ♦ *"Stop, thief," cried John as he ran. Others joined him, and soon there was a hue and cry.* **2.** An excited mass protest, alarm, or outcry of any kind. ♦ *The explosion was so terrible that people at a distance raised a great hue and cry about an earthquake.*

hug the road *v. phr.* To stay firmly on the road; ride smoothly without swinging. ♦ *A heavy car with a low center of gravity will hug the road.* ♦ *At high speeds a car will not hug the road well.*

huh-uh *or* **hum-um** *or* **uh-uh** *adv., informal* No.—Used only in speech or to record dialogue. ♦ *Did Mary come? Huh-uh.* ♦ *Is it raining out? Uh-uh.* Contrast UH-UH.

humble See EAT HUMBLE PIE.

hump See OVER THE HUMP.

hundred See BY THE DOZEN *or* BY THE HUNDRED *or* BY THE THOUSAND.

hunky-dory *adj.* OK; satisfactory; fine. ♦ *The landlord asked about our new apartment and we told him that so far everything was hunky-dory.*

hunt See RUN WITH THE HARE AND HUNT (RIDE) WITH THE HOUNDS.

hunt and peck *n. phr., informal* Picking out typewriter keys by sight, usually with one or two fingers; not memorizing the keys. ♦ *Many newspaper reporters do their typing by hunt and peck.*—Often used, with hyphens, as an adjective. ♦ *Mr. Barr taught himself to type, and he uses the hunt-and-peck system.*

hunt down *v.* **1.** To pursue and capture; look hard for an animal or person until found and caught. ♦ *The police hunted down the escaped prisoner.* Compare TRACK DOWN. **2.** To search for (something) until one finds it. ♦ *Professor Jones hunted down the written manuscript in the Library of Congress.* Syn. TRACK DOWN.

hunting See HAPPY HUNTING GROUND.

hunt up *v.* To find or locate by search. ♦ *When John was in Chicago, he hunted up some old friends.* ♦ *The first thing Fred had to do was to hunt up a hotel room.*

hurry on with *or* **make haste with** *v. phr.* To make rapid progress in an undertaking. ♦ *Sue promised to hurry on with the report and send it out today.*

hurry up *v. phr.* To rush (an emphatic form of hurry). ♦ *Hurry up or we'll miss our plane.*

hurt See CRY BEFORE ONE IS HURT *or* HOLLER BEFORE ONE IS HURT.

hush-hush *adj., informal* Kept secret or hidden; kept from public knowledge; hushed up; concealed. ♦ *The company had a new automobile engine that it was developing, but kept it a hush-hush project until they knew it was successful.*

hush up *v.* **1.** To keep news of (something) from getting out; prevent people from knowing about. ♦ *It isn't always easy to hush up a scandal.* **2.** *informal* To be or make quiet; stop talking, crying, or making some other noise.—Often used as a command. ♦ *"Hush up," Mother said, when we began to repeat ugly gossip.*

ice See BLOOD RUNS COLD or BLOOD TURNS TO ICE, BREAK THE ICE, CUT ICE, ON ICE, SKATE ON THIN ICE.

iceberg See COOL AS AN ICEBERG.

idea See THE IDEA, WHAT'S THE BIG IDEA or WHAT'S THE IDEA.

I declare *interj., dialect* Well; oh my; truly.—Used for emphasis. ♦*I declare, it has been a very warm day!* ♦*Mother said, "I declare, John, you have grown a foot."*

idiot box *n.* A television set. ♦*Phil has been staring at the idiot box all afternoon.*

if See WHAT IF.

if anything *adv. phr.* More likely; instead; rather. ♦*The weather forecast is not for cooler weather; if anything, it is expected to be warmer.* ♦*Joe isn't a bad boy. If anything he's a pretty good one.* Compare MATTER OF FACT.

if it's not one thing it's another If a certain thing doesn't go wrong, another most probably will. ♦*When John lost his keys and his wallet, and his car wouldn't start, he exclaimed in despair, "If it's not one thing it's another."* Compare ONE DAMN THING AFTER ANOTHER (ODTAA).

if need be *adv. phr.* If the need arises. ♦*If need be, I can come early tomorrow and work overtime.*

if only I wish. ♦*If only it would stop raining!* ♦*If only Mother could be here.* Syn. WOULD THAT.

if the hill will not come to Muhammad, Muhammad will go to the hill If one person will not go to the other, then the other must go to him.—A proverb. ♦*Grandfather won't come to visit us, so we must go and visit him. If the hill won't come to Muhammad, then Muhammad will go to the hill.*

if the shoe fits, wear it If what is said describes you, you are meant.—A proverb. ♦*I won't say who, but some children are always late. If the shoe fits, wear it.*

if worst comes to worst If the worst thing happens that be imagined; if the worst possible thing happens; if troubles grow worse. ♦*If worst comes to worst and Mr. Jones loses the house, he will send his family to his mother's farm.* ♦*If worst comes to worst, we shall close the school for a few days.*

if you can't lick them, join them If you cannot defeat an opponent or get him to change his attitude, plans, or ways of doing things, the best thing to do is to change your ideas, plans, etc. ♦*"The small car manufacturers are winning over the big car makers," the president of an American car factory said. "If we want to stay in business, we must do as they do. In other words, if you can't lick them, join them."*

I'll bet you my bottom dollar *interj., informal* An exaggerated assertion of assurance. ♦*I'll bet you my bottom dollar that the Cubs will win this year.*

I'll say or **I tell you** *interj., informal* I agree with this completely.—Used for emphasis. ♦*Did the children all enjoy Aunt Sally's pecan pie? I'll say!* ♦*I'll say this is a good movie!*

I'll tell you what or **tell you what** *informal* Here is an idea. ♦*The hamburger stand is closed, but I'll tell you what, let's go to my house and cook some hot dogs.*

ill See IT'S AN ILL WIND THAT BLOWS NOBODY GOOD, TAKE ILL.

ill at ease *adj. phr.* Not feeling at ease or comfortable; anxious; worried; unhappy. ♦*Donald had never been to a big party before and he was ill at ease.* ♦*When Joe first went to dancing school, he was ill at ease, not knowing how to act.* Contrast AT EASE 2.

ill-favored *adj.* Ugly; unprepossessing. ♦*Oddly enough, the father had less trouble in marrying off his ill-favored daughter than her prettier sister.*

ill-gotten gains *n. phr.* Goods or money obtained in an illegal or immoral fashion. ♦*The jailed criminal had plenty of time to think about his ill-gotten gains.*

image See SPITTING IMAGE or SPIT AND IMAGE.

impose on *v.* To try to get more from (a person who is helping you) than he or she intended to give. ♦*Don't you think you are imposing on your neighbor when you use his telephone for half an* hour? ♦ *You may swim in the Allens' pool so long as you do not impose on them by bringing all your friends.* Compare TAKE ADVANTAGE.

improve on *or* **improve upon** *v.* To make or get one that is better than (another). ♦ *Dick made good marks the first year, but he thought he could improve on them.* ♦ *Charles built a new model racer for the derby race, because he knew he could improve upon his old one.*

I'm telling you *informal* It is important to listen to what I am saying. ♦ *Marian is a smart girl but I'm telling you, she doesn't always do what she promises.*

in a bad frame of mind *adv. phr.* In an unhappy mood. ♦ *Make sure the boss is not in a bad frame of mind when you ask him for a raise.* Contrast IN A GOOD FRAME OF MIND.

in a bad way *adv. phr., informal* In trouble or likely to have trouble. ♦ *If you have only those two girls to help you, you are in a bad way.* ♦ *Jerry has written only one sentence of his term paper that is due tomorrow, and he knows he is in a bad way.* ♦ *Mrs. Jones has cancer and is in a bad way.* ♦ *A new supermarket opened across the street, and the Peters' grocery business was soon in a bad way.*

in a big way *adv. phr., informal* As fully as possible; with much ceremony. ♦ *Our family celebrates birthdays in a big way.* ♦ *John likes to entertain his dates in a big way.*

in a bind *or* **in a box** *adv. phr., informal* Likely to have trouble whether you do one thing or another. ♦ *Sam is in a bind because if he carries home his aunt's groceries, his teacher will be angry because he is late, and if he doesn't, his aunt will complain.* Compare BETWEEN THE DEVIL AND THE DEEP BLUE SEA, HORNS OF A DILEMMA.

in a breeze See WIN IN A WALK *or* WIN IN A BREEZE.

in absentia *adv. phr., formal* When the person is absent.—Used in graduation exercises when presenting diplomas to an absent student or during a court case. ♦ *On Commencement Day, Joe was sick in bed and the college gave him his bachelor's degree in absentia.* [Latin, meaning "in absence."]

in accordance with *adv. phr.* In consonance with something; conforming to something. ♦ *Employees at this firm are expected to always behave in accordance with the rules.*

in a circle *or* **in circles** *adv. phr.* Without any progress; without getting anywhere; uselessly. ♦ *The committee debated for two hours, just talking in circles.* ♦ *If you don't have a clear aim, you can work a long time and still be going in circles.* ♦ *He seemed to be working hard, but was just running around in circles.*

in addition *adv. phr.* As something extra; besides. ♦ *We saw a Mickey Mouse cartoon in addition to the cowboy movie.* ♦ *Aunt Mary gave us sandwiches for our picnic and a bag of cookies in addition.* ♦ *He has two cars and in addition a motorboat.*

in advance *or* **in advance of** *adv. phr.* **1.** In front; ahead (of the others); first. ♦ *In the parade, the band will march in advance of the football team.* ♦ *The soldiers rode out of the fort with the scouts in advance.* **2.** Before doing or getting something. ♦ *The motel man told Mr. Williams he would have to pay in advance.* ♦ *The paperhanger mixed his paste quite a while in advance so it would have time to cool.* ♦ *It will be easier to decorate the snack bar if we cut the streamers in advance of the actual decorating.*

in a family way *or* **in the family way** *adj. phr., informal* Going to have a baby. ♦ *Sue and Liz are happy because their mother is in the family way.* ♦ *The Ferguson children are promising kittens to everyone because their cat is in a family way.* Compare WITH CHILD.

in a fix *adv. phr.* In trouble. ♦ *Last night Jack wrecked his car and now he is in a fix.* Compare IN A JAM, IN A PICKLE.

in a flash *also* **in a trice** *adv. phr.* Very suddenly. ♦ *We were watching the bird eat the crumbs; then I sneezed, and he was gone in a flash.* ♦ *Bob was looking over his notes for English class and in a flash he knew what he would write his paper about.*

in a flutter *adv. phr., informal* In a state of nervous excitement. ♦ *Whenever Norm and Cathy are near one another, both are in a flutter; they must be in love.*

in a fog *or* **in a haze** *adv. phr.* Mentally confused; not sure what is happening. ♦*I didn't vote for Alice because she always seems to be in a fog.* ♦*I was so upset that for two days I went around in a haze, not even answering when people spoke to me.* Contrast ALL THERE, HIT ON ALL CYLINDERS.

in a good frame of mind *adv. phr.* In a happy mood. ♦*After a relaxing holiday in the Bahamas, the boss was in a very good frame of mind.* Contrast IN A BAD FRAME OF MIND.

in a hole *or* **in a spot** *adj. phr., informal* In an embarrassing or difficult position; in some trouble. ♦*When the restaurant cook left at the beginning of the busy season, it put the restaurant owner in a hole.* Compare BEHIND THE EIGHT BALL, IN THE HOLE.

in a huff *adv. phr., informal* Angrily. ♦*Ellen went off in a huff because she didn't get elected class president.*

in a jam *adv. phr., informal* In a predicament; in a situation fraught with difficulty. ♦*If you continue to disregard the university instructions on how to take a test, you'll wind up in a jam with the head of the department.* Compare IN A PICKLE, IN DEEP SHIT.

in a jiffy *adv. phr., informal* Immediately; right away; in a moment. ♦*Wait for me; I'll be back in a jiffy.*

in a kind of way See IN A WAY 1.

in a lather *adj., slang* In great excitement; all worked up; extremely agitated. ♦*I couldn't get across to Joe, he was all in a lather.*

in all *adv. phr.* **1.** All being counted; altogether. ♦*You have four apples and I have three bananas, making seven pieces of fruit in all.* ♦*In all we did very well.* **2.** See ALL IN ALL 2.

in and out *adv. phr.* **1.** Coming in and going out often. ♦*He was very busy Saturday and was in and out all day.* **2.** See INSIDE OUT 2.

in another's place See PUT ONESELF IN ANOTHER'S PLACE.

in a nutshell *adv. phr., informal* In a few words; briefly; without telling all about it. ♦*We are in a hurry, so I'll give you the story in a nutshell.* ♦*In a nutshell, the car is no bargain.* Compare IN SHORT.

in any case *also* **in any event** *or* **at all events** *adv. phr.* **1.** No matter what happens; surely; without fail; certainly; anyhow; anyway. ♦*It may rain tomorrow, but we are going home in any case.* ♦*I may not go to Europe, but in any event, I will visit you during the summer.* **2.** Regardless of anything else; whatever else may be true; anyhow; anyway. ♦*Tom was not handsome and he was not brilliant, but at all events he worked hard and was loyal to his boss.* ♦*I don't know if it is a white house or a brown house. At all events, it is a big house on Main Street.* Compare AT ANY RATE, AT LEAST 2.

in any event See IN ANY CASE.

in a pickle *adv. phr., informal* In a quandary; in a difficult situation. ♦*I was certainly in a pickle when my front tire blew out.*

in a pig's eye *adv., slang, informal* Hardly; unlikely; not so. ♦*Would I marry him? In a pig's eye.*

in a pinch *adv. phr., informal* In an emergency. ♦*Dave is a good friend who will always help out in a pinch.*

in arms *adv. phr.* Having guns and being ready to fight; armed. ♦*When our country is at war, we have many men in arms.* Syn. UP IN ARMS!

in a row See GET ONE'S DUCKS IN A ROW.

in arrears *adv. phr.* Late or behind in payment of money or in finishing something.—Usually used of a legal debt or formal obligation. ♦*Poor Mr. Brown! He is in arrears on his rent.* ♦*He is in arrears on the story he promised to write for the magazine.*

in a sense *adv. phr.* In some ways but not in all; somewhat. ♦*Mr. Smith said our school is the best in the state, and in a sense that is true.* ♦*In a sense, arithmetic is a language.*

inasmuch as *conj.* **1.** See INSOFAR AS. **2.** *also* **for as much as** *formal* Because; for the reason that; since. ♦*Inasmuch as this is your team, you have the right to choose your own captain.* ♦*Inasmuch as the waves are high, I shall not go out in the boat.*

in a sort of way See IN A WAY 1.

in a spot See ON THE SPOT 2.

in a trice See IN A FLASH.

in at the kill *adj. phr., informal* Watching or taking part, usually with pleasure, at the end of a struggle; present at the finish. ♦*Frank and John* *have been quarreling for a long time and tonight they are having a fight. Bill says he wants to be in at the kill, because he is Frank's friend.*

in a walk See WIN IN A WALK.

in a way *adv. phr.* **1.** *also informal* **in a kind of way** *or informal* **in a sort of way** To a certain extent; a little; somewhat. ♦ *I like Jane in a way, but she is very proud.* Compare AFTER A FASHION, MORE OR LESS. **2.** In one thing. ♦ *In a way, this book is easier; it is much shorter.*

in awe of See STAND IN AWE OF.

in a while See AFTER A WHILE, EVERY NOW AND THEN *or* EVERY ONCE IN A WHILE.

in a whole skin See WITH A WHOLE SKIN.

in a word See IN BRIEF.

in a world of one's own *or* **in a world by oneself** **1.** In the place where you belong; in your own personal surroundings; apart from other people. ♦ *They are in a little world of their own in their house on the mountain.* **2a.** In deep thought or concentration. ♦ *Mary is in a world of her own when she is playing the piano.* Compare LOSE ONESELF. **2b.** *slang* Not caring about or connected with other people in thoughts or actions.—Usually used sarcastically. ♦ *That boy is in a world all by himself. He never knows what is happening around him.*

in a zone *adv., slang, informal* In a daze; in a daydream; in a state of being unable to concentrate. ♦ *Professor Smith puts everyone in a zone.*

in back of See BACK OF.

in bad *adv. phr., substandard* Out of favor; unpopular; in difficulty; in trouble. ♦ *No, I can't go swimming today. Father told me to stay home, and I don't want to get in bad.* —Usually used with *with.* ♦ *Mary is in bad with the teacher for cheating on the test.* ♦ *The boy is in bad with the police for breaking windows.* Contrast IN GOOD, IN ONE'S FAVOR.

in bad form *adv. phr.* Violating social custom or accepted behavior. ♦ *When Bob went to the opera in blue jeans and without a tie, his father-in-law told him that it was in bad form.* Contrast IN GOOD FORM.

in behalf of *or* **on behalf of** *prep., formal* **1.** In place of; as a representative of;

for. ♦ *John accepted the championship award on behalf of the team.* **2.** As a help to; for the good of. ♦ *The minister worked hard all his life in behalf of the poor.* Compare IN ONE'S BEHALF, IN ONE'S FAVOR.

in black and white See BLACK AND WHITE.

in brief *or* **in short** *or* **in a word** *adv. phr.* Briefly; to give the meaning of what has been said or written in a word or in a few words; in summary. ♦ *The children could play as long as they liked, they had no work to do, and nobody scolded them; in short, they were happy.* ♦ *The speaker didn't know his subject, nor did he speak well; in brief, he was disappointing.* ♦ *John is smart, polite, and well-behaved. In a word, he is admirable.*

in cahoots with See IN LEAGUE WITH.

in case *adv. phr., informal* **1.** In order to be prepared; as a precaution; if there is need.—Usually used in the phrase *just in case.* ♦ *The bus is usually on time, but start early, just in case.* ♦ *The big dog was tied up, but John carried a stick, just in case.* **2. in case** *or* **in the event** *conj.* If it happens that; if it should happen that; if; lest. ♦ *Tom took his skates in case they found a place to skate.* ♦ *Let me know in case you're not coming.* ♦ *The night watchman is in the store in case there is ever a fire.* ♦ *Keep the window closed in case it rains.* ♦ *I stayed home in case you called.* ♦ *In the event that our team wins, there will be a big celebration.* ♦ *What shall we do in case it snows?*

in case of *also* **in the event of** *prep.* In order to meet the possibility of; lest there is; if there is; if there should be. ♦ *Take your umbrellas in case of rain.* ♦ *The wall was built along the river in case of floods.*

inch See BY INCHES, EVERY INCH, GIVE ONE AN INCH AND HE WILL TAKE A MILE, WITHIN AN ACE OF *or* WITHIN AN INCH OF, WITHIN AN INCH OF ONE'S LIFE.

inch (one's way) along *v. phr.* To proceed slowly and with difficulty. ♦ *When the electricity failed, it took John half an hour to inch his way along the corridors of the office building.*

in character *adv. or adj. phr.* **1.** In agreement with a person's character or personality; in the way that a person usually behaves or is supposed to behave; as usual; characteristic; typical; suitable. ♦*John was very rude at the party, and that was not in character because he is usually very polite.* ♦*The way Judy comforted the little girl was in character. She did it gently and kindly.* **2.** Suitable for the part or the kind of part being acted; natural to the way a character in a book or play is supposed to act. ♦*The fat actor in the movie was in character because the character he played was supposed to be fat and jolly.* ♦*It would not have been in character for Robin Hood to steal from a poor man.* Contrast OUT OF CHARACTER.

in charge *adv. or adj. phr.* **1.** In authority or control; in a position to care for or supervise; responsible. ♦*If you have any questions, ask the boss. He's in charge.* **2.** Under care or supervision. ♦*The sick man was taken in charge by the doctor.* ♦*During your visit to the library, you will be in the librarian's charge.* Compare TAKE CARE OF.

in charge of *prep.* **1.** Responsible for; having supervision or care of. ♦*Marian is in charge of selling tickets.* ♦*The girl in charge of refreshments forgot to order the ice cream for the party.* ♦*When our class had a play, the teacher put Harold in charge of the stage curtain.* **2.** *or* **in the charge of** Under the care or supervision of. ♦*Mother puts the baby in the charge of the baby-sitter while she is out.* ♦*The money was given in charge of Mr. Jackson for safekeeping.*

in check *adv. phr.* In a position where movement or action is not allowed or stopped; under control; kept quiet or back. ♦*The boy was too small to keep the big dog in check, and the dog broke away from his leash.* ♦*The soldiers tried to keep the attacking Indians in check until help came.* ♦*Mary couldn't hold her feelings in check any longer and began to cry.*

in circles See IN A CIRCLE.

in circulation *or* **into circulation** *adj. phr., informal* Going around and doing things as usual; joining what others are doing. ♦*John broke his leg and was out of school for several weeks, but now he is back in circulation again.*

♦*Mary's mother punished her by stopping her from dating for two weeks, but then she got back into circulation.* Contrast OUT OF CIRCULATION.

inclined to *adj. phr.* Having a tendency to; positively disposed toward. ♦*I am inclined to fall asleep after a heavy meal.*

in clover *or* **in the clover** *adv. or adj. phr., informal* In rich comfort; rich or successful; having a pleasant or easy life. ♦*They live in clover because their father is rich.* ♦*When we finish the hard part we'll be in the clover.* Compare BED OF ROSES, LIFE OF RILEY, LIVE HIGH OFF THE HOG, ON EASY STREET.

in cold blood *adv. phr.* Without feeling or pity; in a purposely cruel way; coolly and deliberately. ♦*The bank robbers planned to shoot in cold blood anyone who got in their way.* ♦*The bandits planned to murder in cold blood all farmers in the village by the river.*

in command *adv. phr.* In control of; in charge. ♦*Helen is in command of the situation.*

in commission *or* **into commission** *adv. or adj. phr.* **1.** On duty or ready to be put on duty by a naval or military service; in active service. ♦*The old battleship has been in commission for twenty years.* ♦*It took many months to build the new bomber, and now it is ready to be put into commission.* **2.** In proper condition; in use or ready for use; working; running. ♦*The wheel of my bicycle was broken, but it is back in commission now.* Compare IN ORDER 2. Contrast OUT OF COMMISSION 2.

in common *adv. phr.* Shared together or equally; in use or ownership by all. ♦*Mr. and Mrs. Smith own the store in common.* ♦*The four boys grew up together and have a lot in common.* ♦*The swimming pool is used in common by all the children in the neighborhood.* Compare COMMON GROUND.

in condition See IN SHAPE.

in consequence *adv. phr.* As a result; therefore; so. ♦*Jennie got up late, and in consequence she missed the bus.* ♦*You studied hard, and in consequence you passed the test.*

in consequence of *prep., formal* As a result of. ♦*In consequence of the deep* *snow, school will not open today.* ♦ *In consequence of his promise to pay for the broken window, Bill was not punished.* Compare BECAUSE OF, ON ACCOUNT OF.

in consideration of *adv. phr.* **1.** After thinking about and weighing; because of. ♦ *In consideration of the boy's young age, the judge did not put him in jail for carrying a gun.* **2.** In exchange for; because of; in payment for. ♦ *In consideration of the extra work Joe had done, his boss gave him an extra week's pay.* Compare IN RETURN.

in days *or* **weeks** *or* **years to come** *adv. phr.* In the future. ♦ *In the years to come I will be thinking of my father's advice about life.*

in deep *adj. phr.* Seriously mixed up in something, especially trouble. ♦ *George began borrowing small sums of money to bet on horses, and before he knew it he was in deep.* Compare DEEP WATER, UP TO THE CHIN IN.

in deep water See DEEP WATER.

in defiance of *prep.* Acting against; in disobedience to. ♦ *The girl chewed gum in defiance of the teacher's rule.* ♦ *Bob stayed up late in defiance of the coach's orders.*

in demand *adj. phr.* Needed; wanted. ♦ *Men to shovel snow were in demand after the snow storm.* ♦ *The book about dogs was much in demand in the library.*

Indian See CIGAR-STORE INDIAN.

Indian giver *n. phr.* A person who gives one something, but later asks for it back.—An ethnic slur; avoidable. ♦ *John gave me a beautiful fountain pen, but a week later, like an Indian giver, he wanted it back.*

Indian sign *n., informal* A magic spell that is thought to bring bad luck; curse; jinx; hoo-doo.—Used with *the,* usually after *have* or *with;* and often used in a joking way. ♦ *Bill is a good player, but Ted has the Indian sign on him and always beats him.* ♦ *Father says that he always wins our checker games because he has put the Indian sign on me, but I think he is joking.* Compare GET ONE'S NUMBER.

Indian summer *n. phr.* A dry and warm period of time late in the fall, usually in October. ♦ *After the cold and foggy weather, we had a brief Indian summer,* *during which the temperature was up in the high seventies.*

in dispute *adj. phr.* Disagreed about; being argued. ♦ *The penalty ordered by the referee was in dispute by one of the teams.* ♦ *Everyone in the class wanted to say something about the subject in dispute.*

in doubt *adv. phr.* In the dark; having some question or uncertainty. ♦ *When in doubt about any of the words you're using, consult a good dictionary.*

in due course *or* **in due season** *or* **in due time** See IN GOOD TIME 2.

in due season *or* **in due time** See IN GOOD TIME.

industrial park *n.* A complex of industrial buildings and/or businesses usually located far from the center of a city in a setting especially landscaped to make such buildings look better. ♦ *The nearest supermarket that sells car tires is at the industrial park twenty miles from downtown.*

in Dutch *adj. phr., slang* In trouble. ♦ *George got in Dutch with his father when he broke a window.* ♦ *John was in Dutch with his mother because he tore his new jacket.*

in earnest *adv. or adj. phr.* Seriously; in a determined way. ♦ *The beaver was building his dam in earnest.* ♦ *Bill did his homework in earnest.*—Often used like a predicate adjective. Sometimes used with *dead,* for emphasis. ♦ *Betty's friends thought she was joking when she said she wanted to be a doctor, but she was in dead earnest.*

in effect *adv. or adj. phr.* **1.** The same in meaning or result. ♦ *The teacher gave the same assignment, in effect, that she gave yesterday.* ♦ *Helping your mother with the dishes is in effect earning your allowance.* **2.** Necessary to obey; being enforced. ♦ *The coach says that players must be in bed by midnight, and that rule is in effect tonight.* Syn. IN FORCE.

in effigy See HANG IN EFFIGY *or* BURN IN EFFIGY.

in error *adv. phr.* Wrong; mistaken. ♦ *You were in error when you assumed that he would wait for us.*

in evidence *adj. phr.* Easily seen; noticeable. ♦ *The little boy's measles were very much in evidence.* ♦ *The tulips were blooming; spring was in evidence.*

in fact *also* **in point of fact** *adv. phr.* Really truthfully.—Often used for emphasis. ◆*No one believed it but, in fact, Mary did get an A on her book report.* ◆*It was a very hot day; in fact, it was 100 degrees.* Compare MATTER OF FACT.

in favor of *prep.* On the side of; in agreement with. ◆*Everyone in the class voted in favor of the party.* ◆*Most girls are in favor of wearing lipstick.* Compare IN BACK OF 2.

in fear and trembling See FEAR AND TREMBLING.

in fear of *adj. phr.* Fearful of; afraid of. ◆*They live so close to the border that they are constantly in fear of an enemy attack.*

in for *prep., informal* Unable to avoid; sure to get. ◆*The naughty puppy was in for a spanking.* ◆*On Christmas morning we are in for some surprises.* ◆*We saw Father looking angrily out of the broken window, and we knew we were in for it.* Compare HAVE IT IN FOR.

in force *adj. phr.* **1.** To be obeyed. ◆*New times for eating meals are now in force.* Syn. IN EFFECT. **2.** In a large group. ◆*People went to see the parade in force.* Syn. EN MASSE.

in front of *prep.* Ahead of; before. ◆*The rabbit was running in front of the dog.* ◆*A big oak tree stood in front of the building.* Contrast IN BACK OF 1.

in full swing *adj. phr.* Actively going on; in full action. ◆*The Valentine party was in full swing.* ◆*All of the children were planting seeds; the gardening project was in full swing.*

in fun See FOR FUN.

in general[1] *adv. phr.* Usually; very often. ◆*In general, mother makes good cookies.* ◆*The weather in Florida is warm in general.* Compare ON THE WHOLE 2.

in general[2] *adj. phr.* Most; with few exceptions. ◆*Women in general like to shop for new clothes.* ◆*Boys in general like active sports more than girls do.* Contrast IN PARTICULAR.

in glass houses See PEOPLE WHO LIVE IN GLASS HOUSES SHOULD NOT THROW STONES.

in good *adj. phr., informal* Well liked; accepted.—Used with *with.* ◆*The boy washed the blackboards so that he would get in good with his teacher.* ◆*Although Tom was younger, he was in good with the older boys.* Compare ON ONE'S GOOD SIDE. Contrast IN BAD.

in good faith See GOOD FAITH.

in good form Contrast IN BAD FORM.

in good season See IN GOOD TIME.

in good stead See STAND IN GOOD STEAD.

in good time *or* **in good season** *adv. phr.* **1.** A little early; sooner than necessary. ◆*The school bus arrived in good time.* ◆*The students finished their school work in good time.* ◆*We reached the station in good season to catch the 9:15 bus for New York.* **2.** *or* **in due course** *or* **in due season** *or* **in due time** In the usual amount of time; at the right time; in the end. ◆*Spring and summer will arrive in due course.* ◆*Sally finished her spelling in due course.*

in great measure *adv. phr.* To a great extent; largely. ◆*The Japanese attack on Hawaii was in great measure a contributing factor to President Roosevelt's decision to enter World War II.* Compare TO A LARGE EXTENT.

in half *adv. phr.* **1.** Into two equal parts. ◆*The ticket taker at the football game tore the tickets in half.* ◆*Mother cut the apple in half so each child could have an equal share.* Syn. IN TWO. **2.** To half the size before; to one half as big. ◆*As a punishment, Father cut Bob's allowance in half.*

in hand *adv. or adj. phr.* **1.** Under control. ◆*The principal was happy to find that the new teacher had her class in hand.* ◆*The baby-sitter kept the children well in hand.* ◆*Mabel was frightened when the barking dog ran at her, but she soon got herself in hand and walked on.* Contrast OUT OF HAND. **2.** In your possession; with you.—Often used in the phrase *cash in hand.* ◆*Tom figured that his cash in hand with his weekly pay would be enough to buy a car.* Compare ON HAND. **3.** Being worked on; with you to do. ◆*We should finish the work we have in hand before we begin something new.*

in honor of *prep.* As an honor to; for showing respect or thanks to. ◆*We celebrate Mother's Day in honor of our mothers.* ◆*The city dedicated a monument in honor of the general.*

in hopes *adj. phr.* Hopeful; hoping. ♦ *The Mayor was in hopes of having a good day for the parade.* ♦ *Mother was in hopes that the cake would be good to eat.*

in horror See THROW UP ONE'S HANDS IN HORROR.

in hot water See HOT WATER.

in *or* **into orbit** *adj. phr.* Thrilled; exuberantly happy; in very high spirits. ♦ *When Carol won the lottery she went right into orbit.*

in *or* **into the clear** *adj. phr.* Free; cleared of all responsibility and guilt. ♦ *Because of the new evidence found, Sam is still in the clear, but Harry is still behind bars.*

in *or* **into the doldrums** *adj. phr.* Inactive; sluggish; depressed. ♦ *The news of our factory's going out of business put all of us in the doldrums.*

in *or* **into the limelight** *ad . phr.* In the center of attention. ♦ *Some people will do almost anything to be able to step into the limelight.* Compare IN THE SPOTLIGHT.

in itself See END IN ITSELF.

injury See ADD INSULT TO INJURY.

in keeping *adj. phr.* Going well together; agreeing; similar. ♦ *Mary's hair style was in keeping with the latest fashion.* ♦ *Having an assembly on Friday morning was in keeping with the school program.* Contrast OUT OF KEEPING.

in kind *adv. phr.* In a similar way; with the same kind of thing. ♦ *My neighbor pays me in kind for walking her dog.* ♦ *Lois returned Mary's insult in kind.*

in knots See TIE IN KNOTS.

in league with *or informal* **in cahoots with** *prep.* In secret agreement or partnership with (someone); working together secretly with, especially for harm. ♦ *People once believed that some women were witches in league with the devil.* ♦ *The mayor's enemies spread a rumor that he was in cahoots with gangsters.*

in left field See OUT IN LEFT FIELD.

in lieu of See INSTEAD OF.

in light of *also* **in the light of** *adj. phr.* **1.** As a result of new information; by means of new ideas. ♦ *The teacher changed John's grade in the light of the extra work in the workbook.* **2.** Because of. ♦ *In light of the muddy*

field, the football team wore their old uniforms. Syn. IN VIEW OF.

in line¹ *adv. phr.* In or into a straight line. ♦ *The boys stood in line to buy their tickets.* ♦ *Tom set the chairs in line along the wall.* ♦ *The carpenter put the edges of the boards in line.*

in line² *adj. phr.* **1.** In a position in a series or after someone else. ♦ *John is in line for the presidency of the club next year.* ♦ *Mary is fourth in line to be admitted to the sorority.* **2.** Obeying or agreeing with what is right or usual; doing or being what people expect or accept; within ordinary or proper limits. ♦ *The coach kept the excited team in line.* ♦ *When the teacher came back into the room, she quickly brought the class back in line.* ♦ *The government passed a new law to keep prices in line.* Compare IN HAND. Contrast OUT OF LINE.

in line with *prep.* In agreement with. ♦ *Behavior at school parties must be in line with school rules.* ♦ *In line with the custom of the school, the students had a holiday between Christmas and New Year's Day.*

in love *adj. phr.* Liking very much; loving. ♦ *John is in love with Helen.* ♦ *Tom and Ellen are in love.* ♦ *Mary is in love with her new wristwatch.*

in luck *adj. phr.* Being lucky; having good luck; finding something good by chance. ♦ *Bill was in luck when he found the money on the street.* ♦ *Mary dropped her glasses and they did not break. She was in luck.*

in memory of *prep.* As something that makes people remember (a person or thing); as a reminder of; as a memorial to. ♦ *The building was named Ford Hall in memory of a man named James Ford.* ♦ *Many special ceremonies are in memory of famous men.*

in midair See UP IN THE AIR 2.

in mind *adv. phr.* **1.** In the center of your thought; in your close attention. ♦ *You have to be home by 11 o'clock. Keep that in mind, Bob.* ♦ *Mary is studying hard with a good grade in mind.* ♦ *Bear in mind the rules of safety when you swim.* Compare ON ONE'S MIND. **2.** See PUT IN MIND OF.

in mint condition *adj. phr.* Excellent; as good as new. ♦ *Grandma seldom uses* *her car; it is already ten years old, but it is still in mint condition.*

in my book See BY MY BOOK.

in name *adj. or adv. phr.* Having a title, but not really doing what someone with the title is expected to do. ◆ *The old man is a doctor in name only. He does not have patients now.* ◆ *He was the captain of the team in name only.*

in need of *adj. phr.* Destitute; lacking something. ◆ *The young girl is so ill that she is seriously in need of medical attention.*

inner city *n., colloquial* Densely populated neighborhoods in large metropolitan areas inhabited by low income families usually of minority backgrounds, such as Mexicans, Puerto Ricans, or African Americans; characterized by slums and government-owned high rises. ◆ *Joe comes from the inner city—he may need help with his reading.*

in nothing flat See IN NO TIME.

in no time *or* **in nothing flat** *adv. phr., informal* In a very little time; soon; quickly. ◆ *When the entire class worked together they finished the project in no time.* ◆ *The bus filled with students in nothing flat.*

in no uncertain terms See IN SO MANY WORDS 2.

in on *prep.* **1.** Joining together for. ◆ *The children collected money from their classmates and went in on a present for their teacher.* **2.** Told about; having knowledge of. ◆ *Bob was in on the secret.* ◆ *The other girls wouldn't let Mary in on what they knew.*

in one ear and out the other See GO IN ONE EAR AND OUT THE OTHER.

in one fell swoop *or* **at one fell swoop** *adv. phr.* **1.** *literary* In one attack or accident; in one bad blow. ◆ *The millionaire lost his money and his friends at one fell swoop.* **2.** At one time; at the same time. ◆ *Three cars drove into the driveway, and Mrs. Crane's dinner guests all arrived at one fell swoop.*

in one's bad graces *adj. phr.* Not approved by; not liked by. ◆ *John was in his mother's bad graces because he spilled his milk on the tablecloth.* ◆ *Don got in the bad graces of the teacher by laughing at her hat.* Compare DOWN ON, IN BAD, OUT OF FAVOR. Contrast IN ONE'S GOOD GRACES.

in one's behalf *or* **on one's behalf** *adv. phr., informal* **1.** For someone else; in your place. ◆ *My husband could not be here tonight, but I want to thank you on his behalf.* **2.** For the good of another person or group; as a help to someone. ◆ *My teacher went to the factory and spoke in my behalf when I was looking for a job.* Compare IN BEHALF OF, ON ONE'S ACCOUNT.

in one's blood *or* **into one's blood** *adv. phr.* Agreeing perfectly with one's sympathies, feelings, and desires. ◆ *Living in a warm section of the country gets in your blood.* ◆ *The woods got into Jim's blood.* Contrast OUT OF ONE'S BLOOD.

in one's bones See FEEL IN ONE'S BONES.

in one's boots See DIE IN ONE'S BOOTS *or* DIE WITH ONE'S BOOTS ON, IN ONE'S SHOES *also* IN ONE'S BOOTS.

in one's craw *or* **in one's crop** See STICK IN ONE'S CRAW *or* STICK IN ONE'S CROP.

in one's cups *adj. phr., literary* Drunk. ◆ *The man was in his cups and talking very loudly.*

in one's element *adv. phr.* **1.** In one's natural surroundings. ◆ *The deep-sea fish is in his element in deep ocean water.* **2.** Where you can do your best. ◆ *John is in his element working on the farm.* Compare AT HOME 2. Contrast OUT OF ONE'S ELEMENT.

in one's face *adv. phr.* **1.** Against your face. ◆ *The trick cigar blew up in the clown's face.* ◆ *A cold wind was in our faces as we walked to school.* **2.** In front of you. ◆ *The maid slammed the door in the salesman's face.* ◆ *I told the boys that they were wrong, but they laughed in my face.* Compare IN THE FACE OF, THROW SOMETHING IN ONE'S FACE, TO ONE'S FACE, UNDER ONE'S NOSE.

in one's favor *adv. or adj. phr.* In a way that is good for you. ◆ *Both teams claimed the point, but the referee decided in our favor.* ◆ *Bob made good grades in high school, and that was in his favor when he looked for a job.* Compare COME ONE'S WAY.

in one's footsteps See FOLLOW IN ONE'S FOOTSTEPS.

in one's glory *adj. phr.* Pleased and contented with yourself. ◆ *When John won the race, he was in his glory.* ◆ *Tom is* *very vain, and praise puts him in his glory.*

in one's good books See IN ONE'S GOOD GRACES.

in one's good graces *or* **in one's good books** *adv. phr.* Approved of by you; liked by someone. ♦*Ruth is in her mother's good graces because she ate all her supper.* ♦*Bill is back in the good graces of his girlfriend because he gave her a box of candy.* Compare IN GOOD. Contrast IN ONE'S BAD GRACES.

in one's grave See TURN IN ONE'S GRAVE *or* TURN OVER IN ONE'S GRAVE.

in one's hair *adj. phr., informal* Bothering you again and again; always annoying. ♦*Johnny got in Father's hair when he was trying to read the paper by running and shouting.* ♦*The grown-ups sent the children out to play so that the children wouldn't be in their hair while they were talking.* Compare GIVE A HARD TIME, IN ONE'S WAY. Contrast OUT OF ONE'S HAIR.

in one's hands See TAKE ONE'S LIFE IN ONE'S HANDS.

in one's heart of hearts *adv. phr.* Deep down where it really matters; in one's innermost feelings. ♦*In my heart of hearts, I think you're the nicest person in the whole world.*

in one's mind's eye *adv. phr.* In the memory; in the imagination. ♦*In his mind's eye he saw again the house he had lived in when he was a child.* ♦*In his mind's eye, he could see just what the vacation was going to be like.*

in one's mouth See BUTTER WOULDN'T MELT IN ONE'S MOUTH, MELT IN ONE'S MOUTH.

in one's own juice See STEW IN ONE'S OWN JUICE.

in one's right mind *adj. phr.* Accountable; sane and sober. ♦*If you were in your right mind, you wouldn't be saying such stupid things to our boss.*

in one's shell *or* **into one's shell** *adv. or adj. phr., informal* In or into bashfulness; into silence; not sociable; unfriendly. ♦*After Mary's mother scolded her, she went into her shell.* ♦*The teacher tried to get Rose to talk to her, but she stayed in her shell.* Contrast OUT OF ONE'S SHELL.

in one's shoes *also* **in one's boots** *adv. phr.* In or into one's place or position.

♦*How would you like to be in a lion tamer's boots?* Compare PUT ONESELF IN ANOTHER'S PLACE, STEP INTO ONE'S SHOES.

in one's sleeve See UP ONE'S SLEEVE.

in one's tracks *adv. phr., informal* **1.** Just where one is at the moment; abruptly; immediately. ♦*The hunter's rifle cracked and the rabbit dropped in his tracks.* ♦*Mary stopped dead in her tracks, turned around, and ran back home.* Syn. ON THE SPOT 1, THEN AND THERE. **2.** See FOLLOW IN ONE'S FOOT-STEPS.

in one's way *adv. or adj. phr.* **1.** Within reach; likely to be met; before you. ♦*The chance to work for a printer was put in my way.* Compare PUT IN THE WAY OF. **2.** *or* **in the way** In your path as a hindrance; placed so as to block the way. ♦*Fred tried to get to the door, but the table was in the way.* ♦*A tree had fallen across the street and was in Jim's way as he drove.* ♦*Mary tried to clean the house, but the baby was always in the way.*

in order *adv. or adj. phr.* **1.** In arrangement; in the proper way of following one another. ♦*Come to my desk in alphabetical order as I call your names.* ♦*Line up and walk to the door in order.* ♦*Name all the presidents in order.* Compare IN TURN. **2.** In proper condition. ♦*The car was in good working order when I bought it.* ♦*The club leader looked at the club treasurer's records of money collected and spent, and found them all in order.* Compare IN COMMISSION 2, PUT ONE'S HOUSE IN ORDER. **3.** Following the rules; proper; suitable. ♦*Is it in order to ask the speaker questions at the meeting?* ♦*At the end of a program, applause for the performers is in order.* Compare IN PLACE. Contrast OUT OF ORDER. **4.** See PUT ONE'S HOUSE IN ORDER *or* SET ONE'S HOUSE IN ORDER.

in order that See SO THAT 1.

in order to *or* **so as to** *conj.* For the purpose of; to.—Used with an infinitive. ♦*In order to follow the buffalo, the Indians often had to move their camps.* ♦*We picked apples so as to make a pie.* Compare SO THAT.

in part *adv. phr.* To some extent; partly; not wholly.—Often used with *large* or *small.* ♦ *We planted the garden in part with flowers. But in large part we planted vegetables.* ♦ *Tom was only in small part responsible.*

in particular *adv. phr.* In a way apart from others; more than others; particularly; especially. ♦ *The speaker talked about sports in general and about football in particular.* ♦ *All the boys played well and Bill in particular.* ♦ *Margaret liked all her classes, but she liked sewing class in particular.* Contrast IN GENERAL.

in passing *adv. phr.* While talking about that subject; as extra information; also. ♦ *Our teacher showed us different kinds of flowers and told us in passing that those flowers came from her garden.* ♦ *The writer of the story says he grew up in New York and mentions in passing that his parents came from Italy.* Compare BY THE WAY.

in person *also* **in the flesh** *adv. phr.* Yourself; personally. ♦ *A TV actor appeared in person today in school.* ♦ *The governor cannot march in the parade in person today, but his wife will march.* Compare FACE-TO-FACE 2. Contrast INSTEAD OF.

in place¹ *adv. phr.* **1a.** In the right or usual place or position. ♦ *Nothing is in place after the earthquake. Even trees and houses are turned over.* ♦ *The picture is not in place on the wall. It is crooked.* **1b.** In one place. ♦ *Our first exercise in gym class was running in place.* **2.** In proper order. ♦ *Stay in place in line, children.* Compare IN ORDER. Contrast OUT OF PLACE.

in place² *adj. phr.* In the right place or at the right time; suitable; timely. ♦ *A dog is not in place in a church.* ♦ *Linda wondered if it would be in place to wish the bride good luck after the wedding.* Compare IN ORDER 1. Contrast OUT OF PLACE.

in place of See INSTEAD OF.

in plain English *adv. phr.* Plainly; simply; in clear language. ♦ *Stop beating around the bush and saying that John "prevaricates"; in plain English he is a liar.*

in poor shape *adv. phr.* In a bad condition. ♦ *Most of the streets of Chicago are in poor shape due to the heavy snow and frost during the winters.*

in practice¹ *also* **into practice** *adv. phr.* In actual doing. ♦ *The idea sounds good but will it work in practice?* ♦ *It is easy to say that we will be good. It is harder to put the saying into practice.*

in practice² *adj. phr.* In proper condition to do something well through practice. ♦ *A pianist gets his fingers in practice by playing scales.* ♦ *An ice-skater keeps in practice by skating every day.* Compare IN SHAPE. Contrast OUT OF PRACTICE.

in print *adj. phr.* Obtainable in printed form from a printer or publisher; printed. ♦ *The author has finished writing his book but it is not yet in print.* ♦ *The story of the students' trip to Washington appeared in print in the newspaper.* ♦ *It is a very old book and no longer in print.* Contrast OUT OF PRINT.

in private *adj. or adv. phr.* Not openly or in public; apart from others; confidentially; secretly. ♦ *Mr. Jones waited until they were home in private before he punished his son.* ♦ *The teacher told Susan that she wanted to talk to her in private after class.* Compare IN SECRET. Contrast IN PUBLIC.

in progress *adj. phr.* Going ahead; being made or done; happening. ♦ *Plans are in progress to build a new school next year.* ♦ *A dog ran out on the playing field while the game was in progress.* Contrast IN CHECK.

in public *adv. phr.* **1.** In a place open to the people; in such a way that the public may see, hear, or know; not secretly; openly. ♦ *Two boys down the street are dancing in public for pennies.* ♦ *Actors are used to appearing in public.* ♦ *The mayor has told his friends that he is sick but will not admit it in public.* Contrast IN PRIVATE. **2.** See AIR ONE'S DIRTY LINEN IN PUBLIC *or* WASH ONE'S DIRTY LINEN IN PUBLIC.

in question *adj. phr.* **1.** In doubt; in dispute; being argued about or examined. ♦ *I know Bill would be a good captain for the team. That is not in question. But does he want to be captain?* Contrast BEYOND QUESTION. **2.** Under discussion; being talked or thought about. ♦ *The girls in question are not in school today.* ♦ *On the Christmas Day in question, we could not go to*

Grandmother's house, as we do every year.

in quest of See IN SEARCH OF.

in reason *adv. phr., formal* Following the rules of reasoning; sensibly; reasonably. ♦ *One cannot in reason doubt that freedom is better than slavery.*

in reference to *or* **with reference to** *or* **in regard to** *or* **with regard to** *prep.* In connection with; from the standpoint of; concerning; regarding; about. ♦ *I am writing with reference to your last letter.* ♦ *He spoke in reference to the Boy Scouts.* ♦ *I spoke to him with regard to his low marks.* ♦ *In regard to the test tomorrow, it is postponed.* Compare IN RELATION TO, IN RESPECT TO.

in regard to See IN REFERENCE TO.

in relation to *or* **with relation to** *prep.* In connection with; in dealing with; as concerns; in comparison to; respecting; about. ♦ *Father spoke about school in relation to finding a job when we are older.* ♦ *What did you say in relation to what happened yesterday?* ♦ *With relation to his job, skill is very important.* ♦ *In relation to Texas, Rhode Island is quite a small state.* Compare IN REFERENCE TO, IN RESPECT TO.

in respect to *or* **with respect to** In connection with; related to; about; on. ♦ *The teacher told stories about Washington and Lincoln in respect to the importance of being honest.* ♦ *In respect to your visit with us, we hope you can come before September.* ♦ *There was no shortage in respect to food.* Compare AS TO, IN REFERENCE TO, IN RELATION TO.

in return *adv. phr.* In order to give back something; as payment; in recognition or exchange.—Often used with *for.* ♦ *Bud gave me his knife and I gave him marbles in return.* ♦ *The lady helped Mother when she was sick and in return Mother often invited her to dinner.* ♦ *How much did John give you in return for your bicycle?* ♦ *I hit him in return for the time he hit me.* ♦ *I wrote Dad a letter and got a package in return.*

in reverse *adj. or adv. phr.* In a backward direction; backward. ♦ *John hit the tree behind him when he put the car in reverse without looking first.* ♦ *The*

first of the year Bob did well in school, but then he started moving in reverse.

in round figures *adv. phr.* As an estimated number; as a rounded-off figure containing no decimals or fractions. ♦ *Skip the cents and just tell me in round figures how much this car repair will cost.*

in round numbers See IN ROUND FIGURES.

ins and outs *n. phr.* The special ways of going somewhere or doing something; the different parts. ♦ *The janitor knows all the ins and outs of the big school building.* ♦ *Jerry's father is a good life insurance salesman; he knows all the ins and outs of the business.*

in search of *or literary* **in quest of** *prep.* Seeking or looking for; in pursuit of. ♦ *Many men went West in search of gold.* ♦ *The hunter stayed in the woods all day in quest of game.* ♦ *We looked everywhere in search of our dog.*

in season *adv. or adj. phr.* **1.** *literary* At the proper or best time. ♦ *Fred's father told him that he was not old enough yet but that he would learn to drive in season.* **2a.** At the right or lawful time for hunting or catching. ♦ *Deer will be in season next week.* ♦ *In spring we'll go fishing when trout are in season.* **2b.** At the right time or condition for using, eating, or marketing; in a ripe or eatable condition. ♦ *Christmas trees will be sold at the store in season.* ♦ *Native tomatoes will be in season soon.* ♦ *Oysters are in season during the "R" months.* Compare IN GOOD TIME. Contrast OUT OF SEASON.

in secret *adv. phr.* In a private or secret way; in a hidden place. ♦ *The miser buried his gold in secret and no one knows where it is.* ♦ *The robbers went away in secret after dark.* Compare IN PRIVATE.

in shape *or* **in condition** *adj. phr.* In good condition; able to perform well. ♦ *The football team will be in shape for the first game of the season.* ♦ *Mary was putting her French in shape for the test.* Compare IN PRACTICE. Contrast OUT OF SHAPE.

in short See IN BRIEF.

in short order *adv. phr.* Without delay; quickly. ♦ *Johnny got ready in short order after his father said that he could* *come to the ball game if he was ready in time.*

in short supply *adj. phr.* Not enough; in too small a quantity or amount; in less than the amount or number needed. ♦ *The cookies are in short supply, so don't eat them all up.* ♦ *We have five people and only four beds, so the beds are in short supply.*

inside See STEP INSIDE.

inside and out See INS AND OUTS, INSIDE OUT 2.

inside of *prep.* In; within; on or in an inside part of; not beyond; before the end of. ♦ *There is a broom inside of the closet.* ♦ *There is a label on the inside of the box.* ♦ *Hand your papers in to me inside of three days.* Contrast OUTSIDE OF.

inside out *adv.* **1.** So that the inside is turned outside. ♦ *Mother turns the stockings inside out when she washes them.* **2.** *or* **inside and out** *also* **in and out** In every part; throughout; completely. ♦ *David knows the parts of his bicycle inside out.* ♦ *We searched the house inside and out for the kitten.* Compare BACKWARDS AND FORWARDS, INS AND OUTS, THROUGH AND THROUGH.

inside track *n. phr.* **1.** The inside, shortest distance around a curved racetrack; the place that is closest to the inside fence. ♦ *A big white horse had the inside track at the start of the race.* **2.** *informal* An advantage due to special connections or information. ♦ *I would probably get that job if I could get the inside track.*

insofar as *conj.* To the extent that; to the point that; as much as. ♦ *You will learn your lessons only insofar as you are willing to keep studying them.*

in so many words *adv. phr.* **1.** In those exact words. ♦ *He hinted that he thought we were foolish but did not say so in so many words.* **2.** *or* **in no uncertain terms** In an outspoken way; plainly; directly. ♦ *I told him in so many words that he was crazy.* ♦ *Bob was very late for their date, and Mary told Bob in no uncertain terms what she thought of him.* Compare WORDS OF ONE SYLLABLE.

in someone else's shoes See IN ONE'S SHOES.

insomuch as See INASMUCH AS.

in spite of *prep. phr.* Against the influence or effect of; in opposition to; defying the effect of; despite. ♦ *In spite of the bad storm John delivered his papers on time.* ♦ *In spite of all their differences, Joan and Ann remain friends.*

instance See FOR EXAMPLE *or* FOR INSTANCE.

in state See LIE IN STATE.

instead of *or* **in place of** *also formal* **in lieu of** *prep.* In the place of; in substitution for; in preference to; rather than. ♦ *I wore mittens instead of gloves.* ♦ *The grown-ups had coffee but the children wanted milk in place of coffee.* ♦ *The boys went fishing instead of going to school.* ♦ *The Vice-President talked at the meeting in place of the President, because the President was sick.* ♦ *The magician appeared on the program in lieu of a singer.* Compare IN PERSON.

in step *adv. or adj. phr.* **1.** With the left or right foot stepping at the same time as another's or to the beat of music; in matching strides with another person or persons. ♦ *The long line of soldiers marched all in step: Left, right! Left, right!* ♦ *Johnny marched behind the band in step to the music.* **2.** In agreement; abreast.—Often followed by with. ♦ *Mary wanted to stay in step with her friends and have a doll too.* Contrast OUT OF STEP.

in stitches *adj. phr., informal* Laughing so hard that the sides ache; in a fit of laughing hard. ♦ *The comedian was so funny that he had everyone who was watching him in stitches.*

in stock *adj. phr.* Having something ready to sell or use; in present possession or supply; to be sold. ♦ *The store had no more red shoes in stock, so Mary chose brown ones instead.* Compare IN STORE, ON HAND. Contrast OUT OF STOCK.

in store *adj. or adv. phr.* **1.** Saved up in case of need; ready for use or for some purpose. ♦ *If the electricity goes off, we have candles in store in the closet.* ♦ *The squirrel has plenty of nuts in store for the winter.* Compare IN RESERVE, IN STOCK, ON HAND. **2.** Ready to happen; waiting.—Often used in the phrase *hold* or *have in store.* ♦ *What does the future hold in store for the boy who ran away?* ♦ *There is a surprise in store for Helen when she gets home.*

in stride See TAKE IN STRIDE.

in substance *adv. phr.* In important facts; in the main or basic parts; basically; really. ♦ *In substance the weather report said that it will be a nice day tomorrow.* ♦ *The two cars are the same in substance, except one is red and the other is red and white.*

insult See ADD INSULT TO INJURY.

intent See TO ALL INTENTS AND PURPOSES.

in terms of *prep.* **1.** In the matter of; on the subject of; especially about; about. ♦ *He spoke about books in terms of their publication.* ♦ *What have you done in terms of fixing the house?* ♦ *The children ate a great many hot dogs at the party. In terms of money, they ate $20 worth.* **2.** As to the amount or number of. ♦ *We swam a great distance. In terms of miles, it was three.*

in that *conj.* For the reason that; because. ♦ *I like the city, but I like the country better in that I have more friends in the country.*

in the air *adv. phr.* **1.** In everyone's thoughts. ♦ *Christmas was in the air for weeks before.* ♦ *The war filled people's thoughts every day; it was in the air.* Compare IN THE WIND. **2.** Meeting the bodily senses; surrounding you so as to be smelled or felt. ♦ *Spring is in the air.* ♦ *Rain is in the air.* **3.** See LEAVE HANGING, UP IN THE AIR.

in the back See STAB IN THE BACK.

in the bag *adj. phr., informal* Sure to be won or gotten; certain. ♦ *Jones had the election in the bag after the shameful news about his opponent came out.* ♦ *We thought we had the game in the bag.* Compare SEWED UP.

in the balance See HANG IN THE BALANCE.

in the bargain *or* **into the bargain** *adv. phr.* In addition; besides; also. ♦ *Frank is a teacher, and an artist into the bargain.* ♦ *The heat failed, and then the roof began to leak in the bargain.* Compare TO BOOT, FOR GOOD MEASURE.

in the black *adv. or adj. phr., informal* In a successful or profitable way; so as to make money. ♦ *The big store was running in the black.* ♦ *A business must stay in the black to keep on.* Contrast IN THE RED.

in the blood See RUN IN THE BLOOD *or* RUN IN THE FAMILY.

in the bud See NIP IN THE BUD.

in the can *adj., slang, movie jargon* Ready; finished; completed; about to be duplicated and distributed to exhibitors. ♦ *No sneak previews until it's all in the can!* ♦ *Once my book's in the can, I'll go for a vacation.*

in the cards *also* **on the cards** *adj. phr., informal* To be expected; likely to happen; foreseeable; predictable. ♦ *It was in the cards for the son to succeed his father as head of the business.* ♦ *John finally decided that it wasn't in the cards for him to succeed with that company.*

in the charge of See IN CHARGE OF 2.

in the chips *slang or informal* **in the money** *adj. phr.* Having plenty of money; prosperous; rich. ♦ *After his rich uncle died, Richard was in the chips.* ♦ *After years of struggle and dependence, air transportation is in the money.* Compare ON EASY STREET, WELL-TO-DO.

in the circumstances See UNDER THE CIRCUMSTANCES.

in the clear *adj. phr.* **1.** Free of anything that makes moving or seeing difficult; with nothing to limit action. ♦ *The plane climbed above the clouds and was flying in the clear.* ♦ *Jack passed the ball to Tim, who was in the clear and ran for a touchdown.* **2.** *informal* Free of blame or suspicion; not thought to be guilty. ♦ *After John told the principal that he broke the window, Martin was in the clear.* ♦ *Steve was the last to leave the locker room, and the boys suspected him of stealing Tom's watch, but the coach found the watch and put Steve in the clear.* **3.** Free of debt; not owing money to anyone. ♦ *Bob borrowed a thousand dollars from his father to start his business, but at the end of the first year he was in the clear.* Syn. IN THE BLACK.

in the clouds *adj. phr.* Far from real life; in dreams; in fancy; in thought. ♦ *When Alice agreed to marry Jim, Jim went home in the clouds.*—Often used with *head, mind, thoughts.* ♦ *Mary is looking out the window, not at the chalkboard; her head is in the clouds again.* ♦ *A good teacher should have his head in the clouds sometimes, but his feet always on the ground.* Contrast COME BACK TO EARTH, FEET ON THE GROUND.

in the clover See IN CLOVER.

in the cold See OUT IN THE COLD.

in the cold light of day *adv. phr.* After sleeping on it; after giving it more thought; using common sense and looking at the matter unemotionally and realistically. ♦ *Last night my ideas seemed terrific, but in the cold light of day I realize that they won't work.*

in the dark *adj. phr.* **1.** In ignorance; without information. ♦ *John was in the dark about the job he was being sent to.* ♦ *If the government controls the news, it can keep people in the dark on any topic it chooses.* ♦ *Mary had a letter from Sue yesterday, but she was left in the dark about Sue's plans to visit her.* Contrast IN THE KNOW. See WHISTLE IN THE DARK.

in the doghouse *adj. phr., slang* In disgrace or disfavor. ♦ *Our neighbor got in the doghouse with his wife by coming home drunk.* ♦ *Jerry is in the doghouse because he dropped the ball, and the other team won because of that.* Compare DOWN ON.

in the door See FOOT IN THE DOOR.

in the driver's seat *adv. phr.* In control; having the power to make decisions. ♦ *Stan is in the driver's seat now that he has been made our supervisor at the factory.*

in the dumps See DOWN IN THE DUMPS.

in the event See IN CASE 1.

in the event of See IN CASE OF.

in the eye See LOOK IN THE EYE.

in the face See BLUE IN THE FACE, LOOK IN THE EYE *or* LOOK IN THE FACE, SLAP IN THE FACE, STARE IN THE FACE.

in the face of *adv. phr.* **1.** When met or in the presence of; threatened by. ♦ *He was brave in the face of danger.* ♦ *She began to cry in the face of failure.* **2.** Although opposed by; without being stopped by. ♦ *Talking continued even in the face of the teacher's command to stop.* Syn. IN SPITE OF. Compare FLY IN THE FACE OF, IN ONE'S FACE. **3.** See FLY IN THE FACE OF.

in the family See RUN IN THE BLOOD *or* RUN IN THE FAMILY.

in the first place *adv. phr.* **1.** Before now; in the beginning; first. ♦ *You already ate breakfast! Why didn't you tell me that in the first place instead of saying you didn't want to eat?* ♦ *Carl patched his old football but it soon leaked again. He should have bought a new one in the first place.* **2.** See IN THE PLACE.

in the flesh See IN PERSON.

in the groove *adj. phr., slang* Doing something very well; near perfection; at your best. ♦ *The band was right in the groove that night.* ♦ *It was an exciting football game; every player was really in the groove.*

in the hole *adv. or adj. phr., informal* **1a.** Having a score lower than zero in a game, especially a card game; to a score below zero. ♦ *John went three points in the hole on the first hand of the card game.* **1b.** Behind an opponent; in difficulty in a sport or game. ♦ *We had their pitcher in the hole with the bases full and no one out.* Compare ON THE SPOT. **2.** In debt; behind financially. ♦ *John went in the hole with his hot dog stand.* ♦ *It's a lot easier to get in the hole than to get out again.* Compare IN A HOLE, IN THE RED. Contrast OUT OF THE HOLE.

in the know *adj. phr., informal* Knowing about things that most people do not know about; knowing secrets or understanding a special subject. ♦ *Tina helped Professor Smith make some of the exam questions, and she felt important to be in the know.* ♦ *In a print shop, Mr. Harvey is in the know, but in a kitchen he can't even cook an egg.* Compare GET WISE. Contrast IN THE DARK.

in the lap of luxury *adv. phr.* Well supplied with luxuries; having most things that money can buy. ♦ *Mike grew up in the lap of luxury.* Compare ON EASY STREET, WELL-TO-DO.

in the lap of the gods *also* **on the knees of the gods** *adv. phr., literary* Beyond human control; not to be decided by anyone. ♦ *Frank had worked hard as a candidate, and as election day came he felt that the result was in the lap of the gods.* ♦ *The armies were evenly* *matched and the result of the battle seemed to be on the knees of the gods.*

in the least *adv. phr.* Even a little; in any degree or amount.—Used in negative, interrogative, and conditional sentences. ◆*Sue did not understand physics in the least.* ◆*Are you in the least interested in sewing?* ◆*Mother won't be upset if you come for supper; I'll be surprised if she cares in the least.* ◆*Mike was not upset in the least by the storm.* ◆*It is no trouble to help you. Not in the least.* Compare AT ALL.

in the line of duty *adj. phr.* Done or happening as part of a job. ◆*The policeman was shot in the line of duty.* ◆*The soldier had to clean his rifle in the line of duty.*

in the long run *adv. phr.* In the end; in the final result. ◆*John knew that he could make a success of the little weekly paper in the long run.* ◆*You may make good grades by studying only before examinations, but you will succeed in the long run only by studying hard every day.*

in the lurch See LEAVE IN THE LURCH.

in the main *adv. phr., formal* In most cases; generally; usually. ◆*In the main, small boys and dogs are good friends.* ◆*In the main, the pupils did well on the test.*

in the market for *adj. phr.* Wishing to buy; ready to buy. ◆*Mr. Jones is in the market for a new car.* ◆*People are always in the market for entertainment.*

in the middle *adv. or adj. phr.* In between two sides of an argument; caught between two dangers. ◆*Mary found herself in the middle of the quarrel between Joyce and Ethel.* ◆*John promised Tom to go fishing, but his father wanted him to help at home. John was in the middle.*

in the middle of nowhere *adv. phr.* In a deserted, faraway place. ◆*When my car stopped on the highway in the middle of nowhere, it took forever to get help.*

in the money See IN THE CHIPS.

in the mood (for) *adj. phr.* **1.** Interested in doing something. ◆*Sorry, I'm just not in the mood for a heavy dinner tonight.* **2.** Feeling sexy. ◆*I am sorry, darling, I am just not in the mood tonight.*

in the mouth See LOOK A GIFT HORSE IN THE MOUTH.

in the neck See CATCH IT IN THE NECK *or* GET IT IN THE NECK.

in the nick of time *adv. phr.* Just at the right time; barely soon enough; almost too late. ◆*The doctor arrived in the nick of time to save the child from choking to death.* ◆*Joe saw the other car in the nick of time.* Compare IN TIME.

in the pink *or* **in the pink of condition** *adj. phr., informal* In excellent health; strong and well; in fine shape. ◆*Mr. Merrick had aged well; he was one of those old men who always seem in the pink of condition.* ◆*After a practice and a rubdown, Joe felt in the pink.*

in the ——— place *adv. phr.* As the (first or second or third, etc.) thing in order or importance; first, second, or third, etc.—Used with *first, second, third,* and other ordinal numbers. ◆*No, you cannot go swimming. In the first place, the water is too cold; and, in the second place, there is not time enough before dinner.* ◆*Stealing is wrong, in the first place, because it hurts others, and, in the second place, because it hurts you.* Compare FOR ONE THING.

in the prime of life *adv. phr.* At the peak of one's creative abilities; during the most productive years. ◆*Poor John lost his job due to restructuring when he was in the prime of his life.*

in the public eye *adj. phr.* Widely known; often seen in public activity; much in the news. ◆*The senator's activity kept him in the public eye.* ◆*A big league ballplayer is naturally much in the public eye.*

in the raw *adj. or adv. phr.* **1.** In the simplest or most natural way; with no frills. ◆*Henry enjoyed going into the woods and living life in the raw.* **2.** *informal* Without any clothing; naked. ◆*In the summer the boys slept in the raw.*

in the red *adv. or adj. phr., informal* In an unprofitable way; so as to lose money. ◆*A large number of American radio stations operate in the red.* ◆*A rich man who has a farm or ranch often runs it in the red, but makes his money with his factory or business.* Contrast IN

THE BLACK. [From the fact that people who keep business records usually write in red ink how much money they lose and in black ink how much money they gain.]

in the right *adj. phr.* With moral or legal right or truth on your side; in agreement with justice, truth, or fact; correct. ♦ *When the cars collided, John was clearly in the right.* ♦ *In going before his wife down the stairs, Mr. Franklin was in the right.* ♦ *In many disputes, it is hard to say who is in the right.* Contrast IN THE WRONG.

in the rough See DIAMOND IN THE ROUGH.

in the running *adj. or adv. phr.* Having a chance to win; not to be counted out; among those who might win. ♦ *At the beginning of the last lap of the race, only two horses were still in the running.* ♦ *A month before Joyce married Hal, three of Joyce's boyfriends seemed to be still in the running.* ♦ *Al was in the running for the trophy until the last hole of the golf tournament.* Contrast OUT OF THE RUNNING.

in the saddle *adv. or adj. phr.* In command; in control; in a position to order or boss others. ♦ *Mr. Park was in the saddle when he had over half the company's stock.* ♦ *Getting appointed chief of police put Stevens in the saddle.*

in the same boat *adv. or adj. phr.* In the same trouble; in the same fix; in the same bad situation. ♦ *When the town's one factory closed and hundreds of people lost their jobs, all the storekeepers were in the same boat.* ♦ *Dick was disappointed when Fern refused to marry him, but he knew others were in the same boat.*

in the same breath *adv. phr.* **1.** At the same time; without waiting. ♦ *John would complain about hard times, and in the same breath boast of his prize-winning horses.* ♦ *Jane said Bill was selfish, but in the same breath she said she was sorry to see him leave.* **2.** In the same class; in as high a group—Usually used in the negative with *mention, speak,* or *talk.* ♦ *Mary is a good swimmer, but she should not be mentioned in the same breath with Joan.*

in the same place See LIGHTNING NEVER STRIKES TWICE IN THE SAME PLACE.

in the sand See HIDE ONE'S HEAD IN THE SAND.

in the second place See IN THE ——— PLACE.

in the short run *adv. phr.* In the immediate future. ♦ *We are leasing a car in the short run; later we might buy one.* Contrast IN THE LONG RUN.

in the soup *adj. phr., slang* In serious trouble; in confusion; in disorder. ♦ *When his wife overdrew their bank account without telling him, Mr. Phillips suddenly found himself really in the soup.* ♦ *The police misunderstood Harry's night errand, and arrested him, which put him in the soup with the boss.*

in the spotlight *adv. phr.* In the center of attention, with everybody watching what one is doing. ♦ *It must be difficult for the President to be in the spotlight wherever he goes.* Compare IN THE LIMELIGHT.

in the swim *adj. phr.* Doing the same things that other people are doing; following the fashion (as in business or social affairs); busy with what most people are doing. ♦ *Jim found some college friends at the lake that summer, and soon was in the swim of things.* ♦ *Mary went to New York with introductions to writers and artists, and that winter she was quite in the swim.* Contrast OUT OF THE SWIM.

in the third place See IN THE ——— PLACE.

in the till See ROB THE TILL *or* HAVE ONE'S HAND IN THE TILL.

in the twinkling of an eye See BEFORE ONE CAN SAY JACK ROBINSON.

in the wake of *prep., literary* As a result of; right after; following. ♦ *Many troubles follow in the wake of war.* ♦ *There were heavy losses of property in the wake of the flood.*

in the way See IN ONE'S WAY.

in the way of See PUT IN THE WAY OF.

in the wind *adj. phr.* Seeming probable; being planned; soon to happen. ♦ *Changes in top management of the company had been in the wind for weeks.* ♦ *Tom's close friends knew that marriage was in the wind.* Compare IN THE AIR 1.

in the works *adv. or adj. phr.* In preparation; being planned or worked on; in progress. ♦ *John was told that the paving of his street was in the works.* ♦ *It was reported that the playwright had a new play in the works.* ♦ *The manager told the employees that a raise in wages was in the works.* Compare UNDER WAY.

in the world *or* **on earth** *adv. phr., informal* Of all possible things; ever.— Usually used for emphasis after words that ask questions, as *who, why, what,* etc. ♦ *Where in the world did you find that necktie?* ♦ *The boys wondered how on earth the mouse got out of the cage.* ♦ *Betty could not understand what on earth the teacher meant.*

in the wrong *adj. phr.* With moral or legal right or truth against you; against justice, truth, or fact; wrong. ♦ *In attacking a smaller boy, Jack was plainly in the wrong.* ♦ *Mary was in the wrong to drink from a finger bowl.* ♦ *Since he had put pennies behind the fuses, Bill was in the wrong when fire broke out.* Compare OUT OF THE WAY. Contrast IN THE RIGHT.

in time *adv. or adj. phr.* **1.** Soon enough. ♦ *We got to Washington in time for the cherry blossoms.* ♦ *We got to the station just in time to catch the bus.* ♦ *John liked to get to work in good time and talk to the man who worked on his machine before him.* **2.** In the end; after a while; finally. ♦ *Fred and Jim did not like each other at first, but in time they became friends.* **3.** In the right rhythm; in step. ♦ *The marchers kept in time with the band.* ♦ *Johnny didn't play his piano piece in time.*

into account See TAKE INTO ACCOUNT.

into a nose dive See GO INTO A TAIL SPIN *or* GO INTO A NOSE DIVE.

into a tail spin See GO INTO A TAIL SPIN.

into commission See IN COMMISSION.

into effect *adv. phr.* Into use or operation. ♦ *The new rule was put into effect at once.* ♦ *The judge ordered the old suspended penalty into effect.*

into hot water See HOT WATER.

into line *adv. phr.* **1.** Into agreement. ♦ *The department's spending was brought into line with the budget.* **2.** Under control. ♦ *Independent congressmen were brought into line by warnings that jobs for their friends would be kept back.* ♦ *The players who*

had broken training rules fell into line when the coach warned them that they would be put off the team.

into one's blood See IN ONE'S BLOOD.

into one's head See BEAT INTO ONE'S HEAD, TAKE INTO ONE'S HEAD.

into one's own See COME INTO ONE'S OWN.

into one's own hands See TAKE THE LAW INTO ONE'S OWN HANDS.

into one's shell See IN ONE'S SHELL.

into one's shoes See STEP INTO ONE'S SHOES.

into practice See IN PRACTICE.

into question *adv. phr.* Into doubt or argument.—Usually used with *call, bring* or *come.* ♦ *This soldier's courage has never been called into question.* ♦ *If a boy steals, his parents' teaching comes into question.*

into the bargain See IN THE BARGAIN.

into the fire See OUT OF THE FRYING PAN INTO THE FIRE.

into the ground See RUN INTO THE GROUND.

into the hands of See PLAY INTO THE HANDS OF.

into thin air *adv. phr.* Without anything left; completely. ♦ *When Bob returned to the room, he was surprised to find that his books had vanished into thin air.* Compare OUT OF THIN AIR.

in toto *adv. phr.* As a whole; in its entirety; totally; altogether. ♦ *The store refused the advertising agency's suggestion in toto.* ♦ *They bought the newspaper business in toto.* ♦ *The paving job was accepted in toto.* [Latin, meaning "in the whole."]

in touch *adj. phr.* Talking or writing to each other; giving and getting news. ♦ *John kept in touch with his school friends during the summer.* ♦ *Police anywhere in the U.S. can get in touch instantly with any other police department by teletype.* ♦ *The man claimed to be in touch with people on another planet.* Compare KEEP TRACK. Contrast OUT OF TOUCH.

in tow *adj. phr.* **1.** Being pulled. ♦ *The tugboat had the large ocean liner in tow as they came into the harbor.* ♦ *An engine came with a long string of cars in tow.* **2.** Being taken from place to place; along with someone. ♦ *Janet took the new girl in tow and showed her* *where to go.* ♦ *Mrs. Hayes went to the supermarket with her four little children in tow.*

in trust *adv. or adj. phr.* In safe care for another. ♦ *The money was held by the bank in trust for the widow.* ♦ *At his death Mr. Brown left a large sum in trust for his son until he was twenty-five.*

in tune *adv. or adj. phr.* **1.** At the proper musical pitch; high or low enough in sound. ♦ *The piano is in tune.* **2.** Going well together; in agreement; matching; agreeable.—Often used with *with.* ♦ *In his new job, John felt in tune with his surroundings and his associates.* Contrast OUT OF TUNE.

in turn *adv. phr.* According to a settled order; each following another. ♦ *Each man in turn got up and spoke.* ♦ *Two teachers supervised the lunch hour in turn.* ♦ *Two of the three boys tease their younger brother—John, the biggest, teases Bob, the middle boy; and Bob in turn teases Tim, the youngest.* Compare IN ORDER.

in two *adv. phr.* Into two parts or pieces; into two divisions. ♦ *John and Mary pulled on the wishbone until it came in two.* ♦ *There was only one piece of cake, but we cut it in two.* Syn. IN HALF.

in two shakes of a lamb's tail *adv., informal* Quickly; in no time at all. ♦ *I'll be back in two shakes of a lamb's tail.*

in ——— up to the See UP TO THE ——— IN.

in vain *adv. phr.* **1.** Without effect; without getting the desired result; without success. ♦ *The drowning man called in vain for help.* ♦ *To cry over spilled milk is to cry in vain.* Compare GO FOR NOTHING, NO USE. **2.** See TAKE ONE'S NAME IN VAIN.

in view *adv. or adj. phr.* **1.** In sight; visible. ♦ *We came around a bend and there was the ocean in view.* **2.** As a purpose, hope, or expectation. ♦ *John had his son's education in view when he began to save money.* ♦ *The end that we must keep always in view is peace with justice.* Compare EYE TO.

in view of *prep.* After thinking about; because of. ♦ *Schools were closed for the day in view of the heavy snowstorm.* ♦ *In view of rising labor costs, many companies have turned to automation.* Syn. IN THE LIGHT OF.

in virtue of See BY VIRTUE OF.

in wait See LIE IN WAIT.

in with *prep.* In friendship, favor, or closeness with; in the trust or liking of. ♦ *We trusted on Byrd's being in with the mayor, not knowing that the mayor no longer liked him.* ♦ *It took the new family some time to get in with their neighbors.*

I.O.U. *adj. phr.* I owe you, abbreviated; a promissory note. ♦ *I had to borrow some money from John and, in order to remind both of us, I wrote him an I.O.U. note for $250.*

Irish See GET ONE'S DANDER UP *or* GET ONE'S IRISH UP.

iron horse *n., informal* A railroad locomotive; the engine of a railroad train. ♦ *In its first days, the iron horse frightened many people as it roared across country scattering sparks.*

iron in the fire *n. phr.* Something you are doing; one of the projects with which a person is busy; job. ♦ *John had a number of irons in the fire, and he managed to keep all of them hot.*— Usually used in the phrase *too many irons in the fire.* ♦ *"Ed has a dozen things going all the time, but none of them seem to work out." "No wonder. He has too many irons in the fire."*

iron out *v., informal* To discuss and reach an agreement about (a difference); find a solution for (a problem); remove (a difficulty). ♦ *The company and its workers ironed out their differences over hours and pay.* ♦ *The House and Senate ironed out the differences between their two different tax bills.* Compare MAKE UP 5.

is See SUCH AS IT IS, THAT IS.

island See SAFETY ISLAND.

issue See AT ISSUE, TAKE ISSUE.

is that so *informal* **1.** Oh, indeed? That's interesting.—Used in simple acceptance or reply. ♦ *"The Republicans have pulled a trick at city hall." "Is that so?"* **2.** Surely not?—Used in disbelief or sarcasm. ♦ *"The moon is made of green cheese." "Is that so?"* ♦ *"I'm going to take your girlfriend to the dance," said Bob. "Oh, is that so!" said Dick. "Try it and you'll be sorry."*

itching palm *n., slang* A wish for money; greed. ♦ *He was born with an itching palm.* ♦ *The bellboys in that* *hotel seem always to have itching palms.*

I tell you See I'LL SAY.

I tell you what See I'LL TELL YOU WHAT.

item See COLLECTOR'S ITEM, CONSUMER ITEMS.

it figures *informal sentence* It checks out; it makes sense; it adds up. ♦ *It figures that Bob got the highest raise at our firm; he is the most productive salesman.*

it is an ill wind that blows nobody good No matter how bad a happening is, someone can usually gain something from it.—A proverb. ♦ *When Fred got hurt in the game John got a chance to play. It's an ill wind that blows nobody good.*

it never rains but it pours One good thing or bad thing is often followed by others of the same kind.—A proverb. ♦ *John got sick, then his brothers and sisters all got sick. It never rains but it pours.*

it's a cinch *informal sentence* It is very easy. ♦ *"What about the final*

exam?" Fred asked. "It was a cinch," Sam answered. Compare PIECE OF CAKE.

it's a deal *informal sentence* Consider it done; OK; it is agreed. ♦ *"How much for this used car?" Bill asked. "Two thousand," the man answered. "I'll give $1,500," Bill said. "It's a deal!" the owner answered as they sealed the transaction.*

it's been ———— , it's been real *informal* Shortened form for "it has been real nice (being with you)"—used colloquially between very close friends.

itself See END IN ITSELF.

it's high time *informal sentence* It is overdue. ♦ *It is high time for John Browning to be promoted to full professor; he has written a great deal but his books went unnoticed.*

Ivy League *n.* A small group of the older and more famous eastern U.S. colleges and universities. ♦ *Several Ivy League teams play each other regularly each year.* ♦ *Harvard, Yale, and Princeton were the original Ivy League.*

Jack See ALL WORK AND NO PLAY MAKES JACK A DULL BOY.

jack See EVERY LAST MAN *also* EVERY MAN JACK.

jack of all trades *n., informal* (Often followed by the words "master of none.") A person who is knowledgeable in many areas. Can be used as praise, or as a derogatory remark depending on the context and the intonation. ◆ *Peter is a jack of all trades; he can survive anywhere!* ◆ *"How come Joe did such a sloppy job?" Mary asked. "He's a jack of all trades," Sally answered.*

jackpot See HIT THE JACKPOT.

jack-rabbit start *n., informal* A very sudden start from a still position; a very fast start from a stop. ◆ *Bob made a jack-rabbit start when the traffic light turned green.*

Jack Robinson See BEFORE ONE CAN SAY JACK ROBINSON.

jack up *v.* **1.** To lift with a jack. ◆ *The man jacked up his car to fit a flat tire.* **2.** *informal* To make (a price) higher; raise. ◆ *Just before Christmas, some stores jack up their prices.*

jailbait *n., slang* A girl below the legal age of consent for sex; one who tempts you to intimacy which is punishable by imprisonment. ◆ *Stay away from Arabella, she is a jailbait.*

jailbird *n., informal* A convict; someone who is in jail or has been recently released from prison. ◆ *Because Harry was a jailbird, it was understandably hard for him to find a job after being imprisoned.*

jake flake *n., slang* A boring person whose company is usually not wanted. ◆ *Please don't invite Turner, he is a jake flake.*

jar on *v. phr.* To irritate. ◆ *The constant construction noise was beginning to jar on the nerves of the members of the meeting.*

jaw See GLASS JAW.

jawbreaker *n.* **1.** A large piece of hard candy or bubblegum. ◆ *Billy asked his mother for a quarter to buy some jawbreakers and a chocolate bar.* **2.** *informal* A word or name that is hard to pronounce. ◆ *His name, Nissequogue, is a real jawbreaker.*

jaw drop *or* **jaw drop a mile** *informal* Mouth fall wide open with surprise.—Used with a possessive. ◆ *Tom's jaw dropped a mile when he won the prize.*

jaws tight *adj., slang, informal* Angry; uptight; tense. ◆ *Why are you getting your jaws so tight?*

jazz up *v., slang* To brighten up; add more noise, movement, or color; make more lively or exciting. ◆ *The party was very dull until Pete jazzed it up with his drums.*

Jehu See DRIVE LIKE JEHU.

jerk *or* **jerker** See SODA JERK *or* SODA JERKER.

jerry-built *adj.* **1.** Built poorly or carelessly of cheap materials; easily broken. ◆ *That jerry-built cabin will blow apart in a strong wind.* **2.** Done without careful preparation or thought; planned too quickly. ◆ *When the regular television program didn't come on, a jerry-built program was substituted at the last minute.*

Jesus boots *or* **Jesus shoes** *n., slang* Men's sandals, particularly as worn by hippies and very casually dressed people. ◆ *I dig your Jesus boots, man, they look cool.*

jig's up See GAME'S UP.

jim-dandy *n., slang* Something wonderful; something very good. ◆ *Tommy's new boat is really a jim-dandy! I wish I had one like it.*

jink See HIGH JINKS.

job See DO A JOB ON, FALL DOWN ON THE JOB, LIE DOWN ON THE JOB, ON THE JOB.

Joe Doakes *n.* A name used informally for the average man. ◆ *Let us say that Joe Doakes goes to the movies three times a year.* Compare MAN IN THE STREET, SO-AND-SO.

John Doe *n.* A name used for an unknown person, especially in police and law business. ◆ *The alarm went out for a John Doe who stole the diamonds from the store.*

John Hancock *or* **John Henry** *n., informal* Your signature; your name in writing. ◆ *The man said, "Put your John Hancock on this paper."* ◆ *Joe felt* *proud when he put his John Henry on his very first driver's license.*

Johnny-come-lately *n.* Someone new in a place or group; newcomer; *also:* a new person who takes an active part in group affairs before the group has accepted him; upstart. ♦ *Everybody was amazed when a Johnny-come-lately beat the old favorite in the race.* ♦ *When it looked as though Mr. Brown had a good chance of winning, many Johnny-come-latelies began to support him.*

Johnny-on-the-spot *adj. phr.* At the right place when needed; present and ready to help; very prompt; on time. ♦ *A good waterboy is always Johnny-on-the-spot.* ♦ *The firemen were Johnny-on-the-spot and put out the fire in the house soon after it started.* Compare ON THE JOB.

John Q. Public *n.* A name used informally for the average citizen. ♦ *It is John Q. Public's duty to vote at each election.* Compare JOE DOAKES.

join forces *or* **join hands** *v. phr.* To get together for the same aim; group together for a purpose; unite. ♦ *The students and the graduates joined forces to raise money when the gym burned down.* ♦ *The American soldiers joined hands with the British in the war against Germany.* Compare THROW IN ONE'S LOT WITH.

join hands See JOIN FORCES.

joint See CLIP JOINT, PUT ONE'S NOSE OUT OF JOINT.

joke See CRACK A JOKE.

joking apart See JOKING ASIDE.

joking aside *or* **joking apart** *v. phr., informal* No fooling; without exaggerating; seriously. ♦ *Joking aside, although the conditions were not very comfortable, we had a wonderful time.* ♦ *Joking apart, there must have been over a hundred people in the room.*

Jones See KEEP UP WITH THE JONESES.

jot down *v. phr.* To quickly commit to writing; make a quick note of something. ♦ *Let me jot down your address so that I can send you a postcard from Europe.*

judgment seat *n.* A place where you are judged; a place where justice and punishment are given out. ♦ *Mrs. Smith is so bossy, she always acts as though she is in the judgment seat.*

jug-eared *adj.* With ears that stick out like the handles of a jug. ♦ *Tommy was a redheaded, freckle-faced, jug-eared boy.*

juice See STEW IN ONE'S OWN JUICE.

juice dealer *n., slang* An underworld money lender who charges exorbitant fees to his clientele and frequently collects payment by physical force. ♦ *No matter how broke you are, never go to a juice dealer.*

jump See GET THE JUMP ON *or* HAVE THE JUMP ON, GO JUMP IN THE LAKE, NOT KNOW WHICH WAY TO TURN *or* NOT KNOW WHICH WAY TO JUMP.

jump all over See JUMP ON.

jump at *v.* To take or accept quickly and gladly. ♦ *Johnny jumped at the invitation to go swimming with his brother.* Compare TAKE UP 7.

jump bail *or* **skip bail** *v. phr., informal* To run away and fail to come to trial, and so to give up a certain amount of money already given to a court of law to hold with the promise that you would come. ♦ *The robber paid $2000 bail so he wouldn't be put in jail before his trial, but he jumped bail and escaped to Mexico.* ♦ *The man skipped bail because he was afraid the court might put him in jail for a long time.*

jump ball *n.* The starting of play in basketball by tossing the ball into the air between two opposing players, each of whom jumps and tries to hit the ball to a member of his own team. ♦ *Two players held onto the ball at the same time and the referee called a jump ball.*

jump down one's throat *v. phr.* To suddenly become very angry at someone; scold severely or angrily. ♦ *The teacher jumped down Billy's throat when Billy said he did not do his homework.*

jump from the frying pan into the fire See OUT OF THE FRYING PAN INTO THE FIRE.

jumping-off place *n. phr.* **1.** A place so far away that it seems to be the end of the world. ♦ *Columbus' sailors were afraid they would arrive at the jumping-off place if they sailed farther west.* ♦ *So you visited Little America? That sounds like the jumping-off place!* **2.** The starting place of a long, hard trip or of something difficult or dangerous. ♦ *The jumping-off place for the explorer's trip through the jungle was a little village.*

jump on *or* **jump all over** *or* **land on** *or* **land all over** *v. phr., informal* To scold; criticize; blame. ♦*Tom's boss jumped all over Tom because he made a careless mistake.* ♦*Janice landed on Robert for dressing carelessly for their date.* ♦*"I don't know why Bill is always jumping on me; I just don't understand him," said Bob.* Compare FIND FAULT, GET ON, LAY OUT 7.

jump on the bandwagon *or* **get on the bandwagon** *v. phr., informal* To join a popular cause or movement. ♦*At the last possible moment, the senator jumped on the winning candidate's bandwagon.*

jump out of one's skin *v. phr., informal* To be badly frightened; be very much surprised. ♦*The lightning struck so close to Bill that he almost jumped out of his skin.* Compare HAIR STAND ON END.

jump pass *n.* A pass (as in football or basketball) made by a player while jumping. ♦*The Bruins scored when the quarterback tossed a jump pass to the left end.*

jump the gun *also* **beat the gun** *v. phr.* **1.** To start before the starter's gun in a race. ♦*The runners were called back because one of them jumped the gun.* **2.** *informal* To start before you should; start before anyone else. ♦*The new students were not supposed to come before noon, but one boy jumped the gun and came to school at eight in the morning.* ♦*The students planned to say happy birthday to the principal when the teacher raised her hand, but Sarah jumped the gun and said it when he came into the room.*

jump the traces See KICK OVER THE TRACES.

jump the track *v. phr.* **1.** To go off rails; go or run the wrong way. ♦*The train jumped the track and there was a terrible accident.* ♦*The pulley of the clothesline jumped the track and Mother's washing fell down.* **2.** *informal* To change from one thought or idea to another without plan or reason; change the thought or idea you are talking about to something different. ♦*Bob didn't finish his algebra homework because his mind kept jumping the track to think about the new girl in class.* Compare OFF THE TRACK.*

jump through a hoop *v. phr., informal* To do whatever you are told to do; obey any order. ♦*Bob would jump through a hoop for Mary.* Compare TWIST AROUND ONE'S LITTLE FINGER, UNDER ONE'S THUMB.

jump to a conclusion *v. phr.* To decide too quickly or without thinking or finding the facts. ♦*Jerry saw his dog limping on a bloody leg and jumped to the conclusion that it had been shot.* Contrast LOOK BEFORE YOU LEAP.

junked up *adj. or v. phr., slang, drug culture* To be under the influence of drugs, especially heroine. ♦*You can't talk to Billy, he's all junked up.*

just about *adv., informal* Nearly; almost; practically. ♦*Just about everyone in town came to hear the mayor speak.* ♦*The dress came down to just about the middle of her knee.* ♦*Has Mary finished peeling the potatoes? Just about.*

just for the fun of it *adv. phr.* Merely as a matter of amusement. ♦*"I'll bring a goat to class," Bob said to his classmates, "just for the fun of it; I want to see what kind of a face Professor Brown will make."*

just for the hell of it See JUST FOR THE FUN OF IT.

justice See DO JUSTICE TO.

just in case *adv. phr.* For an emergency; in order to be protected. ♦*"Here are my house keys, Sue," Tom said. "I'll be back in two weeks, but you should have them, just in case...."* See IN CASE.

just in time See IN TIME.

just now *adv. phr.* **1.** Just at this moment; at this time. ♦*Mr. Johnson isn't here just now. Will you phone back later?* **2.** *informal* A very short time ago; only a moment ago; only a little while ago. ♦*"Where could that boy have gone so quickly? He was here just now!"* Compare WHILE AGO.

just so¹ *adj.* Exact; exactly right. ♦*Mrs. Robinson likes to keep her house just so, and she makes the children take off their shoes when they come in the house.*

just so² *conj.* Provided; if. ♦*Take as much food as you want, just so you don't waste any food.* Syn. AS LONG AS 2.

just so³ *adv. phr.* With great care; very carefully. ◆*In order to raise healthy African violets you must treat them just so.*

just the other way *or* **the other way around** *adv. phr.* Just the opposite. ◆*One would have thought that Goliath would defeat David, but it was the other way around.*

just the same See ALL THE SAME.

just what the doctor ordered *n. phr.,* *informal* Exactly what is needed or wanted. ◆*"Ah! Just what the doctor ordered!" exclaimed Joe when Mary brought him a cold soda.*

kangaroo court *n.* A self-appointed group that decides what to do to someone who is supposed to have done wrong. ♦ *The Chicago mob held a kangaroo court and shot the gangster who competed with Al Capone.*

keel See ON AN EVEN KEEL.

keel over *v.* **1.** To turn upside down; tip over; overturn.—Usually refers to a boat. ♦ *The strong wind made the sailboat keel over and the passengers fell into the water.* **2.** *informal* To fall over in a faint; faint. ♦ *It was so hot during the assembly program that two girls who were standing on the stage keeled over.* ♦ *When the principal told the girl her father died, she keeled right over.*

keen about *or* **on** *adj. phr.* Very enthusiastic about someone or something. ♦ *It is well known that Queen Elizabeth is keen on horses.*

keep abreast (of) someone *or* **something** *v. phr.* To be informed of the latest developments. ♦ *It is difficult to keep abreast of all the various wars that are being waged on planet Earth.* Compare KEEP STEP WITH.

keep a civil tongue in one's head *v. phr.* To be polite in speaking. ♦ *He was very angry with his boss, but he kept a civil tongue in his head.* ♦ *The bus driver began yelling at the woman and she told him to keep a civil tongue in his head.*

keep a close check on See KEEP TAB(S) ON.

keep after *v., informal* To speak to (someone) about something again and again; remind over and over again. ♦ *Some pupils will do sloppy work unless the teacher keeps after them to write neatly.* ♦ *Sue's mother had to keep after her to clean her bedroom.*

keep an ear to the ground See EAR TO THE GROUND.

keep an eye on *or* **keep one's eye on** *or* **have one's eye on** *v. phr.* **1.** To watch carefully; not stop paying attention to. ♦ *Keep an eye on the stove in case the coffee boils.* ♦ *You must keep your eye on the ball when you play tennis.* ♦ *A good driver keeps his eye on the road.* ♦ *The teacher had her eye on me* because she thought I was cheating. ♦ *Billy keeps a jealous eye on his toys.* ♦ *The lion tamer keeps a sharp eye on the lions when he is in the cage.* Compare LOOK OUT, LOOK OVER. **2.** To watch and do what is needed for; mind. ♦ *Mother told Jane to keep an eye on the baby while she was in the store.* ♦ *Mr. Brown told John to keep an eye on the store while he was out.* Syn. TAKE CARE OF 1.

keep an eye open *or* **keep an eye out for** See KEEP AN EYE ON.

keep an eye out See EYE OUT.

keep a stiff upper lip *v. phr.* To be brave; face trouble bravely. ♦ *He was very much worried about his sick daughter, but he kept a stiff upper lip.* ♦ *Although he was having some trouble with the engine, the pilot kept a stiff upper lip and landed the plane safely.* Compare KEEP ONE'S CHIN UP.

keep a straight face See STRAIGHT FACE, DEADPAN.

keep at *v.* To continue to do; go on with. ♦ *Mary kept at her homework until she finished it.* Compare KEEP ON 1, KEEP UP 1b.

keep away *v. phr.* To remain at a distance from. ♦ *Her mother advised Diane to keep away from men offering a ride.*

keep back *v. phr.* To refrain or be restrained from entering; remain back. ♦ *The police had a hard time keeping back the crowd when the astronauts came to town after walking on the moon.*

keep body and soul together *v. phr.* To keep alive; survive. ♦ *John was unemployed most of the year and hardly made enough money to keep body and soul together.* Compare KEEP THE WOLF FROM THE DOOR.

keep books *v. phr.* To keep records of money gained and spent; do the work of a bookkeeper. ♦ *Miss Jones keeps the company's books.*

keep company *v. phr.* **1.** To stay or go along with (someone) so that he will not be lonely to visit with (someone). ♦ *John kept Andy company while his parents went to the movies.* ♦ *I'll go* shopping with you just to keep you company. **2.** To go places together as a couple; date just one person. ♦*After keeping company for one year, Mary and John decided to marry.* ♦*Who is Bill keeping company with now?* Compare GO STEADY.

keep cool *v. phr.* Remain calm; remain unexcited. ♦*The main thing to remember in an emergency situation is to not lose one's head and keep cool.*

keep down *v.* Keep from progressing or growing; keep within limits; control. ♦*The children could not keep their voices down.* ♦*We hoe the garden to keep down the weeds.* ♦*You can't keep a good man down.* Compare GET AHEAD.

keeper See FINDERS KEEPERS.

keep from *v., informal* To hold yourself back from; stop or prevent yourself from (doing something). ♦*Can you keep from repeating gossip?* ♦*Jill can't keep from talking about her trip.*— Usually used with *can* in the negative. ♦*You can't keep from liking Jim.* Compare CAN HELP.

keep good time See KEEP TIME.

keep house[1] *v. phr.* To do the necessary things in a household; do the cooking and cleaning. ♦*Since their mother died, Mary and her brother keep house for their father.*

keep house[2] also **play house** *v. phr., informal* To live together without being married. ♦*Bob and Nancy keep house these days.*

keeping See IN KEEPING, OUT OF KEEPING.

keep in mind See IN MIND.

keep in touch with *v. phr.* To remain in communication with; maintain contact with. ♦*Don't forget to keep in touch, either by letter or phone, when you're in Europe!*

keep late hours *v. phr.* To go to bed late; habitually stay up (and work) late. ♦*"If you always keep such late hours, your health might suffer," Tom's doctor said.*

keep off *v. phr.* To refrain from entering; stay away from. ♦*"Keep off the grass,"* the sign in the park indicated.

keep on *v.* **1.** To go ahead; not stop; continue. ♦*The neighbors asked them to stop making noise, but they kept right on.* ♦*Columbus kept on until he saw land.*—Often used before a present participle. ♦*Relentlessly, the boy kept on asking about the birds and the bees.* ♦*The boy kept on talking even though the teacher had asked him to stop.* Syn. GO ON. Compare KEEP AT, KEEP UP. **2.** To allow to continue working for you. ♦*The new owner kept Fred on as gardener.*

keep one at a distance *or* **keep one at arm's length** *v. phr.* To avoid (someone's) company; not become too friendly toward. ♦*Mr. Smith is kind to the workers in his store but after work he keeps them at a distance.* ♦*Betty likes Bill and is trying to be friendly, but he keeps her at arm's length.* Compare KEEP ONE'S DISTANCE, HOLD OFF 1a.

keep (one) posted *v. phr.* To receive current information; inform oneself. ♦*My associates phoned me every day and kept me posted on new developments in our business.*

keep one's balance *v. phr.* To stay even-tempered; not become overexcited. ♦*Mike has the best personality to run our office; he always keeps his balance.* Contrast LOSE ONE'S BALANCE.

keep one's chin up *v. phr.* To be brave; be determined; face trouble with courage. ♦*He didn't think that he would ever get out of the jungle alive, but he kept his chin up.* Compare KEEP A STIFF UPPER LIP.

keep one's distance *v. phr.* To be cool toward someone; avoid being friendly. ♦*Mary did not like her co-worker, Betty, and kept her distance from her.* Compare KEEP ONE AT A DISTANCE.

keep one's end up See HOLD ONE'S END UP.

keep one's eye on See KEEP AN EYE ON.

keep one's eye on the ball *v. phr.* **1.** To watch the ball at all times in a sport, usually in order to hit it or get it; not stop watching the ball. ♦*Keep your eye on the baseball or you won't be able to hit it.* **2.** *informal* To be watchful and ready; be wide-awake and ready to win or succeed; be smart.♦*Tom is just starting on the job but if he keeps his eye on the ball, he will be promoted.* Compare ON THE BALL, KEEP AN EYE ON *or* KEEP ONE'S EYE ON *or* HAVE ONE'S EYE ON.

keep one's eyes open See EYES OPEN.

keep one's eyes peeled *or* **keep one's eyes skinned** *v. phr., informal* To watch carefully; be always looking. ♦ *The bird-watcher kept his eyes peeled for bluebirds.* ♦ *When the boys walked through the roads, they kept their eyes skinned for snakes.* Compare EYES OPEN 1, EYE OUT.

keep one's feet *v. phr.* To keep from falling or slipping down; keep your balance; remain standing. ♦ *The boy stumbled on the stairs but was able to keep his feet.* Compare REGAIN ONE'S FEET.

keep one's feet on the ground See FEET ON THE GROUND.

keep one's fingers crossed See CROSS ONE'S FINGERS 1b.

keep one's hand in *v. phr.* To keep in practice; continue to take part. ♦ *After he retired from teaching, Mr. Brown kept his hand in by giving a lecture once in a while.* ♦ *Mr. Smith left the planning of the trip to his wife, but he kept his hand in, too.* Compare KEEP UP.

keep one's head *also* **keep one's wits about one** *v. phr.* To stay calm when there is trouble or danger. ♦ *When Tim heard the fire alarm he kept his head and looked for the nearest exit.* Compare COUNT TO TEN. Contrast LOSE ONE'S HEAD.

keep one's head above water *v. phr.* To remain solvent; manage to stay out of debt. ♦ *Herb's income declined so drastically that he now has difficulty keeping his head above water.*

keep one's mouth shut *v. phr., informal* To be or stay silent.—A rude expression when used as a command. ♦ *When the crooks were captured by the police, their leader warned them to keep their mouths shut.* ♦ *Charles began to tell Barry how to kick the ball, and Barry said angrily, "Keep your mouth shut!"* Syn. SHUT UP 1.

keep one's nose clean *v. phr., slang* To stay out of trouble; do only what you should do. ♦ *The boss said Jim could have the job as long as he kept his nose clean and worked hard.* ♦ *The policeman warned the boys to keep their noses clean unless they wanted to go to jail.* Compare STEER CLEAR OF 2.

keep one's nose to the grindstone *or* **have one's nose to the grindstone** *or*

hold one's nose to the grindstone *v. phr., informal* To work hard all the time; keep busy with boring or tiresome work. ♦ *Sarah keeps her nose to the grindstone and saves as much as possible to start her own business.*

keep one's own counsel *v. phr., formal* To keep your ideas and plans to yourself. ♦ *John listened to what everyone had to say in the discussion, but he kept his own counsel.* ♦ *Although everybody gave Mrs. O'Connor advice about what to do with her house, she kept her own counsel.*

keep one's shirt on *v. phr., slang* To calm down; keep from losing your temper or getting impatient or excited. ♦ *Bob got very angry when John accidentally bumped into him, but John told him to keep his shirt on.*—Usually used as a command; may be considered impolite. ♦ *John said to Bob, "Keep your shirt on."* Contrast GET ONE'S DANDER UP.

keep one's temper See HOLD ONE'S TEMPER.

keep one's weather eye open See WEATHER EYE.

keep one's wits about one See KEEP ONE'S HEAD.

keep one's word *v. phr.* To do what one has promised; fulfill one's promise. ♦ *Paul kept his word and paid me the $250 that he owed me right on time.*

keep on the good side of See ON ONE'S GOOD SIDE.

keep open house *v. phr.* To offer hospitality and entertain those who come at any given time on a certain day or afternoon. ♦ *Beth and Charlie have a cottage by the lake where they keep open house on Saturday afternoons during the summer.*

keep out (of) *v. phr.* **1.** To stay out; remain out of. ♦ *The sign on the fence said, "Danger! Keep out!"* **2.** To stave off; not allow in. ♦ *The border patrol near El Paso, Texas, is trying to keep illegal immigrants out of the United States.*

keep pace *v. phr.* To go as fast; go at the same rate; not get behind. ♦ *When they go for a walk, Johnny has to take long steps to keep pace with his father.* ♦ *When Billy was moved to a more advanced class, he had to work hard to keep pace.* Compare KEEP UP 2a.

keep plugging along *v. phr., informal* To continue to work diligently and with great effort, often against hardship. ♦*Bob was not particularly talented but he kept plugging along year after year, and eventually became vice president.*

keeps See FOR KEEPS.

keep step with *v. phr.* To maintain the same degree of progress as someone else. ♦*The United States has no choice but to keep step with potential enemies in terms of modern defense systems.*

keep tab on *or* **keep tabs on** *v. phr., informal* **1.** To keep a record of. ♦*The government tries to keep tabs on all the animals in the park.* **2.** To keep a watch on; check. ♦*The house mother kept tabs on the girls to be sure they were clean and neat.* Compare KEEP TRACK OF.

keep the ball rolling *v. phr., informal* To keep up an activity or action; not allow something that is happening to slow or stop. ♦*Clyde kept the ball rolling at the party by dancing with a lamp shade on his head.* Compare GET THE BALL ROLLING.

keep the faith *v. phr.* To not abandon hope; stay committed to the cause of democracy and racial equality. ♦*"Keep the faith, Baby," my neighbor said as he raised his fingers to show the "V" for victory sign.*

keep the home fires burning *v. phr.* To keep things going as usual while someone is away; wait at home to welcome someone back. ♦*While John was in the army, Mary kept the home fires burning.*

keep the wolf (wolves) from the door *v. phr.* To avoid hunger, poverty, and/or creditors. ♦*"I don't like my job," Mike complained, "but I must do something to keep the wolves from the door."* Compare KEEP BODY AND SOUL TOGETHER.

keep things humming *v. phr.* To cause thing to perform smoothly and efficiently. ♦*Until Mr. Long joined our computer center, we had all sorts of problems, but he has corrected them and really keeps things humming.*

keep time *v. phr.* **1.** To show the right time. ♦*My watch has not kept good time since I dropped it.* **2.** To keep the beat; keep the same rhythm; keep in step. ♦*Many people are surprised at how well deaf people keep time with the music when they dance.*

keep to oneself See TO ONESELF 2.

keep track *v. phr.* To know about changes; stay informed or up-to-date; keep a count or record. ♦*What day of the week is it? I can't keep track.*— Usually used with *of.* ♦*Mr. Stevens kept track of his business by telephone when he was in the hospital.* ♦*The farmer has so many chickens, he can hardly keep track of them all.* Compare IN TOUCH, KEEP UP 3. Contrast LOSE TRACK.

keep under one's hat *v. phr., informal* To keep secret; not tell. ♦*Mr. Jones knew who had won the contest, but he kept it under his hat until it was announced publicly.*—Often used as a command. ♦*Keep it under your hat.* Syn. KEEP TO ONESELF.

keep up *v.* **1a.** To go on; not stop; continue. ♦*The rain kept up for two days and the roads were flooded.* Compare KEEP ON. **1b.** To go on with (something); continue steadily; never stop. ♦*Mrs. Smith told John to keep up the good work.* ♦*The teacher asked Dick to stop bothering Mary, but he kept it up.* ♦Compare KEEP AT. **2a.** To go at the same rate as others. ♦*John had to work hard to keep up.* ♦*Billy was the youngest boy on the hike, but he kept up with the others.* Compare CATCH UP, KEEP PACE. Contrast FALL BEHIND, GET BEHIND 1. **2b.** To keep (something) at the same level or rate or in good condition. ♦*The shortage of tomatoes kept the prices up.* ♦*Grandfather was too poor to keep up his house.* **3.** To keep informed.—Usually used with *on* or *with.* ♦*Mary is interested in politics and always keeps up with the news.* Compare KEEP TRACK.

keep up appearances *v. phr.* To maintain an outward show of prosperity in spite of financial problems. ♦*Mr. Smith's widow had a hard time keeping up appearances after her husband's death.*

keep up one's end See HOLD ONE'S END UP.

keep up with See KEEP STEP WITH, KEEP ABREAST OF.

keep up with the Joneses *v. phr.* To follow the latest fashion; try to be equal with your neighbors. ♦ *Mrs. Smith kept buying every new thing that was advertised. Finally Mr. Smith told her to stop trying to keep up with the Joneses and to start thinking for herself.*

keep watch *v. phr.* To be vigilant; be alert; guard. ♦ *The police have asked the neighborhood to keep watch against an escaped convict.*

keep your fingers crossed See CROSS ONE'S FINGERS.

kettle See KETTLE OF FISH, POT CALLS THE KETTLE BLACK.

kettle of fish *v. phr., informal* Something to be considered; how things are; a happening; business. ♦ *I thought he needed money, but it was another kettle of fish—his car had disappeared.*—Usually used with *pretty, fine, nice,* but meaning bad trouble. ♦ *He had two flat tires and no spare on a country road at night, which was certainly a pretty kettle of fish.* ♦ *This is a fine kettle of fish! I forgot my book.* Compare CUP OF TEA 2.

key See LOW KEY, OFF-KEY.

keyed up *adj., informal* Excited; nervous; anxious to do something. ♦ *Mary was all keyed up about the exam.* ♦ *Mother would not let Tom read a ghost story at bedtime; she said it would get him keyed up.*

kick about See KICK AROUND 3.

kick against the pricks *v. phr., literary* To fight against rules or authority in a way that just hurts yourself. ♦ *Johnny kicked against the pricks in his foster home until he learned that he could trust his new family.*

kick around *v., informal* **1.** To act roughly or badly to; treat badly; bully. ♦ *John likes to kick around the little boys.* ♦ *Mr. Jones is always kicking his dog around.* Syn. PUSH AROUND. **2.** To lie around or in a place; be treated carelessly; be neglected. ♦ *This old coat has been kicking around the closet for years.* ♦ *The letter kicked around on my desk for days.* **3.** *slang* To talk easily or carelessly back and forth about; examine in a careless or easygoing way. ♦ *Bob and I kicked around the idea of going swimming, but it was hot and we were too lazy.* Compare TRY

OUT, TALK OVER. **4.** To move about often; go from one job or place to another; become experienced. ♦ *Harry has kicked around all over the world as a merchant seaman.* Compare HAS BEEN AROUND.

kick back *v., slang, informal* To pay money illegally for favorable contract arrangements. ♦ *I will do it if you kick back a few hundred for my firm.*

kickback *n., slang, informal* Money paid illegally for favorable treatment. ♦ *He was arrested for making kickback payments.*

kick down *v. phr., slang* To shift an automobile, jeep, or truck into lower gear by hand-shifting. ♦ *Joe kicked the jeep down from third to second, and we slowed down.*

kick in See CHIP IN.

kick in the pants *or* **kick in the teeth** *n. phr., informal* Unexpected scorn or insult when praise was expected; rejection. ♦ *Mary worked hard to clean up John's room, but all she got for her trouble was a kick in the teeth.* Compare SLAP IN THE FACE.

kick it *v. phr., slang* To end a bad or unwanted habit such as drinking, smoking, or drug addiction. ♦ *Farnsworth finally kicked it; he's in good shape.*

kickoff *n.* The start of something, like a new venture, a business, a sports event, or a concert season. ♦ *Beethoven's Ninth will be the kickoff for this summer season at Ravinia.*

kick off *v. phr.* **1.** To make the kick that begins a football game. ♦ *John kicked off and the football game started.* **2.** *informal* To begin; launch; start. ♦ *The candidate kicked off his campaign with a speech on television.* ♦ *The fund raising drive was kicked off with a theater party.* **3.** *slang* To die. ♦ *Mr. Jones was almost ninety years old when he kicked off.* Syn. KICK THE BUCKET.

kick oneself *v. phr., informal* To be sorry or ashamed; regret. ♦ *When John missed the train, he kicked himself for not having left earlier.* ♦ *Mary could have kicked herself for letting the secret out before it was announced officially.*

kick out *or* **boot out** *v., informal* To make (someone) go or leave; get rid of; dismiss. ♦ *The boys made so much* noise at the movie that the manager kicked them out. ◆ *The chief of police was booted out of office because he was a crook.* Syn. THROW OUT 3.

kick over *v.* **1.** *Of a motor:* To begin to work. ◆ *He had not used his car for two months and when he tried to start it, the motor would not kick over.* **2.** *slang* To pay; contribute. ◆ *The gang forced all the storekeepers on the block to kick over $5 a week.* **3.** *slang* To die. ◆ *Mrs. O'Leary's cow kicked over this morning.*

kick over the traces *also* **jump the traces** *v. phr.* To break the rules; behave badly. ◆ *When their teacher was absent and they had a substitute, the children kicked over the traces.* Compare ACT UP, CUT UP, LET LOOSE, OUT OF HAND, RAISE CAIN.

kick the bucket *v. phr., slang* To die. ◆ *Old Mr. Jones kicked the bucket just two days before his ninety-fourth birthday.* Compare KICK OFF 3.

kick up *v., informal* To show signs of not working right. ◆ *John had had too much to eat and his stomach started to kick up.* ◆ *After working well for a year the air conditioner suddenly started kicking up.*

kick up a fuss *or* **kick up a row** *or* **raise a row** *also* **kick up a dust** *v. phr., informal* To make trouble; make a disturbance. ◆ *When the teacher gave the class five more hours of homework, the class kicked up a fuss.* ◆ *When the teacher left the room, two boys kicked up a row.* Compare RAISE CAIN, RAISE THE ROOF.

kick up one's heels *v. phr., informal* To have a merry time; celebrate. ◆ *When exams were over the students went to town to kick up their heels.* ◆ *Mary was usually very quiet but at the farewell party she kicked up her heels and had a wonderful time.*

kid See HANDLE WITH GLOVES *or* HANDLE WITH KID GLOVES, HANDLE WITHOUT GLOVES *or* HANDLE WITHOUT KID GLOVES.

kiddie car *n., slang, citizen's band radio jargon* A school bus. ◆ *Watch out for that kiddie car coming up behind you!*

kill See CURIOSITY KILLED THE CAT, IN AT THE KILL.

kill off *v.* To kill or end completely; destroy. ◆ *The factory dumped poison-ous wastes into the river and killed off the fish.* ◆ *The president suggested a new law to Congress but many members of Congress were against the idea and they killed it off.* ◆ *Mother made Nancy practice her dancing an hour every day; Nancy got tired of dancing and that killed off her interest.*

kill the goose that laid the golden egg To spoil something that is good or something that you have, by being greedy.—A proverb. ◆ *Mrs. Jones gives you an apple from her tree whenever you go by her house, but don't kill the goose that laid the golden egg by bothering her too much.*

kill time *v. phr.* To cause the time to pass more rapidly; waste time. ◆ *The plane trip to Hong Kong was long and tiring, but we managed to kill time by watching several movies.*

kill two birds with one stone *v. phr.* To succeed in doing two things by only one action; get two results from one effort. ◆ *Mother stopped at the supermarket to buy bread and then went to get Jane at dancing class; she killed two birds with one stone.* ◆ *The history teacher told us that making an outline kills two birds with one stone; it makes us study the lesson till we understand it, and it gives us notes to review before the test.*

kilter See OUT OF KILTER.

kind See IN A WAY *also* IN A KIND OF WAY, IN KIND.

kindly See TAKE KINDLY TO.

kind of *or* **sort of** *adv. phr., informal* Almost but not quite; rather. ◆ *A guinea pig looks kind of like a rabbit, but it has short ears.* ◆ *Bob was kind of tired when he finished the job.* ◆ *The teacher sort of frowned but then smiled.* ◆ *Mary wouldn't tell what she wanted to be when she grew up; it was sort of a secret.*

kindred spirits *n. phr.* People who resemble each other in numerous ways, including their ways of thinking and feeling. ◆ *They are kindred spirits; they both like to go on long walks in the forest.*

king's ransom *n. phr.* **1.** An excessively large sum of money extorted by kidnappers to let someone go free. ◆ *The Smith family had to pay a king's ransom for the freedom of their seven-*

year-old son, Tommy. **2.** An exorbitant fee one is forced to pay. ♦ *The realtors exacted a king's ransom for that choice lot on the corner.*

kiss someone *or* **something goodbye** *v. phr.* To lose or give up someone or something forever. ♦ *"If you won't marry Jane," Peter said to Tom, "you might as well kiss her goodbye." ♦ People who bet on a losing horse at the races might as well kiss their money goodbye.*

kite See GO FLY A KITE.

kitten See HAVE KITTENS.

knee See BRING TO ONE'S KNEES, IN THE LAP OF THE GODS *also* ON THE KNEES OF THE GODS, ON ONE'S KNEES, UP TO THE CHIN IN *or* UP TO THE KNEE IN.

knee-deep *or* **neck-deep** *adv. or adj. phr.* **1.** Very much; deeply; having a big part in. ♦ *Johnny was knee-deep in trouble.* **2.** Very busy; working hard at. ♦ *We were neck-deep in homework before the exams.* **3.** Getting or having many or much. ♦ *The television station was knee-deep in phone calls.* Compare UP TO THE CHIN IN.

knee-high to a grasshopper *also* **knee-high to a duck** *adj. phr., informal* As tall as a very small child; very young. ♦ *Charles started reading when he was knee-high to a grasshopper.* ♦ *I've known Mary ever since she was knee-high to a duck.*

kneeling bus *n., informal* A bus equipped with a hydraulic device to enable it to drop almost to curb level for greater ease of boarding and leaving vehicle, as a convenience for elderly or handicapped passengers. ♦ *The man on crutches was pleased to see the kneeling bus.*

knell See DEATH KNELL.

knit See CLOSE-KNIT.

knitting See STICK TO ONE'S KNITTING *or* TEND TO ONE'S KNITTING.

knock See SCHOOL OF HARD KNOCKS.

knock about *or* **knock around** *v.* To travel without a plan; go where you please. ♦ *After he graduated from college, Joe knocked about for a year seeing the country before he went to work in his father's business.* Compare KICK AROUND.

knock back on one's heels See SET BACK ON ONE'S HEELS.

knock cold *v. phr., informal* To render unconscious. ♦ *The blow on the chin knocked Harry cold.*

knock down *v. phr.* To reduce; lower. ♦ *The realtors said that if we decided to buy the house, they would knock the price down by 10%.*

knocked out *adj., slang* Intoxicated; drugged; out of one's mind. ♦ *Jim sounds so incoherent, he must be knocked out.*

knock for a loop *or* **throw for a loop** *v. phr., slang* To surprise very much. ♦ *When I heard they were moving, I was really knocked for a loop.* ♦ *The news of their marriage threw me for a loop.*

knock it off *v. phr., slang, informal* **1.** To stop talking about something considered not appropriate or nonsensical by the listener.—Used frequently as an imperative. ♦ *Come on, Joe, knock it off, you're not making any sense at all!* **2.** To cease doing something; to quit.—Heavily favored in the imperative. ♦ *Come on boys, knock it off, you're breaking the furniture in my room!*

knock off *v. phr., slang* **1.** To burglarize someone. ♦ *They knocked off the Manning residence.* **2.** To murder someone. ♦ *The gangsters knocked off Herman.*

knock off one's feet *v. phr.* To surprise (someone) so much that he does not know what to do. ♦ *Her husband's death knocked Mrs. Jones off her feet.* ♦ *When Charlie was given the prize, it knocked him off his feet for a few minutes.* Compare BOWL OVER 2, SWEEP OFF ONE'S FEET.

knock one's block off *v. phr., slang* To hit someone very hard; beat someone up. ♦ *Stay out of my yard or I'll knock your block off.* ♦ *Jim will knock your block off if he catches you riding his bike.*

knock oneself out *v. phr., informal* To work very hard; make a great effort. ♦ *Mrs. Ross knocked herself out planning her daughter's wedding.* ♦ *Tom knocked himself out to give his guests a good time.* Compare BREAK ONE'S NECK, FALL OVER BACKWARDS, OUT OF ONE'S WAY.

knock on wood *v. phr.* To knock on something made of wood to keep from having bad luck.—Many people believe that you will have bad luck if you talk about good luck or brag about something, unless you knock on wood; often used in a joking way. ♦ *Charles said, "I haven't been sick all winter." Grandfather said, "You'd better knock on wood when you say that."*

knockout *n., slang* **1.** Strikingly beautiful woman. ♦ *Sue is a regular knockout.* **2.** A straight punch in boxing that causes one's opponent to fall and lose consciousness. ♦ *The champion won the fight with a straight knockout.*

knock out *v. phr.* To make helpless, unworkable, or unusable. ♦ *The champion knocked out the challenger in the third round.* ♦ *The soldier knocked out two enemy tanks with his bazooka.*

knock over *v. phr.* To overturn; upset. ♦ *I accidentally knocked over the Chinese lamp that fell on the floor and broke.*

knock the living daylights out of *v. phr., slang, informal* To render (someone) unconscious (said in exaggeration). ♦ *The news almost knocked the living daylights out of me.*

knock the stuffing out of See KNOCK THE LIVING DAYLIGHTS OUT OF.

knot See TIE IN KNOTS, TIE THE KNOT.

knotty problem *n. phr.* A very complicated and difficult problem to solve. ♦ *Doing one's income tax properly can present a knotty problem.*

know See FOR ALL ONE KNOWS, GOD KNOWS *or* GOODNESS KNOWS *or* HEAVEN KNOWS, IN THE KNOW, NOT KNOW WHICH WAY TO TURN *or* NOT KNOW WHICH WAY TO JUMP.

know a thing or two about *v. phr.* To be experienced in; have a fairly considerable knowledge of. ♦ *Tom has dealt with many foreign traders; he knows a thing or two about stocks and bonds.*

know enough to come in out of the rain *v. phr.* To have good sense; know how to take care of yourself.—Usually used in the negative. ♦ *Bob does so many foolish things that his mother says he doesn't know enough to come in out of the rain.* ♦ *Sally may look stupid, but she knows enough to come in out of the rain.*

know-how *n., slang* Expertise; ability to devise and construct. ♦ *The United States had the know-how to beat the Soviet Union to the moon in 1969.*

know if one is coming or going *or* **know whether one is coming or going** *v. phr.* To feel able to think clearly; know what to do.—Usually used in the negative or with limiters. ♦ *On Monday, the car broke down; on Tuesday, Mother broke her arm; on Wednesday, the children all became ill with the mumps; by Thursday, poor Father didn't know if he was coming or going.* ♦ *My cousin is so much in love that she scarcely knows whether she's coming or going.* Compare IN A FOG.

know in one's bones See FEEL IN ONE'S BONES.

know-it-all *n.* A person who acts as if he knows all about everything; someone who thinks no one can tell him anything new. ♦ *After George was elected as class president, he wouldn't take suggestions from anyone; he became a know-it-all.*—Also used like an adjective. ♦ *The other students didn't like George's know-it-all attitude.*

knowledge See A LITTLE KNOWLEDGE IS A DANGEROUS THING, TO THE BEST OF YOUR KNOWLEDGE.

know one in high places *v. phr.* To be connected with people in power. ♦ *Ted's grandfather was the mayor of Chicago so he knows people in high places.*

know one is alive *v. phr.* Not to notice a person.—Used with negative or limiting words and in questions. ♦ *She was a good-looking girl but she didn't know I was alive.* Compare GIVE A HANG.

know one's own mind *v. phr.* To not hesitate or vacillate; be definite in one's ideas or plans. ♦ *It is impossible to do business with Fred, because he doesn't know his own mind.*

know one's place *v. phr.* To be deferential to one's elders or superiors. ♦ *Ken is a talented teaching assistant, but he has a tendency to tell the head of the department how to run things. Somebody ought to teach him to know his place.*

know one's way around *or* **know one's way about** *v. phr.* **1.** To understand how things happen in the world; be experienced in the ways of the world. ♦ *The sailor had been in the wildest ports in the world. He knew his way around.* Compare HAVE BEEN AROUND. **2.** *or informal* **know one's onions** *or*

know one's stuff To have experience and skill in an activity. ♦ *Before trying to make any pottery, it is better to get advice from someone who knows his stuff in ceramics.* Compare DRY BEHIND THE EARS.

know something inside out *v. phr.* To be extremely well conversant with something; be an expert in; have thorough knowledge of. ♦ *Tom knows the stock market inside out.*

know the ropes See THE ROPES.

know the score See THE SCORE.

know what's what See KNOW SOMETHING INSIDE OUT.

know which side one's bread is buttered on *v. phr.* To know who can help you and try to please him; know what is for your own gain. ♦ *Dick was always polite to the boss; he knew which side his bread was buttered on.*

know which way to turn See NOT KNOW WHICH WAY TO TURN.

knuckle See BUCKLE DOWN *or* KNUCKLE DOWN, RAP ONE'S KNUCKLES.

knuckle down See BUCKLE DOWN.

knuckle under *v. phr.* To do something because you are forced to do it. ♦ *Bobby refused to knuckle under to the bully.* Compare GIVE IN.

labor movement *n.* Groups which form, strengthen, and increase membership in labor unions. ♦ *His father was connected with the labor movement in the 1920's.*

labor of love *n. phr.* Something done for personal pleasure and not pay or profit. ♦ *Building the model railroad was a labor of love for the retired engineer.*

labor the point See BELABOR THE POINT.

labor under *v. phr.* To be the victim of; suffer from. ♦ *Ken is obviously laboring under the delusion that Jennifer will marry him out of love.*

lace into *or* **tie into** *v., informal* To attack physically or with words; begin to hit or criticize. ♦ *The boxer laced into his opponent.* ♦ *The critics laced into the new movie.* Syn. LAY INTO, RIP INTO. Compare GIVE IT TO.

ladies' room *n. phr.* A public toilet and restroom for women. ♦ *Can you please tell me where the ladies' room is?*

lady friend *n.* **1.** A woman friend. ♦ *His aunt stays with a lady friend in Florida during the winter.* **2.** A woman who is the lover of a man.—Used by people trying to appear more polite, but not often used by careful speakers. ♦ *The lawyer took his lady friend to dinner.* Syn. GIRLFRIEND.

lady-killer *n., informal* **1.** Any man who has strong sex appeal toward women. ♦ *Joe is a regular lady-killer.* **2.** A man who relentlessly pursues amorous conquests, is successful at it, and then abandons his heartbroken victims. ♦ *The legendary Don Juan of Spain is the most famous lady-killer of recorded history.* Compare LADY'S MAN.

lady of the house *n. phr.* Female owner, or wife of the owner, of the house; the hostess. ♦ *"Dinner is served," the lady of the house announced to her guests.*

lady's man *n.* A man or boy who likes to be with women or girls very much and is popular with them. ♦ *Charlie is quite a lady's man now.*

lake See GO JUMP IN THE LAKE.

laid out *adj.* Arranged. ♦ *Her house is very conveniently laid out.*

laid up *adj.* Sick; confined to bed. ♦ *I was laid up for a couple of weeks with an ear infection.*

lam See ON THE LAM.

lamb See GOD TEMPERS THE WIND TO THE SHORN LAMB, IN TWO SHAKES OF A LAMB'S TAIL.

lame duck *n., informal* An elected public official who has been either defeated in a new election or whose term cannot be renewed, but who has a short period of time left in office during which he can still perform certain duties, though with somewhat diminished powers. ♦ *In the last year of their second terms, American presidents are lame ducks.*

land See FAT OF THE LAND, LAY OF THE LAND *also* HOW THE LAND LIES.

land all over See JUMP ON.

landing ship *n.* A ship built to land troops and army equipment on a beach for an invasion. ♦ *The landing ship came near the beach, doors in the bow opened, and marines ran out.*

land-office business *n., informal* A great rush of business. ♦ *It was a hot day, and the drive-ins were doing a land-office business in ice cream and cold drinks.*

land of nod *n. phr.* Sleep. ♦ *The little girl went off to the land of nod.*

land on See JUMP ON.

land on one's feet *also* **land on both feet** *v. phr., informal* To get yourself out of trouble without damage or injury and sometimes with a gain; be successful no matter what happens. ♦ *No matter what trouble he gets into, he always seems to land on his feet.* ♦ *Mary lost her first job because she was always late to work, but she landed on her feet and soon had a better job.*

landslide *n.* An overwhelming victory during a political election. ♦ *Ronald Reagan won the election of 1980 in a landslide.*

lane See LOVERS' LANE.

lap See IN THE LAP OF LUXURY, IN THE LAP OF THE GODS.

lap up *v.* **1.** To eat or drink with the tip of the tongue. ♦ *The kitten laps up its milk.* **2.** *informal* To take in eagerly. ♦ *She flatters him all the time and he just laps it up.* ♦ *William is interested in rockets and space, and he laps up all he can read about them.* Syn. EAT UP 3.

lardhead *n., slang* A stupid or slow-witted person. ♦ *You'll never convince Donald; he's a lardhead.*

large See AT LARGE, BY AND LARGE.

large as life See BIG AS LIFE.

large-eyed See ROUND-EYED.

large order *n. phr.* Difficult job; a difficult task to fulfill. ♦ *It is a large order to educate three children in college at the same time.* Compare TALL ORDER.

lash See TONGUE LASHING.

lash out *v.* **1.** To kick. ♦ *The horse lashed out at the man behind him.* **2.** To try suddenly to hit. ♦ *The woman lashed out at the crowd with her umbrella.* **3.** To attack with words. ♦ *The senator lashed out at the administration.* ♦ *The school newspaper lashed out at the unfriendly way some students treated the visiting team.*

last See AT LAST, EVERY LAST MAN, EVERY SINGLE *or* EVERY LAST, FIRST AND LAST, HE LAUGHS BEST WHO LAUGHS LAST, HAVE THE LAST LAUGH, ON ONE'S LAST LEGS, TILL THE LAST GUN IS FIRED *or* UNTIL THE LAST GUN IS FIRED.

last but not least *adv. phr.* In the last place but not the least important. ♦ *Billy will bring sandwiches, Alice will bring cake, Susan will bring cookies, John will bring potato chips, and last but not least, Sally will bring the lemonade.*

last ditch *n.* The last place that can be defended; the last resort. ♦ *They will fight reform to the last ditch.*

last-ditch *adj.* Made or done as a last chance to keep from losing or failing. ♦ *He threw away his cigarettes in a last-ditch effort to stop smoking.* Compare BACK TO THE WALL.

last-ditch effort See LAST DITCH.

last lap *n. phr.* The final stage. ♦ *Although the trip had been very interesting, we were glad that we were on the last lap of our tiring journey.* See LAST LEG.

last laugh See HAVE THE LAST LAUGH.

last leg *n. phr.* **1.** Final stages of physical weakness before dying. ♦ *The poor old man was on his last leg in the nursing home.* **2.** The final stage of a journey. ♦ *The last leg of our round-the-world trip was Paris to Chicago.* See LAST LAP.

last out *v.* **1.** To be enough until the end of. ♦ *There is enough food in the house to last out the snowstorm.* ♦ *Our candles won't last out the night.* **2.** To continue to the end of; continue to live after; live or go through. ♦ *The old man is dying; he won't last out the night.* ♦ *This car will never last out the winter.* Compare HOLD OUT.

last stand *n. phr.* See LAST DITCH.

last straw *or* **straw that breaks the camel's back** *n. phr.* A small trouble which follows other troubles and makes one lose patience and be unable to bear them. ♦ *Bill had a bad day in school yesterday. He lost his knife on the way home, then he fell down, and when he broke a shoe lace, that was the last straw and he began to cry.* ♦ *Mary didn't like it when the other girls said she was proud and lazy, but when they said she told fibs it was the straw that broke the camel's back and she told the teacher.*

last word *n.* **1.** The last remark in an argument. ♦ *I never win an argument with her. She always has the last word.* **2.** The final say in deciding something. ♦ *The superintendent has the last word in ordering new desks.* **3.** *informal* The most modern thing. ♦ *Mrs. Green's stove is the last word in stoves.*

latch on *or* **latch onto** *v., informal* **1.** To get hold of; grasp or grab; catch. ♦ *He looked for something to latch onto and keep from falling.* ♦ *The football player latched onto a pass.* **2.** *slang* To get into your possession. ♦ *The banker latched onto a thousand shares of stock.* **3.** *slang* To understand. ♦ *The teacher explained the idea of jet engines until the students latched onto it.* Syn. CATCH ON. **4.** *informal* To keep; to hold. ♦ *The poor woman latched onto the little money she had left.* **5.** *slang* To stay with; not leave. ♦ *Marie and Dick wanted to go to the movies by themselves, but Marie's little brother latched onto them.*

latch string *n.* **1.** A string that opens an old-fashioned door by lifting a small bar. ♦ *The early settlers kept the latch string outside the door when they were working around the house, but at night they pulled it to the inside.* **2.** *informal* A warm welcome; a friendly greeting. —Used in such phrases as *the latch* *string is out.* ♦ *Mary has her latch string out for everyone who comes.* Syn. WELCOME MAT 2.

late See BETTER LATE THAN NEVER, OF LATE.

lately See JOHNNY-COME-LATELY.

later See SOONER OR LATER.

later on *adv.* Later; not now. ♦ *Finish your lessons. Later on, we may have a surprise.* ♦ *Bill couldn't stand on his head when school started, but later on he learned how.*

lather See IN A LATHER.

laugh See HE LAUGHS BEST WHO LAUGHS LAST, HAVE THE LAST LAUGH.

laugh all the way to the bank *v. phr.* To have made a substantial amount of money either by lucky investment or by some fraudulent deal and rejoice over one's gains. ♦ *If you had done what I suggested, you, too, could be laughing all the way to the bank.*

laughing matter *n.* A funny happening; a silly situation.—Usually used with *no.* ♦ *John's failing the test is no laughing matter!* ♦ *We were amused when our neighbor's cat had five kittens, but when our own cat had six kittens it was no laughing matter.*

laugh in one's beard See LAUGH UP ONE'S SLEEVE.

laugh in one's sleeve See LAUGH UP ONE'S SLEEVE.

laugh off *v.* To dismiss with a laugh as not important or not serious; not take seriously. ♦ *He had a bad fall while ice skating but he laughed it off.* ♦ *You can't laugh off a ticket for speeding.* Compare MAKE LIGHT OF.

laugh one out of *v. phr.* To cause another to forget his/her worries and sorrows by joking. ♦ *Jack was worried about getting airsick, but his son and daughter laughed him out of it.*

laugh one's head off *v. phr., informal* To laugh very hard; be unable to stop laughing. ♦ *Paul's stories are so wildly funny that I laugh my head off whenever he starts telling one of them.*

laugh on the wrong side of one's mouth *or* **laugh on the other side of one's mouth** *or* **laugh out of the other side of one's mouth** *v. phr., informal* To be made sorry; to feel annoyance or disappointment; cry. ♦ *Paul boasted that he was a good skater, but after he fell,* he laughed out of the other side of his mouth.

laugh up one's sleeve *or* **laugh in one's sleeve** *or* **laugh in one's beard** To be amused but not show it; hide your laughter. ♦ *He was laughing up his sleeve when Joe answered the phone because he knew the call would be a joke.*

launch window *n., Space English; informal* **1.** A period of time when the line-up of planets, Sun, and Moon are such as to make favorable conditions for a specific space launch. ♦ *The mission was canceled until the next launch window which will be exactly six weeks from today.* **2.** A favorable time for starting some kind of ambitious adventure. ♦ *My next launch window for a European trip isn't until school is over in June.*

laurel See LOOK TO ONE'S LAURELS, REST ON ONE'S LAURELS.

lavender See LAY OUT 7.

law See LAY DOWN THE LAW, PARLIAMENTARY LAW, TAKE THE LAW INTO ONE'S OWN HANDS.

law-abiding *adj.* Obeying or following the law. ♦ *Michael had been a law-abiding citizen all his life.*

lawful age See LEGAL AGE.

law of averages *n. phr.* The idea that you can't win all the time or lose all the time. ♦ *The Celtics have won 10 games in a row but the law of averages will catch up with them soon.*

law unto oneself *n. phr., literary* A person who does only what he wishes; a person who ignores or breaks the law when he doesn't like it. ♦ *Everybody in Germany feared Hitler because he was a law unto himself.* ♦ *Mr. Brown told Johnny that he must stop trying to be a law unto himself.* Compare TAKE THE LAW INTO ONE'S OWN HANDS.

lay See KILL THE GOOSE THAT LAID THE GOLDEN EGG.

lay about one *v. phr.* To hit out in all directions.—Used with a reflexive object: *her, him,* or *them.* ♦ *The bandits surrounded the sheriff, but he laid about him so hard, with his gun used as a club, that they stepped back and let him escape.* ♦ *Mrs. Franklin didn't kill the mouse, but she laid about her so hard with the broom that she scared it away.*

lay a finger on *v. phr.* To touch or bother, even a little.—Used in negative, interrogative, and conditional sentences. ♦ *Don't you dare lay a finger on the vase!* ♦ *Suppose Billy takes his brother with him; will the mean, tough boy down the street dare lay a finger on him?* ♦ *If you so much as lay a finger on my boy, I'll call the police.* Compare LAY HANDS ON, PUT ONE'S FINGER ON.

lay an egg *v. phr., slang* To fail to win the interest or favor of an audience. ♦ *His joke laid an egg.* ♦ *Sometimes he is a successful speaker, but sometimes he lays an egg.*

lay aside *v. phr.* **1.** To put off until another time; interrupt an activity. ♦ *The president laid aside politics to turn to foreign affairs.* **2.** To save. ♦ *They tried to lay aside a little money each week for their vacation.*

lay at one's door *v. phr., literary* To blame (something) on a person. ♦ *The failure of the plan was laid at his door.* Compare LAY TO 1.

lay away *v.* **1.** To save. ♦ *She laid a little of her pay away each week.* **2.** To bury (a person).—Used to avoid the word *bury*, which some people think is unpleasant. ♦ *He was laid away in his favorite spot on the hill.*

lay-away plan *n.* A plan for buying something that you can't pay cash for; a plan in which you pay some money down and pay a little more when you can, and the store holds the article until you have paid the full price. ♦ *She could not afford to pay for the coat all at once, so she used the lay-away plan.*

lay bare *v. phr.* To expose; reveal; divulge. ♦ *During his testimony the witness laid bare the whole story of his involvement with the accused.*

lay by *v.* To save, especially a little at a time. ♦ *The students laid a little money by every week till they had enough for a trip to Florida.* ♦ *The farmer laid by some of his best corn to use the next year for seed.*

lay down *v.* **1.** To let (something) be taken; give up or surrender (something). ♦ *The general told the troops to lay down their arms.* ♦ *He was willing to lay down his life for his country.* Compare GIVE UP. **2.** To ask people to

follow; tell someone to obey; make (a rule or principle). ♦ *The committee laid down rules about the size of tennis courts.* **3.** To declare; say positively; say surely; state. ♦ *She laid it down as always true that "a fool and his money are soon parted."* **4.** To store or save for future use, especially in a cellar. ♦ *They laid down several barrels of cider.*

lay down one's arms *v. phr.* To cease fighting; surrender. ♦ *The Civil War ended when the Confederate army finally laid down its arms.*

lay down one's cards See LAY ONE'S CARDS ON THE TABLE.

lay down one's life *v. phr.* To sacrifice one's life for a cause or person; suffer martyrdom. ♦ *The early Christians often laid down their lives for their faith.*

lay down the law *v. phr.* **1.** To give strict orders. ♦ *The teacher lays down the law about homework every afternoon.* **2.** To speak severely or seriously about a wrongdoing; scold. ♦ *The principal called in the students and laid down the law to them about skipping classes.* Compare TELL ONE WHERE TO GET OFF.

lay eyes on *or* **set eyes on** *v. phr.* To see. ♦ *She knew he was different as soon as she laid eyes on him.* ♦ *I didn't know the man; in fact, I had never set eyes on him.*

lay for *v., informal* To hide and wait for in order to catch or attack; to lie in wait for. ♦ *The bandits laid for him along the road.* ♦ *I knew he had the marks for the exam, so I was laying for him outside his office.*

lay hands on *v. phr.* **1.** To get hold of; find; catch. ♦ *The treasure hunters can keep any treasure they can lay hands on.* ♦ *If the police can lay hands on him, they will put him in jail.* Compare LAY ONE'S HAND ON 2. **2.** To do violence to; harm; hurt. ♦ *They were afraid that if they left him alone in his disturbed condition he would lay hands on himself.*

lay hold of *v. phr.* **1.** To take hold of; grasp; grab. ♦ *He laid hold of the rope and pulled the boat ashore.* **2.** To get possession of. ♦ *He sold every washing machine he could lay hold of.* **3.** *Chiefly British* To understand. ♦ *Some* *ideas in this science book are hard to lay hold of.*

lay in *v.* To store up a supply of; to get and keep for future use. ♦*Mrs. Mason heard that the price of sugar might go up, so she laid in a hundred pounds of it.* ♦*Before school starts, the principal will lay in plenty of paper for the students' written work.* Compare LAY UP.

lay into *or* **light into** *v., informal* **1.** To attack physically; go at vigorously. ♦*The two fighters laid into each other as soon as the bell rang.* ♦*John loves Italian food and he really laid into the spaghetti.* Syn. PITCH INTO, SAIL INTO. **2.** *slang* To attack with words. ♦*The senator laid into the opponents of his bill.* Syn. LACE INTO, RIP INTO. Compare BAWL OUT, TELL OFF.

lay it on *or* **lay it on thick** *also* **put it on thick** *or* **spread it on thick** *or* **lay it on with a trowel** *v. phr., informal* To persuade someone by using very much flattery; flatter. ♦*Bob wanted to go to the movies. He laid it on thick to his mother.* ♦*Mary was caught fibbing. She sure spread it on thick.* Compare PUT ON 2b.

lay it on the line See LAY ON THE LINE 2.

lay low *v.* **1.** To knock down; to force into a lying position; to put out of action. ♦*Many trees were laid low by the storm.* ♦*Jane was laid low by the flu.* **2.** To kill. ♦*The hunters laid low seven pheasants.* **3.** See LIE LOW.

layoff *n.* A systematic or periodical dismissal of employees from a factory or a firm. ♦*Due to the poor economy, the car manufacturer announced a major layoff starting next month.*

lay off *v. phr.* **1.** To mark out the boundaries or limits. ♦*He laid off a baseball diamond on the vacant lot.* Compare LAY OUT 5. **2.** To put out of work. ♦*The company lost the contract for making the shoes and laid off half its workers.* **3.** *slang* To stop bothering; leave alone.—Usually used in the imperative. ♦*Lay off me, will you? I have to study for a test.* **4.** *slang* To stop using or taking. ♦*His doctor told him to lay off cigarettes.*

lay of the land *also* **how the land lies** *n. phr.* **1.** The natural features of a piece of land, such as hills and valleys. ♦*The style of house the contractor builds*

depends partly on the lay of the land. **2.** The way something is arranged; the important facts about something; how things are. ♦*The banker wanted to check the lay of the land before buying the stock.* ♦*Before the new boy will join our club, he wants to see how the land lies.*

lay on *v.* **1.** To spread on or over a surface; apply. ♦*He told us that we should lay on a second coat of paint for better protection against the weather.* **2.** To beat; to strike. ♦*Little John seized a staff and began to lay on with great energy.* **3.** See LAY IT ON.

lay one's cards on the table *or* **lay down one's cards** *or* **put one's cards on the table** *v. phr., informal* To let someone know your position and interest openly; deal honestly; act without trickery or secrets. ♦*In talking about buying the property, Peterson laid his cards on the table about his plans for it.* ♦*Some of the graduates of the school were unfriendly toward the new superintendent, but he put his cards on the table and won their support.*

lay oneself open to *v. phr.* To make oneself vulnerable to; expose oneself. ♦*If you don't perform your job properly, you will lay yourself open to criticism.*

lay oneself out *v. phr., informal* To make an extra hard effort; try very hard. ♦*Larry wanted to win a medal for his school, so he really laid himself out in the race.*

lay one's finger on See PUT ONE'S FINGER ON.

lay one's hands on *or* **get one's hands on** *v. phr.* **1.** To seize in order to punish or treat roughly. ♦*If I ever lay my hands on that boy he'll be sorry.* Compare LAY A FINGER ON. **2.** To get possession of. ♦*He was unable to lay his hands on a Model T Ford for the school play.* Compare LAY HANDS ON 1. **3.** *or* **lay one's hand on** *or* **put one's hand on** To find; locate. ♦*He keeps a file of letters so he can lay his hands on one whenever he needs it.*

lay on the line *or* **put on the line** *v. phr., informal* **1.** To pay or offer to pay. ♦*The sponsors had to lay nearly a million dollars on the line to keep the show on TV.* ♦*The bank is putting $5,000 on the line as a reward to anyone who*

catches the robber. Compare PUT UP.
2. To say plainly so that there can be no doubt; tell truthfully. ♦ *I'm going to lay it on the line for you, Paul. You must work harder if you want to pass.* **3.** To take a chance of losing; risk. ♦ *The champion is laying his title on the line in the fight tonight.* ♦ *Frank decided to lay his job on the line and tell the boss that he thought he was wrong.*

lay out *v. phr.* **1.** To prepare (a dead body) for burial. ♦ *The corpse was laid out by the undertaker.* **2.** *slang* To knock down flat; to hit unconscious. ♦ *A stiff right to the jaw laid the boxer out in the second round.* **3.** To plan. ♦ *Come here, Fred, I have a job laid out for you.* **4.** To mark or show where work is to be done. ♦ *The foreman laid out the job for the new machinist.* **5.** To plan the building or arrangement of; design. ♦ *The architect laid out the interior of the building.* ♦ *The early colonists laid out towns in the wilderness.* Compare LAY OFF 1. **6.** *slang* To spend; pay. ♦ *How much did you have to lay out for your new car?* **7.** *or* **lay out in lavender** *slang* To scold; lecture. ♦ *He was laid out in lavender for arriving an hour late for the dance.* Compare JUMP ON, LAY INTO 2, LET HAVE IT 1c.

layout *n.* General situation; arrangement; plan. ♦ *The layout of their apartment overlooking Lake Michigan was strikingly unusual.* Compare LAID OUT.

layover *n.* A stopover, usually at an airport or in a hotel due to interrupted air travel. ♦ *There were several layovers at O'Hare last month due to bad weather.*

lay over *v.* **1.** To put off until later; delay; postpone. ♦ *We voted to lay the question over to our next meeting for decision.* **2.** To arrive in one place and wait some time before continuing the journey. ♦ *We had to lay over in St. Louis for two hours waiting for a plane to Seattle.*

lay rubber *or* **lay a patch** *v. phr., slang* To take off in a car or a motorcycle so fast that the tires (made of rubber) leave a mark on the pavement. ♦ *Look at those crazy drag racers; they laid rubber in front of my house.*

lay the blame at one's door *v. phr.* To say that another person or group is

responsible for one's own failure. ♦ *The angry coach laid the blame at the door of the players when our college lost the basketball game.*

lay the fault at one's door See LAY THE BLAME AT ONE'S DOOR.

lay their heads together See PUT THEIR HEADS TOGETHER.

lay to *v.* **1.** To give the blame or credit to; to name as cause. ♦ *He was unpopular and when he made money, it was laid to his dishonesty, but when he lost money, it was laid to his stupidity.* Compare LAY AT ONE'S DOOR. **2.** To hold a ship or boat still against the wind. ♦ *The pirates decided to lay to that night and go ashore in the morning.* Compare LIE TO. **3.** To exert oneself; to work hard. ♦ *He picked up a shovel and laid to with the rest of the gang.*

lay to heart See TAKE TO HEART.

lay to rest *v. phr., informal* **1.** To put a dead person into a grave or tomb; bury. ♦ *President Kennedy was laid to rest in Arlington National Cemetery.* **2.** To get rid of; put away permanently; stop. ♦ *The Scoutmaster's fears that Tom had drowned were laid to rest when Tom came back and said he had gone for a boat ride.* ♦ *The rumor that the principal had accepted another job was laid to rest when he said it wasn't true.*

lay up *v.* **1.** To collect a supply of; save for future use; store. ♦ *Bees lay up honey for the winter.* **2.** To keep in the house or in bed because of sickness or injury; disable. ♦ *Jack was laid up with a twisted knee and couldn't play in the final game.* **3.** To take out of active service; put in a boat dock or a garage. ♦ *Bill had to lay up his boat when school started.* ♦ *If you lay up a car for the winter, you should take out the battery.*

lay waste *v. phr., literary* To cause wide and great damage to; destroy and leave in ruins; wreck. ♦ *Enemy soldiers laid waste the land.*

lead See ALL ROADS LEAD TO ROME, BLIND LEADING THE BLIND.

lead See GET THE LEAD OUT OF ONE'S PANTS.

lead a dog's life *v. phr., informal* To live a hard life, work hard, and be treated unkindly. ♦ *A new college student of long ago led a dog's life.*

lead a merry chase *v. phr.* To delay or escape capture by (someone) skillfully; make (a pursuer) work hard. ♦ *The deer led the hunter a merry chase.* ♦ *Valerie is leading her boyfriend a merry chase.*

lead by the nose *v. phr., informal* To have full control of; make or persuade (someone) to do anything whatever. ♦ *Many people are easily influenced and a smart politician can lead them by the nose.* ♦ *Don't let anyone lead you by the nose; use your own judgment and do the right thing.*

leader See MAJORITY LEADER, MINORITY LEADER.

lead-footed See HEAVY-FOOTED.

leading light *n. phr.* A prominent person in a community, company, or group. ♦ *Alan is the leading light of our discussion group on music.*

lead off *v.* To begin; start; open. ♦ *Richardson led off the inning with a double.* ♦ *We always let Henry lead off.* ♦ *Mr. Jones led off with the jack of diamonds.* ♦ *When the teacher asked if the film helped them to understand, Phil led off by saying that he learned a lot from it.*

lead on *v. phr.* To encourage you to believe something untrue or mistaken. ♦ *Tom led us on to believe that he was a world traveler, but we found out that he had never been outside our state.* ♦ *We were led on to think that Jeanne and Jim were engaged to be married.*

lead one a merry dance *v. phr.* To cause someone unusual discomfort or expense; tire someone by causing one to overdo. ♦ *With her personal extravagances and constant social activities that cost a fortune, Carol led her husband a merry dance.*

lead the way *v. phr.* To go before and show how to go somewhere; guide. ♦ *The boys need someone to lead the way on their hike.* ♦ *The men hired an Indian to lead the way to the Pueblo ruins.* ♦ *That school led the way in finding methods to teach reading.*

lead to *v. phr.* To result in. ♦ *Such a heavy arms race can only lead to war.*

leaf See TURN OVER A NEW LEAF.

leaf through *v. phr.* To scan or glance through a book or other reading matter. ♦ *I only had time to leaf through the program before the concert started.*

league See IN LEAGUE WITH, IVY LEAGUE.

leaguer See TEXAS LEAGUER.

leak out *v. phr.* To become known; escape. ♦ *The famous beauty queen tried to keep her marriage a secret, but news of it soon leaked out.*

leak to *v. phr.* To purposely let a secret be known, as if conveying it in the strictest confidence. ♦ *The movie star's secret divorce was leaked to the tabloids by her housekeeper.*

lean on *v. phr., slang, informal* To pressure (someone) by blackmailing, threats, physical violence, or the withholding of some favor in order to make the person comply with a wish or request. ♦ *I would gladly do what you ask if you only stopped leaning on me so hard!*

lean over backward See BEND OVER BACKWARD.

lean-to *n.* **1.** A shed for tools, such as spades, hoes, etc., attached to the wall of a house. ♦ *Jo looked for the garden hose in the lean-to.* **2.** A small cabin in the country. ♦ *They spend their weekends in their modest lean-to in Wisconsin.*

leap See BY LEAPS AND BOUNDS.

leap year *n.* Every fourth year during which the month of February contains 29 rather than 28 days. ♦ *During a leap year one must wait a day longer for one's February paycheck.*

learn See LIVE AND LEARN.

learn by heart See BY HEART.

learn by rote *v. phr.* To blindly memorize what was taught without thinking about it. ♦ *If you learn a subject by rote, it will be difficult to say anything original about it.*

learn one's way around See KNOW ONE'S WAY AROUND.

learn the hard way See HARD WAY.

learn the ropes See THE ROPES.

least See AT LEAST, IN THE LEAST, LAST BUT NOT LEAST, LINE OF LEAST RESISTANCE.

leatherneck *n., slang, informal* A member of the United States Marine Corps. ♦ *I didn't know your son Joe became a leatherneck.*

leave See SHORE LEAVE, TAKE IT OR LEAVE IT, TAKE LEAVE OF, TAKE ONE'S LEAVE.

leave a bad taste in one's mouth *v. phr.* To feel a bad impression; make you feel disgusted. ♦ *Seeing a man beat his horse leaves a bad taste in your mouth.* ♦ *His rudeness to the teacher left a bad taste in my mouth.*

leave alone See LET ALONE.

leave at the altar *v. phr.* **1.** To decide not to marry someone in the last minute; jilt. ♦ *Ed left poor Susan at the altar.* **2.** To overlook and skip for promotion; not fulfill deserved expectation. ♦ *Once again I didn't get my promotion and was left at the altar.*

leave behind *v. phr.* **1.** Abandon. ♦ *Refugees on the run must sometimes leave old and sick people behind.* **2.** To forget; go away without. ♦ *We had reached our car when we noticed that we had left our keys behind.*

leave flat *v. phr., informal* To quit or leave suddenly without warning when wanted or needed; desert; forsake; abandon. ♦ *Sam found that being a member of the trail-clearing group was a lot of hard work, so he left them flat.* ♦ *My car ran out of gas and left me flat, ten miles from town.* Compare LEAVE IN THE LURCH, WALK OUT 2.

leave hanging *or* **leave hanging in the air** *v. phr.* To leave undecided or unsettled. ♦ *Because the committee could not decide on a time and place, the matter of the spring dance was left hanging.* ♦ *Ted's mother didn't know what to do about the broken window, so his punishment was left hanging in the air until his father came home.* Compare UP IN THE AIR.

leave high and dry See HIGH AND DRY.

leave holding the bag *or* **leave holding the sack** *v. phr., informal* **1.** To cause (someone) not to have something needed; leave without anything. ♦ *In the rush for seats, Joe was left holding the bag.* **2.** To force (someone) to take the whole responsibility or blame for something that others should share. ♦ *When the ball hit the glass, the team scattered and left George holding the bag.* ♦ *After the party, the other girls on the clean-up committee went away with their dates, and left Mary holding the bag.*

leave in the lurch *v. phr.* To desert or leave alone in trouble; refuse to help or support. ♦ *The town bully caught Eddie, and Tom left him in the lurch.* ♦ *Bill quit his job, leaving his boss in the lurch.* Compare LEAVE FLAT, HIGH AND DRY 2, WALK OUT 2.

leave it at that *v. phr.* To avoid further and more acrimonious disagreement; not argue or discuss any further. ♦ *Our opinion on health care is obviously different, so let's just leave it at that.*

leave no stone unturned *v. phr.* To try in every way; miss no chance; do everything possible.—Usually used in the negative. ♦ *The police will leave no stone unturned in their search for the bank robbers.* Compare ALL OUT, BEND HEAVEN AND EARTH, FINE-TOOTH COMB.

leave off *v.* To come or put to an end; stop. ♦ *There is a high fence where the school yard leaves off and the woods begin.* ♦ *Don told the boys to leave off teasing his little brother.* ♦ *Marion put a marker in her book so that she would know where she left off.* Contrast TAKE UP.

leave one's mark *v. phr.* To leave an impression upon; influence someone. ♦ *Tolstoy never won the Nobel Prize, but he left his mark on world literature.* See MAKE ONE'S MARK.

leave open *v. phr.* To remain temporarily unsettled; subject to further discussion. ♦ *Brad said that the question of health insurance would be left open until some future date.*

leave out *v. phr.* To skip; omit. ♦ *The printer accidentally left out two paragraphs from Alan's novel.*

leave out in the cold See OUT IN THE COLD.

leave out of account *v. phr.* To fail to consider; forget about. ♦ *The picnic planners left out of account that it might rain.* Contrast TAKE INTO ACCOUNT.

leave-taking See TAKE ONE'S LEAVE.

leave the matter open See LEAVE OPEN.

leave well enough alone See LET WELL ENOUGH ALONE.

leave without a leg to stand on See LEG TO STAND ON.

leave word with *v. phr.* To leave a message. ♦ *Hank left word with his secretary where he could be reached by* *phone while he was away from his office.*

left See OUT IN LEFT FIELD, RIGHT AND LEFT.

left field *n.* **1.** The part of a baseball outfield to the batter's left. ♦*Right-handed batters usually hit to left field.* Compare CENTER FIELD, RIGHT FIELD. **2.** See OUT IN LEFT FIELD. **left fielder** *n.* The player in baseball who plays in left field. ♦*The scoreboard in the ball park is on the fence behind the left fielder.*

left-handed *adj., informal* **1.** Using the left hand habitually. **2.** Crooked; phoney; homosexual. ♦*Morris is such a left-handed guy.* **3.** Clumsy; untoward; awkward. ♦*Grab that hammer and stop acting so left-handed.*

left-handed compliment An ambiguous compliment which is interpretable as an offense. ♦*I didn't know you could look so pretty! Is that a wig you're wearing?*

left-wing *adj.* That which is or belongs to a group of people in politics that favors radical change in the direction of socialism or communism. ♦*The left-wing faction called for an immediate strike.*

leg See ON ONE'S LAST LEGS, PULL ONE'S LEG, SHAKE A LEG, TAIL BETWEEN ONE'S LEGS.

legal age *or* **lawful age** The age at which a person is allowed to do a certain thing or is held responsible for an action. ♦*In most states the legal age for voting is 21.* ♦*He could not get a driver's license because he was not of lawful age.*

leg man *n., informal* **1.** An errand boy; one who performs messenger services, or the like. ♦*Joe hired a leg man for the office.* **2.** *Slang, semi-vulgar, avoidable* A man who is particularly attracted to good looking female legs and pays less attention to other parts of the female anatomy. ♦*Herb is a leg man.*

leg-pulling See PULL ONE'S LEG.

Legree See SIMON LEGREE.

leg to stand on *n. phr.* A firm foundation of facts; facts to support your claim.—Usually used in the negative. ♦*Jerry's answering speech left his opponent without a leg to stand on.* ♦*Amos sued for damages, but did not*

have a leg to stand on.

leg work *n., informal* The physical end of a project, such as the typing of research reports; the physical investigating of a criminal affair; the carrying of books to and from libraries; etc. ♦*Joe, my research assistant, does a lot of leg work for me.*

leisure See AT LEISURE *or* AT ONE'S LEISURE.

lend a hand *or* **give a hand** *also* **bear a hand** *v. phr.* To give help; make yourself useful; help. ♦*The stage manager asked some of the boys to lend a hand with the scenery.* ♦*Dick saw a woman with a flat tire and offered to give her a hand with it.* Compare LIFT A FINGER.

lend an ear to See GIVE AN EAR TO.

lend color to See GIVE COLOR TO.

lend itself to *v. phr.* To give a chance for or be useful for; to be possible or right for. ♦*Bob was sick and did not go to Jane's party, but his absence lent itself to misunderstanding.* ♦*The teacher's paperweight was a heavy piece of metal which sometimes lent itself to use as a hammer.* ♦*This poem lends itself to our program very well.* Compare LEND ONESELF TO.

lend oneself to *v. phr.* To give help or approval to; encourage; assist. ♦*Alice wouldn't lend herself to the plot to hide the teacher's chalk.*

length See AT LENGTH, GO TO ANY LENGTH, KEEP AT A DISTANCE *or* KEEP AT ARM'S LENGTH.

less See MORE OR LESS, MUCH LESS.

lesson See TEACH A LESSON.

less than *adv.* Not; little. ♦*We were busy and less than delighted to have company that day.* ♦*The boys were less than happy about having a party.* Contrast MORE THAN.

less than no time *n. phr., informal* Very quickly. ♦*We can be ready to go in less than no time.* ♦*It took Sally less than no time to get dinner ready.*

let See LIVE AND LET LIVE.

let alone *conj. phr.* **1.** Even less; certainly not.—Used after a negative clause. ♦*I can't add two and two, let alone do fractions.* ♦*Jim can't drive a car, let alone a truck.* Compare MUCH LESS, NOT TO MENTION. **2. let alone** *or* **leave alone** *v.* To stay away from; keep hands off; avoid. ♦*When Joel gets* mad, just let him alone. ♦ *Little Patsy was warned to leave the birthday cake alone.* Compare LET BE.

let be *v.* To pay no attention to; disregard; forget. ♦ *Let her be; she has a headache.* Compare LET ALONE.

let bygones be bygones *v. phr.* To let the past be forgotten. ♦ *After a long, angry quarrel the two boys agreed to let bygones be bygones and made friends again.* ♦ *We should let bygones be bygones and try to get along with each other.* Syn. FORGIVE AND FORGET. Compare BURY THE HATCHET, LIVE AND LET LIVE.

letdown *n.* A disappointment; a heartbreak. ♦ *It was a major letdown for John when Mary refused to marry him.*

let down *v. phr.* **1.** To allow to descend; lower. ♦ *Harry let the chain saw down on a rope and then climbed down himself.* **2.** To relax; stop trying so hard; take it easy. ♦ *The horse let down near the end of the race and lost.* ♦ *The team let down in the fourth quarter because they were far ahead.* Compare LET GO. **3.** To fail to do as well as (someone) expected; disappoint. ♦ *The team felt they had let the coach down.*

let down easy *v. phr.* To refuse or say no to (someone) in a pleasant manner; to tell bad news about a refusal or disappointment in a kindly way. ♦ *The teacher had to tell George that he had failed his college examinations, but she tried to let him down easy.* ♦ *The boss tried to let Jim down easy when he had to tell him he was too young for the job.*

let down one's hair See LET ONE'S HAIR DOWN.

let drop *v. phr.* **1.** To cease to talk about; set aside; forget. ♦ *This is such an unpleasant subject that I suggest we let it drop for a few days.* **2.** To disclose; hint. ♦ *He unexpectedly let drop that he was resigning and joining another firm.*

let fall See LET DROP.

let George do it *v. phr., informal* To expect someone else to do the work or take the responsibility. ♦ *Many people expect to let George do it when they are on a committee.* Compare PASS THE BUCK.

let go *v.* **1a.** To stop holding something; loosen your hold; release. ♦ *The boy grabbed Jack's coat and would not let go.*—Often used with *of.* ♦ *When the*

child let go of her mother's hand, she fell down. Compare GIVE UP 1a, LET LOOSE. **1b.** To weaken and break under pressure. ♦ *The old water pipe suddenly let go and water poured out of it.* Syn. GIVE WAY. Contrast HOLD ON TO. **2.** To pay no attention to; neglect. ♦ *Robert let his teeth go when he was young and now he has to go to the dentist often.* ♦ *After she was married, Jane let herself go and was not pretty anymore.* **3.** To allow something to pass; do nothing about. ♦ *When Charles was tardy, the teacher scolded him and let it go at that.* ♦ *The children teased Frank, but he smiled and let it go.* Compare LET OFF 2, LET RIDE. **4.** To discharge from a job; fire. ♦ *Mr. Wilson got into a quarrel with his boss and was let go.* **5.** To make (something) go out quickly; shoot; fire. ♦ *The soldiers let go a number of shots.* ♦ *Robin Hood let go an arrow at the deer.* ♦ *Paul was so angry that he let go a blow at the boy.* ♦ *The truck driver saw the flat tire and let go a loud curse.* ♦ *The pitcher let go a fast ball and the batter swung and missed.* Compare CUT LOOSE, LET OUT. **6.** *or* **let oneself go** *informal* To be free in one's actions or talk; relax. ♦ *Judge Brown let go at the reunion of his old class and had a good time.* ♦ *The cowboys worked hard all week, but on Saturday night they went to town and let themselves go.* Syn. CUT LOOSE, LET LOOSE 3, LET OFF STEAM 2.

let go hang See GO HANG.

let go of *v. phr.* To release one's grasp. ♦ *As soon as Sally let go of the leash, her dog ran away.*

let go of one's mother's apron strings See TIED TO ONE'S MOTHER'S APRON STRINGS.

let grass grow under one's feet *v. phr.* To be idle; be lazy; waste time.—Used in negative, conditional, and interrogative sentences. ♦ *The new boy joined the football team, made the honor roll, and found a girlfriend during the first month of school. He certainly did not let any grass grow under his feet.*

let it all hang out *v. phr., slang, informal* Not to disguise anything; to let the truth be known. ♦ *Sue can't deceive anyone; she just lets it all hang out.*

let it lay *v. phr., used imperatively, slang*

Forget it; leave it alone; do not be concerned or involved. ♦ *Don't get involved with Max again—just let it lay.*

let it rip *v. phr., used imperatively, slang* Don't be concerned; pay no attention to what happens. ♦ *Why get involved? Forget about it and let it rip.* **2.** (Imperatively) Do become involved and make the most of it; get in there and really try to win. ♦ *Come on man, give it all you've got and let it rip!*

let know *v. phr.* To inform. ♦ *Please let us know the time of your arrival.*

let loose *v.* **1a.** *or* **set loose** *or* **turn loose** To set free; loosen or give up your hold on. ♦ *The farmer opened the gate and let the bull loose in the pasture.* ♦ *They turned the balloon loose to let it rise in the air.* **1b.** *or* **turn loose** To give freedom (to someone) to do something; to allow (someone) to do what he wants. ♦ *Mother let Jim loose on the apple pie.* ♦ *The children were turned loose in the toy store to pick the toys they wanted.* **1c.** To stop holding something; loosen your hold. ♦ *Jim caught Ruth's arm and would not let loose.* Compare LET GO, LET OUT. **2a.** *informal* To let or make (something) move fast or hard; release. ♦ *The fielder let loose a long throw to home plate after catching the ball.* **2b.** *informal* To release something held. ♦ *Those dark clouds are going to let loose any minute.* Syn. CUT LOOSE, LET GO. **3.** *informal* To speak or act freely; disregard ordinary limits. ♦ *The teacher told Jim that some day she was going to let loose and tell him what she thought of him.* ♦ *Mother let loose on her shopping trip today and bought things for all of us.* Syn. CUT LOOSE, LET GO.

let me see *or* **let us see** *informal* **1.** Let us find out by trying or performing an action. ♦ *Let me see if you can jump over the fence.* **2.** Give me time to think or remember. ♦ *I can't come today. Let me see. How about Friday?* ♦ *Let's see. Where did I put the key?*

let off *v.* **1.** To discharge (a gun); explode; fire. ♦ *Willie accidentally let off his father's shotgun and made a hole in the wall.* Syn. GO OFF, LET LOOSE 2. **2.** To permit to go or escape; excuse from a penalty, a duty, or a promise.

♦ *Two boys were caught smoking in school but the principal let them off with a warning.* ♦ *Mary's mother said that she would let Mary off from drying the supper dishes.* ♦ *The factory closed for a month in the summer and let the workers off.* Compare LET GO. **3.** *or informal* **let off the hook** To miss a chance to defeat or score against, especially in sports or games. ♦ *We almost scored a touchdown in the first play against Tech but we let them off the hook by fumbling the ball.* ♦ *The boxer let his opponent off the hook many times.*

let off steam *or* **blow off steam** *v. phr.* **1.** To let or make steam escape; send out steam. ♦ *The janitor let off some steam because the pressure was too high.* **2.** *informal* To get rid of physical energy or strong feeling through activity; talk or be very active physically after forced quiet. ♦ *After the long ride on the bus, the children let off steam with a race to the lake.* ♦ *When the rain stopped, the boys let off steam with a ball game.* ♦ *Bill's mother was very angry when he was late in coming home, and let off steam by walking around and around.* ♦ *Bill had to take his foreman's rough criticisms all day and he would blow off steam at home by scolding the children.* Compare BLOW ONE'S TOP, LET GO 6.

let off the hook See LET OFF 3.

let on *v. informal* **1.** To tell or admit what you know.—Usually used in the negative. ♦ *Frank lost a quarter but he didn't let on to his mother.* **2.** To try to make people believe; pretend. ♦ *The old man likes to let on that he is rich.*

let one have it *v. phr.* **1a.** *slang* To hit hard. ♦ *He drew back his fist and let the man have it.* ♦ *Give him a kick in the pants; let him have it!* Syn. GIVE IT TO. **1b.** *slang* To use a weapon on; to shoot or knife. ♦ *The guard pulled his gun and let the robber have it in the leg.* Compare OPEN UP. **1c.** *or* **let one have it with both barrels** *slang* To attack with words; scold; criticize. ♦ *Mary kept talking in class until the teacher became angry and let her have it.* Syn. LIGHT INTO 2. **2.** *informal* To tell about it.—Used in the imperative phrase, *let's have it.* ♦ *Now, Mary, let's have it* *from the beginning.* ♦ *We will take turns reading; John, let's have it from page one.*

let one in on *v. phr.* To reveal a secret to; permit someone to share in. ♦ *If I let you in on something big we're planning, will you promise not to mention it to anyone?*

let oneself go See LET GO 6.

let one's hair down *or* **let down one's hair** *v. phr., informal* Act freely and naturally; be informal; relax. ♦ *Kings and queens can seldom let their hair down.* ♦ *After the dance, the college girls let their hair down and compared dates.* Compare LET GO 6.

let one's left hand know what one's right hand is doing *v. phr.* **1.** To make a show of your kindness or help to others.—Used in the negative. ♦ *The Bible tells us not to let the left hand know what the right hand is doing when we give to the poor.* **2.** *informal* To let everyone taking part in something know what each is doing; encourage cooperation in working. ♦ *Tom told Fred and Bill to meet him in town, but he forgot to tell them where. Next time he'll let his left hand know what his right hand is doing.*—Often used in the negative. ♦ *Our team lost today because the coach and captain did not let the left hand know what the right was doing, and the players were all mixed up.*

let out *v.* **1a.** To allow to go out or escape. ♦ *The guard let the prisoners out of jail to work in the garden.* ♦ *Mother won't let us out when it rains.* Compare LET LOOSE. **1b.** *informal* To make (a sound) come out of the mouth; utter. ♦ *A bee stung Charles. He let out a yell and ran home.* ♦ *Father told Betty to sit still and not let out a peep during church.* **2.** To allow to be known; tell. ♦ *I'll never tell you another secret if you let this one out.* Compare LET THE CAT OUT OF THE BAG. **3.** To make larger (as clothing) or looser; allow to slip out (as a rope). ♦ *Mary's mother had to let out her dress because Mary is growing so tall.* ♦ *Father hooked a big fish on his line. He had to let the line out so the fish wouldn't break it.* Compare PIECE OUT. Contrast TAKE IN. **4.** *informal* To allow to move at higher speed. ♦ *The rider let out his horse to try to beat the horse*

ahead of him. **5.** *informal* To free from blame, responsibility, or duty.—Often used with *of.* ♦ *Last time I let you out of it when you were late. I'll have to punish you this time.* ♦ *Frank has shoveled the snow from the sidewalk. That lets me out.* Compare LET GO, LET OFF. **6.** *informal* To discharge from a job; fire. ♦ *The shop closed down and all the men were let out.* **7.** *informal* To dismiss or be dismissed. ♦ *The coach let us out from practice at 3 o'clock.* ♦ *I'll meet you after school lets out.*

let pass *v. phr.* To disregard; overlook. ♦ *Herb may have overheard what was said about him, but he decided to let it pass.*

let ride *v. phr., informal* To allow to go on without change; accept (a situation or action) for the present. ♦ *The committee could not decide what to do about Bob's idea, so they let the matter ride for a month or so.* ♦ *The class was rather noisy but the teacher let it ride because it was near Christmas.* ♦ *Ruth's paper was not very good, but the teacher let it ride because she knew Ruth had tried.* Compare LET GO 3, LET WELL ENOUGH ALONE.

let's don't *also* **don't let's** *substandard* Let's not; let us not; I suggest that we don't. ♦ *"Let's go out and play," said Fred. "Let's don't until the rain stops," said Mary.* ♦ *Don't let's go now. Let's go tomorrow instead.*

let's have it See LET HAVE IT.

let sleeping dogs lie Do not make (someone) angry and cause trouble or danger; do not make trouble if you do not have to.—A proverb. ♦ *Don't tell Father that you broke the window. Let sleeping dogs lie.*

let slip *v. phr.* To unintentionally reveal. ♦ *Ellen let it slip that she had been a witness to the accident.*

letter See CHAIN LETTER, NIGHT LETTER, TO THE LETTER.

letter-perfect *adj. phr.* Memorized perfectly; perfect to the last letter. ♦ *The actor was letter-perfect in his role.*

let the cat out of the bag *v. phr., informal* To tell about something that is supposed to be a secret. ♦ *We wanted to surprise Mary with a birthday gift, but Allen let the cat out of the bag by asking her what she would like.—*

Sometimes used in another form. ♦ *Well, the cat is out of the bag—everybody knows about their marriage.* Compare GIVE AWAY 3, LET OUT 2, SPILL THE BEANS.

let the chips fall where they may *v. phr.* To pay no attention to the displeasure caused others by your actions. ♦ *The senator decided to vote against the bill and let the chips fall where they may.* ♦ *The police chief told his men to give tickets to all speeders and let the chips fall where they may.* Compare COME WHAT MAY.

let the grass grow under one's feet *v. phr., informal* To waste time; be slow or idle. ♦ *Grandpa spends so much time sitting and thinking that Grandma accuses him of letting the grass grow under his feet.*

let up *v., informal* **1.** To become less, weaker, or quiet; become slower or stop. ♦ *It's raining as hard as ever. It's not letting up at all.* ♦ *It snowed for three days before it let up and we could go outdoors.* **2.** To do less or go slower or stop; relax; stop working or working hard. ♦ *Grandfather has been working all his life. When is he going to let up?* ♦ *Let up for a minute. You can't work hard all day.* ♦ *Jim ran all the way home without letting up once.* Compare SLOW DOWN. Contrast BEAR DOWN. **3.** To become easier, kinder, or less strict.— Usually used with *on.* ♦ *Let up on Jane. She is sick.* Syn. EASE UP. **4.** *or* **change up** To pitch a ball at less than full speed in baseball.—Usually used with *on.* ♦ *John pitched a ball that was very fast and the batter missed it. Then he let up on the next pitch and the batter was badly fooled.*

let well enough alone *or* **leave well enough alone** *v. phr.* To be satisfied with what is good enough; not try to improve something because often that might cause more trouble. ♦ *John wanted to make his kite go higher, but his father told him to let well enough alone because it was too windy.* ♦ *Ed polished up his car until his friends warned him to leave well enough alone.* ♦ *Ethel made a lot of changes in her test paper after she finished. She should have let well enough alone, because she made several new mistakes.* Compare

LET RIDE.

level See ON THE LEVEL.

level best *adj. phr.* One's utmost; one's very best. ♦ *Eric refused to stay in school although his parents did their level best to make him finish.*

levelheaded *adj. phr.* Having good common sense; practical; reasonable. ♦ *What our office needs is a good, levelheaded manager.*

level off *or* **level out** *v.* **1.** To make flat or level. ♦ *The steamroller leveled out the gravel roadbed and then the concrete was poured.* **2.** To move on an even level. ♦ *The airplane leveled out at 2,000 feet.* ♦ *After going up for six months, the cost of living leveled off in September.*

level with *v. phr.* To tell someone the truth; not engage in lies and subterfuge. ♦ *"You can level with me," his father said. "Did you break that window?"*

liberty See TAKE LIBERTIES.

lick and a promise *n. phr., informal* A careless, hasty job; an unsatisfactory piece of work. ♦ *You didn't wash your hands. You just gave them a lick and a promise.* ♦ *The boys didn't cut the grass properly. All it got was a lick and a promise.*

lickety-split *also* **lickety-cut** *adv., informal* At full speed; with a rush. ♦ *As soon as school was out the boys ran lickety-split to the swimming pool.*

lick into shape *v. phr.* To make perfect; drill; train. ♦ *The sergeant licked the new volunteer army into shape in three months.*

lick one's boots *v. phr.* To flatter or act like a slave; do anything to please another. ♦ *She wanted her boyfriend to lick her boots all the time.* ♦ *A wise king would not want his friends and officials to lick his boots.*

lick one's chops *v. phr., informal* To think about something pleasant; enjoy the thought of something. ♦ *John is licking his chops about the steak dinner tonight.* ♦ *Tom is licking his chops about the lifeguard job he will have at the beach next summer.* ♦ *Our team is licking its chops because we beat the champions last night.* [From the fact that some animals lick their mouths when they expect to be fed or when they see food, and after eating.] Compare LOOK FORWARD TO, MAKE ONE'S MOUTH WATER.

lick the ——— out of See BEAT THE —— —— OUT OF.

lid See FLIP ONE'S LID, THE LID.

lie See GIVE THE LIE TO, LET SLEEPING DOGS LIE, MAKE ONE'S BED AND LIE IN IT.

lie around *v. phr.* To be unused; inert. ♦ *This old typewriter has been lying around ever since Grandpa died.*

lie down on the job *v. phr., informal* To purposely fail to do your job; neglect a task; loaf. ♦ *Bill isn't trying to learn his lessons. He is lying down on the job.* ♦ *If you lie down on your job, you will lose it.*

lief See AS SOON *also* AS LIEF, HAD AS SOON *also* HAD AS LIEF.

lie in state *v. phr.* Of a dead person: To lie in a place of honor, usually in an open coffin, and be seen by the public before burial. ♦ *When the president died, thousands of people saw his body lying in state.*

lie in wait *v. phr.* To watch from hiding in order to attack or surprise someone; to ambush. ♦ *The driver of the stagecoach knew that the thieves were lying in wait somewhere along the road.*

lie low *or nonstandard* **lay low** *v., informal* **1.** To stay quietly out of sight; try not to attract attention; hide. ♦ *After holding up the bank, the robbers lay low for a while.* **2.** To keep secret one's thoughts or plans. ♦ *I think he wants to be elected president, but he is lying low and not saying anything.*

lie through one's teeth *v. phr.* To lie uninhibitedly and unashamedly. ♦ *Everyone in the courtroom could sense that the accused was lying through his teeth.*

lie to *v.* Of a ship: To stay in one place facing against the wind; stop. ♦ *Our ship will lie to outside the harbor until daylight.* Compare LAY TO 2.

lieu See INSTEAD OF *also* IN LIEU OF.

life See BETWEEN LIFE AND DEATH, BIG AS LIFE, CAT HAS NINE LIVES, CHARMED LIFE, COME ALIVE *or* COME TO LIFE, FACTS OF LIFE, FOR DEAR LIFE, FOR THE LIFE OF ONE, LEAD A DOG'S LIFE, NIGHT LIFE, NOT ON YOUR LIFE OR ONE'S LIFE, TAKE ONE'S LIFE IN ONE'S HANDS, TIME OF ONE'S LIFE, YOU BET *or* YOU BET YOUR LIFE, WALK OF LIFE, WITHIN AN INCH OF ONE'S LIFE.

life of Riley *n. phr., informal* A soft easy life; pleasant or rich way of living. ♦ *He's living the life of Riley. He doesn't have to work anymore.* Compare BED OF ROSES, IN CLOVER, LIVE HIGH OFF THE HOG.

life of the party *n. phr.* A person who makes things enjoyable or interesting for a group of people. ♦ *Bill is the life of the party at school. He is always making us laugh.*

lift a finger *or* **lift a hand** *also* **raise a hand** *v. phr.* **1.** To do something; do your share; to help.—Usually used in the negative. ♦ *We all worked hard except Joe. He wouldn't lift a finger.* ♦ *The king did not lift a hand when his people were hungry.* Compare LEND A HAND.

light See BRING TO LIGHT, COME TO LIGHT, DASH LIGHT, HIDE ONE'S LIGHT UNDER A BUSHEL, IN THE LIGHT OF, MAKE LIGHT OF, MANY HANDS MAKE LIGHT WORK, OUT LIKE A LIGHT, SEE THE LIGHT, TRAVEL LIGHT.

light-fingered *adj.* Given to stealing; having a tendency to be dishonest or a kleptomaniac. ♦ *I always suspected that Freddie might be lightfingered and my suspicions were confirmed when he was arrested for shoplifting.*

light housekeeping *n., slang* An arrangement in which an unmarried couple live together. ♦ *Are Joe and Sue married?—Oh, no,—it's just a case of light housekeeping.* See SHACK UP WITH.

light into See LAY INTO.

lightly See ONCE OVER LIGHTLY *at* ONCE OVER 2.

lightning never strikes twice in the same place The same accident does not happen twice; the same person does not have the same luck again.—A proverb. ♦ *Billy won a pony in the contest last year, but lightning never strikes twice in the same place.*

light on *also* **light upon** *v.* To pick out by sight from among others; see; notice. ♦ *His eyes lighted on the cookies and he remembered how hungry he was.* ♦ *Her eyes lighted upon the row of boxes, and she asked what was in them.*

light out *v., slang* **1.** To run as fast as you

can. ♦ *The boy lit out for home with the bully chasing him.* ♦ *On the next pitch the runner will light out for second.* **2.** To go away in a hurry; leave suddenly.— Often used with *for.* ♦ *Jack won't be in town long. He wants to light out as soon as he has enough money saved.* ♦ *The robbers lit out for Mexico.* Syn. BEAT IT, TAKE OFF 1, HEAD FOR THE HILLS.

light up *v.* Suddenly to look pleased and happy. ♦ *Martha's face lit up when she saw her old friend.* ♦ *Tom will really light up when he sees his new bike!*

like See EAT LIKE A BIRD, FEEL LIKE, LOOK LIKE THE CAT THAT ATE THE CANARY, NOTHING LIKE, THE LIKES OF *or* THE LIKE.

like a bird See EAT LIKE A BIRD.

like a book See READ ONE LIKE A BOOK.

like a fish out of water See FISH OUT OF WATER.

like a glove See FIT LIKE A GLOVE.

like a hole in the head *adv. phr.* Not at all; scarcely; grudgingly; in an unwelcome manner. ♦ *Joan needs her mother-in-law to stay with her for a week like a hole in the head.*

like a horse See EAT LIKE A HORSE.

like a light See OUT LIKE A LIGHT.

like a million See FEEL LIKE A MILLION.

like a million dollars See LOOK LIKE A MILLION DOLLARS.

like anything *adv. phr.* To an extreme degree. ♦ *He swore like anything when he found out that he hadn't been promoted.*

like a steel trap See MIND LIKE A STEEL TRAP.

like clockwork See GO LIKE CLOCKWORK *or* GO OFF LIKE CLOCKWORK.

like crazy See LIKE MAD.

like father, like son A son is usually like his father in the way he acts.—A proverb. ♦ *Frank's father has been on the city council; he is now the mayor, and is running for governor. Frank is on the student council and is likely to be class president. Like father, like son.* ♦ *Mr. Jones and Tommy are both quiet and shy. Like father, like son.* Compare SPITTING IMAGE, FOLLOW IN ONE'S FOOTSTEPS.

like hell *adv., slang, vulgar, avoidable* **1.** With great vigor. ♦ *As soon as they saw the cops, they ran like hell.* **2.** *interj.* Not so; untrue; indicates the speaker's lack of belief in what he heard. ♦ *Like hell you're gonna bring me my dough!*

like it is See TELL IT LIKE IT IS.

like looking for a needle in a haystack See NEEDLE IN A HAYSTACK.

like mad *or* **like crazy** *adv., slang, informal* With great enthusiasm and vigor; very fast. ♦ *We had to drive like mad (like crazy) to get there on time.* See LIKE HELL 1.

like two peas in a pod *adj. phr.* Closely similar; almost exactly alike. ♦ *The twin sisters Eve and Agnes are like two peas in a pod.*

like water *adv. phr.* As something easily poured out or wasted; freely.—Usually used in the phrase *spend money like water.* ♦ *Sailors on shore leave often spend money like water.* ♦ *During the World Wars, the United States spent money like water.*

like water off a duck's back *adv. phr., informal* Without changing your feelings or opinion; without effect. ♦ *Advice and correction roll off him like water off a duck's back.* ♦ *Many people showed him they didn't like what he was doing, but their disapproval passed off him like water off a duck's back.*

lily See GILD THE LILY *also* PAINT THE LILY.

limb See OUT ON A LIMB.

line See BLOW ONE'S LINES *or* FLUFF ONE'S LINES, CHOW LINE, DOWN THE LINE, DRAW A LINE *or* DRAW THE LINE, DROP A LINE, END OF THE ROAD *or* END OF THE LINE, FOUL LINE, GOAL LINE, GOAL LINE STAND, HOLD THE LINE, HOOK, LINE AND SINKER, IN LINE, IN LINE WITH, INTO LINE, LAY ON THE LINE *or* PUT ON THE LINE, ON THE LINE, OUT OF LINE, OUT OF LINE WITH, READ BETWEEN THE LINES, TOE THE LINE, WALK THE CHALK *or* WALK THE CHALK LINE.

line drive *n.* A batted baseball that is usually hit hard and travels in the air not far above the ground. ♦ *The batter hit a line drive to left field for a single.*

linen See AIR ONE'S DIRTY LINEN IN PUBLIC *or* WASH ONE'S DIRTY LINEN IN PUBLIC.

line of fire *n. phr.* The path that something fired or thrown takes. ♦ *When the* bandit and the police began to shoot, John was almost in their line of fire. Compare CROSS FIRE.

line of least resistance *or* **path of least resistance** *n. phr.* The easiest way; the way that takes least effort. ♦ *In becoming a doctor like his father John had really just followed the line of least resistance.* ♦ *Some parents take the path of least resistance with their children and let them do as they please.*

line of scrimmage *n. phr.* An imaginary line on a football field parallel to the goal lines where each play except the kickoff begins. ♦ *The play was stopped at the line of scrimmage.*

line one's pockets *also* **line one's purse** *v. phr., informal* To get a lot of money unfairly; get rich by being dishonest. ♦ *The policeman lined his pockets by taking bribes.* ♦ *The inspector lined his pockets by permitting contractors to use poor building materials.* Compare FEATHER ONE'S NEST.

lineup *n.* **1.** An alignment of objects in a straight line. ♦ *A lineup of Venus and the moon can be a very beautiful sight in the night sky.* **2.** An arrangement of suspects through a one-way mirror so that the victim or the witness of a crime can identify the wanted person. ♦ *She picked out her attacker from a police lineup.*

line up *v. phr.* **1.** To take places in a line or formation; stand side by side or one behind another; form a line or pattern. ♦ *The boys lined up and took turns diving off the springboard.* ♦ *The football team lined up in a "T" formation.* **2.** To put in line. ♦ *John lined up the pool balls.* **3.** To adjust correctly. ♦ *The garage man lined up the car's wheels.* **4a.** *informal* To make ready for action; complete a plan or agreement for; arrange. ♦ *Henry's friends lined up so many votes for him that he won the election.* ♦ *Roger lined up a summer job before school was out.* ♦ *The superintendent lined up all the new teachers he needed before he went on vacation.* **4b.** *informal* To become ready for action; come together in preparation or agreement. ♦ *The football schedule is lining up well; the coach has arranged all games except one.* ♦ *Larry wanted to go to the seashore for the family vacation,* but the rest of the family lined up against him. Compare GANG UP, SHAPE UP, TAKE SIDES.

lining See EVERY CLOUD HAS A SILVER LINING.

link See MISSING LINK.

lion's share *n. phr.* A disproportionate share; the largest part. ♦ *The manager always gets the lion's share of the company's profits.*

lip See BUTTON ONE'S LIP *or* ZIP ONE'S LIP, HANG ON THE WORDS OF *or* HANG ON THE LIPS OF, KEEP A STIFF UPPER LIP, SLIP OF THE TONGUE *also* SLIP OF THE LIP.

lip service *n.* Support shown by words only and not by actions; a show of loyalty that is not proven in action.— Usually used with *pay.* ♦ *By holding elections, communism pays lip service to democracy, but it offers only one candidate per office.* ♦ *Some people pay lip service to education, but don't vote taxes for better schools.*

liquid assets *n. phr.* Those belongings that can be easily converted into cash. ♦ *Herb asked for a loan and the bank manager told him to bring in proof of all his liquid assets.*

liquor up *v. phr., slang* To drink an excessive amount of liquor before engaging in some activity as if comparing oneself to a car that needs to be filled before a journey. ♦ *Joe always liquors up before he takes Sue for a dance.*

list See SUCKER LIST, WAITING LIST.

listen in *v.* **1.** To listen to a radio broadcast. ♦ *We found them listening in to the president's speech.* **2.** To listen to the talk of others, often to talk that is not intended for your ears; eavesdrop. ♦ *When Mary talked to her boyfriend on the telephone, her little brother listened in.*

listen to reason *v. phr.* To listen to and think about advice that you are given. ♦ *Joe was stubborn and would not listen to reason.* ♦ *It will save you a lot of trouble if you will just listen to reason.*

litterbug *n., slang, informal* A person who leaves garbage in a public place, such as a park or beach or a street; one who litters. ♦ *Don't be a litterbug; keep the city clean!*

little See A LITTLE, A LITTLE KNOWL-

EDGE IS A DANGEROUS THING, GREAT OAKS FROM LITTLE ACORNS GROW, LITTLE FROG IN A BIG POND, MAKE LITTLE OF, NOT A LITTLE, QUITE A LITTLE *or* QUITE A LITTLE BIT, THINK LITTLE OF, TWIST AROUND ONE'S LITTLE FINGER.

little does one think *v. phr.* To not realize; not expect; be hardly aware of. ♦ *Little did Ed think that very soon he would be the father of twin daughters.*

little folk *or* **little people** See WEE FOLK.

little frog in a big pond *or* **small frog in a big pond** *n. phr.* An unimportant person in a large group or organization. ♦ *In a large company, even a fairly successful man is likely to feel like a little frog in a big pond.* ♦ *When Bill transferred to a larger high school, he found himself a small frog in a big pond.* Contrast BIG FROG IN A SMALL POND.

little pitchers have big ears Little children often overhear things they are not supposed to hear, or things adults do not expect they would notice.—A proverb. ♦ *Be especially careful not to swear in front of little children. Little pitchers have big ears.*

little theater *n.* A theater, usually with nonprofessional actors and actresses, which presents plays more for personal pleasure and practice than for profit. ♦ *Little theater groups are active in all parts of the United States.* ♦ *Many famous actors began in little theaters.*

lit up like a Christmas tree *adj. phr., informal* To be drunk. ♦ *On New Year's Eve Ned was lit up like a Christmas tree.* Compare THREE SHEETS TO THE WIND.

live See PEOPLE WHO LIVE IN GLASS HOUSES SHOULD NOT THROW STONES.

live and learn You learn more new things the longer you live; you learn by experience.—A proverb. ♦ *"Live and learn," said Mother. "I never knew that the Indians once had a camp where our house is."* ♦ *Janet made her new dress from cheap cloth, and when she washed it, it shrank and was too little. Live and learn.*

live and let live To live in the way you prefer and let others live as they wish without being bothered by you. ♦ *Father scolds Mother because she wears her hair in curlers and Mother scolds Father because he smokes a smelly pipe. Grandfather says it's her hair and his pipe; live and let live.* Compare GIVE AND TAKE 1, LET BYGONES BE BYGONES, FORGIVE AND FORGET.

live down *v.* To remove (blame, distrust or unfriendly laughter) by good conduct; cause (a mistake or fault) to be forgiven or forgotten by not repeating it. ♦ *John's business failure hurt him for a long time, but in the end he lived it down.* ♦ *Frank was rather a bad boy, but he lived it down as he grew up.* ♦ *Sandra called her principal the wrong name at the banquet, in front of everyone, and she thought she would never live it down.*

live from hand to mouth *v. phr.* To live on little money and spend it as fast as it comes in; live without saving for the future; have just enough. ♦ *Mr. Johnson got very little pay, and the family lived from hand to mouth when he had no job.* ♦ *These Indians live from hand to mouth on berries, nuts, and roots.*

live high off the hog *or* **eat high on the hog** See EAT (LIVE) HIGH ON THE HOG *or* EAT (LIVE) HIGH OFF THE HOG.

live in *or* **room in** *v., informal* To live in the school you attend or the place where you work. ♦ *Jack decided to live in during his freshman year at college.* ♦ *Many women advertise for mother's helpers to room in with families and help take care of children.*

live in a fool's paradise *v. phr.* To deceive oneself; tell oneself unreal stories. ♦ *His information is based on a lot of misunderstanding—the poor guy is living in a fool's paradise.*

live in an ivory tower *v. phr.* To be blind to real life; live an unrealistically sheltered existence. ♦ *Professor Nebelmacher has no idea of the cost of living; he lives in an ivory tower.*

live in the fast lane *v. phr., informal* To live a full and very active life pursuing wealth and success. ♦ *They have been living in the fast lane ever since they arrived in New York City.*

live it up *v. phr., informal* To pursue pleasure; enjoy games or night life very much; have fun at places of entertainment. ♦ *Joe had had a hard winter* *in lonesome places; now he was in town living it up.* ♦ *The western cowboys usually went to town on Saturdays to live it up.*

live off someone *v. phr.* To be supported by someone. ♦ *Although Eric is already 40 years old, he has no job and continues to live off his elderly parents.*

live off the fat of the land See FAT OF THE LAND.

live on borrowed time *v. phr.* To live or last longer than was expected. ♦ *Ever since his operation, Harvey felt he was living on borrowed time.* ♦ *Mr. Brown was living on borrowed time because a year ago the doctors had told him he would only live six months.*

live out *v.* **1.** To finish (a period of time); spend. ♦ *Smith lived out the year in the North as he had agreed, but then moved to the South again.* ♦ *After retiring, John and his wife lived out their lives in Florida.* **2.** To last through; endure to the end of. ♦ *We lived out the winter on short ration.* ♦ *He lived out the earthquake, but his house was destroyed.*

live out of a suitcase *v. phr.* To have no permanent residence or a permanent place to hang one's clothes. ♦ *When Jennifer accepted her new job, she had no idea that she would have to live out of a suitcase for six months.*

live up to *v.* To act according to; come up to; agree with; follow. ♦ *So far as he could, John had always tried to live up to the example he saw in Lincoln.* ♦ *Bob was a man who lived up to his promises.* ♦ *The new house didn't live up to expectations.*

live wire *n. phr.* **1.** An electrically charged wire, usually uninsulated. ♦ *The electrician was severely burned by the live wire.* **2.** An alert or energetic person. ♦ *To sell the new merchandise, our company needs several salespeople who are live wires.*

living daylights See BEAT THE ⸺ OUT OF, KNOCK THE ⸺ OUT OF.

living end *adj., slang* Great; fantastic; the ultimate. ♦ *That show we saw last night was the living end.*

load See GET A LOAD OF.

loaded for bear *adj. phr., slang* Ready for action; prepared and eager. ♦ *Frank liked the new merchandise and as he set out on his rounds as a*

salesman, he felt really loaded for bear. ♦ *The football team arrived Friday noon, loaded for bear.*

load the bases *or* **fill the bases** *v. phr.* To get men on all three bases in baseball. ♦ *The Mets loaded the bases with two singles and a base on balls.* ♦ *Don hit a home run with the bases loaded.*

loaf See HALF A LOAF IS BETTER THAN NONE *or* HALF A LOAF IS BETTER THAN NO BREAD.

loan shark *n. phr.* A money lender who charges excessive interest. ♦ *Why go to a loan shark when you can borrow from the bank at the legal rate?*

local yokel *n., slang, citizen's band radio jargon* City police officer, as opposed to state police or highway patrol. ♦ *There's a local yokel westbound on the move.*

lock See SCALP LOCK.

lock, stock, and barrel *n. phr.* Everything; completely. ♦ *The robbers emptied the whole house—lock, stock, and barrel.* Compare HOOK, LINE, AND SINKER.

lock the barn door after the horse is stolen To be careful or try to make something safe when it is too late.—A proverb. ♦ *After Mary failed the examination, she said she would study hard after that. She wanted to lock the barn door after the horse was stolen.*

lock up *v. phr., slang* To be assured of success. ♦ *How did your math test go?—I locked it up, I think.*

lodge a complaint *v. phr.* To make a complaint; complain. ♦ *If our neighbors don't stop this constant noise, I will have to lodge a complaint with the management.*

loggerhead See AT LOGGERHEADS.

loin See GIRD UP ONE'S LOINS.

lone wolf *n.* A man who likes to work or live alone. ♦ *The man who paints a picture or establishes a business is often a lone wolf; so is the criminal outlaw.* ♦ *Jones is a good pitcher, but he is a lone wolf.*

long See AT LAST *or* AT LONG LAST, BEFORE LONG, COME A LONG WAY, IN THE LONG RUN, NO LONGER, SO LONG, THE LONG AND THE SHORT.

long and short of it *n. phr.* The essence; the whole story in a nutshell. ♦ *The long and short of it is that he is lazy and* *doesn't really want to find a job.*

long ball *n.* A baseball hit far enough to be a home run. ♦ *The White Sox need a player who can hit the long ball.*

long face *n.* A sad look; disappointed look. ♦ *He told the story with a long face.*—Often used in the phrase *pull a long face.* ♦ *Don't pull a long face when I tell you to go to bed.*

longhair¹ 1. *n., slang* A male hippie. ♦ *Who's that longhair?—It's Joe.* **2.** An intellectual who prefers classical music to jazz or acid rock. ♦ *Catwallender is a regular longhair; he never listens to modern jazz.*

longhair² *adj., slang* Pertaining to classical art forms, primarily in dancing and music. ♦ *Cut out that longhair Mozart Symphony and put on a decent pop record!*

long haul *or* **long pull** *n., informal* **1.** A long distance or trip. ♦ *It is a long haul to drive across the country.* Contrast SHORT HAUL. **2.** A long length of time during which work continues or something is done; a long time of trying. ♦ *A boy crippled by polio may learn to walk again, but it may be a long haul.*—Often used in the phrase *over the long haul.* ♦ *Over the long haul, an expensive pair of shoes may save you money.* Contrast SHORT HAUL.

long pull See LONG HAUL.

long shot *n.* **1.** A bet or other risk taken though not likely to succeed. ♦ *The horse was a long shot, but it came in and paid well.* ♦ *Jones was a long shot for mayor.* ♦ *The business long shot that succeeds often pays extremely well.* **2.** See BY A LONG SHOT.

long-winded *adj.* Tedious; overlong; given to too much talking. ♦ *Everyone was bored by the old man's long-winded stories.*

look See DIRTY LOOK.

look after *also* **see after** *v.* To watch over; attend to. ♦ *John's mother told him to look after his younger brother.* ♦ *When he went to Europe, Mr. Jenkins left his son to see after the business.* Syn. TAKE CARE OF 1. Compare LOOK OUT 3.

look a gift horse in the mouth To complain if a gift is not perfect.—A proverb. Usually used with a negative. ♦ *John gave Joe a baseball but Joe com-* *plained that the ball was old. His father told him not to look a gift horse in the mouth.*

look alive *v.* Act lively; be quick; wake up and work; be busy; hurry.—Often used as a command. ♦ *"Look alive there," the boss called.*

look as if butter wouldn't melt in one's mouth See BUTTER WOULDN'T MELT IN ONE'S MOUTH.

look as if one has come out of a bandbox *v. phr., informal* To look very clean and fresh; look as if you had just had a bath and put on all-new clothing. ♦ *In spite of the long, hot train ride, Jody arrived looking as if she had come out of a bandbox.* ♦ *After a day at the rodeo we were all dusty and tired except for Hope, who looked as if she'd come out of a bandbox.*

look at *v.* To have a way of thinking or feeling toward; think about something in a certain way. ♦ *Is he a hero or a villain? That depends on how you look at it.* ♦ *Depending on how you looked at it, the tea party could be called a pleasure or a bore.*

look at the world through rose-colored glasses *or* **see with rose-colored glasses** *v. phr.* To see everything as good and pleasant; not see anything hard or bad. ♦ *When Jean graduated from high school, she looked at the world through rose-colored glasses.* ♦ *If you see everything through rose-colored glasses, you will often be disappointed.*

look back *v.* To review the past; think of what has happened. ♦ *As John looked back, his life seemed good to him.* ♦ *Murphy looked back on his early struggles as having made him feel especially alive.* ♦ *When Ed applied for a job and asked the school to recommend him, the principal looked back over his records.*

look bleak *v.* To indicate misfortune; appear threatening or ruinous. ♦ *As prices dropped lower and lower, things looked bleak for Henry's company.* ♦ *Many witnesses gave testimony against Jerry and his case looked bleak.* ♦ *The future looked bleak when Father got hurt and could not work.*

look daggers *v. phr.* To show anger with a look; express hate or enmity by a look or stare; look fiercely. ♦ *The other driver looked daggers at Morris for turning in before him.* ♦ *Mary did not dare talk back to her father, but she looked daggers.*

look down on *also* **look down upon** *v.* To think of (a person or thing) as less good or important; feel that (someone) is not as good as you are, or that (something) is not worth having or doing; consider inferior. ♦ *Mary looked down on her classmates because she was better dressed than they were.* ♦ *Jack looked down on Al for his poor manners.* ♦ *Miss Tracy likes tennis but she looks down on football as too rough.*

look down one's nose at *v. phr., informal* To think of as worthless; feel scorn for. ♦ *The banker's wife has beautiful china cups, and she looked down her nose at the plastic cups that Mrs. Brown used.* ♦ *Harry has never had to work, and he looks down his nose at people in business.* ♦ *Jerry was the athlete who looked down his nose at the weak student.*

look for *v.* **1.** To think likely; expect. ♦ *We look for John to arrive any day now.* ♦ *The frost killed many oranges, and housewives can look for an increase in their price.* ♦ *Bob wouldn't go for a ride with the boys because he was looking for a phone call from Julie.* **2.** To try to find; search for; hunt. ♦ *Fred spent all day looking for a job.* ♦ *Mary and Joe looked for the Smiths at the play.* **3.** To do things that cause (your own trouble); make (trouble) for yourself; provoke. ♦ *Joe often gets into fights because he is always looking for trouble.* ♦ *If you say the opposite of everything that others say, you are looking for a quarrel.*

look for a needle in a haystack See NEEDLE IN A HAY STACK.

look forward to *v.* **1.** To expect. ♦ *At breakfast, John looked forward to a difficult day.* **2.** To expect with hope or pleasure. ♦ *Frank was looking forward to that evening's date.*

look high and low for *v. phr.* To look everywhere; search all over. ♦ *Everyone has been looking high and low for the lost key but no one could find it.*

look-in *n., informal* A chance or hope.—

Usually used with a negative. ♦ *It wasn't much of a look-in, but it was the only chance they let him have.* ♦ *Charlie didn't realize it, but he never had a look-in with Bonnie.*

look in on *v.* To go to see; make a short visit with; make a call on. ♦ *On his way downtown, Jim looked in on his aunt.* ♦ *The doctor looked in on Mary each day when he went by.*

look in the eye *or* **look in the face** *v. phr.* To meet with a steady look; to face bravely or without shame. ♦ *Mary looked the gangster in the eye, and he turned away without hurting her.* ♦ *John had looked death in the face many times.* ♦ *We often believe a person who looks us in the eye, but it does not prove he is truthful.* ♦ *I promised Harry to write to him while I was on vacation, and if I don't do it, I won't be able to look him in the eye.*

look into *v.* To find out the facts about; examine; study; inspect. ♦ *The mayor felt he should look into the decrease of income from parking meters.* ♦ *Mr. Jones said he was looking into the possibility of buying a house.* Compare GO INTO 4, SEE ABOUT.

look like a million dollars *v. phr., informal* To look well and prosperous; appear healthy and happy and lucky; look pretty and attractive. ♦ *John came back from Florida driving a fine new car, tanned and glowing with health. He looked like a million dollars.* ♦ *Dressed in the new formal and in a new hairdo, Betty looked like a million dollars.* Compare FEEL LIKE A MILLION.

look like the cat that ate the canary *or* **look like the cat that swallowed the canary** *v. phr.* To seem very self-satisfied; look as if you had just had a great success. ♦ *Peter bet on the poorest horse in the race and when it won, he looked like the cat that ate the canary.* ♦ *When she won the prize, she went home looking like the cat that swallowed the canary.*

look on *or* **look upon** *v.* **1.** To regard; consider; think of. ♦ *The stuff had always been looked on as a worthless factory waste.* ♦ *Until the day Bob made the touchdown, the other boys had looked upon him as rather a sissy.* **2.** To be an observer; watch without taking part. ♦ *Fred had never been able to do more than look on at athletic sports.* ♦ *The children played in the park while their mother looked on.* Compare SIT IN.

look oneself *v. phr.* To appear self-possessed and well; look or seem in full possession of your abilities and in good health; to appear all right or normal. ♦ *Mary had had a long illness, but now she looked quite herself again.* ♦ *It had been a big night, and Uncle John had been drinking freely, but he looked entirely himself after a night's sleep.*— Often used in the negative. ♦ *What's wrong with Larry? He doesn't look himself.*

lookout See ON THE LOOKOUT.

look out *or* **watch out** *v.* **1.** To take care; be careful; be on guard.—Usually used as a command or warning. ♦ *"Look out!" John called, as the car came toward me.* ♦ *"Look out for the train,"* the sign at the railroad crossing warns. **2.** To be alert or watchful; keep watching. ♦ *A collector of antique cars asked Frank to look out for a 1906 gas head lamp.* Compare EYE OUT, ON THE WATCH. **3.** *informal* To watch or keep (a person or thing) and do what is needed; provide protection and care. —Used with *for.* ♦ *Lillian looked out for her sister's children one afternoon a week.* ♦ *Uncle Fred looked out for his brother's orphan son until the boy was through college.* Compare LOOK AFTER.

look out for *v. phr.* To watch out for; be on the alert. ♦ *There were signs along the highway warning drivers to look out for deer crossing.*

look over *v.* To look at and try to learn something about; look at every part or piece of or at every one of; examine; inspect; study. ♦ *I looked hurriedly over the apples in the basket and took one that looked good.* ♦ *Mrs. Jones spent the evening looking over the month's bills and writing checks.* ♦ *When a new boy comes to school, the others usually look him over rather carefully.* ♦ *We looked over several kinds of new cars before deciding.* Compare ONCE-OVER, SIZE UP.

look sharp *v.* To be alert; be very attentive; keep a close watch. ♦ *It pays to*

look sharp in traffic. ♦ *The guide told us to look sharp because there were rattlesnakes around.*

look small See FEEL SMALL.

look to *v.* **1.** To attend to; get ready for; take care of. ♦ *Plans had been prepared that looked to every possibility.* ♦ *The president assigned a man to look to our needs.* **2.** To go for help to; depend on. ♦ *The child looks to his mother to cure his hurts.* **3.** See SEE TO.

look to one's laurels To make sure that your reputation is not spoiled; protect your good name; keep your record from being beaten by others. ♦ *Tom won the broad jump, but he had to look to his laurels.* ♦ *Look to your laurels, Joan. Betty says she is going to run against you for head cheerleader.*

look up *v.* **1.** *informal* To improve in future chances; promise more success. ♦ *The first year was tough, but business looked up after that.* **2.** To search for; hunt for information about; find. ♦ *It is a good habit to look up new words in a dictionary.* **3.** To seek and find. ♦ *While he was in Chicago, Henry looked up a friend of college days.*

look upon See LOOK ON 1.

look up to *v.* To think of (someone) as a good example to copy; honor; respect. ♦ *Mr. Smith had taught for many years, and all the students looked up to him.* ♦ *Young children look up to older ones, so older children should be good examples.*

loop See KNOCK FOR A LOOP *or* THROW FOR A LOOP.

loose See AT LOOSE ENDS, CAST OFF *or* CAST LOOSE, CUT LOOSE, FAST AND LOOSE, HAVE A SCREW LOOSE, LET LOOSE *or* SET LOOSE *or* TURN LOOSE, ON THE LOOSE.

loose ends *n.* **1.** Parts or things that should be finished or put together. ♦ *Mary's composition had many loose ends.* ♦ *When George came home after a long trip, he started picking up the loose ends.* **2.** See AT LOOSE ENDS.

lord it over *v. phr.* To act as the superior and master of; dominate; be bossy over; control. ♦ *John learned early to lord it over other children.* ♦ *The office manager lorded it over the clerks and typists.*

Lord knows See GOD KNOWS.

lose See HEADS I WIN, TAILS YOU LOSE.

lose face *v.* To be embarrassed or shamed by an error or failure; lose dignity, influence or reputation; lose self-respect or the confidence of others. ♦ *Many Japanese soldiers were killed in World War II because they believed that to give up or retreat would make them lose face.* ♦ *John's careless work made him lose face with his employer.* ♦ *The banker lost face when people found out he bet on horse races.*

lose ground **1.** To go backward; retreat. ♦ *The soldiers began to lose ground when their leader was killed.* Compare GIVE GROUND. **2.** To become weaker; get worse; not improve. ♦ *The sick man began to lose ground when his cough grew worse.* ♦ *When the Democrats are in power, the Republicans lose ground.* Contrast GAIN GROUND.

lose heart *v. phr.* To feel discouraged because of failure; to lose hope of success. ♦ *The team had won no games and it lost heart.* Contrast TAKE HEART.

lose one's balance Contrast KEEP ONE'S BALANCE.

lose oneself *v. phr.* **1.** To go wrong; miss your way; become unable to find the right direction. ♦ *Fred lost himself in the confusion of downtown Boston streets.* **2.** To conceal yourself; hide. ♦ *The pickpocket lost himself in the crowd and escaped the police.* **3.** To become deeply interested and forget yourself; become absorbed. ♦ *Sometimes Harry would lose himself in a book for an afternoon at a time.* Compare IN A WORLD OF ONE'S OWN.

lose one's grip *v. phr.* To fail in control or command; lose your strength, force, or ability to lead. ♦ *Mr. Jones began to lose his grip: he no longer wanted the hard jobs, and he left decisions to others.* ♦ *When a locomotive engineer loses his grip, he is no longer trusted with express runs.*

lose one's head (over) *v. phr.* **1.** To panic. ♦ *"Let's not lose our heads," the captain cried. "We have good lifeboats on this vessel."* **2.** To become deeply infatuated with someone. ♦ *Don't lose your head over Jane; she is already married.* Contrast KEEP ONE'S HEAD.

lose one's heart *v. phr.* To fall in love; begin to love. ♦ *She lost her heart to the soldier with the broad shoulders and the deep voice.* ♦ *Bill lost his heart to the puppy the first time he saw it.*

lose one's marbles *v. phr.* To go mad; become crazed. ♦ *Stan must have lost his marbles; he is hopelessly pursuing a happily married woman.*

lose one's shirt *v. phr., slang* To lose all or most of your money. ♦ *Uncle Joe spent his life savings to buy a store, but it failed, and he lost his shirt.* ♦ *Mr. Matthews lost his shirt betting on the horses.*

lose one's temper *v. phr.* To lose control over one's anger; to get angry. ♦ *He lost his temper when he broke the key in the lock.* Compare BLOW A FUSE, FLY OFF THE HANDLE. Contrast HOLD ONE'S TEMPER.

lose one's tongue *v. phr., informal* To be so embarrassed or surprised that you cannot talk. ♦ *The man would always lose his tongue when he was introduced to new people.* Compare CAT GET ONE'S TONGUE.

lose out *v.* To fail to win; miss first place in a contest; lose to a rival. ♦ *John lost out in the rivalry for Mary's hand in marriage.* ♦ *Fred didn't want to lose out to the other salesman.* Compare MISS OUT. Contrast WIN OUT.

loser See FINDERS KEEPERS *or* FINDERS KEEPERS LOSERS WEEPERS.

lose sight of *v. phr.* **1.** Not to be able to see any longer. ♦ *I lost sight of Mary in the crowd.* ♦ *I watched the plane go higher and higher until I lost sight of it.* Contrast CATCH SIGHT OF. **2.** To forget; overlook. ♦ *Johnny was so interested in the game he lost sight of the time.* ♦ *No matter how rich and famous he became, he never lost sight of the fact that he had been born in the slums.*

lose touch *v. phr., informal* To fail to keep in contact or communication.—Usually used with *with.* ♦ *After she moved to another town, she lost touch with her childhood friends.* Compare OUT OF TOUCH.

lose track *v. phr.* To forget about something; not stay informed; fail to keep a count or record. ♦ *What's the score now? I've lost track.*—Usually used with *of.* ♦ *Mary lost track of her friends at camp after summer was over.* ♦ *John lost track of the money he spent at the circus.* Compare OUT OF TOUCH.

Contrast KEEP TRACK.

loss See AT A LOSS, THROW FOR A LOSS.

lost See GET LOST, NO LOVE LOST.

lost cause *n. phr.* A movement that has failed and has no chance to be revived. ♦ *Communism in Eastern Europe has become a lost cause.*

lost upon *adj.* Wasted. ♦ *Tim's generosity is completely lost upon Sue; he can't expect any gratitude from her.*

lot See A LOT, CAST ONE'S LOT WITH, SAND LOT, THINK A GREAT DEAL OF *or* THINK A LOT OF, THROW IN ONE'S LOT WITH *or* CAST IN ONE'S LOT WITH.

loud See ACTIONS SPEAK LOUDER THAN WORDS, FOR CRYING OUT LOUD, OUT LOUD, THINK ALOUD *or* THINK OUT LOUD.

loud mouth *or* **big mouth** *n., slang* A noisy, boastful, or foolish talker. ♦ *Fritz is a loud mouth who cannot be trusted with secrets.* ♦ *When he has had a few drinks, Joe will make empty boasts like any other big mouth.*

loud-mouthed *or* **big-mouthed** *adj., slang* Talking noisily, boastfully, or foolishly. ♦ *Fred was a loud-mouthed fellow, whose talk no one listened to.* ♦ *If I were you, I would not listen to that loud-mouthed boy.*

lounge lizard *n. phr.* A well-dressed male fortune hunter who sits around in bars and other public places, and attends many social events to try to pick up wealthy women through smart conversation. ♦ *Harry has the reputation of being a lounge lizard; he is looking for a rich wife.*

louse up *v., slang* To throw into confusion; make a mess of; spoil; ruin. ♦ *When the man who was considering John's house heard that the basement was wet, that was enough to louse up the sale.* ♦ *Fred's failure in business not only lost him his business but loused him up with his wife.* ♦ *The rain loused up the picnic.* See MESS UP 2, FUCK UP.

love See FOR LOVE OR MONEY, IN LOVE, LABOR OF LOVE, MAKE LOVE, NO LOVE LOST, PUPPY LOVE *also* CALF LOVE.

love affair *n.* A friendship between lovers; a romance or courtship. ♦ *The love affair of Bob and Jane went on for months.* ♦ *Harry had many love affairs, but he never married.*

love game *n.* A game of tennis which is won without the opponent scoring. ♦ *Britain took a love game on Sangster's service.*

love-in *n., slang, informal* A festival or occasion to celebrate life, human sensuality, the beauty of nature, human sexuality, and universal love; affairs so conceived by some frequently deteriorate into obscenity and drug using sessions in parody of their stated purpose. ♦ *The hippies gathered for a big love-in in the Haight-Ashbury district of San Francisco.*

lovers' lane *n.* A hidden road or walk where lovers walk or park in the evening. ♦ *A parked car in a lonely lovers' lane often is a chance for holdup men.*

low See LAY LOW, LIE LOW.

lowbrow *n.* A person of limited culture; a nonintellectual. ♦ *Some people claim that only lowbrows read the comics.* Contrast HIGH BROW.

lowdown *n., slang, informal* The inside facts of a matter; the total truth. ♦ *Nixon never gave the American people the lowdown on Watergate.*

lower the boom *v. phr., informal* To punish strictly; check or stop fully. ♦ *The mayor lowered the boom on outside jobs for city firemen.* ♦ *Father lowered the boom on the girls for staying out after midnight.* Syn. CRACK DOWN. ♦ *The police lowered the boom on open gambling.*

low-key *adj.* Relaxed and easygoing. ♦ *Surprisingly, dinner with the governor was a low-key affair.*

low season Contrast HIGH SEASON.

luck See DOWN ON ONE'S LUCK, LUCK OUT, PRESS ONE'S LUCK *or* PUSH ONE'S LUCK, IN LUCK, OUT OF LUCK.

luck out *v. phr., slang, informal* **1.** Suddenly to get lucky when in fact the odds are against one's succeeding. ♦ *I was sure I was going to miss the train as I was three minutes late, but I lucked out; the train was five minutes late.* **2.** To be extraordinarily fortunate. ♦ *Catwallender really lucked out at Las Vegas last month; he came home with $10,000 in cash.* **3.** (By sarcastic opposition) to be extremely unfortunate; to be killed. ♦ *Those poor marines sure lucked out in Saigon, didn't they?*

lucky See THANK ONE'S LUCKY STARS.

lucky star *n.* A certain star or planet which, by itself or with others, is seriously or jokingly thought to bring a person good luck and success in life. ♦*John was born under a lucky star.* ♦*Ted was unhurt in the car accident, for which he thanked his lucky stars.*

lump in one's throat *n. phr.* A feeling (as of grief or pride) so strong that you almost sob. ♦*John's mother had a lump in her throat at his college graduation.* ♦*All during her husband's funeral, Aunt May had a lump in her throat.* ♦*The bride's mother had a lump in her throat.*

lump sum *n.* The complete amount; a total agreed upon and to be paid at one time. ♦*The case was settled out of court with the plaintiff receiving a lump sum of half a million dollars for damages.*

lunar module (L.M.) *or* **Lem** *n., Space English* That portion of the rocket assemblage on a flight to the Moon in which the astronauts descend to the Moon's surface. ♦*Building the L.M. was one of the most expensive parts of the American space program.*

lung See AT THE TOP OF ONE'S VOICE *or* AT THE TOP OF ONE'S LUNGS.

lurch See LEAVE IN THE LURCH.

lust for *v. phr.* To physically yearn for; hanker after; want something very strongly. ♦*Ed has been lusting after Meg for a very long time.*

luxury See IN THE LAP OF LUXURY.

mackerel See HOLY CATS or HOLY MACK-EREL.

mad about *adj. phr.* **1.** Angry about. ◆*What is Harriet so mad about?* **2.** Enthusiastic about. ◆*Dan is mad about pop music.*

mad as a hatter or **mad as a March hare** *adj. phr.* Not able to think right; crazy. ◆*Anyone who thinks the moon is made of green cheese is mad as a hatter.*

mad as a hornet or **mad as hops** or **mad as a wet hen** *adj. phr., informal* In a fighting mood; very angry. ◆*When my father sees the dent in his fender, he'll be mad as a hornet.* ◆*Bill was mad as hops when the fellows went on without him.* ◆*Mrs. Harris was mad as a wet hen when the rabbits ate her tulips.*

mad as a March hare See MAD AS A HATTER.

mad as hops See MAD AS A HORNET.

made of money *adj. phr.* Very rich; wealthy. ◆*Mr. Jones buys his children everything they want. He must be made of money.* Compare MONEY TO BURN.

made-to-measure or **tailor-made** *adj.* Made to fit a special set of measurements or needs. ◆*John has a new made-to-measure suit.* ◆*The club is tailor-made for Jane.* Syn. MADE TO ORDER.

made to order *adj. phr.* **1.** Made specially in the way the buyer wants instead of all the same in large amounts; made especially for the buyer. ◆*Mr. Black's clothes were all made to order.* Compare MADE-TO-MEASURE. **2.** Just right. ◆*The weather was made to order for the hike.*

made up out of whole cloth See OUT OF WHOLE CLOTH.

magic carpet *n.* **1.** A rug said to be able to transport a person through the air to any place he wishes. ◆*The caliph of Baghdad flew on his magic carpet to Arabia.* **2.** Any form of transportation that is comfortable and easy enough to seem magical. ◆*Flying the Concord from Dallas to London seemed like boarding the magic carpet.* ◆*Mr. Smith's new car drove so smoothly it seemed like a magic carpet.*

maiden speech *n. phr.* One's first public speech, usually before some legislative body. ◆*It was the new congressman's maiden speech and everyone was listening very keenly.*

maiden voyage *n. phr.* The first voyage of a boat. ◆*The* Titanic *sank on her maiden voyage to America from England.*

mail order *n. phr.* A purchase made by mail. ◆*If you don't have a chance to go to a store, you can sometimes make a purchase by mail order.*

main See IN THE MAIN, WITH MIGHT AND MAIN.

main drag *n., colloquial* **1.** The most important street or thoroughfare in a town. ◆*Lincoln Avenue is the main drag of our town.* **2.** The street where the dope pushers and the prostitutes are. ◆*Wells Street is the main drag of Chicago, actionwise.*

main squeeze *n., slang* **1.** The top ranking person in an organization or in a neighborhood; an important person, such as one's boss. ◆*Mr. Bronchard is the main squeeze in this office.* **2.** The top person in charge of an illegal operation, such as drug sales, etc. ◆*Before we can clean up this part of town, we must arrest the main squeeze.* **3.** One's principal romantic or sexual partner. ◆*The singer's main squeeze is a member of the band.*

majority leader *n.* The leader of the political party with the most votes in a legislative house. ◆*The majority leader of the House of Representatives tried to get the members of his party to support the bill.* Compare MINORITY LEADER.

make See ALL WORK AND NO PLAY MAKES JACK A DULL BOY, HAVE IT MADE, MANY HANDS MAKE LIGHT WORK, ON THE MAKE.

make a beeline for *v. phr.* To go in a straight line toward. ◆*The runner made a beeline for first base.* ◆*When the bell rang Ted made a beeline for the door of the classroom.*

make a big deal about *v. phr., informal* To exaggerate an insignificant event. ◆*Jeff said, "I'm sorry I banged into you in the dark. Don't make a big deal out of it."*

make a clean breast of *v. phr.* To admit (your guilt); tell all about (your wrong doing); confess everything. ♦ *The police caught the hit-and-run driver and he made a clean breast of his crime.* ♦ *Arthur worried because he cheated on the test, and finally he went to the teacher and made a clean breast of it.* Compare OFF ONE'S CHEST.

make a clean sweep of *v. phr.* **1.** Achieve a complete victory. ♦ *In 1980 the Reagan Republicans made a clean sweep of the western states.* **2.** To eliminate thoroughly and completely. ♦ *The new attorney general is expected to make a clean sweep of all the old administrative personnel.*

make a clown of See MAKE A FOOL OF.

make a day of it *v. phr., informal* To do something all day. ♦ *When they go to the beach they take a picnic lunch and make a day of it.* Compare MAKE A NIGHT OF.

make a dent in *v. phr., informal* To make less by a very small amount; reduce slightly.—Usually used in the negative or with such qualifying words as *hardly* or *barely.* ♦ *John shoveled and shoveled, but he didn't seem to make a dent in the pile of sand.* ♦ *Mary studied all afternoon and only made a dent in her homework.*

make a difference *or* **make the difference** *v. phr.* To change the nature of something or a situation; be important; matter. ♦ *John's good score on the test made the difference between his passing or failing the course.* ♦ *It doesn't make a bit of difference if you are late to my party. I just want you to come.*

make a face *v. phr., informal* To twist your face; make an ugly expression on your face (as by sticking out your tongue). ♦ *The boy made a face at his teacher when she turned her back.* ♦ *The sick boy swallowed the medicine and made a face.*

make a fast buck See FAST BUCK.

make a federal case out of See MAKE A BIG DEAL ABOUT, MAKE A MOUNTAIN OUT OF A MOLEHILL.

make a fool of *or* (informal) **make a monkey of** *v. phr.* To make (someone) look foolish. ♦ *The boy made a fool of himself.* ♦ *Mary's classmates made a fool of her by telling her the party was to be a masquerade.*

make after *v. phr.* To chase something; run after something. ♦ *The mouse escaped from the kitchen corner and the cat made after it.*

make a fuss over *v. phr.* **1.** To quarrel about something or someone. ♦ *I want you kids to stop fussing about who gets the drumstick.* **2.** To be excessively concerned about someone or something; worry. ♦ *Let's not fuss over such an insignificant problem!* **3.** To show exaggerated care or preoccupation about a person or an animal. ♦ *Aunt Hermione is constantly fussing over her old lapdog.*

make a go of *v. phr.* To turn into a success. ♦ *He is both energetic and highly skilled at trading; he is sure to make a go of any business that holds his interest.*

make a hit *v. phr., informal* To be successful; be well-liked; get along well. ♦ *Mary's new red dress made a hit at the party.* ♦ *Alice was so happy that her boyfriend made a hit with her parents.* Compare GO OVER 6.

make a killing *v. phr.* To earn or suddenly win a very large sum of money. ♦ *Herb bought a lot of soybean stock when the price was low and sold it when the price went up. Small wonder he made a huge killing.*

make a living *v. phr.* To earn one's livelihood. ♦ *If you're good at your job, you can make a better living than if you don't know what you're doing.* ♦ *It is easier to make a living in the United States than in many other countries.*

make allowance *v. phr.* To judge results by the circumstances.—Often used in plural. ♦ *When a small boy is helping you, you must make allowances for his age.*

make a long story short *v. phr.* To summarize a lengthy narrative. ♦ *"So, to make a long story short," he said, "I made a killing on the stock market."* Compare IN A NUTSHELL.

make a match *v. phr.* To bring a man and woman together for the purpose of an engagement or marriage. ♦ *Sheila's aunt is anxious to make a match between her and an attractive, wealthy man.*

make a mess of See SCREW UP.

make a monkey of See MAKE A FOOL OF.

make a motion *v. phr.* To propose in some committee meeting or legislative group that a certain action be taken. ♦ *The secretary made a motion that the minutes of the last meeting be accepted.*

make a mountain out of a molehill To think a small problem is a big one; try to make something unimportant seem important. ♦ *You're not hurt badly, Johnny. Stop trying to make a mountain out of a molehill with crying.* ♦ *Sarah laughed at a mistake Betty made in class, and Betty won't speak to her; Betty is making a mountain out of a molehill.*

make a move *v. phr.* **1.** To budge; change places. ♦ *"If you make a move," the masked gangster said, "I'll start shooting."* **2.** To go home after dinner or a party. ♦ *"I guess it's time to make a move," Roy said at the end of the party.*

make a name for oneself *v. phr.* To become recognized in a field of endeavor; become a celebrity. ♦ *Joe has worked so hard at soybean trading that he made quite a name for himself as a trader.* ♦ *Bill has made a name for himself both as a pianist and as a composer.*

make an appearance See PUT IN AN APPEARANCE.

make an end of *v. phr.* To make (something) end; put a stop to; stop. ♦ *To make an end of rumors that the house was haunted, a reporter spent the night there.*

make an example of *v. phr.* To punish (someone) publicly to show what happens when someone does wrong. ♦ *The teacher made an example of the boy who copied from another student during a test.* ♦ *The Pilgrims made an example of a thief by putting him in the stocks.*

make an exhibition of oneself *v. phr.* To behave foolishly or embarrassingly in public. ♦ *Stop drinking so much and making an exhibition of yourself.*

make a night of it *v. phr., informal* To spend the whole night at an activity. ♦ *The dog found the door unlatched and made a night of it.* ♦ *The boys and girls at the dance made a night of it.* Compare MAKE A DAY OF IT.

make a nuisance of oneself *v. phr.* To constantly bother others. ♦ *The screaming kids made a nuisance of themselves around the swimming pool.*

make a pass at *v. phr., slang, informal* Make advances toward a member of the opposite sex (usually man to a woman) with the goal of seducing the person. ♦ *We've been dating for four weeks but Joe has never even made a pass at me.*

make a pig of oneself *v. phr., informal* To overindulge; eat too much. ♦ *Mary said, "This dessert is so delicious that I am going to make a pig of myself and have some more."*

make a play for *v. phr., slang* To try to get the interest or liking of; flirt with; attract. ♦ *Bob made a play for the pretty new girl.* ♦ *John made a play for the other boys' votes for class president.*

make a point *v. phr.* To try hard; make a special effort.—Used with *of* and a verbal noun. ♦ *He made a point of remembering to get his glasses fixed.* ♦ *He made a point of thanking his hostess before he left the party.*

make a practice of *v. phr.* To make a habit of; do regularly. ♦ *Make a practice of being on time for work.*

make a quick buck See FAST BUCK.

make a racket *v. phr.* To cause a lot of noisy disturbance. ♦ *I wish the kids playing in the street wouldn't make such a racket while I'm trying to take a nap.*

make a scene *v. phr.* To act hysterically; attract unfavorable attention. ♦ *I didn't want Kate to make a scene in front of all of those people, so I gave her the money she wanted.*

make a splash *v. phr.* To cause a sensation. ♦ *The brilliant young pianist, barely 14 years old, made quite a splash on the concert circuit.*

make a stab at *v. phr.* To try doing something at random without sufficient preparation. ♦ *The singer was not familiar with the aria but she decided to make a stab at it anyhow.* Contrast STAB IN THE BACK, STAB IN THE DARK.

make a stand *v. phr.* **1.** To take a firm position on an issue. ♦ *He keeps talking about politics but he never makes a stand for what he believes in.* **2.** To take up a defensive position against the enemy. ♦ *The retreating troops decided to make a stand by the river.* Contrast LAST DITCH, LAST STAND.

make a stir See MAKE A SCENE.

make a touch *v. phr.* To borrow money; try to borrow money. ◆ *He is known to make a touch whenever he is hard up for cash.*

make a virtue of necessity *v. phr.* Make the best of things as they are; do cheerfully what you do. ◆ *After Mr. Wilson lost all his money, he made a virtue of necessity and found a new and interesting life as a teacher.* Compare MAKE THE BEST OF.

make away with *v., informal* Take; carry away; cause to disappear. ◆ *The lumberjack made away with a great stack of pancakes.* ◆ *Two masked men held up the clerk and made away with the payroll.* Compare MAKE OFF.

make-believe *n.* False; untrue; created by illusion. ◆ *The creatures of* Star Wars *are all make-believe.*

make believe *v.* To act as if something is true while one knows it is not; pretend. ◆ *Let's make believe we have a million dollars.* ◆ *Danny made believe he didn't hear his mother calling.*

make book *v. phr.* To serve as a bookmaker taking bets on the horse races. ◆ *The police were out to prosecute anybody who made book illegally.*

make both ends meet See MAKE ENDS MEET.

make bricks without straw *v. phr.* To make something without the wherewithal; do something the hard way; do a job under hard conditions. ◆ *John could not go to a library, and writing the report was a job of making bricks without straw.* ◆ *It was making bricks without straw to put on plays in that old barn.*

make conversation *v. phr.* To talk with someone just so that there will be talk. ◆ *John made conversation with the stranger so that he would not feel left out.* ◆ *Mary didn't really mean what she said about Joan. She was only making conversation.*

make do *v. phr.* To use a poor substitute when one does not have the right thing. ◆ *John did not have a hammer, and he had to make do with a heavy rock.* ◆ *This motel isn't what we wanted, but we must make do.* ◆ *Many families manage to make do on very little income.* Compare GET ALONG.

make ends meet *v. phr.* To have enough money to pay one's bills; earn what it costs to live. ◆ *Both husband and wife had to work to make ends meet.*

make eyes at *v. phr., informal* To look at a girl or boy in a way that tries to attract him to you; flirt. ◆ *The other girls disliked her way of making eyes at their boyfriends instead of finding one of her own.*

make faces at *v. phr.* To grimace; scowl. ◆ *"Stop making faces at each other, you children," my aunt said, "and start eating."*

make for *v.* To go toward; start in the direction of. ◆ *The children took their ice skates and made for the frozen pond.* ◆ *The bee got his load of pollen and made for the hive.*

make free with *v.* **1.** To take or use (things) without asking. ◆ *Bob makes free with his roommate's clothes.* ◆ *A student should not make free with his teacher's first name.* **2.** To act toward (someone) in a rude or impolite way. ◆ *The girls don't like Ted because he makes free with them.* Compare TAKE LIBERTIES.

make friends *v. phr.* To become friends; form a friendship. ◆ *Mrs. Jones invited Bobby to her home to play with Don. She hoped that they would make friends with each other.* ◆ *You can make friends with an elephant by giving him peanuts.*

make fun of *or* **poke fun at** *v. phr., informal* To joke about; laugh at; tease; mock. ◆ *Men like to make fun of the trimmings on women's hats.* ◆ *James poked fun at the new pupil because her speech was not like the other pupils.*

make good *v. phr.* **1.** To do what one promised to do; make something come true. ◆ *Mr. Smith borrowed some money. He promised to pay it back on payday. He made good his promise.* ◆ *Joe made good his boast to swim across the lake.* ◆ *John's mother promised to take him and his friends to the zoo on Saturday. She made good her promise.* Compare CARRY OUT. **2.** To compensate; pay for loss or damage. ◆ *The policeman told the boy's parents that the boy must make good the money he had stolen or go to jail.—*

Often used in the phrase *make it good.* ♦ *The radio was broken while it was being delivered so the store had to make it good and send us a new radio.* Compare MAKE UP. **3.** To do good work at one's job; succeed. ♦ *Kate wanted to be a nurse. She studied and worked hard in school. Then she got a job in the hospital and made good as a nurse.*

make good time *v. phr.* To make unimpeded progress on a journey; arrive at one's destination sooner than estimated. ♦ *There was not much traffic on the expressway so we made good time on our way to the airport.*

make haste *v. phr.* To move fast; hurry.—Rarely used in speaking. ♦ *The dog wriggled into one end of the hollow log, and the rabbit made haste to get out the other end.* ♦ *Mary saw that she had hurt Jane's feelings, and made haste to say she was sorry.* Compare MAKE TRACKS.

make haste with See HURRY ON WITH.

make hay while the sun shines *v. phr.* To do something at the right time; not wait too long. ♦ *Dick had a free hour so he made hay while the sun shone and got his lesson for the next day.* Compare MAKE THE MOST OF.

make head or tail of *v. phr., informal* To see the why of; finding a meaning in; understand.—Used in negative, conditional, and interrogative sentences. ♦ *She could not make head or tail of the directions on the dress pattern.* ♦ *Can you make head or tail of the letter?*

make headway *v. phr.* To move forward; make progress. ♦ *The university is making headway with its campus reorganization project.*

make it hot *v. phr., informal* To bring punishment; cause trouble. ♦ *Dick threatened to make it hot for anyone who tied knots in his pajama legs again.*

make it snappy *v. phr., informal* To move quickly; be fast; hurry.—Usually used as a command. ♦ *"Make it snappy," Mother said, "or we'll be late for the movie."* ♦ *The man hurried into the restaurant and told the waitress, "A cup of coffee, and make it snappy."*

make it with *v. phr., slang, informal* **1.** To be accepted by a group. ♦ *Joe finally made it with the in crowd in*

Hollywood. **2.** *vulgar* To have sex with (someone). ♦ *I wonder if Joe has made it with Sue.*

make light of *v. phr.* To treat an important matter as if it were trivial. ♦ *One ought to know which problems to make light of and which ones to handle seriously.* Compare LAUGH OFF. Contrast MAKE MUCH OF.

make little of *v. phr.* To make (something) seem unimportant; belittle. ♦ *Mary made little of Jane's new bicycle because she was jealous.* ♦ *Tom made little of his saving the drowning boy.* Contrast MAKE MUCH OF.

make love *v. phr.* **1.** To be warm, loving, and tender toward someone of the opposite sex; try to get him or her to love you too. ♦ *There was moonlight on the roses and he made love to her in the porch swing.* **2.** To have sexual relations with (someone). ♦ *It is rumored that Alfred makes love to every girl he hires as a secretary.*

make merry *v. phr., literary* To have fun, laugh, and be happy. ♦ *In Aesop's fable the grasshopper made merry while the ant worked and saved up food.* ♦ *In the Bible story a rich man ate and drank and made merry.*

make mincemeat (out) of *v. phr.* To destroy completely. ♦ *The defense attorney made mincemeat of the prosecution's argument.*

make much of *v. phr.* To make something seem of more worth or importance than it really is; praise. ♦ *Visitors made much of the new collie.* ♦ *The boy made much of the hard things of his mountain climb.* Contrast MAKE LIGHT OF, MAKE LITTLE OF.

make neither head nor tail of *v. phr.* To be unable to figure something out. ♦ *This puzzle is so complicated that I can make neither head nor tail of it.* Compare HEADS OR TAILS.

make no bones *v. phr., informal* **1.** To have no doubts; not to worry about right or wrong; not to be against.—Used with *about.* ♦ *Bill makes no bones about telling a lie to escape punishment.* ♦ *The boss made no bones about hiring extra help for the holidays.* **2.** To make no secret; not keep from talking; admit.—Used with *about* or *of the fact.* ♦ *John thinks being poor is no* disgrace and he makes no bones of the fact. ♦ *Mary made no bones about her love of poetry even after some of her friends laughed at her.*

make of *v. phr.* To interpret; understand. ♦ *What do you make of his sudden decision to go to Africa?*

make off *v.* To go away; run away; leave. ♦ *When the deer saw the hunter it made off at once.* ♦ *A thief stopped John on a dark street and made off with his wallet.* Compare TAKE OFF.

make one feel at home *v. phr.* To be hospitable; welcome; make someone feel at ease. ♦ *They are very popular hosts because they always manage to make their guests feel at home.*

make one out to be *v. phr.* To accuse someone of being something. ♦ *Don't make me out to be such a grouch; I am really quite happy-go-lucky.*

make one's bed and lie in it To be responsible for what you have done and so to have to accept the bad results. ♦ *Billy smoked one of his father's cigars and now he is sick. He made his bed, now let him lie in it.* Compare FACE THE MUSIC 2.

make one's blood boil *or* **make the blood boil** *v. phr., informal* To make someone very angry. ♦ *When someone calls me a liar it makes my blood boil.* ♦ *It made Mary's blood boil to see the children make fun of the crippled girl.* Compare BOILING POINT.

make one's blood run cold See BLOOD RUNS COLD.

make one's ears burn See EARS BURN.

make oneself at home *v. phr.* To feel comfortable; act as if you were in your own home. ♦ *If you get to my house before I do, help yourself to a drink and make yourself at home.* ♦ *John was an outdoor man and could make himself at home in the woods at night.* Compare AT EASE, AT HOME 2.

make oneself scarce *v. phr., slang* To leave quickly; go away. ♦ *The boys made themselves scarce when they saw the principal coming to stop their noise.* ♦ *A wise mouse makes himself scarce when a cat is nearby.*

make one's hair stand on end See HAIR STAND ON END.

make one's head spin *v. phr.* To be bewildered; be confused. ♦ *It makes my head spin to think about the amount of work I still have to do.*

make one's mark *v. phr.* To become known to many people; do well the work you started to do; make a reputation. ♦ *Shakespeare made his mark as a playwright.*

make one's mouth water *v. phr.* 1. To look or smell very good; make you want very much to eat or drink something you see or smell. ♦ *The pies in the store window made Dan's mouth water.* ♦ *The picture of the ice cream soda made his mouth water.* 2. To be attractive; make you want to have something very much. ♦ *Judy collects folk song records, and the records in the store window made her mouth water.* Compare LICK ONE'S CHOPS.

make one's pile *v. phr.* To make one's fortune. ♦ *The rich man made his pile in the stock market.*

make one's way *v. phr.* 1. To go forward with difficulty; find a path for yourself. ♦ *They made their way through the crowd.* 2. To do many hard things to earn a living; make a life work for yourself. ♦ *He was anxious to finish school and make his own way in the world.* Compare SHIFT FOR ONESELF.

make one tick *v. phr.* To cause to operate; to motivate. ♦ *He is so secretive that we are unable to figure out what makes him tick.*

make or break *v. phr.* To bring complete success or failure, victory or defeat. ♦ *Playing the role of Hamlet will make or break the young actor.*

make out *v.* 1. To write the facts asked for (as in an application blank or a report form); fill out. ♦ *The teacher made out the report cards and gave them to the students to take home.* ♦ *Mrs. Smith gave the clerk in the store some money and the clerk made out a receipt.* 2. To see, hear, or understand by trying hard. ♦ *It was dark, and we could not make out who was coming along the road.* ♦ *They could not make out what the child had drawn.* ♦ *The book had many hard words and Anne could not make out what the writer meant.* ♦ *Mr. White does many strange things. No one can make him out.* Syn. FIGURE OUT. 3. *informal* To make someone believe; show; prove. ♦ *Charles and Bob had a* *fight, and Charles tried to make out that Bob started it.* ♦ *The boy said he did not take the money but the teacher found the money in the boy's desk and it made him out to be a liar.* **4.** *informal* Do well enough; succeed. ♦ *John's father wanted John to do well in school and asked the teacher how John was making out.* ♦ *The sick woman could not make out alone in her house, so her friend came and helped her.* **5.** To kiss or pet. ♦ *What are Jack and Jill up to?—They're making out on the back porch.*

make over *v.* **1.** To change by law something from one owner to another owner; change the name on the title (lawful paper) from one owner to another. ♦ *Mr. Brown made over the title to the car to Mr. Jones.* **2.** To make something look different; change the style of. ♦ *He asked the tailor to make over his pants. The tailor cut off the cuffs and put a belt across the back.*

make passes at See MAKE A PASS AT.

make rounds *v. phr.* To travel the same route, making several stops along the way. ♦ *The milkman makes his rounds every morning.* ♦ *The doctor makes the rounds of the hospital rooms.*

make sense *v. phr.* **1.** To be something you can understand or explain; not be difficult or strange. ♦ *The explanation in the school book made no sense because the words were hard.* Compare MAKE HEAD OR TAIL OF. **2.** To seem right to do; sound reasonable or practical. ♦ *Does it make sense to let little children play with matches?*

make short work of *v. phr.* To finish rapidly. ♦ *The cat made short work of the baby rabbit.* ♦ *Tim was anxious to get to the movies so he made short work of his homework.*

make sit up *v. phr.* To shock to attention; surprise; create keen interest. ♦ *Her sudden appearance at the party and her amazingly low-cut dress made us all sit up.*

make something of *v. phr.* **1.** To make (something) seem important. ♦ *When girls see another girl with a boy, they often try to make something of it.* **2.** To start a fight over; use as an excuse to start a quarrel. ♦ *Bob accidentally shoved Bill in the corridor, and Bill made something of it.* ♦ *Ann didn't like what Mary said about her. She tried to make something of what Mary said.* Compare START SOMETHING.

make sport of See MAKE FUN OF.

make sure *v. phr.* To see about something yourself; look at to be sure. ♦ *Father makes sure that all the lights are off before he goes to bed.* ♦ *Mary thought she had time to get to school but she ran all the way just to make sure.* ♦ *Before you write your report on the life of Washington you should make sure of your facts.*

make the best of *v. phr.* To do something you do not like to do and not complain; accept with good humor. ♦ *The girl did not like to wash dishes but she made the best of it.* Compare MAKE A VIRTUE OF NECESSITY.

make the blood boil See MAKE ONE'S BLOOD BOIL.

make the feathers fly *v. phr., informal* **1.** To enjoy working; be strong and work hard. ♦ *When Mrs. Hale did her spring cleaning she made the feathers fly.* **2.** See MAKE THE FUR FLY.

make the fur fly *or* **make the feathers fly** *v. phr., informal* Say or write mean things about someone or to jump on and fight hard. ♦ *A man fooled Mr. Black and got his money. Mr. Black will really make the fur fly when he finds the man.* ♦ *Mrs. Baker's dog dug holes in her neighbor's garden. The neighbor really made the fur fly when she saw Mrs. Baker.*

make the grade *v. phr., informal* **1.** To make good; succeed. ♦ *It was clear that Mr. Baker had made the grade in the insurance business.* ♦ *It takes hard study to make the grade in school.* **2.** To meet a standard; qualify. ♦ *That whole shipment of cattle made the grade as prime beef.*

make the most of *v. phr.* To do the most you can with; get the most from; use to the greatest advantage. ♦ *She planned the weekend in town to make the most of it.* ♦ *George studied hard. He wanted to make the most of his chance to learn.* ♦ *The teacher went out of the room for five minutes and some bad boys made the most of it.* ♦ *Bill liked Mary; he would do anything for her, and Mary made the most of it.* Compare MAKE HAY WHILE THE SUN SHINES.

make the scene *v. phr., slang* To be present; to arrive at a certain place or event. ♦ *I am too tired to make the scene; let's go home.*

make things hum See KEEP THINGS HUMMING.

make time *v. phr., slang* **1.** To be successful in arriving at a designated place in short or good time. ♦ *We're supposed to be there at 6 P.M., and it's only 5:30— we're making good time.* **2.** To be successful in making sexual advances to someone. ♦ *Joe sure is making time with Sue, isn't he?*

make tongues wag See TONGUES TO WAG.

make tracks *v. phr., informal* To go fast; get a speedy start; hurry. ♦ *Man, it's time we made tracks!* ♦ *The boys made tracks for home when it began to get dark.* Compare GET GOING, MAKE HASTE.

makeup *n.* (stress on *make*) **1.** Cosmetics. ♦ *All the actors and actresses put on a lot of makeup.* **2.** Attributive auxiliary in lieu of, or belated. ♦ *The professor gave a makeup to the sick students.*

make up *v.* (stress on *up*) **1.** To make by putting things or parts together. ♦ *A car is made up of many different parts.* **2.** To invent; think and say something that is new or not true. ♦ *Jean makes up stories to amuse her little brother.* **3a.** To do or provide (something lacking or needed); do or supply (something not done, lost, or missed); get back; regain; give back; repay. ♦ *I have to make up the test I missed last week.* ♦ *I want to go to bed early to make up the sleep I lost last night.* ♦ *We have to drive fast to make up the hour we lost in Boston.* ♦ *Vitamin pills make up what you lack in your diet.* ♦ *The toy cost a dollar and Ted only had fifty cents, so Father made up the difference.*—Often used in the phrase *make it up to.* ♦ *Uncle Fred forgot my birthday present but he made it up to me by taking me to the circus.* ♦ *Mrs. Rich spent so much time away from her children that she tried to make it up to them by giving them things.* Compare MAKE GOOD. **3b.** To do what is lacking or needed; do or give what should be done or given; get or give back what has been lost, missed, or not done; get

or give instead; pay back.—Used with *for.* ♦ *We made up for lost time by taking an airplane instead of a train.* ♦ *Saying you are sorry won't make up for the damage of breaking the window.* ♦ *Mary had to make up for the time she missed in school when she was sick, by studying very hard.* ♦ *The beautiful view at the top of the mountain makes up for the hard climb to get there.* **4.** To put on lipstick and face paint powder. ♦ *Clowns always make up before a circus show.* ♦ *Tom watched his sister make up her face for her date.* **5.** To become friends again after a quarrel. ♦ *Mary and Joan quarreled, but made up after a while.* Compare BURY THE HATCHET. **6.** To try to make friends with someone; to win favor.—Followed by *to.* ♦ *The new boy made up to the teacher by sharpening her pencils.*

make up one's mind *v. phr.* To choose what to do; decide. ♦ *They made up their minds to sell the house.* ♦ *Tom couldn't decide whether he should tell Mother about the broken window or let her find it herself.* Contrast ON THE FENCE.

make waves *v. phr., informal* Make one's influence felt; create a disturbance, a sensation. ♦ *Joe Catwallender is the wrong man for the job; he is always trying to make waves.*

make way *v. phr.* To move from in front so someone can go through; stand aside. ♦ *The people made way for the king.* ♦ *When older men retire they make way for younger men to take their places.*

mama's boy *n. phr., informal* A boy who depends too much on his mother; a sissy. ♦ *The other boys called Tommy a mama's boy because he wouldn't come out to play unless his mother stayed near him.*

man See COMPANY MAN, EVERY LAST MAN *also* EVERY MAN JACK, FRONT MAN, HIRED MAN, LADY'S MAN, NEW MAN, SEPARATE THE MEN FROM THE BOYS, TO A MAN, YES-MAN.

man *or* **the man** *n., slang* **1.** The police; a policeman. ♦ *I am gonna turn you in to the man.* **2.** The boss; the leader; the most important figure in an organization or outfit. ♦ *The man will decide.*

man-about-town *n. phr.* A sophisticate; an idler; a member of café society; one who knows where the best plays and concerts are given. ♦*Ask Mark where to go when you're in New York City; he's a real man-about-town.*

manger See DOG IN THE MANGER.

man in the moon *n. phr.* An imaginary or nonexistent person (often used to indicate a person of ignorance). ♦*Stop asking me such difficult questions about nuclear physics; I know as much about it as the man in the moon.*

man in the street *n. phr.* The man who is just like most other men; the average man; the ordinary man. ♦*The newspaper took a poll of the man in the street.* Compare JOE DOAKES, JOHN Q. PUBLIC.

manner See ALL MANNER OF, TO THE MANNER BORN.

man of few words *n. phr.* A man who doesn't talk very much; a man who says only what is needed. ♦*The principal is a man of few words, but the pupils know what he wants.*

man of his word *n. phr.* A man who keeps his promises and does the things he agrees to do; a man who can be trusted. ♦*My uncle is a man of his word.*

man of letters *n. phr.* A writer; an author; a scholar. ♦*Chekhov was not only a practicing physician but also a first-rate man of letters.*

man of means *n. phr.* A rich person. ♦*He became a man of means by successfully playing the stock market.*

man of parts *n. phr., literary* A man who has several different skills, talents, or qualities. ♦*The pianist is a man of parts. He wrote the piece he played, and he also plays the organ and paints well.*

man-of-war *n. phr.* **1.** A stinging jellyfish in the Gulf of Mexico. ♦*"No swimming today," the sign said, "as we have a man-of-war alert."* **2.** A large battleship displaying its national flag or insignia. ♦*The shipwreck victims were picked up by an American man-of-war.* **3.** The albatross bird. ♦*After several days at sea we noticed some men-of-war majestically sailing through the skies.*

man-to-man *adj.* Honest and full in the telling; not hiding anything embar-rassing. ♦*Tom and his father had a man-to-man talk about his smoking pot.* Compare HEART-TO-HEART.

many See GOOD MANY *or* GREAT MANY, IN SO MANY WORDS, SO MANY.

many a *adj.* Many (persons or things)— Used with a singular noun. ♦*Many a boy learns to swim before he can read.* ♦*I have spent many a day in his home.*

many hands make light work If many people work together, even a hard job becomes easier.—A proverb. ♦*Come on boys, many hands make light work. If we work together, we can finish painting the barn.*

many is the There are a great number of (persons or things); many are the (persons or things).—Used at the beginning of a sentence with a singular noun. ♦*Many is the man I have lent money to.* ♦*Many was the time I ate at that restaurant.* Compare MANY A.

many moons ago *adv. phr.* A long, long time ago. ♦*Many moons ago, when I was young, I was able to dance all night.*

map See PUT ON THE MAP.

map out *v. phr.* To arrange; lay out; plan. ♦*The candidate will meet with his campaign manager tomorrow to map out his campaign strategy.*

marble See HAVE ALL ONE'S BUTTONS *or* HAVE ALL ONE'S MARBLES.

March See MAD AS A HATTER *or* MAD AS A MARCH HARE.

march See STEAL A MARCH ON.

mare's nest *n. phr.* Something that doesn't exist; a discovery that proves to be worthless. ♦*He claims that he has discovered a gasoline substitute but we suspect it will turn out to be a mare's nest.*

marine See TELL IT TO THE MARINES.

mark See MAKE ONE'S MARK, TOE THE LINE *or* TOE THE MARK, UP TO THE MARK *at* UP TO PAR 2, WALK THE CHALK *or* WALK THE CHALK LINE *or* WALK THE CHALK MARK, WIDE OF THE MARK.

markdown *n.* A reduction in price. ♦*Joan asked, "Do you like my new sandals? They were markdowns at Marshall Field's."*

mark down *v. phr.* **1.** To lower the price. ♦*The department store marked down their prices on women's sandals.* **2.** To give a poor grade to a student. ♦*Peter* *was marked down for his numerous spelling errors.* **3.** To make a written note of something. ♦ *Here is my phone number; mark it down.*

marked man *n. phr.* A man whose behavior has made him the object of suspicion; a man whose life may be in danger. ♦ *When Dave dared to criticize the dictator openly, he became a marked man.*

market See FLEA MARKET, IN THE MARKET FOR, ON THE MARKET, PLAY THE MARKET.

mark off *v. phr.* Mark with lines; lay out in sections. ♦ *The field will be marked off in accordance with the special track events that will take place tomorrow.*

mark one's words *v. phr.* To pay close attention to what one says; an emphatic expression indicating prophecy. ♦ *"It will certainly rain tomorrow," he said. "Mark my words."*

mark time *v. phr.* **1.** To move the feet up and down as in marching, but not going forward. ♦ *The officer made the soldiers mark time as a punishment.* **2.** To be idle; waiting for something to happen. ♦ *The teacher marked time until all the children were ready for the test.* **3.** To seem to be working or doing something, but really not doing it. ♦ *It was so hot that the workmen just marked time.*

marry money *v. phr.* To marry a rich person. ♦ *Ellen married money when she became Hal's wife.*

masking tape *n.* A paper tape that is stuck around the edges of a surface being painted to keep the paint off the surface next to it. ♦ *The painters put masking tape around the window frames to keep the paint off the glass.*

masse See EN MASSE.

mast See NAIL ONE'S COLORS TO THE MAST.

master copy *n.* **1.** A perfect text to which all copies are made to conform; a corrected version used as a standard by printers. ♦ *The master copy must be right, because if it isn't, the mistakes in it will be repeated all through the edition.* **2.** A stencil from which other copies are made. ♦ *Mr. Brown told his secretary to save the master copy so that they could run off more copies whenever they needed them.* ♦ *The master*

copy was too light so many of the copies didn't come out clear.

master key *n. phr.* A key that opens a set of different locks. ♦ *The building janitor has a master key to all of the apartments in this building.*

mastermind *v.* To create; direct; invent the central plan for several individuals to follow. ♦ *Lenin masterminded the Bolshevik Revolution in Russia.*

mastermind *n.* A person who supplies the intelligence for a project and/or undertakes its management. ♦ *Winston Churchill was the mastermind in the war against Hitler.*

master of ceremonies *or* **M.C.** *or* **emcee** *n.* The person in charge of introducing the various participants in a show or entertainment. ♦ *Bob Hope was the M.C. of many memorable shows.*

mat See WELCOME MAT IS OUT.

matter See FOR THAT MATTER, LAUGHING MATTER, NO MATTER, THE MATTER.

matter of course *n. phr.* Something always done; the usual way; habit; rule. ♦ *It was a matter of course for John to dress carefully when he was meeting his wife.* ♦ *Bank officers ask questions as a matter of course when someone wants to borrow money.*

matter of fact *n. phr.* Something that is really true; something that can be proved. ♦ *The town records showed that it was a matter of fact that the two boys were brothers.* ♦ *It is a matter of fact that the American war against England was successful.*—Often used for emphasis in the phrase *as a matter of fact.* ♦ *I didn't go yesterday, and as a matter of fact, I didn't go all week.* ♦ *Mary wasn't wearing a blue dress. As a matter of fact, she hasn't got a blue dress.* Compare FOR THAT MATTER, IN FACT. Contrast MATTER OF OPINION.

matter-of-fact *adj.* **1.** Simply telling or showing the truth; not explaining or telling more. ♦ *The newspaper gave a matter-of-fact account of the murder trial.* **2.** Showing little feeling or excitement or trouble; seeming not to care much. ♦ *When Mary's father died she acted in a very matter-of-fact way.* ♦ *He was a very matter-of-fact person.*

matter of opinion *n. phr.* Something that may or may not be true; something that people do not all agree on. ♦ *Whether or not he was a good general is a matter of opinion.* Compare MATTER OF FACT.

matter of record *n. phr.* A fact or event that is kept officially as a legal record. ♦ *If you are convicted of speeding it becomes a matter of record.* ♦ *A birth certificate or a marriage license is a matter of record.*

may See BE THAT AS IT MAY, COME WHAT MAY, LET THE CHIPS FALL WHERE THEY MAY.

M.C. *or* **emcee** *v.* To act as master of ceremonies at a show. ♦ *The famous actor emceed the entire television show.*

me See DEAR ME, PICK-ME-UP, SO HELP ME.

mean business *v. phr., informal* To decide strongly to do what you plan to do; really mean it; be serious. ♦ *The boss said he would fire us if we didn't work harder and he means business.* ♦ *When she went to college to study, she meant business.* ♦ *He just liked the company of the other girls he dated, but this time he seems to mean business.*

means See BY ALL MEANS, BY MEANS OF, BY NO MEANS, WAYS AND MEANS.

means to an end *n. phr.* An action leading to some end or purpose. ♦ *Money for him was just a means to an end; actually he wanted power.*

mean well *v. phr.* To have good intentions. ♦ *Fred generally means well, but he has a tendency to be tactless.*

measure See BEYOND MEASURE, FOR GOOD MEASURE, MADE-TO-MEASURE, TAKE ONE'S MEASURE *or* TAKE THE MEASURE OF.

measure off *v. phr.* To mark by measuring. ♦ *She measured off three yards with which to make the new dress.*

measure up *v.* To be equal; be of fully high quality; come up. ♦ *John didn't measure up to the best catchers but he was a good one.* ♦ *Lois' school work didn't measure up to her ability.* Compare UP TO PAR. Contrast FALL SHORT.

meatball *n., slang* A dull, boring, slow-witted, or uninteresting person. ♦ *You'll never get an interesting story out of that meatball—stop inviting him.*

medicine See TAKE ONE'S MEDICINE.

medium See STRIKE A HAPPY MEDIUM.

meet See MAKE ENDS MEET.

meet halfway See GO HALFWAY.

meeting See BEST BIB AND TUCKER *or* SUNDAY-GO-TO-MEETING CLOTHES.

meet one's death *v. phr.* To die. ♦ *Algernon met his death in a car accident.*

meet one's eye *v. phr.* To be in plain view or come into plain view; appear clearly or obviously. ♦ *When John rounded the bend, a clear blue lake met his eye.* ♦ *On a first reading the plan looked good, but there was more to it than met the eye.*

meet one's match *v. phr.* To encounter someone as good as oneself. ♦ *The champion finally met his match and lost the game.*

meet one's Waterloo *v. phr.* To be defeated; lose an important contest. ♦ *After seven straight victories the team met its Waterloo.* ♦ *John fought instead of running, and the bully met his Waterloo.* [After Napoleon's final defeat at Waterloo.]

meet up with *v. phr.* To meet by accident; come upon without planning or expecting to. ♦ *When he ran around the tree, Bob suddenly meet up with a large bear.* ♦ *The family would have arrived on time, but they met up with a flat tire.*

meet with *v.* **1.** To meet (someone), usually by accident. ♦ *In the woods he met with two strangers.* Syn. COME UPON. **2.** To meet together, usually by plan; join; have a meeting with. ♦ *The two scouts met with the officers to talk about plans for the march.* **3.** To experience (as unhappiness); suffer (as bad luck); have (as an accident or mishap). ♦ *The farmer met with misfortune; his crops were destroyed by a storm.* ♦ *The traveler met with an accident on the road.*

melt See BUTTER WOULDN'T MELT IN ONE'S MOUTH, MELT IN ONE'S MOUTH.

melting pot *n. phr.* A country where different nationalities mingle and mix with the result that, in the second generation, most people speak the main language of the country and behave like the majority. ♦ *It is no longer considered entirely true that the United States is a melting pot; many immigrants speak a second language.*

melt in one's mouth *v. phr.* **1.** To be so tender as to seem to need no chewing.

◆ *The chicken was so tender that it melted in your mouth.* **2.** To taste very good; be delicious. ◆ *Mother's apple pie really melts in your mouth.*

memory See IN MEMORY OF.

mend See ON THE MEND.

mend one's fences *v. phr., informal* To do something to make people like or follow you again; strengthen your friendships or influence. ◆ *The senator went home from Washington to mend his fences.* ◆ *John saw that his friends did not like him, so he decided to mend his fences.*

mend one's ways *v. phr.* To reform; change one's behavior from negative to positive. ◆ *He had better mend his ways or he'll wind up in jail.*

mental telepathy *n. phr.* The passing of one person's thoughts to another without any discoverable talking or carrying of signals between them. ◆ *Mrs. Smith knew the moment her husband's ship sank on the other side of the world. It seems like a case of mental telepathy.* ◆ *Most or all men who practice mental telepathy on stage have really trained themselves to detect tiny clues from the audience.*

mention See NOT TO MENTION.

meow See CAT'S MEOW.

mercy See AT THE MERCY OF.

mercy killing *n. phr.* The act of killing a terminally ill patient or animal in order to avoid further suffering. ◆ *Mercy killing of humans is illegal in most countries, yet many doctors practice it secretly.*

merrier See MORE THE MERRIER.

merry See LEAD A MERRY CHASE, MAKE MERRY.

message See GET THE MESSAGE.

mess around *v. phr.* **1.** To engage in idle or purposeless activity. ◆ *Come on, you guys,—start doing some work, don't just mess around all day!* **2.** *vulgar* To be promiscuous; to indulge in sex with little discrimination as to who the partner is. ◆ *Allen needs straightening out; he's been messing around with the whole female population of his class.* Compare FOOL AROUND.

mess up *v. phr., slang, informal* **1.** To cause trouble; to spoil something. ◆ *What did you have to mess up my accounts for?* **2.** To cause someone

emotional trauma. ◆ *Sue will never get married; she got messed up when she was a teenager.* **3.** To beat up someone physically. ◆ *When Joe came in after the fight with the boys, he was all messed up.*

method in (to) one's madness *n. phr.* A plan or organization of ideas hard to perceive at first, but that becomes noticeable after longer and closer examination. ◆ *We thought he was crazy to threaten to resign from the university but, when he was offered a tenured full professorship, we realized that there had been method in his madness.*

mickey mouse[1] *adj., slang* Inferior; second rate; chicken; easy; gimmicky. ◆ *Watch out for Perkins; he's full of mickey mouse ideas.*

mickey mouse[2] *n. (derogatory)* A stupid person; a policeman; a white man (as used by blacks).

midair See UP IN THE AIR 2 *also* IN MIDAIR.

middle See CHANGE HORSES IN THE MIDDLE OF THE STREAM, IN THE MIDDLE.

middle ground *n.* A place halfway between the two sides of an argument; a compromise. ◆ *John wanted to go running. Bill said it was too hot. Tom took the middle ground and suggested a hike.* ◆ *The committee found a middle ground between the two proposals.*

middleman *n.* A person or small business standing in an intermediary position between two parties. ◆ *A retail merchant is the middleman between the factory and the consumer.*

middle of the road *n. phr.* A way of thinking which does not favor one idea or thing too much; being halfway between two different ideas. ◆ *The teacher did not support the boys or the girls in the debate, but stayed in the middle of the road.*

middle-of-the-road *adj.* Favoring action halfway between two opposite movements or ideas; with ideas halfway between two opposite sides; seeing good on both sides. ◆ *The men who wrote the Constitution followed a middle-of-the-road plan on whether greater power belonged to the United States government or to the separate* *states.* ◆ *Senator Jones favors a middle-of-the-road policy in the labor-management dispute.*

midfield stripe *n.* The line across the center of a football field; the 50-yard line. ◆ *The visitors were able to cross the midfield stripe once during the whole game.*

midnight oil See BURN THE MIDNIGHT OIL.

midstream See CHANGE HORSES IN THE MIDDLE OF THE STREAM *or* CHANGE HORSES IN MIDSTREAM.

might See WITH MIGHT AND MAIN.

mighty See HIGH-AND-MIGHTY.

mile See GIVE ONE AN INCH AND HE WILL TAKE A MILE, JAW DROP *or* JAW DROP A MILE, MISS BY A MILE, MISS IS AS GOOD AS A MILE.

mile markers *n., slang, citizen's band radio jargon* Small signs along interstate highways usually bearing a number. ◆ *The Smokey is located at 131 mile marker.*

miles away *adj. phr.* Inattentive; not concentrating. ◆ *When Betty said, "We have theater tickets for tonight," Ken didn't react as his mind was miles away.*

milk See CRY OVER SPILLED MILK.

mill See RUN-OF-THE-MILL, THROUGH THE MILL.

mill around *v. phr.* To move impatiently in no particular direction. ◆ *The crowd milled around, waiting for the arrival of the president.*

million See FEEL LIKE A MILLION, LOOK LIKE A MILLION DOLLARS.

millstone around one's neck *n. phr.* An intolerable burden. ◆ *Max said that his old car was a millstone around his neck.* Compare MONKEY ON ONE'S BACK.

mince words *v. phr.* To choose words carefully for the sake of politeness or deception. ◆ *I like people who speak frankly and truthfully without mincing words.*

mind See CROSS ONE'S MIND *or* PASS THROUGH ONE'S MIND, GIVE A PIECE OF ONE'S MIND, HALF A MIND, IN MIND, IN ONE'S MIND'S EYE, MAKE UP ONE'S MIND, NEVER MIND, ON ONE'S MIND, OUT OF ONE'S HEAD *or* OUT OF ONE'S MIND, PUT IN MIND OF, READ ONE'S MIND.

mind like a steel trap *n. phr.* A very quick and understanding mind, which is quick to catch an idea. ◆ *Henry is not*

fond of sports, but he has a mind like a steel trap. ◆ *A successful lawyer must have a mind like a steel trap.*

mind one's own business *v. phr.* To not interfere in the affairs of others. ◆ *He finally got tired of her criticism and told her to mind her own business.*

mind one's p's and q's *v. phr.* To be very careful what you do or say; not make mistakes. ◆ *When the principal of the school visited the class the students all minded their p's and q's.* ◆ *If you wish to succeed you must mind your p's and q's.* [From the old U.S. Navy when sailors marked on a board in the bar how many Pints and Quarts of liquor they had taken. It was bad manners to cheat.] Syn. WATCH ONE'S STEP.

mind-reader See READ ONE'S MIND.

mind you *v. phr., informal* I want you to notice and understand. ◆ *Mind you, I am not blaming him.*

mine See BACK TO THE SALT MINES, RUN OF THE MILL *or* RUN OF THE MINE.

mine of information *n. phr.* A person, a book, etc., that is a valuable source of information. ◆ *A dictionary can be a mine of information.* ◆ *He is a mine of information on the stock market.*

minority leader *n. phr.* The leader of the political party that has fewer votes in a legislative house. ◆ *The minority leader of the Senate supported the bill.* ◆ *The minority leader in the House of Representatives held a caucus.* Compare MAJORITY LEADER.

mint money See COIN MONEY.

minutes of the meeting *n. phr.* The notes taken by the recording secretary of an official body or an association recording of what was said and transacted during the given session. ◆ *"Shall we accept the minutes of our last meeting as read by the secretary?" the chairman asked.*

misfire *v.* To fail to appeal; fall flat. ◆ *The standup comic's jokes misfired with the audience.* Compare GO OVER LIKE A LEAD BALLOON.

miss See HEART SKIP A BEAT *or* HEART MISS A BEAT.

miss a trick *v. phr.* To fail to see, hear, or notice something of even the slightest importance. ◆ *He never misses a trick when it comes to the stock market.*

miss by a mile *v. phr., informal* **1.** To shoot at something and be far from hitting it; not hit near. ♦*Jack's first shot missed the target by a mile.* **2.** To be very wrong; be far from right. ♦*Lee tried to guess on the examination, but his answers missed by a mile.* **3.** To fail badly; not succeed at all. ♦*John Brown wanted to be governor but in the election he missed by a mile.*

missing link *n.* **1.** Something needed to complete a group; a missing part of a chain of things. ♦*A 1936 penny was the missing link in John's collection of pennies.* ♦*The detective hunted for the fact that was the missing link in the case.* **2.** An unknown extinct animal that was supposed to be a connection between man and lower animals. ♦*The missing link would be half man and half ape.*

miss is as good as a mile It is the same if one fails or misses something by much or by little.—A proverb. ♦*We thought Tom had a home run but the ball went foul by inches. A miss is as good as a mile.*

Missouri See FROM MISSOURI.

miss out *v., informal* To fail; lose or not take a good chance; miss something good. ♦*Jim's mother told him he missed out on a chance to go fishing with his father because he came home late.* ♦*You missed out by not coming with us; we had a great time.* Compare LOSE OUT.

miss the boat *also* **miss the bus** *v. phr., informal* To fail through slowness; to put something off until too late; do the wrong thing and lose the chance. ♦*Mr. Brown missed the boat when he decided not to buy the house.* ♦*In college he didn't study enough so he missed the boat and failed to pass.* ♦*Ted could have married Lena but he put off asking her and missed the boat.*

miss the point *v. phr.* To be unable to comprehend the essence of what was meant. ♦*The student didn't get a passing grade on the exam because, although he wrote three pages, he actually missed the point.*

mistake See BY MISTAKE.

misty-eyed *or* **dewey-eyed** *adj. phr.* **1.** Having eyes damp with tears; emotional. ♦*The teacher was misty-eyed when the school gave her a retirement gift.* **2.** Of the kind who cries easily; sentimental. ♦*The movie appealed to dewey-eyed girls.*

mixed bag *n. phr.* A varied set of people, ideas, objects, or circumstances, including both the good and the bad. ♦*This report is a mixed bag of opinions.* ♦*There was a mixed bag of people at the press conference.*

mixed blessing *n.* Something good that has bad features. ♦*John's new bicycle was a mixed blessing. The other boys were always asking John to ride it.*

mixed up *adj. phr.* **1.** *informal* Confused in mind; puzzled. ♦*Bob was all mixed up after the accident.* Compare BALL UP 1. **2.** Disordered; disarranged; not neat. ♦*The papers on his desk were mixed up.* **3.** *informal* Joined or connected (with someone or something bad). ♦*Harry was mixed up in a fight after the game.* ♦*Mary's father told her not to get mixed up with the students that always break school rules.*

mix up *v.* To confuse; make a mistake about. ♦*Jimmy doesn't know colors yet; he mixes up purple with blue.* ♦*Even the twins' mother mixes them up.* Compare MIXED UP.

molehill See MAKE A MOUNTAIN OUT OF A MOLEHILL.

moment See ON THE SPUR OF THE MOMENT.

Monday See BLUE MONDAY.

money See COIN MONEY *or* MINT MONEY, EASY MONEY, FOOL AND HIS MONEY ARE SOON PARTED, FOR LOVE OR MONEY, IN THE CHIPS *or* IN THE MONEY, MADE OF MONEY, MARRY MONEY, PUT ONE'S MONEY ON A SCRATCHED HORSE, RUN FOR ONE'S MONEY, SEE THE COLOR OF ONE'S MONEY, SPENDING MONEY *or* POCKET MONEY.

money burns a hole in one's pocket See BURN A HOLE IN ONE'S POCKET.

money is no object *informal sentence* The price of something is irrelevant. ♦*Please show me your most beautiful mink coat; money is no object.*

money to burn *n. phr., informal* Very much money, more than is needed. ♦*Dick's uncle died and left him money to burn.* ♦*When Joe is twenty-one he will have money to burn.* ♦*Jean is looking for a husband with money to burn.* Compare MADE OF MONEY.

monkey See GREASE MONKEY, MAKE A FOOL OF or MAKE A MONKEY OF.

monkey around See FUCK AROUND, HORSE AROUND, MESS AROUND.

monkey business *n., slang, informal* **1.** Any unethical, illegitimate, or objectionable activity that is furtive or deceitful, e.g., undercover sexual advances, cheating, misuse of public funds, etc. ♦ *There is a lot of monkey business going on in that firm; you'd better watch out who you deal with!* **2.** Comical or silly actions; goofing off. ♦ *Come on boys, let's cut out the monkey business and get down to work!*

monkey on one's back *n. phr., informal* An unsolved or nagging problem. ♦ *"My math course is a real monkey on my back," Jack complained.* Compare ALBATROSS AROUND ONE'S NECK, MILLSTONE AROUND ONE'S NECK.

monkey wrench See THROW A MONKEY WRENCH.

monster See GREEN-EYED MONSTER.

month in, month out See DAY IN AND DAY OUT.

month of Sundays *n. phr., informal* A very long time.—Used for emphasis after *for* or *in* and usually with a negative verb. ♦ *I have not had devil's food cake in a month of Sundays.* ♦ *When he got her first letter, he felt that he had not heard from her for a month of Sundays.* Syn. DOG'S AGE.

moon See ASK FOR THE MOON or CRY FOR THE MOON, DARK OF THE MOON, FULL OF THE MOON, ONCE IN A BLUE MOON, PROMISE THE MOON.

moonshine *n.* Illegally distilled alcoholic beverage made at home, mostly on a farm. ♦ *Grandpa is at it again in the barn, making moonshine out of plums.*

mop the floor with *or* **mop up the floor with** *or* **wipe the floor with** *or* **wipe up the floor with** *v. phr., slang* To defeat very clearly or quickly; to beat badly. ♦ *The bully threatened to mop up the floor with Billy.* ♦ *Our team wiped the floor with the visiting team.*

mop up *v. phr.* To disperse or liquidate isolated groups or detachments of opposing forces. ♦ *Our forces won the basic battle but there still remain pockets of resistance they must mop up.*

mop up the floor with See MOP THE FLOOR WITH.

more See BITE OFF MORE THAN ONE CAN CHEW.

more often than not *adv. phr.* More than half the time; fifty-one or more times out of a hundred; not quite usually, but fairly regularly. ♦ *Nancy comes over on Saturday more often than not.* ♦ *Ben is a fairly good runner. He wins more often than not.*

more or less *adv. phr.* **1.** Somewhat; rather; mostly; fairly. ♦ *Earl made some mistakes on the test, but his answers were more or less right.* ♦ *Ed is more or less intelligent.* ♦ *Betty believes more or less in fairies.* Compare IN A WAY. **2.** About; nearly; not exactly, but almost. ♦ *The new building cost more or less what the builder figured.* ♦ *It is a mile, more or less, from his home to the school.* ♦ *He has wanted to date her more or less since he first saw her.* Compare OR SO.

more than *adv.* Over what you might expect; very. ♦ *They were more than glad to help.* ♦ *He was more than upset by the accident.* Contrast LESS THAN.

more than one can chew See BITE OFF MORE THAN ONE CAN CHEW.

more than one could shake a stick at *adj. phr., informal* Very many; a great many; more than you can count. ♦ *There were more people at the game than you could shake a stick at.* ♦ *I had more assignments for homework than I could shake a stick at.*

more the merrier *n. phr.* The more people who join in the fun, the better it will be.—Used in welcoming more people to join others in some pleasant activity. ♦ *Come with us on the boat ride; the more the merrier.*

morning after *n., slang* The effects of drinking liquor or staying up late as felt the next morning; a hangover. ♦ *One of the troubles of drinking too much liquor is the morning after.* ♦ *Mr. Smith woke up with a big headache and knew it was the morning after.*

Moses See HOLY CATS or HOLY MOSES.

moss See ROLLING STONE GATHERS NO MOSS.

most See AT MOST, MAKE THE MOST OF.

mother See TIED TO ONE'S MOTHER'S APRON STRINGS.

motion See GO THROUGH THE MOTIONS.

mountain See MAKE A MOUNTAIN OUT OF A MOLEHILL.

mouse See PLAY CAT AND MOUSE WITH.

mouth See BORN WITH A SILVER SPOON IN ONE'S MOUTH, BUTTER WOULDN'T MELT IN ONE'S MOUTH, BY WORD OF MOUTH, DOWN IN THE DUMPS *or* DOWN IN THE MOUTH, FOAM AT THE MOUTH, HEART IN ONE'S MOUTH, KEEP ONE'S MOUTH SHUT, LAUGH ON THE WRONG SIDE OF ONE'S MOUTH, LEAVE A BAD TASTE IN ONE'S MOUTH, LIVE FROM HAND TO MOUTH, LOOK A GIFT HORSE IN THE MOUTH, MAKE ONE'S MOUTH WATER, MELT IN ONE'S MOUTH, PUT ONE'S FOOT IN IT *or* PUT ONE'S FOOT IN ONE'S MOUTH, PUT WORDS INTO ONE'S MOUTH, SHOOT OFF ONE'S MOUTH, STRAIGHT FROM THE HORSE'S MOUTH, TAKE THE BIT IN ONE'S MOUTH, TAKE THE BREAD OUT OF ONE'S MOUTH.

mouthful See SAY A MOUTHFUL.

mouth-watering *adj.* Smelling or looking very good to eat. ♦*It was a mouth-watering meal.*

move See GET A MOVE ON, ON THE MOVE.

move a muscle *v. phr.* To move even a very little.—Used in negative sentences and questions and with *if.* ♦*The deer stood without moving a muscle until the hunter was gone.* ♦*The girls were so startled that they did not move a muscle.* ♦*You're sitting right where you were when I left! Have you moved a muscle?* ♦*The robber said he would shoot the bank worker if he moved a muscle.*

move heaven and earth *v. phr.* To try every way; do everything you can. ♦*Joe moved heaven and earth to be sent to Washington.* Compare LEAVE NO STONE UNTURNED.

move in on *v. phr., slang, colloquial* To take over something that belongs to another. ♦*He moved in on my girlfriend and now we're not talking to each other.*

movement See LABOR MOVEMENT.

moving spirit *n. phr.* The main figure behind a business or an activity; the one who inspires the others. ♦*Mr. Smith is the moving spirit behind our expansion plans.*

much See AS MUCH AS, FOR AS MUCH AS, MAKE MUCH OF, SO MUCH, SO MUCH FOR, THINK A GREAT DEAL OF *or* THINK MUCH OF.

much as See AS MUCH AS 1.

much less *conj.* And also not; and even less able or likely to.—Used after a negative clause. ♦*I never even spoke to the man, much less insulted him.* ♦*John couldn't even pick up the box, much less carry it upstairs.* ♦*George can hardly understand arithmetic, much less algebra.* Compare LET ALONE, NOT TO MENTION.

mud See NAME IS MUD, STICK-IN-THE-MUD.

mud in your eye *n. phr., informal* A cheering exclamation when people drink, much like "cheers!" ♦*Each time John raised his glass he said, "Well, here's mud in your eye!"*

mug shot *n. phr.* A police photograph showing the arrested person's full face and profile. ♦*"Go over these mug shots," Sergeant O'Malley said, "and tell me if you find the person who held up the liquor store!"*

Muhammad See IF THE HILL WON'T COME TO MUHAMMAD, THEN MUHAMMAD MUST COME TO THE HILL.

mull over *v. phr.* To consider; think over. ♦*He mulled over the offer for some time, but finally rejected it.*

mum is the word You must keep the secret; keep silent; don't tell anyone.— Often used as an interjection. ♦*We are planning a surprise party for John and mum is the word.* ♦*"Mum is the word!" the robber captain told his men.*

murder See SCREAM BLOODY MURDER.

muscle See MOVE A MUSCLE.

muscle-bound *adj.* Having your muscles large, hard, and tight from too much exercising; having muscles so developed that you can hardly move. ♦*Bob was big and strong, but he was muscle-bound, and Bill could beat him.* ♦*An athlete must train properly so as not to become muscle-bound.*

muscle in on *v. phr.* To intrude; penetrate; force oneself into another's business or territory. ♦*The eastern Mafia muscled in on the western Mafia's turf and a shooting war was started.*

music See FACE THE MUSIC.

musical chairs *n. phr.* (Originally the name of a children's game.) The transfer of a number of officers in an organization into different jobs, especially each other's jobs. ◆ *The boss regularly played musical chairs with department heads to keep them fresh on the job.*

music to one's ears *n. phr.* Something one likes to hear. ◆ *When the manager phoned to say I got the job, it was music to my ears.*

mustard See CUT THE MUSTARD.

muster See PASS MUSTER.

my God *or* **my goodness** *interj.* Used to express surprise, shock, or dismay. ◆ *My God! What happened to the car?*

my lips are sealed *informal sentence* A promise that one will not give away a secret. ◆ *"You can tell me what happened," Helen said. "My lips are sealed."*

nail See HARD AS NAILS, HIT THE NAIL ON THE HEAD, TOOTH AND NAIL.

nail down *v. phr., informal* To make certain; make sure; settle. ♦*Joe had a hard time selling his car, but he finally nailed the sale down when he got his friend Sam to give him $300.* ♦*The New York Yankees nailed down the American League Championship when they beat the Red Sox 3 to 0 on September 15.*

nail one's colors to the mast *literary* To let everyone know what you think is right and refuse to change. ♦*During the election campaign the candidate nailed his colors to the mast on the question of civil rights.*

name See CALL NAMES, HANDLE TO ONE'S NAME, IN NAME, TAKE ONE'S NAME IN VAIN, TO ONE'S NAME.

name calling See CALL NAMES.

named after *adj. phr.* Given the same name as someone. ♦*Archibald was named after his father.*

name day *n.* The day of the saint for whom a person is named. ♦*Lawrence's name day is August 10, the feast of St. Lawrence.*

namedropper *n. phr.* A person who is always mentioning well-known names. ♦*Since her move to Hollywood she has become a regular namedropper.*

name is mud *informal* (You) are in trouble; a person is blamed or no longer liked.—Used in the possessive. ♦*If you tell your mother I spilled ink on her rug my name will be mud.* ♦*Your name will be mud if you tell the teacher about the bad thing we did.* Compare IN THE DOG HOUSE.

name of the game *n., informal* The crux of the matter; that which actually occurs under the disguise of something else. ♦*Getting medium income families to support the rest of society—that's the name of the game!*

narrow down *v. phr.* To limit within very strict margins. ♦*Of the numerous applicants, the list has been narrowed down to just a few.*

narrow escape *n. phr.* An escape by a very small margin; a near miss. ♦*If the truck that hit his car had been coming faster, it would have killed him; it was certainly a narrow escape that he only had a broken arm!*

narrow-minded *adj. phr.* Limited in outlook; resistant to new ideas; bigoted. ♦*He is generally very open about everything, but when it comes to politics, he is terribly narrow-minded.*

nary a *informal* Not a single; not one; never a. ♦*One afternoon a large dark cloud came in the sky. John thought it would rain so he took his raincoat—but nary a drop fell.* ♦*John went fishing but he caught nary a one.*

nasty-nice *adj.* Unkind in a polite way; disagreeable while pretending to be gracious. ♦*The bus driver has a nasty-nice way of showing his dislike.*

natural See BIG AS LIFE *or* BIG AS LIFE AND TWICE AS NATURAL.

natural-born *adj.* **1.** Being a (citizen) because you were born in the country. ♦*Mr. and Mrs. Schmidt came to the United States from Germany and are naturalized citizens but their children are natural-born citizens.* **2.** Born with great ability to become (something); having great ability (as in a sport or art) almost from the start. ♦*Joe had never played baseball before trying out for the team but he showed that he was a natural-born pitcher and he became the best in the league.* ♦*Mozart was a natural-born musician. He could play the piano well when he was only six years old.*

nature See SECOND NATURE.

naught See GO FOR NOTHING *also* GO FOR NAUGHT.

near See FAR AND NEAR.

near at hand See AT HAND.

necessity See MAKE A VIRTUE OF NECESSITY, OF NECESSITY.

neck See BREATHE DOWN ONE'S NECK, BREAK ONE'S NECK, CATCH IT IN THE NECK *or* GET IT IN THE NECK, PAIN IN THE NECK, SAVE ONE'S NECK, STICK ONE'S NECK OUT.

neck and neck *adj. or adv., informal* Equal or nearly equal in a race or contest; abreast; tied. ♦*At the end of the race the two horses were neck and neck.* ♦*For months John and Harry seemed to be neck and neck in Alice's favor.* Compare NIP AND TUCK.

neck of the woods *n. phr., informal* Part of the country; place; neighborhood; vicinity. ♦ *We visited Illinois and Iowa last summer; in that neck of the woods the corn really grows tall.* ♦ *We were down in your neck of the woods last week.*

necktie party *n., slang* A hanging by a mob; lynching. ♦ *Cattle thieves were stealing the rancher's cattle, but the cowboys caught them and had a necktie party.* Compare STRING UP.

ned See RAISE THE DEVIL.

needle See ON PINS AND NEEDLES.

needle in a haystack *n. phr., informal* Something that will be very hard to find. ♦ *"I lost my class ring somewhere in the front yard," said June. Jim answered, "Too bad. That will be like finding a needle in a haystack."*

neither fish nor fowl *also* **neither fish, flesh, nor fowl** Something or someone that does not belong to a definite group or known class; a strange person or thing; someone or something odd or hard to understand. ♦ *The man is neither fish nor fowl; he votes Democrat or Republican according to which will do him the most good.* ♦ *Mrs. Harris bought a piece of furniture that was both a table and a chair. Mr. Harris said it was neither fish nor fowl.* ♦ *The movie is neither fish nor fowl; it is a funny love story.*

neither here nor there *adj. phr.* Not important to the thing being discussed; off the subject; not mattering. ♦ *Perhaps you did stay up late finishing your homework. That's neither here nor there. You still must come to school on time.* ♦ *The boys all like the coach but that's neither here nor there; the question is, "Does he know how to teach football?"* Compare BESIDE THE POINT. Contrast HAVE TO DO WITH, COME TO THE POINT.

neither hide nor hair See HIDE OR HAIR.

neither rhyme nor reason *n. phr.* No emotional or intellectual substance. ♦ *As far as I am concerned, his proposal makes no sense; it has neither rhyme nor reason.*

Nellie See NICE NELLY *or* NICE NELLIE, NERVOUS NELLIE.

Nelly See NICE NELLY *or* NICE NELLIE, NERVOUS NELLIE.

nerve See GET ON ONE'S NERVES, GET UP THE NERVE.

nervous breakdown *n.* A mild or severe attack of mental illness; a collapse of a person's ability to make decisions and solve problems because of overwork, great mental strain, or the like. ♦ *When the mother saw her baby run over, she suffered a nervous breakdown.*

Nervous Nellie *n., informal* A timid person who lacks determination and courage. ♦ *I say we will never win if we don't stop being Nervous Nellies!*

nervous prostration *n.* An illness of the mind that makes you feel very tired, worried, and bored, and that often causes headaches, upset stomach, and other sickness. ♦ *Aunt Jane said that taking care of us children all day was enough to give any woman nervous prostration.*

nest See FEATHER ONE'S NEST, STIR UP A HORNET'S NEST.

nest egg *n.* Savings set aside to be used in the future. ♦ *Herb says he doesn't have to worry about his old age because he has a nest egg in the bank.*

never See BETTER LATE THAN NEVER, IT NEVER RAINS BUT IT POURS, LIGHTNING NEVER STRIKES TWICE IN THE SAME PLACE.

never mind *v. phr.* Don't trouble about it; don't worry about it; forget it; skip it.—Usually used in speaking or when writing dialogue. ♦ *Never mind preparing a picnic lunch; we'll find a lunchstand when we get to the beach.* ♦ *"What did you say?" "Oh, never mind." ♦ "What about money?" "Never mind that. I'll take care of it."*

never say die *v. phr.* Don't quit; don't be discouraged. ♦ *"Never say die!" John said, as he got on his feet and tried to ice skate again.*

new See TURN OVER A NEW LEAF.

new blood *n.* Something or someone that gives new life or vigor, fresh energy or power. ♦ *New blood was brought into the company through appointment of younger men to important positions.*

new broom sweeps clean A new person makes many changes.—A proverb. ♦ *The new superintendent has changed many of the school rules. A new broom sweeps clean.*

Newcastle See CARRY COALS TO NEWCASTLE.

new deal *n., informal* **1.** A complete change; a fresh start. ♦*People had been on the job too long; a new deal was needed to get things out of the old bad habits.* **2.** Another chance. ♦*The boy asked for a new deal after he had been punished for fighting in school.*

newfangled *adj.* Newly invented or contrived; excessively complex. ♦*Dorothy felt that many newfangled gadgets in Kate's all-electric kitchen weren't really necessary.*

new leaf See TURN OVER A NEW LEAF.

new lease on life *n. phr.* A new chance to live; an improved manner of living. ♦*After his illness and his retirement, living in Hawaii was a new lease on life.*

new man *n.* A person who has become very much better. ♦*Diet and exercise made a new man of him.*

new money *n. phr.* People who have become rich recently. ♦*Since Bobby's father invented a new computer component, Bobby and his family are new money.* Contrast OLD MONEY.

newshawk *n.* A newspaper reporter. ♦*There are always a lot of newshawks following the president.*

next door *adv. or adj.* **1.** In or to the next house or apartment. ♦*He lived next door to me.* ♦*She telephoned next door to ask about John.* ♦*The house next door caught fire.* **2.** Very close.—Used with *to.* ♦*The sick man was next door to death.* ♦*Printing secrets about our country's missiles is next door to treason.*

next to[1] *adv.* Almost; nearly. ♦*It was next to impossible to believe that in a month the grass would be green and flowers would be blooming.* ♦*It was next to unthinkable that the boy would steal.*

next to[2] *prep.* Just after; second to. ♦*Next to his family, baseball was his greatest love.* ♦*Next to pizza, Bob liked hamburger best.*

next to nothing *n. phr.* Very little; almost nothing. ♦*They gave me next to nothing for my old car when I traded it in for a new one.* ♦*When he first started to work, Mr. Black earned next to nothing.*

nice Nelly[1] *or* **nice Nellie** *n., informal* Someone who acts too good to be true; a prude; a prig. ♦*We took him for a nice Nelly when he wouldn't fight.*

nice Nelly[2] *or* **nice Nellie** *adj., informal* Too careful not to say or do anything wrong or improper; too proper; prudish. ♦*Her nice Nelly behavior made her unpopular at school.*

Nick See FULL OF THE OLD NICK.

nick See IN THE NICK OF TIME.

nigger in the woodpile *n. phr., slang.* Something unexpected that changes a situation; a hidden factor or trick.— Racist and offensive, but commonly used in the past. ♦*I knew there had to be a nigger in the woodpile, because the man was being much too generous.* ♦*When the salesman gave him an extra tire for his bike, the boy suspected a nigger in the woodpile.*

night See FLY-BY-NIGHT, MAKE A NIGHT OF IT.

night and day See DAY AND NIGHT.

nightcap *n.* A good-night drink; a drink taken just before bedtime. ♦*Let's have a nightcap and then go to sleep.* ♦*Would you like to come up to my place for a nightcap?*

night letter *n.* A telegram sent at night at a cheaper rate and delivered in the morning. ♦*I waited until after six o'clock in the evening before sending the telegram home because I can say more for the same price in a night letter.*

night life *n. phr.* Entertainment at night. ♦*People in the city are able to find more night life than those who live in the country.*

night owl *n. phr.* One who sleeps during the day and stays up or works during the night. ♦*Tom hardly ever sleeps at night; he prefers to work by lamp light and has become a regular night owl.* Compare GRAVEYARD SHIFT.

nine See CAT HAS NINE LIVES, ON CLOUD NINE.

nine-to-five job *n. phr.* A typical office job that starts at 9 A.M. and ends at 5 P.M. with a one-hour lunch break at 12 noon or 1 P.M. ♦*We professors are not too well paid but I could never get used to a nine-to-five job.*

ninety See GAY NINETIES.

nip and tuck *adj. or adv., informal* Evenly matched; hard fought to the finish. ♦*The game was nip and tuck until the last minute.* ♦*It was a nip and* tuck race right to the finish line. ♦ The two salesmen fought nip and tuck for the contract all the way. Compare NECK AND NECK.

nip in the bud v. phr. To check at the outset; prevent at the start; block or destroy in the beginning. ♦ The police nipped the plot in the bud. ♦ The teacher nipped the disorder in the bud.

no account[1] adj. Of no importance. ♦ The lowly clerk's opinion is of no account in this matter.

no account[2] n. phr. A person of low social station. ♦ Fred was first considered a no account but he soon proved himself to be a person of great ability.

nobody See IT'S AN ILL WIND THAT BLOWS NOBODY GOOD.

nobody home slang 1. Your attention is somewhere else, not on what is being said or done here; you are absent-minded. ♦ The teacher asked him a question three times but he still looked out the window. She gave up, saying, "Nobody home." 2. You are feeble-minded or insane. ♦ He pointed to the woman, tapped his head, and said, "Nobody home."

nobody's fool n. phr. A smart person; a person who knows what he is doing; a person who can take care of himself. ♦ In the classroom and on the football field, Henry was nobody's fool. Contrast BORN YESTERDAY.

nod See LAND OF NOD.

nodding acquaintance n. Less than casual acquaintance. ♦ I have never spoken to the chancellor; we have only a nodding acquaintance.

no deal or **no dice** or **no go** or **no sale** or **no soap** slang Not agreed to; refused or useless; without success or result; no; certainly not.—Used in the predicate or to refuse something. ♦ Billy wanted to let Bob join the team, but I said that it was no deal because Bob was too young. ♦ "Let me have a dollar." "No dice!" answered Joe. ♦ I tried to get Mary on the telephone but it was no go. ♦ "Let's go to the beach tomorrow." "No sale, I have my music lesson tomorrow." ♦ I asked Dad for a new bicycle but it was no soap. Compare NOTHING DOING, NO USE.

no doubt adv. 1. Without doubt; doubtless; surely; certainly. ♦ No doubt

Susan was the smartest girl in her class. 2. Probably. ♦ John will no doubt telephone us if he comes to town.

no end adv., informal 1. Very much; exceedingly. ♦ Jim was no end upset because he couldn't go swimming. 2. Almost without stopping; continually. ♦ The baby cried no end.

no end to or informal **no end of** So many, or so much of, as to seem almost endless; very many or very much. ♦ There was no end to the letters pouring into the post office. ♦ Bob and Dick became close friends and had no end of fun together.

no frills n. phr. A firm or product that offers no extras; a generic product that carries no expensive label. ♦ We went on a no frills trip to Europe with few luxuries.

noggin See USE ONE'S HEAD or USE ONE'S NOGGIN.

no go See NO DEAL.

no good adj. phr. Not satisfactory; not adequate; not approved. ♦ "That's no good," I told him when he began to cry. ♦ He was no good at arithmetic. ♦ He tried appealing to the man's pride, but it did no good.

no great shakes adj., informal Mediocre; unimportant. ♦ Joe Wilson is no great shakes.

no hard feelings n. phr. A lack of resentment or anger; a state of peace and forgiveness. ♦ "No hard feelings," he said. "You should feel free to make constructive criticism any time."

no kidding n. phr. Without jokes or teasing; honestly spoken. ♦ "You actually won the lottery?" Dick asked. "No kidding," Joe replied. "I really did."

no longer adv. Not any more; not at the present time. ♦ He could no longer be trusted and they had to let him go. ♦ The shore was no longer in sight.

no love lost n. phr. Bad feeling; ill will. ♦ Bob and Dick both wanted to be elected captain of the team, and there was no love lost between them. ♦ There was no love lost between the sales and the accounting departments.

no matter 1. Not anything important. ♦ I wanted to see him before he left but it's no matter. 2. It makes no difference; regardless of. ♦ She was going to be a singer no matter what difficulties she *met.* ♦*He had to get the car fixed no matter how much it cost.* ♦*No matter what you try to do, it is important to be able to speak well.* ♦*You can't go in no matter who you are.* ♦*Mary wanted to get to school on time, no matter if she went without breakfast.*

no matter what *adv. phr.* Under any circumstances. ♦*We will go to Europe this summer, no matter what.* ♦*Charles had decided to go to the football game and he felt he must go no matter what.* Compare COME HELL OR HIGH WATER.

nonce See FOR THE TIME BEING *also* FOR THE NONCE.

none See HALF A LOAF IS BETTER THAN NONE, HAVE NONE OF.

none too *adv.* Not very; not at all. ♦*The doctor arrived none too soon as Lucy's fever was alarmingly high.*

nonsense See STUFF AND NONSENSE.

nonstarter *n.* An idea, plan, or project that doesn't work or is obviously no good. ♦*His plan to start a new private school is a nonstarter because he is unable to organize anything.*

noodle See USE ONE'S HEAD *or* USE ONE'S NOODLE.

no picnic *n. phr.* Something arduous; something that requires great effort to accomplish. ♦*It is no picnic to climb Mount Everest.* Contrast A PIECE OF CAKE, A CINCH, EASY AS APPLE PIE.

nor See NEITHER FISH NOR FOWL, NEITHER HERE NOR THERE, NEITHER HIDE NOR HAIR.

no sale See NO DEAL.

nose See COUNT HEADS *or* COUNT NOSES, CUT OFF ONE'S NOSE TO SPITE ONE'S FACE, FOLLOW ONE'S NOSE, GO INTO A TAIL SPIN *or* GO INTO A NOSE DIVE, HARD-NOSED, KEEP ONE'S NOSE CLEAN, KEEP ONE'S NOSE TO THE GRINDSTONE, LEAD BY THE NOSE, LOOK DOWN ONE'S NOSE AT, ON THE NOSE, PAY THROUGH THE NOSE, PUT ONE'S NOSE OUT OF JOINT, SEE BEYOND ONE'S NOSE, SKIN OFF ONE'S NOSE, THUMB ONE'S NOSE, TURN UP ONE'S NOSE AT, UNDER ONE'S NOSE.

nose about *or* **nose around** *v. phr., informal* To look for something kept private or secret; poke about; explore; inquire; pry. ♦*In Grandmother's attic, Sally spent a while nosing about in the old family pictures.* ♦*The detective was* nosing around in the crowd looking for pickpockets.

nose down *v., of an aircraft* To head down; bring down the nose of. ♦*The big airliner began to nose down for a landing.* ♦*The pilot nosed the plane down toward the runway.*

nose in[1] *or* **nose into**[1] *informal* Prying or pestering interest in; unwelcome interest in; impolite curiosity. ♦*He always had his nose in other people's business.* Contrast NOSE OUT OF.

nose in[2] *or* **nose into**[2] *v.* To move in close; move slowly in with the front first. ♦*The ship nosed into the pier.* ♦*The car nosed into the curb.*

nose in a book *n. phr.* Busy interest in reading.—Used with a possessive. ♦*Mother can't get Mary to help do the housework; she always has her nose in a book.*

nose is out of joint See PUT ONE'S NOSE OUT OF JOINT.

nose out *v., informal* **1.** To learn by effort (something private or secret); uncover. ♦*The principal nosed out the truth about the stolen examination.* **2.** To defeat by a nose length; come in a little ahead of in a race or contest. ♦*The horse we liked nosed out the second horse in a very close finish.* ♦*The Democratic candidate nosed out his rival for Congress by a few hundred votes.*

nose out of *informal* Curious attention; bothering.—Usually used with a possessive and usually used with *keep.* ♦*When Billy asked his sister where she was going she told him to keep his nose out of her business.* Contrast NOSE IN.

nose over *v.* To turn over on the nose so as to land upside down. ♦*The airplane made a faulty landing approach and nosed over.*

nose up *v.* To head up; incline the forward end upwards; move up. ♦*The airplane nosed up through the cloud bank.* ♦*The pilot nosed the plane up from the field.*

no-show *n., informal* A person who makes a reservation, e.g., at a hotel or at an airline, and then neither claims nor cancels it. ♦*The airlines were messed up because of a great number of no-show passengers.*

no sooner ——— than As soon as; at once when; immediately when. ♦*No* *sooner did he signal to turn than the other car turned in front of him.* ♦ *No sooner were the picnic baskets unpacked than it began to rain.*

no spring chicken *n. phr.* A person who is no longer young. ♦ *Even though she is no spring chicken anymore, men still turn their heads to look at her.*

no sweat[1] *adj., slang, informal* Easily accomplished, uncomplicated. ♦ *That job was no sweat.*

no sweat[2] *adv.* Easily. ♦ *We did it no sweat.*

not a few See QUITE A FEW.

not a leg to stand on *n. phr., informal* No good proof or excuse; no good evidence or defense to offer. ♦ *The man with a gun and $300 in his pocket was accused of robbing an oil station. He did not have a leg to stand on.*

not a little See QUITE A LITTLE.

not all there *adj. phr.* Not completely alert mentally; absentminded; not together. ♦ *Bill is a wonderful guy but he is just not all there.*

not at all See AT ALL.

not bad *or* **not so bad** *or* **not half bad** *adj., informal* Pretty good; all right; good enough. ♦ *The party last night was not bad.* ♦ *It was not so bad, as inexpensive vacations go.* ♦ *The show was not half bad.*

not by a long shot See BY A LONG SHOT.

not by any means See BY NO MEANS.

notch See TIGHTEN ONE'S BELT.

note See COMPARE NOTES, TAKE NOTE OF.

not for all the coffee in Brazil *or* **not for all the tea in China** *or* **not for anything in the world** *or* **not for love or money** See NOT FOR THE WORLD.

not for the world *or* **not for worlds** *adv. phr.* Not at any price; not for anything. ♦ *I wouldn't hurt his feelings for the world.* ♦ *Not for worlds would he let his children go hungry.*

not half bad See NOT BAD.

not have anything on See HAVE NOTHING ON.

not have the heart to *v. phr.* To not be insensitive or cruel. ♦ *My boss did not have the heart to lay off two pregnant women when they most needed their jobs.*

nothing See GO FOR NOTHING, HAVE NOTHING ON, HERE GOES NOTHING, IN

NO TIME *or* IN NOTHING FLAT, NOT TO MENTION *or* TO SAY NOTHING OF.

nothing doing *adv. phr., informal* I will not do it; certainly not; no indeed; no. ♦ *"Will you lend me a dollar?" "Nothing doing!"* ♦ *"Let's go for a boat ride!" "Nothing doing!"* Compare NO DEAL.

nothing if not *adv. phr.* Without doubt; certainly. ♦ *With its bright furnishings, flowers, and sunny windows, the new hospital dayroom is nothing if not cheerful.*

nothing like See ANYTHING LIKE.

nothing of the kind *adv. phr.* On the contrary. ♦ *"Did you quit your job?" he asked. "No, I did nothing of the kind," she answered.*

nothing short of *adv. phr.* Absolutely; thoroughly; completely. ♦ *Olivier's performance in* Hamlet *was nothing short of magnificent.*

nothing succeeds like success Success in one thing makes success in other things easier; people like a successful person.—A proverb. ♦ *The girls all like Bob because he is football captain. Nothing succeeds like success.*

nothing to it *adj. phr.* Presenting no serious challenge; easily accomplished. ♦ *Once you learn how to tread water, swimming is really easy; there is nothing to it.* Compare EASY AS APPLE PIE, A CINCH, A PIECE OF CAKE.

nothing to sneeze at See SNEEZE AT.

notice See SIT UP AND TAKE NOTICE, TAKE NOTE OF *or* TAKE NOTICE OF.

not in the least *adv. phr.* Not at all. ♦ *She was not in the least interested in listening to a long lecture on ethics.*

notion See HALF A MIND *also* HALF A NOTION, TAKE INTO ONE'S HEAD *or* TAKE A NOTION.

not know which way to turn *or* **not know which way to jump** *v. phr.* To be puzzled about getting out of a difficulty; not know what to do to get out of trouble. ♦ *When Jane missed the last bus home, she didn't know which way to turn.* ♦ *After Mr. Brown died, Mrs. Brown had no money to pay the bills. When the landlord told her to pay the rent or move out, she didn't know which way to jump.*

not let any grass grow under one's feet See LET GRASS GROW UNDER ONE'S FEET.

not one's cup of tea See CUP OF TEA.

not one's scene See CUP OF TEA.

not on your life *adv. phr., informal* Certainly not; not ever; not for any reason.—Used for emphasis. ♦ *I wouldn't drive a car with brakes like that—not on your life.* ♦ *Did he thank me for my advice? Not on your life.*

not see beyond one's nose See SEE BEYOND ONE'S NOSE.

not so bad See NOT BAD.

not so hot *or* **not too hot** *adj. phr.* Ineffective; not very good. ♦ *His plans to rebuild the house in a hurry obviously weren't so hot.*

not the only fish in the sea *n. phr.* One of many; not the only one of the kind; not the only one available. ♦ *He said he could find other girls—she was not the only fish in the sea.* Compare NOT THE ONLY PEBBLE ON THE BEACH.

not the only pebble on the beach *n. phr.* Not the only person to be considered; one of many. ♦ *George was acting pretty self-important and we finally had to tell him that he wasn't the only pebble on the beach.* Compare NOT THE ONLY FISH IN THE SEA.

not the thing *n. phr.* Not the accepted form of action; something socially improper. ♦ *It is simply not the thing to wear blue jeans to the opera.*

not to get to first base *v. phr.* To fail to make initial progress; have no success at all. ♦ *I tried various ways to make Mary interested in me as a potential husband, but I couldn't even get to first base.*

not to give one the time of day *v. phr., slang, informal* To dislike someone strongly enough so as to totally ignore him. ♦ *Sue wouldn't give Helen the time of day.*

not to give quarter *v. phr.* **1.** To be utterly unwilling to show mercy; not to allow a weaker or defeated party the chance to save themselves through escape. ♦ *The occupying foreign army gave no quarter—they took no prisoners, shot everyone, and made escape impossible.* **2.** To argue so forcefully during a negotiation or in a court of law as to make any counter-argument or counter-proposal impossible. ♦ *The District Attorney hammered away at the witnesses and gave no quarter to the attorney for the defense.*

not to know one from Adam *v. phr.* To not know a person; be unable to recognize someone. ♦ *I have no idea who that guy is that Jane just walked in with; I don't know him from Adam.*

not to know the first thing about *v. phr.* To be totally ignorant about a certain issue. ♦ *Al assured us that he didn't know the first thing about Mary's whereabouts.*

not to know what to make of *v. phr.* To be unable to decipher; be unable to identify; not know how to decide what something really is. ♦ *I got a mysterious letter asking me to meet Santa Claus at 6 P.M. at the supermarket. Is this a joke? I don't know what to make of it.*

not to know whether one is coming or going *v. phr.* To be completely confused. ♦ *He was so perplexed he didn't know whether he was coming or going.* Compare AT SEA 2.

not to lift a finger *v. phr.* To not help in the slightest degree. ♦ *"My husband won't lift a finger to help me," she complained, "although we have 12 people coming for dinner."*

not to mention *or* **not to speak of** *or* **to say nothing of** Without ever needing to speak of; in addition to; besides.— Used to add something to what you have said or explained. ♦ *Dave is handsome and smart not to mention being a good athlete.* ♦ *They have three fine sons, not to speak of their two lovely daughters.* ♦ *Sally takes singing and dancing lessons to say nothing of swimming and tennis lessons.* Compare LET ALONE, TO SPEAK OF.

not to speak of See NOT TO MENTION.

not to touch (something) with a ten-foot pole *v. phr.* To consider something completely undesirable or uninteresting. ♦ *Some people won't touch spinach with a ten-foot pole.* ♦ *Kids who wouldn't touch an encyclopedia with a ten-foot pole love to find information with this computer program.*

not worth a dime See NOT WORTH A TINKER'S DAMN.

not worth a hill of beans See NOT WORTH A TINKER'S DAMN.

not worth a red cent See NOT WORTH A TINKER'S DAMN.

not worth a tinker's damn *or* **not worth a tinker's dam** *adj. phr., informal* Not worth anything; valueless. ♦ *As a bricklayer he was not worth a tinker's damn.* ♦ *I am not familiar with the subject so my opinion would not be worth a tinker's dam.*

no two ways about it *n. phr.* No other choice; no alternative. ♦ *The boss said there were no two ways about it; we would all have to work late to finish the job.*

no use *n.* **1.** No purpose; no object; no gain. ♦ *There's no use in crying about your broken bicycle.* ♦ *Bob said, "Let's try again." Dick answered, "It's no use."* **2.** Bad opinion; no respect; no liking.—Usually used after *have.* ♦ *He had no use for dogs after a dog bit him.* ♦ *Jimmy had no use for arithmetic because it was hard for him.*

no use crying over spilled milk *or* **no use crying over spilt milk** See CRY OVER SPILLED MILK.

now See EVERY NOW AND THEN *or* EVERY NOW AND AGAIN, HERE AND NOW, JUST NOW.

now and then *or* **now and again** *adv. phr.* Not often; not regularly; occasionally; sometimes. ♦ *Now and then he goes to a ball game.* ♦ *The maid broke a dish now and then.* Syn. AT TIMES, FROM TIME TO TIME, ONCE IN A WHILE. Compare EVERY NOW AND THEN, OFF AND ON.

nowhere See OUT OF NOWHERE.

nowhere near See ANYTHING LIKE.

now ——— now *coord. adv.* Sometimes... sometimes; by turns; at one time...then at another.—Often used with adjectives that are very different or opposite, especially to show change. ♦ *The weather changed every day; it was now hot, now cool.* ♦ *The band played different songs, now fast, now slow; now soft, now loud.* ♦ *Billy ran so quickly he seemed to be all over the field; he was now here and now there.*

no way *adv.* Not at all; never; under no circumstances. ♦ *Do you think I will do the house chores alone? No way!*

no wonder *also* **small wonder** *adj.* Not surprising; to be expected. ♦ *It is no wonder that the children love to visit the farm.* ♦ *The Browns didn't go to the fair. Small wonder—they dislike large noisy crowds.*

now or never *adv. phr.* Exclusively at the present time. ♦ *Mike said, "Now that Paul has resigned, there is a perfect place for you. It is now or never!"*

now that *conj.* Since; because; now. ♦ *Now that dinner is ready, wash your hands.* ♦ *You came early, but now that you're here, take off your coat.* Syn. INASMUCH AS.

nth See TO THE NTH DEGREE.

nuisance See PUBLIC NUISANCE.

nuke *v.* To fix any meal in a microwave oven. ♦ *When we are in a hurry, we nuke some beef.*

nuke a tater *v. phr.* **1.** To bake a potato in a microwave oven. ♦ *"We have no time for standard baked potatoes in the oven," she said. "We'll just have to nuke a tater."*

null and void *adj.* Not worth anything; no longer valid. ♦ *Both the seller and the buyer agreed to forget about their previous contract and to consider it null and void.*

number See A NUMBER, ANY NUMBER, DAYS ARE NUMBERED, GET ONE'S NUMBER, HOT NUMBER, QUITE A FEW *or* QUITE A NUMBER.

number among *v. phr.* Consider as one of; consider to be a part of. ♦ *I number Al among my best friends.*

number one[1] *or* **Number One**[1] *n. phr., informal* Yourself; your own interests; your private or selfish advantage. Usually used in the phrase *look out for number one.* ♦ *He was well known for his habit of always looking out for number one.*

number one[2] *adj. phr.* **1.** Of first rank or importance; foremost; principal. ♦ *He is easily America's number one golfer.* **2.** Of first grade; of top quality; best. ♦ *That is number one western steer beef.*

nurse See VISITING NURSE.

nurse a drink *v. phr., informal* To hold a drink in one's hand at a party, pretending to be drinking it or taking extremely small sips only. ♦ *John's been nursing that drink all evening.*

nurse a grudge *v. phr.* To keep a feeling of envy or dislike toward some person; remember something bad that a person said or did to you, and dislike the person because of that. ♦ *Tom nursed a grudge against John because John took his place on the basketball team.* ♦ *Mary nursed a grudge against her teacher because she thought she* *deserved a better grade in English.*

nursing home See CONVALESCENT HOME.

nut See HARD NUT TO CRACK *or* TOUGH NUT TO CRACK.

nut case *n. phr.* A very silly, crazy, or foolish person. ♦*I am going to be a nut case if I don't go on a vacation pretty soon.*

nuts about See CRAZY ABOUT.

nuts and bolts of *n. phr.* The basic facts or important details of something. ♦*"Ted will be an excellent trader," his millionaire grandfather said, "once he learns the nuts and bolts of the profession."*

nutshell See IN A NUTSHELL.

nutty as a fruitcake *adj. phr., slang* Very crazy; entirely mad. ♦*He looked all right, as we watched him approach, but when he began to talk, we saw that he was as nutty as a fruitcake.*

oak See GREAT OAKS FROM LITTLE ACORNS GROW.

oars See REST ON ONE'S OARS.

oath See TAKE OATH.

oats See FEEL ONE'S OATS, SOW ONE'S WILD OATS.

obey the call of nature See ANSWER THE CALL OF NATURE.

occasion See ON OCCASION.

occupy oneself *v. phr.* To make oneself busy with. ◆*Having retired from business, he now occupies himself with his stamp collection.*

oddball *n., slang, informal* An eccentric person; one who doesn't act like everyone else. ◆*John is an oddball—he never invites anyone.*

odd jobs *n. phr.* Work that is not steady or regular in nature; small, isolated tasks. ◆*Dan does odd jobs for his neighbors, barely making enough to eat.*

odds See BY ALL ODDS.

odds and ends *n. phr.* Miscellaneous items; remnants. ◆*After the great annual clearance sale there were only a few odds and ends left in the store.*

odds are against *v. phr.* The likelihood of success is not probable; the chances of success are poor. ◆*The odds are against her getting here before Monday.*

odds-on *adj., informal* Almost certain; almost sure; probable. ◆*Ed is the odds-on choice for class president, because he has good sense and good humor.*

of age *adj. phr.* **1a.** Old enough to be allowed to do or manage something. ◆*Mary will be of driving age on her next birthday.* Contrast OVER AGE, UNDER AGE. **1b.** Old enough to vote; having the privileges of adulthood. ◆*The age at which one is considered of age to vote, or of age to buy alcoholic drinks, or of age to be prosecuted as an adult, varies within the United States.* **2.** Fully developed; mature. ◆*Education for the foreign born came of age when bilingual education was accepted as a necessary part of the public school system.*

of a piece *adj. phr.* Of the same kind; in line.—Usually used with *with.* ◆*His* quitting the job is of a piece with his dropping out of school.

of course *adv. phr.* **1.** As you would expect; naturally. ◆*Bob hit Herman, and Herman hit him back, of course.* ◆*The rain came pouring down, and of course the track meet was canceled.* **2.** Without a doubt; certainly; surely. ◆*Of course you know that girl; she's in your class.*

off a duck's back See LIKE WATER OFF A DUCK'S BACK.

off-again, on-again *or* **on-again, off-again** *adj. phr., informal* Not settled; changeable; uncertain. ◆*John and Susan had an off-again, on-again romance.* ◆*I don't like this off-again, on-again business. Are we going to have the party or not?*

off and on *also* **on and off** *adv.* Not regularly; occasionally; sometimes. ◆*Joan wrote to a pen pal in England off and on for several years.* ◆*It rained off and on all day.*—Sometimes used with hyphens like an adjective. ◆*A worn-out cord may make a hearing aid work in an off-and-on way.* Compare BY FITS AND STARTS, FROM TIME TO TIME, NOW AND THEN.

off balance *adj. phr.* **1.** Not in balance; not able to stand up straight and not fall; not able to keep from turning over or falling; unsteady. ◆*Never stand up in a canoe; it will get off balance and turn over.* ◆*Paul was speeding along on his bicycle, when an unexpected hole in the road caught him off balance and he fell over.* **2.** Not prepared; not ready; unable to meet something unexpected. ◆*Our quarterback kept the other team off balance by changing often from line plays to passes and tricky end runs.* ◆*The teacher's surprise test caught the class off balance, and nearly everyone got a poor mark.*

off base *adj. phr., informal* Not agreeing with fact; wrong. ◆*The idea that touching a toad causes warts is off base.* ◆*When Tom said that the teacher's explanation did not agree with the book, the teacher was embarrassed at being caught off base.*

offbeat *adj., informal* Nonconventional; different from the usual; odd.

♦ *Linguistics used to be an offbeat field, but nowadays every self-respecting university has a linguistics department.*

off center *adv. phr.* Not exactly in the middle. ♦ *Mary hung the picture off center, because it was more interesting that way.*

off-center *adj., informal* Different from the usual pattern; not quite like most others; odd. ♦ *Roger's sense of humor was a bit off-center.* Compare OFF-KEY.

off-color or **off-colored** *adj.* **1.** Not of the proper hue or shade; not matching a standard color sample. ♦ *The librarian complained that the painter had used an off-color green on the walls.* **2.** *informal* Not of the proper kind for polite society; in bad taste; dirty. ♦ *When Joe finished his off-color story, no one was pleased.*

off day *n. phr.* A period when one is not functioning at his or her best; a period of weakness. ♦ *The champion was obviously having an off day; otherwise she would have been able to defeat her opponent.* Contrast DAY OFF.

off duty *adj.* Not supposed to be at work; having free time; not working. ♦ *Sailors like to go sight-seeing, when they are off duty in a foreign port.* ♦ *It seems that all the taxis in New York are off duty whenever it rains.*—Often used with hyphens, before a noun. ♦ *The bank robber was captured by an off-duty policeman.* Contrast ON DUTY.

off feed or **off one's feed** *adj. phr., informal* Not feeling well; lacking in vitality; droopy; moody. ♦ *Mary was worried; her canary was off feed.* ♦ *Jerry seemed to be off his feed; he did not joke and laugh with the others.*

off (one/he/she/it) **goes!** *v. phr.* Said of a person, a vehicle, or a memorable thing who/which has started leaving or moving, both as a statement of fact (declarative assertion) or as a command (imperative). ♦ *When the boat hit the water in the formal launching ceremony, they cried out simultaneously, "Off she goes!"*

off guard *adj.* In a careless attitude; not alert to coming danger; not watching. ♦ *In the second that the boxer was off guard, his opponent landed a knockout punch.* ♦ *Timmy's question caught Jean off guard, and she told him the secret*

before she knew it. Contrast ON GUARD.

offhand *adj.* **1.** Informal; casual; careless. ♦ *Dick found Bob's offhand manner inappropriate for business.* **2.** In an improvised fashion. ♦ *Offhand, I would guess that at least five thousand people attended the festival.*

off in a flash See IN A FLASH.

off-key *adj., informal* **1.** Not proper; queer. ♦ *When George told jokes at the funeral, everyone thought his action was off-key.* **2.** In a false key. ♦ *John always sings off-key.* Compare OUT OF LINE.

off limits See OUT OF BOUNDS.

off one's back *adj. phr.* **1.** *informal* Stopped from bothering one; removed as an annoyance or pest. ♦ *"Having a kid brother always following me is a nuisance," Mary told her mother. "Can't you get him off my back?"* ♦ *The singer was so popular with teenagers that he took a secret vacation, to keep them off his back.* Contrast ON ONE'S BACK **2.** See GIVE THE SHIRT OFF ONE'S BACK.

off one's chest *adj. phr., informal* Told to someone and so not bothering you anymore; not making you feel worried or upset, because you have talked about it. ♦ *After Dave told the principal that he had cheated on the test, he was glad because it was off his chest.* ♦ *Father felt that Tom wasn't helping enough around the house, so he got it off his chest by giving Tom a list of things to do.* Compare MAKE A CLEAN BREAST OF. Contrast ON ONE'S CHEST.

off one's feet See KNOCK OFF ONE'S FEET, SWEEP OFF ONE'S FEET.

off one's hands *adv. phr.* No longer in your care or possession. ♦ *Ginny was glad to have the sick dog taken off her hands by the doctor.* Contrast ON ONE'S HANDS.

off one's head *adj. phr.* Crazy; mad. ♦ *We had no doubt that the old man was off his head when we saw him jumping into the lake with his winter coat on.*

off one's high horse *adj. phr., informal* **1.** Not acting proud and scornful; humble and agreeable. ♦ *The girls were so kind to Nancy after her mother died that she came down off her high horse* *and made friends with them.* **2.** Acting friendly again; not angry and unpleasant any more; agreeable. ♦*Sally wouldn't speak to anyone all afternoon because she couldn't go to the movies, but she's off her high horse now.* Contrast ON ONE'S HIGH HORSE.

off one's nut See OFF ONE'S HEAD.

off one's rocker *or* **off one's trolley** *adj. phr., informal* Not thinking correctly; crazy; silly; foolish. ♦*Tom is off his rocker if he thinks he can run faster than Bob can.* ♦*If you think you can learn to figure skate in one lesson, you're off your trolley.* Syn. OUT OF ONE'S HEAD.

off one's trolley See OFF ONE'S ROCKER.

off season See LOW SEASON. Contrast HIGH SEASON, ON SEASON.

offshoot *n.* A derivative; a side product. ♦*The discovery of nuclear reactors was an offshoot of research in quantum physics.*

off the air *adj. phr.* Not broadcasting; observing radio silence. ♦*The talk show is off the air on Wednesdays and Fridays.*

off the bat See RIGHT AWAY *or* RIGHT OFF THE BAT.

off the beam *adv. or adj. phr.* **1.** *(Of an airplane)* Not in the radio beam that marks the path to follow between airports; flying in the wrong direction. ♦*A radio signal tells the pilot of an airplane when his plane is off the beam.* **2.** *slang* Wrong; mistaken. ♦*Maud was off the beam when she said that the girls didn't like her.* Contrast ON THE BEAM.

off the beaten track *adv. phr.* Not well known or often used; not gone to or seen by many people; unusual. ♦*This theater is off the beaten track.* ♦*We are looking for a vacation spot that is off the beaten track.* Compare OUT OF THE WAY.

off the cuff *adv. phr., informal* Without preparing ahead of time what you will say; without preparation. ♦*Some presidents like to speak off the cuff to newspaper reporters but others prefer to think questions over and write their answers.*

off-the-cuff *adj., informal* Not prepared ahead of time.—Used of a speech or remarks. ♦*Jack was made master of ceremonies because he was a good off-the-cuff speaker.*

off the ground   See GET OFF THE GROUND.

off the handle See FLY OFF THE HANDLE.

off the hog See LIVE HIGH OFF THE HOG.

off the hook *adv. phr.* Out of trouble; out of an awkward or embarrassing situation. ♦*Thelma found she had made two dates for the same night; she asked Sally to get her off the hook by going out with one of the boys.*

off the record[1] *adv. phr.* Confidentially. ♦*"Off the record," the boss said, "you will get a good raise for next year, but you'll have to wait for the official letter."* Contrast ON RECORD, GO ON RECORD, JUST FOR THE RECORD.

off the record[2] *adj. phr.* Not to be published or told; secret; confidential. ♦*The president told the reporters his remarks were strictly off the record.—* Sometimes used with hyphens, before the noun. ♦*The governor was angry when a newspaper printed his off-the-record comments.*

off the top of one's head *adv. or adj. phr., informal* Without thinking hard; quickly. ♦*Vin answered the teacher's question off the top of his head.* ♦*When Lorraine was asked to recite, she talked off the top of her head.*

off the wagon *adj. phr., slang* No longer refusing to drink whiskey or other alcoholic beverages; drinking liquor again, after stopping for a while. ♦*When a heavy drinker quits he must really quit. One little drink of whiskey is enough to drive him off the wagon.* Contrast ON THE WAGON.

off the wall *adj. phr.* Strange; out of the ordinary; stupid. ♦*He has been making off-the-wall remarks all day; something must be the matter with him.*

of it See WHAT OF IT.

of late *adv. phr., formal* In the recent past; not long ago; a short time ago; lately; recently. ♦*There have been too many high school dropouts of late.*

of necessity *adv. phr.* Because there is no other way; because it must be; necessarily. ♦*Being a professional actor of necessity means working nights and Sundays.*

of no avail See TO NO AVAIL.

of old[1] *adj. phr.* Of ancient times; of long ago. ♦*Knights of old had to wear armor in battle.*

of old² *adv. phr.* From earlier experience. ♦ *You won't get any money from Freddie. I know him of old.*

of oneself See GIVE OF ONESELF.

of one's life *adj. phr.* The best or worst; greatest.—Usually describing a time or effort. ♦ *At Disneyland, Tommy had the time of his life.* ♦ *His race for the presidency was the political fight of his life.*

of one's own accord *or* **of one's own free will** *adv. phr.* Without suggestion or help from anyone else; without being told; voluntarily. ♦ *On her mother's birthday, Betsy did the dishes of her own accord.* ♦ *But Johnny hates baths. I can't believe he would take one of his own free will.*

of one's own free will See OF ONE'S OWN ACCORD.

of service *adj. phr.* Valuable as a source of aid; helpful; useful. ♦ *When a visitor seems lost or confused, the courteous student will ask "May I be of service?"* ♦ *A good jackknife is often of service to a camper.*

of sorts *or* **of a sort** *adj. phr.* Not especially good; not very good; of common quality. ♦ *Joel was a magician of sorts, and popular at parties.*

often See EVERY NOW AND THEN *or* EVERY SO OFTEN, MORE OFTEN THAN NOT.

of the devil See SPEAK OF THE DEVIL AND HE APPEARS.

of the first water *adj. phr., informal* Of the finest quality; superior; very good; best. ♦ *The jeweler chose diamonds of the first water for the queen's crown.* ♦ *The dance program at graduation was of the first water.* Compare FIRST-CLASS.

of the same mind *adv. phr.* In agreement; in consonance. ♦ *It is a good thing when father and son are of the same mind regarding business and politics.*

oil See POUR OIL ON TROUBLED WATERS.

oil the wheels See GREASE THE WHEELS.

ointment See FLY IN THE OINTMENT.

old See CHIP OFF THE OLD BLOCK, COMFORTABLE AS AN OLD SHOE, COMMON AS AN OLD SHOE, OF OLD.

old as the hills *adj. phr.* Very old; ancient. ♦ *"Why didn't you laugh?" she asked. "Because that joke is as old as the hills," he answered.*

old boy network *n. phr.* A system whereby men who went to the same school help each other to get good jobs, regardless of their ability or training. ♦ *Peter got his lucrative job thanks to the old boy network rather than because of his qualifications.* Compare OLD COLLEGE TRY.

old boy *or* **old chap** *n., chiefly British* One of the men educated at the same institution and bound by strong ties of loyalty to each other. ♦ *He got the job because the boss was another old boy.*

old college try *n. phr.* An attempt to win a favor from another by mentioning the fact that one had gone to the same college or university as the party from whom the favor is requested. ♦ *Since he needed a job, he decided to use the old college try when he contacted Jerry, but it didn't work.* Compare OLD BOY NETWORK.

old country *n. phr.* Primarily Europe, but also any country other than the United States where one originally came from. ♦ *Al's wife was born in Chicago but Al himself is from the old country, Ireland.*

old flame *n. phr.* An erstwhile lover. ♦ *Did you know that Meg was one of Howard's old flames?*

old guard *n. phr.* People whose ideas may be out of date, but who have been in power for a long time. ♦ *There will not be any change in policy at the company, as long as the old guard still works here.*

old hand *n. phr.* An experienced and highly skilled expert at some particular job. ♦ *Uncle Joe is an old hand at repairing car engines.*

old hat *adj., informal* Old-fashioned; not new or different. ♦ *By now, putting satellites in orbit is old hat to space scientists.* ♦ *Andrea thought her mother's ideas about dating were old hat.*

old maid *n. phr.* A spinster; a woman who has never married. ♦ *Because my old maid aunt is a terrific cook as well as a good-looking woman, nobody understands why she never married.*

old money Contrast NEW MONEY.

Old Nick See FULL OF THE OLD NICK.

old school tie See OLD BOY NETWORK, OLD COLLEGE TRY.

old story *n.* An everyday occurrence; something that often happens. ♦ *Jane's* temper tantrums were an old story. ♦It's an old story when a woman divorces her husband for too much drinking.

old-timer n. An old person who remembers bygone days, matters, and personalities. ♦ There was an old-timer at the party who told us interesting details about World War II. Contrast OLD GUARD, OLD HAND.

old world n. phr. Europe, the continent; a continental manner. ♦ Tom had an old world manner that thoroughly charmed all the ladies. Compare OLD COUNTRY.

olive branch n. phr. An overture; a symbol of peace. ♦ Tired of the constant fighting, the majority government extended an olive branch to the militant minority.

on account adv. phr. As part payment of a debt; to lessen the amount owed. ♦John paid $10 down and $5 on account each month for his bicycle.

on account of prep. As a result of; because of. ♦ The picnic was held in the gym on account of the rain. Compare ON ONE'S ACCOUNT, OF ONE'S OWN ACCORD.

on a dime adv. phr., informal In a very small space. ♦ Bob can turn that car on a dime. ♦ Tom says his new sports car will stop on a dime.

on-again, off-again See OFF-AGAIN, ON-AGAIN.

on air See WALK ON AIR.

on a limb See OUT ON A LIMB.

on all four See HIT ON ALL FOUR.

on all fours adv. phr. **1.** On all four legs; on hands and knees. ♦ Fido sat up to "beg" but dropped down on all fours to eat the dog biscuit Sam gave him. ♦ Billy's father got down on all fours and gave the baby a ride. **2.** informal On a level of equality; of the same value. ♦ Wigs may be widely used, but they are still not on all fours with beautiful natural hair.

on an average or **on the average** adv. phr. In most cases; usually. ♦ On an average Dan's mother has to ask him three times before he helps with the dishes. ♦ On the average, Mr. Blank trades in his car for a new one every three years.

on and off See OFF AND ON.

on an even keel adv. phr., informal In a well-ordered way or condition; orderly. ♦ When the football rally seemed almost ready to become a riot, the principal stepped to the platform and got things back on an even keel.

on a pedestal adv. phr. Lovingly honored and cared for. ♦ Mrs. Raymond's children served her breakfast in bed on Mother's Day and later took her out to dinner. She felt on a pedestal. ♦ Bill is always waiting on his fiancee and bringing her flowers and candy. He has certainly put her on a pedestal.

on approval adv. phr. With the understanding that the thing may be refused. ♦ Mr. Grey bought his camera on approval. ♦ The company offered to send a package of stamps on approval.

on a scratched horse See PUT ONE'S MONEY ON A SCRATCHED HORSE.

on a shoestring adv. phr. With little money to spend; on a very low budget. ♦ The couple was seeing Europe on a shoestring.

on a volcano See SIT ON A VOLCANO.

on behalf of See IN BEHALF OF.

on board[1] prep. On (a ship). ♦Joan was not on board the ship when it sailed.

on board[2] adv. or adj. phr. On a ship. ♦ The captain was not on board when the S.S. Flandre sailed. ♦A ship was leaving the harbor, and we saw the people on board waving.

on borrowed time See LIVE ON BORROWED TIME.

on call adj. phr. **1.** Having to be paid on demand. ♦Jim didn't have the money ready even though he knew the bill was on call. **2.** Ready and available. ♦ This is Dr. Kent's day to be on call at the hospital. ♦ The nurse is on call for emergency cases.

once See AT ONCE, EVERY NOW AND THEN or EVERY ONCE IN A WHILE.

once and for all adv. phr. **1.** One time and never again; without any doubt; surely; certainly; definitely. ♦Let me say, for once and for all, you may not go to the party Saturday. ♦For once and for all, I will not go swimming with you. **2.** Permanently. ♦ Bill and Tom asked the teacher to settle the argument once and for all. ♦ The general decided that two bombs would destroy the enemy and end the war once and for all.

once bitten, twice shy See BURNT CHILD DREADS THE FIRE.

once for all See ONCE AND FOR ALL.

once in a blue moon *adv. phr.* Very rarely; very seldom; almost never. ♦ *Coin collecting is interesting, but you find a valuable coin only once in a blue moon.* ♦ *Once in a blue moon someone grows a very pale marigold, but no truly white marigolds have been raised.*

once in a while *adv. phr.* Not often; not regularly; sometimes; occasionally. ♦ *We go for a picnic in the park once in a while.* ♦ *Once in a while the puppy would run away, but usually he stayed in the yard.* Syn. AT TIMES, FROM TIME TO TIME, NOW AND THEN.

once-over *n., slang* **1.** A quick look; a swift examination of someone or something.—Usually used with *give* or *get.* ♦ *The new boy got the once-over from the rest of the class when he came in.* ♦ *Bob gave his paper the once-over before handing it in.* **2.** *or* **once-over-lightly** A quick or careless job, especially of cleaning or straightening; work done hastily for now. ♦ *Ann gave her room a quick once-over-lightly with the broom and dust cloth.* ♦ *"Just give my hair the once-over," Al said to the barber.* Compare LICK AND A PROMISE.

once upon a time *adv. phr.* Sometime before now, long ago. ♦ *Once upon a time she was thought to be the most talented actress in the country.*—Often used at the beginning of fairy stories. ♦ *Once upon a time there lived a king who had an ugly daughter.*

on cloud nine *adj. phr., slang* Too happy to think of anything else; very happy. ♦ *Ada has been on cloud nine since the magazine printed the story she wrote.* ♦ *We were all on cloud nine when our team won the state championship.* Compare ON TOP OF THE WORLD, WALK ON AIR.

on condition that *conj.* Providing that; if. ♦ *I will lend you the money on condition that you pay it back in one month.* ♦ *She agreed to act in the play on condition that she could keep her costumes.*

on deck *adv. or adj. phr.* **1.** On a floor of a ship open to the outdoors. ♦ *The passengers were playing shuffleboard on deck.* ♦ *The sailors kept busy cleaning and painting on deck.* **2.** *informal* Ready to do something; present. ♦ *The scout leader told the boys to be on deck at 8:00 Saturday morning for the hike.* ♦ *Dick was at bat, and Bob was on deck.*

on deposit *adv. phr.* In a bank. ♦ *I have almost $500 on deposit in my account.* ♦ *The children save their pennies and each month place them on deposit.*

on duty *adj. phr.* Doing one's job; supervising. ♦ *Two soldiers are on duty guarding the gates.* ♦ *There is always one teacher on duty during study hour.* Contrast OFF DUTY.

one See AT ONE, FOR ONE, GO IN ONE EAR AND OUT THE OTHER, HANG ONE ON, HOLE IN ONE, KILL TWO BIRDS WITH ONE STONE, NUMBER ONE, SIX OF ONE AND HALF-A-DOZEN OF THE OTHER, SLIP ONE OVER ON, TEN TO ONE, TWO TO ONE, WORDS OF ONE SYLLABLE.

one and the same *adj. phr.* The same; identical. ♦ *Erle Stanley Gardner and A. A. Fair are one and the same person.* ♦ *The spider lily and the Peruvian Daffodil are one and the same.*

one-armed bandit *n., slang* A slot machine, like those used in Las Vegas and other gambling places. ♦ *Joe was playing the one-armed bandit all day—and he lost everything he had.*

on earth See IN THE WORLD.

on easy street *adj. phr., informal* Having enough money to live very comfortably; rather rich. ♦ *After years of hard work, the Grants found themselves on easy street.* ♦ *Jim's novel was a success and put him on easy street.* Compare IN CLOVER, IN THE CHIPS, WELL-TO-DO.

one damn thing after another *or* **ODTAA** (pronounced owed-tay) *n. phr.* If there is one problem, there will be more. ♦ *First I lost my wallet, then a kid broke the window, and, lastly, my car refused to start. It was just one damn thing after another!* Compare IF IT'S NOT ONE THING IT'S ANOTHER.

on edge *adj. phr.* Excited or nervous; impatient. ♦ *The magician kept the children on edge all through his show.* ♦ *We were all on edge as we listened to the TV for news of the election results.* ♦ *Father was on edge after driving home through the heavy holiday traffic.* See SET ONE'S TEETH ON EDGE. Contrast AT EASE 2.

one eye on *informal* Watching or minding (a person or thing) while doing something else; part of your attention on.—Used after *have, keep,* or *with.* ♦ *Jane had one eye on the baby as she ironed.* ♦ *Bill kept one eye on his books and the other on the clock.* ♦ *Chris tried to study with one eye on the TV set.* Compare KEEP AN EYE ON.

one foot in the grave *n. phr.* Near to death. ♦ *The dog is fourteen years old, blind, and feeble. He has one foot in the grave.* ♦ *Grandfather has never been sick a day in his life, but Mother cares for him as if he had one foot in the grave.*

one for the books *n. phr., informal* Very unusual; a remarkable something. ♦ *The newspaper reporter turned in a story that was one for the books.* ♦ *Their trip through the Rocky Mountains was one for the books.*

one-horse *adj. phr.* Insignificant; modest; provincial. ♦ *Arnold's business is a one-horse operation; he never had a single employee.*

one man's meat is another man's poison What is good for one person is not necessarily good for another.—A proverb. ♦ *Even though Jeff likes to swim in ice cold water, his brother Tim hates it. This is understandable, however, because one's man's meat is another man's poison.* Contrast WHAT'S SAUCE FOR THE GOOSE IS SAUCE FOR THE GANDER.

on end *adj. phr.* Seemingly endless.— Used with plural nouns of time. ♦ *Judy spent hours on end writing and re-writing her essay.* ♦ *During July and August there was no rain for weeks on end.*

one-night stand *n. phr.* **1.** A single performance given by a traveling company while on a tour. ♦ *After they went bankrupt in the big cities, the traveling jazz quartet played one-night stands in the country.* **2.** A brief affair or sexual encounter. ♦ *"With AIDS all around us?" said Jane. "Nobody is having one-night stands anymore."*

one of these days *or* **some of these days** *adv. phr.* Someday; sometime soon. ♦ *One of these days Herbert will be famous.* ♦ *I'm going to do that sewing some of these days.*

one on the city *n., slang* A glass of water (which is provided free of charge, as a free gift from the city). ♦ *What will you have?—Oh, just give me one on the city.*

one's money's worth *n. phr.* A fair return on one's money spent or invested. ♦ *I wouldn't say that the trip was a great bargain, but I feel that we got our money's worth.*

one's own row See HOE ONE'S OWN ROW.

one-two *n.* **1.** A succession of two punches, the first a short left, followed by a hard right punch, usually in the jaw. ♦ *Ali gave Frazier the one-two.* **2.** Any quick or decisive action which takes the opposition by surprise, thereby ensuring victory. ♦ *He gave us the old one-two and won the game.*

one up *adj. phr.* Having an advantage; being one step ahead. ♦ *John graduated from high school; he is one up on Bob, who dropped out.* ♦ *The Platters are one up on their neighbors. They own the only color television set in their neighborhood.*

one-upmanship *v., informal* Always keeping ahead of others; trying to keep an advantage. ♦ *No matter what I do, I find that Jim has already done it better. He's an expert at one-upmanship.* ♦ *Jack took the news to the principal while we were still talking about it. He's very quick to practice one-upmanship.* Compare ONE UP. [The word *one-upmanship* was made up by a British humorist, Stephen Potter, on the pattern of such words as *sportsmanship* and *workmanship.*]

on faith *adv. phr.* Without question or proof. ♦ *He said he was twenty-one years old and the employment agency took him on faith.* ♦ *He looked so honest that we accepted his story on faith.*

on file *adv. phr.* Placed in a written or electronic file; on record. ♦ *We are sorry we cannot hire you right now but we will keep your application on file.*

on fire See SET THE WORLD ON FIRE.

on foot *adv. or adj. phr.* **1.** By walking. ♦ *Sally's bicycle broke and she had to return home on foot.* **2.** Being planned. ♦ *The reporter said that a civil rights demonstration was on foot.* ♦ *Plans have been set on foot for a party for Miss Jackson, because she is retiring.*

on guard *adj. phr.* Watchful; watching. ♦ *The police warned people to be on guard for pickpockets during the Christmas rush.* ♦ *Two men are on guard at the door.* Contrast OFF GUARD.

on hand *adv. phr.* **1a.** Nearby; within reach. ♦ *Always have your dictionary on hand when you study.* **1b.** Here. ♦ *Soon school will end and vacation will be on hand.* **2.** Present. ♦ *Mr. Blake's secretary is always on hand when he appears in public.* **3.** In your possession; ready. ♦ *The Girl Scouts have plenty of cookies on hand.* ♦ *Tim had no cash on hand to pay for the gas.* Compare IN STORE.

on high cotton See ON TOP OF THE WORLD *also* SITTING ON HIGH COTTON.

on hold *adv. phr.* **1.** Left waiting while making a telephone call. ♦ *"Sorry sir,"* the secretary said, *"I'll have to put you on hold for a minute."* **2.** Waiting; temporarily halted. ♦ *"Put your marriage plans on hold, son, and wait until after graduation,"* his father said seriously.

on ice *adv. or adj. phr., slang* **1.** The same as won; sure to be won. ♦ *The score was 20–10 in the last inning, and our team had the game on ice.* **2.** Away for safekeeping or later use; aside. ♦ *You will have to put your vacation plans on ice until your debts are paid.* ♦ *The senator was voted out of office. He is on ice until the next election.*

on in years See ALONG IN YEARS.

onion See KNOW ONE'S WAY AROUND 2.

only See HAVE EYES ONLY FOR, IF ONLY.

on occasion *adv. phr.* Sometimes; occasionally. ♦ *We go to New York on occasion.* ♦ *On occasion we feel like celebrating and have a party.* Compare ONCE IN A WHILE, FROM TIME TO TIME.

on one hand *adv. phr.* Looking at a thing in one of two possible ways; from one point of view.—Usually used with *on the other hand.* ♦ *John wants to be a printer or a teacher; on one hand, printing pays better; on the other hand, schools need good teachers.*

on one's account *adv. phr.* For your good; because you want to help or please someone. ♦ *Barry studied hard on his mother's account.* ♦ *I hope you didn't bring tea to the picnic just on my account.* ♦ *The teacher stayed in school a little late on Tom's account.* Compare OF ONE'S OWN ACCORD, ON ACCOUNT OF.

on one's back *adj. phr., informal* Making insistent demands of you; being an annoyance or bother. ♦ *My wife has been on my back for weeks to fix the front door screen.* ♦ *I can't get any work done with the children on my back from morning until night.* ♦ *Jim could do a better job if his boss weren't on his back so often.* Contrast OFF ONE'S BACK.

on one's bad side *or* **on the bad side of one** *adj. phr., informal* Not liked by someone; not friendly with a person. ♦ *Sally's boyfriend got on Father's bad side by keeping Sally out too late after the dance.* Contrast ON ONE'S GOOD SIDE.

on one's behalf See ON BEHALF OF.

on one's chest *adj. phr., informal* Hidden in your thoughts or feelings and bothering you; making you feel worried or upset; that is something you want to talk to someone about. ♦ *Jane looks unhappy because she has the quarrel with Susan on her chest.* ♦ *"Well, Dave," said the coach, "You look sad—what's on your chest?"* Compare ON ONE'S MIND. Contrast OFF ONE'S CHEST.

on one's coattails *adv. phr.* Because of another's merits, success, or popularity. ♦ *Bob and Jim are best friends. When Jim was invited to join a fraternity, Bob rode in on his coattails.* ♦ *Many people vote straight for all the candidates in the same political party. Most people voted for President K., so Governor B. rode in on K.'s coattails.*

on oneself See TAKE ON ONESELF.

on one's feet *adv. phr.* **1.** Standing or walking; not sitting or lying down; up. ♦ *Before the teacher finished asking the question, George was on his feet ready to answer it.* ♦ *In a busy gasoline station, the attendant is on his feet all day.* Compare TO ONE'S FEET. Contrast OFF ONE'S FEET. **2.** Recovering; getting better from sickness or trouble. ♦ *Jack is back on his feet after a long illness.* ♦ *Susan was on her feet soon after the operation.* ♦ *The bank loaned the store money to get it back on its feet after the fire.* **3.** See LAND ON ONE'S FEET, STAND ON ONE'S OWN FEET, THINK ON ONE'S FEET.

on one's good behavior *adv. phr.* Behaving right to make a good impression. ◆ *While his father was around the boy was on his good behavior, but when the father left the boy soon got into mischief.* ◆ *The minister is coming to dinner, and Mother wants us to be on our good behavior.*

on one's good side *or* **on the good side of one** *adj. phr., informal* Friendly with someone; liked by a person. ◆ *John thought that he would get a good grade if he got on the good side of the teacher.* ◆ *Successful workers stay on the good side of their bosses.* Contrast ON ONE'S BAD SIDE.

on one's hands *adv. or adj. phr.* In your care or responsibility; that you must do something about. ◆ *Mrs. Blake left her five children with me while she shopped. I could not get anything done with the children on my hands.* ◆ *After everyone bought tickets to the dance, the club treasurer had over $100 on his hands.* ◆ *The electricity went off while Mother was cooking supper, and she had a problem on her hands.* ◆ *I had time on my hands before the bus came, so I bought a newspaper to read.* Contrast OFF ONE'S HANDS. See SIT ON ONE'S HANDS. Compare HANG HEAVY *or* HANG HEAVY ON ONE'S HANDS.

on one's head *or* **upon one's head** *adv. phr.* On one's self. ◆ *When the school board fired the superintendent of schools, they brought the anger of the parents upon their heads.* ◆ *Billy had been naughty all day, but he really brought his parents' anger down on his head by pushing his little sister into a mud puddle.* Compare ABOUT ONE'S EARS.

on one's heel See TURN ON ONE'S HEEL.

on one's high horse *adj. phr., informal* **1.** Acting as if you are better than others; being very proud and scornful. ◆ *Martha was chairman of the picnic committee, and at the picnic she was on her high horse, telling everyone what to do.* ◆ *Mrs. Jones asked to see a less expensive hat. The salesgirl got up on her high horse and said the shop did not sell cheap merchandise.* **2.** Refusing to be friendly because you are angry; in a bad temper. ◆ *Joe was on his high horse because he felt Mary wasn't giving him*

enough attention. Contrast OFF ONE'S HIGH HORSE.

on one's honor *adj. phr.* Bound by one's honesty; trusted. ◆ *The students were not supervised during the examination. They were on their honor not to cheat.* ◆ *The house father put the boys on their honor not to smoke in the dormitory.*

on one's knees *adj. phr.* **1.** Pleading; begging very hard. ◆ *The boys were on their knees for hours before their parents agreed to their camping plans.* ◆ *The Jacksons won't contribute to the Red Cross unless you get on your knees.* **2.** In a very weak condition; near failure. ◆ *When the graduates of the school heard that it was on its knees they gave money generously so that it would not close.*

on one's last legs *adj. phr.* Failing; near the end. ◆ *The blacksmith's business is on its last legs.* ◆ *The dog is old and sick. He is on his last legs.* Compare ONE FOOT IN THE GRAVE, ON ONE'S KNEES 2.

on one's mind *adv. phr.* In one's thoughts. ◆ *I'm glad you want to talk about this. It's been on my mind for weeks.* ◆ *What's on your mind?* Compare IN MIND.

on one's nerves See GET ON ONE'S NERVES.

on one's own *adj. phr.* With no help from others. ◆ *It is a happy day when you're allowed to drive a car on your own.* ◆ *Being on your own may be a frightening experience.* Compare GO IT 2.

on one's own account *or informal* **on one's own hook** *adv. phr.* **1.** For yourself; as a free agent; independently. ◆ *After they had picked out the class gift, members of the committee did some shopping on their own account.* **2.** See OF ONE'S OWN ACCORD.

on one's own feet See STAND ON ONE'S OWN FEET.

on one's own hook See ON ONE'S OWN ACCOUNT.

on one's own time *adv. phr.* During one's free time; not during working or school hours. ◆ *If you want to play football, you'll have to do it on your own time.*

on one's part *or* **on the part of one** *adj. phr.* **1.** Of or by you; of someone's.

♦ *When Miss Brown said I was a good student, that was pure kindness on her part.* ♦ *The other team blamed their defeat on unfairness on the part of the referee.* **2.** See FOR ONE'S PART.

on one's shoulders *adv. or adj. phr.* In your care; as your responsibility. ♦ *The success of the program rests on your shoulders.* ♦ *He acts as if he had the cares of the world on his shoulders.*

on one's toes *adj. phr., informal* Alert; ready to act. ♦ *The successful ball player is always on his toes.* Compare HEADS-UP, ON THE BALL.

on one's uppers *adj. phr., informal* Very poor. ♦ *Mr. White had been out of work for several months and was on his uppers.* Compare DOWN ON ONE'S LUCK.

on one's way See ON THE WAY.

on pain of *also* **under pain of** *prep., formal* At the risk of; under penalty of. ♦ *The workers went on strike on pain of losing their jobs.* ♦ *The rebels had to swear under pain of death never to confess where their comrades were hiding.*

on paper *adv. or adj. phr.* Judging by appearances only and not by past performance; in theory; theoretically. ♦ *On paper, the American colonies should have lost the Revolutionary War.* ♦ *The football team lost many games, even though they looked good on paper.*

on pins and needles *adj. phr., informal* Worried; nervous. ♦ *Jane's mother was on pins and needles because Jane was very late getting home from school.* ♦ *Many famous actors are on pins and needles before the curtain opens for a play.*

on purpose *adv. phr.* For a reason; because you want to; not accidentally. ♦ *Jane did not forget her coat; she left it in the locker on purpose.* ♦ *The clown fell down on purpose.*

on record *adj. phr.* **1.** An official or recorded statement or fact; said for everyone to know. ♦ *We do not know when the famous writer was born, but the date of his death is on record.* ♦ *The two candidates went on television to put their ideas on record.* **2.** Known to have said or done a certain thing.—Usually used with *as.* ♦ *The mayor went on record as opposing a tax raise.* ♦ *The governor is on record as favoring the new highway.* ♦ *That congressman is on record as an enemy of waste in government.* Contrast OFF THE RECORD.

on sale *adj. phr.* Selling for a special low price. ♦ *Tomato soup that is usually sold for sixty cents a can is now on sale for fifty cents.* ♦ *John and Mary couldn't sell all of the lemonade at twenty cents a cup so they have it on sale for ten cents a cup.*

on schedule¹ *adv. phr.* As planned or expected; at the right time. ♦ *The school bus arrived at school on schedule.* ♦ *The four seasons arrive on schedule each year.* Compare ON TIME.

on schedule² *adj. phr.* Punctual; as planned. ♦ *The new airline claims to have more on schedule arrivals than the competition.*

on season See HIGH SEASON. Contrast OFF SEASON.

on second thought See SECOND THOUGHT.

on sight See AT SIGHT.

on table See WAIT AT TABLE *or* WAIT ON TABLE.

on the air *adj. or adv. phr.* Broadcasting or being broadcast on radio or TV. ♦ *His show is on the air at six o'clock.* ♦ *The ball game is on the air now.*

on the alert *adj. phr.* Alert; watchful; careful. ♦ *Campers must be on the alert for poison ivy and poison oak.* ♦ *Drivers must be on the alert for traffic signals.* Compare ON ONE'S TOES.

on the average See ON AN AVERAGE.

on the back See PAT ON THE BACK.

on the ball *adj. phr., informal* **1.** Paying attention and doing things well.— Used after *is* or *get.* ♦ *Ben is really on the ball in school.* ♦ *The coach told Jim he must get on the ball or he cannot stay on the team.* Compare GET WITH IT, HEADS-UP, KEEP ONE'S EYE ON THE BALL. **2.** That is a skill or ability; making you good at things.—Used after *have.* ♦ *John will succeed in life; he has a lot on the ball.* ♦ *The coach was eager to try out his new team and see what they had on the ball.*

on the bandwagon *adj. phr., informal* In or into the newest popular group or activity; in or into something you join just because many others are joining it.—Often used after *climb, get,* or *jump.* ◆ *When all George's friends decided to vote for Bill, George climbed on the bandwagon too.* See JUMP ON THE BANDWAGON.

on the barrelhead See CASH ON THE BARRELHEAD.

on the beam *adv. or adj. phr.* **1.** (Of an airplane) In the radio beam that marks the path to follow between airports; flying in the right direction. ◆ *A radio signal tells the pilot of an airplane when he is flying on the beam.* **2.** *slang* Doing well; just right; good or correct. ◆ *Kenneth's answer was right on the beam.* Contrast OFF THE BEAM.

on the bench 1. Sitting in a law court as a judge. ◆ *Judge Wyzanski is on the bench this morning.* **2.** Sitting among the substitute players. ◆ *The coach had to keep his star player on the bench with a sprained ankle.* Compare BENCH WARMER.

on the blink *adj. phr.* Faulty; malfunctioning; inoperative. ◆ *I need to call a competent repairman because my computer is on the blink again.*

on the block *adj. phr.* To be sold; for sale. ◆ *The vacant house was on the block.* ◆ *Young cattle are grown and sent to market to be placed on the block.*

on the brain *adj. phr., slang* Filling your thoughts; too much thought about; almost always in mind. ◆ *Mary Ann has boys on the brain.* ◆ *Joe's hobby is ham radio and he has radio on the brain most of the time.*

on the brink of *adv. phr.* Facing a new event that's about to happen. ◆ *"I am on the brink of a new discovery,"* our physics professor proudly announced.

on the button *adv., adj., slang* At the right place; at the heart of the matter. ◆ *John's remark was right on the button.* Compare ON THE DOT.

on the cards See IN THE CARDS.

on the carpet See CALL ON THE CARPET.

on the cheap *adv. phr.* Inexpensively; on a tight budget. ◆ *She buys most of her clothes on the cheap in secondhand stores.*

on the chin See TAKE IT ON THE CHIN.

on the contrary *adv. phr.* Exactly the opposite; rather; instead. ◆ *The principal thought that the children went to* the zoo; on the contrary, they went to the bakery. ◆ *"You don't like football, do you?" "On the contrary, I like it very much."* Compare TO THE CONTRARY.

on the cuff *adj. or adv. phr., informal* Agreeing to pay later; to be paid for later; on credit. ◆ *Peter lost the money that Mother gave him to buy meat, and the store would not let him have meat on the cuff.* ◆ *Many people buy cars and television sets on the cuff.*

on the dole *adv. phr.* Drawing unemployment benefits. ◆ *When Jim lost his job he got on the dole and is still on it.*

on the dot also **on the button** *adv. phr., informal* Exactly on time; not early and not late. ◆ *Susan arrived at the party at 2:00 P.M. on the dot.* ◆ *Ben's plane arrived on the dot.*

on the double! *adv. phr.* Hurry up! ◆ *"Let's go! On the double!"* the pilot cried, as he started up the engine of the small plane.

on the eve of *prep.* Just before (an event). ◆ *On the eve of the election, the president proposed a plan to cut taxes.*

on the face of it *adv. phr.* Apparently; as it seems. ◆ *On the face of it, Joe's claim that he can swim five miles is true.* ◆ *His statement that he is a millionaire is, on the face of it, false.*

on the fence *adj. or adv. phr.* Not able, or not wanting to choose; in doubt; undecided.—Often used with *sit.* ◆ *Jack sat on the fence for a week last spring before he finally joined the track team instead of the baseball team.* ◆ *Mrs. Jones has decided to vote for the Democrats, but Mr. Jones is still on the fence.* See FENCE-SITTER *or* FENCE-SITTING.

on the fly¹ *adv. phr.* **1.** While in the air; in flight. ◆ *The bird caught a bug on the fly.* ◆ *Joe was called out because the catcher caught the ball on the fly.* **2.** *informal* Between other activities; while busy with many things. ◆ *The president was so busy that he had to dictate letters on the fly.* ◆ *John is very busy, and people who want to talk to him have to catch him on the fly.* Compare ON THE GO, ON THE WING 2.

on the fly² *adj. phr., informal* Busy; going somewhere in a hurry; going about doing things. ◆ *Getting the house ready for the visitors kept Mother on* *the fly all day.* ♦ *The housekeeper of our school is always on the fly.*

on the go *adj. phr., informal* Active and busy. ♦ *Successful businessmen are on the go most of the time.* ♦ *Healthy, happy people are usually on the go.* Compare ON THE MOVE.

on the heels of *prep.* Just after; following (something, especially an event).—Often used with *hard* for emphasis. ♦ *Hard on the heels of the women's liberation parade, homosexuals declared a "gay pride week."*

on the hog See LIVE HIGH OFF THE HOG *or* EAT HIGH ON THE HOG.

on the hour *adv. phr.* Each time the hour has zero minutes and zero seconds. ♦ *The uptown bus goes past the school on the hour.* ♦ *The woman must take her pill on the hour.*

on the house *adj. phr., informal* Paid for by the owner. ♦ *At the opening of the new hotel, the champagne was on the house.* ♦ *Oscar was the first customer at the diner, so his lunch was on the house.*

on the increase See ON THE WAX. Contrast ON THE DECREASE, ON THE WANE.

on the job *adj. phr., informal* Working hard; not wasting time. ♦ *Joe was on the job all of the time that he was at work.* ♦ *The school paper came out on time because the editors were on the job.*

on the knees of the gods See IN THE LAP OF THE GODS.

on the lam *adj. or adv. phr., slang* Running away, especially from the law; in flight. ♦ *The bank robber was on the lam for ten months before the police caught him.*—Sometimes used in the phrase *take it on the lam.* ♦ *After a big quarrel with her father, the girl took it on the lam.*

on the level *adj. phr., informal* Honest and fair; telling the whole truth. ♦ *Our teacher respects the students who are on the level with her.* ♦ *Joyce wondered if the fortune-teller was on the level.*

on the line See LAY ON THE LINE *or* PUT ON THE LINE.

on the lips See HANG ON THE WORDS OF *or* HANG ON THE LIPS OF.

on the lookout *adj. phr.* Watching closely. ♦ *The little boy was on the lookout for his father.* ♦ *Forest rangers are always on the lookout for forest fires.* ♦ *The doctor is on the lookout for a new secretary.*

on the loose *adj. phr., informal* Free to go; not shut in or stopped by anything. ♦ *The zookeeper forgot to close the gate to the monkey cage and the monkeys were on the loose.* ♦ *All of the seniors were on the loose on "Senior Skip Day."*

on the make *adj., slang* **1.** Promiscuous or aggressive in one's sexual advances. ♦ *I can't stand Murray; he's always on the make.* **2.** Pushing to get ahead in one's career; doing anything to succeed. ♦ *The new department head is a young man on the make, who expects to be company president in ten years.*

on the map See PUT ON THE MAP.

on the market *adj. phr.* For sale. ♦ *In the summer many fresh vegetables are on the market.* ♦ *The Goodwins put their house on the market in January, but they did not sell it till August.*

on the mend *adj. phr.* Healing; becoming better. ♦ *John's broken leg is on the mend.* ♦ *Mary's relationship with Joan is on the mend.*

on the money *adv. phr.* Exactly right; exactly accurate. ♦ *Algernon won the lottery; the numbers he picked were right on the money.* Compare ON THE NOSE.

on the move *adj. or adv. phr.* **1.** Moving around from place to place; in motion. ♦ *It was a very cold day, and the teacher watching the playground kept on the move to stay warm.* ♦ *It was vacation time, and the highways were full of families on the move.* **2.** Moving forward; going somewhere. ♦ *The candidate promised that if people would make him president, he would get the country on the move.*

on the nose *adv. phr., informal* Just right; exactly. ♦ *Stanley hit the ball on the nose.* ♦ *The airplane pilot found the small landing field on the nose.*

on the other foot See SHOE ON THE OTHER FOOT.

on the other hand *adv. phr.* Looking at the other side; from another point of view.—Used to introduce an opposite or different fact or idea. ♦ *Jim wanted to go to the movies; his wife, on the other hand, wanted to stay home and read.* ♦ *Mr. Harris may still want a boy* to mow his lawn; on the other hand, he may have found someone to do it. Compare ON ONE HAND.

on the outs *adj. phr., informal* Not friendly; having a quarrel. ♦ *Mary and Sue were on the outs.* ♦ *Being on the outs with a classmate is very upsetting.* Syn. AT ODDS.

on the point of *prep.* Ready to begin; very near to.—Usually used with a verbal noun. ♦ *The coach was on the point of giving up the game when our team scored two points.* ♦ *The baby was on the point of crying when her mother finally came home.* Compare ABOUT TO, AT THE POINT OF.

on the Q.T. *adv. phr., informal* Secretly; without anyone's knowing. ♦ *George and Paul formed a club on the Q.T.* ♦ *The teachers got the principal a present strictly on the Q.T.* [from quiet.]

on the road *adv. or adj. phr.* **1.** Traveling; moving from one place to another. ♦ *When we go on vacation, we take a lunch to eat while on the road.* ♦ *Mr. Smith is on the road for his insurance company.* **2.** Changing; going from one condition to another. ♦ *Mary was very sick for several weeks, but now she is on the road to recovery.* ♦ *Hard study in school put John on the road to success.*

on the rocks *adj. phr.* **1.** *informal* Wrecked or ruined. ♦ *Mr. Jones' business and marriage were both on the rocks.* **2.** With ice only. ♦ *At the restaurant, Sally ordered orange juice on the rocks.*

on the ropes *adv. or adj. phr.* **1.** Against the ropes of a boxing ring and almost not able to stand up. ♦ *The fighter was on the ropes and could hardly lift his gloves.* **2.** Almost defeated; helpless; near failure. ♦ *The new supermarket took most of the business from Mr. Thomas's grocery, and the little store was soon on the ropes.*

on the run *adv. or adj. phr.* **1.** In a hurry; hurrying. ♦ *Jane called "Help!" and Tom came on the run.* ♦ *Modern mothers are usually on the run.* **2.** Going away from a fight; in retreat; retreating. ♦ *The enemy soldiers were on the run.*

on the safe side *adv. phr.* Provided for against a possible emergency; well prepared. ♦ *"Please double-check these proofs, Mr. Brown," the printer said, "just to be on the safe side."*

on the shelf *adv. or adj. phr., informal* Laid aside; not useful anymore. ♦ *When a girl grows up, she puts childish habits on the shelf.* ♦ *Mr. Myron's company put him on the shelf when he reached the age of 65.*

on the side *adv. phr., informal* **1.** In addition to a main thing, amount or quantity; extra. ♦ *He ordered a hamburger with onions and French fries on the side.* ♦ *His job at the hospital did not pay much, so he found another on the side.* ♦ *The cowboys in the rodeo competed for prize money and also made bets on the side.* **2.** *or* **on the ——— side** Tending toward; rather. ♦ *Grandmother thought Jane's new skirt was on the short side.*

on the sly *adv. phr.* So that other people won't know; secretly. ♦ *The boys smoked on the sly.* ♦ *Mary's mother did not approve of lipstick, but Mary used it on the sly.*

on the spot *adv. or adj. phr.* **1.** *or* **upon the spot** At that exact time and at the same time or place; without waiting or leaving. ♦ *The news of important events is often broadcast on the spot over television.* ♦ *When Tom ruined an expensive machine, his boss fired him on the spot.* Compare AT ONCE, IN ONE'S TRACKS, THEN AND THERE. **2.** *informal also* **in a spot** In trouble, difficulty, or embarrassment. ♦ *Mr. Jones is on the spot because he cannot pay back the money he borrowed.* ♦ *Bill is on the spot; he invited George to visit him, but Bill's parents said no.* Compare BACK TO THE WALL. **3.** *slang* In danger of murder; named or listed for death. ♦ *After he talked to the police, the gangsters put him on the spot.*

on the spur of the moment *adv. phr.* On a sudden wish or decision; suddenly; without thought or preparation. ♦ *John had not planned to take the trip; he just left on the spur of the moment.* ♦ *Mary saw a help-wanted advertisement and applied for the job on the spur of the moment.*

on the stage *adv. or adj. phr.* In or into the work of being an actor or actress. ♦ *John's brother is on the stage.* ♦ *Mary went on the stage.*

on the strength of *prep.* With faith or trust in; depending upon; with the support of. ♦ *On the strength of Jim's promise to guide us, we decided to climb the mountain.* ♦ *Bill started a restaurant on the strength of his experience as a cook in the army.*

on the string *or* **on a string** *adv. phr., informal* Under your influence or control; obedient to every wish. ♦ *The baby had his mother on a string.* ♦ *She was pretty and popular, with two or three boys on the string all the time.*

on the take *adv. phr.* Bribable; corrupt. ♦ *Officer O'Keefe was put on three months' probation because it was alleged that he was on the take.*

on the tip of one's tongue *adv. phr.* About to say something, such as a name, a telephone number, etc., but unable to remember it for the moment. ♦ *"His name is on the tip of my tongue," Tom said. "It will come to me in a minute."*

on the town *adv. or adj. phr., informal* In or into a town to celebrate; having a good time or enjoying the amusements in a town. ♦ *When the sailors got off their ship they went out on the town.* Compare PAINT THE TOWN RED.

on the track of *or* **on the trail of** Hunting or looking for; trying to find; following. ♦ *The hunter is on the track of a deer.* ♦ *The lawyer is on the trail of new proof in the case.* ♦ *Jim collects old stamps; he is on the track of one in Midville this afternoon.*

on the trail of See ON THE TRACK OF.

on the trigger See QUICK ON THE TRIGGER.

on the up and up *adj. phr., informal* Honest; trustworthy; sincere. ♦ *We felt that he was honest and could be trusted. This information is on the up and up.* Compare ON THE LEVEL.

on the vine See DIE ON THE VINE *or* WITHER ON THE VINE.

on the wagon *adv. phr.* Participating in an alcohol addiction program; not touching any alcoholic beverage. ♦ *Jim's doctor and his family finally managed to convince him that he was an alcoholic and should go on the wagon.* Contrast FALL OFF THE WAGON.

on the wane and on the wax *adv. phr.* Decreasing and increasing.—Said of the moon. ♦ *The moon is regularly on the wane and on the wax at regular intervals lasting half a month.*

on the warpath *adj. phr., informal* **1.** Very angry. ♦ *When Mother saw the mess in the kitchen she went on the warpath.* ♦ *Betty has been on the warpath ever since she found out she was not invited to the party.* **2.** Making an attack; fighting. ♦ *The government is on the warpath against narcotics.* ♦ *The police are on the warpath against speeders.*

on the watch *adj. phr.* Alert; watchful. ♦ *The customs inspector was on the watch for diamond smugglers.* ♦ *Mary was on the watch for bargains at the auction.* Compare EYE OUT, LOOK OUT 2.

on the way *or* **on one's way** *adv. or adj. phr.* Coming; going toward a place or goal; started. ♦ *Help was on the way.* ♦ *The train left and Bill was on his way to New York.* ♦ *He is well on the way to becoming a fine mechanic.*

on the whole *adv. phr.* **1.** In the most important things; in most ways. ♦ *On the whole, Billy did very well in school this year.* ♦ *Everybody agreed that on the whole it was a good show.* Syn. IN ALL 2, FOR THE MOST PART. **2.** In most cases; usually. ♦ *On the whole, men are stronger than women.* ♦ *On the whole, children begin walking when they are about one year old.* Syn. BY AND LARGE, IN GENERAL.

on the wing *adv. or adj. phr.* **1.** In the air; while flying. ♦ *The duck flew away, but John shot it on the wing.* **2.** *informal* In constant motion; always very busy. ♦ *Susan was on the wing doing things to get ready for her trip.* ♦ *Mr. Jones had a busy schedule and his secretary had to catch him on the wing to sign the letters.* Syn. ON THE FLY. **3.** *informal* Moving from one place to another; traveling; going somewhere. ♦ *Mary's husband is a traveling salesman and he's always on the wing.* ♦ *They stayed in France for a week and then they were on the wing again.* Syn. ON THE GO, ON THE MOVE.

on the words See HANG ON THE WORDS OF.

on the wrong foot See GET OFF ON THE WRONG FOOT.

on the wrong side of the bed See GET UP ON THE WRONG SIDE OF THE BED.

on the wrong track *adv. phr.* Lost; pursuing the wrong lead. ♦*Professor MacAlister confessed that his chemical experiments were on the wrong track.* Contrast BARK UP THE WRONG TREE.

on time *adv. or adj. phr.* **1.** At the time arranged; not late; promptly. ♦*The train left on time.* ♦*Mary is always on time for an appointment.* Contrast AHEAD OF TIME, BEHIND TIME. **2.** On the installment plan; on credit, paying a little at a time. ♦*John bought a car on time.* ♦*You can buy things at the department store on time.*

on top *adv. or adj. phr., informal* In the lead; with success; with victory. ♦*The horse that everyone had expected would be on top actually came in third.* ♦*Although John had been afraid that he was not prepared for the exam, he came out on top.*

on top of *prep.* **1.** On the top of; standing or lying on; on. ♦*When the player on the other team dropped the ball, Bill fell on top of it.* ♦*That high hill has a tower on top of it.* **2.** *informal* Very close to. ♦*The elevator was so crowded that everybody was on top of each other.* ♦*I couldn't find my umbrella and then I realized I was almost on top of it.* **3.** *informal* In addition to; along with. ♦*Mrs. Lane had many expenses and on top of everything else, her baby became ill.* ♦*Mary worked at the store all day and on top of that she had to baby-sit with her brother.* **4.** *informal* Managing very well; in control of. ♦*Although his new job was very complicated, John was on top of it within a few weeks.* ♦*No matter what goes wrong, Mary always stays on top of it.* **5.** Knowing all about; not falling behind in information about; up-to-date on. ♦*Mary stays on top of the news by reading newspapers and magazines.* ♦*When he was in California, Mr. Jones kept on top of things in his office by telephoning every day.*

on top of the world *or* **sitting on top of the world** *also (Southern)* **sitting on high cotton** *adj. phr., informal* Feeling pleased and happy; feeling successful. ♦*John was on top of the world when he found out that he got into college.* ♦*When Ruth won first prize in the contest, she felt as though she was sitting on top of the world.* ♦*The girls were sitting on high cotton because their basketball team had won the trophy.* Compare FLYING HIGH, WALK ON AIR.

on trial *adv. or adj. phr.* **1.** For testing or trying out for a time before making a decision. ♦*I was lucky that I had bought the machine on trial because I didn't like it and was able to return it.* ♦*Mother bought a new dishwasher on trial and was trying it out before deciding whether to keep it.* **2.** In a court being tried for a crime before a judge or jury. ♦*John White was on trial for murder.* ♦*Mary was on trial before the Student Committee for spoiling school property.*

on words See PLAY ON WORDS.

on your life See NOT ON YOUR LIFE.

open See EYES OPEN, THROW OPEN.

open and aboveboard *adj. phr.* Honest. ♦*Jacob felt that the firm he was doing business with wasn't entirely open and aboveboard.*

open and shut See CUT AND DRIED.

open arms See RECEIVE WITH OPEN ARMS.

open-door policy *n. phr.* A policy that states that newcomers are welcome to join the company, firm, or country in question. ♦*During the nineteenth century the United States had an open-door policy regarding immigration.*

open fire *v. phr.* To begin shooting. ♦*The big warship turned its guns toward the enemy ship and opened fire.* ♦*When the policeman called to the robber to stop, he turned and suddenly opened fire.*

openhanded *adj.* Generous; liberal. ♦*Although not wealthy himself, Bob was always very openhanded with those who needed help.*

open heart *n.* **1.** No hiding of your feelings; frankness; freedom. ♦*She spoke with an open heart of her warm feelings for her pupils.* ♦*She told her troubles with an open heart.* Compare HEART ON ONE'S SLEEVE. **2.** Kindness; generosity. ♦*She contributed to the fund with an open heart.* ♦*Mr. Jones has an open heart for underprivileged children.* Compare OPEN ONE'S HEART.

open its doors *v. phr.* **1.** To allow someone or something to enter or join;

become open. ♦ *That college was started for women only, but a few years ago it opened its doors to men.* **2.** To begin doing business; open. ♦ *Proffitts Department Store is having a birthday sale; it first opened its doors fifty years ago this month.* Contrast CLOSE ITS DOORS.

open letter *n. phr.* A public message in the form of a letter addressed to a particular person or to a group. ♦ *There was an open letter to the president of the United States in today's morning paper.*

open market *n. phr.* Goods or securities available for purchase by all. ♦ *The stocks of certain companies are on the open market.*

open marriage *n. phr.* An arrangement by mutual agreement between husband and wife whereby they are both allowed to have extramarital affairs. ♦ *Chances are the open marriage arrangement they had didn't work out too well so they are getting a divorce.*

open-minded *adj.* Having no dogmatic or biased views on matters of theory, religion, politics, etc. ♦ *Fred is easy to talk to about anything; he is a highly intelligent and open-minded person.*

open one's eyes *or* **open up one's eyes** *v. phr.* To make a person see or understand the truth; make a person realize; tell a person what is really happening or what really exists. ♦ *Mary didn't believe that her cousin could be mean until the cousin opened Mary's eyes by scratching and biting her.* ♦ *John's eyes were opened up to the world of nature when he visited his grandfather's farm.* Compare EYES OPEN, WISE UP.—**eye opener** *n.* Something that makes you understand the truth. ♦ *Pam's first visit to school was a real eye-opener.*

open one's heart *v. phr.* **1.** To talk about your feelings honestly; confide in someone. ♦ *After going around worrying, Mary opened her heart to her mother.* ♦ *John felt much better after he opened his heart to Betty.* **2.** To be sympathetic to; give love or help generously. ♦ *Mrs. Smith opened her heart to the poor little boy.* ♦ *After the moving speech by the UN official, the people opened their hearts to the poor people of India.* Compare OPEN HEART, WEAR ONE'S HEART ON ONE'S SLEEVE.

open onto *v. phr.* To have a view of. ♦ *Our apartment in Chicago has a set of windows that open onto Lake Michigan.*

open Pandora's box See PANDORA'S BOX.

open question *n. phr.* A debatable issue. ♦ *Whether assisted suicide is legal and moral or not is still an open question, recent publicity on the matter notwithstanding.*

open secret *n.* Something that is supposed to be a secret but that everyone knows. ♦ *It is an open secret that Mary and John are engaged.* ♦ *Who will be appointed as the next president of the college is an open secret.*

open sesame *n. phr., literary* Immediate means of entrance, or unobstructed access to something. ♦ *Tom mistakenly believed that his wealth would be an open sesame to the world of creative arts.*

open shop *n. phr.* A factory or firm that employs both union and non-union labor. ♦ *The firm refuses to adopt an open shop policy.* Contrast CLOSED SHOP.

open the door *v. phr.* To allow more action or discussion; give a chance. ♦ *Learning to read and write opens the door to a better job and better living conditions.* ♦ *Raising the tax rates will open the door to more help for older people.* Contrast CLOSE THE DOOR. Compare OPEN ITS DOORS.

open the floodgates *v. phr.* To let loose an outburst of human activity or emotion. ♦ *It would open the floodgates of anger and discontent if the university raised tuition too soon.*

open up *v.* **1.** To show for the first time; make clear; reveal. ♦ *The story of Helen Keller's life opened up a whole new world to Mary.* ♦ *Einstein's theories opened up a whole new area for study.* **2.** To make available; present an opportunity; offer. ♦ *The building of the railroad opened up new lands to the pioneers.* ♦ *John opened up a whole new section of the Scrabble board.* **3.** *informal* To go faster. ♦ *When they got out on the highway John opened up and drove at 65 miles per hour.* **4.** *informal* To begin to shoot. ♦ *When they got close to the enemy lines, they opened up with all they had.* **5.** *informal* To begin to talk frankly. ♦ *After John learned to trust Mr. Jones, he opened up and told him how he felt.* **6.** To spread out. ♦ *After a while the road opened up and they traveled more quickly.* **7.** To become available. ♦ *When she got her college diploma, many new jobs opened up.*

open up one's eyes See OPEN ONE'S EYES.

opinion See MATTER OF OPINION.

opposite number *n. phr.* A person occupying the same position as somone in a different group, organization, or country. ♦ *The opposite number of the President of the United States in Germany is the Chancellor of the Federal Republic.*

opposite sex *n. phr.* The sex different from the one being discussed or mentioned. ♦ *Fred came out and said he was gay, having never had any interest in the opposite sex.*

optional origin *n.* Stipulation in international commodities contract whereby the seller may ship from either his foreign or his domestic resources. ♦ *Be sure to enter that in the books as an optional origin order.*

orbit See GO INTO ORBIT.

order See APPLE-PIE-ORDER, CALL TO ORDER, IN ORDER, IN ORDER TO, IN SHORT ORDER, JUST WHAT THE DOCTOR ORDERED, MADE TO ORDER, OUT OF ORDER, PUT ONE'S HOUSE IN ORDER *or* SET ONE'S HOUSE IN ORDER, SHORT ORDER COOK, TO ORDER, WALKING PAPERS *or* WALKING ORDERS.

order about *or* **around** *v. phr.* To dictate arrogantly to someone; domineer. ♦ *Dan orders his younger colleagues around in a most unpleasant way.*

ordinary See OUT OF THE ORDINARY.

or other *adv.*—Used to emphasize indefinite words or phrases beginning with *some* (as *someone, something, somewhere, somehow, sometime*). ♦ *Somehow or other, Linda managed to get to the show on time.* ♦ *I'll think of something or other for the program.* ♦ *She found a beautiful cup and saucer somewhere or other.* ♦ *I'll get around to cleaning the closets sometime or other.* ♦ *Someone or other will take the letters to the post office.*

or so *adv.* About; or a little more. ♦ *Mr. Brown will be back in a day or so.* ♦ *The book cost $5 or so.* ♦ *There will be twenty or so people at the party.* Compare MORE OR LESS.

other See EACH OTHER, EVERY OTHER, GRASS IS ALWAYS GREENER ON THE OTHER SIDE OF THE FENCE *or* GRASS IS ALWAYS GREENER ON THE OTHER SIDE OF THE HILL, GO IN ONE EAR AND OUT THE OTHER, LAUGH ON THE WRONG SIDE OF ONE'S MOUTH *or* LAUGH ON THE OTHER SIDE OF ONE'S MOUTH, ON THE OTHER HAND, OR OTHER, SHOE ON THE OTHER FOOT, SIX OF ONE AND HALF-A-DOZEN OF THE OTHER, THIS AND THAT *also* THIS, THAT, AND THE OTHER, TURN THE OTHER CHEEK.

other fish to fry *n. phr., informal* Other things to do; other plans. ♦ *They wanted John to be the secretary, but he had other fish to fry.* ♦ *Mary was invited to the party but she refused because she had other fish to fry.*

other side of the tracks See WRONG SIDE OF THE TRACKS.

out and about See UP AND ABOUT.

out-and-out *adj.* Extreme; complete; thorough. ♦ *The candidate was an out-and-out conservative.* ♦ *It was out-and-out robbery to charge twice the usual price for eggs just because they were scarce.* Compare THROUGH AND THROUGH.

out at the elbows *adj. phr.* Poorly or shabbily dressed. ♦ *Roy walks around out at the elbows, but it's not because he is penniless, but more in imitation of a certain style.*

out back *adv. phr.* In one's backyard. ♦ *On the Fourth of July they were out back making preparations for their holiday barbecue.*

outback *n.* **1.** The remote and uncultivated wilderness areas of Australia or New Zealand, with very few inhabitants. ♦ *Mike and Barbara roughed it in the Australian outback for nearly two years.* **2.** Any remote, sparsely populated region. ♦ *Tom's old ranch in Texas is next to an arid outback.*

out cold *adv. or adj., informal* Unconscious; in a faint. ♦ *The ball hit Dick in the head and knocked him out cold for ten minutes.* ♦ *They tried to lift Mary when she fell down, but she was out cold.* Syn. OUT LIKE A LIGHT 2. Compare PASS OUT.

outer space *n.* What is outside of the

earth's air. ♦ *An astronaut cannot live without oxygen when he goes into outer space.*

out for *prep.* Joining, or planning to join; taking part in; competing for a place in. ♦ *John is out for the basketball team.* ♦ *Mary is going out for the school newspaper.* Compare TRY OUT.

out from under *adj. phr., informal* Free from something that worries you; seeing the end; finished.—Usually used with *be* or *get.* ♦ *Mary had so much to do in the new house she felt as though she would never be out from under.* ♦ *John had so many debts, he couldn't get out from under.*

out in force *adv. phr.* Present in very large numbers; en masse. ♦ *On the Fourth of July the police cars are out in force in the Chicago area.*

out in left field *adj. phr., informal* Far from the right answer; wrong; astray. ♦ *Johnny tried to answer the teacher's question but he was way out in left field.* ♦ *Susan tried to guess what the surprise was but she was way out in left field.* **2.** Speaking or acting very queerly; crazy. ♦ *The girl next door was always queer, but after her father died, she was really out in left field and had to go to a hospital.* Compare OUT OF ONE'S HEAD.

out in the cold *adj. phr., informal* Alone; not included. ♦ *All the other children were chosen for parts in the play, but Johnny was left out in the cold.* ♦ *Everybody made plans for Christmas Day and Mary found herself out in the cold.* Compare HIGH AND DRY.

out in the open See COME OUT IN THE OPEN.

out like a light *adj. phr., informal* **1.** Fast asleep; to sleep very quickly. ♦ *Tom got so much fresh air and exercise that he went out like a light as soon as he lay down.* ♦ *As soon as the lights were turned off, Johnny was out like a light.* **2.** In a faint; unconscious. ♦ *Johnny was hit by a ball and went out like a light.* ♦ *After she read that Tom had married another girl Jean was out like a light for several minutes.* Compare OUT COLD.

out loud *adv. phr.* In an ordinary speaking voice and not whispering or talking quietly; so everybody can hear; aloud. ♦ *The teacher read the final*

grades out loud. ♦ *Mary spoke out loud so the people standing nearby would hear.* ♦ *Sometimes I find it helpful to think out loud.*

out of *prep.* **1a.** From the inside to the outside of. ♦ *John took the apple out of the bag.* ♦ *Get out of the car!* ♦ *The teacher has gone out of town.* **1b.** In a place away from. ♦ *No, you can't see Mr. Jones; he is out of the office today.* ♦ *Our house is ten miles out of town.* **2.** From a particular condition or situation; not in; from; in a way changed from being in. ♦ *The drugstore is going out of business.* ♦ *The sick man is out of danger at last.* ♦ *Bob is never out of trouble.* **3.** Beyond the range of. ♦ *The plane is out of sight now.* ♦ *If you can't swim, don't go out of your depth.* **4.** From (a source). ♦ *Mother asked Billy who started the fight, but she couldn't get anything out of him.* ♦ *The teacher gave a test to see what the students got out of the lesson.* ♦ *Mr. Jones made a fortune out of cotton.* **5.** Because of; as a result of. ♦ *Mary scolded Joan out of jealousy.* ♦ *The cat ran away out of fear of the dog.* **6.** Without; not having. ♦ *The store is out of coffee.* ♦ *John's father is out of work.* **7.** From (a material). ♦ *The house is built out of stone.* ♦ *His suit is made out of cotton and is cool.* **8.** From among. ♦ *The man picked Joe out of the crowd.* ♦ *Our team won eight out of ten games last season.*

out of a bandbox See LOOK AS IF ONE HAS COME OUT OF A BANDBOX.

out of account See LEAVE OUT OF ACCOUNT.

out of a clear sky *or* **out of a clear blue sky** See OUT OF THE BLUE.

out of action *adv. phr.* Useless; crippled; damaged so as to be quiescent. ♦ *American bombers put Nazi heavy industry out of action during World War II.* ♦ *When I broke my leg I was out of action for the entire football season.*

out of all proportion *adv. phr.* Disproportionate; lopsided. ♦ *The news coverage of the sensational celebrity double murder has grown out of all proportion, obscuring the international news.*

out of bounds *adv. or adj. phr.* **1.** Outside

of the boundary lines in a game; not on or inside the playing field. ♦ *Bill thought he had scored a touchdown, but he had stepped out of bounds before he reached the goal line.* **2.** Outside of a circumscribed area for a certain kind of work, such as construction or military site. ♦ *The principal told the students that the new gymnasium being built on the school grounds was out of bounds.* ♦ *The captain's cabin is out of bounds to the passengers on the ship.* Contrast WITHIN BOUNDS. **3.** Outside of safe or proper limits; not doing what is proper; breaking the rules of good behavior. ♦*John was out of bounds when he called Tom a liar in the meeting.* ♦ *His request for a 25% salary raise was totally out of bounds.*

out of breath *adj. or adv. phr.* Not breathing easily or regularly; gasping; panting. ♦ *The fat man was out of breath after climbing the stairs.* ♦ *The mile run left Bill out of breath.*

out of character *adv. or adj. phr.* **1.** Not in agreement with a person's character or personality; not in the way that a person usually behaves or is expected to behave; not usual; unsuitable; uncharacteristic. ♦ *Mary is a nice girl. Her fit of temper was out of character.* **2.** Not in character; unsuitable for a part or character. ♦ *It isn't always out of character for a young actor to play an old man, if he is a good actor.* Contrast IN CHARACTER.

out of circulation *adj. phr., informal* Not out in the company of friends, other people, and groups; not active; not joining in what others are doing. ♦*John has a job after school and is out of circulation with his friends.* Contrast IN CIRCULATION.

out of commission *adj. phr.* **1.** Retired from active military service; no longer on active duty. ♦*When the war was over, many warships were placed out of commission.* Contrast IN COMMISSION 1. **2.** Not in use or not working; so that it cannot work or be used. ♦ *The strike put the airline out of commission for a week.* ♦*John will have to walk to the store. His bicycle is out of commission.* Compare OUT OF ORDER. Contrast IN COMMISSION 2.

out of condition See OUT OF SHAPE *or* OUT OF CONDITION.

out of date *adj. phr.* Old fashioned; superseded; no longer valid; too old to be used. ♦ *Father's suit is out of date; he needs a new one.* ♦ *The news magazines in the doctor's office were all out of date.*

out of fashion *adj. phr.* Having passed from vogue; out of the current mode. ♦ *The miniskirt is now out of fashion in most quarters, but it may very well come back some day.*

out of gas *adv. phr.* **1.** Out of fuel (said of automobiles). ♦ *Be sure you don't run out of gas when you go on a long distance trip by car.* **2.** Rundown; depleted of energy; in poor physical condition. ♦ *Mary said she had to take a break from her job as she was running totally out of gas.*

out of gear See THROW OUT OF GEAR.

out of hand *adv. phr.* **1.** Out of control. ♦ *Bobby's birthday party got out of hand and the children were naughty.* ♦ *Small puppies often get out of hand.* **2.** Suddenly, quickly without examination of possible truth or merit; without any consideration.—Often used after *dismiss* or *reject.* ♦ *The senator rejected out of hand the critics' call for his resignation.* Compare OUT OF LINE. Contrast IN HAND.

out of hot water See HOT WATER.

out of keeping *adj. phr.* Not going well together; not agreeing; not proper. ♦ *Loud talk was out of keeping in the library.* ♦ *It was out of keeping for the kind man to kick the dog.* Contrast IN KEEPING.

out of kilter *adj. phr., informal* **1.** Not balanced right; not in a straight line or lined up right. ♦ *The scale must be out of kilter because when I weighed myself on it, it said 300 pounds.* ♦ *The wheels of my bicycle were out of kilter after it hit the tree.* Contrast IN BALANCE. **2.** Needing repair; not working right. ♦ *My watch runs too slowly; it must be out of kilter.* Syn. OUT OF ORDER 2.

out of line[1] *adv. phr.* Not in a straight line; away from a true line. ♦ *The two edges were out of line and there was a space between them.* ♦ *The sergeant ordered the soldier who was out of line to get properly lined up.*

out of line[2] *adj. phr.* Not obeying or

agreeing with what is right or usual; doing or being what people do not expect or accept; outside ordinary or proper limits; not usual, right, or proper. ♦ *Little Mary got out of line and was rude to Aunt Elizabeth.* ♦ *The teacher asked Charlie not to tell one of the jokes because it was out of line.* ♦ *Mrs. Green thought the repair man's charge was out of line.* Compare OUT OF HAND, OUT OF ORDER. Contrast IN LINE 2.

out of line with *prep.* Not in agreement with. ♦ *The price of the bicycle was out of line with what Bill could afford.*

out of luck *adj. phr.* Being unlucky; having bad luck; having something bad happen to you. ♦ *Mr. Jones missed his train and was out of luck in getting to the ball game on time.* ♦ *All of the girls had dates so Ben was out of luck.*

out of mind See OUT OF SIGHT, OUT OF MIND.

out of nowhere *adv. phr.* Without having been seen before; suddenly and unexpectedly. ♦ *Mr. Jones was driving too fast on the express highway when a police patrol car appeared out of nowhere and stopped him.* Syn. OUT OF THE BLUE.

out of one's blood *adv. phr.* Separate from one's feelings, interests, or desires. ♦ *When Tom moved to the city, he couldn't get the country out of his blood.* ♦ *Mary is having a hard job getting summer laziness out of her blood.* Contrast IN ONE'S BLOOD.

out of one's element *adv. phr.* Outside of your natural surroundings; where you do not belong or fit in. ♦ *Wild animals are out of their element in cages.* ♦ *Chris is out of his element in singing class.* Compare OUT OF PLACE, BEYOND ONE'S DEPTH. Contrast IN ONE'S ELEMENT.

out of one's hair *adj. phr., informal* Rid of as a nuisance; relieved of as an annoyance. ♦ *Harry got the boys out of his hair so he could study.* Compare OUT OF ONE'S WAY. Contrast IN ONE'S HAIR.

out of one's hand See EAT OUT OF ONE'S HAND.

out of one's head *or* **out of one's mind** *or* **out of one's senses** *also* **off one's head** *adj. phr., informal* Acting in a crazy way; especially, wildly crazy. ♦ *The patient was feverish and out of his head and had to be watched.* ♦ *Her friends thought she was out of her mind to marry that man.* Compare OFF ONE'S ROCKER. Contrast COME TO ONE'S SENSES.

out of one's mind See OUT OF ONE'S HEAD.

out of one's mouth See TAKE THE BREAD OUT OF ONE'S MOUTH, TAKE THE WORDS OUT OF ONE'S MOUTH.

out of one's pocket *adv. phr.* Having sustained a financial loss; poorer by a said amount. ♦ *The show was so bad that, besides having a lousy time, I was also $35 out of my pocket.*

out of one's sails See TAKE THE WIND OUT OF ONE'S SAILS.

out of one's senses See OUT OF ONE'S HEAD.

out of one's shell *adv. phr., informal* Out of one's bashfulness or silence; into friendly conversation—Usually used after *come.* ♦ *John wouldn't come out of his shell and talk to the boys and girls at the party.* ♦ *The other girls tried to draw Ella out of her shell, but without success.* Contrast IN ONE'S SHELL.

out of one's skin See JUMP OUT OF ONE'S SKIN.

out of one's way See OUT OF THE WAY 3.

out of one's wits See SCARE OUT OF ONE'S WITS.

out of (one's) reach *adv. phr.* Unreachable; unattainable; unobtainable. ♦ *Sam wanted to be a United States senator but he came to realize that such a dream was out of his reach.*

out of order *adv. or adj. phr.* **1.** In the wrong order; not coming after one another in the right way. ♦ *Peter wrote the words of the sentence out of order.* ♦ *Don't get out of order, children. Stay in your places in line.* Contrast IN ORDER. **2.** In poor condition; not working properly. ♦ *Our television set is out of order.* **3.** Against the rules; not suitable. ♦ *The judge told the people in the courtroom that they were out of order because they were so noisy.* ♦ *The children's whispering was out of order in the church.* Compare OUT OF LINE, OUT OF PLACE, OUT OF THE WAY, OUT OF TURN, OUT OF COMMISSION 2.

Contrast IN ORDER.

out of place¹ *adv. phr.* Not in the right or usual place or position. ♦ *Harry fell and knocked one of his teeth out of place.* ♦ *The teacher lined up the class and told them not to get out of place.* Compare OUT OF ORDER. Contrast IN PLACE.

out of place² *adj. phr.* In the wrong place or at the wrong time; not suitable; improper. ♦ *Joan was the only girl who wore a formal at the party, and she felt out of place.* ♦ *It was out of place for Russell to laugh at the old lady.* Compare OUT OF ONE'S ELEMENT, OUT OF ORDER, OUT OF THE WAY. Contrast IN PLACE.

out-of-pocket expenses *n. phr.* Expenses one has to pay for oneself, not the company that sends one on a given assignment, such as tips for waiters, cab drivers, etc. ♦ *Luckily, my out-of-pocket expenses didn't amount to more than $15.*

out of practice *adj. phr.* Not in proper condition; unable to do something well because of lack of practice. ♦ *The basketball team got out of practice during the Christmas holidays.* Compare OUT OF SHAPE. Contrast IN PRACTICE.

out of print *adj. phr.* No longer obtainable from the publisher because the printed copies have been sold out; no longer printed. ♦ *The book is out of print. An edition of one thousand copies was sold and no more copies were printed.* Compare OUT OF STOCK. Contrast IN PRINT.

out of school See TELL TALES OUT OF SCHOOL.

out of season *adv. phr.* **1.** Not at the right or lawful time for hunting or catching. ♦ *The boys were caught fishing out of season.* **2.** Not at the usual time for growing and selling. ♦ *The corn we get out of season is different from the kind we grow here.* Contrast IN SEASON.

out of shape *or* **out of condition** *adj. phr.* **1.** Not in good condition; not able to perform well. ♦ *Father was out of shape when he took a long hike with the boys, and he was stiff and sore the next day.* ♦ *Jack's pitching arm got out of condition during the winter, when he wasn't using it.* Compare OUT OF PRAC-

TICE. **2.** Not look the same; changed. ♦ *Someone sat on father's new hat and mashed it. It is now out of shape.* Contrast IN SHAPE.

out of sight *adv. phr.* **1.** Not within one's field of vision. ♦ *The sailboat disappeared out of sight over the horizon.* **2.** Extremely expensive. ♦ *The builder's estimate was so high that it was out of sight.* **3.** Unbelievable; fantastic; incredible (both in the positive and the negative sense; an exaggeration.) ♦ *Roxanne is such a stunning beauty, it's simply out of sight.* ♦ *Mr. Gargoyle is so repulsive, it's out of sight.* **4.** Unreachable; unrealizable; belonging to the world of fiction and fantasy. ♦ *Max's dreams about winning the Senatorial election are really out of sight; he admits it himself.* Compare PIPE DREAM.

out of sight, out of mind If one doesn't see something for an extended period of time, one tends to forget about it.—A proverb. ♦ *After Caroline moved out of town, Ray soon found other women to date. As the saying goes, "out of sight, out of mind."*

out of sorts *adj. phr.* In an angry or unhappy mood; in a bad temper; grouchy. ♦ *Mary was out of sorts and wouldn't say good morning.* ♦ *Bob was out of sorts because he didn't get a bicycle for his birthday.*

out of step *adv. or adj. phr.* **1.** Not in step; not matching strides or keeping pace with another or others. ♦ *George always marches out of step with the music.* **2.** Out of harmony; not keeping up.—Often followed by *with.* ♦ *Just because you don't smoke, it doesn't mean you are out of step with other boys and girls your age.* Contrast IN STEP.

out of stock *adj. phr.* Having none for sale or use; no longer in supply; sold out. ♦ *When Father tried to get tires for an old car, the man in the store said that size was out of stock and were not sold anymore.* ♦ *So many children have bought balloons that the store is now out of stock.* Compare OUT OF PRINT. Contrast IN STOCK.

out of the blue *or* **out of a clear sky** *or* **out of a clear blue sky** *adv. phr., informal* Without any warning; by surprise; unexpectedly. ♦ *At the last minute Johnny came out of the blue to catch the pass and score a touchdown.* ♦ *The cowboy thought he was alone but suddenly out of a clear sky there were bandits all around him.* Syn. OUT OF NOWHERE. Compare BOLT FROM THE BLUE.

out of the corner of one's eye *adv. phr.* Without looking at a person or thing directly or openly; secretly; without being noticed. ♦ *The cat looked at the mouse out of the corner of his eye.* ♦ *Mike watched the boys across the street out of the corner of his eye as he mowed the lawn.*

out of the frying pan into the fire Out of one trouble into worse trouble; from something bad to something worse.—A proverb. ♦ *The movie cowboy was out of the frying pan into the fire. After he escaped from the robbers, he was captured by Indians.*

out of the hole *adv. or adj. phr., informal* **1a.** With a score better than zero in a game; especially a card game, to a score above zero. ♦ *It took us a long time to get out of the hole in the card game.* **1b.** Even with an opponent after being behind; out of trouble in a sport or game. ♦ *The team played very hard, but could not get out of the hole.* **2.** Out of debt; ahead financially. ♦ *It was a small business, but it was wisely managed, and it kept out of the hole.* ♦ *The first year was bad, but after that Fred got out of the hole.* Contrast IN THE HOLE.

out of the ordinary *adj. phr.* Outside or beyond common experience; unusual; wonderful; extraordinary. ♦ *The parade will be something out of the ordinary because a real king will be there.* ♦ *This juggler was out of the ordinary because he could juggle with his feet as well as his hands.*

out of the picture *adv. phr.* No longer a possibility or in the running; rejected. ♦ *Mark assured Carol that his ex-wife was completely out of the picture.*

out of the question *adj. phr.* Not worth considering; unthinkable; impossible. ♦ *It sometimes snows as late as June in the mountains, but the summer campers thought that snow was out of the question.* ♦ *The boys had no money,* so it was out of the question for them to go to the movies.

out of the rain See KNOW ENOUGH TO COME IN OUT OF THE RAIN.

out of the red *adv. phr.* Having reached solvency; no longer in debt. ♦ *Under the new management, our company finally got out of the red.* Contrast IN THE HOLE, IN THE RED. Compare IN THE BLACK.

out of the running *adj. or adv. phr.* Having no chance to win; not among the real contenders; not among those to be considered. ♦ *John had been out of the running since his first date with Mary, but he didn't realize it.* ♦ *Jones's horse was put out of the running early in the race.* Contrast IN THE RUNNING.

out of the swim *adj. phr.* Not doing what others are doing; not active in business or social affairs. ♦ *Mary had to stay home and take care of Mother while she was sick, and soon felt out of the swim.* ♦ *The toy manufacturer who is out of the swim will lose money.* Contrast IN THE SWIM.

out of the way *adv. phr.* **1.** Not where people usually go; difficult to reach. ♦ *When little Tommy comes to visit her, Aunt Sally puts her lamps and vases out of the way.*—Often used with hyphens before a noun. ♦ *Gold was found in an out-of-the-way village in the mountains, and soon a good road and airfield were built.* ♦ *Jack and Fred found an old gun in an out-of-the-way corner of the empty house.* Compare OFF THE BEATEN TRACK. **2.** Not what is usual or proper; strange. ♦ *To leave before the guest of honor would be out of the way.* ♦ *I'm sorry if I said something out of the way.* ♦ *The night watchman looked around the building, but he saw nothing out of the way.* Compare OUT OF PLACE. **3.** *or* **out of one's way** Not able to stop or bother you. ♦ *Tommy wished the visitors were out of the way so that he could have the candy for himself.* Compare OUT OF ONE'S HAIR, PUT OUT OF THE WAY.

out of the woods See CROW BEFORE ONE IS OUT OF THE WOODS.

out of thin air *adv. phr.* Out of nothing or from nowhere. ♦ *The teacher scolded Dick because his story was made out of thin air.* ♦ *On the way home from town,*

Tom saw a house standing on the lot that had been empty that morning; it seemed to have appeared out of thin air. Compare INTO THIN AIR.

out of this world *adj. phr., slang* Wonderfully good or satisfying; terrific; super. ♦ *The dress in the store window was out of this world!* ♦ *Mother was on TV last night. Isn't that out of this world?*

out of touch *adj. phr.* Not writing or talking with each other; not getting news anymore. ♦ *Fred had got out of touch with people in his hometown.* ♦ *On his island Robinson Crusoe was out of touch with world news.* Compare LOSE TOUCH, LOSE TRACK. Contrast IN TOUCH.

out of town *adv. phr.* Having left one's usual residence or place of work on a longer trip. ♦ *"Mr. Smith is out of town until Monday," the secretary said. "May I take a message?"*

out of tune *adv. or adj. phr.* **1.** Out of proper musical pitch; too low or high in sound. ♦ *The band sounded terrible, because the instruments were out of tune.* **2.** Not in agreement; in disagreement; not going well together.—Often used with *with.* ♦ *What Jack said was out of tune with how he looked; he said he was happy, but he looked unhappy.* Compare OFF-KEY. Contrast IN TUNE.

out of turn *adv. phr.* **1.** Not in regular order; at the wrong time. ♦ *John played out of turn.* ♦ *By taking a day off out of turn, Bob got the schedule mixed up.* **2.** Too hastily or wrongly; at the wrong time or place; so as to annoy others. ♦ *Dick loses friends by speaking out of turn.*

out of wedlock See BORN OUT OF WED-LOCK.

out of whack *adj. phr., slang* **1.** Needing repair; not working right. ♦ *Ben was glad the lawn mower got out of whack, because he didn't have to mow the lawn.* Syn. OUT OF ORDER. **2.** Not going together well; not in agreement. ♦ *The things Mr. Black does are out of whack with what he says.* ♦ *George's earnings and his spending were out of whack.* Compare OUT OF LINE.

out of work *adv. phr.* Having no income-producing job; unemployed. ♦ *When too many people are out of*

work, it is a sign that the economy is in a recession.

out on a limb *adv. phr.* With your beliefs and opinions openly stated; in a dangerous position that can't be changed. ♦ *The president went out on a limb and supported a foreign aid bill that many people were against.* ♦ *Grandfather went out on a limb before the summer was over and said that the next winter would be long and cold with many snowstorms.*

out on bail *adv. phr.* Released from prison because a security deposit known as "bail" has been put up by an individual or a bail bond broker. ♦ *The murder suspect was out on a one million dollar bail awaiting trial.*

out on parole *adv. phr.* Released from prison but still under the supervision of the police. ♦ *Although Henry is out on parole he must watch his step very carefully. If he commits another burglary he may have to go to jail for a very long time.*

out on the town *adv. phr.* Going from one bar or restaurant to the next in order to celebrate an event. ♦ *They all went out on the town to celebrate his promotion to vice president.*

outside of *prep.* **1.** Not in; outside. ♦ *I would not want to meet a lion outside of a zoo.* Contrast INSIDE OF. **2.** Except for; not including. ♦ *Outside of Johnny, all the boys on the basketball team are over six feet tall.* ♦ *Mrs. Cox had no jewelry outside of her wedding ring.* Syn. APART FROM.

out to lunch *adj., slang, informal* **1.** Gone for the midday meal. **2.** Inattentive; daydreaming; inefficient; stupid. ♦ *Neil Bender is just out to lunch today.*

overall *adj.* All inclusive; comprehensive. ♦ *What our department needs is an overall revamping of our undergraduate curriculum.*

over a barrel *also* **over the barrel** *adv. phr., informal* In the power of your enemies; not able to do anything about what happens to you; in a helpless condition; trapped. ♦ *Bill had Tom over a barrel because Tom owed him money.* ♦ *Ralph has me over a barrel; I need five dollars, and he won't lend it to me unless I let him use my bicycle.*

Compare ON THE ROPES.

over age *adj. phr.* Too old; not young enough; above the legal age. ♦ *Grandfather wanted to fight in World War II, but he could not because he was over age.* Contrast UNDER AGE.

over and done with *adj. phr.* Finished; completed; forgotten. ♦ *Norm and Meg's affair has been over and done with for a long time.*

overboard See GO OFF THE DEEP END *or* GO OVERBOARD.

overhead *n.* Expenses incurred in the upkeep of one's plant and premises, employees' salaries, etc., which are not due to the cost of individual items or products. ♦ *"Our overhead is killing us!" the used car lot owner complained. "We have to move to a cheaper place."*

overnight *adj.* **1.** From one evening until the next morning. ♦ *We could drive from Chicago to Detroit in one day, but it would be more comfortable if we stayed overnight in a motel.* **2.** Rapidly. ♦ *When Tom won the lottery he became a rich man overnight.*

over one's dead body *adv. phr., informal* Not having the ability to stop something undesirable from taking place. ♦ *"You will get married at age sixteen over my dead body!" Jane's father cried.*

over one's head *adv. or adj. phr.* **1.** Not understandable; beyond your ability to understand; too hard or strange for you to understand. ♦ *Mary laughed just to be polite, but the joke was really over her head.* ♦ *The lesson today was hard; it went over my head.* Compare BEYOND ONE'S DEPTH. **2.** To a more important person in charge; to a higher official. ♦ *When Mary's supervisor said no, Mary went over her head to the person in charge of the whole department.* ♦ *If Johnny can't get what he wants from his big sister, he goes over her head and asks his mother.* **3.** See HANG OVER ONE'S HEAD.

over spilled milk See CRY OVER SPILLED MILK.

over the coals See HAUL OVER THE COALS *or* RAKE OVER THE COALS.

over the hill *adj., informal* Past one's prime; unable to function as one used to; senile. ♦ *Poor Mr. Jones is sure not like he used to be; well, he's over the hill.*

over the hump *adj. phr., informal* Past

the most difficult part; past the crisis; out of danger. ♦ *Mary was failing math, but she is over the hump now.* ♦ *John was very sick after his accident, but he's over the hump.* ♦ *When Mr. Smith was out of work it looked as if his family would have to go on relief, but they got over the hump.*

over the long haul See IN THE LONG RUN. Contrast OVER THE SHORT HAUL.

over the short haul See IN THE SHORT RUN. Contrast OVER THE LONG HAUL.

over the top *adv. phr.* **1.** Out of the trenches and against the enemy. ♦ *The plan was to spend the night in the trenches and go over the top at dawn.* ♦ *Johnny found that he was braver than he thought he would be when his company went over the top.* **2.** Over the goal. ♦ *Our goal was to collect a half million dollars for the new school building, but we went over the top.* ♦ *Mary was asked to sell twenty tickets, and she went over the top.*

over the traces See KICK OVER THE TRACES.

over with[1] *prep.* At the end of; finished with; through with. ♦ *They were over with the meeting by ten o'clock.* ♦ *By Saturday Mary will be over with the measles.*

over with[2] *adj., informal* At an end; finished. ♦ *John knew his mother would scold him for losing the money, and he wanted to get it over with.* ♦ *After the hard test, Jerry said, "I'm glad that's over with!"*

own See COME INTO ONE'S OWN, DOSE OF ONE'S OWN MEDICINE, HOLD ONE'S OWN, IN A WORLD OF ONE'S OWN, KEEP ONE'S OWN COUNSEL, OF ONE'S OWN ACCORD *or* OF ONE'S OWN FREE WILL, ON ONE'S OWN ACCOUNT *or* ON ONE'S OWN HOOK, ON ONE'S OWN TIME, SIGN ONE'S OWN DEATH WARRANT, TAKE THE LAW INTO ONE'S OWN HANDS, UNDER ONE'S OWN STEAM.

own up *v., informal* To take the blame; admit your guilt; confess. ♦ *When Mr. Jones asked who broke the window, Johnny owned up.* ♦ *Mary owned up to having borrowed her sister's sweater.* ♦ *When Mother saw that someone had broken the vase, Billy owned up to it.* See COME CLEAN.

oyster See WORLD IS ONE'S OYSTER.

p See MIND ONE'S P'S AND Q'S.

pace See CHANGE OF PACE, KEEP PACE, PUT THROUGH ONE'S PACES, SNAIL'S PACE.

pace off See STEP OFF 2.

pace-setter, pace-setting See SET THE PACE.

pack a punch *or* **pack a wallop** *v. phr., slang* **1.** To be able to give a powerful blow; have a dangerous fist. ◆*He packed a mean punch.* **2.** To have a violent effect; be powerful. ◆*It was vodka, and it packed quite a wallop.*

pack off *v., informal* To send away; dismiss abruptly. ◆*When an Englishman got in trouble long ago, his family would pack him off to Australia or some other distant land.* ◆*Jane couldn't really get started on her homework until she had packed the children off to school.*

pack rat *n., informal* A person who cannot part with old, useless objects; an avid collector of useless things; a junk hoarder. ◆*"Why are there so many things in this room?" John asked. "It is my brother's room, and he is a pack rat; he is unable to throw stuff away."*

packed (in) like sardines *adj. phr.* So tightly crowded that there is hardly room to turn. ◆*The trains are so full during rush hour that we must go to work packed in like sardines.*

pack of lies *n. phr.* An unbelievable story; unprovable allegations. ◆*What Al told us about his new girlfriend was nothing but a pack of lies.*

pack one's bag *v. phr.* To leave a place out of anger, annoyance, or disagreement. ◆*"This place is beginning to irritate me," she said to her friend. "I want to pack my bags and get out of here."*

pack up *v. phr.* To pack one's suitcase for traveling; prepare a package. ◆*Without saying a single word, the unhappy husband packed up and left.*

paddle See UP THE CREEK *or* UP THE CREEK WITHOUT A PADDLE.

paddle one's own canoe *v. phr., informal* To work without help; earn your own living; support yourself. ◆*After his father died, John had to paddle his own*

canoe. Syn. HOE ONE'S OWN ROW. Compare MAKE ONE'S WAY.

paddy wagon *n., informal* A police van used for transporting prisoners to jail or the police station. ◆*The police threw the demonstrators into the paddy wagon.*

pad the bill *v. phr.* To add false expenses to a bill; make a bill larger than it really was. ◆*The salesman padded the bill for his traveling expenses by exaggerating his food expenses.*

pain See AT PAINS, FEEL NO PAIN, GIVE A PAIN, GROWING PAINS, ON PAIN OF, TAKE PAINS.

pain in the ass *or* **pain in the neck** *n., slang, vulgar with ass* An obnoxious or bothersome person or event. ◆*Phoebe Hochrichter is a regular pain in the neck/ass.*

paint a gloomy picture *v. phr.* To describe something in a gloomy, pessimistic way. ◆*We are sad because the weather forecast has painted a gloomy picture for all of next week when we go on vacation.*

paint oneself into a corner *v. phr.* To get oneself into a bad situation that is difficult or impossible to get out of. ◆*By promising to both lower taxes and raise the defense budget, the president has painted himself into a corner.*

paint the lily See GILD THE LILY.

paint the town red *or* **paint the town** *v. phr., slang* To go out to drink and have a good time; celebrate wildly; carouse. ◆*It was the sailors' first night ashore; they painted the town red.* Compare ON THE TOWN 2.

pair See TAKE TO ONE'S HEELS *also* SHOW A CLEAN PAIR OF HEELS.

pair off *v.* **1.** To make a pair of; put two together; associate; match. ◆*Mrs. Smith paired off her guests by age and tastes.* **2.** To belong to a pair; become one of a pair. ◆*Jane paired off with Alice in a tennis doubles match.* **3.** To divide or join into pairs. ◆*Later in the day the picnic crowd paired off for walks and boat rides.*

pair up *v.* **1.** To make a pair of; match. ◆*When she finished the mending, she* *paired up the socks.* **2.** To form a pair; to be or become one of a pair. ♦*Not all the socks would pair up.* ♦*Joe paired up with Charlie to work on the lesson.*

pajamas See CAT'S MEOW *or* CAT'S PAJAMAS.

pal See PEN PAL.

pale See BEYOND THE PALE.

pale around the gills See GREEN AROUND THE GILLS.

palm See CARRY OFF THE PALM, GREASE ONE'S PALM, ITCHING PALM.

palm off *v., informal* **1.** To sell or give (something) by pretending it is something more valuable; to sell or give by trickery. ♦*He palmed off his own painting as a Rembrandt.* ♦*The salesman palmed off pine wood floors as oak.* Syn. FOB OFF, PASS OFF. **2.** To deceive (someone) by a trick or lie. ♦*He palmed his creditors off with a great show of prosperity.* Syn. PUT OFF. **3.** To introduce someone as a person he isn't; present in a false pretense. ♦*He palmed the girl off as a real Broadway actress.*

pan See FLASH IN THE PAN, OUT OF THE FRYING PAN INTO THE FIRE.

Pandora's box *n. phr., literary* A thing or problem that, if activated, will give rise to many unmanageable problems. ♦*If they insist on having that inquiry, they will open up a Pandora's box.* Compare CAN OF WORMS.

pan gravy *n.* Gravy made with meat drippings with seasoning and often a little water. ♦*His wife liked cream gravy, but he preferred pan gravy.* ♦*Pan gravy from country ham is often called red-eye gravy.*

panic See PUSH THE PANIC BUTTON.

pan out *v., informal* To have a result, especially a good result; result favorably; succeed. ♦*Suppose the class tried to make money by selling candy. How would that pan out?* ♦*Edison's efforts to invent an electric light bulb did not pan out until he used tungsten wires.*

pant for *v. phr.* To desire something very deeply. ♦*He is panting for his girlfriend, who went out of town to see her family.*

pants See ANTS IN ONE'S PANTS, CATCH ONE WITH ONE'S PANTS DOWN, FANCY PANTS, FLY BY THE SEAT OF ONE'S PANTS, GET THE LEAD OUT OF ONE'S PANTS, KICK IN THE PANTS, WEAR THE TROUSERS *or* WEAR THE PANTS.

paper See ON PAPER, WALKING PAPERS.

par See UP TO PAR.

parade See HIT PARADE.

parade rest *n.* A position in which soldiers stand still, with feet apart and hands behind their backs. ♦*The marines were at parade rest in front of the officials' platform.* Compare AT EASE 3.

parallel bars *n.* Two horizontal bars the same distance apart, that are a few feet above the floor of a gymnasium. ♦*The boys exercised on the parallel bars in the gym.*

parcel See PART AND PARCEL.

parcel out *v.* To give out in parts or shares; divide. ♦*He parceled out the remaining food to the workers.*

par for the course *n. phr., informal* Just what was expected; nothing unusual; a typical happening.—Usually refers to things going wrong. ♦*Mary is very clumsy so it was par for the course when she bumped into the table and broke the vase.* ♦*When John came late again, Mary said, "That's par for the course."* Compare ALL IN A DAY'S WORK, RUNNING TRUE TO FORM.

pare down *v. phr.* To limit; economize; reduce. ♦*With a smaller income per month, the family had to pare down their household expenses.*

parliamentary law *n.* The rules for legislative or other meetings. ♦*The club followed parliamentary law at the business meeting.*

parrot-fashion *adv.* Like a parrot; by rote memorization and without any understanding. ♦*The candidate delivered a speech that was prepared for him and he read it parrot-fashion.*

part See DISCRETION IS THE BETTER PART OF VALOR, FOOL AND HIS MONEY ARE SOON PARTED, FOR MY PART, FOR ONE'S PART *also* ON ONE'S PART, FOR THE MOST PART, IN PART, MAN OF PARTS, TAKE PART.

partake of *v., formal* **1.** To take some of; receive a share of; eat. ♦*He partook of ordinary country fare as he traveled.* **2.** To have the same qualities as; show the characteristics of. ♦*Her way of cooking partook of both Italian and American habits.*

part and parcel *n. phr.* A necessary or important part; something necessary to a larger thing.—Usually followed by *of.* ♦ *Freedom of speech is part and parcel of the liberty of a free man.*

part company *v. phr.* **1.** To part with someone; leave each other; separate. ♦ *The boys parted company as they came from the park.* ♦ *George parted company with the others at his front door.* **2.** To be different from someone in opinion or action; follow your own way; disagree; differ. ♦ *They parted company on where the new highway should be built.* ♦ *The mayor parted company with the newspapers on raising taxes.*

partial to *v. phr.* Having a weakness for; favorable toward. ♦ *He seems to be partial to blondes while his brother is partial to redheads.*

particular See IN PARTICULAR.

parting of the ways *n. phr.* **1.** The point where a road or path divides; a fork. ♦ *They stood undecided at a parting of the ways, where a forest path forked.* **2.** A time or place where a choice must be made; a deciding point. ♦ *He had come to a parting of the ways: he had to choose the high school courses that would prepare him for college, or the courses that would prepare him for business.*

part of the furniture *n. phr.* In a job or position for so long that one is taken entirely for granted, like a part of the physical surroundings. ♦ *He has been working in the same office for so many years now that people consider him to be a part of the furniture.*

part with *v.* **1.** To separate from; leave. ♦ *He parted with us at the end of the trip.* Compare PART COMPANY. **2.** To let go. *They were sorry to part with the old house.* ♦ *He had to part with his secretary when she got married.* Compare GIVE UP.

party See HEN PARTY, LIFE OF THE PARTY, NECK-TIE PARTY, THROW A PARTY.

party line *n. phr.* Ideas, policies, and goals set forth by the leadership of a group or organization. ♦ *Dan seldom has an original idea but he keeps faithfully repeating his company's party line.*

party to *adj. phr.* Concerned with; participating in. ♦ *The prosecution has been trying to show that the defendant was party to a fraud.*

pass See BRING TO PASS, COME TO PASS, FORWARD PASS, JUMP PASS, SCREEN PASS.

pass around *v. phr.* To circulate from one to another; distribute something among a group of people. ♦ *Why doesn't he pass around the appetizers to the guests?*

pass away *v.* **1.** To slip by; go by; pass. ♦ *We had so much fun that the weekend passed away before we realized it.* ♦ *Forty years had passed away since they had met.* **2.** To cease to exist; end; disappear; vanish ♦ *When automobiles became popular, the use of the horse and buggy passed away.* **3.** To have your life stop; die. ♦ *He passed away at eighty.* Syn. PASS ON 3, PASS OUT 3.

pass by See PASS OVER.

pass by the board See GO BY THE BOARD.

passed ball *n.* A pitched baseball missed by the catcher when he should have been able to catch it. ♦ *The batter singled and went to second on a passed ball.*

pass for *v. phr.* To be taken for; be considered as. ♦ *Charles speaks Arabic so fluently that he could easily pass for an Arab.*

passing See IN PASSING.

pass muster *v. phr., informal* To pass a test or check-up; be good enough. ♦ *After a practice period, Sam found that he was able to pass muster as a lathe operator.* ♦ *His work was done carefully, so it always passed muster.* Compare MEASURE UP.

pass off *v.* **1.** To sell or give (something) by false claims; offer (something fake) as genuine. ♦ *The dishonest builder passed off a poorly built house by pretending it was well constructed.* Syn. FOB OFF, PALM OFF **2.** To claim to be someone you are not; pretend to be someone else. ♦ *He passed himself off as a doctor until someone checked his record.* **3.** To go away gradually; disappear. ♦ *Mrs. White's morning headache had passed off by that night.* **4.** To reach an end; run its course from beginning to end. ♦ *The party passed off well.* Syn. GO OFF.

pass on *v.* **1.** To give an opinion about; judge; settle. ♦ *The college passed on his application and found him acceptable.* ♦ *The committee recommended three people for the job and the president passed on them.* **2.** To give away (something that has been outgrown.) ♦ *As he grew up, he passed on his clothes to his younger brother.* Compare HAND DOWN. **3.** To die. ♦ *Mary was very sorry to hear that her first grade teacher had passed on.* Syn. PASS AWAY 3, PASS OUT 3.

pass out *v., informal* **1.** To lose consciousness; faint. ♦ *She went back to work while she was still sick, and finally she just passed out.* Compare GIVE OUT 3. **2.** *or slang* **pass out cold** To drop into a drunken stupor; become unconscious from drink. ♦ *After three drinks, the man passed out.* **3.** To die. ♦ *Life came and went weakly in him for hours after surgery; then he passed out.* Syn. PASS AWAY 3, PASS ON 3.

pass over *or* **pass by** *v.* To give no attention to; not notice; ignore. ♦ *I can pass over the disorderliness of the troops, but their disobedience is serious.* ♦ *In choosing men to be given a salary raise, the foreman passed Mr. Hart by.* ♦ *She was unattractive, the kind of a girl that everybody would pass by.*

pass the buck *v. phr., informal* To make another person decide something or accept a responsibility or give orders instead of doing it yourself; shift or escape responsibility or blame; put the duty or blame on someone else. ♦ *Mrs. Brown complained to the man who sold her the bad meat, but he only passed the buck and told her to see the manager.* ♦ *If you break a window, do not pass the buck; admit that you did it.* Compare LET GEORGE DO IT.—**buck-passer** *n. phr.* A person who passes the buck. ♦ *Mr. Jones was a buck-passer even at home, and tried to make his wife make all the decisions.*—**buck-passing** *n. or adj.* ♦ *Buck-passing clerks in stores make customers angry.*

pass the hat *v. phr.* To solicit money; take up collections for a cause. ♦ *The businessmen's club frequently passes the hat for contributions toward scholarships.*

pass the time of day *v. phr.* To exchange greetings; stop for a chat. ♦ *They met at the corner and paused to pass the time of day.*

pass through one's mind See CROSS ONE'S MIND.

pass up *v.* To let (something) go by; refuse. ♦ *Mary passed up the dessert because she was on a diet.* ♦ *John was offered a good job in California, but he passed it up because he didn't want to move.* Compare TURN DOWN.

pass upon *v. phr.* To express an opinion about; judge. ♦ *George said he wanted his wife to pass up the new house before he decided to buy it.*

pass with flying colors See WITH FLYING COLORS.

past master *n. phr.* An expert. ♦ *Alan wins so often because he is a past master at chess.*

past one's peak *adj. phr.* No longer as strong, efficient, or able as one once was, usually because of advanced age and decreased ability. ♦ *He used to be a terrific athlete but we're afraid he is past his peak.*

pat See PIT-A-PAT, STAND PAT.

pat-a-cake *n.* A clapping game that keeps time to a nursery rhyme. ♦ *Mother played pat-a-cake with the baby.*

patch up *v.* **1.** To mend a hole or break; repair; fix. ♦ *He patched up a couple of old tires.* ♦ *The lovers patched up their quarrel.* **2.** To put together in a hurried or shaky way. ♦ *They patched up a hasty peace.*

pat on the back[1] *v. phr.* **1.** To clap lightly on the back in support, encouragement, or praise. ♦ *The coach patted the player on the back and said a few encouraging words.* **2.** To make your support or encouragement for (someone) felt; praise. ♦ *After he won the game, everyone patted him on the back for days.*

pat on the back[2] *n. phr.* **1.** An encouraging tap of the hand on someone's back; a show of sympathy or support. ♦ *I gave her a pat on the back and told her she had done fine work.* **2.** A word or gesture of praise or other encouragement; applause. ♦ *Pats on the back weren't enough; he wanted hard cash.*

patrol See SHORE PATROL.

Paul See ROB PETER TO PAY PAUL.

pause See GIVE PAUSE.

pavement See POUND THE PAVEMENT.

pave the way *v. phr.* To make preparation; make easy. ♦*Aviation paved the way for space travel.* ♦*A good education paves the way to success.*

pay See DEVIL TO PAY.

pay a call *v. phr.* To visit someone. ♦*"Come and pay us a call some time, when you're in town," Sue said to Henry.*

pay as one goes *v. phr.* To pay cash; to pay at once; to avoid charging anything bought; to avoid debt entirely by paying cash.—Usually used with *you.* ♦*It is best to pay as you go; then you will not have to worry about paying debts later.*

pay attention *v. phr.* To listen to someone; hear and understand someone alertly. ♦*"Pay attention, children!" the teacher cried. "Here is your homework for next week!"*

pay court to *v. phr.* To woo; to shower with attention. ♦*He had been paying court to her for three long years before he worked up the courage to ask her to marry him.*

pay dirt *n., slang* **1.** The dirt in which much gold is found. ♦*The man searched for gold many years before he found pay dirt.* **2.** *informal* A valuable discovery.—Often used in the phrase *strike pay dirt.* ♦*When Bill joined the team, the coach struck pay dirt.* ♦*Jean looked in many books for facts about her hometown, and finally she struck pay dirt.* Compare STRIKE IT RICH.

pay down *v. phr.* **1.** To give as a deposit on some purchase, the rest of which is to be paid in periodic installments. ♦*"How much can you pay down on the house, sir?" the realtor asked.* **2.** To decrease a debt with periodical payments. ♦*I'd like to pay down the charges on my credit cards.* Compare DOWN PAYMENT.

pay for *v.* To have trouble because of (something you did wrong or did not do); be punished or suffer because of. ♦*When Bob could not get a good job, he realized he had to pay for all the years of fooling around instead of working in school.* ♦*Mary was very mean to John because she wanted to*
make him pay for all the years in which he had ignored her. Compare MAKE UP 3b, PAY OFF.

pay in advance See IN ADVANCE.

pay lip service to See LIP SERVICE.

payoff *n.* Culmination point; climax. ♦*After many months of patient labor on your book, the payoff comes when you see the first printed copy.*

pay off *v. phr.* **1.** To pay the wages of. ♦*The men were paid off just before quitting time, the last day before the holiday.* **2.** To pay and discharge from a job. ♦*When the building was completed he paid off the laborers.* **3.** To hurt (someone) who has done wrong to you; get revenge on. ♦*When Bob tripped Dick, Dick paid Bob off by punching him in the nose.* Syn. PAY BACK. **4.** *informal* To bring a return; make profit. ♦*At first Mr. Harrison lost money on his investments, but finally one paid off.* **5.** *informal* To prove successful, rewarding, or worthwhile. ♦*Ben's friendship with the old man who lived beside him paid off in pleasant hours and broadened interests.* ♦*John studied hard before the examination, and it paid off. He made an A.*

pay one a left-handed compliment See LEFT-HANDED COMPLIMENT.

pay one back in his own coin *v. phr.* To retaliate. ♦*Jim refused to help Bob when he needed it most, so Bob decided to pay him back in his own coin and told him to go and look for help elsewhere.*

pay one's respect to *v. phr.* To discharge one's social obligations by visiting someone or by calling them on the phone. ♦*The newly arrived people paid their respects to their various neighbors during their first couple of weeks in town.*

pay one's way *v. phr.* **1.** To pay in cash or labor for your expenses. ♦*He paid his way by acting as a guide.* **2.** To be profitable; earn as much as you cost someone; be valuable to an employer; to yield a return above expenses. ♦*The bigger truck paid its way from the start.* ♦*We had to offer our new manager a large salary, but he was a capable man, and paid his way.* Compare WORTH ONE'S SALT.

pay out See PAY OFF.

pay the piper *or* **pay the fiddler** *v. phr.* To suffer the results of being foolish; pay or suffer because of your foolish acts or wasting money. ♦ *Bob had spent all his money and got into debt, so now he must pay the piper.* ♦ *Fred had a fight, broke a window, and quarreled with his counselor so now he must pay the fiddler.* Compare FACE THE MUSIC 2. [From the proverb "He who dances must pay the piper (or the fiddler)."]

pay through the nose *v. phr., informal* To pay at a very high rate; pay too much. ♦ *He had wanted experience, but this job seemed like paying through the nose for it.* ♦ *There was a shortage of cars; if you found one for sale, you had to pay through the nose.*

pay up *v.* To pay in full; pay the amount of; pay what is owed. ♦ *The monthly installments on the car were paid up.* ♦ *He pays his dues up promptly.* ♦ *He gets behind when he is out of work but always pays up when he is working again.*

peace See HOLD ONE'S PEACE.

pearl See CAST PEARLS BEFORE SWINE *or* CAST ONE'S PEARLS BEFORE SWINE.

pebble See NOT THE ONLY PEBBLE ON THE BEACH.

peck See HUNT AND PECK.

pecking order *n.* The way people are ranked in relation to each other (for honor, privilege, or power); status classification; hierarchy. ♦ *After the president was in office several months, his staff developed a pecking order.*

pedestal See ON A PEDESTAL.

peel See KEEP ONE'S EYES PEELED.

peel off *v.* To dive away from a group of airplanes in a flight formation; bring one plane down from a group. ♦ *As the group neared the home base, pilot after pilot peeled off for a landing.*

peeping Tom *n.* A man or boy who likes sly peeping. ♦ *He was picked up by the police as a peeping Tom.*

peg See SQUARE PEG IN A ROUND HOLE, TAKE DOWN A PEG.

peg away *v.* To work methodically, industriously, or steadily. ♦ *Thomson pegged away for years at a shoe repair business.* ♦ *Jones kept pegging away, and finally recognition came.*

pen See POISON-PEN, SLIP OF THE PEN.

penalty box *n.* A place where penalized hockey players are required to go to wait until the penalty is over. ♦ *Two players got into a fight and were sent to the penalty box for two minutes.*

penny for one's thoughts Please tell me what you are thinking about; what's your daydream. ♦ *"A penny for your thoughts!" he exclaimed.*

penny pincher, penny pinching See PINCH PENNIES.

penny wise and pound foolish Wise or careful in small things but not careful enough in important things.—A proverb. ♦ *Mr. Smith's fence is rotting and falling down because he wouldn't spend money to paint it. He is penny wise and pound foolish.*

pen pal *n.* A friend who is known to someone through an exchange of letters. ♦ *John's pen pal writes him letters about school in Alaska.*

people who live in glass houses should not throw stones Do not complain about other people if you are as bad as they are.—A proverb. ♦ *Mary says that Betty is jealous, but Mary is more jealous herself. People who live in glass houses should not throw stones.*

pep talk *n., informal* A speech that makes people feel good so they will try harder and not give up. ♦ *The football coach gave the team a pep talk.* ♦ *Mary was worried about her exams, but felt better after the teacher's pep talk.*

period of grace See GRACE PERIOD.

perish the thought *v. phr.* Let us not even think of it; may it never come true.—Used as an exclamation. ♦ *If John fails the college entrance exam—perish the thought—he will go back to high school for one more year.* ♦ *Perish the thought that Mary should have cancer.* Compare GOD FORBID.

perk up *v.* To get or give back pep, vigor, health, or spirit; become or make more lively; liven up. ♦ *He perked up quickly after his illness.* ♦ *The rain perked up the flowers wonderfully.*

person See IN PERSON.

pet name *n. phr.* A special or abbreviated name indicating affection. ♦ *He never calls his wife her real name, "Elizabeth," but only such pet names as "honey," "honey bunch," "sweetheart," and "sugar."*

petard See HOIST WITH ONE'S OWN PETARD.

Peter See ROB PETER TO PAY PAUL.

peter out *v., informal* To fail or die down gradually; grow less; become exhausted. ◆*After the factory closed, the town pretty well petered out.* ◆*The mine once had a rich vein of silver, but it petered out.* ◆*But as he thought of her, his anger slowly petered out.* Compare GIVE OUT.

photo finish *n. phr.* A close finish in a race of people or animals, where the camera must decide the actual result, sometimes by millimeters. ◆*The black horse was declared the winner in a photo finish.*

pick See BONE TO PICK *or* CROW TO PICK.

pick a bone See BONE TO PICK.

pick a fight See PICK A QUARREL.

pick a hole in *or* **pick holes in** *v. phr., informal* To find a mistake in or things wrong with; criticize; blame. ◆*The witness said he had been walking in the moonlight last Sunday, but the lawyer picked a hole in what he said by proving that there was no moon and that it rained Sunday night.* ◆*Mary is always picking holes in what the other girls do.* Compare FIND FAULT.

pick and choose *v.* To select with much care; choose in a fussy way; take a long time before choosing. ◆*He was never one to pick and choose.* ◆*Some people pick and choose to get something perfect, and some just because they can't make up their minds.*

pick apart *or* **pick to pieces** *v. phr.* To criticize harshly; find things wrong with; find fault with. ◆*After the dance, the girls picked Susan apart.* ◆*They picked the play to pieces.*

pick a pocket *v. phr.* To steal by removing from the pocket of another. ◆*While in the train, somebody picked his pocket and took the last dollar he had.*

pick a/the lock *v. phr.* To burglarize; open illegally; open a lock without the regular key. ◆*The robber got into the house by picking the lock.*

pick a quarrel *v. phr.* To seek the opportunity for a fight or a quarrel. ◆*When Charlie has too much to drink, he has a tendency to pick a quarrel with whomever happens to be around.* See PICK A FIGHT.

pick at *v.* **1.** To reach or grasp for repeatedly. ◆*The baby kept picking at the coverlet.* **2.** To eat without appetite; choose a small piece every little while to eat. ◆*He picked at his food.* **3.** To annoy or bother continually; find fault with. ◆*They showed their displeasure by continually picking at her.* Syn. PICK ON.

pick holes in *v. phr.* To criticize or find fault with something, such as a speech, a statement, a theory, etc. ◆*It is easier to pick holes in someone else's argument than to make a good one yourself.*

pick-me-up *n. phr.* Something you take when you feel tired or weak. ◆*John stopped at a drugstore for a pick-me-up after working three hours overtime.* ◆*Mary always carried a bar of chocolate in her pocketbook for a pick-me-up.*

pickpocket *n.* A thief; a petty criminal who steals things and money out of people's pockets on a bus, train, etc. ◆*In some big cities many poor children become pickpockets out of poverty.*

pick off *v.* **1.** To pull off; remove with the fingers. ◆*He picked off the burs that had stuck to his overcoat.* **2.** To shoot, one at a time; knock down one by one. ◆*The sniper picked off the slower soldiers as they came out into the road.* **3.** To catch a base runner off base by throwing the ball quickly to a fielder who tags him out. ◆*The pitcher turned around suddenly and threw to the second baseman to pick the runner off second base.* Compare OFF BASE. **4.** To catch and, especially in football, to intercept. ◆*Alert defenders picked off three of Jack's passes.*

pick on *v.* **1.** *informal* To make a habit of annoying or bothering (someone); do or say bad things to (someone). ◆*Other boys picked on him until he decided to fight them.* Syn. PICK AT 3. **2.** To single out; choose; select. ◆*He visited a lot of colleges, and finally picked on Stanford.*

pick one's teeth *v. phr.* To clean one's teeth with a toothpick. ◆*It is considered poor manners to pick one's teeth in public.*

pick one's way *v. phr.* To go ahead carefully in difficult or unfamiliar places; advance with care. ◆*After nightfall we* *drove slowly along, picking our way until we found the right turn.* ♦ *He picked his way across the rough and rocky hillside.*

pick out *v.* **1.** To choose. ♦ *It took Mary a long time to pick out a dress at the store.* **2.** To see among others; recognize; tell from others. ♦ *We could pick out different places in the city from the airplane.* ♦ *We could not pick Bob out in the big crowd.* Syn. MAKE OUT 2. **3.** To find by examining or trying; tell the meaning. ♦ *The box was so dirty we couldn't pick out the directions on the label.* Compare FIND OUT.

pick over *v.* To select the best of; look at and take what is good from; choose from. ♦ *She picked the apples over and threw out the bad ones.* ♦ *We hurried to the big sale, but we were late and everything had already been picked over.*

pick the brains of *v. phr.* To get ideas or information about a particular subject by asking an expert. ♦ *If you have time, I'd like to pick your brains about home computers.*

pick to pieces See PICK APART, PICK HOLES IN.

pickup *n.,* (stress on *pick*) **1.** A rugged, small truck. ♦ *When he got into the lumber business, Max traded in his comfortable two-door sedan for a pickup.* **2.** Scheduled meeting in order to transfer merchandise or stolen goods. ♦ *The pickup goes down at 7 A.M. every day by the loading dock.* ♦ *The dope pushers usually make their pickup on Rush Street.* **3.** A person who is easy to persuade to go home with the suitor. ♦ *Sue is said to be an easy pickup.*

pick up *v.* **1.** To take up; lift. ♦ *During the morning Mrs. Carter picked up sticks in the yard.* **2.** *informal* To pay for someone else. ♦ *After lunch, in the restaurant, Uncle Bob picked up the check.* **3.** To take on or away; receive; get. ♦ *At the next corner the bus stopped and picked up three people.* **4.** To get from different places at different times; a little at a time; collect. ♦ *He had picked up rare coins in seaports all over the world.* **5.** To get without trying; get accidentally. ♦ *He picked up knowledge of radio just by staying around the radio station.* ♦ *Billy*

picked up a cold at school. **6a.** To gather together; collect. ♦ *When the carpenter finished making the cabinet, he began picking up his tools.* **6b.** To make neat and tidy; tidy up; put in order. ♦ *Pick up your room before Mother sees it.* **6c.** To gather things together; tidy a place up. ♦ *It's almost dinner time, children. Time to pick up and get ready.* **7.** To catch the sound of. ♦ *He picked up Chicago on the radio.* **8.** To get acquainted with (someone) without an introduction; make friends with (a person of the other sex). ♦ *Mother told Mary not to walk home by herself from the party because some stranger might try to pick her up.* **9.** *informal* To take to the police station or jail; arrest. ♦ *Police picked the man up for burglary.* **10.** To recognize the trail of a hunted person or animal; find. ♦ *State police picked up the bandit's trail.* ♦ *The dogs picked up the fox's smell.* **11.** To make (someone) feel better; refresh. ♦ *A little food will pick you up.* **12a.** To increase (the speed); make (the speed) faster. ♦ *The teacher told her singing class to pick up the tempo.* ♦ *The car picked up speed.* **12b.** To become faster; become livelier. ♦ *The speed of the train began to pick up.* ♦ *After the band practiced for a while, the music began to pick up.* **13.** To start again after interruption; go on with. ♦ *The class picked up the story where they had left it before the holiday.* ♦ *They met after five years, and picked up their friendship as if there had been no interruption.* **14.** *informal* To become better; recover; gain. ♦ *She picked up in her schoolwork.* ♦ *He picked up gradually after a long illness.* ♦ *His spirits picked up as he came near home.*

pick up the tab *v. phr.* To pay the bill in a restaurant; be the one who underwrites financially what others are doing. ♦ *"I am always the one who picks up the tab," Charlie complained bitterly. "Others get away with being freeloaders."* Compare FOOT THE BILL.

Pidgin English *n. phr.* A jargon that consists of some mispronounced English words and some foreign words used by Orientals in talking with Westerners. ♦ *You can conduct a lot of* *business in Pidgin English in the Far East.*

pie See EAT HUMBLE PIE, FINGER IN THE PIE, PIE IN THE SKY, SWEETIE PIE.

piece See BY THE PIECE, CONVERSATION PIECE, GIVE A PIECE OF ONE'S MIND, GO TO PIECES, OF A PIECE, PIECE OF CAKE, SAY ONE'S PIECE *or* SPEAK ONE'S PIECE, TO PIECES.

piece of cake *adj., slang* Easy. ♦ *The final exam was a piece of cake.*

piece out *v.* **1.** To put together from many different pieces; put together from odd parts; patch. ♦ *They pieced out a meal from leftovers.* ♦ *He pieced out the machine with scrap parts.* ♦ *The detective pieced out the story from a stray fact here, a clue there, and a hint somewhere else.* **2.** To make larger or longer by adding one or more pieces. ♦ *The girl grew so fast that her mother had to piece out her dresses.*

piecework *n.* Work paid for in accordance with the quantity produced. ♦ *Al prefers working on a piecework basis to being on a regular salary because he feels he makes more that way.*

pie in the sky *n. phr., informal* An unrealistic wish or hope. ♦ *Our trip to Hawaii is still only a pie in the sky.* Compare PIPE DREAM.

pigeonhole *v.* **1.** To set aside; defer consideration of. ♦ *The plan was pigeonholed until the next committee meeting.* **2.** To typecast; give a stereotypical characterization to someone. ♦ *It was unfair of the committee to pigeonhole him as a left-wing troublemaker.*

pigeonhole *n.* **1.** Small compartment for internal mail in an office or a department. ♦ *"You can just put your late exam into my pigeonhole," said Professor Brown to the concerned student.* **2.** One of the small compartments in a desk or cabinet. ♦ *He keeps his cufflinks in a pigeonhole in his desk.*

piggy-back *adj. or adv.* Sitting or being carried on the shoulders. ♦ *Little John loved to go for a piggy-back ride on his father's shoulders.* ♦ *When Mary sprained her ankle, John carried her piggy-back to the doctor.*

piggy bank *n.* A small bank, sometimes in the shape of a pig, for saving coins. ♦ *John's father gave him a piggy bank.*

pigheaded *adj.* Stubborn; unwilling to compromise. ♦ *"Stop being so pigheaded!" she cried. "I, too, can be right sometimes!"*

pig in a poke *n. phr.* An unseen bargain; something accepted or bought without looking at it carefully. ♦ *Buying land by mail is buying a pig in a poke: sometimes the land turns out to be under water.*

pig out *v. phr.* **1.** To eat a tremendous amount of food. ♦ *"I always pig out on my birthday," she confessed.* **2.** To peruse; have great fun with; indulge in for a longer period of time. ♦ *"Go to bed and pig out on a good mystery story," the doctor recommended.*

pile up *v. phr.* **1.** To grow into a big heap. ♦ *He didn't go into his office for three days and his work kept piling up.* **2.** To run aground. ♦ *Boats often pile up on the rocks in the shallow water.* **3.** To crash. ♦ *One car made a sudden stop and the two cars behind it piled up.*

pile-up *n.* **1.** A heap; a deposit of one object on top of another. ♦ *There is a huge pile-up of junked cars in this vacant lot.* **2.** A large number of objects in the same place, said of traffic. ♦ *I was late because of the traffic pile-up on the highway.*

pill See BITTER PILL.

pillar of society *n. phr.* A leading figure who contributes to the support and the well-being of his/her society; a person of irreproachable character. ♦ *Mrs. Brown, the director of our classical symphony fund, is a true pillar of society.*

pillar to post See FROM PILLAR TO POST.

pimple See GOOSE BUMPS *or* GOOSE PIMPLES.

pin See ON PINS AND NEEDLES.

pinch See TAKE WITH A GRAIN OF SALT *also* TAKE WITH A PINCH OF SALT, WHERE THE SHOE PINCHES.

pinch and scrape *v. phr.* To save as much money as possible by spending as little as possible. ♦ *They are trying to buy their first house so they are pinching and scraping every penny they can.*

pinch-hit *v.* **1.** To substitute for another player at bat in a baseball game. ♦ *Smith was sent in to pinch-hit for Jones.* **2.** *informal* To act for a while, or in an emergency, for another person; take someone's place for a while. ♦ *I asked him to pinch-hit for me while I was away.* ♦ *The president of the City Council pinch-hits for the mayor when the mayor is out of town.*— **pinch-hitter** *n.* ♦ *Jones was hit by a pitched ball and Smith came in as a pinch-hitter.* ♦ *When our teacher was sick, Mrs. Harris was called as a pinch-hitter.*—**pinch-hitting** *adj. or n.* ♦ *Pinch-hitting for another teacher is a hard job.*

pinch pennies *v. phr., informal* Not spend a penny more than necessary; be very saving or thrifty. ♦ *When Tom and Mary were saving money to buy a house, they had to pinch pennies.*— **penny-pincher** *n., informal* A stingy or selfish person; miser. ♦ *He spent so little money that he began to get the name of a penny-pincher.*—**penny-pinching** *adj. or n., informal* ♦ *Bob saved enough money by penny-pinching to buy a bicycle.*

pin curl *n.* A curl made with a hair clip or bobby pin. ♦ *Mary washed her hair and put it up in pin curls.* ♦ *All the girls had their hair in pin curls to get ready for the party.*

pin down *v.* **1a.** To keep (someone) from moving; make stay in a place or position; trap. ♦ *Mr. Jones' leg was pinned down under the car after the accident.* ♦ *The soldier was pinned down in the hole because rifle bullets were flying over his head.* **1b.** To keep (someone) from changing what (he) says or means; make (someone) admit the truth; make (someone) agree to something. ♦ *Mary didn't like the book but I couldn't pin her down to say what she didn't like about it.* ♦ *I tried to pin Bob down to fix my bicycle tomorrow, but he wouldn't say that he could.* **2.** To tell clearly and exactly; explain so that there is no doubt. ♦ *The police tried to pin down the blame for the fire in the school.*

pine away *v. phr.* To waste away with grief. ♦ *After George was sent abroad, his wife pined away for him so much that she became ill.*

pink See IN THE PINK, TICKLE PINK.

pink around the gills See GREEN AROUND THE GILLS.

pin money *n. phr.* Extra money used for incidentals. ♦ *She has a regular full-time job but she earns extra pin money by doing a lot of baby-sitting.*

pin one's ears back *v. phr., slang* **1.** To beat; defeat. ♦ *After winning three games in a row, the Reds had their ears pinned back by the Blues.* **2.** To scold. ♦ *Mrs. Smith pinned Mary's ears back for not doing her homework.*

pin one's faith on *v. phr.* To depend upon; trust. ♦ *We pinned our faith on our home basketball team to win the state finals, and they did!*

pin one's heart on one's sleeve See WEAR ONE'S HEART ON ONE'S SLEEVE.

pint-size *adj., informal* Very small. ♦ *The new pint-size, portable TV sets have a very clear picture.* ♦ *It was funny to hear a pint-size voice coming out of a great big man.*

pinup girl *v. phr.* An attractive girl whose picture is pinned or tacked to the wall by an admirer. ♦ *Some Hollywood actresses are understandably very popular pinup girls among male soldiers.*

pipe See PUT THAT IN YOUR PIPE AND SMOKE IT.

pipe down *v.* **1.** To call (sailors) away from work with a whistle. ♦ *He piped the men down after boat drill.* **2.** *slang* To stop talking; shut up; be quiet. ♦ *"Oh, pipe down," he called.*—Often considered rude.

pipe dream *n., informal* An unrealizable, financially unsound, wishful way of thinking; an unrealistic plan. ♦ *Joe went through the motions of pretending that he wanted to buy that $250,000 house, but his wife candidly told the real estate lady that it was just a pipe dream.* Compare PIE IN THE SKY.

piper See PAY THE PIPER.

pipe up *v., informal* To speak up; to be heard. ♦ *Mary is so shy, everyone was surprised when she piped up with a complaint at the club meeting.* ♦ *Everyone was afraid to talk to the police, but a small child piped up.*

pip-squeak *n., informal* A small, unimportant person. ♦ *If the club is really democratic, then every little pip-squeak has the right to say what he thinks.* ♦ *When the smallest boy was chosen to be the monitor, the class bully said he would not obey a little pip-squeak.*

piss off *v., slang, vulgar, avoidable* To bother; annoy; irritate. ♦ *You really piss me off when you talk like that.*— **pissed off** *adj.* ♦ *Why act so pissed off just because I made a pass at you?*

pit against *v.* To match against; oppose to; put in opposition to; place in competition or rivalry with. ♦ *The game pits two of the best pro football teams in the East against each other.* ♦ *He pitted his endurance against the other man's speed.* ♦ *He was pitted against an opponent just as smart as he was.*

pit-a-pat *adv.* With a series of quick pats. ♦ *When John asked Mary to marry him, her heart went pit-a-pat.* ♦ *The little boy ran pit-a-pat down the hall.*

pitch See WILD PITCH.

pitch a curve *or* **a curve ball** *v. phr.* To catch someone unawares; confront someone with an unexpected event or act. ♦ *My professor pitched me a curve ball when he unexpectedly confronted me with a complicated mathematical equation that was way over my head.*

pitch dark *adj.* Totally, completely dark. ♦ *A starless and moonless night in the country can be pitch dark.*

pitcher See LITTLE PITCHERS HAVE BIG EARS, RELIEF PITCHER, STARTING PITCHER.

pitchfork See RAIN CATS AND DOGS *or* RAIN PITCHFORKS.

pitch in *v., informal* **1.** To begin something with much energy; start work eagerly. ♦ *Pitch in and we will finish the job as soon as possible.* **2.** To give help or money for something; contribute. ♦ *Everyone must pitch in and work together.* ♦ *We all pitched in a quarter to buy Nancy a present.* Syn. CHIP IN. Compare FALL TO.

pitch into *v., informal* **1.** To attack with blows or words. ♦ *He pitched into me with his fists.* ♦ *He pitched into the idea of raising taxes.* Syn. LAY INTO 1, 2, RIP INTO. **2.** To get to work at; work hard at. ♦ *She pitched into the work and had the house cleaned up by noon.* ♦ *He pitched into his homework right after dinner.* Compare LAY INTO, SAIL INTO.

pitch out *v.* **1.** To deliberately throw a pitch outside of the home plate in baseball so that the batter cannot hit the ball and the catcher can make a quick throw. ♦ *The catcher wanted the pitcher to pitch out and see if they could catch the runner stealing.* **2.** To toss the ball easily to a football back. ♦ *The quarterback faked to the fullback and pitched out to the halfback going wide.*

pitch woo *v. phr., slang* To kiss and hug; make love. ♦ *Mary and John pitched woo in the movies.* ♦ *While Bob drove, Betty and Jim sat in the back pitching woo.*

pity See TAKE PITY ON *or* TAKE PITY UPON.

place See HEART IN THE RIGHT PLACE, HIGH PLACE, IN PLACE, INSTEAD OF *or* IN PLACE OF, IN THE FIRST PLACE, JUMPING-OFF PLACE, LIGHTNING NEVER STRIKES TWICE IN THE SAME PLACE, OUT OF PLACE, PUT IN ONE'S PLACE, PUT ONESELF IN ANOTHER'S PLACE, TAKE PLACE.

plague on both your houses *or* **plague o' both your houses** Bad luck to both of you!—Used to show disgust at those who won't stop quarreling. ♦ *The bus drivers went on strike because the bus company would not raise their pay. After several weeks, the people who needed to ride the bus to work said, "A plague on both your houses."*

plain Jane *n. phr.* A common or simple looking young woman or girl. ♦ *When we were in school, Ann was a plain Jane, but she blossomed out and even won the title of Miss Indiana.*

plain *or* **smooth sailing** *n. phr.* An uncomplicated, unhampered, or easy course. ♦ *For a graduate of such a famous university as he was, that assignment was plain sailing.*

plain white wrapper *n., slang, citizen's band radio jargon* Unmarked police car. ♦ *There's a plain white wrapper at your rear door!* See BROWN PAPER BAG.

plan See LAY AWAY PLAN.

plank See WALK THE PLANK.

plan on *v.* **1.** To have the plan of; have in mind.—Used with a verbal noun. ♦ *I plan on going to the movies after I finish my homework.* ♦ *Mary was planning on seeing John at the baseball game.* Syn. FIGURE ON. **2.** To think you will do or have; be sure about; expect. ♦ *I'm hoping to go away for the weekend, but I'm not planning on it.*

♦ *We can't order the food for the party until we know how many people to plan on.* ♦ *We planned on Mary for the decorations, but she is sick.*

plate See HOME PLATE.

platonic love *n. phr.* Great affection toward another person without sex. ♦ *They are platonic lovers; they do everything together except make love.*

platter See HAND SOMETHING TO ONE ON A SILVER PLATTER.

play See ALL WORK AND NO PLAY MAKES JACK A DULL BOY, DOUBLE PLAY, FAIR PLAY, FORCE PLAY, GAME AT WHICH TWO CAN PLAY, MAKE A PLAY FOR, TURN ABOUT IS FAIR PLAY.

play along (with) *v.* Cooperate; make no trouble. ♦ *The honest jockey refused to play along with the bookmaker's illegal plan.*

play a part in *v. phr.* To be instrumental in; have a role in; be concerned with. ♦ *Some First Ladies play a greater part in political life than others.*

play around See FOOL AROUND.

play around with See TOY WITH.

play a waiting game *v. phr.* To withhold action until one's chances for success improve. ♦ *Ray would like to be vice president of the company so he is playing a waiting game in the hope that the president will soon recognize his abilities.*

play ball *v. phr.* **1.** To begin play in a ball game. ♦ *When the umpire calls "Play ball," the game begins.* **2.** *informal* To join in an effort with others; cooperate. ♦ *To get along during Prohibition, many men felt that they had to play ball with gangsters.* ♦ *It is often good business to play ball with a political machine.*

play by ear *v. phr.* **1.** To play a musical instrument by remembering the tune, not by reading music. ♦ *Mary does not know how to read music. She plays the piano by ear.* ♦ *Joe doesn't need any music sheets when he plays his guitar; he knows many songs well and can play them by ear.* **2.** *informal* To decide what to do as you go along; to fit the situation.—Used with *it.* ♦ *John decided to play it by ear when he went for his interview.* ♦ *It was her first job and she didn't know what to expect, so she had to play it by ear.*

play cat and mouse with *v. phr.* To tease or fool (someone) by pretending to let him go free and then catching him again. ♦ *Joe's uncle had fun playing cat and mouse with him.* ♦ *The policeman decided to play cat and mouse when he saw the woman steal the dress in the store.*

play down *v.* To give less emphasis to; make (something) seem less important; divert attention from; draw notice away from. ♦ *The newspaper stories played down the actor's unattractive past.* ♦ *A salesman's job is to emphasize the good points of his merchandise; he must play down any faults it has.*

played out *adj. phr.* Tired out; worn out; finished; exhausted. ♦ *It had been a hard day, and by night he was played out.* ♦ *For a while, at least, it seemed the interest in great speed was played out.* Compare ALL IN.

play fair *v. phr.* To do what is right to others; act in a fair and truthful way. ♦ *The boys like the principal because he always plays fair.* ♦ *Mary would not date any other boys while Jim, her favorite boyfriend, was away; she said that would not be playing fair.*

play fast and loose *v. phr.* To do as you please without caring what will happen to other people; act so carelessly or unfairly that people cannot depend on you; be very unreliable. ♦ *He played fast and loose with the girl's affections.* ♦ *He played fast and loose with the company's good name.*

play footsie *v. phr., slang, informal* **1.** Touch the feet of a member of the opposite sex under the table as an act of flirtation. ♦ *Have you at least played footsie with her?* **2.** To engage in any sort of flirtation or collaboration, especially in a political situation. ♦ *The mayor was suspected of playing footsie with the Syndicate.*

play for keeps *v. phr.* To take an action of finality and irreversibility. ♦ *"Are you serious about me?" she asked. "Yes," he replied. "I want to marry you. I play for keeps."*

play hard to get *v. phr.* To act as if one weren't interested; be fickle; be coy. ♦ *"Professor Brown is playing very hard to get," our dean said, "but I know he will accept our offer and come to teach here."*

play havoc with *or* **raise havoc with** *v. phr.* To cause destruction; ruin; injure badly. ♦*The storm played havoc with the apple orchard.* ♦*When Ralph was arrested for stealing the car, it played havoc with his plans for going to college.* ♦*When Mr. White poisoned the cat, it played havoc with his reputation in the neighborhood.*

play hooky *v. phr., informal* To stay out of school to play. ♦*Carl is failing in school because he has played hooky so many times during the year.*

play into one's hands *v. phr.* To be or do something that another person can use against you; help an opponent against yourself. ♦*In the basketball game, Jerry's foul played into the opponents' hands.* ♦*Mary and Bobby both wanted the last piece of cake, but Bobby played into Mary's hands by trying to grab it.*

play off *v.* **1.** To match opposing persons, forces, or interests so that they balance each other. ♦*The girl played off her admirers against each other.* ♦*Britain tried to play off European nations against each other so that she would have a balance of power.* **2.** To finish the playing of (an interrupted contest.) ♦*The visitors came back the next Saturday to play off the game stopped by rain.* **3.** To settle (a tie score) between contestants by more play. ♦*When each player had won two matches, the championship was decided by playing off the tie.*

play on *or* **play upon** *v.* **1.** To cause an effect on; influence. ♦*A heavy diet of television drama played on his feelings.* **2.** To work upon for a planned effect; excite to a desired action by cunning plans; manage. ♦*The makeup salesman played on the woman's wish to look beautiful.* ♦*In some places, leaders play upon people's superstitious fears.* ♦*He played on the man's ambition and love of honor.*

play one false *v. phr., literary* To act disloyally toward (a person); betray; cheat; deceive. ♦*Good faith was not in him: he played anyone false who trusted him.* ♦*His hopes had played him false.*

play one for *v., informal* To treat (someone) as; act toward (someone) as; handle (someone) as; handle as. ♦*He played the man for a sucker.*

play one's cards right *or* **play one's cards well** *v. phr., informal* To use abilities and opportunities so as to be successful; act cleverly; make the best use of your place or skills. ♦*That millionaire started with very little but showed a skill in playing his cards right.* ♦*People liked Harold, and he played his cards well—and soon he began to get ahead rapidly.*

play ostrich *v. phr.* To refuse to face painful facts or unpleasant truths. ♦*She plays ostrich when it comes to her husband's drinking problem.*

play politics *v. phr.* To make secret agreements for your own gain; handle different groups for your own advantage. ♦*In order to get elected, he had to play politics with both the unions and the bosses.* ♦*Mary always gets what she wants by playing office politics.*

play possum *v. phr., informal* **1.** To pretend to be asleep. ♦*Johnny seemed to be fully asleep, but his mother knew that he was playing possum.* **2.** To stay quiet for self-protection; try to escape attention by inactivity. ♦*The rabbit played possum under the bushes, hoping the hunter would not see him.* ♦*Bob played possum when the teacher looked around.*

play safe *or* **play it safe** *v. phr., informal* To be very careful; accept small gains or none to avoid loss; avoid danger for the sake of safety. ♦*He got tired as the game went on, and began to play safe.* ♦*Tom didn't know what the other driver would do, so he played it safe and stopped his own car.*

play second fiddle *v. phr., informal* To act a smaller part; follow another's lead; be less noticed. ♦*His wife had the stronger mind and he played second fiddle to her.* ♦*During the tournament, lessons played second fiddle to basketball.*

play the devil with *or* **play hob with** *v. phr., informal* To cause confusion in; upset. ♦*Uncle Bob's unexpected visit played the devil with our own plans to travel.* ♦*Mother's illness played hob with our party.*

play the field *v. phr., informal* To date many different people; not always have dates with the same person. ♦*Al had a steady girlfriend, but John was* *playing the field.* ♦ *Jim was crazy about Mary, but she was still playing the field.* Contrast GO STEADY.

play the game *v. phr., informal* To obey the rules; do right; act fairly. ♦ *"That's not playing the game," we told him when he wanted to desert his wife.* ♦ *"Oh, let's play the game," he said, when his partner suggested a way to keep from paying some of their debts.* ♦ *Your parents want you to play the game in life.*

play the market *v. phr.* To try to make money on the stock market by buying and selling stocks. ♦ *John lost all his savings playing the market.* ♦ *Sometimes Mr. Smith makes a lot of money when he plays the market, and sometimes he loses.*

play to the gallery *v. phr.* To try to get the approval of the audience. ♦ *Whenever John recites in class he seems to be playing to the gallery.* ♦ *The lawyer for the defense was more interested in playing to the gallery than in winning the case.* Compare SHOW OFF.

play tricks on *v. phr.* To make another the victim of some trick or joke. ♦ *Al got angry when his classmates played a trick on him by hiding his clothes while he was swimming.*

play up *v.* To call attention to; talk more about; emphasize. ♦ *The coach played up the possibilities, and kept our minds off our weaknesses.* ♦ *The director played up the woman's glamor to conceal her lack of acting ability.*

play upon See PLAY ON.

play up to *v. phr., slang* **1.** To try to gain the favor of, especially for selfish reasons; act to win the approval of; try to please. ♦ *He played up to the boss.* **2.** To use (something) to gain an end; to attend to (a weakness). ♦ *He played up to the old lady's vanity to get her support.*

play with fire *v. phr.* To put oneself in danger; to take risks. ♦ *Leaving your door unlocked in New York City is playing with fire.* ♦ *The doctor told Mr. Smith that he must watch his diet if he doesn't want to play with fire.* Compare SKATE ON THIN ICE.

plough *or* **plow through** *v. phr.* Pass through laboriously. ♦ *Sam had to plough through hundreds of pages of* American history to get ready for his test.

plow See PUT ONE'S HAND TO THE PLOW.

plow into *v.* **1.** To attack vigorously. ♦ *He plowed into his work and finished it in a few hours.* **2.** To crash into with force. ♦ *A truck plowed into my car and smashed the fender.*

pluck up *v.* **1.** To have (courage) by your own effort; make yourself have (courage). ♦ *In spite of failure, he plucked up heart to continue.* ♦ *He plucked up courage when he saw a glimmer of hope.* **2.** To become happier; feel better; cheer up. ♦ *He plucked up when his wife recovered.*

pluck up one's courage See SCREW UP ONE'S COURAGE.

plug away See PEG AWAY.

plug in *v. phr.* To connect (an electrical appliance) to a power wire by putting its plug into a receptacle or hole. ♦ *The integrated circuit has multiplied the number of small radios that need not be plugged in.*

plug into *v.* To connect (an electrical appliance) to a power wire by inserting its plug into a receptacle or hole. ♦ *He thought he had left the lamp plugged into the wall, and so was puzzled when it wouldn't light that night.*

plume oneself *v. phr., literary* To be proud of yourself; boast. ♦ *He plumed himself on having the belle of the ball as his date.* ♦ *He plumed himself on his successful planning in the election.* ♦ *She plumed herself on the grace with which she sat on a horse.* Compare PRIDE ONESELF.

plunk down *v., informal* **1.** To drop down; fall. ♦ *After walking a mile we plunked down on a bench to rest.* **2.** To drop something noisily or firmly. ♦ *He plunked the heavy suitcase down at the station.* **3.** To pay out, primarily an excessive amount ♦ *I had to plunk down $55 for a concert ticket.*

please See AS YOU PLEASE.

pocket See BURN A HOLE IN ONE'S POCKET, LINE ONE'S POCKETS.

pocket money See SPENDING MONEY.

pocket one's pride See SWALLOW ONE'S PRIDE.

point See AT SWORDS' POINTS, AT THE POINT OF, BESIDE THE POINT, BOILING POINT, CASE IN POINT, COME TO THE

POINT, EXTRA POINT, MAKE A POINT, ON THE POINT OF, SORE SPOT *or* SORE POINT, STRETCH A POINT *or* STRAIN A POINT, TALKING POINT.

point-blank *adv.* Straightforwardly; bluntly; directly. ◆ *Sue refused point-blank to discuss marriage with Sam.*

point of view *n.* Attitude; opinion. ◆ *From the American point of view, Fidel Castro is a bad neighbor to have.*

point out *v.* **1.** To show by pointing with the finger; point to; make clear the location of. ◆ *The guide pointed out the principal sights of the city.* **2.** To bring to notice; call to attention; explain. ◆ *The policeman pointed out that the law forbids public sale of firecrackers.* ◆ *The school secretary pointed out that the closing date for making applications had passed.*

point up *v.* To show clearly; emphasize. ◆ *The increase in crime points up the need for greater police protection.* ◆ *Johnny's report card points up his talent for math.*

poison-pen *adj.* Containing threats or false accusations; written in spite or to get revenge, and usually unsigned. ◆ *Mrs. Smith received a poison-pen letter telling her that her husband was untrue.* ◆ *To get revenge on Mary, Alice wrote a poison-pen letter to the teacher and signed Mary's name to it.*

poke See PIG IN A POKE, TAKE A PUNCH AT *or* TAKE A POKE AT.

poke around *or* **poke about** *v.* **1.** To search about; look into and under things. ◆ *The detective poked around in the missing man's office.* **2.** To move slowly or aimlessly; do little things. ◆ *He didn't feel well, and poked around the house.*

poke fun at See MAKE FUN OF.

poles apart *adj.* Completely different. ◆ *The two brothers were poles apart in personality.* ◆ *It was hard for the members to make any decisions because their ideas were poles apart.*

polish off *v., informal* **1.** To defeat easily. ◆ *The Dodgers polished off the Yankees in four straight games in the 1963 World Series.* **2.** To finish completely; finish doing quickly, often in order to do something else. ◆ *The boys were hungry and polished off a big steak.* ◆ *Mary polished off her homework early so that she could watch TV.*

polish the apple *v. phr., slang* To try to make someone like you; to try to win favor by flattery. ◆ *Mary polished the apple at work because she wanted a day off.* ◆ *Susan is the teacher's pet because she always polishes the apple.*—**apple polisher** *n., slang* A person who is nice to the one in charge in order to be liked or treated better; a person who does favors for a superior. ◆ *Jane is an apple polisher. She is always helping the teacher and talking to him.* ◆ *Joe is an apple-polisher. He will do anything for the boss.* Compare EAGER BEAVER, YES-MAN.—**apple polishing** *n., slang* Trying to win someone's good-will by small acts currying favor; the behavior of an apple polisher. ◆ *When John brought his teacher flowers, everyone thought he was apple polishing.*

politics See PLAY POLITICS.

pond See LITTLE FROG IN A BIG POND.

pool See CAR POOL.

pooped out *adj., slang* Worn out; exhausted. ◆ *Everyone was pooped out after the hike.* ◆ *The heat made them feel pooped out.*

poor as a church mouse *adj. phr., informal* Penniless; broke; extremely poor. ◆ *The newly arrived boat people were poor as church mice.*

poor-mouth *v.* To be constantly complaining about one's poverty; keep saying how one cannot afford the better things in life. ◆ *Uncle Jack indulges in an awful lot of poor-mouthing, but we know that he has half a million dollars stashed away in a secret savings account.*

pop See EYES POP OUT.

pop fly *n.* A baseball batted high into the air but not very far from the plate. ◆ *The batter hit a pop fly to the shortstop.*

pop in *v. phr.* To suddenly appear without announcement. ◆ *"Just pop into my office any time you're on campus," Professor Brown said.*

pop one's cork See BLOW A FUSE, FLY OFF THE HANDLE, LOSE ONE'S MARBLES, LOSE ONE'S TEMPER.

pop the question *v. phr., slang* To ask someone to marry you. ◆ *After the dance he popped the question.* ◆ *A man is often too bashful to pop the question.*

pop up *v.* **1.** *or* **bob up** To appear suddenly or unexpectedly; show up; come out. ♦ *Just when the coach thought he had everything under control, a new problem bobbed up.* ♦ *After no one had heard from him for years, John popped up in town again.* **2.** To hit a pop fly in baseball. ♦ *Jim popped the pitch up.*

pork See SALT PORK.

port of call *n. phr.* **1.** Any of the ports that a ship visits after the start of a voyage and before the end; a port where passengers or cargo may be taken on or put off; an in-between port. ♦ *Savannah is a port of call for many Atlantic coasting vessels.* **2.** A place you visit regularly or often; a stop included on your usual way of going. ♦ *It was an obscure little restaurant which I had made something of a port of call.* ♦ *His home had become one of my regular ports of call in Boston.*

port of entry *n. phr.* **1.** A port where things brought into the country to sell may pass through customs. ♦ *Other ports of entry have been taking business from New York.* **2.** A port where a citizen of another country may legally enter a country; a port having passport and immigration facilities. ♦ *Airports have joined seaports as ports of entry for the visiting foreigner.*

position See SCORING POSITION.

possessed of *adj. phr., formal* In possession of; having; owning. ♦ *He was possessed of great wealth.* ♦ *He was possessed of great self-confidence.*

possum See PLAY POSSUM.

post See FROM PILLAR TO POST.

pot See GO TO POT.

potato See HOT POTATO.

potboiler *n.* A book, play, or film written for the primary purpose of earning money for the author. ♦ *"Reading a cheap potboiler helps me go to sleep,"* the professor wryly remarked.

pot call the kettle black *informal* The person who is criticizing someone else is as guilty as the person he accuses; the charge is as true of the person who makes it as of the one he makes it against. ♦ *When the commissioner accused the road builder of bribery, the contractor said the pot was calling the kettle black.* ♦ *Bill said John was cheating at a game but John replied that the pot was calling the kettle black.*

potluck See TAKE POTLUCK.

potluck supper See COVERED-DISH SUPPER.

potshot *n.* A direct shot at an easy, stationary target from behind a protected position or camouflage; criticism. ♦ *Modern journalists like to take potshots at the president of the United States.*

pound See PENNY WISE AND POUND FOOLISH.

pound away at *v. phr.* **1.** To attack; criticize. ♦ *In his campaign speeches the candidate kept pounding away at the administration's foreign policy.* **2.** To work industriously. ♦ *Mike was pounding away at the foundation of his new house with shovels and pickaxes.*

pound of flesh *n. phr., literary* The maximum payment authorized by law. ♦ *He had hoped that Peter would be lenient regarding the interest they had agreed on, but Peter demanded his full pound of flesh.*

pound out *v. phr.* **1.** To play a piece of music very loudly on a percussion instrument. ♦ *The boy was pounding out the tune "Mary had a little lamb" on the marimba.* **2.** To flatten something with a hammer. ♦ *The bodyshop uses special hammers to pound out the indentations in the bodies of cars.* **3.** To produce a piece of writing on a typewriter in haste and without much care. ♦ *She hurriedly pounded out a letter of recommendation for the foreign graduate student.*

pound the pavement *v. phr., informal* To walk up and down the streets; tramp about. ♦ *John pounded the pavement looking for a job.* ♦ *Mary and Bill pounded the pavement to find an apartment.*

pour See IT NEVER RAINS BUT IT POURS.

pour cold water on See THROW COLD WATER ON.

pour it on thick See LAY IT ON THICK.

pour money down the drain *v. phr.* To spend one's money unwisely; to waste one's funds. ♦ *"Stop supporting Harry's drug habit," Ralph said. "You're just pouring money down the drain."*

pour oil on troubled waters *v. phr.* To quiet a quarrel; say something to lessen anger and bring peace. ♦ *The troops were nearing a bitter quarrel* *until the leader poured oil on the troubled waters.*

pour out *v.* **1.** To tell everything about; talk all about. ♦ *Mary poured out her troubles to her pal.* **2.** To come out in great quantity; stream out. ♦ *The people poured out of the building when they heard the fire alarm.*

powder See TAKE A POWDER.

powder room *n.* The ladies' rest room. ♦ *When they got to the restaurant, Mary went to the powder room to wash up.*

power behind the throne *n. phr.* The person with the real power backing up the more visible partner (usually said about the wives of public figures). ♦ *It is rumored that the First Lady is the power behind the throne in the White House.*

practice See IN PRACTICE *also* INTO PRACTICE, MAKE A PRACTICE OF, OUT OF PRACTICE.

presence of mind *n. phr.* Effective and quick decision-making ability in times of crisis. ♦ *When Jimmy fell into the river, his father had the presence of mind to dive in after him and save him from drowning.*

present See AT PRESENT.

press box *n.* The place or room high in a sports stadium that is for newspaper men and radio and television announcers. ♦ *In baseball the official scorer sits in the press box.*

press conference *n. phr.* A meeting with news reporters. ♦ *The reporters questioned the president about foreign affairs at the press conference.* ♦ *The press conference with the senator was broadcast on television.*

press one's luck *or* **push one's luck** *v. phr.* To depend too much on luck; expect to continue to be lucky. ♦ *When John won his first two bets at the race track, he pressed his luck and increased his bets.* ♦ *If you're lucky at first, don't press your luck.*

press the flesh *v., slang* To shake hands with total strangers by the hundreds, keeping an artificial smile all the way, in order to raise one's popularity during political elections. ♦ *Incumbent Governor Maxwell was pressing the flesh all day long at six different hotels.* Compare BABY KISSER.

pressure group *n. phr.* An organization whose goal it is to create changes by lobbying for the benefit of its own members. ♦ *Certain unscrupulous pressure groups stop at nothing to achieve their selfish aims.*

pretty See SITTING PRETTY.

pretty kettle of fish See KETTLE OF FISH.

pretty penny *n. phr.* A large amount of money. ♦ *Their new house is so big and modern that we're sure it must have cost them a pretty penny.*

prevail upon *or* **prevail on** *v.* To bring to an act or belief; cause a change in; persuade. ♦ *He prevailed upon the musician to entertain instead of the absent speaker.* ♦ *He prevailed upon me to believe in his innocence.*

prey on *or* **prey upon** *v.* **1.** To habitually kill and eat; catch for food. ♦ *Cats prey on mice.* **2.** To capture or take in spoils of war or robbery. ♦ *Pirates preyed on American ships in the years just after the Revolutionary War.* **3.** To cheat; rob. ♦ *Gangsters preyed on businesses of many kinds while the sale of liquor was prohibited.* **4.** To have a tiring and weakening effect on; weaken. ♦ *Ill health had preyed on him for years.* ♦ *Business worries preyed on his mind.*

prey on one's mind *v. phr.* To afflict; worry. ♦ *He couldn't sleep because his many debts were preying on his mind.*

price on one's head *n. phr.* Reward offered to anyone who catches a thief or a murderer. ♦ *The hotel manager learned that the quiet man taken from his room by the police was a murderer with a price on his head.*

prick See KICK AGAINST THE PRICKS.

prick up one's ears *v. phr., informal* To come to interested attention; begin to listen closely; try to hear. ♦ *The woman pricked up her ears when she heard them talking about her.*

pride See SWALLOW ONE'S PRIDE.

pride must take a pinch One must endure the minor pains and hardships one encounters while being made pretty.—A proverb. ♦ *"Mother," Sue cried, "stop pulling my hair!" "Just a moment, young lady," the mother answered, while combing her hair. "Don't you know that pride must take a pinch?"*

pride oneself on *v. phr.* To be proud of; take satisfaction in; be much pleased by. ♦ *She prided herself on her beauty.*

♦*He prided himself on his strength and toughness.* Compare PLUME ONESELF.

print See FINE PRINT, IN PRINT, OUT OF PRINT.

private See IN PRIVATE.

private eye *n., colloquial* A private investigator; a detective. ♦*Buddy Ebsen played a private eye on "Barnaby Jones."*

progress See IN PROGRESS.

promise See AS GOOD AS ONE'S WORD, LICK AND A PROMISE.

promise the moon *v. phr.* To promise something impossible. ♦*A politician who promises the moon during a campaign loses the voters' respect.* ♦*I can't promise you the moon, but I'll do the best job I can.* Compare ASK FOR THE MOON.

proof of the pudding is in the eating Only through actual experience can the value of something be tested.—A proverb. ♦*He was intrigued by the ads about the new high mileage sports cars. "Drive one, sir," the salesman said. "The proof of the pudding is in the eating."*

prune See FULL OF BEANS *or* FULL OF PRUNES.

psyched up *adj., informal* Mentally alert; ready to do something. ♦*The students were all psyched up for their final exams.*

psych out *v. phr., slang, informal* **1.** To find out the real motives of (someone). ♦*Sue sure has got Joe psyched out.* **2.** To go berserk; to lose one's nerve. ♦*Joe says he doesn't ride his motorcycle on the highway anymore because he's psyched out.* ♦*Jim psyched out and robbed a liquor store, when he has all he needs and wants!*

Public See JOHN Q. PUBLIC.

public See AIR ONE'S DIRTY LINEN IN PUBLIC *or* WASH ONE'S DIRTY LINEN IN PUBLIC, IN PUBLIC, IN THE PUBLIC EYE.

public-address system *n.* A set of devices for making a speaker's voice louder so that he can be heard by more people. ♦*The public-address system broke down during the senator's speech.* ♦*The news was announced over the public-address system.*

public enemy *n. phr.* A famous criminal. ♦*Al Capone of Chicago used to be Public Enemy Number One during Prohibition.*

public speaker *n.* A person who speaks to the public. ♦*A public speaker must appeal to all kinds of people.*

puffed up *adj.* Elated; proud; conceited. ♦*Just because Bob inherited some money from his father is no reason for him to act so puffed up.*

pull See LONG HAUL *or* LONG PULL.

pull a fast one *v. phr.* To gain the advantage over one's opponent unfairly; deceive; trick. ♦*When Smith was told by his boss that he might be fired, he called the company president, his father-in-law, and pulled a fast one by having his boss demoted.*

pull a long face See LONG FACE.

pull date *n., informal* The date stamped on baked goods, dairy products, or other perishable foods indicating the last day on which they may be sold before they must be removed from the shelves in a retail store. ♦*This pie is way past the pull date—small wonder it's rotten.*

pull down *v., informal* **1.** To catch (a ball) after a hard run. ♦*The outfielder pulled down a long drive to center field.* **2.** To earn. ♦*Mr. Blake pulls down $500 a week.* ♦*John pulled down an A in algebra by studying hard.* Compare HAUL DOWN.

pull down about one's ears *or* **pull down around one's ears** See ABOUT ONE'S EARS.

pull in See HAUL IN.

pull in one's horns *or* **draw in one's horns** *v. phr., informal* **1.** To reduce your boasts; calm down from a quarrel; back down on a promise. ♦*He said he could beat any man there single-handed, but he pulled in his horns when Jack came forward.* **2.** To cut back from one's usual way of living; reduce spending or activities; save. ♦*After the business failed, Father had to pull in his horns.* ♦*As one advances in years, it is prudent to pull in one's horns more and more as to physical activity.*

pull off *v., informal* To succeed in (something thought difficult or impossible); do. *Ben Hogan pulled off the impossible by winning three golf tournaments in one year.* ♦*The bandits pulled off a daring bank robbery.* Compare PUT ACROSS 2.

pull one's chestnuts out of the fire To do someone else a great favor which they don't really deserve, doing oneself a disfavor in the process. ♦ *Small countries often have to pull the chestnuts out of the fire for their more powerful neighbors.*

pull oneself together *v. phr.* To become calm after being excited or disturbed; recover self-command; control yourself. ♦ *It had been a disturbing moment, but he was able to pull himself together.*

pull oneself up by the bootstraps *or* **pull oneself up by one's own bootstraps** *adv. phr.* To succeed without help; succeed by your own efforts. ♦ *He had to pull himself up by the bootstraps.*

pull one's leg *v. phr., informal* To get someone to accept a ridiculous story as true; fool someone with a humorous account of something; trick. ♦ *For a moment, I actually believed that his wife had royal blood. Then I realized he was pulling my leg.* ♦ *Western cowboys loved to pull a stranger's leg.* Compare STRING ALONG.—**leg-pulling** *n.* ♦ *Strangers were often fooled by the cowboys' leg-pulling.*

pull one's punches *v. phr., informal* **1.** Not to hit as hard as you can. ♦ *Jimmy pulled his punches and let Paul win the boxing match.* **2.** To hide unpleasant facts or make them seem good.— Usually used in the negative. ♦ *The mayor spoke bluntly; he didn't pull any punches.* Contrast STRAIGHT FROM THE SHOULDER.

pull one's teeth *v. phr.* To take power away from; make powerless. ♦ *The general pulled the teeth of the rebel army by blocking its ammunition supply line.* ♦ *The student government council was so irresponsible that the principal pulled its teeth.*

pull one's weight *v. phr.* To do your full share of work; do your part. ♦ *In a small shop, it is important that each man pull his weight.* ♦ *When Mother was sick in the hospital, Father said each child must pull his own weight.* Compare WORTH ONE'S SALT.

pullout *n.* An evacuation. ♦ *The pullout of the American military proceeded on schedule.*

pull out *v. phr.* **1.** To withdraw; leave unceremoniously. ♦ *The defeated army hastily pulled out of the occupied territories.* **2.** To leave (said about trains). ♦ *The train pulled out of Grand Central Station just as the foreign students got there.* **3.** To remove by order; evacuate. ♦ *Napoleon pulled his beaten troops out of Russia.*

pull out of a hat *v. phr., informal* To get as if by magic; invent; imagine. ♦ *When the introduction to a dictionary tells you how many hours went into its making, these figures were not pulled out of a hat.* ♦ *Let's see you pull an excuse out of your hat.*

pull over *v.* To drive to the side of the road and stop. ♦ *The policeman told the speeder to pull over.* ♦ *Everyone pulled over to let the ambulance pass.*

pull rank *v. phr., slang, informal* To assert one's superior position or authority on a person of lower rank as in exacting a privilege or a favor. ♦ *How come you always get the night duty?—Phineas Leman pulled rank on me.*

pull something on one *v. phr.* To perpetrate something prejudicial; deceive. ♦ *Larry pulled a very dirty trick on Ann when, after going with her for three years, he suddenly married another girl.*

pull strings *or* **pull wires** *v. phr., informal* To secretly use influence and power, especially with people in charge or in important jobs to do or get something; make use of friends to gain your wishes. ♦ *If you want to see the governor, Mr. Root can pull strings for you.* ♦ *Jack pulled wires and got us a room at the crowded hotel.*—**wire-puller** *n.* ♦ *Bill got a ticket for speeding, but his father is a wire-puller and got it fixed.*—**wire-pulling** *n.* ♦ *It took some wire-pulling to get the mayor to come to the party.*

pull the plug on *v. phr., slang* To expose (someone's) secret activities. ♦ *The citizens' committee pulled the plug on the mayor, and he lost his election.*

pull the rug out from under *v. phr., informal* To withdraw support unexpectedly from; to spoil the plans of. ♦ *Bill thought he would be elected, but his friends pulled the rug out from under him and voted for Vin.* ♦ *We were planning a vacation, but the baby's illness pulled the rug out from under us.*

pull the wool over one's eyes *v. phr., informal* To fool someone into thinking well of you; deceive. ♦ *The businessman had pulled the wool over his partner's eyes about their financial position.* ♦ *Bob tried to pull the wool over his teacher's eyes, but she was too smart for him.*

pull through *v.* **1.** To help through; bring safely through a difficulty or sudden trouble; save. ♦ *A generous loan showed the bank's faith in Father and pulled him through the business trouble.* **2.** To recover from an illness or misfortune; conquer a disaster; escape death or failure. ♦ *By a near-miracle, he pulled through after the smashup.*

pull together *v.* To join your efforts with those of others; work on a task together; cooperate. ♦ *Many men must pull together if a large business is to succeed.* ♦ *Tim was a good football captain because he always got his teammates to pull together.*

pull up *v.* **1.** To check the forward motion of; halt; stop. ♦ *He pulled up his horse at the gate.* **2.** To tell (someone) to stop doing something; say (someone) is doing wrong and must stop; scold. ♦ *Jim talked rudely to Mother, and Father pulled him up.* ♦ *Ann said in her report that America was discovered in 1634, and the teacher pulled her up.* **3.** To stop moving forward; halt. ♦ *The car slowed down and pulled up at the curb.* **4.** To come even with; move up beside. ♦ *The other boat pulled up alongside us.*

pull up one's socks *v. phr.* To try to do better, either in terms of one's behavior or at a task one is performing. ♦ *I'll have to pull up my socks if I am going to finish my work today.*

pull up short *v. phr.* To suddenly stop. ♦ *He pulled up short in his red car at the corner when he saw a pregnant lady crossing.* ♦ *When Mark saw that he was hurting Jill's feelings, he pulled up short and started to talk about something entirely different.*

pull up stakes *v. phr., informal* To leave the place where you have been living. ♦ *We are going to pull up stakes and move to California.* ♦ *The Jones family pulled up stakes three times in two years.*

pull wires See PULL STRINGS.

punch See BEAT TO THE PUNCH, PACK A PUNCH, PULL ONE'S PUNCHES, TAKE A PUNCH AT.

punch-drunk *adj.* **1.** Dazed or become dulled in the mind from being hit in the head. ♦ *He was a punch-drunk boxer who made his living shining shoes.* **2.** In a foggy state of mind; groggy. ♦ *Mary was so thrilled at winning the contest she acted punch-drunk.* ♦ *Mark was punch-drunk for a few minutes after he fell off his bicycle.*

puppy love *also* **calf love** *n., informal* The first love of very young people. ♦ *When John and Mary began going around together in junior high school, their parents said it was just puppy love.*

pure and simple *adj.* Simply stated; basic.—Follows the noun it modifies and is used for emphasis. ♦ *The problem, pure and simple, is finding a baby-sitter.* ♦ *The question, pure and simple, is whether you will support me.* Compare BOIL DOWN 3.

purpose See AT CROSS PURPOSES, ON PURPOSE, TO ALL INTENTS AND PURPOSES.

purse See LINE ONE'S POCKETS *also* LINE ONE'S PURSE.

purse strings *n.* Care or control of money. ♦ *Dad holds the purse strings in our family.* ♦ *The treasurer refused to let go of the club's purse strings.*

push around *v., informal* To be bossy with; bully. ♦ *Don't try to push me around!* ♦ *Paul is always pushing the smaller children around.*

push off *or* **shove off** *v.* **1.** To push a boat away from the shore. ♦ *Before Tom could reach the boat, Jake had shoved off.* **2.** *slang* To start; leave. ♦ *We were ready to push off at ten o'clock, but had to wait for Jill.* ♦ *Jim was planning to stay at the beach all day, but when the crowds arrived he shoved off.*

push on *v. phr.* To press forward; proceed forward laboriously. ♦ *The exhausted mountain climbers pushed on, despite the rough weather, as the peak was already in sight.*

push one's luck See PRESS ONE'S LUCK.

pushover *n.* **1.** Something easy to accomplish or overcome. ♦ *For Howard steering a boat is a pushover as he was raised on a tropical island.* **2.** A person easily seduced. ♦ *It is rumored that she is a pushover when she has a bit to drink.*

push over *v. phr.* To upset; overthrow. ♦ *She is standing on her feet very solidly; a little criticism from you certainly won't push her over.* ♦ *The wind in Chicago can be so strong that sometimes I'm afraid I'll get pushed over.*

push the panic button *v. phr., slang* To become very much frightened; nervous or excited, especially at a time of danger or worry. ♦ *John thought he saw a ghost and pushed the panic button.* ♦ *Keep cool; don't hit the panic button!* Syn. LOSE ONE'S HEAD.

push-up *n.* An exercise to build strong arms and shoulders, in which you lie on your stomach and push your body up on your hands and toes. ♦ *At the age of seventy, Grandpa still does twenty push-ups every day.* ♦ *The football team does push-ups every day.*

push up daisies *v. phr., slang* To be dead and buried. ♦ *I'll be around when you're pushing up daisies.* ♦ *Don't play with guns or you may push up the daisies.*

put See HARD PUT *or* HARD PUT TO IT, STAY PUT.

put about *v. phr.*—Nautical usage. To turn in the opposite direction; turn around. ♦ *When we saw the storm clouds thickening in the sky, we put about quickly and raced ashore.*

put a bee in one's bonnet See BEE IN ONE'S BONNET.

put a bug in one's ear *or* **put a flea in one's ear** See BUG IN ONE'S EAR.

put across *v.* **1.** To explain clearly; make yourself understood; communicate. ♦ *He knew how to put his ideas across.* Compare GET ACROSS. **2.** *informal* To get (something) done successfully; bring to success; make real. ♦ *He put across a big sales campaign.* ♦ *The new librarian put across a fine new library building.* Syn. PUT OVER 2. Compare PULL OFF.

put all one's eggs in one basket *v. phr.* To place all your efforts, interests, or hopes in a single person or thing. ♦ *Going steady in high school is putting all your eggs in one basket too soon.* ♦ *To buy stock in a single company is to put all your eggs in one basket.* ♦ *He*

has decided to specialize in lathe work, although he knows it is risky to put all his eggs in one basket.

put a new face on *v. phr.* To alter the aspect of something; change. ♦ *Mr. Merryman's announcement of his candidacy for governor puts an entirely new face on the political scene in our state.*

put an end to *or* **put a stop to** *v. phr.* **1.** To make (something) end; stop; end. ♦ *The farmer built an electric fence around his field to put an end to trespassing.* ♦ *The principal said that running in the halls was dangerous, and told the teachers to put a stop to it.* **2.** To destroy or kill. ♦ *The new highway took most of the traffic from the old road and put an end to Mr. Hanson's motel business.* ♦ *When the horse broke his leg, the farmer put an end to him.*

put aside *v. phr.* **1.** To save; put something aside for a special purpose. ♦ *Peter puts $100 aside every week.* **2.** To let go of; put away. ♦ *The teacher to the students, "Put your books aside and start writing your tests!"*

put away *v.* **1.** To put in the right place or out of sight. ♦ *She put away the towels.* **2.** To lay aside; stop thinking about. ♦ *He put his worries away for the weekend.* **3.** *informal* To eat or drink. ♦ *He put away a big supper and three cups of coffee.* Compare STOW AWAY. **4.** *informal* To put in a mental hospital. ♦ *He had to put his wife away when she became mentally ill.* **5.** To put to death for a reason; kill. ♦ *He had his dog put away when it became too old and unhappy.*

put back the clock *or* **turn back the clock** *v. phr.* To go back in time; relive the past. ♦ *If I could put back the clock, I'd give more thought to preparing for a career.* ♦ *Richard wishes that he had lived in frontier days, but he can't turn back the clock.*

put by *v.* To save for the future; lay aside. ♦ *He had put by a good sum during a working lifetime.*

putdown *n.* An insult. ♦ *It was a nasty putdown when John called his sister a fat cow.*

put down *v. phr.* **1.** To stop by force; crush. ♦ *In 24 hours the general had entirely put down the rebellion.* **2.** To put a stop to; check. ♦ *She had patiently put down unkind talk by living a good life.* **3.** To write a record of; write down. ♦ *He put down the story while it was fresh in his mind.* **4.** To write a name in a list as agreeing to do something. ♦ *The banker put himself down for $1000.* ♦ *Sheila put Barbara down for the decorations.* **5.** To decide the kind or class of; characterize. ♦ *He put the man down as a bum.* ♦ *He put it down as a piece of bad luck.* **6.** To name as a cause; attribute. ♦ *He put the odd weather down to nuclear explosions.* **7.** To dig; drill; sink. *He put down a new well.*

put forth *v. phr.* To produce; issue; send out. ♦ *In the spring the apple trees put forth beautiful white blossoms.* ♦ *The chairman of the board put forth an innovative proposal that was circulated by mail.*

put ideas into one's head *v. phr.* To persuade someone to do something negative; put one up to something. ♦ *Billy would never have poured glue into his father's shoes if the neighbor's son hadn't been putting ideas into his head.*

put in *v.* **1.** To add to what has been said; say (something) in addition to what others say. ♦ *While the boys were discussing the car accident, Ben put in that the road was icy.* ♦ *My father put in a word for me and I got the job.* **2.** To buy and keep in a store to sell. ♦ *He put in a full stock of drugs.* **3.** To spend (time). ♦ *He put in many years as a printer.* ♦ *He put in an hour a day reading.* **4.** To plant. ♦ *He put in a row of radishes.* **5.** To stop at a port on a journey by water. ♦ *After the fire, the ship put in for repairs.* **6.** To apply; ask.—Used with *for.* ♦ *When a better job was open, he put in for it.* ♦ *The sailor put in for time to visit his family before the ship went to sea.*

put in a word for *v. phr.* To speak in favor of someone; recommend someone. ♦ *"Don't worry about your job application," Sam said to Tim. "I'll put in a word for you with the selection committee."*

put in an appearance *also* **make an appearance** *v. phr.* To be present, esp. for a short time; visit; appear. ♦ *He put in an appearance at work, but he was*

too ill to stay. ♦ *The president put in an appearance at several dances the evening after he was sworn in.*

put in mind of *v. phr., nonstandard* To remind of; suggest to; call up the memory of. ♦ *She puts me in mind of my sister.* ♦ *That puts me in mind of a story.*

put in one's place *v. phr., informal* To criticize someone for impolite boldness; remind someone of low rank or position; reduce someone's unsuitable pride; deflate. ♦ *The assistant was trying to take command when the professor put him in his place by saying, "No, I'm the boss here."* ♦ *She was a teacher who could put a troublemaker in his place with just a glance.* Syn. CUT DOWN TO SIZE.

put in one's two cents worth See TWO CENTS 2.

put in one's way See PUT IN THE WAY OF.

put in the way of *or* **put in one's way** *v. phr.* To set before (someone); give to (someone); show the way to; help toward. ♦ *After Joe graduated, the coach put him in the way of a good job.* ♦ *The librarian put me in the way of a lot of new material on the subject of my report.*

put (it) in black and white See BLACK AND WHITE.

put (it) in writing See BLACK AND WHITE.

put it on thick See LAY IT ON.

put off *v.* **1.** *informal* To cause confusion in; embarrass; displease. ♦ *I was rather put off by the shamelessness of his proposal.* ♦ *The man's slovenliness put me off.* **2.** To wait and have (something) at a later time; postpone. ♦ *They put off the picnic because of the rain.* **3.** To make (someone) wait; turn aside. ♦ *When he asked her to name a day for their wedding, she put him off.* ♦ *When the bill collector called, Mrs. Smith managed to put him off.* **4.** To draw away the attention; turn aside; distract. ♦ *Little Jeannie began to tell the guests some family secrets, but Father was able to put her off.* **5.** To move out to sea; leave shore. ♦ *They put off in small boats to meet the coming ship.* Syn. PUT OUT.

put on *v. phr.* **1.** To dress in. ♦ *The boy took off his clothes and put on his* *pajamas.* ♦ *Mother put a coat on the baby.* **2a.** To pretend; assume; show. ♦ *Mary isn't really sick; she's only putting on.* ♦ *He put on a smile.* ♦ *The child was putting on airs.* **2b.** To exaggerate; make too much of. ♦ *That's rather putting it on* Compare LAY IT ON. **3.** To begin to have more (body weight); gain (weight). ♦ *Mary was thin from sickness, and the doctor said she must put on ten pounds.* ♦ *Too many sweets and not enough exercise will make you put on weight.* **4a.** To plan and prepare; produce; arrange; give; stage. ♦ *The senior class put on a dance.* ♦ *The actor put on a fine performance.* **4b.** To make (an effort). ♦ *The runner put on an extra burst of speed and won the race.* **5.** To choose to send; employ on a job. ♦ *The school put on extra men to get the new building ready.*

put-on *n.* An act of teasing; the playing of a practical joke on someone. ♦ *Eric didn't realize that it was a put-on when his friends phoned him that he won the lottery.*

put on airs *v. phr.* To show conceit; act in a superior or condescending manner. ♦ *The fact that her parents own a villa in Capri is no reason for Amanda to keep putting on airs.*

put on an act *v. phr.* **1.** To perform a play. ♦ *The seventh grade put on a lovely act for Christmas for the parents.* **2.** To pretend. ♦ *"If you always put on an act," her father said, "people will never know who you really are."*

put on ice See ON ICE 2.

put one in one's place See CUT DOWN TO SIZE.

put one in the picture *v. phr.* To inform someone of all the facts about a given situation. ♦ *Once you're back from your overseas trip, we'll put you in the picture about recent developments at home.*

put one on a pedestal *v. phr.* To exaggeratedly worship or admire a person. ♦ *Daniel puts Elaine on a pedestal and caters to her every whim.*

put one on one's feet See ON ONE'S FEET 2.

put one out of the way See OUT OF THE WAY 3.

put one through one's paces *v. phr.* To train and discipline someone; test one's abilities. ♦ *The new recruits were certainly put through their paces by the drill sergeant.*

put one wise *v. phr.* To bring one up-to-date; inform someone; explain. ♦ *Our old friend David put us wise as to where the best used cars could be found in Chicago.*

put one's back to it *v. phr.* To make a real effort; to try. ♦ *You can finish the job by noon if you put your back to it.* ♦ *I'm sure you can make the football team if you put your back to it.*

put one's best foot forward *v. phr., informal* To try to make a good impression; try to make a good appearance; do one's best. ♦ *During courtship, it is natural to put your best foot forward.* ♦ *When Ted applied for the job he put his best foot forward.*

put one's cards on the table See LAY ONE'S CARDS ON THE TABLE.

put oneself in another's place *or* **put oneself in another's shoes** *v. phr.* To understand another person's feeling imaginatively; try to know his feelings and reasons with understanding; enter into his trouble. ♦ *It seemed like a dreadful thing for Bob to do, but I tried to put myself in his place.* ♦ *If you will put yourself in the customer's shoes you may realize why the thing isn't selling.*

put one's finger on *also* **lay one's finger on** *v. phr.* To find exactly. ♦ *The engineers couldn't put their fingers on the reason for the rocket's failure to orbit.* ♦ *We called in an electrician hoping he could put a finger on the cause of the short circuit.*

put one's foot down *v. phr., informal* To take a decided stand; be stubborn in decision. ♦ *John didn't want to practice his piano lesson, but his teacher put his foot down.* ♦ *When it came to smoking pot at parties, our parents put their foot down.*

put one's foot in it *or* **put one's foot in one's mouth** *v. phr., informal* To speak carelessly and rudely; hurt another's feelings without intending to; make a rude mistake. ♦ *He put his foot in it with his remark about self-made men because Jones was one of them.* ♦ *She put her foot in her mouth with her joke about that church, not knowing that one of the guests belonged to it.*

put one's hand on See LAY ONE'S HANDS ON 3.

put one's hand to or **set one's hand to** or **turn one's hand to** v. phr. To start working at; try to do. ◆ Hal does a good job at everything that he turns his hand to. ◆ After Mr. Sullivan found farming unprofitable, he moved to town and turned his hand to carpentry.

put one's hand to the plow or **set one's hand to the plow** v. phr. To start doing something of importance; give yourself to a big job. ◆ We felt that he had put his hand to the plow, and we didn't like it when he quit.

put one's head in the sand See HIDE ONE'S HEAD IN THE SAND.

put one's heart on one's sleeve See HEART ON ONE'S SLEEVE.

put one's money on a scratched horse v. phr., informal To bet on a certain failure; to gamble without a chance of winning. ◆ You bet on the New York Mets to win the World Series? Why put your money on a scratched horse? Compare STACK THE CARDS.

put one's nose out of joint v. phr., informal **1.** To make you jealous; leave you out of favor. ◆ When Jane accepted Tom's invitation it put Jack's nose out of joint. **2.** To ruin your plans; cause you disappointment. ◆ Joe's mother put his nose out of joint by not letting him go to the movie.

put one's house in order or **set one's house in order** v. phr. To arrange your affairs in good order. ◆ Grandfather knew he would not live long and set his house in order. ◆ When Mr. Black died, his lawyer helped the widow put her house in order.

put one's shoulder to the wheel v. phr. To make a great effort yourself or with others; try hard; cooperate. ◆ The effort to get a new high school succeeded because everyone put his shoulder to the wheel. ◆ The company was failing in business until a new manager put his shoulder to the wheel.

put on one's thinking cap v. phr. To think hard and long about some problem or question. ◆ Miss Stone told her pupils to put on their thinking caps before answering the question.

put on paper See BLACK AND WHITE.

put on the back burner See ON ICE.

put on the dog v. phr. To behave ostentatiously in terms of dress and manner. ◆ "Stop putting on the dog with me," Sue cried at Roy. "I knew the real you from way back!"

put on the line See LAY ON THE LINE.

put on the map v. phr. To make (a place) well known. ◆ The first successful climb of Mount Matterhorn put Zermatt, Switzerland, on the map. ◆ Shakespeare put his hometown of Stratford-on-Avon on the map.

put out v. **1.** To make a flame or light stop burning; extinguish; turn off. ◆ Please put the light out when you leave the room. ◆ The firemen put out the blaze. **2.** To prepare for the public; produce; make. ◆ For years he had put out a weekly newspaper. ◆ It is a small restaurant, which puts out an excellent dinner. **3.** To invest or loan money. ◆ He put out all his spare money at 4 percent or better. **4.** To make angry; irritate; annoy. ◆ It puts the teacher out to be lied to. ◆ Father was put out when Jane spilled grape juice on his new suit. **5.** informal To cause inconvenience to; bother. ◆ He put himself out to make things pleasant for us. ◆ Will it put you out if I borrow your pen? Compare GO OUT OF ONE'S WAY. **6.** To retire from play in baseball. ◆ The runner was put out at first base. **7.** To go from shore; leave. ◆ A Coast Guard boat put out through the waves. **8.** vulgar, avoidable Said of women easy and ready to engage in sexual intercourse. ◆ It is rumored that Hermione gets her promotions as fast as she does because she puts out.

put out of action See OUT OF ACTION.

put out of the way v. phr. To kill. ◆ When people spoke against the dictator, he had them put out of the way. ◆ The old dog was very sick, and Father had the animal doctor put him out of the way.

put over v. **1.** To wait to a later time; postpone. ◆ They put over the meeting to the following Tuesday. Syn. PUT OFF. **2.** informal To make a success of; complete. ◆ He put over a complex and difficult business deal. Syn. BRING OFF, PUT ACROSS, SLIP OVER. **3.** informal To practice deception; trick; fool.—Used with on. ◆ George thought he was putting *something over on the teacher when he said he was absent the day before because his mother was sick and needed him.* ♦ *Tom really slipped one over on us when he came to the Halloween party dressed as a witch.*

put someone on   *v.* To play a joke on someone by saying or doing things that are only pretense; kid. ♦ *When the voice on the phone told Mrs. Jones she had won a $10,000 prize, she thought someone was putting her on.*

put that in your pipe and smoke it   *v. phr., informal* To understand something told you; accept something as fact or reality; not try to change it.— Usually used as a command, normally only in speech, and often considered rude. ♦ *People don't vote against Santa Claus, and you might as well put that in your pipe and smoke it.* ♦ *I am not going to do that and you can put that in your pipe and smoke it.*

put the bite on   *v. phr., slang* To ask (for money, favors, etc.) ♦ *John put the bite on his friend for several tickets to the dance.* ♦ *Willie Mays put the bite on the Giants for a large raise.*

put the cart before the horse   See CART BEFORE THE HORSE.

put their heads together *or* **lay their heads together**   *v. phr., informal* To plan or consider things together; discuss something as a group; talk it over. ♦ *They put their heads together and decided on a gift.* ♦ *We laid our heads together and decided to have a picnic.*

put through   *v. phr.* **1.** To carry out; arrange. ♦ *If Jim can put through one more financial transaction like this one, we will be rich.* **2.** To connect. (said of telephone calls) ♦ *The telephone operator had to put me through to Zambia as there is no direct dialing there yet.*

put through one's paces   *v. phr., informal* To test the different abilities and skills of a person or a thing; call for a show of what one can do. ♦ *He put his new car through its paces.* ♦ *Many different problems put the new mayor through his paces in the first months of his term.*

put to bed   *v. phr.* **1.** To put to rest for the night. ♦ *Father put the three children to bed.* ♦ *The boy seemed ill, so the nurse put him to bed.* **2.** *informal* To com-

plete preparations and print. ♦ *The newspaper was put to bed at 1:15 A.M.* ♦ *The pressroom was late in putting the sports section to bed.*

put to it   *adj. phr.* Hard pressed; having trouble; in difficulty; puzzled. ♦ *When he lost his job, he was rather put to it for a while to provide for his family.* ♦ *The boy was put to it to answer the teacher's question.*

put to rights *or* **set to rights**   *v. phr., informal* To put in good order; clean up. *It took the company a long time to put the office to rights after the fire.* ♦ *It took Mrs. Smith an hour to set the room to rights after the party.*

put to sea   *v. phr.* To start a voyage. ♦ *The captain said the ship would put to sea at six in the morning.* ♦ *In the days of sailing ships, putting to sea depended on the tides.*

put to shame   *v. phr.* **1.** To disgrace. ♦ *The cleanliness of European cities puts our cities to shame.* ♦ *That filthy dump puts our town to shame.* **2.** To do much better than surpass. ♦ *Einstein put other physicists to shame when he proved his theory of relativity correct.*

put to sleep   *v. phr.* **1.** To cause to fall asleep. ♦ *Mother used to put us to sleep by telling us a good-night story and giving us a kiss.* **2.** To kill with an injection (said of animals). ♦ *Dr. Murphy, the veterinarian, put our sick, old dog to sleep.*

put to the sword   *v. phr., literary* To kill (people) in war, especially with a sword. ♦ *The Romans put their enemies to the sword.* ♦ *In some wars captives have been put to the sword.*

put to use   *v. phr.* To use. ♦ *During the early part of the Korean war the cooks and office workers of the U.S. Army were put to use in battle.* ♦ *Henry decided to put his dictionary to use.* ♦ *I wish you'd put the lawn mower to use!*

put two and two together   *v. phr.* To make decisions based on available proofs; reason from the known facts; conclude; decide. ♦ *He had put two and two together and decided where they had probably gone.* ♦ *It was just a mater of putting two and two together: the facts seemed to permit only one decision.*

put up   *v.* **1a.** To make and pack (especially a lunch or medicine); get ready;

prepare. ◆ *Every morning Mother puts up lunches for the three children.* ◆ *The druggist put up the medicine that the doctor had prescribed.* Compare MAKE UP 1. **1b.** To put food into jars or cans to save; can. ◆ *Mother is putting up peaches in jars.* **1c.** To store away for later use. ◆ *The farmer put up three tons of hay for the winter.* **2.** To put in place; put (something) where it belongs. ◆ *After he unpacked the car, John put it up.* ◆ *After the hard ride, the doctor gave the horse to the stable boy to put up.* ◆ *After the battle, the knight put up his sword.* Syn. PUT AWAY. **3.** To suggest that (someone) be chosen a member, officer, or official. ◆ *The club decided to take in another member, and Bill put up Charles.*— Often used with *for.* ◆ *The Republicans put Mr. Williams up for mayor.* **4.** To put (hair) a special way; arrange. ◆ *Aunt May puts up her hair in curlers every night.* Compare DO UP 3a. **5.** To place on sale; offer for sale. ◆ *She put the house up for sale.* **6a.** To provide lodging for; furnish a room to. ◆ *The visitor was put up in the home of Mr. Wilson.* ◆ *They put Frank up at a good hotel.* **6b.** To rent or get shelter; take lodging; stay in a place to sleep. ◆ *The traveler put up at a motel.* ◆ *We put up with friends on our trip to Canada.* **7.** To make; engage in. *He put up a good fight against his sickness.* Compare CARRY ON. **8.** To furnish (money) or something needed; pay for. ◆ *He put up the money to build a hotel.*

put-up *adj.* Artificially arranged; plotted; phony; illegal. ◆ *The FBI was sure that the bank robbers worked together with an insider and that the whole affair was a put-up job.*

put up a (brave, good, etc.**) fight** *v. phr.* To resist. ◆ *He put up a good fight but he was bound to lose in the end to the older, more experienced chess player.*

put up a (brave or **good) front** *v. phr.* To act courageously, even though one is actually afraid. ◆ *When Joe was taken in for his open heart surgery, he put up a brave front, although his hands were shaking.*

put up or shut up *v. phr. informal* **1.** To bet your money on what you say or stop saying it. —Often used as a command; often considered rude. ◆ *The man from out of town kept saying their team would beat ours and finally John told him "Put up or shut up."* **2.** To prove something or stop saying it.—Often used as a command; often considered rude. ◆ *George told Al that he could run faster than the school champion and Al told George to put up or shut up.*

put upon *v.* To use (someone) unfairly; expect too much from.—Used in the passive or in the past participle. ◆ *Martha was put upon by the bigger girls.* ◆ *Arthur was a much put-upon person.*

put up to *v. phr., informal* To talk to and make do; persuade to; get to do. ◆ *Older boys put us up to painting the statue red.* Compare EGG ON.

put up with *v.* To accept patiently; bear. ◆ *We had to put up with Jim's poor table manners because he refused to change.* ◆ *The mother told her children, "I refuse to put up with your tracking in mud!"* Compare STAND FOR.

put wise *v., slang* To tell (someone) facts that will give him an advantage over others or make him alert to opportunity or danger. ◆ *The new boy did not know that Jim was playing a trick on him, so I put him wise.* —Often used with *to.* ◆ *Someone put the police wise to the plan of the bank robbers, and when the robbers went into the bank, the police were waiting to catch them.* Compare TIP OFF.

put words into one's mouth *v. phr.* To say without proof that another person has certain feelings or opinions; claim a stand or an idea is another's without asking; speak for another without right. ◆ *When he said "John here is in favor of the idea." I told him not to put words in my mouth.*

q See MIND ONE'S P'S AND Q'S.

Q.T. See ON THE Q.T.

qualms See HAVE (NO) QUALMS ABOUT.

quantity See UNKNOWN QUANTITY.

quarterback sneak *n.* A football play in which the quarterback takes the ball from the center and dives straight ahead in an attempt to gain a very short distance. ◆*Johnson took the ball over on a quarterback sneak for a touchdown.*

queen See HOMECOMING QUEEN.

queer fish *n.* A strange or unusual person who does odd things. ◆*Uncle Algernon dresses in heavy furs in the summer and short-sleeved shirts in the winter. No wonder everyone considers him a queer fish.*

queer oneself *v. phr.* To act in such a manner as to offend others and thus one's own chances or position. ◆*Phil has queered himself with many girls by his erratic behavior.*

quest See IN SEARCH OF *also* IN QUEST OF.

question See BEG THE QUESTION, BESIDE THE POINT *or* BESIDE THE QUESTION, BEYOND QUESTION *also* WITHOUT QUESTION, CALL IN QUESTION, IN QUESTION, INTO QUESTION, OUT OF THE QUESTION, POP THE QUESTION.

quick buck See FAST BUCK.

quick on the draw See QUICK ON THE TRIGGER.

quick on the trigger *or* **trigger happy** *adj. phr.* Ready to shoot without warning; fast with a gun. ◆*He's a dangerous criminal quick on the trigger.* **2.** *informal* Fast at answering questions or solving problems. ◆*In class discussions John is always quick on the trigger.*

quick on the uptake *adj. phr.* Smart; intelligent. ◆*Eleanor is very witty and quick on the uptake.*

quick study *n. phr.* One who acquires new skills and habits in record time. ◆*Sue is new at her job but people have confidence in her because she is a quick study.*

quit See CALL IT QUITS.

quite a bit See QUITE A LITTLE.

quite a few *or* **quite a number** *also formal* **not a few** *n. or adj. phr.* Rather a large number; more than a few. ◆*Quite a few went to the game.* ◆*The basket had quite a few rotten apples in it.*—The phrase *quite a number* is used like an adjective only before *less, more.* ◆*Few people saw the play on the first night but quite a number more came on the second night.*—Sometimes used like an adverb. ◆*We still have quite a few more miles to go before we reach New York.* Syn. GOOD MANY; NOT A FEW. Compare A FEW; A NUMBER.

quite a little *or informal* **quite a bit** *also formal* **not a little** *n. or adj. phr.* Rather a large amount; rather much; more than a little. ◆*We are not finished; quite a little is left to do.* ◆*Cleaning the backyard needed quite a little work.*—The phrase *quite a bit* is used like an adjective only before *less, more.* ◆*Six inches of snow fell today, and quite a bit more is coming tonight.*—Sometimes used like an adverb. ◆*Harry was sick quite a little last winter.* Compare A LITTLE, A LOT, QUITE A FEW.

quite a number See QUITE A FEW.

quite the thing *n. phr.* The socially proper thing to do. ◆*In polite society it is quite the thing to send a written thank you note to one's host or hostess after a dinner party.*

rabbit See JACK-RABBIT START.

race See DRAG RACE, RAT RACE.

race against time *v. phr.* To be in a great hurry to finish a given project by a specified deadline. ◆ *The workers were racing against time to finish the campus modernization project.*

race to stand still *v. phr.* To be so far behind in one's work that one must exert an effort similar to that needed to win a race in order simply not to fall even further behind. ◆ *"Could you review this book for us, Professor Brown?" the editor asked. "Unfortunately, no," the professor answered. "I'm so behind in my work that I am racing to stand still."*

rack and ruin *n. phr.* Complete decay; condition of decline. ◆ *The entire house had been so neglected that it had gone to rack and ruin.*

rack one's brain *v. phr.* To try your best to think; make a great mental effort; especially: to try to remember something you have known. ◆ *Bob racked his brain trying to remember where he left the book.* ◆ *Susan racked her brain trying to guess whom the valentine came from.* ◆ *John racked his brain during the test trying to solve the problem.*

radio ham *n. phr.* Someone whose hobby is the operating of shortwave radio. ◆ *The code letters C.Q. are used by radio hams to invite other radio hams to join in the conversation.*

rag See CHEW THE FAT *or* CHEW THE RAG, GLAD RAGS.

rag doll *n.* A doll made of cloth and filled with soft stuffing. ◆ *My baby brother won't go to bed without his rag doll.*

ragged See RUN RAGGED.

rag trade *n. phr.* The clothing industry. ◆ *My brother is working in the rag trade, manufacturing dresses.*

railroad *v.* To force through; push through by force. ◆ *The bill was railroaded through the state legislature due to the influence of some very wealthy sponsors.*

rain See IT NEVER RAINS BUT IT POURS, KNOW ENOUGH TO COME IN OUT OF THE RAIN.

rain cats and dogs *or* **rain buckets** *or* **rain pitchforks** *v. phr., informal* To rain very hard; come down in torrents. ◆ *In the middle of the picnic it started to rain cats and dogs, and everybody got soaked.* ◆ *Terry looked out of the window and said, "It's raining pitchforks, so we can't go out to play right now."*

rain check *n.* **1.** A special free ticket to another game or show which will be given in place of one canceled because of rain. ◆ *When the drizzle turned into a heavy rain the manager announced that the baseball game would be replayed the next day. He told the crowd that they would be given rain checks for tomorrow's game as they went out through the gates.* **2.** *informal* A promise to repeat an invitation at a later time. ◆ *Bob said, "I'm sorry you can't come to dinner this evening, Dave. I'll give you a rain check."*

rained out *adj.* Stopped by rain. ◆ *The ball game was rained out in the seventh inning.* ◆ *The Friday night rally in the stadium was rained out.*

rain on *v. phr., slang* To bring misfortune to (someone); to complain to (someone) about one's bad luck. ◆ *Don't rain on me.*

rain or shine *adv. phr.* **1.** If the weather is stormy or if it is fair. ◆ *The parade will start promptly, rain or shine.* **2.** No matter; if your luck is good or bad. ◆ *Sam knows he can depend on his family, rain or shine.*

rainproof *adj.* Resistant to rain; something that will not soak in water; referring to a material that repels water. ◆ *"I don't need an umbrella," she said, "as my coat is rainproof."*

rainy day *n.* A time of need; especially: a time when you really need money. ◆ *Squirrels gather acorns for a rainy day.* ◆ *Each week Mrs. Carlson saved a little money for a rainy day.*

raise a hand See LIFT A FINGER.

raise a row *v. phr.* To cause a disturbance, a fuss, or a scene. ◆ *He raised quite a row when he noticed that someone had scratched his brand new car.*

raise a stink *v. phr.* To cause a disturbance; complain; protest strongly.

♦ *Quite a stink was raised in the office when the boss discovered that several employees had left early.*

raise Cain *v. phr., slang* To be noisy; cause trouble. ♦ *When John couldn't go on the basketball trip with the team he raised Cain.* ♦ *The children raised Cain in the living room.* Compare KICK UP A FUSS, RAISE THE DEVIL.

raise eyebrows *v. phr.* To shock people; cause surprise or disapproval. ♦ *The news that the princess was engaged to a commoner raised eyebrows all over the kingdom.*

raise funds *or* **money** *v. phr.* To solicit donations for a charity or a specific project. ♦ *Our church is trying to raise the funds for a new organ.*

raise hackles *or* **raise one's hackles** *v. phr.* To make (someone) upset or annoyed; arouse hostility. ♦ *Attempts to add new ingredients to the beer raised hackles among all the old brew masters.*

raise havoc See PLAY HAVOC WITH.

raise heck See RAISE THE DEVIL.

raise hob See RAISE THE DEVIL.

raise one's sights *v. phr.* To aim high; be ambitious. ♦ *Teenage boys sometimes think too much of themselves and have a tendency to raise their sights too high.*

raise one's voice *v. phr.* To speak loudly, as if in anger or in protest. ♦ *"I'm sorry, Mom," Peter said. "I didn't mean to raise my voice."*

raise the devil *or* **raise heck** *or* **raise hob** *or* **raise ned** *v. phr., informal* To make trouble; start a fight or an argument. ♦ *Mr. Black raised heck when he saw the dented fender. He blamed the other driver.* ♦ *Some teenage boys raised the devil in town on Halloween night and damaged a lot of property.* Compare KICK UP A FUSS.

raise the roof *v. phr., informal* **1.** To make a lot of noise; be happy and noisy. ♦ *The gang raised the roof with their singing.* **2.** To scold loudly. ♦ *Mother raised the roof when she saw the dog's muddy footprints on her new bedspread.* Compare KICK UP A FUSS, RAISE CAIN.

rake in *v. phr.* To realize great profits; take in money. ♦ *Because of the heavy snowfall, ski lodge operators in the Rocky Mountains have been raking in the dough this winter season.*

rake off *v. phr.* To illegally expropriate part of a sum paid. ♦ *The secretary-treasurer of the association has been caught raking off some of the membership dues.*

rake-off See KICKBACK.

rake over the coals See HAUL OVER THE COALS.

rake up *v. phr.* To expose; gather; bring to light. ♦ *Let's forget about the past; there's no need to rake up all those old memories.*

ramble on about *v. phr.* To chatter on idly and without a purpose. ♦ *When Ted has too much to drink, he always rambles on about the good old days.*

ram down one's throat See SHOVE DOWN ONE'S THROAT.

random See AT RANDOM.

rank See CLOSE RANKS, PULL RANK.

rank and file *n. phr.* Ordinary people; the regular membership of an organization; the enlisted privates in the Army. ♦ *The general usually inspects the rank and file on specific national holidays.* ♦ *The secretary of the association sends letters annually to the rank and file.*

rap See TAKE THE RAP.

rap one's knuckles *v. phr.* To scold or punish. ♦ *The principal rapped our knuckles for cheating on the test.* ♦ *If you talk back to Dad, you'll get your knuckles rapped.* ♦ *The club got its knuckles rapped by the principal for hazing new members.* ♦ *Why rap my knuckles? It wasn't my fault.* Compare DRESSING DOWN, GIVE IT TO 2.

rat See SMELL A RAT.

rate See AT ANY RATE, FIRST RATE.

rather See HAD RATHER.

rat on See BLOW THE WHISTLE, RAT OUT.

rat out *or* **rat out on** *v. phr., slang* To desert; to leave at a critical time. ♦ *Joe ratted out on Sue when she was seven months pregnant.*

rat race *n., slang* A very confusing, crowded, or disorderly rush; a confusing scramble, struggle, or way of living that does not seem to have a purpose. ♦ *The dance last night was a rat race. It was too noisy and crowded.* ♦ *School can be a rat race if you don't keep up with your studies.* ♦ *This job is a rat race. The faster you work, the faster the boss wants you to work.*

rate with someone *v. phr.* To be esteemed highly by another. ♦ *The professor really rates with both the graduate students and the undergraduates.*

rattle See SABRE RATTLING.

rattle off *or* **reel off** *v.* To say quickly without having to stop to think; recite easily and rapidly. ♦ *When Roger was seven he could rattle off the names of all the states in alphabetical order.* ♦ *Joan memorized the "Gettysburg Address" so well that she could reel it off.* ♦ *We asked the waitress what flavors of ice cream she had, and she rattled them off.*

rattle one's saber *v. phr.* To threaten another government or country without subsequent acts of war. ♦ *It is considered an act of demagoguery on the part of politicians to rattle their sabers.* Compare YELLOW JOURNALISM.

rave about *v. phr.* To talk very enthusiastically about someone or something. ♦ *Hank praised the new TV show very highly but we didn't think it was anything to rave about.*

raw See IN THE RAW.

raw deal *n. phr.* Unfair treatment; inequity. ♦ *Barry got a raw deal when he was sent to teach the class on advanced nuclear physics; he's an inexperienced graduate student.*

razzle-dazzle *n., slang* Fancy display; showing off. ♦ *He is such a good player that he doesn't have to add razzle-dazzle to his game.* ♦ *Do we need all this razzle-dazzle to advertise our fair?*

reach See BOARDING HOUSE REACH.

reach first base See GET TO FIRST BASE.

reach for the sky *v. phr., slang* **1.** To put your hands high above your head or be shot.—Usually used as a command. ♦ *A holdup man walked into a gas station last night and told the attendant "Reach for the sky!"* Syn. HANDS UP. **2.** To set one's aims high. ♦ *"Why medical technician?" asked her father. "Reach for the sky! Become a physician!"*

read between the lines *v. phr.* To understand all of a writer's meaning by guessing at what he has left unsaid. ♦ *Some kinds of poetry make you read between the lines.* ♦ *A clever foreign correspondent can often avoid censorship by careful wording, leaving his audience to read between the lines.*

read into *v. phr.* To attribute extra meaning to; deduce from; consider to be implicit in. ♦ *Just because Fred's letters sounded so friendly Mary was wrong to read anything serious into them.*

read off *v. phr.* To read in a speaking voice from a list. ♦ *The secretary read off the names of those present in alphabetical order.*

read one like a book *v. phr., informal* To understand someone completely; know what he will think or do at any time. ♦ *John's girlfriend could read him like a book.* Compare READ ONE'S MIND.

read one one's rights *v. phr.* To give to an arrested person the legally required statement regarding the rights of such a person. ♦ *"Read him his rights," Sergeant," the captain said, "and book him for breaking and entering."*

read one's mind *v. phr.* To know what someone else is thinking. ♦ *I have known John so long that I can read his mind.—**mind reader** n.* ♦ *That's exactly what I was going to say. You must be a mind reader!* Compare READ LIKE A BOOK.

read the riot act *v. phr.* To give someone a strong warning or scolding. ♦ *Three boys were late to class and the teacher read the riot act to them.*

read over *v. phr.* To read hurriedly in a rather superficial manner. ♦ *The professor said he had no time to read my essay thoroughly but that he had read it over and would comment later in detail.*

read up on *v. phr.* To study carefully in preparation for an examination or other special purpose. ♦ *Since Mr. and Mrs. Lee are going to take their American citizenship exams soon, they must read up on the Constitution and the three branches of government.*

ready See AT THE READY, ROUGH-AND-READY.

ready-made *adj.* Mass-produced; machine made. ♦ *I buy all my dresses ready-made because I can't afford to have them made to order.*

ready money *n. phr.* Cash on hand. ♦ *Frank refuses to buy things on credit, but, if he had the ready money, he would buy that lovely old house.*

real See FOR REAL, IT'S BEEN REAL.

rear See BRING UP THE REAR.

rear end *n.* **1.** The back part (usually of a vehicle) ♦ *The rear end of our car was smashed when we stopped suddenly and the car behind us hit us.*—Often used like an adjective, with a hyphen. ♦ *A head-on crash is more likely to kill the passengers than a rear-end crash.* Contrast HEAD-ON. **2.** Rump; backside. ♦ *Bobby's mother was so annoyed with his teasing that she swatted his rear end.*

rear its head *v. phr.* To appear; emerge. ♦ *After decades of certainty that tuberculosis had been eradicated globally, it suddenly reared its ugly head right here in the United States.*

reason See IN REASON, LISTEN TO REASON, RHYME OR REASON, STAND TO REASON, WITHIN REASON.

receive with open arms See WITH OPEN ARMS.

reckon with *v.* To consider as one of the things which may change a situation; consider (something) that will make a difference in the results. ♦ *The coach said the opposing pitcher had a fast ball to be reckoned with.* Syn. TAKE INTO ACCOUNT.

reckon without *v.* To fail to consider as one of the things which might change a situation; not think about. ♦ *The committee for the class picnic party made careful plans for a beach party but they reckoned without a sudden change in the weather.*

record See MATTER OF RECORD, OFF THE RECORD, ON RECORD.

red See IN THE RED, PAINT THE TOWN RED, SEE RED.

redcap *n.* A porter at an airport or at a railroad station. ♦ *Mr. Smith works as a redcap at Chicago's O'Hare Airport.*

red carpet See ROLL OUT THE RED CARPET.

red cent *n. phr.* The one-cent coin; a copper coin; very little money. ♦ *Poor Oscar is so broke he doesn't have a red cent to his name.*

red eye *adj. phr.* Bloodshot eyes that are strained from too much reading. ♦ *Poor Tim has a red eye; he must have been studying too late again.*

red eye *n. phr., informal* A night flight. ♦ *The company refused to pay for him to take a more expensive daytime flight, so he had to come in on the red eye.*

red-handed *adj.* In the very act; while committing a crime or evil action. ♦ *The criminal was caught red-handed while holding up the neighborhood bank at gunpoint.*

red herring *n. phr.* A false scent laid down in order to deceive; a phony or misleading story designed to cause confusion. ♦ *That story about the president having an affair was a red herring created by the opposition in order to discredit him.*

red-letter day *n. phr.* A holiday; memorable day (usually printed in red on calendars). ♦ *The Fourth of July is a red-letter day.* ♦ *It was a red-letter day for Felix, when he won the lottery.*

red-light district *n. phr.* A district of brothels or where prostitutes hang out. ♦ *Most unwisely, the young sailor decided to spend his leave on shore by haunting the red-light districts of the port of call.*

red tape *n. phr.* Unnecessary bureaucratic routine; needless but official delays. ♦ *If you want to get anything accomplished in a hurry, you have to find someone in power who can cut through all that red tape.*

reel off See RATTLE OFF.

reference See IN REFERENCE TO *or* WITH REFERENCE TO.

refine on *or* **refine upon** *v.* **1.** To make better; improve. ♦ *Mary was asked to refine on her first outline to make it clearer and more exact.* **2.** To be better than; surpass. ♦ *Modern medical techniques refine on those of the past.*

regain one's feet *v. phr.* To get back up again after falling down. ♦ *Tom fell while he skied down the hill but he regained his feet quickly.* Compare TO ONE'S FEET.

regard See IN REFERENCE TO *or* IN REGARD TO *or* WITH REGARD TO.

regular guy *or* **regular fellow** *n., informal* A friendly person who is easy to get along with; a good sport. ♦ *You'll like Tom. He's a regular guy.* Syn. GOOD EGG.

rein See FREE REIN, GIVE REIN TO *or* GIVE FREE REIN TO.

relation See IN RELATION TO *or* WITH RELATION TO.

relative to 1. On the subject of; about. ♦ *Relative to school athletics, the prin-*

cipal said the students should not allow athletics to interfere with homework. **2.** In comparison with; in proportion to. ♦ *Relative to the size of an ant, a blade of grass is as tall as a tree.*

repeat oneself *v. phr.* To say the same thing over again, often in the same words; repeat ideas because you forget what you said or because you want to stress their importance. ♦ *Grandfather is forgetful and often repeats himself when he tells a story.* ♦ *A teacher often has to repeat herself several times before her pupils remember what she tells them.*

resign oneself *v. phr.* To stop arguing; accept something which cannot be changed. ♦ *When Jane's father explained that he could not afford to buy her a new bicycle, she finally resigned herself to riding the old one.* Compare GIVE UP.

resistance See LINE OF LEAST RESISTANCE.

rest See LAY TO REST, PARADE REST.

rest assured *v. phr.* To be convinced; persuaded; certain and unworried. ♦ *"Please rest assured," he said seriously, "that I will keep all of my promises."*

rest home See CONVALESCENT HOME.

rest on one's laurels *v. phr.* To be satisfied with the success you have already won; stop trying to win new honors. ♦ *Getting an A in chemistry almost caused Mike to rest on his laurels.*

rest on one's oars *v. phr.* To stop trying; stop working for a while; rest. ♦ *The man who wants to become a millionaire can never rest on his oars.* ♦ *A high school student who wants to go to college cannot rest on his oars.*

rest room *n.* A room or series of rooms in a public building which has things for personal comfort and grooming, such as toilets, washbowls, mirrors, and often chairs or couches. ♦ *Sally went to the rest room to powder her nose.* Compare POWDER ROOM.

retreat See BEAT A RETREAT.

return See IN RETURN.

return the compliment *v. phr.* To say or do the same to someone that he has said or done to you; pay someone back. ♦ *Mary said, "I love your new hairdo" and Suzy returned the compli-*

ment with "What a pretty dress you're wearing, Mary." ♦ *John punched Jerry in the nose, and Jerry returned the compliment.*

reverse See DOUBLE REVERSE, IN REVERSE.

rev up *v. phr., informal, slang* **1.** To press down sharply several times on the accelerator of an idling car in order to get maximum acceleration. ♦ *The race driver revved up his car by pumping his accelerator.* **2.** To get oneself ready in order to accomplish a demanding or difficult task. ♦ *The boys were getting all revved up for the football game.* See PSYCHED UP.

rhyme or reason *n. phr.* A good plan or reason; a reasonable purpose or explanation.—Used in negative, interrogative, or conditional sentences. ♦ *Don could see no rhyme or reason to the plot of the play.* ♦ *It seemed to Ruth that her little brother had temper tantrums without rhyme or reason.*

rib See STICK TO ONE'S RIBS *or* STICK TO THE RIBS.

rich See STRIKE IT RICH.

ride See ALONG FOR THE RIDE, LET RIDE, RUN WITH HARE AND HUNT (RIDE) WITH THE HOUNDS, TAKE FOR A RIDE, THUMB A RIDE.

ride herd on *v. phr.* **1.** To patrol on horseback around a herd of animals to see that none of them wanders away. ♦ *Two cowboys rode herd on the cattle being driven to market.* **2.** *informal* To watch closely and control; take care of. ♦ *A special legislative assistant rides herd on the bills the president is anxious to have congress pass.* ♦ *Mary rode herd on the small children walking home from school to keep them from running into the street.*

ride on one's coattails *v. phr.* To succeed in a certain endeavor by attaching oneself to the greater weight of another person or corporate body. ♦ *"We will never get our Ph.D. program approved on our own," said the head of the modern dance department, "but we might succeed if we stay in the Division of Fine Arts, riding on their coattails, as it were."*

ride out *v.* To survive safely; endure. ♦ *The captain ordered all sails lowered so the ship could ride out the storm.*

♦*Jack decided to ride out his troubles by saying that he had made a mistake but that he had learned his lesson.*

ride roughshod over *v. phr.* To do as you wish without considering the wishes of (another person); treat with scorn or lack of courtesy; show no sympathy for. ♦*The city officials rode roughshod over the people who did not want their homes torn down for a new school.* ♦*The boss rode roughshod over the men when they asked for higher wages.*

ride the brake *or* **ride the clutch** *v. phr., informal* To keep your foot on the pedal. ♦*Riding the brake is a bad habit for a driver to form.*

ride the gravy train *v. phr.* To live a life of plenty and luxury. ♦*Those who have a wealthy executive or heir to a fortune for a spouse can ride the gravy train without doing any work.*

ride up *or* **crawl up** *v.* To slip gradually upward on the body. ♦*Shorts that ride up can be very uncomfortable.*

riding for a fall *adj. phr.* Behaving in an overconfident way that is likely to lead to trouble; being too sure of yourself; doing something dangerous. ♦*The student who does not study for exams is riding for a fall.* ♦*Mr. Smith has borrowed too much money on his home. He is riding for a fall.* Compare COME A CROPPER 2.

riding high *adj.* Attracting attention; enjoying great popularity. ♦*After scoring the winning touchdown, John is riding high with his classmates.*

rid of Free of; away from; without the care or trouble. ♦*The puppy is finally rid of worms.* ♦*If I could be rid of the children for the day, I would go.* ♦*I wish you'd get rid of that cat!* Compare DO AWAY WITH, THROW AWAY 1, THROW OFF 1.

right See ALL RIGHT, ALL RIGHT FOR YOU, DEAD TO RIGHTS, GIVE ONE'S RIGHT ARM, HEART IN THE RIGHT PLACE, IN THE RIGHT, PLAY ONE'S CARDS RIGHT, PUT TO RIGHTS *or* SET TO RIGHTS, SERVE RIGHT, TO RIGHTS.

right along *adv. phr., informal* **1a.** On your way satisfactorily or without trouble. ♦*They fixed the engine and the train ran right along.* **1b.** On your way without delay. ♦*Don't wait for me. Go right along.* **2.** See ALL ALONG.

right and left *adv. phr.* In or from every direction; all around; on all sides. ♦*The knight rode into battle striking at the enemy right and left with his broadsword.* ♦*When the talk ended, questions were thrown at the speaker right and left.*

right away *or informal* **right off** *also informal* **right off the bat** *adv. phr.* Immediately; as the next thing in order; without delay. ♦*Phil's mother told him to do his homework right away so that he could enjoy the weekend.* ♦*The Red Cross aids disaster victims right away.* ♦*Jill knew the answer right off.* ♦*The teacher said he could not think of the title of the book right off the bat.* Syn. AT ONCE 2. Compare HERE AND NOW, ON THE SPOT. Contrast AFTER A WHILE.

right down *or* **up one's alley** *adv. phr.* In accordance with one's specialty or predilection. ♦*This kind of preclassical music is right up Bill's alley; after all, he wrote his Ph.D. on Bach.*

right field *n.* The part of a baseball outfield to the batter's right. ♦*Left-handed batters usually hit to right field.* Compare CENTER FIELD, LEFT FIELD.— **right fielder** *n.* The outfielder in baseball who plays in right field. ♦*The batter hit a high fly ball and the right fielder caught it easily.*

right-hand man *v. phr.* A valued and indispensable assistant. ♦*The chancellor of the university never goes anywhere without the vice chancellor, his right-hand man, whose judgment he greatly trusts.*

right on *adj., interj., slang, informal* **1.** Exclamation of animated approval "Yes," "That's correct," "You're telling the truth," "we believe you," etc. ♦*Orator: And we shall see the promised land! Crowd: Right on!* **2.** Correct; to the point; accurate. ♦*The reverend's remark was right on!*

right out *or* **straight out** *adv.* Plainly; in a way that hides nothing; without waiting or keeping back anything. ♦*When Mother asked who broke the window, Jimmie told her right out that he did it.* ♦*When Ann entered the beauty contest her little brother told her straight out that she was crazy.*

right side of the tracks See THE TRACKS.

right-wing *adj.* Being or belonging to a political group which opposes any important change in the way the country is run. ♦*Some countries with right-wing governments have dictators.* Contrast LEFT-WING.

rig out *v. phr.* To overdecorate; doll up; dress up. ♦*Ann arrived all rigged out in her newest Parisian summer outfit.*

Riley See LIFE OF RILEY.

ring See GIVE A RING, RUN CIRCLES AROUND *or* RUN RINGS AROUND, THREE-RING CIRCUS, THROW ONE'S HAT IN THE RING.

ring a bell *v. phr.* To make you remember something; sound familiar. ♦*Not even the cat's meowing seemed to ring a bell with Judy. She still forgot to feed him.* ♦*When Ann told Jim the name of the new teacher it rang a bell, and Jim said, "I went to school with a James Carson."*

ring in *v. phr., informal* **1.** To bring in (someone or something) from the outside dishonestly or without telling; often: hire and introduce under a false name. ♦*Bob offered to ring him in on the party by pretending he was a cousin from out of town.* ♦*No wonder their team beat us; they rang in a professional to pitch for them under the name of Dan Smith.* **2.** To ring a special clock that records the time you work. ♦*We have to ring in at the shop before eight o'clock in the morning.*

ringleader *n. phr.* The chief of an unsavory group; a higher-up. ♦*The FBI finally caught up with the ringleader of the dope smugglers from South America.*

ring out *v.* To ring a special clock that records the time you leave work. ♦*Charles can't leave early in his new job; he has to ring out.*

ring the changes *v. phr.* To say or do the same thing in different ways; repeat the same idea in many ways. ♦*David wanted a new bicycle and he kept ringing the changes on it all day until his parents got angry at him.* ♦*A smart girl saves money on clothes by learning to ring the changes on a few dresses and clothes.*

ring true *v. phr.* To have a tone of genuineness; sound convincing. ♦*I believed his sob story about how he lost his fortune, because somehow it all rang true.*

ring up *v.* **1.** To add and record on a cash register. ♦*The supermarket clerk rang up Mrs. Smith's purchases and told her she owed $33.* ♦*Business was bad Tuesday; we didn't ring up a sale all morning.* **2.** *informal* To telephone. ♦*Sally rang up Sue and told her the news.*

riot See READ THE RIOT ACT, RUN RIOT.

ripe See TIME IS RIPE.

rip into *or* **tear into** *v., informal* **1.** To start a fight with; attack. ♦*The puppy is tearing into the big dog.* Syn. PITCH INTO. **2.** To quarrel with; scold. ♦*Mrs. Brown ripped into her daughter for coming home late.* Syn. BAWL OUT, LACE INTO, LAY OUT, LET HAVE IT.

rip off *v., slang* (Stress on *off*) Steal. ♦*The hippies ripped off the grocery store.*

rip-off *n., slang* (Stress on *rip*) An act of stealing or burglary. ♦*Those food prices are so high, it's almost a rip-off.*

rise See GET A RISE OUT OF, GIVE RISE TO.

rise from the ashes *v. phr.* To rise from ruin; start anew. ♦*A year after flunking out of medical school, Don rose from the ashes and passed his qualifying exams for the M.D. with honors.*

rise in the world See COME UP IN THE WORLD.

rise to *v.* To succeed in doing what is expected by trying especially hard in or on; show that you are able to do or say what is needed or proper in or on. ♦*Jane was surprised when the principal handed her the prize, but she rose to the occasion with a speech of thanks.* ♦*When Michael became sick on the day before the program, Paul rose to the need and learned Michael's part.*

rise up *v. phr.* To stage a rebellion; revolt. ♦*The people finally rose up and communism came to an end in Eastern Europe.*

risk See CALCULATED RISK, RUN A RISK.

road See ALL ROADS LEAD TO ROME, BURN UP THE ROAD, END OF THE ROAD, GET THE SHOW ON THE ROAD, HIT THE ROAD, HUG THE ROAD, MIDDLE OF THE ROAD, ON THE ROAD.

road gang *n.* A group of men who work at road construction. ♦*Football players* *often work with road gangs during summer vacations.*

road hog *n ., informal* A car driver who takes more than his share of the road. ♦ *A road hog forced John's car into the ditch.*

road show *n.* A theatrical play that is performed for a few days in one town and then moves to other towns. ♦ *Many actors get their start in road shows.* ♦ *The road show is often not as good as the original play on Broadway.*

road sign *n.* A sign on which there is information about a road or places; a sign with directions to drivers. ♦ *The road sign read, "25 MPH LIMIT" but Jack drove along at fifty miles an hour.* ♦ *The road sign said Westwood was four miles away.*

road test *n.* **1.** A test to see if you can drive a car. ♦ *Jim took the road test and got his driver's license last week.* **2.** A test to see if a car works all right on the road. ♦ *Most new cars are given road tests before they are put on the market.* ♦ *After he repaired the car, the mechanic gave it a road test.*

roast See WEINER ROAST *or* HOT DOG ROAST.

roasting ear *n.* An ear of corn young and tender enough to be cooked and eaten; *also* corn cooked on the cob. ♦ *The scouts buried the roasting ears in the coals of their campfire.* ♦ *At the Fourth of July picnic we had fried chicken and roasting ears.*

robbery See HIGHWAY ROBBERY.

robin See ROUND ROBIN.

rob Peter to pay Paul *v. phr.* To change one duty or need for another; take from one person or thing to pay another. ♦ *Bill owed Sam a dollar, so he borrowed another from Joe to pay Sam back. He robbed Peter to pay Paul.* ♦ *Trying to study a lesson for one class during another class is like robbing Peter to pay Paul.*

rob the cradle *v. phr., informal* To have dates with or marry a person much younger than yourself. ♦ *When the old woman married a young man, everyone said she was robbing the cradle.*—**cradle-robber** *n.* ♦ *The judge died when he was seventy. He was a real cradle-robber because he left a thirty-year-old widow.*—**cradle-rob-**

bing *adj. or n.* ♦ *Bob is seventeen and I just saw him with a girl about twelve years old. Has he started cradle-robbing? No, that girl was his sister, not his date!*

rob the till *or* **have one's hand in the till** *v. phr., informal* To steal money in your trust or for which you are responsible. ♦ *The supermarket manager suspected that one of the clerks was robbing the till.* ♦ *Mr. Jones deposited one thousand dollars in their joint savings account and told his wife not to rob the till.* ♦ *The store owner thought his business was failing until he discovered that the treasurer had his hand in the till.*

rock See HAVE ROCKS IN ONE'S HEAD, ON THE ROCKS.

rock and roll See ROCK 'N' ROLL.

rock-bottom *n.* The lowest possible point. ♦ *The nation's morale hit rock bottom in the hours following the president's assassination.*—Often used like an adjective, with a hyphen. ♦ *The rock-bottom price of this radio is $25.*

rocker See OFF ONE'S ROCKER.

rock hound *n., slang* A person who studies and collects rocks for a hobby. ♦ *Many young rock hounds grow up to be geologists.* ♦ *Tony is an eager rock hound, and we have rocks all through our house.*

rock 'n' roll *or* **rock and roll** *n.* A style of popular music with heavily accented rhythm. ♦ *Rock 'n' roll appeals mostly to youngsters nine to sixteen years old.* ♦ *Rock and roll became popular for dances about 1954.*

rock the boat *v. phr., informal* To make trouble and risk losing or upsetting something; cause a disturbance that may spoil a plan. ♦ *The other boys said that Henry was rocking the boat by wanting to let girls into their club.* ♦ *Politicians don't like to rock the boat around election time.* Compare UPSET THE APPLE CART. Contrast LET WELL ENOUGH ALONE.

rod See HOT ROD.

roll See GET THE BALL ROLLING, KEEP THE BALL ROLLING, ROCK 'N' ROLL *or* ROCK AND ROLL.

roll around *v., informal* To return at a regular or usual time; come back. ♦ *When winter rolls around, out come the skis and skates.*

rolling stone gathers no moss A person who changes jobs or where he lives often will not be able to save money or things of his own.—A proverb. ♦ *Uncle Willie was a rolling stone that gathered no moss. He worked in different jobs all over the country.*

roll out the red carpet *v. phr.* **1.** To welcome an important guest by putting a red carpet down for him to walk on. ♦ *They rolled out the red carpet for the Queen when she arrived in Australia.* **2.** To greet a person with great respect and honor; give a hearty welcome. ♦ *Margaret's family rolled out the red carpet for her teacher when she came to dinner.* Compare WELCOME MAT.—**red-carpet** *adj.* ♦ *When the president visited the foreign country, he was given the red-carpet treatment and welcomed by a great crowd.* ♦ *We gave Uncle Willie the red-carpet treatment when he returned from Hong Kong.*

roll up one's sleeves To get ready for a hard job; prepare to work hard or seriously. ♦ *When Paul took his science examination, he saw how little he knew about science. He rolled up his sleeves and went to work.*

Roman collar *n.* The high, plain, white collar worn by priests and clergymen. ♦ *The man with the Roman collar is the new Episcopalian preacher.* ♦ *Many Protestant churches do not require their ministers to wear Roman collars.*

Rome See ALL ROADS LEAD TO ROME.

Rome wasn't built in a day Great things are not accomplished overnight; great deeds take a long time.—A proverb. ♦ *It takes a long time to write a successful novel, but don't worry; Rome wasn't built in a day, as the saying goes.*

roof See HIT THE CEILING *or* HIT THE ROOF, RAISE THE ROOF.

rooftop See SHOUT FROM THE HOUSE-TOPS *or* SHOUT FROM THE ROOFTOPS.

room See CONTROL ROOM, POWDER ROOM, UTILITY ROOM.

room and board *n. phr.* A room for rent with meals included. ♦ *A room alone in that country costs only $10 a day, but room and board together run $22 a day.*

room clerk *or* **desk clerk** *n.* A person who is responsible for assigning rooms and providing service to guests in hotels, motels, inns, etc. ♦ *At first-class* *hotels, room clerks are trained to be at the service of every guest.* ♦ *Sometimes resort hotels in the mountains hire college students as room clerks during the summer.*

room in See LIVE IN.

room service *n.* Service provided to hotel guests in their rooms. *Also:* The hotel workers who give this service. ♦ *We called for room service when we wanted ice.* ♦ *Room service will install a TV set in your room upon demand.*

room with *v. phr.* **1.** To live in a furnished room with someone as a roommate without having an affair. ♦ *I roomed with him in college for four years.* **2.** To live together as husband and wife without the benefit of marriage. ♦ *Dan and Sue have been rooming together for quite a while and people are wondering if they will ever get married.*

roost See CHICKENS COME HOME TO ROOST, RULE THE ROOST.

root See TAKE ROOT.

root-bound *adj.* **1.** Having a limited amount of space for root growth. ♦ *After seven or eight years day lilies become root-bound and will not bloom well unless they are divided.* **2.** Liking the familiar place where you live and not wanting to go away from it; having a sentimental attachment to one place. ♦ *Mr. Jones has lived in Connecticut all his life. He is too root-bound to consider moving to another state.*

root for *v. phr.* To cheer for; applaud; support. ♦ *During the Olympics one usually roots for the team of one's own country.*

rope See END OF ONE'S ROPE, GIVE ONE ENOUGH ROPE AND HE WILL HANG HIMSELF, ON THE ROPES, THE ROPES.

rope in *v., informal* **1.** To use a trick to make (someone) do something; deceive; fool. ♦ *The company ropes in high school students to sell magazine subscriptions by telling them big stories of how much money they can earn.* Syn. TAKE UP 5a. **2.** To get (someone to join or help); persuade to do something. ♦ *Martha roped in Charles to help her decorate the gym for the party.* ♦ *I didn't want the job of selling tickets for the dance, but I was roped in because everyone else was too busy to do it.*

rope into *v., informal* **1.** To trick into; persuade dishonestly. ♦ *Jerry let the big boys rope him into stealing some apples.* **2.** To get (someone) to join in; persuade to work at. ♦ *It was Sue's job to bathe the dog but she roped Sam into helping her.* ♦ *Mother did not go to the first meeting of the club because she was afraid she would be roped into something.* Compare TALK INTO.

rope off *v. phr.* To divide into sections by use of a rope. ♦ *The police roped off the section of the street where the president was expected to jog.*

rose See BED OF ROSES, LOOK AT THE WORLD THROUGH ROSE-COLORED GLASSES.

rose-colored glasses See LOOK AT THE WORLD THROUGH ROSE-COLORED GLASSES.

rotten egg *n., informal* A person whose character or way of acting is not good. ♦ *His friends have all learned he is a rotten egg.* Often used by children in fun, as of someone who is slow in doing something. ♦ *The boys ran to the river to go swimming and Dick cried, "Last one in is a rotten egg!"*

rotten to the core *adj. phr.* **1.** Thoroughly decayed or spoiled. ♦ *This apple is inedible; it is brown and soft and rotten to the core.* **2.** In total moral collapse. ♦ *The Communist government of Cuba is rotten to the core.*

rough See DIAMOND IN THE ROUGH.

rough-and-ready *adj.* **1.** Not finished in detail; not perfected; rough but ready for use now. ♦ *We asked Mr. Brown how long it would take to drive to Chicago and his rough-and-ready answer was two days.* **2.** Not having nice manners but full of energy and ability. ♦ *Jim is a rough-and-ready character; he'd rather fight than talk things over.*

rough-and-tumble **1.** *n.* Very rough, hard fighting or arguing that does not follow any rules. ♦ *There was a rough-and-tumble on the street last night between some soldiers and sailors.* ♦ *Many people don't like the rough-and-tumble of politics.* **2.** *adj.* Fighting or arguing in a very rough and reckless way; struggling hard; not following rules or laws. ♦ *It took strong men to stay alive in the rough-and-tumble life of the western frontier.*

rough diamond See DIAMOND IN THE ROUGH.

roughhouse *n.* Riotous play or commotion. ♦ *I told the boys they can play in the attic if there is no roughhouse.*

roughhouse *v.* To play very wildly; be running around as young boys usually do. ♦ *"Stop roughhousing this minute," Grandma cried. "Your father will be home soon."*

rough it *v. phr.* To live like primitive people; live with little of the comfort and equipment of civilization. ♦ *Scouts like to rough it in the woods on weekend hikes.*

roughneck *n.* A low, coarse fellow. ♦ *The only boys in the neighborhood are a bunch of roughnecks, and Mrs. Smith is unhappy about the fact that her son is rapidly becoming one of them.*

rough-shod See RIDE ROUGH-SHOD OVER.

rough sledding See HARD SLEDDING.

rough up *v.* To attack or hurt physically; treat roughly; beat. ♦ *Three boys were sent home for a week because they roughed up a player on the visiting team.* ♦ *While Pete was walking in a strange part of town some boys roughed him up and told him to stay out of their territory.*

roughly speaking *adv. phr.* Approximately; in general terms. ♦ *Roughly speaking, about 250 people attended the annual convention of the Dictionary Society of America.*

roulette See RUSSIAN ROULETTE.

round See BRING AROUND *or* BRING ROUND, COME ROUND, GO THE ROUNDS, MAKE ROUNDS, SQUARE PEG IN A ROUND HOLE, YEAR-ROUND.

round-eyed *or* **wide-eyed** *also* **large-eyed** *adj.* Very much surprised; astonished; awed. ♦ *The people were round-eyed when they learned what the computer could do.* ♦ *The children were wide-eyed at the sight of the Christmas tree and didn't make a sound.*

round off *v.* **1.** To make round or curved. ♦ *John decided to round off the corners of the table he was making so that no one would be hurt by bumping them.* **2.** To change to the nearest whole number. ♦ *The teacher said to round off the averages.* **3.** To end in a satisfactory way; put a finishing touch on; finish nicely. ♦*We rounded off the dinner with mixed nuts.* ♦*A boat ride in the moonlight rounded off the day at the lake.* Compare TOP OFF.

round out *v. phr.* To complete; make whole. ♦*He needs only one or two more rare compact discs to round out his collection of Vivaldi.*

round robin *n. phr.* **1.** Something written, especially a request or protest that is signed by a group of people.—Often used like an adjective. ♦*The people in our neighborhood are sending a round robin to the Air Force to protest the noise the jet planes make flying over our houses.* **2.** A letter written by a group of people each writing one or two paragraphs and then sending the letter to another person, who adds a paragraph, and so on. ♦*The class sent a round-robin letter to Bill in the hospital.* **3.** A meeting in which each one in a group of people takes part; a talk between various members of a group.—Often used like an adjective. ♦*There is a round-robin meeting of expert fishermen on the radio, giving advice on how to catch fish.* **4.** A contest or games in which each player or team plays every other player or team in turn.—Often used like an adjective. ♦*The tournament will be a round robin for all the high school teams in the city.*

rounds See GO THE ROUNDS.

round the clock See AROUND THE CLOCK.

round trip *n.* A return trip; passage to a place and back. ♦*The ticket agent explained that a ticket for a round trip to Hawaii at certain times of the year may cost less than a one-way ticket during the high season.*

roundup *n.* A muster; an inspection; a gathering together. ♦*The farmer and his son decided to hold a major roundup of all their cattle to see that none had been stolen by the bandits.* ♦*The police roundup of all suspected drug dealers took place early in the morning.*

round up *v.* **1.** To bring together (cattle or horses). ♦*Cowboys round up their cattle in the springtime to brand the new calves.* **2.** *informal* To collect; gather. ♦*Dave rounded up many names for his petition.*

row See HARD ROW TO HOE *or* TOUGH ROW TO HOE, HOE ONE'S OWN ROW, SKID ROW.

royal road *n. phr.* A quick means of accomplishment; an easy path. ♦*There is no royal road to learning in order to obtain a university degree.*

rubdown *n.* A massage. ♦*The chiropractor gave his patient a powerful rubdown.*

rub-a-dub *n.* The sound made by beating a drum. ♦*We heard a great rub-a-dub as the parade marched into view.*

rubber check *n., informal* A check written without enough money in the bank to make it good. ♦*Bill got into trouble when he paid his bills with rubber checks.* ♦*By the time we knew he had paid us with a rubber check, the man had left the state.* ♦*The rubber check bounced.*

rub down *v., phr.* **1.** To dry the body of (an animal or person) by rubbing. ♦*Stablemen rub down a horse after a race.* **2.** To rub and press with the fingers on the body of (a person) to loosen muscles or prevent stiffness; massage. ♦*Trainers rub down an athlete after hard exercise.*

rub elbows *also* **rub shoulders** *v. phr.* To be in the same place (with others); meet and mix. ♦*City people and country people, old and young, rub elbows at the horse show.* ♦*On a visit to the United Nations Building in New York, you may rub elbows with people from faraway lands.*

rub it in *v. phr., slang* To remind a person again and again of an error or short-coming; tease; nag. ♦*Jerry was already unhappy because he fumbled the ball, but his teammates kept rubbing it in.* ♦*I know my black eye looks funny. You don't need to rub it in.*

rub off *v.* **1.** To remove or be removed by rubbing; erase. ♦*The teacher rubs the problem off the chalkboard.* ♦*After Ann shook hands with the president, she would not shake hands with anyone else because she thought that the good luck would rub off.* **2.** To stick to something touched; come off. ♦*Don't touch that charcoal, it will rub off.* ♦*Mary's dress touched the door that Father was painting, and some paint* *rubbed off on her dress.* **3.** To pass to someone near as if by touching. ♦*Jimmy is very lucky; I wish some of his luck would rub off on me.*

rub out *v. slang* To destroy completely; kill; eliminate. ♦*The gangsters rubbed out four policemen before they were caught.* ♦*The gangsters told the storekeeper that if he did not pay them to protect him, someone would rub him out.* Compare WIPE OUT, RID OF.

rub salt into one's wounds *v. phr., informal* To deliberately add pain when one feels shame, regret, or defeat. ♦*Must you rub salt into my wounds by telling me how much fun I missed by not going to the party?*

rub shoulders See RUB ELBOWS.

rub the wrong way *v. phr., informal* To make (someone) a little angry; do something not liked by (someone); annoy; bother. ♦*John's bragging rubbed the other boys the wrong way.* ♦*Mother's friend called Harold a little boy, and that rubbed Harold the wrong way.* Compare AGAINST THE GRAIN 2.

rub up against *v. phr.* To come into contact with. ♦*In that business one naturally has to rub up against all kinds of people.*

rub up to *v. phr.* To do nice things for one; flatter a person; gain attention or rewards. ♦*Mona has the ability to rub up to the right kinds of people, so it's no wonder she is so popular at her work.*

ruffle feathers *or* **ruffle one's feathers** *v. phr.* Insult or disturb slightly; offend. ♦*The author ruffled some feathers by his portrait of his hometown.*

rug See PULL THE RUG OUT FROM UNDER, SWEEP UNDER THE RUG.

rule See EXCEPTION PROVES THE RULE, GROUND RULE.

rule of thumb *n. phr.* A simple and practical method that has proven successful or useful in the past. ♦*It is a very good rule of thumb to look up all unfamiliar words in a good dictionary.*

rule out *v.* **1.** To say that (something) must not be done; not allow; *also:* decide against. ♦*The principal ruled out dances on school nights.* ♦*The play was ruled out by the referee.* ♦*Jean probably will not go to college, but she has not ruled that out.* **2.** To show that (someone or something) is not a possi-bility; make it unnecessary to think about; remove (a chance). ♦*We have to find a baby-sitter for tonight; Betsy has a date, so that rules her out.* ♦*The doctor took X rays to rule out the chance of broken bones.* **3.** To make impossible; prevent. *Father's death seems to rule out college for Jean.* ♦*Betsy's date for the dance ruled out any baby-sitting that evening.*

rule the roost *v. phr., informal* To be leader or boss; be in charge. ♦*Jim is very bossy; he always wants to rule the roost.* ♦*Who rules the roost in the Smith's house?* Compare WEAR THE TROUSERS.

run See BLOOD RUNS COLD, END RUN, CUT AND RUN, FIRST-RUN, HOME RUN, IN THE LONG RUN, IN THE RUNNING, ON THE RUN, OUT OF THE RUNNING, SECOND-RUN.

run across See COME ACROSS 1.

run after *or* **chase after** *v.* **1.** To try to find; look for; hunt. ♦*The Dramatic Club has to run all over town after things for setting the stage when it puts on a play.* **2.** *informal* To seek the company of; chase. ♦*Some boys spend a lot of time and money running after girls.*

run along *v.* To go away; leave. ♦*Joan said she had errands to do and must run along.*

run a risk *or* **take a risk** *v. phr.* To be open to danger or loss; put yourself in danger; be unprotected. ♦*A baseball umpire wears a mask and chest protector so he won't run the risk of being hit by the ball.* ♦*Billy takes a risk of being hit by a car when he runs into the street without looking.* ♦*I was afraid to run the risk of betting on the game.* Compare TAKE A CHANCE.

run around in circles *v. phr.* To waste time in repetitious movements; be confused. ♦*There was such a crowd in the lobby that I ran around in circles trying to find my group.*

run around *or* **chase around** *v., informal* To go to different places for company and pleasure; be friends. ♦*Tim hasn't been to a dance all year; with school work and his job, he hasn't time to run around.* ♦*Chuck and Jim chase around a lot together.*—Often used with *with. Ruth runs around with girls who like to go dancing.* Compare GO AROUND, HANG AROUND.

run around like a chicken with its head cut off See RUN AROUND IN CIRCLES.

run a temperature *v. phr.* To have a body temperature that is above normal; have a fever. ♦*Jimmy didn't look ill, although he was running a temperature.* ♦*We took the baby to the doctor because he was running a temperature.*

run a tight ship *v. phr.* To run an organization with a firm hand, with strict rules and regulations. ♦*Our dean of the college runs a very tight ship; he tolerates no mistakes.*

run away *or* **run off** *v.* To leave and not plan to come back; go without permission; escape. ♦*Many times Tommy said he would run away from home, but he never did.* ♦*The guards in jail make sure that none of the prisoners run away.* Compare GET AWAY.

run away with *v.* **1a.** To take quickly and secretly, especially without permission; steal. ♦*A thief ran away with Grandma's silver teapot.* Syn. MAKE OFF. **1b.** To go away with; elope. ♦*Mary said that if her parents wouldn't let her marry Phil, she would run away with him.* **1c.** To take hold of; seize. ♦*The boys thought they saw a ghost in the old house last night; they let their imagination run away with them.* Compare GET THE BETTER OF. **2.** To be much better or more noticeable than others in; win easily. ♦*Our team ran away with the game in the last half.* ♦*The fat comedian ran away with the TV show.* Compare STEAL THE SHOW.

run circles around *also* **run rings around** *v. phr.* To show that you can do a task much better than; do better than (someone) very easily. ♦*In spelling, Ruth could run circles around Barbara any day.* ♦*Frank ran rings around the other boys on the basketball team.*

run down *v.* (stress on *down*) **1.** To crash against and knock down or sink. ♦*Jack rode his bicycle too fast and almost ran down his little brother.* ♦*It was so foggy that the steamship almost ran down a small boat leaving port.* Compare RUN INTO 3a. **2a.** To chase until exhausted or caught. ♦*The dogs ran down the wounded deer.* **2b.** To find by hard and thorough search; *also:* trace to its cause or beginning. ♦*The policeman ran down proof that the burglar had robbed the store.* Compare HUNT DOWN. **2c.** To catch (a base runner) between bases and tag out in baseball. ♦*The pitcher saw that the base runner was not on base, so he surprised him by throwing the ball to the first baseman, who ran him down before he reached second base.* **3.** *informal* To say bad things about; criticize. ♦*Suzy ran down the club because the girls wouldn't let her join.* Compare FIND FAULT. **4.** To stop working; not run or go. ♦*The battery in Father's car ran down this morning.* ♦*The kitchen clock ran down because we forgot to wind it.* **5.** To get into poor condition; look bad. ♦*A neighborhood runs down when the people don't take care of their houses.*

run-down *adj.* (stress on *run*) In poor health or condition; weak or needing much work. ♦*Grandma caught a cold because she was very run-down from loss of sleep.* ♦*The houses near the center of the city get more run-down every year.*

run dry *v. phr.* To dry up; lose the water content. ♦*After many years of use, our well ran dry.*

run errands *v. phr.* To carry messages or perform similar minor tasks. ♦*Peter runs errands for our entire neighborhood to make some extra money.*

run for it *or* **make a run for it** *v. phr.* To dash for safety; make a speedy escape. ♦*The bridge the soldiers were on started to fall down and they had to run for it.* ♦*The policeman shouted for the robber to stop, but the robber made a run for it.*

run for one's money *n. phr.* **1.** A good fight; a hard struggle.—Usually used with *give* or *get.* ♦*Our team didn't win the game, but they gave the other team a run for their money.* **2.** Satisfaction; interest; excitement.—Usually used with *give* or *get.* ♦*People like to watch the champion fight because they get a good run for their money from him.* ♦*A good student gives a teacher more than a run for his money.*

run in *v. phr.* **1.** *informal* To take to jail; arrest. ♦*The policeman ran the man in for peddling without a license.* **2.** To make a brief visit. ♦*The neighbor boy* *ran in for a minute to see Bob's newest model rocket.* Syn. DROP IN. Compare STOP OFF.

run-in *n.* **1.** A traffic accident. ◆*My car was wrecked when I had a run-in with a small truck.* **2.** A violent quarrel. ◆*John had a nasty run-in with his boss and was fired.*

run in the blood *or* **run in the family** *v. phr.* To be a common family characteristic; be learned or inherited from your family. ◆*A great interest in gardening runs in his family.* ◆*Red hair runs in the family.*

run into *v.* **1.** To mix with; join with. ◆*If the paint brush is too wet, the red paint will run into the white on the house.* ◆*This small brook runs into a big river in the valley below.* **2.** To add up to; reach; total. ◆*Car repairs can run into a lot of money.* ◆*The number of people killed on the highways during holidays runs into hundreds.* ◆*A good dictionary may run into several editions.* **3a.** Bump; crash into; hit. ◆*Joe lost control of his bike and ran into a tree.* Compare RUN DOWN. **3b.** To meet by chance. ◆*I ran into Joe yesterday on Main Street.* Compare BUMP INTO, CHANCE ON, COME ACROSS 2. **3c.** Be affected by; get into. ◆*I ran into trouble on the last problem on the test.* ◆*When I ran into a problem while making my model airplane, I asked Uncle Mark for help.*

run into a brick wall *or* **run into a stone wall** See STONE WALL.

run into the ground *v. phr., informal* **1.** To do or use (something) more than is wanted or needed. ◆*It's all right to borrow my hammer once in a while, but don't run it into the ground.* **2.** To win over or defeat (someone) completely. ◆*We lost the game today, but tomorrow we'll run them into the ground.*

run its course *v. phr.* To fulfill a normal development; terminate a normal period. ◆*Your flu will run its course; in a few days you'll be back on your feet.*

run off *v., phr.* **1.** To produce with a printing press or duplicating machine. ◆*The print shop ran off a thousand copies of the newspaper.* **2.** To drive away. ◆*The boys saw a dog digging in mother's flower bed, and they ran him off.* ◆*When the salesman tried to cheat*

the farmer, the farmer ran him off the farm with a shotgun. **3.** See RUN AWAY.

run-off *n.* A second election held to determine the winner when the results of the first one were inconclusive. ◆*The senatorial race was so close that the candidates will have to hold a run-off.*

run off at the mouth *v. phr.* To talk too much; be unable to stop talking. ◆*"Shut up, John," our father cried. "You are always running off at the mouth.*

run of luck *n. phr.* A period of good luck. ◆*I had a run of luck last Saturday when I went fishing and caught seven big trout within one hour.*

run-of-the-mill *or* **run-of-the-mine** *adj.* Of a common kind; ordinary; usual. ◆*Frank is a very good bowler, but Joe is just run-of-the-mill.* ◆*It was just a run-of-the-mine movie.*

runner-up *n.* The person who finishes second in a race or contest; the one next after the winner. ◆*Tom won the race and Jack was runner-up.* ◆*Joan was runner-up in the contest for class secretary.* Compare SECOND-BEST.

running start *n. phr.* Good progress at the beginning. ◆*The team was off to a running start, having won the first two games.* ◆*Contributions of $5000 before the drive began gave the charity fund a running start.* Compare HEAD START.

run out *v.* **1a.** To come to an end; be used up. ◆*Jerry almost got across the brook on the slippery stones but his luck ran out and he slipped and fell.* ◆*We'd better do our Christmas shopping; time is running out.* Syn. GIVE OUT 5. **1b.** To use all of the supply; be troubled by not having enough. ◆*The car ran out of gas three miles from town.* ◆*Millie never runs out of ideas for clever party decorations.* Compare RUN SHORT. **2.** *informal* To force to leave; expel. ◆*Federal agents ran the spies out of the country.* Syn. KICK OUT, RUN OFF.

run out on *v. phr.* To leave someone in the lurch; abandon another. ◆*When Ted ran out on Delores, she got so angry that she sued him for divorce.*

run over *v.* **1.** To be too full and flow over the edge; spill over. ◆*Billy forgot he had left the water on, and the tub ran* *over.* **2.** To try or go over (something) quickly; practice briefly. ♦ *During the lunch hour, Mary ran over her history facts so she would remember them for the test.* ♦ *The coach ran over the signals for the trick play with the team just before game time.* **3.** To drive on top of; ride over. ♦ *At night cars often run over small animals that are blinded by the headlights.* Syn. RUN DOWN.

run ragged *v. phr.* To tire out; make nervous by too much worry or work. ♦ *Trying to keep up with too many clubs, sports, and activities in addition to his homework ran Tom ragged.* ♦ *On a rainy day the children sometimes ran Mother ragged.* Compare WEAR OUT.

run rings around See RUN CIRCLES AROUND.

run riot *v. phr.* **1.** To act freely or wildly; not control yourself. ♦ *The monkey got out of his cage and ran riot in the pet shop.* ♦ *John let his imagination run riot, thinking he was hunting lions in Africa.* **2.** To be or grow in great numbers or large amounts. ♦ *Daisies ran riot in the meadow.* Compare RUN WILD.

run scared *v. phr.* To expect defeat, as in a political campaign. ♦ *The one-vote defeat caused him to run scared in every race thereafter.*

run short *v. phr.* **1.** To not have enough. ♦ *Bob asked Jack to lend him five dollars because he was running short.* ♦ *We are running short of sugar.* Compare RUN OUT. **2.** To be not enough in quantity. ♦ *We are out of potatoes and the flour is running short.*

run that by me again! *v. phr., informal command* Repeat what you just said, as I couldn't understand you. ♦ *"Run that by me again," he cried. "This telephone connection is very bad."*

run the gauntlet *also* **gantlet** *v. phr.* **1.** To be made to run between two lines of people facing each other and be hit by them with clubs or other weapons. ♦ *Joe had to run the gauntlet as part of his initiation into the club.* **2.** To face a hard test; bear a painful experience. ♦ *Ginny had to run the gauntlet of her mother's questions about how the ink spot got on the dining room rug.*

run through *v.* **1.** To make a hole through, especially with a sword; pierce. ♦ *The pirate was a good swordsman, but the hero finally ran him through.* **2.** To spend recklessly; use up wastefully. ♦ *The rich man's son quickly ran through his money.* Syn. GO THROUGH 4. **3.** To read or practice from beginning to end without stopping. ♦ *The visiting singer ran through his numbers with the orchestra just before the program.*

run to *v. phr.* To approximate; reach. ♦ *It has been estimated that the casualties will run to over 300,000 killed by cholera and starvation in the crowded refugee camps.*

run to seed See GO TO SEED.

run true to form *v. phr.* To follow a usual way; act as expected; agree with how a person usually acts. ♦ *The little boy's actions ran true to form. He bothered his mother until she gave him his way.* Compare PAR FOR THE COURSE.

run up *v. phr.* **1.** To add to the amount of; increase. ♦ *Karl ran up a big bill at the bookstore.* **2.** To put together or make hastily; sew quickly together. ♦ *Jill ran up a costume for the party on her sewing machine.* **3.** To pull (something) upward on a rope; put (something) up quickly. ♦ *The pirates ran up the black flag.*

run up against See UP AGAINST.

run wild *v. phr.* To be or go out of control. ♦ *The students ran wild during spring vacation.* ♦ *The new supervisor lets the children run wild.* ♦ *The violets are running wild in the flower bed.* Compare RUN RIOT.

run with the hare and hunt (ride) with the hounds *v. phr.* To appear to support both parties in a conflict; to conduct things in ambiguous ways. ♦ *Critics accused the king of running with the hare and hunting with the hounds.*

running commentary *n. phr.* A continual series of remarks. ♦ *My chiropractor gives me a running commentary on the health care debate while he is giving me a rubdown.*

rush See BUM'S RUSH.

Russian roulette *n.* A game of chance in which one bullet is placed in a revolver, the cartridge cylinder is spun, and the player aims the gun at his own head and pulls the trigger. ♦ *Only a fool would risk playing Russian roulette.*

rust away *v. phr.* To disappear gradually through the process of rust or corrosion. ◆*If you refuse to paint those metal bars on the window, they will soon rust away.*

rustproof *adj.* Free from rusting or corrosion; permeated with anti-rust chemical agents. ◆*My new watch is rustproof and waterproof and I can wear it while swimming or taking a shower.*

saber rattling *or* **sword rattling** *n.* A show of military strength usually to frighten; a threat of military force. ♦ *The dictator marched his troops and tanks along the border of our country and did some saber rattling.*

sack See GET THE SACK *at* GET THE BOUNCE 2, GIVE THE SACK *at* GIVE THE BOUNCE 2, HIT THE HAY *or* HIT THE SACK, LEAVE HOLDING THE BAG *or* LEAVE HOLDING THE SACK.

sack in/out *v., slang* To go to sleep for a prolonged period (as in from night to morning). ♦ *Where are you guys going to sack in/sack out?*

sacred cow *n.* A person or thing that is never criticized, laughed at, or insulted even if it deserves such treatment. ♦ *Motherhood is a sacred cow to most politicians.* ♦ *The bold young governor had no respect for the state's sacred cows.* ♦ *Television respects too many sacred cows.*

sacrifice fly *n.* A baseball hit high in the air that helps a runner score after it is caught. ♦ *Mantle drove in two runs with a single and a sacrifice fly.*

saddle See IN THE SADDLE.

saddled with *adj. phr.* Burdened with; handicapped. ♦ *The business was so saddled with debt that the new owner had a hard time making a go of it for a couple of years.*

saddle shoe *n.* A white shoe with a black or brown piece of leather shaped like a saddle across the top of the shoe. ♦ *Mary wore bobby socks and saddle shoes.*

safe See PLAY SAFE.

safe and sound *adj. phr.* Not harmed; not hurt; safe and not damaged. ♦ *The package arrived safe and sound.* ♦ *The children returned from their trip safe and sound.* Compare WITH A WHOLE SKIN.

safety blitz *n.* A defensive play in football in which the defensive safety man makes a quick run to tackle the offensive quarterback. ♦ *Bob's safety blitz kept Tom from making a touchdown.*

safety glass *n.* Two panes of glass with a sheet of plastic between them so that the glass will not break into pieces. ♦ *Safety glass is used in cars because it does not break into pieces.*

safety in numbers *n. phr.* Protection against trouble by being in a group. ♦ *Peter said, "Stay in a group; there is safety in numbers."*

safety island *or* **safety zone** *n.* A raised area in a highway or road to be used only by people walking. ♦ *John was half-way across the street when the light changed. He stayed on the safety island until it changed again.*

sail See SET SAIL, RAKE THE WIND OUT OF ONE'S SAILS.

sail close to the wind *v. phr.* To be on the borderline between legality and illegality. ♦ *The wealthy tycoon sailed close to the wind during Prohibition.*

sail into *v., informal* **1.** To attack with great strength; begin hitting hard. ♦ *George grabbed a stick and sailed into the dog.* Compare LAY INTO, PITCH INTO. **2.** To scold or criticize very hard. ♦ *The coach really sailed into Bob for dropping the pass.* Syn. BAWL OUT, LAY INTO.

sail (right) through *v. phr.* To conclude easily and rapidly; finish something. ♦ *The bright young man sailed through the bar exam in record time.*

sailor collar *n.* A large square collar like those worn by sailors. ♦ *Little Timmy's suit has a sailor collar.* ♦ *Mary's blouse has a sailor collar.*

sail under false colors *v. phr.* **1.** To sail a ship, often pirate, under the flag of another country. ♦ *The pirate ship flew the American flag until it got near, then raised the black flag.* **2.** To pretend to be what you are not; masquerade. ♦ *The garage hired Jones as a mechanic, but fired him when they found he was sailing under false colors.* ♦ *They found out that Smith was an escaped convict who had been sailing under false colors as a lawyer.*

sake See FOR ONE'S SAKE.

salad days *n. phr., informal* The period of one's youth; a period of inexperience. ♦ *He was silly and immature during his salad days in high school.*

sale See NO DEAL *or* NO SALE, ON SALE, WHITE SALE.

sales check *or* **sales slip** *n.* A paper which the clerk gives the person who bought something; a paper that shows what you bought in a store and how much you paid for it. ♦ *Mrs. Smith checked the sales slip with what she bought.* ♦ *Mary brought the sales check when she returned the dress so she could get her money back.*

sales talk *n.* A speech made to point out all the good reasons why the sale would help someone who might buy the product. ♦ *Mrs. Goldsmith gave the man a good sales talk about the new house.* ♦ *The coach gave a sales talk on exercise in the school assembly.*

salisbury steak *n.* A broiled or fried hamburger patty sometimes containing eggs, milk, bread crumbs, and seasoning. ♦ *James ordered a salisbury steak for lunch.*

salt See BACK TO THE SALT MINES, TAKE WITH A GRAIN OF SALT *also* TAKE WITH A PINCH OF SALT, WORTH ONE'S SALT.

salt away *v., informal* To save (money) for the future. ♦ *Every week Joe salts away half of his pay.*

salt pork *n.* Very fat pork that has been packed in salt or dipped in brine for curing. ♦ *Mother cooked beans with salt pork for supper.*

same See AT THE SAME TIME, ALL THE SAME, *or* JUST THE SAME, IN THE SAME BREATH, LIGHTNING NEVER STRIKES TWICE IN THE SAME PLACE, ONE AND THE SAME.

same here *informal* And it is the same with me; and the same for me.—Used only in speech. ♦ *Mary ordered an ice cream soda, and Jill said, "Same here."* ♦ *Tom said he was too tired to run any further, and Bill said, "Same here."*

sand See HIDE ONE'S HEAD IN THE SAND.

sand lot *n.* A field, vacant lot, or other open place used as a sports playing field, usually by younger teams or by amateurs who can't afford to use anything better. ♦ *Rogers Hornsby, who was National League baseball batting champion six times, first started playing on Texas sand lots.*

sand-lot *adj.* Of the kind seen on sand lots; not professional. ♦ *The professional football team was so confused by their opponents' fast play that they acted like a bunch of sand-lot amateurs.*

sand trap *n.* A low place on a golf course that is filled with sand to stop the ball. ♦ *The golfer lost four strokes trying to get the ball out of the sand trap.*

sandwich board *n.* Two advertising signs worn by a man, one on his chest and the other on his back. ♦ *The man walking along Main Street wore a sandwich board saying "Eat at Joe's."*

salt of the earth *n. phr., informal* One who helps to make society good and wholesome; a basically good or valuable person. ♦ *Everyone here considers Syd and Susan the salt of the earth because they are so generous.*

sauce See HIT THE SAUCE.

save face *v. phr.* To save your good reputation, popularity, or dignity when something has happened or may happen to hurt you; hide something that may cause you shame. ♦ *The policeman was caught accepting a bribe; he tried to save face by claiming it was money owed to him.* ♦ *Bill would not play in the game because he knew he could not do well and he wanted to save face.* ♦ *The colonel who lost the battle saved face by showing his orders from the general.* Contrast LOSE FACE.—**face-saver** *n.* ♦ *The shop teacher's note was a face-saver when another teacher thought John and Bill were playing hookey in town.*—**face-saving** *adj.* ♦ *The note was a face-saving idea.*—**face-saving** *n.* ♦ *Face-saving is not helped by too many invented excuses.*

save for a rainy day See RAINY DAY.

save one's breath *v. phr., informal* To keep silent because talking will not help; not talk because it will do no good. ♦ *Save your breath; the boss will never give you the day off.*

save one's neck *or* **save one's skin** *v. phr., slang* To save from danger or trouble. ♦ *The fighter planes saved our skins while the army was landing from the ships.* ♦ *Betty saved Tim's neck by typing his report for him; without her help he could not have finished on time.*

save the day *v. phr.* To bring about victory or success, especially when defeat is likely. ♦ *The forest fire was nearly out of control when suddenly it rained heavily and saved the day.* ♦ *The team* *was behind, but at the last minute Sam saved the day with a touchdown.*

save up *v. phr.* To put away for future use; keep as savings; save. ♦*John was saving up for a new bicycle.* ♦*Mary saved up pieces of cloth to make a quilt.*

saving grace *n. phr.* A single good attribute; a redeeming quality. ♦*Felicity is not very attractive but her intelligence and wit are her saving grace.*

savings account *n.* An account in a bank, where people put money to save it, and the bank uses the money and pays interest every year. ♦*If you leave your money in your savings account for six months or a year, the bank will pay interest on it.* Compare CHECKING ACCOUNT.

savings bond *n.* A government certificate given for money and saved for a number of years so that the government will pay back the money with interest. ♦*Mary bought a $25 savings bond for $18.75.* ♦*John's father gave him a savings bond for graduation.*

sawed-off *adj., informal* Shorter than usual; small of its kind. ♦*The riot police carried sawed-off shotguns.* ♦*Jimmy was a sawed-off, skinny runt.*

saw wood *also Southern* **saw gourds** *v. phr., slang* To breathe loudly through the nose while sleeping; snore. *John was sawing wood.* ♦*In Alabama a boy who snores saws gourds.*

say See DARE SAY, GO WITHOUT SAYING, I'LL SAY, NEVER SAY DIE, NOT TO MENTION *or* TO SAY NOTHING OF, STRANGE TO SAY, THAT IS *or* THAT IS TO SAY, YOU DON'T SAY, YOU SAID IT *or* YOU CAN SAY THAT AGAIN.

say a mouthful 1. *v. phr., slang* To say something of great importance or meaning; say more by a sentence than the words usually mean.—Usually in past tense. ♦*Tom said a mouthful when he guessed that company was coming to visit. A dozen people came.* **2.** *v. phr., informal* To vent one's honest opinion, even in anger. ♦*He sure said a mouthful when he told his boss what was wrong with our business.* Contrast GET AN EARFUL.

say one's peace *or* **speak one's piece** *v. phr.* To say openly what you think; say, especially in public, what you usually

say or are expected to say. ♦*John told the boss that he thought he was wrong and the boss got angry. He said, "You've said your little piece, so go on home."* ♦*Every politician got up and said his piece about how good the mayor was and then sat down.*

says who *or* **says you** *v. phr., slang* I don't believe or accept that.—An expression of rebuff often used to make fun of someone or oppose him. ♦*"I am the strongest boy on the block." "Says you." ♦"That brook is full of trout." "Says who? I never saw anybody catch trout there." ♦"You can't take Mary to the party—she's my girl." "Says who?"*

say-so *n.* Approval; permission; word. ♦*Father got angry because I took his new car out without his say-so.*

say the word *v. phr., informal* To say or show that you want something or agree to something; show a wish, willingness, or readiness; give a sign; say yes; say so. ♦*Just say the word and I will lend you the money.* ♦*I will do anything you want; just say the word.* ♦*If you get tired of those pictures, say the word.*

say uncle *also* **cry uncle** *v. phr., informal* To say that you surrender; admit that you have lost; admit a defeat; give up. ♦*Bob fought for five minutes, but he had to say uncle.* ♦*The bully twisted Jerry's arm and said, "Cry uncle."* ♦*The other team was beating us, but we wouldn't say uncle.* Compare GIVE IN.

scale See TO SCALE.

scale down *v.* To make smaller or less; decrease. ♦*John scaled down each boy's share of food after a bear robbed the camp.* ♦*Tom built a scaled down model of the plane.* Compare CUT DOWN.

scandal sheet *n.* A newspaper that prints much shocking news and scandal. ♦*Bob wanted to find out who won the election, but he could find only a scandal sheet.* ♦*The scandal sheet carried big headlines about the murder.*

scarcely any See HARDLY ANY.

scarcely ever See HARDLY EVER.

scaredy-cat *or* **scared-cat** See FRAIDY-CAT.

scare away *or* **off** *v. phr.* To cause to flee; frighten away. ♦*Jake is a confirmed* *bachelor; the best way to scare him off is to start talking about marriage.*

scare out of one's wits *or* **scare stiff** *or* **scare the daylights out of** *v. phr., informal* To frighten very much. ♦ *The owl's hooting scared him out of his wits.* ♦ *The child was scared stiff in the dentist's chair.* ♦ *Pete's ghost story scared the daylights out of the smaller boys.*

scare to death See TO DEATH.

scare up *or* **scrape up** *v., informal* To find, collect, or get together with some effort when needed. ♦ *The boy scared up enough money to go to college.* ♦ *"Will you stay for supper?" she asked. "I can scare up enough for us all."* ♦ *He managed to scrape up the money for his speeding fine.*

scene See BEHIND THE SCENES.

scent See THROW OFF THE SCENT.

schedule See ON SCHEDULE.

scheme See COLOR SCHEME.

school See TELL TALES OUT OF SCHOOL.

school of hard knocks *n. phr.* Life outside of school or college; life out in the world; the ordinary experience of learning from work and troubles. ♦ *He never went to high school; he was educated in the school of hard knocks.*

score See SETTLE A SCORE *also* WIPE OUT AN OLD SCORE, THE SCORE.

scot-free *adj. phr.* Without punishment; completely free. ♦ *In spite of his obvious guilt, the jury acquitted him and he got off scot-free.*

scotch broth *n.* A thick barley soup with vegetables and mutton or beef. ♦ *Mother cooked a hearty scotch broth for dinner.*

Scott See GREAT GODFREY *or* GREAT SCOTT.

scout See GOOD EGG *or* GOOD SCOUT.

scout around *v. phr.* To search for; look around. ♦ *When we first came to town, we had to scout around for a suitable apartment.*

scrape See BOW AND SCRAPE.

scrape the bottom of the barrel *v. phr., informal* To use or take whatever is left after the most or the best has been taken; accept the leftovers. ♦ *At first they took out quarters, but they had so little money that they had to scrape the bottom of the barrel and paid with nickels and pennies for their lunch.* ♦ *The garage owner had to scrape the*

bottom of the barrel to find a qualified mechanic to work for him.

scrape together *v. phr.* To quickly assemble, usually from scanty ingredients. ♦ *We were so hungry we had to scrape together some lunch from all kinds of frozen leftovers.*

scrape up See SCARE UP.

scratch See FROM SCRATCH, PUT ONE'S MONEY ON A SCRATCHED HORSE, UP TO PAR *or* UP TO SCRATCH.

scratch around for *v. phr.* To search randomly for something. ♦ *If you scratch around for a more reliable used car, maybe you'll feel more confident on the road.*

scratch one's back *v. phr., informal* To do something kind and helpful for someone or to flatter him in the hope that he will do something for you. Usually used in the expression *"You scratch my back and I'll scratch yours."* ♦ *Mary asked Jean to introduce her to her brother. Jean said, "You scratch my back and I'll scratch yours."*

scratch the surface *v. phr.* To learn or understand very little about something.—Usually used with a limiting adverb (as *only, hardly*). ♦ *We thought we understood Africa but when we made a trip there we found we had only scratched the surface.* ♦ *High school students have only scratched the surface of their subjects, and even after college graduation, they still find there is much more to learn.*

scream bloody murder *v. phr., informal* To yell or protest as strongly as one can. ♦ *When the thief grabbed her purse, the woman screamed bloody murder.* ♦ *When the city doubled property taxes, home owners screamed bloody murder.*

screen test *n.* A short movie made to see if an actor or actress is good enough or the right one to play a part. ♦ *Ellen acted well on the stage, but she failed her screen test.*

screw See HAVE A SCREW LOOSE, PUT ON THE SCREWS.

screw around *v. phr., vulgar, avoidable* To hang around idly without accomplishing anything, to loaf about, to beat or hack around. ♦ *You guys are no longer welcome here; all you do is screw around all day.*

screws See TIGHTEN THE SCREWS.

screw up *v. phr., slang, semi-vulgar, best avoided* **1.** To make a mess of, to make an error which causes confusion. ♦ *The treasurer screwed up the accounts of the Society so badly that he had to be fired.* **2.** To cause someone to be neurotic or maladjusted. ♦ *Her divorce screwed her up so badly that she had to go to a shrink.*

screw-up *n.* A mistake; an error; a confusing mess. ♦ *"What a screw-up!" the manager cried, when he realized that the bills were sent to the wrong customers.*

screw up one's courage *or* **pluck up one's courage** *v. phr.* To force yourself to be brave. ♦ *The small boy screwed up his courage and went upstairs in the dark.* ♦ *When his father came home in a bad mood, it took Pete some time to screw up his courage and ask him for a dollar.* Compare WHISTLE IN THE DARK.

scrimmage See LINE OF SCRIMMAGE.

scrounge around *v. phr., slang* **1.** To search for an object aimlessly without having one clearly in mind. ♦ *I don't know what's the matter with him, he is just scrounging around all day long.* **2.** To look around for a way to get a free drink or a free meal. ♦ *Sue and her husband are so broke they never eat properly; they just scrounge around from one place to the next until someone offers them something.*

sea See AT SEA, BETWEEN THE DEVIL AND THE DEEP BLUE SEA, HIGH SEAS, NOT THE ONLY FISH IN THE SEA, PUT TO SEA.

sea legs *n. phr.* **1.** Adjustment to being in a boat that is rocking on the sea. ♦ *This is my first transatlantic trip so give me a day to get my sea legs before you make me dance.* **2.** Adjustment to a new job or situation. ♦ *"I have just been transferred here and I haven't found my sea legs yet," the new colleague joked.*

seam See BURST AT THE SEAMS.

search See IN SEARCH OF.

search me *informal* I don't know; how should I know?—May be considered rude. ♦ *When I asked her what time it was, she said, "Search me, I have no watch."*

search one's heart *or* **search one's soul** *v. phr., formal* To study your reasons and acts; try to discover if you have been fair and honest. ♦ *The teacher searched his heart trying to decide if he had been unfair in failing Tom.*— **heart-searching** *or* **soul-searching** *n. or adj.* ♦ *After much heart-searching, Jean told Beth she was sorry for the unkind things she had said.* ♦ *The minister preached a soul-searching sermon about the thoughtless ways people hurt each other.*

search out *v.* To search for and discover; find or learn by hunting. ♦ *The police were trying to search out the real murderer.*

search with a fine-tooth comb See FINE-TOOTH COMB.

season See HIGH SEASON, IN SEASON, LOW SEASON, OUT OF SEASON.

seat See BACK SEAT DRIVER, FLY BY THE SEAT OF ONE'S PANTS, HOT SEAT, JUDGMENT SEAT, TAKE A BACK SEAT.

seat belt *n.* A strong strap used to protect a person in a moving car or other vehicle by holding him in his seat. ♦ *When the plane began to land, Billy and his mother fastened their seat belts.* ♦ *Passengers in automobiles should wear seat belts for safety.*

second See PLAY SECOND FIDDLE, SPLIT SECOND.

second best *n.* Something that is lower than or not quite as good as the best. ♦ *Tom liked the deluxe model bicycle; but he could afford only a second best.* ♦ *Joan chose the best and Mary had to take the second best.* ♦ *There were ten boys in the race. Jack won and Fred was a close second best.* Compare RUNNER UP.

second best *adv.* Second; in second place. ♦ *The team came off second best in the game.*

second-best *adj.* Next to best; second in rank. ♦ *Mary wore her second-best dress.* ♦ *Bob was the second-best player on the team.* ♦ *"I am the second-best student in this school because I was second best in the Milwaukee competition."*

second childhood *n. phr.* Senility; dotage. ♦ *"Grandpa is in his second childhood; we must make allowances for him at the dinner table," my mother said, as Grandpa dropped food all over* *the place.*

second class *n.* **1.** The second best or highest group; the class next after the first. ◆*Joe was good enough in arithmetic to be put in the second class but was not good enough for the first.* Compare FIRST CLASS. **2.** The place or quarters, especially on a ship, train, or airplane which people travel who pay the next to the highest fare. ◆*Aunt May bought a ticket to travel in the second class on the boat trip.* Compare FIRST CLASS, THIRD CLASS. **3.** A class of mail that includes magazines and newspapers published at least four times a year and costs less for mailing than first class mail. Compare FIRST CLASS.

second-class[1] *adj.* **1.** Belonging in the class that is next to the highest or next best. ◆*He was only a second-class math student.* ◆*His parents traveled as second-class passengers on the boat.* ◆*The periodical came as second-class mail.* Compare FIRST-CLASS, THIRD-CLASS. **2.** Not so good as others; second-rate. ◆*They were never given full democratic rights but were always treated as second-class citizens.*

second-class[2] *adv.* By second class. ◆*We went second-class on the train to New York.* ◆*I mailed the newspaper second-class.*

second cousin *n.* A child of your father's or mother's first cousin. ◆*Mary and Jane are second cousins.*

second-guess *v. phr.* **1.** To criticize another's decision with advantage of hindsight. ◆*The losing team's coach is always second-guessed.* **2.** To guess what someone else intends or would think or do. ◆*Television planners try to second-guess the public.*

secondhand *adj.* Used; not new; pre-owned. ◆*Sometimes a secondhand car is just as reliable as a brand new one.*

second nature *n.* Something done without any special effort, as if by natural instinct. ◆*Cutting tall trees has become second nature to the experienced lumberjack.*

second-rate *adj.* Of mediocre or inferior quality. ◆*The movie received a bad review; it was second-rate at best.*

second-run *adj.* Of a movie: Shown in many movie theaters before, and allowed to be shown later in other movie theaters. ◆*Tickets to second-run movies cost much less.*

second sight *n. phr.* Intuition; prescience; clairvoyance. ◆*Some police departments employ psychics to find missing persons or objects as they are said to have second sight.*

second thought *n.* A change of ideas or opinions resulting from more thought or study. ◆*Your second thoughts are very often wiser than your first ideas.* ◆*We decided to climb the mountain, but on second thought realized that it was too dangerous.* Compare THINK BETTER OF.

second to none *adj. phr.* Excellent; first rate; peerless. ◆*Our new State University campus is second to none. There is no need to pay all that high tuition at a private college.*

second wind *also* **second breath** *n.* **1.** The easier breathing that follows difficult breathing when one makes a severe physical effort, as in running or swimming. ◆*After the first quarter mile, a mile runner usually gets his second wind and can breathe better.* ◆*We climbed with labored breathing for half an hour, but then got our second wind and went up more easily.* **2.** *informal* The refreshed feeling you get after first becoming tired while doing something and then becoming used to it. ◆*Tom became very tired of working at his algebra, but after a while he got his second wind and began to enjoy it.*

secret See IN SECRET, OPEN SECRET.

section gang *or* **section crew** *n.* A group of railroad workers who watch and repair a number of miles of track. ◆*The section crew was called out to fix the broken bridge.*

section hand *n.* A worker who repairs railway track; one of the men in a section gang. ◆*The section hands moved off the track while the train went by.*

security blanket *n., slang, colloquial* An idea, person, or object that one holds on to for psychological reassurance or comfort as infants usually hang on to the edge of a pillow, a towel, or a blanket. ◆*Sue has gone to Aunt Mathilda for a chat; she is her security blanket.*

see See CAN'T SEE THE WOODS FOR THE TREES, LET ME SEE *or* LET'S SEE.

see a lot of *v. phr.* To go out regularly with someone; have an affair with someone. *♦ They have been seeing a lot of each other lately.*

see about *v.* **1.** To find out about; attend to. *♦ If you are too busy, I'll see about the train tickets.* **2.** *informal* To consider; study. *♦ I cannot take time now but I'll see about your plan when I have time.* Compare SEE TO, LOOK INTO, THINK OVER.

see after See LOOK AFTER.

see better days *v. phr.* **1.** To enjoy a better or happier life. *♦ Mr. Smith is poor now, but he will see better days.* **2.** To become old, damaged, or useless. Used in the perfect tense. *♦ My blue coat is ten years old. It has seen better days. ♦ Our car wasn't old, but it had seen better days.*

see beyond one's nose *or* **see beyond the end of one's nose** *v. phr.* To make wise judgments about questions of importance to yourself and others; act with farseeing understanding. Used in negative, conditional, and interrogative sentences. *♦ He couldn't save money or make plans for the future; he just never saw beyond the end of his nose. ♦ People who always complain about school taxes would stop it if they could see beyond their noses and understand the importance of first-class schools.*

seed See GO TO SEED *or* RUN TO SEED.

see daylight *v. phr., informal* To know that an end or success is near. *♦ We thought we would never finish building the house, but now we can see daylight. ♦ Sarah thought it would take forever to read the book for her report, but finally she saw daylight.*

see eye to eye *v. phr.* To agree fully; hold exactly the same opinion. *♦ Though we did not usually agree, we saw eye to eye in the matter of reducing taxes. ♦ Jim did not see eye to eye with Sally on where they would go for their vacation.*

see fit *or* **think fit** *v. phr.* To decide that an action is necessary, wise, or advisable; choose. *♦ Jim asked "Dad, what time should I come home after the dance?" His father answered, "You may do as you see fit."*—Often used with an infinitive. *♦ After much thought, we did not see fit to join the Smiths on their Caribbean cruise. ♦ The boys were angry because Ed thought fit to report the fight to the principal.*

see how the land lies *v. phr., informal* To reconnoiter; investigate. *♦ Before going there in person to ask for a job, you had better see how the land lies and who does what.* Compare CASE THE JOINT.

seeing is believing Seeing something is good proof. *♦ Bill told Joe he had passed his test, but Joe said, "Seeing is believing."*

see into *v.* To know or understand the real nature or meaning of. *♦ Suddenly the teacher saw into Linda's strange actions.*

see off *v.* To go to say or wave goodbye to. *♦ His brother went to the train with him to see him off. ♦ When Marsha flew to Paris, Flo saw her off at the airport.*

see one home *v. phr.* To walk a person home. *♦ "Let me see you home, dear," Nick said to Jenny at the end of the party.*

see one's way clear *v. phr.* To know no reason for not doing something; feel that you are free. *♦ John finally saw his way clear to help his friends. ♦ Mary had to do her homework and help her mother before she could see her way clear to go to the movies with Jane.*

see out *v.* **1.** To go with to an outer door. *♦ A polite man sees his company out after a party.* **2.** To stay with and finish; not quit. *♦ Pete's assignment was hard but he saw it out to the end.*

see reason *v. phr.* To think or act sensibly, especially after realizing what the facts are on a certain matter and accepting advice about it. *♦ He finally saw reason and reshaped his sales strategy by lowering the prices as his older brother had suggested.*

see red *v. phr., informal* To become very angry. *♦ Whenever anyone teased John about his weight, he saw red.*

see service *v. phr.* **1.** To be used over a considerable period of time. *♦ This old camera of mine has already seen six years of service.* **2.** To serve in a military sense. *♦ Colonel Hutchins has seen service in World War II, Korea, Vietnam, and the Persian Gulf.*

see stars *v. phr., informal* To imagine you are seeing stars as a result of being hit on the head. ♦ *When Ted was hit on the head by the ball, he saw stars.* ♦ *The boxer's head hit the floor, making him see stars.*

see the beat See HEAR THE BEAT.

see the color of one's money *v. phr., informal* To know that you have money to spend. ♦ *The realtor would not show us a house until he saw the color of our money.* ♦ *Before I show you the diamond, let me see the color of your money.*

see the last of *v. phr.* To say good-bye to someone or something; get rid of something. ♦ *We were glad to see the last of the winter.*

see the light *v. phr., informal* To understand or agree, often suddenly; accept another's explanation or decision. ♦ *I did not approve of his action, but he explained his reason and then I saw the light.* ♦ *Bill wanted Harry to help him, but Harry wasn't in the mood until Bill offered to pay him. Then Harry saw the light.* ♦ *Mary thought it was fun to date older boys but when they started drinking, she saw the light.*

see the light at the end of the tunnel *v. phr., informal* To anticipate the happy resolution of a prolonged period of problems. ♦ *We've been paying on our house mortgage for many years, but at long last we can see the light at the end of the tunnel.*

see the light of day *v. phr.* To be born or begun. ♦ *The children visited the old house where their great-grandfather first saw the light of day.* ♦ *The party was a failure, and Mathilda wished her plan had never seen the light of day.*

see the sights See SIGHTSEE.

see things *v. phr., informal* To imagine sights which are not real; think you see what is not there. ♦ *I had not seen him for twenty years and when we met on the street I thought I was seeing things.* ♦ *She woke her husband to tell him she had seen a face at the window, but he told her she was seeing things.*

see through *v.* **1.** To understand the real meaning of or reason for; realize the falseness of. ♦ *Mother saw through Johnny's excuses not to go to bed on Christmas Eve. She knew he wanted to stay up to see Santa Claus.* ♦ *The teacher saw through the boy's story of having to help at home.* **2.** To do (something) until finished; stay with until the end. ♦ *Once Charles started a job, he saw it through till it was finished.* **3.** To help and encourage (a person) through trouble or difficulty. ♦ *Mrs. Miller saw Jane through her sickness.* ♦ *When Mr. and Mrs. Brown lost their little girl, their friends saw them through with help and sympathy.* ♦ *His business was about to fail, but his banker saw him through.* **4.** To be enough for; last. ♦ *This money will see us through the week.* ♦ *Here is a long report to type. Do you have enough paper to see you through?* Compare TIDE OVER.

see to *also* **look to** *v.* To attend to; take care of; do whatever needs to be done about. ♦ *While Donna bought the theatre tickets, I saw to the parking of the car.* Compare SEE ABOUT.

see to it *v. phr.* To take care; take the responsibility; make sure.—Usually used with a noun clause. ♦ *We saw to it that the child was fed and bathed.*

see with rose-colored glasses See LOOK AT THE WORLD THROUGH ROSE-COLORED GLASSES.

seed money *n. phr.* A small grant or donation for others to be able to start a new venture. ♦ *All you need is some seed money and you can set up your own desk-top publishing firm.*

seize on *v.* To make use of (a happening or idea.) ♦ *Bob seized on the rain as an excuse for missing school.*

seize on *or* **upon** *v. phr.* To latch onto. ♦ *Whenever Herb is in a romantic mood, Irene seizes on it and starts talking about marriage, which is not what Herb had in mind.*

seize the opportunity *v. phr.* To exploit a chance. ♦ *His wealthy uncle offered to send him to Harvard and he wisely seized the opportunity.*

self-conscious *adj.* Embarrassed; shy. ♦ *Edith has a freckled face and sometimes she is very self-conscious about it.*

self-made *adj.* Having achieved wealth, fame, and success on one's own without outside help. ♦ *John D. Rockefeller is one of the most famous self-made men in America.*

self-possessed *adj.* Confident; sure of one self. ♦ *Before he made his first million, he used to be shy, but afterwards he became very self-possessed.*

self-seeking *adj.* Given to egotism and self-aggrandizement. ♦ *Al is the most self-seeking person I've ever met, he is not fun to be around.*

sell down the river *v. phr.* To give harmful information about someone or something to one's enemies; betray. ♦ *The traitor sold his country down the river to the enemy army.* ♦ *The criminal told the hiding place of his companions and sold them down the river.* Compare SELL OUT 2.

sell off *v. phr.* To liquidate one's holdings of certain set items. ♦ *The retired professor had to sell off his rare butterfly collection to meet his health expenses.*

sell one a bill of goods *v. phr.* To persuade another to acquire something useless; defraud. ♦ *We were sure sold a bill of goods when Alfred persuaded us to buy his custom-built car for which replacement parts weren't available anywhere.*

sell one on *v. phr.* To persuade someone to do something. ♦ *We were able to sell our wealthy uncle on the idea of having a joint family vacation in Hawaii.*

sellout *n.* **1.** A betrayal or act of treason. ♦ *The spy's behavior during the Cold War was a classical sellout.*

sell out *v.* **1a.** To sell all of a certain thing which a store has in stock. ♦ *In the store's January white sale the sheets and pillowcases were sold out in two days.* **1b.** To sell all the stock and close the store; go out of business. ♦ *The local hardware store sold out last month and was replaced by a cafe.* **2.** *informal* To be unfaithful to your country for money or other reward; be disloyal; sell a secret; accept a bribe. ♦ *In the Revolutionary War, Benedict Arnold sold out to the British.* ♦ *The dishonest wrestler sold out to his opponent for a hundred dollars.*

sell short *v.* To think (a person or thing) less good or valuable than is true; underestimate. ♦ *Don't sell the team short; the players are better than you think.* ♦ *Some teachers sold John short.*

sell snow to the Eskimos *v. phr.* To sell something to people who already have a large quantity of the same or similar goods. ♦ *My Alaskan friend said, "One of the hottest businesses in Alaska is refrigeration. You could say that I, as a refrigerator expert, am selling snow to the Eskimos."* See CARRY COALS TO NEWCASTLE.

send C.O.D. See C.O.D.

send off *v. phr.* To say good-bye to someone ceremoniously. ♦ *They sent us off to the Mainland from our first visit to Hawaii with an elaborate champagne party at the pier.*

send-off *n. phr.* A demonstration of affection or respect at someone's departure, as a retirement ceremony. ♦ *When our colleague retired after 35 years of teaching, we all got together at the Faculty Club and gave him a terrific send-off.*

send one about one's business *v. phr.* To dismiss someone summarily; tell one off. ♦ *When Mrs. Atwater discovered that her daughter's French tutor was an ordinary fortune hunter, she sent him about his business.* Compare SEND ONE PACKING.

send one packing *v. phr.* To fire someone summarily. ♦ *When the boss caught Smith stealing from the cash register, he sent him packing.* Compare SEND ONE ABOUT ONE'S BUSINESS.

send to the minors *v. phr.* To dismiss someone; tell them off; terminate a relationship.—A baseball term. ♦ *"What did you do to your girlfriend?" Ernie asked Bert, when Bert started dating Jane. "I sent her to the minors," Bert answered with a sneer.*

send up *v. phr., colloquial* To sentence (someone) to prison. ♦ *Did you know that Milton Shaeffer was sent up for fifteen years?*

send word *v. phr.* To send notification to; advise. ♦ *When his father fell seriously ill, we sent word to Mike to come home as quickly as possible.*

senior citizen *n.* An older person, often one who has retired from active work or employment. *Mrs. North, the history teacher, is a senior citizen.*

sense See COME TO ONE'S SENSES, HORSE SENSE, MAKE SENSE, OUT OF ONE'S HEAD *or* OUT OF ONE'S SENSES.

separate the men from the boys *v. phr.,*

informal To show who has strength, courage and loyalty and find who do not. ♦ *When the ship hit an iceberg and sank, it separated the men from the boys.* ♦ *The mile run separates the men from the boys.*

separate the sheep from the goats See SEPARATE THE MEN FROM THE BOYS.

serve See FIRST COME, FIRST SERVED.

serve a sentence *v. phr.* To be in jail. ♦ *Charlie served four years of an eight-year sentence, after which he was paroled and released.*

serve notice *v. phr.* **1.** To notify one's employer in a formal or legal manner that one is quitting the former's employment. ♦ *She gave notice to her boss that she was quitting because of marriage.* **2.** To notify an employee or a tenant that one no longer needs their services or wishes to have them as tenants. ♦ *The new landlady gave notice to several families in our building because they were late in paying their rent.*

serve one right *v. phr.* To be what (someone) really deserves as a punishment; be a fair exchange for what (someone) has done or said or failed to do or say. ♦ *He failed his exam; it served him right because he had not studied.* ♦ *Bob said it served Sally right when she cut her finger; she had taken his knife without asking him.* Compare ASK FOR, HAVE IT COMING.

serve time See SERVE A SENTENCE.

serve up *v.* To prepare and serve (as a food). ♦ *Father caught a trout and Mother served it up at dinner.*

service See AT ONE'S SERVICE, CURB SERVICE, LIP SERVICE, OF SERVICE, ROOM SERVICE.

session See BULL SESSION.

set See GET SET.

set ablaze *v. phr.* To cause to burn by lighting with a match or other incendiary device. ♦ *The criminals poured gasoline on the house and set it ablaze with a small lighter.*

set about *v.* To begin; start. ♦ *Benjamin Franklin set about learning the printer's trade at an early age.* ♦ *After breakfast, Mother set about her household duties.*

set afire *or* **set on fire** See SET ABLAZE.

set aside *v.* **1.** To separate from the others in a group or collection. ♦ *She set aside the things in the old trunk*

which she wanted to keep. **2.** To select or choose from others for some purpose. ♦ *The governor set aside a day for thanksgiving.* **3.** To pay no attention to (something); leave out. ♦ *The complaint was set aside as of no importance.* **4.** *formal* To refuse to accept; annul; cancel as worthless or wrong. ♦ *The Supreme Court set aside the decision of the lower courts.*

setback *n.* A disadvantage; a delay. ♦ *We suffered a major setback when my wife lost her job.*

set back *v.* **1.** To cause to put off or get behind schedule; slow up; check. ♦ *The cold weather set back the planting by two weeks.* **2.** *informal* To cause to pay out or to lose (a sum of money); cost. ♦ *His new car set him back over $3000.*

set back on one's heels *or* **knock back on one's heels** *v. phr., informal* To give an unpleasant surprise; upset suddenly; stop or turn back (someone's) progress. ♦ *Jack brags too much and it set him back on his heels when the coach told him he wasn't as good a player as he thought he was.* ♦ *Jean was doing very well in school until sickness knocked her back on her heels.* Compare KNOCK FOR A LOOP, THROW FOR A LOSS.

set down *v.* **1.** To write; record. ♦ *He set down all his important thoughts in his dairy.* ♦ *At the beginning of his letter Dan set down the date.* Syn. PUT DOWN. **2.** To stop a bus or other vehicle and let (someone) get off. ♦ *The bus driver set her down at the corner.* **3.** To put into some group; classify; consider. ♦ *When he heard the man speak, he set him down as a fool.* **4.** To explain; think a reason for. ♦ *The teacher set down the boy's poor English to his foreign birth.*

set eyes on See LAY EYES ON.

set fire to *v. phr.* To cause to burn; start a fire in. ♦ *The sparks set fire to the oily rags.* Compare CATCH FIRE.

set foot *v. phr.* To step; walk; go.—Used with a negative. ♦ *She would not let him set foot across her threshold.* ♦ *She told the boy not to set foot out of the house until he had finished supper.*

set forth *v., formal* **1.** To explain exactly or clearly. ♦ *The President set forth his plans in a television talk.* **2.** To start to go somewhere; begin a trip. ♦ *The troop set forth on their ten-mile hike early.* Compare SET OUT.

set free *v. phr.* To liberate. ♦ *The trapper set all the small animals free before the snowstorm hit.*

set great store by See SET STORE BY.

set in *v.* To begin; start; develop. ♦ *Before the boat could reach shore, a storm had set in.* ♦ *He did not keep the cut clean and infection set in.* ♦ *The wind set in from the east.*

set in one's ways *adj. phr.* Stubborn; opinionated; unchangeable. ♦ *My grandfather is so old and set in his ways that he'll eat nothing new.*

set loose See LET LOOSE 1a.

set off *v.* **1.** To decorate through contrast; balance by difference. ♦ *The bright colors of the birds were set off by the white snow.* ♦ *A small gold pin set off her plain dark dress.* **2.** To balance; make somewhat equal. ♦ *Her great wealth, as he thought, set off her plain face.* **3a.** To begin to go. ♦ *They set off for the West in a covered wagon.* Compare SET OUT. **3b.** To cause to begin. ♦ *A letter from home set off an attack of homesickness.* ♦ *An atomic explosion is created by setting off a chain reaction in the atom.* Compare TOUCH OFF. **3c.** To cause to explode. ♦ *On July 4 we set off firecrackers in many places.*

set of new threads *n. phr.* New men's suit. ♦ *"Nice set of new threads!" Ed said, when he saw Dave in his new tailor-made outfit.*

set on *also* **set upon** *v.* **1.** To begin suddenly to fight against; attack fiercely. ♦ *Tom was walking through the park when a gang of boys set on him.* **2.** To cause to attack. ♦ *Some boys went to steal melons but the farmer set his dog on them.*

set one's cap for *v. phr., informal* To attempt to win the love of or to marry. —Usually used of a girl or woman. ♦ *The young girl set her cap for the new town doctor, who was a bachelor.*

set one's face against *v. phr., literary* To be very much against; strongly disapprove. ♦ *The banker's daughter wanted to marry a poor boy, but her father set his face against it.*

set one's hand to See PUT ONE'S HAND TO.

set one's hand to the plow See PUT ONE'S HAND TO THE PLOW.

set one's heart on *v. phr.* To want very much. ♦ *He set his heart on that bike.* *also:* To be very desirous of; hope very much to succeed in.—Used with a verbal noun. ♦ *He set his heart on winning the race.*

set one's house in order See PUT ONE'S HOUSE IN ORDER.

set one's mind at rest *v. phr.* To relieve someone's anxieties; reassure someone. ♦ *"Let me set your mind at rest about the operation," Dr. Vanek said. "You'll be back on your feet in a week."*

set one's mind on *v. phr.* To be determined to; decide to. ♦ *He has set his mind on buying an old chateau in France.*

set one's sights *v. phr.* **1.** To want to reach; aim for. ♦ *John has set his sights higher than the job he has now.* **2.** To wish to get or win. ♦ *Owen set his sights on the championship.*

set one's teeth on edge *v. phr.* **1.** To have a sharp sour taste that makes you rub your teeth together. ♦ *The lemon juice set my teeth on edge.* **2.** To make one feel nervous or annoyed. ♦ *She looks so mean that her face sets my teeth on edge.*

set on foot See ON FOOT.

set out *v.* **1.** To leave on a journey or voyage. ♦ *The Pilgrims set out for the New World.* Compare SET FORTH 2, SET OFF 4, START OUT. **2.** To decide and begin to try; attempt. ♦ *George set out to improve his pitching.* **3.** To plant in the ground. ♦ *The gardener set out some tomato seedlings.*

set right *v. phr.* To discipline; correct; indicate the correct procedure. ♦ *"Your bookkeeping is all messed up," the accountant said. "Let me set it right for you, once and for all."*

set sail *v. phr.* To begin a sea voyage; start sailing. ♦ *The ship set sail for Europe.*

set store by *v. phr., informal* To like or value; want to keep. Used with a qualifying word between *set* and *store*. ♦ *George sets great store by that old tennis racket.* ♦ *Pat doesn't set much store by Mike's advice.*

set the ball rolling See GET THE BALL ROLLING.

set the pace *v. phr.* To decide on a rate of speed of travel or rules that are followed by others. ♦ *The scoutmaster set the pace so that the shorter boys would not get tired trying to keep up.* ♦ *Louise set the pace in selling tickets for the school play.*—**pace-setter** *n.* ♦ *John is the pace-setter of the class.*—**pace-setting** *adj.* ♦ *Bob's time in the cross-country race was pace-setting.* ♦ *The country is growing at a pace-setting rate.*

set the stage for *v. phr.* To prepare the way or situation for (an event); to make a situation ready for something to happen. ♦ *The country's economic problems set the stage for a depression.*

set the world on fire *v. phr., informal* To do something outstanding; act in a way that attracts much attention or makes you famous. ♦ *John works hard, but he will never set the world on fire.* ♦ *Mary could set the world on fire with her piano playing.*

setting-up *adj.* Done early in the morning to make you fresh and feel strong for the day. ♦ *Tom jumped out of bed and did his setting-up exercises.* Compare DAILY DOZEN.

settle a score *also* **wipe out an old score** To hurt (someone) in return for a wrong or loss. ♦ *John settled an old score with Bob by beating him.* Compare GET BACK AT, GET EVEN.

settle down *v.* **1.** To live more quietly and sensibly; have a regular place to live and a regular job; stop acting wildly or carelessly, especially by growing up. ♦ *John will settle down after he gets a job and gets married.* **2.** To become quiet, calm, or comfortable. ♦ *Father settled down with the newspaper.* ♦ *The house settled down for the night after the children were put to bed.* ♦ *The teacher told the students to settle down and study the lesson.*

settle for *v.* To be satisfied with (less) agree to; accept. ♦ *Jim wanted $200 for his old car, but he settled for $100.*

settle on *v. phr.* To decide which one to choose among various alternatives. ♦ *My parents have been debating what kind of a car to get and have finally settled on a BMW from Germany.*

settle up *v. phr.* To pay up; conclude monetary or other transactions. ♦ *"Let's settle up," Carol's attorney said, when she sued Don for a hefty sum of money after their divorce.*

set to *v.* **1.** To make a serious beginning. ♦ *Charlie took a helping of turkey, grabbed his knife and fork, and set to.* **2.** To start to fight. ♦ *One man called the other a liar and they set to.*

set to music *v. phr.* To compose a musical accompaniment to verse. ♦ *Schubert and Beethoven both set to music many a famous poem by Goethe and Schiller.*

set to rights See PUT TO RIGHTS.

set tongues wagging See TONGUES WAG.

set up *v.* **1.** To provide the money for the necessities for. ♦ *When he was twenty-one, his father set him up in the clothing business.* **2.** To establish; start. ♦ *The government has set up many hospitals for veterans of the armed forces.* **3.** To make ready for use by putting the parts together or into their right place. ♦ *The men set up the new printing press.* **4.** To bring into being; cause. ♦ *Ocean tides are set up by the pull between earth and the moon.* **5.** To claim; pretend. ♦ *He set himself up to be a graduate of a medical school, but he was not.* **6.** To harm someone by entrapment or some other ruse. ♦ *Joe was actually innocent of the robbery, but his "trusted friends" set him up, so the police found the gun in his car.*

setup *n. phr.* (stress on *set*) **1.** Arrangement, management, circumstances. ♦ *Boy, you really have a wonderful setup in your office!* ♦ *I just can't do my work in such a messy setup!* **2.** Financial arrangement. ♦ *It is a fairly generous setup sending your uncle $1,000 a month.*

set upon See SET ON.

seven See AT SIXES AND SEVENS.

seventh heaven *n. phr., literary* The pinnacle of happiness. ♦ *We were in seventh heaven when the helicopter flew us over the magnificent Grand Canyon.*

sewed up *adj. phr., informal* Won or arranged as you wish; decided. ♦ *They thought they had the game sewed up, but the other team won it with a touchdown in the last quarter.* ♦ *Dick thought he had the job sewed up, but another* *boy got it.* Compare IN THE BAG.

sexual harassment *n. phr.* The act of constantly making unwanted advances of a sexual nature for which the offended party may seek legal redress. ◆ *The court fined Wilbur Catwallender $750,000 for sexual harassment of two of his female employees.*

shack up with *v. phr., slang* To move in with (someone) of the opposite sex without marrying the person. ◆ *Did you know that Ollie and Sue aren't married? They just decided to shack up for a while.* See LIGHT HOUSEKEEPING.

shadow See AFRAID OF ONE'S SHADOW, EYE SHADOW.

shaggy dog (story) *n. phr.* A special kind of joke whose long and often convoluted introduction and development delay the effect of the punch line. ◆ *Uncle Joe only seems to bore his audiences with his long shaggy dog jokes, for when he comes to the long-awaited punch line, he gets very few laughs.*

shake See MORE THAN ONE COULD SHAKE A STICK AT.

shake a leg *v. phr., slang* To go fast; hurry. ◆ *Shake a leg! The bus won't wait.* Compare STEP ON IT.

shakedown *n.* **1.** A test. ◆ *Let's take the new car out and give it a shakedown.* **2.** An act of extorting money by threatening. ◆ *It was a nasty shakedown, to get $500 from the old man, promising to protect him.*

shake down *v. phr.* **1.** To cause to fall by shaking. ◆ *He shook some pears down from the tree.* **2.** *informal* To test, practice, get running smoothly (a ship or ship's crew). ◆ *The captain shook down his new ship on a voyage to the Mediterranean Sea.* **3.** *slang* To get money from by threats. ◆ *The gangsters shook the store owner down every month.*

shake in one's shoes *or* **shake in one's boots** *v. phr., informal* To be very much afraid. ◆ *The robber shook in his boots when the police knocked on his door.*

shake off *v., informal* To get away from when followed; get rid of; escape from. ◆ *A convict escaped from prison and shook off the officers trying to follow him.* ◆ *Tom could not shake off his*

cold.

shake the dust from one's feet *v. phr.* To depart or leave with some measure of disgust or displeasure. ◆ *Jim was so unhappy in our small, provincial town that he was glad to shake the dust from his feet and move to New York.*

shake up *v., informal* To bother; worry; disturb. ◆ *The notice about a cut in pay shook up everybody in the office.*

shake-up *n.* A change; a reorganization. ◆ *After the scandal there was a major shake-up in the Cabinet.*

shame See FOR SHAME, PUT TO SHAME.

shape See IN SHAPE, OUT OF SHAPE, TAKE SHAPE.

shape up *v. phr., informal* **1.** To begin to act or work right; get along satisfactorily. ◆ *If the new boy doesn't begin to shape up soon, he'll have to leave school.* ◆ *"How is the building of the new gym coming along?" "Fine. It's shaping up very well."* **2.** To show promise. ◆ *Plans for our picnic are shaping up very well.*

shape up or ship out *v. phr., informal* To either improve one's disposition or behavior, or quit or leave. ◆ *When Paul neglected to carry out his part of the research work that Professor Brown had assigned him with for the fifth time, the professor cried, "Shape up, or ship out, Paul. I have lost my patience with you!"*

sharp See LOOK SHARP.

sharp as a tack *adj. phr.* **1.** Very neatly and stylishly dressed ◆ *That new boy always looks sharp as a tack in class.* **2.** Very intelligent; smart; quick-witted. ◆ *Tom is sharp as a tack; he got 100 on every test.*

shed light on *or* **upon** See CAST LIGHT ON; THROW LIGHT ON.

sheep See WOLF IN SHEEP'S CLOTHING.

sheepskin *n.* Diploma. ◆ *Dr. Miller has half a dozen different sheepskins hanging on the wall of his office.*

sheet See SCANDAL SHEET, THREE SHEETS IN THE WIND *or* THREE SHEETS TO THE WIND.

shelf See ON THE SHELF.

shell See IN ONE'S SHELL *or* INTO ONE'S SHELL, OUT OF ONE'S SHELL.

shell out *v., informal* To pay or spend. ◆ *Dick had to shell out a lot of money for his new car.*

shift for oneself *v. phr.* To live or act independently with no help, guidance or protection from others; take care of yourself. ♦ *Mrs. McCarthy was forced to shift for herself after her husband died.*

shine See RAIN OR SHINE, TAKE A SHINE TO.

shine up to *v., slang* To try to please; try to make friends with. ♦ *Smedley shines up to all the pretty girls.*

shingle See HANG OUT ONE'S SHINGLE.

ship See GIVE UP THE SHIP, LANDING SHIP.

ship come in All the money a person has wished for is received; wealth comes to a person. Used with a possessive. ♦ *When my ship comes in, I will take a trip to Norway.* ♦ *Mr. Brown is just waiting for his ship to come in.*

ship out *v.* To begin a journey; leave. ♦ *The army group shipped out for the Far East today.*

shipshape *adj.* In perfect condition; in good order. ♦ *After we left the islands, we left the rented car shipshape for the next driver.*

shirk one's duty *v. phr.* To be negligent or irresponsible. ♦ *If you continue to shirk your duty, you can expect to be fired.*

shirt See GIVE THE SHIRT OFF ONE'S BACK, KEEP ONE'S SHIRT ON, LOSE ONE'S SHIRT.

shoe See COMFORTABLE AS AN OLD SHOE, COMMON AS AN OLD SHOE, FILL ONE'S SHOES, IF THE SHOE FITS, WEAR IT, IN ONE'S SHOES, SHAKE IN ONE'S SHOES, SADDLE SHOE, STEP INTO ONE'S SHOES, WHERE THE SHOE PINCHES.

shoe on the other foot The opposite is true; places are changed. ♦ *He was my captain in the army but now the shoe is on the other foot.*

shoestring See ON A SHOESTRING.

shoestring catch *n.* A catch of a hit baseball just before it hits the ground. ♦ *The left fielder made a shoestring catch of a line drive to end the inning.*

shoo away *v. phr.* To frighten or chase away. ♦ *When the children gathered around the new sports car, we shooed them away.*

shoo-in *n., informal* Someone or something that is expected to win; a favorite; sure winner. ♦ *Chris is a shoo-*

in to win a scholarship. ♦ *Do you think he will win the election? He's a shoo-in.* ♦ *This horse is a shoo-in. He can't miss winning.* Syn. SURE THING 1.

shoot ahead of *or* **past** *or* **through** *or* **alongside of** *v. phr.* To move or drive ahead rapidly. ♦ *As we had to slow down before the tunnel, a red sports car shot ahead of us.*

shoot a line See DROP A LINE.

shoot from the hip *v. phr., informal* **1.** To fire a gun held at the hip without aiming by aligning the barrel with one's eye. ♦ *In many Western movies the heroic sheriff defeats the villains by shooting from the hip.* **2.** To speak sincerely, frankly, and without subterfuge. ♦ *"What kind of an administrator will Mr. Brown be?" the head of the search committee asked. "He shoots straight from the hip," he was assured.*

shoot off one's mouth *or* **shoot off one's face** *v. phr., slang* To give opinions without knowing all the facts; talk as if you know everything. ♦ *Tom has never been to Florida, but he's always shooting his mouth off about how superior Florida is to California.* ♦ *I want to study the problem before I shoot off my face.* ♦ *The editor of the newspaper is always shooting his mouth off about the trouble in Africa.*

shoot one's wad *v. phr. slang, colloquial* **1.** To spend all of one's money. ♦ *We've shot our wad for the summer and can't buy any new garden furniture.* **2.** To say everything that is on one's mind. ♦ *Joe feels a lot better now that he's shot his wad at the meeting.*

shoot out *v.* **1.** To fight with guns until one person or side is wounded or killed; settle a fight by shooting.— Used with *it.* ♦ *The cornered bank robbers decided to shoot it out with the police.* ♦ *The moment she opened the door, the cat shot out and ran around the house.* ♦ *During the last half-minute of the race, Dick shot out in front of the other runners.*

shoot questions at *v. phr.* To interrogate rapidly and vigorously. ♦ *The attorney for the prosecution shot one question after another at the nervous witness.*

shoot straight *or* **shoot square** *v., informal* To act fairly; deal honestly. ♦ *You can trust that salesman; he shoots* straight with his customers. ♦ We get along well because we always shoot square with each other.—**straight shooter** or **square shooter** n., informal Bill is a square-shooter.—**straight-shooting** adj. ♦ The boys all liked the straight-shooting coach.

shoot the breeze or **bat the breeze** or **fan the breeze** or **shoot the bull** v. phr., slang To talk. ♦ Jim shot the breeze with his neighbor while the children were playing. ♦ Come into the kitchen and we'll bat the breeze over a cup of coffee. ♦ The women were shooting the breeze about Jim's latest trouble with the police. ♦ The fishermen were shooting the bull about the school of sailfish they had seen.

shoot the works v. phr., slang 1. To spare no expense or effort; get or give everything. ♦ Billy shot the works when he bought his bicycle; he got a bell, a light, a basket, and chrome trimmings on it, too. ♦ The Greens shot the works on their daughter's wedding reception. 2. To go the limit; take a risk. ♦ The motor of Tom's boat was dangerously hot, but he decided to shoot the works and try to win the race.

shoot up v. 1. To grow quickly. ♦ Billy had always been a small boy, but when he was thirteen years old he began to shoot up. 2. To arise suddenly. ♦ As we watched, flames shot up from the roof of the barn. 3. informal To shoot or shoot at recklessly; shoot and hurt badly. ♦ The cowboys got drunk and shot up the bar room. ♦ The soldier was shot up very badly. 4. To take drugs by injection. ♦ A heroin addict will shoot up as often as he can.

shop See CLOSE UP SHOP, TALK SHOP.

shop around for v. phr. To make the rounds of various commercial establishments in order to find the most economical answer for one's needs. ♦ We've been shopping around for a larger condominium that is affordable, and near the university.

shoplifter n. A thief who steals things from a store. ♦ The TV camera identified the shoplifter, who was then arrested and sentenced to jail.

shopping center n. A place usually for neighborhood shopping, where there is a group of stores and shops inside of a large parking lot. ♦ There is a bowling alley at the nearest shopping center. ♦ All the stores in our shopping center stay open until nine o'clock on Friday evenings.

shopworn adj. A piece of merchandise that is offered below the usual price because it is slightly damaged or soiled. ♦ Although shopworn, the jacket was perfectly usable, so he eagerly bought it.

shore leave n. Permission given to a man in the Navy to leave his ship and go where he wants for a certain length of time. ♦ Jim went to visit New York when he was given three days' shore leave. ♦ The ship did not dock long enough for the sailors to get shore leave.

shore patrol n. The police of a navy. ♦ The sailors who were fighting in town were arrested by the shore patrol. ♦ The shore patrol was ordered to search every sailor who went on board the ship.

shore up v. To add support to (something) where weakness is shown; make (something) stronger where support is needed; support. ♦ When the flood waters weakened the bridge. it was shored up with steel beams and sandbags until it could be rebuilt. ♦ The coach sent in a substitute guard to shore up the line when Fitchburg began to break through.

shorn See GOD TEMPERS THE WIND TO THE SHORN LAMB.

short See CAUGHT SHORT, FALL SHORT, FOR SHORT, IN BRIEF or IN SHORT, IN SHORT ORDER, IN SHORT SUPPLY, MAKE SHORT WORK OF, RUN SHORT, SELL SHORT, THE LONG AND THE SHORT.

short and sweet adj. Brief and to the point. ♦ Henry's note to his father was short and sweet. He wrote, "Dear Dad, please send me $5. Love, Henry."

shortchange v. phr. To return less money to a customer in a store than is coming to him or her; cheat. ♦ I was shortchanged by the cashier when I got seven dollars back instead of eight.

shortcut n. A road shorter than the one that people normally take. ♦ We can save twenty minutes if we take this shortcut over the hill.

short end n. The worst or most unpleasant part. ♦ The new boy got the *short end of it because all the comfortable beds in the dormitory had been taken before he arrived.* ♦ *The girls who served refreshments at the party got the short end of it. When everybody had been served, there was no cake left for them.*

shorthanded *adj.* Understaffed; short on workers. ♦ *With several employees gone for the holiday weekend and two dozen people in line, the rent-a-car agency suddenly found itself terribly shorthanded.*

short haul *n.* A short distance; a short trip. ♦ *The Scoutmaster said that it was just a short haul to the lake.* ♦ *The man from the moving company said they did not make short hauls, so we hired a truck to move our furniture three blocks to our new house.* Contrast LONG HAUL.

short list *or* **short-listed** *v. phr.* To place on the list of select finalists for a job. ♦ *Only three of the twenty-seven applicants were short-listed for the assistant professorial vacancy in our department.*

short of[1] *adj. phr.* **1.** Less or worse than. ♦ *Don't do anything short of your best.* **2.** Not having enough. ♦ *We did not buy anything because we were short of money.* ♦ *The girls were asked to wait on tables because the kitchen was short of help.*

short of[2] *adv. phr.* Away from; at a distance from. ♦ *The day's drive still left us a hundred miles short of the ocean.* ♦ *The golfer's shot fell far short of the hole.*

short of breath *adj.* Panting and wheezing. ♦ *He ran up six flights of stairs so rapidly that he was short of breath for several minutes.*

short-order cook *n.* A person who prepares food that cooks quickly. ♦ *Bruce found a summer job as a short-order cook in a drive-in restaurant.* ♦ *The new diner needs another short-order cook.* Compare SLING HASH.

short shrift *n.* Little or no attention.— Usually used with *get* or *give.* ♦ *In books about jobs, women's work is consistently given short shrift.*

short-spoken *adj.* Using so few words that you seem impatient or angry; speaking in a short impatient way; saying as little as possible in an

unfriendly way. ♦ *Jim is always short-spoken when he is tired.* ♦ *We were hoping to borrow Dad's car, but he was so short-spoken when he came home that we were afraid to ask.*

shot See BIG CHEESE *or* BIG SHOT, BY A LONG SHOT, CALL ONE'S SHOT, CALL THE SHOTS, FOUL SHOT, LONG SHOT.

shot in the arm *n. phr., informal* Something inspiring or encouraging. ♦ *The general's appearance was a shot in the arm for the weary soldiers.* ♦ *We were ready to quit, but the coach's talk was a shot in the arm.*

shot in the dark *n. phr.* An attempt without much hope or chance of succeeding; a wild guess. ♦ *It was just a shot in the dark, but I got the right answer to the teacher's question.*

shot through with Full of. ♦ *His speech was shot through with praise for the president.* ♦ *Jane's letter was shot through with hints for a pony.*

shoulder See CHIP ON ONE'S SHOULDER, COLD SHOULDER, GOOD HEAD ON ONE'S SHOULDERS, HEAD AND SHOULDERS, PUT ONE'S SHOULDER TO THE WHEEL, ON ONE'S SHOULDERS, RUB ELBOWS *or* RUB SHOULDERS, SQUARE ONE'S SHOULDERS, WEIGHT OF THE WORLD ON ONE'S SHOULDERS.

shoulder to cry on *or* **to lean on** *n. phr.* A sympathetic person who is willing to listen to one's complaints and troubles. ♦ *When Ken left her, Donna needed a shoulder to lean on, and Bob was right there to fill the role.*

shoulder to shoulder *adv. phr.* **1.** One beside the other; together. ♦ *The three boys were shoulder to shoulder all during the working hours.* Compare SIDE BY SIDE. **2.** Each helping the other; in agreement; together.—Often used with *stand.* ♦ *We can win the fight if we all stand shoulder to shoulder.* Compare SEE EYE TO EYE.

shoulder to the wheel See PUT ONE'S SHOULDER TO THE WHEEL.

shout down *v.* To object loudly to; defeat by shouting. ♦ *Grace suggested that we give our club money to charity, but she was shouted down.* ♦ *The crowd shouted down the Mayor's suggestions.*

shout from the housetops *or* **shout from the rooftops** *v. phr., informal* To tell everyone; broadcast, especially one's own personal business. ♦*Mr. Clark was so happy when his son was born that he shouted the news from the housetops.* ♦*When Mary bleached her hair, her neighbors shouted it from the housetops.*

shouting See ALL OVER BUT THE SHOUTING.

shove down one's throat *or* **ram down one's throat** *v. phr., informal* To force you to do or agree to (something not wanted or liked.) ♦*We didn't want Mr. Bly to speak at our banquet, but the planning committee shoved him down our throats.* ♦*The president was against the idea, but the club members rammed it down his throat.*

shove off See PUSH OFF.

show See GET THE SHOW ON THE ROAD, GO TO SHOW *or* GO TO PROVE, ROAD SHOW, STEAL THE SHOW, TALENT SHOW, VARIETY SHOW, WHOLE CHEESE *or* WHOLE SHOW.

show a clean pair of heels See TAKE TO ONE'S HEELS.

show around *v. phr.* To act as a host or guide to someone; to show newly arrived people or strangers what's what and where. ♦*When Gordon and Rose arrived in Hawaii for the first time, their host showed them around the islands.*

show cause *v. phr.* To give a reason or explanation. ♦*The judge asked the defendants to show cause why they should not be held without bail.*

showdown *n.* A final challenge or confrontation during which both sides have to use all of their resources. ♦*You cannot know a country's military strength until a final showdown occurs.*

showgirl *n.* One who works as an entertainer in a bar or nightclub, musical show, etc. ♦*Several famous Hollywood stars actually started their careers as showgirls.*

show in *or* **out** *or* **up** *or* **to the door** *v. phr.* To usher; conduct; accompany. ♦*"My husband will show you in,"* Mary *said to the guests when they arrived at the door.*

showoff *n.* A boastful person. ♦*Jim always has to be the center of attention; he is an insufferable showoff.*

show off *v. phr.* **1.** To put out nicely for people to see; display; exhibit. ♦*The Science Fair gave Julia a chance to show off her shell collection.* ♦*The girls couldn't wait to show off their fine needlework to our visitors.* **2.** *informal* To try to attract attention; *also,* try to attract attention to. ♦*The children always show off when we have company.* ♦*Joe hasn't missed a chance to show off his muscles since that pretty girl moved in next door.*

show of hands *n. phr.* An open vote during a meeting when those who vote "yes" and those who vote "no" hold up their hands to be counted. ♦*The chairman said, "I'd like to see a show of hands if we're ready for the vote."*

show one's colors *v. phr.* **1.** To show what you are really like. ♦*We thought Toby was timid, but he showed his colors when he rescued the ponies from the burning barn.* **2.** To make known what you think or plan to do. ♦*Mr. Ryder is afraid that he will lose the election if he shows his colors on civil rights.* ♦*We would not help Jim until he showed his colors.*

show one's face *v. phr.* To be seen; appear. ♦*Bill is afraid to show his face since Tom threatened to beat him up.* ♦*Judy is a wonderful mimic but she is too shy to show her face on stage.* ♦*After cheating on the test, Chris was ashamed to show his face.*

show one's hand *v. phr.* To reveal or exhibit one's true and hitherto hidden purpose. ♦*Only after becoming Chancellor of Germany did Adolf Hitler really show his hand and reveal that he intended to take over other countries.*

show one's teeth *v. phr.* To show anger; show belligerence. ♦*He is a very mild, private person, but during a tough business negotiation he knows how to show his teeth.*

show signs See GIVE SIGNS.

show the door *v. phr.* To ask (someone) to go away. ♦*Ruth was upsetting the other children, so I showed her the door.* ♦*Our neighbors invited themselves to the party and stayed until Harry showed them the door.*

show up *v.* **1.** To make known the real truth about (someone). ♦*The man said he was a mind reader, but he was shown up as a fake.* **2.** To come or bring out;

become or make easy to see. ♦ *The detective put a chemical on the paper, and the fingertips showed up.* ♦ *This test shows up your weaknesses in arithmetic.* **3.** *informal* To come; appear. ♦ *We had agreed to meet at the gym, but Larry didn't show up.* ♦ *Only five students showed up for the class meeting.* Compare TURN UP 2.

shrift See SHORT SHRIFT.

shrink See HEAD SHRINKER.

shrug off *or* **shrug away** *v.* To act as if you are not interested and do not care about something; not mind; not let yourself be bothered or hurt by. ♦ *Alan shrugged off our questions; he would not tell us what had happened.* ♦ *Muriel shrugged away every attempt to comfort her.* ♦ *The ballplayer shrugged off the booing of the fans.* ♦ *Jim cut his hand but he tied a cloth around it and shrugged it away.*

shudder to think *v. phr.* To be afraid; hate to think about something. ♦ *The professor is so strict I shudder to think what his final exam questions will be like.*

shut See KEEP ONE'S MOUTH SHUT, PUT UP *or* SHUT UP, CLOSE ONE'S EYES.

shut down See CLOSE DOWN.

shut-eye *n., slang* Sleep. ♦ *It's very late. We'd better get some shut-eye.* ♦ *I'm going to get some shut-eye before the game.* Compare FORTY WINKS.

shut off *v.* **1.** To make (something like water or electricity) stop coming. ♦ *Please shut off the hose before the grass gets too wet.* Compare TURN OFF 1. **2.** To be apart; be separated from; *also* to separate from. ♦ *Our camp is so far from the highway we feel shut off from the world when we are there.* ♦ *The sow is so bad tempered we had to shut it off from its piglets.*

shut one's eyes See CLOSE ONE'S EYES.

shut out *v.* **1.** To prevent from coming in; block. ♦ *During World War II, Malta managed to shut out most of the Italian and German bombers by throwing up an effective anti-aircraft screen.* ♦ *The boys were annoyed by Tom's telling club secrets and shut him out of their meeting.* **2.** To prevent (an opposing team) from scoring throughout an entire game. ♦ *The Dodgers shut out the Reds, 5–0.*

shut the door See CLOSE THE DOOR.

shut up *v.* **1.** *informal* To stop talking. ♦ *Little Ruthie told Father about his birthday surprise before Mother could shut her up.*—Often used as a command; usually considered rude. *Shut up and let Joe say something.* ♦ *If you'll shut up for a minute, I'll tell you our plan.* Syn. BUTTON YOUR LIP, DRY UP 3, KEEP ONE'S MOUTH SHUT. **2.** To close the doors and windows of. ♦ *We got the house shut up only minutes before the storm hit.* **3.** To close and lock for a definite period of time. ♦ *The Smiths always spend Labor Day shutting up their summer home for the year.* ♦ *We got to the store only to find that the owner had shut up shop for the weekend.* **4.** To confine. ♦ *That dog bites. It should be shut up.* ♦ *John has been shut up with a cold all week.*

shy See ONCE BITTEN, TWICE SHY *and* BURNT CHILD DREADS THE FIRE.

shy away *or* **shy off** *v.* To avoid; seem frightened or nervous. ♦ *The boys shied away from our questions.* ♦ *The horse shied off when Johnny tried to mount it.*

sick See TAKE ILL *or* TAKE SICK.

sick and tired *adj.* **1.** Feeling strong dislike for something repeated or continued too long; exasperated; annoyed. ♦ *Jane was sick and tired of always having to wait for Bill, so when he didn't arrive on time she left without him.* ♦ *John is sick and tired of having his studies interrupted.* ♦ *I've been studying all day, and I'm sick and tired of it.* Compare FED UP.

side See CHOOSE UP SIDES, FROM SIDE TO SIDE, GET UP ON THE WRONG SIDE OF THE BED, GRASS IS ALWAYS GREENER ON THE OTHER SIDE OF THE FENCE *or* GRASS IS ALWAYS GREENER ON THE OTHER SIDE OF THE HILL, LAUGH ON THE WRONG SIDE OF ONE'S MOUTH, ON ONE'S BAD SIDE, ON ONE'S GOOD SIDE, ON THE SIDE, SUNNY-SIDE UP, TAKE SIDES, THORN IN THE FLESH *or* THORN IN THE SIDE.

side against *v.* To join or be on the side that is against; disagree with; oppose. ♦ *Bill and Joe sided against me in the argument. We sided against the plan to go by plane.* Contrast SIDE WITH.

side by side *adv.* **1.** One beside the other

in a row. ♦*Alice's dolls were lined up side by side on the window seat.* ♦*Charles and John are neighbors; they live side by side on Elm Street.* Compare SHOULDER TO SHOULDER. **2.** Close together. ♦*The two boys played side by side all afternoon.*

sidekick *n.* A companion; a close friend of lesser status. ♦*Wherever you see Dr. Howell, Dr. Percy, his youthful sidekick is sure to be present as well.*

side of the tracks See THE TRACKS.

side street *n.* A street that runs into and ends at a main street. ♦*The store is on a side street just off Main Street.* ♦*The Spellmans bought a house on a side street that runs off Broad Street.* Compare BACK STREET, CROSS STREET.

side with *v.* To agree with; help. ♦*Alan always sides with Johnny in an argument.* ♦*Gerald sided with the plan to move the club.* Contrast SIDE AGAINST.

sight See AT FIRST GLANCE *or* AT FIRST SIGHT, AT SIGHT *or* ON SIGHT, CATCH SIGHT OF, HEAVE IN SIGHT, LOSE SIGHT OF, ON SIGHT, SET ONE'S SIGHTS.

sight for sore eyes *n. phr., informal* A welcome sight. ♦*After our long, dusty hike, the pond was a sight for sore eyes.* *"Jack! You're a sight for sore eyes!"*

sight-read *v.* To be able to play music without memorization by reading the sheet music and immediately playing it. ♦*Experienced, good musicians are expected to be able to sight-read.*

sight unseen *adv. phr.* Before seeing it; before seeing her, him, or them. ♦*Tom read an ad about a car and sent the money for it sight unseen.*

sign See HIGH SIGN, INDIAN SIGN, ROAD SIGN.

sign in *v.* To write your name on a special list or in a record book to show that you are present. ♦*Every worker must sign in when coming back to work.* ♦*Teachers go to the office and sign in each morning before going to their classrooms.* Contrast SIGN OUT.

sign off *v.* **1.** To end a program on radio or television. ♦*That TV newscaster always signs off by saluting.* **2.** To stop broadcasting for the day. ♦*That TV station always signs off after the late movie.*

sign of the times *n. phr.* A characteristic of the times in which one lives. ♦*It is a sad sign of the times that all the major lakes and rivers are badly polluted and fish in them are poisoned.*

sign on *v. phr.* **1.** To sign an agreement to become an employee. ♦*The new cowboys signed on with the wealthy rancher in Nevada.* **2.** To start a radio or television broadcast. ♦*Station WLAK signs on every morning at 6 A.M.* Contrast SIGN OFF.

sign one's own death warrant *v. phr.* To cause your own death or the loss of something you want very much. ♦*Mr. Carter had lung trouble, and the doctor told him he would sign his own death warrant if he didn't stop smoking.* ♦*When Jim's fiancée saw him on a date with another girl, he signed his own death warrant.*

sign on the dotted line *v. phr.* To attach one's signature on an important document, such as a contract, a bill of sales, etc. ♦*The seller said to the buyer, "All you need to do is sign on the dotted line."*

sign out *v.* To write your name on a special list or in a record book to show that you are leaving a place. ♦*Most of the students sign out on Friday.* Contrast SIGN IN.

sign over *v.* To give legally by signing your name. ♦*He signed his house over to his wife.*

sign up *v.* **1.** To promise to do something by signing your name; join; sign an agreement. ♦*We will not have the picnic unless more people sign up.* ♦*John wants to sign up for the contest.* ♦*Miss Carter has signed up to be the chaperone at the dance.* **2.** To write the name of (a person or thing) to be in an activity; also, to persuade (someone) to do something. ♦*Betty decided to sign up her dog for obedience training.* ♦*The superintendent has signed up three new teachers for next year.*

signed, sealed, and delivered *adj. phr.* Finished; completed; in a state of completion. ♦*"How is the campus renovation plan for the governor's office coming along?" the dean of the college asked. "Signed, sealed, and delivered," his assistant answered.* Compare CUT AND DRIED; HOOK, LINE AND SINKER.

silence gives consent If you say nothing or do not say no to something, it means that you agree.—A proverb. ♦*Don't be afraid to say, if you don't like something. Silence gives consent.*

silent majority *n., informal* The large majority of people who, unlike the militants, do not make their political and social views known by marching and demonstrating and who, presumably, can swing an election one way or the other. ♦*Sidney Miltner is a member of the silent majority.*

silver See BORN WITH A SILVER SPOON IN ONE'S MOUTH, EVERY CLOUD HAS A SILVER LINING, HAND SOMETHING TO ONE ON A SILVER PLATTER.

silver anniversary *or* **wedding** *n. phr.* The twenty-fifth wedding anniversary of a couple; the twenty-fifth anniversary of a business or an association, etc. ♦*"The day after tomorrow is Mom and Dad's silver anniversary," Sue said to her brother. "I hope you have a nice present picked out."*

simmer down *v., informal* To become less angry or excited; become calmer. ♦*Tom got mad, but soon simmered down.*

Simon Legree *n., informal* A strict person, especially a boss, who makes others work very hard. ♦*Don't talk on the job; the boss is a real Simon Legree.* ♦*Everybody avoids the foreman. IIe acts like a Simon Legree.*

simple See PURE AND SIMPLE.

sing a different tune *or* **whistle a different tune** *also* **sing a new tune** *v. phr., informal* To talk or act in the opposite way; contradict something said before. ♦*Charles said that all smokers should be expelled from the team but he sang a different tune after the coach caught him smoking.* Syn. CHANGE ONE'S TUNE, DANCE TO ANOTHER TUNE. Compare LAUGH OUT OF THE OTHER SIDE OF ONE'S MOUTH.

sing for one's supper *v. phr., informal* To have to work for what one desires. ♦*I realized a long time ago that I had to sing for my supper if I wanted to get ahead in my profession.*

sing in tune See IN TUNE.

single See EVERY SINGLE.

single out *v. phr.* To select or choose one from among many. ♦*There were a lot of pretty girls at the high school prom but Don immediately singled out Sally.*

sing one's praises *v. phr.* To extol or praise continuously. ♦*The audience left the concert with everyone singing the praises of the young piano virtuoso.*

sing out of tune See OUT OF TUNE.

sink See HEART SINKS.

sinker See HOOK, LINE AND SINKER.

sink in *or* **soak in** *v., informal* To be completely understood; be fully realized or felt. ♦*Everybody laughed at the joke but Joe; it took a moment for it to sink in before he laughed too.* ♦*When Frank heard that war had started, it didn't sink in for a long time until his father was drafted into the army.* Compare BRING HOME.

sink one's teeth into See GET ONE'S TEETH INTO.

sink or swim *v. phr.* To succeed or fail by your own efforts, without help or interference from anyone else; fail if you don't work hard to succeed. ♦*When Joe was fourteen, his parents died, and he was left by himself to sink or swim.* ♦*Tom's new job was confusing and no one had time to help him learn, so he had to sink or swim.*

sit See GO SIT ON A TACK, ON THE FENCE *also* FENCE-SITTING.

sit back *v.* **1.** To be built a distance away; stand away (as from a street). ♦*Our house sits back from the road.* **2.** To relax; rest, often while others are working; take time out. ♦*Sit back for a minute and think about what you have done.*

sit by *v.* **1.** To stay near; watch and care for. ♦*The nurse was told to sit by the patient until he woke up.* ♦*Mother sat by her sick baby all night.* **2.** To sit and watch or rest especially while others work ♦*Don't just sit idly by while the other children are all busy.*

sit down *v.* To sit on a seat or resting place. ♦*After gym class Jim was tired and was glad to sit down and rest.*

sit in *v.* **1.** To be a member; participate. ♦*We're having a conference and we'd like you to sit in. also* **sit in on:** To be a member of; participate in. ♦*We want you to sit in on the meeting.* **2.** To attend but not participate. Often used with *on.* ♦*Our teacher was invited to sit in on the conference.* Compare LOOK ON.

sit on *v.* **1.** To be a member of (a jury, board, commission), etc. ♦ *Mr. Brown sat on the jury at the trial.* **2.** *informal* To prevent from starting or doing something; squelch. ♦ *The teacher sat on Fred before he could get started with the long story.* ♦ *The teacher sat on Joe as soon as he began showing off.*

sit on a bomb *or* **bombshell** *v. phr., informal* To be in possession of anything that is potentially disastrous or dangerous. ♦ *The finance department will be sitting on a bomb unless it finds a way to cut overhead expenses.*

sit on a volcano *v., informal* **1.** To be in a place where trouble may start or danger may come suddenly. ♦ *Bob was in that part of South America before the revolution began. He knew he was sitting on a volcano.* ♦ *The policemen who patrolled the big city slum area that summer were sitting on a volcano.*

sit on one's hands *v. phr., informal* To do nothing; fail or refuse to do anything. ♦ *We asked Bill for help with our project, but he sat on his hands.*

sit on the fence See ON THE FENCE.

sit out *v.* To not take part in. ♦ *The next dance is a polka. Let's sit it out.* ♦ *Toby had to sit out the last half of the game because his knee hurt.*

sitter See ON THE FENCE *also* FENCE-SITTER.

sitting on a powder keg See SIT ON A VOLCANO.

sit through *v.* To watch or listen until (something) is finished. ♦ *The show was so boring that we could hardly sit through the first act.* ♦ *Elaine liked the movie so much that she sat through three showings.*

sit tight *v. phr., informal* To make no move *or* change; stay where you are.— Often used as a command. ♦ *Sit tight; I'll be ready to go in a few minutes.* ♦ *The doctor said to sit tight until he arrived.* ♦ *The gangsters sat tight in the mountains while the police looked for them.* Compare STAND PAT.

sitting on top of the world See ON TOP OF THE WORLD.

sitting pretty *adj., slang* To be in a lucky position. ♦ *The new library is sitting pretty because a wealthy woman gave it $10,000 worth of reference books.* ♦ *Mr. Jones was sitting pretty until his* $25,000-a-year job was dropped by the company.

sit up *v.* **1.** To move into a sitting position. ♦ *Joe sat up when he heard the knock on his bedroom door.* **2.** To stay awake instead of going to bed. ♦ *Mrs. Jones will sit up until both of her daughters get home from the dance.* ♦ *We sat up until two* A.M. *hoping for news from Alaska.* **3.** *informal* To be surprised. ♦ *Janice really sat up when I told her the gossip about Tom.*

sit-up *n.* A vigorous exercise in which the abdominal muscles are strengthened by locking one's feet in a fastening device and sitting up numerous times. ♦ *Do a few sit-ups if you want to reduce your waist.*

sit up and take notice *v. phr., informal* To be surprised into noticing something. ♦ *Grace had never impressed her teachers. Hearing that she had won the essay contest made them sit up and take notice.* ♦ *George's sudden success made the town sit up and take notice.*

sit up for *v. phr.* To wait until after the usual bedtime for someone's return. ♦ *Mrs. Smith always sits up for her two daughters, no matter how late it is.*

sit up with *v. phr.* To be with; particularly to keep someone ill company. ♦ *Mrs. Brown sat up with her sick husband all night in the hospital room.*

sit well (with) *v.* Find favor with; please. ♦ *The reduced school budget did not sit well with the teachers.*

sit with *v., informal* To be accepted by; affect.—Used in interrogative sentences and in negative sentences modified by *well.* ♦ *How did your story sit with your mother?* ♦ *Bob's poor sportsmanship doesn't sit well with the coach.*

six See AT SIXES AND SEVENS, DEEP-SIX.

six bits *n., slang* Seventy-five cents. ♦ *"Lend me six bits till Friday, Sam,"* said Jim. *"I've spent all my allowance."* Compare TWO BITS.

six of one and half-a-dozen of the other *n,. phr.* Two things the same; not a real choice; no difference. ♦ *Which coat do you like better, the brown or the blue? It's six of one and half-a-dozen of the other.* ♦ *Johnny says it's six of one and half-a-dozen of the other whether he does the job tonight or tomorrow night.*

size See CUT DOWN TO SIZE, PINT-SIZE.

size up *v., informal* To decide what one thinks about (something); to form an opinion about (something). ◆ *Give Joe an hour to size up the situation and he'll tell you what to do next.* ◆ *Our coach went to New York to size up the team we'll face in our homecoming game.* Compare TAKE STOCK 2.

skate See CHEAP SKATE.

skate on thin ice *v. phr.* To take a chance; risk danger, disapproval or anger. ◆ *You'll be skating on thin ice if you ask Dad to increase your allowance again.* ◆ *John knew he was skating on thin ice, but he could not resist teasing his sister about her boyfriend.*

skating rink *n., slang, citizen's band radio jargon* Slippery road. ◆ *Attention all units—there's a skating rink ahead!*

skeleton in the closet *n. phr.* A shameful secret; someone or something kept hidden, especially by a family. ◆ *The skeleton in our family closet was Uncle Willie. No one mentioned him because he drank too much.*

skid lid *n., slang* A crash helmet worn by motorcyclists and race drivers. ◆ *How much did you pay for that handsome skid lid?*

skid row *n.* The poor part of a city where men live who have no jobs and drink too much liquor. ◆ *That man was once rich, but he drank and gambled too much, and ended his life living on skid row.* ◆ *The Bowery is New York City's skid row.*

skim the surface *v. phr.* To do something very superficially. ◆ *He seems knowledgeable in many different areas but his familiarity is very superficial, since he only skims the surface of everything he touches.*

skin See BY THE SKIN OF ONE'S TEETH, GET UNDER ONE'S SKIN, JUMP OUT OF ONE'S SKIN, KEEP ONE'S EYES PEELED *or* KEEP ONE'S EYES SKINNED, SAVE ONE'S NECK *or* SAVE ONE'S SKIN, WITH A WHOLE SKIN *or* IN A WHOLE SKIN.

skin alive *v. phr.* **1.** *informal* To scold angrily. ◆ *Mother will skin you alive when she sees your torn pants.* **2.** *informal* To spank or beat. ◆ *Dad was ready to skin us alive when he found we had ruined his saw.* **3.** *slang* To defeat. ◆ *We all did our best, but the visiting gymnastic team skinned us alive.*

skin and bones *n.* A person or animal that is very thin; someone very skinny. ◆ *The puppy is healthy now, but when we found him he was just skin and bones.* ◆ *Have you been dieting? You're nothing but skin and bones!*

skin-deep *adj.* Only on the surface; not having any deep or honest meaning; not really or closely connected with what it seems to belong to. ◆ *Mary's friendliness with Joan is only skin-deep.* ◆ *Ralph crammed for the test and got a good grade, but his knowledge of the lesson is only skin-deep.* Contrast BRED IN THE BONE.

skin off one's nose *n. phr., slang* Matter of interest, concern, or trouble to you. Normally used in the negative. ◆ *Go to Jake's party if you wish. It's no skin off my nose.* ◆ *Grace didn't pay any attention to our argument. It wasn't any skin off her nose.* ◆ *You could at least say hello to our visitor. It's no skin off your nose.*

skip See HEART SKIP A BEAT.

skip bail See JUMP BAIL.

skip it *v. phr., informal* To forget all about it. ◆ *When Jack tried to reward him for returning his lost dog, the man said to skip it.* ◆ *I asked what the fight was about, but the boys said to skip it.*

skip out *v., informal* To leave in a hurry; especially after cheating or taking money dishonestly; sneak away; leave without permission. ◆ *The man skipped out of the hotel without paying his bill.* ◆ *"How did you get out of the house after supper, Harry?" "I skipped out!"*

skirt around *v. phr.* To avoid something. ◆ *"Let's not skirt around the facts," said the attorney to his client. "You must tell me the truth."*

sky See OUT OF THE BLUE *or* OUT OF A CLEAR SKY *or* OUT OF A CLEAR BLUE SKY, REACH FOR THE SKY.

sky is the limit There is no upper limit to something. ◆ *"Buy me the fastest racehorse in Hong Kong," Mr. Lee instructed his broker. "Spend whatever is necessary; the sky is the limit."*

slack off *v. phr.* **1.** To become less active; grow lazy. ◆ *Since construction work has been slacking off toward the end of the summer, many workers were* *dismissed.* **2.** To gradually reduce; taper off. ♦ *The snowstorms tend to slack off over the Great Lakes by the first of April.*

slam See GRAND SLAM.

slap down *v., slang* **1.** To stop (someone, usually in a lower position or job) from doing or saying something, in a rough way or with a scolding; silence. ♦ *When Billy talked back, the teacher slapped him down.* **2.** To put a quick stop to; refuse roughly. ♦ *The boss slapped down our idea of taking a nap on the job every afternoon.*

slap in the face[1] *n.* An insult; a disappointment. ♦ *We felt that it was a slap in the face when our gift was returned unopened.* ♦ *Doris thought it was a slap in the face when her boyfriend invited another girl to the dance.* Compare KICK IN THE PANTS.

slap in the face[2] *v. phr.* To insult; embarrass; make feel bad. ♦ *John slapped our club in the face by saying that everyone in it was stupid.* ♦ *I don't want to slap her in the face by not coming to her party.*

slap one's wrist *v. phr.* To receive a light punishment. ♦ *She could have been fired for contradicting the company president in public, but all she got was a slap on the wrist.*

slap together See THROW TOGETHER 1.

slate See CLEAN SLATE.

slated for *or* **slated to be** Going to be; planned or intended for. ♦ *People think the governor is slated to be president.* ♦ *That subject is slated for debate at the next meeting.*

slave driver *n.* A cruel, merciless boss or employer who makes the people under him work extremely hard for little compensation. ♦ *Mr. Catwallender is such a slave driver that nobody cares to work for him anymore.*

sledding See HARD SLEDDING *or* ROUGH SLEDDING *or* TOUGH SLEDDING.

sleep See BEAUTY SLEEP, LET SLEEPING DOGS LIE, SLEEP A WINK.

sleep around *v. phr., slang, vulgar, avoidable* To be free with one's sexual favors; to behave promiscuously. ♦ *Sue Catwallender is a nice girl but she sleeps around an awful lot with all sorts of guys.*

sleep a wink *v. phr.* To get a moment's sleep; enjoy a bit of sleep.—Used in negative and conditional statements and in questions. ♦ *I didn't sleep a wink all night.*

sleep like a log *v. phr.* To sleep very deeply and soundly. ♦ *Although I am usually a light sleeper, I was so exhausted from the sixteen-hour transpacific flight that, once we got home, I slept like a log for twelve hours.*

sleep off *v. phr.* To sleep until the effect of too much alcohol or drugs passes. ♦ *George had too many beers last night and he is now sleeping off the effects.*

sleep on *v.* To postpone a decision about. ♦ *We asked Judy if she would join our club and she answered that she would sleep on it.* ♦ *We will have to sleep on your invitation until we know whether we will be free Monday night.*

sleep out *v.* **1.** To sleep outdoors. ♦ *The Scouts plan to sleep out next Saturday.* **2.** To go home at night instead of sleeping at the place where you work. ♦ *Mrs. Jones' maid sleeps in, but her cook sleeps out.*

sleep with *v. phr.* To have a sexual affair with someone; have sex; copulate. ♦ *It has been rumored in the office that the boss sleeps with all the girls he hires.*

sleeve See CARD UP ONE'S SLEEVE, LAUGH UP ONE'S SLEEVE *or* LAUGH IN ONE'S SLEEVE, ROLL UP ONE'S SLEEVES, UP ONE'S SLEEVE *or* IN ONE'S SLEEVE, WEAR ONE'S HEART ON ONE'S SLEEVE *also* PIN ONE'S HEART ON ONE'S SLEEVE.

sling hash *v., slang* To serve food, especially in a cheap, small diner, a drive-in, or short-order restaurant. ♦ *Jake got a job slinging hash at the new drive-in restaurant.* ♦ *Jody earned money for college by slinging hash in a restaurant during the summer.* Compare SHORT-ORDER COOK.

slinging match *n. phr.* A loud, angry quarrel. ♦ *The debate deteriorated into a most unseemly slinging match.*

slip See GIVE THE SLIP, SALES CHECK *or* SALES SLIP.

slip a cog *or* **slip a gear** *v. phr., slang* To make a mistake. ♦ *I must have been slipping a cog when I said that I would run for mayor.* ♦ *Jim hates to sleep outdoors. He's slipping his gears if he's promised to take the boys camping.* Compare SLIP UP.

slip away *v. phr.* To leave unnoticed. ♦ *The party was such a bore that we decided to quietly slip away.*

slip off *v. phr.* **1.** To slide off something. ♦ *The children climbed up the hill but when it was time to come down, they didn't walk, but slipped off the smooth, old ledges.* **2.** See SLIP AWAY.

slip of the lip See SLIP OF THE TONGUE.

slip of the pen *n. phr.* The mistake of writing something different from what you should or what you planned. ♦ *That was a slip of the pen. I meant to write September, not November.* ♦ *I wish you would forget it. That was a slip of the pen.*

slip of the tongue *also* **slip of the lip** *n. phr.* The mistake of saying something you had not wanted or planned to say; an error of speech. ♦ *No one would have known our plans if Kay hadn't made a slip of the tongue.* ♦ *She didn't mean to tell our secret; it was a slip of the lip.*

slip one's mind *v. phr.* To forget something. ♦ *I meant to mail those letters but it entirely slipped my mind.*

slip over See PUT OVER 2.

slip through one's fingers *v. phr.* To escape without someone's knowing how. ♦ *Policemen surrounded the building, but the thief managed to slip through their fingers.* ♦ *Mike earns a good wage, but he doesn't save a penny. Money just slips through his fingers.*

slipup *n.* A mistake. ♦ *"I'm sorry, sir. That was an unfortunate slipup," the barber said when he scratched the client's face.*

slip up *v. phr.* To make a mistake. ♦ *Someone at the bank slipped up. There are only 48 pennies in this 50¢ roll of coins.* ♦ *If he hadn't slipped up on the last questions, his score on the test would have been perfect.*

slow burn *n., informal* A slowly increasing feeling of anger. ♦ *The boys kept teasing John, and watched him do a slow burn.* ♦ *Barbara's slow burn ended only when Mary explained the misunderstanding.*

slowdown *n.* A period of lesser activity, usually in the economic sphere. ♦ *We all hope the current slowdown in the economy will soon be over.*

slow down *v. phr.* To go more slowly than usual. ♦ *The road was slippery, so Mr. Jones slowed down the car.* ♦ *Pat once could run a mile in five minutes, but now that he's older he's slowing down.* Compare LET UP 2. STEP DOWN. Contrast SPEED UP.

slow on the draw *adj. phr.* Not very smart; having difficulty figuring things out. ♦ *Poor Eric doesn't get very good grades in physics; when it comes to problem-solving, he is rather slow on the draw.*

slow on the uptake See SLOW ON THE DRAW.

slow time See STANDARD TIME.

slow up *v.* **1.** To go more slowly. ♦ *The truck slowed up as it approached the toll gate.* ♦ *Construction on the road slows up traffic.* **2.** To become less busy. ♦ *Business slows up at the stores after Christmas.*

slug it out *v. phr.* To have a strong verbal or physical battle with someone; to contest something most vigorously. ♦ *The two contenders for the lightweight boxing championship were slugging it out in the ring.* ♦ *The two candidates for Congress were slugging it out on radio and on television.*

sly See ON THE SLY.

smack-dab *also Southern* **smack-to-dab** *adv., informal* Exactly; squarely. ♦ *The ball landed smack-dab at our feet.* ♦ *The plane landed smack-to-dab in the middle of the hayfield.*

smack one's lips *v. phr.* To reveal an appetite for; show enjoyment of. ♦ *Eleanor smacked her lips over the dessert of strawberries and whipped cream.*

small See BIG FROG IN A SMALL POND.

small frog in a big pond See LITTLE FROG IN A BIG POND.

small fry *n.* **1.** Young children. ♦ *In the park, a sandbox is provided for the small fry.* **2.** Something or someone of little importance. ♦ *Large dairies ignore the competition from the small fry who make only a few hundred pounds of cheese a year.*

small *or* **wee hours** *n. phr.* The very early hours of the morning between 1 and 4 A.M. ♦ *My brother was in trouble for coming home in the small hours.* See WEE HOURS.

small talk *n. phr.* General idle conversation. ♦*At the party there was the usual kind of small talk about the cost of living increase and the war in Africa.*

small-time *adj., informal* Unimportant; minor; with little power or importance. ♦*He has a job as a drummer with a small-time band.* ♦*It is a small-time business, but it may grow.* Contrast BIG-TIME.

small wonder See NO WONDER.

smash hit *n., informal* A very successful play, movie or opera. ♦*The school play was a smash hit.*

smell a rat *v. phr., informal* To be suspicious; feel that something is wrong. ♦*Every time Tom visits me, one of my ashtrays disappears. I'm beginning to smell a rat.* ♦*When the policeman saw a light go on in the store at midnight, he smelled a rat.*

smell out See FERRET OUT.

smell up *v., informal* To make a bad smell. ♦*A skunk smelled up our yard last night.* ♦*Mr. Brodsky's cigar smelled up the living room.*

smile See CRACK A SMILE.

smoke See CHAIN-SMOKE, GO UP IN FLAMES *or* GO UP IN SMOKE, PUT THAT IN YOUR PIPE AND SMOKE IT, WATCH ONE'S DUST *or* WATCH ONE'S SMOKE.

smoke like a chimney *v. phr., informal* To smoke very heavily and continuously. ♦*"If you continue smoking like a chimney" the doctor told my uncle, "you'll wind up in the hospital with lung cancer."*

smoke out *v. phr.* **1.** To force out with smoke. ♦*The boys smoked a squirrel out of a hollow tree.* ♦*The farmer tried to smoke some gophers out of their burrows.* **2.** *informal* To find out the facts about. ♦*It took the reporter three weeks to smoke out the whole story.*

smoke-out *n.* A successful conclusion of an act of investigative journalism revealing some long-kept secrets. ♦*Journalist Bob Woodward was the hero of the Watergate smoke-out.*

smoke screen *n. phr.* A camouflage; a veil; something used to cover or hide something. ♦*June hides her commercial interests behind a smoke screen of religious piety.*

Smokey Bear *or* **Smokey-the-Bear** *or* **the Smokies** *n., slang, citizen's band radio jargon* A policeman; a patrol

car; frequently abbreviated as *Smokey.* ♦*Slow down, Smokey's ahead!* ♦*A Smokey is on the move, heading east.*

smooth away *v.* To remove; (unpleasant feelings) take away. ♦*Mr. Jones' new job smoothed away his worry about money.*

smooth down *v.* To make calm; calm down. ♦*Mrs. Smith's feelings were hurt and we couldn't smooth her down.*

smooth over *v.* To make something seem better or more pleasant; try to excuse. ♦*Bill tried to smooth over his argument with Mary by making her laugh.* Syn. GLOSS OVER. Compare PATCH UP.

smooth sailing See PLAIN SAILING.

snail's pace *n.* A very slow movement forward. ♦*Time moved at a snail's pace before the holidays.* ♦*The donkey on which he was riding moved at a snail's pace.*

snake in the grass *n. phr., informal* A person who cannot be trusted; an unfaithful traitor; rascal. ♦*Did Harry tell you that? He's a snake in the grass!* ♦*Some snake in the grass told the teacher our plans.*

snap See COLD SNAP.

snap it off See MAKE IT SNAPPY.

snap one's fingers at *v. phr.* To show contempt for; show no respect for; pay no attention to; scorn; disregard. ♦*John snapped his fingers at the sign that said "Do not enter," and he went in the door.* ♦*The highway sign said "Speed limit, 35 miles per hour," but when a driver snapped his fingers at it by going 55 miles an hour, a motorcycle policeman arrested him.*

snap out of *v., informal* To change quickly from a bad habit, mood, or feeling to a better one.—Often used with *it.* ♦*Mary was unhappy when her fiancé abandoned her, but she snapped out of it when she met a new young man.* ♦*The coach told the lazy player to snap out of it.*

snappy See MAKE IT SNAPPY.

snapshot *n.* A small photograph, unlike a professional portrait. ♦*We took several snapshots of the scenery while driving around the island.*

snap up *v., informal* To take or accept eagerly. ♦*Eggs were on sale cheap, and the shoppers snapped up the bargain.*

♦ *Mr. Hayes told Bob that he would take him skiing, and Bob snapped up the offer.*

sneak See QUARTERBACK SNEAK.

sneak away See SLIP AWAY.

sneak up on See CREEP UP ON.

sneeze at *v., informal* To think of as not important; not take seriously.—Used with negative or limiting words and in questions. ♦ *Mr. Jones was chosen by his party to run for President. He was not elected, but to be chosen to run is not to be sneezed at.* ♦ *If you think Mrs. Green's tests are things to be sneezed at, you have a surprise coming.* ♦ *Is a thousand dollars anything to sneeze at?* ♦ *John finished third in a race with twenty other runners. That is nothing to sneeze at.*

sniff out See FERRET OUT.

snow in *v.* To block up or trap by much snow; keep inside. ♦ *After the storm the farmer and his family were snowed in for three days.* ♦ *The train went off the track and the passengers were snowed in for several days.*

snow job *n., slang, informal* **1.** Insincere or exaggerated talk designed to gain the favors of someone. ♦ *Joe gave Sue a snow job and she believed every word of it.* **2.** The skillful display of technical vocabulary and prestige terminology in order to pass oneself off as an expert in a specialized field without really being a knowledgeable worker in that area. ♦ *That talk by Nielsen on pharmaceuticals sounded very impressive, but I will not hire him because it was essentially a snow job.*

snow under *v.* **1.** To cover over with snow. ♦ *The doghouse was snowed under during the blizzard.* **2.** *informal* To give so much of something that it cannot be taken care of; to weigh down by so much of something that you cannot do anything about it.— Usually used in the passive. ♦ *The factory received so many orders that it was snowed under with work.* ♦ *The disabled girl was snowed under with Christmas letters.*

snuff See UP TO PAR *or* UP TO SNUFF.

snug as a bug in a rug *adj. phr.* Comfortable; cozy. ♦ *"Are you warm enough?" the boy's mother asked. "Yeah," he replied, "I'm snug as a bug in a rug."*

so See AND SO FORTH *or* AND SO ON, EVEN SO, EVERY NOW AND THEN *or* EVERY SO OFTEN, HOW SO, IN SO MANY WORDS, IS THAT SO, OR SO, THUS AND SO.

soak in See SINK IN.

soak up *v.* **1.** To take up water or other liquid as a sponge does. ♦ *The rag soaked up the water that I spilled.* **2.** To use a sponge or something like a sponge to take up liquid. ♦ *John soaked up the water with the rag.* **3.** *informal* To take up into yourself in the way a sponge takes up water. ♦ *Mary was lying on the beach soaking up the sun.* ♦ *Charles soaks up facts as fast as the teacher gives them.*

so-and-so[1] *pronoun, informal* Someone whose name is not given. ♦ *Don't tell me what so-and-so thinks. Tell me what you think.*

so-and-so[2] *n., informal* A person of a special kind and usually of a very bad kind.—This word is used in place of a more unacceptable word or swear word. ♦ *I wish that old so-and-so who thinks digging is easy work was right here digging now.* ♦ *He called me a dirty so-and-so and I hit him in the mouth.* Sometimes used in a joking way. ♦ *Peter met his friend John and said, "Hello there, you old so-and-so."*

so ——— as to—Used with an adjective or adverb before an infinitive to show a result. ♦ *Who could be so mean as to do a thing like that?* ♦ *Ruth wouldn't be so careless as to forget her pen.* Compare SO ——— THAT.

soap opera *n. phr.* Radio or television serialized stories of a sentimental nature, often involving sex, crime, and social intrigue. These shows often advertise soap products, hence their name. ♦ *The two longest running soap operas in the United States were "Dallas" and "Knot's Landing."*

so as to See IN ORDER TO.

sob all the way to the bank See CRY ALL THE WAY TO THE BANK. Contrast LAUGH ALL THE WAY TO THE BANK.

so bad See NOT BAD.

so be it *also* **be it so** *adv. phr., formal* **1.** Let it be that way; may it be so. *So be it.* ♦ *We shall smoke the pipe of peace.* **2.** Very well; all right. ♦ *Will the com-*

pany lose money by doing this? So be it, then.

sob story *n.* A story that makes you feel pity or sorrow; a tale that makes you tearful. ◆ *The beggar told us a long sob story before he asked for money.* ◆ *The movie is based on a sob story, but people love it.*

social climber *n.* A person who tries to mix with rich or well-known people and be accepted by them as friends and equals. ◆ *People do not like Mrs. Brown very well; she is known as a social climber.* ◆ *Social climbers are usually soon known and they are not accepted by those they run after.*

sock See TAKE A PUNCH AT *or* TAKE A SOCK AT.

sock it *v. phr., also interj., slang, informal* To give one's utmost; everything one is capable of; to give all one is capable of. ◆ *Right on, Joe, sock it to 'em!* ◆ *I was watching the debate on television and more than once Bill Buckley really socked it to them.*

soda jerk *or* **soda jerker** *n., informal* A person who serves soda and ice cream to customers, usually in a drug store or ice cream parlor. ◆ *Bob worked as a soda jerk at the drug store all summer.* ◆ *He is just a soda jerker with no future.*

so far *also* **thus far** *adv.* Until this time or to this place. ◆ *The weather has been hot so far this summer.* ◆ *This is a lonely road. We have not met another car so far.*

so far as See AS FAR AS.

so far, so good *informal* Until now things have gone well. ◆ *So far, so good; I hope we keep on with such good luck.*

soft drink *n. phr.* A nonalcoholic beverage such as 7-Up, Coca-Cola, etc. ◆ *She drinks no alcohol; she always orders a soft drink.*

softhearted *adj.* Generous; sympathetic. ◆ *Street beggars tend to exploit the softhearted nature of passersby.*

soft touch *n.* A person with a sympathetic disposition from whom it is easy to get help, primarily money. ◆ *My Uncle Herb is a soft touch; whenever I'm in need I ask him for a quick twenty bucks.*

so help me *interj., informal* I promise; I swear; may I be punished if I lie. ◆ *I've*

told you the truth, so help me. ◆ *So help me, there was nothing else I could do.*

soil one's hands See DIRTY ONE'S HANDS.

so it goes Akin to the French *c'est la vie!* This exclamation means "that's life." ◆ *Too bad Jim has lost his job but there are lots of people who are better qualified; well, so it goes!*

sold on *adj.* Approving of; well disposed toward; convinced of the value of. ◆ *When Japanese cars first appeared on the market Andy was hesitant to drive one but now he is sold on them.*

so long *interj., informal* Good-bye.— Used when you are leaving someone or he is leaving you. ◆ *So long, I will be back tomorrow.*

so long as See AS LONG AS.

so many¹ *adj.* **1.** A limited number of; some ◆ *Our school auditorium will hold only so many people.* **2.** A group of.—Often used for emphasis. ◆ *The children were all sitting very quietly in their chairs, like so many dolls.* Compare SO MUCH. *(adj.)* ◆ *Bob is always bragging; his stories are just so many lies.*

so many² *pron.* A limited number; some. ◆ *Many people want to come to the prom; but the gymnasium will hold only so many.* ◆ *Don't give the boys all the cookies they want; give so many to Tom, so many to Dick, and so many to Bob.* Compare SO MUCH.

some See AND THEN SOME.

somebody up there loves/hates me *slang* An expression intimating that an unseen power in heaven, such as God, has been favorable or unfavorable to the one making the exclamation. ◆ *Look at all the money I won! I say somebody up there sure loves me!* ◆ *Look at all the money I've lost! I say somebody up there sure hates me!*

some of these days See ONE OF THESE DAYS.

something See HAVE SOMETHING GOING FOR ONE, HAVE SOMETHING ON, MAKE SOMETHING OF, START SOMETHING.

something else *adj., slang, informal* So good as to be beyond description; the ultimate; stupendous. ◆ *Janet Hopper is really something else.*

something else again *n. phr.* A different kind of thing; something different. ◆ *I* *don't care if you borrow my dictionary sometimes, but taking it without asking and keeping it is something else again.* ♦ *"But I don't want a new car," Charles said to the car dealer. "I want a used car." "Oh," said the car dealer, "that's something else again."*

so much[1] *adj.* **1.** A limited amount of; some. ♦ *Sometimes students wonder if the teacher knows they have only so much time to do their lessons.* ♦ *If you can't give everyone a full glass of milk, just put so much milk in each glass.* **2.** Equally or amounting to; only amounting to.—Often used for emphasis. ♦ *Charley spends money as if it were so much paper.* ♦ *What Mary said was so much nonsense; there wasn't a word of truth in it.* Compare SO MANY 1.

so much[2] *pron.* A limited amount; some; a price or amount that is agreed or will be agreed on. ♦ *You can do only so much in a day.* ♦ *Milk costs so much a quart but cream costs so much a pint.* Compare SO MANY 2.

so much[3] *adv.* By that much; by the amount shown; even.—Used with the comparative and usually followed by the. ♦ *I can't go tomorrow. So much the better; we'll go today.* ♦ *John isn't coming to the picnic. So much the more for us to eat!* ♦ *So much the worse for you if you break the rules.* Syn. ALL THE 2.

so much as *adv. phr.* **1.** Even.—Usually used in negative sentences and questions. ♦ *He didn't so much as thank me for returning his money that I found.* ♦ *Would you so much as get me a glass of water? No, you wouldn't.* **2.** See AS MUCH AS 2.

so much for Enough has been said or done about.—Used to point out that you have finished with one thing or are going to take up something else. ♦ *So much for the geography of Ireland. We will now talk about the people who live there.* ♦ *"I have nothing more to say to you, Tommy, and so much for that," Mary said angrily.*

son See FAVORITE SON, LIKE FATHER, LIKE SON.

song See FOR A SONG.

song and dance *n., informal* **1.** Foolish or uninteresting talk; dull nonsense. Usually used with *give.* ♦ *I met Nancy today and she gave me a long song and dance about her family.* **2.** A long lie or excuse, often meant to get pity. Usually used with *give.* ♦ *Billy gave the teacher a song and dance about his mother being sick as an excuse for being late.* ♦ *The tramp asked us for money and tried to give us a big song and dance about having to buy a bus ticket to Chicago.*

sonic boom *n.* A loud noise and vibration in the air, made when a jet plane passes the speed of sound (1087 feet per second). ♦ *Fast jet planes sometimes cause a sonic boom, which can break windows and crack the plaster in houses below them.* ♦ *We thought there was an explosion or earthquake, but it was only a sonic boom that shook the house.*

son of a bitch *or* **sunuvabitch** *also* **S.O.B.** *n. phr., vulgar, avoidable (but becoming more and more acceptable, especially if said with a positive or loving intonation).* Fellow, character, guy, individual. Negatively: ♦ *Get out of here you filthy, miserable sunuvabitch!* Positively: ♦ *So you won ten million dollars at the lottery, you lucky son of a bitch (or sunuvabitch)!* Compare SON OF A GUN.

son of a gun *n. phr., slang* **1.** A bad person; a person not liked. ♦ *I don't like Charley; keep that son of a gun out of here.* Syn. BAD ACTOR. **2.** A mischievous rascal; a lively guy.—Often used in a joking way. ♦ *The farmer said he would catch the son of a gun who let the cows out of the barn.* ♦ *Hello Bill, you old son of a gun!* Compare SO AND SO. **3.** Something troublesome; a hard job. ♦ *The test today was a son of a gun.* Used as an exclamation, usually to show surprise or disappointment. ♦ *Son of a gun! I lost my car keys.* Compare SON OF A BITCH.

soon See AS SOON, FOOL AND HIS MONEY ARE SOON PARTED.

sooner See HAD RATHER *or* HAD SOONER, NO SOONER ——— THAN.

sooner or later *adv. phr.* At some unknown time in the future; sometime. ♦ *John will come back sooner or later.* ♦ *Grandpa is very slow about fixing things around the house, but he always* *does it sooner or later.* Compare OR OTHER.

sore See SIGHT FOR SORE EYES.

sore spot *or* **sore point** *n.* A weak or sensitive part; a subject or thing about which someone becomes angry or upset easily. ♦ *Don't ask Uncle John why his business failed; it's a sore spot with him.* Compare WHERE THE SHOE PINCHES.

sorrow See DROWN ONE'S SORROWS.

sort See OF SORTS, IN A WAY *also* IN A SORT OF WAY.

sort of See KIND OF.

sort out *v. phr.* **1.** To alphabetize; arrange in numerical order. ♦ *The secretary helped Professor Brown sort out his numerous index cards.* **2.** To clarify. ♦ *"Help me sort out these bills,"* *she begged her husband.*

so-so *adj.* Fair; neither good nor bad. ♦ *The children's grades were just so-so on the test.* ♦ *How is the fishing today? So-so.*

so that *conj.* **1.** *or* in order that; for the purpose that; so.—"So that" is usually followed by *can* or *could;* "in order that" is usually followed by *may* or *might.* ♦ *Let's get ready now so that we can leave when Father comes.* ♦ *Betty saved her money in order that she might buy a doll.* Compare IN ORDER TO. **2.** With the result that; so. ♦ *My pencil fell under my desk, so that I couldn't see it.* ♦ *George often told stories that weren't true, so that no one believed him when he told about a deer in the school yard.*

so ——— that—Used with an adjective or adverb before a clause of result. ♦ *The bus was so full that I could hardly turn around.* ♦ *Billy pitched so well that everyone cheered him at the end of the game.*

so to speak *adv. phr.* To say it in this way. ♦ *John was, so to speak, the leader of the club, but he was officially only the club's secretary.* ♦ *The horse, so to speak, danced on his hind legs.* Compare AS IT WERE.

sought after *adj.* Wanted by many buyers; searched for. ♦ *Antiques are much sought after nowadays.* Syn. IN DEMAND.

soul See HEART AND SOUL, KEEP BODY AND SOUL TOGETHER.

soul-searching See SEARCH ONE'S

HEART *or* SEARCH ONE'S SOUL.

sound See HIGH-SOUNDING, SAFE AND SOUND.

sound effects *n.* The noises made to imitate real sounds in a play, movie, or program. ♦ *Greg agreed to plan the sound effects for the class play.* ♦ *The movie was good but the sound effects were not very true to life.*

sound off *v.* **1.** To say your name or count "One! Two! Three! Four!" as you march.—Used as orders in U.S. military service. ♦ *"Sound off!" said the sergeant, and the soldiers shouted, "One! Two! Three! Four!" with each step as they marched.* **2.** *informal* To tell what you know or think in a loud clear voice, especially to brag or complain. ♦ *If you don't like the way we're doing the job, sound off!* ♦ *George sounded off about how the game should have been played.* ♦ *The teacher is always sounding off about the students not doing their homework.* Compare SPEAK ONE'S PIECE, SPEAK OUT.

sound out *v.* To try to find out how a person feels about something usually by careful questions. ♦ *Alfred sounded out his boss about a day off from his job.* ♦ *When you see the coach, sound him out about my chances of getting on the basketball team.* Syn. FEEL OUT.

sound sheet *n., slang, informal* A thin low-quality phonograph recording frequently bound into books and magazines for use as promotional or advertising material; it may have either a spoken or a musical message. ♦ *Don't throw that away; Sue is collecting sound sheets for her market research course.*

sound truck *n. phr.* A truck equipped with loudspeakers. ♦ *During the senatorial campaign, the streets of the big city were full of sound trucks blaring out messages.*

soup See IN THE SOUP.

souped-up *adj., informal* More powerful or faster because of changes and additions. ♦ *Many teen-aged boys like to drive souped-up cars.* ♦ *The basketball team won the last five games with souped-up plays.*

so what *informal* Used as an impolite reply showing that you don't care about what another has said. ♦*Roy boasted that he was in the sixth grade, but Ted said, "So what? I am in Junior High."* Syn. WHAT OF IT.

sow one's wild oats *v. phr.* To do bad or foolish things, especially while you are young. ♦*Mr. Jones sowed his wild oats while he was in college, but now he is a wiser and better man.*

space See OUTER SPACE.

spaced out *adj., slang, informal* Having gaps in one's train of thought, confused, incoherent; resembling the behavior of someone who is under the influence of drugs. ♦*Joe's been acting funny lately—spaced out, you might say.*

space probe *n., Space English* An unmanned spacecraft other than an Earth satellite fitted with instruments which gather and transmit information about other planets in the solar system (e.g., Venus, Mars, and Jupiter) on what are called fly-by missions, i.e., without the craft landing on any of these bodies. ♦*Both the U.S.A. and Russia have sent up many a space probe in the past decade.*

spade See CALL A SPADE A SPADE.

Spain See BUILD CASTLES IN THE AIR *or* BUILD CASTLES IN SPAIN.

spar with See FENCE WITH.

speak See ACTIONS SPEAK LOUDER THAN WORDS, CHILDREN AND FOOLS SPEAK THE TRUTH, NOT TO MENTION *or* NOT TO SPEAK OF, SHORT-SPOKEN, SO TO SPEAK, TO SPEAK OF.

speakeasy *n.* A bar during Prohibition where illegal alcoholic beverages were sold. ♦*Al Capone's associates met in a Chicago speakeasy to drink and discuss business.*

speaker See PUBLIC SPEAKER.

speak for *v.* **1.** To speak in favor of or in support of. ♦*At the meeting John spoke for the change in the rules.* ♦*The other girls made jokes about Jane, but Mary spoke for her.* **2.** To make a request for; to ask for. ♦*The teacher was giving away some books. Fred and Charlie spoke for the same one.* **3.** To give an impression of; be evidence that (something) is or will be said.—Used with the words *well* or *ill*. ♦*It seems that it will rain today. That speaks ill for the picnic this afternoon.* ♦*Who robbed*

the cookie jar? The crumbs on your shirt speak ill for you, Billy. ♦*John wore a clean shirt and a tie when he went to ask for a job, and that spoke well for him.* ♦*It speaks well for Mary that she always does her homework.*

speak of the devil and he appears A person comes just when you are talking about him.—A proverb. ♦*We were just talking about Bill when he came in the door. Speak of the devil and he appears.*

speak one's mind *v. phr.* To say openly what you think; give advice that may not be liked. ♦*John thought it was wrong to keep George out of the club and he spoke his mind about it.* Compare SOUND OFF.

speak one's piece See SAY ONE'S PIECE.

speak out of turn *v. phr.* To say something tactless; commit an indiscretion. ♦*You spoke out of turn in criticizing Aunt Hermione's old furniture; she considers herself quite a connoisseur on the subject.*

speak out *or* **speak up** *v.* **1.** To speak in a loud or clear voice. ♦*The trucker told the shy boy to speak up.* **2.** To speak in support of or against someone or something. ♦*Willie spoke up for Dan as club president.* ♦*Ed spoke up against letting girls join the club.*

speak the same language *v. phr.* To have similar feelings, thoughts, and tastes; have a mutual understanding with another person. ♦*We both love listening to Mozart. Obviously, we speak the same language.*

speak volumes *v. phr.* To tell or show much in a way other than speaking; be full of meaning. ♦*The nice present she gave you spoke volumes for what she thinks of you.* ♦*A child's choice of hobbies speaks volumes.* Compare READ BETWEEN THE LINES.

speak well of *v. phr.* To approve of; praise. ♦*Everyone always speaks well of my sister because she's so kind.*

speak with a forked tongue *v. phr., literary* To lie; to say one thing while thinking of the opposite. ♦*I have learned not to trust Peter's promises because he speaks with a forked tongue.*

speed trap *n.* A place where police hide and wait to catch drivers who are going even a little faster than the speed limit. ♦ *Mr. Jones was caught in a speed trap.*

speed up *v.* To go faster than before; *also,* to make go faster. ♦ *The car speeded up when it reached the country.* ♦ *Push in the throttle to speed up the engine.* Compare PICK UP 12. Contrast SLOW DOWN.

spell out *v.* **1.** To say or read aloud the letters of a word, one by one; spell. ♦ *John could not understand the word the teacher was saying, so she spelled it out on the blackboard.* **2.** To read slowly, have trouble in understanding. ♦ *The little boy spelled out the printed words.* **3.** *informal* To explain something in very simple words; explain very clearly. ♦ *The class could not understand the problem, so the teacher spelled it out for them.* ♦ *Before the game the coach spelled out to the players what he wanted them to do.* Compare WORDS OF ONE SYLLABLE.

spell trouble *v. phr.* To signify major difficulties ahead. ♦ *The note we just received from the Chancellor seems to spell trouble.*

spending money *or* **pocket money** *n.* Money that is given to a person to spend. ♦ *When the seniors went to New York City on a trip, each was given $10 in spending money.* ♦ *Father gave John a nickel in pocket money when he went to the store with Mother.*

spend the night *v. phr.* To sleep somewhere. ♦ *It was so late after the party that we decided to spend the night at our friends' house.*

spick-and-span *adj.* Sparkling clean; having a brand new look. ♦ *She is such a good housekeeper that her kitchen is always spick-and-span.*

spill See CRY OVER SPILLED MILK.

spill the beans *v. phr., informal* To tell a secret to someone who is not supposed to know about it. ♦ *John's friends were going to have a surprise party for him, but Tom spilled the beans.* Compare GIVE AWAY 3, LET THE CAT OUT OF THE BAG, TELL TALES OUT OF SCHOOL.

spin a yarn *v. phr.* To tell a story of adventure with some exaggeration mixed in; embellish and protract such a tale. ♦ *Uncle Fred, who used be a sailor, knows how to spin a fascinating yarn, but don't always believe everything he says.*

spine-chilling *adj.* Terrifying; causing great fear. ♦ *Many children find the movie, "Frankenstein," spine-chilling.* ♦ *It was spine-chilling to learn that a murderer was in our neighborhood.* Compare HAIR STAND ON END.

spine-tingling *adj.* Very exciting; thrilling. ♦ *Our ride up the mountain in a chair lift was spine-tingling.* ♦ *The children's plane ride was a spine-tingling adventure to them.*

spinoff *n.* A byproduct of something else. ♦ *The television soap opera "Knot's Landing" was considered a spinoff of "Dallas," with many of the same characters featured in both.*

spin off *v. phr.* To bring something into existence as a byproduct of something that already exists. ♦ *When Dr. Catwallender opened his medical practice, he also spun off a small dispensary beside it where patients could get their prescriptions filled.*

spin one's wheels *v. phr.* **1.** Said of cars stuck in snow or mud whose wheels are turning without the car moving forward. ♦ *There was so much snow on the driveway that my car's wheels were spinning in it and we couldn't get going.* **2.** To exert effort in a job without making any progress. ♦ *I've been working for the firm for two decades, but I feel I am merely spinning my wheels.*

spin out *v. phr.* **1.** To go out of control. ♦ *The bus spun out on the icy road and fell into the ditch.* **2.** To make something go out of control. ♦ *Tom stepped on the breaks so fast that he spun his car out of control and went off the road.*

spirit away *v. phr.* To hide or smuggle something out; abduct. ♦ *The famous actress was spirited away by her bodyguards as soon as she emerged from the door.*

spite See CUT OFF ONE'S NOSE TO SPITE ONE'S FACE.

spit *or* **piss into the wedding cake** *v. phr., vulgar, avoidable* To spoil someone's pleasure or celebration by doing or saying something harsh or unseemly in an otherwise happy gathering; bring up depressing or unhappy subjects at a supposedly happy time.

♦*Stuart really spit into the wedding cake when he told Burt in a bragging fashion that Lucy, Burt's bride, used to be his girlfriend.*

spitting image *n.* **spit and image** *informal* An exact likeness; a duplicate. ♦*John is the spitting image of his grandfather.* ♦*That vase is the spitting image of one I wanted to buy in Boston.* Compare LIKE FATHER, LIKE SON.

spit up *v.* To vomit a little. ♦*The baby always spits up when he is burped.* ♦*Put a bib on the baby. I don't want him to spit up on his clean clothes.*

split end *n.* An end in football who plays five to ten yards out from the tackle in the line. ♦*The split end is one of the quarterback's most important targets for passes.* Contrast TIGHT END.

split hairs *v. phr.* To find and argue about small and unimportant differences as if the differences are important. ♦*John is always splitting hairs; he often starts an argument about something small and unimportant.* ♦*Don't split hairs about whose turn it is to wash the dishes and make the beds; let's work together and finish sooner.*

split second *n.* A very short time; less than a second. ♦*The lightning flash lasted a split second, and then disappeared.*

split the difference *v. phr., informal* To settle a money disagreement by dividing the difference, each person giving up half. ♦*Bob offered $25 for Bill's bicycle and Bill wanted $35; they split the difference.*

split ticket *n.* A vote for candidates from more than one party. ♦*Mr. Jones voted a split ticket.* ♦*An independent voter likes a split ticket.* Contrast STRAIGHT TICKET.

split up *v. phr.* **1.** To separate; get a divorce. ♦*After three years of marriage, the unhappy couple finally split up.* **2.** To separate something; divide into portions. ♦*The brothers split up their father's fortune among themselves after his death.*

split-up *n.* A separation or division into two or many smaller parts. ♦*The split-up of our company was due to the founder's untimely death.*

spoil for *v. phr.* To want something very badly; be belligerent or pugnacious about something. ♦*After a few drinks it became embarrassingly evident that Hal was spoiling for a fight.* Compare HANKER AFTER, LUST FOR.

spoken for *adj.* Occupied; reserved; taken; already engaged or married. ♦*"Sorry, my boy," Mr. Jones said condescendingly, "but my daughter is already spoken for. She will marry Fred Wilcox next month."*

sponge See THROW IN THE SPONGE.

sponge bath *n.* A bath with a cloth or sponge and a little water. ♦*During the drought the family had only sponge baths.* ♦*The family took sponge baths because they had no bathtub.*

sponge on *or* **off** *v. phr.* To exploit parasitically; depend upon for support. ♦*He is already forty years old, but he refuses to go to work and sponges off his retired parents.*

spoon See BORN WITH A SILVER SPOON IN ONE'S MOUTH.

spoon-feed *v.* **1.** To feed with a spoon. ♦*Mothers spoon-feed their babies.* **2a.** To make something too easy for (a person). ♦*Bill's mother spoon-fed him and never let him think for himself.* ♦*Alice depended on her mother for all decisions because she had been spoon-fed.* **2b.** To make (something) too easy for someone. ♦*Some students want the teacher to spoon-feed the lessons.*

sporting blood *n.* Willingness to take risks; spirit of adventure. ♦*The cowboy's sporting blood tempted him to try to ride the wild horse.* ♦*The boy's sporting blood caused him to run away with a circus.*

spot See HIT THE HIGH SPOTS, HIT THE SPOT, JOHNNY-ON-THE-SPOT, ON THE SPOT *or* UPON THE SPOT *also* IN A SPOT, SORE SPOT.

spot check *n. phr.* A sample check or investigation. ♦*Internal Revenue Service employees often conduct a spot check of individual returns when the figures don't add up.*

spotlight See STEAL THE SPOTLIGHT.

spread it on thick See LAY IT ON *or* LAY IT ON THICK.

spread like wildfire *v. phr.* To spread uncontrollably and rapidly. ♦*Bad news has a tendency to spread like wildfire.*

spread oneself too thin *v. phr.* To try to do too many things at one time. ♦*As* *the owner, chef, waiter, and dishwasher of his restaurant, Pierre was spreading himself too thin.*

spring a leak *v. phr.* **1.** To develop a hole (said of boats) through which water can enter, threatening the boat to sink. ♦ *When our small boat sprang a leak, we rapidly returned to shore to fix it.* **2.** To be threatened by some oncoming danger. ♦ *Our firm sprang a leak when the vice president suddenly died of a heart attack.*

spring chicken *n., slang* A young person.—Usually used with *no.* ♦ *Mr. Brown is no spring chicken, but he can still play tennis well.* ♦ *The coach is no spring chicken, but he can show the players what to do.*

spring on one *v. phr.* To approach someone unexpectedly with an unpleasant idea or project. ♦ *Our firm was merely six weeks old when they sprang the news on me that I had to go to Algiers to open a new branch there.*

spring up *v. phr.* To arise suddenly. ♦ *Small purple flowers were springing up all over our backyard.*

sprout wings *v. phr.* **1.** To enter the stage after a period of development when wings appear (said of larvae that turn into butterflies). ♦ *The dragonflies suddenly sprouted wings and are flying all about in the park.* **2.** To become good and virtuous (as if airborne). ♦ *Joe has helped many colleagues in need; he seems to have sprouted wings.*

spruce up *v., informal* To make clean or neat. ♦ *Mary spruced up the house before her company came.* ♦ *John spruced himself up before he went out on his date.*

spur See ON THE SPUR OF THE MOMENT, WIN ONE'S SPURS.

squad See FIRING SQUAD.

square See FAIR AND SQUARE, SHOOT STRAIGHT *or* SHOOT SQUARE.

square away *v. phr.* **1.** To arrange the sails of a ship so that the wind blows from behind. ♦ *The captain ordered the crew to square away and sail before the wind.* **2.** *informal* To put right for use or action.—Often used in the passive or participle. ♦ *The living room was squared away for the guests.* ♦ *Harry got into trouble, but his scoutmaster talked with him and got him squared*

away. Syn. STRAIGHTEN OUT. **3.** *informal* To stand ready to fight; put up your fists. ♦ *Jack and Lee squared away.* Syn. SQUARE OFF.

squared away *adj. phr.* Looked after properly; tucked away; arranged. ♦ *My first two daughters are happily married, but my third one, Jennifer, isn't squared away yet.*

square deal *n. phr.* **1.** Equitable or fair treatment. ♦ *We are proud to say that at this firm every employee gets a square deal.* Contrast NEW DEAL; RAW DEAL.

square meal *n. phr.* A full, nourishing well-balanced meal. ♦ *The refugees looked as if they hadn't had a square meal in months.*

square off *v. phr., informal* To stand ready for fighting with the fists. ♦ *The two boxers squared off when the bell rang.*

square oneself with *v. phr.* To apologize; re-establish friendship with; make amends. ♦ *"Mr. Allen is very angry with you for leaving the firm,"* Bob said. *"It will take more than a few words and a drink to square yourself with him."*

square one's shoulders *v. phr.* To stand strong and ready to give battle; be brave. ♦ *Jack squared his shoulders and entered the game.* ♦ *Graduates must square their shoulders and face the world.*

square peg in a round hole *n., informal* A person who does not fit into a job or position; someone who does not belong where he is. ♦ *Arthur is a square peg in a round hole when he is playing ball.* ♦ *George likes to work with his hands. When it comes to books, he's a square peg in a round hole.*—Sometimes used in a short form, **square peg.**

square shooter See SHOOT STRAIGHT.

square up *v. phr.* To liquidate debts and other obligations. ♦ *I want to square up my medical bills before I accept my new teaching assignment in Africa.*

squeak See PIP-SQUEAK.

squeak by *v. phr.* **1.** To barely succeed. ♦ *He was so poorly prepared for his bar exam that he barely squeaked by.* **2.** To clear with difficulty. ♦ *The entrance to the corridor in the old Italian castle was so narrow that I barely managed to* *squeak by it.*

squeak through *v., informal* To be successful but almost fail; win by a small score. *Susan squeaked through the history examination.* ♦ *The football team squeaked through 7–6.* Compare BY THE SKIN OF ONE'S TEETH.

squeeze out of *v. phr.* To apply pressure to someone in order to obtain what one desires. ♦ *The police were interrogating the suspect to squeeze information out of him.*

stab in the back[1] *v. phr., slang* To say or do something unfair that harms (a friend or someone who trusts you). ♦ *Owen stabbed his friend Max in the back by telling lies about him.*

stab in the back[2] *n. phr., slang* An act or a lie that hurts a friend or trusting person; a promise not kept, especially to a friend. ♦ *John stabbed his own friend in the back by stealing from his store.* ♦ *My friend stabbed me in the back by telling the teacher I was playing hooky when I was home sick.*

stab in the dark *n. phr.* A random attempt or guess at something without previous experience or knowledge of the subject. ♦ *"You're asking me who could have hidden grandpa's will,"* Fred said. *"I really have no idea, but let me make a stab in the dark—I think my sister Hermione has it."*

stack See BLOW A FUSE *or* BLOW ONE'S STACK.

stack the cards *v. phr.* **1.** To arrange cards secretly and dishonestly for the purpose of cheating. ♦ *The gambler had stacked the cards against Bill.* **2.** To arrange things unfairly for or against a person; have things so that a person has an unfair advantage or disadvantage; make sure in an unfair way that things will happen.—Usually used in the passive with "in one's favor" or "against one." ♦ *A tall basketball player has the cards stacked in his favor.* ♦ *The cards are stacked against a poor boy who wants to go to college.*

stage See AT ——— STAGE OF THE GAME, HOLD THE STAGE, ON THE STAGE, SET THE STAGE.

stage fright *n. phr.* The fear one feels before appearing in front of an audience. ♦ *Many famous actors and actresses admit that they often have stage fright before the curtain goes up.*

stagestruck *adj.* Desirous of becoming an actor or actress; enamored of the acting profession. ♦ *Milly is so stagestruck that she waits for actresses at the stage door after each performance to get their signatures.*

stage whisper *n. phr.* A loud whisper intended to reach other ears than those of the person(s) addressed. ♦ *Some jokes should be told in a stage whisper.*

stag party Contrast HEN PARTY. See GO STAG.

stake See AT STAKE, PULL UP STAKES.

stake a claim *v. phr.* **1.** To claim ownership of land by driving stakes to show boundaries. ♦ *The gold hunters staked claims in the West.* **2.** *informal* To claim a person or thing as your own by some sign. Usually used with *on.* ♦ *George staked a claim on Dianne by giving her his class ring.*

stamp See SAVINGS STAMP, TRADING STAMP.

stamping ground *n., informal* A place where a person spends much of his time. ♦ *Pete's soda fountain is an after-school stamping ground.* ♦ *When John returned to his hometown many years later, he visited all of his old stamping grounds.*

stamp out *v.* To destroy completely and make disappear. ♦ *In the last few years, we have nearly stamped out polio by using vaccine.* ♦ *The police and judges are trying to stamp out crime.* Compare WIPE OUT.

stand See GOAL LINE STAND, HAIR STAND ON END, HEART STAND STILL, LEG TO STAND ON.

stand a chance *or* **stand a show** *n. phr.* To have a possibility or opportunity; be likely to do or get something. ♦ *Fred doesn't stand a chance of being elected.* ♦ *We stand a good chance of seeing Mary at the party.*

standard time *also* **slow time** *n.* Clock time that is set by law or agreement in a country or in part of a country; *especially, in the United States:* the clock time used between fall and spring, which is an hour slower than the time used in the summer.—Abbreviation ST. ♦ *When we go to bed Saturday night, we will set our clocks back an* *hour, because Sunday we will be on standard time again.* ♦ *Next week it will get dark an hour earlier, because we will be on standard time.* Contrast DAYLIGHT SAVING TIME.

stand by *v.* **1.** To be close beside or near. ♦ *Mary could not tell Jane the secret with her little brother standing by.* ♦ *Would you just stand by and watch the big boys beat your little brother?* **2.** To be near, waiting to do something when needed. ♦ *The policeman in the patrol car radioed the station about the robbery, and then stood by for orders.* ♦ *Lee stood by with a fire extinguisher while the trash was burning.* **3.** To follow or keep (one's promise). *He is a boy who always stands by his promises.* **4.** To be loyal to; support; help. *When three big boys attacked Bill, Ed stood by him.* ♦ *Some people blamed Harry when he got into trouble, but Joe stood by him.* Compare BACK UP, HANG TOGETHER, STAND UP FOR.

stand by one's guns See STICK TO ONE'S GUNS.

stand for *v.* **1.** To be a sign of; make you think of; mean. ♦ *The letters "U.S.A." stand for "United States of America."* ♦ *The written sign "=" in an arithmetic problem stands for "equals."* ♦ *Our flag stands for our country.* ♦ *The owl stands for wisdom.* **2.** To speak in favor of something, or show that you support it. ♦ *The new President stood for honest government.* ♦ *John always stands for what is right.* **3.** *Chiefly British* To try to be elected for. ♦ *Three men from London are standing for parliament.* ♦ *The governor did not stand for reelection.* **4.** *informal* To allow to happen or to be done; permit.— Usually used in the negative. ♦ *The teacher will not stand for fooling in the classroom.* Compare HAVE IT 4, PUT UP WITH.

stand in awe of *v. phr.* To look upon with wonder; feel very respectful to. ♦ *Janet always stands in awe of the superintendent.* ♦ *The soldier stood in awe to his officers.*

stand in for *v. phr.* To substitute for someone. ♦ *The famous brain surgeon was called out of town so his assistant had to stand in for him during the operation.*

stand in one's way See IN ONE'S WAY.

stand in with *v. phr., informal* To be liked by or friendly with.—Usually used with *well.* ♦ *John stands in well with the teacher.*

stand off *v.* **1.** To stay at a distance; stay apart. ♦ *At parties, Mr. Jones goes around talking to everyone, but Mrs. Jones is shy and stands off.* **2.** To keep (someone or something) from coming near or winning. ♦ *The soldiers defending the fort stood off a large band of Indians.* ♦ *The other schools wanted to beat our team and win the championship, but our boys stood them all off.* Contrast GIVE GROUND.

standoffish *adj.* Stiff; aloof; reserved in manner. ♦ *The famous chess player is hard to get to know because he is so standoffish.*

stand on ceremony *v. phr.* To follow strict rules of politeness; be very formal with other people.—Usually used with a helping verb in the negative. ♦ *Grandmother does not stand on ceremony when her grandchildren call.*

stand one in good stead *v. phr.* To be helpful or useful to. ♦ *A boy scout knife will stand you in good stead when you do not have other tools.* ♦ *Julia knew how to typewrite, and that stood her in good stead when she looked for a job.*

stand one's ground *also* **hold one's ground** *v. phr.* **1.** To stay and fight instead of running away. ♦ *The enemy attacked in great numbers but our men stood their ground.* Compare GAIN GROUND. Contrast GIVE GROUND, LOSE GROUND. **2.** To defend a belief or statement; refuse to weaken when opposed; insist you are right. ♦ *John's friends said he was mistaken but he stood his ground.* Compare STICK TO ONE'S GUNS.

stand on one's own feet *or* **stand on one's own two feet** *v. phr.* To depend on yourself; do things yourself; earn your own living; be independent. ♦ *After his father died, John had to stand on his own feet and earn his own living.* ♦ *You should learn to stand on your own two feet.*

stand out *v.* **1.** To go farther out than a nearby surface; project. ♦ *A mole stood out on her cheek.* Compare STICK OUT

1b. **2.** To be more noticeable in some way than those around you; be higher, bigger, or better. ♦*Fred was very tall and stood out in the crowd.* ♦*John stood out as a track star.*

stand over *v.* **1.** To watch closely; keep checking all the time. ♦*Ted's mother had to stand over him to get him to do his homework.* **2.** To be held over for later action; be postponed; wait. ♦*The committee decided to let the proposal stand over until its next meeting.*

stand pat *v., informal* To be satisfied with things and be against a change. ♦*Bill had made up his mind on the question and when his friends tried to change his mind, he stood pat.* Compare STAND ONE'S GROUND 2.

stand the gaff *v. phr., informal* To stand rough treatment; do well in spite of great physical or mental hardship. ♦*An athlete must learn to stand the gaff.* ♦*No person running for office gets far unless he can stand the gaff.* Compare HOLD OUT 2, STICK OUT 2.

stand to reason *v. phr.* To seem very likely from the known facts. ♦*If you have a driver's license, it stands to reason you can drive.* ♦*Joe is intelligent and studies hard; it stands to reason that he will pass the examination.*

stand trial *v. phr.* To submit to a trial by court. ♦*The case has been postponed and he may not have to stand trial until next April.*

stand up *v.* **1.** To rise to a standing position; get up on your feet. ♦*A gentleman stands up when a lady enters a room.* **2.** To be strong enough to use hard or for a long time. ♦*A rocket must be built strongly to stand up under the blast-off.* ♦*The old car has already stood up for twenty years.* Compare WEAR WELL. **3.** *informal* To make a date and then fail to keep it. ♦*June cried when Bill stood her up on their first date.*

stand up and be counted *v. phr.* To be willing to say what you think in public; let people know that you are for or against something. ♦*The equal rights movement needs people who are willing to stand up and be counted.* ♦*If you disagree with the group, you should be ready to stand up and be counted.*

stand up for *or informal* **stick up for** *v.*

To defend against attack; fight for. ♦*John always stands up for his rights.* ♦*When Mary was being criticized, Jane stuck up for her.* Compare BACK UP, GO TO BAT FOR, STAND BY, STAND ONE'S GROUND, STICK TO ONE'S GUNS, GO TO BAT FOR.

stand up to *v.* To meet with courage. ♦*Mary stood up to the snarling dog that leaped toward her.* ♦*A soldier must stand up to danger.*

stand up with *v., informal* To be best man or maid of honor at a wedding. ♦*A groom often chooses his brother to stand up with him.*

star See FIVE-STAR, SEE STARS, HITCH ONE'S WAGON TO A STAR, LUCKY STAR, THANK ONE'S LUCKY STARS.

starch See TAKE THE STARCH OUT OF.

stare in the face *n. phr.* **1.** To be about to meet or to happen to (you.) ♦*Grandmother became very sick and death was staring her in the face.* ♦*Defeat stared them in the face, but the soldiers fought on bravely.* **2.** To be easy to see; be plain. ♦*Are you looking for your pencil? It's on your desk, staring you in the face.* ♦*Their friends all knew that Mary loved John, but John did not see it even though it was staring him in the face.*

stars in one's eyes *n. phr.* **1.** An appearance or feeling of very great happiness or expectation of happiness. ♦*Mary gets stars in her eyes when she thinks of her boyfriend.* **2.** A belief in the possibility of quick and lasting reforms in people and life and an eagerness to make such changes. ♦*Some inexperienced people get stars in their eyes when they think of improving the world.*—**starry-eyed** *adj.* Very happy and excited, perhaps with little reason; eager and self-confident about improving human nature and general conditions of life. ♦*Young people are often starry-eyed and eager to improve the world; they do not know how hard it is.*

start See BY FITS AND STARTS, HEAD START, JACK-RABBIT START, RUNNING START.

start from scratch See FROM SCRATCH.

start in *v., informal* **1.** To begin to do something; start. ♦*Fred started in weeding the garden. The family started* *in eating supper.* Compare GO AT. **2.** To begin a career. ♦ *Bob started in as an office boy and became president.* **3.** To give a first job to. ♦ *The bank started him in as a clerk.*

start out *v.* **1.** To begin to go somewhere. *Bill started out for school on his bicycle.* ♦ *Art started out on a voyage around the world.* Compare SET OUT. **2.** To begin a career or life. *Harry started out as an errand boy in a business office.* ♦ *We all start out in life as helpless infants.* Syn. START IN. **3.** *informal* To give one a first job. ♦ *The garage man started Pete out as a grease rack man.* Syn. START IN 3.

start something *v. phr., informal* To make trouble; cause a quarrel or fight. ♦ *John is always starting something.* ♦ *Jack likes to play tricks on the other boys to start something.* Compare MAKE SOMETHING OF.

start the ball rolling See GET THE BALL ROLLING.

start up *v.* **1.** To begin operating. ♦ *The driver started up the motor of the car.* ♦ *The engine started up with a roar.* **2.** To begin to play (music). ♦ *The conductor waved his baton, and the band started up.* ♦ *The orchestra started up a waltz.* Compare STRIKE UP. **3.** To rise or stand suddenly. ♦ *When he heard the bell, he started up from his chair.*

stash bag *or* **stuff bag** *n., slang, informal* **1.** A small bag containing marijuana cigarettes or the ingredients for making them. ♦ *The police are holding John because they found a stash bag full of the stuff on him.* **2.** Any small bag resembling a stash bag used for small personal items such as lipstick, driver's license, etc. ♦ *Do you have any room for my keys in your stash bag?*

state See LIE IN STATE.

state-of-the-art *adj. phr.* The best and the latest any field of research can offer; modern; the latest; the most advanced. ♦ *State-of-the-art personal computers may cost a little more than older models, but may be worth the cost for those who need them.* Compare UP TO DATE.

status symbol *v. phr.* Signs of wealth and prestige. ♦ *A new yacht or airplane might be a status symbol to a bank manager.*

stead See STAND IN GOOD STEAD.

stave off *v., literary* To keep from touching or hurting you. Syn. WARD OFF. ♦ *The white knight struck with his sword. The black knight staved it off with his own sword.* ♦ *Bill's warm new coat staved off the cold.* ♦ *They staved off starvation by eating two of the sled dogs.*

stay in *v. phr.* To remain at home. ♦ *The weather was so bad that we decided to stay in all day.*

stay out *v. phr.* To stay away from home. ♦ *Her father was very upset because Mary stayed out until 3 A.M. last night.*

stay put *v. phr.* To stay in place; not leave. ♦ *Harry's father told him to stay put until he came back.* ♦ *The rocks can be glued to the bulletin board to make them stay put.* ♦ *After Grandmother came home from her trip to visit Aunt May, she said she wanted to stay put for a while.*

stay up late *v. phr.* To not go to bed until very late. ♦ *Peter has to stay up late these days as he is preparing for his comprehensive exams.* See BURN THE MIDNIGHT OIL.

stay with See STICK WITH.

steady See GO STEADY.

steak See SALISBURY STEAK, T-BONE STEAK.

steal See LOCK THE BARN DOOR AFTER THE HORSE IS STOLEN.

steal a march on *v. phr.* To get ahead of someone by doing a thing unnoticed; get an advantage over. ♦ *The army stole a march on the enemy by marching at night and attacking them in the morning.* ♦ *Jack got the job by getting up earlier than Bill. He stole a march on him.* Compare GET THE JUMP ON, GET THE BETTER OF, TAKE BY SURPRISE.

steal away See SLIP AWAY.

steal one's thunder *v. phr.* To do or say something, intentionally or not, that another person has planned to say or do. ♦ *Fred intended to nominate Bill for president, but John got up first and stole Fred's thunder.* ♦ *Mary was going to sing "Oh! Susanna," but Ellen did it first and Mary said Ellen had stolen her thunder.* ♦ *Smith heard that Jones was going to offer a new law which people wanted, so he himself proposed the law* *first, stealing Jones' thunder.*

steal the show *v. phr.* To act or do so well in a performance that you get most of the attention and the other performers are unnoticed. ♦*Mary was in only one scene of the play, but she stole the show from the stars.*

steal the spotlight *v. phr.* To attract attention away from a person or thing that people should be watching. ♦*When the maid walked on the stage and tripped over a rug, she stole the spotlight from the leading players.* ♦*Just as the speaker began, a little dog ran up the aisle, and stole the spotlight from him.*

steal up on *v. phr.* To stealthily approach one; sneak up on someone. ♦*The thief stole up on his victim, snatched her purse, and ran away.*

steam See LET OFF STEAM *or* BLOW OFF STEAM, UNDER ONE'S OWN STEAM.

steamed up *adj., informal* Excited or angry about or eager to do something. ♦*The coach gave the team a pep talk before the game, and he got them all steamed up to win the game.* ♦*When Mary found out that Jane had not kept their secret, she became all steamed up.* ♦*Bill was all steamed up about the movie he had just seen.*

steel See MIND LIKE A STEEL TRAP.

steer clear of *v.* **1.** To steer a safe distance from; go around without touching. ♦*A ship steers clear of a rocky shore in stormy weather.* **2.** *informal* To stay away from; keep from going near. ♦*Fred was angry at Bill, and Bill was steering clear of him.* ♦*Some words Martha always spells wrong. She tries to steer clear of them.*

stem the tide *v. phr.* To resist; hold back something of great pressure or strength. ♦*The way to stem the tide of juvenile delinquency is to strengthen education and to pass a stiff gun control law.*

step See IN STEP, OUT OF STEP, TAKE STEPS.

step all over See WALK OVER.

step down *v.* **1.** To come down in one move from a higher position to a lower. ♦*As soon as the train stopped, the conductor stepped down to help the passengers off.* **2.** To make go slower little by little. ♦*The train was*

approaching the station, so the engineer stepped it down. Compare SLOW DOWN, STEP UP. **3.** To leave a job as an official or some other important position. ♦*When the judge became ill, he had to step down.*

step in *v.* **1.** To go inside for a quick visit. ♦*It was a cold night, and when the policeman passed, we invited him to step in for a cup of coffee.* **2.** To begin to take part in a continuing action or discussion, especially without being asked. ♦*When the dogs began to fight, John stepped in to stop it before they were hurt.* ♦*When Bill had done as much as he was able to on his model plane, his father stepped in to help him.*

step inside *v.* To come or go inside. ♦*Mother invited the callers to step inside.*

step into *v.* **1.** To come or go into. ♦*The taxi stopped, and we stepped into it.* ♦*Mr. Jones called to his secretary to step into his office.* **2.** To begin to do, undertake. *When the star became sick, his understudy stepped into his part.* ♦*When Bill graduates from college, he will step into a job in his father's bank.*

step into one's shoes *v. phr.* To do what someone else usually does after he has stopped doing it. ♦*When Bill's father died, Bill had to step into his father's shoes to support his mother.* ♦*A coach trains the junior varsity to step into the shoes of the members of the varsity team when they graduate.* ♦*When the boss retires, his son will step into his shoes.* Compare IN ONE'S SHOES.

step off *v.* **1.** To walk or march quickly. ♦*The drum major lowered his baton and the band stepped off.* **2.** *or* **pace off.** To measure by taking a series of steps in a line. ♦*The farmer stepped off the edge of the field to see how much fencing he would need.* ♦*The referee stepped off a five-yard penalty against our team.*

step on it *or* **step on the gas** *v. phr.* **1.** To push down on the gas pedal to make a car go faster. ♦*Be very careful when you step on the gas. Don't go too fast.* Compare GIVE IT THE GUN. **2.** *informal* To go faster; hurry. ♦*Step on it, or we'll be late for school.* ♦*John is a slow starter, but he can step on the gas when it looks as if he might lose the race.*

♦ *Lee was wasting time at breakfast and his father told him to step on it or they would miss the bus.*

step on one's toes *or* **tread on one's toes** *v. phr.* To do something that embarrasses or offends someone else. ♦ *If you break in when other people are talking, you may step on their toes.* ♦ *Mary is pretty, and she often treads on the toes of the girls by stealing their boyfriend.*

step on the gas See STEP ON IT.

step out *v. phr.* **1.** To go out, particularly socially, as on a date. ♦ *Paul said to Sylvia, "You look so dressed up tonight—you must be stepping out, eh?"* **2.** To leave for a short period during the work day to go to the lavatory or to get a cup of coffee. (Frequently said by secretaries over the phone.) ♦ *"May I speak to Mr. Kotz?" Roy asked. "I'm sorry, sir. He just stepped out for a minute," the secretary answered.*

step out on *v. phr.* To be unfaithful to one's marriage partner or steady lover. ♦ *It is rumored that he has been stepping out on his wife. That's why she's so upset.*

stepped up *adj.* Carried on at a faster or more active rate; increased. ♦ *To fill the increase in orders, the factory had to operate at a stepped-up rate.*

step up *v.* **1.** To go from a lower to a higher place. ♦ *John stepped up onto the platform and began to speak.* **2.** To come towards or near; approach. ♦ *The sergeant called for volunteers and Private Jones stepped up to volunteer.* ♦ *John waited until the teacher had finished speaking to Mary, and then he stepped up.* **3.** To go or to make (something) go faster or more actively. ♦ *When John found he was going to be late, he stepped up his pace.* ♦ *After we had reached the outskirts of town, we stepped up the engine.* ♦ *The enemy was near, and the army stepped up its patrols to find them before they got too close.* **4.** To rise to a higher or more important position; be promoted. ♦ *This year Mary is secretary of the club, but I am sure she will step up to president next year.* Contrast STEP DOWN 3.

sterling character *n. phr.* A person of irreproachable character; one of the highest professional standards. ♦ *The nominee for the Supreme Court must be a sterling character in every possible way.*

stew in one's own juice *v. phr., informal* To suffer from something that you have caused to happen yourself. ♦ *John lied to Tom, but Tom found out. Now Tom is making John stew in his own juice.* ♦ *I warned you not to steal those apples. You got caught, and you can stew in your own juice.*

stick See CARROT AND STICK, MORE THAN ONE COULD SHAKE A STICK AT.

stick around *v., informal* To stay or wait nearby. ♦ *John's father told him to stick around and they would go fishing.* ♦ *After work Mr. Harris stuck around to ride home with his friend.*

stick by one *v. phr.* To support; remain loyal to. ♦ *All of Peter's friends stuck by him faithfully, in spite of what has been said about him in the press.*

stick in one's craw *or* **stuck in one's crop** *v. phr.* To make you angry; bother you; annoy you. ♦ *His parents' praise of his brother stuck in Jerry's craw.* ♦ *Sue's failure to get a better grade than Ann stuck in her crop.*

stick in one's throat *v. phr.* To be something you do not want to say; be hard to say. ♦ *Jean wanted to ask the teacher's pardon, but the words stuck in her throat.*

stick-in-the-mud *n., informal* An overcareful person; someone who is old-fashioned and fights change. ♦ *Mabel said her mother was a real stick-in-the-mud to make a rule that she must be home by 10 o'clock on weeknights and 11:30 Saturdays.* ♦ *Mr. Thomas is a stick-in-the-mud who plows with mules; he won't buy a tractor.*

stick one's neck out *or* **stick one's chin out** *v. phr., informal* To do something dangerous or risky. ♦ *When I was in trouble, Paul was the only one who would stick his neck out to help me.* ♦ *John is always sticking his chin out by saying something he shouldn't.*

stick one's nose into See NOSE INTO.

stick out *v.* **1a.** To stand out from a wall or other surface; project; extend. ♦ *The limb stuck out from the trunk of the tree.* **1b.** To be seen or noticed more easily or quickly than others; be noticeable. ♦ *My house is the only brick one on the street. It sticks out and you can't miss it.* ♦ *Mary plays basketball very well. The others on the team are good, but she really sticks out.* **1c.** Often used in the informal phrase *stick out like a sore thumb.* ♦ *John is so shy and awkward that he sticks out like a sore thumb.* Syn. STAND OUT. **2.** *informal* To keep on doing something until it is done no matter how long, hard, or unpleasant. ♦ *Bill is not a fast runner and he doesn't have a chance of winning the marathon, but he will stick out the race even if he finishes last.*— Often used in the phrase *stick it out.* ♦ *Mathematics is hard, but if you stick it out you will understand it.* Compare HANG ON 2, STICK WITH 1.

stick out like a sore thumb *v. phr.* To be conspicuous; be different from the rest. ♦ *When the foreign student was placed in an advanced English grammar class by mistake, it was no wonder that he stuck out like a sore thumb.*

stick together *v.* To remain close together in a situation. ♦ *Stick together in the cave so that no one gets lost.* ♦ *The gang stuck together after the game.* ♦ *Bill and Bob stick together in a game or in a fight.* Syn. HANG TOGETHER 1.

stick to one's guns *or* **stand by one's guns** *v. phr.* To hold to an aim or an opinion even though people try to stop you or say you are wrong. ♦ *People laughed at Columbus when he said the world was round. He stuck to his guns and proved he was right.* ♦ *At first the boss would not give Jane the raise in pay she wanted, but she stood by her guns and he gave it to her.* Compare STAND ONE'S GROUND.

stick to one's knitting *or* **tend to one's knitting** *v. phr., informal* To do your own job and not bother other people. ♦ *The trouble with Henry is that he is always telling other people what to do; he can't stick to his knitting.*

stick to one's ribs *or* **stick to the ribs** *v. phr., informal* To keep you from getting hungry again too quickly. ♦ *Doctors say you should eat a good breakfast that sticks to your ribs.*

♦ *Farmers eat food that sticks to the ribs.*

stick to the point *v. phr.* To stay on course during a discussion; adhere to the topic; not talk about extraneous matters. ♦ *Stick to the point and stop telling us your life history!* See COME TO THE POINT.

stick up *v., informal* To rob with a gun. ♦ *When the messenger left the bank, a man jumped out of an alley and stuck him up.* Syn. HOLD UP. ♦ *In the old West, outlaws sometimes stuck up the stagecoaches.*

stick-up *n., informal* A robbery by a man with a gun. ♦ *Mr. Smith was the victim of a stick-up last night.*

stick up for See STAND UP FOR.

stick with *v., informal* **1.** *or* **stay with** To continue doing; not quit. ♦ *Fred stayed with his homework until it was done.* ♦ *Practicing is tiresome, but stick with it and some day you will be a good pianist.* Compare STICK TO. **2.** To stay with; not leave. ♦ *Stick with me until we get out of the crowd.* ♦ *For two months Bill's boss could not pay his salary, but Bill stuck with him because he thought the company would soon succeed.* **3.** To sell (someone) something poor or worthless; cheat. ♦ *Father said that the man in the store tried to stick him with a bad TV set.* **4.** To leave (someone) with (something unpleasant); force to do or keep something because others cannot or will not.—Usually used in the passive. ♦ *When Harry and I went to the store to buy ice cream cones, Harry ran out with his cone without paying and I was stuck with paying for it.* ♦ *Mary didn't wash the dishes before she left so I'm stuck with it.* ♦ *Mr. Jones bought a house that is too big and expensive, but now he's stuck with it.*

stick with *v. phr.* To unfairly thrust upon; encumber one with. ♦ *In the restaurant my friends stuck me with the bill although it was supposed to be Dutch treat.*

sticky fingers *n. phr., slang* **1.** The habit of stealing things you see and want. ♦ *Don't leave money in your locker; some of the boys have sticky fingers.* ♦ *Don't leave that girl alone in the room with so many valuable objects around, because she has sticky fingers.* **2.**

Ability to catch a ball, especially football forward passes. ◆*Jack is very tall and has sticky fingers. He is an end on the football team.*

stiff See KEEP A STIFF UPPER LIP, SCARE OUT OF ONE'S WITS *or* SCARE STIFF.

still See HEART STAND STILL.

still life *n. phr.* A term used by artists to describe a motionless picture of a bowl of fruit, flowers, etc. ◆*One of van Gogh's most famous still lifes is a vase of yellow flowers.*

still waters run deep Quiet people probably are profound thinkers.—A proverb. ◆*He doesn't say much, but he sure looks smart. Well, still waters run deep, isn't that true?*

stir up *v.* **1.** To bring (something) into being, often by great exertion or activity; cause. ◆*It was a quiet afternoon, and John tried to stir up some excitement.* ◆*Bob stirred up a fight between Tom and Bill.* Compare WHIP UP 2. **2.** To cause (someone) to act; incite to action or movement; rouse. ◆*The coach's pep talk stirred up the team to win.* ◆*When Mary heard what Betty said about her, she became stirred up.*

stir up a hornet's nest *v. phr.* To make many people angry; do something that many people don't like. ◆*The principal stirred up a hornet's nest by changing the rules at school.*

stitch See IN STITCHES.

stock See IN STOCK, OUT OF STOCK, TAKE STOCK, TAKE STOCK IN.

stock-in-trade *n. phr.* The materials which one customarily deals, sells, or offers. ◆*Imported silk blouses from the Orient are the stock-in-trade of their small shop.* ◆*Anecdotes are often an after-dinner speaker's stock-in-trade.*

stomach See EYES BIGGER THAN ONE'S STOMACH, BUTTERFLIES IN YOUR STOMACH, TURN ONE'S STOMACH.

stone See CAST THE FIRST STONE, HAVE A HEART OF STONE, KILL TWO BIRDS WITH ONE STONE, LEAVE NO STONE UNTURNED, PEOPLE WHO LIVE IN GLASS HOUSES SHOULD NOT THROW STONES, ROLLING STONE GATHERS NO MOSS.

stone-blind *adj. phr.* **1.** Completely blind. ◆*Poor Al is stone-blind and needs help to get across the street carefully.* **2.** Highly intoxicated. ◆*George*

drank too much and got stone-blind at the office party. See GET STONED, THREE SHEETS TO THE WIND.

stone-broke *or* **dead broke** *or* **flat broke** *adj., informal* having no money; penniless. ◆*Jill wanted to go to the movies but she was stone-broke.* ◆*The man gambled and was soon flat broke.*

stone-cold *adj.* Having no warmth; completely cold.—Used to describe things that are better when warm. ◆*The boys who got up late found their breakfast stone-cold.* ◆*The furnace went off and the radiators were stone-cold.*

stone-dead *adj., informal* Showing no signs of life; completely dead. ◆*Barry tried to revive the frozen robin but it was stone-dead.*

stone-deaf *adj. phr.* Completely deaf. ◆*Sam is stone-deaf so let him read your lips if you know no sign language.*

stone wall *or* **brick wall** *adj.* Something hard to overcome; an idea or belief that is hard to change. ◆*The students ran into a brick wall when they asked the principal to put off the examination.* ◆*Dick tried to change Father's mind about letting him use the car Saturday night, but he was up against a stone wall.*

stone's throw *or* **within a stone's throw** *adv. phr.* Within a very short distance. ◆*They live across the street from us, just within a stone's throw.* See HOP, SKIP AND A JUMP.

stool pigeon *n.* A criminal who informs on his associates. ◆*The detective was able to solve the crime mainly through information obtained from a stool pigeon.*

stop See PUT AN END TO 1, *or* PUT A STOP TO.

stop at nothing *v. phr.* To be unscrupulous. ◆*Al will stop at nothing to get Nancy to go out with him.*

stop by See DROP BY.

stop cold *or* **stop dead** *or* **stop in one's tracks** *v. phr., informal* To stop very quickly or with great force. ◆*The hunter pulled the trigger and stopped the deer cold.* ◆*When I saw Mary on the street, I was so surprised I stopped dead.* ◆*The deer heard a noise and he stopped in his tracks.*

stop off *v.* To stop at a place for a short

time while going somewhere. ♦ *We stopped off after school at the soda fountain before going home.* ♦ *On our trip to California we stopped off in Las Vegas for two days.*

stop over *v.* To stay at a place overnight or for some other short time while on a trip elsewhere. ♦ *When we came back from California, we stopped over one night near the Grand Canyon.*

stop short *v. phr.* To suddenly stop. ♦ *Jake stopped short when he heard somebody yell out his name loud but there was no one in sight.*

stop street *n.* A street where cars must come to a full stop before crossing another street. *Johnny was late because he traveled on a stop street.* Contrast THROUGH STREET.

stop the show *v. phr.* To elicit such a strong applause from the audience that the show is interrupted. ♦ *Pavarotti's rendition of "O sole mio" always stops the show.*

stop up *v. phr.* To block; close. ♦ *If you want to get rid of the leak, you must stop up the two holes you have in the ceiling.*

store See DIME STORE, IN STORE, SET STORE BY, VARIETY STORE.

storm See TAKE BY STORM.

story See OLD STORY, SOB STORY, UPPER STORY.

stow away *v.* **1.** *informal* To pack or store away. ♦ *After New Year's Day the Christmas decorations were stowed away until another season.* **2.** To hide on a ship or another kind of transportation to get a free ride. ♦ *John ran away from home and stowed away on a freighter going to Jamaica.*

straight See GO STRAIGHT, SHOOT STRAIGHT.

straighten out *v.* To correct a mistake; make you realize you are wrong. ♦ *The teacher saw Jim's awkward sentence on the board and asked for volunteers to straighten it out.* ♦ *Sometimes only a good spanking will straighten out a naughty child.* Syn. SQUARE AWAY 2.

straighten up *v.* To put in order; make neat. ♦ *Vic had to straighten up his room before he could go swimming.* ♦ *Mrs. Johnson straightened up the house before company came.* Compare PICK UP 6b, SQUARE AWAY.

straight face *n.* A face that is not laughing or smiling. ♦ *Mary told all the funny stories she knew to try to make Joan laugh, but Joan kept a straight face.* ♦ *It is hard to tell when Jim is teasing you. He can tell a fib with a straight face.* ♦ *When Bob fell into the water, he looked funny and I could hardly keep a straight face.*

straight from the horse's mouth *slang* Directly from the person or place where it began; from a reliable source or a person that cannot be doubted. ♦ *They are going to be married. I got the news straight from the horse's mouth—their minister.* ♦ *John found out about the painting straight from the horse's mouth, from the painter himself.*

straight from the shoulder *adv. phr., informal* In an open and honest way of speaking; without holding back anything because of fear or politeness or respect for someone's feelings; frankly. ♦ *John asked what he had done wrong. Bob told him straight from the shoulder.* ♦ *The candidate for Congress spoke out against his opponent's dishonesty straight from the shoulder.* Contrast PULL ONE'S PUNCHES.

straightlaced *adj.* Of very strict morals and manners. ♦ *She is so straightlaced that she won't even go out with a man unless she senses that he is serious about her.*

straight off *adv. phr.* At once; immediately. ♦ *After school is over, you come home straight off, and don't waste time.* ♦ *He asked his father for the car, but his father said straight off that he couldn't have it.*

straight out See RIGHT OUT.

straight shooters See SHOOT STRAIGHT.

straight ticket *n.* A vote for all the candidates of a single party. ♦ *Uncle Fred was a loyal member of his party. He always voted the straight ticket.* Contrast SPLIT TICKET.

strain a point See STRETCH A POINT.

strange to say *adv. phr.* Not what you might think; surprisingly.—Used for emphasis. ♦ *Strange to say, Jerry doesn't like candy.* ♦ *Strange to say, the Indians didn't kill Daniel Boone.*

strapped for *adj.* Broke; out of funds. ♦ *My brother is so extravagant that he is* *always strapped for cash.*

straw See GIVE A HANG, GRASP AT A STRAW, GRASP AT STRAWS, LAST STRAW *or* STRAW THAT BREAKS THE CAMEL'S BACK, MAKE BRICKS WITHOUT STRAW.

straw boss *n.* **1.** The boss of a few workers who is himself under another boss or foreman. ♦ *The straw boss told Jim he would have to see the foreman about a job.* **2.** A man who works himself and also bosses a few other workers. *Smith worked better than the other men, so the foreman made him straw boss, too.*

straw in the wind *n. phr.* A small sign of what may happen. ♦ *The doctor's worried face was a straw in the wind.* ♦ *The quickly-called meeting of the President and his cabinet was a straw in the wind.*

straw poll *n. phr.* An informal survey taken in order to get an opinion. ♦ *The results of our straw poll show that most faculty members prefer to teach between 9 and 11 A.M.*

straw that breaks the camel's back See LAST STRAW.

straw vote See STRAW POLL.

streak See WINNING STREAK.

streak of luck See RUN OF LUCK.

stream See CHANGE HORSES IN THE MIDDLE OF THE STREAM, SWIM AGAINST THE CURRENT *or* SWIM AGAINST THE STREAM.

street See BACK STREET, CROSS STREET, MAN IN THE STREET, ON EASY STREET, SIDE STREET, STOP STREET, THROUGH STREET.

strength See ON THE STRENGTH OF.

stretch a point *or* **strain a point** *v. phr.* To permit something different or more than usual; not tell the exact truth or make an exception. ♦ *Mother stretched a point because it was Christmas time and let the children stay up later than usual.* ♦ *It's straining a point to call Joe a hero just because he saved the kitten from drowning in the bathtub.*

stretch of the imagination *n. phr.* Imaginative attempt or effort. ♦ *By no stretch of the imagination can I see Al as a successful lawyer.*

stride See HIT ONE'S STRIDE, TAKE IN STRIDE.

strike See CALLED STRIKE, HAVE TWO STRIKES AGAINST ONE, LIGHTNING NEVER STRIKES TWICE IN THE SAME PLACE, TWO STRIKES AGAINST ONE.

strike a bargain *v. phr.* To arrive at a price satisfactory to both the buyer and the seller. ♦ *After a great deal of haggling, they managed to strike a bargain.*

strike a happy medium *v. phr.* To find an answer to a problem that is halfway between two unsatisfactory answers. ♦ *Mary said the dress was blue. Jane said it was green. They finally struck a happy medium and decided it was blue-green.* ♦ *Two teaspoons of sugar made the cup of coffee too sweet, and one not sweet enough. One heaping teaspoon struck a happy medium.*

strike all of a heap See ALL OF A HEAP.

strikebreaker *n.* One who takes the place of workers on strike or one who recruits such people. ♦ *The striking workers threw rotten eggs at the strikebreakers.*

strike gold *v. phr.* **1.** To find gold. ♦ *Ted struck gold near an abandoned mine in California.* **2.** To find suddenly the answer to an old puzzle. ♦ *Professor Brown's assistant struck gold when he came up with an equation that explained the irregular motions of a double star.* See PAY DIRT.

strike home See HIT HOME.

strike it rich *v. phr., informal* **1.** To discover oil, or a large vein of minerals to be mined, or a buried treasure. ♦ *The old prospector panned gold for years before he struck it rich.* **2.** To become rich or successful suddenly or without expecting to. ♦ *Everyone wanted to buy one of the new gadgets, and their inventor struck it rich.* ♦ *John did not know that he had a rich Uncle John in Australia. John struck it rich when his uncle left his money to John.* Compare PAY DIRT 2.

strike one funny *v. phr.* To appear or seem laughable, curious, ironic, or entertaining. ♦ *"It strikes me funny," he said, "that you should refuse my invitation to visit my chateau in France. After all, you love both red wine and old castles."*

strike one's colors See HAUL DOWN ONE'S COLORS.

strike one's fancy *v. phr.* To please one's predilections; appeal to one. ♦ *The red* *tie with the yellow dragon on it happened to strike my fancy, so I bought it.*

strike *or* **hit a sour note** *v. phr.* To spoil the mood at a gathering by hearing some bad news. ♦ *The news of Mr. Brown's sudden illness struck a sour note during our New Year's Eve party.* Compare SPIT INTO THE WEDDING CAKE.

strike out *v.* **1.** To destroy something that has been written or drawn by drawing a line or cross through it or by erasing it. ♦ *John misspelled "corollary." He struck it out and wrote it correctly.* **2.** To begin to follow a new path or a course of action that you have never tried. ♦ *The boy scouts struck out at daybreak over the mountain pass.* ♦ *John quit his job and struck out on his own as a traveling salesman.* **3.** To put (a batter) out of play by making him miss the ball three times; *also:* To be put out of play by missing the ball three times. ♦ *The pitcher struck out three men in the game.* ♦ *The batter struck out twice.* **4.** To push out an arm suddenly in a hitting motion. ♦ *The boxer saw his chance and struck out at his opponent's jaw.*

strike out at *v. phr.* To attack someone verbally or physically. ♦ *She was so angry that she struck out at him every occasion she got.*

strike the hour *v. phr.* To mark or toll the hour (said of clocks or bells). ♦ *We heard the church clock strike the hour of two.*

strike up *v.* **1a.** To start to sing or play. ♦ *We were sitting around the campfire. Someone struck up a song, and we all joined in.* ♦ *The President took his place on the platform, and the band struck up the national anthem.* **1b.** To give a signal to start (a band) playing. ♦ *When the team ran on the field, the band director struck up the band.* **2.** To bring about; begin; start. ♦ *The policeman struck up a conversation with John while they were waiting for the bus.* ♦ *It did not take Mary long to strike up acquaintances in her new school.*

strike while the iron is hot See MAKE HAY WHILE THE SUN SHINES.

string See FIRST STRING, LATCH STRING, ON THE STRING *or* ON A STRING, PULL STRINGS, PURSE STRINGS, SHOE-STRING CATCH, TIED TO ONE'S MOTHER'S APRON STRINGS.

string along *v., informal* **1.** To deceive; fool; lead on dishonestly. ♦ *Mary was stringing John along for years but she didn't mean to marry him.* ♦ *George told the new boy that he must always call the teacher "Sir," but the new boy soon saw that George was stringing him along.* Compare ON A STRING. **2.** To follow someone's leadership; join his group. ♦ *Those of you who want to learn about wild flowers, string along with Jake.*

string out *v.* To make (something) extend over a great distance or a long stretch of time. ♦ *The telephone poles were strung out along the road as far as we could see.* ♦ *Mary and Ann did not have much to say but they did not want to go home. They strung out their gossip for a long time.*

string up *v., slang* To put a rope around the neck of a person and choke him to death; hang. ♦ *The posse strung up the rustler without a trial.* Compare NECKTIE PARTY.

strings attached *adv. phr.* With some special proviso or condition that is a handicap. ♦ *John inherited a large fortune but with the string attached that he could not touch a penny of it before his 28th birthday.*

strip See DRAG STRIP.

stripe See MIDFIELD STRIPE.

stroke See AT A STROKE *or* AT ONE'S STROKE.

stroke of luck See RUN OF LUCK.

strong language *n. phr.* Cursing; swearing. ♦ *When Ned learned that he had been fired, he used some very strong language about his boss.*

strung out *adj., slang, colloquial* **1.** Nervous, jittery, jumpy; generally ill because of drug use or withdrawal symptoms. ♦ *The only explanation I can think of for Max's behavior is that he must be strung out.* **2.** To suffer because of a lack of something previously accustomed to, such as the love and affection of someone. ♦ *Sue is all strung out for Jim; they've just split up.* Compare SPACED OUT.

stuck on *slang* Very much in love with; crazy about. ♦ *Judy thinks she is very* *pretty and very smart. She is stuck on herself.* ♦ *Lucy is stuck on the football captain.*

stuck-up *adj., informal* Acting as if other people are not as good as you are; conceited; snobbish. ♦ *Mary is very stuck-up, and will not speak to the poor children in her class.*

stuck with *adj. phr.* Left in a predicament; left having to take care of a problem caused by another. ♦ *Our neighbors vanished without a trace and we got stuck with their cat and dog.*

study See BROWN STUDY.

stuff See KNOW ONE'S WAY AROUND 2.

stuff and nonsense *n.* Foolish or empty writing or talk; nonsense. ♦ *Fred told a long story about his adventures in Africa, but it was all stuff and nonsense.* Often used as an interjection. ♦ *When Jane said she was too sick to go to school, her mother answered, "Stuff and nonsense! I know there's a test today."*

stuff the ballot box *v. phr.* To give more votes to a candidate in an election than there are people who actually voted for him. ♦ *It is a crime to stuff the ballot box.*—**ballot-stuffing** *adj. phr.*

stuffed shirt *n. phr.* A pretentious bore; a pompous, empty person. ♦ *I think that Howard is a terrible stuffed shirt with no sense of humor.*

stuffed up *adj. phr.* Impeded; blocked. ♦ *Our kitchen sink is all stuffed up so I have to call the plumber.*

stumble across *v. phr.* To encounter a person or thing, mostly by accident. ♦ *I gave up looking for my old hat when I accidentally stumbled across it in a dark corner of the closet.*

stump See TAKE THE STUMP *or* TAKE TO THE STUMP, UP A STUMP.

style See CRAMP ONE'S STYLE, HIGH STYLE.

subject to *adj. phr.* **1.** Under the government or control of; in the power of. ♦ *The English colonies in America were subject to the English king.* ♦ *The principal and the teachers of a school are subject to the school board.* **2.** Likely to get or have; liable. ♦ *John is in rather poor health and is subject to colds.* ♦ *The western plains are subject to tornadoes.* **3.** Depending on some change, happening, or need. ♦ *The*

company and the union agreed that the workers' wages should be subject to changes in the cost of living. ♦ *Agreements made by the President with other countries are subject to the approval of the Senate.*

substance See IN SUBSTANCE.

succeed See HOWLING SUCCESS, NOTHING SUCCEEDS LIKE SUCCESS.

such and such *pron.* Something whose name is not mentioned because it does not need to be mentioned. ♦ *George's argument tries to prove such and such to be true, but it does not convince me.*

such-and-such *adj. phr.* Being one whose name has been forgotten or whose name does not need to be mentioned. ♦ *She told me to go to such-and-such a street and turn right.* ♦ *Suppose, now, that we have such-and-such a group coming to the school, and we don't have enough chairs. What do we do then?*

such as *conj.* **1.** Of a kind or amount shown or named; of a kind like. ♦ *The explorer took only such men and things as he really needed into the jungle with him.* ♦ *They felt such heat in the jungle as they had never felt before.* ♦ *Many different pies were in the bakery such as apple, cherry, and blueberry pies.* **2.** Of the average or ordinary kind; poor; humble. ♦ *Such as the food was, there was plenty of it.* ♦ *The room is not very nice, but such as it is, you may stay there for the night.*

such as it is Just as it appears or is presented, not being any better or worse than most others of its kind; being average or mediocre. ♦ *This pie, such as it is, is the best I can make.* ♦ *Jane told her grandmother her grades, such as they were.*

such that *conj.* Of a kind or amount that; so great or so little that; enough that. ♦ *There was such a big line at the movie that we had to wait before we could get in.* ♦ *Jimmy made such noise that his sister told him to be quiet.* ♦ *Mother's answer was such that she didn't say yes and she didn't say no.*

sucker list *n., slang* A list of easily-fooled people, especially people who are easily persuaded to buy things or give money. ♦ *The crook got hold of a sucker list and started out to sell his* *worthless stock.* ♦ *Mr. Smith gets so many advertisements in his mail that he says he is on every sucker list in the country.*

suck in *v.* **1.** *informal* To pull in by taking a deep breath and tightening the muscles; flatten. ♦ *"Suck in those stomachs," the gym teacher said.* **2.** *slang* To make a fool of; cheat. ♦ *The uneducated farmer was sucked in by a clever crook.*

sugar daddy *n., slang, semi-vulgar, avoidable* An older, well-to-do man, who gives money and gifts to a younger woman or girls usually in exchange for sexual favors. ♦ *Betty Morgan got a mink coat from her sugar daddy.*

suit See BIRTHDAY SUIT, FOLLOW SUIT.

suit to a T See TO A T.

suit up *v. phr.* To don a uniform or sports outfit. ♦ *The veterans like to suit up for the Fourth of July parade.*

suit yourself *v. phr., informal* To do what one likes or prefers. ♦ *"I don't care where you want to sleep," he said. "Suit yourself!"*

sum total *n.* The final amount; everything taken together; total. ♦ *The sum total of expenses for the trip was $450.* ♦ *Ten years was the sum total of John's education.*

sum up *v.* To put something into a few words; shorten into a brief summary; summarize. ♦ *The teacher summed up the lesson in three rules.* ♦ *The mailman's job, in all kinds of weather, is summed up in the phrase "Deliver the mail."*

sun See UNDER THE SUN.

sunbelt *n., informal* A portion of the southern United States where the winter is very mild in comparison to other states. ♦ *The Simpsons left Chicago for the sunbelt because of Jeff's rheumatism.*

Sunday See MONTH OF SUNDAYS.

Sunday best *or* **Sunday-go-to-meeting clothes** See BEST BIB AND TUCKER.

sunny-side up *adj.* Fried on one side only. ♦ *Barbara likes her eggs sunny-side up.*

supper See COVERED-DISH SUPPER *or* POTLUCK SUPPER.

supply See IN SHORT SUPPLY.

sure See FOR SURE, MAKE SURE, TO BE SURE.

sure enough *adv.* As expected. ♦ *Charles was afraid he had done badly on the test, and sure enough, his grade was failing.* ♦ *The children saw a familiar shape coming up the street and hoped it was their lost dog. When it came near, sure enough, it was Spot.* Compare SURE THING 2.

sure-enough *adj.* Real; genuine. ♦ *Rick found a sure-enough nickel.* ♦ *Martha's uncle gave her a sure-enough pearl on a little gold chain.* ♦ *Jane's uncle is a sure-enough cowboy.*

surefire *adj.* Without fail; effective; bringing actual results. ♦ *During a campaign the only surefire way to get the sympathy of the voters is to mingle with them in person.*

sure thing **1.** *n., informal* Something sure to happen; something about which there is no doubt. ♦ *It's no fun betting on a sure thing.*—**sure thing** **2.** *adv.* Of course; certainly. ♦ *Sure thing, I'll be glad to do it for you.* Compare FOR SURE 2, SURE ENOUGH.

surface See SCRATCH THE SURFACE.

surprise See TAKE BY SURPRISE.

survival of the fittest *n. phr.* The staying alive or in action of the best prepared; often: idea that those living things best able to adjust to life survive and those unable to adjust die out. ♦ *Life in the old West was often a case of survival of the fittest.* ♦ *With changes in the world's climate, dinosaurs died but many smaller animals lived on. It was survival of the fittest.* ♦ *On the 50-mile hike it was survival of the fittest; only 12 out of 25 Scouts finished.*

suspicion See ABOVE SUSPICION.

swallow See LOOK LIKE THE CAT THAT ATE THE CANARY.

swallow hook, line, and sinker See HOOK, LINE, AND SINKER.

swallow one's pride *v. phr.* To bring your pride under control; humble yourself. ♦ *After Bill lost the race, he swallowed his pride and shook hands with the winner.* Compare EAT ONE'S WORDS.

swallow one's words **1.** To speak unclearly; fail to put enough breath into your words. ♦ *Phyllis was hard to understand because she swallowed her words.* **2.** See EAT ONE'S WORDS.

swallow up *v. phr.* To do away with;

absorb; engulf. ♦ *My expenses are so great that they swallow up my modest salary.*

swan song *n. phr., literary* A farewell or last appearance. ♦ *The famous soprano gave her swan song in* La Traviata *before she retired.*

swat team *n., informal* Police unit trained for especially hazardous or sensitive law-enforcement assignments; short for Special Weapons and Tactics. ♦ *Joe made the SWAT team of the NYPD due to his athletic skills.*

swathe See CUT A SWATHE.

swear by *v.* **1.** To use as the support or authority that what you are saying is truthful; take an oath upon. ♦ *A witness swears by the Bible that he will tell the truth.* ♦ *In ancient Greece a doctor swore by Apollo, the god of healing, that he would be a good doctor.* ♦ *John swore by his honor he would return the bike.* **2.** To have complete confidence in; be sure of; trust completely. ♦ *When John has to go somewhere fast, he swears by his bike to get there.* ♦ *We can be sure that Fred will come on time, since his friend Tom swears by him.*

swear in *or* **swear into** *v.* To have a person swear or promise to do his duty as a member or an officer of an organization, government department, or similar group.—*Swear into* is used when the name of the group is given. ♦ *Mary and Ann will be sworn into the club tonight.* ♦ *Fred was sworn in as class president.* ♦ *Many new men were sworn into the army last month.* ♦ *At the inauguration, the Chief Justice of the Supreme Court swore in the new President.*

swear off *v., informal* To give up something you like or you have got in the habit of using by making a promise. ♦ *Mary swore off candy until she lost ten pounds.* ♦ *John has sworn off dessert for Lent.*

swear out *v.* To get (a written order to do something) by swearing that a person has broken the law. ♦ *The policeman swore out a warrant for the suspect's arrest.* ♦ *The detectives swore out a search warrant.*

sweat See BY THE SWEAT OF ONE'S BROW.

sweat blood *v. phr., slang* **1.** To be very much worried. ♦ *The engine of the air-*

plane stopped, and the pilot sweated blood as he glided to a safe landing. **2.** To work very hard. ♦ *Jim sweated blood to finish his composition on time.*

sweat out *v., informal* To wait anxiously; worry while waiting. ♦ *Karl was sweating out the results of the college exams.* ♦ *The search plane signaled that help was on the way. The men in the lifeboat just had to sweat it out.*

Sweeney See TELL IT TO THE MARINES *or* TELL IT TO SWEENEY.

sweep See NEW BROOM SWEEPS CLEAN.

sweep off one's feet *v. phr.* To make (someone) have feelings (as love or happiness) too strong to control; overcome with strong feeling; win sudden and complete acceptance by (someone) through the feelings. ♦ *The handsome football captain swept Joan off her feet when he said so many things to her at the dance.* ♦ *Joan was swept off her feet when the football captain started flirting with her.* ♦ *Mary is swept off her feet whenever she hears a band start playing.* ♦ *John was swept off his feet when he won the contest.* Compare BOWL OVER 2, CARRY AWAY.

sweep out of *v. phr.* To leave in an impressive, majestic manner. ♦ *Offended by Tim's remark, Mary swept out of the room with her head high in the air.*

sweep the city *or* **country** *or* **nation** *or* **world** *v. phr.* To gain great attention or popularity throughout the city, country, etc. ♦ *Pavarotti's unmatched tenor voice swept the world in an unprecedented manner.*

sweep under the rug *v. phr.* To hide or dismiss casually (something one is ashamed of or does not know what to do about). ♦ *In many places, drug abuse by school children is swept under the rug.*

sweet See SHORT AND SWEET.

sweetie pie *n., informal* A person who is loved; darling; sweetheart. ♦ *Arnold blushed with pleasure when Annie called him her sweetie pie.* ♦ *Nancy is Bill's sweetie pie.*

sweet on *adj. phr., informal* In love with; very fond of. ♦ *John is sweet on Alice.*

sweet talk **1.** *n., informal* Too much praise; flattery. ♦ *Sometimes a girl's better judgment is overcome by sweet talk.* **2.** *v., informal* To get what you want by great praise; flatter. ♦*Polly could sweet talk her husband into anything.*

sweet tooth *n. phr.* A great weakness or predilection for sweets. ♦*Sue has such a sweet tooth that she hardly eats anything else but cake.*

swelled head *n., informal* A feeling that you are very important or more important than you really are. ♦*When John won the race, he got a swelled head.* ♦*Pretty girls shouldn't get a swelled head about it.*—**swell-headed** *adj. phr.* ♦*After he was elected captain of the team, Bob became swell-headed.* Compare BIG HEAD.

swell-headed See SWELLED HEAD.

swim See IN THE SWIM, SINK OR SWIM.

swim against the current *or* **swim against the stream** *v. phr.* To do the opposite of what most people want to do; go against the way things are happening; struggle upstream. ♦*The boy who tries to succeed today without an education is swimming against the stream.*

swine See CAST PEARLS BEFORE SWINE *or* CAST ONE'S PEARLS BEFORE SWINE.

swing See IN FULL SWING.

swing one's weight *v. phr.* To use your personal power to get something done. ♦*The President swings his weight to get laws passed.* ♦*Mr. Thomas swung his weight to get his son a job with the company.*

switch See ASLEEP AT THE SWITCH.

switched on *adj., slang* **1.** In tune with the latest fads, ideas, and fashions. ♦*I dig Sarah, she is really switched on.* **2.** Stimulated; as if under the influence of alcohol or drugs. ♦*How come you're talking so fast? Are you switched on or something?*

swoop See AT ONE FELL SWOOP.

sword See AT SWORDS' POINTS, PUT TO THE SWORD.

sword rattling See SABER RATTLING.

sworn enemies *n. phr.* People or groups or nations that have a long-standing dislike for each other. ♦*The Israelis and the Arabs used to be sworn enemies but hopefully they will sign a lasting peace accord.*

syllable See WORDS OF ONE SYLLABLE.

system See PUBLIC-ADDRESS SYSTEM.

T See TO A T.

tab See KEEP TAB ON *or* KEEP TABS ON.

table See AT THE TABLE *or* AT TABLE, COFFEE TABLE, PUT ONE'S CARDS ON THE TABLE *or* LAY ONE'S CARDS ON THE TABLE, TURN THE TABLES, WAIT AT TABLE *or* WAIT ON TABLE.

tack See GET DOWN TO BRASS TACKS, GO SIT ON A TACK, SHARP AS A TACK.

tackle See FLYING TACKLE

tack on *v. phr.* To append; add. ◆*We were about to sign the contract when we discovered that the lawyer had tacked on a codicil that was not acceptable to us.*

tag end *or* **tail end** *n., informal* The end, farthest to the rear, last in line, nearest the bottom, or least important. ◆*John was at the tail end of his class.* ◆*Mary's part in the play came at the tag end, and she got bored waiting.* ◆*Bill waited at the crossing for the tag end of a freight to go by.*

tail See COW'S TAIL, HEADS I WIN, TAILS YOU LOSE, MAKE HEAD OR TAIL OF, TURN TAIL.

tail between one's legs *n. phr.* State of feeling beaten, ashamed, or very obedient, as after a scolding or a whipping. ◆*The army sent the enemy home with their tails between their legs.* ◆*The boys on the team had boasted they would win the tournament, but they went home with their tails between their legs.* [So called because a beaten dog usually puts his tail down between his legs and slinks away.]

tail end See TAG END.

taillight *n.* The rear red light of a car. ◆*My father was fined $15 for driving without a taillight.*

tailor-made See MADE-TO-MEASURE.

tailspin See GO INTO A TAILSPIN.

tail wags the dog Said of situations in which a minor part is in control of the whole. ◆*He is just a minor employee at the firm, yet he gives everyone orders, a case of the tail wagging the dog.*

take See CAN TAKE IT WITH ONE, GIVE-AND TAKE, GIVE ONE AN INCH AND HE WILL TAKE A MILE, GIVE OR TAKE, SIT UP AND TAKE NOTICE.

take aback See TAKEN BACK.

take a back seat *v. phr., informal* To accept a poorer or lower position; be second to something or someone else. ◆*During the war all manufacturing had to take a back seat to military needs.* ◆*She does not have to take a back seat to any singer alive.* Compare PLAY SECOND FIDDLE.

take a bath *v. phr., informal* To come to financial ruin. ◆*Boy, did we ever take a bath on that merger with Brown & Brown, Inc.*

take a bow *v. phr.* To stand up or come on a stage to be clapped for or praised for success. ◆*The audience shouted for the author of the play to take a bow.* ◆*The basketball team should take a bow for fine work this season.*

take a break *v. phr.* To have a brief rest period during the course of one's work. ◆*"You've worked hard. It's time to take a break," the boss said.*

take a chance *v. phr.* To accept the risk of failure or loss ◆*We will take a chance on the weather and have the party outdoors.*

take a crack at *v. phr.* To try doing something. ◆*It was a difficult challenge to reorganize our antiquated campus, but the resident architect decided to take a crack at it.*

take a dig at *v. phr.* To attack verbally; offend; denigrate. ◆*If you keep taking digs at me all the time, our relationship will be a short one.*

take a dim view of *v. phr.* **1.** To have doubts about; feel unsure or anxious about. ◆*Tom took a dim view of his chances of passing the exam.* ◆*Betty hoped to go on a picnic, but she took a dim view of the weather.* **2.** To be against; disapprove. ◆*John's father took a dim view of his wanting to borrow the car.* ◆*The teacher took a dim view of the class's behavior.*

take a dislike to Contrast TAKE A FANCY TO.

take a drop *v. phr.* **1.** To indulge in alcoholic drinks. ◆*Aunt Liz doesn't really drink; she just takes a drop every now and then.* **2.** To lose value; decrease in price. ◆*Stocks took a big drop yesterday due to the international crisis.*

take advantage of *v. phr.* **1.** To make good use of. ♦ *The cat took advantage of the high grass to creep up on the bird.* ♦ *Jean took advantage of the lunch hour to finish her homework.* **2.** To treat (someone) unfairly for your own gain or help; make unfair use of. ♦ *He took advantage of his friend's kindness.* ♦ *The little children did not know how much to pay for the candy, and Ralph took advantage of them.* Syn. IMPOSE ON.

take after *v.* To be like because of family relationship; to have the same looks or ways as (a parent or ancestor). ♦ *He takes after his father in mathematical ability.* ♦ *She takes after her father's side of the family in looks.* Compare LIKE FATHER, LIKE SON; RUN IN THE FAMILY.

take a fancy to *v. phr.* To become fond of; cultivate a predilection for. ♦ *Aunt Hermione has taken a fancy to antique furniture.*

take a flop *v. phr.* To fall heavily. ♦ *I took a nasty flop on the ice-covered sidewalk.*

take aim *v. phr.* To get ready to hit, throw at, or shoot at by sighting carefully. ♦ *When the captain orders "Take aim," raise your gun to your shoulder and sight along the barrel at the target.* ♦ *Before the hunter could take aim, the deer jumped out of sight.*

take a hand in *v. phr.* To assist in the direction of; participate. ♦ *The University Faculty Club decided to take a hand in helping the recent refugees.*

take a hard line with See HARD LINE, HARD-LINER.

take a hike See GO FLY A KITE.

take a hint *v. phr.* To understand an allusion or a suggestion and behave accordingly. ♦ *"I don't like people who smoke," she said. "Can't you take a hint and either quit smoking or seeing me?"*

take a joke *v. phr.* Accept in good spirit some derision directed at oneself. ♦ *My brother has a good sense of humor when teasing others, but he cannot take a joke on himself.*

take a liking to See TAKE A FANCY TO.

take a load off one's feet *v. phr.* To alleviate one's fatigue by sitting down during some taxing work. ♦ *"You've been standing there for hours, Jake,"* John said. *"Why don't you take a load off your feet?"*

take a long breath See DRAW A LONG BREATH.

take amiss *or* **the wrong way** *v. phr.* To become offended due to a misunderstanding. ♦ *"I hope you won't take it amiss," the boss said to Jane, "that I find you irresistibly attractive."*

take a new turn *v. phr.* To start a new course; decide upon a new direction. ♦ *The company took a new turn under Jack's directorship.*

take a nose dive *v. phr.* To plummet; fall sharply. ♦ *The stock market took a nose dive after the news of the President's heart attack.*

take a notion See TAKE INTO ONE'S HEAD.

take apart *v. phr.* To dismantle; disassemble. ♦ *Boys like taking radios and watches apart, but they seldom know how to put them back together again.*

take a poke at See TAKE A PUNCH AT.

take a pot shot at See POTSHOT.

take a powder *v. phr., slang* To leave hurriedly; run out or away; desert, flee. ♦ *All the gang except one had taken a powder when the police arrived.*

take a punch at *or* **take a poke at** *or* **take a sock at** *v. phr.* To try to hit (someone) with the fist; swing or strike at; attack with the fists. ♦ *Bob was very angry and suddenly he took a punch at Fred.* ♦ *Johnny knocked my hat off, so I took a poke at him.* ♦ *I felt like taking a sock at Joe, but I kept my temper.*

take a risk See RUN A RISK.

take a shine to *v. phr., slang* To have or show a quick liking for. ♦ *He took a shine to his new teacher the very first day.* Compare TAKE A FANCY TO.

take a shot at *v. phr.* To try casually; attempt to do. ♦ *"Can you handle all these new book orders?" Tom asked. "I haven't done it before," Sally replied, "but I can sure take a shot at it."*

take a sock at See TAKE A PUNCH AT.

take a spill *v. phr.* To fall down; tip over. ♦ *During the harsh winter, when the sidewalk is covered with ice, many people take a spill.*

take at one's word *v. phr.* To believe everything (someone) says; to act on what is said. ♦ *If you say you don't want this coat, I'll take you at your* word and throw it away. ♦ *When the king said he wished to be rid of his advisor, a friend took him at his word and murdered the councillor.*

take a stand *v. phr.* To assert one's point of view; declare one's position. ♦ *It is time for American society to take a stand against crime.*

take a turn *v. phr.* To become different; change. ♦ *Mary's fever suddenly took a bad turn.* ♦ *The story took an odd turn.* Often used with *for the better* or *for the worse.* ♦ *In the afternoon the weather took a turn for the better.* ♦ *Suddenly the battle took a turn for the worse.*

take a turn for the better *v. phr.* To start improving; start to get better. ♦ *Aunt Hermione was very ill for a long time, but last week she suddenly took a turn for the better.*

take a turn for the worse See FOR THE WORSE. Contrast TAKE A TURN FOR THE BETTER.

take a whack at See TAKE A SHOT AT.

take back *v.* To change or deny something offered, promised, or stated; admit to making a wrong statement. ♦ *I take back my offer to buy the house now that I've had a good look at it.* ♦ *I want you to take back the unkind things you said about Kenneth.*

take by storm *v. phr.* **1.** To capture by a sudden or very bold attack. ♦ *The army did not hesitate. They took the town by storm.* **2.** To win the favor or liking of; make (a group of people) like or believe you. ♦ *The comic took the audience by storm.* ♦ *John gave Jane so much attention that he took her by storm, and she said she would marry him.* Compare MAKE A HIT.

take by surprise *v. phr.* **1.** To appear in front of someone suddenly or to suddenly discover him before he discovers you; come before (someone) is ready; appear before (someone) unexpectedly. ♦ *The policeman took the burglar by surprise as he opened the window.* ♦ *When Mrs. Green's dinner guests came half an hour early, they took her by surprise.* **2.** To fill with surprise or amazement; astonish. ♦ *Ellen was taken by surprise when the birthday cake was brought in.* ♦ *When our teacher quit in the middle of the year to work for the government, it took us all by surprise.*

take by the scruff *v. phr.* **1.** To assert authority over a person. ♦ *Tim's mother took him by the scruff and told him to get cleaned up.* **2.** To punish a person. ♦ *The boss took us by the scruff when he found us chatting idly by the coffee machine.* **3.** To assume firm control over a job or a situation that has been causing some difficulty. ♦ *Someone had better take the post office by the scruff; there are too many customer complaints pouring in.*

take care *v. phr.* To be careful; use wisdom or caution. ♦ *Take care that you don't spill that coffee!* ♦ *We must take care to let nobody hear about this.*

take care of *v. phr.* **1.** To attend to; supply the needs of. ♦ *She stayed home to take care of the baby.* Syn. KEEP AN EYE ON 2, LOOK AFTER. Compare IN CHARGE 2. **2.** *informal* To deal with; do what is needed with. ♦ *I will take care of that letter.* ♦ *The coach told Jim to take care of the opposing player.* Compare SEE TO.

take charge *v. phr.* To begin to lead or control; take control or responsibility; undertake the care or management (of persons or things). ♦ *When Mrs. Jackson was in the hospital, her sister took charge of the Jackson children until Mrs. Jackson could care for them.* ♦ *The child care class gave a party for the nursery children, and Mary took charge of the games.* ♦ *John was elected the new president of the club and took charge at the next meeting.* ♦ *Bob is a natural leader, and can take charge in an emergency.* Compare IN CHARGE 2.

take cold See CATCH COLD.

take cover *v. phr.* To seek shelter or protection. ♦ *The rain began so suddenly that we had to take cover in a doorway.*

take down *v.* **1.** To write or record (what is said). ♦ *I will tell you how to get to the place; you had better take it down.* **2.** To pull to pieces; take apart. ♦ *It will be a big job to take that tree down.* ♦ *In the evening the campers put up a tent, and the next morning they took it down.* **3.** *informal* To reduce the pride or spirit of; humble. ♦ *Bob thought he was a good wrestler, but Henry took him down.* Syn. TAKE DOWN A NOTCH.

take down a notch *or* **take down a peg** *v. phr., informal* To make (someone) less proud or sure of himself. ♦ *The team was feeling proud of its record, but last week the boys were taken down a peg by a bad defeat.*

take effect *v. phr.* **1.** To have an unexpected or intended result; cause a change. ♦ *It was nearly an hour before the sleeping pill took effect.* **2.** To become lawfully right, or operative. ♦ *The new tax law will not take effect until January.*

take exception to *v. phr.* To speak against; find fault with; be displeased or angered by; criticize. ♦ *There was nothing in the speech that you could take exception to.* ♦ *Did she take exception to my remarks about her cooking.*

take five *v. phr.* To take a five-minute break during some work or theatrical rehearsal. ♦ *"All right, everyone," the director cried. "Let's take five."*

take for *v.* To suppose to be; mistake for. ♦ *Do you take me for a fool?* ♦ *At first sight you would take him for a football player, not a poet.*

take for a ride *v. phr., slang* **1.** To take out in a car intending to murder. ♦ *The gang leader decided that the informer must be taken for a ride.* **2.** To play a trick on; fool. ♦ *The girls told Linda that a movie star was visiting the school, but she did not believe them; she thought they were taking her for a ride.* Compare STRING ALONG. **3.** To take unfair advantage of; fool for your own gain. ♦ *His girlfriend really took him for a ride before he stopped dating her.*

take for granted *v. phr.* **1.** To suppose or understand to be true. ♦ *Mr. Harper took for granted that the invitation included his wife.* ♦ *A teacher cannot take it for granted that students always do their homework.* Compare BEG THE QUESTION. **2.** To accept or become used to (something) without noticing especially or saying anything. ♦ *George took for granted all that his parents did for him.* ♦ *No girl likes to have her boyfriend take her for granted; instead, he should always try to make her like him better.*

take French leave *v. phr.* To leave secretly; abscond. ♦ *The party was so boring that we decided to take French leave.* ♦ *While the Smith family was in Europe, the house-sitter packed up all the silver and took French leave.* See SLIP AWAY.

take heart *v. phr.* To be encouraged; feel braver and want to try. ♦ *The men took heart from their leader's words and went on to win the battle.* ♦ *When we are in trouble we can take heart from the fact that things often seem worse than they are.* Contrast LOSE HEART.

take heed *v. phr., literary* To pay attention; watch or listen carefully; notice. ♦ *Take heed not to spill coffee on the rug.*

take hold of *v. phr.* To grasp. ♦ *The old man tried to keep himself from falling down the stairs, but there was no railing to take hold of.*

take ill *or* **take sick** *v.* To become sick. ♦ *Father took sick just before his birthday.*—Used in the passive with the same meaning. ♦ *The man was taken ill on the train.*

take in *v.* **1.** To include. ♦ *The country's boundaries were changed to take in a piece of land beyond the river.* ♦ *The class of mammals takes in nearly all warm-blooded animals except the birds.* **2.** To go and see; visit. ♦ *The students decided to take in a movie while they were in town.* ♦ *We planned to take in Niagara Falls and Yellowstone Park on our trip.* **3.** To make smaller. ♦ *This waistband is too big; it must be taken in about an inch.* ♦ *They had to take in some sail to keep the ship from turning over in the storm.* **4.** To grasp with the mind; understand. ♦ *He didn't take in what he read because his mind was on something else.* ♦ *He took in the situation at a glance.* **5a.** To deceive; cheat; fool. ♦ *The teacher was taken in by the boy's innocent manner.* Compare PUT OVER, ROPE IN. **5b.** To accept without question; believe. ♦ *The magician did many tricks, and the children took it all in.* **6a.** To receive; get. ♦ *The senior class held a dance to make money and took in over a hundred dollars.* **6b.** Let come in; admit. ♦ *The farmer took in the lost travelers for the night.* ♦ *When her husband died, Mrs. Smith took in boarders.* **7.** To see or hear with interest; pay close attention to. ♦ *When Bill told about his adventures, the other boys took it all in.*

take in stride *v. phr.* To meet happenings without too much surprise; accept good or bad luck and go on. ♦ *He learned to take disappointments in stride.*

take in tow *v. phr.* To take charge of; lead; conduct. ♦ *Brian and Kate took a group of children in tow when they went to see the circus.*

take into account *v. phr.* To remember and understand while judging someone or something; consider. ♦ *How much time will we need to get to the lake? You have to take the bad road into account.* ♦ *His acting in the play was remarkable, taking into account his youth and inexperience.* Syn. RECKON WITH. Contrast LEAVE OUT OF ACCOUNT.

take issue with *v. phr.* To be openly against; speak against; disagree with. ♦ *He thought his boss was wrong but was afraid to take issue with him on the matter.*

take it *v. phr.* **1.** To get an idea or impression; understand from what is said or done.— Usually used with *I.* ♦ *I take it from your silence that you don't want to go.* **2.** *informal* To bear trouble, hard work, criticism; not give up or weaken. ♦ *Henry could criticize and tease other boys, but he couldn't take it himself.* ♦ *Bob lost his job and his girl in the same week, and we all admired the way he took it.*

take it all in *v. phr.* To absorb completely; listen attentively. ♦ *Bill's piano music filled the room and we took it all in with admiration.*

take it away *v. phr., informal* Theatrical expression You're on; it's your turn; you're next. ♦ *And here comes that wonderful comedian, Bob Hope. The announcer said, "Take it away, Bob."*

take it easy *v. phr., informal* **1.** *or* **go easy** *or* **take things easy** To go or act slowly, carefully, and gently.—Often used with *on.* ♦ *Take it easy. The roads are icy.* ♦ *"Go easy," said Billy to the other boys carrying the table down the stairs.* ♦ *"Take it easy on John and don't scold him too much," said Mrs. Jones to Mr. Jones.* ♦ *Go easy on the cake.*

There isn't much left. **2.** *or* **take things easy** To avoid hard work or worry; have an easy time; live in comfort. ♦ *The doctor said that Bob would have to take things easy for awhile after he had his tonsils out.* ♦ *Barbara likes to take it easy.* ♦ *Grandfather will retire from his job next year and take things easy.* ♦ *Mr. Wilson has just made a lot of money and can take things easy now.*

take it from the top *v. phr., informal* Musical and theatrical expression To start again from the beginning. ♦ *The conductor said, "We must try it once again. Take it from the top and watch my baton."*

take it into one's head *or informal* **take a notion** *v. phr.* To get a sudden idea; decide without thinking. ♦ *The boy suddenly took it into his head to leave school and get a job.* ♦ *Grandmother keeps a bag packed so that she can go visiting whenever she takes a notion.*

take it on the chin *v. phr., informal* **1.** To be badly beaten or hurt. ♦ *Our football team really took it on the chin today. They are all bumps and bruises.* ♦ *Mother and I took it on the chin in the card game.* **2.** To accept without complaint something bad that happens to you; accept trouble or defeat calmly. ♦ *A good football player can take it on the chin when his team loses.*

take it or leave it *v. phr., informal* To accept something without change or refuse it; decide yes or no.—Often used like a command. ♦ *He said the price of the house was $10,000, take it or leave it.*

take it out on *v. phr., informal* To be unpleasant or unkind to (someone) because you are angry or upset; get rid of upset feelings by being mean to.— Often used with the name of the feeling instead of "it." ♦ *The teacher was angry and took it out on the class.* ♦ *Bob was angry because Father would not let him use the car, and he took it out on his little brother.*

take its toll *v. phr.* To cause loss or damage. ♦ *The bombs had taken their toll on the little town.* ♦ *The budget cut took its toll of teachers.*

take kindly to *v.* To be pleased by; like.—Usually used in negative, interrogative, and conditional sentences.

♦ *He doesn't take kindly to any suggestions about running his business.* ♦ *Will your father take kindly to the idea of your leaving college?*

take leave of *v. phr.* **1.** To abandon, go away from, or become separated from.—Usually used in the phrase *take leave of one's senses.* ♦ *Come down from the roof, Billy! Have you taken leave of your senses?* **2.** See TAKE ONE'S LEAVE.

take leave of one's senses *v. phr.* To go mad; become crazy. ♦ *"Have you taken leave of your senses?" Jake cried, when he saw Andy swallow a live goldfish.*

take liberties *v. phr.* To act toward in too close or friendly a manner; use as you would use a close friend or something of your own. ♦ *Mary would not let any boy take liberties with her.* ♦ *Bill took liberties with Tom's bicycle.* Compare MAKE FREE WITH.

take lying down *v. phr.* To accept something without defense or protest. ♦ *If you take such insults lying down, you will only encourage more of the same.*

taken aback *also* **taken back** *adj.* Unpleasantly surprised; suddenly puzzled or shocked. ♦ *When he came to pay for his dinner he was taken aback to find that he had left his wallet at home.*

taken by *or* **with** *v. phr.* To be impressed by; intrigued by. ♦ *Ned was much taken by the elegance of Sophie's manners.*

take no stock in See TAKE STOCK IN.

take note of *or* **take notice of** *v. phr.* **1.** To look carefully at; pay close attention to; observe well. ♦ *A detective is trained to take note of people and things.* **2.** To notice and act in response; pay attention. ♦ *Two boys were talking together in the back of the room but the teacher took no notice of them.* ♦ *The principal thanked everyone who helped in the program, and took note of the decorations made by the art class.*

take oath *v. phr.* To promise to tell the truth or to do some task honestly, calling on God or some person or thing as a witness. ♦ *Mary took her oath that she did not steal the watch.* ♦ *John took oath that he would fill the office of president faithfully.*

takeoff *n.* **1.** Departure of an airplane; the act of becoming airborne. ♦ *The nervous passenger was relieved that we had such a wonderfully smooth takeoff.* **2.** Imitation; a parody. ♦ *Vaughn Meader used to do a wonderful takeoff on President Kennedy's speech.*

take off *v. phr.* **1a.** To leave fast; depart suddenly; run away. ♦ *The dog took off after a rabbit.* Compare LIGHT OUT. **1b.** *informal* To go away; leave. ♦ *The six boys got into the car and took off for the drug store.* **2.** To leave on a flight, begin going up. ♦ *A helicopter is able to take off and land straight up or down.* **3.** *informal* To imitate amusingly; copy another person's habitual actions or speech. ♦ *He made a career of taking off famous people for nightclub audiences.* ♦ *At the party, Charlie took off the principal and some of the teachers.* **4.** To take (time) to be absent from work. ♦ *When his wife was sick he took off from work.* ♦ *Bill was tired out so he took the day off.*

take off one's hat to *v. phr.* To give honor, praise, and respect to. ♦ *He is my enemy, but I take off my hat to him for his courage.* Compare HAND IT TO.

take offense at *v. phr.* To become indignant; become angry. ♦ *Why do you always take offense at everything I say?*

take off one's hands *v. phr.* **1.** To abdicate one's responsibility of a person or matter. ♦ *"I am herewith taking my hand off your affairs," Lou's father said. "See how you succeed on your own."* **2.** To buy; relieve someone of something. ♦ *He offered to take my old car off my hands for $350.*

take off the edge See TAKE THE EDGE OFF.

take on *v.* **1.** To receive for carrying; be loaded with. ♦ *A big ship was at the dock taking on automobiles in crates to carry overseas for sale.* ♦ *The bus driver stopped at the curb to take the woman on.* **2.** To begin to have (the look of); take (the appearance of). ♦ *Others joined the fistfight until it took on the look of a riot.* ♦ *After the students put up Christmas decorations, the classroom took on a holiday appearance.* **3a.** To give a job to; hire; employ. ♦ *The factory has opened and is beginning to take on new workers.* Contrast LET GO 4. LET OFF, LET OUT 6. **3b.** To accept in business or a contest. ♦ *The big man took on two opponents at once.* ♦ *After his father died, Bill took on the management of the factory.* ♦ *We knew their football team was bigger and stronger, but we took them on anyway and beat them.* **4.** *informal* To show great excitement, grief, or anger. ♦ *At the news of her husband's death she took on like a madwoman.* Compare CARRY-ON.

take one at one's word *v. phr.* To naively lend credence to what one tells one. ♦ *It's a bad idea to take street vendors at their word in large, crowded cities.*

take one's breath away *v. phr.* To surprise greatly; impress very much; leave speechless with surprise or wonder or delight; astonish. ♦ *The sunset is so beautiful it takes our breath away.* ♦ *His refusal was so unexpected it took my breath away.* Compare CATCH ONE'S BREATH 1.

take one's death of See CATCH ONE'S DEATH OF.

take one's leave *or* **take leave of** *v. phr., formal* To say good-bye and leave. ♦ *He stayed on after most of the guests had taken their leave.* ♦ *The messenger bowed and took leave of the queen.—* **leave-taking** *n.* *The end of school in June is a time of leave-taking.*

take one's life in one's hands *v. phr.* To face great danger or take great risk. ♦ *Driving that car with those worn tires would be taking your life in your hands.* ♦ *He took his life in his hands when he tried to capture the wild horse.*

take one's measure *or* **take the measure of** *v. phr.* To judge the character, quality, or nature of; try to guess about something—how hard or easy, dangerous or safe, good or bad, etc. ♦ *The boxers sparred for a while taking each other's measure.* ♦ *John took the measure of the cliff before he climbed it.* Compare SIZE UP.

take one's medicine *v. phr.* To accept punishment without complaining. ♦ *The boy said he was sorry he broke the window and was ready to take his medicine.* Compare FACE THE MUSIC 2.

take one's name in vain *v. phr.* **1.** To call upon (God) as a witness to your truth or honesty when you are lying; swear by (God) untruthfully. ♦ *You shall not*

take the name of the Lord your God in vain. **2.** *informal* To talk about a person or mention his name. ♦ *"Did I hear someone taking my name in vain?" asked Bill as he joined his friends.*

take one's time *v. phr.* To avoid haste; act in an unhurried way. ♦ *He liked to take his time over breakfast.* ♦ *It is better to take your time at this job than to hurry and make mistakes.*

take one's word *v. phr.* To believe one's promise. ♦ *Herb took Eric's word when he promised to pay up his debt.*

take on faith *v. phr.* To lend credence to something due to one's confidence in the source, rather than based on evidence. ♦ *One should never take on faith what one hears about Washington politics.*

take on oneself *or* **take upon oneself** *v. phr.* **1.** To accept as a duty or responsibility. ♦ *He took it on himself to see that the packages were delivered.* **2.** To assume wrongfully or without permission as a right or privilege. ♦ *You should not have taken it upon yourself to accept the invitation for the whole family.*

take one wrong See GET ONE WRONG.

take on the chin *v. phr.* To gracefully accept criticism. ♦ *It's good to be able to tell people what they do wrong, but it is equally important to be able to take it on the chin when they tell you what you have done wrong.*

take out *v. phr.* **1.** To ask for and fill in. ♦ *Mary and John took out a marriage license.* **2.** To begin to run. ♦ *When the window broke, the boys took out in all directions.* ♦ *When the wind blew the man's hat off, Charlie took out after it.* See TAKE IT OUT ON.

take out after *v. phr.* To start pursuing one. ♦ *The watchdog took out after the burglars.*

take out on *v. phr.* To vent one's sadness, frustration, or anger on someone who is usually innocent of the problem at hand. ♦ *"Why are you always taking out your frustrations on me?" Jane asked Tom, when he slammed the door.*

take-out order *n. phr.* An order in a restaurant that one does not eat on the premises, but takes home. ♦ *The new Chinese restaurant on the corner sells* *nice take-out orders.*

take over *v.* **1a.** To take control or possession of. ♦ *He expects to take over the business when his father retires.* **1b.** To take charge or responsibility. ♦ *The airplane pilot fainted and his co-pilot had to take over.* **2.** To borrow, imitate, or adopt. ♦ *The Japanese have taken over many European ways of life.*

take pains *v. phr.* To do something very carefully and thoroughly. ♦ *She had taken pains to see that her guests had everything that they could possibly want.* ♦ *She always takes pains with her appearance.*

take part *v. phr.* To have a part or share; join. ♦ *Jim saw the new boy watching the game and asked him to take part.* ♦ *The Swiss did not take part in the two World Wars.*

take pity on *also* **take pity upon** *v. phr.* To feel sympathy or pity and do something for. ♦ *Mary took pity on the orphan kittens.* ♦ *The farmer took pity upon the campers, and let them stay in his barn during the rain.*

take place *v. phr.* To happen; occur. ♦ *The accident took place only a block from his home.* ♦ *The action of the play takes place in ancient Rome.* ♦ *The dance will take place after the graduation exercises.* Compare GO ON 3.

take potluck *v. phr.* To share as a guest an everyday meal without special preparation. ♦ *You are welcome to stay for dinner if you will take potluck.* ♦ *They were about to have lunch when he phoned and they asked him to take potluck with them.*

take root *v. phr.* **1.** To form roots so as to be able to live and grow. ♦ *We hope the transplanted apple trees will take root.* **2.** To be accepted; to be adopted; to live and succeed in a new place. ♦ *Many European customs failed to take root in the New World.* ♦ *The immigrants to our country took root and began to think of themselves as Native Americans.*

take shape *v. phr.* To grow or develop into a certain fixed form. ♦ *Plans for our vacation are beginning to take shape.* ♦ *Their new home took shape as the weeks went by.* Compare SHAPE UP.

take sick See TAKE ILL.

take sides *v. phr.* To join one group against another in a debate or quarrel. ♦ *Switzerland refused to take sides in the two World Wars.* ♦ *Tom wanted to go fishing. Dick wanted to take a hike. Bob took sides with Tom so they all went fishing.* Compare LINE UP 4b. Contrast ON THE FENCE.

take someone for a ride *v. phr., informal* **1.** To cheat or swindle someone. ♦ *Poor Joe Catwallender was taken for a ride.* **2.** To kill someone after kidnapping. ♦ *The criminals took the man for a ride.*

take steps *v. phr.* To begin to make plans or arrangements; make preparations; give orders.—Usually used with *to* and an infinitive. ♦ *The city is taking steps to replace its streetcars with busses.*

take stock *v. phr.* **1.** To count exactly the items of merchandise or supplies in stock; take inventory. ♦ *The grocery store took stock every week on Monday mornings.* **2.** To study carefully a situation, or a number of possibilities or opportunities. ♦ *During the battle the commander paused to take stock of the situation.* Compare SIZE UP.

take stock in *v. phr., informal* To have faith in; trust; believe.—Usually used in the negative. ♦ *He took no stock in the idea that women were better cooks than men.* ♦ *They took little or no stock in the boy's story that he had lost the money.* ♦ *Do you take any stock in the gossip about Joan?*

take the bit in one's mouth *also* **take the bit in one's teeth** *adv. phr.* To have your own way; take charge of things; take control of something. ♦ *When Mary wanted something, she was likely to take the bit in her teeth and her parents could do nothing with her.* Compare TAKE THE BULL BY THE HORNS, TAKE THE LAW INTO ONE'S OWN HANDS.

take the bread out of one's mouth *v. phr.* To take away or not give your rightful support, especially through selfish pleasure. ♦ *She accused her husband of drinking and gambling—taking bread out of his children's mouths.*

take the bull by the horns *v. phr., informal* To take definite action and not care about risks; act bravely in a difficulty. ♦ *He decided to take the bull* *by the horns and demand a raise in salary even though it might cost him his job.* Compare TAKE THE BIT IN ONE'S MOUTH, TAKE THE LAW INTO ONE'S OWN HANDS.

take the cake *v. phr., slang* **1.** To take the first prize; be the best; rank first. ♦ *Mr. Jones takes the cake as a story-teller.* **2.** To be the limit; to be the worst; have a lot of nerve; be a very rude, bold, or surprising action. ♦ *I let Jack borrow my baseball and he never gave it back. Doesn't that take the cake?* ♦ *For being absent-minded, Mr. Smith takes the cake.* Compare BEAT ALL.

take the day off See DAY OFF.

take the defensive Contrast TAKE THE OFFENSIVE.

take the edge off *also* **take off the edge** *v. phr.* To lessen, weaken, soften or make dull. ♦ *Eating a candy bar before dinner has taken the edge off Becky's appetite.* ♦ *Bob was sorry for hurting Tom and that took the edge off Tom's anger.* ♦ *A headache took the edge off Dick's pleasure in the movie.*

take the fifth *v. phr., informal* **1.** Taking refuge behind the Fifth Amendment of the Constitution of the United States which guarantees any witness the right not to incriminate himself while testifying at a trial. ♦ *Alger Hiss took the Fifth when asked whether he was a member of the Communist Party.* **2.** Not to answer any question in an informal setting. ♦ *Have you been married before?—I take the Fifth.*

take the floor *v. phr.* To get up and make a speech in a meeting. ♦ *The audience became very attentive the moment the president took the floor.*

take the law into one's own hands *v. phr.* To protect one's supposed rights or punish a suspected wrongdoer without reference to a court.—An overused expression. ♦ *When the men of the settlement caught the suspected murderer, they took the law into their own hands and hanged him to a tree.* ♦ *His farm was going to be sold for taxes, but he took the law into his own hands and drove the sheriff away with a shotgun.* Compare LAW UNTO ONESELF, TAKE THE BIT IN ONE'S MOUTH.

take the lid off *v. phr.* **1.** To let out in the open; divulge. ♦ *It's about time to*

take the lid off the question of how many prisoners of war are still in enemy hands. **2.** To start to face an issue. ♦ *"The best way to deal with your divorce," the doctor said to Fran "is to take the lid off of it."* Compare BLOW THE LID OFF, LET THE CAT OUT OF THE BAG.

take the measure of See TAKE ONE'S MEASURE.

take the offensive *v. phr.* To make one-self the attacking party. ♦ *After many months of preparation, the freedom fighters were ready to take the offensive.* Contrast TAKE THE DEFENSIVE.

take the pledge *v. phr.* To swear to give up drinking, smoking, or using drugs. ♦ *Gary finally took the pledge and he has kept it thus far.*

take the plunge *v. phr.* To take a fatal or decisive step; venture. ♦ *When I asked Don when he and Melissa were going to get married, he answered that they'll take the plunge in September.*

take the rap *v. phr., slang* To receive punishment; to be accused and punished. ♦ *All of the boys took apples, but only John took the rap.* ♦ *Joe took the burglary rap for his brother and went to prison for two years.*

take the stand *v. phr.* To assume one's position in the witness box during a trial. ♦ *The judge asked the defendant to take the stand.*

take the starch out of *v. phr., informal* **1.** To make (someone) feel weak or tired. ♦ *The hot weather took the starch out of Mrs. Jones, and she didn't feel like doing a thing.* ♦ *The cross-country run took all the starch out of the boys.* **2.** See TAKE THE WIND OUT OF ONE'S SAILS.

take the stump *or* **take to the stump** *v. phr.* To travel around to different places making political speeches. ♦ *The men running for president took to the stump to attract votes.*

take the trouble See GO TO THE TROUBLE.

take the wind out of one's sails *v. phr.* To surprise someone by doing better or by catching him in an error. ♦ *John came home boasting about the fish he had caught; it took the wind out of his sails when he found his little sister had caught a bigger one.* ♦ *Dick took the* *wind out of Bob's sails by showing him where he was wrong.* Compare TAKE THE STARCH OUT OF 2.

take the words out of one's mouth *v. phr.* To say what another is just going to say; to put another's thought into words. ♦ *"Let's go to the beach tomorrow." "You took the words right out of my mouth; I was thinking of that."* ♦ *I was going to suggest a movie, but she took the words out of my mouth and said she would like to see one.*

take things easy See TAKE IT EASY 2.

take time off See TIME OFF; Compare DAY OFF.

take time out See TIME OUT.

take to *v.* **1.** To go to or into; get yourself quickly to.—Often used in the imperative. ♦ *Take to the hills! The bandits are coming!* ♦ *We took to the woods during the day so no one would see us.* ♦ *Take to the boats! The ship is sinking.* ♦ *We stopped at a hotel for the night but took to the road again the next morning.* **2.** To begin the work or job of; make a habit of. ♦ *He took to repairing watches in his spare time.* ♦ *She took to knitting when she got older.* ♦ *Grandfather took to smoking cigars when he was young and he still smokes them.* ♦ *Uncle Willie took to drink while he was a sailor.* ♦ *The cat took to jumping on the table at mealtime.* **3.** To learn easily; do well at. ♦ *Father tried to teach John to swim, but John didn't take to it.* ♦ *Mary takes to mathematics like a duck takes to water.* **4.** To like at first meeting; be pleased by or attracted to; accept quickly. ♦ *Our dog always takes to children quickly.* ♦ *Mary didn't take kindly to the new rule that her mother made of being home at 6 o'clock.*

take to heart *also* **lay to heart** *v. phr.* To be seriously affected by; to feel deeply. ♦ *He took his brother's death very much to heart.* ♦ *He took his friend's advice to heart.*

take to one's heels *also* **show a clean pair of heels** *v. phr.* To begin to run or run away. *When he heard the police coming, the thief took to his heels.*

take to task *v. phr.* To reprove or scold for a fault or error. ♦ *He took his wife to task for her foolish wastefulness.* ♦ *The principal took Bill to task for*

breaking the window.

take to the cleaners *v. phr., slang* **1.** To win all the money another person has (as in poker). ♦ *Watch out if you play poker with Joe; he'll take you to the cleaners.* **2.** To cheat a person out of his money and possessions by means of a crooked business transaction or other means of dishonest conduct. ♦ *I'll never forgive myself for becoming associated with Joe; he took me to the cleaners.*

take to the woods *v. phr., informal* To run away and hide. ♦ *When John saw the girls coming, he took to the woods.* ♦ *Bob took to the woods so he would not have to mow the grass.* Compare HEAD FOR THE HILLS.

take turns *v. phr.* To do something one after another instead of doing it all at the same time. ♦ *In class we should not talk all at the same time; we should take turns.* ♦ *Jean and Beth took turns on the swing.* ♦ *The two boys took turns at digging the hole.* ♦ *The three men took turns driving so one would not be too tired.*

take under one's wing See UNDER ONE'S WING.

take up *v.* **1.** To remove by taking in. ♦ *Use a blotter to take up the spilled ink.* ♦ *When the vacuum cleaner bag is full, it will not take up dirt from the rug.* **2.** To fill or to occupy. ♦ *All his evenings were taken up with study.* ♦ *The oceans take up the greater part of the earth's surface.* ♦ *The mayor has taken up residence on State Street.* **3.** To gather together; collect. ♦ *We are taking up a collection to buy flowers for John because he is in the hospital.* **4.** To take away. ♦ *John had his driver's license taken up for speeding.* **5a.** To begin; start. ♦ *The teacher took up the lesson where she left off yesterday.* **5b.** To begin to do or learn; go into as a job or hobby. ♦ *He recently took up gardening.* ♦ *He took up the carpenter's trade as a boy.* Compare GO INTO 3, GO IN FOR, TAKE TO. **6.** To pull and make tight or shorter; shorten. ♦ *The tailor took up the legs of the trousers.* ♦ *Take up the slack on the rope!* Compare TAKE IN 3. **7.** To take or accept something that is offered. ♦ *The boss offered me a $5 raise and I took him up.* ♦ *I took John* *up on his bet.* Compare JUMP AT.

take up arms   *v. phr., literary.* To get ready to fight; fight or make war. ♦ *The people were quick to take up arms to defend their freedom.* ♦ *The President called on people to take up arms against poverty.* Contrast LAY DOWN ONE'S ARMS.

take upon oneself   See TAKE ON ONESELF.

take up the cudgels for   *v. phr., literary* To come to the defense of; to support or fight for. ♦ *He was the first to take up the cudgels for his friend.* Compare STAND UP FOR.

take up with   *v.* To begin to go around with (someone); see a lot of. ♦ *Frank has taken up with Lucy lately.*

take with a grain of salt *also* **take with a pinch of salt**   *v. phr.* To accept or believe only in part; not accept too much. ♦ *A man who says he is not a candidate for President should usually have his statement taken with a grain of salt.* ♦ *We took Uncle George's stories of the war with a pinch of salt.*

taking pictures   *v. phr., slang, citizen's band radio jargon* To use a radar-operated speed indicator in order to enforce the 55 MPH speed limit. ♦ *The Smokeys are taking pictures!*

tale   See TELL TALES OUT OF SCHOOL.

talent scout   *n. phr.* A person employed by a large organization to seek out promising and gifted individuals. ♦ *Gordon has been working as a talent scout for a television program.* Compare HEAD HUNTING 2.

talent show   *n.* An entertainment in which new entertainers try to win a prize. ♦ *Mary won the talent show by her dancing.* ♦ *The people liked Bill's singing in the talent show.*

talk   See DOUBLE-TALK, PEP TALK, SALES TALK, SWEET TALK.

talk a blue streak   *v. phr., informal* To talk on and on, usually very fast. ♦ *Sue is a nice girl but after one drink she talks a blue streak and won't stop.*

talk back *also* **answer back** *v., informal* To answer rudely; reply in a disrespectful way; be fresh. ♦ *When the teacher told the boy to sit down, he talked back to her and said she couldn't make him.* ♦ *Mary talked back when her mother told her to stop watching*

television; she said, "I don't have to if I don't want to." ♦ *Russell was going somewhere with some bad boys, when his father told him it was wrong, Russell answered him back, "Mind your own business."*

talk big   *v., informal* To talk boastfully; brag. ♦ *He talks big about his pitching, but he hasn't won a game.*

talk down   *v.* **1.** To make (someone) silent by talking louder or longer. ♦ *Sue tried to give her ideas, but the other girls talked her down.* Compare SHOUT DOWN **2.** To use words or ideas that are too easy. ♦ *The speaker talked down to the students, and they were bored.*

talking book   *n.* A book recorded by voice on phonograph records for blind people. ♦ *Billy, who was blind, learned history from a talking book.*

talking point   *n.* Something good about a person or thing that can be talked about in selling it. ♦ *The streamlined shape of the car was one of its talking points.* ♦ *John tried to get Mary to date Bill. One of his talking points was that Bill was captain of the football team.*

talk in circles   *v. phr.* To waste time by saying words that don't mean very much. ♦ *After three hours at the negotiating table, the parties decided to call it quits because they realized that they had been talking in circles.*

talk into   *v.* **1.** To get (someone) to agree to; make (someone) decide on (doing something) by talking; persuade to.— Used with a verbal noun. ♦ *Bob talked us into walking home with him.* Compare TALK OVER 2. Contrast TALK OUT OF. **2.** To cause to be in or to get into by talking. ♦ *You talked us into this mess. Now get us out!* ♦ *Mr. Jones lost the customer in his store by arguing with him. "You'll talk us into the poor house yet!" said Mrs. Jones.* Contrast TALK OUT OF.

talk of the town   *n. phr.* Something that has become so popular or prominent that everyone is discussing it. ♦ *Even after three decades, Picasso's famous metal statue is still the talk of the town in Chicago.*

talk out   *v.* To talk all about and leave nothing out; discuss until everything is agreed on; settle. ♦ *After their quarrel,*

Jill and John talked things out and reached full agreement.

talk out of *v.* **1.** To persuade not to; make agree or decide not to.—Used with a verbal noun. ♦ *Mary's mother talked her out of quitting school.* Contrast TALK INTO. **2.** To allow to go or get out by talking; let escape by talking. ♦ *Johnny is good at talking his way out of trouble.* Contrast TALK INTO.

talk out of turn See SPEAK OUT OF TURN.

talk over *v.* **1.** To talk together about; try to agree about or decide by talking; discuss. ♦ *Tom talked his plan over with his father before he bought the car.* ♦ *The boys settled their argument by talking it over.* **2.** To persuade; make agree or willing; talk and change the mind of. ♦ *Fred is trying to talk Bill over to our side.* Compare TALK INTO.

talk rot *v. phr.* To say silly things; talk nonsense. ♦ *He's talking rot when he says that our company is almost bankrupt.*

talk shop *v. phr., informal* To talk about things in your work or trade. ♦ *Two chemists were talking shop, and I hardly understood a word they said.*

talk through one's hat *v. phr., informal* To say something without knowing or understanding the facts; talk foolishly or ignorantly. ♦ *John said that the earth is nearer the sun in summer, but the teacher said he was talking through his hat.*

talk turkey *v. phr., informal* To talk about something in a really businesslike way; talk with the aim of getting things done. ♦ *Charles said, "Now, let's talk turkey about the bus trip. The fact is, it will cost each student $1.50."* ♦ *The father always spoke gently to his son, but when the son broke the windshield of the car, the father talked turkey to him.*

talk up *v.* **1.** To speak in favor or support of. ♦ *Let's talk up the game and get a big crowd.* **2.** To speak plainly or clearly. ♦ *The teacher asked the student to talk up.* Syn. SPEAK UP. **3.** *informal* To say what you want or think; say what someone may not like. ♦ *Talk up if you want more pie.* ♦ *George isn't afraid to talk up when he disagrees with the teacher.* Syn. SPEAK UP. Compare SPEAK OUT.

tall order See LARGE ORDER.

tall story *or* **tale** *n. phr.* See FISH STORY.

tamper with *v.* **1.** To meddle with (something); handle ignorantly or foolishly. ♦ *He tampered with the insides of his watch and ruined it.* **2.** To secretly get someone to do or say wrong things, especially by giving him money, or by threatening to hurt him. ♦ *A friend of the man being tried in court tampered with a witness.*

tank See THINK TANK.

tan one's hide *v. phr., informal* To give a beating to; spank hard. ♦ *Bob's father tanned his hide for staying out too late.*

tape See FRICTION TAPE, MASKING TAPE.

taper down *adj. phr.* To decrease; reduce. ♦ *He has tapered down his drinking from three martinis to one beer a day.*

taper off *v.* **1.** To come to an end little by little; become smaller toward the end. ♦ *The river tapers off here and becomes a brook.* **2.** To stop a habit gradually; do something less and less often. ♦ *Robert gave up smoking all at once instead of tapering off.* Contrast COLD TURKEY.

tar See BEAT THE ——— OUT OF.

tar and feather *v.* To pour heated tar on and cover with feathers as a punishment. ♦ *In the Old West bad men were sometimes tarred and feathered and driven out of town.*

task See TAKE TO TASK.

taste See LEAVE A BAD TASTE IN ONE'S MOUTH.

tat See TIT FOR TAT.

tax trap *n., informal* Predicament in which taxpayers in middle-income brackets are required to pay steeply progressive rates of taxation as their earnings rise with inflation but their personal exemptions remain fixed, resulting in a loss of real disposable income. ♦ *Everybody in my neighborhood has been caught in a tax trap.*

T-bone steak *n.* A steak with a bone in it which looks like a "T". ♦ *On Jim's birthday we had T-bone steak for supper.*

tea See CUP OF TEA *also* DISH OF TEA.

teach a lesson *v. phr.* To show that bad behavior can be harmful. ♦ *When Johnny pulled Mary's hair, she taught*

him a lesson by breaking his toy boat.
♦ *The burns Tommy got from playing with matches taught him a lesson.*

teach the ropes See THE ROPES.

team up with *v. phr.* To join with; enter into companionship with. ♦ *My brother prefers to do business by himself rather than to team up with anybody else.*

teapot See TEMPEST IN A TEAPOT.

tear around *v. phr.* To be constantly on the go; dash around. ♦ *No one can understand how she manages to tear around from one social event to another and yet be a good mother to her children.*

tear down *v.* **1.** To take all down in pieces; destroy. ♦ *The workmen tore down the old house and built a new house in its place.* **2.** To take to pieces or parts. ♦ *The mechanics had to tear down the engine, and fix it, and put it together again.* **3.** To say bad things about; criticize. ♦ *"Why do you always tear people down? Why don't you try to say nice things about them?"* ♦ *Dorothy doesn't like Sandra, and at the class meeting she tore down every idea Sandra suggested.*

tear into *v. phr.* To attack vigorously, physically or verbally. ♦ *The anxious buyers tore into the wedding gowns on sale at the famous department store.* See RIP INTO.

tearjerker *n.* A sentimental novel or movie that makes one cry. ♦ *Love Story,* both in its novel form and as a movie, *was a famous tearjerker.*

tear oneself away *v. phr.* To force oneself to leave; leave reluctantly. ♦ *The beaches in Hawaii are so lovely that I had to tear myself away from them in order to get back to my job in Chicago.*

tear one's hair *v. phr.* To show sorrow, anger, or defeat. ♦ *Ben tore his hair when he saw the wrecked car.* ♦ *The teacher tore his hair at the boy's stupid answer.* ♦ *It was time to go to class, but Mary had not finished the report she had to give, and she began tearing her hair.*

tears See BORE TO TEARS, CROCODILE TEARS.

tear up *v.* **1.** To dig a hole in; remove the surface of; remove from the surface. ♦ *The city tore up the street to lay a new water pipe.* ♦ *Mother tore up the car-*

peting in the living room and had a new rug put in. **2.** To tear into pieces. ♦ *Mary tore up the old sheets and made costumes for the play out of the pieces.* ♦ *John tore up his test paper so that his mother wouldn't see his low grade.*

tee off *v.* **1.** To hit the golf ball from a small wooden peg or tee to begin play for each hole. ♦ *We got to the golf course just in time to see the champion tee off.* **2.** *slang* To hit a ball, especially a baseball very hard or far. ♦ *He teed off on the first pitch.* **3.** *slang* To attack vigorously. ♦ *The governor teed off on his opponent's speech.* **4.** *slang* To make (someone) angry or disgusted. ♦ *It teed me off when Billy stole my candy.* ♦ *Joe was teed off because he had to wait so long.*

teeth See TOOTH.

tee up *v.* To set the golf ball on the tee in preparation for hitting it toward the green. ♦ *Arnold Palmer teed the ball up for the final hole.*

telepathy See MENTAL TELEPATHY.

tell See DO TELL, I'LL SAY *or* I TELL YOU, I'LL TELL YOU WHAT, I'M TELLING YOU, YOU'RE TELLING ME, YOU TELL 'EM.

tell apart *v. phr.* To see the difference between; know each of. ♦ *The teacher could not tell the twins apart.*

tell a thing or two *v. phr., informal* To tell in plain or angry words; scold. ♦ *When John complained about the hard work, his father told him a thing or two.* ♦ *If Bert thinks he would like to join the army, I'll tell him a thing or two that will make him change his mind.* Compare BAWL OUT, GIVE A PIECE OF ONE'S MIND, TELL OFF, THING OR TWO.

tell it like it is *v. phr., slang, informal* To be honest, sincere; to tell the truth. ♦ *Joe is the leader of our commune; he tells it like it is.*

tell it to the marines *or* **tell it to Sweeney** *slang* I don't believe you; stop trying to fool me. ♦ *John said, "My father knows the President of the United States." Dick answered, "Tell it to the marines."*

tell off *v.* **1.** To name or count one by one and give some special duty to; give a share to. ♦ *Five boy scouts were told off to clean the camp.* **2.** *informal* To speak to angrily or sharply; attack with words; scold. ♦ *Mr. Black got angry* and told off the boss. ♦ *Bobby kept pulling Sally's hair; finally she got angry and told him where to get off.* Syn. TELL ONE WHERE TO GET OFF. Compare GIVE A PIECE OF ONE'S MIND, LAY DOWN THE LAW, TELL A THING OR TWO.

tell on v. **1.** To tire; wear out; make weak. ♦ *The ten-mile hike told on Bill.* **2.** *informal* To tell someone about another's wrong or naughty acts.— Used mainly by children. ♦ *Andy hit a little girl and John told the teacher on Andy.* ♦ *If you hit me, I'll tell Mother on you.*

tell tales out of school v. phr. To tell something that is secret; tell others something that is not meant to be known. ♦ *Don't tell Jane anything. She is always telling tales out of school.* Compare LET THE CAT OUT OF THE BAG, SPILL THE BEANS.

tell one where to get off *or* **tell one where to head in** v. phr., informal To talk angrily to; speak to or answer with rough language; scold. ♦ *Bob told Ted to get out of his way. Ted told Bob where to get off.* ♦ *Mary laughed at Barbara's hairdo. Barbara told Mary where to head in.* Compare TELL A THING OR TWO, TELL OFF.

tell time v. phr. To read a clock or watch. ♦ *Although Johnny is only three years old, he is already able to tell time.*

tell you what See I'LL TELL YOU WHAT.

temper See GOD TEMPERS THE WIND TO THE SHORN LAMB, HOLD ONE'S TEMPER *or* KEEP ONE'S TEMPER, LOSE ONE'S TEMPER.

temperature See RUN A TEMPERATURE.

tempest in a teapot n. phr. Great excitement about something not important. ♦ *Bess tore her skirt a little and made a tempest in a teapot.*

tempt fate *or* **tempt the fates** v. phr. To take a chance; run a risk; gamble. ♦ *You're tempting fate every time you drive that old wreck of a car.*

ten See DIME STORE *or* FIVE-AND-TEN, COUNT TO TEN.

ten-four? v. phr., interrog., slang, citizen's band radio jargon Do you understand? ♦ *Is that a ten-four?*

ten gallon hat n., informal A tall felt hat with a wide, rolled brim worn by men in the western part of the U.S. ♦ *Men from the southwest usually wear ten gallon hats.*

ten roger v. phr., slang, citizen's band radio jargon I acknowledge. ♦ *That's a ten roger.*

ten to one *or* **two to one** adv. or adj. phr., informal Almost certainly, nearly sure to be true; very likely to happen. ♦ *Ten to one it will rain tomorrow.* ♦ *It is ten to one that Bill will be late.*

term See BRING TO TERMS, COME TO TERMS, IN SO MANY WORDS **2.** *or* IN NO UNCERTAIN TERMS, IN TERMS OF.

terror See HOLY TERROR.

test See ROAD TEST, SCREEN TEST.

tether See END OF ONE'S ROPE *or* END OF ONE'S TETHER.

than See LESS THAN, LESS THAN NO TIME, MORE THAN.

thank one's lucky stars v. phr., informal To be thankful for good luck; think oneself lucky. ♦ *You can thank your lucky stars you didn't fall in the hole.*

thanks to prep. With the help of. ♦ *Thanks to a good teacher, John passed the examination.* ♦ *I finally finished washing the dishes, no thanks to you.* **2.** Owing to; because of. ♦ *Thanks to a sudden rain, the children came home with wet clothes.*

that is *or* **that is to say** I mean; that means; in other words. ♦ *John is a New Yorker; that is, he lives in New York.* ♦ *Susan is a good student; that is to say, she gets good grades in school.*

that is that *or* **that's that** informal The matter is decided; there is nothing more to be said; it is done. ♦ *Jim, you will go to school this morning, and that is that.*

that'll be the day informal That will never happen. ♦ *Joe wanted me to lend him money to take my girl to the movies. That'll be the day!* ♦ *"Wouldn't it be nice if we had to go to school only one day a week?" "That'll be the day!"*

That makes two of us! Informal way to say, "I am in agreement with what you are saying or doing." ♦ *So you voted for Senator Aldridge? So did I—that makes two of us.*

That takes care of that! Informal way to say, "That concludes our business." ♦ *I paid my ex-wife the last alimony check and that takes care of that!*

That will do! Informal expression of

impatience meaning "stop," "no more." ♦ *"That will do, Tommy,"* his *mother cried. "I've had just about enough of your drumming on the table."*

that's ——— **for you** That's the way (someone or something) is; (someone or something) is like that. ♦ *John tried hard, but he lost the game. That's life for you.* ♦ *Mary changed her mind about going. That's a girl for you.*

That's about the size of it! Informal way to say, "What you said is true; the rumor or the news is true." ♦ *"I am told you're leaving our firm for Japan,"* Fred said to Tom. "That's about the size of it," Tom replied with a grin.*

That's the story of my life… Usually spoken when something goes wrong. ♦ *I spent seven years writing a novel, but no publisher wants to accept it. That's the story of my life.*

That's the ticket! Informal way to say, "excellent; correct." ♦ *"First we'll go up the Sears Tower, and then we'll take a night sightseeing tour on the lake,"* Fran said. "That's the ticket!" Stan, an old inhabitant of Chicago, replied.*

That's the way the ball bounces or the cookie crumbles! Nothing unusual about that. Said of unpleasant things. ♦ *"Susan left me for a heavyweight boxer, and then I got drunk and wrecked my car,"* Bob bitterly complained. "Well, that's the way the cookie crumbles," Pam answered philosophically.*

theater See LITTLE THEATER.

the business *n., slang*—Usually used with *give* or *get*. **1.** All that you are able to do; greatest effort. ♦ *Johnny gave the tryouts the business but he failed to make the team.* **2.** The most harm possible; the greatest damage or hurt. ♦ *Fred got the business when Tom caught him with his bicycle.* **3.** A harsh scolding. ♦ *The teacher gave Walter the business when he came to school late again.* ♦ *Mike thought he was the star of the team until he got the business from the coach.* Compare THE WORKS.

The cat did it! A humorous and convenient way to pass the blame. ♦ *"My vase is broken!" Mother shrieked in horror. "Well," Dad smirked cynically, "I guess the cat did it!"*

the creeps *n., informal* **1.** An uncomfortable tightening of the skin caused by fear or shock. ♦ *Reading the story of a ghost gave Joe the creeps.* ♦ *The queer noises in the old house gave Mary the creeps.* **2.** A strong feeling of fear or disgust. ♦ *The cold, damp, lonely swamp gave John the creeps.* ♦ *The dog was so ugly it gave Mary the creeps.*

the devil to pay *n. phr.* A severe penalty. ♦ *If we don't finish the work by next Monday, there will be the devil to pay.*

the edge *n., informal* The advantage.— Usually used in the phrases *get the edge on, have the edge on.* ♦ *In the last quarter of the game, our team got the edge on the other team and kept it.* ♦ *Mary has the edge on Jane in the beauty contest.*

the fickle finger of fate See ACT OF GOD.

the idea *or* **the very idea** *n. phr.*—Used in exclamations to show that you do not like something. ♦ *The idea! Thinking Mother was my sister!* ♦ *The very idea of Tom bringing that dirty dog into my clean house!*

the lid *n., slang* Something that holds back or holds out of sight. ♦ *The police blew the lid off the gambling operations.* ♦ *John kept the lid on his plans until he was ready to run for class president.* ♦ *The chief of police placed the lid on gambling in the town.*

the likes of *informal* Something like or similar to; something of the same kind as. ♦ *I have never seen the likes of John.* ♦ *It was a chocolate sundae the likes of which Mary would never see again.*

the long and the short *or* **the long and short** *n. phr.* All that needs to be said; the basic fact; point. ♦ *The long and the short of the matter is that the man is no actor.* ♦ *The money isn't there, and that's the long and short of it.*

the matter *adj.* Not as it should be; wrong.—Used in questions or with negatives or *if.* ♦ *Why don't you answer me? What's the matter?* ♦ *John may be slow in arithmetic, but nothing's the matter with his pitching arm.* ♦ *If anything is the matter, please tell me.*

the more ——— **the more——** *or the* ——— **er the** ——— **er**—Used in two halves of a sentence to show that when there is more of the first, there is more of the second too. ♦ *The more you eat,* *the fatter you will get.* ◆ *Get your report in when you can; the sooner, the better.* ◆ *The bigger they are, the harder they fall.* ◆ *The more Bill worked on the arithmetic problem, the more confused he became.*

then See AND THEN SOME, EVERY NOW AND THEN, NOW AND THEN.

then again *adv.* As an opposite possibility; another thing. ◆ *He may be here tomorrow. Then again, he may not come until next week.* ◆ *I thought you told me about the fire, but then again it could have been Bill.*

then and there *adv. phr.* At that very time and place in the past; right then. ◆ *He said he wanted his dime back then and there, so I had to give it to him.* Compare IN ONE'S TRACKS, ON THE SPOT, HERE AND NOW.

the other day *adv. phr.* In the recent past. ◆ *I saw an incredible parade of elephants along Michigan Avenue the other day on my way to work.*

the other way around *adv. phr.* See JUST THE OTHER WAY.

the picture *n.* The way things are or were; the facts about something; the situation; what happened or happens. ◆ *Where does Susan come into the picture.* ◆ *When you are looking for a job your education enters into the picture.* ◆ *Old Mr. Brown is out of the picture now and his son runs the store.* ◆ *After the fight on the playground, the principal talked to the boys who were watching, until he got the whole picture.* Compare GET THE MESSAGE.

the pits *n., slang* **1.** A low class, blighted and ill-maintained place, motel room or apartment. ◆ *Max, this motel is the pits, I will not sleep here!* **2.** The end of the road, the point of no return, the point of total ruin of one's health *(from the drug anticulture referring to the arm-pits as the only place that had veins for injections).* ◆ *John flunked high school this year for the third time; he will never get to college; it's the pits for him.* **3.** A very depressed state of mind. ◆ *Poor Marcy is down in the pits over her recent divorce.*

the powers that be *n. phr.* Constituted authority; those in power. ◆ *I have done all I can; the rest is up to the powers that be.*

there See ALL THERE, HERE AND THERE, NEITHER HERE NOR THERE, THEN AND THERE.

There *or* **here you are! 1.** Informal way to say, "Here is what you wanted." ◆ *The doorman politely opened the door of the taxi and said, "There you are, sir!"* ◆ *The clerk wrapped up the package and handed it to the customer saying, "Here you are, ma'am!"* **2.** You have found the correct answer; you are correct. ◆ *"The reason for the violent crime rate is the all too easy availability of handguns," he said. "Yeah, there you are!" Officer Maloney replied.*

there is more than one way to get a pig to market *or* **flay a fox** *or* **skin a cat** There are always new and different ways to accomplish a difficult task.—A proverb. ◆ *"How did you get Tommy to study so hard?" Eleanor asked. "I simply disconnected the television set," Tommy's mother answered. "There's more than one way to get a pig to market."*

there is nothing to it Informal way to say, "It is easy." ◆ *Cooking stir-fried Chinese food is really not difficult at all; in fact, there's nothing to it.*

There you go! 1. Informal way to say, "You are doing it already and you are doing it well." ◆ *"Is roller skating hard?" Freddie asked. "No," Beth replied, "let me show you how to do it. There you go!"* **2.** See THERE *or* HERE YOU ARE 2.

the ropes *n. plural, informal* Thorough or special knowledge of a job; how to do something; the ways of people or the world. ◆ *On a newspaper a cub reporter learns his job from an older reporter who knows the ropes.* ◆ *When you go to a new school it takes a while to learn the ropes.* ◆ *Betty showed Jane the ropes when she was learning to make a dress.* ◆ *Mr. Jones was an orphan and he had to learn the ropes when he was young to make his way in the world.* Compare BE AROUND, INS AND OUTS, TRICK OF THE TRADE.

the score *n., slang* The truth; the real story or information; what is really happening; the way people and the world really are. ◆ *Very few people know the score in politics.* ◆ *You are too* *young to know the score yet.* ◆ *What's the score anyhow? When will the program begin?* Compare KNOW ONE'S STUFF, KNOW ONE'S WAY AROUND, THE ROPES.

these See ONE OF THESE DAYS *or* SOME OF THESE DAYS.

the three R's *n. phr.* (W)riting, reading, and (a)rithmetic, the three basic skills of an elementary education. ◆ *Barry has completed the three R's, but otherwise he has had little formal education.*

the ticket *n.* Exactly what is needed.— Often used with *just.* ◆ *This airtight locker is just the ticket for storing your winter clothes.*

the tracks *n.* The line between the rich or fashionable part of town and the poor or unfashionable part of town. ◆ *The poor children knew they would not be welcome on the other side of the tracks.* ◆ *Mary's mother did not want her to date Jack, because he came from across the tracks.*—Often used in the expression *the wrong side of the tracks.* ◆ *The mayor was born on the wrong side of the tracks, but he worked hard and became successful.*

the whole way See ALL THE WAY.

the wiser *adj.* Knowing about something which might be embarrassing of knowing.—Usually used with *nobody* or *no one.* ◆ *Mary took the teacher's book home by mistake, but early the next morning she returned it with nobody the wiser.*

the works *n., plural, slang* **1.** Everything that can be had or that you have; everything of this kind, all that goes with it. ◆ *When the tramp found $100, he went into a fine restaurant and ordered the works with a steak dinner.* **1b.** See SHOOT THE WORKS. **2.** Rough handling or treatment; a bad beating or scolding; killing; murder.—Usually used with *get* or *give.* ◆ *The boy said that Joe was going to get the works if he ever came back to that neighborhood again.* ◆ *The newspaper gave the police department the works when they let the burglars get away.* ◆ *The gangster told his friend he would give him the works if he double-crossed him.* Compare THE BUSINESS.

they See LET THE CHIPS FALL WHERE THEY MAY.

thick See BLOOD IS THICKER THAN WATER, LAY IT ON *or* LAY IT ON THICK, THROUGH THICK AND THIN.

thicker See BLOOD IS THICKER THAN WATER.

thin See INTO THIN AIR, OUT OF THIN AIR, SIT ON THIN ICE, SPREAD ONESELF TOO THIN, THROUGH THICK AND THIN, WEAR THIN.

thing See A LITTLE KNOWLEDGE IS A DANGEROUS THING, DO ONE'S THING *or* DO ONE'S OWN THING, FIRST THINGS COME FIRST, FOR ONE THING, SEE THINGS, SURE THING, TAKE IT EASY *or* TAKE THINGS EASY, TELL A THING OR TWO.

thing or two *n. phr., informal* **1.** Facts not generally known, or not known to the hearer or reader; unusual or important information. ◆ *Mary told Joan a thing or two about Betty's real feelings.* **2.** A lot; much. ◆ *Bob knows a thing or two about sailing.* Compare TELL A THING OR TWO.

Things are looking up! Informal way to say that conditions are improving. ◆ *Things are looking up at our university as the governor promised a 5% salary raise.*

think See COME TO THINK OF IT.

think a great deal of *or* **think a lot of** *also* **think much of** *v. phr.* To consider to be very worthy, valuable, or important; to esteem highly. ◆ *Mary thinks a great deal of Tim.* ◆ *The teacher thought a lot of Joe's project.*—The phrase *think much of* is usually used in negative sentences. ◆ *Father didn't think much of Paul's idea of buying a goat to save lawn mowing.* Contrast THINK LITTLE OF.

think a lot of See THINK A GREAT DEAL OF.

think aloud *or* **think out loud** *v.* To say what you are thinking. ◆ *"I wish I had more money for Christmas presents," Father thought aloud. "What did you say?" said Mother. Father answered, "I'm sorry. I wasn't talking to you. I was thinking out loud."*

think better of *v.* To change your mind about; to consider again and make a better decision about. ◆ *John told his mother he wanted to leave school, but later he thought better of it.* Compare SECOND THOUGHT, THINK TWICE.

Think big! *v. phr., informal* To believe in one's ability, purpose, or power to perform or succeed. ♦ *Be confident; be positive; tell yourself you are the greatest; above all, think big!*

think fit See FIT.

thinking cap See PUT ON ONE'S THINKING CAP.

think little of *v. phr.* Think that (something or someone) is not important or valuable. ♦ *John thought little of Ted's plan for the party.* ♦ *Joan thought little of walking two miles to school.* Contrast THINK A GREAT DEAL OF.

think much of See THINK A GREAT DEAL OF.

think nothing of *v. phr.* To think or consider easy, simple, or usual. ♦ *Jim thinks nothing of hiking ten miles in one day.*

think nothing of it *v. phr., informal*— Used as a courteous phrase in replying to thanks. *"Thank you very much for your help." "Think nothing of it."* Compare YOU'RE WELCOME.

think on one's feet *v. phr.* To think quickly; answer or act without waiting; know what to do or say right away. ♦ *A good basketball player can think on his feet.* ♦ *Our teacher can think on his feet; he always has an answer ready when we ask him questions.*

think out *v.* **1.** To find out or discover by thinking; study and understand. ♦ *Andy thought out a way of climbing to the top of the pole.* Compare FIGURE OUT, WORK OUT. **2.** To think through to the end; to understand what would come at last. ♦ *Bill wanted to quit school, but he thought out the matter and decided not to.*

think out loud See THINK ALOUD.

think over *v.* To think carefully about; consider; study. ♦ *When Charles asked Betty to marry him, she asked him for time to think it over.* ♦ *Think over what we studied in history this year and write a lesson on the thing that interested you most.* Compare MAKE UP ONE'S MIND, SEE ABOUT.

think piece *n., slang* **1.** The human brain. ♦ *Lou's got one powerful think piece, man.* **2.** Any provocative essay or article that, by stating a strong opinion, arouses the reader to think about it and react to it by agreeing or disagreeing. ♦ *That article by Charles Fenyvesi on Vietnamese refugees in the Washington Post sure was a think piece!*

think tank *n.* A company of researchers who spend their time developing ideas and concepts. ♦ *The government hired a think tank to study the country's need for coins, and was advised to stop making pennies.*

think twice *v.* To think again carefully; reconsider; hesitate. ♦ *The teacher advised Lou to think twice before deciding to quit school.* Compare THINK BETTER OF.

think up *v.* To invent or discover by thinking; have a new idea of. ♦ *Mary thought up a funny game for the children to play.*

third base *n.* The base to be touched third in baseball. ♦ *He reached third base standing up on a long triple.*

third class *n.* **1.** The third best or highest group; the class next after the second class. ♦ *Mary won the pie-making contest in the third class, for the youngest girls.* **2.** Mail that is printed, other than magazines and newspapers that are published regularly, and packages that are not sealed and weigh less than a pound. ♦ *The company uses third class to mail free samples of soap.* **3.** The least expensive class of travel. ♦ *I couldn't afford anything better than the third class on the ship coming home from France.* Compare FIRST CLASS, SECOND CLASS.

third-class[1] *adj.* Belonging to the third class; of the third highest or best class. *Much advertising is sent by third-class mail.* ♦ *I bought a third-class airline ticket to Hawaii.*

third-class[2] *adv.* By third class. ♦ *How did you send the package? Third class.* ♦ *We traveled third-class on the train.*

third degree *n. phr.* A method of severe grilling used to extract information from an arrested suspect. ♦ *"Why give me the third degree?" he asked indignantly. "All I did was come home late because I had a drink with my friends."*

third sex *n., euphemism, slang, informal* Homosexual individuals who are either men or women. ♦ *Billy is rumored to belong to the third sex.*

third world *n.* **1.** The countries not

aligned with either the former U.S.S.R.-dominated Communist bloc or the U.S.A.-dominated capitalist countries. ♦ *New Zealand made a move toward third country status when it disallowed American nuclear submarines in its harbors.* **2.** The developing nations of the world where the industrial revolution has not yet been completed. ♦ *Africa and the rest of the third world must be freed from starvation and illiteracy.*

this See OUT OF THIS WORLD.

this and that *also* **this, that, and the other** *n. phr.* Various things; different things; miscellaneous things. ♦ *When the old friends met they would talk about this and that.* ♦ *The quilt was made of this, that, and the other.*

this, that, and the other See THIS AND THAT.

this is how the cookie crumbles *or* **that's how the cookie crumbles** *v. phr.,* *informal* That's how things are; that's life. ♦ *It's too bad about John and Mary getting divorced, but then that's how the cookie crumbles.*

thither See HITHER AND THITHER.

thorn in the flesh *or* **thorn in one's side** *n. phr.* Something that causes stubborn trouble; a constant bother; a vexation. ♦ *The new voter organization soon became the biggest thorn in the senator's side.* ♦ *The guerrilla band was a thorn in the flesh of the invaders.*

though See AS IF *or* AS THOUGH.

thought See FOOD FOR THOUGHT, PENNY FOR ONE'S THOUGHTS, PERISH THE THOUGHT, SECOND THOUGHT.

thousand See BY THE DOZEN *or* BY THE THOUSAND.

thrash out *v. phr.* To discuss fully; confer about something until a decision is reached. ♦ *They met to thrash out their differences concerning how to run the office.*

thread See HANG BY A THREAD.

threat See TRIPLE THREAT.

three-ring circus *n.* A scene of much confusion or activity. ♦ *The street was a three-ring circus of cars, people, noise, and lights.* ♦ *It is a three-ring circus to watch that silly dog play.*

three sheets in the wind *or* **three sheets to the wind** *adj. phr., informal* Unsteady from too much liquor; drunk. ♦ *The sailor came down the street, three sheets in the wind.*

thrill one to death *or* **pieces** See TICKLE PINK.

throat See CUT ONE'S THROAT, FLY AT ONE'S THROAT, JUMP DOWN ONE'S THROAT, LUMP IN ONE'S THROAT, RAM DOWN ONE'S THROAT *and* SHOVE DOWN ONE'S THROAT.

through a hoop See JUMP THROUGH A HOOP.

through and through *adv.* Completely; entirely; whole-heartedly. ♦ *Bob was a ball player through and through.* ♦ *Mary was hurt through and through by Betty's remarks.* Compare OUT-AND-OUT.

through hell and high water See HELL AND HIGH WATER.

through one's hat See TALK THROUGH ONE'S HAT.

through one's head See GET THROUGH ONE'S HEAD.

through one's mind See CROSS ONE'S MIND *or* PASS THROUGH ONE'S MIND.

through one's paces See PUT THROUGH ONE'S PACES.

through street *n.* **1.** A street on which cars can move without stopping at intersections, but cars on streets crossing it have to stop at the intersection. ♦ *You have to be especially careful crossing a through street.* ♦ *Mr. Jones stopped his car when he came to the through street. He waited until there were no cars on it, and drove across it.* Contrast STOP STREET. **2.** A street that is open to other streets at both ends; a street that has a passage through it, so that it is not necessary to come back to get out of it. ♦ *We thought we could get through to Main St. by going up a side street but there was a sign that said "Not a through street."*

through the mill *adv. phr.* **1.** Experienced. ♦ *You could tell immediately that the new employee had been through the mill.* **2.** Through real experience of the difficulties of a certain way of life. ♦ *Poor Jerry has had three operations in one year, and now he's back in the hospital. He's really gone through the mill.* Compare GO THROUGH HELL AND HIGH WATER, COME HELL OR HIGH WATER.

through the motions See GO THROUGH

THE MOTIONS.

through the nose See PAY THROUGH THE NOSE .

through thick and thin *adv. phr.* Through all difficulties and troubles; through good times and bad times. ♦ *The friends were faithful through thick and thin.* ♦ *George stayed in college through thick and thin, because he wanted an education.*

through train *n. phr.* A direct train that doesn't necessitate any changes. ♦ *We'll take the through train from Chicago to New York because it's the most convenient.*

throw See FREE THROW, PEOPLE WHO LIVE IN GLASS HOUSES SHOULD NOT THROW STONES.

throw a curve *v. phr., slang, informal* **1.** To mislead or deceive someone; to lie. ♦ *John threw me a curve about the hiring.* **2.** To take someone by surprise in an unpleasant way. ♦ *Mr. Weiner's announcement threw the whole company a curve.*

throw a fit See HAVE A FIT.

throw a monkey wrench *or* **throw a wrench** *v. phr., informal* To cause something that is going smoothly to stop. ♦ *The game was going smoothly until you threw a monkey wrench into the works by fussing about the rules.* ♦ *The Michigan tacklers threw a wrench into the Wisconsin team's offense.* ♦ *He hoped to see the class plan fail and looked for a chance to throw a wrench in the machinery.*

throw a party *v. phr., informal* To hold a party; have a party. ♦ *The club is throwing a party in the high school gym Saturday night.* ♦ *The Seniors threw a masquerade party on Halloween.*

throw a punch *v. phr.* To strike at someone with your fist; hit; punch. ♦ *Bob became so mad at Fred that he threw a punch at him.* ♦ *The bell rang and the boxers started throwing punches.* Compare TAKE A PUNCH AT.

throw away *v.* **1.** To get rid of as unwanted or not needed; junk. ♦ *Before they moved they threw away everything they didn't want to take with them.* ♦ *I never save those coupons; I just throw them away.* Syn. THROW OUT. **2.** To waste. ♦ *The senator criticized the government for throwing away bil-*

lions on the space program. **3.** To fail to make use of. ♦ *She threw away a good chance for a better job.*

throw a wet blanket See WET BLANKET.

throw caution to the winds *also* **throw discretion to the winds** *v. phr.* To be daring; make a bold or risky move. ♦ *Hearing that Apaches were planning to start a war, the whites decided to throw caution to the winds and attack the Apaches first.*

throw cold water on *also* **dash cold water on** *or* **pour cold water on** *v. phr.* To discourage; say or do something to discourage. ♦ *We had high hopes of victory but our opponents soon threw cold water on them.* ♦ *Henry's father threw cold water on his plans to go to college by saying he could not afford it.*

throw a loop See KNOCK FOR A LOOP.

throw down the gauntlet *v. phr.* To challenge, especially to a fight. ♦ *Another candidate for the presidency has thrown down the gauntlet.*

throw for a loss *v. phr.* **1.** To tackle a member of the opposing football team behind the place where his team had the ball at the beginning of the play; push the other team back so that they lose yardage in football. ♦ *The Blues' quarterback ran back and tried to pass, but before he could, the Reds' end threw him for a loss.* Compare LOSE GROUND. **2.** *informal* To surprise or shock (someone); upset; make worry greatly; cause trouble. ♦ *It threw Jim for a loss when he failed the test.* ♦ *Mr. Simpson was thrown for a loss when he lost his job.* Compare KNOCK FOR A LOOP, SET BACK ON ONE'S HEELS.

throw in *v.* **1.** To give or put in as an addition; to give to or with something else. ♦ *John threw in a couple of tires when he sold Bill his bicycle.* ♦ *Mary and Tess were talking about the prom, and Joan threw in that she was going with Fred.* Compare FOR GOOD MEASURE. **2.** To push into operating position. ♦ *Mr. Jones threw in the clutch and shifted the gears.*

throw light on See CAST LIGHT ON, SHED LIGHT ON.

throw something in one's face *or* **throw something in one's teeth** *v. phr.* To blame a person for (something wrong); not allow someone to forget (a mistake or failure).—Often used with *back.* ♦ *Bob came home late for dinner last week, and his mother keeps throwing it back in his face.* ♦ *I made a mistake in the ball game and the boys keep throwing it back in my teeth.* Compare IN ONE'S FACE.

throw in one's lot with *or literary* **cast in one's lot with** *v. phr.* To decide to share or take part in anything that happens to; join. ♦ *The thief decided to throw in his lot with the gang when he heard their plans.* ♦ *Washington was rich, but he decided to cast in his lot with the colonies against Britain.* ♦ *When Carl was old enough to vote, he threw in his lot with the Democrats.* Syn. JOIN FORCES.

throw in the sponge *or* **throw up the sponge** *or* **throw in the towel** *v. phr., informal* To admit defeat; accept loss. ♦ *After taking a beating for five rounds, the fighter's seconds threw in the sponge.* ♦ *When Harold saw his arguments were not being accepted, he threw in the towel and left.* Syn GIVE UP.

throw off *v.* **1.** To get free from. ♦ *He was healthy enough to throw off his cold easily.* Compare RID OF. **2.** To mislead; confuse; fool. ♦ *They went by a different route to throw the hostile bandits off their track.* **3.** To produce easily or as if without effort. ♦ *She could throw off a dozen poems in a night.*

throw off the scent *v. phr.* To mislead; confuse. ♦ *The robbers went different ways hoping to throw the sheriff's men off the scent.* Syn. THROW OFF 2.

throw off the track *v. phr.* To divert; mislead; confuse. ♦ *The clever criminals threw the detective off the track by changing their names and faces.* Contrast OFF THE BEATEN TRACK.

throw oneself at someone's feet *v. phr.* To make a public display of serving, loving, or worshiping someone. ♦ *When Arthur became king, almost all of the nobles threw themselves at his feet and promised to obey and serve him.* ♦ *When the new girl entered school, several boys threw themselves at her feet.*

throw oneself at someone's head *or* **fling oneself at someone's head** *v. phr., informal* To try hard and openly to make a person love you. ♦ *She threw herself at his head, but he was interested in another girl.* Compare AT ONE'S FEET.

throw one's hat in the ring *or* **toss one's hat in the ring** *v. phr., informal* To announce that you are going to try to be elected to an official position; become a candidate for office. ♦ *Bill tossed his hat in the ring for class president.* ♦ *The senator threw his hat in the ring for re-election.*

throw one's weight around *v. phr., informal* To use one's influence or position in a showy or noisy manner. ♦ *John was the star of the class play, and he was throwing his weight around telling the director how the scene should be played.* ♦ *Bob was stronger than the other boys, and he threw his weight around.* Compare PULL RANK.

throw open **1.** To open wide with a sudden or strong movement. ♦ *He dashed in and threw open the windows.* **2.** To remove limits from. ♦ *The Homestead Act threw open the West.* ♦ *When a hurricane and flood left many people homeless, public buildings were thrown open to shelter them.*

throw *or* **feed one to the wolves** *v. phr.* **1.** To turn someone into a scapegoat. ♦ *In order to explain the situation to the media, the governor blamed the mayor and threw him to the wolves.* **2.** To send into danger without protection. ♦ *Mary was very shy. Her friends did not come to speak before the club in her place. They threw her to the wolves.* ♦ *The boys on the football team were so small that when they played a good team they were thrown to the wolves.*

throw out *or* **toss out** *v.* **1.** To put somewhere to be destroyed because not wanted. ♦ *He didn't need the brush anymore so he threw it out.* Syn. THROW AWAY 1. **2.** To refuse to accept. ♦ *The inspector tossed out all the parts that didn't work.* **3.** To force to leave; dismiss. ♦ *When the employees complained too loudly, the owner threw them out.* Syn. KICK OUT, TURN OUT 1. **4.** To cause to be out in baseball by throwing the ball. ♦ *The shortstop tossed the runner out.*

throw out of gear *v. phr.* **1.** To separate the gears of (a car or some other machine) when you want to stop it. ♦ *When John wanted to stop, he threw the car out of gear and braked sharply.* **2.** To stop or bother (what someone is doing or planning); confuse; upset. ♦ *The whole country was thrown out of gear by the assassination of the President.* ♦ *My mother's illness threw my plans for the summer out of gear.*

throw over *v.* To give up for another; break your loyalty or attachment to. ♦ *Bob threw Mary over for a new girlfriend.* ♦ *Tom threw over those who helped him run for class president after he was elected.*

throw the baby out with the bath (bathwater) *v. phr.* To reject all of something because part is faulty. ♦ *God knows that there are weaknesses in the program, but if they act too hastily they may cause the baby to be thrown out with the bathwater.*

throw the book at *v. phr., informal* To give the most severe penalty to (someone) for breaking the law or rules. ♦ *Because it was the third time he had been caught speeding that month, the judge threw the book at him.*

throw together *v.* **1.** *also* **slap together** To make in a hurry and without care. ♦ *Bill and Bob threw together a cabin out of old lumber.* ♦ *The party was planned suddenly, and Mary threw together a meal out of leftovers.* **2.** To put in with other people by chance. ♦ *The group of strangers was thrown together when the storm trapped them on the highway.* ♦ *Bill and Tom became friends when they were thrown together in the same cabin at camp.*

throw up *v.* **1.** *informal or slang* **heave up**. To vomit. ♦ *The heat made him feel sick and he thought he would throw up.* ♦ *He took the medicine but threw it up a minute later.* **2.** *informal* To quit; leave; let go; give up. ♦ *When she broke their engagement he threw up his job and left town.* **3.** To build in a hurry. ♦ *The contractor threw up some temporary sheds to hold the new equipment.* **4.** To mention often as an insult. ♦ *His father threw up John's wastefulness to him.*

throw up one's hands *v. phr.* To give up trying; admit that you cannot succeed. ♦ *Mrs. Jones threw up her hands when* the children messed up the living room for the third time. ♦ *When Mary saw the number of dishes to be washed, she threw up her hands in dismay.*

throw up one's hands in horror *v. phr.* To be horrified; feel alarmed; give up hope of straightening things out; be shocked by something terrible. ♦ *When Mrs. Brown saw the mess the children were making in her living room, she threw up her hands in horror.* ♦ *Everybody threw up their hands in horror at the destruction caused by the hurricane.*

throw up the sponge See THROW IN THE SPONGE.

thumb See ALL THUMBS, GREEN THUMB, TURN THUMBS DOWN, TWIDDLE ONE'S THUMBS, UNDER ONE'S THUMB *or* UNDER THE THUMB OF.

thumb a ride *v. phr., informal* To get a ride by hitchhiking; hitchhike. ♦ *Not having much money, Carl decided to thumb a ride to New York.*

thumb one's nose *v. phr.* **1.** To hold one's open hand in front of one's face with one's thumb pointed at one's nose as a sign of scorn or dislike. ♦ *After Bob ran into the house he thumbed his nose at Tom through the window.* **2.** *informal* To look with disfavor or dislike; regard with scorn; refuse to obey.—Used with *at.* ♦ *Betty thumbed her nose at her mother's command to stay home.* Compare LOOK DOWN ON. ♦ *Mary thumbed her nose at convention by wearing odd clothes.*

thumb through *v. phr.* To examine superficially; read cursorily. ♦ *I have read* War and Peace *but Fran has only thumbed through it.*

thunder See BLOOD AND THUNDER, STEAL ONE'S THUNDER.

thus and so *also* **thus and thus** *adv. phr.* In a particular way; according to directions that have been given. ♦ *The teacher is very fussy about the way you write your report. If you don't do it thus and so, she gives you a lower mark.*

thus far See SO FAR.

ticket See SPLIT TICKET, STRAIGHT TICKET, THE TICKET, WALKING PAPERS *also* WALKING TICKET .

tickle pink *v. phr., informal* To please very much; thrill; delight. Usually used in the passive participle. ♦ *Nancy was*

tickled pink with her new dress.
tickle to death See TO DEATH.
tick off *v.* **1.** To mention one after the other; list. ♦ *The teacher ticked off the assignments that Jane had to do.* **2.** To scold; rebuke. ♦ *The boss ticked off the waitress for dropping her tray.* **3.** To anger or upset. Usually used as *ticked off.* ♦ *She was ticked off at him for breaking their dinner date again.*
tide See TURN THE TIDE.
tide over *v.* To carry past a difficulty or danger; help in bad times or in trouble. ♦ *He was out of work last winter but he had saved enough money to tide him over until spring.* ♦ *An ice cream cone in the afternoon tided her over until supper.* Compare SEE THROUGH.
tide turn See TURN THE TIDE.
tidy sum *n. phr.* A large amount of money. ♦ *The Smith's big new home cost them a tidy sum.* Compare PRETTY PENNY.
tie See FIT TO BE TIED.
tie down *v.* To keep (someone) from going somewhere or doing something; prevent from leaving; keep in. ♦ *Mrs. Brown can't come to the party. She's tied down at home with the children sick.* ♦ *The navy tied the enemy down with big gunfire while the marines landed on the beach.* ♦ *I can't help you with history now! I'm tied down with these algebra problems.*
tied to one's mother's apron strings Not independent of your mother; not able to do anything without asking your mother. ♦ *Even after he grew up he was still tied to his mother's apron strings.*
tie in *v.* To connect with something else; make a connection for.—Often used with *with.* ♦ *The teacher tied in what she said with last week's lesson.* ♦ *The English teacher sometimes gives compositions that tie in with things we are studying in other classes.* ♦ *The detectives tied in the fingerprints on the man's gun with those found on the safe, so they knew that he was the thief.*
tie-in *n.* A connection; a point of meeting. ♦ *John's essay on World War II provides a perfect tie-in with his earlier work on World War I.*
tie in knots *v. phr.* To make (someone) very nervous or worried. ♦ *The thought of having her tooth pulled tied Joan in knots.* ♦ *The little boy's experience with the kidnapper tied him in knots and it was hard for him to sleep well for a long time.*
tie into See LACE INTO.
tie one's hands *v. phr.* To make (a person) unable to do anything.— Usually used in the passive. ♦ *Since Mary would not tell her mother what was bothering her, her mother's hands were tied.* ♦ *Charles wanted to help John get elected president of the class, but his promise to another boy tied his hands.* ♦ *Father hoped Jim would not quit school, but his hands were tied; Jim was old enough to quit if he wanted to.*
tie the knot *v. phr., informal* To get married; *also* to perform a wedding ceremony. ♦ *Diane and Bill tied the knot yesterday.* ♦ *The minister tied the knot for Diane and Bill yesterday.*
tie up *v. phr.* **1.** To show or stop the movement or action of; hinder; tangle. ♦ *The crash of the two trucks tied up all traffic in the center of town.* ♦ *The strike tied up the factory.* **2.** To take all the time of. ♦ *The meeting will tie the President up until noon.* ♦ *The Senate didn't vote because a debate on a small point kept it tied up all week.* ♦ *He can't see you now. He's tied up on the telephone.* **3.** To limit or prevent the use of. ♦ *His money is tied up in a trust fund and he can't take it out.* ♦ *Susan tied up the bathroom for an hour.* **4.** To enter into an association or partnership; join. ♦ *Our company has tied up with another firm to support the show.* **5.** To dock. ♦ *The ships tied up at New York.* **6.** *slang* To finish; complete. ♦ *We've talked long enough; let's tie up these plans and start doing things.*
tie-up *n.* A congestion; a stoppage of the normal flow of traffic, business or correspondence. ♦ *There was a two-hour traffic tie-up on the highway. No pay checks were delivered because of the mail service tie-up.*
tight See SIT TIGHT.
tight end *n.* An end in football who plays close to the tackle in the line. ♦ *The tight end is used to catch passes but most often to block.* Contrast SPLIT END.
tighten one's belt *v. phr.* To live on less money than usual; use less food and

other things. ♦ *When father lost his job we had to tighten our belts.* Often used in the expression tighten one's belt another notch. ♦ *When the husband lost his job, the Smiths had to do without many things, but when their savings were all spent, they had to tighten their belts another notch.*

tighten the screws *v. phr.* To try to make someone do something by making it more and more difficult not to do it; apply pressure. ♦ *When many students still missed class after he began giving daily quizzes, the teacher tightened the screws by failing anyone absent four times.*

tight-lipped *adj.* A taciturn person; one who doesn't say much. ♦ *The witness was tight-lipped about what she saw for fear of physical retaliation by the mob.*

tight money *n. phr.* The opposite of inflation, when money is hard to borrow from the banks. ♦ *The government decided that tight money is the way to bring down inflation.*

tight squeeze *n. phr.* A difficult situation; financial troubles. ♦ *The Browns aren't going out to dinner these days; they are in a tight squeeze.*

tightwad *n. phr.* A stingy person. ♦ *My father is such a tightwad that he won't give me an allowance.*

Tijuana taxi *n., slang, citizen's band radio jargon* A police car. ♦ *I've got a Tijuana taxi in sight.*

till See ROB THE TILL *or* HAVE ONE'S HAND IN THE TILL.

till the cows come home *adv. phr.* Until sunset; until the last. ♦ *The women in the country used to sit in the spinning room making yarn out of skeins of wool, usually till the cows came home.*

till the last gun is fired *or* **until the last gun is fired** *adv. phr.* Until the end; until everything is finished or decided. ♦ *Fred always liked to stay at parties until the last gun was fired.* ♦ *The candidate didn't give up hope of being elected until the last gun was fired.*

tilt See FULL TILT.

tilt at windmills *v. phr., literary* To do battle with an imaginary foe (after Cervantes' Don Quixote). ♦ *John is a nice guy but when it comes to departmental meetings he wastes everybody's time by constantly tilting at windmills.*

time See ABOUT TIME, AGAINST TIME, AT A TIME, AT ONE TIME, AT THE SAME TIME, AT TIMES, BEHIND THE TIMES, BEHIND TIME, BIDE ONE'S TIME, BIG TIME, EVERY TIME ONE TURNS AROUND, FOR THE TIME BEING, FROM TIME TO TIME, GIVE A HARD TIME, HAVE A TIME, HIGH TIME, IN GOOD TIME, IN NO TIME, IN THE NICK OF TIME, IN TIME, KEEP TIME, LESS THAN NO TIME, LIVE ON BORROWED TIME, MAKE TIME, MARK TIME, ONCE UPON A TIME, ON ONE'S OWN TIME, ON TIME, PASS THE TIME OF DAY, SMALL-TIME, TAKE ONE'S TIME, TWO-TIME.

time and again *or* **time and time again** *adv.* Many times; repeatedly; very often. ♦ *I've told you time and again not to touch the vase!* ♦ *Children are forgetful and must be told time and time again how to behave.*

time and a half *n. phr.* Pay given to a worker at a rate half again as much as he usually gets. ♦ *John got time and a half when he worked beyond his usual quitting time.* ♦ *Tom gets one dollar for regular pay and a dollar and a half for time and a half.*

time is ripe The best time has come for doing something. ♦ *The Prime Minister will hold elections when the time is ripe.* ♦ *Lee saw his mother was upset, so he decided the time was not ripe to tell her about the broken window.*

time of day See NOT TO GIVE ONE THE TIME OF DAY.

time off *n. phr.* A period of release from work. ♦ *If I had some time off this afternoon, I would finish writing the letters I promised to my family.*

time of one's life *n. phr.* A very happy or wonderful time. ♦ *John had the time of his life at the party.* ♦ *I could see that she was having the time of her life.*

time out *n. phr.* Time during which a game, a lecture, a discussion or other activity is stopped for a while for some extra questions or informal discussion, or some other reason. ♦ *He took a time out from studying to go to a movie.* ♦ *The player called time out so he could tie his shoe.* ♦ *"Time out!"—The students said, "Could you explain that again?"*

tin ear *n. phr.* **1.** A lack of sensitivity to noise. ♦ *The construction noise doesn't* *bother Fred; he's got a tin ear.* **2.** A lack of musical ability; state of being tone deaf. ♦ *People with a tin ear make poor choir members.*

tingle See SPINE-TINGLING.

tinker's damn See NOT WORTH A TINKER'S DAMN.

Tin Pan Alley *n. phr.* The pop music industry. ♦ *What kind of music will Tin Pan Alley come up with this year?*

tip See AT THE TIP OF ONE'S TONGUE, FROM TIP TO TIP.

tip off *v., informal* To tell something not generally known; tell secret facts to; warn. ♦ *The class president tipped off the class that it was the superintendent's birthday.* ♦ *The thieves did not rob the bank as planned because someone tipped them off that it was being watched by the police.* Compare PUT WISE.

tip the balance See TIP THE SCALES 2.

tip the scales *v. phr., informal* **1.** To weigh. ♦ *Martin tips the scales at 180 pounds.* **2.** *or* **tip the balance** To have important or decisive influence; make a decision go for or against you; decide. ♦ *John's vote tipped the scales in our favor, and we won the election.* Compare TURN THE TIDE.

tired See DEAD TIRED, SICK AND TIRED.

tire out See WEAR OUT 2.

tit for tat *n. phr.* Equal treatment in return; a fair exchange. ♦ *Billy hit me, so I gave him tit for tat.* ♦ *I told him if he did me any harm I would return tit for tat.* ♦ *They had a warm debate and the two boys gave each other tit for tat.* Compare GET BACK AT, EYE FOR AN EYE AND A TOOTH FOR A TOOTH.

to a conclusion See JUMP TO A CONCLUSION.

to a crisp See BURN TO A CRISP.

to a degree *adv. phr.* **1.** *Chiefly British* Very; to a large extent. ♦ *In some things I am ignorant to a degree.* **2.** Somewhat; slightly; in a small way; rather. ♦ *His anger was, to a degree, a confession of defeat.* ♦ *To a degree, Mary was to blame for Bob's failing mathematics, because he spent much time with her when he should have been studying.*

to advantage *adv. phr.* So as to bring out the good qualities of; favorably; in a flattering way. ♦ *The jeweler's window showed the diamonds to advantage.* ♦ *The green dress showed up to advantage with her red hair.*

to a fault *adv. phr.* So very well that it is in a way bad; to the point of being rather foolish; too well; too much. ♦ *Aunt May wants everything in her house to be exactly right; she is neat to a fault.* ♦ *Mary acts her part to a fault.* ♦ *John carries thoroughness to a fault; he spends many hours writing his reports.*

to a halt See GRIND TO A HALT.

to a large extent See IN GREAT MEASURE.

to all intents and purposes *adv. phr.* In most ways; in fact. ♦ *The president is called the head of state, but the prime minister, to all intents and purposes, is the chief executive.*

to a man *adv. phr.* Without exception; with all agreeing. ♦ *The workers voted to a man to go on strike.* ♦ *To a man John's friends stood by him in his trouble.* Compare EVERY LAST MAN.

to and fro *adv. phr.* Forward and back again and again. ♦ *Father pushed Judy in the swing, and she went to and fro.* ♦ *Busses go to and fro between the center of the city and the city limits.* ♦ *The man walked to and fro while he waited for his phone call.* Compare BACK AND FORTH.

to another tune See DANCE TO ANOTHER TUNE.

to a T *or* **to a turn** *adv. phr.* Just right; to perfection; exactly. ♦ *The roast was done to a turn.* ♦ *His nickname, Tiny, suited him to a T.* Compare TO THE LETTER.

to bat See GO TO BAT FOR.

to bay See BRING TO BAY.

to-be *adj.* That is going to be; about to become.—Used after the noun it modifies. ♦ *Bob kissed his bride-to-be.* ♦ *The principal of the high school greeted the high school students-to-be on their last day in junior high.*

to bed See PUT TO BED, PUT TO BED WITH A SHOVEL.

to be on the safe side *adv. phr.* To take extra precautions; reduce or eliminate the possibility of a mistake, an error, or even danger. ♦ *Dad always keeps his valuables in a bank's safe deposit box, just to be on the safe side.* Compare JUST IN CASE.

to be sure *adv. phr.* Without a doubt; certainly; surely. ♦*"Didn't you say Mr. Smith would take us home?" "Oh, yes. To be sure, I did."*—Often used before a clause beginning with *but.* ♦*He works slowly, to be sure, but he does a good job.* ♦*To be sure, Jim is a fast skater, but he is not good at doing figures.* Syn. OF COURSE.

to blame *adj. phr.* Having done something wrong; to be blamed; responsible. ♦*John was to blame for the broken window.* ♦*The teacher tried to find out who was to blame in the fight.*

to boot *adv. phr.* In addition; besides; as something extra. ♦*He not only got fifty dollars, but they bought him dinner to boot.* Compare FOR GOOD MEASURE, IN THE BARGAIN, THROW IN.

to date *adv. or adj. phr.* Up to the present time; until now. ♦*To date twenty students have been accepted into the school.* ♦*The police have not found the runaway to date.* ♦*Jim is shoveling snow to earn money, but his earnings to date are small.* Syn. SO FAR.

to death *adv. phr., informal* To the limit; to the greatest degree possible.—Used for emphasis with verbs such as *scare, frighten, bore.* ♦*Cowboy stories bore me to death, but I like mysteries.* ♦*Sara is scared to death of snakes.* ♦*John is tickled to death with his new bike.*

to do See HAVE TO DO WITH.

toe See CURL ONE'S HAIR *or* CURL ONE'S TOES, ON ONE'S TOES, STEP ON THE TOES OF.

toe the line *or* **toe the mark** *v. phr.* To be very careful to do just what you are supposed to do; obey the rules and do your duties. ♦*The new teacher will make Joe toe the line.* ♦*Bill's father is strict with him and he has to toe the mark.* Compare WALK THE CHALK.

to first base See GET TO FIRST BASE.

together See GET IT ALL TOGETHER.

together with *prep.* In addition to; in the company of; along with. ♦*John, together with his brother, has gone to the party.* ♦*The police found a knife, together with the stolen money, hidden in a hollow tree.*

to grips See COME TO GRIPS WITH.

to heart See TAKE TO HEART *also* LAY TO HEART.

to heel *adj. phr.* **1.** Close behind. ♦*The dog ran after a rabbit, but Jack brought him to heel.* **2.** Under control; to obedience. ♦*When Peter was sixteen, he thought he could do as he pleased, but his father cut off his allowance, and Peter soon came to heel.*

to hell with *or* **the hell with** *prep. phr., informal*—Used to express disgusted rejection of something. ♦*It's slop; the hell with what the cook calls it.* Compare FED UP, GIVE A HANG.

to it See PUT ONE'S BACK TO IT.

to light See BRING TO LIGHT, COME TO LIGHT.

toll See TAKE ITS TOLL.

toll call *n. phr.* A long distance telephone call for which one has to pay. ♦*We had several toll calls on last month's telephone bill.*

toll free *adv. phr.* Calling an (800) telephone number with the call paid by the business whose number one has dialed. ♦*You can call us day and night, seven days a week, toll free.*

Tom See PEEPING TOM.

Tom, Dick, and Harry *n. phr.* People in general; anyone; everyone.—Usually preceded by *every* and used to show scorn or disrespect. ♦*The drunk told his troubles to every Tom, Dick and Harry who passed by.*

tone down *v.* To make softer or quieter; make less harsh or strong; moderate. ♦*He toned down the sound of the TV.* ♦*She wanted the bright colors in her house toned down.* ♦*When the ladies arrived, he toned down his language.* ♦*The strikers were asked to tone down their demands for higher pay so that there might be a quicker agreement and an end to the strike.*

tong See GO AT IT HAMMER AND TONGS.

tongue See AT THE TIP OF ONE'S TONGUE, CAT GET ONE'S TONGUE, HOLD ONE'S TONGUE, KEEP A CIVIL TONGUE IN ONE'S HEAD, SLIP OF THE TONGUE.

tongue-in-cheek *adj. phr.* In an ironic or insincere manner. ♦*When the faculty complained about the poor salary increments, the university's president said that he was not a psychiatrist, thus making an inappropriate tongue-in-cheek remark.*

tongue-lashing *n.* A sharp scolding or criticism. ♦*Jim's mother gave him a tongue-lashing for telling family* *secrets.* Syn. PIECE OF ONE'S MIND.

tongues wag *informal* People speak in an excited or gossipy manner; people spread rumors. ♦ *If married women go out with other men, tongues will wag.* ♦ *When the bank clerk showed up in an expensive new car, tongues wagged.*

tongue-tied See TIGHT-LIPPED.

tongue twister *n.* A word or group of words difficult to pronounce whose meaning is irrelevant compared to the difficulty of enunciation. ♦ *"She sells sea shells by the seashore" is a popular American tongue twister.*

to no avail *or* **of no avail**[1] *adj. phr., formal* Having no effect; useless, unsuccessful. ♦ *Tom's practicing was of no avail. He was sick on the day of the game.* ♦ *Mary's attempts to learn embroidering were to no avail.*

to no avail[2] *adv. phr., formal* Without result; unsuccessfully. ♦ *John tried to pull the heavy cart, but to no avail.* ♦ *Mary studied hard for the test but to no avail.* Compare IN VAIN.

too See EAT ONE'S CAKE AND HAVE IT TOO.

too bad *adj.* To be regretted; worthy of sorrow or regret; regrettable.—Used as a predicate. ♦ *It is too bad that we are so often lazy.* ♦ *It was too bad Bill had measles when the circus came to town.*

too big for one's breeches *or* **too big for one's boots** *adj. phr.* Too sure of your own importance; feeling more important than you really are. ♦ *That boy had grown too big for his breeches. I'll have to put him back in his place.* ♦ *When the teacher made Bob a monitor, he got too big for his boots and she had to warn him.*

too ——— by half *adj. (princ. British)* Much too; excessively. ♦ *The heroine of the story is too nice by half; she is not believable.*

too close for comfort *adj. phr.* Perilously near (said of bad things). ♦ *When the sniper's bullet hit the road the journalist exclaimed, "Gosh, that was too close for comfort!"* Compare CLOSE CALL, CLOSE SHAVE.

too many cooks spoil the broth *or* **stew** A project is likely to go bad if managed by a multiplicity of primary movers.—A proverb. ♦ *When several* people acted all at once in trying to reshape the company's investment policy, Tom spoke up and said, "Let me do this by myself! Don't you know that too many cooks spoil the broth?"

too many irons in the fire See IRONS IN THE FIRE.

to one See TEN TO ONE, TWO TO ONE.

to oneself[1] *adv. phr.* **1.** Silently; in the thoughts; without making a sign that others can see; secretly. ♦ *Tom thought to himself that he could win.* ♦ *Mary said to herself that Joan was prettier than Ann.* ♦ *Bill laughed to himself when John fell down.* **2.** Without telling others; in private; as a secret.—Used after *keep.* ♦ *Mary keeps her affairs to herself.* ♦ *John knew the answer to the problem, but he kept it to himself.*

to oneself[2] *adj. phr.* **1.** Without company; away from others; alone; deserted. ♦ *The boys went home and John was left to himself.* ♦ *When Mary first moved to her new neighborhood she was very shy and kept to herself.* **2.** Following one's own beliefs or wishes; not stopped by others. ♦ *When John insisted on going, Fred left him to himself.* ♦ *The teacher left Mary to herself to solve the problem.*

to one's face *adv. phr.* Directly to you; in your presence. ♦ *I told him to his face that I didn't like the idea.* ♦ *I called him a coward to his face.* Compare IN ONE'S FACE. Contrast BEHIND ONE'S BACK.

to one's feet *adv. phr.* To a standing position; up. ♦ *After Henry had been tackled hard by four big players, he got to his feet slowly and painfully.* ♦ *When Sally saw the bus coming, she jumped to her feet and ran out.* Compare ON ONE'S FEET.

to one's guns See STICK TO ONE'S GUNS.

to one's heart's content *adv. phr.* To the extent of one's wishes; one's complete satisfaction. ♦ *There is a wonderful small restaurant nearby where you can eat to your heart's content.*

to one's heels See TAKE TO ONE'S HEELS.

to one's name *adv. phr.* In your ownership; of your own; as part of your belongings. ♦ *David did not have a book to his name.* ♦ *Ed had only one suit to his name.*

to one's ribs See STICK TO ONE'S RIBS.

to one's senses See COME TO ONE'S SENSES.

to order *adv. phr.* According to directions given in an order in the way and size wanted. ♦ *The manufacturer built the machine to order.* ♦ *A very big man often has his suits made to order.* **2.** See CALL TO ORDER .

tooth See BY THE SKIN OF ONE'S TEETH, CUT TEETH OR CUT EYETEETH, EYE FOR AN EYE AND A TOOTH FOR A TOOTH, FED TO THE GILLS *or* FED TO THE TEETH, GET ONE'S TEETH INTO OR SINK ONE'S TEETH INTO, KICK IN THE PANTS *or* KICK IN THE TEETH, PULL ONE'S TEETH, SET ONE'S TEETH ON EDGE, TAKE THE BIT IN ONE'S TEETH, THROW SOMETHING IN ONE'S FACE *or* THROW SOMETHING IN ONE'S TEETH.

tooth and nail See HAMMER AND TONGS.

tooth and nail *adv. phr.* With all weapons or ways of fighting as hard as possible; fiercely.—Used after *fight* or a similar word. ♦ *When the Indian girl was captured, she fought tooth and nail to get away.* ♦ *The farmers fought tooth and nail to save their crops from the grasshoppers.* ♦ *His friends fought tooth and nail to elect him to Congress.*

toot one's own horn See BLOW ONE'S OWN HORN.

top See AT THE TOP OF ONE'S VOICE, BIG TOP, BLOW A FUSE *or* BLOW ONE'S TOP, HARD-TOP, OFF THE TOP OF ONE'S HEAD, ON TOP, ON TOP OF, ON TOP OF THE WORLD, OVER THE TOP.

top banana *or* **top dog** *n., slang informal* The head of any business or organization; the most influential or most prestigious person in an establishment. ♦ *Who's the top banana/dog in this outfit?* See MAIN SQUEEZE.

to pass See COME TO PASS.

top-drawer *adj., informal* Of the best; or most important kind. ♦ *Mary's art work was top-drawer material.* ♦ *Mr. Rogers is a top-drawer executive and gets a very high salary.*

topflight *or* **topnotch** See TOP DRAWER.

to pieces *adv. phr.* **1.** Into broken pieces or fragments; destroyed. ♦ *The cannon shot the town to pieces.* ♦ *The vase fell to pieces in Mary's hand.* **2.** *informal* So as not to work; into a state of not operating. ♦ *After 100,000 miles the car* went to pieces. ♦ *When Mary heard of her mother's death, she went to pieces.* **3.** *informal* Very much; greatly; exceedingly. ♦ *Joan was thrilled to pieces to see Mary.* ♦ *The noise scared Bob to pieces.* **4.** See PICK APART.

top off *v.* To come or bring to a special or unexpected ending; climax. ♦ *John batted three runs and topped off the game with a home run.* ♦ *Mary hadn't finished her homework, she was late to school, and to top it all off she missed a surprise test.* ♦ *George had steak for dinner and topped it off with a fudge sundae.*

to put it mildly See TO SAY THE LEAST.

torch See CARRY A TORCH.

to reason See STAND TO REASON.

to rest See LAY TO REST.

to rights See PUT TO RIGHTS *or* SET TO RIGHTS.

to Rome See ALL ROADS LEAD TO ROME.

to say nothing of See NOT TO MENTION.

to say the least *v. phr.* To understate; express as mildly as possible. ♦ *After all we did for him, his behavior toward us, to say the least, was a poor way to show his appreciation.*

to scale *adv. phr.* In the same proportions as in the true size; in the same shape, but not the same size. ♦ *The statue was made to scale, one inch to a foot.* ♦ *He drew the map to scale, making one inch represent fifty miles.*

to sea See PUT TO SEA.

to shame See PUT TO SHAME.

to size See CUT DOWN TO SIZE.

to speak of *adj. phr., informal* Important; worth talking about; worth noticing.—Usually used in negative sentences. ♦ *Did it rain yesterday? Not to speak of.* ♦ *What happened at the meeting? Nothing to speak of.* ♦ *Judy's injuries were nothing to speak of; just a few scratches.* Compare NOT TO MENTION.

to spite one's face See CUT OFF ONE'S NOSE TO SPITE ONE'S FACE.

toss off *v. phr.* **1.** To drink rapidly; drain. ♦ *He tossed off two drinks and left.* **2.** To make or say easily without trying or thinking hard. ♦ *She tossed off smart remarks all during dinner.* ♦ *He thinks a reporter should be able to toss off an article every few hours.*

toss one to the sharks See THROW ONE

TO THE WOLVES.

toss out See THROW OUT.

total See SUM TOTAL.

to task See TAKE TO TASK.

to terms See BRING TO TERMS, COME TO TERMS.

to that effect *adj. or adv. phr.* With that meaning. ♦ *She said she hated spinach, or words to that effect.* ♦ *When I leave, I will write you to that effect so you will know.*

to the best of one's knowledge As far as you know; to the extent of your knowledge. ♦ *He has never won a game, to the best of my knowledge.* ♦ *To the best of my knowledge he is a college man, but I may be mistaken.*

to the bitter end *adv. phr.* To the point of completion or conclusion.—Used especially of a very painful or unpleasant task or experience. ♦ *Although Mrs. Smith was bored by the lecture, she stayed to the bitter end.* ♦ *They knew the war would be lost, but the men fought to the bitter end.*

to the bone *adv., slang, informal* Thoroughly, entirely, to the core, through all layers. ♦ *I am dreadfully tired; I've worked my fingers to the bone.* See ALSO WORK ONE'S FINGERS TO THE BONE.

to the bottom See GET TO THE BOTTOM OF.

to the contrary *adv. or adj. phr.* With an opposite result or effect; just the opposite; in disagreement; saying the opposite. ♦ *Although Bill was going to the movies, he told Joe to the contrary.* ♦ *We will expect you for dinner unless we get word to the contrary.* ♦ *School gossip to the contrary, Mary is not engaged to be married.* Compare ON THE CONTRARY.

to the effect that *adj. phr.* With the meaning or purpose; to say that. ♦ *He made a speech to the effect that we would all keep our jobs even if the factory were sold.* ♦ *The new governor would do his best in the office to which he had been elected.*

to the eye *adv. phr.* As it is seen; as a person or thing first seems; apparently. ♦ *That girl looks to the eye like a nice girl to know, but she is really rather mean.* ♦ *That suit appears to the eye to be a good buy, but it may not be.*

Compare AT FIRST GLANCE.

to the fore *adv. or adj. phr.* Into leadership; out into notice or view; forward. ♦ *The hidden skill of the lawyer came to the fore during the trial.* ♦ *In the progress of the war some new leaders came to the fore.*

to the full *adv. phr.* Very much; fully. ♦ *The campers enjoyed their trip to the full.* ♦ *We appreciated to the full the teacher's help.* Compare TO THE HILT.

to the gallery See PLAY TO THE GALLERY.

to the good *adv. phr.* On the side of profit or advantage; in one's favor; to one's benefit; ahead. ♦ *After I sold my stamp collection, I was ten dollars to the good.* ♦ *The teacher did not see him come in late, which was all to the good.*

to the grindstone See KEEP ONE'S NOSE TO THE GRINDSTONE.

to the heart See GET TO THE HEART OF.

to the hilt *or* **up to the hilt** *adv. phr.* To the limit; as far as possible; completely. ♦ *The other boys on the team told Tom he couldn't quit. They said, "You're in this to the hilt."* ♦ *The Smith's house is mortgaged up to the hilt.* Compare HEART AND SOUL, TO THE FULL, UP TO THE ———— IN.

to the kings taste *or* **to the queen's taste** *adv. phr.* Perfectly; just as anyone could want it; very satisfactorily. ♦ *The rooms in her new home were painted and decorated to the queen's taste.* ♦ *The soldiers dressed and marched to the king's taste.*

to the letter *adv. phr.* With nothing done wrong or left undone; exactly; precisely. ♦ *He carried out his orders to the letter.* ♦ *When writing a test you should follow the instructions to the letter.* Compare TO A T.

to the manner born *adj. phr.* At ease with something because of lifelong familiarity with it. ♦ *She says her English is the best because she is to the manner born.*

to the nth degree *adv. phr.* To the greatest degree possible; extremely; very much so. ♦ *Scales must be accurate to the nth degree.* ♦ *His choice of words was exactly to the nth degree.*

to the point See COME TO THE POINT.

to the punch See BEAT TO THE PUNCH.

to the ribs See STICK TO ONE'S RIBS *or* STICK TO THE RIBS.

to the salt mines See BACK TO THE SALT MINES.

to the stump See TAKE THE STUMP *or* TAKE TO THE STUMP.

to the sword See PUT TO THE SWORD.

to the tune of *adv. phr., informal* To the amount or extent of; in the amount of. ◆*He had to pay to the tune of fifty dollars for seeing how fast the car would go.* ◆*When she left the race track she had profited to the tune of ten dollars.*

to the wall *adv. phr.* Into a place from which there is no escape; into a trap or corner.—Usually used after *drive* or a similar word. ◆*John's failing the last test drove him to the wall.* ◆*The score was 12–12 in the last minute of play, but a touchdown forced the visitors to the wall.* ◆*Bill had to sell his five Great Danes. The high cost of feeding them was driving him to the wall.*

to the wolves See THROW TO THE WOLVES.

to the woods See TAKE TO THE WOODS.

to the world See DEAD TO THE WORLD.

to think of it See COME TO THINK OF IT.

toto See IN TOTO.

touch See COMMON TOUCH, IN TOUCH, LOSE TOUCH, OUT OF TOUCH.

touch and go *adj. phr.* Very dangerous or uncertain in situation. ◆*Our team won the game, all right, but it was touch and go for a while.* ◆*At one time while they were climbing the cliff it was touch and go whether they could do it.*

touch base with *v. phr.* To confer or consult with one. ◆*Before we make a decision, I'd like to touch base with our financial department.*

touch bottom See HIT BOTTOM.

touch off *v.* **1.** To cause to fire or explode by lighting the priming or the fuse. ◆*The boy touched off a firecracker.* Compare SET OFF. **2.** To start something as if by lighting a fuse. ◆*The coach's resignation touched off a quarrel.* Compare SET OFF.

touch on *or* **touch upon** *v.* To speak of or write of briefly. ◆*The speaker touched on several other subjects in the course of his talk but mostly kept himself to the main topic.* Contrast DWELL ON.

touch to the quick *v. phr.* To hurt someone's feelings very deeply; offend. ◆*His remark about her lack of education touched her to the quick.*

touchup *n.* **1.** A small repair; a small amount of paint. ◆*Just a small touchup here and there and your novel may be publishable.* **2.** Redoing the color of one's hair. ◆*My roots are showing; I need a touchup.*

touch up *v.* **1.** To paint over (small imperfections.) ◆*I want to touch up that scratch on the fender.* ◆*The woodwork is done, but there are a few places he has to touch up.* **2.** To improve with small additions or changes. ◆*He touched up the photographic negative to make a sharper print.* ◆*It's a good speech, but it needs a little touching up.* **3.** *slang* To talk into lending; wheedle from. ◆*He touched George up for five bucks.*

tough act to follow *n. phr.* A speech, performance, or activity of such superior quality that the person next in line feels and thinks that it would be very difficult to match it in quality. ◆*Sir Lawrence Olivier's performance of* Hamlet *was a tough act to follow in every sense.*

tough break See TOUGH LUCK, TOUGH SHIT.

tough cat *n., slang* A man who is very individualistic and, as a result, highly successful with women. ◆*Joe is a real tough cat, man.*

tough cookie *n. phr.* An extremely determined, hardheaded person, or someone with whom it is unusually difficult to deal. ◆*Marjorie is a very pretty girl, but when it comes to business she sure is one tough cookie.*

tough it out *v. phr.* To live through and endure a trying situation. ◆*The tourists got lost in the desert without a compass, and they had to tough it out for three days on a single bottle of water.*

tough luck *n. phr.* An informal way to say that one had that coming; it serves one right. ◆*So your date didn't show up, eh? Tough luck, fellow.*

tough nut to crack See HARD NUT TO CRACK.

tough row to hoe See HARD ROW TO HOE.

tough shit *n. phr., vulgar, avoidable* See HARD CHEESE, TOUGH LUCK.

tough sledding See HARD SLEDDING.

tourist trap See CLIP JOINT.

to use See PUT TO USE.

tow See IN TOW.

towel See THROW IN THE SPONGE *or* THROW IN THE TOWEL.

tower of strength *n. phr.* Someone who is strong, helpful, and sympathetic, and can always be relied on in times of trouble. ♦ *John was a veritable tower of strength to our family while my father was in the war and my mother lay ill in the hospital.*

town See GO TO TOWN, ON THE TOWN, PAINT THE TOWN RED.

town and gown *n.* The residents of a college town and the students and teachers of the college. ♦ *The senator made a speech attended by both town and gown.* ♦ *There were fights between town and gown.*

toy with an *or* **the idea** *v. phr.* To consider an idea or an offer periodically without coming to a decision. ♦ *He was toying with the idea of accepting the company's offer of the vice presidency in Tokyo, but he was unable to decide.*

to your hat See HANG ON TO YOUR HAT *or* HOLD ON TO YOUR HAT.

trace See KICK OVER THE TRACES *also* JUMP THE TRACES.

track See COVER ONE'S TRACKS, IN ONE'S TRACKS, INSIDE TRACK, JUMP THE TRACK, KEEP TRACK, LOSE TRACK, MAKE TRACKS, OFF THE BEATEN TRACK, ON THE TRACK OF, THE TRACKS.

track down *v.* To find by or as if by following tracks or a trail. ♦ *The hunters tracked down game in the forest.* ♦ *She spent weeks in the library tracking the reference down in all their books on the subject.* Compare HUNT DOWN.

trade See CARRIAGE TRADE, HORSE TRADE, TRICKS OF THE TRADE.

trade in *v.* To give something to a seller as part payment for another thing of greater value. ♦ *The Browns traded their old car in on a new one.* Syn. TURN IN 3.

trade-in *n.* Something given as part payment on something better. ♦ *The dealer took our old car as a trade-in.*—Often used like an adjective. ♦ *We cleaned up the car at trade-in time.*

trade on *v.* To use as a way of helping yourself. ♦ *The coach traded on the pitcher's weakness for left-handed batters by using all his southpaws.* ♦ *The senator's son traded on his father's*

name when he ran for mayor.

trading stamp *n.* One of the stamps that you get (as from a store or gas station) because you buy something there; a stamp you get with a purchase and save in special books until you have enough to take to a special store and trade for something you want. ♦ *Mother always buys things in stores where they give trading stamps.*

trail See BLAZE A TRAIL, ON THE TRACK OF *or* ON THE TRAIL OF.

trail-blazer See BLAZE A TRAIL.

trap See MIND LIKE A STEEL TRAP, SAND TRAP, SPEED TRAP.

travel light *v. phr.* To travel with very little luggage or with very little to carry. ♦ *Plane passengers must travel light.* ♦ *Tom and Fred traveled light on their camping trip.*

tread on the toes of *or* **tread on one's toes** See STEP ON THE TOES OF *or* STEP ON ONE'S TOES.

tread water *v. phr.* To keep the head above water with the body in an upright position by moving the feet as if walking. ♦ *He kept afloat by treading water.*

treat See TRICK OR TREAT.

tree See BARK UP THE WRONG TREE, CAN'T SEE THE WOOD FOR THE TREES, UP A TREE.

trembling See FEAR AND TREMBLING.

trial See ON TRIAL.

trial and error *n.* A way of solving problems by trying different possible solutions until you find one that works. ♦ *John found the short circuit by trial and error.* ♦ *The only way Tom could solve the algebra problem was by the method of trial and error.*

trial balloon *n.* A hint about a plan of action that is given out to find out what people will say. ♦ *John mentioned the class presidency to Bill as a trial balloon to see if Bill might be interested in running.* ♦ *The editorial was a trial balloon to test the public's reaction to a change in the school day.*

trice See IN A FLASH *also* IN A TRICE.

trick See DO THE TRICK, TURN THE TRICK.

trick of the trade *n. phr., usually in plural, informal* **1.** A piece of expert knowledge; a smart, quick, or skillful way of working at a trade or job. ♦ *Mr. Olson spent years learning the tricks of* *the trade as a carpenter.* ♦*Anyone can learn how to hang wallpaper, but only an expert can show you the tricks of the trade.* **2.** A smart and sometimes tricky or dishonest way of doing something in order to succeed or win. ♦*The champion knows all the tricks of the boxing trade; he knows many ways to hurt his opponent and to get him mixed up.*

trick or treat *n.* The custom of going from house to house on Halloween asking for small gifts and playing tricks on people who refuse to give. ♦*When Mrs. Jones answered the doorbell, the children yelled "Trick or treat." Mrs. Jones gave them all some candy.* ♦*On Halloween Bill and Tom went out playing trick or treat.*

trigger See QUICK ON THE TRIGGER.

trigger happy See QUICK ON THE TRIGGER 1.

triple threat *n.* A football player who is able to pass, kick, and run all very well. ♦*The triple threat halfback was the star of the team.*

tripped out *adj., slang, informal* Incoherent, confused, faulty of speech, illogical; as if under the influence of drugs or alcohol. ♦*It was hard to make sense of anything Fred said yesterday, he sounded so tripped out.* See SPACED OUT.

trip up *v.* **1.** To make (someone) unsteady on the feet; cause to miss a step, stumble, or fall. ♦*A root tripped Billy up while he was running in the woods, and he fell and hurt his ankle.* **2.** To cause (someone) to make a mistake. ♦*The teacher asked tricky questions in the test to trip up students who were not alert.*

trolley See OFF ONE'S ROCKER *or* OFF ONE'S TROLLEY.

trot out *v. phr.* To bring out for inspection; display. ♦*Don't mention compact disks to Joe, or he'll trot out his entire collection and we'll be stuck here all night.*

trouble See BORROW TROUBLE, GO TO THE TROUBLE *or* TAKE THE TROUBLE.

troubled waters See POUR OIL ON TROUBLED WATERS .

trousers See WEAR THE TROUSERS.

trowel See LAY IT ON.

truck See PANEL TRUCK.

true See COME TRUE, HOLD TRUE, RUN TRUE TO FORM.

trump See HOLD ALL THE TRUMPS.

trump card *n.* Something kept back to be used to win success if nothing else works. ♦*The coach saved his star pitcher for a trump card.* ♦*Mary had several ways to get Joan to come to her party. Her trump card was that the football captain would be there.*

trump up *v.* To make up (something untrue); invent in the mind. ♦*Every time Tom is late getting home he trumps up some new excuse.* ♦*The Russians were afraid he was a spy, so they arrested him on a trumped-up charge and made him leave the country.*

trust See IN TRUST.

truth See CHILDREN AND FOOLS SPEAK THE TRUTH.

try on *v.* To put (clothing) on to see if it fits. ♦*She tried on several pairs of shoes before she found one she liked.* ♦*The clerk told him to try the coat on.*

try one's hand *v. phr.* To make an inexperienced attempt (at something unfamiliar.) ♦*I thought I would try my hand at bowling, although I had never bowled before.*

try one's wings *v. phr.* To try out a recently acquired ability. ♦*Marjorie just had her twelfth French lesson and wants to try her wings by speaking with our visitors from Paris.*

tryout *n.* An audience at a theater or opera for would-be actors and singers. ♦*The Civic Opera is holding tryouts throughout all of next week. Maybe I'll go and see if I can sing in the chorus.*

try out *v. phr.* **1.** To test by trial or by experimenting. ♦*He tried golf out to see if he would like it.* ♦*The scientists tried out thousands of chemicals before they found the right one.* ♦*The coach wants to try the new play out in the first game.* **2.** To try for a place on a team or in a group. ♦*Tom tried out for the basketball team.* ♦*Shirley will try out for the lead in the play.* Compare OUT FOR.

tuck See NIP AND TUCK.

tucker See BEST BIB AND TUCKER.

tuck in *v. phr.* To place the covers carefully around the person (usually a child) in bed. ♦*When I was a child, my mother used to tuck me into bed every night.*

tug-of-war *n.* **1.** A game in which two teams pull on opposite ends of a rope, trying to pull the other team over a line marked on the ground. ♦ *The tug-of-war ended when both teams tumbled in a heap.* **2.** A contest in which two sides try to defeat each other; struggle. ♦ *A tug-of-war developed between the boys who wanted to go fishing and those who wanted to go hiking.* ♦ *Betty felt a tug-of-war between her wish to go to the movies and her realizing she had to do her homework.* ♦ *The tug of war between the union men and management ended in a long strike.*

tune See CALL THE TUNE, CHANGE ONE'S TUNE, IN TUNE, SING A DIFFERENT TUNE *or* WHISTLE A DIFFERENT TUNE *also* SING A NEW TUNE, TO THE TUNE OF.

tune in To adjust a radio or television set to pick up a certain station. ♦ *Bob tuned in his portable radio to a record show.* ♦ *Tom tuned in to Channel 11 to hear the news.*

tune out *v. phr.* To not listen to something. ♦ *"How can you work in such a noisy environment?" Jane asked Sue. "Well, I simply tune it out," she answered.*

tune up *v.* **1a.** To adjust (a musical instrument) to make the right sound. ♦ *Before he began to play, Harry tuned up his banjo.* **1b.** To adjust a musical instrument or a group of musical instruments to the right sound. ♦ *The orchestra came in and began to tune up for the concert.* **2.** To adjust many parts of (car engine) which must work together so that it will run properly. ♦ *He took his car to the garage to have the engine tuned up.*

tune-up *n.* **1.** The adjusting or fixing of something (as a motor) to make it work safely and well. ♦ *Father says the car needs a tune-up before winter begins.* **2.** Exercise or practicing for the purpose of getting ready; a trial before something. ♦ *The team went to the practice field for their last tune-up before the game tomorrow.* Syn. WARM UP.

turkey See TALK TURKEY.

turn See AT EVERY TURN, BLOOD RUN COLD *or* BLOOD TURNS TO ICE, BY TURNS, CALL THE TURN *at* CALL ONE'S SHOTS 2, EVERY TIME ONE TURNS AROUND, IN TURN, NOT KNOW WHICH WAY TO TURN, OUT OF TURN, TAKE A TURN, TAKE TURNS, TO A T *or* TO A TURN.

turn a blind eye *v. phr.* To pretend not to see; not pay attention. ♦ *The corrupt police chief turned a blind eye to the open gambling in the town.* ♦ *Bob turned a blind eye to the "No Fishing" sign.* Compare CLOSE ONE'S EYES.

turn a cold shoulder See COLD SHOULDER.

turn a deaf ear to *v. phr.* To pretend not to hear; refuse to hear; not pay attention. ♦ *Mary turned a deaf ear to Lois's asking to ride her bicycle.* ♦ *The teacher turned a deaf ear to Bob's excuse.* Compare COLD SHOULDER.

turn a hand *v. phr.* To do anything to help.—Usually used in the negative. ♦ *When we were all hurrying to get the house ready for company, Mary sat reading and wouldn't turn a hand.* Syn. LIFT A FINGER.

turn an honest penny *v. phr.* To realize a good profit. ♦ *Tom turned an honest penny in the soybean trading business.* Compare PRETTY PENNY.

turn back the clock See PUT BACK THE CLOCK.

turn color *v. phr.* To become a different color. ♦ *In the fall the leaves turn color.* ♦ *When the dye was added the solution turned color.*

turn down *v.* **1.** To reduce the loudness, brightness, or force of. ♦ *The theater lights were turned down.* ♦ *Turn down that radio, will you?* ♦ *The hose was throwing too much water so I turned down the water a little bit.* **2.** To refuse to accept; reject. ♦ *His request for a raise was turned down.* ♦ *If she offers to help, I'll turn her down.* ♦ *Many boys courted Lynn, but she turned them all down.*

turn for the worse See FOR THE WORSE.

turn in *v.* **1.** *or* **hand in** To give to someone; deliver to someone. ♦ *I want you to turn in a good history paper.* ♦ *When the football season was over, we turned in our uniforms.* **2.** To inform on; report. ♦ *She turned them in to the police for breaking the street light.* **3.** To give in return for something. ♦ *They turned in their old money for new.* ♦ *We turned our car in on a* *new model.* Syn. TRADE IN. **4.** *informal* To go to bed. ♦*We were tired, so we turned in about nine o'clock.* Contrast TURN OUT 4.

turn in one's grave *or* **turn over in one's grave** *v. phr.* To be so grieved or angry that you would not rest quietly in your grave. ♦*If your grandfather could see what you're doing now, he would turn over in his grave.*

turn loose See LET LOOSE 1a.

turn off *v.* **1.** To stop by turning a knob or handle or by working a switch; to cause to be off. ♦*He turned the water off.* ♦*He turned off the light.* **2.** To leave by turning right or left onto another way. ♦*Turn off the highway at exit 5.* ♦*The car turned off on Bridge Street. slang* **3.** To disgust, bore, or repel (someone) by being intellectually, emotionally, socially, or sexually unattractive. ♦*I won't date Linda Bell anymore—she just turns me off.* Contrast TURN ON.

turn of the century *n. phr.* The time at the end of one century and the beginning of the next century; *especially:* The time when the 1800's became the 1900's; the early 1900's. ♦*Automobiles were strange things to see at the turn of the century.*

turn on *v.* **1.** To start by turning a knob or handle or working a switch; cause to be on. ♦*Jack turned on the water.* ♦*Who turned the lights on?* **2.** *informal* To put forth or succeed with as easily as turning on water. ♦*She really turns on the charm when that new boy is around.* **3.** To attack. ♦*The lion tamer was afraid the lions would turn on him.* ♦*After Joe fumbled the ball and lost the big game, his friends turned on him.* **4.** *slang* The opposite of turning someone off; to become greatly interested in an idea, person, or undertaking; to arouse the senses pleasantly. ♦*Mozart's music always turns me on.* **5.** Introducing someone to a new experience, or set of values. ♦*Benjamin turned me on to transcendental meditation, and ever since I've been feeling great!* Contrast TURN OFF.

turn on a dime *v. phr.* To be able to turn in a very narrow spot comparable to a small coin. ♦*This new sports car can turn on a dime.*

turn one around one's little finger See TWIST ONE AROUND ONE'S LITTLE FINGER.

turn one's back on *v. phr.* To refuse to help (someone in trouble or need.) ♦*He turned his back on his own family when they needed help.* ♦*The poorer nations are often not grateful for our help, but still we can not turn our back on them.* Compare GO BACK ON 1.

turn one's hand to See PUT ONE'S HAND TO.

turn one's head *v. phr., informal* To make you lose your good judgment. ♦*The first pretty girl he saw turned his head.* ♦*Winning the class election turned his head.*

turn one's nose up at *v. phr.* To scorn; snub; look down at somebody or something. ♦*I don't understand why Sue has to turn her nose up at everyone who didn't go to an Ivy League college.*

turn one's stomach *v. phr., informal* To make you feel sick. ♦*The smell of that cigar was enough to turn your stomach.* ♦*The sight of blood turns my stomach.*

turn on one's heel *v. phr.* To turn around suddenly. ♦*When John saw Fred approaching him, he turned on his heel.* ♦*When little Tommy's big brother showed up, the bully turned on his heel.*

turnout *n.* The number of people in attendance at a gathering. ♦*This is a terrific turnout for Tim's poetry reading.*

turn out *v.* **1.** To make leave or go away. ♦*His father turned him out of the house.* ♦*If you don't behave, you will be turned out.* Compare THROW OUT. **2.** To turn inside out; empty. ♦*He turned out his pockets looking for the money.* ♦*Robbers turned out all the drawers in the house in a search for jewels.* **3.** To make; produce. ♦*The printing press turns out a thousand books an hour.* ♦*Sally can turn out a cake in no time.* ♦*Martin turns out a poem each week for the school paper.* **4.** *informal* To get out of bed. ♦*At camp the boys had to turn out early and go to bed early too.* Contrast TURN IN 4. **5.** *informal* To come or go out to see or do something. ♦*Everybody turned out for the big parade.* ♦*Many boys turned out for football practice.* Compare FALL OUT. **6.** To prove to be;

be in the end; be found to be. ♦ *The noise turned out to be just the dog scratching at the door.* ♦ *Her guess turned out to be right.* ♦ *Everything turned out all right.* **7.** To make (a light) go out. ♦ *Please turn out the lights.* Syn. TURN OFF 1.

turnover *n.* **1.** The proportion of expenditure and income realized in a business; the volume of traffic in a business. ♦ *Our turnover is so great that in two short years we tripled our original investment and are expanding at a great rate.* **2.** Triangular baked pastry filled with some fruit. ♦ *John's favorite dessert is apple turnovers.* **3.** The number of employees coming and going in a company. ♦ *The boss is so strict in our office that the turnover in personnel is very large.*

turn over *v.* **1.** To roll, tip, or turn from one side to the other; overturn; upset. ♦ *He's going to turn over the page.* ♦ *The bike hit a rock and turned over.* **2.** To think about carefully; to consider. ♦ *He turned the problem over in his mind for three days before he did anything about it.* **3.** To give to someone for use or care. ♦ *I turned my library books over to the librarian.* ♦ *Mrs. Jackson brought her boy to the school and turned him over to the house father.* ♦ *Bob turns over most of the money he earns to his mother.* **4.** Of an engine or motor; to start. ♦ *The battery is dead and the motor won't turn over.* **5a.** To buy and then sell to customers. ♦ *The store turned over $5,000 worth of skiing equipment in January.* **5b.** To be bought in large enough amounts; sell. ♦ *In a shoe store, shoes of medium width turn over quickly, because many people wear that size, but a pair of narrow shoes may not be sold for years.*

turn over a new leaf *v. phr.* To start afresh; to have a new beginning. ♦ *"Don't be sad, Jane," Sue said. "A divorce is not the end of the world. Just turn over a new leaf and you will soon be happy again."* Compare CLEAN SLATE.

turn over in one's grave See TURN IN ONE'S GRAVE .

turn over in one's mind *v. phr.* To carefully consider. ♦ *I will have to turn it over in my mind whether to accept the new job offer from Japan.*

turn tail *v. phr., informal* To run away from trouble or danger. ♦ *When the bully saw my big brother, he turned tail and ran.*

turn the clock back *v. phr.* To return to an earlier period. ♦ *Mother wished she could turn the clock back to the days before the children grew up and left home.* ♦ *Will repealing the minimum wage for workers under age eighteen turn the clock back to the abuses of the last century?*

turn the other cheek *v. phr.* To let someone do something to you and not to do it in return; not hit back when hit; be patient when injured or insulted by someone; not try to get even. ♦ *Joe turned the other cheek when he was hit with a snowball.*

turn the scales *v. phr.* To affect the balance in favor of one party or group against the other. ♦ *It could well be that the speech he made turned the scales in their favor.*

turn the tables *v. phr.* To make something happen just the opposite of how it is supposed to happen. ♦ *The boys turned the tables on John when they took his squirt gun away and squirted him.*

turn the tide *v. phr.* To change what looks like defeat into victory. ♦ *We were losing the game until Jack got there. His coming turned the tide for us, and we won.* Compare TIP THE SCALES.

turn the trick *v. phr., informal* To bring about the result you want; succeed in what you plan to do. ♦ *Jerry wanted to win both the swimming and diving contests, but he couldn't quite turn the trick.* Compare DO THE TRICK.

turn thumbs down *v. phr.* To disapprove or reject; say no.—Usually used with *on.* ♦ *The company turned thumbs down on Mr. Smith's sales plan. The men turned thumbs down on a strike at that time.*

turn to *v.* To begin working with much energy. ♦ *All the boys turned to and cleaned the cabin in a few minutes.* ♦ *Mary turned to and studied for the test.* Syn. FALL TO.

turn turtle *v. phr.* To turn upside down. ♦ *The car skidded on the ice and turned turtle.*

turn up v. **1.** To find; discover. ♦ *The police searched the house hoping to turn up more clues.* **2.** To appear or be found suddenly or unexpectedly. ♦ *The missing boy turned up an hour later.* ♦ *A man without training works at whatever jobs turn up.* Compare SHOW UP 3.

turn up one's nose at v. phr. To refuse as not being good enough for you. ♦ *He thinks he should only get steak, and he turns up his nose at hamburger.*

turn up one's toes v. phr., slang To die. ♦ *One morning the children found that their pet mouse had turned up his toes, so they had a funeral for him.* Compare PUSH UP THE DAISIES.

turtle See TURN TURTLE.

tut-tut interj., informal—Used to express mild disapproval. ♦ *"Tut-tut," said the teacher. "You shouldn't cross the street without looking."* ♦ *Tut-tut, put that piece of candy back. You've already had three pieces.*

twice See BIG AS LIFE 2, LIGHTNING NEVER STRIKES TWICE IN THE SAME PLACE, THINK TWICE, ONCE BITTEN, TWICE SHY and BURNT CHILD DREADS THE FIRE.

twice as natural See BIG AS LIFE or BIG AS LIFE AND TWICE AS NATURAL.

twiddle one's thumbs v. phr. To do nothing; be idle. ♦ *I'd rather work than stand around here twiddling my thumbs.*

twist one around one's little finger also **turn one around one's little finger** or **wrap one around one's finger** v. phr. To have complete control over; to be able to make (someone) do anything you want. ♦ *Sue can twist any of the boys around her little finger.* Compare JUMP THROUGH A HOOP.

twist one's arm v. phr., informal To force someone; threaten someone to make him do something.—Usually used jokingly. ♦ *Will you dance with the prettiest girl in school? Stop, you're twisting my arm!* ♦ *I had to twist Tom's arm to make him eat the candy!*

two See BETWEEN THE DEVIL AND THE DEEP BLUE SEA or BETWEEN TWO FIRES, TWO CENTS, BIRD IN THE HAND IS WORTH TWO IN THE BUSH, CUT BOTH WAYS or CUT TWO WAYS, HAVE TWO STRIKES AGAINST ONE, IN TWO, KILL TWO BIRDS WITH ONE STONE, NO TWO WAYS ABOUT IT, PUT TWO AND TWO TOGETHER, STAND ON ONE'S OWN FEET or STAND ON ONE'S OWN TWO FEET, TELL A THING OR TWO, THING OR TWO.

two bits n., slang Twenty-five cents; a quarter of a dollar. ♦ *A haircut only cost two bits when Grandfather was young.* Compare FOUR BITS, SIX BITS.

two cents n. informal **1.** Something not important or very small; almost nothing. ♦ *Paul was so angry that he said for two cents he would quit the team.* ♦ *When John saw that the girl he was scolding was lame, he felt like two cents.* **2.** or **two cents worth** Something you want to say; opinion.—Used with a possessive. ♦ *The boys were talking about baseball, and Harry put in his two cents worth, even though he didn't know much about baseball.* ♦ *If we want your two cents, we'll ask for it.*

two-faced adj. Insincere; disloyal; deceitful. ♦ *Don't confide too much in him as he has the reputation of being two-faced.* Compare SPEAK WITH A FORKED TONGUE.

Two's company; three's a crowd An informal way to express a situation when two people desire privacy and a third one is present.—A proverb. ♦ *Beth and Carl wanted to be alone so when Maggie joined them they said, "Two's company; three's a crowd."*

two strikes against one n. phr.—From baseball. Two opportunities wasted in some undertaking, so that only one chance is left. ♦ *Poor John has two strikes against him when it comes to his love for Frances: first, he is too fat, and, second, he is bald.*

two-time v., slang To go out with a second boy or girlfriend and keep it a secret from the first. ♦ *Joan was two-timing Jim with Fred.* ♦ *Mary cried when she found that Joe was two-timing her.* Compare DOUBLE-CROSS.

two to one See TEN TO ONE.

two ways about it See NO TWO WAYS ABOUT IT.

U.F.O. *n. phr.* Unidentified Flying Object. ◆*Some people think that the U.F.O.s are extraterrestrial beings of higher than human development who pay periodic visits to Earth to warn us of our self-destructive tendencies.*

ugly duckling *n.* An ugly or plain child who grows up to be pretty and attractive. ◆*Mary was the ugly duckling in her family, until she grew up.*

uh-huh *or* **um-hum** *adv., informal* Yes.—Used only in speech or when recording dialogue. ◆*Are you going to the Fair? Uh-huh.* ◆*We were in Alaska, um-hum, but that was long before the earthquakes.* ◆*When I asked for an appointment, the nurse said, "Um-hum, I have an opening at four o'clock on Friday."* Contrast HUH-UH.

um-hum See UH-HUH.

unbosom oneself *v. phr.* To confess one's personal thoughts or feelings; disclose private information to a confidante. ◆*Once she was at home with her mother, she unbosomed herself of all her troubles.*

uncertain See IN SO MANY WORDS 2. or IN NO UNCERTAIN TERMS.

uncle See SAY UNCLE *also* CRY UNCLE.

under See CUT THE GROUND FROM UNDER, GO UNDER, OUT FROM UNDER, SNOW UNDER.

under a bushel See HIDE ONE'S LIGHT UNDER A BUSHEL.

under a cloud *adj. phr.* **1.** Under suspicion; not trusted. ◆*Joyce has been under a cloud since her roommate's bracelet disappeared.* ◆*The butcher is under a cloud because the inspectors found his scales were not honest.* **2.** Depressed, sad, discouraged. ◆*Joe has been under a cloud since his dog died.*

under age *adj. phr.* Too young; not old enough; below legal age. ◆*He could not enlist in the army because he was under age.* ◆*Rose was not allowed to enroll in the Life Saving Course because she was under age.* Contrast OF AGE 1.

under arrest *adj. phr.* Held by the police. ◆*The man believed to have robbed the bank was placed under arrest.* ◆*The three boys were seen breaking into the school building and soon found themselves under arrest.*

under construction *adv. phr.* In the process of being built or repaired. ◆*It is a good idea to take the train to work while the expressway is under construction.*

under cover *adv. or adj. phr.* Hidden; concealed. ◆*The prisoners escaped under cover of darkness.* ◆*He kept his invention under cover until it was patented.* Compare UNDER WRAPS.

under false colors See SAIL UNDER FALSE COLORS.

under fire *adv. phr.* Being shot at or being attacked; hit by attacks or accusations; under attack. ◆*The soldiers stood firm under fire of the enemy.* ◆*The principal was under fire for not sending the boys home who stole the car.*

under lock and key *adv. phr.* Secured; locked up; well protected. ◆*Dad keeps all his valuables under lock and key.*

under one's belt *adv. phr., informal* **1.** In your stomach; eaten; or absorbed. ◆*Once he had a good meal under his belt, the man loosened his tie and fell asleep.* ◆*Jones is talkative when he has a few drinks under his belt.* **2.** In your experience, memory or possession; learned or gotten successfully; gained by effort and skill. ◆*Jim has to get a lot of algebra under his belt before the examination.* ◆*With three straight victories under their belts, the team went on to win the championship.*

under one's breath *adv. phr.* In a whisper; with a low voice. ◆*The teacher heard the boy say something under his breath and she asked him to repeat it aloud.* ◆*I told Lucy the news under my breath, but Joyce overheard me.*

under one's hat See KEEP UNDER ONE'S HAT.

under one's heel *adv. phr.* In one's power or control. ◆*If one marriage partner always wants to keep the other person under his or her heel, it is not a happy or democratic arrangement and may lead to a divorce.*

under one's nose *or* **under the nose of**

adv. phr., informal In sight of; in an easily seen or noticeable place. ◆ *The thief walked out of the museum with the painting, right under the nose of the guards.* ◆ *When Jim gave up trying to find a pen, he saw three right under his nose on the desk.*

under one's own steam *adv. phr., informal* By one's own efforts; without help. ◆ *The boys got to Boston under their own steam and took a bus the rest of the way.* ◆ *We didn't think he could do it, but Bobby finished his homework under his own steam.*

under one's skin See GET UNDER ONE'S SKIN.

under one's spell *adv. phr.* Unable to resist one's influence. ◆ *From the first moment they saw each other, Peter was under Nancy's spell.*

under one's thumb *or* **under the thumb** *adj. or adv. phr.* Obedient to you; controlled by you; under your power. ◆ *The Jones family is under the thumb of the mother.* ◆ *Jack is a bully. He keeps all the younger children under his thumb.* ◆ *The mayor is so popular that he has the whole town under his thumb.* Compare JUMP THROUGH THE HOOP.

under one's wing *adv. phr.* Under the care or protection of. ◆ *Helen took the new puppy under her wing.* ◆ *The boys stopped teasing the new student when Bill took him under his wing.* Compare IN TOW.

under orders *adv. phr.* Not out of one's own desire or one's own free will; obligatorily; not freely. ◆ *"So you were a Nazi prison guard?" the judge asked. "Yes, your Honor," the man answered, "but I was acting under orders and not because I wished to harm anyone."*

under pain of See ON PAIN OF *also* UNDER PAIN OF.

under protest *adv. phr.* Against one's wish; unwillingly. ◆ *"I'll go with you all right," she said to the kidnapper, "but I want it clearly understood that I do so under protest."*

understand See GIVE ONE TO UNDERSTAND.

under the circumstances *also* **in the circumstances** *adv. phr.* In the existing situation; in the present condition; as things are. ◆ *In the circumstances, Father couldn't risk giving up his job.*

◆ *Under the circumstances, the stagecoach passengers had to give the robbers their money.*

under the collar See HOT UNDER THE COLLAR.

under the counter *adv. phr., informal* Secretly (bought or sold). ◆ *That book has been banned, but there is one place you can get it under the counter.* ◆ *The liquor dealer was arrested for selling beer under the counter to teenagers.*— Also used like an adjective, with hyphens. ◆ *During World War II, some stores kept scarce things hidden for under-the-counter-sales to good customers.*

under the hammer *adv. phr.* Up for sale at auction ◆ *The Brights auctioned off the entire contents of their home. Mrs. Bright cried when her pewter collection went under the hammer.* ◆ *The picture I wanted to bid on came under the hammer soon after I arrived.*

under the nose of See UNDER ONE'S NOSE.

under the sun *adj. or adv. phr.* On earth; in the world.—Used for emphasis. ◆ *The President's assassination shocked everyone under the sun.* ◆ *Where under the sun could I have put my purse?*

under the table See UNDER THE COUNTER.

under the thumb of See UNDER ONE'S THUMB.

under the weather *adv. phr.* In bad health or low spirits. ◆ *Mary called in today asking for a sick day as she is under the weather.*

under the wire *adv. phr.* With a narrow time limit; in the last minute. ◆ *The journalist's new lead article on Russia was due in press at 5 P.M., and he got it in at 4:57, just under the wire.*

underway *adv. phr.* In progress; in motion. ◆ *The yearly fund-raising campaign for the renovation of our university campus is already underway.*

under wraps *adv. or adj. phr.* Not allowed to be seen until the right time; not allowed to act or speak freely; in secrecy; hidden.—Usually used with *keep.* ◆ *We have a new player, but we are keeping him under wraps until the game.* ◆ *What the President is planning will be kept under wraps until* *tomorrow.* ♦ *The spy was kept under wraps and not allowed to talk to newspapermen.* Compare UNDER COVER.

unknown quantity *n.* Someone or something whose value and importance are not known, especially in a certain situation, time or place; a new and untested person or thing. ♦ *What we would find if we could fly to the moon is an unknown quantity.* ♦ *The new player is still an unknown quantity. We'll find out how good he is in the game.*

unseen See SIGHT UNSEEN.

until all hours *adv. phr.* Until very late at night. ♦ *He is so anxious to pass his exams with flying colors that he stays up studying until all hours.*

until hell freezes over *adv. phr., slang* Forever, for an eternity. ♦ *He can argue until hell freezes over; nobody will believe him.* Contrast WHEN HELL FREEZES OVER.

until the last gun is fired See TILL THE LAST GUN IS FIRED.

unturned See LEAVE NO STONE UNTURNED.

up against *prep. phr.* Blocked or threatened by. ♦ *When she applied to medical school, the black woman wondered whether she was up against barriers of sex and race prejudice.*

up against it *adj. phr., informal* Faced with a great difficulty or problem; badly in need. ♦ *The Smith family is up against it because Mr. Smith cannot find a job.* ♦ *You will be up against it if you don't pass the test. You will probably fail arithmetic.* Compare HARD UP, END OF ONE'S ROPE, BACK TO THE WALL 2.

up and about *or* **around** *adv. phr.* Recovered and able to move about; once again in good health after an illness. ♦ *My sister was ill for several weeks, but is now up and about again.*

up and at them 1. *adv. phr.* Actively engaged in a task as if doing combat. ♦ *"You want to know whether he will make a diligent worker?" Dick asked. "Well, I can tell you that most of the time he is up and at them like no one else I know."* **2.** *v. phr.* To become aggressively engaged in doing something; (useable as a command). ♦ *Come on, up and at them, you guys.*

We still have a lot of work to get done.

up-and-coming *adj. phr.* Bound toward success; upwardly mobile; progressive; ambitious. ♦ *The newly elected state senator is an up-and-coming young politician who is expected to be highly successful in national politics in the future.*

up a stump *adj. phr., slang* Stumped; blocked; mixed up or confused in what you are trying to do. ♦ *Jimmy knows how to add and subtract but fractions have him up a stump.*

up a tree *adv. or adj. phr.* **1.** Hunted or chased into a tree; treed. ♦ *The dog drove the coon up a tree so the hunter could shoot him.* **2.** *informal* in trouble; having problems; in a difficulty that it is hard to escape or think of a way out of. ♦ *John's father has him up a tree in the checker game.* Compare UP THE CREEK.

up for grabs *adj. phr., informal* Available for anyone to try to get; ready to be compctcd for; there for the taking. ♦ *When the captain of the football team moved out of town, his place was up for grabs.*

up front[1] *n., slang, informal* The managerial section of a corporation or firm. ♦ *Joe Catwallender finally made it (with the) up front.*

up front[2] *adj., slang, informal* Open, sincere, hiding nothing. ♦ *Sue was completely up front about why she didn't want to see him anymore.*

up in arms *adj. phr.* **1.** Equipped with guns or weapons and ready to fight. ♦ *All of the colonies were up in arms against the Redcoats.* Syn. IN ARMS. **2.** Very angry and wanting to fight. ♦ *Robert is up in arms because John said he was stupid.* ♦ *The students were up in arms over the new rule against food in the dormitory.*

up in the air *adj. or adv. phr.* **1.** *informal* In great anger or excitement. ♦ *My father went straight up in the air when he heard I damaged the car.* ♦ *The Jones family are all up in the air because they are taking a trip around the world.* Compare HIT THE CEILING, BLOW A FUSE. **2.** *also* **in midair** Not settled; uncertain; undecided. ♦ *Plans for the next meeting have been left up in the air until Jane gets better.* ♦ *The* *result of the game was left hanging in midair because it rained before the finish.* Compare LEAVE HANGING .

up one's alley See DOWN ONE'S ALLEY.

up one's sleeve *or* **in one's sleeve** *adv. phr.* **1.** Hidden in the sleeve of one's shirt or coat and ready for secret or wrongful use. ♦ *The crooked gambler hid aces up his sleeve during the card game so that he would win.* **2.** *informal* Kept secretly ready for the right time or for a time when needed. ♦ *Jimmy knew that his father had some trick up his sleeve because he was smiling to himself during the checker game.* Compare CARD UP ONE'S SLEEVE. **3.** SEE LAUGH UP ONE'S SLEEVE.

upon oneself See TAKE ON ONESELF *also* TAKE UPON ONESELF.

upon one's head See ON ONE'S HEAD.

upon the spot See ON THE SPOT 1.

upper See KEEP A STIFF UPPER LIP, ON ONE'S UPPERS.

upper crust *n., informal* The richest, most famous, or important people in a certain place; the highest class. ♦ *It is a school that only the children of the upper crust can afford.*

upper hand *or* **whip hand** *n.* Controlling power; advantage. ♦ *In the third round the champion got the upper hand over his opponent and knocked him out.* ♦ *The cowboy trained the wild horse so that he finally got the whip hand and tamed the horse.*

upper story *n.* **1.** A floor or level of a building above the first floor. ♦ *The apartment house where Gene lives is five stories high and he lives in one of the upper stories.* **2.** *slang* A person's head or brain. ♦ *Lulu has nobody home in the upper story.* ♦ *Bill's sister says he is weak in the upper story.*

Upsadaisy! *or* **Upsee-daisy!** *or* **Upsy-daisy!** *adv. phr.*—A popular exclamation used when just about anything is lifted, particularly a small child raised to his or her highchair or bed. ♦ *"Upsee-daisy!" the nurse said with a smile on her face, as she lifted the baby from its bed.*

ups and downs *n. phr.* Vicissitudes; alternating periods between good and bad times; changes in fortune. ♦ *He is now a wealthy stock trader, but at the beginning of his career he, too, had*

many ups and downs.

upset the applecart *or* **upset one's applecart** *v. phr., informal* To ruin a plan or what is being done, often by surprise or accident; change how things are or are being done, often unexpectedly; ruin or mix up another person's success or plan for success. ♦ *John upset the other team's applecart by hitting a home run in the last inning and we won the game.* ♦ *We are planning a surprise party for Bill, so don't let Mary upset the applecart by telling him before the party.* ♦ *Frank thinks he is going to be the boss, but I'll upset his applecart the first chance I get.* Compare ROCK THE BOAT.

upside down *adv. phr.* Overturned so that the bottom is up and the top is down. ♦ *The ladybug lay upside down in the sand and was unable to take off.* ♦ *The problem with this company is that everything is upside down; we need a new C.E.O.*

upstairs See NOBODY HOME UPSTAIRS.

up the creek *or* **up the creek without a paddle** *adj. phr., informal* In trouble or difficulty and unable to do anything about it; stuck. ♦ *Father said that if the car ran out of gas in the middle of the desert, we would be up the creek without a paddle.* ♦ *I'll be up the creek if I don't pass this history test.* Compare DEEP WATER, IN THE SOUP, UP A TREE, OUT OF LUCK.

up tight *or* **uptight** *adj., slang, informal* Worried, irritated, excessively eager or anxious. ♦ *Why are you so uptight about getting that job? The more you worry, the less you'll succeed.*

up to *prep.* **1.** As far as, as deep as, or as high as. ♦ *The water in the pond was only up to John's knees.* ♦ *Mary is small and just comes up to Bill's chest.* ♦ *The shovel sank in the soft mud all the way up to the handle.* **2.** Close to; approaching. ♦ *The team did not play up to its best today.* ♦ *Because of the rain, the number of people at the party didn't come up to the number we expected.* **3.** As high as; not more than; as much or as many as. ♦ *Pick any number up to ten.* ♦ *There were up to eight fire engines at the fire.* **4.** *or* **up till** *or* **up until**—Until; till. ♦ *Up to her fourth birthday, the baby slept in a crib.*

♦ *Up to now I always thought John was honest.* ♦ *We went swimming up till breakfast time.* ♦ *Up until last summer we always went to the beach for our vacation.* **5.** Capable of; fit for; equal to; strong or well enough for. ♦ *We chose Harry to be captain because we thought he was up to the job.* ♦ *Mother is sick and not up to going out to the store.* **6.** Doing or planning secretly; ready for mischief. ♦ *What are you up to with the matches, John?* ♦ *Mrs. Watson was sure that the boys were up to no good, because they ran when they saw her coming.* **7.** Facing as a duty; to be chosen or decided by; depending on. ♦ *It's up to you to get to school on time.* ♦ *I don't care when you cut the grass. When you do it is up to you.*

up-to-date *adj.* Modern; contemporary; the latest that technology can offer. ♦ *"I want an up-to-date dictionary of American idioms," Mr. Lee said, "that has all the latest Americanisms in it."* Contrast STATE-OF-THE-ART.

up to no good *adv. phr.* Intending to do something bad; perpetrating an illicit act. ♦ *We could tell from the look on Dennis the Menace's face that he was once again up to no good.*

up to one's ears *adv. phr.* Immersed in; covered with. ♦ *"Around final examination time," Professor Brown explained, "I am always up to my ears in work."*

up to one's neck *adv. phr.* Overwhelmed with; submerged in. ♦ *"During the summer season in our cottage by the lake," the Allens complained, "we are usually up to our necks in uninvited guests."* Compare UP TO ONE'S EARS.

up to par *or informal* **up to scratch** *or informal* **up to snuff** **1.** In good or normal health or physical condition. ♦ *I have a cold and don't feel up to par.* ♦ *The boxer is training for the fight but he isn't up to scratch yet.* **2.** *or* **up to the mark** As good as usual; up to the usual level or quality. ♦ *The TV program was not up to par tonight.* ♦ *John will have to work hard to bring his grades up to snuff.* Compare MEASURE UP.

up to scratch See UP TO PAR.

up to snuff See UP TO PAR.

up to the chin in *or* **in———up to the chin** *adj. phr., informal* Used also with

ears, elbows, eyes or knees instead of chin, and with a possessive instead of the. **1.** Having a big or important part in; guilty of; not innocent of; deeply in. ♦ *Was Tom mixed up in that trouble last night? He was up to his ears in it.* ♦ *Mr. Johnson is up to the eyes in debt.* ♦ *Mrs. Smith is in debt up to her chin.* Compare TO THE HILT. **2.** Very busy with; working hard at. ♦ *Bob is up to his neck in homework.* ♦ *They are up to their elbows in business before Christmas.* **3.** Having very much or many of; flooded with. ♦ *Mary was up to her knees in invitations to go to parties.* Compare KNEE-DEEP.

up to the hilt See TO THE HILT.

up to the last minute *adv. phr.* Until the last possible moment; until the very end. ♦ *When I try to send in an important eyewitness report from the scene of a major accident, I must keep working up to the last minute.* Compare TO THE BITTER END, UNDER THE WIRE.

up to the mark See UP TO PAR 2.

up-to-the-minute See UP-TO-DATE.

urban homesteading *n., informal* Renovation and occupation through cooperative ownership by tenants of previously abandoned city apartment buildings. ♦ *Urban homesteading is on the rise in many big American cities these days.*

use See NO USE, PUT TO USE.

used to¹ *adj. phr.* In the habit of or familiar with. ♦ *People get used to smoking and it is hard for them to stop.* ♦ *Farmers are used to working outdoors in the winter.* ♦ *After my eyes became used to the dim light in the cave, I saw an old shovel on the ground.* ♦ *On the hike Bob soon got tired, but Dick did not because he was used to walking.*

used to² *or* **did use to** *v. phr.* Did formerly; did in the past.—Usually used with an infinitive to tell about something past. ♦ *Uncle Henry used to have a beard, but he shaved it off.* ♦ *Did your father use to work at the bank?* ♦ *People used to say that tomatoes were poison.*—Sometimes used without the infinitive. ♦ *I don't go to that school any more, but I used to.* ♦ *We don't visit Helen as much as we used to.* ♦ *I used to go to the movies often. Did you use to?*

used to be *or* **did use to be** *v. phr.*
Formerly or once was. ♦*Mary used to be small; but she has grown up.* ♦*Dick used to be the best pitcher on the team last year; now two other pitchers are better than he is.*

use every trick in the book *v. phr., informal* To avail oneself of any means at all in order to achieve one's goal, not exclusive of possibly immoral or illegal acts. ♦*Algernon used every trick in the book to get Maxine to go out with him, but she kept refusing.*

use one's head *or slang* **use one's bean** *or slang* **use one's noodle** *or slang* **use one's noggin** *v. phr.* To use your brain or mind; think; have common sense.— Often used as a command. ♦*If you used your bean you wouldn't be in trouble now.* ♦*Never point a gun at anybody, John. Use your head!*

use up *v. phr.* **1.** To use until nothing is left; spend or consume completely. ♦*Don't use up all the soap. Leave me some to wash with.* ♦*Jack used up his last dollar to see the movies.* Compare GIVE OUT 5. **2.** *informal* To tire completely; make very tired; exhaust; leave no strength or force in.—Usually used in the passive. ♦*After rowing the boat across the lake, Robert was used up.* Compare GIVE OUT 4, WEAR OUT.

utility room *n.* A room in a house or building for machinery and other things important in the daily use of the building and the work of the people in it. ♦*There is a utility room upstairs where Mother does the laundry.* ♦*The oil burner is kept in the utility room in the basement.*

vain See IN VAIN, TAKE ONE'S NAME IN VAIN.

valor See DISCRETION IS THE BETTER PART OF VALOR.

value See FACE VALUE.

vanish into thin air See DISAPPEAR INTO THIN AIR.

vanishing cream *n.* A cosmetic cream for the skin that is used chiefly before face powder. ♦ *Mrs. Jones spread vanishing cream on her face before applying her face powder.*

vanity case *n.* **1.** A small case containing face powder, lipstick, and other things and usually carried in a woman's handbag; a compact. ♦ *She took out her vanity case and put lipstick on.* **2.** A handbag or a small bag carried by a woman and holding various toilet articles. ♦ *She had the porter carry her big bags and she herself carried her vanity case.*

variety show *n.* A program that includes several different kinds of entertainment (as songs, dances, comic skits and little dramas). ♦ *Jane's father was the master of ceremonies of a variety show on TV.*

variety store *n.* A store that sells many different kinds of things, especially items that are fairly small and in everyday use. ♦ *I went into a variety store and bought some paint.* ♦ *Five-and-ten cent stores are a kind of variety store.*

vein See FREEZE ONE'S BLOOD *or* FREEZE THE BLOOD IN ONE'S VEINS, FREEZE ONE'S VEINS.

verbal diarrhea *n. phr.* The inability to keep silent; over-talkativeness. ♦ *Archibald is a nice guy but he's got verbal diarrhea and he can't shut up for a single minute.*

very See ALL VERY WELL.

very well *interj., formal* Agreed; all right.—Used to show agreement or approval. ♦ *Very well. You may go.* ♦ *Very well, I will do as you say.* Compare ALL RIGHT 2.

vibrations *or* **vibes** *n.* Psychic emanations radiating from an object, situation, or person. ♦ *I don't think this relationship will work out—this guy has given me bad vibes.*

vicious circle *n. phr.* A kind of circular or chain reaction in which one negative thing leads to another. ♦ *Some people take so many different kinds of medicine to cure an illness that they develop other illnesses from the medicine and are thus caught in a vicious circle.*

Vietnam syndrome *n., informal* An attitude in government circles that diplomacy may be more effective in solving local political problems in other countries than the use of military force, stemming from the failure of the U.S. military intervention in Vietnam. ♦ *The pundits of Foggy Bottom display the Vietnam syndrome these days when it comes to Iran.*

view See IN VIEW, IN VIEW OF, TAKE A DIM VIEW OF.

vine See DIE ON THE VINE *or* WITHER ON THE VINE, CLINGING VINE.

virtue See BY VIRTUE OF, MAKE A VIRTUE OF NECESSITY.

visiting nurse *n.* A nurse who goes from home to home taking care of sick people or giving help with other health problems. ♦ *After John returned home from the hospital, the visiting nurse came each day to change his bandages.*

voice See AT THE TOP OF ONE'S VOICE, GIVE VOICE.

voice box *n.* The part of the throat where the sound of your voice is made; the larynx. ♦ *Mr. Smith's voice box was taken out in an operation, and he could not talk after that.*

voiceprint *n., technological, colloquial* The graphic pattern derived from converting an individual's voice into a visible graph used by the police for identification purposes, much as fingerprints. ♦ *They have succeeded in identifying the murderer by using a voiceprint.*

volcano See SIT ON A VOLCANO.

volume See SPEAK VOLUMES.

vote a straight ticket *v. phr.* To not differentiate one's ballot according to individual names and posts, but to vote for all candidates for all positions of the same party. ♦ *"I never have time to study the ballot in detail," Marie said,* *"and so I tend to vote a straight Republican ticket."*

vote in *v. phr.* To elevate to the status of "Law of the Land" by special or general ballot. ♦ *Congress has finally voted in the Brady Law that requires that prospective gun owners wait a special period of time before making their purchase.*

vote one out *v. phr.* To terminate one's elected office by casting a negative vote about that person (judge, congressman, etc.), mostly so that someone else might occupy the same position. ♦ *Congressman Smith was voted out last November in favor of Congresswoman Bradley.*

wade in or **wade into** v., informal **1.** To go busily to work. ♦ *The house was a mess after the party, but Mother waded in and soon had it clean again.* **2.** To attack. ♦ *When Bill had heard Jim's argument, he waded in and took it apart.* ♦ *Jack waded into the boys with his fists flying.*

wade through v. phr. To read through something long and laborious. ♦ *It took John six months to read through Tolstoy's* War and Peace *in the original Russian.*

wag See TONGUES TO WAG or TONGUES WAG.

wagon See FIX SOMEONE'S WAGON, HITCH ONE'S WAGON TO A STAR, JUMP ON THE BAND WAGON, OFF THE WAGON, ON THE WAGON.

wag one's chin See BEAT ONE'S GUMS, CHEW THE FAT, CHEW THE RAG, SHOOT THE BREEZE.

wait See LIE IN WAIT.

wait at table or **wait on table** or **wait table** v. phr. To serve food. ♦ *Mrs. Lake had to teach her new maid to wait on table properly.* ♦ *The girls earn spending money by waiting at table in the school dining rooms.*

waiting list n. A list of persons waiting to get into something (as a school). ♦ *The nursery school enrollment was complete, so the director put our child's name on the waiting list.* ♦ *The landlord said there were no vacant apartments available, but that he would put the Rogers' name on the waiting list.*

waiting room n. phr. The sitting area in a doctor's, lawyer's, accountant's, etc. office, or in a hospital, or other workplace, where people wait their turn. ♦ *Some doctor's offices have elegantly furnished waiting rooms with magazines, newspapers, and coffee for the patients.*

wait on or **wait upon** v. **1.** To serve. ♦ *Sue has a summer job waiting on an invalid.* ♦ *The clerk in the store asked if we had been waited upon.* **2.** formal To visit as a courtesy or for business. ♦ *We waited upon the widow out of respect for her husband.* ♦ *John waited upon the President with a letter of intro-*duction. **3.** To follow. ♦ *Success waits on hard work.*

wait on hand and foot v. phr. To serve in every possible way; do everything for (someone). ♦ *Sally is spoiled because her mother waits on her hand and foot.* ♦ *The gentlemen had a valet to wait on him hand and foot.* Compare HAND AND FOOT.

wait on table See WAIT AT TABLE.

wait up v. phr. To not go to bed until a person one is worried about comes home (said by parents and marriage partners). ♦ *My mother always waited up for me when I went out as a young student.* ♦ *She always waits up for her husband when he's out late.*

wait upon See WAIT ON.

wake See IN THE WAKE OF.

walk See WIN IN A WALK.

walk all over See WALK OVER.

walk a tightrope v. phr. To be in a dangerous or awkward situation where one cannot afford to make a single mistake. ♦ *"When we landed on the moon in 1969," Armstrong explained, "we were walking a tightrope till the very end."*

walk away with or **walk off with** v. **1.** To take and go away with; take away; often: steal. ♦ *When Father went to work, he accidentally walked off with Mother's umbrella.* ♦ *How can a thief walk off with a safe in broad daylight?* **2.** To take, get, or win easily. ♦ *Jim walked away with all the honors on Class Night.* ♦ *Our team walked off with the championship.*

walking dictionary n. phr. A person highly knowledgeable in matters of language use. ♦ *If you want to know what "serendipity" means, ask my Uncle Fred. He is a professor of English and is also a walking dictionary.*

walking encyclopedia n. phr. A polymath; a person very well versed in a number of different disciplines. ♦ *My uncle is a veritable walking encyclopedia when it comes to the history of World War II.* Contrast WALKING DICTIONARY.

walking papers or **walking orders** also **walking ticket** n., informal A statement that you are fired from your job; dismissal. ♦ *The boss was not satisfied with Paul's work and gave him his walking papers.* ♦ *George is out of work. He picked up his walking ticket last Friday.*

walk off with See WALK AWAY WITH.

walk of life   *n. phr.*   Way of living; manner in which people live. ♦ *Many rich people have yachts; people in their walk of life can afford them.* ♦ *The banker did not want his son to marry a girl in a different walk of life.* ♦ *People from every walk of life enjoy television.* Compare THE TRACKS.

walk on air   *v. phr., informal*   To feel happy and excited. ♦ *Sue has been walking on air since she won the prize.* ♦ *His father's compliment left Jed walking on air.* Compare ON CLOUD NINE, ON TOP OF THE WORLD.

walk on eggs   *v. phr.*   To act with utmost caution due to being in a precarious position. ♦ *Tom has been walking on eggs ever since he started working for a new boss in Cincinnati.*

walk out   *v.*   **1.** To go on strike. ♦ *When the company would not give them higher pay, the workers walked out.* **2.** To leave suddenly; especially to desert. ♦ *He didn't say he wasn't coming back; he just walked out.*—Often used informally with *on.* ♦ *The man walked out on his wife and children.* Compare LEAVE FLAT; LEAVE IN THE LURCH.

walk over *or* **walk all over** *or* **step all over**   *v. phr, informal*   To make (someone) do whatever you wish; make selfish use of; treat like a slave; impose upon. ♦ *Jill is so friendly and helpful that people walk all over her.* ♦ *We wanted the man's business, so we let him step all over us.* Compare TAKE ADVANTAGE OF.

walk the chalk *or* **walk the chalk line** *or* **walk the chalk mark**   To act exactly as you are supposed to; behave properly; obey. ♦ *That new teacher really makes the students walk the chalk.* ♦ *In some classes the students play and talk, but Mr. Parker makes them walk the chalk.* ♦ *That theater owner wants his place to be orderly, and if boys and girls don't walk the chalk, he puts them out.* [From the fact that sailors used to be asked to walk a chalk line along the deck of the

ship to prove they were not drunk.] Compare TOE THE MARK.

walk the floor   *v. phr.*   To walk one direction and then the other across the floor, again and again; pace. ♦ *Mr. Black walked the floor, trying to reach a decision.* ♦ *The sick baby had his mother walking the floor all night.* ♦ *Mrs. Black's toothache hurt so much that she got up and walked the floor.*

walk the plank   *v. phr.*   **1.** To walk off a board extended over the side of a ship and be drowned. ♦ *The pirates captured the ship and forced the crew to walk the plank.* **2.** *informal* To resign from a job because someone makes you do it. ♦ *When a new owner bought the store, the manager had to walk the plank.*

wall See BACK TO THE WALL, BEAT ONE'S HEAD AGAINST A WALL, CLIMB THE WALL, FORWARD WALL, HANDWRITING ON THE WALL, HOLE-IN-THE-WALL, STONE WALL *or* BRICK WALL, TO THE WALL.

wallflower   *n.*   A girl who has to sit out dances because nobody is asking her to dance. ♦ *"I used to be a wallflower during my high school days,"* Valerie complained, *"but my luck changed for better once I got into college."*

wallop See PACK A PUNCH *or* PACK A WALLOP .

walls have ears   Sometimes one's most confidential conversations are overheard. ♦ *"Be careful what you say,"* he whispered. *"Remember that walls have ears."*

want ad   *n.*   A small advertisement on a special page in a newspaper that offers employment opportunities and merchandise. ♦ *"You want a temporary job?"* he asked the recent arrival in town. *"Go and look at the want ads!"*

war See COLD WAR, TUG OF WAR.

war baby   *n., informal*   A person born during a war. ♦ *War babies began to increase college enrollments early in the 1960s.* ♦ *The war babies forced many towns to build new schools.*

ward off   *v. phr.*   To deflect; avert. ♦ *Vitamin C is known to ward off the common cold.*

warmer See BENCH WARMER.

warm one's blood   *v. phr.*   To make you feel warm or excited. ♦ *When the*

Bakers came to visit on a cold night, Mr. Harmon offered them a drink to warm their blood.

warm the bench *v. phr., informal* To act as a substitute on an athletic team. ♦ *Bill has been warming the bench for three football seasons; he hopes that the coach will let him play this year.*— **bench warmer** *n., informal* A substitute player. ♦ *Last year Ted was only a bench warmer, but this year he is the team's star pitcher.*

warm up *v.* **1.** To reheat cooked food. ♦ *Mr. Jones was so late that his dinner got cold; his wife had to warm it up.* ♦ *When the children had left for school, their mother warmed up the breakfast coffee.* **2.** To become friendly or interested. ♦ *It takes an hour or so for some children to warm up to strangers.* ♦ *As he warmed up to his subject, Tom forgot his bashfulness.* **3.** To get ready for a game or other event by exercising or practicing. ♦ *The dancers began to warm up fifteen minutes before the performance.* ♦ *The coach told us to warm up before entering the pool.*

warm-up *n.* A period of exercise or practice in preparation for a game or other event. ♦ *During the warm-up the baseball players were throwing the ball around and running up and down the side of the field.* ♦ *Before the television quiz program, there was a warm-up to prepare the contestants.*

warpath See ON THE WARPATH.

warrant See SIGN ONE'S OWN DEATH WARRANT.

wash and wear *adj.* Not needing to be ironed.—Refers especially to synthetic and synthetic blend fabrics. ♦ *Dick bought three wash and wear shirts to take on his trip.* ♦ *Sally's dress is made of a wash and wear fabric.*

washed out *adj.* Listless in appearance; pale, wan. ♦ *Small wonder Harry looks so washed out; he has just recovered from major surgery.*

washed up *adj.* Ruined; finished; a failure. ♦ *Harry is looking awfully sad. I hear his business has collapsed and he is all washed up.*

wash one's dirty linen in public See AIR ONE'S DIRTY LINEN IN PUBLIC.

wash one's hands of *v. phr.* To withdraw from or refuse to be responsible for.

♦ *We washed our hands of politics long ago.* ♦ *The school washed its hands of the students' behavior during spring recess.*

washout *n.* A dismal failure. ♦ *As far as investments were concerned, Dick and his precious advice turned out to be a total washout.*

wash out *v. phr.* To disappear; vanish. ♦ *Do you think this stain will wash out?*

waste See GO TO WASTE, LAY WASTE.

waste away *v.* To become more thin and weak every day. ♦ *Jane is wasting away with tuberculosis.* ♦ *After Mrs. Barnes died, her husband wasted away with grief.*

waste one's breath *v. phr.* To speak or to argue with no result; do nothing by talking. ♦ *The teacher saw that she was wasting her breath; the children refused to believe her.* ♦ *I know what I want. You're wasting your breath.*

watch See BIRD WATCHER, BEAR WATCHING, ON THE WATCH.

watched pot never boils If you watch or wait for something to get done or to happen, it seems to take forever.—A proverb. ♦ *Jane was nine months pregnant and Tom hovered over her anxiously. She said, "You might as well go away and play some golf. A watched pot never boils, you know!"*

watcher See CLOCK WATCHER.

watch every penny See PINCH PENNIES.

watch it *v. phr. informal* To be careful.—Usually used as a command. ♦ *You'd better watch it. If you get into trouble again, you'll be expelled.* ♦ *Watch it—the bottom stair is loose!*

watch one's dust *or* **watch one's smoke** *v. phr. slang* To notice your quick action; watch you do something quickly. ♦ *Offer Bill a dollar to shovel your sidewalk, and watch his smoke!* ♦ *"We'll have your yard cleaned in a jiffy," the Boy Scouts told Mr. Truitt." "Watch our smoke!"* ♦ *I can go to the store and be back in five minutes," bragged Tom. "Just watch my dust."*

watch one's language *v. phr.* To be careful of how one speaks; avoid saying impolite or vulgar things. ♦ *"You boys watch your language,"* Mother said, *"or you won't be watching television for a whole week!"*

watch one's step *v. phr.* To mend one's

ways; exercise prudence, tact, and care. ♦ *I have to watch my step with the new boss as he is a very proud and sensitive individual.*

watch out See LOOK OUT.

watch over *v. phr.* To guard; take care of. ♦ *The museum guards carefully watch over the world-famous paintings.*

water See BLOOD IS THICKER THAN WATER, COME HELL OR HIGH WATER, DEEP WATER, FISH OUT OF WATER, GO THROUGH HELL AND HIGH WATER, HEAD ABOVE WATER, HOLD WATER, HELL AND HIGH WATER, HOT WATER, LIKE WATER, LIKE WATER OFF A DUCK'S BACK, MAKE ONE'S MOUTH WATER, OF THE FIRST WATER, POUR OIL ON TROUBLED WATERS, THROW COLD WATER ON, TREAD WATER.

water down *v.* To change and make weaker; weaken. ♦ *The Senator argued that the House should water down the bill before passing it.* ♦ *The African American did not accept watered down Civil Rights legislation.* ♦ *After talking with the management about their demands, the workers agreed to water them down.* ♦ *The teacher had to water down the course for a slow-learning class.*

watered down *adj.* Weakened; diluted. ♦ *The play was a disappointing, watered down version of Shakespeare's* Othello.

waterfront See COVER THE WATERFRONT.

watering hole *or* **place** *n. phr.* A bar, pub, or nightclub where people gather to drink and socialize. ♦ *I like "The Silver Dollar"—it is my favorite watering hole in all of Sidney, Nebraska.*

Waterloo See MEET ONE'S WATERLOO.

water over the dam *or* **water under the bridge** *n. phr.* Something that happened in the past and cannot be changed. ♦ *Since the sweater is too small already, don't worry about its shrinking; that's water over the dam.* Compare CRY OVER SPILLED MILK.

water under the bridge See WATER OVER THE DAM.

water wagon See ON THE WAGON.

way See ALL THE WAY *or* THE WHOLE WAY, BY THE WAY, BY WAY OF, COME A LONG WAY, CUT BOTH WAYS *or* CUT TWO WAYS, EVERY WHICH WAY, FROM WAY BACK, GO OUT OF ONE'S WAY, HARD WAY, HAVE A WAY WITH, IN A BAD WAY, IN A BIG WAY, IN A FAMILY WAY, IN A WAY, IN ONE'S WAY *or* IN THE WAY, KNOW ONE'S WAY AROUND *or* KNOW ONE'S WAY ABOUT, LEAD THE WAY, MAKE ONE'S WAY, MAKE WAY, NOT KNOW WHICH WAY TO TURN, NO TWO WAYS ABOUT IT, ON THE WAY, *or* ON ONE'S WAY, PARTING OF THE WAYS, PUT IN THE WAY OF *or* PUT IN ONE'S WAY, PUT OUT OF THE WAY, RUB THE WRONG WAY, SEE ONE'S WAY CLEAR.

way off *adj. phr.* At a great distance from a particular point (said of a discrepancy). ♦ *We were way off on our calculations; the house cost us twice as much as we had thought.*

wayside See FALL BY THE WAYSIDE.

way the wind blows *or* **how the wind blows** *n. phr.* The direction or course something may go; how things are; what may happen. ♦ *Most senators find out which way the wind blows in their home state before voting on bills in Congress.*

ways and means *n. plural* Methods of getting something done or getting money; how something can be done and paid for. ♦ *The boys were trying to think of ways and means to go camping for the weekend.* ♦ *The United States Senate has a committee on ways and means.*

wear See IF THE SHOE FITS—WEAR IT, WASH AND WEAR, WORSE FOR WEAR.

wear and tear *n. phr.* Deterioration through use. ♦ *After 75,000 miles there is usually a lot of wear and tear on any car.*

wear away See WEAR DOWN.

wear blinders *or* **blinkers** *v. phr.* To refuse or be unable to consider alternative ways of thinking or acting. ♦ *Anybody who disputes the importance of learning languages is wearing blinders.*

wear down, wear off *or* **wear away** *v.* **1.** To remove or disappear little by little through use, time, or the action of weather. ♦ *Time and weather have worn off the name on the gravestone.* ♦ *The eraser has worn off my pencil.* ♦ *The grass has worn away from the path near the house.* **2.** To lessen;

become less little by little. ◆*The people went home as the excitement of the fire wore off.* ◆*John could feel the pain again as the dentist's medicine wore away.* **3.** To exhaust; tire out, win over or persuade by making tired. ◆*Mary wore her mother down by begging so that she let Mary go to the movies.* Compare DIE OUT.

wear on *v.* **1.** To anger or annoy; tire. ◆*Having to stay indoors all day long is tiresome for the children and wears on their mother's nerves.* **2.** To drag on; pass gradually or slowly; continue in the same old way. ◆*Johnny tried to wait up for Santa Claus but as the night wore on, he couldn't keep his eyes open.* ◆*As the years wore on, the man in prison grew old.* ◆*The boys' quarrel wore on all afternoon.*

wear one's heart on one's sleeve *also* **pin one's heart on one's sleeve** *v. phr.* To show your feelings openly; show everyone how you feel; not hide your feelings. ◆*She wears her heart on her sleeve. It's easy to see if she is sad or happy.* ◆*Sometimes it is better not to pin your heart on your sleeve.* Compare OPEN ONE'S HEART.

wear out *v.* **1a.** To use or wear until useless. ◆*Bobby got a toy truck that would run on a battery, and he used it so much that he soon wore it out.* ◆*The stockings are so worn out that they can't be mended any more.* Compare GIVE OUT 4, USE UP. **1b.** To become useless from use or wear. ◆*The old clock finally wore out.* ◆*One shoe wore out before the other.* **2.** *or* **tire out** To make very tired; weaken. ◆*The children played inside when it rained, and they soon wore out their mother.* ◆*When Dick got home from the long walk, he was all worn out.*—Often used with *oneself.* ◆*Don't wear yourself out by playing too hard.* Compare GIVE OUT 4. **3.** To make by rubbing, scraping, or washing. ◆*The waterfall has worn out a hole in the stone beneath it.*

wear out one's welcome *v. phr., informal* To visit somewhere too long or come back too often so that you are not welcome any more. ◆*The Smith children have worn out their welcome at our house because they never want to go home.* ◆*This hot weather has worn out its welcome with us.*

wear the trousers *or* **wear the pants** *v. phr., informal* To have a man's authority; be the boss of a family or household. ◆*Mr. Wilson is henpecked by his wife; she wears the trousers in that family.* ◆*Mrs. Jones talks a lot but Mr. Jones wears the pants in their house.* Compare RULE THE ROOST.

wear thin *v.* **1.** To become thin from use, wearing, or the passing of time. ◆*My old pair of pants has worn thin at the knees.* ◆*This old dime has worn very thin.* **2.** To grow less, or less interesting; decrease. ◆*The joke began to wear thin when you heard it too many times.* ◆*The teacher's patience began to wear thin when he saw that no one knew the lesson.*

wear well *v.* **1.** To continue to be satisfactory, useful, or liked for a long time. ◆*My old overcoat has worn very well.* ◆*Their marriage has worn well.* ◆*That author wears well.* Compare STAND UP 2. **2.** To carry, accept, or treat properly or well. ◆*Grandfather wears his years well.* ◆*Tommy has won many honors but he wears them well.*

weasel out *v. phr.* To renege on a previous promise; not keep an obligation for some not always straight reason. ◆*I'm so tired I think I am going to weasel my way out of going to that meeting this afternoon.*

weasel word *n., informal* A word which has more than one meaning and may be used to deceive others. ◆*When the thief was being questioned by the police, he tried to fool them with weasel words.*

weather See FAIR-WEATHER FRIEND.

weather eye *n.* **1.** Eyes that can tell what the weather will be. ◆*Grandfather's weather eye always tells him when it will rain.* **2.** Eyes ready or quick to see; careful watch.—Usually used in phrases like *keep a weather eye on, open,* or *out for.* ◆*Mrs. Brown kept a weather eye on the children so they wouldn't hurt each other.* ◆*Keep a weather eye out for Uncle George at the store.* ◆*Keep a weather eye open for deer.* ◆*The police have a weather eye out for the robbers.* Compare LOOK OUT.

weather the storm *v. phr.* To survive

some disaster. ◆ *When Peter and Sue started their business they had very little money, but in a year they weathered the storm.*

wedge See FLYING WEDGE.

wedlock See BORN OUT OF WEDLOCK.

wee hours The crack of dawn, or just before it, usually between 1 A.M. and 4 A.M. or 2 A.M. and 5 A.M. ◆ *He stayed up all night when they were expecting their first child; finally, a boy was born in the wee hours of the morning.* Compare SMALL HOURS.

weeper See FINDERS KEEPERS *or* FINDERS KEEPERS LOSERS WEEPERS.

weed out *v.* **1.** To remove what is unwanted, harmful, or not good enough from. ◆ *Mother weeded out the library because there were too many books.* ◆ *Many colleges and universities weed out their freshman classes to make room for better students.* **2.** To take (what is not wanted) from a collection or group; remove (a part) for the purpose of improving a collection or group; get rid of. ◆ *The coach is weeding out the weak players this week.* ◆ *The teacher told Elizabeth to read over her English composition and weed out every sentence that was not about the subject.*

wee folk *or* **little folk** *or* **little people** *n. pl.* Fairy people; brownies; elves; fairies; or goblins. ◆ *Mother read me a story about the wee folk who lived in the forest and came out at night.* ◆ *There are many stories about little people dancing in the moonlight.*

week in, week out See DAY IN, AND DAY OUT.

week of Sundays *n. phr.* A long time; seven weeks. ◆ *I haven't seen them in a week of Sundays.*

weigh anchor *v. phr.* To set sail; get going. ◆ *After a week in Hawaii, we weighed anchor and sailed south toward Tahiti.*

weigh down *also* **weight down** **1.** To make heavy; cause to go down or bend with weight; overload. ◆ *The evergreens are weighed down by the deep snow.*—Often used with *with* or *by.* ◆ *There are so many children in the back seat that they are weighing down the back of the car.* **2a.** To overload with care or worry; make sad or low in

spirits.—Usually used in the passive. ◆ *The family is weighed down by sorrow.* ◆ *The company is weighed down by debt.* **2b.** To make heavy, hard, or slow; make dull or uninteresting.—Often in the passive used with *by* or *with.* ◆ *The book is weighted down with footnotes.* ◆ *The TV program is weighed down by commercials.*

weigh in *v.* **1a.** To take the weight of; weigh. ◆ *The man at the airport counter weighed in our bags and took our plane tickets.* ◆ *A doctor weighed in the wrestlers.* **1b.** To have yourself or something that you own weighed.—Often used with *at.* ◆ *I weighed in at 100 pounds on the scale today.* ◆ *We took our bags to the airport counter to weigh in.* **1c.** To have yourself weighed as a boxer or wrestler by a doctor before a match.—Often used with *at.* ◆ *The champion didn't want to weigh in at more than 160 pounds.* **2.** *slang* To join or interfere in a fight, argument, or discussion. ◆ *We told Jack that if we wanted him to weigh in with his opinion we would ask him.* Compare TAKE PART.

weigh on *or* **weigh upon** *v.* **1.** To be a weight or pressure on; be heavy on. ◆ *The pack weighed heavily on the soldier's back.* **2.** To make sad or worried; trouble; disturb; upset. ◆ *Sadness weighed on Mary's heart when her kitten died.* ◆ *John's wrongdoing weighed upon his conscience.* ◆ *The teacher's advice weighed upon Tom's mind.* **3.** To be a burden to. ◆ *His guilt weighed heavily upon him.*

weigh on one's mind See WEIGH ON 2.

weigh one's words *v. phr.* To choose your words carefully; be careful to use the right words. ◆ *When a teacher explains about religion, he must weigh his words because his pupils may be of several different faiths.* ◆ *When old Mr. Jones talked to the students about becoming teachers, he spoke slowly, weighing his words.* ◆ *In a debate, a political candidate has little time to weigh his words, and may say something foolish.*

weight See PULL ONE'S WEIGHT, SWING ONE'S WEIGHT, THROW ONE'S WEIGHT AROUND.

weight down See WEIGH DOWN.

weight of the world on one's shoulders *or* **world on one's shoulders** *or* **world on one's back** *n. phr.* A very heavy load of worry or responsibility; very tired or worried behavior, as if carrying the world; behavior as if you are very important. ♦*Don't look as if you had the weight of the world on your shoulders, Henry, just because you have to mow the lawn.* ♦*John acts as if he were carrying the world on his back because he has a paper route.*

weigh upon See WEIGH ON.

welcome See WEAR OUT ONE'S WELCOME.

welcome mat *n.* **1.** A mat for wiping your shoes on, often with the word *welcome* on it, that is placed in front of a door. ♦*Mother bought a welcome mat for our new house.* **2.** *informal* A warm welcome; a friendly greeting.— Used in such phrases as *the welcome mat is out* and *put out the welcome mat.* ♦*Our welcome mat is always out to our friends.* ♦*Spread out the welcome mat, children, because Uncle Bill is visiting us tonight.* Syn. LATCH STRING 2. Compare ROLL OUT THE RED CARPET, WITH OPEN ARMS.

welcome with open arms See WITH OPEN ARMS.

well See ALL VERY WELL, AS WELL, AS WELL AS, HAIL FELLOW WELL MET, LET WELL ENOUGH ALONE, PLAY ONE'S CARDS RIGHT *or* PLAY ONE'S CARDS WELL, VERY WELL, WEAR WELL.

well and good *adj. phr.* Good; satisfactory. ♦*If my daughter finishes high school, I will call that well and good.*— Often used without a verb to show agreement or understanding. ♦*Well and good; I will come to your house tomorrow.* Compare ALL RIGHT, ALL VERY WELL, VERY WELL.

well-heeled *adj., slang* Wealthy; having plenty of money. ♦*Bob's father, who is well-heeled, gave him a sports car.* Compare IN CLOVER, ON EASY STREET.

well-off *adj. phr.* **1.** Rich. ♦*They may not be millionaires, but they are sufficiently well-off.* **2.** In good condition; free of problems or difficulties. ♦*He is pleased that his business is well-off.*

well put *adj. phr.* Well expressed or defined. ♦*His remarks about too much violence on television were extremely well put.*

well-to-do *adj.* Having or making enough money to live comfortably; prosperous. ♦*John's father owns a company and his family is well-to-do.*—Often used with *the* like a plural noun. ♦*This is the part of town where the well-to-do live.* Compare IN THE LAP OF LUXURY, IN THE CHIPS, ON EASY STREET.

wet See ALL WET, GET ONE'S FEET WET, MAD AS A WET HEN, WRINGING WET.

wet behind the ears *adj. phr., informal* Not experienced; not knowing how to do something; new in a job or place. ♦*The new student is still wet behind the ears; he has not yet learned the tricks that the boys play on each other.* Compare DRY BEHIND THE EARS.

wet blanket *n. informal* A person or thing that keeps others from enjoying life. ♦*The teenagers don't invite Bob to their parties because he is a wet blanket.* ♦*The weatherman throws a wet blanket on picnic plans when he forecasts rain.* Compare CREPE HANGER.

wet one's whistle *v. phr., slang* To have a drink, especially of liquor. ♦*Uncle Willie told John to wait outside for a minute while he went in to the cafe to wet his whistle.*

whack See OUT OF WHACK.

whale away *v., informal* **1.** To beat or hit hard; strike again and again.—Often used with *at.* ♦*The boxer is whaling away at his opponent with both fists.* **2.** To attack severely or again and again; go on without stopping or with great force; pound away. ♦*Mary has been whaling away on the typewriter for an hour.*—Often used with *at.* ♦*During the election the Mayor whaled away at the other party in his speeches.*

whale the ——— out of See BEAT THE ——— OUT OF.

what See COME WHAT MAY, GET WHAT'S COMING TO ONE, I'LL TELL YOU WHAT, JUST WHAT THE DOCTOR ORDERED, SO WHAT.

what about *interrog.* **1.** About *or* concerning what; in connection with what.—Often used alone as a question. ♦*"I want to talk to you." "What about?"* Compare WHAT FOR. **2.** See WHAT OF IT. **3.** SEE HOW ABOUT.

what about that See HOW ABOUT THAT.

What a pity! How unfortunate! What a shame! ♦*What a pity that he couldn't join us on our Hawaiian trip.*

what for¹ *interrog.* For what reason; why? ♦*I told Mary what I was going to town for.* ♦*What are you running for?*—Often used alone as a question. ♦*Billy's mother told him to wear his hat. "What for?" he asked.* Compare HOW COME.

what for² *n. phr., informal* A scolding, or other punishment.—Usually used with *get* or *give.* ♦*Tom got what for from his father for answering him rudely, and I heard him crying in the house.* ♦*The teacher gave me what for because I was late.*

what have you *or* **what not** *n. phr., informal* Whatever you like or want; anything else like that. ♦*The store sells big ones, small ones, medium ones, or what have you.* ♦*We found suits, coats, hats and what not in the closet.* Syn. AND SO FORTH.

what if What would, or will, happen if; what is the difference if; suppose that. ♦*What if you go instead of me?* ♦*What if we paint it red. How will it look?* ♦*"You can't go now" said mother. "What if I do?" Dick asked.* ♦*What if Jack scores a touchdown?*

what is what See WHAT'S WHAT.

what of it *or* **what about it** *interj., informal* What is wrong with it; what do you care. ♦*Martha said "That boy is wearing a green coat." Jan answered, "What of it?"* ♦*"John missed the bus." "What of it?"* Syn. SO WHAT.

what not See WHAT HAVE YOU.

what's cooking See WHAT'S UP.

what's doing See WHAT'S UP.

what's sauce for the goose, is sauce for the gander What goes for the one, also goes for the other—A proverb. ♦*If Herb gets a speeding ticket, so should Erica, who was right behind him; after all, what's sauce for the goose is sauce for the gander.*

what's the big idea *or* **what's the idea** *informal* What is the purpose; what do you have in mind; why did you do that; what are you doing; how dare you.—Often used to question someone or something that is not welcome. ♦*The Smith family painted their house red, white, and blue. What's the big idea?*

♦*What's the idea of coming in here after I told you not to?* ♦*I heard you are spreading false rumors about me, what's the big idea?*

what's the idea See WHAT'S THE BIG IDEA.

what's up *or* **what's cooking** *also* **what's doing** *slang* What is happening or planned; what is wrong.—Often used as a greeting. ♦*"What's up?" asked Bob as he joined his friends. "Are you going to the movies?"* ♦*What's cooking? Why is the crowd in the street?* ♦*What's doing tonight at the club?* ♦*Hello Bob, what's up?* Compare WHAT'S WITH.

what's what *or* **what is what** *n. phr., informal* **1.** What each thing is in a group; one thing from another. ♦*The weeds and the flowers are coming up together, and we can't tell what is what.* **2.** All that needs to be known about something; the important facts or skills. ♦*Richard did the wrong thing, because he is new here and doesn't yet know what's what.* ♦*When Bob started his new job, it took him several weeks to learn what was what.* ♦*When it comes to cooking, Jenny knows what's what.* ♦*Harold began to tell the teacher how to teach the class, and the teacher told him what was what.* Compare WHICH IS, WHICH, WHO'S WHO.

what's with *or* **what's up with** *also* **what's by** *slang* What is happening to; what is wrong; how is everything; what can you tell me about. ♦*Mary looks worried. What's with her?* ♦*What's with our old friends?* ♦*I'm fine. What's with you?*

what with *prep.* Because; as a result of. ♦*I couldn't visit you, what with the snowstorm and the cold I had.* ♦*What with dishes to wash and children to put to bed, mother was late to the meeting.* Compare ON ACCOUNT OF.

wheel See BIG CHEESE *or* BIG WHEEL, GREASE THE WHEELS, PUT ONE'S SHOULDER TO THE WHEEL.

wheel and deal *v. phr., slang* To make many big plans or schemes; especially with important people in government and business; in matters of money and influence; handle money or power for your own advantage; plan important matters in a smart or skillful way and sometimes in a tricky, or not strictly honest way. ♦ *Mr. Smith made a fortune by wheeling and dealing on the stock market.* ♦ *The senator got this law passed by wheeling and dealing in Congress.*—**wheeler-dealer** *n. phr., slang* A person with power and control. ♦ *The biggest wheeler-dealer in the state has many friends in high places in business and government and is a rich man himself.*

wheelhorse *n. phr.* A reliable and industrious worker on whom one may depend. ♦ *Jake is such a good worker that he is the wheelhorse of our tiny firm.*

when hell freezes over *adv. phr., slang* Never. ♦ *I'll believe you when hell freezes over.* Contrast UNTIL HELL FREEZES OVER.

when it comes to See COME TO 4.

when one's ship comes in See SHIP COME IN.

when push comes to shove *adv. phr.* A time when a touchy situation becomes actively hostile or a quarrel turns into a fight. ♦ *Can we count on the boss' goodwill, when push comes to shove?*

when the chips are down *adv. cl., informal* When the winner and loser of a bet or a game are decided; at the most important or dangerous time. ♦ *Tom hit a home run in the last inning of the game when the chips were down.* ♦ *When the chips were down, the two countries decided not to have war.* [From the fact that in gambling games, a person puts chips or money down in front of him to show that he is willing to risk an amount in a bet.]

where See TELL ONE WHERE TO GET OFF *or* TELL ONE WHERE TO HEAD IN.

wherefore See WHY AND WHEREFORE.

where it's at *adv. phr., informal* That which is important; that which is at the forefront of on-going social, personal, or scientific undertakings. ♦ *Young, talented and black, that's where it's at.* ♦ *We send sophisticated machines to Mars instead of people, that's where it's at.*

where the shoe pinches *n. phr., informal* Where or what the discomfort or trouble is. ♦ *Johnny thinks the job is easy, but he will find out where the shoe pinches when he tries it.* ♦ *The coach*

said he wasn't worried about any position except quarterback; that was where the shoe pinched.

whether one is coming or going See KNOW IF ONE IS COMING OR GOING.

whether——or *or* **whether——or whether 1.** *coord. conj.* Used to introduce an indirect question. ♦ *You must decide whether you should go or stay.* ♦ *I don't know whether Jack or Bill is a better player.* Compare EITHER—— OR **2.** Used to show a choice of things, or that different things are possible. ♦ *Whether the bicycle was blue or red, it didn't matter to Frank.*

which See GAME AT WHICH TWO CAN PLAY.

which is which *n. phr.* Which is one person or thing and which is the other; one from another; what the difference is between different ones; what the name of each one is. ♦ *Joe's coat and mine are so nearly alike that I can't tell which is which.* ♦ *Mr. Hadley hadn't seen his friend's daughters in such a long time that he couldn't remember which was which.* Compare WHAT'S WHAT, WHO'S WHO.

which was which See WHICH IS WHICH.

while See AFTER A WHILE *or* IN A WHILE, ALL THE TIME 1, EVERY NOW AND THEN *or* EVERY ONCE IN A WHILE, ONCE IN A WHILE.

while ago *adv.* At a time several minutes in the past; a few minutes ago; a short time ago.—Used with *a.* ♦ *I laid my glasses on this table a while ago; and now they're gone.* ♦ *A while ago, Mary was tired and wanted to go home; now she's dancing with Bob as if she could dance all night.* Compare JUST NOW 2.

while away *v.* To make time go by pleasantly or without being bored; pass or spend. ♦ *We whiled away the time that we were waiting by talking and playing cards.* ♦ *We whiled away the summer swimming and fishing.*

while back *adv.* At a time several weeks or months in the past.—Used with *a.* ♦ *We had a good rain a while back, but we need more now.* ♦ *Grandfather is well now, but a while back he was in the hospital for three weeks.* See CRACK THE WHIP.

whip hand See UPPER HAND.

whipping boy *n. phr.* The person who gets punished for someone else's mistake. ♦ *"I used to be the whipping boy during my early days at the company,"* he musingly remembered.

whip up *v., informal* **1.** To make or do quickly or easily. ♦ *Mary whipped up a lunch for the picnic.* ♦ *The reporter whipped up a story about the fire for his paper.* **2.** To make active; stir to action; excite. ♦ *The girls are trying to whip up interest for a dance Saturday night.* Compare STIR UP, WHOOP IT UP 2.

whispering campaign *n.* The spreading of false rumors, or saying bad things, about a person or group, especially in politics or public life. ♦ *A bad man has started a whispering campaign against the mayor, saying that he isn't honest.*

whistle See BLOW THE WHISTLE ON, WET ONE'S WHISTLE.

whistle a different tune See SING A DIFFERENT TUNE.

whistle for *v., informal* To try to get (something) but fail; look for (something) that will not come. ♦ *Mary didn't even thank us for helping her, so the next time she needs help she can whistle for it.*

whistle in the dark *v. phr., informal* To try to stay brave and forget your fear. ♦ *Tom said he could fight the bully with one hand, but we knew that he was just whistling in the dark.* [From the fact that people sometimes whistle when walking in a dark, scary place to keep up their courage.]

whistle-stop *n.* A small town where the trains only stop on a special signal. ♦ *President Truman made excellent use of the whistle-stop during his 1948 campaign for the presidency.*

white See BLACK AND WHITE, IN BLACK AND WHITE .

white around the gills See GREEN AROUND THE GILLS.

white-collar workers *n. phr.* Workers employed in offices and at desks as opposed to those who work as manual workers; the middle class. ♦ *It is a well-known fact that white-collar workers are less well organized than unionized manual workers.* Contrast BLUE-COLLAR WORKERS.

white elephant *n. phr.* Unwanted property, such as real estate, that is hard to

sell. ♦ *That big house of theirs on the corner sure is a white elephant.*

white lie *n. phr.* An innocent social excuse. ♦ *I am too busy to go to their house for dinner tonight. I will call them and tell a little white lie about having the flu.*

white sale *n.* The selling, especially at lower prices, of goods or clothing usually made of white cloth. ♦ *Mother always buys many things at the January white sale to save money.*

whitewash *n., informal* A soothing official report that attempts to tranquilize the public. ♦ *Some people believe that the Warren Commission's report on the Kennedy assassination was a whitewash.*

whitewash something *v., informal* To explain a major, national scandal in soothing official terms so as to assure the public that things are under control and there is no need to panic. ♦ *Many people in the United States believe that President Kennedy's assassination was whitewashed by the Warren Commission.* See WHITEWASH, *n.*

whiz See GEE WHIZ.

who See SAYS WHO.

whodunit *n.* A detective story; a murder story; a thriller. ♦ *Agatha Christie was a true master of the whodunit.*

who is who See WHO'S WHO.

who laughs last laughs best See HE LAUGHS BEST WHO LAUGHS LAST.

whole See ALL THE WAY *or* THE WHOLE WAY, GO THE WHOLE HOG, ON THE WHOLE, WITH A WHOLE SKIN *or* IN A WHOLE SKIN.

whole cheese *slang or informal* **whole show** *n., informal* The only important person; big boss. ♦ *Joe thought he was the whole cheese in the game because he owned the ball.* ♦ *You're not the whole show just because you got all A's.* Compare BIG CHEESE.

whole hog See GO THE WHOLE HOG.

whole lot See A LOT.

whole show See WHOLE CHEESE.

whoop it up *v. phr., slang* **1.** To make a loud noise; have a noisy celebration; enjoy yourself noisily. ♦ *The team whooped it up after winning the game.* **2.** To praise something enthusiastically; encourage enthusiasm or support—Often used with *for.* ♦ *Father* *wanted to go to the country, but the children whooped it up for the beach.*

who's who *or* **who is who** *informal* **1.** Who this one is and who that one is; who the different ones in a group of people are or what their names or positions are. ♦*It is hard to tell who is who in the parade because everyone in the band looks alike.* ♦*It took the new teacher a few days to remember who was who in the class.* Compare WHICH IS WHICH. **2.** Who the important people are. ♦*John didn't recognize the champion on television. He doesn't know who is who in boxing.* ♦*After about a year, Mr. Thompson had lived in this town long enough to know who was who.* Compare WHAT'S WHAT .

why and wherefore *n.* The answer to a question or problem. Usually used in the plural. ♦*Father told him not to always ask the whys and wherefores when he was told to do something.*

wide See FAR AND WIDE, GIVE A WIDE BERTH.

wide-eyed See ROUND-EYED.

wide of the mark *adv. or adj. phr.* **1.** Far from the target or the thing aimed at. ♦*James threw a stone at the cat but it went wide of the mark.* **2.** Far from the truth; incorrect. ♦*You were wide of the mark when you said I did it, because Bill did it.* Contrast HIT THE BULL'S-EYE, HIT THE NAIL ON THE HEAD.

widow See GOLF WIDOW.

wiener roast *or* **hot dog roast** *n.* A party where frankfurters are cooked and eaten over an outdoor fire. ♦*For his birthday party, John had a wiener roast in his backyard.* ♦*Mary's Girl Scout troop had a hot dog roast on their overnight hike.*

wig See BIG CHEESE *or* BIG WIG.

wild see RUN WILD, SOW ONE'S WILD OATS.

wildcat strike *n. informal* A strike not ordered by a labor union; a strike spontaneously arranged by a group of workers. ♦*The garbage collectors have gone on a wildcat strike, but the union is going to stop it.*

wild goose chase *n. phr.* An absurd and completely futile errand. ♦*I was on a wild goose chase when I was sent to find a man who never really existed.*

wild pitch *n.* A pitch in baseball that is so high, so low, or so far from the plate that the catcher cannot catch it and a base runner can move to the next base. ♦*The runner went to second base on a wild pitch.*

will See AT WILL, OF ONE'S OWN ACCORD *or* OF ONE'S OWN FREE WILL.

will not hear of *v. phr.* Will not allow or consider, refuse attention to or permission for. ♦*I want to go to the show tonight, but I know my mother will not hear of it.* ♦*Mary needs another day to finish her book report, but the teacher won't hear of any delay.* ♦*John's father told him he would not hear of his having a car.*

win See HEADS I WIN, TAILS YOU LOSE.

wind See GET WIND OF, GOD TEMPERS THE WIND TO THE SHORN LAMB, GONE WITH THE WIND, IN THE WIND, IT'S AN ILL WIND THAT BLOWS NOBODY GOOD, SECOND WIND, STRAW IN THE WIND, TAKE THE WIND OUT OF ONE'S SAILS, THREE SHEETS IN THE WIND *or* THREE SHEETS TO THE WIND, THROW CAUTION TO THE WIND, WAY THE WIND BLOWS *or* HOW THE WIND BLOWS.

windbag *n.* Someone who talks too much; a boring person. ♦*Uncle Joe goes on and on; he is a boring windbag.*

windfall *n.* An unexpected gift or gain of sizeable proportion. ♦*The unexpected retroactive pay raise was a most welcome windfall.*

window See GO OUT THE WINDOW.

window dressing *n. phr.* An elaborate exterior, sometimes designed to conceal one's real motives. ♦*All those fancy invitations turned out to be nothing but window dressing.* ♦*All he really wanted was to be introduced to my influential father-in-law.*

wind up *v.* **1.** To tighten the spring of a machine; to make it work or run. ♦*Mary wound up the toy car and let it run across the room.* ♦*He doesn't have to wind up his watch because it is run by a battery.* **2.** To make very excited, nervous, upset.—Usually used in the past participle. ♦*The excitement of her birthday party got Jane all wound up so she could not sleep.* **3.** *informal* To bring or come to an end; finish; stop. ♦*John got two hits and wound his afternoon up with a home run.* ♦*Before Jim knew it, he had spent all his money* *and he wound up broke.* ♦ *The boys followed the path to the left and wound up where they started.* Syn. END UP. Compare FINISH OFF, TURN OUT 6. **4.** To put (your business or personal affairs) in order; arrange; settle. ♦ *Fred wound up his business and personal affairs before joining the Navy.* **5.** To swing your arm with the ball just before pitching to a batter. ♦ *The pitcher wound up quickly and then threw a curve.*

wing See CLIP ONE'S WINGS, LEFT-WING, ON THE WING, RIGHT-WING, UNDER ONE'S WING.

win hands down *v. phr.* To win conclusively and without external help. ♦ *The opposition was so weak that Dan won the election hands down.*

win in a walk *or* **win in a breeze** *v. phr., informal* To win very easily; win without having to try hard. ♦ *Joe ran for class president and won in a walk.* ♦ *Our team won the game in a breeze.* Compare HANDS DOWN.

wink See FORTY WINKS, SLEEP A WINK.

wink at *v.* To allow and pretend not to know about (a rule or law being broken). ♦ *John was not allowed to stay out late at night, but his parents winked at his being five minutes late.* ♦ *A judge should never wink at any law-breaking.*

winning streak *n.* A series of several wins one after the other. ♦ *The team extended their winning streak to ten.*

win one's spurs *v. phr.* **1.** In old times, to be named a knight with the right to wear little sharp spikes on your heels. ♦ *A young squire won his spurs in battle.* **2.** To win fame or honor. ♦ *The young lieutenant won his spurs by leading an attack on enemy machine guns.* ♦ *Edison won his spurs as an inventor while rather young.* ♦ *He has yet to win his spurs as a big league ball player.*

win out *v. phr.* To win after a rather protracted struggle. ♦ *The lawsuit lasted a long time, but we finally won out.*

win over *v. phr.* To convert to one's position or point of view. ♦ *The Democrats offered him a high-level executive position and thus way won him over to their side.*

wipeout *n.* A total failure. ♦ *The guy is so bad at his job that he is a total wipeout.*

wipe out *v.* **1.** To remove or erase by wiping or rubbing. ♦ *The teacher wiped out with an eraser what she had written on the board.* Compare RUB OUT. **2.** *informal* To remove, kill, or destroy completely. ♦ *The earthquake wiped out the town.* ♦ *Doctors are searching for a cure that will wipe out cancer.* ♦ *The Indians wiped out the soldiers who were sent to stop their attacks.* Compare RUB OUT, STAMP OUT.

wipe out an old score See SETTLE A SCORE.

wipe the floor with *or* **wipe up the floor with** See MOP THE FLOOR WITH.

wire See ACROSS THE WIRE, DOWN TO THE WIRE, PULL STRINGS *or* PULL WIRES.

wise See GET WISE, PENNY WISE AND POUND FOOLISH, PUT WISE, THE WISER.

wisecrack *n.* A joke or witty remark usually made at someone else's expense. ♦ *The comedians kept up a steady stream of wisecracks.*

wise guy *n. phr., informal* A person who acts as if he were smarter than other people; a person who jokes or shows off too much ♦ *Bill is a wise guy and displeases others by what he says.*

wise up to *v. phr., slang* To finally understand what is really going on after a period of ignorance. ♦ *Joe immediately quit his job when he wised up to what was really going on.*

wish on *v.* **1.** To use as a lucky charm while making a wish. ♦ *Mary wished on a star that she could go to the dance.* ♦ *Bob wished on his lucky rabbit's foot that he could pass the test.* **2.** *or* **wish off on** *informal* To get rid of (something unwanted) by passing it on to someone else. ♦ *Martha did not like to do the dishes and wished the job on to her little sister.* ♦ *Tom got a very ugly tie for his birthday and when Billy's birthday came, Tom wished the tie off on Billy.*

wit See AT ONE'S WITS' END, KEEP ONE'S HEAD *or* KEEP ONE'S WITS ABOUT ONE, SCARE OUT OF ONE'S WITS.

witch-hunt *n. phr.* A hysterical movement during which people are persecuted for having views (political or religious) considered different or unpopular. ♦ *During the McCarthy era many innocent Americans were* *accused of being Communists, as Republican patriotism deteriorated into a witch-hunt.*

with a free hand See FREE HAND.

with a grain of salt *or* **with a pinch of salt** See TAKE WITH A GRAIN OF SALT.

with all one's heart See FROM THE BOTTOM OF ONE'S HEART.

with an eye to See EYE TO.

with a silver spoon in one's mouth See BORN WITH A SILVER SPOON IN ONE'S MOUTH.

with a whole skin *also* **in a whole skin** *adv. phr.* With no injury; unhurt; safely. ◆*The boy was lucky to escape with a whole skin when the car went off the road.* ◆*Jack came through the game with a whole skin.* ◆*The horse threw him off, but he got away in a whole skin.* Syn. SAFE AND SOUND.

with bad grace *or* **with a bad grace** *adv. phr.* In an unpleasant or discourteous way; unwillingly, ◆*Fred takes defeat with bad grace.* ◆*Tom shouted "Hello" to Bill. Bill was in a sour mood and replied with a bad grace.* Contrast WITH GOOD GRACE .

with bells on *adv. phr., informal* With enthusiasm; eager or ready and in the best of spirits for an event. ◆*"Will you come to the farewell party I'm giving for Billy?" asked Jerry. "I'll be there with bells on," replied Ed.*

with child *adv. phr., literary* Going to have a baby; pregnant. ◆*The angel told Mary she was with child.* Compare IN A FAMILY WAY *or* IN THE FAMILY WAY.

wither on the vine See DIE ON THE VINE.

with fire See PLAY WITH FIRE.

with flying colors *adv. phr.* With great or total success; victoriously. ◆*Tom finished the race with flying colors.* ◆*Mary came through the examination with flying colors.*

with good grace *adv. phr.* With pleasant and courteous behavior; politely; willingly; without complaining. ◆*The boys had been well-coached; they took the loss of the game with good grace.* ◆*The principal scolded Nora, who accepted his criticism with good grace.* Contrast WITH BAD GRACE.

with heart and soul See HEART AND SOUL.

within an ace of *informal or* **within an inch of** *adv. phr.* Almost but not quite; very close to; nearly. ◆*Tim came within an ace of losing the election.* ◆*John was within an inch of drowning before he was pulled out of the water.* Compare BY THE SKIN OF ONE'S TEETH.

within an inch of one's life *adv. phr.* Until you are almost dead; near to dying. ◆*The bear clawed the hunter within an inch of his life.* Often used after *to*. ◆*The prize fighter was beaten to within an inch of his life.*

within bounds *adv. or adj. phr.* **1.** Inside of the boundary lines in a game; on or inside of the playing field. ◆*You must hit the ball inside the lines of the tennis court or it will not be within bounds.* ◆*If you kick the football over a sideline, it will not be in bounds.* **2.** Inside of a place where one is allowed to go or be. ◆*The soldiers are within bounds on one side of the city, but are out of bounds on the other side.* **3.** Inside of safe or proper limits; allowable. ◆*If you ask Father for a quarter, he might give it to you, but a dollar would not be within bounds.* ◆*He succeeded in keeping his temper within bounds.* Contrast OUT OF BOUNDS.

within call *or* **within hail** *adv. phr.* **1.** Near enough to hear each other's voices. ◆*When the two ships were within hail, their officers exchanged messages.* ◆*Billy's mother told him to stay within call because supper was nearly ready.* **2.** In a place where you can be reached by phone, radio, or TV and be called. ◆*The sick man was very low and the doctor stayed within call.* ◆*The soldiers were allowed to leave the base by day, but had to stay within call.*

within reason *adv. or adj. phr.* Within the limits of good sense; in reasonable control or check; moderate. ◆*I want you to have a good time tonight, within reason.* ◆*If Tom wants to go to the fair, he must keep his expenses within reason.* ◆*Jean's plans are quite within reason.*

with it See GET WITH IT.

with might and main *adv. phr.* With full strength or complete effort. ◆*The sailors pulled the rope with might and main.* ◆*John tried with all his might and main to solve the problem.*

with one's boots on See DIE IN ONE'S BOOTS *or* DIE WITH ONE'S BOOTS ON.

with one's pants down See CATCH ONE WITH ONE'S PANTS DOWN.

with open arms *adv. phr.* **1.** With the arms spread wide for hugging or catching. ♦ *When Father came home from work, little Sally ran out to meet him with open arms.* ♦ *Dick stood under the window with open arms, and Jean dropped the bag of laundry down to him.* **2.** With words or actions showing that you are glad to see someone; gladly, warmly, eagerly. ♦ *When Grandmother came to visit us at Christmas, we welcomed her with open arms.* ♦ *After his pioneering flight in the Friendship VII, Col. John Glenn was welcomed with open arms by the people of his hometown.*

without See DO WITHOUT *or* GO WITHOUT, MAKE BRICKS WITHOUT STRAW, RECKON WITHOUT.

without a paddle See UP THE CREEK *or* UP THE CREEK WITHOUT A PADDLE.

without batting an eye *or* **without batting an eyelash** See BAT AN EYE.

without fail *adv. phr.* Without failing to do it or failing in the doing of it; certainly, surely. ♦ *Be here at 8 o'clock sharp, without fail.* ♦ *Ben promised to return the bike at a certain time without fail.*

without number See BEYOND NUMBER.

without rhyme or reason See RHYME OR REASON.

with reference to See IN REFERENCE TO.

with regard to See IN REFERENCE TO.

with relation to See IN RELATION TO.

with respect to See IN RESPECT TO.

with the best *or* **with the best of them** *adv. phr.* As well as anyone. ♦ *Bob could horseback ride with the best of them, but he never boasted about it.* ♦ *John can bowl with the best of them.*

with the Joneses See KEEP UP WITH THE JONESES.

wolf See CRY WOLF, KEEP THE WOLF FROM THE DOOR, LONE WOLF, THROW TO THE WOLVES .

wolf in sheep's clothing *n. phr.* A person who pretends to be good but really is bad. ♦ *Mrs. Martin trusted the lawyer until she realized that he was a wolf in sheep's clothing.* ♦ *Mr. Black was fooled by the salesman's manners until he showed that he was really a wolf in sheep's clothing by selling Mr.*

Black a car that was falling apart.

wonder See NO WONDER *also* SMALL WONDER .

woo See PITCH WOO.

wood See CAN'T SEE THE WOOD FOR THE TREES, KNOCK ON WOOD, SAW WOOD.

woodpile See NIGGER IN THE WOODPILE.

woods See BABE IN THE WOODS, CROW BEFORE ONE IS OUT OF THE WOODS, NECK OF THE WOODS, TAKE TO THE WOODS.

wool See ALL WOOL AND A YARD WIDE, PULL THE WOOL OVER ONE'S EYES.

word See ACTIONS SPEAK LOUDER THAN WORDS, AS GOOD AS ONE'S WORD, BY WORD OF MOUTH, EAT ONE'S WORDS, FROM THE WORD "GO", GET A WORD IN, GET THE MESSAGE *or* GET THE WORD, HANG ON THE WORDS OF, IN BRIEF *or* IN A WORD, IN SO MANY WORDS, LAST WORD, MAN OF FEW WORDS, MAN OF HIS WORD, MUM IS THE WORD, PLAY ON WORDS, PUT WORDS INTO ONE'S MOUTH, SAY THE WORD, SWALLOW ONE'S WORDS, TAKE AT ONE'S WORD, TAKE THE WORDS OUT OF ONE'S MOUTH, WEASEL WORD, WEIGH ONE'S WORDS.

word for word *adv. phr.* In exactly the same words. ♦ *Mary copied Sally's composition word for word.* ♦ *Joan repeated the conversation word for word.* ♦ *She learned the poem many years ago but she recited it word for word.*

word of mouth *n. phr.* Communication by oral rather than written means. ♦ *The merchant told us that the best customers he had were recommended to him by word of mouth.*

words of one syllable *n. phr.* Language that makes the meaning very clear; simple, or frank language.—Usually used after *in.* ♦ *Mary explained the job to Ann in words of one syllable so that she would be sure to understand.* ♦ *Some people say that John is cute and mischievous, but in words of one syllable, he's just a brat.* Compare IN SO MANY WORDS, SPELL OUT.

word to the wise *n. phr.* A word of warning or advice which the intelligent person is expected to follow.—A proverb. ♦ *I had once spoken to him about being late all the time, and thought that a word to the wise was enough.*

work See ALL IN A DAY'S WORK, ALL WORK AND NO PLAY MAKES JACK A DULL BOY, AT WORK, BUSY WORK, IN THE WORKS, MAKE SHORT WORK OF, MANY HANDS MAKE LIGHT WORK, SHOOT THE WORKS, THE WORKS, IN THE WORKS.

work cut out See CUT OUT 2 *adj.* 1.

worked up *also* **wrought up** *adj., literary* Feeling strongly; excited; angry; worried. ♦ *Mary was all worked up about the exam.* ♦ *John got worked up when they blamed him for losing the game.* Compare ON EDGE.

work in *v.* **1.** To rub in. ♦ *The nurse told Mary to put some cream on her skin and to work it in gently with her fingers.* **2.** To slip in; mix in; put in; ♦ *When Mary was planning the show, she worked a part in for her friend Susan.*

working girl *n., slang* **1.** *(vulgar, avoidable)* A prostitute. ♦ *I didn't know Roxanne was a working girl.* **2.** A girl, usually single, who supports herself by working in an honest job, such as in an office, etc. ♦ *The average working girl can't afford such a fancy car.*

work into *v.* **1.** Force into little by little. ♦ *John worked his foot into the boot by pushing and pulling.* **2.** Put into; mix into. ♦ *Mary worked some blue into the rug she was weaving.*

work off *v.* To make (something) go away, especially by working. ♦ *John worked off the fat around his waist by doing exercise every morning.* ♦ *Mr. Smith worked off his anger by chopping wood.*

work on *also* **work upon** *v.* **1.** Have an effect on; influence. ♦ *Some pills work on the nerves and make people feel more relaxed.* **2.** To try to influence or convince. ♦ *Senator Smith worked on the other committee members to vote for the bill.*

work one's fingers to the bone *v. phr.* To work very hard. ♦ *"I have to work my fingers to the bone for a measly pittance of a salary," Fred complained.*

workout *n.* A physical exercise session. ♦ *My morning workout consists of sit-ups and push-ups.*

work out *v. phr.* **1.** To find an answer to. ♦ *John worked out his math problems all by himself.* ♦ *Mary had trouble getting along with her roommate, but they*

worked it out. Compare FIGURE OUT. **2.** To plan; develop. ♦ *Mary worked out a beautiful design for a sweater.* ♦ *Alice worked out a new hair-do.* **3.** To accomplish; arrange. ♦ *The engineers worked out a system for getting electricity to the factory.* **4.** To be efficient; get results. ♦ *If the traffic plan works out, it will be used in other cities too.* **5.** To exercise. ♦ *John works out in the gym two hours every day.*

work over *v. phr., slang* To beat someone up very roughly in order to intimidate him or extort payment, etc. ♦ *Matthew was worked over by the hoodlums in the park right after midnight.*

work through channels *v. phr.* To go through the proper procedures and officials. ♦ *At a state university everybody must work through channels to get things done.*

work up *v.* **1.** To stir up; arouse; excite. ♦ *I can't work up any interest in this book.* ♦ *He worked up a sweat weeding the garden.* **2.** To develop; originate. ♦ *He worked up an interesting plot for a play.*

work upon See WORK ON.

world See COME UP IN THE WORLD *or* RISE IN THE WORLD, DEAD TO THE WORLD, FOR ALL THE WORLD, IN A WORLD OF ONE'S OWN *or* IN A WORLD BY ONESELF, IN THE WORLD, LOOK AT THE WORLD THROUGH ROSE-COLORED GLASSES, NOT FOR THE WORLD, ON TOP OF THE WORLD *or* SITTING ON TOP OF THE WORLD, OUT OF THIS WORLD, SET THE WORLD ON FIRE, THIRD WORLD.

world is one's oyster Everything is possible for you; the world belongs to you; you can get anything you want. ♦ *When John won the scholarship, he felt as though the world was his oyster.* ♦ *The rich girl acts as though the world is her oyster.*

world on one's shoulders See WEIGHT OF THE WORLD ON ONE'S SHOULDERS.

world on one's back See WEIGHT OF THE WORLD ON ONE'S SHOULDERS.

world without end *adv. phr., literary* Endlessly; forever; eternally. ♦ *Each human being has to die, but mankind goes on world without end.*

worlds apart *adj. phr.* Completely different; in total disagreement. ♦ *Jack* *and Al never agree on anything; they are worlds apart in their thinking.*

worm See EARLY BIRD CATCHES THE WORM *or* EARLY BIRD GETS THE WORM.

worm in *v. phr.* To insinuate oneself; penetrate gradually. ♦ *By cultivating the friendship of a few of the prominent merchants, Peter hoped to worm his way into that exclusive elite of export magnates.*

worm may turn Even the meek will ultimately rebel if always maltreated. ♦ *Sam may think that he can continue to mistreat his wife, but, knowing her, I think that some day the worm may turn.*

worm out *v. phr.* To learn through persistent questioning; draw out from. ♦ *I finally wormed out of her the reason she broke off her engagement to Larry.*

worn to a frazzle *adj. phr.* To be fatigued; be exhausted. ♦ *I'm worn to a frazzle cooking for all these guests.*

worrywart *n. phr.* A person who always worries. ♦ *"Stop being such a worrywart," Bob said to Alice, who was constantly weighing herself on the bathroom scale.*

worse See BARK WORSE THAN ONE'S BITE, FOR BETTER OR WORSE *or* FOR BETTER OR FOR WORSE, FOR THE WORSE, GO FROM BAD TO WORSE.

worse for wear *adj. phr.* Not as good as new; worn out; damaged by use.— Used with *the*. ♦ *Her favorite tablecloth was beginning to look the worse for wear.*—Often used with *none* to mean: as good as new. ♦ *The doll was Mary's favorite toy but it was none the worse for wear.*

worst See GET THE WORST OF *also* HAVE THE WORST OF, IF WORST COMES TO WORST.

worth See BIRD IN THE HAND IS WORTH TWO IN THE BUSH, FOR ALL ONE IS WORTH, GAME IS NOT WORTH THE CANDLE, NOT WORTH A TINKER'S DAMN, WORTH A CENT.

worth a cent *adj. phr.* Worth anything; of any value.—Used in negative, interrogative, and conditional sentences. ♦ *The book was old and it was not worth a cent.*

worth one's salt *adj. phr.* Being a good worker, or a productive person; worth what you cost. ♦ *Mr. Brown showed that he was worth his salt as a salesman when he got the highest sales record for the year.*—Often used with *not* or *hardly*. ♦ *When the basketball team did so poorly, people felt that the coach was hardly worth his salt.* Compare PAY ONE'S WAY 2.

would-be *adj.* Aspiring. ♦ *The Broadway casting offices are always full of would-be actors.*

would that *or* **I would that** *or* **would God** *or* **would heaven** *literary* I wish that.—Used at the beginning of a sentence expressing a wish; followed by a verb in the subjunctive; found mostly in poetry and older literature. ♦ *Would that I could only drop everything and join you.* ♦ *Would that my mother were alive to see me married.* Syn. IF ONLY.

wouldn't put it past one *v. phr.* To think that someone is quite capable or likely to have done something undesirable or illegal. ♦ *Congressman Alfonso is insisting that he didn't violate congressional ethics, but knowing both his expensive habits and his amorous escapades, many of us wouldn't put it past him that he might have helped himself to funds illegally.*

wrack See GO TO WRACK AND RUIN.

wrap See UNDER WRAPS.

wrap one around one's finger See TWIST ONE AROUND ONE'S LITTLE FINGER.

wrapped up in *adj. phr.* Thinking only of; interested only in. ♦ *John has no time for sports because he is all wrapped up in his work.* ♦ *Mary was so wrapped up in her book she didn't hear her mother calling her.* ♦ *Jean is so wrapped up in herself, she never thinks of helping others.* ♦ *Mrs. Brown gave up her career because her life was all wrapped up in her children.* Compare IN A WORLD OF ONE'S OWN 2b.

wrap up *or* **bundle up** *v. phr.* **1.** To put on warm clothes; dress warmly. ♦ *Mother told Mary to wrap up before going out into the cold.* **2.** *informal* To finish (a job). ♦ *Let's wrap up the job and go home.* **3.** *informal* To win a game. ♦ *The Mets wrapped up the baseball game in the seventh inning.*

wreak havoc with *v. phr.* To cause damage; ruin something. ♦ *His rebellious attitude is bound to wreak havoc at the company.*

wrench See THROW A MONKEY WRENCH.

wringing wet *adj.* Wet through and through; soaked; dripping. ♦*He was wringing wet because he was caught in the rain without an umbrella.* ♦*He was wringing wet after working in the fields in the hot sun.*

write home about *v. phr.* To become especially enthusiastic or excited about; boast about.—Often used after *to.* ♦*Mary's trip to the World's Fair was something to write home about.* ♦*Joe did a good enough job of painting but it was nothing to write home about.* ♦*"That was a dinner worth writing home about!" said Bill coming out of the restaurant.*

write off *v. phr.* **1.** To remove (an amount) from a business record; cancel (a debt); accept as a loss. ♦*If a customer dies when he owes the store money, the store must often write it off.* Compare CHARGE OFF. **2.** To accept (a loss or trouble) and not worry anymore about it; forget. ♦*Mr. Brown had so much trouble with the new TV set that he finally wrote it off and bought a new one.* ♦*Jim's mistake cost him time and money, but he wrote it off to experience.* Compare CHARGE OFF 2. Contrast CHALK UP 2. To say that (something) will fail or not be good; believe worthless. ♦*Just because the boys on the team are young, don't write the team off.* Compare COUNT OUT.

write-off *n.* A loss. ♦*This last unfortunate business venture of ours is an obvious write-off.*

writer's cramp *n* . Pain in the fingers or hand caused by too much writing. ♦*Holding your pencil too tightly for too long often gives you writer's cramp.* Often used humorously to stress the idea that you have been doing a lot of writing. ♦*By the time Mary finished* her Christmas cards she complained of writer's cramp.

writer's block *n. phr.* A condition of being unable to write; a period when the words just won't come. ♦*One of the more common problems writers occasionally experience is a writer's block that may last a shorter or a longer time.* ♦*They say that the reason for Ernest Hemingway's suicide was a severe and seemingly endless writer's block.*

write-up *n.* A report or story in a newspaper or magazine. ♦*There was a write-up of the accident in the newspaper.* ♦*I read an interesting write-up about the President in a new magazine.*

write up *v.* **1.** To write the story of; describe in writing; give a full account of. ♦*Reporters from many newspapers are here to write up the game.* ♦*The magazine is writing up the life of the President.* **2.** To put something thought or talked about into writing; finish writing (something). ♦*John took notes of what the teacher said in class and he wrote them up when he got home.* ♦*The author had an idea for a story when he saw the old house, and he wrote it up later.*

writing or **handwriting on the wall** *n. phr., literary* A warning; a message of some urgency. ♦*"This nuclear plant is about to explode, I think," the chief engineer said. "We'd better get out of here in a hurry, the handwriting is on the wall."*

wrong See BARK UP THE WRONG TREE, BET ON THE WRONG HORSE, GET OFF ON THE WRONG FOOT, GET UP ON THE WRONG SIDE OF THE BED, IN THE WRONG, LAUGH ON THE WRONG SIDE OF ONE'S MOUTH, RUB THE WRONG WAY.

wrong side of the tracks See THE TRACKS.

wrought up See WORKED UP.

• X •

x-double minus *adj., slang, informal* Extremely poorly done, bad, inferior (said mostly about theatrical or musical performances). ♦ *Patsy gave an x-double minus performance at the audition and lost her chance for the lead role.*

X marks the spot. An indication made on maps or documents of importance to call attention to a place or a feature of some importance. ♦ *The treasure hunter said to his companion, "Here it is; X marks the spot."*

x-rated *adj., slang informal* Pertaining to movies, magazines, and literature judged pornographic and therefore off limits for minors. ♦ *My son celebrated his 21st birthday by going to an x-rated movie.*

x-raying machine *n., slang, citizen's band radio jargon* Speed detection device by radar used by the police. ♦ *The smokies are using the x-raying machine under the bridge!*

· Y ·

yak-yak *or* **yakety-yak** *or* **yakib-yak** *n., slang* Much talk about little things; talking all the time about unimportant things. ♦ *Tom sat behind two girls on the bus and he got tired of their silly yak-yak.*

year See ALONG IN YEARS *or* ON IN YEARS.

year in, year out See DAY IN AND DAY OUT.

year-round *or* **year-around** *adj.* Usable, effective, or operating all the year. ♦ *Colorado is a year-round resort; there is fishing in the summer and skiing in the winter.*

yellow around the gills See GREEN AROUND THE GILLS.

yellow-bellied *adj., slang* Extremely timid, cowardly. ♦ *Joe Bennett is a yellow-bellied guy, don't send him on such a tough assignment!*

yellow journalism *n. phr.* Cheap and sensational newspaper writing; inflammatory language designed to stir up popular sentiment against another country. ♦ *Yellow journalism is hardly ever truly informative.*

yellow-livered *adj.* Cowardly. ♦ *The young boy greatly resented being called yellow-livered and started to fight right away.*

yeoman service *n. phr.* Help in time of need; serviceable and good assistance. ♦ *Sam was pressed into yeoman service in organizing our annual fundraiser for cerebral palsy victims.*

yes-man *n., informal* A person who tries to be liked by agreeing with everything said; especially, someone who always agrees with a boss or the one in charge. ♦ *John tries to get ahead on his job by being a yes-man.*

yesterday See BORN YESTERDAY.

yon See HITHER AND THITHER *or* HITHER AND YON.

yoo-hoo *interj.*—Used as an informal call or shout to a person to attract his attention. ♦ *Louise opened the door and called "Yoo-hoo, Mother—are you home?"* See ALL RIGHT FOR YOU, I'M TELLING YOU, SAYS WHO *or* SAYS YOU, THAT'S————FOR YOU, WHAT HAVE YOU.

you bet *or* **you bet your boots** *or* **you bet your life** *informal* Most certainly; yes, indeed; without any doubt.—Used to declare with emphasis that a thing is really so. ♦ *Do I like to ski? You bet your life I do.* ♦ *You bet I will be at the party.* ♦ *You can bet your boots that Johnny will come home when his money is gone.* Compare BET ONE'S BOTTOM DOLLAR.

you can say that again See YOU SAID IT.

you can't teach an old dog new tricks It is very hard or almost impossible to train an older person to acquire some new skill.—A proverb. ♦ *You'll never teach your grandfather how to do his income tax on a personal computer. You can't teach an old dog new tricks.*

you don't say *interj., informal*—Used to show surprise at what is said. ♦ *Your ring is a real diamond? You don't say!* ♦ *"Bill and Jean are going to get married." "You don't say!"* Syn. DO TELL.

your See HANG ON TO YOUR IIAT *or* HOLD ON TO YOUR HAT *or* HOLD YOUR HAT, YOU BET YOUR BOOTS *or* YOU BET YOUR LIFE.

you're telling me *interj., informal*—Used to show that a thing is so clear that it need not be said, or just to show strong agreement. ♦ *"You're late." "You're telling me!"* Compare YOU BET, YOU SAID IT.

you said it *or* **you can say that again** *interj., slang*—Used to show strong agreement with what another person has said. ♦ *"That sure was a good show." "You said it!"* ♦ *"It sure is hot!" "You can say that again!"* Compare SAY A MOUTHFUL.

you tell 'em *interj., slang*—Used to agree with or encourage someone in what he is saying. ♦ *The drunk was arguing with the bartenders and a man cried, "You tell 'em!"*

yours truly *adv. phr.* **1.** Signing off at the end of letters. ♦ *Yours truly, Tom Smith.* **2.** I, the first person singular pronoun, frequently abbreviated as t.y. ♦ *As t.y. has often pointed out...T.y. is not really interested in the offer.*

yum-yum *interj., informal*—Used usually by or to children, to express great delight, especially in the taste of food. ♦ *"Yum-Yum! That pie is good!"*

zero hour *n.* **1.** The exact time when an attack or other military action is supposed to start. ♦*Zero hour for the bombers to take off was midnight.* **2.** The time when an important decision or change is supposed to come; the time for a dangerous action. ♦*It was zero hour and the doctor began the operation on the man.* ♦*On the day of the championship game, as the zero hour came near, the players grew nervous.*

zero in on *v.* **1.** To adjust a gun so that it will exactly hit (a target); aim at. ♦*Big guns were zeroed in on the enemy fort.* ♦*American missiles have been zeroed in on certain targets, to be fired if necessary.* **2.** *slang* To give your full attention to. ♦*The Senate zeroed in on the Latin-American problems.* ♦*Let's zero in on grammar tonight.*

zip one's lip See BUTTON ONE'S LIP.

zone defense *n.* A defense in a sport (as basketball or football) in which each player has to defend a certain area. ♦*The coach taught his team a zone defense because he thought his players weren't fast enough to defend against individual opponents.*

zonk out *v. phr., slang* **1.** To fall asleep very quickly. ♦*Can I talk to Joe?—Call back tomorrow, he zonked out.* **2.** To pass out from fatigue, or alcohol. ♦*You won't get a coherent word out of Joe, he has zonked out.*

zoom in *v. phr.* **1.** To rapidly close in on (said of airplanes and birds of prey). ♦*The fighter planes zoomed in on the enemy target.* **2.** To make a closeup of someone or something with a camera. ♦*The photographer zoomed in on the tiny colibri as it hovered over a lovely tropical flower.*

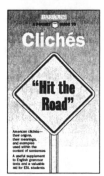